The Blue Ribbon Country Cookbook

The Blue Ribbon Country Cookbook

By Diane Roupe

ILLUSTRATIONS BY SHARON K. SODER

PHOTOGRAPHS BY MIKE DIETER

THOMAS NELSON
Since 1798

NASHVILLE   DALLAS   MEXICO CITY   RIO DE JANEIRO   BEIJING

Published in Nashville, Tennessee, by Thomas Nelson. Thomas Nelson is a trademark of Thomas Nelson, Inc..

Thomas Nelson books may be purchased in bulk for educational, business, fund-raising, or sales promotional use. For information, please e-mail SpecialMarkets@ThomasNelson.com.

Library of Congress Cataloging-in-Publication Data

Roupe, Diane.
  The blue ribbon country cookbook: the new standard of American cooking / by Diane Roupe; illustrations by Sharon K. Soder; photographs by Mike Dieter
    Includes index.
  1. Cooker, American—Midwestern style. 2. Cookery—Middle West. I. Title.
  TX715.2.M53R68   1998
  641.5977—dc21   97-43569

  ISBN-10: 1-4016-0360-2
  ISBN-13: 978-1-4016-0360-1

Printed in the United States of America
07 08 09 10 11—5 4 3

Contents

Recipes Tagged with Winning Ribbons

RECIPES FOR MY WINNING ENTRIES AT THE IOWA STATE
FAIR ARE TAGGED AS FOLLOWS:

 RECIPE FOR A BLUE RIBBON WINNER (FIRST PLACE)
AT THE IOWA STATE FAIR.

 RECIPE FOR A RED RIBBON WINNER (SECOND PLACE)
AT THE IOWA STATE FAIR.

IN ADDITION, TWO RECIPES FOR OTHER PEOPLE'S WINNING
ENTRIES ARE INCLUDED AND TAGGED. THOSE RECIPES ARE:

Pat Berry's JULEKAKE (NORWEGIAN CHRISTMAS
BREAD) (PAGE 355).

Joy McFarland's MILE-HIGH TORTE (PAGE 496).

Introduction

America is a unique political and social amalgamation of people and cultures from around the world. Our food is a rich reflection of this diversity interwoven with the copious bounty of our magnificent, fruitful land. American food rightfully can be counted as one of the grand cuisines of the world.

The first edition of *The Blue Ribbon Country Cookbook* presented Midwest food—deriving from the twelve-state stretch of our nation's land that harbors some of the most fertile, productive soil on the planet—as uniquely supreme and the genesis of a blue ribbon, American cooking style. The recipes contained in this new edition of the cookbook remain predominantly of the Midwest American persuasion—a distillation of this nation's bountiful land and opulent ethnicity, and at the heart of the American food and cooking style.

The Blue Ribbon Country Cookbook was written to be much used in everyday cookery. It is a practical book containing recipes for foods that Americans love to eat—everything from boiling potatoes to preparing standing rib roast and baking pineapple upside-down cake. I call it "the real world."

The recipes call for familiar ingredients, and the procedures are written clearly and in detail. Featured are more than 100 explicitly written techniques, ranging from how to make flaky piecrust to the basics of yeast-bread baking to directions for making dried and fresh bread crumbs. One can learn to cook from *The Blue Ribbon Country Cookbook*, and experienced cooks will welcome the easy-to-follow, dependable recipes for a broad range of traditional and contemporary American foods.

It is hoped that you find *The Blue Ribbon Country Cookbook* to be one of your kitchen standbys on which you rely for wonderful American food recipes.

Happy blue ribbon cooking!

Special Information

Notes About Recipe Ingredients

HIGH-QUALITY PRODUCTS. Prepared foods are only as good as the products that go into them. The whole equals the sum of its parts. Select fresh, high-quality foods to bring into your kitchen. Neither the combining of inferior products with other foods nor the cooking process will disguise poor-quality products.

EGGS. Recipes are based on the use of extra-large eggs unless otherwise specified. For best results with the recipes herein, extra-large eggs should be used unless otherwise specified; however, if extra-large eggs are not available, large eggs may be substituted in most recipes. A few recipes, in which the volume of eggs is critical, specify the number of large eggs that may be used in substitution for extra-large eggs.

BUTTER. Use lightly salted butter unless otherwise specified.

SUBSTITUTION OF MARGARINE FOR BUTTER. Margarine may be substituted for butter in most recipes; however, in my opinion, the flavor of the end product will be adversely affected in most cases. For example, cakes and cookies made with butter have a deep, rich taste, which is missing when margarine is substituted in the same recipes.

MILK. In general, when whole milk is specified in a recipe, fat-free (skim) milk or lowfat (1% or 2%) milk should not be substituted. While fat-free (skim) milk is a good-tasting, nonfat, healthful product for drinking, the use of whole milk in baked goods and for most cooking results in finer end products. Try to select ways other than eliminating whole milk from cooking to reduce fat in the family diet.

PURE VANILLA EXTRACT. Use of pure vanilla extract is specified in the recipes. Imitation vanilla results in inferior flavor.

BAKING POWDER. Remember to watch the expiration date on the container and discard after that date.

WINE AND ALCOHOLIC LIQUOR. Use good wine and alcoholic liquor for cooking. Poor-quality wine and spirits produce second-class flavor in finished dishes.

GROUND BEEF. Lean ground beef is called for in these recipes. The ground beef should be 97% lean, pure ground beef containing no fillers, such as carrageenin or oat bran, and no additives, such as salt or hydrolyzed vegetable protein.

MUSHROOMS. Unless otherwise designated, "mushrooms" specified as an ingredient refers to the common, cultivated white mushrooms (*Agaricus bisporus*) generally available in most supermarkets. Cultivated white mushrooms are sometimes called "button" mushrooms, generally referring to small white mushrooms.

HAZELNUTS. Hazelnuts are also known as filberts.

COMMERCIAL CAN SIZES. The sizes of commercial cans of food often change (generally becoming smaller). In many cases, using a can of food which varies slightly in size from that specified in a recipe will not affect the outcome of the prepared food. The cook will have to make this determination. If there is a significant variation in can size from the recipe specification, it may necessitate using a portion of food from a second can or reducing the amount of food used from a single, larger can.

FLOUR STORAGE. For convenient use, all-purpose flour may be stored in an airtight canister placed in a dry, cool place on the kitchen counter. Surplus all-purpose flour may be stored in a dry place at cool, room temperature. For storage, place the paper package of remaining flour in a zipper-seal plastic bag. Flour stored at room temperature should be used within 6 months.

   Wheat germ and flour containing part germ, such as whole wheat flour, should be stored in the refrigerator or freezer to prevent rancidity caused by oil in the germ. For refrigeration or freezing, wheat germ and small quantities of flour may be placed in glass jars with tight lids; larger quantities of flour may be left in their original paper packages and sealed tightly in zipper-seal plastic bags.

   Refrigerated or frozen wheat germ and flour should be brought to room temperature before being used in a baked product.

Glossary

N.=NOUN, V.=VERB, ADJ.=ADJECTIVE

ALMOND PASTE: *N.* Blanched almonds blended to an oily consistency, then mixed with a sugar and water syrup that has been cooked to 240°F and then kneaded.

AMANDINE: *ADJ.* Prepared or garnished with almonds.

AMARETTO: *N.* An almond-flavored liqueur, although apricot pits are often used to flavor it rather than almonds. Amaretto di Saronno, the original Amaretto, comes from Saronno, Italy.

APPLEJACK: *N.* Apple brandy.

ARROWROOT: *N.* The starch from the root of a tropical plant used to thicken glazes and sauces. Flavorless and colorless, it produces exceptionally clear, smooth glazes and sauces. Ideal for use in mixtures which should not boil because, unlike cornstarch and flour, it requires no cooking and reaches its maximum capability as a thickener at a temperature below the boiling point.

ASPIC: *N.* Jellied meat, poultry, fish, or vegetable broth used to mold or coat foods—usually meat, poultry, fish, or vegetables. Unflavored aspic is gelatinized water.

BAKE: *V.* To cook a food product, covered or uncovered, in an oven.

BARBECUE: *V.* (1) To cook, primarily, meats, poultry, fish, shellfish, or wild game by indirect heat in an outdoor smoker or grill. (2) To cook, primarily, meats, poultry, fish, shellfish, or wild game indoors, using barbecue sauce.

BARBECUE SAUCE: *N.* A highly seasoned, traditionally tomato-based sauce containing vinegar and/ or wine and a sweetener; generally used on foods grilled or smoked outdoors, but may also be used on foods prepared indoors.

BASTE: *V.* To spoon or brush a liquid or sauce over a food while it is cooking for one or more of the following purposes: (1) to keep the food moist, (2) to help cook the top surface of the food, or (3) to add flavor. The liquid or sauce may or may not be from the pan or other container in which the food is cooking. A bulb baster is an efficient utensil for drawing liquid from around cooking food and expelling it over the food to baste.

BATTER: *N.* A thick but pourable raw mixture of ingredients, usually including flour.

BEAT: *V.* To rapidly move a single food or a mixture of foods for the purpose of smoothing, blending or combining, and/or incorporating air, using (1) an electric mixer, (2) a hand-operated rotary beater (sometimes referred to as an eggbeater), or (3) a spoon, fork, or whisk by repeatedly lifting the food(s) in a circular motion from the bottom to the top of the bowl or sauce dish.

BLANCH: *V.* To dip briefly in boiling water, generally for the purpose of loosening the skin of a food for peeling or for the purpose of cooking briefly (see To Blanch, page 29).

BLEND: *V.* To mix two or more ingredients together until the separate ingredients are indistinguishable.

BOIL: *V.* (1) To heat a liquid until it reaches a temperature at which large vapor bubbles form rapidly, rise and burst below the surface of the liquid, and leave the liquid, agitating the surface. At sea level, water boils at 212°F. Due to less atmospheric pressure in higher altitudes, the boiling point of water decreases as the altitude above sea level increases. To a lesser extent, weather conditions are another factor which causes fluctuations in the temperature at which water boils (see Boiling Point of Water at Various Altitudes, page 9). (2) To cook food in a boiling liquid.

BOUQUET GARNI: *N.* A small bunch of flavorful herbs—usually assorted and preferably fresh—tied together, added to foods (such as soups, stews, and sauces) during cooking, and removed before serving. A bouquet garni traditionally consists of parsley, thyme, and a bay leaf; however, any single herb or combination of herbs may be used. The herbs may be tied in a cheesecloth bag, if desired. Dried herbs may also be placed in a cheesecloth bag and used in substitution for fresh herbs. (See To Make a Fresh Bouquet Garni, page 26.)

BRAISE: *V.* To cook a food in a small amount of liquid at a low simmer in a covered skillet or pan.

BRANDY: *N.* An alcoholic liquor distilled from wine.

BREAD: *V.* To coat food with ground, dry bread or a ground, dry, breadlike product, such as cracker crumbs, cornmeal, or cornflake crumbs, in preparation for cooking. Often, the food to be breaded is first dipped in beaten egg and/or milk, or some other liquid, to help achieve adherence of the crumbs.

BRINE: *N.* A strong salt and water solution used in pickling, curing, and fermenting food for the purpose of preserving it and/or imparting flavor.

BROIL: *V.* To cook food by direct exposure beneath a dry heat source.

BROTH: *N.* The strained liquid produced by the long, slow simmering of meat, poultry, fish, bones, and vegetables—alone or in combination. Used in making sauces, soups, and other dishes. Usually clarified when served as a thin soup. Also known as stock.

BROWN: *V.* As a first step in cooking a food (often meat), to cook it quickly on all sides in a small amount of fat over medium to high heat until a golden to deep-brown color for the purpose of sealing in the juices and enhancing the flavor and color of the finished, cooked food.

BUN: *N.* A round and rather flat plain or sweet yeast roll.

BUTTERFLY: *V.* To split—usually meat or shrimp—nearly in two and lay open, making the product resemble a butterfly. The butterflied product may be cooked open or may be stuffed, with the butterfly "wings" encasing the stuffing.

CANAPÉ: *N.* A small, attractively cut piece of

bread (untoasted or toasted) or a small cracker topped with a tasty spread or other food and often an eye-appealing decoration or garnish; served as an hors d'oeuvre. "Canapé" is a French word meaning "couch."

CANDIED: *ADJ.* (1) Fruit—especially the peel—or ginger which has been cooked in a syrup until tender and translucent and then drained. Candied foods are used in cooking, or some are eaten alone as a candylike product, such as candied orange peel. (2) Sweet potatoes or other foods cooked in a syrup or with a sweet glaze.

CAPERS: *N.* Flower buds of the caper plant, a Mediterranean shrub, which are pickled and used in cooking for flavoring or garnish.

CASSEROLE: *N.* (1) A container, usually glass, in which food is baked and served. It generally has built-in handles and a lid. (2) The dish baked and served in a casserole.

CAVIAR: *N.* The roe (eggs) of large fish. True caviar—and the finest—is the black roe of the beluga sturgeon, which is imported from Russia and Iran. Red caviar is the roe of salmon. Yellow caviar is also marketed.

CELERY HEARTS: *N.* The small, tender, pale green to nearly white celery stalks (and leaves) at the very center of a bunch of celery.

CHOP: *V.* To cut into small, usually irregular, pieces, using a knife or other sharp implement.

CHUTNEY: *N.* A highly spiced, thick relish of Indian origin, containing fruits, spices (usually including ginger), vinegar, sugar (often brown sugar), often raisins, and often onions and/or garlic; used primarily as a condiment (see definition), especially with curry dishes, but also used as an ingredient in other dishes.

CLARIFIED BUTTER: *N.* The clear, yellow liquid which rises to the top of slowly melted butter, separated from the milk solids which settle on the bottom of the pan. The fat floating on top of the clarified butter is skimmed off, and,

using a baster, the clarified butter is drawn off, leaving the milk solids on the pan bottom.

COBBLER: *N.* A baked fruit dessert covered with a biscuitlike crust.

CODDLE: *V.* To cook food (usually unshelled eggs) in liquid at just below the boiling point.

COGNAC: *N.* A brandy (see definition) produced in the Cognac region of France.

COMBINE: *V.* To mix two or more ingredients or combination of ingredients together until the separate and/or combination ingredients are evenly distributed but still distinguishable, as in adding nuts to cake batter.

CONDIMENT: *N.* A sauce, relish, or seasoning placed on or beside food, usually at the table, to enhance flavor.

CONSERVE: *N.* A sweet spread similar to jam, with the same consistency. Conserves generally—but not always—contain two or more fruits, one of which is usually a citrus fruit. They contain nuts and/or raisins and/or coconut. In their purest form, conserves contain both nuts and raisins. They are favored for meat and poultry accompaniments; however, they also may be used as spreads on bread products.

CORE: *V.* To remove the central, often inedible, part of some fruits such as apples.

COURT BOUILLON: *N.* A well-seasoned liquid, usually consisting of water, wine and/or vinegar, vegetables, and seasoning, in which fish or shellfish is poached.

CREAM: *V.* To beat, usually using an electric mixer on high speed, a fat (generally butter, margarine, or shortening) until smooth, fluffy, and completely blended if creamed with another product such as sugar.

CRÈME DE CASSIS: *N.* A black currant-flavored liqueur.

CROQUETTE: *N.* A mixture of ground or minced foods, usually meat, fish, and/or vegetables, molded into a cone shape, coated with beaten egg and crumbs, and deep-fat fried or baked.

CROUTONS: *N.* Small cubes of toasted bread, seasoned or unseasoned, used as an ingredient or garnish in salads and other dishes.

CRUDITÉS: *N.* Raw vegetables cut into small strips or pieces and served, usually with a dip, as an hors d'oeuvre or first-course appetizer.

CUBE: *V.* To cut food into chunks with 6 equal square sides greater than $\frac{1}{4}$ inch square.

CURRANTS: *N.* (1) Any of several varieties of a tiny, acid berry which grows on shrubs of the genus *Ribes*. There are red, black, and white currants, red currants being the most common. Gooseberries are related to currants. (2) Dried Black Corinth grapes, called Zante currants (unrelated to the fruit in the first definition).

CURRY POWDER: *N.* Various blends of several ground, pungent spices and herbs. Originated in India.

CUT IN: *V.* To cut solid fat, such as butter or lard, into particles and/or small pieces while simultaneously mixing it with a dry ingredient, usually flour or a flour mixture, using a wire pastry blender or two knives.

DASH: *N.* Less than $\frac{1}{8}$ teaspoon.

DEEP-FAT FRY: *V.* To cook a food by immersing in hot fat. Also known as French fry.

DEGLAZE: *V.* To release food particles stuck to the bottom of a pan in which food has been cooked by adding liquid to the pan, placing it over low heat, and scraping the bottom with a spoon or spatula.

DEVILED: *ADJ.* Seasoned highly with spices and/or condiments such as mustard.

DICE: *V.* To cut food into small pieces with 6 equal sides $\frac{1}{4}$ inch square or less.

DOLLOP: *N.* A spoonful of soft food, such as whipped cream, usually informally placed on the top of another food.

DOUGH: *N.* A very thick, unpourable raw mixture of ingredients, usually including flour, which is stiff enough to be kneaded or shaped.

DREDGE: *V.* To coat a solid food with a fine, dry ingredient, such as flour, or a mixture of dry ingredients, by pulling the food across the ingredient or mixture or by sprinkling the ingredient or mixture over the food.

DRESS: *V.* To eviscerate and otherwise prepare an animal, fowl, or fish for cooking after killing.

DRIPPINGS: *N.* Juices and fat which run off meats and fowl during cooking.

DUMPLING: *N.* (1) A bread product that is a portion of batter dropped (dumped) onto boiling liquid, such as soup, stew, or water, and cooked, covered, by low-boiling/steaming (see Dumplings, page 382). (2) A formed ball of dough that may include various foods, such as chopped, riced, or ground vegetables and/or meats, dropped into boiling liquid, such as broth or water, to cook; for example, Potato Dumplings (page 281), matzoh balls, and liver dumplings. (3) A vegetable, fruit, meat, fish, or shellfish dipped in batter and deep-fat fried; for example, tempura and some fritters (not the Corn Fritters or Apple Fritters on page 390 of this cookbook, which are fried in a small amount of oil in a skillet). (4) A whole fruit or large pieces of fruit wrapped in pastry and baked usually in a syrup; for example, Apple Dumplings (page 575). (5) Food encased in pasta or other dough and cooked in boiling liquid or deep-fat fried; for example, ravioli and egg rolls.

DUTCH OVEN: *N.* A heavy—often aluminum—round pot with small side handles and a tight-fitting, domed lid, both usually made of the same metal as the pot; sometimes equipped with a rack. Commonly 4- or 6-quart capacity. Generally used for browning, braising, and roasting.

FILLET: *N.* A strip, piece, or slice of boneless meat or fish, especially the tenderloin of beef, and the strip or piece of flesh from either side of a fish.

FILLET: *V.* To cut fillets.

FILET MIGNON: *N.* A thick steak cut from the small end of a tenderloin of beef.

FLUTED: *ADJ.* In the shape of a continuous series of scallops or rounded grooves.

FOLD: *V.* To move a utensil, usually a spoon, briefly and carefully through a mixture in a vertical circular motion (down the back of the bowl, across the bottom, up, and over) to blend or combine an ingredient(s) with the mixture while (1) retaining the air in both the new ingredient(s) and the mixture and (2) incorporating new air.

FOWL: *N.* Any bird, domestic or wild.

FRITTER: *N.* A small amount of batter, usually containing a vegetable, fruit, or meat, which is deep-fat fried or sautéed.

FRY: *V.* To cook a food in fat in a skillet, pan, or griddle over heat. (See definitions for Deep-Fat Fry and Sauté.)

GIBLETS: *N.* The liver, heart, and gizzard of poultry.

GLAZE: *N.* (1) A thin, translucent, sweet, soft-gel coating usually brushed on or drizzled over fruit fillings in pies, tarts, and desserts to give a smooth sheen and add flavor. (2) A thin, translucent mixture used to coat foods before serving to give a glossy appearance and add flavor. (3) A very thin frosting (usually powdered sugar frosting) used to coat certain doughnuts and ice certain cakes and breads. (4) Concentrated meat stock.

GLAZE: *V.* To apply glaze.

GLUTEN: *N.* The viscous (or thick) and elastic proteins, particularly in wheat flour, which, when mixed with liquid and manipulated (stirred/kneaded), develop into strands.

These help retain, in doughs and batters, gas bubbles created by leavening agents such as yeast, baking powder, and steam. This allows doughs and batters to rise, resulting in light baked products.

GRAND MARNIER: *N.* A French orange-flavored liqueur with a cognac brandy base (see definition for Cognac).

GRATE: *V.* To break down a semi-hard product to a texture resembling finely rolled cracker crumbs, usually by rubbing the product against a sharp, densely pronged, metal kitchen tool made for this purpose, or by processing it in a food processor or blender.

GRAVY SKIMMER: *N.* A spouted liquid measuring cup designed for separating and pouring off the drippings from the fat in meat pan juices.

GREEN ONION: *N.* A young onion pulled before the bulb has enlarged. Also known as a "scallion."

GRILL: *V.* To cook food by direct exposure over direct heat, as in cooking food on a grate directly over charcoal in an outdoor grill.

GRIND: *V.* To reduce food to small fragments or powder with the use of a grinder or other kitchen implement or tool.

HERBS: *N.* The fresh or dried green leaves of certain plants used for flavoring foods.

HORS D'OEUVRES: *N.* Small, attractive savories served as appetizers, usually with cocktails, before a meal and before proceeding to the table.

HULL: *V.* (1) To remove the green, leafy sepals at the stem end of a fruit, plus the pith (the central strand of tissue) of strawberries. (2) To remove the outer covering of a fruit or seed.

INTERMEZZO: *N.* A minor course in a meal, usually consisting of a small serving of sorbet or sherbet, served between principal courses for the purpose of cleansing the palate.

JULIENNE: *V.* To cut into very narrow, square or rectangular matchstick-like strips, usually not exceeding ¼ inch wide by 2 to 2½ inches long.

KAHLÚA: *N.* A brand of coffee-flavored liqueur (see definition) produced in Mexico.

KIRSCHWASSER: *N.* Cherry brandy. A German word meaning "cherry water." It is pronounced "keersh-vahser."

KNEAD: *V.* To manipulate dough—for the purposes of gaining cohesiveness and developing the gluten—by placing it on a lightly floured surface, folding the dough in half toward you, pushing the dough with the heels of your hands, turning it one-quarter, and repeating this procedure for a specific time or until the dough is smooth and elastic. (See Kneading Dough, page 348.)

LARD: *N.* A soft, solid fat rendered from the fatty tissue of pork. Leaf lard, from leaf fat around the kidneys, is the finest lard.

LEAVENING AGENT: *N.* A gas—air, steam, or carbon dioxide—which is incorporated into, or forms in, a batter or dough, causing it to rise, increase in volume, and become light and porous during preparation and cooking. Baking soda (sodium bicarbonate), baking powder, and yeast are products used in cooking which, when activated, produce carbon dioxide by a chemical or biological reaction. (See Leavening, page 18.)

LIQUEUR: *N.* A sweetened, alcoholic liquor, such as brandy, flavored with fruit, nuts, spices, herbs, or seeds. The best liqueurs usually are made with a cognac (see definition) base.

LIQUOR: *N.* (1) A distilled alcoholic beverage, usually whiskey, vodka, gin, rum, and brandy. (2) A natural (as in oysters) or other concentrated liquid surrounding food.

LUKEWARM: *ADJ.* Approximately 97 to 100°F. (body temperature); tepid.

LYONNAISE: *ADJ.* Prepared with onions, as in lyonnaise potatoes.

MACAROON: *N.* A cookie made principally of egg whites, sugar, coconut or almond paste, and flavoring.

MARINADE: *N.* A liquid consisting of one or more ingredients, usually with seasonings, in which a food, usually meat, fowl, or fish, is immersed for a period of time prior to cooking for the purpose of imparting flavor and/or tenderizing.

MARINATE: *V.* To let food stand in a marinade.

MARZIPAN: *N.* A candy made with sweetened almond paste, which is often colored and molded into miniature fruits and vegetables, animals, flowers, and other forms.

MERINGUE: *N.* A mixture of stiffly beaten egg whites and sugar which is (1) piled high on top of pies or other desserts and baked until golden (a soft product), or (2) used to make pie or other dessert shells (a hard product).

MINCE: *V.* To chop into tiny pieces.

MOCHA: *ADJ.* Flavored with coffee, often in combination with chocolate.

MOUSSE: *N.* A light, airy, molded dish, usually a dessert or an appetizer, made with gelatin and/or egg whites, and often whipped cream. Dessert mousses are usually smooth in texture; solid ingredients in appetizer mousses are usually ground, minced, or chopped.

NONPAREILS: *N.* Tiny sugar pellets, in various colors, used to decorate cookies, cakes, doughnuts, candies, and other sweet foods.

PARBOIL: *V.* To partially cook in boiling water, preliminary to additional cooking by a different method.

PARE: *V.* To cut the skin or outer layer off a tight-skinned product, such as a potato. (In contrast to "peel"—see definition.)

PARFAIT: *N.* A dessert made by layering variously

flavored ice creams and/or sherbets, fruit sauces, syrups, and whipped cream in a special, tall, narrow, short-stemmed parfait glass. Eaten with an iced-tea spoon.

PÂTÉ: *N.* (1) Ground or diced meat, fish, or fowl, usually highly seasoned and sometimes with added ingredients, which is packed into a loaf pan and baked. May have an aspic and/or pastry covering. Served cold, thinly sliced, and usually as a first course. (2) A spread made of seasoned, finely ground or pureed meat, fish, or fowl.

PECTIN: *N.* Water-soluble substances found in the cell walls and intercellular layers of fruits. Combined with sugar and acid in correct proportions, pectin forms a gel which is the basis for jellied sweet spreads such as jelly and jam. Commercially packaged powdered or liquid fruit pectin is often used in making these jellied products.

PEEL: *N.* The skin or outer layer of a loose-skinned product such as a banana or a blanched tomato (see definition for Blanch), which can be stripped off with little or no cutting.

PEEL: *V.* To strip the skin or outer layer off a loose-skinned product, such as a banana, with little or no cutting. (In contrast to "pare"—see definition.)

PETIT FOUR: *N.* A fancy, dainty sweet consisting of a very small, usually square, piece of cake covered with icing glaze and usually decorated with a piped flower or other piped decoration. The cake may be layered with a filling(s).

PHYLLO: *N.* Also known as "filo." A paper-thin pastry dough which is usually layered when used in making desserts and other dishes, producing a flaky pastry when baked. Usually available, frozen, in supermarkets. "Phyllo" is from the Greek word meaning "leaf."

PICKLE: *N.* A food prepared in a seasoned vinegar mixture or a brine solution to preserve it and/or impart flavor.

PILAF: *N.* Seasoned rice, often browned, with added meat, poultry, shellfish, and/or vegetables.

PINFEATHER: *N.* An undeveloped, new feather just coming through the skin of a fowl.

PIT: *N.* The centralized seed of certain one-seeded fruits. Also known as a stone.

PIT: *V.* To remove the pit (also known as the stone) from certain one-seeded fruits.

POACH: *V.* To cook in liquid at a simmer. A cooking method used especially when care is to be taken to retain the shape of the food product.

POULTRY: *N.* Domestic birds raised for eggs and/or meat.

PUFF PASTRY: *N.* A light, flaky, high-rising pastry made of many thin, alternating layers of flour dough and butter. Usually available, frozen, in supermarkets.

PUREE: *V.* To whip, press, or mash a solid or semisolid food to a smooth, thick consistency, but not liquefied. A blender, food processor, food mill, or sieve is often used to puree a food.

REDUCE: *V.* To boil or simmer a liquid or thin mixture, uncovered, for the purpose of condensing it by evaporation.

RELISH: *N.* (1) A chopped vegetable(s) and/or fruit(s) cooked in vinegar and seasonings; eaten as a complement to other food. (2) Raw vegetables, olives, and other such food, commonly finger-type, served as an hors d'oeuvre or an appetizer at the table.

RIND: *N.* A usually tough outer layer; for example, the peel of a fruit.

ROAST: *V.* To cook, uncovered, by dry heat in an oven or on an outdoor grill using indirect heat. Also, to cook food products in hot coals or ashes.

ROASTER: *N.* Similar to a Dutch oven (see definition) except oval shaped and usually larger; 8-quart capacity is common for a large roaster.

ROLLING BOIL: *N.* A full, rapid boil, when water-vapor bubbles continuously and rapidly burst below the surface of the liquid, causing extreme agitation over the entire surface as they leave the liquid. A full rolling boil cannot be stirred down.

ROULADE: *N.* A thin piece of meat or other food that is rolled around vegetables or another filling; usually browned and then baked or braised.

RUB: *N.* A dry mixture of ground spices, herbs, and other seasonings that is rubbed on the surface primarily of meats, poultry, fish, and wild game before barbecuing, grilling, or roasting for the purpose of enhancing flavor.

SALT PORK: *N.* Exceptionally fat pork which has been cured in salt; generally used in foods to add flavor.

SAUTÉ: *V.* To cook in a small amount of fat in a skillet over heat.

SCALD: *V.* (1) To heat liquid to just under the boiling point. Milk reaches the scalding point when tiny bubbles appear at the edge of the pan. (2) To dip a food briefly in boiling water. Also known as blanch (see definition).

SCALLION: *N.* Same as a "green onion" (see definition).

SCALLOP: *N.* Any of a number of bivalve mollusks of the family *Pectinidae.* In the United States, the large adductor muscle which closes the valves is the part eaten. The most commonly eaten species are the large sea scallop (*Placopecten magellanicus*) and the tiny bay scallop (*Aequipecten irradians*), although other species are available in various regions of the United States.

SCALLOP: *V.* To bake a food or a combination of foods in a sauce or liquid, usually with a crumb topping.

SCORE: *V.* To cut shallow slits, often in a diamond pattern, in the surface of meats or other foods, to prevent surface fat from curling during cooking, to tenderize, to mark for later cutting, or for decorative purposes.

SHERBET: *N.* Sorbet (see definition) that contains milk or cream.

SHRED: *V.* To cut a semi-hard food into tiny or small strips, usually by rubbing it against a sharp, perforated metal kitchen tool made for this purpose, or by cutting it very thinly with a knife.

SHUCK: *V.* (1) To remove the husks from some foods such as corn. (2) To remove the shells from mollusks, such as oysters.

SIFT: *V.* To put one or more dry ingredients, such as flour, baking powder, and baking soda, through a wire-mesh sifter or sieve for the purpose of removing any lumps and/or mixing the ingredients and/or incorporating air.

SIMMER: *N.* When liquid reaches a temperature just below the boiling point, at which time small water-vapor bubbles, which form principally on the bottom of the pan, slowly rise to the surface and break.

SMOKING: *V.* To cook primarily meats, poultry, fish, shellfish, and wild game by indirect heat in an outdoor smoker or covered grill using hardwood of choice to infuse a smoked flavor. In noncommercial smoking, hardwood is used to produce the desired smoke flavor while charcoal (see Charcoal, 204) generally is used to provide the heat source.

SORBET: *N.* An ice usually made with fruit juice and/or pureed or very finely chopped fruit pulp, and a sugar and water syrup. Egg white or gelatin may also be ingredients.

SOUFFLÉ: *N.* A very light, airy, high-rising, baked dessert or savory usually made with a sauce or mixture containing egg yolks, beaten egg whites, and sometimes pureed or ground food. Special round, straight-sided dishes are generally used for baking soufflés. Soufflés must be served immediately after removal from the oven, before they lose their height and puffiness due to the escape of air.

SPICES: *N.* The pungently flavored roots, stems, bark, seeds, buds, or fruit of certain plants and trees used for seasoning foods.

STEAM: *V.* (1) To cook food in steam by placing it in a perforated, metal container suspended over boiling or simmering water in a covered pan. (2) To cook food in an airtight container lowered into low-simmering water, as in steamed puddings.

STIR: *V.* To move a utensil, usually a spoon, through a liquid or a pliable mixture, principally in a circular motion around a bowl or pan, for the purpose of mixing ingredients or preventing a mixture from sticking to the bottom of a pan during cooking.

STIR-FRY: *V.* To cook, in a wok (see definition) or skillet, bite-sized slices or pieces of meat and/or vegetables in a small amount of oil over medium-high to high heat, stirring and turning constantly. The vegetables are cooked until just tender but still crisp.

STOCK: *N.* Same as broth (see definition).

TAPIOCA: *N.* A starch from the root of the tropical cassava plant. Available in granular form (quick-cooking tapioca) and two sizes of small, round pellets (small pearl and large pearl tapioca). Most commonly used to make tapioca pudding and as a thickener in fruit pies and other fruit desserts. Also available in flour form.

TEPID: *ADJ.* Moderately warm; lukewarm (see definition).

TOAST: *V.* To brown a food by exposure to dry heat.

TRIPLE SEC: *N.* An orange-flavored liqueur (see definition).

TRUSS: *V.* To bind the legs and wings of a fowl close to the carcass, and to bind the carcass cavities, usually with poultry skewers and/or cotton string, in preparation for cooking.

VINAIGRETTE: *N.* A salad dressing (or sauce) made of oil and vinegar. Seasonings and other additions may be used. Variations on vinaigrette substitute lemon juice or wine for the vinegar. (See headnotes for Vinaigrette Dressings and Basic Vinaigrette Dressing, page 129.)

VINEGAR: *N.* An acetic and other acid solution produced by fermentation. Four common types of vinegar are cider, distilled white, wine, and malt. Herb, fruit, nut, and other flavored vinegars usually are made by flavoring wine vinegars.

WHIP: *V.* To beat (see definition) very rapidly and vigorously for the purpose of incorporating air and increasing volume, as in whipped cream.

WINE: *N.* The fermented juice of grapes. Also, the fermented juice of other fruits or other plant products.

WOK: *N.* A bowl-shaped, Asian cooking utensil used like a skillet; especially good for stir-frying (see definition for Stir-Fry).

ZEST: *N.* Very small, thin curls or pieces of the colored, outer part of the peel of citrus fruits; used for flavoring or decoration.

Boiling Point of Water at Various Altitudes

As altitude increases, atmospheric pressure decreases due to a thinner blanket of air. As the atmospheric pressure decreases, causing less weight of air on the surface of water, the boiling point of water also decreases. At sea level, water boils at 212° F. The following chart shows the boiling point of water at higher altitudes.

Altitude	Boiling Point of Water
Sea Level	212° F.
1,000 ft.	210° F.
2,000 ft.	208° F.
3,000 ft.	206° F.

4,000 ft.	204° F.
5,000 ft.	203° F.
6,000 ft.	201° F.
7,000 ft.	199° F.
8,000 ft.	197° F.

To find out the altitude of the location in which you live, call the local Extension Service office serving your county or your local district conservationist with the U.S. Department of Agriculture, Natural Resources Conservation Service.

Weather conditions also affect the boiling point of water, but to a far less extent than altitude. At a given altitude, high barometric pressure causes water to boil at a somewhat higher temperature and low barometric pressure causes water to boil at a somewhat lower temperature. Therefore, when recipes call for cooking foods to a specific number of degrees above the boiling point of water, it is a good idea to check the boiling point of water with a candy thermometer just before making these products.

Food Safety

There is greater prevalence of foodborne illness than most people realize. It is estimated that 33 million cases of food poisoning occur in the United States each year. It is further estimated that 85 percent of these cases could have been avoided if consumers had followed safe food storage, handling, and cooking practices.

Food poisoning, caused by harmful bacteria, parasites, and viruses, normally produces intestinal flu-like symptoms which last a few hours to several days. However, in the case of botulism, or when foodborne illness strikes infants and young people, pregnant women, elderly people, ill persons, or people with weakened immune systems, it can be serious or sometimes fatal.

You are usually unaware that harmful bacteria are present. They are microscopic in size, and you normally can't taste, smell, or see them. Of course, when food has an unusual odor or appearance, it should be discarded immediately, untasted. Most moldy food should be discarded. The poisons that molds can form are found *under* the surface of food. Hard cheeses, salamis, and firm fruits and vegetables can sometimes be safely saved if a large section of the food around and under the mold is cut away.

Safe storage, sanitation, and proper cooking are critical factors in food safety. Below are general food safety guidelines, as well as particular food safety procedures for packed lunches, picnics, and microwave ovens. Food safety guidelines for several specific foods are found in other sections of *The Blue Ribbon Country Cookbook,* as follows:

Meat Safety, page 134
Meat Safety for Outdoor Cooking, page 204
Poultry and Stuffings (Dressings) Safety,
    page 168
Fish and Shellfish Safety, page 184
Egg Safety, page 220

- When you are doing errands, do your grocery shopping last—just before you return home. At the grocery store, select perishable foods requiring refrigeration after you have selected the nonperishable items on your list. Transport perishable foods home and get them under refrigeration as soon as possible.

- Do not purchase any food you will not use by the expiration date given on the packaging.

- Refrigerate perishable foods at 40° F. or below. Keep your refrigerator as cold as possible without freezing stored milk and fresh vegetables. Keep your freezer and the freezing compartment of your refrigerator at 0° F. or below. At 0° F. bacterial growth is stopped. Use an appliance thermometer to check the temperatures of your refrigerator and freezer.

- Thaw food in the refrigerator or in the microwave oven (see Microwave Ovens [page 15–16] for procedural information), not on the kitchen counter or in the sink. Thawing

EQUIVALENCIES

Food	Quantity	Approximate Equivalency	Food	Quantity	Approximate Equivalency
Apples	1 lb.	3 c. sliced	**Cream**		
Beans, navy, dried	½ lb. (1 c.)	2½ c. cooked	sour cream (commercial)	8 oz.	1 c.
Bran flakes crumbs	2 c. unrolled flakes	1 c. rolled crumbs	sour cream (homemade)	8 oz.	1 c.
Bread crumbs			whipping cream	1 c. (½ pint)	2 c. whipped
dry bread	1 slice	¼ c. processed or rolled crumbs	**Gelatin, unflavored**	¼-oz. envelope	2 tsp.
fresh bread	1 slice	½ c. crumbs	**Honey**	16 oz.	1⅓ c.
Butter	¼ lb. (1 stick)	½ c. or 8 tbsp.	**Mandarin orange segments, canned**	11-oz. can, drained	1 c.
Carrots, fresh	1 lb.	3 c. shredded		11-oz. can, drained; segments cut in half widthwise	¾+ c.
Cheese					
cheddar	4 oz.	1 c. shredded			
cottage cheese	8 oz.	1 c.		15-oz. can, drained	1½ c.
cream cheese	3 oz.	¼ c. plus 2 tbsp.		15-oz. can, drained; segments cut in half widthwise	1¼ c.
Parmesan	4 oz.	1 c. grated			
Romano	4 oz.	1 c. grated			
Swiss	4 oz.	1 c. shredded			
Chocolate			**Milk**		
baking squares	1 oz.	1 square	evaporated	5-oz. can	½ c. plus 2 tbsp.
chips	6 oz.	1 c.		12-oz. can	1½ c.
Coconut			sweetened condensed	14-oz. can	1¼ c.
flaked	7 oz.	2⅔ c.			
Cookie crumbs			**Mushrooms, fresh**	8 oz.	3 c. sliced
chocolate wafers	15 2¼-inch wafers	1 c. rolled crumbs	**Nuts**		
vanilla wafers	22 wafers	1 c. rolled crumbs	almonds	1 lb. in shells	1 c. shelled
			Brazil nuts	1 lb. in shells	1½ c. shelled
Cracker crumbs			cashews	1 lb. shelled	3¼ c.
graham crackers	20 squares	1½ c. finely rolled crumbs	hazelnuts	1 lb. in shells	1½ c. shelled
			hickory nuts	1 lb. in shells	⅔ c. shelled
Ritz crackers	12 crackers	½ c. rolled crumbs	peanuts	1 lb. in shells	2 c. shelled
saltines	10 crackers	½ c. rolled crumbs	pecans	1 lb. in shells	2 c. halves, shelled

Food	Quantity	Approximate Equivalency	Food	Quantity	Approximate Equivalency
Nuts (*cont.*)			**Sugar**		
walnuts, black	1 lb. in shells	½ c. shelled	brown, light or dark	1 lb.	2¼ c. packed
walnuts, English	1 lb. in shells	1¾ c. halves, shelled	granulated	1 lb.	2¼ c.
Pasta			powdered	1 lb. unsifted	4 c.
macaroni, elbow	7 oz. (2 c.)	4 c. cooked	**Syrup, corn, light or dark**	16 oz. (1 pint)	2 c.
noodles, egg	8 oz.	6 c. cooked	**Water chestnuts, sliced, canned**	8-oz. can, drained	1 c.
spaghetti	8 oz.	4 c. cooked			
Popcorn	¼ c.	8 c. popped			
Rice, white, long-grain	1 c.	3½ c. cooked			
Rice, wild	1¼ c.	4 c. cooked			
Shortening, vegetable	1 lb.	2⅓ c.			
Soup, condensed, canned	10¾-oz. can	1½ c.			

THICKENER EQUIVALENCIES

2 tablespoons flour =
2 tablespoons quick-cooking tapioca =
1 tablespoon cornstarch =
1 tablespoon arrowroot

proceeds from the outside in, so surface bacteria can multiply to illness-causing levels before food is thawed all the way through.

• Before storing packages of raw meat, poultry, fish, and shellfish in the refrigerator, place the packages on plates to prevent raw juices from dripping onto other foods.

• The danger temperature zone for the growth of foodborne bacteria is between 40 and 140°F. In this temperature range, foodborne bacteria can double in number every 20 minutes. The rule is: never leave either raw or cooked perishable foods unrefrigerated for more than 2 hours. Normally, bacteria do not multiply to dangerous levels in less than 2 hours.

• Promptly refrigerate leftovers. When refrigerating a large quantity of food, divide it among small, shallow containers for quick cooling. Avoid packing the refrigerator. To keep food at a safe temperature, it is necessary for the cool refrigerator air to circulate.

• Hot cooking temperatures kill most bacteria found in raw foods. For information on safe cooking temperatures for meats, poultry and stuffings (dressings), fish, shellfish, and eggs, refer to the other food safety sections listed above.

• Use a meat thermometer or instant thermometer (page 28) to gauge the internal temperature of meats, poultry, and other foods.

• Properly refrigerated, leftover cooked foods may safely be served cold. When reheating leftover cooked foods, bring gravies, sauces, and soups to a boil. Thoroughly heat other leftover foods to at least 165°F (steaming hot).

• An astonishing number of bacteria are carried by hands. Wash your hands with soap and hot water immediately before commencing to prepare food. Wash your hands again with soap and hot water after handling raw or cooked meat, poultry, fish, shellfish, and eggs, before you handle other food. Use a utensil, rather than your hands, to mix meat, salads, and other foods.

• Wash kitchen tools and equipment, cutting boards and other work surfaces, sink, and faucet handles with hot, soapy water after they come in contact with raw or cooked meat, poultry, fish, shellfish, and eggs, and before they come in contact with other food.

• Use clean utensils and a clean platter or bowl to serve cooked meat, poultry, fish, shellfish, and eggs. Do not reuse utensils, platters, or bowls that came in contact with these foods before they were cooked unless they are first washed in hot, soapy water.

• Do not use food from damaged containers. Check cans for dents and bulging lids, and glass jars for cracks. Check paper packages for leaks and stains.

• Do not purchase refrigerated foods that are not cold to the touch. Frozen foods should be completely solid.

• Wash fresh fruits and vegetables well to remove soil as well as bacteria, viruses, and insecticide sprays.

• Wash kitchen towels, dishcloths, and sponges often. When washing the cloth items, use the hottest water setting on the washer.

• When entertaining, keep perishable foods which will be served cold, refrigerated until serving time. Remove perishable foods from serving tables when they have been unrefrigerated more than 2 hours, or serve cold perishable foods on ice. Hot foods left on serving tables for consumption by guests over a period of time should be kept heated to 145°F or above, by use of chafing dishes or other suitable methods.

• Keep pets and insects away from food, kitchen counters and sinks, and dining tables.

• For additional information on the safe storage, handling, and preparation of meat and poultry products, as well as information on the labeling of these foods, call the Meat and Poultry Hotline, a service of the U.S. Department of Agriculture's Food Safety and Inspection Service at 888-674-6854 (TTY at 800-256-7072), Monday through Friday, 10:00 A.M. –4:00 P.M. Eastern time; or visit the Food Safety and Inspection Service Web site at www.fsis.usda.gov; or email at mphotline.fsis@usda.gov.

PACKED LUNCHES

• Keep perishable foods cold. If a refrigerator is not available for storage of your packed lunch, pack it in a small, lunch-sized, insulated cooler or bag. Place a zipper-seal plastic bag filled with ice cubes or a frozen packet of ice or ice substitute in the cooler or bag to keep the contents cold. A thermos may be used to keep milk or juice cold.

• If you prepare your lunch the night before, refrigerate the perishables, such as meat, poultry, fish, and shellfish, and sandwiches and foods containing perishables such as eggs and mayonnaise. Pack your lunch the next morning just before leaving.

• Good food choices for packed lunches are:

~ Canned meats, poultry, and fish which can be opened and eaten immediately. If the can does not have a self-opener, make sure that the can opener you use has been washed.

~ Commercially precooked and ready-to-eat meats such as bologna, salami, and corned beef.

~ Fresh fruits and vegetables.

• Keep perishable foods that will be microwaved at lunchtime in a refrigerator or in an insulated cooler or bag.

• Do not leave lunch containers in the sun or near a warm radiator or other heat source.

• Wash your hands with soap and hot water before eating lunch, or use disposable wet wipes.

- Wash the lunch container after each use to prevent bacteria from growing. An occasional washing with baking soda will help eliminate odors.

PICNICS

- Pack all perishable foods in an insulated cooler kept cool with sufficient ice cubes or frozen packets of ice or ice substitute.

- Thoroughly chill perishable foods before placing them in the cooler. Cans or bottles of beverages should be cold before placing them in the same cooler with perishable foods.

- If you are packing a large quantity of cold beverages for a number of people, pack the beverages in one insulated container and the perishable foods in another. This will help avert the danger of perishable foods being exposed to warm air by frequent opening of the cooler lid.

- Salads with commercial mayonnaise are safe if kept cold. Avoid cream and custard pies, cream puffs, cream-filled rolls, and other pudding- and custard-like foods.

- When driving to and from the picnic site, try to avoid transporting the coolers in the hot trunk of the car. If possible, carry the coolers in the passenger area.

- At the picnic site, keep the coolers in the shade. Avoid opening the lid of the cooler holding perishable foods too often. If possible, replenish melting ice in the cooler.

- If running water is not available for picnickers responsible for the final preparation and serving of the food to wash their hands, take along disposable wet wipes.

- In hot weather of 85°F or above, do not leave food out more than 1 hour (not including cooking time for items grilled at the picnic site).

- Put leftover, perishable foods back in the cooler as soon as you finish eating. The leftovers should be safe to save if you are gone from home no longer than 4 to 5 hours, and the perishable foods are kept cold in the cooler except when cooked and/or served.

MICROWAVE OVENS

Unique characteristics of microwave cooking present problems in achieving the uniform cooking or reheating of food. Uneven cooking in microwave ovens can leave cool or cold spots in food where foodborne pathogens can survive and cause illness.

When food is cooked or reheated in a microwave oven, cold spots in the food can occur because of the irregular way in which the microwaves enter the oven and are absorbed by the food. Further, microwaves cook food from the outside to the inside; therefore, outer portions of food may become fully cooked or reheated while inner portions remain cool. Additionally, microwaves heat fats, sugars, and liquids more quickly than other food elements. These factors and others create food safety hazards which can be alleviated with the application of special microwaving procedures.

- Use only containers approved for microwave use. Glass and glass ceramic dishes are safe for use in a microwave oven. Do not reuse containers and trays provided with microwavable foods. They have been designed for one-time use with a particular food product.

Avoid using metal-trimmed dishes and containers, and metal twist ties. TV dinners in aluminum foil trays no deeper than $3/4$ inch may be microwaved. Large pieces of aluminum foil should not be used; however, small pieces of foil may be used to cover poultry legs and other small areas over food, provided the foil ends are wrapped smoothly over the food or area being covered. Any aluminum foil should be kept at least 1 inch from the sides of the oven.

Do not use dairy cartons, margarine tubs, and other such containers designed for cold storage. The high heat of a microwave oven could cause chemicals from these containers to invade cooking food.

Carefully follow the instructions in the manufacturer's manual that accompanies your microwave.

- Cover the food container used for micro-waving food with a glass lid or plastic wrap. Vent the plastic wrap and make certain it does not touch the food. (Unless plastic wrap is heavy duty, it could melt when coming in contact with hot food.) Covering food in this manner helps retain steam, which aids in obtaining thorough and even cooking, and in destroying bacteria and other pathogens. A small amount of water added to the food assists to create addi-tional steam.

Waxed paper is also safe for covering food in the microwave. Plain white paper towels and napkins may be used to cover food pro-vided they have not been made from re-cycled material.

- Rotate the food container during cooking to achieve even cooking. If your microwave does not have a turntable, rotate the food container by hand once or twice during cooking. Move food inside the container several times during cooking; stir soups, stews, and sauces.

- Adhere to the standing time called for in the recipe or package instructions. Food contin-ues to cook during the standing time. Speci-fied standing times are usually about $\frac{1}{3}$ the length of cooking times.

- Use the microwave oven temperature probe, a meat thermometer, or an instant thermome-ter to make certain that food has reached a safe temperature. Check the internal temper-ature of the food at several places.

- Debone large pieces of meat before cooking. Bone can prevent meat around it from cook-ing thoroughly.

- Cook large pieces of meat at 50 percent power for longer time periods. This will help achieve proper cooking of inner areas of the meat without overcooking the outer por-tions. Commercial oven bags are safe for use in the microwave and are useful in helping to secure even cooking and a tender final product.

- Do not use the microwave oven for cooking whole, stuffed poultry. Poultry bones and density of the stuffing (dressing) prevent even and thorough cooking.

- Before commencing to thaw food in the microwave oven, remove the food from its store wrap. Plastic trays, paper wrapping, and other packaging material not designed for microwaving may contain chemicals which could transfer to the food under the high heat of a microwave oven.

- Do not defrost or hold food at room tem-perature in the microwave for longer than 2 hours.

- After thawing food in the microwave, immediately proceed to finish cooking it. The heat of the microwave may cause outer portions of the food to commence cooking, raising the outer temperature of the food to a level conducive to quick bacteria multiplication.

- If the microwave oven is used to partially cook food, immediately transfer the partially cooked food to a conventional oven, broiler, or grill for completion of the cooking. Do not partially cook food and then complete the cooking at a later time (even if the par-tially cooked food will be stored in the refrigerator).

- Heat leftovers and other cooked foods to at least 165°F (steaming hot).

The Functions of Ingredients in Batters and Doughs

Flour, liquid, fat, sugar, eggs, leavening, and salt are the basic ingredients used in batters and doughs. The quality of home-baked products depends on the proportions of ingredients, how they are mixed, and the cooking temperatures and times. These relationships affect the color, flavor, texture, shape, and volume of the final product.

FLOUR

Flour contains proteins that combine with liquid to form gluten. This sticky, elastic material gets stronger and more elastic as the batter is stirred or the dough is kneaded. These strands of gluten form a network of cells that expand when heated. Baking "sets" this framework.

Flour also contains starch, which absorbs liquid and swells. When heated, this adds body to the framework of baked foods.

Three common types of flour are:

All-purpose flour. A blend of hard and soft wheat flours, which makes it versatile for many products. It is usually enriched, and may be bleached or unbleached.

Bread flour. Made from hard wheat and is rich in protein, which forms strong gluten. It is desirable for yeast breads.

Cake flour. Made from soft wheat. As it is lower in protein, less gluten is developed. Thus, it produces more tender cakes.

When the same amount of liquid is used, both all-purpose flour and bread flour produce a stiffer dough than cake flour.

Whole wheat, buckwheat, rye, barley, and soy are among other types of flours used in batters and doughs.

LIQUID

Some type of liquid is needed to develop the gluten, gelatinize the starch, activate the leavening agent, and dissolve the sugar and salt to distribute them through the batter or dough.

The proportion of water and flour helps determine the amount of gluten formed.

Milk is the most commonly used liquid, although fruit juice and water also can be used. Whole milk is 87.69 percent water and also contains protein. Milk tends to give baked products a finer texture, better color, and somewhat different flavor than water.

FAT

Shortening, cooking oil, butter, and margarine make baked products tender and rich. They also help retain freshness and serve to blend and distribute flavorings. When butter is used, it gives a special flavor to the final product.

Since fat is insoluble in any of the other ingredients, it separates the particles of dough. During baking, the fat melts while other ingredients are setting up. It is easy for the leavening gas to expand into the tiny areas of melted fat. However, excess fat weakens the gluten structure and can cause the product to decrease in volume or fall.

Vegetable shortenings and oils are 100 percent fat. By contrast, butter and margarine combine 80 percent fat with 20 percent water and milk solids.

SUGAR

Although primarily added for sweetening, sugar has additional functions. As it caramelizes with heat, sugar helps the product brown during baking. It also increases the tenderness of the product.

Honey, corn syrup, and molasses are sugars and can be substituted for granulated sugar. However, the amount of liquid used also must be adjusted.

Noncaloric sweetening agents require special

recipes. They contribute a sweet flavor but do not tenderize or increase browning. Sometimes they lose their sweetening power and become bitter with heat.

EGGS

By their emulsifying action, egg yolks bring about even distribution of fat in batters and doughs. They promote tenderness and a fine texture. The egg proteins, along with gluten, form the structure of the product.

Beaten eggs, particularly beaten egg whites, aid in leavening because of the formation of tiny air cells. The air expands on heating and steam is formed from the moisture of the egg. As the egg proteins coagulate with heating, the cell walls become set.

LEAVENING

Leavening is produced by the release and/or expansion of gas within a batter or dough. A variety of substances contribute to lighten the batter or dough.

Air is incorporated in baking mixtures in several ways. The most common is folding beaten egg whites into the batter. Other ways include beating whole eggs, creaming sugar and fat, and beating the batter itself.

Heating the batter or dough causes the air bubbles to expand, making the batter light. Angel food cakes depend on the incorporation of air for one-half to two-thirds of their leavening.

Baking powder releases gas during mixing and/or baking and is used in most cakes and quick breads. Baking powder contains baking soda (sodium bicarbonate) and acid-reacting ingredients. In the presence of moisture and heat, these components react to form carbon dioxide gas, which expands and leavens.

Baking powder contains cornstarch to keep the mixture dry by absorbing moisture, and to standardize measuring.

Baking soda is required to neutralize an acid ingredient such as buttermilk, sour cream, sour milk, or molasses. The combination releases carbon dioxide gas, which leavens the batter or dough.

Steam provides the leavening in batters containing large proportions of liquid, such as popovers and cream puffs. When water is heated, it produces more than 1,600 times its volume in steam.

Yeast is a microscopic plant that grows rapidly in a warm, moist medium. It ferments sugar and/or starch to form carbon dioxide gas and alcohol. The gas is the principal leavener, but the alcohol vaporizes during baking and also helps in leavening. During baking, the heat expands the gas, stops the yeast action in the raised dough, evaporates the alcohol, and sets the gluten.

SALT

The major function of salt in baked products is to add and enhance flavor. In yeast breads, it helps to control the action of the yeast, thus improving texture.

This section consists of edited extractions from Publication N-2857: What's in a Recipe? *published by Iowa State University, Cooperative Extension Service, Ames, Iowa, in March 1986, and prepared by Phyllis Olson and Diane Nelson.*

For additional information on the function of ingredients in yeast dough, see Yeast Breads and Rolls, page 346.

Techniques

TO COOK AND BAKE AT HIGH ALTITUDES

Atmospheric pressure decreases as altitude increases. This fact has several ramifications which affect cooking and baking. As altitude increases:

- water and other liquids boil at lower temperatures;

- water and other liquids evaporate faster at a given temperature;

- leavening gases expand more.

These principles necessitate adjustments in ingredients, temperature, time, and procedures in the cooking and baking of many foods at high altitudes. Most cookbook recipes, including those herein, are written for use at sea level. (see Note, page 21). This section gives some guidelines for adjusting sea-level recipes for use at higher altitudes. While adjustments for altitude are definitive in the preparation of some food products such as the processing of home-canned foods, exact formulas cannot be given for modifications of sea-level recipes for many items, such as cakes, quick and yeast breads, and cookies. Cooks and bakers will need to experiment with adjustments to specific recipes for these products in order to fine-tune modifications—if modifications are needed at all.

At sea level, the temperature of boiling water is 212°F. For each 500 feet above sea level, the boiling point of water decreases approximately 1°F. See Boiling Point of Water at Various Altitudes (page 10) for a chart and a more complete explanation.

GENERAL COOKING: Because water boils at lower temperatures at higher altitudes, it often takes longer to cook foods at high elevations. In addition, it may be necessary to increase liquid due to greater vaporization before foods are fully cooked.

BOILED CANDIES AND FROSTINGS: When making boiled candies and frostings, the temperature of the boiling sugar mixture (syrup) exceeds the temperature of boiling water as the water in the syrup evaporates. The less water in the syrup, the higher the temperature rises above the boiling point of water. The temperature of the boiling syrup, gauged by a candy thermometer, is the most accurate way of determining when sufficient water has evaporated.

In principle, for each 500 feet above sea level, the temperature to which candies and frostings are boiled should be decreased 1°F. from the temperature called for in sea-level recipes. However, another factor should be taken into account: at any given altitude, the atmospheric pressure frequently varies somewhat due to changing weather conditions. Thus, atmospheric conditions also affect the boiling point of water (see page 10). Therefore, it is a good practice to test the temperature of boiling water immediately before commencing to make boiled candy or frosting.

To test for the boiling point of water, attach the candy thermometer to a saucepan of water. Bring the water to a boil and let it boil for a few minutes, or until the thermometer indicator stops rising. The thermometer reading will give the current boiling point of water from which any necessary adjustments in the recipe can be calculated. For example, if the thermometer registers 210°F (2°F below 212°F, the boiling point of water at sea level) and the sea-level candy recipe to be followed calls for the syrup to be brought to 234°F, the temperature to which the syrup should be boiled will be decreased 2°F, or to 232°F.

It should be noted that candy thermometers are not always precisely accurate. Testing for the boiling point of water will accommodate any inaccuracy in the thermometer.

SHORTENED CAKES: Most sea-level cake recipes do not require adjustment when used at alti-

GUIDELINE ADJUSTMENTS TO SEA-LEVEL RECIPES
FOR SHORTENED CAKES BAKED AT HIGH ALTITUDES

Adjustment	Altitude of Baking Location		
	3,000 feet	5,000 feet	7,000 feet
Baking Powder For each teaspoon, decrease	1/8 teaspoon	1/8 to 1/4 teaspoon	1/4 teaspoon
Sugar For each cup, decrease	0 to 1 tablespoon	0 to 2 tablespoons	1 to 3 tablespoons
Liquid For each cup, increase	1 to 2 tablespoons	2 to 4 tablespoons	3 to 4 tablespoons

tudes of less than 3,000 feet above sea level. At altitudes of 3,000 feet and above, adjustments may be necessary.

At high altitudes, cakes made using sea-level recipes may rise excessively due to less atmospheric pressure. This overexpansion stretches the cell structure of the cake, causing coarse texture or causing the cake to fall if the cells break. A decrease in the leavening agent usually will correct this problem. Also, an increase in baking temperature by 15°F to 25°F will help set the cake structure before it collapses.

Faster and excessive evaporation of liquid in cakes baked at high altitudes causes dryness and a higher concentration of sugar, resulting in a weakened cell structure. (One of the functions of sugar in cake batter is to increase tenderness; see The Functions of Ingredients in Batters and Doughs, page 17.) This problem may be alleviated by a reduction in sugar and/or an increase in liquid. Because eggs help strengthen cell structure, the addition of an egg or an egg yolk may be warranted.

Fat, like sugar, weakens cell structure. Therefore, in a very rich cake, a reduction of fat by 1 to 2 tablespoons per cup may be part of the solution.

The chart, above, gives ranges for adjustments in baking powder, sugar, and liquid for shortened cakes baked at designated high altitudes. It is suggested that the smaller adjustments be used when first modifying a recipe.

ANGEL FOOD AND SPONGE CAKES: Air is one of the primary leavening agents in angel food and sponge cakes (see page 448). Much of the air in these cakes is incorporated by the inclusion of numerous beaten egg whites. At high altitudes, air incorporation can be reduced in these cakes by beating the egg whites only until soft peaks fall over, and not until they are stiff. An increase in flour by 1 or 2 tablespoons, a reduction in sugar by 1 or 2 tablespoons, and an increase in baking temperature are other suggested modifications.

QUICK BREADS: To adjust sea-level recipes for baking cake-type quick breads at high altitudes, follow the recommendations for Shortened Cakes, above.

Biscuit and muffin-type quick bread recipes generally need no alteration for use in high altitudes due to the resilience of their cell structure, which deters overexpansion. However, due to inadequate neutralization, baking powder and baking soda can sometimes produce a bitter or alkaline taste in these products baked at high altitudes. If this occurs, flavor generally can be enhanced by a slight decrease in these leavening agents.

YEAST BREADS: Yeast breads rise more rapidly at

high altitudes. As a shorter rising period reduces the desired time for development of flavor, it is particularly advisable to let the dough rise twice before shaping. Be careful to allow the dough to rise only until doubled in bulk (see Raising Dough, page 348).

Flour is generally drier in high, dry locations, making the flour capable of greater liquid absorption. As a result, less flour may be required at higher elevations.

COOKIES: While many sea-level cookie recipes may be used without adjustment at high altitudes, slight adjustments often improve the quality of the end results. Possible adjustments include slight increases in baking temperature, liquid, and flour; and slight decreases in baking powder or baking soda, sugar, and fat.

PIECRUST: Sea-level piecrust recipes usually do not require modification for use at high altitudes. However, slightly more liquid may be needed due to the general occurrence of drier flour in higher elevations.

PUDDINGS AND CREAM PIE FILLINGS: At altitudes above 5,000 feet, puddings and cream pie fillings made in a double boiler do not reach a high enough temperature to achieve maximum gelatinization of cornstarch or flour ingredients used as thickeners. Therefore, in locations above 5,000 feet, these products should be made in a saucepan over direct heat.

HOME-CANNED PRODUCTS: Altitude is a critical factor in the safe canning of foods at every altitude. Length of processing time in boiling-water bath canning and pounds of pressure in pressure canning are determined, in part, by the altitude of the canning location.

NOTE: Recipes specifically written for use at high altitudes are available. Contact the local Cooperative Extension Service office serving your county for assistance in securing such recipes.

Several excellent high-altitude recipe booklets have been published by Colorado State University Cooperative Extension. Copies may be secured at reasonable prices. For information, visit their Web site at www.cerc.colostate.edu/titles.html#food or write:

Cooperative Extension Resource Center
115 General Services Building
Colorado State University
Fort Collins, Colorado 80523

TO USE HERBS

WHAT ARE HERBS? There is not a clear-cut consensus as to the definition of an herb (pronounced "erb" in the United States and "herb" in England). Herbalists, lexicographers, botanists, and culinarians vary in their opinions as to what makes an herb an herb—particularly when contrasting herbs with spices.

As applied to culinary use, I define herbs and spices as follows:

Herbs: The fresh or dried green leaves of certain plants used for flavoring foods.

Spices: The pungently flavored roots, stems, bark, seeds, buds, or fruit of certain plants and trees used for seasoning foods.

Strictly speaking, by these definitions dill-weed and fennel weed are herbs, while dill seed and fennel seed are spices. However, dill seed and fennel seed often are categorized as herbs along with the leaves of these plants. I plead "culinary license" in siding with these exceptions in my own definitions.

Herbalists frequently label certain flowers as herbs based upon their aromatic, cosmetic, or medicinal utility. However, for culinary purposes, I prefer to exclude edible flowers from designation as herbs (see Edible Flowers, page 316).

Since ancient times, both herbs and spices have been highly valued for their medicinal, aromatic, cosmetic, and culinary uses as well as for their beauty. In early history, they also were employed in religious rites and were steeped in symbolism. Herbs, an essential part of Roman gardens, were

(Article continues on page 26)

HERB CHART

	SOUPS STEWS	SALADS	MEATS	POULTRY
BASIL	Tomato, Vegetable, Chicken, and Minestrone Soups; Beef, Pork, Veal and Bratwurst Stews	Greens; Vegetable; Tomato and Onion; Chicken; Shellfish; Italian and Vinaigrette Salad Dressings	Beef, Pork, Veal, and Lamb; Meat Casseroles; Swiss Steak; Italian Meat and Sauce Dishes	Baked Chicken; Sautéed Chicken Breasts; Turkey Dishes
BAY LEAVES	Vegetable Beef Soup; Beef and Chicken Broth; Corn Chowder; Bratwurst, Beef, and Fish Stews	Seldom Used	Beef; Beef and Noodles; Sauerbraten; Italian Meat Sauces; Lamb	Certain Chicken Dishes such as Chicken Cacciatore
CHERVIL	Vegetable and Cream Soups; Broths; Decoration for Most Soups; Fish Soups and Stews; Meat and Vegetable Stews	Vegetable; Chicken; Turkey; Greens; Sliced Tomatoes; Cottage Cheese; Egg; Potato	Beef; Veal; Béarnaise Sauce	Baked Chicken; Chicken Casseroles; Cornish Game Hens; Turkey Dishes; Stuffings
CHIVES	Vegetable and Chicken Noodle Soups; Soup Topping; Decoration for Many Soups and Stews	Greens; Vegetable; Cucumber; Potato; Cottage Cheese; Avocado; Vinaigrette Salad Dressing	Ground Beef and Pork Dishes; Ham Salad; Veal	Chicken Breasts; Turkey Casseroles
CORIANDER (Cilantro; Chinese Parsley)	Tomato Soup; Garnish for Chicken and Pea Soups	Greens; Vegetable; Bell Pepper; Tomato	Garnish for Beef and Pork; Lamb; Smoked Meats	Cornish Game Hens; Chicken
DILLWEED	Cucumber, Vegetable, Tomato, Split Pea, and Chicken Soups; Chowders	Cucumber; Shrimp; Cottage Cheese; Cabbage; Potato; Vegetable; Fish; Salad Dressings	Cold Sliced Beef; Veal; Lamb	Chicken Casseroles; Turkey Dishes
FENNEL WEED	Tomato, Cucumber, and Lentil Soups; Meat and Fish Stews	Shrimp; Other Shellfish; Fish; Green Bean; Pasta; Greens; Salad Dressings	Beef; Pork; Lamb	Chicken; Goose; Duck
MARJORAM	Chicken, Onion, Fish, Tomato, and Potato Soups; Meat and Vegetable Stews	Greens; Vegetable; Cottage Cheese; Cabbage; Fish; Shellfish; Chicken; Salad Dressings	Veal; Ground Beef Dishes; Braised Beef Dishes; Lamb; Meat Sauces	Baked Chicken; Turkey; Chicken and Turkey Casseroles; Duck; Stuffings

FISH SHELLFISH	WILD GAME	VEGETABLES	EGGS CHEESE	BREADS
Halibut; Baked and Poached Fish; Salmon; Tuna; All Shellfish	Quail; Venison; Rabbit; Duck; Moose	Tomatoes; Zucchini; Potatoes; Lima Beans; Peas; Corn; Carrots; Asparagus; Broccoli	Scrambled Eggs; Omelets; Pasta and Cheese Dishes; Cheese Spreads; Combined with Grated Parmesan or Romano Cheese; Cottage Cheese; Cream Cheese; Cheese Sauces	Yeast Breads; Muffins; Toasted Herb Bread; Sautéed Toast Points
Poached Salmon; Poached Shellfish; Shrimp Dishes	Braised Pheasant; Venison; Rabbit; Antelope; Grouse; Partridge; Quail	Potatoes; Tomatoes; Beets; Sauerkraut	Rarely Used	Not Used
Mild Fish Fillets; Baked Fish Dishes; Fish Sauces	Partridge; Quail; Pheasant; Woodcock; Wild Turkey; Stuffings	Carrots; Spinach; Potatoes; Peas; Zucchini; Tomatoes; Cabbage; Squash	Omelets; Scrambled Eggs; Baked Egg Dishes; Cottage Cheese; Cream Cheese; Cheese Dips and Spreads; Cheese Sauces	Toasted Herb Bread
Salmon; Most Baked and Broiled Fish; Shellfish Dishes; Green Sauce	Quail; Rabbit; Partridge; Wild Turkey	Potatoes; Creamed Peas; Tomatoes; Lima Beans; Corn; Onions; Artichokes	Omelets; All Egg Dishes; Cheese Sauces; Cottage Cheese; Cream Cheese	Toasted Herb Bread
All Shellfish	Quail; Grouse	Corn; Tomatoes; Onions; Beets; Potatoes; Salsa	Cream Cheese Spreads; Cottage Cheese	Quick Breads
Salmon; Tuna; All Fish and Shellfish; Green Sauce	Prairie Chicken; Wild Turkey Breast	Potatoes; Parsnips; Carrots; Cucumbers; Peas; Green Beans; Brussels Sprouts; Cauliflower	Baked Egg Dishes; Creamed Eggs; Cottage Cheese; Casseroles with Cheese Sauces; Swiss and Cheddar Cheese Spreads; Cheese Sauces	Yeast Breads; Bagels; Croutons; Toasted Herb Bread; Sautéed Toast Points
Broiled Fish Fillets; Salmon; Mackerel; Shellfish; Fish Sauces	Duck; Goose; Moose	Tomatoes; Cucumbers; Green Beans; Cabbage; Onions; Zucchini; Potatoes	Vegetable Omelets; Baked Egg Dishes; Cottage Cheese; Cheese Spreads	Yeast Breads; Toasted Herb Bread
Tuna, Swordfish, and Halibut Steaks; Salmon; Lobster; Crab Dishes; Fish Sauces	Duck; Goose; Wild Turkey; Venison; Rabbit; Elk; Stuffings	Green Beans; Broccoli; Asparagus; Brussels Sprouts; Eggplant; Sauerkraut; Corn; Carrots	Egg Dishes; Scrambled Eggs; Omelets; Cheese Dishes; Cheese Spreads	Bagels; Toasted Herb Bread

HERB CHART (continued)

	SOUPS STEWS	SALADS	MEATS	POULTRY
MINT	Split Pea, Cold Cucumber, Lentil, Black Bean, and Cream of Vegetable Soups	Decoration for Fruit Salads; Melon; Cucumber; Fish; Mint-flavored Mayonnaise for Fruit Salads	Lamb and Lamb Sauces; Veal Sauces; Mint Jelly for Lamb Garnish	Cold Sliced Chicken and Turkey
OREGANO	Cream of Broccoli, Tomato, Vegetable Beef, and Minestrone Soups; Chowders; Gumbos; Meat Stews	Vegetable; Fish; Shellfish	Meat Loaf; Spanish Rice; Italian Meatballs and Sauces; Veal; Pork; Meat Stuffings	Chicken
PARSLEY	Potato, Vegetable, Wild Rice, and Tomato Soups; Beef and Chicken Broth; Corn Chowder; Chili; Beef, Pork, and Veal Stews	Greens; Vegetable; Wild Rice; Chicken; Turkey; Fish; Egg; Italian and Vinaigrette Salad Dressings	All Meats; Meat Roulades; Ground Beef, Veal, Pork, and Ham Dishes; Swiss Steak; Italian Meat and Sauce Dishes; Béarnaise Sauce	Baked Chicken; Chicken and Turkey Dishes; Duck; Goose; Plate Decoration for All Poultry
ROSEMARY	Pea, Chicken, and Potato Soups; Fish Chowder; Bratwurst Stews; Meat and Vegetable Stews	Beef, Pork, and Lamb; Vegetable; Greens; Fish; Shellfish; Salad Dressings	Beef; Roast Pork; Lamb; Ham; Meat Sauces and Gravies	Chicken; Turkey; Duck; Cornish Game Hens; Stuffings
SAGE	Chicken, Turkey; Tomato, and Fish Soups; Chowders; Pork Stews	Cottage Cheese; Chicken; Turkey; Duck; Goose; Pork; Asparagus; Artichoke; Salad Dressings	Pork Sausage; Roast Pork; Ground Pork Dishes; Lamb; Sauces and Gravies	Stuffings for Chicken and Turkey; Chicken and Turkey Casseroles; Duck; Goose; Sauces and Gravies
SUMMER SAVORY	Vegetable, Onion, Pea, Lentil, and Chicken Noodle Soups; Broths; Meat and Vegetable Stews	Vegetable; Greens; Cabbage; Potato; Tomato; Cucumber; Poultry	Pork Sausage; Beef; Pork; Veal; Lamb; Calf's Liver; Sauces and Gravies	Baked Chicken; Turkey Casseroles; Cornish Game Hens; Stuffings
TARRAGON	Tomato, Vegetable, Chicken, Dried Bean, Pea, and Cream Soups; Chowders; Meat Stews	Zucchini; Green Bean; Lettuce and Vegetable; Tomato; Fish; Shellfish; Salad Dressings	Beef; Pork; Veal; Lamb; Béarnaise Sauce	Baked and Creamed Chicken; Turkey Dishes; Duck; Goose; Sauces and Gravies
THYME	Vegetable, Pea, Chicken, Beef, and Tomato Soups; Fish Chowders; Gumbos	Greens; Fish; Shellfish; Green Bean; Tomato; Chicken; Turkey; Vegetable; Salad Dressing	Beef; Stuffed Cabbage Leaves and Stuffed Onions using Ground Beef; Lamb; Veal; Barbecue Sauce; Sauces and Gravies	Scalloped Chicken; Turkey Casseroles; Baked Chicken; Corn Bread Dressing; Wild Rice Dressing

FISH SHELLFISH	WILD GAME	VEGETABLES	EGGS CHEESE	BREADS
Baked and Broiled Fish; Fish Sauces; Salmon	Cold Sliced Wild Turkey Breast	Peas; Celery; Carrots; Potatoes; Green Beans; Spinach; Eggplant	Cottage Cheese; Cream Cheese	Seldom Used
All Fish; Fish Sauces; Scalloped Oysters	Venison; Pheasant; Dove; Antelope	Tomatoes; Mushrooms; Eggplant; Onions; Asparagus; Broccoli; Potatoes; Squash; Bell Peppers	Scrambled Eggs; Omelets; Pizza; Cheese Sauces; Cheese Spreads	Yeast Breads
Baked Fish; Tuna; Salmon; Swordfish and Halibut Steaks; Escargots; Scalloped Oysters; Most Shellfish; Green Sauce; Caper Sauce	Goose, Duck, and Venison Pâtés; Woodcock; Quail; Pheasant; Baked Duck; Goose; Grouse; Stuffings	Carrots; Potatoes; Tomatoes; Beets; Cauliflower; Sautéed Onions and Mushrooms; Most Vegetables	Garnish for Deviled Eggs and Egg Dishes; All Egg Dishes; Cottage Cheese; Cheese Dips and Spreads; All Cheese Dishes; Combined with Grated Parmesan or Romano Cheese	Yeast Breads; Dumplings; Toasted Sesame Bread; Toasted Parmesan-Parsley Bread; Toasted Herb Bread; Sautéed Toast Points
Full-flavored Fish; Halibut; Tuna; Salmon; All Shellfish	Venison; Elk; Moose; Goose; Antelope; Duck; Rabbit; Dove	Cauliflower; Kohlrabi; Carrots; Onions; Zucchini; Red Bell Peppers; Turnips	Baked Egg Dishes; Selected Cheese Dishes; Cheese Sauces	Yeast Breads; Corn Bread; Biscuits; Dumplings; Toasted Herb Bread
All Fish; Stuffings for Fish; Special Flavoring for Shellfish	Partridge; Prairie Chicken; Grouse; Pheasant; Quail; Duck; Goose; Stuffings	Brussels Sprouts; Tomatoes; Green Beans; Artichokes; Eggplant; Zucchini; Carrots; Celery	Creamed Eggs; Egg Casseroles; Cheese Spreads; Baked Dishes with Cheese; Swiss Cheese Sauces	Yeast Breads; Buns; Dumplings; Corn Bread, Corn Fritters
All Baked and Broiled Fish; All Shellfish; Fish Sauces	Partridge; Quail; Grouse; Prairie Chicken; Pheasant	Carrots; Peas; Green Beans; Zucchini; Cauliflower; Rutabagas; Asparagus; Lima Beans; Artichokes	Scrambled Eggs; Omelets; Soufflés; Cream Cheese; Cheese Dips; Casseroles with Cheese	Dumplings; Biscuits; Toasted Herb Bread
Baked and Broiled Fish; Poached Fish; Lobster; Fish Sauces	Elk; Moose; Duck; Goose; Pheasant; Partridge	Green Beans; Tomatoes; Asparagus; Kohlrabi; Sautéed Onions and Mushrooms; Spinach; Beets	Egg Dishes; Soufflés; Cheese Casseroles; Cottage Cheese; Cheese Spreads	Croutons; Toasted Herb Bread
Poached Salmon; Baked and Broiled Fish; Shellfish Dishes; Fish Sauces; Fish and Shellfish Spreads	Venison; Duck; Quail; Goose; Rabbit; Pheasant; Partridge; Wild Turkey; Stuffings	Onions; Potatoes; Carrots; Tomatoes; Asparagus; Eggplant; Sauerkraut; Spinach; Cauliflower	Egg Dishes; Scrambled Eggs; Cottage Cheese; Casseroles with Cheese; Cheese Dips and Spreads	Yeast Breads; Muffins; Dumplings; Rolls; Corn Bread; Biscuits; Toasted Herb Bread

cultivated, studied, and widely used in monasteries for many centuries. By the 1400's, herb gardens had become quite widespread.

Herbs and spices continue to play a central role in modern-day life, primarily as flavor-enhancers for food. While spices have been consistently prized and heavily used, especially in sweet, baked goods and desserts, herbs are enjoying a groundswell of new popularity in everyday cooking.

In the agricultural Heartland, the pleasure of herb gardening is undergoing a renaissance, buoyed by herb study clubs which focus on both the cultivation of herbs and their use in cooking. The nutritional benefits derived from the substitution of herbs for food flavorings high in fat and cholesterol have given further impetus to the resurgent interest in herb cookery.

COOKING WITH HERBS: In cooking, herbs may be used fresh or dried. Fresh herbs are definitely preferable because a measure of characteristic flavor and aroma, as well as potency, is lost when herbs are dried. This is particularly apparent when subtle, delicately flavored herbs, such as chervil and summer savory, are dried. Another hazard in using dried herbs is their relatively short shelf life of approximately 9 to 12 months. When kept too long, herbs lose much of their individualistic flavor and aroma, deteriorating to a grasslike state. To best retard this deterioration, freshly dried and crushed herbs should be placed in tightly covered jars or bottles and stored in a dark, dry, cool place.

In general, fresh and dried herbs may be used interchangeably if the proportions are altered. Use 3 portions of fresh herbs to 1 portion of dried herbs; in other words:

3 teaspoons (1 tablespoon) fresh herbs =
   1 teaspoon dried herbs.

Be prudent and cautious about using multiple herbs to flavor the same dish. While many herbs such as parsley, chives, and chervil, are successfully used in combination with other herbs, be careful when it comes to using more than one predominant herb in a single dish.

And avoid overwhelming the flavor of a dish with too great a quantity of herbs. Properly used, herbs should complement, not overtake.

To use dried, crushed (not ground) herbs that can be removed from a dish after cooking, place them in a cheesecloth bag (page 28).

The Herb Chart on pages 22–25 suggests some of the foods which popularly used herbs complement.

TO SNIP FRESH HERBS: Fresh herbs are commonly snipped into tiny pieces for use in cooking. First, wash the sprigs of herbs in cold water and place them in a colander to drain. Bounce the herbs in the colander to expel as much water as possible. Place the herbs, single layer, between layers of paper towels to dry.

Using your fingers or kitchen scissors, remove the leaves from the stems of the herbs; discard the stems. Place the leaves on a cutting board, the top of which is at least 1¼ inches higher than the counter surface (to allow space for the scissoring procedure, to follow). Holding the kitchen scissors parallel with the top of the cutting board, while containing the herb leaves with your free hand, snip the leaves to the desired fineness, cutting through the entire little pile of herbs with each cut of the scissors.

An exception to this procedure is the method used to snip chives. The structure of chive leaves allows them to be cut into uniform pieces using standard scissor-cutting procedure.

Snipped fresh herbs may be stored in the refrigerator in small, airtight containers for 2 to 4 days.

TO MAKE A FRESH BOUQUET GARNI: A fresh bouquet garni is an assortment of selected fresh herb sprigs, tied together and added during cooking to dishes, such as soups and stews, for flavor enhancement. It is removed from the dish and discarded after the cooking period.

While the traditional bouquet garni usually consists of parsley, thyme, and a bay leaf, any single herb or combination of herbs may be used, and any number of sprigs may be included. Commonly, bouquets garnis are made of 2 to 10 sprigs. Among the herbs often included in bouquets garnis are:

Parsley	Marjoram
Thyme	Savory
Bay leaves	Chervil
Chives	Tarragon
Basil	Celery leaves

(Note: Celery leaves are usually classified nowadays as a vegetable.)

To make a bouquet garni, gather the herb sprigs in your hand as you would a bouquet of flowers. Using white cotton string, securely tie the bouquet together at the stem end of the herb sprigs. When preparing herb sprigs for inclusion in a bouquet garni, leave sufficiently long stems for tying so the leafy ends of the sprigs can fan out, allowing the cooking liquids to flow more freely through the herbs.

Alternatively, the fresh herbs may be tied loosely in a cheesecloth bag (page 28).

TO DRY HERBS: While it is preferable to use fresh herbs, the relatively short Midwest growing season permits fresh herbs from the garden only during a few summer months. Even though a greater variety of fresh herbs is available nowadays in good supermarkets, the quality is often disappointing and the price quite high. Midwest herb gardeners rely heavily upon their supply of dried summer herbs for use in cold-weather dishes. Anyway, preparing dried herbs is fun and the extra supply makes much-appreciated holiday gifts.

While herbs may be dried in an electric dehydrator, the instructions that follow are for drying herbs by hanging. In addition to the fact that most households are not equipped with an electric dehydrator, the hanging procedure results in equally fine herbs for cooking and is a more satisfactory method of handling large quantities of harvested herbs. Most herbs, except chives, may be successfully dried by hanging.

Herbs are at their height of flavor when the plants are mature, but just *before* they bloom. The flower buds should be pruned. Despite vigilance, if herb plants are allowed to bloom, the blooms should be snipped off (unless being reserved for use as edible flowers (see page 316–318).

To prepare herbs for drying, cut off branches of the plants and use extra-long pieces of twine to tie them in small bundles. Tie the bundles near the bottom of the branches in order to allow as much air as possible to circulate around the leaves while drying. The diameter of the branch bundles, where tied, should not exceed approximately $2\frac{1}{2}$ inches after tying. Leave the long ends of twine uncut, and use them to tie each bundle *upside down* on a clothesline located preferably in the basement, or, alternatively, in the garage. The bundles should not be in direct sunlight which might cause fading, and should be protected from dust which would cause the final product to be dirty.

Allow the bundles to hang until the leaves are dry and brittle—approximately one month, depending upon the dryness of the basement (or other hanging location). Keep the basement well ventilated and as free as possible from dampness. Let the bundles hang only as long as it takes the leaves to thoroughly dry. A measure of flavor, color, and aroma will be lost each week they are allowed to hang thereafter.

Process one bundle at a time on a large table covered with waxed paper. Use kitchen scissors or your fingers to carefully remove the leaves, discarding the stems. Place a small quantity of leaves in a large bowl and crush them in your hands repeatedly until crumbled to tiny pieces. Transfer the processed herbs to another bowl.

Repeat the procedure until all the dried leaves are processed. Place a small quantity of the processed herbs in a small airtight bottle to keep in the kitchen for immediate use. Place the remainder in airtight, glass jars or bottles and store them in a dark, dry, cool place such as a metal cabinet in the basement. A large plateful of charcoal placed in the cabinet will help to retain dryness. After 9 to 12 months, stored dried herbs lose their original potency and flavor.

TO MAKE A CHEESECLOTH BAG FOR HERBS OR SPICES

To make a cheesecloth bag to hold herbs or spices that are to be removed from the dish after cooking and then discarded, cut 4 layers of plain, untreated cheesecloth into a square large enough to hold the herbs or spices to be used (usually about 7 inches square). Draw the corners of the cheesecloth together and tie the bag very securely with white, cotton sewing thread. Do not pull the bag too tightly, leaving space for the liquid to flow freely through the herbs or spices.

TO USE A MEAT THERMOMETER

Meat thermometers are used to gauge the internal temperature of meats and fowl during roasting or baking to determine degree of doneness.

LARGE MEAT CUTS: Insert the meat thermometer into the meat—preferably before commencing to cook—positioning the pointed tip of the thermometer at the center of the thickest part of the meat, not touching bone or fat.

To help in determining how deep to insert the thermometer, hold the thermometer against the side of the meat with the pointed tip at the depth which will reach the center of the thickest part of the meat; then, place your thumb on the thermometer stem at the top surface of the meat. While continuing to hold your thumb on the thermometer stem, insert the thermometer into the thickest part of the meat to the depth of your thumb.

WHOLE FOWL: Insert the meat thermometer into one of the inner thigh areas near the breast—preferably before commencing to cook—making certain that the tip of the thermometer is not touching bone.

POSITION ADJUSTMENT: During cooking, meat thermometers often work away from their original position. Therefore, when the thermometer reaches the temperature for desired doneness, push it deeper into the meat or fowl and watch the gauge to see whether or not the temperature drops. If it does, additional cooking time will be required.

INSTANT THERMOMETERS: Small, instant thermometers are convenient and helpful for certain applications. They register the temperature of meats, fowl, and other foods in just a few seconds and are used toward the end of cooking. They are not left in food in the oven.

The best and most common type of instant thermometer has a 1-inch dial head and a very thin probe, allowing a minimum loss of juices when the flesh of meats or fowl is pierced. Instant thermometers make it easy to quickly find the temperature at two or more locations in a piece of meat or a fowl.

In general, a regular meat thermometer is the most practical for use with many meats and with whole fowl as it allows the internal temperature to be monitored throughout the cooking period with only one invasion of the flesh.

BURGERS: To secure the accurate internal temperature reading of a burger, insert an instant thermometer into the edge of the burger, parallel to the surface of the burger and halfway between the top and bottom of the burger. For an accurate reading on many instant thermometers, you must push the thermometer into the burger at least 2 inches; however, it is important to read the instructions accompanying the instant thermometer being used as the temperature-reading mechanism on instant thermometers varies.

ENCASED SAUSAGES: To secure the accurate internal temperature reading of an encased sausage, such as a bratwurst, insert an instant thermometer into the center of one of the ends of the sausage. For an accurate reading on many instant thermometers, you must push the thermometer into the sausage at least 2 inches;

however, it is important to read the instructions accompanying the instant thermometer being used as the temperature-reading mechanism on instant thermometers varies.

TO BLANCH

"Blanch" means to dip briefly in boiling water, generally for the purpose of loosening the skin of a food for peeling or for the purpose of cooking briefly. To blanch a food, bring water to a rapid boil in the bottom of a blancher or in a saucepan or kettle. If using a blancher, place the food in the top of the blancher and lower it into the boiling water. If using a saucepan or kettle, drop the food directly into the boiling water. Leave the boiling water over heat, and use a timer to accurately time the blanching process. Follow the recipe for suggested blanching time.

To blanch for peeling, tomatoes require approximately 45 seconds and peaches require approximately 1 minute in boiling water. Blanching times will vary somewhat, depending upon the ripeness and variety of the produce. During the blanching process, use a wooden mixing spoon to turn over foods that float in order that the boiling water reaches all surfaces.

When the blanching time is completed, immediately remove the food from the boiling water and immerse it in cold water to stop the cooking.

TO SEED AND CORE TOMATOES

In general, when seeded and cored tomatoes are used in food preparation, the tomatoes should be blanched (29) and peeled prior to seeding and coring.

To seed and core tomatoes, first quarter the tomatoes lengthwise. Then, using your thumb, remove and discard the seeds and the pouches containing them. Using a small paring knife, cut away and discard all white and greenish core and membrane. Only red tomato flesh should remain.

TO PARE CARROTS

The quickest and best way to remove the thin outer skin of carrots is to use a vegetable parer. When carrots are pared with a vegetable parer, their round shape is retained, the pared surface of the carrots is smooth, and very little of the flesh is pared away. When a vegetable parer is not available, carrots may also be pared by scraping them with the blade of a sharp paring knife.

TO PARE AND CORE CUCUMBERS

TO PARE CUCUMBERS: Cut a slice off both ends of the cucumbers to trim. Then, use a vegetable parer to pare.

TO CORE CUCUMBERS: Cut the cucumbers in half lengthwise. Using a serrated-type apple corer, scoop out the seeds and cores, leaving only the cucumber flesh.

TO PEEL PEARL ONIONS

Place pearl onions in a saucepan; cover with boiling water and let stand 2 minutes. Drain the onions and immediately immerse them in cold water to halt the cooking process. Drain the onions in a colander. With the aid of a small paring knife, peel the onions.

TO EXTRACT ONION JUICE

Over waxed paper, rub a peeled onion back and forth over a very fine metal grater. Pour off and save the onion juice that accumulates on the waxed paper. Reserve the remaining grated onion pulp for other uses.

TO CHOP RAISINS AND OTHER DRIED AND CANDIED FRUITS

Use a wet knife or wet kitchen scissors to chop raisins and other dried and candied fruits. A wet cutting tool will minimize the problem of stickiness.

TO DUST NUTS, RAISINS, AND FRUITS WITH FLOUR

To help prevent nuts, raisins, and chopped fruits from sinking to the bottom of cakes and breads, dust them with flour before adding them to the batter. For dusting, use flour from the *measured* flour in the recipe before any other ingredients, such as baking soda or baking powder, are added. Measure 1 tablespoon flour to dust 2 cups nuts and/or raisins. To dust damp, chopped fruit, measure 2 tablespoons flour for each 2 cups chopped fruit. Place nuts and/or raisins and/or chopped fruit in a mixing bowl; sprinkle with flour and stir until evenly coated.

TO PLUMP RAISINS AND OTHER DRIED FRUITS

Place measured raisins or other dried fruit in a saucepan; add hot water to cover. Cover the pan. Bring to a boil over high heat. Immediately remove from the heat. Let stand, covered, until cool. Drain in a colander or sieve. The juice may be retained for serving over fresh fruit, braising pork, or other uses.

Dark baking raisins are now available at the supermarket. They are moist and are ready for use in most baked goods without plumping. Golden raisins are generally more moist than dark raisins and may not require plumping before inclusion in baked goods.

TO GRATE PARMESAN AND ROMANO CHEESES

Use a food processor to grate Parmesan and Romano cheeses. Cut the cheese into 1-inch-square chunks; using the steel blade, grate 1 cup at a time, using on/off turns until the cheese is of desired fineness.

A hand-operated, drum-style grater (see illustration, page 32) is sometimes used to "grate" Parmesan and Romano cheeses. While this kitchen tool reduces the cheese to a consistency generally compatible with its intended use, the tool actually finely shreds the cheese rather than grating it.

TO SHRED FRESH HORSERADISH

Purchase firm horseradish root which is not sprouting and does not have greenish tinges. Pare only as much of the root as you plan to use. Shred the pared root medium-finely to finely. Freshly shredded horseradish quickly loses some of its pungency and browns in color; therefore, it should be shredded shortly before serving unless it is to be prepared with vinegar (see To Make Prepared Horseradish, below) or added to a sauce. To store unpared horseradish root, dampen it very slightly, wrap it tightly in plastic wrap, and refrigerate.

TO MAKE PREPARED HORSERADISH

Cut horseradish root into 1-inch pieces. In a food processor, mince the horseradish root (see Note). Uncover the processor bowl away from your face to avoid the pungent aroma. Place the minced horseradish root in a small glass mixing bowl. Add enough white wine vinegar to moisten the horseradish. Add a dash of sugar and a dash of salt; stir to combine.

Place the Prepared Horseradish in a glass jar;

cover and refrigerate. Best when eaten within 1 to 2 weeks.

NOTE: If a food processor is not available, the horseradish root may be grated or shredded finely by hand, using a simple grater/shredder kitchen tool.

CREAMED PREPARED HORSERADISH: Follow Prepared Horseradish recipe, above, adding unwhipped whipping cream to the other ingredients to moisten the horseradish.

TO USE
FRESH GINGER

To use fresh ginger, pare the ginger root and then grate or slice it. Fresh ginger may be stored in the refrigerator in a zipper-seal plastic bag up to approximately 1 month.

TO CUT
CITRUS ZEST

Zest (see definition, page 10) is cut from the thin, colored, outer part of the peel of citrus fruits. To cut citrus zest, first wash the fruit well, removing any brand names or other markings which may be stamped on the surface. Pull a citrus zesting tool (see illustration) firmly across the unpeeled fruit to cut tiny curls of zest. If a citrus zester is not available, a small, handheld, metal shredder may be used. When cutting zest, try to exclude any of the white membrane which lies underneath the colored, outer portion of the peel. Not only does the white membrane have a bitter taste, but also, inclusion of any of it will generally make the zest too thick.

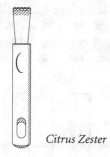

Citrus Zester

To cut pieces of zest rather than tiny curls, use a vegetable parer or a sharp paring knife.

If not using zest immediately, place it in a very small sauce dish, cover securely with plastic wrap, and refrigerate to retain its moisture, pliability, and color. Zest may be satisfactorily stored in this manner only for a brief period of time—no longer than 1 day.

TO GRATE
CITRUS RIND

Select unblemished fruit to use for grating citrus rind (see definition, page 8). Wash the fruit well, removing any brand names or other markings which may be stamped on the surface. Leave the fruit whole, and use a small, handheld, metal, prong-type grater to grate (see definition, page 6) the rind. Grate only the thin, colored, outer part of the fruit's peel. Try not to include any of the white membrane beneath the outer, colored portion of the peel. The white membrane has a bitter taste and is not the flavor desired when grated citrus rind is called for in a recipe.

When finely grated rind is specified, as is often the case, use a very finely pronged grater (see illustration). Grate over waxed paper and use a paring knife or a tiny kitchen brush (such as a toothbrush reserved only for use as a kitchen tool) to help remove grated rind that does not fall onto the waxed paper and builds up between the tiny prongs.

Instead of a finely pronged grater, an ultra-fine Microplane® (see illustration) may be used. A Microplane® actually shreds (see definition, page 9) extremely finely rather than grates; however, the planed citrus rind very closely resembles grated rind.

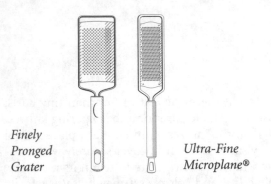

Finely Pronged Grater

Ultra-Fine Microplane®

One medium-sized lemon or 1 very small orange will yield about 1 teaspoon of finely grated or planed rind.

If grated citrus rind will not be used immediately, place it in a very small sauce dish, cover securely with plastic wrap, and refrigerate to retain its moisture and color. Grated citrus rind may be satisfactorily stored in this manner up to 1 day.

TO SECTION ORANGES AND GRAPEFRUIT

Using a small, sharp, thin-bladed knife, cut a small slice off both the stem and blossom ends of the fruit. Then, cut away the peel, including all white membrane on the outer surface of the fruit meat, cutting circularly around the fruit to preserve its round shape.

To cut away sections, make lengthwise cuts along both sides of the membranes which divide the sections, cutting to the core of the fruit. Carefully remove each released section as it is cut away; remove any seeds. Properly sectioned fruit should be free of all membrane.

Cut away the sections over a bowl in order to retain any juice which may be released from the fruit during the cutting process. With your hands, squeeze the fruit which remains after

the sections have been removed to extract additional juice.

TO MAKE DRIED BREAD CUBES

To make dried bread cubes, use a type of sliced, fresh bread which is rather firm. Do not use the very soft-style bread. Lay the bread slices single layer on waxed paper to dry slightly before cutting into cubes. This will help prevent crushing the bread when slicing and will aid in cutting more uniform cubes. Using a very sharp, thin-bladed knife, cut each slice into $\frac{1}{2}$-inch-square cubes. The bread crusts may or may not be cut away before cutting the cubes. (Generally, the crusts are not removed when preparing bread cubes for stuffings.) Place the bread cubes single layer on waxed paper. Let stand (uncovered) to dry at least 24 hours, turning the cubes with a spatula at least 3 times. When completely dry, use immediately or store in an airtight container for up to 3 days at room temperature.

Approximately 12 slices of bread (with crusts) make 7 cups of dried cubes.

TO MAKE CROUTONS

PLAIN CROUTONS

1 cup $\frac{1}{2}$-inch-square fresh, white bread cubes
with crusts removed (about 2 slices bread)
2 tablespoons butter, melted

Spread the fresh bread cubes single layer on waxed paper; let stand to dry at least 24 hours, turning occasionally with a spatula.

Preheat the broiler.

In a small saucepan, melt the butter over low heat. Remove from the heat. Add the dried bread cubes; using a spoon, toss lightly. Place the croutons single layer in a small, shallow baking pan; toast under the broiler until golden brown, turning several times to toast all sides of the cubes. Remove from the broiler and place pan on a wire rack; cool croutons, uncovered. Store in a covered jar up to 1 week in the refrigerator or up to 3 months in the freezer.

GARLIC CROUTONS: Follow the Plain Croutons recipe, above, except: simmer, briefly, $\frac{1}{2}$ pressed garlic clove in the butter prior to tossing with the dried bread cubes. Or, add $\frac{1}{8}$ teaspoon garlic powder to the melted butter.

ONION CROUTONS: Follow the Plain Croutons recipe, above, except: simmer, briefly, 1 teaspoon grated onions in the butter prior to tossing with the dried bread cubes. Or, add $\frac{1}{8}$ teaspoon onion powder to the melted butter.

HERB CROUTONS: Follow the Plain Croutons recipe, above, except: add $\frac{1}{4}$ teaspoon dried parsley, leaf basil, leaf thyme, leaf tarragon, leaf chervil, dillweed, or other dried herb to the melted butter; stir to combine. If fresh herbs are used, add $\frac{3}{4}$ teaspoon fresh herbs to the melted butter. More than 1 herb may be used. Herbs may also be added to the melted butter just prior to tossing Garlic Croutons and Onion Croutons (recipes above).

TO MAKE
BREAD CRUMBS

DRIED BREAD CRUMBS

Cut fresh bread, including the crust, into small cubes. Spread single layer on waxed paper; let stand (uncovered) to dry at least 24 hours. Using a spatula, turn the bread cubes 2 or 3 times during the drying period. When the cubes are very dry, crumb them in a food processor or blender, or roll them with a rolling pin. One slice of bread makes approximately $\frac{1}{4}$ cup dried crumbs. Store in a covered jar up to 3 days at room temperature, up to 1 week in the refrigerator, or up to 3 months in the freezer.

FRESH BREAD CRUMBS

Tear slices of fresh bread into pieces approximately 1 inch square. Place up to 3 slices torn bread at a time in a food processor and process until crumbled finely. If a food processor is not available, pull small pieces of bread from the slices or from an unsliced loaf and crumble them between your fingers.

Use of the crust is optional, depending upon its softness. One slice of bread makes approximately $\frac{1}{2}$ cup fresh crumbs. Use immediately or store in a covered jar up to 1 week in the refrigerator or up to 3 months in the freezer.

TO MAKE,
STORE, AND USE
BUTTERED CRUMBS

BUTTERED CRACKER CRUMBS

$\frac{1}{4}$ cup rolled cracker crumbs
   (6 Ritz crackers or 5 saltines)
1 tablespoon butter

Using a rolling pin, roll the crackers medium-finely; set aside. In a small saucepan, melt the butter over low heat. Remove from the heat; add the crumbs and stir until the crumbs are evenly coated with butter.

BUTTERED BREAD CRUMBS: Follow the Buttered Cracker Crumbs recipe, substituting $\frac{1}{4}$ cup Dried Bread Crumbs (page 33) for rolled cracker crumbs.

STORING BUTTERED CRUMBS: For use within 3 days, buttered crumbs may be stored in a covered jar in the refrigerator. Otherwise, buttered crumbs store well in the freezer. Store in a tightly covered, labeled jar up to 3 months.

USING BUTTERED CRUMBS TO TOP CASSEROLE DISHES: When preparing casserole dishes topped with buttered crumbs, add the buttered-crumb topping just before baking to prevent the crumbs from becoming soggy. Approximately $\frac{1}{4}$ cup buttered crumbs will top a dish to be baked in a 2-quart round baking dish or a 7 × 11-inch baking dish.

TO CRUMB CORNFLAKES

Measure the cornflakes; transfer to a food processor or blender. Process a few seconds until the cornflakes are of desired texture. If using a blender, it may be necessary to stop the blender once or twice and shake the covered beaker to redistribute the unprocessed flakes. Approximately 2½ cups cornflakes makes ½ cup crumbs.

TO GRIND MOST FOODS OTHER THAN NUTS AND COFFEE BEANS

To grind (see definition, page 6) most foods other than nuts and coffee beans, use a hand-cranked food grinder, generally called a "meat grinder" although it is used to grind many foods in addition to meats (see illustration). Meat grinders come with coarse- and fine-blade fittings for adaptation to specific uses. Some meat grinders come with additional fittings such as a sausage stuffer.

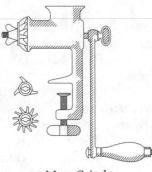

Meat Grinder

Meat grinders reduce foods to small, fairly uniform fragments. Meat grinders do not shred or splinter food during grinding, and the ground food retains its original consistency quite well. For uniform size, shape, and texture, and for an attractive finished food, a meat grinder is a requisite tool in the preparation of many foods.

Although food processors often are used to chop foods, they generally are not well suited for grinding foods because often they do not cut foods into a uniform size and shape, and some foods may become paste-like or partially liquefy during processing.

TO PREPARE BROKEN, CHOPPED, GROUND, AND GRATED NUTS

BROKEN NUTS: Break nuts into pieces with your fingers. Broken nuts are more coarse in size than chopped nuts.

CHOPPED NUTS: Most nuts can be chopped in a hand-operated, rotary nut chopper with metal (not plastic) blades (see illustration). If you desire more finely chopped nuts, run the nuts through the chopper two or more times.

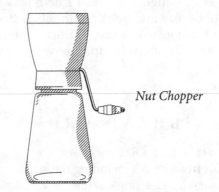

Nut Chopper

Almonds are very firm; therefore the use of slivered almonds for chopping simplifies the process and produces chopped pieces of more uniform size. Chop slivered almonds in a hand-operated, rotary nut chopper. Run the nuts through the chopper twice if necessary.

Whole almonds, **Brazil nuts**, and **hazelnuts** are too firm to chop in a hand-operated, rotary nut chopper. Chop these nuts in a food processor.

GROUND NUTS: Grind nuts in a food processor until very fine. Do not overprocess or nuts will form a butter. Nuts may also be ground in a blender, although it is more difficult to achieve a consistent coarseness (some large pieces of nuts may remain unground while, simultaneously, other very small pieces turn to butter).

GRATED NUTS: Grate nuts in a hand-operated, drum-style grater (see illustration). Use a grater made of heavy-duty metal or plastic. Flimsy metal graters are not sturdy enough to grate nuts successfully. Ground nuts (see above) often may be substituted for grated nuts if they are ground carefully to prevent their becoming too oily and butterlike. Very firm nuts, such as almonds, Brazil nuts, and hazelnuts—especially when they are whole— are difficult to grate in a hand-operated grater, and it is recommended that they be ground in a food processor.

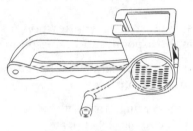

Drum-Style Grater

TO TOAST NUTS AND SEEDS

To toast shelled almonds, pine nuts, sesame seeds, or other nuts and seeds, spread the nuts or seeds in a shallow baking pan. Bake 6 minutes, until lightly browned, at 350°F, turning once or twice with a spatula during the baking period. Watch closely during baking to prevent overbrowning.

TO TOAST HAZELNUTS AND REMOVE SKINS: Shell hazelnuts and place them in a shallow baking pan. Bake 20 minutes at 350°F, turning once or twice with a spatula during the baking period. When cool enough to handle, remove the skins by rubbing the warm hazelnuts between your fingers or in a tea towel. It is extremely difficult (and for most uses, unnecessary) to remove every bit of skin covering the hazelnuts; however, perfectionists may use a small paring knife to help remove little pieces of skin that do not rub off easily.

TO SHELL, SKIN, AND BOIL CHESTNUTS

To shell and skin chestnuts, use a small, sharp knife to cut a cross on the flat side of the chestnuts. Place, single layer, in a baking pan. Bake 15 minutes at 450°F. Remove the shells and inner skin while the chestnuts are still warm.

To boil chestnuts, place shelled and skinned chestnuts in a saucepan; add water to cover. Boil, covered, about 20 minutes until tender; drain.

TO BLANCH ALMONDS

Shelled almonds may be blanched for the purpose of removing the skin that tightly covers the nutmeats.

To blanch shelled almonds, place the nuts in a mixing bowl or saucepan. Pour boiling water over the nuts until covered; let stand 1 minute. Then, immediately drain the nuts in a sieve. Briefly run cold water over the nuts to halt the heating. Pinch each almond between your thumb and index finger to slip off the skin. Place the skinned almonds between two layers of paper towels to partially dry. When the excess water covering the nuts has been absorbed by the paper towels, place the almonds single layer on two layers of clean, dry paper towels; let stand, uncovered, until thoroughly dry.

TO STORE NUTS

Stale nuts have spoiled many a batch of cookies and brownies, as well as other dishes. Even in state fair food competitions, a surprising number of entries containing less-than-fresh nuts are encountered in a day of cookie judging.

Light, air, warmth, and moisture all cause

nuts to become rancid quite quickly. Unless used immediately upon purchase, nuts should be stored in the freezer either in their unopened bag, or if opened, in a tightly covered glass jar or plastic container or in a zipper-seal plastic bag.

Nuts defrost rapidly and may be broken, chopped, ground, or grated just a few minutes after removal from the freezer. After preparing and measuring partially thawed nuts, it is best to leave them in an *uncovered* bowl as they continue to warm at room temperature. If covered, condensation can cause the nuts to become slightly damp and lose some of their snap. Hurry unused nuts back to the freezer.

Broken and chopped nuts may be stored in the freezer satisfactorily. If more than one kind of chopped nuts is stored, use freezer tape to label the containers because it is sometimes difficult to distinguish types of nuts after they have been chopped.

Nuts may be stored in the freezer for approximately 6 to 8 months. After that, they begin to lose their flavor. The freezer life of nuts depends, to a degree, upon how fresh they were when purchased. In many cases, the consumer has no way of knowing how long nuts have been sitting on the grocery shelf or stored in a warehouse. Expiration dates, which are given on some packages, are an indication of age; however, some observed expiration dates allow for nuts to remain on unrefrigerated, bright grocery shelves for many months. It is not unusual to purchase nuts found to be past their prime when tasted at home.

Before using nuts which have been frozen for 6 or more months, it is best to taste them before using to determine if they still have their characteristic and full flavor.

TO MEASURE
INGREDIENTS

The accurate measurement of ingredients is critical to the successful production of many prepared foods such as breads, pastry, cakes, cookies, and sauces. In fact, consistent, reliable cookery leans heavily on the dependability of measuring. The rigid overtones of this statement are not meant to throw cold water on the important and satisfying works of culinary art created by inventive cooks who assemble a little of this, some of that, and a wee bit of the other to culminate in one-of-a-kind *chefs d'oeuvre*. However, soon after the creative high begins to fade, best that the *artiste de cuisine* take pencil and paper in hand and translate the inspired dish into measurable portions or, alas, it may be lost to ephemeral memory. All of the traditional foods we love were born of inspired minds, but they were also reduced to notations (recipes) so they could be enjoyed more than once.

MEASURING UTENSILS: There are three fundamental sets of measuring utensils that are standard in a well-equipped kitchen:

- Measuring spoons ($\frac{1}{4}$ teaspoon, $\frac{1}{2}$ teaspoon, 1 teaspoon, and 1 tablespoon).

- Fractional measuring cups ($\frac{1}{4}$ cup, $\frac{1}{3}$ cup, $\frac{1}{2}$ cup, and 1 cup).

- Glass measuring cups with pouring spouts (1 cup, 2 cups, and 4 cups).

PREPARATION FOR MEASURING: Before commencing to measure and prepare a food, assemble all the measuring utensils and other kitchen tools and cooking equipment which will be needed.

Place a piece of waxed paper on the counter before beginning the measuring process. Measuring over waxed paper expedites kitchen cleanup.

TO MEASURE DRY INGREDIENTS: For correct measurement, dry ingredients must be measured in fractional measuring cups or measuring spoons which are overfilled and then leveled. Accurate measurement of dry ingredients cannot be achieved by filling fractional measuring cups or measuring spoons less than overfull before leveling, or by using glass measuring cups with pouring spouts due to the fact that their capacity is greater than the amount of dry ingredients to be measured.

Stir dry ingredients, such as flour, cornmeal, baking powder, baking soda, and spices, before they are measured for the purpose of aerating.

Use a scoop or spoon to lightly place flour, cornmeal, and other such prestirred dry ingredients in a fractional measuring cup or a measuring spoon, filling it to slightly overflowing. Do not cause the dry ingredient to settle or pack in the measuring utensil by touching the top surface of the mounded ingredient with the scoop or spoon, or by shaking the measuring utensil, tapping the side of the utensil, or rapping the bottom of the utensil on the counter. To level the dry ingredient with the top of the measuring utensil, draw the flat side of a table knife blade across the top of the measuring cup or measuring spoon, letting the excess drop onto the waxed paper. Use the table knife or a spoon to gather the excess and return it to the storage package or canister.

Many recipes call for flour to be sifted *before* it is measured. See To Sift Flour (page 40) for sifting and measuring procedures.

Prestirred baking powder, baking soda, and spices may be measured by lightly dipping a measuring spoon directly into their containers. Slightly overfill the measuring spoon; then, draw the flat side of a table knife blade across the spoon, letting the excess drop back into the container or onto the waxed paper. Most baking powder containers are designed with a strip of thin metal across one side of the top for use in leveling measuring spoons dipped into the container. This is a completely satisfactory method of leveling.

To measure $\frac{1}{8}$ teaspoon of a dry ingredient, measure $\frac{1}{4}$ teaspoon of the ingredient and then use a knife to divide the measured portion in half.

TO MEASURE BROWN SUGAR: Contrary to the procedure used to measure most other dry ingredients, brown sugar is packed into a fractional measuring cup or a measuring spoon before it is measured. Use a spoon to place brown sugar in a fractional measuring cup, intermittently packing it firmly into the cup with your thumbs. Measuring spoons may be dipped directly into the brown sugar and then packed into the spoon with your thumbs. To level the cup or measuring spoon, draw the flat side of a table knife blade across the top, letting the excess brown sugar drop onto the waxed paper.

After a package of brown sugar has been opened, transfer the sugar to a quart-sized glass jar with a tight-fitting lid for storage at room temperature in the cupboard. Improperly stored brown sugar quickly dries out, making it difficult, if not impossible, to measure and evenly combine with other ingredients.

TO MEASURE LIQUID INGREDIENTS: All three types of measuring utensils—measuring spoons, fractional measuring cups, and glass measuring cups with pouring spouts—may be used to measure liquid ingredients. I prefer using measuring spoons or fractional measuring cups in most cases. To measure liquids in a glass measuring cup with a pouring spout, the measuring cup must be placed on a level counter—not held in the hand. Then, while measuring the liquid, the measuring line of the cup must be viewed at *eye level*, which requires the cook to do a deep knee bend in front of the counter.

The top surface of contained liquid, called the "meniscus," is not level. It is crescent-shaped. The liquid at the center of a filled measuring utensil is higher than at the edges of the utensil. Liquid is measured at the outside edge, or brim, of the top surface. Therefore, to measure liquid in a measuring spoon or fractional measuring cup, *completely* fill the utensil to the outside brim. When measuring liquid in a glass measuring cup with a pouring spout, the liquid should be even with the line on the measuring cup which designates the amount to be measured.

Some liquid is retained on the inside surface of measuring utensils after the liquid is poured from them. For this reason, when a glass measuring cup with a pouring spout is used to measure liquid, a measuring cup as close as possible in size to the amount of liquid to be measured should be used. An inaccurate measurement will occur if measured liquid is poured from a proportionately oversized glass measuring cup.

For accurate measurement, it is necessary to use a small, rubber spatula to empty measured viscous liquids such as honey, corn syrup, and molasses from the measuring utensil. (See To Measure and Store Honey, page 38.)

TO MEASURE PLASTIC FATS (butter, margarine, vegetable shortening, and lard): The measurement lines printed on most wrappings covering ¼-pound sticks of butter and margarine may be relied upon for measuring tablespoons and teaspoons (1 stick = ½ cup = 8 tablespoons = 24 teaspoons). Use a small, sharp knife to cut through the wrapping and butter or margarine at the desired measurement line.

Similar to measured sticks of butter and margarine but twice the size, 1-cup sticks of vegetable shortening with fractional measurement lines on the foil wrappers are now available on supermarket shelves. This packaging provides a reliable, convenient way of measuring vegetable shortening. To my knowledge, premeasured lard is unavailable.

To measure vegetable shortening or lard not purchased in premeasured packaging, it must be packed into a fractional measuring cup or a measuring spoon and then leveled. Cold, hardened vegetable shortening or lard is somewhat difficult to pack in measuring utensils as air spaces between the pieces of hard fat must be eliminated if an accurate measurement is to be achieved. To measure cold vegetable shortening or lard, use a table knife to cut medium chunks of the fat for placement in a fractional measuring cup, or small pieces for placement in a measuring spoon. Very firmly press the fat into the measuring utensil, a portion at a time, with your thumbs. When the utensil is packed slightly more than full, draw the flat side of a table knife blade across the top of the utensil to remove the excess. In the process of packing, the warmth of your thumbs will slightly soften the fat. When it is important to use very cold fat in the preparation of a food such as pastry piecrust, it is advisable to measure the lard (or vegetable shortening) a little in advance of use,

and then to refrigerate it until just ready for incorporation in the product being prepared.

When recipes do not call for the use of cold vegetable shortening or lard, the fat may be softened at room temperature, making it easier to measure. Lard or vegetable shortening to be used in pastry piecrust and other foods in which very cold fat is to be cut into other ingredients, may also be softened prior to measuring if, after measurement, it is refrigerated for a lengthy period of time until it cools to refrigerator temperature throughout and rehardens.

TO MEASURE AND STORE HONEY: When measuring honey, use a wet measuring spoon or cup to avoid sticking. Also, use a wet, small rubber spatula to empty the measuring utensil. Store honey at room temperature, not in the refrigerator.

TO MEASURE OTHER FOODS: Other foods—whole, grated, shredded, chopped, cubed, or prepared in any other designated fashion—may be measured using any of the three types of measuring utensils (see Measuring Utensils, page 36). Selection of the measuring utensil is dependent upon the quantity and makeup of the food to be measured and the preference of the cook.

TO USE A PASTRY CLOTH AND A STOCKINET-COVERED ROLLING PIN

The purpose of using a pastry cloth and a stockinet-covered rolling pin is to provide surfaces which help prevent pastry and dough from sticking when they are rolled, kneaded, or otherwise handled. While some good pie and cookie bakers roll their pastry and dough on wooden boards, I have always achieved better results, with less effort, using a pastry cloth and stockinet-covered rolling pin, and I recommend their use.

Pastry cloths and stockinet covers for rolling pins are usually sold together. The best pastry cloths are made of preshrunk canvas and come equipped with a frame to keep the cloth from shifting. The frame consists of two narrow, wooden slats which slide into the hemmed top and bottom of the pastry cloth, and two metal rods which run along the sides of the pastry cloth and loop over the ends of the wooden slats to hold the cloth tightly. The front of each metal rod hangs over the edge of the kitchen counter or other work surface to prevent the frame and pastry cloth from slipping. A taut, secure pastry cloth greatly assists in the production of evenly rolled pastry and dough. Stockinet rolling pin covers are fairly standard. They are made of knit material and fit any regular rolling pin (see illustration).

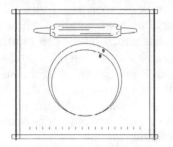

Pastry Cloth and Stockinet-Covered Rolling Pin

If a pastry cloth with a frame is not available at a local cookware store, one may be ordered from Sweet Celebrations Inc. (see Product Sources, page 631).

Pastry cloths without frames are more commonly available. They also usually come with a knit stockinet rolling pin cover. When using a pastry cloth without a frame, the pastry cloth can be held more securely by placing a flour canister (or other heavy object) on one of the upper corners of the pastry cloth, and a sugar canister (or other heavy object) on the other upper corner of the pastry cloth.

Pastry cloths and stockinet-covered rolling pins nearly always are floured immediately before use. Often they are floured lightly, but sometimes more heavily, depending upon the consistency of the pastry or dough in a particular recipe and the task to be performed (rolling, kneading, etc.).

To flour a pastry cloth, use a flour scoop to sprinkle flour over the area of the pastry cloth to be used (generally, most of the cloth). Then, with your hand, spread the flour evenly over the cloth, exerting slight downward pressure to press a little of the flour into the fabric. This helps produce an evenly floured, nonstick surface. When rolling pastry and cookie dough, it is desirable to have only as much loose flour on the pastry cloth as required to prevent sticking. When pastry and dough are rolled over loose flour, a portion of the flour assimilates into the pastry or dough, thereby causing the rolled product to become more dry. The same general technique used in flouring a pastry cloth is used to flour a stockinet-covered rolling pin.

It is usually necessary to lightly reflour the pastry cloth and/or stockinet covering on the rolling pin before rolling, kneading, or handling each portion of pastry or dough. If little pieces of moistened flour are left on the surface of the pastry cloth after rolling a portion of pastry or dough, before proceeding to roll the next portion, lightly flour the pastry cloth and use the back of a spatula to clear the pastry cloth surface, pushing the flour to the extreme top of the pastry cloth in the same manner that you would use to clean a griddle surface. Then, lightly reflour the pastry cloth. Sometimes, bits of pastry or dough cling to the stockinet covering the rolling pin. When this happens, lightly reflour the spot of pastry or dough and then use your fingernail or a knife to remove it. It will be necessary to reflour the cleared spot on the stockinet.

When rolling pastry or dough of proper consistency on a properly floured pastry cloth using a stockinet-covered, then properly floured rolling pin, the pastry or dough will virtually glide over the pastry cloth as it spreads. A few well-executed rolls outward from the center of the pastry or dough to the edges, and the job is done. Especially in the case of pastry, where minimum handling is critical, use of a pastry cloth and stockinet-covered rolling pin can significantly improve the finished baked product.

I also use a pastry cloth for kneading and handling yeast-bread and yeast-roll dough, although I call for use of either a pastry cloth or a wooden board in the yeast-bread and yeast-roll recipes in this book. Some bread bakers prefer to work on a wooden board; however, I get better results using a pastry cloth.

Recipes in this book specify when the use of a pastry cloth and/or stockinet-covered rolling pin is recommended. Sometimes, when a perfectly flat finish is desired on rolled dough (unmarked by the thread pattern of a knit stockinet), such as in Springerle cookies (page 562), a pastry cloth and an uncovered rolling pin are used.

Pastry cloths and stockinets should be washed after use. I do not put pastry cloths in the dryer, but hang them over a clothesline or rod until thoroughly dry.

Rolling pins should not be washed by immersing them in water because water will seep inside around the handles and cause damage. After use, simply wipe the rolling pin with a warm, damp sponge, and wipe it dry with a clean tea towel.

TO GREASE AND FLOUR BAKING PANS

TRADITIONAL METHOD
To grease and flour a baking pan, use a pastry brush to spread a thin application of room-temperature vegetable shortening over the entire inside of the pan, including the bottom and sides. Then, sprinkle about 2 tablespoons of all-purpose flour over the bottom of the pan. Over the kitchen sink, tilt the pan back and forth until all the greased surfaces are coated with flour. Turn the pan upside down and tap it on the rim of the sink to expel excess flour.

SPECIAL GREASE
½ cup vegetable shortening, softened
½ cup vegetable oil
½ cup all-purpose flour

Place the ingredients in a medium mixing bowl. Using an electric mixer, beat on high speed until perfectly smooth. Place in an airtight plastic container; store in the refrigerator. Special Grease will keep in the refrigerator for several months.

Special Grease replaces both the grease and flour when used to prepare a pan. (Do not flour the pan after applying Special Grease.)

WHEN TO USE SPECIAL GREASE: Special Grease helps prevent many cakes and certain other baked products from sticking to the pans in which they are baked. Many cake recipes in this cookbook specify the recommended use of Special Grease on the pans. It is also excellent for use in baking muffins and casserole dishes.

Most cookies which require baking on greased cookie sheets are best when baked on cookie sheets which have been lightly greased with vegetable shortening or vegetable oil. The flour in Special Grease can cause a slight residue on the bottoms of baked cookies; however, this cookbook specifies the use of Special Grease in certain cookie recipes because of its unique nonstick quality.

When recipes in this cookbook call for the pans to be *greased and floured,* Special Grease should not be used either in total substitution or in substitution for the grease. Rather, the procedure given under Traditional Method, above, should be used.

TO SIFT FLOUR

There are three purposes for sifting flour:

• To pulverize any lumps in the flour or other ingredients with which the flour is sifted.

• To help evenly combine the flour with other dry ingredients with which it is sifted; most commonly, these include leavens (baking powder and/or baking soda); seasonings, such as salt and spices; and flavorings, such as powdered cocoa.

• To incorporate air, helping to make the end product lighter.

Recipe ingredient lists give instructions about flour sifting in one of three ways:

- 1 cup sifted flour (flour is to be sifted *before* measuring).

- 1 cup flour, sifted (flour is to be sifted *after* measuring).

- 1 cup flour (if flour is to be sifted at all, instructions are given in the recipe procedures).

If the flour is to be sifted *before* measuring, a simple, small 1-cup sifter is a very convenient and workable means of accomplishing the task. On a large piece of waxed paper, hold the small sifter over the properly sized fractional measuring cup (1 cup in the above examples), scoop flour lightly into the sifter, and sift it into the measuring cup until the cup is slightly more than full. Without shaking the cupful of sifted flour, causing it to settle or pack, draw the flat side of a table knife blade across the top of the measuring cup, letting the excess flour drop onto the waxed paper (see To Measure Dry Ingredients, page 36). Generally, recipes call for sifted and measured flour to be subsequently sifted with other ingredients, in which case, the sifted, measured flour can be placed immediately in the top of a regular-sized sifter, ready for sifting with other ingredients. For convenience and conservation of counter space, one large piece of waxed paper may be used for all the flour-sifting procedures involved in most recipes, using the left side of the paper for the initial sifting and measuring, and situating the large sifter on the right side of the paper for the final sifting. After placing sifted and measured flour in the large sifter, use the table knife to remove all flour which has spilled onto the waxed paper during the measuring process. The waxed paper will then be free of any unmeasured flour and may be used for the final sifting procedure.

When recipes call for the flour to be sifted *after* it is measured, measure the flour and place it directly in the large sifter for sifting.

Recipe procedures for baked goods often call for unsifted, measured flour to be sifted with other ingredients. In general cooking (in contrast to baking), flour usually is measured and used directly in the dish, with no sifting involved.

There are two common types of regular-sized (5-cup is preferable) kitchen sifters. One type looks like a wire mesh, basket-type sieve and operates with a rotary crank. The other type is cylindrical in shape, with three tiers of wire mesh which serve to sift the ingredients three times in a single operation. This latter type sifter is operated by repeatedly gripping and releasing the handle, and is my preference. Triple sifting better achieves all three purposes for sifting stated above. Particularly in cake baking, when evenly combined ingredients and optimal air incorporation are important factors, triple sifting is a must. It saves time and energy to triple sift in one operation.

Whichever type sifter is used, during the sifting process the bottom of the sifter should be held about 6 inches above the waxed paper or top of the sifted pile of ingredients. This will help incorporate air into the flour and other sifted ingredients.

When a large quantity of ingredients is placed in a triple sifter, the gripping handle is more difficult to operate and the ingredients are somewhat slow in working through the three screens of wire mesh. To overcome this sluggishness, continue holding the sifter by the handle with one hand, and beat against the side of the sifter with the other hand until some of the ingredients have sifted, at which time the gripping-releasing procedure may be resumed. Sifting quality is not diminished by using the beating methodology.

Because the incorporation of air is one of the purposes of sifting, the final sifting of flour and other ingredients should be delayed until these ingredients are about to be added to the batter or dough.

Use a scoop to transfer sifted ingredients from the waxed paper to the mixing bowl. Scoop beneath the pyramid of sifted ingredients in order not to crush the light, airy flour or flour mixture.

Do not wash flour sifters as it is difficult to expel wet flour from the fine, wire mesh. After using, firmly tap both ends of the sifter against the kitchen sink rim to remove excess flour. Then, wipe the inside and outside of the sifter with a clean, barely damp towel. Store in a dry kitchen cabinet. Sifters made of stainless steel are preferable as they will not rust and are usually constructed more sturdily.

If food requiring the sifting of whole-wheat flour is prepared often, it is a good practice to equip the kitchen with two sifters—one for white flour and one for whole-wheat and dark rye flours as well as other fibrous and/or darker-colored flours and food products. This will preclude small particles of coarse grain, which may become trapped in the sifter, from infusing sifted white flour, and will prevent any discoloration of sifted white flour due to previously sifted darker flours or food products.

Commercial flours labeled "presifted" should be sifted anyway, if sifting is called for in the recipe. While presifted flour may virtually be void of lumps, thus fulfilling the first purpose for sifting, sifting is still necessary to accomplish the second and third purposes—to thoroughly combine the flour with other dry ingredients, and to incorporate air. Proper sifting of flour and other ingredients is one of the elements that makes the difference between "okay baking" and "exceptional baking."

TO SIFT POWDERED SUGAR

Over a piece of waxed paper, place powdered sugar in a medium (about 6 inches in diameter) sieve. Hold the sieve by the handle and use short, quick, back and forth, and up and down motions of the hand and arm to sift the powdered sugar onto the waxed paper. To sift powdered sugar directly onto the top of cakes, cookies, and other desserts, use a very small, handheld strainer. Powdered sugar does not sift satisfactorily through most flour sifters.

TO MAKE SOUR MILK AND SOUR CREAM

1 CUP SOUR MILK
Pour 1 tablespoon freshly squeezed, strained lemon juice into a 1-cup glass measuring cup with pouring spout. Add whole milk to fill the measuring cup to the 1-cup measuring line. Let stand 5 minutes. Stir briefly to blend. Use immediately.

$\frac{1}{2}$ CUP SOUR MILK
Pour $1\frac{1}{2}$ teaspoons freshly squeezed, strained lemon juice into a 1-cup glass measuring cup with pouring spout. Add whole milk to fill the measuring cup to the $\frac{1}{2}$-cup measuring line. Let stand 5 minutes. Stir briefly to blend. Use immediately.

SOUR CREAM
Follow either Sour Milk recipe above, substituting unwhipped whipping cream for whole milk.

TO MAKE SEASONED SALT

Some commercially purchased seasoned salt contains MSG (monosodium glutamate), which many people prefer to avoid eating. The following is a recipe for seasoned salt which may be used in lieu of the commercial product.

SEASONED SALT
$\frac{3}{4}$ teaspoon salt
$\frac{1}{2}$ teaspoon garlic powder
$\frac{1}{4}$ teaspoon pepper
$\frac{1}{4}$ teaspoon ground thyme
$\frac{1}{4}$ teaspoon ground sage
$\frac{1}{4}$ teaspoon ground cardamom
$\frac{1}{4}$ teaspoon sugar
$\frac{1}{8}$ teaspoon paprika
$\frac{1}{8}$ teaspoon cayenne pepper
$\frac{1}{8}$ teaspoon ground cumin
$\frac{1}{8}$ teaspoon ground turmeric

Place all ingredients in a small mixing bowl; stir to combine.

MAKES 1 TABLESPOON

Hors d'Oeuvres,
First-Course Appetizers,
and Snacks

Cold Hors d'Oeuvres

CHUTNEY DIP

3 ounces cream cheese, softened
8 ounces commercial sour cream
1 tablespoon finely grated onions
¾ teaspoon curry powder
⅛ teaspoon chili powder
⅛ teaspoon salt
½ cup commercially canned chutney, large pieces chopped
Paprika for decoration
Ridged potato chips or crackers

In a medium mixing bowl, place the cream cheese, sour cream, onions, curry powder, chili powder, and salt; using an electric mixer, beat on high speed until no lumps of cream cheese remain. Add the chutney; using a spoon, fold in to combine. Turn into a serving bowl and sprinkle sparingly with paprika. Serve with potato chips or crackers.

MAKES ABOUT 2 CUPS
(4 DOZEN HORS D'OEUVRES)

RAW VEGETABLE PLATTER WITH VEGETABLE DIP

On a platter, attractively arrange a selection of raw vegetables around a bowl of Vegetable Dip (recipe follows). The following vegetables, as well as others of choice, may be used:

Beet strips*
Broccoli flowerets*
Carrot strips
Cauliflower flowerets*
Celery strips
Cherry tomatoes
Cucumber slices
Yellow summer squash and zucchini slices or strips
Green onions
Green, red, yellow, orange, and purple bell pepper strips
Radish roses (page 339)
Turnip strips

*May be steamed (page 252) 1 minute to bring out color and enhance flavor. Immediately after steaming, place the steamer basket containing the vegetables under cold, running water to stop the cooking. Drain well. Place carefully in a zipper-seal plastic bag; refrigerate until completely cold. Vegetables should be steamed and prepared separately to preserve their individual colors and tastes.

VEGETABLE DIP

1 cup mayonnaise
1 tablespoon finely grated onions
1 tablespoon cider vinegar
1 tablespoon prepared horseradish, homemade (page 30) or commercially canned
½ teaspoon curry powder
Finely snipped, fresh chives for garnish

In a small mixing bowl, place the mayonnaise, onions, vinegar, horseradish, and curry powder; stir well. Transfer the dip to a serving bowl and garnish with chives.

MAKES ABOUT 1 CUP

VARIATION: Hot Swiss Cheese Sauce (page 303) makes a tasty and different dip for raw vegetables

SPINACH SPREAD

(See photo insert page A-1)

1 10-ounce package frozen chopped spinach
16 ounces commercial sour cream
1.8 ounces (2 envelopes) vegetable soup mix
1 8-ounce can sliced bamboo shoots, drained
    and chopped very coarsely
1 tablespoon white wine vinegar
1 teaspoon soy sauce
1 teaspoon sugar
Assorted crackers

AT LEAST 6 HOURS BEFORE SERVING: In the sink, place the spinach in a colander and defrost, allowing the liquid to drain off.

When defrosted, press the spinach in the colander to extract any remaining liquid. In a medium mixing bowl, place the spinach, sour cream, soup mix, bamboo shoots, vinegar, soy sauce, and sugar; using a spoon, stir until well combined. Cover and refrigerate at least 6 hours to allow the soup mix to soften and the flavors to blend. Serve in a bowl and surround with crackers; supply a small knife for spreading.

MAKES ABOUT 3 CUPS
(7 DOZEN HORS D'OEUVRES)

KALE SPREAD

1 10-ounce package frozen chopped kale*

*Frozen chopped kale is not always available
    at the supermarket.*

Follow the Spinach Spread recipe above, substituting the frozen chopped kale for the frozen chopped spinach. After pressing the defrosted kale to extract any remaining liquid, chop the kale into somewhat smaller pieces to make the dip easier to spread and eat.

MAKES ABOUT 3 CUPS
(7 DOZEN HORS D'OEUVRES)

ABC DIP

⅓ cup sliced almonds, chopped coarsely
3 strips bacon, fried crisply, drained between
    paper towels, and crumbled
1½ cups shredded sharp cheddar cheese
1 tablespoon plus 1 teaspoon finely grated onions
¾ cup Miracle Whip dressing
Paprika for decoration
Assorted crackers

In a small mixing bowl, place the almonds, bacon, cheese, onions, and dressing; stir lightly to combine. Turn into a serving bowl; sprinkle with paprika to decorate. Place the bowl on a doily-lined plate. Arrange the crackers on plate around the bowl of dip.

MAKES ABOUT 2 CUPS
(4 DOZEN HORS D'OEUVRES)

SUMMER SAUSAGE-HORSERADISH DIP

8 ounces regular cream cheese spread
½ cup mayonnaise
3 tablespoons honey
¼ teaspoon salt
⅛ teaspoon dry mustard
1 cup finely ground (page 16), fully cooked
    cervelat summer sausage*
2 tablespoons undrained, prepared
    horseradish, homemade (page 30) or
    commercially canned
¾ cup finely chopped green bell peppers
2 tablespoons finely grated onions
Low-sodium whole-wheat crackers

*Cervelat is the name given to a classification
    of semi-dry, mildly seasoned, smoked
    summer sausages. Most cervelats are made
    with both pork and beef. Thuringer is
    probably the most popular. Other cervelats
    include Farmer, Goettinger, Goteborg,
    Gothaer (made with pork only),*

(Recipe continues on next page)

Holsteiner, and Landjaeger. Any of these cervelats may be used in this recipe.

In a medium mixing bowl, place the cream cheese, mayonnaise, honey, salt, and dry mustard; using a spoon, stir vigorously until completely smooth and blended. Add the summer sausage, horseradish, green peppers, and onions; stir to combine. Serve with crackers.

MAKES ABOUT 3 CUPS
(6 DOZEN HORS D'OEUVRES)

SHRIMP WITH DIPS

Boil fresh shrimp (page 191); shell, leaving the tails on, and devein (page 191). Refrigerate in a covered container until cold. Arrange attractively on a platter and serve with one or more of the following sauces for dipping:

Cocktail Sauce (page 296)
Louis Dressing (page 128)
Hot Swiss Cheese Sauce (page 303)

GUACAMOLE

The dressing in this version of guacamole not only adds a zingy flavor, but also allows advance preparation of the hors d'oeuvre by using the dressing to spread over the avocado mixture, thus sealing it and preventing it from darkening. You stir the guacamole just before serving. Bacon also adds a new, delicious twist to this ever-popular savory.

2 large ripe avocados
1 tablespoon minced onions
1 garlic clove, pressed
1/4 teaspoon chili powder
1/2 cup Miracle Whip dressing
4 slices bacon
1 medium tomato
Tortilla chips

Peel, pit, and cut the avocados into small chunks; place the chunks in a blender. Add the onions, garlic, and chili powder; process the mixture in the blender until pureed. Place the mixture in a glass mixing bowl. Using a small, narrow, angled spatula, spread evenly and smoothly in the bowl. Spoon the dressing over the avocado mixture; using a clean, small, narrow, angled spatula, carefully spread until smooth, sealing in the avocado mixture to prevent it from discoloring. Using plastic wrap, cover the bowl tightly and refrigerate.

Fry the bacon until crisp; drain well between paper towels. Using your fingers, crumble the bacon into small pieces. Place the pieces in a covered container and refrigerate. Blanch the tomato for 45 seconds (page 29); stem, peel, quarter, seed, and core it (page 29). Then chop it finely. Measure 1/2 cup chopped tomato; place in a covered container and refrigerate. Reserve the remaining chopped tomato for other uses.

At serving time, add the bacon and chopped tomato to the bowl containing the avocado mixture and dressing. Using a tablespoon, stir together the avocado mixture, dressing, bacon, and tomatoes until evenly combined. Transfer the guacamole to a medium- shallow serving bowl. Serve it with tortilla chips for dipping.

MAKES ABOUT 2 CUPS
(4 DOZEN HORS D'OEUVRES)

TACO SPREAD

(See photo insert page A-1)

11 ounces cream cheese, softened
1/2 cup commercial sour cream
2 tablespoons plus 1 teaspoon commercial
   taco seasoning mix
1 tablespoon vegetable oil
1 pound lean, pure ground beef
1/2 cup finely chopped onions
1 garlic clove, pressed
16 ounces (2 cups) commercially canned
   mild salsa

8 ounces (2 cups) shredded cheese for tacos
½ cup sliced, pitted ripe olives
1¾ cups coarsely chopped iceberg lettuce, well dried
2 cups blanched (page 29), peeled, stemmed, quartered, seeded and cored (page 29), and diced (about ¼-inch square) tomatoes
1 10-ounce bag tortilla chips

In a small mixing bowl, place the cream cheese, sour cream, and taco seasoning mix; using an electric mixer, beat on high speed until smooth and blended. Using a tablespoon and a small, narrow spatula, press the cream cheese mixture evenly onto the bottom of a 9 × 13-inch baking dish; cover and refrigerate.

Place the vegetable oil in an electric skillet or a skillet on the range over medium heat (350°F in an electric skillet); using a spatula, distribute the oil over the bottom of the skillet. Add the ground beef; using a large spoon, break up the chunks of meat as it begins to brown. Add the onions and garlic; sauté until the contents are lightly browned, stirring often. Cool to room temperature; spread evenly over the cream cheese mixture in the baking dish; press *very lightly*. Spread evenly in layers over the beef mixture in the following order: salsa, shredded cheese, olives, lettuce, and tomatoes. Cover and refrigerate.

To serve, place tortilla chips in an attractive basket or bowl next to the Taco Spread. Provide 1 or 2 small knives for spreading.

MAKES ABOUT 9 CUPS
(11 DOZEN HORS D'OEUVRES)

LAST-MINUTE CHEESE SPREAD

A good-tasting hors d'oeuvre you can prepare in a jiffy after a quick trip to the grocery store. A simple sprig of parsley will doll up the top of the spread.

12 ounces (1¼ cups) regular cream cheese spread
2 tablespoons whole milk*
1 cup shredded sharp cheddar cheese

4 ounces blue cheese, crumbled
Assorted crackers

Lowfat or skim milk may be substituted.

In a medium mixing bowl, place the cream cheese and milk; using a spoon, stir until blended. Add the cheddar cheese and blue cheese; stir until evenly combined. Serve the spread in an attractive bowl surrounded by assorted crackers. Supply a small knife for spreading.

MAKES ABOUT 2½ CUPS
(5 DOZEN HORS D'OEUVRES)

BRAUNSCHWEIGER SPREAD

Braunschweiger is a soft, smooth, smoked pork liver sausage. Its name derives from the German town of Braunschweig.

8 ounces braunschweiger
16 ounces commercial sour cream
1 1-ounce envelope onion soup mix
Cocktail-sized pumpernickel bread

AT LEAST 6 HOURS BEFORE SERVING: Place the braunschweiger in a medium mixing bowl; let it stand at room temperature until slightly softened.

Using a tablespoon, mash the braunschweiger. Add the sour cream; using an electric mixer, beat on medium speed until blended. Add the onion soup mix; using a spoon, stir to combine. Cover and refrigerate at least 6 hours to allow the soup mix to soften and the flavors to blend.

Spoon the Braunschweiger Spread into a serving bowl; place it on a doily-lined plate and surround it with slices of pumpernickel bread. Provide a small knife for spreading.

MAKES ABOUT 3 CUPS
(6 DOZEN HORS D'OEUVRES)

ALTERNATIVE SERVING SUGGESTION: Spread Braunschweiger Spread on cocktail-sized pumpernickel bread slices prior to serving; garnish each canapé with a small, fresh parsley leaf or a thin slice of tiny, sweet gherkin pickle.

DRIED BEEF AND GREEN PEPPER SPREAD

This is one of my sister-in-law's standbys served at family gatherings for years. We love it! Hope you do too. The recipe has been in Dee's files for so long, she can't remember the source. This is often the case with many Midwest recipes handed down and exchanged over the years (and generations).

16 ounces cream cheese, softened
3 tablespoons finely grated onions
2 garlic cloves, pressed
1 tablespoon white wine Worcestershire sauce
5 ounces sliced dried beef, chopped finely
    (about 1⅓ cups)
1½ cups finely chopped green bell peppers
    (about 1½ medium green peppers)
Low-sodium whole-wheat crackers

Preheat the oven to 300°F.

In a medium mixing bowl, place the cream cheese, onions, garlic, and Worcestershire sauce; using an electric mixer, beat on high speed until creamy. Add the dried beef and green peppers; using a spoon, stir until evenly combined. Turn the mixture into a 1-quart round baking dish. Cover the dish and heat the mixture in the oven until *warm,* not hot, stirring twice during the warming period (about 30 minutes). The purpose of warming the mixture is to blend the flavors while retaining the crispness of the green peppers. Do not allow the mixture to become hot and begin to bubble. Transfer the warm mixture to a serving bowl; cover and refrigerate it until cold. Serve with crackers; provide a knife for spreading.

MAKES ABOUT 3½ CUPS
(7 DOZEN HORS D'OEUVRES)

TRIPLE-LAYER CAVIAR SPREAD

½ cup (¼ pound) butter, softened
3 extra-large eggs, hard-cooked (page 222)
    and chopped
8 ounces commercial sour cream
¾ cup finely chopped onions
3½ ounces caviar
Small, plain water crackers

AT LEAST 6 HOURS BEFORE SERVING: In a blender, place the butter and chopped eggs; process until the mixture is a smooth, buttery consistency. Using a small, narrow, angled spatula, spread the mixture evenly over the bottom of a 7- or 8-inch flat-bottomed crystal serving plate with short sides (or an 8-inch glass pie plate). In a small mixing bowl, place the sour cream and onions; stir to combine. Spoon the sour cream mixture over the egg-butter layer in the serving plate; using a clean small, narrow, angled spatula, spread evenly and smoothly. Cover well with plastic wrap and then aluminum foil; refrigerate at least 6 hours.

Shortly before serving, carefully spoon the caviar over the sour cream layer in the serving dish and spread evenly. Place the serving dish on a round, silver or crystal plate; surround the caviar serving dish with crackers. Provide a small serving knife.

MAKES ABOUT 3 CUPS
(6 DOZEN HORS D'OEUVRES)

BOK CHOY STUFFED WITH RED CAVIAR

1 bunch bok choy* (page 256)
8 ounces regular cream cheese spread
1 tablespoon finely grated onions
2 ounces red salmon caviar
3 hard-cooked, extra-large egg yolks, finely
    grated

If bok choy is not available, celery may be substituted.

Clean the bok choy thoroughly. Split the white stalks in half lengthwise. Cut the split stalks into 2-inch-long pieces; dry with paper towels; set aside. In a small mixing bowl, place the cream cheese and onions; stir to blend. Add ⅔ of the caviar; stir carefully to combine. Using a knife, stuff the bok choy pieces with the cream cheese mixture. Sprinkle the stuffed bok choy with the grated egg yolks; garnish the tops with the remaining caviar. Cover carefully; refrigerate until ready to serve.

MAKES ABOUT 4 DOZEN

CUCUMBER WHEELS

2 seedless cucumbers, about 1 foot long each
1 5-ounce jar prepared horseradish
½ teaspoon finely snipped, fresh dillweed
2 teaspoons sugar
¼ teaspoon salt
⅛ teaspoon white pepper
½ cup whipping cream, whipped
Tiny sprigs of fresh dillweed for decoration

Pare 1 cucumber (page 17). Cut evenly into ⅜-inch slices (about 30 slices). Using a tiny, ⅜-inch melon baller, carefully scoop out a well in the center seed section of each cucumber slice, leaving the bottom of each slice intact and uncut. Place the slices, well side down, on 3 layers of paper towels; let stand.

Pare the remaining cucumber. Cut into ½-inch slices; cut each slice into quarters. Measure 4 cups quartered cucumber slices; reserve any remaining slices for other uses. Place the 4 cups quartered cucumber slices in a food processor, ⅓ at a time, and process, using on/off turns, until they reach the consistency of pulp. Be careful not to completely liquefy them. Secure 2 layers of damp cheesecloth in a medium-sized sieve and place over a deep pan. Pour the cucumber pulp into the cheesecloth to strain. When strained, lift the cheesecloth containing the strained pulp off the sieve; pull the 4 corners of the cheesecloth together and twist to make a cheesecloth bag of pulp. Wring and squeeze the bag to extract nearly all liquid until there remains ½ cup measured pulp; set aside.

Place the horseradish in a medium-sized sieve to drain. With your hand, firmly press the horseradish in the sieve to extract as much liquid as possible until there remains ¼ cup measured, drained, packed horseradish. In a medium mixing bowl, place the drained cucumber pulp, drained horseradish, ½ teaspoon dillweed, sugar, salt, and white pepper; stir to combine. Add the whipped cream; fold in.

Using a decorating bag fit with large round tip number 1A (page 325), pipe a mound of horseradish mixture into the well in each cucumber slice. Gently tuck a tiny sprig of fresh dillweed (using a pair of kitchen tweezers, if you have them) into the top of each mound of horseradish mixture for decoration. Place the Cucumber Wheels in a dome-covered container and refrigerate them until serving time.

MAKES 30

CUCUMBER AND CHEESE CANAPÉS

3 ounces cream cheese, softened
2 teaspoons chili sauce
2 teaspoons light rum
3 slices thinly sliced white bread
12 thin, seedless cucumber slices

In a small mixing bowl, place the cream cheese, chili sauce, and light rum; using an electric mixer, beat on high speed until smooth and blended; set aside. Toast the bread. Using a sharp knife, cut off the crusts. Cut each piece of toast into 4 squares. Spread the cream cheese mixture on the toast squares. Place a slice of cucumber on top of each square. Cover and refrigerate them until serving time.

MAKES ONE DOZEN

CHERRY TOMATOES STUFFED WITH CURRIED CHICKEN SALAD

(See photo insert page A-2)

3 dozen uniformly sized cherry tomatoes
4 cups finely ground (page 16), cooked
   chicken breasts (page 169)
1½ cups minced celery
2 teaspoons finely grated onions
¾ cup mayonnaise
½ cup Miracle Whip dressing
1 tablespoon curry powder
½ teaspoon salt
½ teaspoon white pepper
3 ounces cream cheese, softened
Yellow paste food coloring (optional)

Using a very sharp, thin-bladed paring knife, cut a generous slice off the stem end of the tomatoes; discard the slices. Using the knife, carefully remove the seeds and cores from the tomatoes; as they are prepared, place them upside down on paper towels to drain. After preparing all the tomatoes, turn them right side up and place them in an airtight container; refrigerate until ready to stuff.

In a medium mixing bowl, place the chicken, celery, and onions; stir to combine and set aside. In a small mixing bowl, place the mayonnaise, dressing, curry powder, salt, and white pepper; stir until well combined. Add the mayonnaise mixture to the chicken mixture; stir to combine.

Using a demitasse spoon, mound the chicken salad in the tomatoes and pack it with your thumb. Set the filled tomatoes aside. Place the cream cheese in a small mixing bowl; using an electric mixer, beat on high speed until smooth. Add a tiny amount of food coloring to tint yellow; beat the mixture until evenly blended. Using a decorating bag fit with small open-star tip number 15 (page 319), pipe a small star (page 324) on top of each stuffed tomato.

MAKES 6 DOZEN

PETITE POTATOES

2½ dozen tiny, unpared, new red potatoes,
   steamed (page 276)
Vegetable oil
16 ounces commercial sour cream
¼ cup very finely grated onions
Black caviar
Red caviar

Place the steamed potatoes on 2 layers of paper towels to drain and cool. When cool, dampen a paper towel with vegetable oil and rub the potatoes to lightly oil the skins. Using a sharp, thin-bladed knife, cut the potatoes in half lengthwise. Using a ⅞-inch melon baller, scoop a ⅞-inch-diameter and ¼-inch-deep round section of potato flesh out of the center of each potato half to form a cup. Place the potatoes on plastic wrap in a flat-bottomed dish; cover and refrigerate them until cold.

In a small mixing bowl, place the sour cream and onions; stir to combine. Using a decorating bag fit with medium round tip number 8 (page 319), pipe a mound of the sour cream mixture into the cup in each potato half (or use 2 demitasse spoons to mound the mixture in the potatoes). Refrigerate the filled potatoes on plastic wrap in a dome-covered container until shortly before serving.

Close to the time of serving, place the black caviar and red caviar separately on 4 layers of paper towels to drain. Using a tiny ⅜-inch melon baller or 2 demitasse spoons, place a small amount of caviar on top of each mound of sour cream mixture in the potatoes. Place the black caviar on half of the potatoes and the red caviar on the remaining half. Placing the caviar on the sour cream mixture too far in advance of serving may result in the caviar running slightly.

MAKES 5 DOZEN

RED AND GREEN VEGETABLE TRAY

Red bell peppers, cut into ¼-inch strips
Radish Roses (page 339)
Cherry tomatoes
Pimiento-stuffed green olives
Fresh snow peas, steamed 30 seconds
  (page 252)
Fresh green asparagus spears, blanched
  (page 29) 1 minute
Bite-sized, fresh broccoli flowerets, steamed
  (page 252) 1 minute
Small, fresh Brussels sprouts, steamed
  (page 252) 2 minutes
Fresh green beans, steamed (page 252)
  2 minutes
Fresh, frozen, or canned (in water) artichoke
  hearts, cooked (if fresh or frozen) and cut
  in half lengthwise
1 recipe Vegetable Dip (page 44)

Steam, blanch, or cook the vegetables separately (to preserve their individual colors and flavors), as specified above. Then, immediately place each vegetable in a colander and rinse under cold, running water to stop the cooking. Drain well. Place the vegetables carefully in separate zipper-seal plastic bags and refrigerate until completely cold.

To serve, spoon Vegetable Dip into a bowl and place it in the center of a round tray. Arrange the vegetables in pinwheel fashion around the bowl of dip.

VARIATIONS: Any other red or green vegetables may be added or substituted.

MINI BAGELS WITH SMOKED SALMON

20 presliced mini bagels, about 2½ inches in
  diameter (available at most supermarkets)
11 ounces cream cheese, softened
8 ounces thinly sliced smoked salmon
About 5 ounces alfalfa sprouts

Separate the halves of the bagels (each half is to be an individual hors d'oeuvre). Spread each bagel half with approximately 1½ teaspoons cream cheese. Cut slices of the smoked salmon to fit on the bagel halves; place 1 slice on each half. Sprinkle alfalfa sprouts atop the smoked salmon on each hors d'oeuvre. Keep refrigerated in an airtight container until ready to serve.

MAKES 40

TARTLETS WITH CRABMEAT FILLING

1 cup boiled, fresh or frozen Alaskan
  king crabmeat (page 192),* chilled and
  finely chopped
¼ cup finely diced, pimiento-stuffed green
  olives
¼ cup chopped pecans
2 tablespoons minced celery
2 teaspoons finely minced onions
1½ teaspoons freshly squeezed, strained
  lemon juice
¼ cup Miracle Whip dressing
1 recipe Tartlet Shells (page 402)
36 thin slices of small, pimiento-stuffed green
  olives for decoration

**Canned and drained crabmeat may be
  substituted.*

In a medium mixing bowl, place the crabmeat, ¼ cup diced olives, pecans, celery, onions, and lemon juice; stir to combine. Add the dressing; stir to combine. Using a demitasse

(Recipe continues on next page)

spoon, mound the crabmeat mixture in the Tartlet Shells. Decorate the top of each filled tartlet with an olive slice.

MAKES ABOUT 3 DOZEN

VARIATIONS: The Tartlet Shells may also be filled with finely chopped Lobster Salad (page 116) or other fillings of your choice and invention.

DILL PICKLE ROLL-UPS

5 2-ounce packages lean beef (3¾-inch squares of thin, pressed beef found in the cold-cut section of the grocery store)
1 32-ounce jar Gedney kosher baby dills (small dill pickles)
8 ounces cream cheese, softened

THE DAY BEFORE SERVING: On a cutting board, place 2 pieces of the lean beef on top of each other symmetrically. Place a dill pickle lengthwise along the bottom edge of the stacked beef, lining up one end of the pickle evenly with the left side of the beef. Cut the right side of the beef, from top to bottom, evenly with the right end of the pickle. Reserve the cutaway portion of the meat to make small roll-ups or for other uses. Remove the pickle from the top of the beef. Spread a moderately thin layer of cream cheese over the beef. Replace the pickle on the beef. Roll the beef, jelly-roll fashion, around the pickle; place, seam down, in a flat-bottomed glass dish; cover lightly and refrigerate.

SHORTLY BEFORE SERVING: Using a small, sharp knife, cut the rolls into ¼- to ½-inch slices. Arrange in a single layer on a serving plate.

MAKES ABOUT 13 DOZEN

CHRISTMAS CHEESE BALL

8 ounces cream cheese, softened
1 tablespoon minced onions
1 teaspoon Worcestershire sauce
2 ounces blue cheese, finely crumbled
4 ounces medium cheddar cheese, finely shredded
2 tablespoons finely chopped green bell peppers
1 tablespoon finely chopped pimientos
¾ cup broken English walnuts
Assorted crackers

In a small mixing bowl, place the cream cheese, onions, and Worcestershire sauce; using an electric mixer, beat on high speed until creamy and smooth. Add the blue cheese; resume beating on high speed until creamed. Add the cheddar cheese; beat on medium speed until mixed, leaving some visible pieces of yellow cheddar cheese; set aside. In a small bowl, place the green peppers and pimientos; stir to combine. Add the peppers and pimientos to the cheese mixture; using a spoon, stir until evenly distributed. Cover and refrigerate 1 hour.

Scatter the walnuts on waxed paper. Remove the cheese mixture from the refrigerator; form it into a ball and roll it in the walnuts until evenly covered. Wrap the cheese ball in plastic wrap; refrigerate. Serve with assorted crackers of choice.

MAKES ABOUT 2½ CUPS
(5 DOZEN HORS D'OEUVRES)

CHRISTMAS CRACKERS

2½ dozen small, plain water crackers
8 ounces regular cream cheese spread
Mint jelly
Canned wild lingonberries in sugar

Spread the crackers generously with cream cheese, forming a slight mound in the center of each cracker. Using the back of a melon baller, make a cup in the center of the cream cheese. Fill each cream cheese cup in half of the crackers with ½ teaspoon mint jelly. Fill each cream cheese cup in the remaining half of the crackers with ½ teaspoon lingonberries. Arrange on a white doily-lined plate.

MAKES 2½ DOZEN

VARIATIONS: Cherry jelly and strawberry jelly may also be used as fillings.

CHUTNEY CHEESE BALL

8 ounces cream cheese, softened
2 ounces blue cheese, softened
⅓ cup commercially canned chutney, chopped
½ cup chopped, toasted unblanched almonds
   (chop, page 4; then toast, page 10)
Assorted crackers

THE DAY BEFORE SERVING: In a small mixing bowl, place the cream cheese and blue cheese; using an electric mixer, beat on high speed until well blended. Add the chutney; using a spoon, stir to combine. Cover and refrigerate at least 3 hours until firm enough to form into a ball.

Scatter the almonds on waxed paper. Remove the cheese mixture from the refrigerator; form into a ball and roll in the almonds until evenly covered. Wrap the cheese ball in plastic wrap; refrigerate overnight.

TO SERVE: Reshape the ball, flatten slightly, and place on a small plate. Serve with crackers.

MAKES ABOUT 2 CUPS
(4 DOZEN HORS D'OEUVRES)

COLD POACHED WHOLE SALMON

Talk about elegance—a cold, poached whole salmon gorgeously decorated and shimmering with an aspic glaze is hard to top. Place a crystal bowl of Green Sauce (Sauce Verte) (page 299) next to this sublime offering on the buffet, and you have a stunning delicacy fit for the most sophisticated of epicures. (Plus, you'll have great fun preparing it.)

This recipe calls for the salmon to be poached in a court bouillon, which is a flavored broth generally used for poaching fish and shellfish. Court bouillon consists of a water base in which vegetables such as onions, carrots, and celery; herbs (a bouquet garni [page 26]); and wine, vinegar, or lemon juice (an acid) are simmered for a short period of time to impart flavor. Very often, thyme, parsley, and a bay leaf are among the herbs. In this court bouillon, I used white wine (chardonnay); in fact, I used one whole bottle of it.

1 5- to 6-pound whole salmon, skin, head, and tail left on; scales and fins removed
Court Bouillon (see headnote)
   3 large sprigs fresh thyme
   3 large sprigs fresh parsley
   1 bay leaf
   3 quarts water
   1 750mL bottle (slightly more than 3 cups)
      chardonnay wine
   1 stalk celery with green leaves, sliced into
      ½-inch pieces
   1 medium carrot, pared and sliced into
      ½-inch pieces
   1 small, yellow onion studded with 3 whole
      cloves
   1 ¼-inch slice lemon (including peel)
   8 black peppercorns (whole black pepper)
   ¾ teaspoon salt

(Recipe continues on next page)

Unflavored Aspic (recipe follows)
Optional decorations for salmon and platter
  (see Optional Decoration Suggestions below)
3 recipes Green Sauce (Sauce Verte) (page 299)
Deluxe Crackers, room temperature (page 382)

If frozen, thaw the salmon in the refrigerator. Do not thaw the salmon unrefrigerated.

Place the salmon on one of its sides and precisely measure it at the thickest part; make a note of the measurement. Then, wash the salmon under cold, running water. Wrap the salmon in cheesecloth; using cotton string, tie it widthwise, somewhat securely, in 3 places. Place the wrapped salmon (on one of its sides) on the rack of a 24 × 7 × 4 ½-inch fish poacher; set aside.

Using the thyme and parsley sprigs, make a bouquet garni (page 26); set aside. The bay leaf may be included in the bouquet garni or added to the court bouillon separately. (I added it separately.)

Situate the poacher on the range so it covers 2 burners to achieve sufficient and as even heat as possible. Pour the water and wine into the poacher (see Note). Add the bouquet garni, bay leaf (if not included in the bouquet garni), celery, carrots, onion, lemon slice, peppercorns, and salt. Cover the poacher. Over high heat, bring the court bouillon to a low boil; reduce the heat and simmer the mixture moderately to slowly for 15 minutes.

Then, carefully lower the rack containing the salmon into the poacher. If the liquid does not entirely cover the salmon, add more water. It is important that the salmon be covered with liquid. Return the court bouillon to a simmer and poach the salmon 10 minutes for each inch of its thickness as measured. It is very important not to overcook the salmon, as overcooking will cause it to fall apart. Do not allow the court bouillon to come to a full boil, as this, too, will cause the salmon to overcook.

When the cooking time has expired, remove the rack containing the wrapped salmon from the poacher and place the rack containing the salmon across the sink to drain briefly; let stand.

Lay an unfolded tea towel on a flat counter surface. Place the rack (with the salmon) on the tea towel. Move the wrapped salmon from the rack onto the center of the tea towel. Very carefully, unwrap the salmon to expose one side of it. Leaving the salmon on the tea towel, use a small, sharp paring knife to remove the skin and scrape away the underlying dark flesh from the exposed side of the salmon. (Removing the dark flesh will require a little time and patience. Try not to roughen the red/pink salmon flesh.) Then, pull the front and back of the tea towel together to encase the salmon; roll the salmon over on its other side. Turn back the tea towel; remove and discard the cheesecloth. Then, remove the skin and dark flesh from the other side of the salmon, leaving the salmon on the tea towel.

Next to the salmon, place a long, narrow fish platter made especially for serving whole fish (available at commercial kitchen supply stores). Holding the far side of the tea towel, roll the salmon onto its side on the serving platter. Cover the salmon and platter with plastic wrap; refrigerate.

When cold, remove the salmon from the refrigerator; remove the plastic wrap. Pour some of the Unflavored Aspic (syrup consistency) into a small pitcher or measuring cup. Pour a fairly thin layer of aspic over the salmon. A very soft pastry brush may be used sparingly to assist in covering all the exposed parts of the salmon, including the head and tail, with aspic. The underside of the salmon will not be covered with aspic. Then, decorate the salmon, if desired. After decorating, pour additional aspic over the salmon. Using a damp sponge and cotton swabs, remove any aspic that has dripped onto the platter.

Near serving time, remove the salmon from the refrigerator and decorate the platter around the salmon, if desired; refrigerate until serving time.

To serve, place the salmon platter on the buffet or serving table; provide a serving fork and small, sharp knife. Spoon the Green Sauce into a crystal or other glass bowl and place it on a doily-lined plate; provide a small spoon. (Refill the bowl with Green Sauce, as needed.) Arrange the Deluxe Crackers in a napkin-lined, silver or other attractive dish. Place the plate with Green Sauce and the dish of Deluxe Crackers next to the salmon platter. Diners use the serving fork (and possibly the knife) to remove small servings of salmon from the whole fish and place it on a cracker. Then, they add Green Sauce, if desired. Or, diners may place servings of salmon directly on a small plate and spoon Green Sauce either directly on the salmon or on their plate.

NOTE: After pouring the water and wine into the poacher, the rack containing the wrapped salmon may be lowered into the poacher to assure that the water and wine are sufficient to cover the fish. This step is advisable if a different size salmon or poacher from that called for in this recipe is used. Remove the rack (and salmon) before proceeding to add the other ingredients to the poacher.

The rule of thumb is 1 cup of wine to 1 quart of water. While the amount of liquid called for in this court bouillon recipe may be altered to some extent, amounts of the other court bouillon ingredients may remain the same when making the approximate amount of court bouillon this recipe yields.

SERVES 25 AS AN HORS D'OEUVRE

UNFLAVORED ASPIC

½ cup cold water
1 tablespoon plus 1 teaspoon (2 envelopes) unflavored gelatin
1 cup water

Pour ½ cup cold water into a small sauce dish; sprinkle the gelatin over the water; let stand 15 minutes.

Into a small saucepan, pour 1 cup water. Over high heat, bring the water to a boil. Remove from the heat. Add the gelatin mixture; stir until completely dissolved.

Refrigerate until the consistency of syrup. If the aspic begins to gel, it may be reheated briefly over medium-low heat until it returns to a syrup consistency.

OPTIONAL DECORATION SUGGESTIONS: (see illustration) The following are merely suggestions for rendering fairly simple salmon and platter decorations. If you are so inclined, use your imagination and finesse to create more intricate decorations appropriate to the dish.

SALMON DECORATION

3 thin, grooved, seedless cucumber slices (see Grooved Cucumber Slices, page 334)
2 small, round flower centers made from yellow bell pepper flesh (see Bell Pepper Leaves and Flower Petals, page 338)
1 small, round flower center made from red bell pepper flesh (see Bell Pepper Leaves and Flower Petals, page 338)
3 flower stems plus leaves fashioned from green onion leaves (see Ribbons and Outline Designs from Green Onion Leaves, page 336)

Arrange the 3 cucumber slices like flower blossoms over the freshly aspic-coated salmon. Using decorating tip number 12, if available, (see page 319) or another small, sharp, round implement, stamp out the 2 yellow and 1 red flower centers from the processed bell peppers. Add the centers to the 3 cucumber flowers on the salmon. Then, using the pliable green onion leaves, arrange stems with leaves on the cucumber flowers to simulate a bouquet. (Then, add the last coat of aspic over the salmon and decorations.)

PLATTER DECORATION

Grooved, seedless cucumber slices (see Grooved Cucumber Slices, page 334)
Grooved lemon slices (see Grooved Citrus Slices, page 334)
Curly-leaf and Italian parsley sprigs

Decoratively arrange the cucumber slices, lemon slices, and parsley sprigs around the salmon on the platter (see illustration).

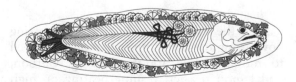

Other Cold Hors d'Oeuvre Recipes

Deviled Eggs (page 224)
Hickory-Smoked Ham Mousse (page 65)
Shrimp Mousse with Dill (page 63)

Hot Hors d'Oeuvres

HOT BOURBON-CHEESE DIP

8 ounces cream cheese, softened
½ cup Miracle Whip dressing
1 tablespoon bourbon
1 teaspoon lemon pepper
1 cup (4 ounces) shredded brick cheese
1 cup (4 ounces) shredded Swiss cheese
3 tablespoons minced onions
6 slices bacon, fried crisply, drained well
  between paper towels, and crumbled
¼ cup chopped pecans
¼ cup rolled Ritz crackers
Onion-flavored melba rounds

Preheat the oven to 350°F.

Place the cream cheese in a medium mixing bowl; using an electric mixer, beat on high speed to smooth slightly. Add the dressing, bourbon, and lemon pepper; resume beating on high speed until very smooth. Add the brick cheese, Swiss cheese, and onions; using a spoon, stir to

combine. Place the mixture in a 9-inch glass pie plate; using a small, narrow spatula, spread evenly. Distribute the bacon evenly over the surface of the mixture. Sprinkle the pecans evenly over the bacon. Just before baking, sprinkle the cracker crumbs over the top. Bake, uncovered, 20 minutes. Remove from the oven and place on a wire rack; let stand 5 minutes to cool slightly before serving. Serve with onion-flavored melba rounds. Provide a small knife.

MAKES ABOUT 2¾ CUPS
(5 DOZEN HORS D'OEUVRES)

ARTICHOKE DIP

1 9-ounce package frozen artichoke hearts
  cooked well, drained, and chopped (about
  1½ cups chopped artichoke hearts)*
1 cup mayonnaise
1 cup freshly grated Parmesan cheese
  (page 30)
1 very small garlic clove, pressed
1 tablespoon very finely chopped onions
Assorted crackers

*Fresh or canned (in water) artichoke hearts
  may be substituted. Canned artichoke
  hearts are precooked and do not require
  additional cooking for this recipe.*

Preheat the oven to 350°F. Grease a 1-quart round baking dish.

In a medium mixing bowl, place the artichoke hearts, mayonnaise, Parmesan cheese, garlic, and onions; stir well to combine. Place the mixture in the prepared baking dish; bake 20 minutes or until bubbly. Serve warm with crackers. Provide a small knife.

MAKES ABOUT 3 CUPS
(6 DOZEN HORS D'OEUVRES)

ASPARAGUS ROLLS

(See photo insert page A-2)

I receive more recipe requests from friends for this simple hors d'oeuvre than for any other hors d'oeuvre I serve.

36 medium-small fresh asparagus spears*
1 pound sliced bacon
36 slices of thinly sliced, soft-style, very fresh, white sandwich bread (the least expensive kind of bread works best with this recipe)
1½ cups Miracle Whip dressing
½ cup plus 2 tablespoons butter, softened

If desired, 1½ 15-ounce commercial cans of extra-long green asparagus spears, drained, may be substituted. Canned asparagus spears are precooked and do not require additional cooking for this recipe.

Wash the asparagus spears and cut them exactly 4 inches long; discard the cutaway stalks or reserve for other use. Boil the asparagus spears (page 252) 3 minutes; rinse them in cold water to stop the cooking. Drain the spears well. Place the spears on a plate; cover and refrigerate. Fry the bacon until crisp; drain well between paper towels. With your fingers, crumble the bacon. Place the bacon in a small storage container; cover and refrigerate.

Assemble the Asparagus Rolls no longer than 2 hours before serving. To assemble, cut the crusts off the bread slices. Keep the bread slices covered to retain softness. Using a small, narrow, angled spatula, spread dressing liberally on one side of each slice of bread (about 2 teaspoons per slice) to within about ¼ inch of the edges. Sprinkle about 1 tablespoon crumbled bacon over the dressing on each bread slice. Place 1 asparagus spear diagonally across the center of each slice. Roll each slice diagonally around the asparagus spear and place in a shallow, ungreased baking pan, with the unsealed corner of bread down. Place the Asparagus Rolls side by side, touching each other, in the pan. Using a table knife, spread about ½ teaspoon butter over the top of each roll. Cover the pan tightly with aluminum foil until ready to serve.

When ready to serve, preheat the broiler. Uncover the pan of Asparagus Rolls and place under the broiler, 6 inches from the heat. Leave under the broiler just a few minutes until the tops of the rolls are golden brown. Watch constantly as they can overbrown very quickly. Using a spatula, transfer the Asparagus Rolls to a doily-lined tray and serve immediately.

MAKES 3 DOZEN

CRABMEAT SUPREME WITH SAUTÉED TOAST POINTS

1 pound cooked lump crabmeat, frozen or canned and drained
11 ounces cream cheese, softened
2 tablespoons butter
½ cup finely chopped green bell peppers
¼ cup drained, minced capers
½ cup mayonnaise
1 tablespoon finely snipped, fresh parsley
1 tablespoon drained, prepared horseradish, homemade (page 30) or commercially canned
¼ teaspoon salt
Dash cayenne pepper
2 teaspoons Worcestershire sauce
¼ cup dry white wine
¼ cup Buttered Bread Crumbs (page 33)
Paprika
2 recipes Sautéed Toast Points (page 364)

Preheat the oven to 375° F. Lightly butter a 1-quart round baking dish.

Place the crabmeat in a small mixing bowl. With your fingers, carefully remove any bits of cartilage or shell and discard; set aside. Place the softened cream cheese in a medium mixing bowl; set aside. In a skillet, over medium-low heat, melt the butter; add the green peppers and sauté until soft but not browned (about 3 min-

(Recipe continues on next page)

utes). Add the green peppers, capers, mayonnaise, parsley, horseradish, salt, cayenne pepper, Worcestershire sauce, and white wine to the cream cheese; using an electric mixer, beat on medium-high speed until the ingredients are well blended. Add the crabmeat; using a spoon, fold in. Pour into the prepared baking dish. Sprinkle the bread crumbs on top. Bake uncovered for 30 minutes.

To serve, sprinkle sparingly with paprika. Place the casserole in the center of a serving dish and surround with Sautéed Toast Points. Supply 1 or 2 small knives for serving.

MAKES 4 DOZEN HORS D'OEUVRES

GOUDA IN PUFF PASTRY

1 7-ounce round of Gouda cheese
1 sheet frozen puff pastry (½ of a 17.3-ounce package)
1 extra-large egg
1 teaspoon whole milk
¼ teaspoon garlic powder
1 tablespoon freshly grated Parmesan cheese (page 30)
Plain butter crackers

3 HOURS BEFORE SERVING: Remove the red wax covering from the Gouda cheese. Place the cheese on a small plate; cover with plastic wrap and let stand at room temperature.

1½ HOURS BEFORE SERVING: Remove 1 sheet of frozen puff pastry from the package; place it folded on a floured pastry cloth; let stand 20 minutes to thaw. Unfold the puff pastry carefully on the pastry cloth; let stand an additional 15 minutes to continue thawing.

Meanwhile, in a small mixing bowl, place the egg and milk; using an electric mixer, beat briefly until blended; set aside.

Preheat the oven to 400° F.

Cover a rolling pin with a stockinet (page 38); flour the stockinet lightly. Roll the pastry sheet to a 10½-inch square. Place an inverted 9-inch pie pan on the pastry; using a small, sharp knife, cut the pastry around the periphery of the inverted pie pan to form a circle of pastry. Lift the pie pan from the pastry. Lift the excess pastry from the edges of the circle and reserve for optional cutout decoration (see Note). Place the Gouda cheese, more-rounded side down, in the center of the pastry circle. Sprinkle the garlic powder on the cheese round; using your fingers, rub the powder evenly over the exposed surface of the cheese. Sprinkle the Parmesan cheese over the cheese round. Using the back of a teaspoon, press the Parmesan cheese onto the exposed top of the cheese round.

Using a soft, small pastry brush, brush the egg mixture around the edges of the pastry circle to help seal the pastry in the next step. Pull 2 opposite sides of the pastry circle snugly over the cheese round; using your fingers, pinch the pastry edges together to seal (stretch pastry slightly if necessary). Pull the remaining edges of the pastry snugly over the cheese round, wrapping it like a package. Use your hands to *lightly*—and with minimum handling—press the pastry against the Gouda to retain the circular shape of the round. Using kitchen scissors, cut away ½- to ¾-inch excess pastry from the last edges of pastry pulled over the cheese round; brush the cut pastry edges with the egg mixture and pinch to seal.

Turn over the pastry-wrapped cheese round and place, seam side down, on the pastry cloth. Brush all exposed pastry surfaces with the egg mixture. (Do not brush the underneath seam side.) Decorate the pastry, if desired, using the excess pastry (see Note). Using a spatula, place the pastry-wrapped cheese round on a parchment-paper-lined cookie sheet. (If parchment paper is not available, place it on an ungreased cookie sheet.) Bake 20 minutes.

Remove from the oven; using a spatula, transfer the baked Gouda to a serving plate. Let stand 15 minutes before serving; then serve immediately. Supply a very sharp knife with which guests may cut small wedges of the pastry-wrapped cheese. Arrange crackers in a dish next to the cheese. As warm Gouda runs slightly, it is better to eat this hors d'oeuvre atop a light, buttery cracker.

NOTE: To decorate the top of the pastry-wrapped Gouda, use tiny, flour-dipped cutters in designs or an X-Acto knife to cut a design, such as a flower, out of the rolled, excess puff pastry. Brush the back of each pastry cutout with the egg mixture and very lightly press it onto the unbaked, pastry-wrapped Gouda round, which has been brushed with the egg mixture. When all parts of the decoration have been arranged, brush the top of the decoration with the egg mixture. Follow the baking procedure in the recipe.

MAKES ABOUT 16 HORS D'OEUVRES

SAUSAGE PUFFS

12 ounces sage-seasoned bulk pork sausage
¼ cup fine Dried Bread Crumbs (page 33)
1 tablespoon snipped, fresh parsley
¼ cup minced onions
1 extra-large egg, beaten
1 sheet frozen puff pastry (½ of a 17.3-ounce package)
Sprigs of fresh sage for decoration (optional)
Sprigs of fresh parsley for decoration (optional)

Preheat the oven to 400°F.

In a medium bowl, place the sausage, crumbs, parsley, onions, and egg; stir to combine. Divide the mixture into thirds and shape into 3 rolls, each 7½ inches long. Place the rolls in a shallow, ungreased baking pan; bake 20 minutes. Remove from the oven and transfer the rolls onto 3 layers of paper towels to drain and cool. Meanwhile, place 1 sheet of frozen puff pastry, folded, on a floured pastry cloth; let stand 20 minutes to thaw.

Preheat the oven to 425°F.

Unfold the puff pastry carefully on the pastry cloth; let stand an additional 15 minutes to continue thawing. Using a sharp knife, cut the pastry into quarters (approximately square). Cover

a rolling pin with a stockinet (page 38); flour the stockinet lightly. Roll 3 of the pastry quarters into rectangles approximately 6 × 9 inches; reserve the fourth pastry quarter for other uses. Place 1 roll of sausage along the 9-inch side of 1 of the pastry rectangles; roll the sausage, jelly-roll fashion, in the pastry. With your fingers, seal the side seam and ends of the pastry roll well. Repeat the procedure with the other 2 sausage rolls. Place the pastry rolls in an ungreased 10½ × 15½-inch cookie pan; bake 12 to 15 minutes. Using a sharp, thin-bladed knife, cut each roll widthwise into ½-inch slices. Serve immediately. The serving plate may be decorated with sprigs of fresh sage and parsley.

MAKES 42 HORS D'OEUVRES

PIGS IN A BLANKET
Saucijzebroodjes

A popular, traditional Holland Dutch pastry, Pigs in a Blanket are most often enjoyed at Dutch coffee tijd (time) in the mid-morning or mid-afternoon, when fairly substantial fare may be served. Pigs in a Blanket are most commonly made in approximately 3-inch lengths; however, in this recipe I have shortened them to about 2 inches for serving as hors d'oeuvres.

FILLING
¾ pound seasoned, lean bulk sausage
¾ pound lean, pure ground beef
¾ teaspoon salt
¼ teaspoon pepper
2 teaspoons finely crushed, dried leaf sage
½ cup Dutch rusk crumbs*
1 tablespoon half-and-half or whole milk

***Dried Bread Crumbs (page 33) may be substituted.**

In a medium mixing bowl, place the sausage, ground beef, salt, pepper, sage, rusk crumbs, and half-and-half; stir until thoroughly combined. Using a 1-inch trigger scoop and

(Recipe continues on next page)

your hands, form the mixture into 1-inch-diameter balls. With the palms of your hands, roll each ball into a 1¾-inch-long by ½-inch-diameter roll; cover and refrigerate.

DOUGH

2 cups all-purpose flour
1 tablespoon baking powder
2 teaspoons sugar
¾ teaspoon salt
½ cup lard, refrigerated
1 extra-large egg, beaten
½ cup whole milk
About ¾ teaspoon lard to top pastries

Preheat the oven to 350° F.

Onto waxed paper, sift together the flour, baking powder, sugar, and salt; place in a large mixing bowl. Using a pastry blender, cut ½ cup lard into the flour mixture until it is the texture of cornmeal, with a few pieces the size of small peas; set aside. Place the egg in a small bowl; using an electric mixer, beat on medium speed. Add the milk; beat briefly to blend. Add the egg mixture to the flour mixture all at once; using a fork, mix *quickly*. Lightly flour your hands; form the dough into a ball and knead 30 seconds on a floured pastry cloth.

Divide the dough in half; wrap one half in plastic wrap and place in the refrigerator while working with the other half. Cover a rolling pin with a stockinet (page 38); flour the stockinet lightly. Roll half of the dough to ⅛-inch thickness. With a sharp, thin-bladed knife, cut the dough into 2 × 2½-inch rectangles. Place one roll of filling on each rectangle; roll the dough around the filling; pinch the side seam and ends to close. Place, side seam down, in an ungreased 10½ × 15½-inch cookie pan. Repeat the procedure with the remaining half of dough. Place a tiny dot of lard (about half the size of a chocolate chip) on top of each pastry. Bake 30 minutes. Serve hot.

MAKES ABOUT 4 DOZEN

VARIATION: Pigs in a Blanket may be made in lengths up to 3 inches.

PIZZA MUSHROOMS

1 pound (about 4 dozen) medium-small (bite-sized), fresh mushrooms
⅓ cup white wine vinegar
⅔ cup water
¼ teaspoon dry mustard
¼ teaspoon salt
⅛ teaspoon white pepper
⅔ cup commercially canned pizza sauce
⅓ cup finely chopped pepperoni
⅓ cup finely chopped green bell peppers
2 tablespoons finely chopped onions
⅔ cup finely shredded mozzarella cheese

THE DAY BEFORE SERVING: Wash the mushrooms and remove the stems by snapping them out of the caps. Set the mushroom caps aside, stem side down, on 3 layers of paper towels; reserve the stems for other uses or discard. In a pint glass jar, place the vinegar, water, dry mustard, salt, and white pepper. Cover and shake vigorously until blended; set aside. Place the mushroom caps in a ½-gallon zipper-seal plastic bag; add the vinegar mixture (marinade) and seal the bag securely. Turn the bag until all the mushrooms are coated with the marinade. Place the bag in a shallow, glass dish (in case of leakage); refrigerate. Turn the bag several times during the 24-hour marinating period.

THE DAY OF SERVING: In a small mixing bowl, place the pizza sauce, pepperoni, green peppers, and onions; stir until combined. Cover and refrigerate.

3 HOURS OR LESS BEFORE SERVING: Drain the mushrooms in a sieve or colander; discard the marinade or reserve for other uses. Place the mushrooms, stem side down, on 3 layers of paper towels to continue draining. Lay another paper towel over the mushrooms and pat dry. Using a teaspoon and your thumb, fill the stem cavities of the mushrooms with the pizza sauce mixture, mounding the mixture generously and patting it until smooth and symmetrical. Place the stuffed mushrooms in a very shallow baking pan. If not ready to serve, cover with plastic wrap and refrigerate.

SERVING TIME: Preheat the oven to 350° F.

Heat the stuffed mushrooms, uncovered, for 8 minutes. Remove from the oven.

Preheat the broiler.

Sprinkle a generous amount of mozzarella cheese over the stuffing in each mushroom. Place the pan of mushrooms under the broiler, 6 inches from the heat; watch carefully and remove from the broiler as soon as the cheese melts. Be careful not to overbroil, causing the cheese to overheat and become less attractive. Immediately remove the stuffed mushrooms from the pan and place them briefly on 3 layers of paper towels to dry the round bottoms of the mushrooms. Arrange the Pizza Mushrooms on a doily-lined serving tray or plate, and serve while hot.

MAKES ABOUT 4 DOZEN

SWEDISH MEATBALLS

1 cup whole milk
1 extra-large egg
2 slices white bread, crusts cut away
1 pound lean, pure ground beef
1 pound lean ground pork
1 pound ground ham
2 tablespoons vegetable shortening
1 cup packed dark brown sugar
1 tablespoon cornstarch
½ cup red wine vinegar
½ cup beef broth, homemade (page 70) or
   commercially canned
1 tablespoon tomato catsup
1 teaspoon dry mustard

Grease a 2-quart round baking dish; set aside.

In a large mixing bowl, place the milk and egg; using an electric mixer, beat on medium speed until blended. Place the bread in the egg mixture and let soak thoroughly; then, using the electric mixer, beat the bread mixture on medium-low speed until the bread is broken into tiny pieces.

Add the beef, pork, and ham; using a mixing spoon, mix until completely and evenly combined. Using a 1-inch trigger scoop or melon baller, measure the meat mixture and roll in the palms of your hands to form small, uniform meatballs. In an electric skillet or skillet on the range, melt the shortening over medium heat (350° F in an electric skillet). Distribute the melted shortening over the bottom of the skillet. Add the meatballs and brown well, rolling often to maintain their round shape. Cook in batches if necessary. Drain the meatballs on 3 layers of paper towels. Place the drained meatballs in the prepared baking dish; set aside.

Preheat the oven to 300° F.

In a small saucepan, place the brown sugar, cornstarch, vinegar, beef broth, catsup, and dry mustard; stir to combine. Over medium heat, bring the mixture to a boil, stirring constantly; pour over the meatballs. Bake, uncovered, 2 hours. Serve in the baking dish or transfer to a chafing dish. Provide fancy toothpicks in an attractive container next to the meatballs and a small plate on which used toothpicks may be discarded.

MAKES ABOUT 9 DOZEN

WATER CHESTNUT ROLL-UPS

1 8-ounce can whole water chestnuts
¼ cup packed dark brown sugar
½ teaspoon dry mustard
¼ cup tomato catsup
8 slices bacon

Preheat the broiler.

Drain the water chestnuts in a small sieve; place on 2 layers of paper towels to dry; set aside. In a small sauce dish, place the brown sugar and dry mustard; stir to combine; set aside. Place the catsup in a small sauce dish; set aside. Cut each bacon slice into thirds widthwise; set aside. Dip each water chestnut in the catsup, roll in the brown sugar mixture to coat, and wrap in a

(Recipe continues on next page)

piece of bacon. Place, seam up, in a shallow baking pan. Broil, 6 inches from the heat, about 6 minutes. Remove from the broiler. Place a cellophane-frilled toothpick in each roll-up. Lift each roll-up from the baking pan, lightly blot it on 2 layers of paper towels, and place it on a doily-lined serving dish. Serve immediately.

MAKES ABOUT 2 DOZEN

BOURBON BANGERS

1¼ cups tomato catsup
½ cup packed dark brown sugar
1 tablespoon finely grated onions
2 teaspoons prepared mustard
½ cup bourbon
1 pound fully cooked, smoked, cocktail-sized
    sausages

In a medium saucepan, place the catsup, brown sugar, onions, mustard, and bourbon; stir to combine. Bring the mixture to a simmer over medium-high heat. Reduce the heat to low and slowly simmer, uncovered, 5 minutes, stirring occasionally. Add the sausages and heat through. Serve in a chafing dish with an attractive holder full of cellophane-frilled toothpicks on the side.

MAKES ABOUT 4 DOZEN

WINGLETS ORIENTAL

1½ pounds (about 16) drumstick sections of
    chicken wings
¼ cup packed light brown sugar
½ teaspoon dry mustard
2 tablespoons butter
¼ cup soy sauce

Preheat the oven to 350°F. Butter an 8 × 8-inch baking dish.

Place the drumsticks in the prepared baking dish; set aside. In a small bowl, place the brown sugar and dry mustard; stir to combine; set aside. Place the butter in a small saucepan; melt over low heat. Add the soy sauce and brown sugar mixture. Bring to a boil over medium heat, stirring constantly; pour over drumsticks. Bake 45 minutes, turning once after 25 minutes baking time. Drain briefly on paper towels.

MAKES ABOUT 16

SPINACH BARS

1 cup all-purpose flour
1 teaspoon baking powder
1 teaspoon salt
2 extra-large eggs
6 tablespoons butter, melted
2 pounds fresh spinach, cooked, well drained,
    and finely chopped (not buttered; page
    285) (about 1 cup)
¼ cup finely grated onions
1 pound Monterey Jack cheese, shredded

Preheat the oven to 350°F. Using a pastry brush, grease a 10½ × 15½ × 1-inch cookie pan with vegetable oil. Using paper towels, remove the excess oil; set aside.

Onto waxed paper, sift together the flour, baking powder, and salt; set aside. Place the eggs in a medium mixing bowl; using an electric mixer, beat lightly on medium speed. Add the butter; beat on medium speed until blended.

Add the flour mixture; beat on low speed only until blended. Add the spinach, onions, and cheese; using a mixing spoon, fold in until evenly combined. Spoon the mixture into the prepared cookie pan; using a large, narrow spatula, spread lightly and evenly. Bake 40 minutes.

Remove from the oven and place on a wire rack; let cool 5 minutes. Then, using a sharp, thin-bladed knife, cut into 64 bars. Using a small spatula, remove the bars from the pan and place momentarily on 3 layers of paper towels to dry the bottom surfaces before transferring to a serving plate. Serve immediately.

MAKES 64

First-Course Appetizers

SHRIMP MOUSSE WITH DILL

¾ pound raw, unshelled shrimp, boiled (page 191), shelled and deveined (page 191), and chilled
½ cup tomato juice
1 tablespoon plus 1 teaspoon (2 envelopes) unflavored gelatin
1 cup tomato juice
2 teaspoons sugar
¼ teaspoon salt
16 ounces commercial sour cream
1 tablespoon freshly squeezed, strained lemon juice
1 tablespoon cider vinegar
2 teaspoons onion juice (page 29)

½ teaspoon Worcestershire sauce
2 dashes Tabasco pepper sauce
1 tablespoon packed, snipped, fresh dillweed
2 recipes Dill Sauce (page 298)
Sprigs of fresh dillweed for decoration

Lightly oil (see To Lightly Oil a Salad Mold, page 89) a 4½ × 8½-inch loaf pan; set aside.

Using a food processor, process the shrimp in 2 batches, pulsing until finely flaked (about 1½ cups finely flaked shrimp). Place the processed shrimp in a bowl; cover and refrigerate. Pour ½ cup tomato juice into a small sauce dish. Sprinkle the gelatin over the juice; stir in; let stand 15 minutes.

Pour 1 cup tomato juice into a small saucepan; bring to a boil over high heat. Turn off the heat; add the gelatin mixture, sugar, and salt; stir until completely dissolved. Remove the saucepan from the range; set aside. In a blender or food processor, place the sour cream, lemon juice, vinegar, onion juice, Worcestershire sauce, and pepper sauce. Add the tomato juice mixture; process in the blender or food processor until completely blended. Add 1 tablespoon dillweed; process very briefly only until evenly distributed. Add the shrimp; process very briefly only until combined. Turn the mixture into the prepared loaf pan. Using a small, narrow spatula, spread smoothly. Refrigerate until cold; then cover with plastic wrap and aluminum foil (over the plastic wrap). Return to the refrigerator; wait until completely set (at least 8 hours) before serving.

To serve, unmold (page 89) on a flat cutting surface. Cut widthwise into 18⅜-inch slices (page 89). Spoon about 1½ tablespoons Dill Sauce into the center of small, individual serving plates; using the back of the spoon, spread the sauce over the center section of each plate. Lay 1 slice of Shrimp Mousse over the sauce on each plate (some of the sauce should be visible beyond the edges of the mousse slice). Decorate the top of each Shrimp Mousse slice with a small, feathery sprig of fresh dillweed.

SERVES 18

(Recipe continues on next page)

VARIATION ~ TO SERVE AS AN HORS D'OEUVRE: Mold the Shrimp Mousse with Dill in a lightly oiled 4-cup curved fish mold (mold the remaining

Shrimp Mousse in a small 1-cup mold for later use). Unmold the mousse (page 89) on an appropriate serving plate; decorate the plate with fresh dill sprigs. Supply a small, wide-bladed knife. Arrange small, plain water crackers on a dish or in a napkin-lined basket and place beside the mousse serving plate. (Eliminate the Dill Sauce.)

SHRIMP COCKTAIL

Leaf lettuce
¼ cup plus 2 tablespoons chopped celery
½ cup chopped boiled, fresh or frozen
    Alaskan king crabmeat (page 192)*
30 to 36 medium-sized, raw, unshelled
    shrimp, boiled (page 191), shelled with the
    tails removed, and deveined
    (page 191)
½ recipe Cocktail Sauce (page 296)

***Canned and drained crabmeat may be
    substituted.***

All ingredients should be cold before assembling the Shrimp Cocktail. Line crystal sherbet glasses with leaf lettuce. Sprinkle 1 tablespoon chopped celery in the bottom of each glass over the lettuce. Distribute 1 tablespoon plus 1 teaspoon chopped crabmeat over the chopped celery in each glass. Arrange 5 or 6 shrimp, depending upon their size and the size of the sherbet glasses, on top of the crabmeat. Spoon Cocktail Sauce over the shrimp.

Place each sherbet glass of Shrimp Cocktail on a small, doily-lined plate. Cocktail forks should be provided with each diner's table service.

SERVES 6

SCALLOPED LOBSTER

¼ cup plus 2 tablespoons all-purpose flour
½ teaspoon salt
Dash of cayenne pepper
¾ cup (¼ pound plus 4 tablespoons) butter
¼ cup plus 2 tablespoons dry sherry
1 quart half-and-half
6 extra-large egg yolks, slightly beaten
2½ cups boiled lobster meat (page 192) cut
    into small, bite-sized pieces (about
    2 pounds uncooked lobster tails)
1 cup Buttered Bread Crumbs (page 33)
Sprigs of fresh lemon thyme (optional)

Preheat the oven to 350° F. Butter twelve 5-inch-diameter by 1-inch-deep round baking dishes appropriate for serving; set aside.

In a small bowl, place the flour, salt, and cayenne pepper; stir to combine; set aside. In the top of a double boiler, over low boiling water, melt the butter. Remove the top of the double boiler from the bottom pan. Add the flour mixture to the melted butter; stir until perfectly smooth. Add the sherry and half-and-half; stir in. Return the top of the double boiler to the bottom pan. Over low boiling water, cook the mixture until heated through. In a small bowl, spoon some of the hot mixture into the egg yolks and stir in. Add the egg yolk mixture to the mixture in the double boiler; stir vigorously to blend. Continue cooking and stirring until the mixture begins to thicken. Add the lobster and cook *just until the mixture thickens,* stirring constantly. Remove the top of the double boiler.

Using a slotted spoon, distribute the hot lobster meat among the 12 prepared baking dishes, spreading the meat evenly on the bottom of each dish. Then, fill each dish with sauce. Top with buttered crumbs. Bake 5 minutes or until hot.

Preheat the broiler.

Place the baking dishes of Scalloped Lobster under the broiler; brown lightly. Garnish the top of each serving with a small sprig of lemon thyme, if desired. Place each baking dish on a doily-lined, salad-sized plate.

SERVES 12

SCALLOPED KING CRAB

Follow the Scalloped Lobster recipe, above, substituting boiled Alaskan king crabmeat (page 192) for the lobster meat.

HICKORY-SMOKED HAM MOUSSE

¼ cup cold water
1 tablespoon plus 1 teaspoon (2 envelopes) unflavored gelatin
⅔ cup boiling water
3 tablespoons Miracle Whip dressing
2 tablespoons beer mustard*
2 tablespoons cream-style, prepared horseradish, homemade (page 30) or commercially canned
¼ teaspoon paprika
2 tablespoons snipped, fresh parsley
3 cups (about 13½ ounces) fully cooked, finely ground, hickory-smoked ham
1 cup (½ pint) whipping cream
2 tablespoons powdered sugar
Sprigs of fresh parsley for decoration
1 recipe Horseradish Sauce (page 297)

If beer mustard is not available, Düsseldorf mustard or a brown mustard with smooth consistency may be substituted.

Lightly oil (see To Lightly Oil a Salad Mold, page 89) a 4½ × 8½-inch loaf pan; set aside.

Pour ¼ cup cold water into a small mixing bowl. Sprinkle the gelatin over the cold water; let stand 15 minutes. Add ⅔ cup boiling water to the gelatin mixture; stir until completely dissolved. Pour the gelatin mixture into a blender or food processor. Add the dressing, beer mustard, horseradish, and paprika; process until fully blended. Add parsley; process briefly to combine. Add ham; process briefly until combined. Set aside.

Pour the whipping cream into a medium mixing bowl; using an electric mixer, beat on high speed until the cream begins to thicken. Add the powdered sugar; beat on medium speed until stiff; set aside. Turn the blender or food processor on, briefly, to recombine the ham mixture. Transfer the ham mixture to a large mixing bowl. Add the whipped cream; using a large mixing spoon, fold in. Turn the mixture into the prepared loaf pan; using a small, narrow spatula, spread smoothly. Refrigerate until cold; then, cover with plastic wrap and aluminum foil (over the plastic wrap). Return to the refrigerator; wait until completely set (at least 8 hours) before serving.

To serve, unmold (page 89) on a flat cutting surface. Cut widthwise into 18 ⅜-inch slices (page 89). Place 1 slice of Ham Mousse on each individual serving plate; decorate with parsley sprigs. Pass the Horseradish Sauce in an attractive crystal or silver serving bowl at the table.

SERVES 18

VARIATION ~ **TO SERVE AS AN HORS D'OEUVRE:** Mold Hickory-Smoked Ham Mousse in a decorative, lightly oiled 4-cup mold. Line a serving plate with red-tip Boston lettuce leaves. Unmold the mousse (page 89) on the lettuce leaves. Serve with stoned rye crackers; provide a small, wide-bladed knife. (Eliminate the Horseradish Sauce.)

Other First-Course Appetizers

Broiled Grapefruit (page 293)
Creamed Mushrooms in tiny rice ring molds (page 272, see Serving Suggestions)
Fettuccine Alfredo (page 236–237)
French-Fried Onion Rings (page 273–274)
Venison Pâté (page 199)
Wild Duck Pâté (page 199)
Wild Goose Pâté (page 197–198)

Snacks

MUNCHIES

11 cups (³/₄ of a 1-pound box) Corn Chex cereal
1¹/₂ cups (about 7 ounces) deluxe, lightly
  salted mixed nuts
³/₄ cup (¹/₄ pound plus 4 tablespoons) butter
1¹/₂ cups packed light brown sugar
¹/₃ cup light corn syrup
¹/₄ teaspoon baking soda

Preheat the oven to 300°F.
  In a very large mixing bowl, place the cereal
and nuts; stir to combine, being careful not to
crumble the cereal; set aside. Place the butter in
a medium, heavy saucepan; melt the butter over
medium heat. Remove from the heat. Add the
brown sugar and corn syrup; stir together.
Bring to a full boil over medium-high heat, stirring constantly. Remove from the heat. Add the
baking soda; stir until well blended. Pour over
the cereal mixture; using a large mixing spoon,
stir until evenly coated. Transfer the mixture to
an ungreased 9 × 13-inch baking pan; distribute evenly. Place in the oven for 15 minutes.
  Remove from the oven; invert the pan of hot
mixture onto a large area of waxed paper. Using
a large mixing spoon, distribute the mixture
over the waxed paper; let stand 1 hour to cool
and dry. Then, using your hands, break into
small clumps; store in an airtight container.
Keeps up to 1 week at room temperature.

MAKES ABOUT 12 CUPS

BEER NUTS

1 cup sugar
¹/₂ cup water
10 ounces raw Spanish peanuts
Salt

Preheat the oven to 300°F. Butter a 9 × 13-inch
baking pan; set aside.
  In a medium skillet, place the sugar and
water; stir together. Over medium-high heat,
bring the mixture to a boil; add the peanuts and
boil 7 minutes (no more). Using a slotted mixing spoon, place the peanuts in the prepared
baking pan; sprinkle with salt. Discard the
syrup. Bake the peanuts 30 minutes, turning 3
times with a spatula. Remove from the oven and
place on a wire rack to cool. Store in a covered
quart jar. Keeps up to 1 month.

MAKES 2 CUPS

OYSTER CRACKER SNACKS

1 10-ounce package oyster crackers
³/₄ cup vegetable oil
1 1-ounce package ranch salad dressing mix
2 tablespoons dried dillweed

Place the crackers in a large mixing bowl; set
aside. In a small mixing bowl, place the vegetable oil and salad dressing mix; using a spoon,
beat until blended. Drizzle over the crackers
and toss. Sprinkle the dillweed over the crackers
and toss again. Let stand several hours at room
temperature, stirring lightly several times. Store
in an airtight container in the refrigerator up to
1 month.

MAKES ABOUT 6 CUPS

GRANOLA

1 18-ounce box (about 6 cups) quick-cooking
   rolled oats, uncooked
¾ cup untoasted (raw) wheat germ
⅓ cup sesame seeds
1 cup coarsely chopped hazelnuts
¾ cup flaked coconut
½ cup packed light brown sugar
½ cup (¼ pound) butter, melted
½ cup honey
1½ teaspoons pure vanilla extract
1½ cups raisins
1 8-ounce package dried mixed fruit, coarsely
   diced (2 cups) (optional)

Preheat the oven to 350°F.

Pour the oats into an ungreased 9 × 13-inch baking pan. Bake 10 minutes, turning once with a spatula after 5 minutes of baking. Meanwhile, in a medium mixing bowl, place the wheat germ, sesame seeds, hazelnuts, coconut, and brown sugar; stir to combine; set aside. Place the butter in a small saucepan; over very low heat, melt the butter. Remove from the heat. Add the honey and vanilla; stir vigorously until completely blended; set aside. Remove the oats from the oven and transfer to a very large mixing bowl. Leave the oven on at 350°F.

Add the wheat germ mixture to the oats; stir until evenly combined. Add the honey mixture; stir until the mixture is evenly dampened. Spoon the mixture equally into two 9 × 13-inch ungreased baking pans. Bake 20 minutes, turning the mixture every 5 minutes to achieve even browning. Remove from the oven and place the pans on wire racks; cool 5 minutes. Add the raisins and mixed fruit (if included), dividing equally between the 2 pans; stir to combine. Keep the pans on the wire racks and stir the Granola occasionally as it cools, breaking up any clumps of mixture sticking together.

When completely cool, store in zipper-seal plastic bags. Keeps up to 2 weeks at room temperature and up to 1 month in the refrigerator.

MAKES ABOUT 10 CUPS

SERVING SUGGESTIONS: Serve dry as a nutritious snack or serve with milk as a breakfast cereal.

Other Snack Recipes

Caramel Corn (page 615)
Spiced Pecans (page 612–613)

Soups and Stews

Soups

BEEF BROTH

Homemade broth discernibly improves the taste of foods in which it is used, and yet the mere idea of taking the time to make homemade broth could be easily dismissed. But broth is so simple to make and can be left to simmer while you carry on other activities around the house or just relax. It is made in large quantities and freezes well, providing a superlative ingredient at your fingertips for weeks to come. Broth may be kept in the freezer (at 0°F or below) up to 6 months.

2 pounds beef shank and 2 pounds beef
    knuckle, together containing a total of
    about ⅓ bone plus some fat
2 tablespoons vegetable shortening
2 cups water
14 cups water
1 large onion, coarsely chopped
½ cup coarsely chopped celery
½ cup pared and sliced carrots
4 large sprigs of fresh parsley
1 small bay leaf
4 whole cloves
5 whole black peppercorns
2 teaspoons salt

Cut the meat into 1-inch cubes, reserving the bones and fat. In a medium, heavy-bottomed skillet, melt the shortening over medium-high heat. Tilt the skillet back and forth to completely cover the bottom with melted shortening. Place ⅓ (only) of the meat in the skillet; brown well on all sides. Reduce the heat to low. Remove the browned meat from the skillet and place it in a kettle at least 8 quart in size; set aside. When the skillet cools, add 2 cups of water and deglaze. Pour the skillet liquid into the kettle with the meat. Add to the kettle the remaining ⅔ meat, bones, fat, 14 cups water, onion, celery, carrots, parsley, bay leaf, cloves, and peppercorns. Cover the kettle and bring the mixture to a boil over high heat. Reduce the heat and simmer the mixture *very slowly* 3½ hours, stirring occasionally. Add the salt; cover and simmer an additional ½ hour.

Using a slotted spoon, remove the beef and vegetables from the broth and reserve for other uses (see Note). Strain the broth through a sieve into a large bowl or plastic container; cover and refrigerate. When cold, spoon off and discard the congealed fat on top of the broth. Wipe the edges of the bowl (or container) with a clean, hot, damp cloth to remove all fat. The broth may be frozen in pint or quart plastic freezer containers.

NOTE: The reserved beef and vegetables may be used in making Cream of Vegetable-Beef Soup (page 75).

MAKES ABOUT 12 CUPS

CHICKEN BROTH

1 4-pound chicken, cut up
12 cups water
3 stalks celery (including 1 leafy top), cut into
    ½-inch pieces
3 carrots, pared and cut into ½ inch pieces
1 large onion, cut into large pieces
4 large sprigs of fresh parsley
1 small bay leaf
2 teaspoons salt
5 whole black peppercorns
½ teaspoon pepper

Wash the chicken under cold, running water. In a kettle at least 8 quart in size, place the chicken, water, celery, carrots, onion, parsley, bay leaf, salt, peppercorns, and pepper. Cover the kettle and bring the mixture to a boil over high heat. Reduce the heat and simmer the mixture very slowly 2 hours, stirring occasionally.

Using a slotted spoon, remove the chicken and vegetables from the broth and reserve for other uses (see Note). Strain the broth through a sieve into a large bowl or plastic container; cover and refrigerate. When cold, spoon off and discard the congealed fat on top of the broth. Wipe the edges of the bowl (or container) with a clean, hot, damp cloth to remove all fat. The broth may be frozen in pint or quart plastic freezer containers.

NOTE: The reserved vegetables may be (1) used in making Cream of Vegetable Soup (page 75), or (2) pressed through a food mill, then pureed in a blender and added to Beef Gravy (page 311–312) for a wonderful flavor-enhancer. Makes about 1¼ cups puréed vegetables.

MAKES ABOUT 10 CUPS

CLARIFIED BEEF OR CHICKEN BROTH

Cooks who have never clarified their homemade beef or chicken broths need not feel the least bit intimidated by this easy task. If the simple instructions are carefully followed, success is almost guaranteed.

4 cups Beef Broth (page 70) or Chicken Broth (page 70–71)
1 extra-large egg, slightly beaten
1 eggshell, crushed

In a kettle or saucepan over medium heat, heat the broth until *just* warm. Add the egg and crushed egg shell; stir in. Increase heat to high and bring the mixture to the boiling point, stirring constantly. Reduce the heat, cover and simmer (do not boil) 15 minutes. Remove from the heat and let stand to settle. When the broth

has settled, strain it through 4 layers of cheesecloth. This recipe may be doubled or tripled.

MAKES ABOUT 4 CUPS

SHERRIED BEEF BROTH

4 cups Clarified Beef Broth (recipe above)
¼ cup dry sherry, or to taste
¼ teaspoon salt, or to taste

Heat the Clarified Beef Broth. Add the sherry and salt. Serve with Rice Crackers (page 383).

MAKES ABOUT 4 CUPS

NOTE: Both recipes above may be doubled or tripled.

HOMEMADE EQUIVALENCIES OF COMMERCIALLY CANNED SOUPS

While very few recipes in this cookbook include the use of commercially canned soups, many casserole recipes call for canned cream soups, especially cream of mushroom and cream of celery. The following recipes may be substituted for one 10¾-ounce commercial can of condensed cream of mushroom soup (undiluted) and one 10¾-ounce commercial can of condensed cream of celery soup (undiluted), respectively, when these commercial soups are called for in recipes.

CREAM OF MUSHROOM SOUP

1 recipe Thick White Sauce (page 301–302)
1 tablespoon butter
½ cup coarsely chopped mushrooms

Make the Thick White Sauce; set aside. In a small, heavy-bottomed skillet, melt the butter over medium heat, being careful not to let it brown. Place the mushrooms in the skillet; sauté until the mushrooms give up their

(Recipe continues on next page)

juices (about 3 minutes). Do not allow the mushrooms to brown. Add the mushrooms and pan juices to the white sauce; stir well.

MAKES 1¹/₂ CUPS

CREAM OF CELERY SOUP

1 recipe Thick White Sauce (page 301–302),
    substituting ¹/₂ teaspoon celery salt for
    ¹/₂ teaspoon salt
1 tablespoon butter
¹/₄ cup minced celery
3 tablespoons minced leeks (whites only)

Make the Thick White Sauce; set aside. In a small, heavy-bottomed skillet, melt the butter over medium heat, being careful not to let it brown. Place the celery in the skillet; sauté 4 minutes. Do not allow the celery to brown. Remove from the heat. Using a slotted spoon, remove the celery (not the pan juices) from the skillet and add to the white sauce. Place the leeks in the same skillet; sauté 3 minutes over medium heat. Do not allow the leeks to brown. Add the leeks and pan juices to the white sauce; stir well.

MAKES 1¹/₂ CUPS

BEAN SOUP

(See photo insert page A-3)

Both smoked pork shank and smoked pork hock are used in this recipe. The shank supplies sufficient meat, and the hock gives additional flavor. Salt causes uncooked beans to become tough, so take care not to add the salt until the very end, after the beans have cooked. Little added salt is required in this recipe as the smoked pork imparts a salty flavor.

1 pound dried Great Northern beans
1¹/₂ pounds smoked pork shank
1 (about ¹/₂ pound) smoked pork hock

1 large onion
¹/₄ cup packed light brown sugar
¹/₄ teaspoon salt
¹/₄ teaspoon plus ¹/₈ teaspoon pepper

Wash and sort the beans. Place the beans (unsoaked), pork shank, pork hock, and onion in an 8-quart kettle; add water to cover (about 10 cups). Cover the kettle and bring the mixture to a simmer over high heat. Reduce the heat and simmer for 1¹/₂ hours or until the beans are tender, stirring occasionally. Do not overcook, causing the beans to become mushy.

Remove from the heat. Remove and discard all the skin, bones, and fat from the meat. Tear the meat into bite-sized pieces and return to the soup. Using a spoon, break the onion into bite-sized pieces against the side of the kettle. Add the brown sugar, salt, and pepper; stir to combine. Cover the kettle; place it over the heat and simmer the mixture 5 minutes.

SERVES 10 AS A MAIN COURSE

ACCOMPANIMENT SUGGESTION: Hot Corn Bread (page 374) is traditionally served with Bean Soup.

TEN-BEAN SOUP

The Bean Mix portion of this recipe calls for mixing a total of 10 pounds of various beans, even though the soup uses only 2 cups of the mix. If you prefer not to have a quantity of leftover Bean Mix, just purchase fewer of the specified beans in equal quantities. My mother and several of her friends who liked and made this soup (I got the recipe from Mom) would bag their extra Bean Mix in 2-cup quantities and share it with each other. This bean-team approach kept everyone's cupboard stocked with ready Bean Mix, resulting in more frequent preparation of this hearty soup with less effort.

BEAN MIX
1 pound dried yellow split peas
1 pound dried green split peas

1 pound barley pearls
1 pound dried black beans
1 pound dried red beans
1 pound dried pinto beans
1 pound dried navy beans
1 pound dried Great Northern beans
1 pound dried lentils
1 pound dried black-eyed peas

Place all beans in a large bowl; stir until evenly distributed. Divide the bean mixture into ten 2-cup portions; place 9 of the 2-cup portions in individual zipper-seal plastic bags and reserve for future use or gift giving.

2 cups Bean Mix
8 cups water
2½ pounds smoked pork shanks
1 large onion, very coarsely chopped
1 garlic clove, pressed
1 14½-ounce can whole, peeled tomatoes, undrained
1 10-ounce can diced tomatoes and green chilies*
3 tablespoons packed dark brown sugar
1¼ teaspoons salt
¼ teaspoon pepper

* *Found in the canned tomatoes or Mexican food section at the supermarket.*

Wash and sort the 2 cups Bean Mix. Place the beans in a large, heavy-bottomed kettle; add cold water to 2 inches above the beans. Cover the kettle and soak the beans overnight.

Drain the beans in a sieve. Return the beans to the kettle; add 8 cups water; set aside. Rinse the pork shanks under cold, running water; add to the bean mixture. Add the onion and garlic. Cover the kettle; bring the mixture to a boil over high heat. Reduce the heat and simmer the mixture 1½ hours, stirring occasionally.

Then, place the tomatoes, with their liquid, in a medium mixing bowl; using the edge of a metal mixing spoon, chop the tomatoes coarsely. Add the cut-up tomatoes, tomatoes and green chilies, brown sugar, salt, and pepper

to the bean mixture. Cover and simmer an additional 30 minutes, stirring occasionally. Remove from the heat. Remove the meat from the pork shanks; discard the bone and fat. Cut or tear the meat into bite-sized pieces and return to the soup. Cover the kettle and return the soup to a simmer; remove from the heat and serve.

SERVES 10

CREAM OF TOMATO SOUP

2 14½-ounce cans whole, peeled tomatoes, undrained
3 tablespoons minced onions
1 teaspoon dried leaf basil
1 teaspoon sugar
¼ teaspoon celery seed
⅛ teaspoon white pepper
¼ teaspoon baking soda
¼ cup all-purpose flour
1 teaspoon salt
¼ teaspoon white pepper
¼ cup (4 tablespoons) butter
2 cups whole milk
2 cups (1 pint) half-and-half
6 sprigs of fresh coriander (cilantro) or 1 teaspoon snipped, fresh parsley for garnish

" *6 cups blanched (page 29), stemmed, peeled, cut-up, and cooked fresh tomatoes may be substituted. To cook, place the tomatoes in a saucepan; do not add water. Cover the saucepan. Bring the tomatoes to a simmer over medium heat; reduce heat and simmer 8 minutes.*

In a medium-large saucepan, place the tomatoes, onions, basil, sugar, celery seed, and ⅛ teaspoon white pepper; stir to combine. Over medium heat, simmer the mixture, uncovered, 30 minutes, until moderately thickened. Press the mixture through a food mill to yield approximately 2½ cups. Add the baking soda; stir until blended; cover and refrigerate.

In small bowl, place the flour, salt, and ¼ teaspoon white pepper; stir to combine; set aside.

(Recipe continues on next page)

In a large saucepan, melt the butter over low heat. Remove from the heat; add the flour mixture and stir until completely smooth. Add the milk and half-and-half; stir to mix. Place over medium-low heat; cook until the milk mixture thickens and is just under boiling, stirring constantly. Do not allow the mixture to boil. Remove from the heat. If not ready to serve the soup immediately, cover the saucepan and refrigerate (separately from the tomato mixture). The milk mixture and tomato mixture may be refrigerated up to 24 hours before completing and serving the soup.

When ready to serve, heat the milk mixture over medium-low heat, stirring constantly (do not allow to boil). Just before serving, add the tomato mixture; heat through, stirring continuously (do not allow to boil). Ladle into soup cups; garnish with the coriander (cilantro) or parsley.

SERVES 6

CREAM OF BROCCOLI SOUP

¼ cup all-purpose flour
1 teaspoon salt
¼ teaspoon white pepper
¾ teaspoon dried leaf oregano
¼ teaspoon curry powder
¼ cup (4 tablespoons) butter
⅔ cup finely chopped onions
3 cups whole milk
2 cups (1 pint) half-and-half
8 cups broccoli flowerets, steamed (page 252)
   until tender

In a small bowl, place the flour, salt, white pepper, oregano, and curry powder; stir to combine; set aside. In a large, heavy-bottomed skillet, melt the butter over medium heat. Place the onions in the skillet; sauté until tender, but not brown (about 5 minutes). Remove from the heat and add the flour mixture; stir until the flour mixture is completely smooth. Add the milk and half-and-half; stir to mix. Place over

medium-low heat and cook until thick, stirring constantly. Do not allow to boil.

In a blender or food processor, place the cooked cream mixture and broccoli; process until smooth. Serve immediately or refrigerate and heat through (do not allow to boil) before serving. Best if served the day it is made.

SERVES 6

CREAM OF VEGETABLE SOUP

2 cups cooked mixed vegetables (such as
   carrots, celery, and onions) which have
   been pressed through a food mill when hot
   (measure after pressing)
¼ cup all-purpose flour
1 teaspoon dried leaf chervil
1 teaspoon celery salt
¼ teaspoon dried dillweed
⅛ teaspoon pepper
¼ cup (4 tablespoons) butter
1 cup whole milk
1 cup half-and-half
1 cup chicken broth, homemade
   (page 70–71) or commercially canned

Prepare the vegetables; set aside. In a small mixing bowl, place the flour, chervil, celery salt, dillweed, and pepper; set aside. In a medium saucepan, melt the butter over low heat. Remove from the heat; add the flour mixture and stir until the mixture is perfectly smooth. Add the milk, half-and-half, and chicken broth; stir to mix. Place over medium-low heat; cook until the mixture thickens and is just under boiling, stirring constantly. Do not allow the mixture to boil. Remove from the heat; add the pressed vegetables. Return to the heat and stir until the soup is hot (do not allow to boil).

SERVES 4

CREAM OF VEGETABLE-BEEF SOUP

Follow the Cream of Vegetable Soup recipe page 74, including very tender, cooked beef with the vegetables pressed through a food mill (2 cups total pressed vegetables and beef).

SERVES 4

VEGETABLE SOUP

2 tablespoons butter
1½ cups coarsely chopped onions
6 cups homemade Chicken Broth (page 70–71) or 3 14-ounce cans commercial chicken broth
1 14½-ounce can Italian-style stewed tomatoes
1 14½-ounce can regular stewed tomatoes
1½ cups pared and sliced carrots
1½ cups pared turnips cut into bite-sized cubes
1½ cups fresh green beans cut into 1¼-inch lengths
1 cup sliced celery
2 teaspoons drained, green peppercorns
1 teaspoon sugar
⅛ teaspoon ground allspice
1 large sprig of fresh parsley
2 sprigs of fresh savory
2 leafy celery tops
1 sprig of fresh basil
1 small bunch of fresh chives
1½ cups pared red potatoes cut into bite-sized cubes
1 cup fresh corn
1½ cups sliced zucchini

In a large, heavy-bottomed kettle, melt the butter over medium heat. Place the onions in the kettle. Sauté the onions until lightly golden (about 7 minutes), stirring often. Remove the kettle from the heat; let stand until the onions cool slightly. Then, add the chicken broth, Italian-style stewed tomatoes, regular stewed tomatoes, carrots, turnips, green beans, celery,

green peppercorns, sugar, and allspice; stir to combine; set aside.

Make a bouquet garni (page 26–27) with the parsley, savory, celery tops, basil, and chives. Immerse the bouquet garni in the vegetable mixture in the kettle. Cover the kettle and place it over high heat. Bring the mixture to a boil; reduce the heat and simmer, slowly, 10 minutes, stirring occasionally. Add the potatoes; stir to combine. Cover the kettle; simmer the mixture an additional 10 minutes. Add the corn and zucchini; stir to combine. Cover the kettle; simmer the mixture an additional 5 minutes. Remove from the heat. Remove and discard the bouquet garni.

SERVES 8 AS A MAIN COURSE

POTATO-LEEK SOUP

2 pounds russet potatoes (enough for 4 cups mashed potatoes; about 4 large potatoes)
¼ cup whole milk
1 tablespoon butter
1½ cups thinly sliced leeks (about 6 leeks)
2 tablespoons butter
2 cups chicken broth, homemade (page 70–71) or 1 14-ounce can commercial chicken broth
1 tablespoon snipped, fresh parsley
2 cups (1 pint) half-and-half
1 tablespoon instant chicken bouillon granules
2 teaspoons salt
¼ teaspoon white pepper
Small, single, fresh parsley leaves for decoration

Pare the potatoes, retaining them in a large saucepan of cold water to prevent discoloration. Drain the potatoes. Cut each potato into 3 pieces and return to the saucepan; add hot water to cover. Cover the pan and bring the potatoes to a boil over high heat; reduce the heat to

(Recipe continues on next page)

medium and boil the potatoes moderately until they are tender (about 25 minutes). Drain well. Add the milk and 1 tablespoon butter; using an electric mixer, beat on high speed until the potatoes are fluffy with no lumps remaining. Measure 4 cups mashed potatoes; set aside.

Trim away and discard the root ends and leaves of the leeks, leaving only the white and greenish-white parts. Slice the leeks in half lengthwise and wash well, making certain all sand has been washed away. Thinly slice the leek halves width-wise; set aside. In a large saucepan, melt 2 table-spoons butter over low heat; add the leeks and sauté lightly about 3 minutes. Do not allow the leeks to brown. Remove from the heat; add the chicken broth and 1 tablespoon parsley. Cover and bring the leek mixture to a boil over medium heat; reduce the heat and simmer 1 hour.

Press the leek mixture through a food mill; then, return it to the saucepan. Add the mashed potatoes, half-and-half, bouillon granules, salt, and white pepper; using a handheld electric mixer, beat on medium-high speed until blended. Over medium heat, heat the soup through, stirring often. Ladle into soup cups or bowls; float parsley leaves on top of each serving.

SERVES 6

Cut each bacon slice widthwise into 6 pieces; place in a small, heavy-bottomed skillet. Over medium heat, fry the bacon pieces until medium done, but not crisp; drain between paper towels. In a large, heavy-bottomed kettle, place the bacon, potatoes, onions, celery, and water; stir to combine. Cover the kettle and bring the potato mixture to a boil over high heat; reduce the heat and cook the mixture at a brisk simmer for 30 minutes. Drain the potato mixture well in a sieve, reserving the cooking liquid; set aside.

Press the potato mixture through a food mill. Place the pressed mixture in the kettle. Add the half-and-half, milk, ½ cup reserved cooking liquid, 2 tablespoons parsley, salt, and white pepper; stir to combine. Cover the kettle and place over medium-low heat. Heat the soup only until hot; do not allow it to boil. Ladle into soup cups or bowls; sprinkle sparingly with snipped, fresh parsley.

SERVES 6

POTATO SOUP

6 slices bacon
2 pounds red potatoes, diced (about 6 medium potatoes)
1½ cups chopped onions
1½ cups chopped celery
5 cups water
1½ cups half-and-half
1 cup whole milk
½ cup cooking liquid (from cooking bacon-vegetable mixture)
2 tablespoons snipped, fresh parsley
2 teaspoons salt
¼ teaspoon plus a dash of white pepper
1 tablespoon snipped, fresh parsley for decoration

WILD RICE SOUP

¾ cup (¼ pound plus 4 tablespoons) butter
3 tablespoons minced onions
1 cup all-purpose flour
6 cups homemade Chicken Broth (page 70–71) or 3 14-ounce cans commercial chicken broth
4 cups cooked wild rice (use 1¼ cups raw wild rice; page 231)
2 cups finely ground, fully cooked ham
2 cups pared and very finely shredded carrots (about 5 medium carrots)
⅓ cup ground, blanched almonds (page 29) (use one 2-ounce package slivered, blanched almonds)
1 teaspoon salt
¼ teaspoon pepper
2 cups (1 pint) half-and-half
¼ cup dry white wine
2 tablespoons minced, fresh parsley for garnish

In a large kettle, melt the butter over low heat. Place the onions in the kettle; sauté 4 minutes, keeping the heat low to avoid burning the butter. Remove from the heat. Add the flour and stir until completely smooth. Return to low heat; cook the mixture for 1 minute, but do not allow it to brown. Gradually add the broth, stirring constantly and combining thoroughly. Increase the heat to medium; bring the mixture to a boil and boil 1 minute. Add the rice, ham, carrots, almonds, salt, and pepper; stir to combine. Cover and simmer 5 minutes. Add the half-and-half and wine; heat through but do not allow to boil.

To serve, ladle the soup into soup bowls or cups and garnish each serving with minced parsley.

SERVES 8

SERVING SUGGESTIONS: This soup may be served as either a main course or an appetizer. When served as an appetizer, you may wish to thin it down with 2 additional cups of chicken broth.

WISCONSIN BEER CHEESE SOUP

(See photo insert page A-3)

¾ cup all-purpose flour
¼ teaspoon salt
¼ teaspoon white pepper
Dash of cayenne pepper
1¾ cups homemade Chicken Broth
  (page 70–71) or 1 14-ounce can
  commercial chicken broth
½ cup pared and very finely shredded carrots
½ cup minced celery
¼ cup plus 3 tablespoons (7 tablespoons)
  butter
½ cup minced onions
2 cups whole milk
1 teaspoon packed light brown sugar
1 pound shredded, sharp cheddar cheese
1 12-ounce can or bottle of beer
Popped popcorn for garnish

In a small mixing bowl, place the flour, salt, white pepper, and cayenne pepper; stir to combine; set aside. In a medium saucepan, place the chicken broth, carrots, and celery; stir to combine. Cover the saucepan. Bring the mixture to a boil over high heat; reduce the heat and simmer 10 minutes until the vegetables are tender. Remove from the heat; set aside.

In a 3½-quart heavy-bottomed saucepan, heat the butter over medium heat. Place the onions in the saucepan; sauté 5 minutes until translucent but not brown. Remove from the heat. Add the flour mixture; stir until blended, with no lumps remaining. Add the chicken broth mixture and milk; stir to combine. Place over medium heat; cook the mixture until thickened and just under boiling, stirring constantly. Do not allow the mixture to boil. Add the brown sugar, cheese, and beer; stir constantly until the cheese melts. Continue cooking to just under boiling, stirring continuously. Do not allow the soup to boil. Remove from the heat.

To serve, ladle the soup into soup cups or bowls. Float a few kernels of popped corn on each serving.

MAKES ABOUT SIX 1-CUP SERVINGS

FISH CHOWDER

4 slices thickly sliced bacon, cut into 1-inch
  pieces
2½ pounds northern pike fillets,* carefully
  boned and cut into ¾-inch cubes
3 pounds red potatoes, pared and cut into
  1-inch cubes
3 cups very coarsely chopped onions
About 5 cups hot water
2 tablespoons butter
1 teaspoon celery salt
¾ teaspoon salt
½ teaspoon pepper
½ teaspoon ground mace
½ cup all-purpose flour
2 12-ounce cans (3 cups) evaporated milk,
  divided

(Recipe continues on next page)

Paprika for decoration
Oyster crackers

* *Fillets of perch, walleye, or any other firm,
mild fish may be substituted.*

Place the bacon in an 8-quart heavy-bottomed
kettle; fry over medium-low heat until done but
not crisp. Remove the kettle from the heat; let
stand until the bacon cools slightly. Add the
fish, potatoes, onions, and enough hot water to
cover. Cover the kettle; place it over high heat
and bring the mixture to a boil. Reduce the heat
and simmer the mixture about 10 minutes until
the potatoes are just tender. Remove from the
heat. Add the butter, celery salt, salt, pepper, and
mace; stir to blend and combine; set aside.

In a glass jar or plastic container with a secure
lid, place the flour and *1 cup* evaporated milk;
cover and shake vigorously until blended. Add
the flour mixture and remaining evaporated
milk to the fish mixture in the kettle; stir well to
blend. Place the kettle over medium heat; cook
the chowder until it thickens and is just under
boiling, stirring constantly. Do not allow the
chowder to boil.

To serve, ladle the chowder into soup bowls
and sprinkle lightly with paprika. Pass a big
bowl of oyster crackers at the table.

SERVES 8

CORN CHOWDER

8 slices bacon
2 tablespoons all-purpose flour
½ teaspoon salt
½ teaspoon pepper
1 teaspoon dried parsley
¼ teaspoon poultry seasoning
¼ cup plus 2 tablespoons (6 tablespoons)
　　butter
½ cup chopped onions
¼ cup chopped green bell peppers
½ bay leaf
4 cups (1 quart) whole milk

2 14¾-ounce cans cream-style corn
1 pound red potatoes, boiled (page 275–276),
　　peeled, and cut into ⅜-inch cubes (about 2
　　cups potatoes)

In a large, heavy-bottomed skillet, fry the bacon
over medium heat until crisp; drain between
paper towels. Using your fingers, break the
bacon into small pieces; place in a small container; cover, and refrigerate. In a small bowl,
place the flour, salt, pepper, parsley, and poultry
seasoning; stir to combine; set aside.

In a large, heavy-bottomed saucepan, melt
the butter over medium heat. Place the onions
and green peppers in the saucepan; sauté until
tender, but not brown (about 5 minutes).
Remove from the heat. Place the flour mixture
in the saucepan; stir until the flour mixture is
smooth. Add ½ bay leaf and milk; stir to mix.
Return to medium heat. While stirring constantly, cook until smooth and slightly thickened, bringing the mixture nearly to a boil, but
not allowing it to boil. Add the corn and potatoes; stir to combine. Heat through.

Just before serving, remove and discard the
bay leaf. Then add the bacon, reserving a small
amount to sprinkle over each serving of chowder for decoration.

SERVES 8

SERVING SUGGESTIONS: May be served as a first
course or a main course.

DEE'S CHILI

*This original recipe of Dee Staples, my sister-in-
law, calls for just the right ingredients in just the
right amounts to culminate in an incredibly good
chili—a menu-must in cold winter months.*

2 tablespoons butter
1½ pounds lean, pure ground beef
¾ cup chopped onions
½ cup chopped green bell peppers
1 large garlic clove, pressed

2 14½-ounce cans stewed tomatoes
1 15-ounce can tomato sauce
1 tablespoon chili powder*
1 teaspoon ground cumin
1 tablespoon dried parsley
2 teaspoons salt
1 teaspoon pepper
1 15-ounce can chili beans in chili sauce, undrained
1 15½-ounce can dark red kidney beans, undrained
8 ounces commercial sour cream (optional)
2 ounces finely shredded, sharp cheddar cheese (optional)

For less spicy chili, reduce the amount of chili powder to 2 teaspoons.

In a large, heavy-bottomed skillet, melt the butter over medium heat. Tilt the skillet back and forth to completely cover the bottom with the melted butter. Place the ground beef in the skillet; brown until medium-browned, using a large, metal mixing spoon to break up the meat during the browning. Add the onions, green peppers, and garlic; continue cooking until the meat is well browned (the onions and green peppers should be barely browned). Remove the skillet from the heat.

When the skillet cools slightly, add the stewed tomatoes and tomato sauce; stir until the skillet is deglazed. Add the chili powder, cumin, parsley, salt, and pepper; stir to combine. Cover and simmer the mixture slowly for 1 hour. Add the chili beans and kidney beans; simmer, uncovered, an additional ½ hour.

To serve, ladle the chili into soup bowls. If desired, spoon a small dollop of sour cream over the center of the chili in each bowl, and sprinkle shredded cheese over the sour cream.

SERVES 8

Stews

BRANDIED PORK STEW WITH THYME DUMPLINGS

Blue Ribbon winner in the Stews of Iowa class, sponsored by the Iowa Farm Bureau, at the 1992 Iowa State Fair.

Ted Yanacek, accomplished gourmet cook, judged the class in which I entered this stew at the fair. He praised the ample amount of pork tenderloin and inclusion of apples, golden raisins, and spices—rare ingredients in Midwest stews. (Although he didn't mention the brandy ingredient, I think it might have helped make this stew a winner.)

1 pound red potatoes
2 cups fresh green beans cut diagonally into 1-inch lengths
½ cup red bell peppers cut into ½-inch cubes
¾ cup water
1 tablespoon sugar
¼ teaspoon ground cinnamon
1½ cups Golden Delicious apples pared, cored, and cut into ¾-inch cubes
¼ cup all-purpose flour
1 teaspoon salt
½ teaspoon pepper
1¾ pounds pork tenderloin (2 whole tenderloins) cut into 1-inch cubes
3 tablespoons butter
2 tablespoons butter
⅓ cup finely chopped onions
½ cup water
4 cups clarified beef broth, homemade (page 70) or 2 14-ounce cans commercial beef broth
1½ cups sliced, fresh mushrooms

(Recipe continues on next page)

2 tablespoons snipped, fresh parsley
1 small bay leaf
1 teaspoon salt
½ teaspoon pepper
10 ounces (about 2 cups) pearl onions, peeled (page 29)
¼ cup golden raisins
1 recipe Thyme Dumplings (page 382)
½ teaspoon ground nutmeg
3 tablespoons good brandy

Pare the potatoes; drop into cold water as they are pared to prevent darkening. Cut the large potatoes in half. Place the potatoes in a large saucepan; add hot water to cover. Cover the pan. Bring the potatoes to a boil over high heat; reduce the heat and boil the potatoes moderately for 15 minutes. Drain the potatoes; immerse in cold water to stop the cooking. Drain and cut the potatoes into ½-inch cubes. Place in a zipper-seal plastic bag; refrigerate.

Place the green beans in a medium saucepan; add water to cover. Cover the pan. Bring the green beans to a boil over high heat; reduce the heat and simmer the beans about 10 minutes until they are just tender. Drain; immerse the beans in cold water to stop the cooking. Drain the beans well in a colander; place in a zipper-seal plastic bag and refrigerate.

Steam the red peppers (page 252) 4 minutes. Immediately remove the steamer basket containing the peppers from the pan. Leave the peppers in the steamer basket and rinse them under cold, running water to stop the cooking. Drain the peppers well; place in a zipper-seal plastic bag and refrigerate.

In a small saucepan, place ¾ cup water, sugar, and cinnamon; stir to combine. Bring the mixture to a boil over high heat, stirring constantly. Add the apples. Return to a simmer; reduce the heat and simmer 3 minutes. Drain the apples well in a colander. (Do not immerse them in cold water.) Place in a bowl or container; cover and refrigerate.

In a small mixing bowl, place the flour, 1 teaspoon salt, and ½ teaspoon pepper; stir to combine. Sprinkle the flour mixture over a piece of waxed paper. Dredge the tenderloin cubes in the flour mixture and then place them on a clean piece of waxed paper; set aside. In an electric skillet or a large, heavy-bottomed skillet on the range, melt 3 tablespoons butter over medium-low heat (320°F in an electric skillet). Tilt the skillet back and forth to completely cover the bottom with the melted butter. Place the tenderloin cubes in the skillet and brown well on all sides. Place the browned meat in a heavy-bottomed kettle; set aside.

Leave the skillet (in which the pork was cooked) over medium-low heat and add 2 additional tablespoons butter. When the butter melts, add ⅓ cup chopped onions. Brown the onions lightly; add to the meat in the kettle. Reduce the skillet heat to very low (220°F in an electric skillet). When the skillet cools to the reduced temperature, add ½ cup water and deglaze.

Pour the skillet liquid into the kettle containing the meat. Add the beef broth, mushrooms, parsley, bay leaf, 1 teaspoon salt, and ½ teaspoon pepper; stir to combine. Cover the kettle and place it over medium heat. Bring the mixture to a low boil; reduce the heat and simmer 15 minutes, stirring occasionally. Add the pearl onions and raisins; stir to combine. Remove from the heat; set aside.

Prepare the Thyme Dumplings batter. Place the kettle of stew mixture over high heat; cover and bring the mixture to a boil. Drop the dumpling batter by the tablespoonful onto the top of the boiling stew. Cover the kettle; reduce the heat slightly, but keep the stew bubbling. Cook 15 minutes. *Do not lift the cover while the dumplings are cooking—not even to peek.* Remove from the heat. Uncover the kettle. Using a small spatula, remove the dumplings and place, single layer, in a pan; cover to keep warm.

Remove the bay leaf from the stew mixture and discard it. Add the nutmeg and brandy; stir to combine. Add the potatoes, green beans, red peppers, and apples; stir carefully to evenly distribute. Place the kettle of stew over medium-high heat. Bring the stew to a simmer; reduce the heat and simmer until heated through. Ladle the stew into a tureen. Using a small spatula, arrange the dumplings on top of the stew around the edge of the tureen.

SERVES 6

OVEN STEW

One would be hard pressed to find a more simple stew to make than this one from the recipe box of Des Moines friend Gayle Hamilton. Quick-cooking tapioca is the thickener.

2¾ pounds round steak, ¾ inch thick
2 large onions, cut into eighths
3 large red potatoes, pared and cut into
   1-inch cubes
4 stalks celery, sliced ½ inch thick
Leafy tops of 2 celery stalks, coarsely chopped
6 carrots, pared and cut, diagonally, into bite-
   sized pieces
3 cups fresh green beans snapped into
   1½-inch lengths
4 cups tomato juice
1 teaspoon salt
½ teaspoon pepper
1 tablespoon sugar
2 tablespoons quick-cooking tapioca
2 teaspoons dried leaf basil

Preheat the oven to 325°F.

Trim the fat and gristle from the round steak; cut it into ¾-inch cubes and spread them over the bottom of a heavy 8-quart roaster. Do not brown the meat. In layers, add the vegetables to the roaster in the following order: onions, potatoes, celery, leafy celery tops, carrots, and green beans; set aside.

In a medium mixing bowl, place the tomato juice, salt, pepper, sugar, tapioca, and basil; stir to combine. Pour evenly over the vegetables and meat; do not stir the stew contents. Cover and bake for 3 hours. Do not baste or stir the stew during the baking period. To serve, stir briefly and ladle into soup bowls.

SERVES 10 TO 12

FARM-STYLE BEEF STEW

½ cup all-purpose flour
¾ teaspoon salt
½ teaspoon pepper
2 pounds boned chuck, cut into 1¼-inch cubes
2 tablespoons butter
1 tablespoon butter
1 cup water
2 cups homemade Beef Broth (page 70) or 1
   14-ounce can commercial beef broth
1 cup water
½ cup dry red wine
2 cups very coarsely chopped onions
¾ cup celery sliced ⅜ inch thick
Green leafy top of 1 celery stalk, chopped
1 garlic clove, pressed
½ bay leaf
¾ teaspoon Worcestershire sauce
1 pound carrots, pared and sliced ½ inch
   thick
2 pounds red potatoes, pared and cut into
   bite-sized cubes
1⅓ cups frozen peas (about ⅔ of a
   10-ounce package)
½ cup water

In a small mixing bowl, place the flour, salt, and pepper; stir to combine. Sprinkle the flour mixture over a piece of waxed paper. Lightly dredge the meat cubes in the flour mixture and then place them on a clean piece of waxed paper. Reserve the remaining flour mixture in a glass jar or plastic container with a secure lid.

In an electric skillet or a large, heavy-bottomed skillet on the range, melt 2 tablespoons butter over medium heat (350°F in an electric skillet). Tilt the skillet back and forth to completely cover the bottom with the melted butter. Place the meat cubes, single layer, in the skillet; brown well on all sides. Add 1 additional tablespoon butter during browning when the skillet becomes dry. Place the browned meat cubes in a heavy-bottomed, 8-quart kettle; set aside. Reduce the skillet heat to very low (220°F in an electric skillet). When the skillet cools to

(Recipe continues on next page)

the reduced temperature, add 1 cup water and deglaze.

Pour the skillet liquid into the kettle containing the browned meat. Add the beef broth, 1 cup water, wine, onions, sliced celery, chopped celery top, garlic, ½ bay leaf, and Worcestershire sauce; stir to combine. Cover the kettle and bring the mixture to a boil over high heat. Reduce the heat and simmer, moderately to slowly, 2 hours, until the meat is very tender, stirring occasionally. Stir more frequently during the last 45 minutes of simmering when the mixture thickens and becomes increasingly prone to stick to the bottom of the kettle.

Meanwhile, place the carrots in a medium saucepan; cover with water. Cover the saucepan and place it over high heat. Bring the carrots to a boil; reduce the heat and boil the carrots about 12 minutes, until they are just tender. Drain the carrots and let stand until cool; then, cover and refrigerate. Using the same procedure, boil the potatoes in a large saucepan for about 10 minutes, until just tender. Drain and let stand until cool; then, cover and refrigerate. Do not overcook the carrots and potatoes, or they will lose their shape in the stew.

When the meat mixture has simmered 2 hours and the meat is tender, remove the kettle from the heat. Add the carrots, potatoes, and frozen peas to the kettle mixture. Cover the kettle; set aside. Add ½ cup water to the reserved flour mixture; cover the jar or container and shake vigorously until blended. Add to the stew mixture in the kettle. Using a wooden mixing spoon, stir the stew contents to combine, being careful not to cut or break up the carrots and potatoes. Remove the ½ bay leaf from the stew and discard it.

Place the kettle over medium heat; bring the stew to a low simmer, stirring often. Simmer 1 to 2 minutes until the stew thickens, stirring constantly. Ladle into soup bowls.

SERVES 8

VEAL STEW WITH HERB DUMPLINGS

¼ cup all-purpose flour
½ teaspoon salt
¼ teaspoon pepper
1¼ pounds boned veal shoulder, cut into 1-inch cubes
2 tablespoons butter
2 tablespoons butter
¼ cup minced onions
1 cup water
1 cup chicken broth, homemade (page 70–71) or commercially canned
1¼ teaspoons salt
¼ teaspoon pepper
1 teaspoon Worcestershire sauce
1 bay leaf
½ cup dry white wine
2½ cups water
1 pound red potatoes, pared and cut into small, bite-sized cubes (about 3 cups)
2 cups carrots pared and sliced ¼ inch thick
½ cup chopped celery
1 recipe Herb Dumplings (page 382)
1 14½-ounce can petite diced tomatoes, undrained
1 14½-ounce can cut wax beans, drained
¾ cup cooked and drained frozen peas

In a small bowl, place the flour, ½ teaspoon salt, and ¼ teaspoon pepper; stir to combine. Sprinkle the flour mixture over a piece of waxed paper. Dredge the veal cubes in the flour mixture and then place them on a clean piece of waxed paper; set aside.

In an electric skillet or a large, heavy-bottomed skillet on the range, melt 2 tablespoons butter over medium heat (350°F in an electric skillet). Tilt the skillet back and forth to completely cover the bottom with the melted butter. Place the veal cubes in the skillet; brown well on all sides. Remove the veal cubes from the skillet and place them in a bowl; set aside. Place an additional 2 tablespoons butter in the skillet; add the onions and brown. Reduce the skillet heat to very low (220°F in an electric skillet). When the skillet cools to the reduced temperature, add 1 cup water and the chicken broth. Deglaze the skillet.

Pour the skillet mixture into a heavy-bottomed kettle. Add 1¼ teaspoons salt, ¼ teaspoon pepper, Worcestershire sauce, bay leaf, wine, and 2½ cups water; stir to combine. Add the veal cubes. Cover the kettle. Bring the mixture to a boil over high heat; reduce the heat and simmer the mixture 1 hour or until the veal is nearly tender. Add the potatoes, carrots, and celery; cover and continue simmering for 10 minutes. Meanwhile, prepare the Herb Dumplings batter; set aside.

Add the tomatoes, wax beans, and peas to the stew; cover and bring to a boil over high heat. Drop the dumpling batter by the tablespoonful onto the top of the boiling stew. Cover the kettle; reduce the heat slightly, but keep the stew bubbling. Cook 15 minutes. *Do not lift the cover while the dumplings are cooking—not even to peek.* Remove from the heat. Uncover the kettle; using a spatula, remove the dumplings and place them on a plate. Remove the bay leaf from the stew and discard it. Ladle the stew into individual soup bowls and place a dumpling on top of the stew in the center of each bowl.

SERVES 6

HEARTLAND STEW

Blue Ribbon winner in the Stews of Iowa class, sponsored by the Iowa Farm Bureau, at the 1988 Iowa State Fair.

½ pound beef tenderloin, ¾ inch thick
½ pound pork tenderloin, ½ inch thick
½ pound veal tenderloin, ¼ inch thick
½ cup all-purpose flour
1½ teaspoons salt
½ teaspoon pepper
¼ cup (4 tablespoons) butter
¼ cup (4 tablespoons) butter
½ cup minced onions

1 garlic clove, pressed
¼ cup water
3½ cups chicken broth, homemade (page 70–71) or commercially canned
½ teaspoon Worcestershire sauce
1 teaspoon salt
⅛ teaspoon pepper
½ teaspoon celery salt
2 tablespoons snipped, fresh parsley
1 tablespoon snipped, fresh basil
4 ounces (about 1½ cups) sliced, fresh mushrooms
¾ cup pearl onions, peeled (page 29)
1 cup fresh snow peas with ends trimmed off and strings removed
¾ cup carrots pared and sliced, diagonally, ¼ inch thick
¾ cup asparagus trimmed and cut, diagonally, into 2-inch lengths
½ cup miniature corn on the cob, frozen or commercially canned
2½ pounds russet potatoes (about 5 medium potatoes)
1 cup half-and-half
¼ cup dry sherry
2 tablespoons butter
¼ teaspoon salt
1 extra-large egg, beaten
½ cup whole milk

Cut the beef into 1½-inch cubes, the pork into 1-inch cubes, and the veal into 1 × 1½-inch strips; set aside. In a small mixing bowl, place the flour, 1½ teaspoons salt, and ½ teaspoon pepper; stir to combine. Sprinkle the flour mixture over a piece of waxed paper. Dredge the meat in the flour mixture and place it on a clean piece of waxed paper; set aside. Reserve the remaining flour mixture in a glass jar or plastic container with a secure lid.

In a deep electric skillet or a Dutch oven, melt 4 tablespoons butter over medium heat (350°F in an electric skillet). Place all the meat in the skillet and brown *very* well on all sides, adding more of the butter as needed. Remove the browned meat from the skillet and place it in a bowl; set aside. Add 4 more tablespoons butter

(Recipe continues on next page)

to the skillet. Place the minced onions and garlic in skillet; sauté until golden brown. Reduce the skillet heat to very low (220°F in an electric skillet).

When the skillet cools to the reduced temperature, add ¼ cup water and deglaze. Return the meat to the skillet. Add the chicken broth, Worcestershire sauce, 1 teaspoon salt, ⅛ teaspoon pepper, celery salt, parsley, and basil; stir to combine. Cover the skillet and increase the heat to medium low (320°F in an electric skillet). Simmer the meat mixture for 15 minutes. Add the mushrooms; cover and simmer an additional 15 minutes or until all the meat is tender.

Meanwhile, briefly steam (page 252) separately the pearl onions until just tender and the snow peas 3 minutes. In a colander, rinse the onions and peas separately under cold running water to stop the cooking. Drain well and place in separate bowls; cover and set aside. Briefly boil (page 252) separately the carrots until just tender and the asparagus about 3 minutes. In a colander, rinse the carrots and asparagus separately under cold running water to stop the cooking. Drain well and place in separate bowls; cover and set aside. Do not cook the miniature corn. If the corn is frozen, thaw; if canned, drain. Place the corn in a bowl; cover and set aside. Pare, boil (page 275–276) and drain the potatoes; cover and keep warm on the back of the range. (Prepare the vegetables separately to preserve their individual colors and flavors.)

Add the pearl onions, snow peas, carrots, asparagus, and miniature corn to the cooked meat mixture in the skillet. Add the half-and-half to the reserved flour mixture; cover and shake vigorously until well blended. Place the stew over medium heat (350°F in an electric skillet). While stirring the stew constantly, add the half-and-half mixture; bring to a boil, stirring continuously. Add the sherry; stir well to blend. Turn the stew into a 2½-quart round, ovenproof casserole; cover and keep warm.

Preheat the broiler.

Using an electric mixer, mash the potatoes on high speed, adding 2 tablespoons butter,

¼ teaspoon salt, beaten egg, and enough milk (approximately ½ cup) to make the potatoes fluffy. Using a decorating bag fit with large open-star tip number 8B (page 319), pipe a wide zigzag border (page 324) of mashed potatoes on top of the stew around the edge of the casserole (see Note). Brown the mashed-potato border under the broiler.

NOTE: If a decorating bag and tip are not available, spoon small mounds of mashed potatoes over the stew around the perimeter of the casserole. (Brown under the broiler.)

SERVES 6

OYSTER STEW

Oyster Stew is quickly and easily prepared. Plan to cook it just before serving, and once you begin the cooking, do not leave the stove unattended as Oyster Stew demands a watchful eye to prevent the butter from browning or burning, to allow the oysters to curl only slightly, and to prevent the stew from boiling after adding the milk and half-and-half.

1½ teaspoons celery salt
1 teaspoon salt
⅛ teaspoon pepper
¼ cup plus 2 tablespoons (6 tablespoons) butter
3 dozen (about 1¾ pounds) shucked, raw oysters with liquor
1 tablespoon plus 2 teaspoons Worcestershire sauce
Dash of Tabasco pepper sauce
2 cups whole milk
2 cups (1 pint) half-and-half
Paprika for decoration
Oyster crackers

In a small sauce dish, place the celery salt, salt, and pepper; stir to combine; set aside. In a heavy-bottomed kettle over medium-low heat, heat the butter until it sizzles, but do not allow the butter to brown. Add the oysters with all their liquor, celery salt mixture, Worcestershire sauce, and pepper sauce; stir to combine. Increase the heat to medium-high and cook until the oysters curl *slightly* (about 5 minutes). Do not allow the butter to burn. Add the milk and half-and-half. Heat the stew, but do not allow it to boil; stir often. Serve immediately. Ladle into soup bowls; sprinkle paprika over each serving. Place oyster crackers in a large serving bowl and pass at the table.

SERVES 4 OR 5

SOYBEAN-BRATWURST STEW

Most people eat soybeans frequently, if not daily, in the form of soybean oil. It is the major oil used in cooking oils called "vegetable oil," and it is also used in many margarines, shortenings, and salad dressings. Another soybean product, soy flour, is sometimes used in combination with wheat flour to make breads, cookies, and other baked goods (see the recipe for Soy Whole-Wheat Muffins, page 377). Despite our significant consumption of soybeans, mainly in the oil form, they are eaten in the whole-bean form rather infrequently. Soybeans can be a nutritious and welcome addition to the more traditional varieties of beans we enjoy serving.

Soybeans are very firm and, due to their high protein content, require lengthy cooking. I have found that dried soybeans are best when cooked in a pressure cooker as this manner of cooking results in softer beans than when they are boiled conventionally. Both methods of cooking are given in the procedures for this recipe.

8 ounces (about 1 cup) dried soybeans
4 cups cooking liquid from soybeans
2 cups 100% vegetable juice
1½ cups tomato juice
1 large onion, cut into eighths
1 garlic clove, pressed
5 slices bacon, cut into 1-inch pieces

½ cup chili sauce
¾ teaspoon dried leaf rosemary
1 tablespoon snipped, fresh basil or
   1 teaspoon dried leaf basil
1 bay leaf
¾ teaspoon pepper
1 12-ounce can or bottle of beer
1 8-ounce package frozen miniature corn on the cob (about 1½ cups corn)*
2 cups carrots pared and sliced diagonally ½ inch thick
1 pound smoked bratwurst, sliced ¾ inch thick
½ cup all-purpose flour
1 cup water
2 teaspoons salt

* *If frozen miniature corn on the cob is not available, about 1½ cups drained, canned miniature corn on the cob may be substituted. Make sure that the canned miniature corn is not pickled. Do not cook commercially canned miniature corn on the cob before adding it to the stew.*

Wash the soybeans well and carefully sort them. Place the soybeans in a mixing bowl and add water to cover. Soak the beans for 12 hours.

In a sieve, drain and rinse the beans well. Cook the beans in a pressure cooker for 30 minutes at 15 pounds, following pressure cooker instructions and adding 1 tablespoon of vegetable oil to prevent frothing (see Note). Drain the soybeans, reserving the cooking liquid. Place the drained soybeans in a bowl or storage container; cover and refrigerate. In a heavy-bottomed kettle, place 4 cups reserved cooking liquid from the soybeans, vegetable juice, tomato juice, onion, garlic, bacon, chili sauce, rosemary, basil, bay leaf, pepper, and beer. Cover the kettle; bring the mixture to a boil over high heat. Reduce the heat and simmer the mixture, covered, 1½ hours.

Meanwhile, pour ½ inch water into a small saucepan. Cover the saucepan and bring the water to a boil over high heat. Add the corn; cover and return to a simmer. Reduce the heat

(Recipe continues on next page)

and cook the corn briefly until just tender. Drain and set aside. Place the carrots in a medium saucepan; add water to cover. Cover the saucepan and bring the carrots to a boil over high heat. Reduce the heat to medium and cook the carrots until just tender (about 6 minutes). Drain and set aside.

After the stew mixture has simmered 1½ hours, add the drained soybeans and bratwurst; simmer, covered, for an additional 10 minutes.

In a glass jar or plastic container with a secure lid, place the flour and 1 cup water; cover and shake vigorously until blended. Slowly add the flour mixture to the stew, stirring constantly. Add the salt; stir to blend. Add the corn and carrots; stir to evenly distribute. Cover and simmer 2 minutes. Remove the bay leaf from the stew and discard it. Ladle the stew into soup bowls.

NOTE: After soaking, draining, and rinsing the soybeans, they may be cooked by the traditional method rather than in a pressure cooker. To cook the beans by the traditional method, place them in a heavy-bottomed kettle. Add 4 cups of fresh water for each cup of soaked and drained beans. Cover the kettle and bring the mixture to a boil over high heat. Reduce the heat and skim off the excess foam. Simmer the beans about 3 hours until tender (the beans will remain somewhat firm). Add additional water during the cooking period if needed. Drain the cooked soybeans, reserving the cooking liquid, and continue to follow the recipe.

SERVES 8

SERVING SUGGESTION: Serve with Soy Whole-Wheat Muffins (page 377), butter, and Strawberry Jam.

Spinach Spread, page 45

Taco Spread, page 46

Asparagus Rolls, page 57;
Cherry Tomatoes Stuffed with Curried Chicken Salad, page 50

Wisconsin Beer Cheese Soup, page 77

Bean Soup, page 72; Corn Bread, page 374

Field of Dreams Salad, page 106

Marinated Cucumbers and Onions, page 108

Perfection Salad, page 114

Seven-Layer Salad, page 118

Stuffed Bell Peppers, page 150

Deviled Eggs, page 224

Scalloped Potatoes, page 277

Salads and
Salad Dressings

Salad as a Separate Course in Home Dining

Serving most salads as a separate, first course could add to the pleasure of home dining. (It requires very little extra effort on the part of the cook.)

Food tastes best when the palate is not over-taxed with too many simultaneous flavors. Eating by courses allows the diner to experience in full measure the taste and texture of each food prepared for the meal. When more than one food is placed on a plate—as normally occurs with the main course—care should be exercised to plan foods and garnishes which complement each other in taste, color, smell, and texture, in order to achieve a combination which provides harmonious sensory satisfaction.

Another benefit of first-course salads at home is that the practice promotes the eating of more fresh vegetables and fruits and less fatty, high-calorie, and sweet foods which may follow in the meal. When a diner brings a healthy appetite to the table, a generous, fresh, appealing salad can go a long way toward assuaging hunger—a real assist in holding down portions of subsequently served, higher-calorie foods.

TO WASH AND PREPARE GREENS FOR SALADS

Greens should be washed and prepared on the day they are to be served. If processed too far in advance, they will tend to wilt and develop brown spots. To wash and prepare greens, other than heads of iceberg lettuce and cabbage (instructions for these greens follow), cut out the core (if the variety you are serving has one), trim back and discard long, tough stems on varieties such as watercress and spinach, separate the leaves or sprigs, and cut away any wilted leaves or brown spots.

Wash individual leaves or sprigs under cold, running water; then, place them in a sink filled with cold water for a second washing. Swish the greens gently in the water. Then, let them stand a few minutes to allow any sand or soil particles to gravitate to the bottom of the sink and away from the greens.

Lift the greens out of the water, lowering your hands into the water only as deeply as necessary to grasp them. Place the greens in a colander to drain. After allowing a few minutes for the greens to drain, rap the colander a few times on the bottom of the sink to expel additional water.

Fold a clean tea towel in half lengthwise, and lay it on the kitchen counter. Distribute the greens, front side up, over the tea towel; roll the towel loosely, starting from one of the short ends. Loosely fold the toweling under the ends of the roll and place it, seam down, in the vegetable storage drawer of the refrigerator. The tea towel will continue to absorb water from the surface of the greens.

As near serving time as possible, unroll the tea towel of greens. If the greens are still somewhat wet, wipe them lightly with a dry tea towel or with paper towels. Greens for salads should be crisp and nearly dry. Tear, cut, or leave greens whole, as called for in the salad recipe being prepared, and depending upon the size of the leaves.

When washing and preparing heads of iceberg lettuce and cabbage, the leaves are usually not separated. Wash and prepare these greens, as follows:

ICEBERG LETTUCE: Core the head and remove any wilted outer leaves. Hold the head upside down under cold, running water, letting the water run into the head. Invert the head and place it in a colander to drain. Rap the colander a few times on the bottom of the sink to expel additional water. Wrap the head of lettuce in a dry tea towel and refrigerate in the vegetable storage drawer.

CABBAGE HEADS: Trim the stem and remove any wilted or discolored outer leaves. Wash the head under cold, running water; dry with a clean towel or with paper towels. Cut the head into quarters lengthwise through the stem end.

Cut away the core from each quarter. No further washing is necessary. Place the cabbage quarters in zipper-seal plastic bags and refrigerate.

MOLDED SALADS

PREPARE MOLDED SALADS ONE DAY IN ADVANCE: To assure that molded salads are completely set, it is best to make them the day before they are to be served. When molded salads have gelled sufficiently to become stationary, cover them, in the refrigerator, with plastic wrap or aluminum foil to retain their fresh appearance and surface texture.

TO LIGHTLY OIL A SALAD MOLD: Brush the inside of the salad mold with a light coat of vegetable oil. Then, wipe nearly dry with paper towels.

TO REMOVE SALADS FROM SMALL, INDIVIDUAL MOLDS: Run a sharp, thin-bladed paring knife around the outer edge (and inner edge, if there is one) of the molded salad, penetrating the salad only ⅛ inch. Then, hold one mold at a time in a bowl of warm water for about 3 seconds, taking care not to get water on the gelatin salad. After removing each mold from the warm water, quickly turn it upside down on an individual salad plate. If the salad does not unmold, dip it again in warm water; or, with the mold upside down and in place slightly above the salad plate, slide a paring knife ½ inch into the outer edge of the mold at a single place. This will sometimes help release the salad.

TO REMOVE SALADS FROM LARGE MOLDS: Run a sharp, thin-bladed paring knife around the outer edge (and inner edge, if there is one) of the molded salad, penetrating the salad only ⅛ inch. Place a serving plate upside down on top of the molded salad; then, holding the serving plate and mold securely, invert. The unmolded salad should now be in place above the serving plate. Place a clean tea towel under hot running water; wring out the towel. Cover the mold with the hot, moist towel and press, with your hands,

against the entire surface of the mold. When the towel feels cool, place it under hot water again, and repeat the process. After 2 or 3 applications of the hot towel, the salad should drop from the mold onto the plate. If the salad continues not to release, *very carefully* lift the edge of the mold and slide a paring knife ½ inch into the outer edge of the mold, at a single place, to help release the salad. This is a hazardous procedure with very large molds, as it can cause the gelatin to split.

TO CUT MOLDED SALADS INTO INDIVIDUAL SERVINGS: Use a small, sharp, thin-bladed knife about the size of a steak knife. Dip the knife blade into a tall glass of very hot water to warm the blade. Quickly wipe the blade dry; then, firmly make the desired cut. Redip the knife into hot water and dry it before making each cut.

To remove cut servings from the dish, use a small spatula as close to the size of the individual servings as possible.

Fruit Salads

APPLE SALAD

2 cups unpared, quartered, cored, and
   sliced (see recipe procedures below) firm red
   apples, such as Delicious or Jonathan (about
   1 large apple or 2 medium-small apples)
½ cup sliced celery
¼ cup broken pecans
1 cup miniature marshmallows
1 recipe Special Mayonnaise Dressing
   (page 131)
Shredded iceberg lettuce

(Recipe continues on next page)

Wash the apples. Quarter and core them, leaving the skin on. Cut each quarter in half lengthwise, and slice ⅜ inch thick. Measure 2 cups apple slices; reserve any remaining slices for other uses. Place 2 cups apple slices in a medium mixing bowl. Add the celery, pecans, marshmallows, and Special Mayonnaise Dressing; stir to combine. Serve on a bed of shredded lettuce arranged on individual salad plates.

SERVES 4

FRESH PEAR SALAD WITH GINGER DRESSING

6 ounces cream cheese, softened
⅓ cup well-drained, commercial crushed pineapple in pineapple juice, reserving juice
3 tablespoons finely broken English walnuts
2 tablespoons ginger preserves
3 ripe, chilled Comice or Bartlett pears
2 tablespoons freshly squeezed, strained lemon juice
Leaf lettuce
Ginger Dressing (recipe follows)
¼ cup plus 2 tablespoons shredded, mild cheddar cheese

Place the cream cheese in a small mixing bowl; using an electric mixer, beat on high speed until creamy. Add the drained pineapple, walnuts, and ginger preserves; stir to combine; cover and refrigerate.

Shortly before serving, halve, core, and pare the pears. Brush the pears lightly with lemon juice to prevent discoloration. Line 6 individual salad plates with leaf lettuce and place one pear half on each plate. Using a 1½-inch trigger scoop, place a ball of the cream cheese mixture in the core cavity of each pear half. Spoon Ginger Dressing over each entire pear half (including the cream cheese filling). Sprinkle 1

tablespoon cheddar cheese over the dressing on each pear half.

SERVES 6

GINGER DRESSING
½ cup mayonnaise
1 tablespoon reserved pineapple juice (from crushed pineapple above)
¾ teaspoon very finely grated fresh ginger (page 6)
½ cup Whipped Cream (page 309) (whip ½ cup whipping cream; then measure ½ cup)

In a small mixing bowl, place the mayonnaise, pineapple juice, and ginger; using an electric mixer, beat on medium speed until smooth and blended. Add the whipped cream; using a spoon, fold in.

PEACH AND COTTAGE CHEESE SALAD

Leaf lettuce
4 chilled, canned peach halves
1 cup small-curd cottage cheese
⅔ cup Poppy Seed Dressing (page 127)
3 red maraschino cherries, cut into eighths, for decoration

Line 4 small, individual salad plates with leaf lettuce. Tear additional leaf lettuce into bite-sized pieces; arrange in the center part of each plate to provide a low platform for the peach and cottage cheese and to make the salad plate look more lush.

Place 1 peach half, pit side up, in the center of each plate. Using a 2¼-inch trigger scoop, place a full scoop (about ¼ cup) of cottage cheese on top of each peach half. If the cottage cheese is especially creamy, drain off some of the liquid before scooping. Spoon about 1 tablespoon plus 1 teaspoon Poppy Seed Dressing over the cottage cheese and peach half on each plate. Sprinkle 5 pieces of maraschino cherry over the cottage cheese in each salad.

SERVES 4

VARIATION ~ HOLIDAY DECORATION: Substitute 2 red and 2 green maraschino cherries for 3 red maraschino cherries. Cut the cherries into eighths; arrange 3 red pieces and 3 green pieces on top of the cottage cheese on each plate.

TWENTY-FOUR-HOUR SALAD

2 extra-large eggs, beaten
¼ cup freshly squeezed, strained lemon juice
¼ cup sugar
2 tablespoons butter
1 cup (½ pint) whipping cream, whipped
2 8-ounce cans pineapple tidbits in their own juice, well drained
1 15-ounce can pitted white cherries, well drained
1½ cups orange sections (page 32) (about 3 medium oranges)
1 cup seedless white grapes
1¼ cups fresh apricots cut into twelfths (about 4 apricots)*
2 cups miniature marshmallows
¼ cup slivered almonds, toasted (page 35)

Or, 1 15-ounce can apricot halves, well drained. Cut each apricot half into 6 pieces.

Place the eggs in the top of a double boiler; using a handheld electric mixer, beat slightly. Add the lemon juice, sugar, and butter; stir. Place the top of the double boiler over boiling water in the bottom pan. Cook the mixture until thick, stirring constantly. Remove the top of the double boiler from the bottom pan and refrigerate until the mixture cools to room temperature, stirring occasionally. Add the whipped cream; using a spoon, fold in; refrigerate.

In a large mixing bowl, place the pineapple, cherries, orange sections, grapes, apricots, marshmallows, and whipped cream mixture; fold carefully to combine. Place the salad in a crystal serving bowl; cover and refrigerate for 24 hours. At serving time, sprinkle the top of the salad with almonds.

SERVES 12

FROSTY CHRISTMAS SALAD

8 ounces cream cheese, softened
1 cup Miracle Whip dressing
1 cup (½ pint) whipping cream, whipped
2 cups fresh red raspberries
1 cup pared, sliced, then quartered kiwis
Thinly sliced, then halved kiwis for garnish
Additional red raspberries for garnish
Green leaf lettuce

In a small mixing bowl, place the cream cheese and dressing; using an electric mixer, beat on high speed until smooth and blended. Place the cream cheese mixture in a large mixing bowl. Add the whipped cream; using a spoon, fold in. Add 2 cups raspberries and 1 cup kiwis; carefully fold in until evenly distributed. Spoon into a 7 × 11-inch baking dish; using a small, narrow, angled spatula, spread evenly. Cover tightly and freeze.

To serve, cut into 15 pieces using a sharp, thin-bladed knife dipped intermittently into a glass of warm water. Serve on individual salad plates over pieces of green leaf lettuce. Garnish the top of each serving with 2 small fans of kiwis and a red raspberry.

SERVES 15

FROSTY FRUIT SALAD

Follow the Frosty Christmas Salad recipe above, substituting 3 cups of any combination of fresh and/or canned fruits for the raspberries and kiwis. Garnish with small, attractive pieces of the fruits used in the salad.

SERVES 15

Molded Fruit Salads

STRAWBERRY-AVOCADO HOLIDAY SALAD

Strawberries and avocados would seem an unlikely combination, but they come together beautifully in this striking red and green holiday salad with a subtle, understated flavor.

1½ cups fresh strawberries quartered
   lengthwise
¼ cup cold water
2 teaspoons (1 envelope) unflavored gelatin
1 3-ounce package lime-flavored gelatin
1 cup boiling water
¼ cup cold water
½ cup mayonnaise
¼ cup freshly squeezed, strained lime juice
2 medium-sized ripe avocados
1 cup (½ pint) whipping cream
Leaf lettuce

Place the strawberries, single layer, randomly but evenly over the bottom of a 6 × 10-inch baking dish, with the outside surface of the berries against the bottom of the dish. Cover the dish

with plastic wrap; refrigerate. Place ¼ cup cold water in a small sauce dish; sprinkle the unflavored gelatin over the water; let stand 10 minutes.

Meanwhile, place the lime-flavored gelatin in a medium mixing bowl. Add the boiling water; stir until the gelatin is completely dissolved. Add ¼ cup cold water; stir to blend. Remove the dish containing the strawberries from the refrigerator; uncover. Measure ½ cup lime gelatin mixture; pour over the strawberries; cover and refrigerate.

Add the unflavored gelatin mixture to the remaining lime gelatin mixture; stir, briskly, until the unflavored gelatin is completely dissolved and blended. Add the mayonnaise; using an electric mixer, beat on medium-high speed until fully blended. Refrigerate until the gelatin mixture is set about 1 inch around the edge of the bowl.

Meanwhile, pour the lime juice into a small bowl. Pit and peel the avocados (see Note); cut into chunks and immediately drop into lime juice and toss to coat to prevent discoloration. Place the avocado chunks and lime juice in a blender or food processor; process until pureed. Using a rubber spatula, scrape the avocado puree into a measuring cup. There should be approximately 1½ cups avocado puree. Cover and refrigerate.

Pour the whipping cream into a medium bowl; using an electric mixer, beat on high speed until softly whipped. Cover and refrigerate.

When the gelatin is set 1 inch around the edge of the bowl, remove it from the refrigerator. Using the electric mixer, beat the gelatin on high speed until fluffy. Add the avocado puree; beat until completely blended. Add the whipped cream; using a mixing spoon, fold in only until the color of the mixture is uniform. Spoon the mixture over the strawberry-gelatin layer in the dish; using a small, narrow, angled spatula, spread evenly. Refrigerate until set; then, cover with plastic wrap.

To serve, use a small, sharp, thin-bladed knife to cut individual servings. Using a small spatula, carefully remove the servings from the dish and invert onto individual salad plates atop a small piece of leaf lettuce. The colorful, red strawberries in clear, green gelatin thus become the attractive top layer of the served salad.

NOTE: Cut the unpeeled avocados in half lengthwise. To separate from the pits, gently twist the avocado halves in opposite directions. Then peel.

SERVES 8 TO 10

ALTERNATIVE SERVING METHOD: To serve buffet style, the entire uncut salad may be unmolded onto a serving platter (page 89). Decorate the platter with leaf lettuce, sprigs of watercress, and unstemmed fresh strawberries.

CHRISTMAS GOOSEBERRY SALAD

2 15-ounce cans gooseberries in light syrup
1 6-ounce package lime-flavored gelatin
2 cups miniature marshmallows
2 cups finely chopped celery
1 cup broken English walnuts
1 cup fresh strawberries cut into ½-inch cubes
Leaf lettuce
1 recipe Thick Special Mayonnaise Dressing (page 131)
Fresh strawberries for decoration

Drain the gooseberries in a sieve, reserving the syrup (about 2 cups drained gooseberries). Place the gooseberries in a bowl; cover with plastic wrap and refrigerate. Add enough water to the reserved gooseberry syrup to make 4 cups liquid; pour into a medium saucepan and set aside. Place the gelatin in a large mixing bowl; set aside.

Over high heat, bring the gooseberry syrup mixture to a boil; pour over the gelatin; stir until the gelatin is completely dissolved. Add the marshmallows; stir until the marshmallows have completely melted. Refrigerate until the mixture begins to set and is the consistency of unbeaten egg whites, intermittently stirring

vigorously to reblend. (The mixture may be placed in the freezer to hasten cooling if watched closely.)

When the mixture cools to egg-white consistency, stir or, using a handheld electric mixer, beat to reblend. Add the gooseberries, celery, walnuts, and 1 cup strawberries; stir until evenly combined. Pour the mixture into a 9 × 13-inch baking dish; refrigerate. When firm, cover tightly with plastic wrap; refrigerate until completely set (at least 4 hours).

Cut into 18 individual servings (page 89). Place each serving on a lettuce-lined individual salad plate. Spoon 2 teaspoons Thick Special Mayonnaise Dressing over the center of each gelatin serving. For decoration, press ¼ or ½ (depending upon size) of a fresh strawberry into the dollop of dressing on each serving.

SERVES 18

MANDARIN ORANGE-GOOSEBERRY SALAD

To serve Gooseberry Salad at times other than Christmas, substitute one 15-ounce can mandarin orange segments in light syrup for the fresh strawberries.

Drain the orange segments in a sieve, reserving the syrup. Cut the orange segments in half widthwise; reserve 18 segment halves to decorate the top of individual salad servings; set aside.

Follow the salad recipe, adding the reserved orange segment syrup to the gooseberry syrup; then, adding enough water to make 4 cups liquid. Continue following the recipe, adding the unreserved segment halves (about 1 cup) to the salad in substitution for 1 cup cubed strawberries.

SERVES 18

RASPBERRY SHIMMER

2 12-ounce bags frozen red raspberries
    without syrup
1 6-ounce package red raspberry-flavored
    gelatin
2 cups boiling water
1 cup cold water
16 ounces red raspberry-flavored, lowfat yogurt
Red-tip leaf lettuce
Fresh red raspberries for garnish

Remove the raspberries from freezer 1 hour
ahead of time. Place a colander in the sink, fill
with raspberries, and thaw.

After 1 hour, place the gelatin in a large mixing
bowl. Add boiling water; stir until gelatin dissolves. Add cold water; stir to blend. Refrigerate
until mixture just begins to set (watch closely).

Remove gelatin from refrigerator. Add the
yogurt; stir to blend . Using an electric mixer, beat
mixture on low speed until completely blended.
Carefully fold in raspberries. Pour the mixture
evenly into a 9 X 13-inch baking dish and smooth
top with spatula. Refrigerate until set. Cut into 18
servings (page 89) and serve on lettuce-lined
places with 3 fresh raspberries on top.

SERVES 4

STRAWBERRY SHIMMER

Follow the Raspberry Shimmer recipe, above,
substituting 1 20-ounce bag of frozen strawberries without syrup, strawberry-flavored gelatin,
and strawberry-flavored lowfat yogurt for the raspberry ingredients. Garnish with fresh strawberries.

CITRUS FRUIT THREE-LAYER PARTY SALAD

BOTTOM LAYER
1 3-ounce package orange-flavored gelatin
¾ cup boiling water
1 cup cold water
2 cups orange sections (page 32)
Orange zest (page 31) for decoration

Place the gelatin in a medium mixing bowl. Add
the boiling water; stir until the gelatin is completely dissolved. Add the cold water; stir to
blend. Refrigerate until the gelatin mixture
begins to set and is the consistency of unbeaten
egg whites (watch closely).

Meanwhile, distribute the orange sections,
single layer, randomly over the bottom of a
7 × 11-inch baking dish. Pour the partially set
gelatin over the orange sections; refrigerate until set (at least 4 hours). Using a citrus zester
(page 32) cut the orange zest and place it in a
small sauce dish; cover and refrigerate, reserving for decoration on the individual salad
servings.

CENTER LAYER
12 ounces regular cream cheese spread
½ cup chopped, slivered blanched almonds
    (page 29)

Prepare the center layer after the bottom layer is
fully set.

Place the cream cheese in a small mixing
bowl; using an electric mixer, beat on high speed
until smooth and creamy. Add the almonds; stir
until evenly distributed. Spoon the cream
cheese mixture evenly and carefully over the
surface of the bottom layer. Using a small, narrow, angled spatula, spread evenly and
smoothly. Refrigerate until cold and set (at least
4 hours).

TOP LAYER
1 3-ounce package lemon-flavored gelatin
¾ cup boiling water
1 cup cold water
2 cups white grapefruit sections (page 32)
Boston lettuce leaves

When the center layer is set, prepare the top
layer. Follow the same procedure for preparing
the gelatin as in the bottom layer, above. Distribute the grapefruit sections, single layer, ran-

domly over the center layer. Pour the partially set gelatin over the grapefruit sections; refrigerate until set (at least 4 hours).

To serve, cut the salad into individual servings (page 89). Using a small spatula, place the servings on individual salad plates atop a small leaf of Boston lettuce (the grapefruit layer will be on top). Sprinkle a few curls of orange zest over the center of each salad serving.

SERVES 8 TO 10

VARIATION ~ HOLIDAY DECORATION
8 ounces regular cream cheese spread
Bright green and red paste food coloring

For an attractive salad decoration for the Christmas holidays, pipe green and red holly near one corner or in the center of each salad serving. Eliminate the orange zest decoration.

To make piped holly, place the cream cheese in a small mixing bowl; using an electric mixer, beat briefly on high speed until smooth and fluffy. Spoon about ⅔ of the cream cheese into a small container or bowl. Using a toothpick, add a tiny amount of green paste food coloring; stir vigorously until completely blended. Spoon the remaining ⅓ cream cheese into another small container or bowl; tint red, using the same procedure. Using a decorating bag fit with medium leaf tip number 68 (page 319), pipe 2 green holly leaves (page 326). Using another decorating bag fit with small round tip number 3, add 3 small red berries (see Dots, page 323) where the stem ends of the holly leaves meet.

APRICOT SALAD

1 30-ounce can peeled or unpeeled apricots in light or heavy syrup
1 8-ounce can pineapple tidbits in their own juice
Additional pineapple juice, if necessary
1 6-ounce package orange-flavored gelatin
2 cups boiling water
2 cups miniature marshmallows

½ cup sugar
3 tablespoons plus 2 teaspoons all-purpose flour
1 extra-large egg
2 tablespoons butter
1 cup (½ pint) whipping cream, whipped
1¼ cups shredded Colby cheese
Lettuce leaves

In a sieve, drain the apricots and pineapple together, reserving the syrup and juice. Measure 2 cups reserved syrup and juice, adding additional pineapple juice, if necessary, to make 2 cups liquid; set aside. Place the drained apricots and pineapple tidbits in a blender or food processor. Chop the fruit finely in the blender or food processor, but do not puree; set aside.

Place the gelatin in a large mixing bowl. Add the boiling water; stir until the gelatin completely dissolves. Add 1 cup of the mixed apricot syrup and pineapple juice; stir to blend. Add the chopped fruit and marshmallows; stir until evenly combined. Pour into a 9 × 13-inch baking dish; refrigerate until firm.

Then, in a small mixing bowl, place the sugar and flour; stir to combine; set aside. Place the egg in the top of a double boiler; using a handheld electric mixer, beat slightly. Add the sugar mixture; stir well. Add the remaining 1 cup of mixed apricot syrup and pineapple juice, and butter; stir. Place the top of the double boiler over simmering water in the bottom pan. Cook the mixture until thick, stirring constantly. Remove the top of the double boiler from the bottom pan; refrigerate until the mixture cools to room temperature, stirring occasionally.

After the mixture cools to room temperature, add the whipped cream; using a spoon, fold in. Spoon the whipped cream mixture over the set gelatin mixture; using a large, narrow, angled spatula, spread evenly and smoothly. Sprinkle the top evenly with shredded cheese. Refrigerate until the whipped cream topping is set (at least 6 hours). Cut into 15 individual serving pieces (page 89). Serve on small salad plates lined with lettuce leaves.

SERVES 15

MANDARIN ORANGE SALAD

Orange frozen yogurt is a refreshing ingredient in this salad, which can also double as a dessert (omit the lettuce and decorate the plate with a sprig of fresh mint). This salad should be made a day in advance to allow sufficient time for it to set solidly.

2 11-ounce cans mandarin orange segments
  in light syrup
1 3-ounce package lemon-flavored gelatin
1 pint orange frozen yogurt
1 banana
Bibb lettuce leaves

Drain the mandarin orange segments in a sieve, reserving the syrup. Reserve 8 orange segments for garnish; cover and refrigerate. Place the remaining orange segments in a bowl; cover and set aside. Measure 1 cup reserved syrup and place in a small saucepan; set aside.

Place the gelatin in a medium mixing bowl; set aside. Place the saucepan containing the syrup over medium-high heat; bring the syrup to a boil. Pour the syrup over the gelatin; stir until the gelatin is completely dissolved. Add the frozen yogurt while the gelatin mixture is still hot; stir until the yogurt completely melts and the mixture is smooth. Refrigerate the mixture exactly 10 minutes (no longer as the melted frozen yogurt has already made the mixture quite cold before you refrigerate it; overrefrigeration at this point will allow the mixture to set too firmly before adding the fruit).

Peel the banana; split in half lengthwise; slice. Add the sliced banana and orange segments to the gelatin mixture; carefully fold in. Ladle into 8 lightly oiled (page 89) individual molds; refrigerate until set (at least 8 hours, but preferably overnight). After the mixture is set, cover each mold with a small piece of aluminum foil.

It is not necessary to dip the molds containing this salad in warm water to unmold. To unmold, run a paring knife around the outer edge of each mold, penetrating the salad about ⅛ inch. Invert each mold over an individual salad plate lined with Bibb lettuce and slide the paring knife about ½ inch into the outer edge of the mold, at a single place, to release the salad. Garnish each salad with one of the reserved orange segments.

SERVES 8

CRANBERRY-ORANGE SALAD

2 cups fresh cranberries
1 medium orange, unpeeled, quartered, and
  seeded
1 8-ounce can crushed pineapple in its own
  juice
1 3-ounce package orange-flavored gelatin
½ cup sugar
1 cup finely diced celery
¾ cup quartered, seedless red grapes
½ cup broken English walnuts
Leaf lettuce
1 recipe Special Mayonnaise Dressing
  (page 131)
Small sprigs of celery leaves for garnish
Orange zest (page 31) for decoration

Wash and drain the cranberries. Using a food grinder fit with a fine blade (page 34), grind the cranberries and orange quarters (including the peel) finely. Then, drain the cranberry-orange mixture in a sieve. Place the drained mixture in a covered container and refrigerate. Drain the crushed pineapple in a sieve, reserving the juice. Cover the drained crushed pineapple; set aside. Add enough water to the pineapple juice to make 2 cups liquid; set aside. In a medium saucepan, place the gelatin and sugar; stir to combine. Add the pineapple juice mixture; stir to combine. Place over medium heat and stir until the gelatin and sugar are completely dissolved; refrigerate until the mixture begins to set and is the consistency of unbeaten egg whites.

Then, add the ground cranberries and oranges, crushed pineapple, celery, grapes, and walnuts; fold in until evenly combined. Ladle into 8 lightly oiled (page 89) individual molds; refrigerate until firm (at least 3 hours).

It is not necessary to dip the molds containing this salad in warm water to unmold if the molds were lightly oiled before filling. To unmold, run a paring knife around the outer edge of each mold, penetrating the salad about 1/8 inch. Invert each mold over an individual salad plate lined with leaf lettuce and slide the paring knife about 1/2 inch into the outer edge of the mold, at a single place, to release the salad. Top each molded salad with a dollop of Special Mayonnaise Dressing. Arrange a small sprig of celery leaves beside the molded salad on each plate and sprinkle a few curls of orange zest over the dressing.

SERVES 8

VARIATION: Substitute 3/4 cup ground (page 16), unpeeled, firm red apples for the grapes.

CINNAMON-APPLE SALAD

2 tablespoons cinnamon imperials (candy red hots)
1/4 cup boiling water
1 3-ounce package lemon-flavored gelatin
Dash of salt
3/4 cup boiling water
2 cups cinnamon applesauce, homemade and pressed through a food mill or commercially canned
Dash of ground nutmeg
8 ounces cream cheese, softened
3 tablespoons Miracle Whip dressing
Ground cinnamon for decoration
Lettuce leaves

In a small bowl, dissolve the cinnamon imperials in 1/4 cup boiling water; set aside. In a medium bowl, place the lemon gelatin and salt; add 3/4 cup boiling water; stir until the gelatin and salt are completely dissolved. Add the cinnamon imperial mixture; stir to blend. Add the applesauce and nutmeg; stir until combined. Pour into an 8 × 8-inch baking dish; refrigerate until set (at least 3 hours).

In a small mixing bowl, place the cream cheese and dressing; using an electric mixer, beat on high speed until blended. Spoon the dressing mixture over the set gelatin mixture; using a small, narrow, angled spatula, spread evenly. Sprinkle lightly with cinnamon. Refrigerate until the topping is set (at least 3 hours). Cut into 9 squares (page 89); place individual servings on lettuce-lined salad plates.

SERVES 9

VARIATION ~ **VALENTINE'S DAY GARNISH:** To serve Cinnamon-Apple Salad on Valentine's Day, add a few drops of red liquid food coloring to the cinnamon imperial and boiling water mixture. Omit the ground cinnamon decoration and decorate the top of each salad serving with additional cinnamon imperials or small, red gumdrop hearts.

MOLDED PEAR SALAD

1 15-ounce can pear halves in light syrup
1 3-ounce package lemon-flavored gelatin
6 ounces cream cheese, softened
1 teaspoon freshly squeezed, strained lemon juice
1/2 cup finely broken pecans
1/3 cup maraschino cherries cut into eighths
1 cup (1/2 pint) whipping cream, whipped
Boston lettuce
2 ounces mild cheddar cheese, shredded (1/2 cup shredded cheese)

Drain the pears in a sieve, reserving the syrup. Cut the pears into 1/2-inch cubes; place in a bowl; cover and refrigerate. Measure 1 cup reserved syrup. (If necessary, add water to make 1 cup liquid.) Pour into a small saucepan; set aside. Place the gelatin in a medium mixing bowl; set aside. Place the saucepan containing the syrup over medium-high heat; bring the syrup to a boil. Pour over the gelatin; stir until the gelatin is completely dissolved.

Pour the gelatin mixture into a blender or

(Recipe continues on next page)

food processor. Add the cream cheese and lemon juice; process until completely blended. Pour the processed mixture into a large mixing bowl; refrigerate until the mixture begins to set. Add the pears, pecans, maraschino cherries, and whipped cream; fold until evenly combined. Turn the mixture into a 7 × 11-inch baking dish; refrigerate until set (at least 5 hours).

To serve, cut into 15 servings (page 89). Using a spatula, place the servings on individual salad plates lined with Boston lettuce. Sprinkle the shredded cheese over the molded salad in each serving.

SERVES 12

MOLDED FRUIT SALAD

1 15-ounce can mandarin orange segments in light syrup
1 15-ounce can pitted Royal Anne white cherries in heavy syrup
1 20-ounce can pineapple tidbits in pineapple juice
1 6-ounce package cherry-flavored gelatin
2 cups boiling water
1 cup (½ pint) whipping cream
Shredded iceberg lettuce
15 additional mandarin orange segments for decoration (optional)

In a sieve, drain the orange segments, cherries, and pineapple, reserving the syrup/juice. Place the drained fruit in a bowl; cover and set aside. Measure 2 cups reserved syrup/juice; set aside. Place the gelatin in a large mixing bowl. Add the boiling water; stir until the gelatin is completely dissolved. Add the syrup/juice; stir to blend. Add the drained fruit; stir until evenly combined. Refrigerate until the gelatin begins to set and is the consistency of unbeaten egg whites.

Meanwhile, place the whipping cream in a medium bowl; using an electric mixer, beat until softly whipped; cover and refrigerate. When the gelatin reaches the consistency of unbeaten egg whites, add the whipped cream.

Stir and fold until the whipped cream is combined and the fruits are evenly distributed. Pour into a 9 × 13-inch baking dish; refrigerate until completely set (at least 6 hours).

To serve, cut into 15 servings (page 89). Using a spatula, place the servings on individual salad plates lined with shredded lettuce. The top of each salad serving may be decorated with a mandarin orange segment.

SERVES 15

PINEAPPLE-CREAM CHEESE SALAD

This is a real old-timer we were always happy to find at our places when we took our chairs at my grandmother's table. In those days, it was called "30 Minute Salad" because—as it was made then—you let the recipe mixture stand 30 minutes after three of the additions. Clever names and unconventional procedures were characteristic of many old recipes. They provided relief from the day in, day out routine of cooking, and engendered much conversation, recipe exchanging, and fun in the kitchen. Wacky Cake (page 474) is another example of this playful cooking humor.

1 20-ounce can crushed pineapple in pineapple juice
1 6-ounce package lemon-flavored gelatin
1 cup boiling water
8 ounces cream cheese, softened
1 4-ounce jar diced pimientos, drained (4 tablespoons)
1 cup chopped pecans
2 cups (1 pint) whipping cream, whipped
Shredded iceberg lettuce
½ cup Cooked Salad Dressing (page 128)
Paprika for decoration

Drain the pineapple in a sieve, reserving the juice. Place the drained pineapple in a bowl;

cover and refrigerate. Measure 1 cup reserved juice. (If necessary, add water to make 1 cup liquid.) Set aside. Place the gelatin in a large mixing bowl. Add the boiling water; stir until the gelatin is completely dissolved. Add the pineapple juice; stir to blend. Refrigerate until the mixture begins to set and is the consistency of unbeaten egg whites.

Meanwhile, place the cream cheese in a medium mixing bowl; using an electric mixer, beat on high speed until smooth and creamy. Add the crushed pineapple; stir to combine. Add the pimientos and pecans; stir until evenly distributed; set aside.

When the gelatin mixture reaches the consistency of unbeaten egg whites, add the pineapple mixture; stir until combined. Add the whipped cream; fold in. Turn the mixture into a 9 × 13-inch baking dish; using a small, narrow, angled spatula, spread evenly. Refrigerate until set (at least 6 hours). When set, cover with plastic wrap.

At serving time, cut into 16 pieces (page 89). Using a spatula, place the servings on a platform of shredded lettuce on individual salad plates. Place a dollop (about 1 teaspoon) of Cooked Salad Dressing atop each molded salad serving. Sprinkle paprika sparingly over the salad dressing.

SERVES 16

FROSTED LIME-WALNUT SALAD

1 cup chopped celery
1 tablespoon drained, diced pimientos
½ cup broken English walnuts
1 20-ounce can (2½ cups) crushed pineapple
   in pineapple juice
1 3-ounce package lime-flavored gelatin
¾ cup boiling water
1 cup small-curd cottage cheese, drained
Frosting (recipe follows)
8 Pineapple Tulips tinted yellow (page 338)
   for decoration (optional; see Alternative
   Decorations below)
Sprigs of watercress or other greens for garnish

Place the celery, pimientos, and walnuts in separate bowls; cover and set aside. Drain the pineapple in a sieve, reserving the juice. Place the drained pineapple in a bowl; cover and refrigerate. Set aside the reserved juice. Place the gelatin in a medium mixing bowl; add the boiling water; stir until the gelatin is completely dissolved. Add the pineapple juice to the gelatin mixture; stir to blend. Refrigerate until the mixture begins to set and is the consistency of unbeaten egg whites.

Then, add the celery, pimientos, walnuts, pineapple, and cottage cheese; stir until evenly combined. Turn into a 6 × 10-inch baking dish; using a small, narrow, angled spatula, spread evenly. Refrigerate until set (at least 5 hours).

Spoon the Frosting over the set gelatin mixture; using a small, narrow, angled spatula, spread evenly over the entire surface. Refrigerate. If desired, after the frosting sets, score the salad into 8 servings using a sharp, thin-bladed knife, and arrange a Pineapple Tulip on top of each serving.

At serving time, cut into 8 servings (page 89). Using a spatula, place the servings on individual salad plates. Garnish the plates with sprigs of watercress or other greens.

SERVES 8

FROSTING

8 ounces cream cheese, softened
2 tablespoons commercial sour cream
2 tablespoons freshly squeezed, strained
   lemon juice

In a small mixing bowl, place the cream cheese, sour cream, and lemon juice; using an electric mixer, beat on high speed until very smooth.

ALTERNATIVE DECORATIONS
• For simpler decoration, sprinkle each salad serving with finely chopped English walnuts.

(Recipe continues on next page)

• For a holiday salad, decorate the top of each salad serving with finely diced pimientos and celery (use greenest outer stalks).

DOUBLE RECIPE: To double the recipe, double all the salad ingredients, including the Frosting. Place in a 9 × 13-inch baking dish.

GINGER ALE FRUIT SALAD

½ cup freshly squeezed, strained orange juice
1 tablespoon plus 1 teaspoon (2 envelopes) unflavored gelatin
1 15-ounce can fruit cocktail in light syrup
¾ cup freshly squeezed, strained orange juice
¼ cup sugar
¼ cup freshly squeezed, strained lemon juice
1 10-ounce bottle (1¼ cups) ginger ale
½ cup broken pecans
Leaf lettuce

Pour ½ cup orange juice into the top of a double boiler. Sprinkle the gelatin over the orange juice; let stand 15 minutes.

Meanwhile, drain the fruit cocktail in a sieve, reserving the syrup. Place the drained fruit cocktail in a bowl; cover and refrigerate. Pour the reserved fruit cocktail syrup into a 1-cup glass measuring cup with pouring spout; add enough of the ¾ cup orange juice to make ¾ cup combined liquid. Pour into a medium mixing bowl; set aside. Reserve the remaining orange juice for other uses.

Add the sugar to the gelatin mixture in the top of the double boiler; stir to combine. Place the top of the double boiler over hot water in the bottom pan; stir the gelatin mixture just until dissolved. Add the gelatin mixture and lemon juice to the combined liquid in the mixing bowl; stir until blended. Add the ginger ale; stir to blend. Refrigerate until the mixture begins to set and is the consistency of unbeaten egg whites.

Then, add the fruit cocktail and pecans; stir to combine. Ladle into 8 lightly oiled (page 89) individual molds; refrigerate until fully set (at least 3 hours).

To serve, unmold (page 89) on leaf lettuce arranged an individual salad plates.

SERVES 8

Vegetable Salads

CAESAR SALAD

½ cup extra-virgin olive oil
2 tablespoons freshly squeezed, strained lemon juice
2 tablespoons balsamic vinegar
2 garlic cloves, pressed
2 ounces anchovy fillets
12 cups romaine lettuce cut into generous bite-sized pieces
½ cup freshly grated Parmesan cheese
1¼ cups Garlic Croutons (page 33)

In a glass jar or plastic container with a secure lid, place the olive oil, lemon juice, vinegar, and garlic; cover and shake vigorously until the dressing ingredients are blended; set aside.

Place the anchovy fillets in a small mixing bowl; using the back of a spoon, mash until paste consistency. Add about ¼ cup of the dressing to the anchovy paste; stir until well combined; cover and refrigerate. Cover and refrigerate the remaining dressing.

Just before serving, place the lettuce in a large crystal or wooden salad bowl. Add the remaining dressing; toss until the lettuce is well coated. Add, in the following order, the anchovy mixture, Parmesan cheese, and Garlic Croutons; toss until combined.

SERVES 6

BIBB LETTUCE, WATERCRESS, AND ARTICHOKE HEARTS SALAD

6 cups Bibb lettuce torn into bite-sized pieces
2 cups watercress sprigs with most of stems removed
1 14-ounce can artichoke hearts (not pickled) (about 8 large artichoke hearts), drained and quartered lengthwise
1½ cups sliced fresh mushrooms
⅔ cup Basic Vinaigrette Dressing (page 129)

In a large mixing bowl, place the lettuce, watercress, artichoke hearts, mushrooms, and Basic Vinaigrette Dressing; toss to combine. Serve on glass salad plates.

SERVES 4

VARIATION: 2 tablespoons pine nuts may be tossed with the other ingredients.

SLICED TOMATOES AND LETTUCE SALAD

4 medium to large ripe tomatoes
Mixed greens of choice, torn into bite-sized pieces
Special Mayonnaise Dressing (page 131)
Paprika for decoration
Sprigs of watercress for garnish

Blanch (page 29), stem, peel, and slice the tomatoes; set aside. Arrange generous beds of greens on individual, chilled salad plates. Over the greens on each plate, place 2 or 3 overlapping slices of tomatoes. Spoon 1 heaping tablespoon of dressing over the tomatoes in each salad. Sprinkle a sparing amount of paprika on the center portion of the dressing. Garnish each plate with a sprig of watercress.

SERVES 6

DUTCH LETTUCE SALAD

4 cups iceberg lettuce torn into bite-sized pieces
6 slices bacon, cut into 1-inch pieces, fried crisply, and drained between paper towels
2 extra-large eggs, hard-cooked (page 222) and chopped
1 cup pared and shredded carrots
1 tablespoon minced onions
¾ cup Cooked Salad Dressing made with ¼ cup plus 1 tablespoon sugar (page 128)

In a large mixing bowl, place the lettuce, bacon, eggs, carrots, onions, and Cooked Salad Dressing; toss to combine.

SERVES 4

BOSTON LETTUCE, HEARTS OF PALM, AND MUSHROOM SALAD

1 cup canned hearts of palm drained and sliced ⅝ inch thick
8 cups Boston lettuce torn into bite-sized pieces
⅔ cup sliced, fresh mushrooms
2 extra-large eggs, hard-cooked (page 222) and coarsely chopped
½ cup Creamy Vinaigrette Dressing (page 129)

(Recipe continues on next page)

Test each heart of palm for tenderness before slicing. Especially if the heart of palm is large in diameter, it may be necessary to remove and discard the tough outer layer before slicing.

In a large mixing bowl, place the hearts of palm, lettuce, mushrooms, eggs, and Creamy Vinaigrette Dressing; toss to combine.

SERVES 4

HEARTS OF PALM–PERSIMMON SALAD

This salad features two delicacies worthy of "company fare" designation, but appropriately flavored for informal dining. Hearts of palm are just that: the center of palmetto (cabbage) palm tree stems. Unless you live in Florida, where they can be purchased fresh, hearts of palm come to us canned from Florida, Brazil, and Costa Rica. They've been one of my favorite salad ingredients ever since I first ate them at the former Well-of-the-Sea restaurant in Chicago when I was in high school.

Persimmons are a shiny, bright orange, Asian fruit, which is also grown in the United States. Persimmons grown in this country are available September through November, but imported persimmons may be found in some produce markets through May. Wild American persimmons, a different species from domestic persimmons, are smaller than domestic persimmons and are extremely sour until fully ripe. The name "persimmon" is derived from the Native American Indian word for this wild fruit.

¾ cup canned hearts of palm drained and
   sliced ¼ inch thick
¾ cup coarsely diced persimmons
¾ cup coarsely chopped celery
¾ cup thinly sliced radishes
1 recipe Sour Cream Salad Dressing
   (page 130–131)
Spinach leaves

Test each heart of palm for tenderness before slicing. Especially if the heart of palm is large in diameter, it may be necessary to remove and discard the tough outer layer before slicing.

In a medium mixing bowl, place the hearts of palm, persimmons, celery, radishes, and Sour Cream Salad Dressing; stir to combine. Arrange the spinach leaves on 4 individual salad plates. Spoon the salad in the center of each plate over the spinach leaves.

SERVES 4

TOSSED SALADS

The following are suggested ingredients to include in tossed salads of your own invention. Toss the salad ingredients with a compatible dressing of your choice (pages 125–132).

GREENS
Arugula
Bibb lettuce
Bok choy
Boston lettuce
Red-tip Boston lettuce
Chinese cabbage
Green cabbage
Red cabbage
Belgian endive
Curly endive
Escarole
Iceberg lettuce
Leaf lettuce
Red-tip leaf lettuce
Radicchio
Romaine
Spinach
Watercress

VEGETABLES
Artichoke hearts (not pickled)
Green and white asparagus, boiled
Garbanzo beans (chickpeas)
Green and wax beans, boiled

Kidney beans, canned, drained, and rinsed
Lima beans, boiled
Beets, boiled
Green, red, yellow, orange, and purple bell
    peppers
Pimientos
Broccoli flowerets
Brussels sprouts, steamed
Carrots
Cauliflower flowerets
Celery
Corn, boiled
Cucumbers
Fennel bulbs
Hearts of palm
Mushrooms
Green onions (scallions)
Red onions
Sweet onions
Green peas, boiled
Snow peas, blanched
Potatoes, pared or unpared, boiled
Radishes
Sauerkraut
Alfalfa sprouts
Bean sprouts
Daikon radish sprouts
Red and yellow cherry tomatoes
Red and yellow tomatoes
Water chestnuts
Zucchini
Yellow summer squash

FRUITS
Apples
Avocados
Dates
Figs
Grapes
Mandarin orange segments
Pineapple tidbits, canned
Prunes
Dark and golden raisins

MEATS, POULTRY, FISH, AND
SHELLFISH
Beef tenderloin
Veal

Pork tenderloin
Bacon
Ham
Lamb
Ring bologna
Summer sausage
Chicken
Duck
Turkey
Anchovy fillets
Mild fish fillets
Salmon
Albacore tuna, solid white packed in water
Crabmeat
Lobster
Shrimp

OTHER INGREDIENTS
Capers
Cheeses, such as cheddar, Swiss, blue, feta,
    chèvre, Monterey Jack, Colby, provolone,
    Edam, Gouda, grated Parmesan, and grated
    Romano
Croutons
Hard-cooked eggs
Herbs, such as parsley, chives, basil, dill,
    chervil, marjoram, cilantro, savory,
    tarragon, and rosemary
Nuts, such as almonds, English walnuts,
    pecans, pine nuts, hickory nuts, and
    chestnuts
Ripe and green olives, pitted; also, pimiento-
    stuffed
Pasta
Rice
Sesame Seeds

ALL-YELLOW VEGETABLE SALAD

1½ cups whole, yellow teardrop tomatoes
1¼ cups cooked, cooled, and drained, fresh
    wax beans (page 254) cut into 1¼-inch
    lengths
1 cup yellow summer squash sliced ⅛ inch
    thick, then cut in half
½ cup coarsely chopped yellow bell peppers
⅔ cup Honey-Mustard Dressing (page 126)
Belgian endive

In a large mixing bowl, place the tomatoes, wax
beans, squash, peppers, and Honey-Mustard
Dressing; using a wooden mixing spoon, toss
until evenly distributed. On each of 6 individual
salad plates, arrange leaves of Belgian endive in
flower-petal fashion (like spokes of a wheel).
Spoon the salad in the center of each plate.

SERVES 6

SOPHISTICATED SALAD

3 cups arugula sprigs
3 cups radicchio torn into generous, bite-
    sized pieces
3 cups Belgian endive cut widthwise into
    generous, bite-sized pieces
1 14-ounce can artichoke hearts (not pickled)
    (about 8 large artichoke hearts), drained
    and quartered lengthwise
⅓ cup pine nuts
¾ cup Basic Vinaigrette Dressing (page 129)

In a large mixing bowl, place the arugula, radicchio, Belgian endive, artichoke hearts, pine
nuts, and Basic Vinaigrette Dressing; toss to
coat and evenly distribute. Serve on individual
salad plates (clear glass salad plates are especially nice).

SERVES 6

SORORITY HOUSE SALAD

*After a morning of classes, this was one of my
favorite items to find on the lunch menu at my
sorority house at Northwestern University in
Evanston, Illinois. I have served it ever since.*

6 cups romaine lettuce cut into generous,
    bite-sized pieces
6 cups iceberg lettuce cut into bite-sized
    pieces
4 extra-large eggs, hard-cooked (page 222)
    and coarsely chopped
1 cup sliced celery
1½ recipes Special Mayonnaise Dressing
    (page 131)
Paprika for decoration

In a large bowl, place the romaine lettuce, iceberg lettuce, eggs, celery, and Special Mayonnaise Dressing; toss until combined. Distribute
among 8 individual salad plates. Sprinkle paprika sparingly over each salad.

SERVES 8

BEET AND WATERCRESS SALAD

2 cups cooked, fresh beets (page 255) cut
    julienne (page 7) or 1 15-ounce can
    julienne beets, drained**
2 cups watercress with large stems removed
1 cup sliced, fresh mushrooms
½ cup diced purple bell peppers*
2 tablespoons thinly sliced green onions
    (scallions)
½ cup Mild Creamy Vinaigrette Dressing
    (page 130)
6 medium-sized leaves of red-tip leaf lettuce
6 sprigs of watercress

 *Yellow bell peppers may be substituted if
  purple bell peppers are not available.*

**If julienne beets are not available, substitute
  1 14½ ounce can sliced beets, drained. Cut
  the beets juliene (page 7).*

In a large mixing bowl, place the beets, 2 cups watercress, mushrooms, purple peppers, onions, and Mild Creamy Vinaigrette Dressing; toss and set aside. Line each of 6 individual salad plates with a leaf of red-tip leaf lettuce. Spoon the Beet and Watercress Salad over the lettuce leaves. Garnish each plate with a sprig of watercress.

SERVES 6

BROCCOLI-CAULIFLOWER SALAD

4 cups fresh broccoli flowerets
4 cups fresh cauliflower flowerets
1½ cups sliced radishes
½ cup sliced green onions (scallions)
1 6-ounce can pitted, medium, ripe olives, drained (1½ cups olives), cut in half widthwise
½ recipe Mild Creamy Vinaigrette Dressing (page 130)

Steam the broccoli flowerets (page 252) for 3 minutes. Immediately remove the steamer basket containing the broccoli from the pan. Leave the broccoli in the steamer basket and rinse under cold running water to stop the cooking. Drain well. Place the broccoli in a zipper-seal plastic bag; refrigerate until completely cold. Steam and store the cauliflower flowerets, following the same procedure as for the broccoli flowerets. Steam and prepare the broccoli and cauliflower separately to preserve their individual colors and flavors.

In a medium mixing bowl, place the broccoli, cauliflower, radishes, green onions, olives, and Mild Creamy Vinaigrette Dressing; using a wooden mixing spoon, toss lightly until the vegetables are coated with dressing and evenly distributed.

SERVES 8

COPPER PENNIES

2 pounds uniformly sized carrots, pared and sliced ¼ inch thick
½ cup sugar
1 teaspoon dry mustard
¾ teaspoon salt
½ teaspoon pepper
1 10¾-ounce can condensed tomato soup (undiluted)
1 teaspoon Worcestershire sauce
½ cup vegetable oil
1 medium to small onion, sliced as thinly as possible, separated into rings
1 medium green bell pepper, sliced into rings ⅛ inch thick, seeds removed, white core cut away, and rings cut into fourths

Place the carrots in a large saucepan; add water to cover. Cover and bring to a boil over high heat; reduce the heat and simmer the carrots gently about 12 minutes, until just tender. Drain in a colander; set aside to cool slightly.

In a large saucepan, place the sugar, dry mustard, salt, and pepper; stir to combine. Add the tomato soup, Worcestershire sauce, and vegetable oil; using a handheld electric mixer, beat on high speed until blended; set aside. In a large glass or pottery bowl, place the carrots, onions, and green peppers; toss lightly until evenly distributed; set aside.

Over medium heat, bring the tomato soup mixture to a simmer; pour evenly over the vegetables. Cool slightly; cover and refrigerate. Let stand 24 hours before serving.

MAKES ABOUT 2 QUARTS

COLORFUL MARINATED VEGETABLES WITH SWEET BASIL DRESSING

2 cups fresh broccoli flowerets
2 cups fresh cauliflower flowerets
¼ pound (about 1¾ cups) fresh snow peas
1 cup carrots pared and sliced diagonally ⅛ inch thick
1 cup small cherry tomatoes
¾ cup yellow bell peppers cut julienne (page 7) ¼ inch wide by 1½ inches long
¾ cup Sweet Basil Dressing (page 128)

Steam the broccoli flowerets (page 252) for 2 minutes. Immediately remove the steamer basket containing the broccoli from the pan. Leave the broccoli in the steamer basket and rinse under cold running water to stop the cooking. Drain well. Place the broccoli in a zipper-seal plastic bag; refrigerate until completely cold. Steam and store the cauliflower flowerets, following the same procedure as for broccoli flowerets.

Remove the strings and ends from the snow peas (page 275). Steam the snow peas 1 minute and follow the same procedure as for preparing the broccoli flowerets. Steam and prepare the vegetables separately to preserve their individual colors and flavors.

In a large mixing bowl, place the broccoli, cauliflower, snow peas, carrots, cherry tomatoes, yellow peppers, and Sweet Basil Dressing; using a wooden mixing spoon, toss until combined. Cover and let stand in the refrigerator at least 1 hour. Toss again and serve.

SERVES 6

FIELD OF DREAMS SALAD

(See photo insert page A-4)

3 large ears yellow corn
1 10-ounce package frozen baby lima beans
¾ cup pared and cored cucumbers (page 29) cut into ⅜-inch cubes
½ cup carrots pared and cut julienne (page 7) 1 inch long
½ cup diced celery
¼ cup diced red bell peppers
1 cup blanched (page 29), stemmed, peeled, seeded, and cored (page 29) tomatoes cut into bite-sized chunks
1 tablespoon snipped, fresh chives
½ cup Honey-Mustard Dressing (page 126)
Boston lettuce

Prepare and boil the corn on the cob (page 263); place the hot ears of corn on a clean towel to cool. When cool enough to handle, cut the kernels off the cobs. Measure 1½ cups corn; cover and refrigerate. Reserve the remaining corn for other uses. Cook the lima beans. Measure ½ cup drained beans; cover and refrigerate. Reserve the remaining lima beans for other uses. Wait until the corn and lima beans are cold to compose the salad.

Then, in a mixing bowl, place 1½ cups corn, ½ cup lima beans, cucumbers, carrots, celery, and peppers; toss to combine. Add the tomatoes, chives, and Honey-Mustard Dressing; toss lightly until evenly distributed. Spoon the salad over leaves of Boston lettuce on individual salad plates.

SERVES 6

ALTERNATIVE SERVING SUGGESTION: Serve the salad in an attractive bowl lined with green leaf lettuce. On top and in the center of the salad, artistically arrange 3 ears of miniature corn on the cob (steamed and cooled if frozen, or without further cooking if commercially canned) with husks fashioned from softened green tops of leeks (page 336).

GARDEN SALAD

⅓ pound fresh snow peas
2 carrots, pared and sliced ⅜ inch thick
1¼ pounds tomatoes (3 medium-large
    tomatoes), blanched (page 29), stemmed,
    peeled, seeded and cored (page 29), and cut
    into bite-sized chunks
1½ cups cucumber slices cut ³⁄₁₆ inch thick
½ cup Basil Vinaigrette Dressing
    (page 130)
Leaf lettuce

Steam the snow peas 1 minute (page 252).
Immediately remove the steamer basket containing the peas from the pan. Leave the peas in
the steamer basket and rinse under cold running water to stop the cooking. Drain well.
Place the snow peas in a zipper-seal plastic bag;
refrigerate until completely cold.

Place the carrots in a small saucepan; add
water to cover. Cover and bring to a boil over
high heat; reduce the heat and simmer 3 minutes. Immediately place the carrots in a colander and rinse under cold running water to stop
the cooking. Drain well. Place the carrots in a
zipper-seal plastic bag; refrigerate until completely cold.

In a large mixing bowl, place the snow peas,
carrots, tomatoes, cucumbers, and Basil Vinaigrette Dressing; toss gently to combine. Line
individual salad plates with leaf lettuce; spoon
the salad atop the lettuce. Or serve family style
in a lettuce-lined serving bowl.

SERVES 6

OPTIONAL DECORATIVE PRESENTATION: For a more
decorative salad, use a fluted garnishing cutter
(see illustration) to slice the carrots, and groove
the cucumbers (page 334) before slicing them.

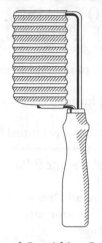

Fluted Garnishing Cutter

VEGETABLE COLLAGE
WITH CHÈVRE

1½ cups tomatoes blanched (page 29),
    stemmed, peeled, quartered, seeded and
    cored (page 29), and cut into uniform, bite-
    sized pieces
1 cup fresh green beans snapped in half or
    into thirds, cooked (page 254), and cooled
⅔ cup coarsely chopped yellow bell peppers
¾ cup celery sliced ¼ inch thick
½ cup chèvre cheese* cut into small, bite-
    sized pieces
2 teaspoons fresh, snipped basil
White Wine Vinaigrette Dressing (page 130)
Boston lettuce

A soft goat's milk cheese.

In a medium bowl, place the tomatoes, green
beans, peppers, celery, cheese, basil, and White
Wine Vinaigrette Dressing; toss to evenly combine. Serve on individual salad plates atop Boston lettuce leaves or in a serving bowl lined with
lettuce leaves.

SERVES 4

CARROT, RAISIN, AND PINEAPPLE SALAD

1 pound carrots, pared and shredded (about 3 cups)
½ cup raisins, plumped (page 30) and drained
½ cup golden raisins, plumped (page 30) and drained
1 8-ounce can pineapple tidbits in their own juice, drained
¾ cup Cooked Salad Dressing made with ¼ cup plus 1 tablespoon sugar (page 128)
Red-tip leaf lettuce
8 sprigs of fresh parsley for garnish

In a medium mixing bowl, place the carrots, raisins, golden raisins, pineapple, and Cooked Salad Dressing; stir to combine and evenly distribute the ingredients. Spoon onto 8 individual salad plates lined with lettuce. Garnish each plate with a sprig of parsley.

SERVES 8

PEA SALAD

This is one of the easiest to make and best-tasting Midwest salads. Keep a can of peas in the refrigerator for making it on the spur of the moment when you have cheese (it can be any cheddar) and celery on hand.

1 15-ounce can peas, drained
1 cup shredded Colby cheese
½ cup coarsely chopped celery
1 recipe Special Mayonnaise Dressing (page 131)
¼ teaspoon salt
⅛ teaspoon pepper

In a medium mixing bowl, place the peas, cheese, and celery; set aside. In a small mixing bowl, place the Special Mayonnaise Dressing, salt, and pepper; stir together. Pour the dressing mixture over the pea mixture; stir to combine.

SERVES 6

MARINATED CUCUMBERS AND ONIONS

(See photo insert page A-5)

4 cups (1½ pounds) seedless cucumbers sliced ⅛ inch thick* (paring is optional)
2 cups (¾ pound) medium-sized white onions sliced ⅛ inch thick, separated into rings
½ cup sugar
1 teaspoon salt
½ teaspoon white pepper
1 cup white vinegar
½ cup extra-virgin olive oil or vegetable oil
1 cup water

If seedless cucumbers are not available, substitute 1½ pounds cucumbers with seeds, pared (optional), cored (page 29), and sliced ⅛ inch thick.

In a large bowl, place the sliced cucumbers and onions; set aside. In a medium mixing bowl, place the sugar, salt, white pepper, vinegar, oil, and water; using an electric mixer, beat on high speed until blended. Pour over the cucumbers and onions; stir to combine and evenly distribute the vegetables. Refrigerate; let stand 24 hours before serving.

To serve, stir the ingredients; then, remove the cucumbers and onions from the marinade with a slotted spoon. Keep leftover cucumbers and onions refrigerated in the marinade. The marinade may be reused to make this dish a second time.

SERVES 4 TO 6

VARIATION: Tomatoes may be added to this recipe. Blanch (page 29), stem, peel, quarter, and seed and core (page 29) the tomatoes.

CUCUMBER SALAD

1½ pounds seedless cucumbers (about
   1½ large cucumbers), pared (page 29) and
   sliced ⅛ inch thick (about 4 cups sliced
   cucumbers)*
¼ cup commercial sour cream
2 tablespoons white vinegar
¼ teaspoon salt
⅛ teaspoon white pepper
1 tablespoon snipped, fresh chives
1 tablespoon snipped, fresh dillweed**

*Or 1½ pounds cucumbers with seeds (about
   2 large cucumbers), pared and cored (page
   29) and sliced ⅛ inch thick.*

**If fresh dillweed is not available, substitute
   1 teaspoon dried dillweed.*

Place the cucumbers in a medium mixing bowl;
set aside. In a separate medium mixing bowl,
place the sour cream, vinegar, salt, white pepper,
chives, and dillweed; stir well to combine. Pour
over the cucumbers; toss lightly to coat. Turn
the salad into a serving bowl.

SERVES 8

SERVING SUGGESTIONS
• Decorate the salad with a Cucumber Rose
  (page 334) and sprigs of fresh dillweed.

• Serve the salad in small, individual sauce
  dishes and decorate each serving with a sprig
  of fresh dillweed.

VARIATION: Substitute 1 tablespoon snipped, fresh
fennel weed for 1 tablespoon snipped, fresh
dillweed. Decorate the salad with sprigs of fresh
fennel weed.

FRESH ASPARAGUS SALAD

Boston lettuce
12 or 16 (depending upon size) fresh
   asparagus spears, boiled (page 253) and
   chilled
2 extra-large eggs, hard-cooked (page 222)
   and sliced
1 tablespoon chopped pimientos
½ cup Honey-Mustard Dressing (page 126)

Line 4 individual salad plates with Boston lettuce leaves. Place additional torn pieces of lettuce evenly over the lettuce lining to form a
platform. Place 3 or 4 asparagus spears, side by
side, diagonally across each plate. Overlap ¼ of
the egg slices in a row on top of the asparagus
spears on each plate. Sprinkle the pimientos
over the egg slices and center portions of the
asparagus spears. Spoon the Honey-Mustard
Dressing over all.

SERVES 4

YELLOW SUMMER SQUASH AND GREEN BEAN SALAD

2 cups yellow summer squash sliced ⅛ inch
   thick, then cut in half
2 cups fresh green beans cut into 1½-inch
   lengths, cooked (page 254) and cooled
¾ cup coarsely chopped radishes
⅔ cup Tarragon Vinaigrette Dressing
   (page 130)
6 medium-sized leaves of Boston lettuce

In a large mixing bowl, place the squash, green
beans, radishes, and Tarragon Vinaigrette
Dressing; toss until evenly distributed. Line 6
individual salad plates with the lettuce leaves;
spoon the salad over the lettuce.

SERVES 6

FANTASIA

¾ pound Roma tomatoes* (about
   4 tomatoes)
1 large cucumber
1 cup chopped celery hearts and leaves (page
   30)
⅓ cup Basil Vinaigrette Dressing (page 130)

  *Also known as plum tomatoes and Italian
  tomatoes.*

Blanch the tomatoes (page 29); immediately
immerse in cold water. Stem, peel, quarter, and
seed and core (page 29) the tomatoes; cut each
quarter in half widthwise. Makes about 2 cups.
Place the tomatoes in a mixing bowl; set aside.
   Pare and core the cucumber (page 29); cut
into bite-sized chunks. Measure 2 cups
cucumber chunks; add to the tomatoes in the
bowl. (Reserve any remaining cucumber
chunks for other uses.) Add the celery hearts
and leaves and Basil Vinaigrette Dressing; toss
to combine. Serve cold on 6 small, chilled salad
plates.

SERVES 6

NASTURTIUM SALAD

*Nasturtium blossoms and leaves are both beauti-
ful and edible. Plant them in your garden to use
in marvelous, tony luncheon and dinner salads
(see Edible Flowers, page 316–318).*

3 cups Bibb lettuce torn into bite-sized pieces
3 cups leaf lettuce torn into bite-sized pieces
½ cup White Wine Vinaigrette Dressing (page
   130)
12 or 20 (optional) freshly picked nasturtium
   blossoms plus leaves

In a large mixing bowl, place the Bibb lettuce
and leaf lettuce. Add the White Wine Vinaigrette Dressing; toss. Place on 4 individual salad

plates. Arrange 3 or 5 freshly picked nasturtium
blossoms plus leaves decoratively over each
salad. Serve immediately.

SERVES 4

KIDNEY BEAN SALAD

1 15½-ounce can dark red kidney beans,
   drained and rinsed
2 extra-large eggs, hard-cooked (page 222)
   and coarsely chopped
1 cup chopped celery
½ cup chopped sweet gherkin pickles
⅛ teaspoon pepper
1 recipe Special Mayonnaise Dressing
   (page 131)
1 extra-large egg, hard-cooked (page 222) and
   sliced, for garnish

In a medium mixing bowl, place the kidney
beans, 2 chopped eggs, celery, pickles, pepper,
and Special Mayonnaise Dressing; toss until
evenly distributed. Place the salad in a serving
bowl; garnish with the sliced egg.

SERVES 5

THREE-BEAN SALAD

⅓ cup sugar
⅔ cup white vinegar
⅓ cup vegetable oil
1 teaspoon salt
½ teaspoon freshly ground pepper
2 cups fresh green beans cut or snapped into
   1½-inch lengths, cooked (page 254) and
   cooled, or 1 14½-ounce can cut green
   beans, drained
2 cups fresh wax beans cut or snapped into
   1½-inch lengths, cooked (page 254) and
   cooled, or 1 14½-ounce can cut wax beans,
   drained

1 15½-ounce can dark red kidney beans, drained and rinsed
½ cup coarsely chopped green bell peppers

In a small mixing bowl, place the sugar, vinegar, vegetable oil, salt, and pepper; using an electric mixer, beat on high speed until blended; set aside. In a medium bowl, place the green beans, wax beans, kidney beans, and green peppers. Add the vinegar marinade; toss lightly. Refrigerate for 24 hours.

To serve, toss again and drain. If serving less than the entire salad, use a slotted spoon to remove the quantity of salad needed from the bowl, leaving the remainder in the marinade for serving at a later time.

SERVES 6 TO 8

COLESLAW

¾ pound cabbage (1 small head)
¾ cup Miracle Whip dressing
2 tablespoons half-and-half or whole milk
¼ teaspoon salt
¼ teaspoon pepper
Paprika for decoration

Wash, dry, and core the cabbage (page 88); chop finely in a food processor or by hand using a sharp knife. Measure 3 cups chopped cabbage and place in a medium mixing bowl; set aside. (Reserve any remaining cabbage for another use.) In a small mixing bowl, place the dressing, half-and-half, salt, and pepper; stir vigorously until blended. Add the dressing to the cabbage; stir to combine. Turn the salad into a serving bowl; sprinkle with paprika. Refrigerate until ready to serve.

SERVES 4

PINEAPPLE COLESLAW

In a sieve, drain one 8-ounce can commercial pineapple chunks in juice, reserving the juice.

Cut the pineapple chunks into quarters; place in a bowl; cover and refrigerate. Cover the reserved juice and set aside.

Follow the Coleslaw recipe, above, substituting 2 tablespoons reserved pineapple juice for 2 tablespoons half-and-half. (Reserve remaining pineapple juice for other uses.) Add the pineapple pieces to the prepared coleslaw and stir to combine before transferring to a serving bowl. Decorate with paprika.

POTATO SALAD

3 pounds red potatoes, boiled (page 275–276); then peeled, quartered lengthwise, and sliced ¼ inch thick (about 5 cups sliced potatoes)
½ cup chopped onions
1 cup coarsely chopped celery
4 extra-large eggs, hard-cooked (page 222) and chopped
½ cup diced sweet gherkin pickles
2 teaspoons celery seed
1½ cups Miracle Whip dressing
1 teaspoon salt
¼ teaspoon white pepper
2 teaspoons sugar
1 tablespoon plus 1 teaspoon prepared mustard
1 extra-large egg, hard-cooked (page 222) and sliced, for garnish
Sprigs of fresh parsley for decoration
Paprika for decoration

In a large mixing bowl, place the potatoes, onions, celery, eggs, and pickles; sprinkle the celery seed over the ingredients; set aside. In a small mixing bowl, place the dressing, salt, white pepper, sugar, and mustard; stir to combine. Pour the dressing mixture over the potato salad ingredients in the bowl; using a wooden mixing spoon, stir carefully to combine.

Turn the Potato Salad into a serving bowl. Arrange the egg slices and parsley sprigs over the salad around the perimeter of the serving

(Recipe continues on next page)

bowl. Sprinkle the center lightly with paprika. Cover and refrigerate until serving time.

SERVES 14

GERTRUD'S GERMAN POTATO SALAD

2½ pounds medium, uniform red potatoes
¼ cup extra-virgin olive oil
2 tablespoons red wine vinegar
1 tablespoon Dijon mustard
1 teaspoon salt
1 teaspoon sugar
½ teaspoon pepper
¾ cup finely chopped onions
½ cup beef broth, homemade (page 70) or commercially canned
2 tablespoons snipped, fresh chives

Boil the potatoes, unpared (page 275–276), about 20 minutes, until just tender (the potatoes will continue cooking as they cool). Immediately drain the potatoes and immerse them briefly in cold water to help stop the cooking; drain. Let the potatoes stand until cooled to medium hot.

Meanwhile, in a covered, *heat-resistant* container or glass jar (such as a canning jar), place the olive oil, vinegar, mustard, salt, sugar, and pepper; cover and shake vigorously until blended; set aside.

When the potatoes have cooled to medium hot, peel and slice them widthwise ³⁄₁₆ to ¼ inch thick. Separate the slices and place them in a large mixing bowl. Sprinkle the onions over the potatoes; cover to keep warm; set aside.

Pour the beef broth into a small saucepan; heat to boiling. Add the hot beef broth to the vinegar mixture; cover the container or jar and shake until blended. Pour back and forth over the potatoes and onions. Using a wooden spoon to help prevent breakage of the potato slices, toss, briefly and carefully, until the onions are combined and the potato slices are coated with

the vinegar mixture. Turn the potato salad into a warmed serving bowl. Sprinkle the chives over the top of the salad to garnish; serve immediately. The salad should be served lukewarm.

SERVES 8

WILD RICE SALAD

1¼ cups raw wild rice, cooked (page 231)
⅓ cup green bell peppers cut into ¼-inch cubes
⅓ cup yellow bell peppers cut into ¼-inch cubes
⅓ cup red bell peppers cut into ¼-inch cubes
⅓ cup carrots pared and cut into ¼-inch cubes
⅔ cup sliced green onions (scallions) including some of the green tops
¼ cup chopped water chestnuts
2 tablespoons small, fresh parsley leaves (snip the single leaves from the stems)
½ cup extra-virgin olive oil
½ cup orange sherry wine vinegar*
½ teaspoon salt
¼ teaspoon coarsely ground pepper
⅔ cup canned mandarin orange segments drained and cut in half widthwise (less than 1 11-ounce can commercial mandarin orange segments)

  If orange sherry wine vinegar is not available, plain sherry wine vinegar or white wine vinegar may be substituted.

Let the cooked wild rice stand in the covered saucepan until cooled to room temperature. Then, place the rice in a large mixing bowl. Add the green peppers, yellow peppers, red peppers, carrots, onions, water chestnuts, and parsley; set aside.

In a pint jar, place the olive oil, vinegar, salt, and pepper; cover and shake vigorously to blend. Pour over the wild rice and vegetables in the mixing bowl. Using a wooden mixing spoon, toss until the vegetables are evenly distributed. Add the orange segments; toss carefully to evenly distribute.

To serve, spoon into a large serving bowl, preferably clear glass. Serve at room temperature.

SERVES 6 TO 8

OPTIONAL DECORATION: Use the remaining whole mandarin orange segments and sprigs of fresh parsley to decorate the top of the salad. Decoratively place the orange segments and parsley sprigs around the edge of the salad bowl. Or, fashion a flower blossom, using the orange segments as petals and parsley leaves as the center of the blossom.

Molded Vegetable Salads

CUCUMBER-DILL RING

1 ½ large seedless cucumbers*
½ cup cold water
1 tablespoon plus 1 teaspoon (2 envelopes)
   unflavored gelatin
1 ½ cups water
2 tablespoons sugar
¼ teaspoon salt
¼ cup plus 2 tablespoons freshly squeezed,
   strained lemon juice

16 ounces cream cheese, softened
16 ounces commercial sour cream
1 cup Miracle Whip dressing
¼ cup finely grated onions
2 tablespoons finely snipped, fresh dillweed**
Leaf lettuce
Cucumber Roses (page 334) for decoration
   (optional)
Sprigs of fresh dillweed for decoration

If seedless cucumbers are not available, substitute cucumbers with seeds (about 2 large cucumbers)

**If fresh dillweed is not available, substitute 2 teaspoons dried dillweed.*

Pare the cucumbers (page 29); slice them widthwise into pieces approximately 1 inch wide. Using a food grinder (page 16), finely grind the cucumber pieces. Place the ground cucumbers in a sieve to drain. With your hand, press the ground cucumbers into the sieve to extract as much liquid as possible. Then, measure 1 ½ cups well-drained cucumbers. (Reserve any remaining drained cucumbers for other purposes.)

Pour ½ cup cold water into a small sauce dish; sprinkle the gelatin over the water; let stand 15 minutes. Pour 1 ½ cups water into a small saucepan. Bring the water to a boil over high heat; remove from the heat. Add the sugar and salt; stir until dissolved. Add the gelatin mixture; stir until completely dissolved. Add the lemon juice; stir to blend; set aside.

In a large mixing bowl, place the cream cheese and sour cream; using an electric mixer, beat on high speed until completely smooth. Add the dressing; beat until blended and fluffy. Add the onions; beat to combine. Add the ground cucumbers and 2 tablespoons dillweed; using a large mixing spoon, fold in. Turn into a lightly oiled (page 89) 10 ½-inch ring mold. Cover and refrigerate overnight.

To serve, unmold (page 89) on a large, round platter. Decorate the platter around the molded salad with leaf lettuce, Cucumber

Roses, and sprigs of dillweed. If a fresh dill head is available, place it in the center of the mold.

SERVES 18

FLUFFY EGG CONFETTI SALAD

1 3-ounce package lemon-flavored gelatin
1 cup boiling water
½ teaspoon salt
½ cup cold water
½ cup Miracle Whip dressing
1 tablespoon plus 1 teaspoon prepared
  mustard
4 extra-large eggs, hard-cooked (page 222)
  and sliced
⅓ cup chopped green bell peppers
½ cup chopped celery
1 2-ounce jar diced pimientos, drained
  (2 tablespoons)
2 tablespoons thinly sliced green onions
  (scallions)
1 cup shredded Colby cheese
Leaf lettuce
2 extra-large eggs, hard-cooked (page 222)
  and sliced, for decoration
Extra diced pimientos for decoration

Place the gelatin in a large mixing bowl. Add the boiling water and salt; stir until the gelatin is completely dissolved. Add the cold water, dressing, and mustard; using an electric mixer, beat on high speed until completely blended. Refrigerate until the mixture is set about 1 inch around the edge of the bowl.

Then, using the electric mixer, beat the gelatin mixture on high speed until light and fluffy. Add the eggs, green peppers, celery, pimientos, onions, and cheese. Using a mixing spoon, fold in until the ingredients are evenly distributed. Pour into a lightly oiled (page 89) 8-inch ring mold. Refrigerate until completely set (at least 6 hours).

At serving time, unmold (page 89) on a serving plate lined with leaf lettuce. Decorate the plate with slices of hard-cooked eggs and pieces of well-drained pimientos fashioned like flower blossoms.

SERVES 8

PERFECTION SALAD

(See photo insert page A-5)

½ cup cold water
1 tablespoon plus 1 teaspoon (2 envelopes)
  unflavored gelatin
½ cup sugar
½ teaspoon salt
2 cups boiling water
½ cup cider vinegar
2 tablespoons freshly squeezed, strained
  lemon juice
1 cup finely shredded cabbage
1 cup finely chopped celery
⅓ cup finely chopped green bell peppers
1 4-ounce jar sliced pimientos, drained
  (¼ cup)
Bibb lettuce leaves
Special Mayonnaise Dressing (page 131)

Pour ½ cup cold water into a small sauce dish; sprinkle the gelatin over the water; let stand 15 minutes.

In a medium mixing bowl, place the sugar, salt, boiling water, and gelatin mixture; stir until the sugar is completely dissolved. Add the vinegar and lemon juice; stir to blend. Refrigerate the mixture until it begins to set and is the consistency of unbeaten egg whites.

Add the cabbage, celery, green peppers, and pimientos; stir until the vegetables are evenly distributed. Ladle into 8 lightly oiled (page 89) individual molds or 1 lightly oiled 1-quart mold. Refrigerate until set (at least 3 hours for individual molds; at least 5 hours for a 1-quart mold).

To serve, unmold (page 89) individual salads on plates lined with Bibb lettuce. If made in a 1-quart mold, unmold (page 89) on a serving platter and arrange lettuce leaves handsomely around the salad. Pass Special Mayonnaise Dressing at the table.

SERVES 8

ZIPPY VEGETABLE SALAD MOLD

1 3-ounce package lemon-flavored gelatin
1 cup boiling water
½ cup Miracle Whip dressing
⅛ teaspoon salt
3 tablespoons cider vinegar
½ cup cold water
1 cup finely chopped cabbage
½ cup pared and grated carrots
½ cup sliced radishes
½ cup chopped celery
¼ cup diced green bell peppers
1 tablespoon finely grated onions
Leaf lettuce
8 Radish Gyroscopes (page 338–339) for garnish (optional)
8 tiny sprigs of celery leaves for garnish

Place the gelatin in a large mixing bowl. Add the boiling water; stir until the gelatin is completely dissolved. Add the dressing, salt, vinegar, and cold water; using an electric mixer, beat lightly until blended. Refrigerate until the mixture is set about 1 inch around the edge of the bowl.

Using an electric mixer, beat the gelatin mixture on high speed until light and fluffy. Add the cabbage, carrots, radishes, celery, green peppers, and onions; using a mixing spoon, fold in until the vegetables are evenly distributed. Ladle into 8 lightly oiled (page 89) individual molds. Refrigerate until set (at least 3 hours).

To serve, unmold (page 89) on individual salad plates lined with leaf lettuce. Garnish the top of each molded salad with a Radish Gyroscope and a tiny sprig of celery leaves.

SERVES 8

Main-Course Salads

SPINACH SALAD

1 pound fresh spinach
½ pound sliced bacon, cut into 1-inch pieces, fried crisply, and drained between paper towels
6 ounces sliced, fresh mushrooms
3 extra-large eggs, hard-cooked (page 222) and chopped
⅔ cup extra-virgin olive oil
¼ cup red wine vinegar
2 tablespoons dry red wine
2 teaspoons soy sauce
1 teaspoon dry mustard
1 teaspoon sugar
¼ teaspoon curry powder
½ teaspoon garlic salt
½ teaspoon freshly ground pepper

Wash the spinach twice, remove stems, and pat dry using a clean tea towel. In a large bowl, place the spinach leaves, bacon, mushrooms, and eggs; set aside. In a pint jar, place the olive oil, vinegar, wine, soy sauce, dry mustard, sugar, curry powder, garlic salt, and pepper; cover and shake vigorously until blended. Pour over the salad; toss until the ingredients are evenly combined.

SERVES 4 AS A MAIN COURSE OR 8 AS A SALAD COURSE

AVOCADO AND BANANA SALAD WITH CURRIED DRESSING

2 ripe avocados
2 teaspoons freshly squeezed, strained lemon
   juice
2 ripe bananas
2 tablespoons raisins, plumped (page 30) and
   drained
¼ cup very coarsely broken English walnuts
Leaf lettuce
Bibb lettuce
1 recipe Curried Mayonnaise Dressing (page
   131)

Cut the avocados in half lengthwise and gently twist the halves apart; remove the pits. Peel the avocado halves and cut each half into thirds lengthwise. Using a soft brush, immediately brush all the surfaces of the avocado slices with lemon juice to prevent discoloration; set aside. Peel the bananas; cut in half widthwise. Then, slice each half in two lengthwise; set aside.

Line 4 luncheon plates with leaf lettuce. Using bite-sized pieces of Bibb lettuce, build a low platform over the central part of each plate. Arrange 3 avocado slices and 2 banana pieces in the center of each plate. Sprinkle the raisins and then walnuts over the fruit. Using a spoon, generously drizzle Curried Mayonnaise Dressing diagonally across the fruit, raisins, and nuts, leaving portions of the salad contents uncovered for a more attractive presentation.

SERVES 4

SERVING SUGGESTIONS: Arrange slices of Apricot Bread (page 366–367) and a small bunch of assorted seedless grapes (on their stems) on each plate. Place a small plate of Butter Roses (page 329) on the table.

CARNIVAL SALAD

¾ pound rotini pasta
1 cup yellow teardrop tomatoes
1 cup canned artichoke hearts (not pickled)
   cut in half lengthwise
1 cup cooked and drained frozen miniature
   corn on the cob*
1 cup fresh snow peas, blanched (page 29)
1 cup pared and diagonally sliced carrots
1 cup avocados cut in half lengthwise,
   pitted,** peeled, and sliced widthwise
¾ cup yellow summer squash cut julienne
   (page 7)
¾ cup whole, giant pitted olives
½ cup sliced, fresh mushrooms
½ cup chopped green bell peppers
½ cup chopped yellow bell peppers
½ cup fresh asparagus diagonally cut into
   4-inch lengths, blanched (page 29)
Dressing (recipe follows)

**If frozen corn on the cob is not available,
1 cup drained commercially canned miniature corn on the cob (not pickled) may be
substituted. Do not cook commercially
canned miniature corn on the cob.*

***To pit the avocados, gently twist the cut
halves in opposite directions; then peel.*

Cook the rotini 12 minutes, until tender, in boiling water to which 1 tablespoon salt has been added; drain in a colander. Rinse the rotini under cold running water; drain well. Place in a large mixing bowl; refrigerate, uncovered, until chilled.

To the chilled rotini, add the tomatoes, artichoke hearts, corn, snow peas, carrots, avocados, squash, olives, mushrooms, green peppers, yellow peppers, asparagus, and Dressing; using a wooden mixing spoon, toss until evenly combined. Serve in a large salad bowl (preferably a clear glass bowl as this salad looks so pretty).

SERVES 10 AS A MAIN COURSE OR 20 AS A SIDE DISH

DRESSING

¾ cup extra-virgin olive oil
¼ cup white wine vinegar
2 tablespoons balsamic vinegar
1 tablespoon snipped, fresh basil
1 tablespoon snipped, fresh parsley
1 teaspoon dry mustard

In a pint jar, place the olive oil, white wine vinegar, balsamic vinegar, basil, parsley, and dry mustard; cover and shake vigorously until blended.

DECORATION SUGGESTION: For a splashy, colorful presentation, place a large Cucumber Rose (page 334) atop the center of the salad. Cut an inverted V at one end of briefly blanched snow peas to simulate ribbons. Place the cut snow peas around the Cucumber Rose in the fashion of spokes. Cut large flower petals from softened and peeled red and yellow bell peppers (page 338). Then, arrange the petals on top of the snow peas in a spoke-like fashion around the Cucumber Rose, alternating petal colors.

MACARONI SALAD

7 ounces (about 1¾ cups) small, elbow
    macaroni
1½ cups mild cheddar cheese cut into
    ⅜-inch cubes
¾ cup chopped green bell peppers
¾ cup chopped celery
⅓ cup sliced, small, pimiento-stuffed green
    olives
¼ cup chopped onions
¾ cup Miracle Whip dressing
1 tablespoon prepared mustard
2 teaspoons sugar
½ teaspoon salt
¼ teaspoon white pepper
2 extra-large eggs, hard-cooked (page 222)
    and sliced, for garnish

Pour 2 quarts water into a kettle; cover and bring to a boil over high heat; uncover and add the macaroni. Boil the macaroni 8 to 10 minutes until tender; drain in a colander; rinse in cold water and *drain well.* Turn the macaroni into a large mixing bowl. Add the cheese, green peppers, celery, olives, and onions; set aside. In a small mixing bowl, place the dressing, mustard, sugar, salt, and white pepper; stir until blended. Add the dressing mixture to the bowl containing the macaroni; fold and stir until the ingredients are evenly combined.

Turn the salad into a large serving bowl. Arrange the egg slices on top of the salad in a circle around the edge of the bowl. Cover with plastic wrap and refrigerate until chilled (about 4 hours). Keeps up to 1 week in the refrigerator.

SERVES 8 AS A MAIN COURSE OR 12 AS A SIDE DISH

ALTERNATIVE INGREDIENTS: While the above recipe calls for ingredients considered by many people generally to be used in traditional Macaroni Salad, many other ingredients may be successfully added or substituted and are favored by some cooks and families. Among these other ingredients are:

Cubed, fully cooked ham
Cooked, drained peas
Steamed broccoli flowerets (page 252)
Diced pimientos
Chopped red bell peppers
Pared, sliced carrots
Sliced radishes
Sliced green onions (scallions), including
    green tops
Diced sweet pickles

SEVEN-LAYER SALAD

(See photo insert page A-6)

This versatile salad works equally well as a main-course or side salad.

1 medium head or ½ extra-large head iceberg
    lettuce, cut into bite-sized pieces
3 cups sliced celery (about 7 stalks)
1 sweet onion (Vidalia or purple Bermuda),
    sliced, then quartered and separated into
    partial rings
2 10-ounce packages frozen peas, cooked
    briefly, drained well, and cooled
12 ounces sharp cheddar cheese, coarsely
    shredded
1 cup freshly grated Parmesan cheese
    (page 30)
1 pound sliced bacon, fried, drained between
    paper towels, and coarsely crumbled
1 quart mayonnaise
1 green bell pepper, cored and cut lengthwise
    into ¼-inch-wide strips, for garnish
Cucumber slices for garnish*

   *For more pizzazz, groove the cucumber slices
   (page 334).*

In a 6-quart glass bowl with straight sides, place
in layers in the order listed: lettuce, celery, onion
rings, peas, cheddar cheese, Parmesan cheese,
and bacon. If the bowl becomes too full, the
ingredients may be gently pressed down as the
layers are added. Spoon the mayonnaise over
the salad; using a small, narrow spatula, spread
as evenly and smoothly as possible.

Arrange the green pepper slices over the mayonnaise in scallop fashion around the edge of
the bowl. Place a cucumber slice in the center of
each scallop. Cover the salad tightly with plastic
wrap and refrigerate at least 6 hours before
serving. May be successfully refrigerated up to
1½ days before serving (the lettuce will not wilt
or become soggy).

SERVES 10 AS A MAIN COURSE OR 20 AS A SIDE DISH

ALTERNATIVE SERVING SUGGESTIONS

• The layers may be arranged in individual
  glass salad bowls with straight sides.

• For a smaller salad, cut the ingredient
  amounts in half. Arrange the salad in a
  smaller (3-quart) glass bowl with straight
  sides.

CHICKEN SALAD

4 cups cold, cooked, skinless chicken-breast
    meat cut into large, bite-sized pieces (cook
    and prepare about 4 pounds split chicken
    breasts *with* skin, page 169)
1 cup chopped celery
2 cups pared, quartered, and cored apples cut
    into bite-sized cubes
2 teaspoons freshly squeezed, strained lemon
    juice
1 cup mayonnaise
Boston lettuce
Fresh pineapple slices, Strawberry Fans (page
    339), coarsely broken English walnuts, and
    fresh orange sections (page 32) for garnish

In a large mixing bowl, place the chicken and
celery; set aside. Place the apple cubes in a
medium mixing bowl. Add the lemon juice; toss
until the apple cubes are evenly coated to prevent discoloration. Add the apple cubes and
mayonnaise to the bowl containing the chicken
and celery; toss until the ingredients are evenly
combined; set aside.

Line 6 individual luncheon plates with
Boston lettuce leaves. Place torn Boston lettuce
leaves in the center of each plate to provide a
platform for the chicken salad. Spoon the salad
over the torn lettuce. Garnish the plates with
pineapple slices, Strawberry Fans, English walnuts, and orange sections.

SERVES 6

MESQUITE-GRILLED CHICKEN SALAD

A wonderful recipe from The Diner in Des Moines, Iowa.

1⅓ pounds cold Mesquite-Grilled Chicken
    Breasts (page 211–212), cut into ¼-inch strips
2 cups green bell peppers cut julienne
    ¼ inch wide (page 7) (about 1 large green
    bell pepper)
1¼ cups chopped celery
⅓ cup chopped green onions (scallions),
    including some of the green tops
1 2-ounce jar diced pimientos, drained (2
    tablespoons)
Dressing (recipe follows)
Iceberg lettuce
Romaine lettuce
4 ⅜-inch-wide, uniform slices honeydew
    melon for garnish
4 ⅜-inch-wide, uniform slices cantaloupe for
    garnish
Whole strawberries for garnish

In a large mixing bowl, place the chicken, green peppers, celery, onions, pimientos, and Dressing; toss until evenly combined; set aside. Line 4 dinner plates with leaves of iceberg and romaine lettuce. Using torn pieces of mixed iceberg and romaine lettuce, build a low platform over the center portion of each plate. Spoon the chicken salad over the lettuce platforms, dividing the salad evenly among the 4 plates. Garnish each plate with a slice of honeydew melon, a slice of cantaloupe, and strawberries.

SERVES 4

DRESSING

1 8-ounce bottle (¾ cup) Catalina salad
    dressing
½ small garlic clove, pressed
1 tablespoon chili powder
⅛ teaspoon ground cumin

In a pint jar, place the salad dressing, garlic, chili powder, and cumin; cover and shake vigorously until combined.

HOT CHICKEN SALAD

3 cups cooked, skinless chicken-breast meat
    cut into bite-sized pieces (cook and prepare
    about 3 pounds split chicken breasts *with*
    skin, page 169)
1½ cups chopped celery
⅓ cup chopped green bell peppers
¼ cup chopped green onions (scallions)
1 2-ounce jar diced pimientos, drained
    (2 tablespoons)
½ cup sliced almonds
⅔ cup Miracle Whip dressing
1 tablespoon freshly squeezed, strained lemon
    juice
⅛ teaspoon white pepper
¾ cup shredded cheddar cheese
1 cup coarsely crushed potato chips

Butter a 6 × 10-inch (1½ quart) baking dish; set aside.

Place the chicken in a large mixing bowl. Add the celery, green peppers, green onions, pimientos, and almonds; set aside. In a small bowl, place the dressing, lemon juice, and white pepper; stir vigorously until blended. Add the dressing mixture to the chicken mixture; toss until evenly combined. Turn the mixture into the prepared baking dish; sprinkle the cheese evenly over top. Cover and refrigerate until ready to heat.

Preheat the oven to 350° F.

Remove the baking dish from the refrigerator; uncover. Just before placing it in the oven, distribute the potato chips evenly over the top of the cheese in the baking dish. Bake, uncovered, 25 to 30 minutes, just until heated through and the cheese has melted. Serve with a spatula or spoon.

MAKES 6 GENEROUS SERVINGS

WARM CHICKEN-VEGETABLE SALAD WITH PISTACHIO NUTS AND RASPBERRY VINAIGRETTE DRESSING

5 cups spinach leaves torn into generous, bite-sized pieces
5 cups romaine cut into bite-sized pieces
½ cup pared and finely shredded carrots
½ cup finely chopped celery
⅔ cup red bell peppers diced ¼-inch square
⅔ cup yellow bell peppers diced ¼-inch square
½ pound Plain Grilled Chicken Breasts (page 212),* cut into ¼-inch strips
⅔ cup extra-virgin olive oil
1¼ cups sliced, fresh mushrooms
¼ cup plus 1 tablespoon minced shallots
1 teaspoon sugar
¼ teaspoon salt
¼ teaspoon pepper
⅓ cup red raspberry vinegar
¼ cup pistachio nuts
Whole spinach leaves

If a grill is not available, the chicken breasts may be sautéed in a heavy-bottomed skillet over medium-high heat on the range. Sauté the breasts 3 minutes on each side in half vegetable oil and half butter.

Preheat the oven to 350° F.

In a large mixing bowl, place the spinach, romaine, carrots, celery, red peppers, and yellow peppers; toss to combine; set aside. Wrap the chicken strips in airtight aluminum foil; place in the oven to heat.

Meanwhile, pour the olive oil into a small, heavy-bottomed skillet; place over medium heat. When the oil has heated, add the mushrooms and shallots; sauté 3 minutes, turning often. Remove the skillet from the heat; add the sugar, salt, and pepper; stir to combine. Let the skillet stand to cool slightly; then, add the vinegar. Return the skillet to medium heat; heat the mixture through, but do not bring it to a sim-

mer. Add the pistachio nuts; stir to combine. Remove the skillet from medium heat; keep warm over very low heat.

Line 4 large, individual salad bowls (see Note) with whole spinach leaves; set aside. Add the heated chicken to the vegetable mixture in the bowl. Add the warm vinegar mixture; toss until evenly combined. Distribute the salad evenly among the 4 spinach-lined bowls. Place the salad bowls on serving plates. Serve immediately.

SERVES 4

NOTE: 8 × 2-inch-high clear glass salad bowls are nice to use for this salad.

ARABESQUE TURKEY SALAD

2 cups cold, cooked, white turkey meat cut into ½-inch cubes*
2 cups cold, cooked, dark turkey meat cut into ½-inch cubes*
¾ cup medium-finely chopped celery
¾ cup quartered, seedless red grapes
½ cup broken English walnuts
1 cup Cooked Salad Dressing (page 128)
Coarsely shredded iceberg lettuce
6 cold, thin, large slices turkey breast
Extra Cooked Salad Dressing
Capers for decoration

4 cups white turkey meat or 4 cups dark turkey meat may be substituted for 2 cups white turkey meat and 2 cups dark turkey meat.

In a large mixing bowl, place the white turkey meat cubes, dark turkey meat cubes, celery, grapes, walnuts, and 1 cup Cooked Salad Dressing; toss to combine; set aside.

Arrange a platform of shredded lettuce on 6 dinner plates. Pack ¾ cup of the turkey salad into a cone-shaped funnel; invert the funnel on the lettuce in the center of 1 of the plates; lift the funnel off the turkey salad. Wrap the cone-shaped turkey salad with 1 of the slices of turkey breast. Place a tiny dollop of dressing on top of the cone and decorate with 3 capers. Prepare the remaining 5 plates, repeating the preparation procedure. Extra Cooked Salad Dressing may be served on the side.

SERVES 6

ACCOMPANIMENT SUGGESTIONS: Place a Spiced Peach, fresh strawberries and blueberries, and a slice of Cranberry Nut Bread (page 367) on each plate. Place a small, crystal dish of Ribbed Butter Balls (page 331) on the table.

TUNA-ALMOND LUNCHEON SALAD

1 3-ounce package lemon-flavored gelatin
½ cup boiling water
1 10½-ounce can condensed chicken with rice soup (undiluted)
2 6-ounce cans solid, white albacore tuna, packed in water
½ cup chopped celery
½ cup chopped, slivered blanched almonds (about 2 ounces almonds)
1 2-ounce jar diced pimientos, drained (2 tablespoons)
8 ounces lemon-flavored, lowfat yogurt
½ cup Miracle Whip dressing
Bibb lettuce leaves
Additional Miracle Whip dressing for decoration
Pale yellow paste food coloring

Place the gelatin in a medium mixing bowl. Add ½ cup boiling water; stir until the gelatin is completely dissolved. Add the soup; stir to combine. Refrigerate until the mixture begins to set and is the consistency of unbeaten egg whites. Drain the tuna and break into small, bite-sized chunks. Add the tuna, celery, almonds, and pimientos to the gelatin mixture; stir until evenly combined. Add the yogurt and dressing; fold in. Turn into a 6 × 10-inch baking dish; refrigerate until set.

To serve, cut into 8 servings (page 89). Using a spatula, place the servings on individual plates lined with Bibb lettuce. Place additional dressing in a small bowl. Using a toothpick, add a tiny amount of paste food coloring; stir until evenly blended. Using a decorator bag fit with medium open-star tip number 18 (page 319), pipe a decoration on the top of each molded salad serving.

SERVES 8

SHRIMP LUNCHEON SALAD WITH FRESH GREEN BEANS AND SHERRIED DRESSING

Boston lettuce
20 large, raw, unshelled shrimp (about 1 pound), boiled (page 191), shelled with the tails removed and deveined (page 191), and chilled
½ pound fresh green beans, cut into 2-inch lengths, cooked (page 254), chilled, and drained
1 dozen yellow cherry tomatoes, cut in half lengthwise
12 small sprigs of fresh fennel weed for decoration
1 recipe Sherried Dressing with Fennel and Thyme (page 127)

Line four 9-inch plates with large, whole, Boston lettuce leaves. Then, generously mound torn Boston lettuce leaves over the entire center portion of the plates. Artistically arrange 5 shrimp, ¼ of the green beans, and 6 tomato halves over the lettuce on each plate. Decorate each plate with 3 sprigs of fresh fennel weed. Serve the Sherried Dressing with Fennel and Thyme on the side in 4 small, individual sauceboats placed on doily-lined plates, or pass the dressing in a large sauceboat at the table.

SERVES 4

MOLDED SHRIMP AND CUCUMBER RING

1 1/2 pounds medium to small, raw, unshelled shrimp
1/4 cup cold water
1/2 teaspoon unflavored gelatin
1 or 2 cucumbers, depending upon size
1/2 cup cold water
1 tablespoon plus 1 teaspoon (2 envelopes) unflavored gelatin
1 extra-large vegetable bouillon cube (or enough cubes for 2 cups bouillon)
3/4 cup Miracle Whip dressing
2 tablespoons plus 1 1/2 teaspoons freshly squeezed, strained lemon juice
1 tablespoon well drained, prepared horseradish, homemade (page 30) or commercially canned
1 cup (1/2 pint) whipping cream
5 drops green liquid food coloring
3 tablespoons finely sliced green onions (scallions) including green tops
Sprigs of watercress and fresh parsley for decoration
Additional boiled, shelled, and deveined shrimp for garnish
Grooved Cucumber Slices (page 334)* for garnish

Plain cucumber slices may be substituted.

Boil the shrimp (page 191); cover and refrigerate. When cold, shell and devein (page 191); cover and refrigerate. Lightly oil (page 89) an 8-inch ring mold; set aside.

Pour 1/4 cup cold water into a very small saucepan; sprinkle 1/2 teaspoon gelatin over the water; let stand 15 minutes. Then, place over medium-low heat and stir until the gelatin is completely dissolved; pour into the prepared ring mold. Place 8 whole shrimp at even intervals on the bottom of the ring mold in the gelatin. The shrimp may not be entirely covered with the gelatin. Refrigerate until completely set (at least 3 hours).

Meanwhile, cut the remaining shrimp into fourths; cover and refrigerate. Pare the cucumber(s) (page 17) and finely shred them down to the seeds and core. (Discard the seeds and core.) Place the shredded cucumbers (and juice) in a small mixing bowl; let stand for at least 1 hour.

Place the shredded cucumbers and accumulated juice in a sieve over a bowl to drain. Press the shredded cucumbers with your hand to extract juice, reserving the strained juice in the bowl. Measure 1 cup shredded, drained cucumbers; cover and refrigerate. Add enough water to the reserved cucumber juice to make 2 cups liquid. Pour into a small saucepan; set aside. Pour 1/2 cup cold water into a small bowl; sprinkle 1 tablespoon plus 1 teaspoon unflavored gelatin over the water; let stand 15 minutes. Then, bring the cucumber juice mixture to a boil over high heat. Add the bouillon cube and gelatin mixture; remove from the heat and stir until dissolved. Pour the gelatin mixture into a medium mixing bowl. Add the dressing, lemon juice, and horseradish; using an electric mixer, beat lightly until blended. Refrigerate until the mixture is set about 1 inch around the edge of the bowl.

Meanwhile, pour the whipping cream into a medium mixing bowl; using the electric mixer with clean blades, beat on high speed until softly whipped; cover and refrigerate. When the gelatin mixture is set about 1 inch around the edge of the bowl, add the food coloring; using the electric mixer, beat on high speed until the mixture is fluffy and the food coloring is evenly blended. Add the shrimp, shredded cucumbers, onions, and whipped cream; using a mixing spoon, fold together until evenly combined and blended. Pour into the ring mold over the set shrimp-gelatin layer; refrigerate until set.

To serve, unmold (page 89) on a serving plate. Arrange sprigs of watercress and parsley around the molded salad. In an eye-appealing fashion, tuck the shrimp and Grooved Cucumber Slices into the greens to garnish.

SERVES 8

CRABMEAT SALAD

3 cups boiled, fresh or frozen Alaskan king
    crabmeat (page 192)* chilled and cut into
    bite-sized chunks
²/₃ cup pared and cored cucumbers
    (page 29) diced ¼-inch square
²/₃ cups chopped celery
1 tablespoon plus 1 teaspoon freshly
    squeezed, strained lemon juice
¼ teaspoon white pepper
½ cup whipping cream
½ cup mayonnaise
Watercress
Capers for decoration

*If fresh or frozen Alaskan king crabmeat is
    not available, canned and drained crabmeat
    may be substituted.

In a medium mixing bowl, place the crabmeat,
cucumbers, celery, lemon juice, and white pepper; toss to combine; set aside.

Place the whipping cream in a small mixing
bowl; using an electric mixer, beat on high
speed until softly whipped. Add the mayonnaise; using a large spoon, fold in. Add the mayonnaise mixture to the crabmeat mixture; stir
lightly until the crabmeat and vegetables are
coated. Arrange beds of watercress on 4 individual plates. Spoon the salad over the watercress. Decorate the top of the salads with a few
capers.

SERVES 4

CRAB LOUIS

Boston lettuce leaves
Shredded iceberg lettuce
5 cups boiled, fresh or frozen Alaskan king
    crabmeat (page 192)* chilled and cut into
    bite-sized chunks
1 recipe Louis Dressing (page 128–129)
5 extra-large eggs, hard-cooked (page 222)
    and sliced (includes 1 sliced egg for
    garnish)
Thin slices of pared (page 29), seedless
    cucumbers for garnish
Ripe olives for garnish

*If fresh or frozen Alaskan king crabmeat is
    not available, canned and drained crabmeat
    may be substituted.

Line 4 dinner or luncheon plates with Boston
lettuce leaves. Arrange a bed of shredded iceberg lettuce in the center of each plate over the
Boston lettuce leaves. Heap the crabmeat over
the beds of shredded lettuce, evenly dividing the
crabmeat among the 4 plates. Spoon the Louis
Dressing liberally over the crabmeat. Artistically
arrange slices of 1 hard-cooked egg on top of
the crabmeat and dressing on each plate. Garnish the plates with the remaining egg slices,
and the cucumber slices and olives.

SERVES 4

LOBSTER LOUIS

Follow the Crab Louis recipe, above, substituting boiled, fresh or frozen lobster meat (page
192) for the crabmeat. If fresh or frozen lobster
meat is not available, canned and drained lobster meat may be substituted.

LOBSTER SALAD

4 cups boiled, fresh or frozen lobster meat
  (page 192)* chilled and cut into bite-sized
  chunks
¼ cup medium-finely chopped celery
½ cup mayonnaise
2 teaspoons freshly squeezed, strained lemon
  juice
Boston lettuce leaves
Tomato wedges for garnish
4 extra-large eggs, hard-cooked (page 222)
  and sliced, for garnish
Thin slices of pared (page 29), seedless
  cucumbers for garnish

  *If fresh or frozen lobster meat is not avail-
  able, canned and drained lobster meat may
  be substituted.

In a medium mixing bowl, place the lobster
meat and celery; set aside. In a small mixing
bowl, place the mayonnaise and lemon juice;
stir vigorously until blended. Pour the mayonnaise mixture over the lobster meat and celery;
stir until evenly combined.

  Line 4 dinner plates with Boston lettuce
leaves. Place a few torn pieces of lettuce in the
center of each plate to make a slightly elevated
bed for the lobster salad. Spoon the lobster
salad on the lettuce beds, evenly dividing the
salad among the 4 plates. Garnish each plate
with tomato wedges, 1 sliced hard-cooked egg,
and cucumber slices.

SERVES 4

LOBSTER-AVOCADO SALAD

2 ripe avocados
¼ cup freshly squeezed, strained lemon juice
Boston lettuce leaves
3 cups boiled, fresh or frozen lobster meat
  (page 192)* chilled and cut into bite-sized
  chunks
8 Deviled Eggs (egg halves) (page 224–225)
  for garnish
Tomato wedges, julienne strips (page 7) of
  carrots and celery, lemon wedges, and
  sprigs of watercress for garnish
1 recipe Creamy Vinaigrette Dressing
  (page 129–130)

  *If fresh or frozen lobster meat is not avail-
  able, canned and drained lobster meat may
  be substituted.

Cut the avocados in half lengthwise and gently
twist the halves apart; remove the pits. Peel the
avocado halves. Using a soft brush, immediately
brush all the surfaces of the avocados with
lemon juice to help prevent discoloration; set
aside.

  Line 4 dinner plates with Boston lettuce
leaves. Place an avocado half, pit side up, on
each plate. Pile the lobster meat on top of each
avocado half, evenly dividing the lobster meat
among the 4 plates. Garnish each plate with
2 Deviled Eggs (halves), tomato wedges, carrot
and celery strips, lemon wedges, and sprigs of
watercress. Serve a small sauceboat of Creamy
Vinaigrette Dressing on the side to each diner,
or pass a large sauceboat of dressing.

SERVES 4

Salad Dressings

THOUSAND ISLAND DRESSING

This is one of the all-time best salad dressings. When it is made from scratch, with plenty of hard-cooked eggs and other fresh ingredients, it's a winner! Because such a great quantity of eggs and vegetables is included in Thousand Island Dressing, it really qualifies as more than a "dressing" and becomes a major part of the salad. For this reason, it is often served with lettuce alone—traditionally, over a wedge of iceberg lettuce. Due to the fact that the dressing is heavy and bulky, a strong, rigid green, such as iceberg lettuce, is necessary to support the weight of the dressing. If you wish to use an additional vegetable in the salad, quartered tomatoes may be placed on the salad plate or, if the salad is served in bowls, on top of the salad near the edge of the bowls.

1 cup Miracle Whip dressing
½ cup chili sauce
1¼ cups medium-finely chopped green bell peppers (about 1 medium pepper)
½ cup medium-finely chopped celery
½ cup minced onions
3 extra-large eggs, hard-cooked (page 222) and chopped

In a medium mixing bowl, place the dressing and chili sauce; stir until combined. Add the green peppers, celery, onions, and eggs; stir until evenly distributed. Place in a container or jar; cover tightly and refrigerate up to 1 week.

MAKES ABOUT 3 CUPS

FRENCH DRESSING

¾ cup vegetable oil
¼ cup cider vinegar
⅔ cup tomato catsup
⅓ cup sugar
1 tablespoon grated onions
1 teaspoon Worcestershire sauce
1 teaspoon prepared mustard
½ teaspoon salt
¼ teaspoon pepper
1 teaspoon paprika

In a pint jar, place the vegetable oil, vinegar, catsup, sugar, onions, Worcestershire sauce, mustard, salt, pepper, and paprika; cover and shake vigorously until blended. Refrigerate up to 3 weeks.

MAKES ABOUT 1¾ CUPS

ITALIAN SALAD DRESSING

1¼ cups extra-virgin olive oil
¼ cup white wine vinegar
2 tablespoons balsamic vinegar
1 large, firm cherry tomato, finely chopped (about 1 tablespoon)
1 tablespoon minced onions
1 tablespoon snipped, fresh parsley
1 garlic clove, sliced in half lengthwise
1½ teaspoons snipped, fresh basil (or ½ teaspoon dried leaf basil)
⅛ teaspoon pepper

In a pint jar, place the olive oil, white wine vinegar, balsamic vinegar, tomato, onions, parsley, garlic, basil, and pepper; cover and shake vigorously to combine. Refrigerate and let stand at least 24 hours to allow flavors to blend. The garlic slices may be removed after 2 days, depending upon desired intensity of garlic flavor. Keep refrigerated up to 1 week.

MAKES ABOUT 1¾ CUPS

LEMON PEPPER DRESSING

Lemon pepper is not only a splendid seasoning for chicken, but also it is a grand addition to dressings used on tossed salads. In this recipe, I softened the tartness, slightly, with a dab of honey.

¾ cup extra-virgin olive oil
¼ cup freshly squeezed, strained lemon juice
2 tablespoons dry white wine
2 tablespoons honey
1 tablespoon lemon pepper
1 teaspoon finely grated onions
¼ teaspoon garlic powder

In a pint jar, place the olive oil, lemon juice, wine, honey, lemon pepper, onions, and garlic powder; cover and shake vigorously until blended. Refrigerate up to 2 weeks.

MAKES ABOUT 1 ¼ CUPS

BLUE CHEESE DRESSING

4 ounces Maytag blue cheese, crumbled
½ cup commercial sour cream
½ cup mayonnaise
2 teaspoons minced shallots
3 tablespoons half-and-half
1 tablespoon cognac

In a blender or food processor, place the blue cheese, sour cream, mayonnaise, shallots, half-and-half, and cognac; process until smooth. Place in a glass jar; cover and refrigerate up to 1 week.

MAKES ABOUT 1 ½ CUPS

HONEY-MUSTARD DRESSING

Popular in recent years, this salad dressing pleases a cross section of palates with its tangy, yet slightly sweet flavor. It complements mixed vegetable salads, such as Field of Dreams Salad (page 106), and is a natural with tossed lettuce and vegetable combinations.

⅔ cup extra-virgin olive oil
⅓ cup white wine vinegar
2 tablespoons honey
1 tablespoon prepared mustard

In a pint jar, place the olive oil, vinegar, honey, and mustard; cover and shake vigorously until blended. Refrigerate up to 1 month.

MAKES ABOUT 1 CUP

MUSTARD DRESSING

¾ cup extra-virgin olive oil
¼ cup white wine vinegar
1 tablespoon Dijon mustard

In a pint jar, place the olive oil, vinegar, and mustard; cover and shake vigorously until blended. Refrigerate up to 1 month.

MAKES ABOUT 1 CUP

PARSLEY DRESSING

¾ cup extra-virgin olive oil
3 tablespoons white wine vinegar
2 tablespoons dry white wine
¼ cup fresh parsley leaves (snip single leaves
    from the stems)
1 tablespoon minced shallots
½ garlic clove, pressed
¼ teaspoon salt
⅛ teaspoon freshly ground pepper

In a pint jar, place the olive oil, vinegar, wine, parsley, shallots, garlic, salt, and pepper; cover and shake vigorously until blended. Refrigerate up to 1 week.

MAKES ABOUT 1 CUP

SHERRIED DRESSING WITH FENNEL AND THYME

The herbs fennel and thyme both complement shellfish, fish, greens, and tomatoes (see Herb Chart, pages 22–25). I used it on the Shrimp Luncheon Salad with Fresh Green Beans and Sherried Dressing (page 127). You may have your own favorite shellfish or fish salads on which you might find this dressing nice to use.

⅓ cup extra-virgin olive oil
⅓ cup orange sherry wine vinegar*
⅓ cup mayonnaise
2 tablespoons cream sherry
1 teaspoon sugar
½ teaspoon coarsely ground pepper
1½ teaspoons snipped, fresh fennel weed
1½ teaspoons snipped, fresh thyme

  If orange sherry wine vinegar is not available, plain sherry wine vinegar or white wine vinegar may be substituted.

In a medium mixing bowl, place the olive oil, vinegar, mayonnaise, sherry, sugar, and pepper;

using an electric mixer, beat on high speed until blended. Add the fennel weed and thyme; beat briefly on low speed to combine. Pour into a glass jar; cover and refrigerate up to 1 week.

MAKES ABOUT 1 CUP

POPPY SEED DRESSING

One of the most widely used and esteemed dressings for fruit salads, Poppy Seed Dressing is also excellent with lettuce and fruit combination salads.

⅔ cup sugar
1½ teaspoons paprika
1 teaspoon dry mustard
1 teaspoon salt
⅛ teaspoon garlic salt
½ cup red wine vinegar
1½ cups vegetable oil
2 tablespoons poppy seeds
2 teaspoons finely grated onions

In a medium mixing bowl, place the sugar, paprika, dry mustard, salt, and garlic salt; stir to combine. Add the vinegar; stir in. Using an electric mixer, beat the vinegar mixture on medium speed while slowly adding the vegetable oil; beat until well blended. Add the poppy seeds and onions; beat until combined. Pour into a glass jar; cover and refrigerate up to 3 weeks.

MAKES ABOUT 2⅓ CUPS

SWEET BASIL DRESSING

If you prefer a lightly sweetened dressing for vegetable salads, this one may be just the ticket. It features a generous amount of fresh basil—one of the more versatile herbs because it harmonizes well with so many different vegetables, meats, and other foods. When it comes to salads, basil is often unduly confined to use with tomatoes. A marinated vegetable salad recipe which combines Sweet Basil Dressing with 5 vegetables in addition to tomatoes may be found on page 108. (To assist in planning salads using various herbs, consult the Herb Chart, pages 22–25).

⅓ cup extra-virgin olive oil
⅓ cup vegetable oil
½ cup cider vinegar
3 tablespoons snipped, fresh basil
3 tablespoons sugar
¼ teaspoon white pepper

In a pint jar, place the olive oil, vegetable oil, vinegar, basil, sugar, and white pepper; cover and shake vigorously until blended. Refrigerate up to 1 week.

MAKES ABOUT 1¼ CUPS

COOKED SALAD DRESSING

While this timeless, ever-good salad dressing is traditionally made with whole milk (or cream), this version is made with evaporated milk, which I think you'll like.

3 tablespoons sugar*
2 tablespoons all-purpose flour
¾ teaspoon dry mustard
½ teaspoon salt
2 extra-large eggs
½ cup cider vinegar
2 tablespoons butter
1 5-ounce can (½ cup plus 2 tablespoons) evaporated milk
Dash of cayenne pepper

*When using this dressing in fruit-intensive salads, the sugar may be increased to ¼ cup plus 1 tablespoon (5 tablespoons).

In a small bowl, place the sugar, flour, dry mustard, and salt; stir to combine; set aside. Place the eggs in the top of a double boiler; using an electric mixer, beat well on high speed. Add the flour mixture; beat until blended. Add the vinegar; beat to blend. Place the top of the double boiler over (not in) boiling water in the bottom pan. Cook the mixture until very thick (about 2 minutes), beating continuously with a hand-held electric mixer on low speed.

Remove the top of the double boiler from the bottom pan and place on a wire rack. Add the butter; stir until melted and blended. Add the evaporated milk and cayenne pepper; stir until completely blended. Then, using the electric mixer, beat very briefly on low speed to assure complete smoothness of the dressing. Pour into a jar; cover and refrigerate up to 2 weeks.

MAKES 1½ CUPS

LOUIS DRESSING

This dressing is most often associated with the dish Crab Louis (page 123), which is generally believed to have been created on the West Coast, probably in San Francisco, around the turn of the twentieth century. For decades, Crab Louis has been faithfully served in elegant hotel dining rooms and restaurants across the country. The dressing is equally fitting and wonderful with lobster in the adapted, traditional dish, Lobster Louis (page 123). Also, I like to serve Louis Dressing as a "new" dip for cold shrimp served as an hors d'oeuvre (page 128).

½ cup whipping cream
1 cup mayonnaise
⅓ cup chili sauce

2 tablespoons finely grated onions
2 teaspoons freshly squeezed, strained lemon
    juice
2 dashes of Tabasco pepper sauce

Pour the whipping cream into a small mixing bowl; using an electric mixer, beat on high speed until moderately stiff; cover and refrigerate.

In a medium mixing bowl, place the mayonnaise, chili sauce, onions, lemon juice, and pepper sauce; using an electric mixer, beat on high speed just until blended. Add the whipped cream; using a small mixing spoon, fold in. Cover and refrigerate up to 5 hours.

MAKES ABOUT 2⅓ CUPS

VINAIGRETTE DRESSINGS

Most people agree that the most fundamental of all salad dressings is vinaigrette in all its forms and flavors (challenged only by ubiquitous mayonnaise). Vinaigrette has 2 basic ingredients: oil and vinegar. But the variations on this theme are nearly endless. The types of oil, vinegar, seasonings, and other ingredients used in vinaigrettes produce a range of flavors as diverse as the plumage on songbirds. Seven variations are given in the vinaigrette recipes that follow.

In all seven recipes, the oil called for is extra-virgin olive oil. It is the finest grade of olive oil, made from the first pressing of olives and containing no more than 1 percent oleic acid. Extra-virgin olive oils vary in flavor, depending upon the regions from which they come and the varieties of olives used in the making. Try various available extra-virgin olive oils and decide which one(s) you prefer.

Wine vinegars are generally considered the best for use in vinaigrettes. As with wine, wine vinegars differ greatly in taste and color. Herb wine vinegars are widely used in vinaigrettes to infuse herb flavorings.

Selecting the best-quality oils and vinegars is of paramount importance in making good vinaigrettes. Although top-flight oils and vinegars may be deemed expensive, they are usually more economical when purchased in larger quantities, and they keep for a long time when properly stored. (Store olive oil up to 6 months in a cool, dark place; store opened vinegar up to 6 months in the refrigerator or in a cool, dark place.)

BASIC VINAIGRETTE DRESSING

This basic vinaigrette is great for any occasion, from family meals at the kitchen table to formal dinner parties. It calls for balsamic vinegar, an exquisite Italian wine vinegar with an incomparable sweet-pungent flavor. Although made from the juice of the white grape Trebbiano, balsamic vinegar is very dark in color because it is aged in wooden barrels.

The basic formula for making vinaigrettes is 3 parts oil to 1 part vinegar, as in this recipe; however, this ratio is dependent upon the pungency of the vinegar used and the flavor desired. When using softer wine vinegars, I sometimes use ⅔ oil to ⅓ vinegar. If you prefer less stringent vinaigrettes, adjust the oil-vinegar ratio in particular recipes to suit your own taste.

¾ cup extra-virgin olive oil
¼ cup balsamic vinegar
½ teaspoon dry mustard

In a pint jar, place the olive oil, vinegar, and mustard; cover and shake vigorously until blended. Refrigerate up to 1 month.

MAKES 1 CUP

CREAMY VINAIGRETTE DRESSING

1 cup Basic Vinaigrette Dressing
    (recipe, above)
1 cup Miracle Whip dressing

In a small mixing bowl, place the Basic Vinaigrette Dressing and the Miracle Whip dressing; using a handheld electric mixer, beat on medium speed until blended. Place in a glass jar; cover and refrigerate up to 2 weeks.

MAKES 2 CUPS

MILD CREAMY VINAIGRETTE DRESSING

1 cup Basic Vinaigrette Dressing
  (recipe, above)
1 cup mayonnaise

In a small mixing bowl, place the Basic Vinaigrette Dressing and the mayonnaise; using a handheld electric mixer, beat on medium speed until blended. Place in a glass jar; cover and refrigerate up to 2 weeks.

MAKES 2 CUPS

MUSTARD-HORSERADISH VINAIGRETTE DRESSING

¾ cup extra-virgin olive oil
¼ cup balsamic vinegar
1 tablespoon Dijon mustard
1½ teaspoons prepared horseradish,
  homemade (page 30) or commercially
  canned

In a pint jar, place the olive oil, vinegar, mustard, and horseradish; cover and shake vigorously until blended. Refrigerate up to 2 weeks.

MAKES ABOUT 1 CUP

BASIL VINAIGRETTE DRESSING

¾ cup extra-virgin olive oil
2 tablespoons cider vinegar
3 tablespoons white wine vinegar
1 tablespoon snipped, fresh basil

In a pint jar, place the olive oil, cider vinegar,

white wine vinegar, and basil; cover and shake vigorously until blended. Refrigerate up to 1 week.

MAKES ABOUT 1 CUP

TARRAGON VINAIGRETTE DRESSING

¾ cup extra-virgin olive oil
¼ cup tarragon white wine vinegar
1 tablespoon freshly squeezed, strained lemon
  juice
1 tablespoon snipped, fresh tarragon
1 tablespoon minced onions
⅛ teaspoon white pepper

In a pint jar, place the olive oil, vinegar, lemon juice, tarragon, onions, and white pepper; cover and shake vigorously until blended. Refrigerate up to 1 week.

MAKES ABOUT 1 CUP

WHITE WINE VINAIGRETTE DRESSING

⅔ cup extra-virgin olive oil
⅓ cup white wine vinegar
¼ teaspoon dry mustard
¼ teaspoon salt
⅛ teaspoon white pepper

In a pint jar, place the olive oil, vinegar, dry mustard, salt, and white pepper; cover and shake vigorously until blended. Refrigerate up to 1 month.

MAKES 1 CUP

SOUR CREAM SALAD DRESSING

This is a refined dressing for subtly flavored salads, such as Hearts of Palm–Persimmon Salad (page 102).

8 ounces commercial sour cream
3 tablespoons dry white wine

1 tablespoon finely grated onions
⅛ teaspoon salt

In a small mixing bowl, place the sour cream, wine, onions, and salt; stir until well combined. Cover and refrigerate up to 1 week.

MAKES ABOUT 1 CUP

YOGURT-TARRAGON SALAD DRESSING

This dressing goes well with a variety of salad ingredients, including lettuce, cabbage, tomatoes, green beans, asparagus, fish, and shellfish. For other salad vegetables and meats compatible with tarragon, consult the Herb Chart on pages 22–25.

8 ounces plain, lowfat yogurt
2 tablespoons tarragon white wine vinegar
1 tablespoon minced onions (optional)
¼ teaspoon dried leaf tarragon
⅛ teaspoon pepper
Dash of cayenne pepper

In a small mixing bowl, place the yogurt, vinegar, onions (if using), tarragon, pepper, and cayenne pepper; stir to combine. Cover and refrigerate up to 1 week.

MAKES ABOUT 1 CUP

SPECIAL MAYONNAISE DRESSING

A standard in our family since I can remember, this dressing is great for molded salads, Sliced Tomatoes and Lettuce Salad (page 101), Kidney Bean Salad (page 110), and lettuce and fruit combination salads.

½ cup Miracle Whip dressing
2 teaspoons sugar
2 teaspoons whole milk

In a small mixing bowl, place the dressing, sugar, and milk; stir vigorously until completely blended. Cover and refrigerate up to 3 days.

THIN SPECIAL MAYONNAISE DRESSING

Follow the Special Mayonnaise Dressing recipe, above, adding 1 additional teaspoon whole milk.

THICK SPECIAL MAYONNAISE DRESSING

¾ cup Miracle Whip dressing
1½ teaspoons sugar
1 teaspoon half-and-half

Follow the mixing procedure for Special Mayonnaise Dressing, above.

CURRIED MAYONNAISE DRESSING

This curried salad dressing pairs lusciously with both bananas and avocados. All three combine deliciously in the main-course salad, Avocado and Banana Salad with Curried Dressing, on page 116.

1/2 cup Miracle Whip dressing
3 teaspoons whole milk
2 teaspoons sugar
1 teaspoon curry powder

In a small mixing bowl, place the dressing, milk, sugar, and curry powder; stir vigorously until completely blended. Cover and refrigerate up to 3 days.

TOMATO SOUP SALAD DRESSING

This is an excellent French dressing made with a surprise ingredient—a can of tomato soup.

1 10¾-ounce can condensed tomato soup
   (undiluted)
1½ cups vegetable oil
¾ cup red wine vinegar
½ cup sugar
½ teaspoon paprika
2 teaspoons finely grated onions
1 garlic clove, pressed
1 teaspoon dry mustard
½ teaspoon salt
2 teaspoons Worcestershire sauce

In a large mixing bowl, place the tomato soup, vegetable oil, vinegar, sugar, paprika, onions, garlic, dry mustard, salt, and Worcestershire sauce; using an electric mixer, beat on medium-high speed until blended. Pour into a quart jar; cover and refrigerate up to 1 week.

MAKES 1 QUART

Meats

Today's Leaner Meats

The meat we consume today is vastly leaner and thus more healthful than only fifteen years ago. This advancement is attributable to improved animal genetics, feeding methods, and management practices, as well as the trimming of substantially more fat from meat by both packers and retailers.

The U.S. Department of Agriculture's 1991 data on pork are particularly startling. The eight most commonly consumed cuts of fresh pork had, on average, 31 percent less total fat, 29 percent less saturated fat, 14 percent fewer calories, and 10 percent less cholesterol, after cooking and trimming, than reported in the USDA's 1983 data.

The National Beef Market Basket Survey, conducted in 1987–1988 and supported by the U.S. Department of Agriculture and the beef industry, revealed that since the late 1970s and early 1980s, the overall average thickness of external fat for all retail beef cuts had been reduced from ½ inch to less than ⅛ inch, with 42.5 percent of the cuts having no external fat at all. The survey showed an overall 27.4 percent decrease in trimmable fat from beef steaks and roasts at the retail level over the same period. A follow-up survey in 1990 showed continued reductions.

The table of USDA statistics, below, shows that various cuts of beef and pork are now very comparable to skinless chicken with regard to calories, total fat, saturated fat, and cholesterol.

Complete bibliographical references for statistics contained in this section may be found on page 626.

Meat Safety

The Food Safety and Inspection Service of the U.S. Department of Agriculture exerts every effort to assure a safe meat supply for the nation. However, it is virtually impossible to produce completely bacteria-free, sterile, raw meat. Therefore, the proper storage, handling, and cooking of meat by consumers is of utmost importance to avoid foodborne illnesses.

Consumer adherence to the following basic

BASED ON 3-OUNCE SERVINGS

	Calories	Total Fat (grams)	Saturated Fatty Acids (grams)	Cholesterol (milligrams)
Beef Eye of Round (roasted)[1]	141	3.99	1.45	59
Pork Tenderloin (roasted)[2]	139	4.09	1.41	67
Skinless Chicken Breast (roasted)	140	3.04	0.86	72
Beef Top Sirloin (broiled)[1]	162	5.78	2.25	76
Pork Boneless Top Loin Chop (broiled)[3]	173	6.60	2.31	68
Skinless Chicken Thigh (roasted)	178	9.25	2.58	81

[1]*Separable lean only, trimmed to 0 inch fat.*
[2]*Separable lean only, trimmed to 0.02 inch fat before cooking.*
[3]*Separable lean only, trimmed to 0.11 inch fat before cooking.*
Sources: USDA Agriculture Handbooks 8-5, 1979; 8-10, 1992; and 8-13, 1990, based on all grades.

practices will help ensure the consumption of safe meat:

- Generally, cook fresh beef, veal, and lamb to an internal temperature of 160°F (medium) or 170°F (well done). Larger cuts may be cooked to as low as 145°F (150°F is medium rare) provided they have not been scored or tenderized before cooking, thereby forcing surface bacteria into the center of the meat. When fresh beef, veal, and lamb are consumed rare (140°F), there is some bacterial risk.

  Always cook ground beef, veal, and lamb to an internal temperature of at least 160°F with no pink meat or juices remaining, as bacteria can spread throughout ground meat during processing.

- Cook fresh pork (including fresh ham and ground pork) to an internal temperature of 160°F (medium) or 170°F (well done).

  Until recent years, a widespread belief prevailed that pork must be cooked until well done, with no pink remaining, to guard against trichinosis infection. Today, the microscopic parasite *Trichinella spiralis* (trichina) is a clinical rarity in hogs due to improved feeding practices by pork producers. Further, it is a scientific fact that trichina is destroyed when pork is cooked to an internal temperature of 137°F. This is well below 160°F, the current recommended temperature for cooking pork. At 160°F, pork is at its maximum tenderness, juiciness, and flavor, and many cuts are pink at the center. Federal regulations require that ready-to-eat pork products be heat-processed above 137°F prior to sale. Freezing raw pork at 5°F or below for 20 days or more also destroys trichina.

  Precooked ham may be reheated to 140°F.

- Use a meat thermometer or instant thermometer (see page 28–29) to assure internal meat temperatures.

- Refrigerate meat as soon as possible after purchase. This is particularly important in hot weather. Do your grocery shopping just before you plan to return home.

- Store both raw and cooked meat in the refrigerator at 40°F or below. A temperature of 40°F or below prevents most bacteria that cause foodborne illnesses from multiplying. Place packages of raw meat on plates before refrigeration to prevent raw meat juices from dripping onto other foods. Raw meat juices often contain bacteria.

- If raw meat will not be cooked within a few days after purchase, freeze it at 0°F or below. Temperatures of 0°F or below stop the growth of bacteria.

- Defrost meat in the refrigerator or in the microwave oven (see Food Safety: Microwave Ovens, page 15–16, for procedural information), not on the kitchen counter or in the sink. When defrosted at room temperature, the outer portions of meat can warm to a temperature which allows bacteria to multiply before the inside of the meat has thawed.

- Do not leave raw or cooked meat unrefrigerated for more than 2 hours (not including cooking time). The danger temperature zone is between 40 and 140°F. At these temperatures, foodborne bacteria can double in number every 20 minutes. Normally, bacteria will not reach dangerous levels in 2 hours, and most healthy people will not be affected.

- Throw away meat packaging material.

- Do not cook meat at an oven temperature lower than 325°F.

- Refrigerate or freeze leftover meat promptly. For rapid cooling, cut large pieces of meat into smaller portions and divide large quantities of food containing meat among several small containers.

- Cooked meat which has been properly refrigerated may safely be eaten unheated. To reheat leftover cooked meat, heat it to at least 165°F (steaming hot).

- Wash your hands with soap and hot water before and after handling raw or cooked meat. Wash kitchen tools and equipment, cutting boards and other work surfaces, sink, and faucet handles with hot, soapy water after they come in contact with raw or cooked meat, and before they come in contact with other food.

For safety guidelines on the preparation of meat on outdoor grills, see Meat Safety for Outdoor Cooking, page 204–205.

For further information and answers to specific questions regarding meat safety, call the U.S. Department of Agriculture's Meat and Poultry Hotline at 888-674-6854 (TTY at 800-256-7072), Monday through Friday, 10:00 A.M.–4:00 P.M. Eastern time; or visit the Food Safety and Inspection Service Web site at www.fsis.usda.gov; or email at mphotline.fsis@usda.gov.

Beef

BEEF AND NOODLES

2 pounds boneless beef chuck, cut into
   1-inch cubes
1 medium (about 1½ pounds) beef soup
   bone
1 carrot, pared and quartered
1 stalk celery with green leaves, cut in half or
   thirds, depending upon size
1 medium onion, quartered
1 bay leaf
1 teaspoon salt
½ teaspoon freshly ground pepper
About 8 cups water
2 cups homemade beef broth (page 70) or
   1 14-ounce can commercial beef broth
12 ounces medium-wide egg noodles
2 tablespoons all-purpose flour
¼ teaspoon salt

¼ teaspoon freshly ground pepper
½ cup water

EARLY IN THE DAY: In a large, heavy-bottomed kettle, place the beef cubes, soup bone, carrot, celery, onion, bay leaf, 1 teaspoon salt, and ½ teaspoon pepper. Add water to cover (about 8 cups). Cover the kettle. Over high heat, bring to a boil; reduce the heat and simmer until the beef cubes are fork-tender (about 1 hour and 15 minutes).

Remove from the heat. Using a slotted spoon, remove the beef cubes from the kettle and place in a bowl. Remove the soup bone from the kettle. Trim any lean meat from the bone; cut into bite-sized pieces and add to the beef cubes. Discard the bone. Cover the meat and refrigerate. Strain the kettle broth in a sieve; discard the vegetables and bay leaf. Measure the broth and keep a note regarding quantity. Pour the measured broth into a large mixing bowl; refrigerate.

When cold, use a tablespoon or spatula to skim the congealed fat off the top of the broth; discard. Cover the skimmed broth and refrigerate.

30 MINUTES BEFORE SERVING: In a large kettle, place the refrigerated kettle broth. Add the beef broth; stir to blend. (The broth should total about 10 cups. If necessary, add additional beef broth.) Cover and bring to a boil over high heat. Add the noodles; boil, uncovered, until nearly tender (about 8 minutes), stirring often to keep the noodles separated. Add the beef cubes; stir to combine. Continue boiling briefly until heated through.

Meanwhile, in a small glass jar or plastic container with a secure lid, place the flour, ¼ teaspoon salt, ¼ teaspoon pepper, and ½ cup water; cover and shake vigorously until completely blended with no lumps remaining. (Use a spoon to break up lumps against the side of the container, if necessary.) Add the flour mixture to the beef and noodles; stir until blended. Simmer briskly until the broth thickens (about 2 minutes). Serve soon, before the noodles begin to stick together.

SERVES 8

SERVING SUGGESTION: Beef and Noodles are often served over Mashed Potatoes (page 279); however, they are also delicious served separately.

SWISS STEAK

If Swiss Steak isn't already in your cooking repertoire, I urge you to consider adding it. It's delectable!

¼ cup all-purpose flour
1 teaspoon salt
½ teaspoon pepper
5 pounds top round steak, butterflied, each half cut 1¾ inches thick
2 to 3 tablespoons vegetable shortening
¾ cup water
2 medium-large onions, sliced ¼ inch thick (about 3½ cups sliced onions)
1 14½-ounce can commercial whole, peeled tomatoes
1 garlic clove, pressed
⅓ cup golden raisins
3 tablespoons snipped, fresh parsley
1 teaspoon dried leaf basil
1 large carrot, pared and cut julienne (page 17) ¼ inch wide by 2 inches long
¾ cup celery sliced ¼ inch thick

In a small bowl, place the flour, salt, and pepper; stir to combine; set aside. Place the round steak on a piece of waxed paper. Sprinkle ½ of the flour mixture over the steak. Using your hand, rub the flour mixture over the entire top surface of the steak. Using a metal-pronged meat tenderizer, lightly pound the flour mixture into the meat. Turn the steak over and repeat procedure, using the remaining ½ flour mixture; set aside. In an electric skillet or a large, heavy skillet on the range, melt 2 tablespoons vegetable shortening over high heat (400° F in an electric skillet). Tilt the skillet back and forth to completely cover the bottom with the melted shortening. Place the steak in the skillet; brown *very well* on both sides, turning once (about 7 to 8 minutes

on each side). If needed, add 1 additional tablespoon shortening to the skillet after turning the meat. Using tongs, transfer the steak to a heavy roaster; set aside. Reduce the skillet heat to low (250° F in an electric skillet).

Preheat the oven to 350° F.

When the skillet cools to the reduced temperature, add ¾ cup water and deglaze. Pour the skillet liquid *around* (not over) the steak in the roaster. Arrange the onions on top of the steak; set aside. Place the tomatoes (undrained) in a medium mixing bowl. Using a metal mixing spoon, break the tomatoes into large chunks. Add the garlic, raisins, parsley, and basil; stir to combine. Pour the tomato mixture over the onions on the steak. Cover the roaster. Bake for 3 hours. Remove from the oven. Baste; then, distribute the carrots and celery evenly over the steak. Cover; return to the oven and bake for an additional 30 minutes.

When done, place the Swiss Steak on a serving platter; cover lightly with aluminum foil to keep warm. Strain the roaster drippings through a sieve; serve in a sauceboat at the table.

SERVES 12

ACCOMPANIMENT SUGGESTIONS: Serve Swiss Steak with Mashed Potatoes (page 279) or buttered egg noodles.

TO CUT THE RECIPE IN HALF: Use one 2½ pound top round steak, 1¾ inches thick (not butterflied). Halve the remaining ingredients in the recipe. Bake for a total of 2½ hours, adding the carrots and celery for the last 30 minutes of baking.

BEEF STROGANOFF

2 pounds beef tenderloin, cut ½ inch thick
1 tablespoon vegetable shortening
2 tablespoons butter, divided
½ teaspoon salt, divided
¼ teaspoon pepper, divided
3 tablespoons butter
¼ cup minced shallots

(Recipe continues on next page)

1 pound fresh mushrooms, sliced
1 recipe Medium White Sauce (page
    301–302), substituting ½ cup beef broth
    (homemade [page 70] or commercially
    canned) and ½ cup half-and-half for 1 cup
    whole milk
¼ cup dry sherry
12 cups water
12 ounces wide (not extra-wide) egg noodles
16 ounces commercial sour cream
2 tablespoons butter, melted

Cut the beef tenderloin widthwise into ½-inch-wide strips. (Each strip will be approximately 2 inches long.) Set aside. In an electric skillet or a heavy skillet on the range, melt the vegetable shortening over medium-high heat (380°F in an electric skillet). Tilt the skillet back and forth to completely cover the bottom with the melted shortening. Add 1 tablespoon butter; melt and spread to blend with the shortening. Place ½ of the tenderloin strips, single layer, in the skillet; sprinkle with ½ of the salt and pepper. Sauté quickly only until very lightly browned, turning often. Place the browned strips in a bowl; set aside. Add 1 additional tablespoon butter to the skillet; melt and spread to cover the bottom of the skillet. Place the remaining ½ tenderloin strips in skillet; sprinkle with the remaining ½ salt and pepper. Sauté lightly and add to the bowl of browned tenderloin strips; set aside.

Reduce the skillet heat to medium-low (300°F in an electric skillet). When the skillet cools to the reduced temperature, add 3 tablespoons butter; melt and spread to cover the bottom of the skillet. Add the shallots and mushrooms; sauté 3 minutes or until the mushrooms give up their juices, stirring often. Turn off the skillet heat (or remove the skillet from the heat). Leave the shallots and mushrooms in the skillet; set aside.

Add the sherry to the Medium White Sauce; stir to blend and set aside. Pour 12 cups water into a small kettle; cover and bring to a boil over high heat. Add the noodles; cook, uncovered, in boiling water for about 10 minutes until tender (page 236), stirring often.

Meanwhile, add the white sauce mixture to the skillet containing the shallots and mushrooms; stir to combine. Over low heat (250°F in an electric skillet), heat the mixture through and completely deglaze the skillet (use a spatula to scrape the bottom of the skillet, if necessary). Do not allow the mixture to boil. Add the sour cream; stir until well blended, but do not allow to boil or simmer. Add the tenderloin strips; stir to combine. Heat the mixture through, but continue not to allow it to boil or simmer; cover and keep warm.

When the noodles are tender, drain in a colander; return the noodles to the kettle and rinse in very hot water. Drain the noodles well in a colander and return to the kettle. Add 2 tablespoons melted butter and toss until the noodles are evenly coated. Place servings of noodles on individual plates; spoon generous amounts of Beef Stroganoff over the noodles.

SERVES 8

VARIATION: Beef Stroganoff may be served over Boiled Rice (page 228) rather than noodles.

ROAST BEEF TENDERLOIN WITH MUSHROOM SAUCE

1 whole beef tenderloin with the small,
    narrow end trimmed off* (about 4 to
    4½ pounds)
1 recipe Beef Gravy/Sauce with Mushrooms
    (page 312)

* *Trimming the narrow end off the tenderloin will make the piece of meat more uniform in thickness to achieve uniform doneness when roasted. Have the butcher remove the tough, silver-colored, membranous tissue over the top of the tenderloin.*

Preheat the oven to 425°F.

Place the tenderloin on a wire rack in a shallow roasting pan. Insert a meat thermometer into the center of the thickest part of the meat. Roast, uncovered, adding no water, until the thermometer reaches 140°F (rare), about 45 to 55 minutes (see Note). Remove the tenderloin from the oven when the thermometer reaches 5°F below the desired temperature, as the meat will continue cooking.

Place the tenderloin on a cutting board and lay a piece of aluminum foil lightly over the top of the meat to help keep it hot. Do not crimp the foil around the tenderloin, since the intensity of the retained heat may cause the meat to continue cooking beyond the desired doneness. Prepare the Beef Gravy/Sauce with Mushrooms; keep hot in the pan.

Cut the tenderloin into ½-inch slices; place 1 or 2 slices on warm, individual dinner plates or arrange all the slices on a warm serving platter. Pour the hot sauce into a sauceboat and pass at the table.

NOTE: While beef tenderloin is traditionally served rare as many diners consider this tender, deluxe cut of meat to be at the height of succulence at this doneness, it may be served more done, if preferred, for reasons of taste or food safety (see Meat Safety, page 134–136). To roast beef tenderloin to stages of doneness greater than rare, use the following guide:

Doneness	Thermometer Reading
Medium Rare	150° F
Medium	160° F
Well Done	170° F

SERVES 8 (⅓ TO ½ POUND PER PERSON)

CHICKEN-FRIED STEAK

This recipe for Chicken-Fried Steak is from The Windrow restaurant located in Creston, Iowa, where both my parents were raised. The restaurant gets its name from a term used in farming. Formerly, all mowed hay was raked into long rows, called "windrows," to dry before it was baled or stored. Nowadays, much hay is put up using systems and new machinery which do not always involve windrowing.

½ cup all-purpose flour
1 tablespoon seasoned salt, homemade (page 42) or commercial*
¼ teaspoon garlic powder
¼ teaspoon white pepper
1 extra-large egg
2 tablespoons whole milk
6 top round steaks (about 2 pounds total) cut ½ inch thick, then put through a tenderizer 4 times by the butcher
1 tablespoon vegetable oil
1 tablespoon butter
1 recipe Milk Gravy (page 310–311) (optional)

* If commercial seasoned salt is used, select one that does not include monosodium glutamate as an ingredient.

Preheat the oven to 275°F.

In a small mixing bowl, place the flour, seasoned salt, garlic powder, and white pepper; stir to combine. Sprinkle the flour mixture over a 1-foot-square piece of waxed paper; set aside. In a small mixing bowl, place the egg and milk; using an electric mixer or a table fork, beat until blended. Pour the egg mixture into a pie pan; set aside. Dredge both sides of the steaks in the flour mixture; shake off the excess. Dip the steaks in the egg mixture; then, redredge in the flour mixture. Place the coated steaks on a clean piece of waxed paper; set aside.

In an electric skillet or a large, heavy skillet on the range, heat the vegetable oil over medium heat (360°F in an electric skillet). Tilt the skillet back and forth to completely cover the bottom with the oil. Add the butter; melt and spread over the bottom of the skillet. Place the steaks in the skillet; fry 3 to 4 minutes on each side until well browned and cooked through, turning once.

Place the fried steaks, single layer, in a shallow pan; cover loosely with aluminum foil. Place the pan in the warm oven to keep the steaks hot while making Milk Gravy. Serve the gravy over or under the steaks, or pass at the table.

SERVES 6

(Recipe continues on next page)

ACCOMPANIMENT SUGGESTION: Mashed Potatoes (page 279) are traditionally served with Chicken-Fried Steak, in which case the gravy is usually passed at the table.

DRIED BEEF GRAVY

½ cup all-purpose flour
¾ teaspoon salt
½ teaspoon white pepper
¼ cup (4 tablespoons) butter
5 ounces sliced dried beef, cut into 1-inch-square pieces
1 quart whole milk

In a small bowl, place the flour, salt, and white pepper; stir to combine; set aside. In a large, heavy skillet, melt the butter over medium heat. Do not allow the butter to brown. Place the dried beef in the skillet; stir until the dried beef is coated with butter. Remove the skillet from the heat.

Sprinkle the flour mixture over the dried beef; stir until the dried beef is coated with the flour mixture and no lumps remain. Add the milk and return the skillet to the heat. Cook the dried beef mixture until the gravy thickens and is just under boiling, stirring constantly. Do not allow the mixture to boil.

SERVES 6

SERVING SUGGESTIONS: Serve over Mashed Potatoes (page 279), toasted and buttered English muffins, or boiled white rice (page 228).

ROUND STEAK BRAISED WITH ONIONS

Top round steak, a less-expensive cut of meat, is transformed into luscious dining when braised slowly with onions.

1 top round steak, ¾ inch thick (about 1⅓ pounds)

¾ teaspoon salt
¼ teaspoon pepper
¼ cup all-purpose flour
1 tablespoon plus 2 teaspoons vegetable shortening
1 cup hot water
1 pound onions, sliced ¼ inch thick and separated into rings (about 2 large onions)
1 cup hot water
1 pound red potatoes, unpared, sliced ⅜ inch thick (about 3 large potatoes)
Additional water, if necessary
⅛ teaspoon pepper
½ 1-ounce envelope onion soup mix

Using a sharp knife, slit the fat every 2 inches around the edge of the steak, being careful not to penetrate the flesh, which would cause a loss of meat juices during cooking. Place the steak on a piece of waxed paper; set aside.

In a small sauce dish, place ¾ teaspoon salt and ¼ teaspoon pepper; stir to combine. Sprinkle ½ of the salt and pepper mixture over the steak; then sprinkle ½ of the flour over the steak. Using your hand, spread the flour over the entire top surface of the steak. Turn the steak over and repeat the procedure, using the remaining salt and pepper mixture and flour; set aside.

In an electric skillet or a large, heavy skillet on the range, melt the vegetable shortening over high heat (400°F in an electric skillet). Tilt the skillet back and forth to completely cover the bottom with the melted shortening. Place the steak in the skillet, letting the excess flour fall onto the waxed paper. Brown the steak well, about 6 minutes on the first side and 5 minutes on the second side.

Reduce the skillet heat to very low (210°F in an electric skillet). When the skillet cools to the reduced temperature, pour 1 cup hot water around (not over) the steak. Cover the skillet tightly; simmer the steak for ½ hour. Then, place the onions over and around the steak. Pour an additional 1 cup hot water around the steak and onions; cover and simmer for ½ hour.

Place overlapping sliced potatoes around the steak and onions. If necessary, add additional hot water to keep a small amount of water in the skillet. Sprinkle ⅛ teaspoon pepper over the potatoes. Sprinkle the soup mix over the meat, onions, and potatoes. Cover and simmer for an additional ½ hour (see Note).

To serve, place the steak on a serving platter; spoon the onions and natural sauce over the steak. Arrange the potatoes around the steak. If desired, the potatoes may be served with the bottom, browned side up.

NOTE: If necessary, add water periodically during cooking to retain a small amount of water on the bottom of the skillet. To achieve a rich flavor and deep brown color, allow the water in the skillet to reduce to a thick, brown sauce at least once during the cooking process, being careful not to allow the sauce to burn.

SERVES 4

BROILED STEAK

Steaks for broiling: tenderloin (fillet and filet mignon), top loin, porterhouse, T-bone, rib eye, rib, sirloin, and chuck eye. 1½ inches is the preferable thickness for most broiled steaks*
Salt or garlic salt (optional)
Pepper (optional)

* Of course, these steaks vary in size naturally, due to their cut. Generally, a full steak should be served to each person, except in the case of sirloin steak—a large steak which is cut into individual servings after broiling. On average, people eat 6 to 8 ounces of steak; however, on occasion some will eat up to a 16-ounce steak.

Preheat the broiler.

To prepare the steaks for broiling, trim away the excess fat. To prevent the steaks from curling during broiling, slit the remaining fat at 2-inch intervals around the edges of the steaks, being careful not to penetrate the flesh, causing loss of meat juices.

Place the steaks on an ungreased broiler rack over the broiler pan. If desired, *just prior to broiling,* the steaks may be lightly seasoned with salt or garlic salt, and pepper.

Broil the steaks 4 inches from the heat. Turn the steaks only once during broiling, using tongs (a fork will pierce the meat and cause loss of juice). Broil the steaks 2 minutes longer on the first side than on the second side. The size and amount of bone and fat vary considerably among steaks; therefore, prescribed broiling times are only approximate (see following chart). Use an instant thermometer (page 28–29) to test for doneness. Or test for doneness by slitting the steak near the bone, using a sharp, thin-bladed knife. For steaks with no bone, make a slit in the center of the steak.

APPROXIMATE BROILING TIMES

Doneness	Minutes	
	1st Side	2nd Side
1½-INCH-THICK STEAKS		
Rare*	9	7
Medium Rare	11	9
Medium	12	10
Well Done	14	12
1-INCH-THICK STEAKS		
Rare*	6	3
Medium Rare	7	5
Medium	8	6
Well Done	11	9

* There is some bacterial risk when beef is consumed rare (140° F) (see Meat Safety, page 134–136).

ACCOMPANIMENT SUGGESTIONS
- Place a cold Onion Butter star (page 304–305) or Garlic Butter ball (page 304) atop each hot steak before serving, or pass molded Garlic Butter at the table. Do not season the steaks otherwise.

- Béarnaise Sauce (page 302) is a nice accompaniment for tenderloin steak. No other seasonings should be used on the steak.

BEEF BRISKET

1 5- to 6-pound beef brisket
1 1.1-ounce package beefy onion soup mix
¼ teaspoon pepper
1 12-ounce bottle or can beer
1 12-ounce bottle chili sauce
¼ cup cornstarch

Preheat the oven to 325°F.

Place the brisket in a heavy roaster; set aside. In a small mixing bowl, place the soup mix and pepper; stir to combine; set aside. Pour the beer over the brisket in the roaster. Use the entire bottle/can of beer even though the beer may partially cover the meat. Sprinkle the top of the brisket evenly with the onion soup mixture. Pour the chili sauce back and forth evenly over the onion soup mixture. Bake, covered, 5 to 6 hours (1 hour per pound of brisket). Do not baste.

Remove the brisket from the roaster and cover with aluminum foil to keep warm. Strain the roaster drippings in a sieve. Measure 2 cups strained drippings and pour into a small saucepan, reserving the remaining drippings; set aside. Place the cornstarch in a glass jar or plastic container with a secure lid; set aside. Measure ½ cup reserved drippings (add water, if necessary, to make ½ cup liquid); add to the cornstarch in the jar/container. Cover and shake vigorously until blended. Add to the drippings in the saucepan; stir to blend. Cook over medium heat until thickened, stirring constantly; cover and keep warm over very low heat.

Slice the brisket ½ inch thick and place on a serving plate. Serve the sauce in a gravy boat.

SERVES 12

SERVING SUGGESTIONS: Small Yukon Gold potatoes, unpared and steamed (page 252); Mashed Potatoes (page 279); or Mashed Potatoes in a Casserole (page 279–280) make a good accompaniment for this meat dish.

RIB ROAST (STANDING OR ROLLED)

1 standing or rolled rib roast (allow
    approximately ½ pound per serving)
Salt (optional)
Pepper (optional)

Preheat the oven to 325°F.

Place the roast, fat side up, on a wire rack in a shallow roasting pan. Salt and pepper the meat, if desired. Insert a meat thermometer to the center of the meat, making certain that the tip of the thermometer is not touching a bone. Do not add water or any other liquid to the meat; do not cover the meat or pan. Roast for approximately the following lengths of time, depending upon the size and shape of the meat and individual ovens:

APPROXIMATE ROASTING TIMES

Doneness	Thermometer Reading	Approx. Minutes per Pound
STANDING RIB ROAST		
Rare*	140° F	18 to 20
Medium Rare	150° F	20 to 25
Medium	160 °F	25
Well Done	170 °F	30
ROLLED RIB ROAST		
Rare*	140° F	23 to 28
Medium Rare	150° F	28 to 30
Medium	160 °F	30 to 35
Well Done	170 °F	35 to 40

* There is some bacterial risk when beef is consumed rare (140° F) (see Meat Safety, page 134–136).

Do not baste the meat. When the roast is close to reaching the desired thermometer reading, press the thermometer deeper into the meat. Very often, the thermometer reading will then fall due to a dislocation of the thermometer during roasting. As the meat will continue roasting after it is removed from the oven, remove the roast from the oven when the thermometer registers 5°F below the desired temperature. Transfer the roast to a heated platter and cover it loosely with aluminum foil. Let the roast stand about 15 minutes before carving, to achieve easier and neater slicing.

SERVING SUGGESTIONS
- Serve with Beef Gravy (page 311–312) made from drippings in the roasting pan.

- Serve with natural juices (au jus) and with freshly shredded horseradish (page 30) over individual servings of meat or served as a garnish on each plate.

- Serve Popovers (page 387–388) as an accompaniment, in which case the roast should be served with natural juices rather than Beef Gravy.

POT ROAST WITH VEGETABLES

(See photo insert page B-3)

A mainstay for Sunday dinner—and the leftovers are a boon when it's time to make Monday and Tuesday nights' dinners.

2 tablespoons vegetable shortening, divided
1 4- to 5-pound boneless beef chuck roast
¼ teaspoon salt, divided
¼ teaspoon pepper, divided
1½ pounds russet potatoes (about 4 to 5 medium potatoes)
6 medium-sized carrots
3 medium-sized yellow onions
Salt and pepper
1 recipe Pot Roast Gravy (page 312)
Sprigs of fresh parsley for decoration

Preheat a large, deep electric skillet (see Note) to 400°F (high heat). Add 1 tablespoon shortening. Tilt the skillet back and forth to completely cover the bottom with the melted shortening. Place the roast in the skillet; sprinkle with ⅛ teaspoon salt and ⅛ teaspoon pepper. Brown the roast *well* on the bottom and all short sides. Add the remaining 1 tablespoon shortening. Turn the roast over; sprinkle with the remaining ⅛ teaspoon salt and

the ⅛ teaspoon pepper; brown the top (which now becomes the bottom of the roast). Brown the roast until a *very deep brown* on all sides, just short of burning (about 20 minutes total browning time). Deep browning enhances the flavor of the meat and gravy. It is important to brown *all* sides of the roast to seal in the natural juices. Use tongs to turn the meat; piercing the meat with a fork will cause loss of juice from the meat. When browning the short sides of the roast, it may be necessary to hold the meat in position with the tongs.

After the roast has been browned, reduce the skillet heat to 220°F (very low heat). When the skillet cools to the reduced temperature, pour hot water around (not over) the roast to a depth of about ⅜ inch. Cover the skillet and slowly simmer the roast 45 minutes per pound, adding additional water if necessary.

Meanwhile, pare and cut the potatoes widthwise in half or into thirds, depending upon the size of the potatoes. As the potatoes are prepared, place them in a large bowl of cold water to prevent discoloration; set aside. Pare the carrots (page 17). Cut the carrots in half widthwise; then cut lengthwise in half or into fourths, depending upon the size of the carrots; set aside. Cut off the ends of the onions and peel; set aside.

One hour before the roast is done, arrange the vegetables around the meat. Salt and pepper the vegetables lightly. To achieve especially rich, brown gravy, allow the liquid in the skillet to reduce to a thick, brown sauce before adding the vegetables; watch carefully to prevent the sauce from burning. After adding the vegetables, add the water to restore the liquid to ⅜--inch depth. Then, allow the liquid to reduce again, which will brown the vegetables and enrich their flavor.

When done, place the pot roast and vegetables on a serving platter; cover with aluminum foil to keep warm. Prepare Pot Roast Gravy and serve in a gravy boat at the table. Just before serving, decorate the serving platter with sprigs of fresh parsley.

NOTE: Pot Roast with Vegetables may be prepared in a large, heavy-bottomed, tightly covered, conventional skillet on the range. The skillet must be deep enough and the lid high enough to accommodate the meat with the lid tightly covering the skillet.

SERVES 6

SUGGESTION FOR USING LEFTOVER POT ROAST: Use leftover meat and potatoes to make Hash (page 147).

SAUERBRATEN WITH POTATO DUMPLINGS

In German, "sauerbraten" means "marinated roast." And marinate it does!—for 3 full days before you cook it. I won a blue ribbon for this dish in the ethnic cooking division at the 1988 Iowa State Fair.

1 4-pound boned rump roast
4 bay leaves
1/2 teaspoon whole black peppercorns
2 large onions, sliced thinly
2 tablespoons sugar
8 whole cloves
1 small carrot, pared and minced
1 teaspoon salt
1 teaspoon mustard seed
1/2 cup dry red wine
1 cup water
1 1/2 cups red wine vinegar
2 tablespoons all-purpose flour
1 1/2 teaspoons salt
1/8 teaspoon ground pepper
1/4 cup vegetable shortening
1 large onion, sliced thinly
6 whole cloves
1/2 teaspoon whole black peppercorns
1/2 teaspoon mustard seeds
1/3 cup rolled gingersnap crumbs
Additional salt (optional)
1 recipe Potato Dumplings (page 281–282)

Place the roast in a large, round baking dish; set aside. In a medium mixing bowl, place the bay leaves, 1/2 teaspoon peppercorns, 2 sliced onions, sugar, 8 whole cloves, carrot, 1 teaspoon salt, 1 tea-spoon mustard seed, and red wine; stir to combine; set aside. Into a small saucepan, pour the water and vinegar; bring to a boil over high heat. Add to the wine mixture; stir to blend. Pour the wine mixture over the roast and let stand several minutes until cool. Then, cover and refrigerate for 3 days, turning the roast twice each day.

Remove the roast from the marinade and dry with paper towels; set aside. Strain the marinade through a sieve; set aside. In a small sauce dish, place the flour, 1 1/2 teaspoons salt, and ground pepper; stir to combine. Sprinkle the flour mixture over a piece of waxed paper; dredge the roast in the flour mixture. In a deep electric skillet (or a Dutch oven on the range), melt the vegetable shortening over high heat (400°F in an electric skillet). Tilt the skillet back and forth to completely cover the bottom with the melted shortening. Place the roast in the skillet, letting the excess flour fall onto the waxed paper. Brown the roast well on all sides.

Reduce the skillet heat to very low (220°F in an electric skillet). When the skillet cools to the reduced temperature, pour 3/4 cup of the marinade over the roast. Cover and refrigerate the remaining marinade. Arrange 1 sliced onion over and around the roast. Add 6 whole cloves, 1/2 teaspoon peppercorns, and 1/2 teaspoon mustard seed to the marinade around the roast. Cover the skillet and simmer the roast for 3 1/2 to 4 hours, or until the meat is tender, adding a little additional marinade, if necessary.

Place the roast on a warm platter; cover loosely with aluminum foil; let stand. Strain the skillet drippings through a sieve. Pour the strained drippings into a gravy skimmer (page 145; see Note). Let stand 2 minutes. Pour off the drippings and discard the fat; return 1/3 cup drippings to the skillet. Add the gingersnap crumbs; stir to combine. Slowly add 2 cups reserved marinade (add water, if necessary, to measure 2 cups liquid); stir to blend. Bring to a boil over medium-low heat (300°F in an electric skillet) and cook until thickened, stirring constantly. Add additional salt, if desired.

Slice the roast and arrange on a warm serving platter. Spoon some gingersnap gravy over the meat and pour the remainder into a gravy boat to pass at the table. Arrange Potato Dumplings around the Sauerbraten.

NOTE: If a gravy skimmer is not available, pour the strained drippings into a regular 1-cup glass liquid measuring cup. Let stand about 2 minutes until the fat rises to the top. Using a baster, draw off the fat and discard.

SERVES 8 TO 10

BRAISED SHORT RIBS WITH DILLED POTATOES

Short ribs are cut from the ends of standing rib roasts. Have the butcher cut them to the specifications suggested in the recipe.

3½ pounds short ribs, 2 × 3½ to 4 inches
 (1 to 1¾ inches thick)
⅔ cup vegetable oil
⅓ cup red wine vinegar
1 teaspoon Worcestershire sauce
¼ teaspoon salt
¼ teaspoon pepper
1 tablespoon vegetable shortening
½ cup chopped onions
½ teaspoon whole black peppercorns
¾ cup water
2 pounds whole, small potatoes, pared Salt
1 recipe Cream Gravy (page 310–311)
1 teaspoon snipped, fresh dillweed

Place the short ribs, single layer, in an 8 × 8-inch ungreased baking dish; set aside. In a glass jar or plastic container with a secure lid, place the vegetable oil, vinegar, Worcestershire sauce, ¼ teaspoon salt, and ¼ teaspoon pepper. Cover and shake vigorously until blended; pour over the meat. Cover with plastic wrap; refrigerate for 1 hour, turning the meat over after 30 minutes.

In an electric skillet or a large, heavy skillet on the range, melt the vegetable shortening over high heat (400°F in an electric skillet). Tilt the skillet back and forth to completely cover the bottom with the melted shortening. Lift the short ribs out of the marinade and place them

in the skillet. (Do not wipe the marinade off the meat.) Discard the remaining marinade. Brown the meat well on all 4 sides. Reduce the skillet heat to very low (210°F in an electric skillet).

When the skillet cools to the reduced temperature, scatter the onions and peppercorns around (not over) the meat. Pour ¾ cup water around the meat. Cover the skillet; simmer slowly for 2¼ hours, adding additional water if necessary. After 1¼ hours cooking time, place the potatoes on the bottom of the skillet around the short ribs. Sprinkle each potato with a dash of salt. Turn the potatoes after 30 minutes cooking time to achieve more even browning.

When done, the meat will be very tender and may fall off the bone of some pieces when removed from the skillet. Place the short ribs in the center of a large serving platter and arrange the potatoes around the meat; cover with aluminum foil to keep warm while making the gravy.

Pour the drippings from the skillet into a bowl; measure 1 tablespoon drippings and pour back into skillet. Increase the skillet heat to medium-low (325°F in an electric skillet) and make Cream Gravy. Strain the gravy in a sieve. Pour the strained gravy into a gravy boat and serve at the table. Remove the foil from the meat and potatoes platter; sprinkle dillweed over the potatoes. Serve immediately.

SERVES 4

ACCOMPANIMENT SUGGESTIONS: Glazed Carrots (page 261) and Sliced Tomatoes and Lettuce Salad (page 101) complement this dish well.

BROILED GROUND BEEF PATTIES

The simple addition of onions, an egg, catsup, and other seasonings elevate this easy-to-fix ground beef fare from ordinary to praiseworthy family dining.

1 pound lean, pure ground beef
¼ cup finely chopped onions
1 extra-large egg

(Recipe continues on next page)

2 tablespoons tomato catsup
¼ teaspoon salt
⅛ teaspoon pepper
Dash of garlic powder

Preheat the broiler.

In a medium mixing bowl, place the ground beef, onions, egg, catsup, salt, pepper, and garlic powder, using a large, metal mixing spoon, break up the ground beef and stir until the ingredients are combined evenly. Form into four 1-inch-thick patties and place on an ungreased broiler rack over the broiler pan.

Broil 6 inches from the heat for the following times, depending upon the desired doneness, turning only once.

BROILING TIMES

| | Minutes | |
Doneness	1st Side	2nd Side
Medium	8	6
Well Done	12	8

SERVES 4

ACCOMPANIMENT SUGGESTIONS: At the table, pass Bell Pepper Relish or Chili Sauce.

HAMBURGER STUFF

Oh, so simple, but oh, so good! This kid- and adult-pleaser, an invention of my mom's and, for lack of a formal name, has always been called "Hamburger Stuff" in our family.

1 pound lean, pure ground beef
1½ pounds pared and coarsely ground (page 16–17) russett potatoes (about 3 large potatoes)
¾ cup coarsely ground onions
1 teaspoon salt
½ teaspoon pepper
1½ cups beef broth, homemade (page 70) or comercially canned
1 recipe (¼ cup) Buttered Cracker Crumbs (page 33)

Preheat the oven to 350° F. Grease a 2-quart round baking dish; set aside.

Place the ground beef in a large, heavy skillet; lightly brown the meat over medium to medium-low heat. Remove from the heat. Add the potatoes, onions, salt, and pepper; stir to combine. Add the beef broth; stir to combine.

Turn the ground beef mixture into the prepared baking dish. Sprinkle the crumbs evenly over the top. Bake, uncovered, for 45 minutes.

SERVES 6

SERVING SUGGESTION: At the table, pass chili sauce.

MOTHER'S MEAT LOAF

1 14½-ounce can whole, peeled tomatoes
1½ pounds lean, pure ground beef
½ teaspoon salt
⅛ teaspoon pepper
¾ cup chopped onions
30 Ritz crackers, rolled finely
2 extra-large eggs
1 recipe Catsup Sauce (page 298)

Preheat the oven to 325° F. Grease a 6 × 10-inch baking dish; set aside.

Drain the tomatoes *well*, reserving the juice for other uses. In a large bowl, place the tomatoes, ground beef, salt, pepper, onions, crackers, and eggs; using a large, metal mixing spoon, combine thoroughly, breaking the tomatoes into small pieces. Form the mixture into an oval loaf and place it in the prepared baking dish. Bake, uncovered, 1 hour.

Meanwhile, make the Catsup Sauce; set aside. After baking 1 hour, remove the meat loaf from the oven and spoon approximately ½ of the hot Catsup Sauce evenly over the top of the loaf. Return the meat loaf to the oven and bake, uncovered, an additional 15 minutes.

To serve, cut the meat loaf into ⅝-inch slices widthwise; then, cut the loaf in half lengthwise, creating 2 pieces of meat loaf per slice. Serve 2 pieces, overlapping, on each plate. Reheat the remaining hot Catsup Sauce, pour into a sauce-boat, and pass at the table.

SERVES 8

HASH

2½ cups cold, coarsely chopped, cooked roast beef, pork, or lamb
2½ cups cold, coarsely chopped, cooked potatoes (about 2 medium potatoes)
1¼ cups chopped onions (about 1 medium onion)
¼ cup all-purpose flour
¾ teaspoon salt
¼ teaspoon pepper
½ cup whole milk
2 tablespoons vegetable oil
Sprigs of fresh parsley for decoration
Tomato catsup

In a large mixing bowl, place the meat, potatoes, and onions; set aside. In a half-pint jar or plastic container with a secure lid, place the flour, salt, pepper, and milk; cover and shake vigorously until blended and smooth. Add the flour mixture to the mixing bowl containing the meat, potatoes, and onions; stir to combine; set aside.

In a large, *heavy-bottomed* skillet, heat the vegetable oil over low heat. Add the meat mixture in an even layer and cook, uncovered, over *low* heat, for 20 minutes. Cover and cook an additional 10 minutes. During the entire cooking time, do not turn the hash or stir, but intermittently run a small spatula under the hash to loosen it and help keep it from sticking to the bottom of the skillet.

When nicely brown and cooked, use a large spatula to fold half of the hash over the other half. Lift to a serving the plate; decorate the plate with parsley. At the table, pass the catsup.

SERVES 6

ALICE'S MEAT AND TATER PIE

Alice Dalbey Bernstein is one of my closest, lifelong friends. In fact, our families' association predates Alice and me—her parents and my mother attended Drake University together. Now living in Baltimore with her husband, Neil, Alice served this yummy dish—a definite reflection of her Midwest heritage—when I was there on a visit. She served it with a crisp, green salad at her always impeccably set dining room table before we headed, with friends, to watch a national tennis tournament. It seemed just the right menu for the occasion. Of course I asked for and received the recipe, which I now pass on with Alice's permission.

1 pound lean, pure ground beef
½ cup whole milk
1 1-ounce package onion soup mix
⅛ teaspoon pepper
⅛ teaspoon ground allspice
Pastry for 1 9-inch, 2-crust pie (Pastry Piecrust, page 392–394)
12 ounces frozen shredded hash brown potatoes, thawed
½ cup shredded onions
1 cup tomato catsup, warmed

Preheat the oven to 350°F.

In a medium bowl, place the ground beef, milk, soup mix, pepper, and allspice; using a large, metal mixing spoon, break up the ground beef and stir until the ingredients are well combined; set aside. Line a 9-inch pie pan with pastry for the bottom crust. Spoon the meat mixture evenly over the bottom-crust pastry; lightly pat. With your fingers, spread the potatoes evenly over the meat mixture. Spoon the onions over the potatoes. Slit and arrange the top piecrust. Flute the edge. Bake for 1 hour and 10 minutes. Pass warmed catsup at the table.

SERVES 6

VARIATIONS: Substitute chili sauce, unheated, for the warmed catsup.

MEAT AND POTATO PATTIES

Here's a simple way to convert leftover roast (of any kind) and mashed potatoes into a new dish. Sometimes this dish is as popular at the dinner table as the original meal served the night before.

3 cups cold, coarsely ground (page 16),
   cooked roast beef, pork, veal, or lamb
½ medium onion, coarsely ground
1½ cups cold mashed potatoes
1 extra-large egg
¾ teaspoon salt
¼ teaspoon pepper
1 tablespoon vegetable oil
1 tablespoon butter

In a medium mixing bowl, place the meat, onions, potatoes, egg, salt, and pepper; stir to combine. Using a ½ cup measuring cup, measure level ½ cups of the meat mixture; with your hands, form the portions into patties and place on a piece of waxed paper; set aside.

In a heavy-bottomed skillet, heat the vegetable oil over medium heat. Tilt the skillet back and forth to completely cover the bottom with the oil. Add the butter; spread to blend with the oil. Place the patties in the skillet; sauté until the patties are brown and the onions in them are cooked. Turn once. Serve the patties directly on individual dinner plates or place them on a serving platter.

MAKES 7 PATTIES

BEEF AND BISCUIT CASSEROLE

1 pound lean, pure ground beef
½ cup chopped onions
1 8-ounce can tomato sauce
¼ cup tomato catsup
½ teaspoon salt
⅛ teaspoon pepper
½ teaspoon dried leaf basil

4 ounces Colby cheese, sliced
1 recipe Baking Powder Biscuits (page 380)
   (see Variation below)

Preheat the oven to 400° F.

In an electric skillet or a heavy skillet on the range, begin browning the ground beef over medium-low heat (325° F in an electric skillet). Using a large, metal mixing spoon, break up the ground beef as it cooks, and stir often. When the ground beef releases enough fat to cover the bottom of the skillet, add the onions. Continue cooking until the ground beef and onions are nicely browned. Turn off the heat and allow the skillet to cool slightly. Then, add the tomato sauce, catsup, salt, pepper, and basil; stir to combine.

In an ungreased 1½-quart round baking dish, place, alternately, 3 layers of the ground beef mixture and 2 layers of cheese slices (beginning and ending with the meat mixture). Bake, uncovered, for 10 minutes.

Remove the baking dish from the oven. Increase the oven temperature to 450° F. Arrange 8 unbaked Baking Powder Biscuits, nearly touching, around the edge of the baking dish, over the ground beef mixture. Arrange the remaining biscuits, nearly touching, in an ungreased round cake pan. Place the baking dish and pan of extra biscuits in the oven. Bake, uncovered, for 10 to 12 minutes until the biscuits are lightly golden.

SERVES 6

VARIATION: For faster preparation, substitute 1 7.5-ounce tube of refrigerated biscuits for the homemade Baking Powder Biscuits. After adding the biscuits to the baking dish, bake for 8 to 10 minutes. (Check the biscuit-tube label for suggested oven temperature and baking time.)

GROUND SIRLOIN-NOODLE CASSEROLE

1 tablespoon butter
1¼ pounds ground sirloin
¾ cup chopped onions
¾ teaspoon salt
½ teaspoon pepper
1 cup chopped celery
2 tablespoons butter
1 cup sliced, fresh mushrooms
¼ cup dry white wine
1½ recipes Medium White Sauce
　　(page 301–302)
2 teaspoons instant beef bouillon granules
¼ cup freshly grated Parmesan cheese
　　(page 30)
10 cups water
8 ounces wide egg noodles
1 tablespoon butter, melted
1 recipe (¼ cup) Buttered Cracker Crumbs
　　(page 33)

In an electric skillet or a skillet on the range, melt 1 tablespoon butter over medium heat (350° F in an electric skillet). Tilt the skillet back and forth to completely cover the bottom with the melted butter. Add the ground sirloin and start to brown it, breaking up the meat with a large, metal mixing spoon, and stirring often. When the meat is slightly brown, add the onions, salt, and pepper. Continue cooking and stirring until the meat is well browned. Turn off the heat under the skillet. Add the celery and stir to combine; cover the skillet and let stand.

In a small, heavy skillet, melt 2 tablespoons butter over medium heat. Place the mushrooms in the skillet; sauté 3 minutes until the mushrooms give up their juices, stirring often. Remove from the heat; let stand until cooled slightly. Add the wine and stir in; cover and set aside.

Make the Medium White Sauce; remove from the heat. Add the bouillon granules; stir until dissolved. Add the Parmesan cheese; stir to blend. Add the mushroom mixture; stir until the liquids are blended; cover and set aside.

Preheat the oven to 350° F. Butter a 2-quart round baking dish; set aside.

Pour 10 cups water into a kettle; cover and bring to a boil over high heat. Add the noodles and boil, uncovered, until tender (about 10 minutes), stirring often. Drain the noodles in a colander. Return the noodles to the cooking kettle; rinse in hot water. Drain the noodles well in the colander.

Place the noodles in a large mixing bowl. Add 1 tablespoon melted butter; toss to coat. Add the ground sirloin mixture and white sauce mixture; stir and fold until evenly combined. Turn the mixture into the prepared baking dish. Sprinkle the crumbs evenly over the top. Bake, uncovered, for 30 minutes.

SERVES 8 GENEROUSLY

STUFFED CABBAGE LEAVES

1 pound lean, pure ground beef
½ cup parboiled* long-grain rice (not instant)
2 extra-large eggs
1 cup minced onions (about 1 medium onion)
2 tablespoons snipped, fresh parsley
¾ teaspoon dried leaf thyme
½ teaspoon salt
¼ teaspoon pepper
1 large head cabbage
1 large onion, sliced
2 28-ounce cans whole, peeled, tomatoes, undrained
1 15-ounce can tomato sauce
¾ cup freshly squeezed, strained lemon juice (about 2 large lemons)
⅓ cup packed light brown sugar
½ teaspoon salt
¼ teaspoon pepper
⅛ teaspoon ground nutmeg

* See Parboiled Rice, page 228.

(Recipe continues on next page)

In a large mixing bowl, place the ground beef, rice, eggs, minced onions, parsley, thyme, ½ teaspoon salt, and ¼ teaspoon pepper; using a large, metal mixing spoon, break up the ground beef and combine the ingredients well. Cover with plastic wrap; set aside.

Wash the cabbage; remove and discard the outer leaves. Using a paring knife, cut out as much of the cabbage core as possible without cutting into the leaves. Fill an 8-quart kettle ¾ full of hot water; cover and bring to a boil over high heat. Remove the cover and dip the cabbage head into the boiling water. After *a few seconds,* remove the cabbage from the kettle with a slotted spoon and place it on several layers of paper towels. With your hands, remove as many whole leaves as will easily separate from the head (usually 2 or 3), being careful not to tear the leaves. Place the separated leaves on several layers of dry paper towels. Redip the cabbage head in boiling water and repeat the process until a total of 17 cabbage leaves has been removed. As the leaves are removed, it likely will be necessary to cut out the remainder of the cabbage core, which had previously been too deep in the head for careful removal.

Blanch the leaves (page 29) 3 minutes, in batches. Drain well on several layers of paper towels. Arrange 5 of the smaller, less green leaves over the bottom of a heavy 8-quart roaster; set aside. Place ¼ cup of the ground beef mixture in the center (cupped side) of each of 11 or 12 of the remaining cabbage leaves. Fold the 2 sides of each leaf over the meat mixture; then, from the thick end of the cabbage leaves, loosely roll the leaves. Place the cabbage rolls, seam down, over the cabbage leaves in the bottom of the roaster. (It will be necessary to arrange some of the rolls in 2 layers.) Distribute the onion slices over the cabbage rolls; set aside.

Preheat the oven to 375° F.

Place the undrained tomatoes in a large saucepan; using a metal mixing spoon, break the tomatoes into large chunks. Add the tomato sauce and lemon juice; stir to blend. Cover the saucepan; bring the tomato mixture to a boil over medium-high heat. Ladle the mixture over the onion slices and cabbage rolls in the roaster. Cover the roaster; set aside. In a small mixing bowl, place the brown sugar, ½ teaspoon salt, ¼ teaspoon pepper, and nutmeg; stir to combine. Sprinkle over all in the roaster. Bake, covered, for 1 hour. Then, baste lightly. Bake, *uncovered,* for an additional 2 hours, basting lightly after 1 hour of baking. Baste lightly again before serving.

SERVES 8

STUFFED BELL PEPPERS

(See photo insert page A-7)

½ cup parboiled* long-grain rice, regular or instant
4 large in color(s) of choice (green, red, yellow, and orange) bell peppers.
1 6-ounce can tomato paste
¾ cup water
1 tablespoon tomato catsup
1 tablespoon cider vinegar
1 tablespoon packed dark brown sugar
1 tablespoon onion juice (page 29) or
    1 teaspoon onion powder
¼ teaspoon salt
⅛ teaspoon pepper
Dash of ground cinnamon
1 pound lean, pure ground beef
½ cup finely chopped celery
¼ cup finely chopped onions
½ teaspoon salt
⅛ teaspoon garlic salt
⅓ cup water
4 small sprigs of fresh rosemary for decoration (optional)

   * *See Parboiled Rice, page 228.*

Boil the rice (see page 228 for boiling *regular* long-grain rice; follow the package instructions for cooking *instant* rice); set aside. Wash the peppers. Cut a thin slice off the top of the peppers; carefully remove the seeds and inner, white parts of the flesh. In a large kettle, bring sufficient water to a boil, over high heat, as will cover the peppers. Place the peppers in the boiling water; cover the kettle and reduce the heat slightly. Boil the peppers 5 minutes. Drain the peppers upside down on several layers of paper towels.

In a medium saucepan, place the tomato paste, water, catsup, vinegar, brown sugar, onion juice, ¼ teaspoon salt, pepper, and cinnamon. Cover the pan. Over medium-low heat, simmer the mixture for 10 minutes. Meanwhile, in a large mixing bowl, place the ground beef, celery, onions, ½ teaspoon salt, and garlic salt; using a large, metal mixing spoon, break up the ground beef and combine the ingredients well.

Preheat the oven to 350°F. Lightly grease an 8 × 8-inch baking dish; set aside.

Stuff the cavities of the green peppers with the meat mixture, patting lightly and filling to slightly above the top of the peppers. Place the stuffed peppers in the prepared baking dish. Pour ½ of the tomato paste mixture over the tops of the peppers (some of the mixture will trickle down the sides of the peppers). Cover the remaining ½ of the tomato paste mixture, and set aside. Pour ⅓ cup water into the bottom of the baking dish. Bake the stuffed peppers for 1 hour and 10 minutes.

At serving time, heat the remaining ½ of the tomato paste mixture over medium-low heat; pour into a sauce dish and pass at the table.

SERVES 4

Other Beef Recipes

Veal

BREADED VEAL CUTLETS WITH LEEKS AND SHIITAKE MUSHROOMS

1 cup commercially packaged corn flake
   crumbs or 5 cups corn flakes crumbed in a
   food processor or blender (page 34–35)
½ teaspoon salt
¼ teaspoon white pepper
1 extra-large egg
2 tablespoons whole milk
1 ¾-inch thick, boneless veal loin strip
   with the back strap removed (about
   2 pounds), cut widthwise into 6 pieces
1 tablespoon vegetable oil
1 tablespoon butter
2 tablespoons butter
¾ cup leeks thinly sliced widthwise (about 2
   medium leeks)
3½ ounces sliced, fresh shiitake mushrooms
   (about 2 cups)
2 recipes Extra-Thin White Sauce (page 301–
   302), substituting 1½ cups whole milk and ½
   cup chicken broth (homemade [page 70-71] or
   commercially canned) for 2 cups whole milk

EARLY IN THE DAY (see Note): Butter a 7 × 11-inch baking dish; set aside.

In a small bowl, place the corn flake crumbs, salt, and white pepper; stir to combine. Sprinkle the mixture over a 1-foot-square piece of waxed paper; set aside. In a small mixing bowl, place the egg and 2 tablespoons milk; using an electric mixer or a table fork, beat until blended. Pour the egg mixture into a pie pan. Dredge each piece of veal in the corn flake crumbs mixture; then, dip in the egg mixture to coat; dredge again in the corn flake crumbs mixture and

(Recipe continues on next page)

place on a clean piece of waxed paper. Let stand for 5 minutes.

In a large electric skillet or a heavy-bottomed skillet on the range, heat the vegetable oil over medium heat (350° F in an electric skillet). Using a spatula, spread the oil over the bottom of the skillet. Add 1 tablespoon butter. Tilt the skillet back and forth to blend the butter with the oil. Place the cutlets in the skillet; sauté 4 to 5 minutes on each side until deeply browned. Arrange, single-layer, in the prepared baking dish. Let cool slightly; then, cover tightly with aluminum foil and refrigerate.

In a medium, heavy-bottomed skillet, melt 2 tablespoons butter over medium heat. Be careful not to let the butter brown. Add the leeks and mushrooms; sauté for 5 to 6 minutes, turning often and not allowing them to brown; set aside. Make the Extra-Thin White Sauce. Add the sautéed leeks and mushrooms plus the pan juices to the white sauce; stir to combine. Cover the saucepan and refrigerate.

1¼ HOURS BEFORE SERVING: Preheat the oven to 325° F.

Mound the white sauce mixture over the veal cutlets. Cover the baking dish lightly with aluminum foil. Bake for 1 hour.

To serve, place the Breaded Veal Cutlets on 6 individual dinner plates. Pour the remaining sauce in the baking dish into a sauceboat; pass at the table.

NOTE: The reason for preparing this dish early in the day is to allow the white sauce mixture to become slightly firm under refrigeration, making it possible to mound the mixture over the cutlets before baking. This procedure eliminates the need for basting and results in a greater quantity of the white sauce mixture remaining on top of the cutlets during baking, thus improving their flavor and appearance.

SERVES 6

VEAL OR CALF'S LIVER WITH BACON AND ONIONS

¼ cup all-purpose flour
½ teaspoon salt
¼ teaspoon pepper
1 pound veal or calf's liver, cut ⅜ inch thick
8 slices (about ½ pound) bacon
1 large onion, thinly sliced and separated into rings
⅛ teaspoon salt
Dash of pepper
1 tablespoon butter, if necessary

In a small mixing bowl, place the flour, ½ teaspoon salt, and ¼ teaspoon pepper; stir to combine. Sprinkle the flour mixture over a piece of waxed paper. Dredge both sides of the liver in the flour mixture; set aside.

In an electric skillet or a heavy-bottomed skillet on the range, fry the bacon over medium-low heat (320° F in an electric skillet); drain between several layers of paper towels. Place the onions in the skillet. Sprinkle ⅛ teaspoon salt and a dash of pepper over the onions. Sauté the onions 3 minutes only, turning occasionally. Move the onions to one side of the skillet and place the liver directly on the bottom of the skillet. If necessary, add 1 tablespoon butter for sufficient grease to sauté the liver. Sauté the liver for 4 to 5 minutes, turning once. Continue sautéing and turning the onions alongside the liver. When done, the liver should be nicely browned on the outside and delicately pink on the inside. Do not overcook, as this will cause toughness.

To serve, pile the onions on the liver and place the bacon next to the liver on the plate

SERVES 4

VARIATION ~ WITHOUT BACON: Follow the recipe through the dredging of the liver. Omit the bacon. In an electric skillet or a heavy-bottomed skillet on the range, heat 1 tablespoon vegetable oil over medium-low heat (320° F in an electric skillet); using a spatula, spread the vegetable oil over the bottom of the skillet. Add 1 tablespoon butter. Tilt the skillet back and forth to blend the butter with the oil. Place the onions in the skillet and resume following the recipe. Add 1 additional tablespoon butter to the skillet just before adding the liver for sautéing.

VEAL TENDERLOIN ROULADES WITH WILD RICE

1 pound fresh spinach
⅓ pound ground veal
⅓ pound mild Italian sausage
⅓ pound lean, pure ground beef
1 2-ounce jar sliced pimientos, drained
    (2 tablespoons)
1 cup fresh, white bread crumbs (page 33)
½ teaspoon salt
½ teaspoon dried leaf marjoram
1 extra-large egg
4 veal tenderloins, ⅔ to ¾ pound each,
    pounded to ¼-inch thickness
1 tablespoon vegetable shortening
2½ cups chicken broth, homemade (page
    70–71) or commercially canned, divided
¼ cup all-purpose flour
½ cup dry white wine
1¼ cups raw wild rice, cooked (page 231)

Cut the stems off the spinach leaves; discard the stems. Wash the spinach leaves twice; then, place in a large kettle and add water to cover. Cover the kettle. Bring the spinach to a boil over high heat. Reduce the heat and simmer for 4 minutes. Drain the spinach well in a colander; with your hand, press the spinach to remove as much liquid as possible. Using a sharp knife, chop the spinach finely. Measure ½ cup chopped spinach.

In a medium mixing bowl, place ½ cup spinach, ground veal, Italian sausage, ground beef, pimientos, bread crumbs, salt, marjoram, and egg; using a large, metal mixing spoon, break up the ground meats and combine the ingredients well. Set aside.

Place the tenderloins on a piece of waxed paper. Divide the meat mixture into fourths

and place ¼ of the mixture on each tenderloin. Distribute the mixture over the surface of the tenderloins; pat down well with the back of a spoon to within ⅜ inch of the edges of the tenderloins. Roll the tenderloins short side to short side. With cotton string, securely tie each roulade twice widthwise to hold it closed; then, tie it lengthwise around the ends and widthwise around the center, as you would tie a package (see illustration).

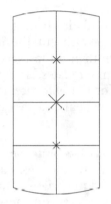

Preheat the oven to 325° F.

In an electric skillet or a heavy skillet on the range, melt the vegetable shortening over medium heat (350° F in an electric skillet). Using a spatula, spread the melted shortening over the entire bottom of the skillet. Place the roulades in the skillet; brown well on all sides. Place the roulades in a heavy roaster, arranging them single layer, seams down; set aside. Reduce the skillet heat to very low (220° F in an electric skillet). When the skillet cools to the reduced temperature, pour 1 cup chicken broth into the skillet and deglaze completely. Pour the skillet liquid over the roulades. Cover the roaster. Bake the roulades for 1 hour, basting 2 or 3 times during the baking period.

Remove the roaster from the oven and baste the roulades. Transfer the roulades to a plate or pan; cover lightly with aluminum foil. Pour the roaster drippings into a 2-cup glass measuring cup. Add enough chicken broth to measure

(Recipe continues on next page)

2 cups liquid; pour into a medium saucepan; set aside. Return the roulades to the roaster; cover to keep warm.

In a small glass jar or plastic container with a secure lid, place the flour and ½ cup chicken broth; cover and shake vigorously until blended. Add the flour mixture to the drippings and broth in the saucepan; stir to blend. Place the saucepan over medium heat and cook the gravy mixture until thick, stirring continuously. Add the wine; heat through. Remove the wine gravy from the heat and strain in a sieve, if necessary; keep warm.

Remove the roulades from the roaster. Remove the strings and cut the roulades into ½-inch slices widthwise. On a serving platter or on individual dinner plates, arrange the roulade slices on a bed of hot wild rice. Pour the wine gravy into a gravy boat and pass at the table.

SERVES 8

SERVING SUGGESTIONS: Decorate the serving platter with a cluster of Tomato Roses and Rosebuds (page 340) nestled in sprigs of flat-leaf parsley. If the roulade is served on individual plates, decorate each plate with one Tomato Rose arranged on one or two small sprigs of flat-leaf parsley.

VEAL PICCATA WITH THYME

½ cup all-purpose flour
1 teaspoon salt
½ teaspoon white pepper
10 slices (about 2¼ pounds) veal top round, cut ¼ inch thick; then, each slice cut in half widthwise to make 20 pieces
1 to 2 tablespoons vegetable oil
1 to 2 tablespoons butter
1¾ cups homemade Chicken Broth (page 70–71) or 1 14-ounce can commercial chicken broth, divided
¼ cup dry white wine
1 tablespoon fresh thyme leaves

¼ cup freshly squeezed, strained lemon juice
¼ cup dry white wine
Thin slices of lemon for garnish

In a small mixing bowl, place the flour, salt, and white pepper; stir to combine. Sprinkle the flour mixture over a piece of waxed paper. Dredge the veal pieces lightly in the mixture; shake to remove all excess flour, and place, single layer, on a clean piece of waxed paper. Measure 2 tablespoons of the remaining flour mixture (add additional flour, if necessary) and place in a small glass jar or plastic container with a secure lid; cover and set aside.

In an electric skillet or a large, heavy-bottomed skillet on the range, heat 1 tablespoon vegetable oil over medium-low heat (320° F in an electric skillet), being careful not to let the heat become warmer. Using a spatula, spread the vegetable oil over the entire bottom of the skillet. Add 1 tablespoon butter. Tilt the skillet back and forth to blend the butter with the oil. Place veal pieces, single layer, a few at a time, in the skillet; sauté about 5 minutes (2 to 3 minutes on each side) until very lightly golden. Place the sautéed veal pieces in a large, shallow pan and set aside. Add 1 additional tablespoon vegetable oil and 1 additional tablespoon butter during sautéing, if necessary. After all the pieces of veal have been sautéed, reduce the skillet heat to very low (220° F in an electric skillet).

When the skillet has cooled to the reduced temperature, return all the veal pieces to the skillet; set aside. Into a small mixing bowl, pour ½ cup chicken broth and ¼ cup white wine; stir to blend. Pour the wine mixture carefully over the veal. Sprinkle the thyme over and around the veal. Cover the skillet. Cook the veal for 15 minutes. Add ½ cup additional chicken broth if liquid depletes during cooking. Do not turn the meat. (See Note.)

Place the veal in a shallow pan; cover lightly with aluminum foil and keep warm. Retain very low skillet heat (220° F in an electric skillet). Pour ½ cup chicken broth, lemon juice, and ¼ cup white wine into the skillet; using a large, metal mixing spoon, stir and scrape until the skillet is completely deglazed. Strain the skillet liquid through a sieve; pour the strained liquid into a small saucepan; set aside.

Add ¼ cup chicken broth to the 2 tablespoons reserved flour; cover the jar/container and shake briskly until blended. Add the flour mixture to the strained skillet juices in the saucepan; stir to blend. Place the saucepan over medium heat. Bring the mixture to a boil, stirring constantly. Boil for 2 minutes, continuing to stir constantly. Remove the sauce from the heat.

To serve, arrange 3 pieces of veal, overlapping slightly, on 6 individual dinner plates (there will be 2 extra pieces). Spoon the sauce over the veal on each plate. Garnish the plates with thin lemon slices.

NOTE: At this point in the preparation, the skillet may be turned off or removed from the heat and the veal may be left in the covered skillet for up to 1 hour until the recipe is completed shortly before serving. In this case, the veal must be reheated in the skillet over very low heat before proceeding with the recipe.

SERVES 6

Pork

CROWN ROAST OF PORK FILLED WITH FRESH MIXED VEGETABLES ROSEMARY

---

1 8- to 10-pound crown roast of pork, with backbone removed*
¼ teaspoon pepper
1 teaspoon snipped, fresh rosemary
1 cup German Spätlese wine,** divided

2 recipes Pork Wine Gravy using German Spätlese wine** (page 313)
1 recipe Mixed Fresh Vegetables with Rosemary (page 269–270)
4½ pounds Oven-Browned Potatoes (page 281)
Tomato Roses (page 340) for decoration
Sprigs of fresh rosemary for decoration

 * *Have the butcher remove the backbone from the meat before he makes the crown roast. Order the exact number of ribs you want in the roast—1 rib per diner plus 2 extra ribs for big eaters. An 18-rib crown roast of pork weighs about 8¾ pounds and will serve 16.*

**German Kabinett or American Johannisberg Riesling wine may be substituted.*

Preheat the oven to 325° F.

Place the roast on a wire rack in a shallow roasting pan. Sprinkle the inside of the crown and the outside of the roast with the pepper and rosemary. Cover the ends of the rib bones firmly with aluminum foil to prevent over-browning. Insert a meat thermometer into the center of the thickest part of the roast near the base, making certain that the tip of the thermometer is not touching a bone. Roast, uncovered, until the thermometer reaches 160° F for medium doneness (approximately 20 to 25 minutes per pound) (see Note). Remove the roast from the oven when the temperature reaches 5° F below the desired temperature, as the meat will continue cooking. After roasting 1 hour, carefully pour ½ cup wine over the roast. After roasting an additional 45 minutes, pour the remaining ½ cup wine over the roast. After roasting another 45 minutes, baste the roast with pan juices.

When the thermometer has reached the desired temperature, remove the roast from the oven and place it into the center of a large, round serving platter. Cover lightly with aluminum foil to keep warm. Make the Pork Wine Gravy.

To serve, remove the aluminum foil from the roast and rib bones. Fill the crown with the mixed vegetables; place the remaining mixed vegetables

(Recipe continues on next page)

in a vegetable serving dish. Place white paper frilled booties over each rib bone. Arrange the potatoes around the roast. Decorate the platter with Tomato Roses and sprigs of fresh rosemary. Cut and serve the roast at the table. Cut between each rib bone and serve 1 rib chop to each diner. Pass the Pork Wine Gravy in a gravy boat.

NOTE: For well done, roast until the thermometer reaches 170°F (approximately 25 to 30 minutes per pound).

SERVES 16

ACCOMPANIMENT SUGGESTION: Scalloped Apples (page 290–291) make an excellent side dish.

IOWA PORK CHOPS

Known throughout the Midwest as the Iowa Pork Chop or the Iowa Chop, this thick, flavorful, and tender cut of pork is like a steak. Specifically, Iowa Pork Chops are center-cut loin pork chops cut 1¼ to 1½ inches thick. They may be prepared in any way desired. During the winter, when it's too cold for outdoor grilling, I like to fix them in this traditional way. When the weather is warmer, these succulent chops are incredibly delicious prepared outdoors on the grill (see Grilled Iowa Pork Chops, page 207). Iowa Chops are so named because Iowa produces more pork than any other state.

4 Iowa Pork Chops (center-cut loin pork
   chops, 1¼ to 1½ inches thick)
Salt
Pepper
All-purpose flour
2 tablespoons vegetable shortening
¼ cup water

Place the pork chops on a piece of waxed paper. Sprinkle the chops lightly on both sides with salt and pepper. Sprinkle flour liberally over the chops. Using your hand, spread the flour over the entire top surface of the chops. Turn the chops over and repeat the procedure; set aside.

Preheat an electric skillet or a heavy skillet on the range to medium-high heat (380°F in an electric skillet). Melt the shortening in the skillet. Tilt the skillet back and forth to completely cover the bottom with the melted shortening. Shake the excess flour off the chops and place them in the skillet. Brown for about 10 minutes on each side, turning once. Reduce the skillet heat to very low (220°F in an electric skillet). When the skillet cools to the lower temperature, add the water. Cover tightly and cook for 30 minutes.

SERVES 4

ACCOMPANIMENT SUGGESTIONS
• Serve with Mashed Potatoes (page 279) and Milk Gravy (page 310–311). The gravy should be served on the mashed potatoes, not over or under the pork chops.

• Ten minutes before the pork chops are done, place unpared, cored, fresh apple slices, or fresh or canned pineapple slices in the skillet and brown for 5 minutes on each side. Serve as a garnish on the plates.

• Serve with homemade Plain Applesauce (page 290).

BARBECUED LOIN BACK RIBS

6 pounds pork loin back ribs (baby backs)*
1 recipe Barbecue Sauce (page 205), divided

* Have the butcher remove the fell (a thin, tough membrane) from the bony side of the ribs.

Preheat the oven to 400°F.

Cut each side of ribs in half, or leave whole. Place the ribs, bony side down, in a heavy roaster. Bake, uncovered, for 30 minutes. Remove the roaster from the oven; reduce the oven heat to 325°F. Using a baster, draw off and discard the excess fat in the roaster.

Pour ½ of the Barbecue Sauce over the ribs,

lifting them with a fork to make certain that all the ribs are coated with sauce. Bake, covered, for 30 minutes. Then, baste each piece of ribs. Bake, covered, for an additional 30 minutes. Pour an additional ¼ of the Barbecue Sauce over the ribs; bake, covered, for an additional 1 hour, basting twice. Pour the remaining ¼ of the Barbecue Sauce over the ribs; bake, uncovered, for an additional 30 minutes, basting after 15 minutes baking time. (Leave the ribs bony side down during the entire baking time.)

SERVES 6
(ALLOW 1 POUND RIBS PER DINER)

LOIN OF PORK

For perfect pork, cook it to 160°F (medium doneness). For more on this subject, see page 134.

½ teaspoon ground sage
½ teaspoon Hungarian paprika
½ teaspoon dry mustard
¼ teaspoon salt
⅛ teaspoon pepper
1 4- to 5-pound center-cut, boneless, *double* pork loin, tied at 1½-inch intervals

Preheat the oven to 325°F.

In a small sauce dish, place the sage, paprika, dry mustard, salt, and pepper; stir to combine; set aside. Place the roast on a wire rack in a shallow roasting pan. Rub the sage mixture over the top of the roast. Insert a meat thermometer into the center of the roast. Roast the meat, uncovered, until the thermometer reaches 160°F for medium doneness (approximately 30 minutes per pound) (see Note). Remove the roast from the oven when the thermometer reaches 5°F below the desired temperature, as the meat will continue cooking.

When the meat thermometer has reached the desired temperature, remove the roast from the oven and cover loosely with aluminum foil; let stand 15 minutes.

To serve, place the sliced or unsliced roast on a warm serving platter.

NOTE: For well done, roast until the thermometer reaches 170°F (approximately 30 to 35 minutes per pound).

A 4-POUND PORK LOIN SERVES 8 TO 12

SINGLE PORK LOIN

To prepare 1 4- to 5-pound center-cut, boneless, single pork loin, tie at 3-inch intervals. Follow the recipe, above, for double pork loin, with the following alterations in roasting times: To reach an internal temperature of 160°F (medium done), roast approximately 20 minutes per pound. To reach an internal temperature of 170°F (well done), roast approximately 25 minutes per pound.

LOIN OF PORK NATURAL JUICE OR GRAVY

To serve loin of pork natural juice, deglaze the roasting pan with 1 cup water; strain the pan juices through a sieve and serve in a small sauceboat. To serve loin of pork gravy, follow the recipe for Roast Pork Gravy (page 312–313).

LOIN OF PORK WITH BRANDIED APPLES

1 recipe Loin of Pork (above)
¼ cup packed light brown sugar
¼ cup granulated sugar
½ teaspoon ground cinnamon
¼ teaspoon ground mace
2 pounds Golden Delicious apples
   (4 medium-large apples)
1 tablespoon freshly squeezed, strained lemon juice
2 teaspoons vegetable oil
2 tablespoons butter
1 teaspoon cornstarch
2 teaspoons good brandy

30 MINUTES BEFORE LOIN OF PORK IS DONE: In a small mixing bowl, place the brown sugar, granulated sugar, cinnamon, and mace; stir to combine; set aside. Wash, quarter, and core the apples; do not pare. Slice the apples ¼ inch thick; place in a

(Recipe continues on next page)

large mixing bowl. Sprinkle the lemon juice over the apples; toss to coat. Add the sugar mixture; toss until the apples are coated; set aside.

Pour the vegetable oil into a medium, heavy-bottomed skillet; using a spatula, distribute the oil over the entire bottom. Place the skillet over medium-high heat. Add the butter. Tilt the skillet back and forth to blend the butter with the oil. Place the apples in the skillet; sauté for 12 minutes until tender, turning intermittently. Remove the skillet from the heat and let the sautéed apples stand, uncovered, in the skillet.

While the Loin of Pork is standing for 15 minutes after removal from the oven, reheat the sautéed apples. Then, using a slotted spoon, transfer the apples to a mixing bowl; cover lightly and set aside. Pour about ¼ cup juice from the skillet into a small mixing bowl; add the cornstarch and stir until blended. Add the cornstarch mixture to the remaining juice in the skillet; stir to blend. Place over medium heat and cook until the mixture thickens, stirring constantly. Add the brandy; heat through. Pour over the apples; toss lightly.

To serve, surround the sliced or unsliced roast on the serving plate with the brandied apples. This recipe makes enough brandied apples to serve as a garnish with the Loin of Pork. If larger portions are desired, double the recipe.

WITH A 4-POUND PORK LOIN, SERVES 8 TO 12

SPARERIBS AND SAUERKRAUT

2 slabs (about 6 pounds) pork spareribs with
   brisket removed*
2 tablespoons butter
1 large onion, sliced and separated into rings
1 cup water
½ teaspoon salt
½ teaspoon pepper
1½ pounds russet potatoes, pared and cut in
   half or into thirds, depending upon size
32 ounces commercial, fresh sauerkraut
1 tablespoon caraway seed

1 tablespoon packed light brown sugar
2 cups pared, quartered, cored, and sliced
   Golden Delicious apples (about 1 large or
   2 medium-small apples)
Paprika for decoration

** Have the butcher cut each slab into 3
approximately equal pieces.*

Parboil (page 7) the spareribs for 10 minutes in a large kettle to remove fat and tenderize. Drain the spareribs; set aside.

Preheat the oven to 350°F.

In a large, heavy roaster, melt the butter over medium-high heat. Tilt the roaster back and forth to completely cover the bottom with the melted butter. Add the onions; sauté until well browned (about 10 minutes), turning often. Remove from the heat; let the roaster stand until cooled slightly. Add 1 cup water to the roaster; stir briefly to combine with the onions; set aside.

In a small sauce dish, place the salt and pepper; stir to combine; set aside. Place the spareribs in the roaster, meaty side up. Sprinkle the combined salt and pepper over each of the 6 pieces of spareribs. Cover the roaster. Bake the spareribs for 1 hour.

Place the potatoes around and over the spareribs; cover the roaster. Bake an additional 1 hour. Meanwhile, in a colander, drain the sauerkraut well. In a large mixing bowl, place the drained sauerkraut, caraway seed, and brown sugar; stir to combine. Cover with plastic wrap; set aside. Near the end of the second hour of baking the spareribs, prepare the apples and add to the sauerkraut mixture; stir to combine. Cover and set aside.

After 2 hours of baking the spareribs, remove the roaster from the oven. Remove the potatoes from the roaster and place in a bowl. Move the spareribs to one side of the roaster. Place the sauerkraut mixture on the other side of the roaster next to the spareribs. Return the potatoes to the roaster, placing them around and over the spareribs. Cover the roaster. Bake for an additional 1 hour.

To serve, place 1 piece of the spareribs on each of 6 individual dinner or oval steak plates. Place 1 or 2 potato pieces on each plate next to the spareribs. Sprinkle the potatoes lightly with paprika for decoration. Remove the remaining potatoes from the roaster and place in a bowl. Stir the sauerkraut together with the onions and juices in the bottom of the roaster. Using a large, slotted spoon, place a serving of drained sauerkraut on each plate. Place the remaining drained sauerkraut in a serving bowl; arrange the remaining potatoes around the periphery of the bowl over the sauerkraut. Pass at the table for additional helpings.

SERVES 6

PORK AND NOODLES CASSEROLE WITH SAGE-Y RED SAUCE

1 pound lean, ground pork
1 15-ounce can tomato sauce
2 teaspoons dried leaf sage
2 teaspoons dried parsley
¾ teaspoon salt
⅛ teaspoon black pepper
Dash of cayenne pepper*
15 ounces ricotta cheese
¼ cup commercial sour cream
¼ cup finely chopped onions
2 tablespoons snipped, fresh chives
2 tablespoons finely chopped green bell peppers
8 cups water
8 ounces (about 4 cups) egg noodles
2 tablespoons butter, melted
Sprig of fresh sage for decoration (optional)

For more spicy flavor, use ⅛ teaspoon cayenne pepper.

In a large, heavy-bottomed skillet, brown the ground pork well over medium heat, using a large, metal mixing spoon to break up the meat and stir often. Remove from the heat. When cooled slightly, add the tomato sauce, sage, parsley, salt, black pepper, and cayenne pepper;

stir to combine; set aside. In a medium bowl, place the ricotta cheese, sour cream, onions, chives, and green peppers; stir until completely combined; set aside.

Preheat the oven to 375°F. Butter a 7 × 11-inch baking dish; set aside.

In a large saucepan, bring 8 cups water to a boil over high heat. Add the noodles and boil until just tender (about 8 minutes), stirring frequently. Drain the noodles in a sieve and rinse well under hot, running water. Rinse and dry the saucepan in which the noodles were cooked; return the noodles to the saucepan. Drizzle the melted butter over the noodles; using a wooden spoon, toss to coat.

Place ½ of the noodles in the prepared baking dish; distribute evenly over the bottom of the dish. Spoon the ricotta cheese mixture over the noodles and spread evenly. Add the remaining ½ noodles; distribute evenly over the ricotta cheese mixture. Spoon the meat mixture evenly over all. Bake, uncovered, for 30 minutes. Cut into 8 servings. Decorate with a sprig of fresh sage, if available. Serve with a spatula.

SERVES 8

BISCUITS AND GRAVY MADEIRA

1 recipe raw sausage mixture (page 160) (do not make sausage mixture into patties and do not cook)
½ cup all-purpose flour
½ teaspoon salt
½ teaspoon pepper
1 cup whole milk
¼ cup (4 tablespoons) butter
2 cups homemade Beef Broth (page 70) or 1 14-ounce can commercial beef broth
1 cup whole milk
¼ cup Madeira wine
1 recipe Baking Powder Biscuits (page 380)

Place the sausage mixture in an electric skillet or a large, heavy skillet on the range over medium-

(Recipe continues on next page)

low heat (300°F in an electric skillet). Using a large, metal mixing spoon, break up the sausage mixture into small pieces as it cooks and stir often. Cook the sausage until completely done, with no pink remaining, and browned slightly. When done, reduce the skillet heat to very low (210°F in an electric skillet). Using a slotted spoon, remove the sausage from the skillet and place it in a small mixing bowl; set aside. In a small glass jar or plastic container with a secure lid, place the flour, salt, and pepper; stir to combine. Add 1 cup milk; cover and shake vigorously until blended; set aside.

When the skillet cools to the reduced temperature, add the butter. When the butter melts, add the beef broth and deglaze the skillet completely. Add 1 cup milk, Madeira wine, and the flour mixture; stir to blend. Bring the mixture to a simmer, stirring constantly (increase the heat very slightly, if necessary). Simmer the mixture 2 minutes, until thick and blended, stirring continuously. Add the sausage and stir to combine; heat through (see Note).

Make the Baking Powder Biscuits as near serving time as possible and serve piping hot in a cloth-lined roll basket. Serve the gravy in an appropriate serving bowl or tureen with a large serving ladle. To eat this dish, diners split 1 or 2 biscuits in half, place the biscuit halves open-faced on their plates, and ladle gravy over the top.

NOTE: At this point in the procedure, the Gravy Madeira may be refrigerated in a covered container and reheated in a skillet at serving time.

SERVES 4

SAUSAGE PATTIES

1 pound ground pork
1½ teaspoons ground sage
¾ teaspoon dried, leaf summer savory
¾ teaspoon salt
¼ teaspoon pepper
Dash of cayenne pepper

Place the ground pork in a medium mixing bowl; set aside. In a small mixing bowl, place the sage, summer savory, salt, pepper, and cayenne pepper; stir to combine. Add the sage mixture to the ground pork; using your hands, mix until thoroughly combined. Pat the mixture in the bottom of the mixing bowl; using a knife, cut into 6 even portions. Using your hands, shape 6 patties ¾ inch thick and 2½ inches in diameter.

Place the patties in an ungreased, 9-inch, heavy-bottomed skillet. Over medium-low heat, fry the patties for 18 minutes, turning once after the first 10 minutes of frying. After frying 18 minutes, cover the skillet and continue cooking for an additional 5 minutes. The patties should be fried to a dark brown, but should not be crispy or burned. They should be well done with no pink remaining.

SERVES 3 TO 6

SMOKED PORK CHOPS WITH PRUNE-APPLE STUFFING

2 pounds yams
6 smoked rib pork chops, 1 to 1¼ inches thick
⅓ cup bite-sized pitted prunes cut into
⅜-inch cubes
1½ cups pared, quartered, cored, and chopped Golden Delicious apples
2 tablespoons packed light brown sugar
2 tablespoons ginger preserves
2 tablespoons freshly squeezed orange juice
1 teaspoon finely grated orange rind
(page 31)

1 tablespoon vegetable shortening
1 tablespoon butter
½ cup water
Dash of salt
Dash of white pepper

Using a vegetable brush, scrub the yams. Place the unpared yams in a large saucepan; add hot water to cover. Cover the saucepan. Bring the yams to a boil over high heat; reduce the heat and cook at a low boil for 15 minutes. Drain the yams and place on a wire rack; let stand to cool. Then, peel the yams, removing the thin layer of flesh under the skin to reveal the bright orange flesh. Cut the yams widthwise into approximately 2-inch slices; set aside.

Using a sharp knife, slit each pork chop laterally through the center from the meaty side to ½ inch from the bone edge to form a pocket; set aside. In a small mixing bowl, place the prunes, apples, brown sugar, ginger preserves, orange juice, and orange rind; stir to combine. Fill the pockets in the pork chops with the prune mixture. Break 6 toothpicks in half and skewer each pocket closed with 2 toothpick halves; set aside. Preheat the oven to 350°F.

In an electric skillet or a large, heavy-bottomed skillet on the range, melt the shortening over medium heat (350°F in an electric skillet). Using a spatula, spread the melted shortening over the entire bottom of the skillet. Add the butter. Tilt the skillet back and forth to blend the butter with the melted shortening. Place the pork chops in the skillet; brown on both sides, turning once (about 7 to 8 minutes on each side). Place the chops in a heavy roaster; set aside. Reduce the skillet heat to very low (220°F in an electric skillet).

When the skillet cools to the reduced temperature, pour ½ cup water into the skillet and deglaze. Pour the skillet liquid over and around the chops. Arrange the yams around the chops. Sprinkle the yams with a dash of salt and white pepper. Cover the roaster.

Bake the pork chops and yams for 35 minutes, basting twice during baking and again just before serving. *Remove all toothpicks before serv-*ing. Pour the drippings in the roaster into a gravy boat and pass at the table as additional sauce for the yams. (If necessary, strain the sauce in a sieve.)

SERVES 6

HAM BAKED IN SHERRY SAUCE

1 8- to 9-pound full-muscle,* boneless, best-quality, fully cooked ham**
1½ cups cream sherry
1 cup (½ pint) apricot jam
1 cup honey
2 tablespoons cornstarch
¼ teaspoon ground cinnamon
2 cups cream sherry

* *Some retail hams consist of smaller pieces of meat pressed together with water and formed. Full-muscle hams are whole, uncut-up sections of meat.*

** *To prepare a 3½- to 4-pound piece of ham, halve the recipe ingredients and reduce the initial baking period from 2 hours to 1½ hours. (Maintain the final baking period of 50 minutes to 1 hour.)*

Preheat the oven to 325°F.

Place the ham in a shallow baking dish. Pour 1½ cups sherry over the ham. Bake, uncovered, for 2 hours, basting occasionally.

Meanwhile, in a medium saucepan, place the apricot jam, honey, cornstarch, cinnamon, and 2 cups sherry; stir to combine. Cook the mixture over medium heat until clear and slightly thickened, stirring constantly; cover and set aside.

At the end of the 2-hour baking period, pour the sherry sauce over the ham. Bake, uncovered, for an additional 50 minutes to 1 hour, basting at least twice.

To serve, slice the ham and arrange on a serving platter. Spoon hot sherry sauce from the baking dish into a sauceboat and pass at the table.

EACH POUND OF HAM SERVES 4

TRADITIONAL BAKED HAM

1 8- to 9-pound full-muscle,* boneless,
  best-quality, fully cooked ham
Whole cloves
1 20-ounce can sliced pineapple in pineapple
  juice
1 cup packed light brown sugar
2 tablespoons prepared mustard
1 tablespoon reserved pineapple juice
Maraschino cherries, cut in half lengthwise

 * *Some retail hams consist of smaller pieces
   of meat pressed together with water and
   formed. Full-muscle hams are whole,
   uncut-up sections of meat.*

Preheat the oven to 350°F.

Using a sharp knife, score the ham by making diagonal cuts, about ⅛ inch deep at ¾-inch intervals, in 2 directions over the surface of the ham, forming a diamond pattern. Insert a whole clove in the ham at each point where the scoring lines cross. Wrap and seal the ham in heavy-duty aluminum foil; place in a shallow baking pan. Bake for 3 hours.

Meanwhile, near the end of the 3-hour baking period, drain the pineapple in a sieve, reserving the juice. Set the juice aside. Place the pineapple slices in a bowl; cover and set aside. In a medium bowl, place the brown sugar, mustard, and 1 tablespoon reserved pineapple juice; stir until blended; set aside. (Reserve the remaining pineapple juice for other uses.)

When the ham has baked 3 hours, remove it from the oven. Reduce the oven temperature to 325°F. Open the aluminum foil and place the pineapple slices, single layer, on top of the ham, securing the slices with short toothpicks, if necessary. (Reserve any remaining pineapple slices for other uses.) Place a maraschino cherry half, cut side down, in the center of each pineapple slice. Pour the brown sugar mixture over the ham.

Return the ham to the oven, leaving the aluminum foil open. Bake an additional 30 minutes, basting 3 or 4 times. *Before serving, remove any toothpicks which may have been used to secure the pineapple slices.*

EACH POUND OF HAM SERVES 4

HAM AND YAM CASSEROLE

1½ pounds yams
2 cups fully cooked ham cut into bite-sized
  pieces
1½ cups pared, quartered, cored, and sliced
  Golden Delicious apples
¼ teaspoon salt
¼ teaspoon paprika
½ cup packed light brown sugar
2 tablespoons bourbon
2 tablespoons butter

Using a vegetable brush, scrub the yams well. Place the unpared yams in a large saucepan; add hot water to cover. Cover the saucepan. Bring the yams to a boil over high heat; reduce the heat to medium and cook at a low boil for 15 minutes. Drain the yams and place them on a wire rack; let stand until cool.

Preheat the oven to 350°F. Butter a 2-quart round baking dish; set aside.

Peel the yams, removing the thin layer of flesh directly beneath the skin to reveal the bright orange flesh. Slice the yams ¾ inch thick (about 4 cups sliced yams). Arrange ½ of the yams in the bottom of the prepared baking dish. Distribute the ham evenly over the yams; then, distribute the apples evenly over the ham. Arrange the remaining yams over the apples; sprinkle with salt and paprika; set aside. In a small mixing bowl, place the brown sugar and bourbon; stir to combine. Sprinkle the brown sugar mixture evenly over the ingredients in the baking dish. Dot with butter.

Bake, covered, for 20 minutes. Baste; then bake, uncovered, for an additional 25 minutes. Baste and serve.

SERVES 6

HAM STEAK WITH GLAZED PINEAPPLE

1 2-pound center-sliced, smoked ham steak,
   ¾ to 1 inch thick
1 tablespoon vegetable shortening
Glazed Pineapple (recipe follows)
Sprigs of fresh parsley for decoration

In an electric skillet or a heavy skillet on the range, melt the shortening over medium-low heat (330°F in an electric skillet). Using a spatula, spread the melted shortening over the entire bottom of the skillet. Place the ham steak in the heated skillet; fry 8 minutes on each side (16 minutes total), turning once. Serve on a platter with Glazed Pineapple. Decorate with sprigs of parsley.

SERVES 4

GLAZED PINEAPPLE

1 8-ounce can pineapple slices in their own
   juice (4 slices)
2 tablespoons packed light brown sugar
1 teaspoon vegetable oil
2 teaspoons butter

Drain the pineapple in a sieve, reserving the juice. Set the pineapple aside. Measure 2 tablespoons reserved juice and place in a small mixing bowl. (Reserve the remaining pineapple juice for other uses.) Add the brown sugar to the 2 tablespoons pineapple juice; stir to combine; set aside.

In a medium-small, heavy skillet, heat the vegetable oil over medium-high heat. Using a spatula, spread the vegetable oil over the entire bottom of the skillet. Add the butter. Tilt the skillet back and forth to blend the butter with the oil. Arrange the pineapple slices, single layer, in the skillet. Spoon the brown sugar mixture over the pineapple; sauté for 10 minutes, turning once or twice with a spatula.

HAM LOAF WITH HORSERADISH SAUCE

1 14½-ounce can whole, peeled tomatoes
1 pound ground, fully cooked ham
½ pound lean, pure ground beef
½ pound lean, ground pork
2 cups bran flakes, rolled (about 1 cup rolled
   flakes)
3 extra-large eggs
¾ cup chopped onions
½ cup chopped green bell peppers
¼ teaspoon pepper
1 recipe Horseradish Sauce (page 297)

Preheat the oven to 350°F. Grease a 9 × 13-inch baking dish; set aside.

In a sieve, drain the tomatoes well; reserve the juice for other uses. In a large mixing bowl, place the drained tomatoes, ground ham, ground beef, ground pork, bran flakes crumbs, eggs, onions, green peppers, and pepper; using a large, metal mixing spoon, break up the ground meats and combine the ingredients well. Using your hands, form the meat mixture into an oval loaf and place it in the prepared dish. Bake, uncovered, for 1½ hours.

To serve, place the ham loaf on a warm, oval serving platter. Cut the loaf into ⅝-inch slices widthwise; then, cut the loaf in half lengthwise, creating 2 pieces of ham loaf per slice. Supply a small serving spatula or a serving fork for serving the ham loaf slices. Pass the Horseradish Sauce in a sauce dish at the table.

SERVES 8

GLAZED HAM LOAF

1½ pounds ground, fully cooked ham
½ pound lean ground pork
½ pound lean, pure ground beef
22 graham cracker squares, rolled finely
   (about 1⅔ cups)
1 cup whole milk

(Recipe continues on next page)

2 extra-large eggs
¼ teaspoon pepper
Glaze (recipe follows)

Preheat the oven to 350°F. Grease a 9 × 13-inch baking dish; set aside.

In a large mixing bowl, place the ground ham, ground pork, ground beef, graham cracker crumbs, milk, eggs, and pepper; using a large, metal mixing spoon, break up the ground meats and combine the ingredients well. Using your hands, form the meat mixture into an oval loaf and place it in the prepared dish. Bake, uncovered, for 1 hour.

Meanwhile, make the glaze; cover and set aside. When the ham loaf has baked 1 hour, remove it from the oven. Using a baster, draw off and discard any excess fat which has accumulated on the bottom of the dish. Pour the glaze over the loaf and continue baking, uncovered, for ½ hour, basting at least 3 times.

To serve, cut the ham loaf into ⅝-inch slices widthwise; then, cut the loaf in half lengthwise, creating 2 pieces of ham loaf per slice. Serve 2 pieces overlapping, on each individual plate. Spoon a little glaze over the ham loaf slices. Pour the remaining glaze into a sauceboat and pass at the table.

SERVES 8

GLAZE

1 cup packed dark brown sugar
2 tablespoons dry mustard
½ cup red wine vinegar
½ cup water
Dash of ground cloves

In a small mixing bowl, place the brown sugar, dry mustard, vinegar, water, and cloves; stir to combine. Do not cook.

ACCOMPANIMENT SUGGESTION: Serve with Carrot Puree (page 260–261). To serve, place the uncut ham loaf on a serving platter. Using a decorating bag fit with large open-star tip number 8B (page 319), pipe small servings of Carrot Puree on the platter around the ham loaf. Decorate the platter with sprigs of fresh parsley. Cut the ham loaf at the table. Provide the server with a small spatula for use in transferring the decorative portions of Carrot Puree from the serving platter to individual dinner plates.

HAM PINWHEELS WITH CHEESE SAUCE

¼ cup plus 2 tablespoons (6 tablespoons) butter, softened
¼ cup plus 1 tablespoon prepared mustard
3 cups ground, fully cooked ham
1 recipe Baking Powder Biscuits dough (page 380)
1 recipe Cheese Sauce (page 303)

Preheat the oven to 450°F. Grease two 7 × 11-inch shallow baking pans; set aside.

In a medium mixing bowl, place the butter and mustard; stir to blend. Add the ham; stir to combine; set aside. Make the Baking Powder Biscuit dough. Using a stockinet-covered and lightly-floured rolling pin (page 38), roll out the biscuit dough on a floured pastry cloth to a rectangle approximately 12 × 15 inches. (The biscuit dough will be a little less than ¼ inch thick.)

Spread the ham mixture evenly over the dough. Starting from one of the short sides of the rectangle, roll the dough and ham mixture jelly-roll fashion. With a sharp, thin-bladed knife, cut the 15-inch-long roll into ten 1½-inch slices. Place the pinwheels on the floured pastry cloth. Using a small, floured spatula, flatten each pinwheel to about 1-inch thickness. Place the pinwheels in the prepared baking pans.

Bake the pinwheels for 12 to 15 minutes. Pass warm Cheese Sauce at the table.

SERVES 8 TO 10

Other Pork Recipes

Deluxe Eggplant Stuffed with Ham (page 266)
Eggplant and Ham Casserole (page 266)
Gary's Hickory-Smoked Pork Ribs (page 208–210)
Grilled Iowa Pork Chops (page 207)
Pigs in a Cornfield (page 263)
Pork Chop Dinner in Foil (page 249–250)
Pork Roast with Tangy Rosemary Sauce (page 211)
Scalloped Potatoes with Ham (page 278)

Lamb

BABY LAMB CHOPS

(See photo insert page B-5)

Baby (spring) loin lamb chops, 1¼ to 1½ inches thick (about ⅓ pound per chop)
1 garlic clove
Dash of garlic salt (optional)

Preheat the broiler.

Using a small, sharp knife, slit the fat on the sides of each chop 2 or 3 times at 1-inch intervals to prevent the meat from curling during broiling. When slitting the fat, be careful not to penetrate the meat flesh, causing loss of meat juices. Rub the broiler rack with a small piece of fat; place the rack over the broiler pan. Cut the garlic clove in half lengthwise. Rub both sides of the chops with the cut sides of the garlic. Arrange the chops on the broiler rack; sprinkle lightly with garlic salt, if desired.

Broil the chops 3 inches from the heat. For medium-done chops, broil 6 minutes on each side. For medium-rare chops, broil 5 minutes on each side. For rare chops (see Note), broil 4 minutes on each side. For well-done chops, broil 7 to 8 minutes on each side.

NOTE: There is some bacterial risk when lamb is consumed rare (140°F) (see Meat Safety, page 134).

ROAST LEG OF LAMB WITH MINT JELLY GLAZE

Shank half of a leg of lamb (4 to 5 pounds)*
1 large garlic clove, cut into 5 slices
½ teaspoon salt
¼ teaspoon pepper
¼ cup mint jelly
⅛ teaspoon garlic salt
1 recipe Roast Lamb Gravy (page 313)
Additional mint jelly, if desired

To roast a full leg of lamb, follow this recipe, making no changes, including ingredient amounts.

Preheat the oven to 325°F.

Using a small knife, cut 5 small gashes, equally spaced, around the top and sides of the lamb. Insert one garlic slice in each gash. If the end of the leg bone has been stripped of meat, cover the bone with aluminum foil to prevent overbrowning. Place the lamb, fat side up, on a wire rack in a shallow roasting pan. Sprinkle salt and pepper over the roast. Insert a meat thermometer into the center of the lamb, making certain that the tip of the thermometer is not touching the bone.

Place the lamb, uncovered, in the oven. For well-done lamb, roast until the meat thermometer reaches 170°F (about 30 to 35 minutes per

(Recipe continues on next page)

pound). For medium-done lamb, roast until the meat thermometer reaches 160°F (about 25 to 30 minutes per pound). For medium-rare lamb, roast until the meat thermometer reaches 150°F (about 20 to 25 minutes per pound). Remove the lamb from the oven when the thermometer reaches 5°F below desired temperature, as the meat will continue cooking.

30 MINUTES BEFORE LAMB IS DONE: In the a small saucepan, place the mint jelly and garlic salt; heat over low heat until the jelly melts, stirring occasionally. Brush the mint glaze over the lamb 3 times during the last 20 minutes of roasting.

TO SERVE LEG OF LAMB: When the meat thermometer registers 5°F below the desired temperature, remove the lamb from the oven and place it on a platter; cover loosely with aluminum foil to keep warm while making Roast Lamb Gravy. The lamb may be sliced at the table or in the kitchen. Pour the gravy into a gravy boat and pass at the table. Unmelted mint jelly may be served at the table, if desired.

SERVES 6

DAY TWO LEG OF LAMB

This dish reflects a common way to turn leftover roast (beef, veal, pork, or lamb), gravy, and vegetables into a tasty new dish for dinner the next evening. In the case of this recipe, there are no leftover vegetables from the preparation of Roast Leg of Lamb with Mint Jelly Glaze (page 165–166), so newly cooked carrots, mushrooms, and onions are combined with the leftover lamb and gravy.

1¼ cups carrots, pared and sliced ⅛ inch
   thick (about 3 carrots)
2 tablespoons butter
1½ cups sliced, fresh mushrooms
2 tablespoons butter
1 cup coarsely chopped onions
1 garlic clove, pressed

4 cups cold, cubed, cooked Leg of Lamb
   (above)
2 cups leftover Roast Lamb Gravy
   (page 313)*

*If there are less than 2 cups of leftover gravy, place ½ cup of the liquid in which the carrots were cooked, and 1 tablespoon flour in a small glass jar or plastic container with a secure lid; cover and shake vigorously until blended. Add to all the ingredients before heating (double the liquid and flour, if needed).

Boil the carrots (page 3); drain (reserve the liquid, if needed [see Note, above]). Set the carrots aside. In a small, heavy-bottomed skillet, melt 2 tablespoons butter over medium heat. Tilt the skillet back and forth to completely cover the bottom with the melted butter. Place the mushrooms in the skillet; sauté until the mushrooms give up their juices (about 5 minutes). Remove from the heat. Using a slotted spoon, remove the mushrooms from the skillet and place in a small bowl; set aside.

Return the skillet to medium heat; add 2 tablespoons butter. When the butter melts, add the onions and garlic; sauté until the onions are transparent and tender (about 5 minutes). Remove from the heat.

In a heavy saucepan, place the cubed lamb, lamb gravy, drained carrots, mushrooms, and onion mixture; stir to combine. Place over medium-high heat; bring to a simmer and cook for 2 minutes, stirring intermittently.

SERVING SUGGESTIONS: Serve Day Two Leg of Lamb over Mashed Potatoes (page 279), egg noodles, or Perfect Boiled Rice (page 228).

Poultry and Stuffings
(Dressings)

Poultry and Stuffings (Dressings) Safety

All poultry sold commercially in the United States must be officially inspected by the Food Safety and Inspection Service of the U.S. Department of Agriculture to ensure that it is wholesome, properly labeled, and not adulterated. Proper handling by the consumer is equally important to ensure that safe poultry is served at the table. To help inform consumers, the USDA requires that safe handling and cooking instructions be placed on all packages of raw poultry, including any poultry product not considered ready-to-eat.

For further assistance, consumers may call the U.S. Department of Agriculture's Meat and Poultry Hotline at 888-674-6854 (TTY at 800-256-7072), Monday through Friday, 10:00 A.M.–4:00 P.M. Eastern time; or visit the Food Safety and Inspection Service Web site at www.fsis.usda.gov; or email at mphotline.fsis@usda.gov.

The following are basic guidelines for the safe storage, handling, and cooking of poultry:

- Cook poultry to the following internal temperatures:

Poultry Product	Internal Temperature and Indication
Whole poultry	180° F—Juices run clear when thigh is pierced with a fork; legs move easily; meat is fork-tender
Poultry breasts, roasts	170° F—Juices run clear; meat is fork-tender
Poultry thighs, drumsticks, and wings	170° F—Juices run clear

- Use a meat thermometer to accurately gauge the internal temperature of whole poultry (see page 28–29) and poultry breasts (roasts).

   Although poultry technically is safe when cooked to an internal temperature of 165°F, most people do not consider the texture or taste to be as palatable as when cooked to the temperatures given above. Always cook ground poultry to 165°F as bacteria can spread throughout ground poultry during processing.

- Keep raw poultry stored in the refrigerator at 40°F or below, or in the freezer at 0°F or below. Cook fresh poultry within 1 or 2 days or freeze it.

- Thaw poultry in the refrigerator, in the microwave oven (see Food Safety: Microwave Ovens, page 15–16, for procedural information), or in cold water, changing the water every 30 minutes. Do not thaw poultry at room temperature on the kitchen counter or in the sink as surface bacteria on thawed portions of the poultry can multiply to illness-causing levels before inner portions have thawed.

   Poultry thawed in the refrigerator may be kept refrigerated 1 to 2 days after thawing. Poultry thawed in the microwave oven or in cold water should be cooked immediately after thawing.

   Keep poultry thawed in cold water in a leakproof package or a zipper-seal plastic bag during thawing to prevent bacteria in the surrounding environment from being introduced into the food, and to prevent the poultry tissues from absorbing water, resulting in a watery product.

- Thoroughly rinse raw, thawed poultry under cold, running water, and dry it with paper towels before cooking.

- Throw away poultry packaging material.

- Completely cook poultry at one time. Do not partially cook it, refrigerate it, and then complete the cooking at a later time.

- Stuff whole poultry *just before* cooking. Mix dry stuffing (dressing) ingredients with other stuffing (dressing) ingredients, such as butter and broth, just before stuffing the bird. Stuff the bird fairly loosely, as the stuffing (dressing) will expand during cooking. Cook stuffing (dressing) in the bird or separately, to 165°F; use a meat thermometer or instant thermometer to check the temperature.

- Place cooked poultry on a clean platter, not on the unwashed platter that held the raw poultry.

- Refrigerate poultry within 2 hours after cooking. Remove the stuffing (dressing) from the bird and refrigerate it in a separate container. For quicker cooling, it is best to remove the meat from the bones before refrigeration. If there is a large quantity of leftover poultry, store it in several shallow containers to expedite cooling.

- Use refrigerated, leftover poultry and stuffing (dressing) within 3 to 4 days, or freeze these foods. If leftover poultry is covered with gravy or broth, use it within 1 to 2 days or freeze it. Eat cooked leftover poultry cold, or reheat it to at least 165°F (steaming hot).

- Wash your hands with soap and hot water before and after handling raw or cooked poultry. Wash kitchen tools and equipment, cutting boards and other work surfaces, sink, and faucet handles with hot, soapy water after they come in contact with raw or cooked poultry, and before they come in contact with other food.

Chicken

COOKED CHICKEN
For Salads and Other Dishes

4 pounds split chicken breasts *with* skin*
  (may have attached ribs)
1 tablespoon butter, melted

*While the breast is the most desirable chicken part to use in salads and most dishes, any other parts of choice may be substituted. Baking chicken pieces with the skin on and then removing the skin after baking results in more moist cut-up chicken.

Preheat the oven to 350°F.

Wash the chicken under cold, running water and place it between several layers of paper towels to dry. When dry, place the chicken breasts, single layer, skin side up, in an ungreased 9 × 13-inch baking dish. Brush the chicken with the melted butter. Cover the baking dish tightly with aluminum foil, leaving space between the foil and the chicken. Bake for 1¼ hours, until fork-tender.

While the chicken is hot, remove the skin and bones; discard. Place the breasts in a container or bowl; cover and refrigerate. When the chicken is cold, cut into desired pieces.

MAKES ABOUT 4 CUPS COOKED, CUT-UP CHICKEN

BAKED CUT-UP CHICKEN

3 to 4 pounds cut-up chicken with skin
  (chicken parts of choice)
2 tablespoons butter
⅛ teaspoon salt
Dash of white pepper
2 teaspoons snipped, fresh summer savory or
  ¾ teaspoon dried leaf summer savory

Preheat the oven to 350°F. Butter lightly a
9 × 13-inch baking dish.

Wash the chicken pieces under cold, running
water and place them between several layers of
paper towels to dry. When dry, place the chicken
pieces, single layer, skin side down, in the prepared
baking dish. Dot the chicken with the butter.

Bake the chicken, uncovered, for 30 minutes.
Turn the chicken pieces over; sprinkle with salt,
pepper, and savory. Bake, uncovered, for an
additional 30 minutes, until fork-tender.

SERVES 6 TO 8

CHICKEN BREASTS STUFFED WITH SPINACH AND MUSHROOMS

A nice party-time entrée for luncheons or dinners.

8 whole, boneless chicken breasts *with* skin,
  cut in half lengthwise
1½ pounds fresh spinach
3 tablespoons butter
⅔ cup finely chopped onions
8 ounces finely chopped, fresh mushrooms
1 tablespoon dry white wine
⅓ cup Ritz cracker crumbs (about 8 finely
  rolled crackers)
1 extra-large egg, slightly beaten
2 teaspoons freshly squeezed, strained lemon
  juice
½ cup fresh parsley leaves (stems removed)
1 teaspoon dried leaf tarragon

¾ teaspoon salt
¼ teaspoon pepper
¼ cup (4 tablespoons) butter, melted

Wash the chicken breasts under cold, running
water and place them between several layers of
paper towels to dry; set aside.

Cut the stems off the spinach leaves; discard
the stems. Wash the spinach leaves twice. Place
the spinach in a large kettle and add water to
cover. Cover the kettle. Bring the spinach to a
boil over high heat. Reduce the heat and simmer 4 minutes. Drain the spinach in a colander;
with your hand, press the spinach to remove as
much liquid as possible. Using a sharp knife,
chop the spinach (about 1 cup cooked and
chopped spinach); set aside.

Preheat the oven to 350°F. Butter a 9 × 13-
inch baking dish; set aside.

In a heavy-bottomed skillet, melt 3 tablespoons butter over medium-high heat. Tilt the
skillet back and forth to completely cover the
bottom with the melted butter. Place the onions
in the skillet; sauté 1 minute. Then, add the
mushrooms; sauté an additional 4 minutes,
until very little liquid remains in the skillet.
Remove the skillet from the heat and let cool
slightly. Add the white wine and stir in; set
aside. In a large mixing bowl, place the spinach,
onion mixture, crumbs, egg, lemon juice, parsley, tarragon, salt, pepper, and ¼ cup melted
butter; stir until well combined; set aside.

Using your fingers, open a 2½-inch-wide
pocket between the skin and flesh on the side
opposite the cut side of each chicken breast.
Stuff the pocket of each breast with 1 heaping
tablespoon of stuffing. Pull the skin over the
stuffing and under the side of each breast; secure
with half a toothpick. Tuck the extra skin on
both ends of each breast under the breast and
place, single layer, in the prepared baking dish.

Bake the chicken breasts, uncovered, for 50
minutes. *Remove the toothpicks before serving.*

SERVES 16

ACCOMPANIMENT SUGGESTION: Serve with Baked
Rice (page 231).

CHICKEN DIVAN

(See photo insert page B-1)

A true American classic that continues to thread across the generations—you just can't go wrong serving Chicken Divan, for luncheons, dinners, suppers, buffets, and family meals.

1 recipe (4 pounds) Cooked Chicken breasts (page 169) skinned, boned (if any bones), and refrigerated. Reserve and refrigerate baking-dish juices in a separate, covered bowl
7 cups fresh broccoli spears
2 recipes Thick White Sauce (page 301–302), substituting 1 cup whole milk and 1 cup chicken broth (homemade, page 70–71, or commercially canned) for 2 cups whole milk
1 cup Miracle Whip dressing
3 tablespoons freshly squeezed, strained lemon juice
½ teaspoon curry powder
2 tablespoons freshly grated Parmesan cheese (page 30)

Preheat the oven to 350°F. Butter lightly a 9 × 13-inch baking dish; set aside.

Cut the cold chicken breasts widthwise into ³⁄₁₆-inch slices; arrange in the bottom of the prepared baking dish; set aside. Steam the broccoli spears (page 252) until just tender (about 5 minutes). Place the steamed broccoli spears in a colander and rinse under cold, running water to stop the cooking; let stand to drain well.

Skim the congealed fat off the top of the cold chicken baking-dish juices and discard; use the remaining chicken broth to make Thick White Sauce (see recipe ingredients, above). If necessary, add homemade (page 70–71) or commercially canned chicken broth to make 1 cup broth. Add the dressing, lemon juice, and curry powder to the white sauce; using a handheld electric mixer, beat on low speed only until blended and smooth. Set aside.

Arrange the drained broccoli spears over the chicken in the baking dish. Pour the white sauce mixture evenly over the broccoli spears. Sprinkle the Parmesan cheese evenly over all. Bake, uncovered, until the Chicken Divan bubbles (about 30 minutes).

SERVES 8

SESAME CHICKEN BREASTS

2 whole, skinless, boneless chicken breasts, cut in half lengthwise (1 to 1¼ pounds total chicken breasts)
⅓ cup chicken broth, homemade (page 70–71) or commercially canned
¼ cup dry white wine
1 tablespoon freshly squeezed, strained lemon juice
1 tablespoon minced green onions (scallions), white part only
2 teaspoons honey
2 teaspoons extra-virgin olive oil
1 tablespoon butter
½ teaspoon lemon pepper, divided
2 tablespoons dry white wine
½ teaspoon cornstarch
1 teaspoon toasted sesame seeds (page 35)

Wash the chicken breasts under cold, running water and place them between several layers of paper towels to dry; set aside. In a small mixing bowl, place the chicken broth, ¼ cup white wine, lemon juice, onions, and honey; stir to combine. Cover with plastic wrap and set aside.

In a large, heavy-bottomed skillet, heat the olive oil over medium-high heat. Using a spatula, spread the olive oil over the entire bottom of the skillet. Add the butter. Tilt the skillet back and forth to blend the butter with the oil. Place the chicken breasts, single layer, skin side down, in the skillet. Sprinkle ¼ teaspoon of the lemon pepper over the breasts. Sauté the chicken breasts 3 minutes. Turn the breasts over and sprinkle with the remaining ¼ teaspoon lemon pepper. Sauté the breasts 3 minutes on the

(Recipe continues on next page)

second side. Reduce the heat to low. Remove the skillet from the heat and let cool slightly. Then, pour the chicken broth mixture around (not over) the breasts.

Cover the skillet and place over low heat. Bring the chicken breasts to a simmer; simmer gently 5 minutes. Do not overcook the breasts, causing them to become tough.

Place the chicken breasts on a platter and cover with aluminum foil to keep warm. Increase the heat under the skillet to high; cook until the skillet liquid reduces to about ⅔ cup. Meanwhile, in a small sauce dish, place 2 tablespoons white wine and cornstarch; stir until blended. Add the cornstarch mixture to the reduced skillet liquid; continue cooking until the sauce thickens, stirring continuously. Spoon the sauce over the chicken breasts; then, sprinkle the sesame seeds over top.

SERVES 4

CHICKEN BREASTS BAKED IN SHERRY SAUCE

4 whole, skinless, boneless chicken breasts,
    cut in half lengthwise (2 to 2½ pounds total
    chicken breasts)
3 tablespoons butter
3 tablespoons all-purpose flour
½ teaspoon celery salt
⅛ teaspoon white pepper
3 tablespoons butter
1 cup whole milk
8 ounces commercial sour cream
1 tablespoon butter
¼ cup minced celery
3 tablespoons minced leeks
1 tablespoon butter
¾ cup sliced, fresh mushrooms
1 teaspoon dried leaf chervil
¼ cup dry sherry

Preheat the oven to 325°F. Butter very lightly a 9 × 13-inch baking dish; set aside.

Wash the chicken breasts under cold, running water and place them between several layers of paper towels to dry; set aside.

In an electric skillet or a large, heavy-bottomed skillet on the range, melt 3 tablespoons butter over medium-low heat (320°F in an electric skillet). Tilt the skillet back and forth to completely cover the bottom with the melted butter. Place the chicken breasts in the skillet; brown lightly (2 minutes on each side). Drain the browned chicken breasts on 3 layers of paper towels. Then, arrange the chicken breasts, single layer, in the prepared baking dish; set aside.

In a small sauce dish, place the flour, celery salt, and white pepper; stir to combine; set aside. In a medium saucepan, melt 3 tablespoons butter over low heat. Remove from the heat. Add the flour mixture; stir until perfectly smooth. Add the milk; stir to combine. Place the saucepan over medium-low heat; cook the mixture until thick and just under boiling, stirring constantly. Do not allow the mixture to boil. Remove from the heat. Add the sour cream; stir until smooth and blended; set aside.

In a small, heavy-bottomed skillet, melt 1 tablespoon butter over medium heat. Do not let the butter brown. Place the celery in the skillet; sauté 4 minutes (do not brown). Remove from the heat. Using a slotted spoon, remove the sautéed celery (excluding pan juices) from the skillet and add to the sour cream mixture; set aside. Place the leeks in the skillet used for sautéing the celery; sauté 3 minutes over medium heat (do not brown). Remove from the heat. Using a slotted spoon, remove the sautéed leeks (excluding pan juices) from the skillet and add to the sour cream mixture; set aside.

Add 1 tablespoon butter to the skillet used for sautéing the celery and leeks. Melt the butter over medium heat. Place the mushrooms in the skillet; sauté 3 minutes, until the mushrooms give up their juices (do not brown). Add the mushrooms and pan juices, and the chervil and sherry to the sour cream mixture; stir until all ingredients are combined. Pour evenly over the chicken breasts. Bake, uncovered, for 40 minutes.

SERVES 8

SERVING SUGGESTION: Serve the chicken breasts on individual dinner plates over Perfect Boiled Rice (page 228). Spoon additional sherry sauce from the baking dish over all.

ROSEMARY CHICKEN BREASTS WITH RED RASPBERRY SAUCE

(See photo insert page B-3)

I hope you try (and like) this contemporary chicken breast recipe. It blends red raspberry vinegar, chicken broth, crème de cassis, and honey in a luscious sauce punctuated with whole, fresh raspberries. The sauce is spooned over boneless chicken breasts which have been sautéed over fresh rosemary.

2 whole, skinless, boneless chicken breasts, cut in half lengthwise (1 to 1¼ pounds total chicken breasts)
⅔ cup chicken broth, homemade (page 70-71) or commercially canned
3 tablespoons red raspberry vinegar
1 tablespoon crème de cassis (page 4)
2 tablespoons honey
2 teaspoons cornstarch
¼ teaspoon salt
⅛ teaspoon white pepper
1 tablespoon vegetable oil
1 tablespoon butter
1 teaspoon snipped, fresh rosemary
5 drops liquid red food coloring (optional)
½ cup fresh red raspberries, washed and well drained
4 sprigs of fresh rosemary for decoration

Wash the chicken breasts under cold, running water and place them between several layers of paper towels to dry; set aside. In a small saucepan, place the chicken broth, vinegar, crème de cassis, honey, cornstarch, salt, and white pepper; stir until blended; set aside.

In a large, heavy-bottomed skillet, heat the vegetable oil over medium-high heat. Using a spatula, spread the vegetable oil over the entire bottom of the skillet. Add the butter. Tilt the skillet back and forth to blend the butter with the oil. Sprinkle the rosemary evenly over the bottom of the skillet. Then, place the chicken breasts, single layer, skin side down, in the skillet. Sauté the breasts 3 minutes on each side, until cooked through, turning once.

Meanwhile, place the saucepan containing the raspberry vinegar mixture over medium heat; bring the mixture to a low boil, stirring constantly. Boil the mixture 5 minutes until clear, thickened, and slightly reduced, stirring often. Remove from the heat; add the food coloring (if used) and stir until blended. Add the raspberries; return to medium heat, and quickly heat through without stirring, to prevent breaking up the raspberries. Remove from the heat; cover to keep warm and set aside.

After the chicken breasts have been sautéed 3 minutes on each side, remove from the heat; cover and let stand 1 minute. To serve, place the chicken breasts, skin side up, on individual dinner plates. Carefully spoon the raspberry sauce over each chicken breast. Decorate each plate with a sprig of fresh rosemary.

SERVES 4

SERVING SUGGESTION: Serve the chicken breasts on individual plates over Perfect Boiled Rice (page 228).

CHICKEN THIGHS WITH PEACH-APRICOT GLAZE

3½ to 4 pounds chicken thighs* with skin
2 tablespoons butter
⅓ cup peach jam
⅓ cup apricot jam
2 teaspoons cider vinegar

(Recipe continues on next page)

2 teaspoons soy sauce
1 teaspoon dry mustard

*Any other chicken parts of choice may be
  substituted.*

Preheat the oven to 350°F. Butter lightly a
9 × 13-inch baking dish; set aside.

Wash the chicken thighs under cold, running water and dry between several layers of
paper towels. Place the chicken thighs, single
layer, skin side down, in the prepared baking
dish; dot with the butter. Bake, uncovered, for
40 minutes.

Meanwhile, in a small mixing bowl, place the
peach jam, apricot jam, vinegar, soy sauce, and
dry mustard; stir until evenly combined.

After 40 minutes baking, turn the chicken
over and spoon ½ of the jam mixture (glaze)
over the thighs. Bake, uncovered, for an additional 10 minutes. Spoon the remaining ½ glaze
over the thighs. Bake for an additional 10 minutes, until fork-tender.

SERVES 6 TO 8

CHICKEN À LA KING

*This is one of those grand old dishes which never
goes out of style. The origin of this refined chicken
fare is a matter of debate. However, published
records verify its existence in the early twentieth
century, and some argue that it dates back to the
last quarter of the nineteenth century. One thing
we can say with certainty: it will remain popular
in this century!*

3 tablespoons butter
3 cups sliced, fresh mushrooms (about
  8 ounces mushrooms)
2 tablespoons very finely chopped onions
½ cup all-purpose flour
1 teaspoon salt
¼ teaspoon white pepper
½ cup (¼ pound) butter
2 cups (1 pint) half-and-half

2 cups chicken broth, homemade (page
  70–71) or commercially canned
4 cups cold, cooked, skinless chicken-breast
  meat cut into bite-sized pieces (cook and
  prepare about 4 pounds split chicken
  breasts *with* skin [may have attached ribs],
  page 169)
1 4-ounce jar sliced pimientos, drained and
  coarsely chopped (¼ cup)
2 extra-large egg yolks, slightly beaten
2 tablespoons dry sherry

In a medium, heavy-bottomed skillet, melt 3
tablespoons butter over medium heat. Tilt the
skillet back and forth to completely cover the
bottom with the melted butter. Place the mushrooms in the skillet; sauté until the mushrooms
give up their juices (about 7 minutes). Using a
slotted spoon, remove the mushrooms from the
skillet and place them in a small mixing bowl;
set aside. Add the onions to the skillet; sauté
lightly for about 2 minutes. Do not allow the
onions to brown. Add the onions and skillet liquid to the sautéed mushrooms in the mixing
bowl; set aside.

In a small mixing bowl, place the flour, salt,
and white pepper; stir to combine; set aside. In
a large saucepan, melt ½ cup butter over low
heat. Remove from the heat. Add the flour mixture and stir until perfectly smooth. Add the
half-and-half and chicken broth; stir to combine. Place the saucepan over medium heat;
cook the mixture until thick and just *under* a
simmer, stirring constantly. Remove from the
heat. Add the mushroom mixture, chicken, and
pimientos; stir to combine. Return to medium
heat; heat through but do not allow the mixture
to simmer. (At this point, the saucepan may be
covered and the chicken mixture refrigerated
until shortly before serving time.)

Just prior to serving time, heat the chicken
mixture over medium-low heat, stirring often.
Spoon about ¾ cup of the hot chicken mixture
over the egg yolks in a small bowl; stir in. Add
the egg yolk mixture to the chicken mixture; stir
well to blend. While stirring constantly, continue cooking over medium-low heat until the

mixture thickens slightly more from addition of the egg yolks, but do not allow it to simmer (about 3 minutes). Add the sherry; stir to blend. Serve immediately.

SERVES 8

SERVING SUGGESTIONS: Serve over Puff Pastry Shells (Patty Shells) (page 402–404), Perfect Boiled Rice (page 228), or Mashed Potatoes (page 279).

CHICKEN AND NOODLES

2 tablespoons butter
8 ounces sliced, fresh mushrooms (about 3 cups)
2 cups chicken broth, homemade (page 70–71) or commercially canned, divided
1 tablespoon all-purpose flour
1 teaspoon salt
½ teaspoon pepper
12 cups water
12 ounces egg noodles
4 cups cold, cooked, skinless white and dark chicken meat cut into bite-sized pieces (cook and prepare about 4 pounds chicken pieces *with* skin, page 169)
2 tablespoons butter, melted

In a medium, heavy-bottomed skillet, melt 2 tablespoons butter over medium heat. Tilt the skillet back and forth to completely cover the bottom with the melted butter. Place the mushrooms in the skillet; sauté until the mushrooms give up their juices (about 5 minutes). Do not let the butter or mushrooms brown. Set aside.

Pour about ⅓ cup of the chicken broth into a small glass jar or plastic container with a secure lid. Add the flour. Cover and shake vigorously until blended and smooth; set aside. In a large saucepan, place the remaining 1⅔ cups chicken broth, salt, and pepper; bring the mixture to a boil over medium-high heat. Add the flour mixture; stir to blend. Return to a simmer and cook until the mixture thickens slightly (about 2 minutes), stirring continuously. Remove from the heat; cover and set aside.

Pour 12 cups water into a small kettle or large saucepan; cover and bring to a boil over high heat. Add the noodles; boil, uncovered, until the noodles are tender (about 10 minutes), stirring often. Meanwhile, add the chicken to the broth mixture and heat through over medium-low heat, stirring often.

Drain the noodles in a sieve; return the noodles to the kettle and rinse in very hot water. Drain the noodles again in the sieve. Return the well-drained noodles to the kettle. Add 2 tablespoons melted butter and toss until the noodles are evenly coated. Add the hot chicken mixture and mushrooms with pan liquids; toss lightly to combine.

SERVES 8

TRADITIONAL SERVING ACCOMPANIMENTS: Chicken and Noodles are traditionally served with Mashed Potatoes (page 279). Diners spoon Chicken and Noodles over their Mashed Potatoes. Baking Powder Biscuits (page 380) also are a favorite accompaniment.

SCALLOPED CHICKEN

When I was a young camper at Clearwater Camp on Tomahawk Lake near Minocqua, Wisconsin, this was my all-time favorite Sunday noon dinner dish, which was often served by the fabulous cook, Andy.

4 cups cold, cooked, skinless, white and dark chicken meat cut into bite-sized pieces (cook and prepare about 4 pounds chicken parts with skin, page 169)
3½ cups chicken broth, homemade (page 70–71) or commercially canned
⅓ cup chopped celery
½ cup finely chopped onions
1 teaspoon dried leaf thyme
½ teaspoon salt
¼ teaspoon pepper
4 extra-large eggs, slightly beaten

(Recipe continues on next page)

2 tablespoons butter

2 cups sliced, fresh mushrooms (5 to 6 ounces mushrooms)

3 cups small, fresh bread cubes, ½ white and ½ whole wheat*

2 recipes Medium White Sauce (page 301–302), substituting 1 cup whole milk and 1 cup chicken broth (homemade, page 70–71, or commercially canned) for 2 cups whole milk

*All white or all whole-wheat fresh bread cubes may be used.

Preheat the oven to 350° F. Grease a 9 × 13-inch baking dish; set aside.

In a large mixing bowl, place the chicken, 3½ cups chicken broth, celery, onions, thyme, salt, pepper, and eggs; do not mix; set aside. In a small skillet, melt the butter over low heat. Tilt the skillet back and forth to completely cover the bottom with the melted butter. Place the mushrooms in the skillet; sauté slowly until the mushrooms give up their juices (about 5 minutes). Keep the heat low to prevent the butter from browning. Add the mushrooms and skillet juices to the chicken mixture. Add the bread cubes. Using a large mixing spoon, fold all the ingredients together; turn into the prepared baking dish and spread evenly. Bake, uncovered, for 45 minutes.

Meanwhile, make the Medium White Sauce.

To serve, cut the Scalloped Chicken into square servings. Using a spatula, place 1 serving on each individual plate. Pour the hot white sauce into a sauce dish and pass at the table.

SERVES 12

FRIED CHICKEN

This is a very popular way to prepare fried chicken (and the way our family has fixed it for three generations). After frying the chicken in vegetable oil and butter over high heat to as deep a brown as possible, reduce the heat to low, pour off all but a little of the skillet liquid, and cover. After

cooking 1 hour undisturbed (don't turn the pieces), the chicken will be succulent and tender, with a deep, rich outer flavoring.

Tip: When I'm preparing a large quantity of Fried Chicken for our family's annual Fourth of July picnic, I take the electric skillet to the garage and do the browning out there on a table covered with paper towels to keep the spattering out of the kitchen. (When you fry chicken over high heat to achieve deep browning, there is considerable and unavoidable spattering). Then, I bring the skilletful of browned chicken back into the house for the final hour of cooking.

1 3- to 4-pound chicken (fryer), cut up

½ cup all-purpose flour

1½ teaspoons salt

¼ teaspoon pepper

1 teaspoon paprika

¼ cup vegetable oil

1 tablespoon butter

Wash the chicken pieces under cold, running water and place them between several layers of paper towels to dry; set aside. In a small mixing bowl, place the flour, salt, pepper, and paprika; stir until combined thoroughly. Sprinkle the flour mixture over a piece of waxed paper; dredge the chicken pieces in the mixture. Shake the chicken pieces to remove excess flour and place, single layer, on a clean piece of waxed paper; set aside.

Preheat an electric skillet or a large, heavy-bottomed skillet on the range to high heat (400° F in an electric skillet). Pour the vegetable oil into the skillet. Tilt the skillet back and forth to completely cover the bottom with the vegetable oil. Add the butter; spread to blend the butter with the oil. Place the chicken pieces, single layer, in the skillet; fry until a deep golden brown (about 10 to 15 minutes), turning once or twice. Reduce the skillet heat to low (250° F in an electric skillet); pour off excess liquid, if necessary, to leave about ¼ inch liquid in the skillet. Cover the skillet and cook the chicken 1 hour, until fork-tender.

NOTE: When browning larger quantities of chicken, it may be necessary intermittently to add more vegetable oil and butter to the skillet. In the final recipe step, pile all of the browned chicken in the skillet, cover, and cook for 1 hour at 250°F, until fork-tender.

SERVES 4 TO 5

SERVING SUGGESTIONS

- In the summer, serve with Potato Salad (page 111–112). During warm months, Fried Chicken may be served at room temperature or chilled. Wonderful for picnics.

- In the winter, serve with Mashed Potatoes (page 279) and Milk Gravy (page 310–311). The gravy should be served on the Mashed Potatoes, and should not be served over or under the Fried Chicken. Spiced Peaches (page 120–121) are an excellent accompaniment.

BARBECUED CHICKEN

1 3-pound chicken (fryer), cut up
2 tablespoons butter
1¼ cups Barbecue Sauce (page 205), divided

Preheat the oven to 350°F. Butter the bottom and 2 inches up the side of a Dutch oven.

Wash the chicken pieces under cold, running water and place them between several layers of paper towels to dry. When dry, place the chicken pieces, skin side down, in the prepared Dutch oven; dot with the butter.

Bake the chicken, uncovered, for 30 minutes. Turn the chicken pieces over; bake, uncovered, for an additional 30 minutes. Reduce the oven heat to 325°F. Pour ¾ cup of the Barbecue Sauce over the chicken; cover and bake for 30 minutes. Then, pour the remaining ½ cup Barbecue Sauce over the chicken; uncover and bake for an additional 30 minutes, until fork-tender.

SERVES 6

Other Chicken Recipes

Turkey

ROAST STUFFED TURKEY

1 6- to 24-pound dressed turkey, fresh or frozen (allow 1 pound per serving for birds 12 pounds or under, and ¾ pound per serving for birds over 12 pounds)
Dressing (stuffing) of choice (page 181)
Vegetable oil
Turkey Gravy (or Turkey Giblet Gravy) (page 313)

TO THAW FROZEN TURKEY: Although a whole turkey purchased frozen may safely be thawed in the refrigerator, in cold water, or in the microwave oven, I prefer thawing in the refrigerator. Procedures for all 3 methods of thawing follow.

(Recipe continues on next page)

To thaw in the refrigerator, keep the turkey wrapped and place it in a pan; let stand about 24 hours for each 5 pounds of turkey. Let large turkeys stand a maximum of 5 days in the refrigerator. The giblets and neck are customarily packed in the neck and body cavities of frozen turkeys. They may be removed from the cavities near the end of the thawing period to expedite complete thawing of the bird. If desired, the giblets and neck may be refrigerated and reserved for use in Giblet Gravy.

To thaw in cold water, make certain that the turkey is in a leakproof package or a zipper-seal plastic bag. This prevents bacteria in the surrounding environment from being introduced into the food and prevents the poultry tissues from absorbing water, resulting in a watery product. Change the cold water every 30 minutes. Approximately 30 minutes per pound of turkey are required for thawing. After thawing in cold water, the turkey should be cooked immediately.

To thaw in the microwave oven, consult the manufacturer's instructions for the size turkey that will fit into your oven, the minutes per pound, and power level to use for thawing. Turkeys thawed in the microwave must be cooked immediately after thawing (see Microwave Ovens, page 15–16, for further information on this food safety guideline).

TO REFRIGERATE FRESH TURKEY: A whole turkey purchased fresh (not frozen) may safely be refrigerated up to 2 days before roasting.

TO PREPARE THE TURKEY FOR ROASTING: *Do not stuff the turkey until immediately before roasting.* When ready to roast the turkey, rinse the outside and cavities of the bird under cold, running water. Cut away and discard any fat remaining on the bird. Place the turkey on several layers of paper towels to drain. Using additional paper towels, pat the outside and cavities dry.

To stuff the turkey, stand the bird on its tail end in a large bowl; using a tablespoon, stuff the neck cavity loosely with dressing. Pull the neck skin over the dressing and fasten it to the body with a poultry skewer. Turn the bird and place the neck end in the bowl; stuff the body cavity loosely with dressing. It is important to stuff the dressing fairly loosely in the bird as dressing expands during cooking.

Remove the turkey from the bowl and lay the bird, breast side up, on a piece of waxed paper or directly on a clean work surface. Pull the legs close to the body and tie the ends together with cotton string. If the tail has been left on the bird, tie the legs to the tail to partially close the body cavity. Some frozen turkeys are packed with a metal clamp to secure the legs, in which case it is not necessary to tie the legs with string. Fold the wings under the bird to provide a platform for roasting.

Place the turkey, breast side up, on a wire rack in a shallow roasting pan. Brush all the exposed surfaces of the bird with vegetable oil. Insert a meat thermometer into one of the inner thigh areas near the breast, making certain the tip of the thermometer is not touching bone. While many commercial turkeys are packed with a disposable thermometer preinserted into the breast which is designed to pop up when the bird is done, a standard meat thermometer, inserted into the thickest part of the thigh at the time the turkey is placed in the oven for roasting, is considered a more reliable means of determining doneness. Also, a standard meat thermometer makes it possible to know how close the turkey is to being done—an aid in timing preparation of the remainder of the meal.

TO ROAST THE TURKEY: Preheat the oven to 325° F.

Cover the turkey loosely with extra-heavy aluminum foil, leaving space between the bird and the foil. Lightly tuck the foil around the front, back, and sides of the bird. Do not add water to the pan. Roast the turkey until the meat thermometer reaches 180° F and the juices run clear, which will take the following approximate time:

APPROXIMATE ROASTING TIMES

Turkey Weight	Hours
6–8 pounds	3–3½
8–12 pounds	3½–4½
12–16 pounds	4½–5½

16–20 pounds	5½–6
20–24 pounds	6–6½

The roasting time may vary up to 30 minutes, depending upon the bird and the oven. Use the meat thermometer to check the temperature of the dressing. The center of the dressing inside the bird (or in a separate baking dish) must reach a temperature of 165°F for food safety.

Remove the aluminum foil about 30 minutes before the turkey is done to complete the browning of the bird.

When done, remove the turkey from the oven and place it on a serving platter or carving board; cover loosely with aluminum foil and let it stand 10 minutes before carving. Meanwhile, make the Turkey Gravy (or Giblet Gravy). Remove all the dressing from the neck and body cavities before carving the turkey. Pour the gravy into a gravy boat and pass at the table.

TRADITIONAL ACCOMPANIMENT: Mashed Potatoes (page 279) are traditionally served with turkey at holiday meals.

ROAST UNSTUFFED TURKEY

Follow the Roast Stuffed Turkey recipe, above, omitting the dressing (stuffing). Roast the turkey until the meat thermometer reaches 180°F, which will take the following approximate time:

APPROXIMATE ROASTING TIMES

Turkey Weight	Hours
6–8 pounds	2½–3
8–12 pounds	3–4
12–16 pounds	4–5
16–20 pounds	5–5½
20–24 pounds	5½–6

ROAST TURKEY BREAST

1 5- to 7-pound fresh (or frozen and thawed) turkey breast
Vegetable oil

Preheat the oven to 325°F.

Brush the turkey breast with vegetable oil. Insert the meat thermometer to the center of the breast. Wrap and seal the breast in extra-heavy aluminum foil, with the face of the meat thermometer on the outside of the foil for viewing. Place on a wire rack in a shallow roasting pan.

Roast the turkey breast until the meat thermometer reaches 170°F (about 2 to 2¾ hours). Open the aluminum foil about 30 minutes before the breast is done and baste 2 times with drippings.

SERVES 12

PRONTO SPICY TURKEY TENDERLOINS

1 cup commercially canned mild salsa
2 tablespoons dry red wine
1 tablespoon peach jam
¼ teaspoon salt
¾ cup zucchini cut into ½-inch cubes
⅔ cup sliced, fresh mushrooms
1 tablespoon vegetable oil
2 5- to 7-ounce turkey tenderloins
½ teaspoon cornstarch

In a medium mixing bowl, place the salsa, wine, jam, and salt; stir to combine. Add the zucchini and mushrooms; stir to combine; set aside. In a medium, heavy-bottomed skillet, heat the vegetable oil over medium heat. Using a spatula, spread the vegetable oil over the entire bottom of the skillet. Place the tenderloins in the skillet; sauté 3 minutes on each side, until lightly browned. Remove the skillet from the heat and let stand until cooled slightly. Reduce the range heat to medium-low.

(Recipe continues on next page)

When the skillet cools, pour the salsa mixture over the tenderloins. Cover the skillet and place over medium-low heat. Bring the tenderloins to a simmer and simmer 12 to 18 minutes (depending upon the thickness of the tenderloins), until no pink color remains in the turkey meat. Remove the skillet from the heat.

Using a spatula, place the tenderloins on individual plates or on a serving plate. Using a slotted spoon, lift the remaining vegetables from the sauce in the skillet and place over the tenderloins. Cover the tenderloins lightly with aluminum foil to keep warm. Add the cornstarch to the sauce in the skillet; stir vigorously until completely blended. Place the skillet over medium heat; bring the sauce to a boil, stirring constantly. Boil for about 30 seconds until the sauce thickens, stirring continuously. Spoon the sauce over the turkey tenderloins and vegetables.

SERVES 2

Other Turkey Recipe

Arabesque Turkey Salad (page 120–121)

Stuffings (Dressings)

SAGE DRESSING

7 cups Dried Bread Cubes (page 32),
  ½ white and ½ whole wheat*
1 cup medium-finely chopped celery
¾ cup chopped onions
1 tablespoon plus 2 teaspoons coarsely
  crushed dried leaf sage
1 teaspoon salt
¼ teaspoon pepper
¼ teaspoon poultry seasoning
½ cup (¼ pound) butter, melted
1 cup hot water

*Although not as desirable in my opinion, all
white or all whole-wheat Dried Bread Cubes
may be used.*

In a very large mixing bowl, place the bread cubes, celery, onions, sage, salt, pepper, and poultry seasoning; stir to combine. Add the butter; toss to coat the ingredients. Drizzle the water evenly over the mixture; toss lightly to moisten.

MAKES ENOUGH DRESSING TO STUFF THE NECK AND BODY CAVITIES OF AN 8-POUND TURKEY (SEE NOTE). OR, PLACE THE UNBAKED DRESSING IN A BUTTERED 2-QUART ROUND BAKING DISH AND BAKE, COVERED, FOR 30 MINUTES AT 350° F. (MAY BE BAKED FOR 45 MINUTES AT 325° F.)

NOTE: For dressing to stuff a larger turkey, increase the recipe ingredients proportionately.

CHESTNUT DRESSING

Shell and skin 2 dozen medium to large chestnuts (page 35). Measure 1½ cups skinned chestnuts. Boil the chestnuts (page 3) and drain; let stand to cool. Chop the chestnuts coarsely; set aside.

Follow the Sage Dressing recipe, above, adding the chopped chestnuts to the ingredients after adding the onions.

OYSTER DRESSING

Follow the Sage Dressing recipe above, reducing the dried leaf sage to 2 teaspoons and reducing the hot water to ¾ cup. Add 1 pint shucked, raw oysters, drained (see Note) and chopped coarsely, to the ingredients after adding the onions. The drained oyster liquor may be heated and substituted for part of the water, if desired.

NOTE: If desired, reserve the drained liquor for use in the dressing.

CORN BREAD DRESSING

1 recipe Corn Bread (page 374–375)
1 cup chicken broth, homemade (page 70–71) or commercially canned
1 cup chopped celery with leaves
1 cup chopped onions
5 slices bacon, fried, drained between paper towels, and crumbled
¼ cup (4 tablespoons) butter, melted
2 extra-large eggs, beaten
1 teaspoon dried leaf thyme (or 1 tablespoon finely snipped, fresh thyme)
½ teaspoon poultry seasoning
½ teaspoon salt
⅛ teaspoon pepper

After baking the Corn Bread, let it stand, uncovered, for 5 hours to dry. Crumble the dried corn bread. Measure 6 cups crumbled corn bread and place in a large mixing bowl; set aside. Pour the broth into a medium saucepan. Cover the saucepan. Bring the broth to a boil over high heat. Add the celery and onions. Cover the saucepan and reduce the heat. Simmer the broth mixture 5 minutes. Remove from the heat; let stand to cool.

Sprinkle the crumbled bacon over the corn bread; set aside. Add the butter, eggs, thyme, poultry seasoning, salt, and pepper to the cooled broth mixture; stir well. Pour the broth mixture evenly over the corn bread and bacon; toss lightly to combine.

MAKES ENOUGH DRESSING TO STUFF THE NECK AND BODY CAVITIES OF AN 8-POUND TURKEY (SEE NOTE). OR, PLACE THE UNBAKED DRESSING IN A BUTTERED 2-QUART ROUND BAKING DISH AND BAKE, COVERED, FOR 40 MINUTES AT 325°F.

NOTE: For dressing to stuff a larger turkey, increase the recipe ingredients proportionately.

WILD RICE DRESSING

⅓ cup raw wild rice, cooked in homemade (page 71) or commercially canned beef broth.
4 slices bacon, cut widthwise into ½-inch pieces
½ cup chopped onions
1¼ cups sliced, fresh mushrooms
½ cup chopped celery
1 cup Dried Bread Crumbs (page 33)
½ teaspoon dried leaf thyme
½ teaspoon dried leaf sage
½ teaspoon salt
⅛ teaspoon pepper
¼ cup beef broth, homemade (page 71) or commercially canned

Place the cooked wild rice in a large mixing bowl; set aside. In a small, heavy-bottomed skillet, fry the bacon over medium heat until crisp, but not too brown. Using a slotted spoon, remove the bacon from the skillet and place in the bowl containing the wild rice; set aside. Place the

(Recipe continues on next page)

onions and mushrooms in the skillet; fry in the bacon grease, over medium heat, until the onions are translucent and the mushrooms give up their juices (about 5 minutes). Using a slotted spoon, remove the onions and mushrooms from the skillet and add to the wild rice. Add the celery, crumbs, thyme, sage, salt, and pepper; stir to combine all the ingredients. Add 1/4 cup beef broth; stir to combine.

MAKES ENOUGH DRESSING TO STUFF THE NECK AND BODY CAVITIES OF A 6-POUND BIRD (SEE NOTE). OR PLACE THE UNBAKED DRESSING IN A BUTTERED 1½-QUART ROUND BAKING DISH AND BAKE, COVERED, FOR 30 MINUTES AT 350°F (MAY BE BAKED FOR 45 MINUTES AT 325°F.)

NOTE: For dressing to stuff a larger bird, increase the recipe ingredients proportionately.

Chicken Divan, page 171

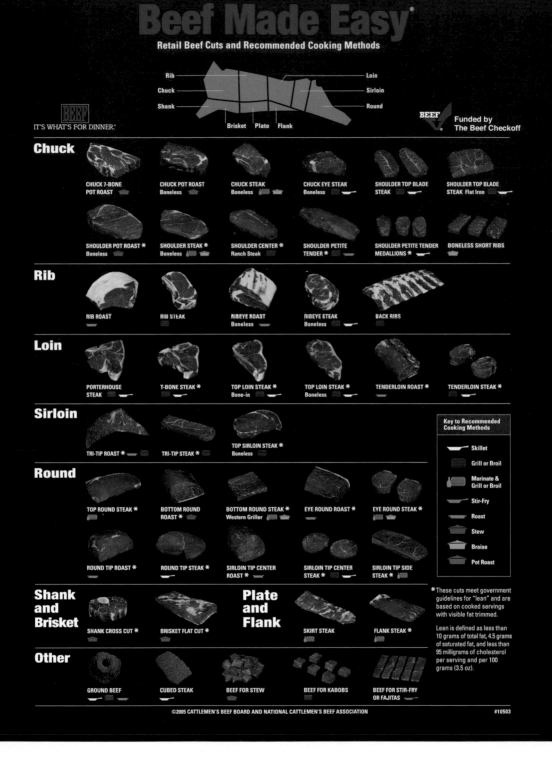

Beef Chart

Pot Roast with Vegetables, page 143; Pot Roast Gravy, page 312

Rosemary Chicken Breasts with Red Raspberry Sauce, page 173

Fettuccine Alfredo, page 236

Baby Lamb Chops, page 165; Vegetable Bundles, page 271

**Perch Fillets with Hazelnuts and White Wine, page 185; Simmered
Fresh Green Beans, page 254; Tomato Roses, page 340**

Pork Basics

The Other White Meat®

Don't be blah.™

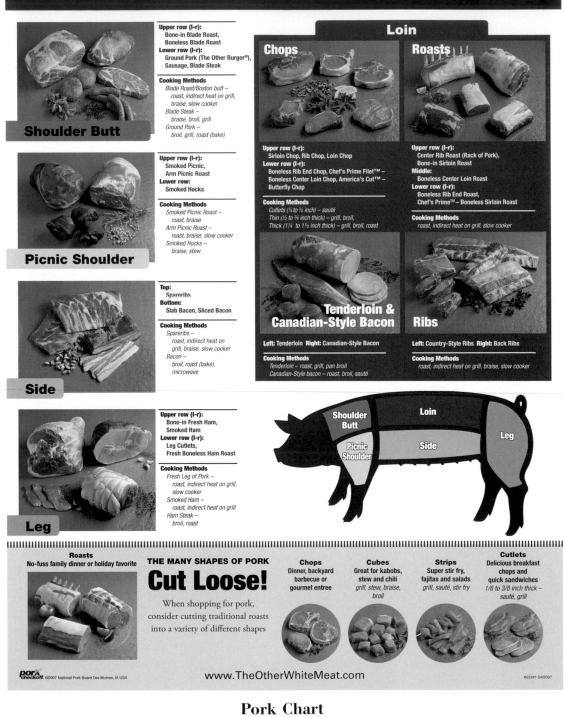

Shoulder Butt

Upper row (l-r):
Bone-in Blade Roast,
Boneless Blade Roast
Lower row (l-r):
Ground Pork (The Other Burger®),
Sausage, Blade Steak

Cooking Methods
Blade Roast/Boston butt –
roast, indirect heat on grill,
braise, slow cooker
Blade Steak –
braise, broil, grill
Ground Pork –
broil, grill, roast (bake)

Picnic Shoulder

Upper row (l-r):
Smoked Picnic,
Arm Picnic Roast
Lower row:
Smoked Hocks

Cooking Methods
Smoked Picnic Roast –
roast, braise
Arm Picnic Roast –
roast, braise, slow cooker
Smoked Hocks –
braise, stew

Side

Top:
Spareribs
Bottom:
Slab Bacon, Sliced Bacon

Cooking Methods
Spareribs –
roast, indirect heat on
grill, braise, slow cooker
Bacon –
broil, roast (bake),
microwave

Leg

Upper row (l-r):
Bone-in Fresh Ham,
Smoked Ham
Lower row (l-r):
Leg Cutlets,
Fresh Boneless Ham Roast

Cooking Methods
Fresh Leg of Pork –
roast, indirect heat on grill,
slow cooker
Smoked Ham –
roast, indirect heat on grill
Ham Steak –
broil, roast

Loin

Chops

Upper row (l-r):
Sirloin Chop, Rib Chop, Loin Chop
Lower row (l-r):
Boneless Rib End Chop, Chef's Prime Filet™ –
Boneless Center Loin Chop, America's Cut™ –
Butterfly Chop

Cooking Methods
Cutlets (⅛ to ⅜ inch) – sauté
Thin (½ to ¾ inch thick) – grill, broil,
Thick (1¼ to 1½ inch thick) – grill, broil, roast

Roasts

Upper row (l-r):
Center Rib Roast (Rack of Pork),
Bone-in Sirloin Roast
Middle:
Boneless Center Loin Roast
Lower row (l-r):
Boneless Rib End Roast,
Chef's Prime™ – Boneless Sirloin Roast

Cooking Methods
roast, indirect heat on grill, slow cooker

Tenderloin & Canadian-Style Bacon

Left: Tenderloin **Right:** Canadian-Style Bacon

Cooking Methods
Tenderloin – roast, grill, pan broil
Canadian-Style bacon – roast, broil, sauté

Ribs

Left: Country-Style Ribs **Right:** Back Ribs

Cooking Methods
roast, indirect heat on grill, braise, slow cooker

THE MANY SHAPES OF PORK
Cut Loose!

When shopping for pork,
consider cutting traditional roasts
into a variety of different shapes

Roasts
No-fuss family dinner or holiday favorite

Chops
Dinner, backyard
barbecue or
gourmet entree

Cubes
Great for kabobs,
stew and chili
grill, stew, braise,
broil

Strips
Super stir fry,
fajitas and salads
grill, sauté, stir fry

Cutlets
Delicious breakfast
chops and
quick sandwiches
1/8 to 3/8 inch thick –
sauté, grill

www.TheOtherWhiteMeat.com

#03341 04/2007

Pork Chart

Pork Chop Dinner in Foil, page 249

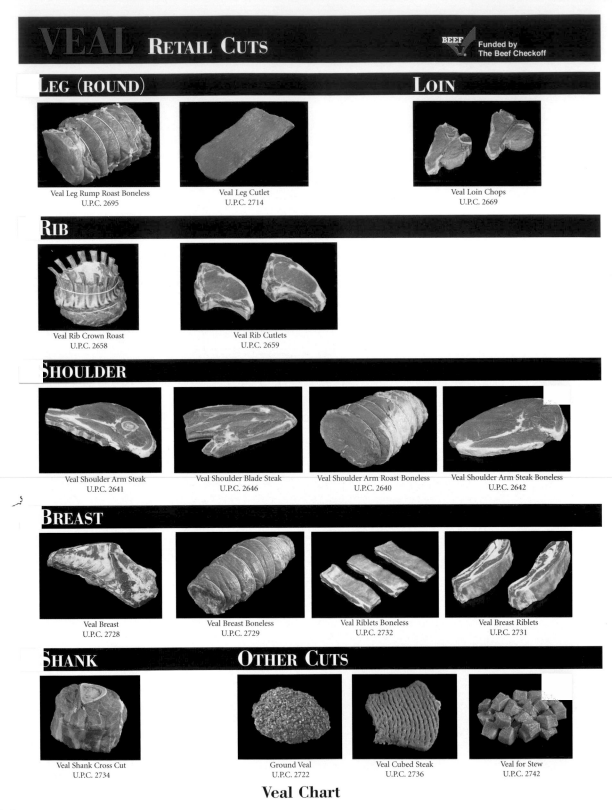

VEAL RETAIL CUTS

BEEF Funded by The Beef Checkoff

LEG (ROUND)

Veal Leg Rump Roast Boneless
U.P.C. 2695

Veal Leg Cutlet
U.P.C. 2714

LOIN

Veal Loin Chops
U.P.C. 2669

RIB

Veal Rib Crown Roast
U.P.C. 2658

Veal Rib Cutlets
U.P.C. 2659

SHOULDER

Veal Shoulder Arm Steak
U.P.C. 2641

Veal Shoulder Blade Steak
U.P.C. 2646

Veal Shoulder Arm Roast Boneless
U.P.C. 2640

Veal Shoulder Arm Steak Boneless
U.P.C. 2642

BREAST

Veal Breast
U.P.C. 2728

Veal Breast Boneless
U.P.C. 2729

Veal Riblets Boneless
U.P.C. 2732

Veal Breast Riblets
U.P.C. 2731

SHANK   OTHER CUTS

Veal Shank Cross Cut
U.P.C. 2734

Ground Veal
U.P.C. 2722

Veal Cubed Steak
U.P.C. 2736

Veal for Stew
U.P.C. 2742

Veal Chart

Fish and Shellfish

Fish and Shellfish Safety

To help ensure against foodborne illnesses, the following procedures should be practiced when securing, storing, handling, and cooking fish and shellfish:

- Oysters, scallops, clams, and mussels are molluscan shellfish. They are filter feeders that process large quantities of water. Illness-causing bacteria and viruses may be present in shellfish harvested in polluted waters which have not been certified as safe, and the safety of waters can change from day to day. Therefore, it is very important to purchase mollusks and other shellfish from reputable sources.

- Fully cook fish and shellfish. Cook fish, filleted or whole, to an internal temperature of 160°F At this temperature, the flesh is opaque and it flakes easily when pricked with a sharp fork. Cook shellfish to an internal temperature of 160°F (steaming hot). The flesh should be opaque. To check the internal temperature of fish and shellfish, use an instant thermometer (page 28–29).

- Refrigerate raw fish and shellfish at 40°F or below for only 1 to 2 days before cooking or freezing. Freeze at 0°F or below.

- Thaw frozen fish and shellfish in the refrigerator or in the microwave oven (see Food Safety: Microwave Ovens, page 15–16, for procedural information), not on the kitchen counter or in the sink.

- Before cooking, rinse raw fish and shellfish under cold, running water, and dry with paper towels.

- Throw away fish and shellfish packaging material.

- Place cooked fish and shellfish on a clean platter, not on an unwashed platter which held the raw product.

- Wash your hands with soap and hot water before and after handling raw and cooked fish or shellfish. Wash kitchen tools and equipment, cutting boards and other work surfaces, sink, and faucet handles with hot, soapy water after they come in contact with raw or cooked fish or shellfish, and before they come in contact with other food.

Fish

BAKED BASS WITH MUSTARD-WINE SAUCE

2 pounds bass fillets
½ cup whole milk
½ teaspoon salt
¾ cup Dried Bread Crumbs (page 33)
¼ cup (4 tablespoons) butter, melted
Mustard-Wine Sauce (recipe follows)

Preheat the oven to 425°F. Grease a 10½ ×15-½-inch shallow baking (cookie) pan; set aside.

Wash the fillets under cold, running water and place them between several layers of paper towels to dry; set aside. In a small, flat-bottomed dish or a pie pan, place the milk and salt; stir to blend; set aside. Sprinkle the bread crumbs over a piece of waxed paper; set aside. Dip the fillets in the milk mixture; then, dredge in the crumbs until fully coated. Place the fillets, single layer, in the prepared baking pan; drizzle with the butter.

Bake uncovered for 15 to 20 minutes, or until the fish flakes easily when pricked with a sharp fork. Place the fillets on individual plates or on a serving platter; spoon hot Mustard-Wine Sauce over top.

SERVES 4

MUSTARD-WINE SAUCE

3 tablespoons all-purpose flour
¼ teaspoon dry mustard
⅛ teaspoon white pepper
2 teaspoons sugar
¼ cup (4 tablespoons) butter
½ cup water (or fish stock)
½ cup dry white wine
1 tablespoon prepared mustard

In a small sauce dish, place the flour, dry mustard, white pepper, and sugar; stir to combine; set aside. In a small saucepan, melt the butter over low heat. Remove from the heat. Add the flour mixture; stir until perfectly smooth. Add the water. Cook over medium-low heat until the mixture thickens, stirring continuously. Add the wine and prepared mustard; stir to blend. Heat through, stirring constantly.

VARIATION: Substitute white Rhine wine for dry white wine and omit the sugar.

PERCH FILLETS WITH HAZELNUTS AND WHITE WINE

(See photo insert page B-5)

Fishermen friends are always asking me for new and different ways to prepare their stringers of fish. They seem to like this one a lot. I hear reports of their taking the chopped hazelnuts, white wine, and chives along on fishing trips to Minnesota and Canada so they can prepare the dish after a good day's catch. Any type of mild fish fillets may be used with this recipe.

2 pounds perch fillets
⅓ cup all-purpose flour
½ teaspoon salt
½ cup chopped hazelnuts (page 34)
¼ cup (4 tablespoons) butter
¼ cup dry white wine
1 tablespoon snipped, fresh chives

Preheat the oven to 450°F. Grease liberally a 10½ × 15½-inch shallow baking (cookie) pan; set aside.

Wash the fillets under cold, running water and place them between several layers of paper towels to dry; set aside. In a small sauce dish, place the flour and salt; stir to combine. Sprinkle the flour mixture over a piece of waxed paper. Dredge the fillets in the flour mixture. Shake off excess flour and place the fillets, single layer, in the prepared baking pan. Distribute the chopped hazelnuts evenly over the fillets; set aside.

In a tiny saucepan, melt the butter over low heat; add the wine and stir to blend. Spoon the wine mixture over the fillets. Distribute the chives evenly over the fillets.

Bake the fillets for 12 to 15 minutes, or until the fish flakes easily when pricked with a sharp fork. Remove from the oven and spoon the pan juices over the fillets.

SERVES 4

BAKED WALLEYE DELUXE

2 pounds walleye fillets (about 4 fillets)
½ cup Caesar salad dressing, homemade
   (including anchovy mixture and Parmesan
   cheese—see Caesar Salad, page 100–101) or
   commercially bottled
2 cups finely rolled potato chips
¼ cup freshly grated Parmesan cheese (page 30)
1 cup finely shredded, extra-sharp cheddar
   cheese
1 tablespoon finely snipped, fresh parsley
¼ teaspoon paprika

Preheat the oven to 450°F. Grease liberally a 10½ × 15½-inch shallow baking (cookie) pan; set aside.

Wash the fillets under cold, running water and place them between several layers of paper towels to dry; set aside. Pour the salad dressing into a shallow, flat-bottomed, glass dish such as a pie pan; set aside. Sprinkle the rolled potato chips over a piece of waxed paper; set aside.

(Recipe continues on next page)

Dip the fillets in the salad dressing; then, dredge in the potato chips until fully coated. Place the fillets, single layer, in the prepared baking pan. Sprinkle the Parmesan cheese over the fillets; then, distribute the cheddar cheese evenly over the fillets. Scatter the parsley over the cheddar cheese. Using your fingers, sprinkle the paprika lightly over all.

Bake uncovered for 12 to 15 minutes, or until the fish flakes easily when pricked with a sharp fork.

SERVES 4

BROILED FISH FILLETS

This is a basic recipe for broiling fish fillets.

1½ to 2 pounds walleye, sauger, crappie, bass, perch, sole, or other fish fillets
¼ cup freshly squeezed, strained lemon juice
3 tablespoons butter
Paprika
Lemon wedges for garnish
1 recipe Tartar Sauce (page 297) (optional)

Preheat the broiler.

Wash the fillets under cold, running water and place them between several layers of paper towels to dry. When dry, arrange the fillets, single layer, in the bottom of a broiler pan (remove and do not use the perforated rack over the broiler pan). Pour the lemon juice over the fillets; dot with the butter and sprinkle lightly with paprika.

Broil the fillets 4 inches from the heat about 5 to 7 minutes, or until the fish flakes easily when pricked with a sharp fork. As a general guide, broil fillets 5 minutes per ½ inch of thickness measured at the thickest part of the fish to be cooked. Small, thin fillets require less cooking time. Baste the fillets with the pan juices halfway through broiling. Do not turn the fillets.

When done, place the fillets on individual plates. Garnish the plates with lemon wedges. If desired, Tartar Sauce may be passed at the table.

SERVES 4

BROILED FISH FILLETS AMANDINE

2 tablespoons butter
⅓ cup sliced, unblanched almonds
Dash of salt
Dash of white pepper

In a small, heavy-bottomed skillet, melt the butter over medium heat. Tilt the skillet back and forth to completely cover the bottom with the melted butter. Place the almonds, salt, and white pepper in the skillet; sauté 3 minutes; set aside and keep warm.

Follow the Broiled Fish Fillets recipe above. After the fillets have been broiled and removed from the broiler pan, add the hot sautéed almonds and skillet liquid to the pan juices in the broiler pan; stir to combine and spoon over the fillets after placing them on individual plates.

BROILED WALLEYE FILLETS WITH CAPER SAUCE

2 pounds walleye fillets (about 4 fillets)
¼ cup freshly squeezed, strained lemon juice
3 tablespoons butter
¼ teaspoon celery salt
1 recipe Caper Sauce (page 299)

Preheat the broiler.

Wash the fillets under cold, running water and place them between several layers of paper towels to dry. When dry, arrange the fillets, single layer, in the bottom of a broiler pan (remove and do not use the perforated rack over the broiler pan). Pour the lemon juice over the fillets; dot with the butter and sprinkle with the celery salt.

Broil the fillets, 4 inches from the heat, for 5 to 7 minutes, or until the fish flakes easily when pricked with a sharp fork. Baste the fillets with the pan juices after 3 minutes of broiling. Do not turn the fillets. When done, place the fillets on individual plates; spoon the Caper Sauce over the fish.

SERVES 4

PANFRIED FISH FILLETS

2 pounds walleye, sauger, crappie, bass, or
   perch fillets
1 extra-large egg
1/4 teaspoon salt
1/8 teaspoon pepper
1 1/2 cups commercial corn flake crumbs or
   7 1/2 cups cornflakes, crumbed (page 34)
1 tablespoon vegetable oil
1 tablespoon butter

Wash the fillets under cold, running water and
place them between several layers of paper towels to dry; set aside. In a flat-bottomed dish or a
pie pan, place the egg, salt, and pepper; using a
table fork, beat well; set aside. Sprinkle the
cornflake crumbs over a piece of waxed paper;
set aside. Dip the fillets in the egg mixture; then,
dredge in the crumbs until fully coated. Place
the dredged fillets on a clean piece of waxed
paper; set aside.

   Preheat an electric skillet or a large, heavy
bottomed skillet on the range to medium high
heat (380°F in an electric skillet). Place the vegetable oil in the skillet. Using a spatula, spread
the vegetable oil over the entire bottom of the
skillet. Add the butter. Tilt the skillet back and
forth to blend the butter with the oil. Place the
fillets, single layer, in the skillet. Fry the fillets 4
minutes on each side, turning only once. Small,
thin fillets require less cooking time. The fish is
done when it flakes easily when pricked with a
sharp fork. Do not overcook. Add additional
vegetable oil and butter during frying, if necessary. Place the fillets directly on individual plates.

SERVES 4

TRADITIONAL ACCOMPANIMENTS: Panfried Fish Fillets are traditionally served with American Fries
(page 277). Tartar Sauce (page 297) is usually
passed at the table for diners who wish it, and
the fish plates are often garnished with lemon
wedges.

SALMON LOAF

2 cups Cold Poached Salmon Steaks (page
   53–55) cut into chunks, or 1 14 3/4-ounce
   can red sockeye salmon
1 tablespoon freshly squeezed, strained lemon
   juice
2 tablespoons butter, melted
2 extra-large eggs, or 1 extra-large egg if using
   canned salmon
20 Ritz crackers, rolled finely
2 tablespoons hot water

Preheat the oven to 350°F Butter an 8 × 8-inch
or a 6 × 10-inch baking dish; set aside.

   Place the salmon (and all salmon juices, if
using canned salmon) in a medium mixing
bowl. Using your fingers and a small paring
knife, carefully remove and discard all the skin,
dark flesh, and bones. Then, using your fingers,
flake the salmon. Add the lemon juice, butter,
eggs (1 egg if using canned salmon), and rolled
crackers; stir to combine. Shape into a round or
oval loaf and place in the prepared baking dish.
Pour 2 tablespoons hot water around (not over)
the loaf. Bake, uncovered, 35 minutes.

SERVES 4

ACCOMPANIMENT SUGGESTION: At the table, serve
Dilled Creamed Peas (page 274) or plain
Creamed Peas (page 274) for diners to ladle
over the Salmon Loaf slices.

POACHED SALMON STEAKS

1 cup chopped onions
2 stalks celery with leaves, cut into 1/2-inch
   slices
1 carrot, pared and cut into 1/8-inch slices
4 sprigs of fresh parsley
1 bay leaf
6 whole black peppercorns
1 whole clove
1 teaspoon salt

(Recipe continues on next page)

¼ teaspoon dried leaf thyme
½ cup dry white wine
¼ cup cider vinegar
6 cups water
4 fresh salmon steaks, 1 inch thick
Sprigs of fresh watercress or parsley for decoration
1 recipe Hollandaise Sauce (page 302–303)

In a large saucepan, place the onions, celery, carrots, 4 sprigs parsley, bay leaf, peppercorns, clove, salt, thyme, wine, vinegar, and water; stir to combine. Cover the saucepan. Bring the mixture to a boil over high heat; reduce the heat and simmer 20 minutes. Pour the mixture into a large skillet; cover and set aside. Wrap each salmon steak in 2 layers of damp cheesecloth (do not tie with string); set aside.

Over high heat, bring the mixture in the skillet to a boil. Lower the salmon steaks into the mixture; cover the skillet and return the mixture to a low boil. Reduce the heat and simmer 10 minutes. When properly done, the salmon steaks should flake when pricked with a sharp fork.

Using a spatula, remove the steaks from the skillet; unwrap. With the aid of a small paring knife, carefully remove the skin and dark flesh under the skin around the steaks. (Discard the mixture in which the steaks were poached.)

Using the spatula, place the salmon steaks on individual plates. Decorate the plates with sprigs of watercress or parsley. Pass Hollandaise Sauce in an attractive sauce dish at the table.

SERVES 4

ACCOMPANIMENT SUGGESTIONS: Serve with Baked Cucumbers (page 265) and plain, steamed new potatoes (page 276) which may be peeled or left unpeeled.

COLD POACHED SALMON STEAKS
Lemon wedges for garnish
Sprigs of watercress for decoration
1 recipe Green Sauce (Sauce Verte) (page 299)

Follow the Poached Salmon Steaks recipe, above, through poaching the steaks. Then, place the wrapped salmon steaks in a flat dish; cover and refrigerate until cold. When ready to serve, unwrap the steaks; carefully remove the skin and place the steaks on individual plates. Garnish the plates with lemon wedges and decorate with sprigs of watercress. Serve with Green Sauce (Sauce Verte) on the side.

ACCOMPANIMENT SUGGESTION: Serve with Cucumber Salad (page 109).

DEVILED TUNA ON PATTY SHELLS

Puff Pastry Shells, often called Patty Shells, make delightful, flaky, cups for creamed foods, such as this Deviled Tuna or Chicken à la King (page 174–175). As the name implies, Puff Pastry Shells are made of puff pastry (the recipe for making them on page 402 uses frozen puff pastry). When time doesn't permit making Patty Shells, serve the Deviled Tuna on toast.

3 tablespoons all-purpose flour
1 teaspoon dry mustard
1 teaspoon onion powder
¾ teaspoon salt
¼ teaspoon white pepper
3 tablespoons butter
2 cups whole milk
½ teaspoon Worcestershire sauce
1 6-ounce can solid, white albacore tuna, packed in water, drained and broken into large chunks
2 extra-large eggs, hard-cooked (page 222) and chopped coarsely
6 Patty Shells (page 402–404), warm
2 teaspoons finely snipped, fresh parsley for garnish

In a small mixing bowl, place the flour, dry mustard, onion powder, salt, and white pepper; stir to combine; set aside. In a small saucepan, melt the butter over low heat. Remove from the heat. Add the flour mixture; stir until perfectly smooth. Add the milk; stir to combine. Place over medium-low heat; cook until the mixture thickens and is just under boiling, stirring constantly. Remove from the heat. Add the Worcestershire sauce; stir until blended. Add the tuna and eggs; stir to evenly distribute. Return to medium-low heat; stir until the mixture is hot. Do not allow to boil.

Place 1 warm Patty Shell on each of 6 individual plates. Spoon Deviled Tuna over the Patty Shells; sprinkle with snipped parsley to garnish.

SERVES 6

VARIATION: Serve the Deviled Tuna over toast rather than over Patty Shells.

Other Fish Recipes

Cold, Poached Whole Salmon (page 187–188)
Fish Chowder (page 77–78)
Marinated Fish Steaks (page 214–215)
Kathy Griffin's Orange Roughy Parmesan (page 215)
Tuna-Almond Luncheon Salad (page 121)
Tuna-Noodle Casserole (page 248)

Shellfish

SHRIMP CURRY

Authentic Shrimp Curry of this type contains fresh coconut milk which is made by processing the liquid and meat of coconuts. In most parts of the country, it is impractical to rely on the availability of usable fresh coconuts; however, the substitution of cream of coconut and coconut-flavored milk, as called for in this recipe, achieves a similar flavor and consistency.

½ teaspoon finely grated fresh ginger (page 31)
½ teaspoon ground turmeric
½ teaspoon ground cardamom
½ teaspoon ground cinnamon
½ teaspoon ground cloves
1 teaspoon salt
¼ cup (4 tablespoons) butter
2½ cups finely chopped onions (about 2 large onions)
1 cup canned cream of coconut*
1 cup Coconut-Flavored Milk (recipe follows)
1½ pounds raw, unshelled 26- to 30-sized shrimp, boiled, shelled, and deveined (page 191)
1½ cups parboiled** long-grain white rice (not instant), boiled (page 228)

* *Available in the mixed beverage or baking section of the supermarket.*

** *See Parboiled Rice, page 228.*

CONDIMENTS
Chutney (the primary condiment served with Shrimp Curry), commercially canned
Raisins, dark and/or golden
Finely chopped, preserved kumquats, commercially canned
Shredded coconut
Salted peanuts
Finely chopped, crystallized ginger
Pickled pearl onions, commercially canned
Snipped, fresh parsley
Fresh tomatoes, blanched (page 29), peeled, quartered, seeded and cored (page 29), and chopped
Chopped, hard-cooked eggs (page 222)
Chopped sweet pickles
Grated lemon rind

In a small sauce dish, place the ginger, turmeric, cardamom, cinnamon, cloves, and salt; set aside. In a large, heavy-bottomed skillet, melt the butter over medium heat. Tilt the skillet back and forth to completely cover the bottom with the melted butter. Place the onions in the skillet; sauté until golden (about 10 minutes). Be careful not to burn the butter nor to brown the onions too deeply. Add the spice mixture and

(Recipe continues on next page)

continue cooking for about 2 minutes, stirring constantly. Remove the skillet from the heat and let stand to cool slightly. Then, add the cream of coconut and coconut-flavored milk; stir in well.

Return the skillet to medium heat. Bring the mixture to a low simmer; cook for 3 to 5 minutes, until the mixture thickens slightly. Add the shrimp and heat through only. The shrimp will become tough if allowed to cook beyond heating.

To serve, place the Shrimp Curry and rice in separate serving bowls. Diners spoon the Shrimp Curry over rice. Place a medium sauce dish of chutney and small sauce dishes of at least 5 additional condiments in the center of the table so diners may conveniently and intermittently spoon various condiments over portions of their Shrimp Curry. For a dazzling table, serve all of the condiments. If more than 6 diners are seated at the table, provide 2 sets of condiments.

SERVES 4

COCONUT-FLAVORED MILK

1 cup whole milk
1 cup packed, raw, chip coconut
  (unsweetened)

Pour the milk into a small saucepan; heat to just under boiling over medium-low heat. Add the coconut; stir to combine. Cover the saucepan; turn off the heat, but leave the saucepan on the burner. Let stand 30 minutes.

Place the mixture in a blender beaker; process to liquify. Strain the mixture through 4 layers of damp cheesecloth secured in a sieve over a deep pan. Wring the cheesecloth to press out as much milk as possible; discard the unstrained pieces of coconut. Refrigerate the coconut-flavored milk in a covered container up to 2 days, ready for use.

ACCOMPANIMENT SUGGESTIONS: For a meal planned around Shrimp Curry, serve Hearts of Palm-Persimmon Salad (page102) for a first course. Pass warm Deluxe Sesame Seed Crackers (page 383) with the Shrimp Curry course. For dessert, serve Fresh Fruit Compote (page 291) and Macadamia Nut Cookies (page 545).

BAKED SCALLOPS WITH SHERRIED GARLIC BUTTER

1½ pounds sea scallops
¼ cup (4 tablespoons) butter
2 garlic cloves, pressed
4 ounces sliced, fresh mushrooms
¼ cup thinly sliced green onions (scallions),
  white part only
1 tablespoon dry sherry
Paprika for decoration

Preheat the oven to 400° F.

Wash the scallops under cold, running water to remove any sand in the crevices; place them between 3 layers of paper towels to dry; set aside. In a medium, heavy-bottomed skillet, melt the butter over medium heat. Tilt the skillet back and forth to completely cover the bottom with the melted butter. Place the garlic, mushrooms, and onions in the skillet; sauté until the mushrooms give up their juices (about 3 minutes), being careful not to let the butter or vegetables brown. Remove from the heat. Add the sherry; stir in.

Using a slotted spoon, remove the *mushrooms* from the skillet and distribute evenly over the bottoms of four 5-inch-diameter by 1-inch-deep round baking dishes appropriate for serving. (Don't worry if some of the sautéed onions and garlic are spooned out and distributed with the mushrooms.) Set the baking dishes aside. Place the scallops in the skillet containing the onions and garlic; stir to coat with the mixture in the skillet.

Using the slotted spoon, remove the coated scallops from the skillet and arrange over the mushrooms, distributing them evenly among the 4 baking dishes. Spoon the remaining skillet mixture evenly over the scallops in each dish. Sprinkle with paprika.

Bake the scallops, uncovered, for 15 minutes. Place each baking dish on a doily-lined, salad-sized plate. Provide a cocktail fork and a fish knife (or other small knife) with each diner's table service.

SERVES 4

SCALLOPED OYSTERS

¼ cup plus 1 tablespoon (5 tablespoons)
  butter
½ cup (about 10) coarsely rolled saltines
½ cup fine Dried Bread Crumbs (page 33)
1 pint medium-sized, shucked, raw oysters
¼ cup half-and-half
¼ teaspoon ground nutmeg
¾ teaspoon dried leaf oregano
½ teaspoon salt
⅛ teaspoon pepper
1 tablespoon snipped, fresh parsley
Paprika

Preheat the oven to 325°F. Butter a 1-quart
round baking dish; set aside.

In a small saucepan, melt the butter over low
heat. Remove from the heat. Add the saltines
and bread crumbs; stir to combine; set aside.
Drain the oysters in a sieve, reserving the liquor.
Set the oysters aside. Measure ¼ cup oyster
liquor and pour into a small mixing bowl. Add
the half-and-half; stir until blended; set aside. In
a small sauce dish, place the nutmeg, oregano,
salt, and pepper; stir to combine; set aside.

Place ½ of the oysters in the prepared baking
dish. Sprinkle ½ of the nutmeg mixture over
the oysters. Spoon ⅓ of the crumb mixture
evenly over the seasoned oysters. Repeat the layers. Pour the half-and-half mixture evenly over
the layers. Add a final layer of crumbs. Scatter
the parsley over the top; sprinkle with paprika.
Bake, uncovered, for 45 minutes.

SERVES 4

BOILED SHRIMP

4 pounds raw, unshelled shrimp
1 3-ounce bag shrimp boil spice*
1 12-ounce bottle or can beer

 * *Ready-filled bags of shrimp boil spice may be
   purchased commercially.*

Rinse the shrimp under cold, running water; set
aside. Into a deep kettle, pour enough water to
generously cover the shrimp when they are
added later. Place the shrimp boil spice in the
kettle. Cover the kettle and bring the mixture to
a boil over high heat. Add the beer; cover and
return to a boil. Add the shrimp and simmer,
uncovered, 2 to 5 minutes, until the shrimp are
pink and curled. *Do not overcook,* as this will
result in tough shrimp. Immediately drain the
shrimp in a colander to retard further cooking.

To serve Boiled Shrimp as a main course, see
the procedure below. If Boiled Shrimp are to
be used in the preparation of another recipe,
such as Shrimp Curry, Shrimp Cocktail, or
other shrimp dishes, hot or cold, proceed to
shell and devein the shrimp (procedure follows), or refrigerate the boiled, unshelled
shrimp for later preparation.

TO SERVE BOILED SHRIMP AS A MAIN COURSE: Boiled
shrimp may be served hot or cold as a main
course. To serve, heap drained, unpeeled shrimp
into a large bowl and place it in the center of the
dining table. If serving a number of people at a
large table, divide the shrimp into 2 bowls for
convenient access by diners throughout the meal.

Let each diner shell and devein his or her own
shrimp. Provide a small knife with each diner's
table service for this purpose, and set the table
with a bowl at each diner's place for discarded
shrimp shells and veins. Provide each diner with
a generous amount of Cocktail Sauce (page 296)
served in an individual ramekin or small sauce
dish. A Boiled Shrimp meal is informal luxury!

ONE POUND RAW, UNSHELLED SHRIMP SERVES 3

TO SHELL AND DEVEIN SHRIMP: To shell shrimp,
place your thumb between the swimmerettes
(small appendages under the abdomen) and pull
off the shell. The tail may be left on or removed.
To remove the black vein which runs along the
center of the back, use a paring knife to make a
⅛-inch cut at the head end of the shrimp. Pull
the vein toward the tail and remove.

BOILED WHOLE LOBSTERS

For average servings, allow one 1- to 2-pound lobster per person. Avid lobster gourmands with hearty appetites may prefer larger lobsters.

Pour sufficient water into a large kettle to completely cover the lobsters when they are added later; cover and bring to a rapid boil over high heat. Plunge the live lobsters headfirst into the boiling water. Cover the kettle. When the water returns to a rapid boil, boil 1- to 2-pound lobsters 10 to 15 minutes. If the water begins to boil over during cooking, remove the kettle cover briefly to release steam. Do not boil more lobsters at a time than can be well covered with the boiling water. When done, the shells will be bright red and the meat will be opaque. Place the cooked lobsters on 4 layers of paper towels to drain. Using kitchen scissors or a sharp knife, slit the underside of the lobsters from end to end. Serve the lobsters with individual, small ramekins of Clarified Butter (page 305) and lemon wedges. Provide a lobster cracker, cocktail fork, and lobster pick (if available) for each diner.

BOILED LOBSTER TAILS
Lobster Meat for Salads and Other Dishes

Purchase African or American lobster tails in the shell weighing about 8 ounces each. Thaw the tails if frozen. Rinse the lobster tails under cold, running water. Drop the tails into a kettle of rapidly boiling water over high heat. When the water returns to a rapid boil, boil the lobster tails, uncovered, about 1 minute per ounce of tail (boil 8-ounce lobster tails about 8 minutes). When done, the shells will be bright red and the meat will be opaque. Place the cooked lobster tails, shell side up, on 4 layers of paper towels to drain.

When cooled sufficiently to handle, use a small knife and kitchen scissors to cut away the underside membrane on each lobster tail. With your fingers, pull the meat from the shells. Place the lobster meat in a bowl or plastic container; cover and refrigerate. Or, proceed to prepare the cooked lobster meat for use in a recipe.

BOILED ALASKAN KING CRAB LEGS
Crabmeat for Salads and Other Dishes

Purchase Alaskan king crab legs. Thaw the crab legs if frozen.

If the crab legs are uncooked, rinse them under cold, running water. Drop the crab legs into a kettle of rapidly boiling water over high heat. When the water returns to a rapid boil, boil the crab legs, uncovered, 5 minutes. *If the crab legs have been precooked,* rinse them under cold, running water and boil them only 3 minutes.

Place the cooked crab legs on 4 layers of paper towels to drain.

When cooled sufficiently to handle, cut the crab leg shells with a small, sharp knife. Use your fingers and a small fork or lobster pick to pull the crabmeat from the shells. Place the crabmeat in a bowl or plastic container; cover and refrigerate. Or, proceed to prepare the cooked crabmeat for use in a recipe.

ONE POUND UNSHELLED ALASKAN KING CRAB LEGS YIELDS ABOUT 2 CUPS FINELY CHOPPED CRABMEAT

Other Shellfish Recipes

Corn-Oyster Casserole (page 265)
Crabmeat Louis (page 123)
Crabmeat Salad (page 123)
Grilled Lobster Tails Basted with Tarragon Butter Sauce (page 216–217)
Lobster-Avocado Salad (page 124)
Lobster Salad (page 124)
Molded Shrimp and Cucumber Ring (page 122)
Oyster Stew (page 84–85)
Shrimp Luncheon Salad with Fresh Green Beans and Sherried Dressing (page 121)

Wild Game

BAKED PHEASANT

1 2- to 3-pound wild pheasant, skinned or
   unskinned, and dressed (page 5)
1 recipe Wild Rice Dressing (page 181–182)
2 slices bacon
¼ cup beef broth, homemade (page 71) or
   commercially canned

Wash the pheasant, inside and outside, under
cold, running water. Using a paring knife, remove
and discard most of the fat and any remaining
gunshot, bits of feathers, and pinfeathers (if
unskinned). Using paper towels, dry the pheasant
on the outside and in the body cavity (also the
neck cavity, if unskinned).

Preheat the oven to 325°F

Stuff the cavity(ies) of the bird loosely with
Wild Rice Dressing (see Note 1); truss (page 10)
and set aside. Cut the bacon slices in half widthwise. Cover the pheasant breast with the bacon
slices; set aside.

Lay a large piece of extra-heavy aluminum
foil over a wire rack in a shallow roasting pan.
Place the pheasant, breast up, on the aluminum
foil. Cover the sharp ends of the poultry skewers (if used) with small pieces of aluminum foil
to prevent piercing of the foil wrapping. Cup
the aluminum foil around the sides of the
pheasant. Pour the beef broth over the pheasant, retaining the broth within the foil. Seal the
pheasant and beef broth in the aluminum foil.

Bake the pheasant for 2 hours. Then, open
the foil to expose the breast. If the pheasant is
unskinned, the bacon slices may be removed to
allow the breast to brown for a more attractive
appearance. (Before serving the pheasant, discard the bacon or reserve it for other uses.) Bake
for an additional 30 minutes (see Note 2).

NOTE 1: Any remaining dressing may be placed
in a buttered, round baking dish and baked,
covered, for 45 minutes at 325°F or 30 minutes
at 350°F. Serve as additional dressing with the
pheasant.

NOTE 2: Allow the pheasant to bake the full 2½
hours even though, in all likelihood, this baking

time will exceed the time required for the bird to
reach an internal temperature of 180°F, the recommended temperature for doneness of whole
poultry (including game birds) (page 168). Game
birds generally must be cooked longer than
domestic poultry to achieve the desired doneness.

SERVES 4

WILD PHEASANT
WITH PORT WINE SAUCE

1 wild pheasant, plucked (not skinned),
   dressed (page 5), and cut into serving pieces
1 cup chicken broth, homemade (page 70–71)
   or commercially canned
½ cup port wine
1 bay leaf
½ cup all-purpose flour
1 teaspoon salt
¼ teaspoon pepper
2 tablespoons vegetable oil
2 tablespoons butter
½ cup currant jelly
1 teaspoon prepared mustard
1 teaspoon finely grated orange rind (page 31)

Wash the pheasant pieces under cold, running
water. Using a paring knife, remove any remaining gunshot, bits of feathers, and pinfeathers. Place the pheasant pieces between several
layers of paper towels to dry; set aside.

In a small mixing bowl, place the chicken
broth, wine, and bay leaf; stir to combine; set
aside. In another small mixing bowl, place the
flour, salt, and pepper; stir to combine. Sprinkle
the flour mixture over a piece of waxed paper.
Dredge the pheasant pieces in the flour mixture
and place on a clean piece of waxed paper; set
aside.

Preheat an electric skillet or a large, heavy-
bottomed skillet on the range to high heat
(400°F in an electric skillet). Place the vegetable
oil in the skillet. Tilt the skillet back and forth to
completely cover the bottom with the vegetable
oil. Add the butter; spread to blend with the oil.

Place the pheasant pieces, single layer, in the skillet and brown well on all sides (about 10 to 15 minutes). Reduce the skillet heat to very low (220°F in an electric skillet). When the skillet cools to the reduced temperature, add the wine mixture. Cover and simmer for 1 hour, or until the pheasant is tender.

Meanwhile, in a small mixing bowl, place the jelly, mustard, and orange rind; stir to combine; set aside. When the pheasant is done, remove it from the skillet and arrange on a heated platter; cover with aluminum foil to keep warm. Remove the bay leaf from the skillet and discard it. Then, place the jelly mixture in the skillet; stir until the jelly dissolves and blends with the skillet juices. Pour the sauce over the pheasant.

SERVES 3 OR 4

HUNGARIAN PARTRIDGE GRAND MARNIER WITH ORANGE-WILD RICE STUFFING

Native to Eurasia, Hungarian or gray partridge (Perdix perdix) were introduced to the United States in the late 1700s by Benjamin Franklin's son-in-law, who released some of the birds on his land in New Jersey. Numerous generally unsuccessful attempts were made to establish Hungarian partridge in many parts of this country in the early 1900s. However, through continual stocking attempts over the years, Hungarian partridge gradually have been established in North America, most successfully on the northern Great Plains, which includes the western portion of the Midwest. (A hunting season for Hungarian partridge was established in Iowa in 1963.)

While Hungarian partridge are increasing in number, they are far less prevalent in the Midwest than ring-necked pheasants and bobwhite quail which, like Hungarian partridge, are members of the Phasianidae family of gallinaceous birds. Gallinaceous birds are ground birds which feed on insects, grain, seeds, berries, and buds. They burst into rapid flight, but do not fly long distances.

Hungarian partridge resemble quail, with a short tail and similar-looking head, but they are larger than quail, averaging about 10 inches long, which makes them especially nice for serving.

1½ cups raw wild rice
1¾ cups homemade Beef Broth (page 71)
   or 1 14-ounce can commercial beef broth
10 wild Hungarian partridge, dressed (page 5)
⅓ cup finely diced orange peel
½ cup water
⅛ teaspoon ground nutmeg
10 slices bacon
1¾ cups homemade Beef Broth (page 71)
   or 1 14-ounce can commercial beef broth
½ cup Grand Marnier
1½ cups freshly squeezed, strained orange
   juice, divided
¼ cup cornstarch
Salt (optional)
White pepper (optional)

Cook the wild rice in 1¾ cups beef broth (see page 231 for procedure). If necessary, add additional broth or water to the rice during cooking.

Wash the partridge, inside and outside, under cold, running water. Using a paring knife, remove any remaining gunshot, bits of feathers, and pinfeathers (if unskinned). Drain the partridge on several layers of paper towels.

Preheat the oven to 350°F.

In a tiny saucepan, place the orange peel and ½ cup water. Bring the mixture to a simmer over medium heat; reduce the heat and simmer, uncovered, 5 minutes. Remove from the heat; drain well in a small sieve. Add the drained orange peel and nutmeg to the rice; stir to combine. Spoon the orange-wild rice stuffing into the cavities of the partridge and pack lightly. With cotton string, tie the ends of the legs of each bird together; then run the string around the body of each bird and tie securely.

Cut the bacon slices in half widthwise; place 2 half slices over the breast of each partridge. Place the birds, single layer, breast up, in 1 or 2 heavy roasters; set aside. In a small mixing bowl, place 1¾ cups beef broth and the Grand

(Recipe continues on next page)

Marnier; stir to blend. Pour over the partridge. Cover and bake for 2¼ hours, basting occasionally (see Note).

Remove the roaster(s) from the oven and transfer the birds to a large pan. Remove the bacon slices from the partridge and reserve. Cut and remove the string from the birds. Replace the bacon slices on the breasts of the partridge. Cover the pan with aluminum foil to keep the birds warm.

Strain the roaster juices in a sieve; then, pour into a medium saucepan. Add *1 cup* orange juice; stir to blend; set aside. In a small glass jar or plastic container with a secure lid, place the cornstarch and the remaining ½ cup orange juice; cover and shake vigorously until blended and smooth; set aside. Place the saucepan containing the roaster-juice mixture over medium heat. Bring the mixture to a simmer, stirring constantly. Add sufficient cornstarch mixture to bring the sauce to a medium-thin consistency, stirring continuously.

If commercial beef broth has been used, it is not necessary to add salt and white pepper to the sauce; if homemade broth has been used, the addition of salt and white pepper may be required, depending upon the seasoning of the broth and individual taste preference.

To serve, place 1 partridge on each individual dinner plate. Ladle a small amount of the sauce over the birds and pass the remainder in a sauceboat at the table.

NOTE: Allow the partridge to bake the full 2¼ hours, even though, in all likelihood, this baking time will exceed the time required for the birds to reach an internal temperature of 180°F, the recommended temperature for doneness of whole poultry (including game birds) (page 168). Game birds generally must be cooked longer than domestic poultry to achieve the desired tenderness.

Allow 2 partridge for diners with big appetites and 1 for diners with lighter appetites

SERVING SUGGESTION: Garnish the plates with Orange Baskets (page 336–337) filled with gooseberry conserve or cranberry relish.

WILD DUCK WITH MERLOT WINE SAUCE

The mallard is generally considered to be the most desirable species of duck for dining from the Midwest flyways. Mallards are among the larger ducks and are surface feeders. Surface-feeding ducks, sometimes called "dabblers," seldom dive. Rather, they feed in shallow water or on dry land and are primarily vegetarians, although they eat some insects, small fish, and mollusks.

2 wild ducks, plucked (not skinned) and
  dressed (page 5)
2 small celery stalks with green leaves
2 medium carrots, pared
1 medium onion, quartered
2 sprigs of dried sage (or 1 tablespoon plus 1
  teaspoon dried leaf sage)
1½ cups merlot wine
¼ cup cognac
8 ounces fresh mushrooms, sliced (3 cups)
½ cup chopped onions
2 tablespoons snipped, fresh parsley
½ teaspoon salt
¼ teaspoon pepper
2 tablespoons all-purpose flour
½ cup merlot wine

Preheat the oven to 375°F.

Wash the ducks, inside and outside, under cold, running water. Using a paring knife, remove any remaining gunshot, bits of feathers, and pinfeathers. Using paper towels, dry the ducks on the outside and in the cavities. In the body cavity of each duck, place 1 celery stalk, 1 carrot, 2 quarters of the onion, and 1 sprig dried sage (or 2 teaspoons dried leaf sage).

Place the ducks, side by side, on a large piece of extra-heavy aluminum foil. Wrap the ducks loosely in the foil and place them on a wire rack in a shallow roasting pan. Bake the ducks for 45 minutes.

Meanwhile, in a medium mixing bowl, place 1½ cups merlot wine, cognac, mushrooms, ½ cup chopped onions, parsley, salt, and pepper; stir to combine; set aside.

After the ducks have baked for 45 minutes, remove them from the oven. Reduce the oven temperature to 325°F. Using a baster, remove and discard any fat which has accumulated in the bottom of the foil. Pour the wine mixture over the ducks, retaining the mixture within the foil. Pull the foil back over the birds, leaving a slight opening at the top. Return the ducks to the oven.

Bake the ducks until cooked medium (160°F internal temperature) to medium rare (150°F internal temperature), depending upon preference (see Note) (about 30 minutes to 1 hour additional baking time, depending upon the size of the ducks and doneness preference), basting frequently.

When done, place the ducks on a cutting board, reserving the wine mixture in the aluminum foil. Remove and discard the vegetables and sage sprigs in the duck cavities. Using game shears, cut each duck in half lengthwise; cover with aluminum foil to keep warm.

Pour the wine mixture from the aluminum foil into a small saucepan; place over low heat. In a small glass jar or plastic container with a secure lid, place the flour and ½ cup merlot wine; cover and shake vigorously until blended. Add to the wine mixture in the saucepan; stir to blend. Increase the heat to medium-high; bring the sauce to a boil, stirring constantly. Reduce the heat to medium and cook 1 minute, until the sauce thickens, stirring continuously. Remove from the heat and cover.

Arrange the duck halves on a warm serving platter, or place on 4 individual dinner plates. Ladle a moderate amount of the wine sauce over the duck halves and pass the remaining sauce in a sauceboat at the table.

NOTE: While there are several schools of thought regarding the degree of doneness at which wild duck is best eaten, I side with the majority of duck hunters/connoisseurs who maintain that duck is at its height of flavor and succulence when served on the medium-rare side. There is some bacterial risk to consuming duck cooked to less than 160°F internal temperature.

SERVES 4

BAKED GOOSE WITH APRICOT-COGNAC DRESSING

1 5- to 8-pound wild goose, plucked (not skinned) and dressed (page 5)
6 ounces chopped, dried apricots (about 1 cup)
3 cups small, fresh, whole-wheat bread cubes (about 5 slices bread; use crusts)
½ cup chopped onions
1 cup unpared, quartered, cored, and chopped Granny Smith apple (about 1 small apple)
½ teaspoon salt
¼ teaspoon pepper
¼ cup (4 tablespoons) butter, melted
2 tablespoons cognac, divided
4 slices bacon
¼ cup beef broth, homemade (page 71) or commercially canned
¼ cup cognac
1 recipe Apricot Sauce (page 300)

Wash the goose, inside and outside, under cold, running water. Using a paring knife, remove any remaining gunshot, bits of feathers, and pinfeathers. Cut away and discard as much fat as possible from the cavity. Using paper towels, dry the goose on the outside and in the cavities; set aside or cover and refrigerate until ready to roast.

Preheat the oven to 325°F.

Prepare the dressing just before stuffing and roasting the goose as follows: in a large mixing bowl, place the apricots, bread cubes, onions, apples, salt, and pepper. Pour the melted butter and 2 tablespoons cognac over the ingredients; toss lightly to combine. Stuff the neck and body cavities of the goose loosely with dressing (see Note 1). Using poultry skewers and cotton string, close the cavities. Tie the ends of the legs together to hold them close to the body. With a sharp fork, prick the breast of the goose 8 times to allow fat to drain during baking. Cut the bacon slices in half widthwise. Cover the goose breast with the bacon slices; set aside.

Lay a large piece of extra-heavy aluminum foil over a wire rack in a shallow roasting pan. Place the goose, breast up, on the aluminum foil. Cover

(Recipe continues on next page)

the sharp ends of the poultry skewers with small pieces of aluminum foil to prevent piercing of the foil wrapping; set aside. In a small bowl, pour the beef broth and 2 tablespoons cognac; stir to blend; set aside. Cup the aluminum foil around the sides of the goose. Pour the beef broth mixture over the goose, retaining the mixture within the foil. Seal the goose and beef broth mixture in the aluminum foil.

Bake the goose for 40 minutes *per pound* (see Note 2). Do not baste. After 1½ hours of baking, open the foil and pour *1 tablespoon* of the cognac over the goose breast; reseal the foil. Repeat the procedure after an additional 1 hour of baking. One-half hour before the goose is done, open the foil to expose the breast; the bacon slices may be left on the breast or removed. The bacon slices help retain moisture; however, if the goose is to be served uncarved at the table, removal of the bacon slices will allow the breast to brown for a more attractive appearance. (Before serving the goose, discard the bacon or reserve it for other uses.)

To serve, spoon hot Apricot Sauce over individual servings of sliced goose. Pass additional Apricot Sauce in a sauce dish at the table.

NOTE 1: Any remaining dressing may be placed in a buttered, round baking dish and baked, covered, for 45 minutes at 325°F or 30 minutes at 350°F. Serve as additional dressing with the goose.

NOTE 2: Allow the goose to bake the full 40 minutes per pound even though, in all likelihood, this baking time will exceed the time required for the bird to reach an internal temperature of 180°F, the recommended temperature for doneness of whole poultry (including game birds) (page 168). Game birds generally must be cooked longer than domestic poultry to achieve the desired tenderness.

SERVES 6 TO 10, DEPENDING UPON SIZE OF GOOSE

WILD GOOSE PÂTÉ

4 cups (1 pound) ground (use coarse grinder
   blade, page 34), cooked wild goose (page 197)
1 pound ground pork
½ pound ground ham
2 extra-large eggs
¼ cup whipping cream, unwhipped
¼ cup cognac
½ cup finely chopped onions
2 tablespoons finely snipped, fresh parsley
1 garlic clove, pressed
2 tablespoons all-purpose flour
¾ teaspoon salt
¾ teaspoon pepper
½ teaspoon ground thyme
¼ teaspoon ground cinnamon
½ pound thickly sliced side pork

A S P I C
½ cup cold water
2 teaspoons (1 envelope) unflavored gelatin
1 cup Clarified Beef Broth (page 71), divided
2 tablespoons cognac, divided
1 tablespoon snipped, fresh parsley
Snipped, fresh parsley for garnish (optional)
Cornichon* Pickle Fans (page 337) for
   garnish
Small, thin slices pumpernickel bread

  * *A type of pickle.*

Set out two 3¾ × 7½ × 2¼-inch loaf pans. Cut 2 pieces of white, corrugated cardboard (cake board) *slightly* smaller in length and width than the top of the loaf pans. Cover the boards smoothly with aluminum foil; set aside. Preheat the oven to 350°F.

In a large mixing bowl, place the goose, pork, and ham; stir until well combined. Place about ⅓ of the meat mixture in a blender or food processor. Add the eggs, whipping cream, cognac, onions, parsley, and garlic. Using the blender or food processor, puree the mixture. Add the pureed mixture to the remaining meat mixture in the mixing bowl; stir to combine; set aside. In a small sauce dish, place the flour, salt, pepper, thyme, and cinnamon; stir to combine.

Add the flour mixture to the meat mixture; stir until thoroughly combined; set aside.

Line the loaf pans with the side pork, laying the pork slices, single layer, widthwise across the bottom of the pans and up the sides, letting the ends of the pork slices hang over the sides of the pans. Pack the meat mixture into the pork-lined pans. Use the back of a tablespoon to smooth the top of the mixture in each pan. Fold overlapping pork slices neatly over the meat mixture in each pan. Cover the pans tightly with heavy-duty aluminum foil. Place the loaf pans of pâté in a 9 × 13-inch baking pan. Pour very hot, but not boiling, water into the baking pan to approximately ½ the height of the loaf pans. Bake for 2 hours.

Remove the pans of pâté from the hot water and place on a wire rack. Remove the aluminum foil from the tops of the pans and discard. Place the foil-covered boards directly on the hot pâté in each pan. Place weights, such as heavy canned goods, directly on top of the foil covered boards. Let stand 15 minutes. Then, transfer the wire racks holding the weighted pâtés to the refrigerator; let stand 8 hours or overnight. Weighting the pâtés during the cooling period will make them firmer in consistency and easier to slice.

After cooling, remove the weights and foil-covered boards. Run a sharp, thin-bladed knife around the inside edges of the pans. To unmold the pâtés, cover the tops of the pans with a large piece of plastic wrap; place a wire rack over 1 pan at a time and invert. Wrap the pâtés in the plastic wrap and refrigerate.

Then, wash, dry, and lightly oil (page 40) the loaf pans in which the pâtés were baked; set aside and proceed to make the aspic.

Pour ½ cup cold water into a small bowl; sprinkle the gelatin over the water; let stand 15 minutes. In a very small saucepan, place ¼ cup plus 2 teaspoons of the beef broth. Cover and refrigerate the remaining beef broth. Place the saucepan over high heat and bring the beef broth mixture to a boil. Remove from the heat. Add 3 tablespoons of the gelatin mixture; stir until completely dissolved. Cover the remaining gelatin mixture; set aside at room temperature. Let the beef broth mixture stand until lukewarm. Then, add 1 tablespoon of the cognac; stir to blend. Pour the beef broth mixture (aspic) over the bottoms of the 2 prepared loaf pans, dividing the mixture evenly between the pans. Refrigerate until the aspic is partially set. Distribute the snipped parsley evenly over the partially set aspic in the 2 pans; refrigerate until completely set (about 3 hours).

Unwrap the pâtés and carefully place them in the loaf pans over the set gelatin. Place the pâtés in the loaf pans as they were baked (do not invert the pâtés in the pans). Refrigerate the pâtés.

Pour the remaining, refrigerated beef broth into a small saucepan; bring to a boil over high heat. Remove from the heat. Add the remaining gelatin mixture; stir until completely dissolved. Let stand until lukewarm. Add the remaining 1 tablespoon cognac; stir to blend. Pour the aspic around and over the pâtés. Aspic should entirely cover the sides of the pâtés. Refrigerate until completely set (about 5 hours). Then, cover lightly with aluminum foil. Keeps in the refrigerator up to 3 days.

To unmold, remove the foil cover and follow the directions for unmolding small, individual salad molds (page 89). Using a sharp, thin-bladed knife, cut each pâté into 16 slices. To serve as a first-course appetizer, arrange 2 slices on each individual plate. Sprinkle snipped parsley sparingly over the pâté slices, if desired. Garnish the plates with Cornichon Pickle Fans. Arrange pumpernickel bread on a bread tray and pass at the table.

SERVES 16

WILD DUCK PÂTÉ: Substitute cooked wild duck for cooked wild goose.

VENISON PÂTÉ: Substitute cooked venison for cooked wild goose.

WILD TURKEY BREAST OVER RICE WITH SPICED GRAPE SAUCE

The native North American wild turkey (Meleagris gallopavo) *is the source of all domesticated turkeys, which explains why wild and domestic turkeys look very much alike. The Eastern wild turkey* (Meleagris gallopavo silvestris), *one of the subspecies of the North American wild turkey, was the turkey of the Pilgrims and became our symbol of Thanksgiving.*

Thanks to the efforts of state departments of natural resources, biologists, and the National Wild Turkey Federation, the North American wild turkey population has been regenerated. By about the early 1970s, wild turkeys had multiplied in the Midwest to the point that there was a harvestable population for hunting (beyond the protected breeding population).

Although wild turkeys roost in trees, they are incredibly fast ground runners, which accounts for their highly muscled legs (which do not make the best eating). While our family occasionally roasts a whole wild turkey on Thanksgiving to authentically celebrate the day, more often we prepare only the good-tasting, more tender breast.

1 8-pound wild turkey breast, skinned
¼ cup (4 tablespoons) butter, melted
¼ cup chicken broth, homemade (page 70–71) or commercially canned
2 cups parboiled* long-grain rice (not instant), boiled (page 228)
Spiced Grape Sauce (recipe follows)

 * *See Parboiled Rice, page 228.*

Preheat the oven to 325° F.

Wash the turkey breast under cold, running water. Using a paring knife, remove any remaining gunshot and bits of feathers; dry with paper towels. Place the breast in the center of a large piece of extra-heavy aluminum foil. Cup the foil around the sides of the breast. Brush the breast with the melted butter. Pour the chicken broth around the base of the

breast, retaining the broth within the foil. Seal the breast and chicken broth in the aluminum foil. Place on a wire rack in a shallow roasting pan. Bake for 4 hours (30 minutes per pound), basting occasionally (see Note).

To serve, slice the breast thinly and serve over the rice. Spoon the Spiced Grape Sauce over the turkey breast slices and pass the remaining sauce in a sauce dish at the table.

NOTE: Allow the breast to bake the full 30 minutes per pound even though, in all likelihood, this baking time will exceed the time required for the breast to reach an internal temperature of 170° F, the recommended temperature for doneness of whole poultry breasts (including game birds) (page 168). Game birds generally must be cooked longer than domestic poultry to achieve the desired tenderness.

SERVES 16

VARIATION: To prepare this recipe using domestic turkey breast, roast the turkey breast following the recipe for Roast Turkey Breast on page 179. Otherwise, follow this recipe for preparation of the rice and Spiced Grape Sauce, and for serving.

SPICED GRAPE SAUCE

4 cups seedless white grapes cut in half lengthwise
6 2½-inch pieces of stick cinnamon
12 whole cloves
4 cups water
1 cup (½ pound) butter
2 tablespoons plus 2 teaspoons cornstarch
⅛ teaspoon ground cloves
2 cups white German Rhine wine or American Johannisberg Riesling
1 cup finely chopped celery hearts
½ cup chopped, fresh mushrooms

In a large saucepan, place the grapes, stick cinnamon, cloves, and water. Cover the saucepan. Bring the mixture to a boil over high heat; reduce the heat and simmer 5 minutes. Drain the mixture in a colander. Remove and discard the cinnamon sticks and cloves; set the grapes aside.

Melt the butter in a clean, dry, large saucepan over low heat. Remove from the heat. Add the cornstarch and ground cloves; stir until the mixture is perfectly smooth. Add the wine, celery, and mushrooms; stir to combine. Bring the mixture to a low simmer over medium heat, stirring constantly; simmer 5 minutes, stirring continuously. Add the drained grapes; heat through.

MAKES ABOUT 8 CUPS

QUAIL IN NESTS

Several species of quail are native to N   er-ica; however, only the bobwhite qua   ius virginianus) is found in the Midwest. Bobwhite quail are named after their call, which sounds like "bob-bob-white." Mottled reddish brown in color, bobwhites nest under brush and in other ground cover, and roost there in groups called coveys. They are small birds, about 8 inches long and only 4 to 6 ounces dressed for cooking. This recipe was the winner of the Game Wardens' Wild Game Cook-Off at the 1990 Iowa State Fair.

½ cup dry white wine
1 cup chopped, fresh mushrooms
12 wild quail, dressed (page 5)
½ cup all-purpose flour
1 teaspoon salt
¼ teaspoon pepper
1 tablespoon vegetable oil
2 tablespoons butter, divided
¼ cup finely chopped shallots
1¾ cups homemade Chicken Broth (page 70–71)
   or 1 14-ounce can commercial chicken broth
¾ cup pared and finely shredded carrots
2 tablespoons snipped, fresh parsley
2 tablespoons finely chopped celery
1 leafy celery-stalk top, chopped
Additional dry white wine, if necessary
½ teaspoon salt
⅛ teaspoon pepper
¼ cup all-purpose flour
½ cup water
12 Nests (recipe follows)

EARLY IN THE DAY: In a small glass bowl, place ½ cup wine and the mushrooms; cover with plastic wrap and refrigerate. Wash the quail, inside and outside, under cold, running water. Using a paring knife, remove any remaining gunshot, bits of feathers, and pinfeathers (if unskinned). Dry the quail on several layers of paper towels.

Slightly cross the legs of each bird and secure the legs close to the body with cotton string wrapped around the ends of the legs and around the bird; tie securely. Arrange the quail, single layer, on several layers of paper towels placed in the bottom of a flat baking dish. Cover the baking dish tightly with plastic wrap; refrigerate until ready to begin cooking the quail, allowing sufficient time for the birds to thoroughly drain.

2½ HOURS BEFORE SERVING TIME: In a small bowl, place ½ cup flour, 1 teaspoon salt, and ¼ teaspoon pepper; stir to combine. Sprinkle the flour mixture over a piece of waxed paper. Dredge the quail in the flour mixture and place on a clean piece of waxed paper; set aside.

Preheat an electric skillet or a heavy skillet on the range to medium-low to medium (330°F in an electric skillet). Place the vegetable oil in the skillet. Using a spatula, spread the vegetable oil over the entire bottom of the skillet. Add 1 tablespoon of the butter. Tilt the skillet back and forth to blend the butter with the oil. (The vegetable oil will help prevent the butter from burning.) Place the quail in the skillet and brown on all sides (approximately 30 minutes). Handle the quail carefully to prevent the string from becoming loose. If necessary, add the remaining 1 tablespoon butter to the skillet during browning. When a nice, deep brown, remove the quail from the skillet and arrange, single layer, breast up, in the center of a heavy roaster; set aside. Reduce the skillet heat to very low (220°F in an electric skillet) and let the skillet cool slightly.

Preheat the oven to 350°F.

Place the shallots in the skillet to simmer just a bit as the skillet continues to lose heat. When the skillet cools to the reduced temperature, add the chicken broth and deglaze. Add the refrigerated wine and mushroom mixture, carrots,

(Recipe continues on next page)

parsley, chopped celery, and chopped celery top; heat through, but do not allow to boil. Spoon the entire skillet mixture over and around the quail.

Cover the roaster and bake the quail 1½ hours. Baste the quail after the first 30 minutes of baking; then, baste every 20 minutes. Add a little additional dry white wine (or water), if necessary (see Note). Meanwhile, prepare the Nests and cover tightly with aluminum foil; place in a shallow baking pan, ready to toast just before serving.

NOTE: Allow the quail to bake the full 1½ hours even though, in all likelihood, this baking time will exceed the time required for the birds to reach an internal temperature of 180° F, the recommended temperature for doneness of whole poultry (including game birds) (page 168). Game birds generally must be cooked longer than domestic poultry to achieve the desired doneness.

SERVING TIME: Remove the quail from the roaster and place them in a baking pan. Leave the strings on the birds and cover the birds with aluminum foil to keep them warm; set aside.

Preheat the broiler.

Press the roaster juices and vegetables through a food mill; then, pour into a small saucepan. Add ½ teaspoon salt and ⅛ teaspoon pepper; stir to combine; set aside. In a small jar or plastic container with a secure lid, place ¼ cup flour and ½ cup water; cover and shake vigorously until well blended. Add about ½ of the flour mixture to the roaster-juice mixture in the saucepan; stir to blend. Bring the mixture to a boil over medium heat, stirring constantly and adding additional flour mixture, if needed, to achieve medium-thin consistency. Remove from the heat and strain the sauce through a sieve. Return the sauce to the pan; cover and keep warm.

Toast the Nests under the broiler until light brown. Remove the strings from the quail. Fit 1 quail into each hot, toasted Nest. Place 1 Quail in Nest on each individual dinner plate. Ladle the sauce moderately over all. Pour the remaining sauce into a gravy boat and pass at the table.

SERVES 6 TO 12
(QUAIL ARE TINY AND MANY DINERS WILL EAT 2)

NESTS

2 large loaves French bread
½ cup (¼ pound) butter, softened
½ teaspoon dried parsley
½ teaspoon dried leaf basil

Select bread slightly larger in diameter than the size of the quail; use only the large center sections of the loaves. Cut 12 slices of bread 1½ inches thick. With your fingers, carefully pull out pieces of bread from the center portion of each slice to form a nest about 1 inch deep, leaving about ½ inch of bread at the base of the Nest. Butter the entire top side of each Nest, including the inside and top edge. Sprinkle the entire top side of each Nest with the parsley and basil. Follow the recipe for completion of the Nests.

ACCOMPANIMENT AND SERVING SUGGESTIONS: Pecan Wild Rice (page 231–232) is a perfect complement to Quail in Nests. Spread a generous bed of Pecan Wild Rice over a large serving platter. Arrange the Quail in Nests on the rice. Garnish the platter with Artichoke Bottoms Filled with Tiny Vegetables (page 331–332) and decorate the platter with A Bunch of Whole Miniature Carrots (page 333–334). Pour all of the sauce into a gravy boat and pass at the table.

Other Wild Game Recipe

Wine-Marinated Venison Steaks (page 217–218)

Outdoor Cooking

Charcoal

Whether cooking outdoors on a grill (using direct heat or indirect heat) or in a smoker, lump charcoal (charwood) is far superior to charcoal briquettes for the heat source. Lump charcoal is irregular pieces of noncompressed, carbonized hardwood, such as oak, hickory, mesquite, apple, and pecan. It is usually available at stores specializing in outdoor cooking supplies.

Lump charcoal tends to burn hotter than charcoal briquettes; therefore, less lump charcoal may be required. Upon first using lump charcoal, close monitoring is required until adjusting to it.

Charcoal briquettes are compressed. Often they are made by carbonizing sawdust through a process that causes the wood flavor to be lost. Fillers such as coal dust may be employed, and the briquettes may contain petroleum-based binders which adversely affect the taste of grilled or smoked foods. "Natural" charcoal briquettes are made by compressing carbonized hardwood and binding it with plant starches.

STARTING CHARCOAL

The most favored way to start charcoal—whether by lump or briquettes—is by the use of a metal chimney starter (see illustration). Crumpled newspaper is placed in the bottom section of the starter, and the charcoal is placed in the top section. A match is used to light the newspaper, thus averting the use of charcoal lighter fluid, which may impart a petroleum taste to the food being prepared.

In a chimney starter, charcoal heats to the desired point quite rapidly (usually 15 to 20 minutes) and is readily transported to the grill or smoker (use insulated mitts). If required, additional batches of charcoal may be heated in the chimney starter ready for use.

Chimney starters must be used on a nonflammable surface. The instructions that accompany the chimney starter should be read and followed.

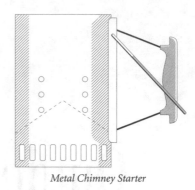

Metal Chimney Starter

Meat Safety for Outdoor Cooking

For basic principles on the safe storage, handling, and cooking of meat, see Meat Safety, page 134. The following are additional safety guidelines which specifically pertain to cooking meat outdoors:

• Marinate meat in a glass dish in the refrigerator, not on the kitchen counter. When preparing marinade, reserve any portion needed for basting or making a sauce; then, combine the remaining marinade with the raw meat. Do not baste meat cooking on the grill with marinade which has been in contact with raw meat unless it has been boiled.

• Wash forks, tongs, brushes, and other tools which come in contact with raw meat in hot, soapy water before reusing them to handle cooked meat.

• When cooking meat ahead in a conventional or microwave oven (see Note), cook it completely to ensure that bacteria throughout the meat are destroyed. Then, quickly cool the cooked meat in the refrigerator. Later, the meat can safely be reheated on the grill to add that distinctive barbecue flavor.

- It is safe to partially cook meat in the oven or microwave, or to parboil it to reduce outdoor cooking time, only if—after partially cooking or parboiling—the meat immediately goes on the grill.

- In hot weather of 85°F or above, do not leave meat out more than 1 hour before cooking and 1 hour after cooking. It is best to take raw meat directly from the refrigerator (or cooler, if picnicking) to the grill. Immediately refrigerate leftovers.

- Cook meat to the safe internal temperatures specified in Meat Safety, page 134, but be careful not to overcook meat on the outdoor grill. Remove visible fat from raw meat before placing it on the grill to avoid flare-ups. Do not consume charred meat.

- Place cooked meat on a clean platter, not on the unwashed platter which held the raw meat.

- Clean the grill after each use.

For further information and answers to specific questions regarding the safe cooking of meat outdoors, call the U.S. Department of Agriculture's Meat and Poultry Hotline at 888-674-6854 (TTY at 800-256-7072), Monday through Friday, 10:00 A.M.–4:00 P.M. Eastern time; or visit the Food Safety and Inspection Service Web site at www.fsis.usda.gov; or email at mphotline.fsis@usda.gov.

NOTE: See Food Safety: Microwave Ovens, page 15–16, for information on safe microwave cooking.

BARBECUE SAUCE FOR OUTDOOR COOKING

1 tablespoon extra-virgin olive oil
1 tablespoon butter
¾ cup finely ground (page 16) onions
 (about 1 large onion)
1 large garlic clove, pressed
About 1½ cups Heinz hot and spicy catsup

½ cup red wine vinegar
½ cup dry red wine
¼ cup unsulphured molasses
3 tablespoons freshly squeezed, strained lemon juice
3 tablespoons Worcestershire sauce
2 tablespoons horseradish mustard
2 tablespoons chili powder
2 teaspoons ground cumin
½ teaspoon celery salt
½ teaspoon dry mustard
½ teaspoon salt
¼ teaspoon pepper
8 dashes Tabasco pepper sauce
1 tablespoon cornstarch
1 tablespoon red wine vinegar

In a medium-large, deep, heavy-bottomed, nonaluminum saucepan, heat the olive oil over medium heat. Tilt the saucepan back and forth to completely cover the bottom with the olive oil. Add the butter; spread to blend with the oil. Place the onions and garlic in the saucepan; sauté 10 minutes, stirring and turning often. Remove from the heat. Add the catsup, ½ cup vinegar, wine, molasses, lemon juice, Worcestershire sauce, horseradish mustard, chili powder, cumin, celery salt, dry mustard, salt, pepper, and pepper sauce; stir to combine. Place over medium heat; bring the mixture to a simmer, stirring often. Reduce the heat and simmer, uncovered, 30 minutes, stirring frequently. Remove from the heat; set aside.

In a very small sauce dish, place the cornstarch and 1 tablespoon vinegar; stir until perfectly smooth. Add to the barbecue sauce mixture; stir to blend. Place over medium heat and bring to a simmer, stirring constantly. Reduce the heat and simmer 5 minutes, stirring nearly constantly as the sauce thickens. Remove from the heat; cool slightly. Pour the Barbecue Sauce into a heatproof quart jar (such as a canning jar); cover and refrigerate.

MAKES ABOUT 2¼ CUPS

Beef

GRILLED STEAK

Steaks for grilling: tenderloin fillet (and filet
mignon), top loin, porterhouse, rib eye,
T-bone, rib, sirloin, and chuck eye*
Salt or garlic salt (optional)
Pepper (optional)

* *1½ inches is the preferable thickness for most
grilled steaks, depending upon the cut.*

Trim away the excess fat from the edges of the
steaks. To prevent the steaks from curling during grilling, slit the remaining fat at 2-inch
intervals around the edges of the steaks, being
careful not to penetrate the flesh, causing loss of
meat juices. If desired, *just prior to grilling*, the
steaks may be seasoned lightly with salt or garlic salt, and pepper.

Place the steaks on the cooking grate in an
outdoor grill, about 4 inches above medium-
hot coals (the coals should be covered with a
thin layer of ash). Grill the steaks uncovered.
Use tongs (a fork will pierce the meat and cause
loss of juice) to turn the steaks only once,
grilling 2 minutes longer on the first side than
on the second side. While the length of grilling
time depends not only upon the desired doneness but also upon the size of the steaks, the
temperature of the coals, and the weather, the
following time chart may serve as a guideline
for grilling 1½-inch steaks:

APPROXIMATE GRILLING TIMES

Doneness	Minutes	
	1st Side	2nd Side
1½-INCH-THICK STEAKS		
Rare*	9	7
Medium Rare	11	9
Medium	13	11
Well Done	16	14

* *There is some bacterial risk when beef is consumed rare (140°F) (see Meat Safety, page 134).*

To grill 1-inch-thick steaks, deduct approximately 5 minutes total from the above grilling
times.

Use an instant thermometer (page 28–29) to
test for doneness. Or, test for doneness by slitting the steak near the bone, using a sharp, thin-
bladed knife. For steaks with no bone, make a
slit in the center of the steak.

GRILLED HAMBURGER STEAK

2¼ pounds lean, pure ground beef
¾ cup finely chopped onions
1 extra-large egg
½ teaspoon salt
¼ teaspoon pepper
6 slices bacon
Chili sauce

In a large mixing bowl, place the ground beef,
onions, egg, salt, and pepper; using a large,
metal mixing spoon, break up the ground beef
and combine all the ingredients well. Form the
ground beef mixture into 6 1-inch-thick patties.
Wrap a strip of bacon around each patty and
secure with half a toothpick.

Place the hamburger steaks on the cooking
grate in an outdoor charcoal or gas grill, about
4 inches above hot coals (the coals should be
barely covered with ash). Grill the hamburger
steaks uncovered. For medium-done hamburger steaks, grill for 3 minutes. Turn the hamburger steaks and grill for 10 minutes. Then,

turn and grill for an additional 10 minutes. For well-done hamburger steaks, turn again and grill another 7 minutes.

Carefully remove the toothpicks before serving. Pass the chili sauce in a sauce dish at the table.

SERVES 6

Pork

PORK RUB

See page 9 for the definition of "rub."

2 tablespoons ground (see recipe procedures below) dried leaf summer savory
4 bay leaves, ground (see recipe procedures below)
2 tablespoons ground thyme
2 teaspoons onion powder
2 teaspoons celery salt
1 teaspoon lemon pepper
1 tablespoon granulated brown sugar*
⅛ teaspoon cayenne pepper

*If granulated brown sugar is not available, regular white sugar may be substituted.

Using a blender on the highest speed, grind the dried leaf summer savory until as close to powder consistency as possible; measure 2 tablespoons and place in a small mixing bowl; set aside. Using the same procedure, grind the bay leaves; add to the measured summer savory. Over waxed paper, place the ground summer savory and bay leaves in a small sieve. Using up and down movements with your hand, bounce the herbs in the sieve over the waxed paper to separate the small quantity of less finely ground fragments from the remainder of the mixture. Then, using your finger, press the separated larger fragments back and fourth against the inside of the sieve to break them into fragments small enough to pass through the sieve. Discard any remaining fragments.

Place the sieved summer savory and bay leaves back in the small mixing bowl. Add the thyme, onion powder, celery salt, lemon pepper, sugar, and cayenne pepper; using a tablespoon, stir until all the ingredients are evenly combined.

Place the rub mixture in a small, glass jar with a secure lid. Best if used within 2 weeks. May be stored in a cool, dark location up to 6 months.

MAKES ENOUGH TO RUB ALL SIDES OF 6 SLABS OF PORK RIBS

GRILLED IOWA PORK CHOPS

As prepared and served annually at the Iowa State Fair by the Iowa Pork Producers. They use Seven Seas Viva Italian salad dressing when grilling these awesome chops.

8 Iowa Pork Chops (center-cut pork loin chops, 1¼ to 1½ inches thick)
Garlic salt
1 8-ounce bottle Italian salad dressing (see headnote)

Place the pork chops on the cooking grate in an outdoor charcoal or gas grill, 4 to 6 inches above medium-hot coals (the coals should be covered with a thin layer of ash). Grill the pork chops for 8 minutes, uncovered. Then, sprinkle the chops lightly with garlic salt. Using a brush, cover the surface of the chops with salad dressing. Turn the chops and immediately repeat the garlic salt and salad dressing additions on the second side of the chops. Grill the chops, uncovered, for an additional 8 minutes or until the internal temperature reaches 160°F (medium done). (Turn the chops only once.)

SERVES 8

GARY'S HICKORY SMOKED PORK RIBS

Smoking succulent pork ribs takes study and practice, but the satisfaction and pleasure accorded the chief barbecuer when friends and family ooh and aah as their sauce-laden fingers reach for yet another serving, add up to fun galore.

"Gary" in this recipe's title is my brother, Gary Staples. Our family is relatively new to tackling the art of smoking, but Gary has marched some platters of mighty tasty ribs into the kitchen following afternoons of vigilant monitoring of his smoker on the patio. He forewarns that directions in this recipe are guidelines. The smoker, fuel, weather, and meat are among the important factors affecting successful results. When all is said and done, experience is the best teacher.

As a certified Kansas City Barbeque Society judge, I have had the opportunity to taste and judge pork ribs supremely barbecued by some of our country's most outstanding, winning teams. Among this corps d'elite, barbecuing is a major hobby. In many cases, years have gone into perfecting their techniques of preparing some of the most luscious meat fathomable.

Onward to the smoker!

10 to 11 pounds natural (unenhanced*), not
　frozen, pork loin back (baby back) ribs
　(about 5 to 6 slabs weighing 1½ to 2¼
　pounds each)**
Lump charcoal (charwood)***
Approximately 4 hickory and 2 apple wood
　chunks about 1½ x 2 x 3 inches each
Apple juice
1½ cups granulated brown sugar****
1 6-ounce squeeze bottle of honey
½ cup butter, melted
2 recipes Barbecue Sauce for Outdoor
　Cooking (page 205)

* Copy on the packaging of fresh pork will indicate if the product has been enhanced. Fresh pork products may be enhanced by immersion or injection of the meat using water, lemon juice, phosphate, and other approved ingredients, including salt, to an optional maximum percentage of 7%, 10%, 12%, or 15% added ingredients. The purpose of adding these ingredients is to improve the tenderness and juiciness of the meat. It is recommended that enhanced pork ribs not be used for this recipe because the texture and flavor of the meat may be adversely affected over the long smoking period.

** Have the butcher remove the fell (a thin, tough membrane) from the bone side of the ribs. Or remove it yourself, as follows: Place one slab of ribs, meat side down, on a flat surface. Using your fingernail or a small, sharp knife, such as a paring knife, loosen the membrane at the small end of the rib slab and, using your hand, pull about 2 inches of the membrane loose. Then, using a paper towel (to help maintain a firm grip on the slippery membrane), pull the membrane down the length of the rib slab and discard it. Should the membrane tear in the process, repeat the procedure from the point of the tear. Repeat the procedure with the remaining rib slabs.

*** Use hardwood (such as oak) lump charcoal, also known as "charwood." It is usually available at outdoor cooking stores. Lump charcoal is far preferable to charcoal briquettes, which may contain a variety of binders and may impart a petroleum or other undesirable taste to the meat (see Charcoal, page 204).

**** If granulated brown sugar is not available, regular light brown sugar (pack to measure) may be substituted.

THE SMOKER: Use a smoker that utilizes charcoal for the heat source rather than gas or electricity. The smoker should have an offset firebox with dampers on the firebox and chimney to help control the temperature, and a reliable thermometer with a gauge that is visible when the smoker is closed. A well-constructed smoker is a requisite for producing top-quality smoked meat of any kind. Shop and study before purchasing.

PREPARATION FOR SMOKING:

1. Clean the smoker to help achieve the goal of clear smoke and good flavor.

2. About 24 hours before commencing to smoke, place the hickory and apple wood chunks in a clean bowl of water. Soaking the wood chunks reduces flaming and lengthens the time of hickory- and apple-smoke emission.

3. Remove the ribs from the refrigerator 30 minutes (no longer) before placing them in the smoker. If not already removed, remove the fell from the rib slabs (see ** above). Then, remove excess fat from the rib slabs, but leave a little fat for self-basting.

4. Place a metal, chimney-type charcoal starter (available at outdoor cooking supply stores) (see illustration, page 204) on a non-flammable surface. In the bottom of the chimney starter, place crumpled newspaper. Then, fill the chimney starter with lump charcoal. Using a match (not charcoal lighter fluid, which may impart an undesirable flavor), light the newspaper. Follow the instructions that accompany the chimney starter. Let the charcoal burn until it is coated with gray ash.

TO SMOKE THE RIBS: Using nonstick cooking spray, lightly spray the clean, cold, cooking grate of the smoker. Place the burning charcoal in the firebox. Bring the smoker temperature to 225° to 250° F. Then, distribute 2 soaked (but not dripping) hickory wood chunks and 1 soaked (but not dripping) apple wood chunk evenly over the charcoal. There usually is considerable visible smoke when first adding fuel to the firebox. Wait until the smoke subsides before placing the ribs in the smoker. The smoke emitting from the smoker should be as clear as possible (barely visible) throughout the smoking time. Place the ribs, meat side up and single layer, on the grate in the smoker.

It is very important to carefully and consistently monitor the temperature of the smoker, maintaining a range of 225° to 250° F (no higher). Add hot charcoal (prepared as previously described) when needed. When you begin to see the temperature drop, preheat charcoal in the chimney starter, readying it for adding to the smoker.

Add the remaining soaked hickory and apple wood chunks to the fire during the first 2 hours of smoking, if desired, noting that hickory imparts a strong flavor. Too much wood smoke will cause the ribs to have a bitter taste. After the surfaces of the ribs seal from cooking, little hickory and apple flavor will infuse them.

After smoking the ribs for 2 hours, pour apple juice into a spray bottle and lightly spray the meat side of the ribs to add moisture and enhance flavor. Then, turn the ribs meat side down and lightly spray apple juice over the bone side of the ribs. Leave the ribs meat side down and smoke them for 1 additional hour.

After smoking the ribs for 3 total hours, remove the ribs from the smoker and place them in a large, clean pan; cover them loosely with aluminum foil to help retain heat; let stand. On a flat surface, place a piece of heavy-duty aluminum foil large enough to wrap 1 slab of ribs securely. Sprinkle, evenly, two tablespoons of brown sugar down the center section of the foil, covering the approximate area of 1 slab of ribs. Over the brown sugar, squeeze about 1 tablespoon of honey back and forth in parallel rows. Then, drizzle about 2 teaspoons of melted butter over the brown sugar and honey. Place 1 slab of ribs, meat side down, over the brown sugar area on the foil. Apply the same measurement of brown sugar, honey, and melted butter onto the bone side of the rib slab.

Then, securely seal the top and one end of the rib slab in the foil, leaving a little space between the foil and the ribs on the top and edge of the slab (for steaming). Before sealing the second end of the foil, spray some apple juice into the packet to provide moisture. Repeat the procedure with the other rib slabs.

Place the aluminum foil-wrapped rib slabs (meat side down and single layer) in the smoker. Cook for 2 hours. Then, remove the rib slabs from the smoker. Remove the slabs from the aluminum foil wrappings and place them,

(Recipe continues on next page)

meat side up, back in the smoker for about 1 hour. Smoke the ribs for a total of approximately 5 to 6 hours (or longer) depending upon the variables such as weather and success in maintaining the 225° to 250° F. smoker temperature. Cook by the maintenance of smoker temperature and doneness of the ribs, not by time. When properly done, the meat will be tender. Generally, when the ribs are done, a small amount of bone (about ¼ inch) will be exposed at the end of each rib. Optimally, a bite of meat should cleanly release from the rib bone at the place where the diner takes a bite, but the meat on the entire side of rib bone should not pull away when the bite is taken.

When the ribs are done, remove them from the smoker and place them, meat side up, in a large, clean pan. Place the Barbecue Sauce in a clean squeeze bottle, and squeeze the sauce generously over the meat side of the ribs. Place the ribs, meat side up, in the smoker. Smoke for 10 minutes. Then, if desired, squeeze additional Barbecue Sauce over the ribs and smoke them for an additional 10 minutes.

Serve the ribs immediately or hold them in a covered pan in a 150° F preheated oven up to 1 hour. In a sauceboat, serve additional heated Barbecue Sauce at the table, if desired.

The smoked ribs may be kept in the refrigerator or freezer for later heating and serving.

SERVES 10 (ALLOW 1 POUND RIBS PER DINER)

VARIATION: Wood chunks other than hickory and apple may be used when smoking ribs. Hickory and mesquite are strongly flavored woods. Also, they are very hard woods, which can cause considerable smoke. Care must be exercised not to create too much smoke when using these woods. Some barbecuers like to start with hickory or mesquite wood chunks and then go to more mild woods, such as apple or pecan.

HICKORY SMOKED, RUBBED PORK RIBS

Apple juice in a spray bottle
1 recipe, Pork Rub (page 207)

Follow Gary's Hickory Smoked Pork Ribs recipe above, except:

After removing the ribs from the refrigerator 30 minutes before placing them in the smoker (and removing the fell and excess fat), spray the slabs lightly on all sides with apple juice. Then, using your fingers, rub all the sides of the rib slabs fairly liberally with the Pork Rub. Place the slabs in a glass baking dish and cover lightly with plastic wrap; let stand until placed in the smoker. (NOTE: Include the brown sugar/honey/butter and Barbecue Sauce steps using the rubbed rib slabs.)

SERVES 10 (ALLOW 1 POUND RIBS PER DINER)

VARIATIONS
• Eliminate the brown sugar/honey/butter applications to the ribs. Simply seal the slabs in the apple-juice-sprayed aluminum foil packets and continue to follow the recipe.

• Eliminate the Barbecue Sauce application(s) to the ribs and otherwise follow the recipe.

• Eliminate both the brown sugar/honey/butter applications and the Barbecue Sauce application(s) to the ribs. Otherwise, follow the recipe, including the procedure of sealing the slabs in the apple-juice-sprayed aluminum foil packets.

PORK ROAST WITH TANGY ROSEMARY SAUCE

Until I began writing this cookbook, our family had never tackled the preparation of a roast on the outdoor grill. I guess we had always envisioned it a demanding task with questionable results. We were wrong. Once you take a few minutes to learn the procedure for roasting by indirect heat on the grill, you find that it's quite simple. The roasts are not only reliably cooked, but they have a unique, tantalizing flavor not achievable in the kitchen oven. Add a sauce, such as the rosemary sauce in this recipe, and you have phenomenal eating with little effort. Roasts prepared on the grill are great to serve when you gather family or friends for a weekend meal in the summertime.

½ cup tomato catsup
¼ cup red wine vinegar
2 tablespoons packed dark brown sugar
2 teaspoons dried leaf rosemary
1 garlic clove, pressed
1 3- to 4-pound boneless pork rib-end roast,
    tied every 1¼ inches

EARLY IN THE DAY: In a small mixing bowl, place the catsup, vinegar, brown sugar, rosemary, and garlic; stir until well combined. Cover and refrigerate.

TO PREPARE THE OUTDOOR GRILL FOR INDIRECT COOKING: Purchase ready-made, or construct out of extra-heavy aluminum foil, a shallow, aluminum foil drip pan slightly larger than the area under the roast during grilling. Place the drip pan on the center of the fuel grate. Although not necessary, if you have them, attach 2 charcoal rails to the outside wires along both sides of the fuel grate (1 rail on each outside wire). These rails will help contain the charcoal when added.

25 MINUTES BEFORE COMMENCING TO COOK THE ROAST (ABOUT 2 HOURS BEFORE SERVING): Ignite a plentiful amount of charcoal in the chimney starter (page 204) and let it burn until the charcoal is lightly coated with gray ash. Then, mound a plentiful and equal amount of charcoal along both of the long sides of the drip pan on the outside of the pan (or along the outside of the rails). Place the cooking grate in the grill, about 4 inches above the coals.

Place the roast on an outdoor-grill roast holder (a V-shaped wire rack available where outdoor cooking equipment is sold). Insert a meat thermometer to the center of the roast.

Place the holder containing the roast on the cooking grate directly above the drip pan. Using a brush, generously baste the roast with the rosemary sauce. Cover the grill.

Roast the meat for 1 to 1¾ hours, or until the meat thermometer reaches 160°F for medium doneness (see Note), brushing the roast with the rosemary sauce every 20 minutes. Remove the roast from the grill when the thermometer reaches 5°F below the desired temperature, as the meat will continue cooking. The length of cooking time depends upon the desired doneness, the size of the roast, and the heat of the coals. If the grill contains a thermometer, try to maintain a grill temperature of 325 to 350°F. If the grill temperature begins to drop, carefully tap some of the ash off the coals with a long-handled implement or add additional heated charcoal.

When the roast has reached the desired doneness, remove it from the grill and let it stand 5 to 10 minutes before slicing.

NOTE: For well done, roast until the thermometer reaches 170°F.

A 4-POUND ROAST SERVES 8

Chicken

MESQUITE-GRILLED CHICKEN BREASTS

3 whole, skinless, boneless chicken breasts, cut
    in half lengthwise (1½ to 2 pounds total)
8 mesquite wood chunks approximately
    1×1×2 inches each

Wash the chicken breasts under cold, running water. Cut away any remaining fat on the breasts. Place the breasts between several layers of paper towels to dry. When dry, place the breasts in a flat-bottomed dish; cover and refrigerate.

Place the wood chips in a large, clean bowl or pan. Cover the chips with water; let stand at least 30 minutes. About 20 minutes before commencing to grill, ignite the charcoal in the chimney starter (page 204); let stand until the coals are medium hot (the coals should be covered with a thin layer of ash). Distribute the medium-hot coals, single layer, over the fuel grate. Drain the wood chips; distribute them over the coals. (If using a gas grill, consult the manufacturer's instructions for using wood chips.)

Spray the clean, cold, outdoor-grill cooking grate with nonstick cooking spray. Just before commencing to grill the chicken breasts, place the cooking grate in the grill, about 4 inches above the coals. Place the chicken breasts on the cooking grate and grill, uncovered, for 4 to 5 minutes per side, depending upon the size of the breasts, the temperature of coals, and the weather. Do not overcook the chicken breasts as they will become tough and dry. Serve hot or refrigerate, covered, for use in other recipes.

SERVES 6

PLAIN GRILLED CHICKEN BREASTS

Follow the Mesquite-Grilled Chicken Breasts recipe, above, eliminating the mesquite wood chips.

GRILLED CHICKEN BREASTS WITH FRESH SUMMER SAVORY AND TOASTED WALNUTS

3 tablespoons finely minced leeks (about
   1 leek) (see recipe procedures below)
2 teaspoons butter

1½ cups chicken broth, homemade (page
   70–71) or commercially canned
2 teaspoons fresh, snipped summer savory
2 teaspoons white balsamic vinegar
2 teaspoons honey
1 teaspoon cornstarch
¼ teaspoon finely grated fresh ginger
¼ teaspoon salt
⅛ teaspoon white pepper
¼ cup broken English walnuts, toasted (page 35)
4 Plain Grilled Chicken Breasts
   (left column)
Sprigs of fresh summer savory for decoration

Trim away and discard the root end and leaves of the leek, leaving only the white and greenish white parts. Slice the leek in half lengthwise and wash it well, making certain all sand has been washed away. Mince the leek finely. Measure 3 tablespoons minced leeks and place in a small sauce dish; set aside.

In a small, heavy-bottomed saucepan, melt the butter over medium-low heat. Add the minced leeks and sauté about 5 minutes, until the leeks are softened. Do not allow the leeks to brown. Remove from the heat. Add the chicken broth; stir to combine. Cover the saucepan. Over high heat, bring the chicken broth mixture to a boil. Uncover the saucepan and reduce the heat to medium. Cook the mixture at a gentle boil until reduced to about 1 cup (about 15 minutes). Remove from the heat.

To the reduced chicken broth mixture, add the summer savory, vinegar, honey, cornstarch, ginger, salt, and white pepper; stir well to combine. Over medium heat, bring the mixture to a gentle boil, stirring constantly. Boil the mixture 5 minutes to blend the flavors and thicken the mixture, continuing to stir constantly. Remove from the heat. Add the walnuts to the hot chicken broth mixture just before serving; stir to combine.

Place the hot Plain Grilled Chicken Breasts on 4 individual plates or on a serving platter. Spoon the sauce over the chicken breasts. Decorate with sprigs of fresh summer savory.

SERVES 4

ROTISSERIE CHICKEN WITH ORANGE-GINGER GLAZE

1 to 3 3-pound whole chickens (fryers)*
1 tablespoon vegetable oil per chicken
½ cup orange marmalade
2 teaspoons ground ginger
2 tablespoons tomato catsup
¼ cup vegetable oil

 * *If cooking only 1 chicken, cut the glaze ingredients in half (use ¼ cup orange marmalade, 1 teaspoon ginger, 1 tablespoon catsup, and 2 tablespoons vegetable oil).*

TO PREPARE THE GRILL AND FIRE: Prepare the outdoor grill for cooking the chicken(s) indirectly by placing a drip pan(s) on the fuel grate, under the rotisserie spit where the chicken(s) will be mounted. About 25 minutes before commencing to cook the chicken(s), ignite a plentiful amount of charcoal in the chimney starter (page 204) and let it burn until the charcoal is lightly coated with gray ash. Then, mound a generous and equal amount of charcoal on either side of the drip pan(s) on the outside of the pan(s). The coals should be about 6 inches from the spit.

TO PREPARE THE CHICKEN(S) FOR THE ROTISSERIE: To prepare each chicken, wash, inside and outside, under cold, running water. Using paper towels, dry the outside and cavities of the chicken. Cut away and discard the neck skin if it has been left on the chicken. Secure the wings close to the body by placing heavy cotton string under the back of the bird widthwise, pulling it tightly around the bird, looping each end of the string around one of the wings, and tying the string over the breast. For further security, the string may be pulled around the body and wings again (omitting looping the wings) and tied over the breast. Leave the string ends uncut. Insert the spit through the chicken lengthwise, and firmly insert the holding fork into the

front end of the bird; tighten the holding-fork screw. Then, insert the second holding fork into the tail end of the bird and tighten the holding-fork screw. Wrap another piece of string around the tail and pull crosswise over the spit to secure the tail to the spit. Loop the ends of the string around the crossed legs of the bird and tie securely. Leave the string ends uncut. Then, pull the wing and leg strings together and tie. Repeat the mounting procedure if cooking 2 or 3 chickens (using 2 holding forks per chicken).

Center the chicken(s) evenly on the spit. Brush each chicken generously with about 1 tablespoon vegetable oil.

NOTE: The procedure for mounting 1 or more chickens on a spit varies with the size and make of the grill. Check the manufacturer's instructions for specific information on using your grill for rotisserie cooking.

TO COOK THE CHICKEN(S): After the coals have been properly arranged in the grill, mount the spit holding the chicken(s) on the rotisserie and cover the grill. The grill temperature should be about 350°F (medium heat). Rotate the chicken(s) on the rotisserie about 1 to 1¼ hours, until an instant thermometer (page 28–29) inserted to the center of the thickest part of the breast registers 180°F. If the cooking time exceeds 1 hour, add some additional hot charcoal that has been heated in the chimney starter. It is not necessary to brush additional vegetable oil on the chicken(s) during cooking as it (they) will self-baste.

Meanwhile, in a small mixing bowl, place the marmalade, ginger, catsup, and ¼ cup vegetable oil; stir until blended. When the chicken reaches 180°F internal temperature, brush the marmalade mixture over the entire body of the bird(s) as it (they) rotates. Then, cover the grill and let the chicken(s) rotate about 1½ minutes. Repeat this glazing procedure 2 more times (about 5 minutes total time for the glazing process), being watchful not to allow the glazed chicken(s) to overbrown.

(Recipe continues on next page)

Remove the chicken(s) from the spit. Remove and discard the string. Using poultry shears or a sharp knife, cut the chicken(s) in half lengthwise. For smaller portions, cut each half in two widthwise.

ONE CHICKEN SERVES 2 TO 4 PERSONS

TO COOK THE CHICKEN(S) ON A ROAST HOLDER: Rather than cooking the chicken(s) on a rotisserie, 1 or 2 chickens may be cooked and glazed on an outdoor-grill roast holder. See the recipe for Pork Roast with Tangy Rosemary Sauce (page 211) for preparation of the outdoor grill and placement of the roast holder.

To prepare each chicken, wash, inside and outside, under cold, running water. Using paper towels, dry the outside and cavities of the chicken. Cut away and discard the neck skin if it has been left on the chicken. Fold the wings under the back. Cross the legs and tie them together securely with cotton string. Brush the bird with vegetable oil as in the rotisserie recipe above. Place the bird, breast up, on the roast holder. Insert a meat thermometer into one of the inner thigh areas near the breast, making certain the tip of the thermometer is not touching bone.

After the heated charcoal has been arranged in the grill, place the roast holder containing the chicken(s) on the cooking grate directly above the drip pan. Cover the grill and cook for approximately the same period of time as in the rotisserie recipe. If needed, add some additional hot charcoal that has been heated in the chimney starter. Do not turn the chicken(s). When the internal temperature reaches 180°F, remove the meat thermometer. Glaze the accessible parts of chicken(s) 3 times, following the procedure in the rotisserie recipe.

Fish

MARINATED FISH STEAKS

(See photo insert page C-1)

6 salmon, tuna, swordfish, or halibut steaks, 1 inch thick
1 cup freshly squeezed, strained orange juice
¼ cup freshly squeezed, strained lemon juice
¼ cup extra-virgin olive oil
¼ cup tomato catsup
¼ cup low-sodium soy sauce
2 tablespoons snipped, fresh parsley
1 tablespoon snipped, fresh marjoram
½ teaspoon white pepper
Lemon wedges for garnish

Wash the fish steaks under cold, running water and place them between several layers of paper towels to dry; set aside. In a quart jar or plastic container with a secure lid, place the orange juice, lemon juice, olive oil, catsup, soy sauce, parsley, marjoram, and white pepper; cover and shake vigorously until blended and smooth. Pour 1/4 cup of the mixture (marinade) into a small glass jar or plastic container; cover, refrigerate, and reserve for later use during grilling. Set the remaining marinade aside.

Arrange the fish steaks, single layer, in a flat-bottomed, glass baking dish. Pour the set-aside, remaining marinade over the fish; cover tightly with plastic wrap and refrigerate for 30 minutes. Turn the fish over; cover and refrigerate an additional 30 minutes.

Meanwhile, ignite the charcoal in the chimney starter (page 204); let stand until the coals are medium-hot (the coals should be covered with a thin layer of ash). Distribute the medium-hot coals, single layer, over the fuel grate.

Spray the clean, cold, outdoor-grill cooking grate and an outdoor-cooking spatula with non-stick cooking spray. Just before commencing to grill the fish steaks, place the cooking grate in the grill, about 4 inches above the coals. Remove the fish steaks from the marinade and place them on the cooking grate. Discard the marinade. Grill the steaks, uncovered, for 5 minutes. Brush the tops of the steaks lightly with a small amount of the ¼ cup reserved, refrigerated marinade. Using the sprayed spatula, carefully turn the steaks over; grill an additional 5 minutes, or until the fish flakes easily when pricked with a sharp fork. Guard against overcooking by staying at the grill while the steaks are cooking. Fish overcooks and chars very easily.

To serve, garnish the serving platter or individual dinner plates with lemon wedges.

SERVES 6

KATHY GRIFFIN'S ORANGE ROUGHY PARMESAN

You never know where or when you'll find a fabulous recipe. This one turned up when I was waiting in the examination room for my dermatologist. His nurse, Kathy, noticed that I was writing recipes on my ever-present yellow legal pad, and we began talking about this cookbook. I could tell instantly that she was a good cook. Here is one of the excellent recipes she shared that day.

4 (about 2 pounds) orange roughy fillets*
1 cup freshly grated Parmesan cheese (page 30)
¼ teaspoon salt
¼ teaspoon white pepper
1 cup thinly sliced leeks
2 tablespoons butter
1 tablespoon capers

* Any mild fish fillets may be substituted.

Wash the fillets under cold, running water and place them between several layers of paper tow-els to dry; set aside. In a small mixing bowl, place the Parmesan cheese, salt, and white pepper; stir to combine; set aside.

Place the fillets, single layer, in the center of a large piece of extra-heavy aluminum foil. Distribute the leeks equally over the fillets; dot with the butter. Scatter the capers equally over the fillets. Spoon the Parmesan cheese mixture evenly over all.

Seal the fillets tightly in the aluminum foil; carefully place on the cooking grate in the outdoor cooking grill, about 4 inches above hot coals (the coals should be barely covered with ash). Grill, uncovered, for 10 minutes. Do not turn.

SERVES 4

GRILLED SALMON FILLETS

When my brother returned from a fishing trip off the west coast of Queen Charlotte Islands, British Columbia, with 70 pounds of beautifully cleaned and frozen salmon and halibut, our family and friends feasted on many luxurious meals centered on offerings from the enviable catch. This simple, easy recipe was one of our favorite ways to prepare the salmon fillets. The touch of smoky flavor complemented by a drizzle of Caper Sauce all added up to glorious dining experiences. (Of course, if you're not so lucky to have a brother who loves to fish, good-quality wild—not farm-raised—salmon fillets may be purchased at better fish markets across the county.)For other ways I prepared this salmon windfall, see Cold, Poached Whole Salmon (page 53–55) and Poached Salmon Steaks (page 187–188).

6 6- to 8-ounce wild salmon fillets, skin on,
    1 to 1 ½ inches thick at the widest part*
Vegetable oil
1 recipe Caper Sauce (page 299)

*These are pieces of salmon fillet cut widthwise from whole fillets.

(Recipe continues on next page)

Wash the fillets under cold, running water and place them between several layers of paper towels to dry. When dry, place the fillets, single layer, in a pan or baking dish. Brush each fillet fairly generously on all sides with vegetable oil; set aside.

Using nonstick cooking spray, spray the clean, cold, outdoor-grill cooking grate and a thin, outdoor-cooking spatula. Just before commencing to grill the salmon fillets, place the cooking grate in the outdoor cooking grill over medium heat. Place the salmon fillets, skin side down, on the cooking grate. Cover the grill. Grill the fillets, covered, approximately 10 minutes, until the fish flakes when pricked with a sharp fork. Do not turn the fillets.

When the fillets are done, remove the grill cover and carefully slide the outdoor-cooking spatula between the skin and the flesh of each fillet, leaving the skin on the cooking grate and placing the fillet on a clean platter. Before leaving the grill, use the spatula to remove the skins from the cooking grate; discard the skins.

Serve 1 salmon fillet per person. Pour the Caper Sauce into a small sauceboat equipped with a small sauce ladle, and pass at the table.

SERVES 6

ACCOMPANIMENT SUGGESTIONS: Serve Grilled Salmon Fillets with New Potatoes with Parsley (page 278); Mixed Fresh Vegetables of choice (page 269–270), eliminating the rosemary; and a tossed salad of greens with sliced, fresh mushrooms and White Wine Vinaigrette Dressing (page 130). For dessert, serve Strawberry "Shortcake" (with Angel Food Cake) (page 484–485).

Shellfish

GRILLED LOBSTER TAILS BASTED WITH TARRAGON BUTTER SAUCE

6 African or American lobster tails in the shell (about 8 ounces each)
1 recipe Tarragon Butter Sauce (recipe follows)
1 cup Clarified Butter (page 305)

If purchased frozen, thaw the lobster tails in the refrigerator. Using a small knife and kitchen scissors, cut away and discard the underside hard membrane. Rinse under cold, running water and place, shell side up, on 2 layers of paper towels to drain.

Insert a long, metal skewer (see Note) lengthwise through each tail to prevent curling during grilling. Or, with your hands, bend each tail backward to crack the shell in several places. Place the tails, shell side down, in a pan; brush generously with Tarragon Butter Sauce.

Spray the clean, cold, outdoor-grill cooking grate with nonstick cooking spray. Just before commencing to grill the lobster tails, place the cooking grate in the grill. Place the lobster tails, shell side up, directly on the grill grate, about 4 inches above medium-hot coals (the coals should be covered with a thin layer of ash). Grill the tails, uncovered, for 7 minutes. Turn the tails over (to shell side down). Brush the tails generously with Tarragon Butter Sauce and continue brushing intermittently with the sauce (use all of the sauce) while the tails grill for 10 minutes on the second side. Exact grilling time depends upon the size of the lobster tails, the temperature of coals, the grill, and the weather. The tails are done when the shells are bright red and the meat is opaque.

Serve 1 lobster tail per person. Place an individual, small ramekin of Clarified Butter on each plate.

NOTE: If using wooden skewers, soak the skewers at least 15 minutes in water before inserting in the lobster tails to help prevent burning on the grill.

SERVES 6

TARRAGON BUTTER SAUCE

½ cup (¼ pound) butter
¼ cup freshly squeezed, strained lemon juice
¼ teaspoon dried leaf tarragon
½ teaspoon onion powder

Melt the butter in a small saucepan. Add the lemon juice, tarragon, and onion powder; stir to combine. Keep warm over very low heat.

ACCOMPANIMENT SUGGESTIONS: Serve Grilled Lobster Tails with Rice Pilaf (page 229–230), Carrot Puree (page 260–261), and a tossed green salad (page 102–103).

Wild Game

WINE-MARINATED VENISON STEAKS

4 venison steaks, ½ inch thick
2 cups blackberry wine*
2 teaspoons dried leaf oregano
2 bay leaves
½ teaspoon whole black peppercorns
¼ cup extra-virgin olive oil
1 recipe Onion Butter stars (page 304)

* If blackberry wine is not available, port wine may be substituted.

18 TO 24 HOURS BEFORE GRILLING THE STEAKS: Wash the steaks under cold, running water and place between several layers of paper towels to dry. When dry, trim away all the fat and connective tissue. Place the steaks in an 8 × 8-inch glass baking dish; set aside. In a small mixing bowl, place the wine, oregano, bay leaves, and peppercorns; stir to combine. Pour the wine mixture over the steaks; the steaks must be entirely covered with liquid. If necessary, add additional wine. Cover the baking dish securely with plastic wrap. Refrigerate 18 to 24 hours. The steaks should not be marinated longer than 24 hours.

30 MINUTES BEFORE GRILLING THE STEAKS: Remove the steaks from the refrigerator. Remove the steaks from the marinade and place them on several layers of paper towels. Pat the steaks dry. Do not remove any leaf oregano which may remain on the surface of the steaks after drying. Discard the marinade; wash and dry the baking dish. Return the steaks to the baking dish; brush generously on both sides with olive oil. Let stand, uncovered, at room temperature until grilled.

(Recipe continues on next page)

TO GRILL THE STEAKS: Place the steaks on the outdoor-grill cooking grate, about 4 inches above hot coals (the coals should be barely covered with ash). Grill the steaks, uncovered, for 14 minutes on the first side; turn and grill for an additional 10 minutes on the second side, until well done (see Note). Transfer the steaks to warmed plates and place an Onion Butter star atop each steak. Serve immediately.

NOTE: Venison steaks may be cooked medium (160°F); however, I believe the flavor of venison is enhanced by cooking it well done (170°F). In addition, the meat is more tender when cooked until well done.

SERVES 4

ACCOMPANIMENT SUGGESTION: Potato Pancakes with Lingonberries (page 282–283) are an excellent taste and visual complement to Wine-Marinated Venison Steaks.

Vegetables

ONIONS IN FOIL

FOR EACH INDIVIDUAL SERVING
1 medium onion
1 tablespoon Italian salad dressing, homemade (page 125) or commercially bottled
¼ teaspoon Worcestershire sauce
Dash of salt
Dash of pepper
2 teaspoons butter

Cut off and discard each end of the onion. Peel the onion and remove the outer layer. Partially quarter the onion by making two cuts at right angles from the top through ¾ of the onion (leaving the bottom ¼ of the onion uncut). Place the onion in the center of two layers of heavy-duty aluminum foil cut 12 inches square. Carefully spread the onion slightly apart. Pour the salad dressing and Worcestershire sauce into the center of the onion. Sprinkle the center lightly with salt and pepper. Place the butter pat inside the onion. Seal the onion and seasonings tightly in the foil. With your hands, press the foil against the onion to form a ball shape.

TO COOK ON AN OUTDOOR COVERED GRILL: Place the onions on the cooking grate, about 4 inches above hot coals (the coals should be barely covered with ash). Cover the grill and cook about 35 minutes, turning the onions to a new side every 5 minutes.

TO COOK ON AN UNCOVERED, OPEN GRILL: Place the onions directly on the hot coals and roast for about 25 minutes, turning the onions to a new side every 5 minutes. Begin checking the onions for doneness about 8 minutes before the end of the cooking period. Exact cooking time depends upon the size of the onions, the temperature of coals, the grill, and the weather.

VARIATION: Add a pinch of snipped, fresh oregano or dried leaf oregano to the seasonings placed in the onion before sealing in aluminum foil.

Other Outdoor Cooking Recipes

Mesquite-Grilled Chicken Salad (page 119)
Warm Chicken-Vegetable Salad with Pistachio Nuts and Raspberry Vinaigrette Dressing (page 120)

Eggs

Egg Sizes

Commercial eggs are sold in six sizes: jumbo, extra large, large, medium, small, and peewee. In the preparation of many foods, it is important to use the size of eggs specified in the recipes. With few exceptions, the recipes in *The Blue Ribbon Country Cookbook* call for extra-large eggs.

Egg Safety

The chance of contracting the illness salmonellosis from raw or undercooked eggs is very minimal. Only a very small percentage of eggs (liberally estimated at 0.005 percent, or 1 in 20,000 eggs produced nationally) might contain the bacteria *Salmonella enteritidis*. The bacteria is inside the egg shell, and scientists as yet have been unable to discover how contamination occurs.

While salmonellosis is an uncomfortable illness, it is usually of short duration and is rarely life-threatening. However, some groups of people are particularly vulnerable to the infection. Those at high risk are very young persons, elderly people, pregnant women (because of risk to the fetus), and persons with serious illnesses or weakened immune systems.

Most cases of salmonellosis have been traced to foods other than eggs, namely, chicken, fish, and beef, as well as to human carriers and to cross-contamination via food preparers, kitchen tools, and other foods during preparation.

Refrigeration of eggs at 40°F or below limits the growth of *Salmonella enteritidis*, and the organism is destroyed when eggs are cooked to a temperature of 160°F. The number of *Salmonella enteritidis* bacteria in freshly laid, contaminated eggs is probably very small; therefore, with proper refrigeration, handling, and cooking of these eggs, there is a good chance that the bacteria will not multiply sufficiently to cause sickness in healthy people.

While *Salmonella enteritidis* may be found in both the yolk and white of eggs, egg whites do not support the growth of the bacteria well, whereas egg yolks provide a good environment for multiplication of the bacteria. Therefore, the inclusion of uncooked, refrigerated egg whites in properly refrigerated foods might be considered a low risk for healthy people. A cautionary note heads recipes in *The Blue Ribbon Country Cookbook* which contain uncooked egg whites. Foods in *The Blue Ribbon Country Cookbook* containing egg yolks should be cooked according to the recipe procedures and the guidelines in this section.

Adherence to the following guidelines will help assure the safe purchase, storage, handling, and cooking of eggs:

- Purchase only refrigerated, grade A or AA eggs with clean, uncracked shells.

   There is no difference in nutritional value between infertile and fertile eggs or between white-shelled and brown-shelled eggs. Shell color results from hen breed.

   Yolk color (pale yellow to deep yellow) results from the type of feed consumed by the hen and is not an indication of nutritional content.

- Keep eggs refrigerated at 40°F or below. Refrigerate eggs as soon as possible after purchase.

   It is best to refrigerate eggs in their carton on an inside shelf of the refrigerator rather than to transfer them to the special egg container in the door of some refrigerators. Repeated opening of the refrigerator door risks fluctuation in the temperature of eggs stored in the door. Storage in the carton helps prevent loss of moisture and carbon dioxide from eggs. This is especially applicable with frost-free refrigerators.

- Do not wash eggs before storing or using them. Eggs are washed as a part of commercial processing; therefore, it is unnecessary to rewash them.

- Raw eggs may safely be kept refrigerated at home up to 3 weeks. Hard-cooked eggs, unpeeled or peeled, may safely be kept refrigerated up to 1 week after cooking.

- When recipes call for the use of raw eggs at room temperature, eggs may be left at room temperature up to 2 hours, including preparation time.

- Cooked eggs and cooked dishes containing eggs should not be unrefrigerated for more than 2 hours (not including cooking time). Refrigerate leftover food containing eggs immediately after serving. When refrigerating large amounts of hot, egg-containing food, place smaller portions in shallow containers for quicker cooling.

  Hard-cooked Easter eggs should not be consumed if unrefrigerated for more than 2 hours.

- Do not eat raw egg yolks or foods containing raw egg yolks. Homemade foods which often contain raw egg yolks are: eggnog, Caesar salad, ice cream, mayonnaise, and hollandaise sauce. When made commercially, these foods contain pasteurized eggs. Pasteurization of eggs destroys microorganisms which are present, including *Salmonella enteritidis*.

  For complete safety, do not eat raw egg whites; however, refrigerated raw egg whites in properly refrigerated foods might be considered a low risk for healthy people (see paragraph 5 of this section).

  Make homemade eggnog, ice cream, and like foods using a cooked custard base. (A pasteurized liquid egg product may be used; however, many of the liquid egg products currently available on the retail market contain 98 percent to 99 percent egg white and no egg yolk. When using pasteurized egg products, carefully follow the package instructions for storage and handling to prevent contamination and spoilage.)

  Do not eat uncooked cake batter or cookie dough containing raw eggs, or taste partially cooked foods containing eggs.

- Cook eggs until the whites are completely set and the yolks begin to thicken. The yolks need not be cooked until they are hard. Cook scrambled eggs and omelets until no visible liquid egg remains. Cook fried eggs on both sides or in a covered frying pan, or baste the eggs. For the greatest safety, and especially when preparing eggs for high-risk groups, cook eggs until both the whites and yolks are completely firm.

  Under all circumstances, cook egg yolks and food containing egg yolks to a temperature of 160° F. An instant thermometer (page 28–29) is an efficient, easy way to gauge the temperature of eggs or dishes containing eggs while they are cooking. Baked goods reach a temperature of more than 160° F when fully cooked. Soft custards reach a temperature above 160° F when the mixtures coat a metal spoon.

- A blood spot in an egg does not affect its safety or nutritional value. Simply use a clean teaspoon to remove it, if desired.

- The cord-type parts of an egg white, called the chalazae, are perfectly edible and do not interfere with the beating of egg whites. The chalazae function to hold the egg yolk in the center of the egg white. Thick chalazae are an indication of an egg's freshness and high quality.

- The U.S. Food and Drug Administration recommends washing hands, utensils, equipment, and work surfaces with hot, soapy water *before* and *after* they come in contact with eggs and egg-containing foods.

For answers to further questions pertaining to egg safety, call the U.S. Department of Agriculture's Meat and Poultry Hotline at 888-674-6854 (TTY at 800-256-7072), Monday through

Friday, 10:00 A.M.–4:00 P.M. Eastern time; or visit the Food Safety and Inspection Service Web site at www.fsis.usda.gov; or email at mphotline.fsis@usda.gov.

TO COOK EGGS
IN THE SHELL

HARD-COOKED EGGS: Purchase eggs 5 to 7 days prior to hard-cooking as very fresh, hard-cooked eggs are difficult to peel. To hard-cook eggs, place the eggs in a saucepan and cover with cold water. Cover the pan. Over medium-high heat, bring the eggs to just boiling. Turn off the heat, but leave the covered pan on the burner. If the eggs continue to boil, remove the pan from the burner for a few moments until the burner cools slightly. Let extra-large eggs stand in the hot water 15 minutes. (Decrease or increase the standing time by 3 minutes per egg size [see Egg Sizes, page 220].) Drain immediately and run cold water over the eggs in the saucepan for about 30 seconds. Drain; refill the saucepan with fresh, cold water. Let the eggs stand in the cold water 15 minutes. Drain; place the eggs in a covered container and refrigerate. Peel when ready to use.

Hard-cooking eggs at too high a temperature, or for too long a time at a low temperature, causes the whites to become tough and rubbery and the yolks to become tough and to possibly darken on the surface.

It is important to cool the eggs in cold water immediately after cooking to help prevent the shells from sticking to the cooked egg whites, making peeling difficult. Quickly cooling hard-cooked eggs also helps prevent the yolk surfaces from darkening.

SOFT-COOKED EGGS: Follow the procedure for Hard-Cooked Eggs, above, letting extra-large eggs stand in the hot water from 3 to 5 minutes, depending upon desired softness. Drain immediately and run cold water over the eggs in the saucepan for about 30 seconds until cool enough to handle.

TO SERVE SOFT-COOKED EGGS: To serve a soft-cooked egg in a small ramekin or other sauce-type serving dish, use a sharp knife to break the shell in half widthwise around the egg. Cut the egg in half where the shell was broken. Using a teaspoon, scoop the egg from each shell half into the dish.

To serve a soft-cooked egg in an egg cup, place the unshelled egg, small end down, in the egg cup. Using egg scissors—sometimes called an egg topper—made especially for the purpose (see illustration), cut the shell circularly near the top of the large end of the egg. (If you don't have egg scissors, use a butter knife to tap around the top of the egg and crack the shell.) Using a sharp knife, cut off the top of the egg at the place where the shell was cut (or cracked). Discard the egg top. Supply a small teaspoon for the diner to eat the egg directly from the shell.

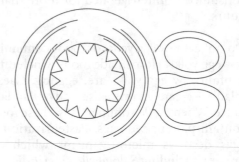

Egg Scissors

BRUNCH EGGS

2 cups (8 ounces) shredded, sharp cheddar
   cheese
2 tablespoons butter
2 tablespoons butter
2 cups sliced, fresh mushrooms
8 ounces commercial sour cream
2 teaspoons Worcestershire sauce
1 cup half-and-half
2 tablespoons Dijon mustard
¼ teaspoon salt
¼ teaspoon white pepper
1 dozen extra-large eggs
1 2-ounce jar diced pimientos, drained
   (2 tablespoons)
2 tablespoons freshly grated Parmesan cheese
   (page 30)

Preheat the oven to 325°F. Butter a 9 × 13-inch
baking dish.

Distribute the cheese evenly over the bottom
of the prepared baking dish; dot with 2 tablespoons butter; set aside. In a small, heavy-
bottomed skillet, melt 2 tablespoons butter over
medium heat. Tilt the skillet back and forth to
completely cover the bottom with the melted
butter. Place the mushrooms in the skillet; sauté
until the mushrooms give up their juices and
the pan liquid reduces to a small quantity covering the bottom of the skillet (about 6 to 7
minutes). In a small mixing bowl, place the
mushrooms and remaining pan liquid, sour
cream, and Worcestershire sauce; stir to
combine.

Spoon the mushroom mixture over the
shredded cheese and butter in the baking dish;
using a small, narrow spatula, spread evenly; set
aside. In a small mixing bowl, place the half-
and-half, mustard, salt, and white pepper; stir
to combine. Pour ½ of the mustard mixture
evenly over the mushroom mixture in the baking dish. Set the remaining ½ of the mustard
mixture aside.

Place the eggs in a medium mixing bowl; using
an electric mixer, beat slightly on medium speed.

Add the pimientos; stir to evenly distribute. Pour
the egg mixture over the mustard mixture in the
baking dish. Pour the remaining ½ of the mustard mixture evenly over the egg mixture. Sprinkle the Parmesan cheese over all. Bake, uncovered,
for 45 minutes, until set.

Using a sharp, thin-bladed knife, cut the
Brunch Eggs into serving pieces. Remove the
serving pieces from the baking dish with a
spatula.

SERVES 8 TO 10

SCRAMBLED EGGS WITH FRESH SAVORY

4 extra-large eggs
¼ cup plus 1 tablespoon whole milk
Dash of salt
1 tablespoon butter
1 teaspoon finely snipped, fresh savory

In a small mixing bowl, place the eggs, milk, and
salt; set aside. In a medium skillet, melt the butter over medium to medium-high heat. While
the butter is melting, beat the egg mixture very
vigorously with a table fork. When the butter just
begins to sizzle (do not let it brown, even faintly),
beat the egg mixture again and immediately
pour it into the skillet. It is important to beat the
egg mixture right up to the moment of pouring
it into the skillet to produce light and airy scrambled eggs.

After pouring the egg mixture into the skillet,
sprinkle it evenly with the savory. Let the egg
mixture cook undisturbed until it begins to con-
geal around the edge of the skillet. Then, using
the table fork or a spatula, turn the egg mixture
over to expose the uncooked portions to the
direct heat of the skillet. After a few seconds,
move and turn the egg mixture again. Continue
moving and turning the mixture until no visible
liquid egg remains. Minimum movement and
turning of the mixture will produce the lightest

(Recipe continues on next page)

scrambled eggs. Do not allow the eggs to brown at all. Serve immediately.

SERVES 2 OR 3, DEPENDING UPON APPETITES

TO REDUCE OR INCREASE THE RECIPE: The recipe may be reduced to as little as 1 egg (use 1 tablespoon plus 1 teaspoon milk, a dash of salt, ¼ teaspoon savory, and about 2 teaspoons butter to grease a small skillet), or the recipe may be increased for more servings.

VARIATIONS

- To make plain scrambled eggs, eliminate the savory.

- Substitute ¼ cup fried and drained bacon pieces for the savory.

FRIED EGGS

1 tablespoon butter, bacon drippings, or
   sausage drippings
4 extra-large eggs
1 tablespoon water

In a 9-inch, heavy-bottomed skillet, melt 1 tablespoon butter over medium heat. If bacon or sausage has just been fried in the skillet, pour the drippings into a small, heatproof bowl. Using a spatula, scrape away and discard any meat particles remaining on the bottom of the skillet. Measure 1 tablespoon of the drippings and return to the skillet; omit the butter. Tilt the skillet back and forth to completely cover the bottom with the melted butter or drippings.

When the fat is sizzling, break the eggs, one at a time, into the skillet. Avoid placing the eggs in the skillet before the fat is hot, as the egg whites will not begin to solidify quickly enough to prevent them from spreading too thinly. When the egg whites have partially solidified, add 1 tablespoon water to the skillet and cover. The steam resulting from the addition of the water will help cook the tops of the eggs without turning them over.

After adding the water and covering the skillet, avoid removing the lid to check the eggs as much as possible, as the steam will escape each time the lid is removed, and the cooking of the top of the eggs will be interrupted. For medium-well doneness, cook the eggs a total of about 5 minutes. When done, serve immediately.

MAKES 4 FRIED EGGS

NOTE: Adjust the size of the skillet and the amount of fat and water to the number of eggs to be fried. Adjust the cooking time to the preference for doneness of eggs (see Egg Safety, page 220).

DEVILED EGGS

(See photo insert page A-8)

1½ dozen small eggs or 1 dozen extra-large
   eggs, hard-cooked (page 222)
¼ teaspoon salt
⅛ teaspoon white pepper
½ teaspoon dry mustard
1 teaspoon sugar
1 tablespoon prepared mustard
⅓ cup Miracle Whip dressing
Paprika and/or single, fresh parsley leaves for
   decoration

Peel the eggs (see Note 1). Cut the eggs in half lengthwise (see Note 2). Remove the yolks and place them in a small mixing bowl; place the egg whites on a piece of waxed paper and set aside. Using a table fork, mash the egg yolks against the side of the mixing bowl until they are of fine consistency. Then, add the salt, white pepper, dry mustard, sugar, prepared mustard, and dressing; using a spoon, stir until blended well.

Using a decorating bag fit with large open-star tip number 6B (page 319), fill the egg whites with the egg-yolk mixture (see Note 3). For simple decoration, sprinkle the egg-yolk fillings with paprika or decorate the top of each filling with a tiny, fresh parsley leaf.

NOTE 1: To peel a hard-cooked egg, softly tap it against the kitchen sink rim to crack the shell. Then, using your fingers, carefully peel away the shell, taking care not to nick the egg white.

NOTE 2: The eggs may be cut widthwise if preferred. Deviled Eggs cut widthwise may be cut sawtooth fashion.

NOTE 3: The egg whites may be filled using a table knife. Then, using your thumb, pat the egg-yolk mixture smoothly into the yolk cavities.

MAKES 3 DOZEN SMALL OR 2 DOZEN EXTRA-LARGE DEVILED EGGS

ALTERNATIVE DECORATIONS

- Decorate each Deviled Egg with a thin slice of cold, Boiled Shrimp (page 191), about ½ inch long, and 3 capers. Six medium shrimp will decorate 3 dozen Deviled Eggs.

- Arrange a tiny sprig of fresh dillweed and 3 capers on top of the egg-yolk filling in each Deviled Egg.

- Decorate the Deviled Eggs with caviar, pieces of smoked salmon, thin slices of stuffed olives, strips of pimiento, or slices of truffles.

EGGS GOLDENROD

Eggs Goldenrod is an old dish which is equally appropriate for sophisticated or simple dining. It is nice to serve for a late-night buffet supper, a brunch, or a family lunch.

2 recipes Medium White Sauce (page 301–302), adding 1 teaspoon sugar, ¾ teaspoon dry mustard, and a dash of cayenne pepper to the total flour mixture for 2 recipes
6 extra-large eggs, hard-cooked
4 slices warm, white toast,* buttered
Sprigs of fresh parsley for garnish

* *Whole-wheat toast may be substituted.*

Prepare the Medium White Sauce; cover and set aside. Peel the eggs. Remove and reserve 2 egg yolks. Chop coarsely the remainder of the eggs, including the 2 extra egg whites; set aside. Grate the 2 reserved egg yolks finely; set aside. Add the chopped eggs to the white sauce; stir to combine. Over medium-low heat, heat the white sauce mixture through, but do not allow it to boil.

Place 1 piece of toast on each of 4 individual plates. Spoon the white sauce mixture over the toast. Sprinkle the grated egg yolks over the white sauce mixture. Decorate the plates with parsley sprigs.

SERVES 4

EGGSOTIC EGGS

10 extra-large eggs, hard-cooked (page 222)
2 13¾-ounce cans artichoke bottoms, drained
3 recipes Thin White Sauce (page 301–302), adding 1½ teaspoons dry mustard and 1½ teaspoons sugar to the total flour mixture for 3 recipes
½ cup Miracle Whip dressing
4 ounces dried beef, cut into ¾-inch squares
½ pound carrots, pared, sliced ¼ inch thick, boiled (page 3), and drained
2 ounces (¾ cup) sliced, fresh mushrooms
2 recipes 4½-Inch-Square Puff Pastry Shells (page 402–404) (16 Puff Pastry Shells)
Garnish (optional; instructions follow)

Butter a 7 × 11-inch baking dish; set aside.

Use 10 yolks and 9 whites of the 10 hard-cooked eggs to make 18 Deviled Eggs (reserve the remaining egg white for other uses). Follow the Deviled Eggs recipe on page 224, using the same amount of ingredients (other than the eggs) as for 1 dozen extra-large eggs, and omitting the decoration. Cut the eggs widthwise in sawtooth fashion. Use large open-star tip number 6B (page 319) to fill the eggs; set aside.

Place 17 artichoke bottoms, stem side down,

(Recipe continues on next page)

in the prepared baking dish (reserving 1 artichoke bottom for garnish). If necessary, cut a small slice off the stem side of the artichoke bottoms so they stand stably in the baking dish. Place 1 Deviled Egg in each artichoke bottom (reserving 1 Deviled Egg for garnish). If necessary, trim a small slice off the bottom of the Deviled Eggs so they rest securely in the artichoke bottoms; set aside.

Preheat the oven to 350°F.

Make the Thin White Sauce; remove from the heat. Add the dressing; using a handheld electric mixer, beat on high speed until blended. Add the dried beef, carrots, and mushrooms; stir to combine. Pour the dried beef mixture over the Deviled Eggs and artichokes in the baking dish. Arrange the partial garnish, if used (see Garnish instructions that follow). Bake, uncovered, for 30 minutes.

Remove from the oven and arrange the remainder of the garnish, if used. Serve Eggsotic Eggs at the table or on the buffet, placing 1 hot Puff Pastry Shell on each individual plate, and spooning 1 artichoke bottom and Deviled Egg with dried beef sauce into each shell.

SERVES 8 (2 FOR EACH DINER)

GARNISH (See Illustration)
1 artichoke bottom, reserved from recipe
    above
1 Deviled Egg, reserved from recipe above
Carrots, pared and boiled (page 3); then, cut
    julienne (page 7) into 20 2-inch-long sticks
Individual pieces of dried beef, rolled tightly
    and cut into 12 1¾-inch-long rolls
Vegetable oil
Small sprigs of fresh parsley leaves
1 Cutout Tomato Star (page 341)

Eggsotic Eggs Garnish

Before baking the Eggsotic Eggs, place an artichoke bottom in the center of the filled baking dish; place the Deviled Egg in the artichoke bottom. Alternate the carrot strips and dried-beef rolls in spoke-like fashion around the artichoke bottom. Brush all the garnish very lightly with vegetable oil.

After baking, arrange the parsley sprigs around the Deviled Egg and place the Cutout Tomato Star in the center of the Deviled Egg filling.

Rice and Beans

Rice

PARBOILED RICE

Parboiled rice, also called converted rice, is a white rice that has been soaked in water, drained, pressure-steamed, and dried before it is milled. This process helps retain the nutrients in the rice, and produces rice that is more fluffy and has greater separation of the kernels after it is cooked.

PERFECT BOILED RICE

For the fluffiest, driest rice imaginable, try this recipe—it really isn't difficult. Once you make boiled rice this way, you will see how easy it is to do and how wonderful the results are.

2 quarts water
1 teaspoon salt
1 cup parboiled* long-grain rice (not instant)

See Parboiled Rice, above

In a kettle or large saucepan, bring the water and salt to a boil over high heat. Add the rice gradually so the water continues to boil. Boil briskly, uncovered, for 20 minutes until the rice is completely tender, stirring occasionally.

Turn the rice into a sieve and rinse it under hot, running water. Place a clean, cotton tea towel, folded into several layers, over the sieve and rice; set aside. Pour very hot water (from the teakettle) into a large saucepan; place the covered sieve in the saucepan *over* the hot water. Make certain that the rice is not touching the water. Do not place the saucepan over heat.

In about 15 minutes, the rice will be fluffy and dry, ready for serving.

MAKES ABOUT 3½ CUPS

BROCCOLI-RICE CASSEROLE

2½ cups water
1 cup parboiled* long-grain rice (not instant)
1 tablespoon butter
4 cups fresh broccoli flowerets
1½ recipes Thick White Sauce (page 301–302)
2 teaspoons instant chicken bouillon granules
¼ teaspoon celery salt
1 8-ounce jar Cheez Whiz pasteurized process cheese sauce
1 tablespoon butter
¾ cup chopped onions
1 tablespoon butter
¼ cup coarsely chopped, fresh mushrooms
¼ cup sliced, then quartered, fresh mushrooms
4 ounces (1 cup) shredded, mild cheddar cheese

See Parboiled Rice, above.

Pour 2½ cups water into a medium saucepan. Cover the saucepan and bring the water to a boil over high heat. Add the rice and 1 tablespoon butter; stir to combine. Cover the saucepan. Reduce the heat and simmer the rice 20 minutes, stirring occasionally. Remove from the heat; let stand, covered, 5 minutes or until all the water is absorbed.

Steam the broccoli flowerets (page 252) 3 minutes. Immediately remove the steamer basket (or top of the steamer pan) containing the broccoli from the saucepan (or bottom of the steamer pan). Leave the broccoli in the steamer basket (pan) and rinse it under cold, running water to stop the cooking; set aside.

Make the Thick White Sauce. Remove from the heat. Add the bouillon granules and celery salt; stir until the granules dissolve. Then, add the process cheese sauce and stir until blended; cover and set aside.

Preheat the oven to 350°F. Grease a 7 × 11-inch baking dish; set aside.

In a small, heavy-bottomed skillet, melt 1 tablespoon butter over medium to medium-high heat. Tilt the skillet back and forth to completely cover the bottom with the melted butter.

Place the onions in the skillet; sauté 5 minutes until pale golden. Add the onions to the white sauce mixture; stir to combine; cover and set aside.

In a clean, small, heavy-bottomed skillet, melt 1 tablespoon butter over medium heat. Place ¼ cup chopped mushrooms and ¼ cup sliced, then quartered mushrooms in the skillet; sauté 3 minutes. Add the sautéed mushrooms and pan liquids to the white sauce mixture; stir to combine; set aside. Drain any water remaining on the rice. Add the white sauce mixture to the rice; stir until combined; set aside.

Arrange the broccoli over the bottom of the prepared baking dish. Spoon the rice mixture evenly over the broccoli. Scatter the shredded cheese over the top. Bake, uncovered, for 30 minutes.

SERVES 14

RICE IN RING MOLD

A lovely way to serve rice.

1½ cups parboiled* long-grain rice (not instant)
2 tablespoons butter, melted
2 tablespoons snipped, fresh parsley
2 tablespoons pine nuts

See Parboiled Rice, page 228.

Butter a 1-quart ring mold; set aside.

Boil the rice, following the procedure in the recipe for Perfect Boiled Rice (page 228). Place the hot, boiled rice in a medium mixing bowl. Add the butter, parsley, and pine nuts; toss until evenly combined. Place the rice mixture in the prepared ring mold; press lightly into the mold. Let stand about 2 minutes. Invert the mold onto a warm, flat serving platter.

SERVES 6

RICE PILAF

Pilaf (also called pilaff, pilau, and pilaw) is a dish of Middle East origin which has been known to the English-speaking world since at least as far back as the seventeenth century. Although it has enjoyed popularity in the southern part of the United States for decades (there, usually called pilau and often pronounced "perlew"), and ethnic groups across the nation have perpetuated traditional versions of the dish, pilaf has undergone a general, American reincarnation in recent years.

While there are many ways to prepare it, pilaf is most commonly made with rice that is first browned in butter or oil and then cooked in broth with seasonings and, often, vegetables. When meat, fowl, fish, or shellfish are added, it becomes a main dish. The version that follows is meant to be a side dish; however, it can be converted into a main dish by adding cooked beef, veal, or lamb.

¼ cup (4 tablespoons) butter
1 cup parboiled* long-grain rice (not instant)
1 tablespoon butter
⅓ cup chopped celery
1 tablespoon butter
½ cup chopped leeks (white and greenish white parts)
¾ cup chopped, fresh mushrooms
1 tablespoon chopped celery leaves
¼ teaspoon salt
⅛ teaspoon pepper
1¾ cups homemade Chicken Broth (page 70–71) or 1 14-ounce can commercial chicken broth
½ cup dry white wine
2 tablespoons snipped, fresh parsley

See Parboiled Rice, page 228

In a small, heavy-bottomed skillet, melt ¼ cup butter over medium heat. Place the rice in the skillet; sauté 5 minutes until it is a deep caramel color, stirring often. Place the rice in a large saucepan; set aside.

Wipe the skillet with a paper towel. Place 1 tablespoon butter in the skillet; melt the butter

(Recipe continues on next page)

over medium heat. Tilt the skillet back and forth to completely cover the bottom with the melted butter. Place the celery in the skillet; sauté 4 minutes, stirring occasionally. Do not let the celery brown. Place the sautéed celery in the saucepan containing the rice; set aside. Add 1 tablespoon butter to the skillet; melt the butter over medium heat. Spread the melted butter over the skillet bottom. Place the leeks and mushrooms in the skillet; sauté 3 minutes, stirring often. Do not let the leeks and mushrooms brown. Add the sautéed leeks and mushrooms with pan juices to the rice. Add the celery leaves, salt, pepper, broth, and wine to the rice; stir to combine all the ingredients in the saucepan. Cover the saucepan.

Bring the rice mixture to a boil over high heat; reduce the heat to low and simmer 20 minutes, stirring occasionally. Most of the liquid will have been absorbed. Remove from the heat; uncover. Quickly add the parsley and stir to evenly distribute. Place a clean, cotton tea towel, folded into several layers, over the pan. Make certain that the entire pan is covered. Move the saucepan to the back of the range (not over direct heat) and let stand 10 minutes or more until no liquid remains. Then, if not served immediately, the saucepan may be placed in a warm (not hotter) oven for a brief period of time to keep the Rice Pilaf warm. Remove the tea towel and place the regular cover on the saucepan before placing it in the oven.

SERVES 6

SPANISH RICE

Serve a tossed salad alongside this dish, and you have a meal. Well, almost. Some of us dessert lovers will want a brownie to top it off.

1 pound lean, pure ground beef
1 tablespoon butter
1 cup chopped onions
1 cup chopped green bell peppers
1 garlic clove, pressed
½ cup water
1 28-ounce can whole, peeled tomatoes, undrained
¾ teaspoon dried leaf oregano
¾ teaspoon chili powder
1 teaspoon sugar
¾ teaspoon salt
½ teaspoon pepper
2 dashes Tabasco pepper sauce
1¼ cups uncooked instant rice

Place the ground beef in an electric skillet or a large, heavy-bottomed skillet on the range. Brown the ground beef over medium to medium-low heat (340° F in an electric skillet) until the meat loses its red color. Using a large, metal mixing spoon, break up the ground beef as it browns. Add the butter, onions, green peppers, and garlic; continue cooking until the onions and green peppers are tender but barely browned. Remove the skillet from the heat and let the mixture cool slightly. Then, add the water, tomatoes, oregano, chili powder, sugar, salt, pepper, and pepper sauce; using the mixing spoon, break the tomatoes into small chunks and stir to combine the ingredients.

Return the skillet heat to medium to medium-low (340° F in an electric skillet). Bring the mixture to a boil. Add the rice; stir to combine. Remove from the heat. Cover the skillet and let stand 7 minutes undisturbed. Then, stir the mixture. If the liquid has not been completely absorbed, simmer the mixture, uncovered, over low heat (250° F in an electric skillet) until the liquid has been reduced sufficiently to achieve the desired consistency of the mixture. Spanish Rice should be moist but not runny.

SERVES 6

BAKED RICE

When time is a factor, one would be hard-pressed to find a more simple rice recipe than this one. It's mighty good, too—one of those "put it in a dish, put it in the oven, and it comes out great" miracle dishes. We all love them!

1¼ cups parboiled* long-grain rice (not instant)
4 cups homemade Chicken Broth (page 70–71) or 2 14-ounce cans commercial chicken broth*
1 medium bay leaf
3 dashes Tabasco pepper sauce
⅛ teaspoon white pepper
¼ cup plus 2 tablespoons (6 tablespoons) butter, melted

See Parboiled Rice, page 228.

**Beef broth may be substituted for chicken broth if the rice is to be served as an accom paniment to a meat dish.*

Preheat the oven to 350° F. Butter a 2-quart round baking dish or a 7 × 11 inch baking dish; set aside.

In a large mixing bowl, place the rice, broth, bay leaf, pepper sauce, white pepper, and butter; stir to combine. Pour the mixture into the prepared baking dish. Bake, uncovered, for 1 hour, until the rice is tender and golden. Stir once or twice during the early part of baking before the rice begins to set.

SERVES 8

VARIATION: Add ¼ cup thinly sliced green onions (scallions) when combining all the ingredients.

TO COOK WILD RICE

Place the raw wild rice in a sieve. Wash the rice *well* under cold, running water. Place the rice in a saucepan; cover with water ½ inch above the rice. Cover the saucepan. Bring the rice to a boil over high heat; reduce the heat and simmer 35 minutes, until all the rice has opened. The water will have been all, or nearly all, absorbed. Stir the rice 2 or 3 times during the cooking period, adding a little additional water if necessary. Wild rice is done when all the kernels have opened.

When the rice is done, remove the saucepan from the heat and move it to the back of the range. Let stand, covered, 1 hour or more to allow any remaining water to be absorbed by the rice.

Just before serving, warm the rice, covered, over very low heat.

1¼ CUPS RAW WILD RICE YIELDS ABOUT 4 CUPS COOKED RICE

VARIATION: Wild rice may be cooked in beef broth or chicken broth rather than water. For 1¼ cups raw wild rice, cook in 2 cups broth. It generally takes longer for wild rice to open when cooked in broth. Add more broth during cooking if necessary.

PECAN WILD RICE

(See photo insert page C-2)

1¼ cups raw wild rice
2 cups homemade chicken broth (page 70–71) or 1 14-ounce can commercial chicken broth
3 tablespoons butter
½ cup chopped pecans
¾ cup chopped onions
½ teaspoon salt
2 tablespoons snipped, fresh parsley

Cook the wild rice in the chicken broth (see To Cook Wild Rice and Variation, above); set aside.

(Recipe continues on next page)

In a small, heavy skillet, melt the butter over medium heat. Tilt the skillet back and forth to completely cover the bottom with the melted butter. Place the pecans and onions in the skillet; sauté lightly until the onions are tender, being careful not to let the butter burn. Add the salt and parsley; stir to combine. Remove from the heat. Add the pecan mixture, including the pan juices, to the wild rice; stir to combine.

SERVES 7 TO 8

WILD RICE CASSEROLE

1 ½ cups raw wild rice
1 pound sliced bacon
1 tablespoon instant chicken bouillon
   granules
⅓ cup boiling water
¾ cup chopped onions
1 cup sliced, fresh mushrooms
8 ounces commercial sour cream
¼ cup Worcestershire sauce
2 tablespoons butter, melted
½ teaspoon salt
¼ teaspoon freshly ground pepper
⅓ cup slivered almonds

Cook the wild rice in water (see To Cook Wild Rice, page 231); set aside.

Preheat the oven to 350°F. Butter a 2-quart round baking dish; set aside.

In a large, heavy-bottomed skillet, fry the bacon over medium heat until crisp; drain well between paper towels. With your fingers, break the bacon into small pieces; set aside. Place the bouillon granules in ⅓ cup boiling water; stir until dissolved; set aside.

In a large mixing bowl, place the wild rice, bacon pieces, bouillon, onions, mushrooms, sour cream, Worcestershire sauce, melted butter, salt, pepper, and almonds; stir until combined. Place the mixture in the prepared baking dish. Bake, uncovered, for 1 hour.

SERVES 8

WILD RICE WITH BACON AND ONIONS

1 ¼ cups raw wild rice
¼ pound (5 slices) bacon, cut widthwise into
   1-inch pieces
1 ¼ cups chopped onions

Cook the wild rice in water (See To Cook Wild Rice, page 231); set aside.

In a medium, heavy-bottomed skillet, fry the bacon pieces over medium heat until crisp. Using a slotted spoon, remove the bacon from the skillet and add to the wild rice; set aside. Place the onions in the skillet; fry in the bacon grease over medium heat until tender and golden in color (about 5 minutes). Add the onions and remaining skillet grease to the wild rice; stir to combine the ingredients. Then, heat the wild rice mixture, covered, over warm heat, stirring 2 or 3 times.

Wild Rice with Bacon and Onions may be prepared up to 1 day before serving and refrigerated in the covered saucepan. Before heating the cold rice mixture over warm heat, add a very small amount of water to barely cover the bottom of the pan.

SERVES 8

Other Rice Recipes

Beans

BAKED BEANS

⅔ cup packed dark brown sugar
1 teaspoon dry mustard
1 31-ounce can Van Camp's pork and beans, undrained
½ cup tomato catsup
1 medium onion
2 slices bacon, cut in half widthwise

Preheat the oven to 325°F. Grease a 1½-quart round baking dish; set aside.

In a small mixing bowl, place the brown sugar and dry mustard; stir to combine; set aside. Spoon ½ of the pork and beans into the prepared baking dish. Sprinkle ½ of the brown sugar mixture evenly over the beans. Repeat the layers with the remaining ½ pork and beans and ½ brown sugar mixture. Pour the catsup back and forth over the top of the beans and brown sugar mixture; using a small, narrow spatula, spread evenly to cover the surface of the beans and brown sugar mixture.

Place the onion in the center of the dish over the catsup. Arrange the bacon slices over the catsup. Bake, uncovered, for 2½ hours.

SERVES 8

CALICO BEANS

Perfect for taking to a potluck.

1 pound lean, pure ground beef
½ teaspoon salt
¼ teaspoon pepper
½ pound sliced bacon
½ cup chopped onions
1 31-ounce can pork and beans, undrained
1 15½-ounce can dark red kidney beans, drained
1 15½-ounce can butter beans, undrained
½ cup packed dark brown sugar
¼ cup granulated sugar
1 teaspoon dry mustard
⅓ cup tomato catsup
2 tablespoons dark molasses

Preheat the oven to 325°F. Grease a 3-quart round baking dish; set aside.

In a large, heavy-bottomed skillet, place the ground beef, salt, and pepper. Over medium to medium-low heat, brown the ground beef lightly. Using a large, metal mixing spoon, break up the ground beef as it browns. Spoon the browned ground beef into a very large mixing bowl; set aside.

Cut 4 slices of bacon widthwise into 1-inch pieces; add to the ground beef; set aside. Cut the remaining slices of bacon widthwise into 1-inch pieces and place in the skillet used to brown the ground beef; fry lightly over medium to medium-low heat. Using a slotted spoon, remove the bacon from the skillet and add to the ground beef; set aside. Place the onions in the skillet used to fry the bacon; brown lightly in the bacon grease over medium heat. Using the slotted spoon, remove the onions from the skillet and add to the ground beef. Add the pork and beans, kidney beans, and butter beans to the ground beef. Do not stir; set aside.

In a small mixing bowl, place the brown sugar, granulated sugar, and dry mustard; stir to combine. Add the catsup and molasses to the

(Recipe continues on next page)

sugar mixture; stir until well combined. Add the sugar mixture to the ground beef and beans; using a large, wooden mixing spoon, stir and fold until all the ingredients are combined and evenly distributed. In the stirring process, try to avoid cutting the beans with the spoon.

Turn the mixture into the prepared baking dish. Bake for 2 hours, covered. Then, remove the cover and continue baking, uncovered, for an additional 1½ hours.

SERVES 12

ACCOMPANIMENT SUGGESTIONS
- In the summer, serve with Corn on the Cob (page 263), Potato Salad (page 111–112), and Marinated Cucumbers and Onions (page 108). For dessert, serve a compote of fresh, summer fruit, and Peanut Cookies (page 554–555).

- In the winter, serve with Iowa Pork Chops (page 156), Coleslaw (page 111), and Deviled Eggs (page 224–225). For dessert, serve Apple Pie (page 409) à la mode.

BAKED BEANS AND POLISH SAUSAGE WITH SAUERKRAUT AND APPLESAUCE

1 15-ounce can pork and beans
2 cups or (16 ounces) commercial, fresh sauerkraut, drained
2 cups homemade extra-thick Plain Applesauce (page 290) or canned commercial plain applesauce
⅓ cup packed dark brown sugar
¼ teaspoon ground allspice
½ pound (2 to 4, depending upon size) Polish sausages, sliced ⅜ inch thick

Preheat the oven to 325°F. Grease a 1½-quart round baking dish; set aside.

In a large mixing bowl, place the pork and beans, sauerkraut, and applesauce; stir to combine; set aside. In a small mixing bowl, place the brown sugar and allspice; stir to combine. Add the brown sugar mixture to the bean mixture; stir to combine. Add the Polish sausage slices; stir until evenly distributed. Place the mixture in the prepared baking dish. Bake, uncovered, for 2 hours.

SERVES 8

Other Bean Recipes

Bean Soup (page 72)
Lima Bean and Ground Sirloin Casserole (page 246)
Succotash (page 271)
Ten-Bean Soup (page 72–73)

Pasta

TO COOK DRIED PASTA

In a large, covered kettle or saucepan, bring sufficient water to a boil, over high heat, as will cover by 2 inches the quantity of pasta to be cooked (approximately 5 quarts of water per pound of pasta). Salt may be added optionally to the water (up to 1 tablespoon per pound of pasta). When the water comes to a rolling boil, uncover the kettle and add the pasta all at once. Cook the pasta uncovered. Return the water (with pasta) to a rolling boil, stirring frequently to prevent the pasta from sticking to the kettle and the pieces of pasta from sticking together. Keep the cooking temperature sufficiently high during the cooking process to retain a rapid boil. Continue to stir frequently during the cooking process. Cook the pasta until it reaches the desired tenderness (approximately 8 to 15 minutes) depending upon the type of pasta and the amount being cooked. Thinner pasta and lesser quantities of pasta require less cooking time.

To check for doneness, use a spoon to cut a piece of the pasta against the inside of the kettle. When done, pasta should be firm and retain its shape, but cut easily. Do not overcook. When done, drain the pasta in a colander or sieve and rinse it under hot, running water. Drain well. Rinse the cooking kettle with hot water and dry the kettle. Return the pasta to the kettle. Melted butter may be added and tossed with the pasta to prevent the pasta from sticking together and to add flavor (about 2 tablespoons of butter per pound of pasta). Or, add the desired sauce and toss. If pasta is to be served cold, rinse it in cold water, drain well, and return it to a cold kettle.

The quantity of pasta required per serving varies widely with the dish to be served and the appetites of the diners; however, ⅛ to ¼ pound per serving is an average range for pasta-intensive dishes.

FETTUCCINE ALFREDO

Main dish, side dish, or first course, this one's rich beyond reason. (Every now and then we're entitled to throw open the gate.) My introduction to this dish was in Rome in 1954, when it was tossed high above the pasta bowl and served by the Alfredo.

1 pound dried fettuccine, cooked, rinsed in
   hot water, and drained (left column)
1 cup (½ pint) whipping cream, unwhipped
½ teaspoon white pepper
¼ teaspoon salt
½ cup (¼ pound) butter, melted
2 cups freshly grated Parmesan cheese
   (page 30)

After cooking, rinsing, and draining the fettuccine, return the hot fettuccine to the rinsed and dried cooking kettle; cover and set aside. Pour the whipping cream into a small saucepan; warm over low heat. Remove from the heat and add the white pepper and salt; stir to combine. Add the cream mixture and butter to the fettuccine; toss until the pasta is evenly coated. Add the Parmesan cheese; toss *well*. Turn into a warm, pasta serving bowl; serve immediately.

SERVES 4 AS A MAIN DISH OR 6 AS A SIDE DISH OR FIRST COURSE

VARIATIONS

- After adding the Parmesan cheese and tossing, add 6 slices bacon, fried crisply, drained, and crumbled; toss until evenly distributed. Or, sprinkle the crumbled bacon over the top of the dish before serving.

- After adding the Parmesan cheese and tossing, add 1½ cups small broccoli flowerets, steamed (page 252) 3 minutes; toss carefully to evenly distribute.

PASTA RIPIENA

½ pound lean, pure ground beef
¾ cup freshly grated Romano cheese
   (page 30)
½ cup commercially packaged, seasoned,
   Italian-style bread crumbs
1 tablespoon plus 1 teaspoon snipped, fresh
   basil
1 large garlic clove, pressed
½ teaspoon salt
¼ teaspoon pepper
2 extra-large eggs
2 tablespoons whole milk
½ cup extra-virgin olive oil
2 garlic cloves, pressed
½ cup water
1 12-ounce can tomato paste
1 8-ounce can tomato sauce
2¾ cups water
1 tablespoon plus 1 teaspoon snipped, fresh
   basil
½ bay leaf
½ teaspoon salt
¼ teaspoon pepper
3 extra-large eggs, hard-cooked (page 222)
2 quarts water
8 ounces rigatoni
⅔ cup freshly grated Romano cheese
   (page 30), divided
1 cup shredded, mild cheddar cheese, divided

In a medium mixing bowl, place the ground beef, ¾ cup Romano cheese, bread crumbs, 1 tablespoon plus 1 teaspoon basil, 1 large pressed garlic clove, ½ teaspoon salt, ¼ teaspoon pepper, eggs, and milk. Using a large, metal mixing spoon, break up the ground beef and stir until the ingredients are completely combined and evenly distributed. Using a 1-inch trigger scoop or melon baller to apportion the meat mixture, roll tiny, 1-inch meatballs in your hands and set aside on a piece of waxed paper. (Makes about 5 dozen meatballs.)

In an electric skillet or a large, heavy-bottomed skillet on the range, heat the olive oil over medium heat (350°F in an electric skillet). Brown ⅓ of the meatballs at a time in the hot olive oil, turning them several times with a very small spatula to achieve even browning and retain their round shape. (It is difficult to turn more than ⅓ of the meatballs at a time in a timely manner.) When properly browned, the meatballs should be medium brown in color and not crusty. Place the browned meatballs in a bowl; cover and refrigerate.

Heat the skillet in which the meatballs were browned to medium heat (350°F in an electric skillet), leaving the olive oil and pan juices in the skillet. Place the 2 pressed garlic cloves in the skillet; sauté the garlic about 1 minute until very slightly browned. Reduce the skillet heat to low (250°F in an electric skillet).

When the skillet cools to the reduced temperature, pour ½ cup water into the skillet and completely deglaze. Pour the skillet liquid into a large (about 8-quart), heavy-bottomed kettle. Add the tomato paste and tomato sauce; stir until the olive oil is completely blended. Add 2¾ cups water, 1 tablespoon plus 1 teaspoon basil, ⅓ bay leaf, ⅓ teaspoon salt, and ¼ teaspoon pepper; stir well to blend and combine.

Cover the kettle; bring the sauce to a fast simmer over medium high heat, stirring often. Reduce the heat to low and maintain a fast *simmer*. Cook for 1 hour, stirring frequently and keeping the vent on the kettle lid open. If the lid does not have a vent, tilt the lid to partially cover the kettle during the last 15 minutes of cooking.

Add the meatballs to the sauce in the kettle; using a wooden spoon to help avoid cutting the meatballs, stir to combine. Cover the kettle and continue simmering the mixture for 1 additional hour, stirring often. Continue to keep the lid vent open, or tilt the kettle lid during the last 15 minutes of cooking. If the sauce reduces to the desired thickness before the cooking time has elapsed, close the vent on the lid and keep the kettle tightly covered except when stirring. A small amount of water may be added if necessary. When the cooking time has elapsed, remove from the heat. Remove and discard the bay leaf. Cover the kettle and set aside.

(Recipe continues on next page)

Peel the eggs. Cut three ⅜-inch egg slices for decoration; set aside. Chop the remaining eggs; set aside. Pour 2 quarts water into a medium kettle. Cover the kettle and bring the water to a rolling boil over high heat. Drop the rigatoni into the boiling water and boil, uncovered, 12 to 14 minutes, until tender, stirring frequently. Do not overcook. Drain the rigatoni in a colander. Return the rigatoni to the kettle in which it was cooked; add hot water to rinse. Drain well in the colander. Turn the rigatoni into a large mixing bowl. Add ½ cup of the sauce (no meatballs) from the kettle and 2 tablespoons of the Romano cheese; toss to combine; set aside.

In an ungreased, 2½-quart, 3-inch-deep, rectangular baking casserole, place ½ cup of the sauce (no meatballs) from the kettle; spread to thinly cover the bottom of the casserole. Add ½ of the rigatoni mixture; spread evenly. Sprinkle ½ of the remaining Romano cheese over the rigatoni mixture. Distribute ½ of the cheddar cheese over the Romano cheese. Spoon ½ of the chopped eggs evenly over the cheddar cheese. Add ½ of the meatballs and ½ of the remaining sauce; distribute evenly. Repeat the layers of rigatoni mixture, Romano cheese, cheddar cheese, chopped eggs, meatballs, and sauce, using the remainder of the ingredients. Decoratively arrange the 3 reserved egg slices on top and in the center of the casserole.

Bake, uncovered, for 25 minutes, until just hot. If the casserole has been refrigerated prior to baking, the baking time will be slightly longer.

SERVES 6 OR 7

MACARONI AND CHEESE

2 quarts water
1¾ cups dried small-elbow macaroni
⅓ cup diced green bell peppers
1 4-ounce jar diced pimientos, drained (¼ cup)
1 12-ounce can (1½ cups) evaporated milk
½ teaspoon salt
½ pound pasteurized process sharp American cheese, cut into approximately ½-inch cubes
2 teaspoons Worcestershire sauce
½ teaspoon dry mustard

Preheat the oven to 350°F. Grease a 2-quart round baking dish; set aside.

Pour 2 quarts water into a medium kettle; cover the kettle and bring the water to a rolling boil over high heat. Drop the macaroni into the boiling water and boil, uncovered, 8 to 10 minutes, until tender, stirring frequently. Do not overcook. Drain the macaroni in a colander; rinse under hot, running water and drain well. Turn the macaroni into a large mixing bowl. Add the green peppers and pimientos; toss to distribute evenly. Place the macaroni mixture in the prepared baking dish; set aside.

In a small saucepan, place the evaporated milk and salt; stir to combine. Place the saucepan, uncovered, over medium heat; scald the milk (page 9). Remove from the heat. Add the cheese, Worcestershire sauce, and dry mustard. Place over low heat and stir until the cheese melts and the mixture is completely blended. Do not allow the mixture to boil. Pour the cheese mixture evenly over the macaroni. Bake, uncovered, for 25 minutes.

SERVES 8

CHICKEN AND BROCCOLI PASTA

2 cups dried rotini, cooked, rinsed in hot
 water, and drained (page 236)
¼ cup (4 tablespoons) butter
1 cup (½ pint) whipping cream, unwhipped
⅛ teaspoon salt
½ teaspoon white pepper
2 cups freshly grated Parmesan cheese
 (page 30)
2 cups cooked, skinless chicken-breast meat
 cut into bite-sized pieces (page 169), hot
2 cups hot, steamed broccoli flowerets
 (page 252)
1 cup sliced, fresh mushrooms (uncooked)
Additional freshly grated Parmesan cheese
 (page 30)

After cooking, rinsing, and draining the rotini,
return the hot rotini to the rinsed and dried
cooking kettle. Add the butter, whipping cream,
salt, white pepper, and 2 cups Parmesan cheese;
using a wooden mixing spoon, toss to combine.
Add the hot chicken, hot broccoli, and mushrooms; toss lightly to evenly distribute. Pass
additional Parmesan cheese at the table.

SERVES 4

VARIATIONS

• Substitute the following meat and vegetable
 combinations, or other combinations of
 your choice, for the chicken, broccoli, and
 mushrooms, making the substitutions in
 amounts and proportions to suit your taste
 preferences:

 ~ Crisply fried bacon pieces, cooked peas,
  and cooked carrot slices.

 ~ Bite-sized pieces of medium-rare beef tenderloin (see Meat Safety, page 134),
  steamed zucchini sliced ½ inch thick and
  cut in half, and fresh tomato pieces with
  seeds and cores removed (page 29).

 ~ Hot ring bologna slices, cooked green
  beans, and bite-sized pieces of steamed red
  bell peppers.

• Substitute spinach or rainbow rotini for the
 plain rotini.

GRACE MONTOGNESE'S BRACIOLE
Italian Steak Rolls

STEAK ROLLS

4 boneless, top round steaks, about
 ½ pound each, cut ¼ inch thick
6 slices bacon
1 cup minced celery hearts (with leaves)
 (page 7)
¾ cup freshly grated Romano cheese
 (page 30)
¾ cup commercially packaged, seasoned,
 Italian-style bread crumbs
1 large or 2 small garlic cloves, pressed
1 teaspoon dried leaf basil
1 tablespoon plus 1 teaspoon finely snipped,
 fresh parsley
½ teaspoon salt
¼ teaspoon pepper
2 extra-large eggs

SAUCE

2 cups water
3 cups water
2 18-ounce cans tomato paste
1 15-ounce can tomato sauce
1 garlic clove, pressed
1 bay leaf
1 teaspoon dried leaf basil
½ teaspoon dried leaf oregano
1 teaspoon dried parsley
½ teaspoon salt
¼ teaspoon pepper

PASTA

1 pound dried linguini
¾ cup freshly grated Romano cheese (page 30),
 divided
Additional freshly grated Romano cheese
 (page 30)

Cut each round steak in half widthwise. Using a
sharp knife, slit any fat on the sides of the meat
diagonally at 2-inch intervals, being careful not
to cut into the flesh (causing loss of meat juice);
set aside. Cut major portions of fat from the

(Recipe continues on next page)

bacon. Place the bacon fat inan electric skillet or a large, heavy-bottomed skillet on the range. Melt the bacon fat over low heat (250°F in an electric skillet). Meanwhile, cut the remaining bacon into ¼-inch-square pieces. In a large mixing bowl, place the bacon, celery, ¾ cup Romano cheese, bread crumbs, 1 large or 2 small pressed garlic cloves, 1 teaspoon basil, fresh parsley, ½ teaspoon salt, ¼ teaspoon pepper, and eggs; stir until thoroughly combined; set aside.

Remove the skillet from heat. Using a slotted spoon, remove the unmelted bacon pieces from the skillet and discard. Set the skillet aside (do not remove the bacon grease).

Lay the 8 pieces of round steak on a piece of waxed paper resting on a flat work surface. Spoon the bacon mixture, evenly divided, onto the meat pieces. Using a spoon, spread the bacon mixture evenly over each piece of meat to within ½ inch of the edges. Roll each piece of meat widthwise, jelly-roll fashion, and tie securely with cotton string, making certain the filling is sealed in; set aside.

Heat the skillet containing the bacon grease to medium (350°F in an electric skillet). When hot, place the braciole (steak rolls) in the skillet; brown well on all sides (about 15 minutes). Add some olive oil to the skillet if additional fat is needed. When brown, place the braciole in a flat pan and reduce the skillet heat to low (250°F in an electric skillet).

When the skillet cools to the reduced temperature, add 2 cups water and deglaze completely. Pour the skillet liquid into a large, *heavy-bottomed* kettle. To the kettle, add 3 cups water and the tomato paste, tomato sauce, 1 pressed garlic clove, bay leaf, 1 teaspoon basil, oregano, dried parsley, ½ teaspoon salt, and ¼ teaspoon pepper; stir to combine. Bring the sauce to a simmer over medium-high heat, stirring constantly. Reduce the heat to low and add the braciole; cover and simmer slowly 2½ hours. During the cooking period, occasionally run a large mixing spoon or spatula under the braciole to help prevent them from sticking to the bottom of the kettle.

20 MINUTES BEFORE SERVING TIME: Cook the linguini, rinse in hot water, and drain (page 236). Return the hot linguine to the rinsed and dried cooking kettle; cover to keep warm; set aside. Remove the braciole from the kettle and carefully remove the string. Place the braciole on a heated serving platter; cover with aluminum foil to keep warm. Remove the bay leaf from the cooked sauce and discard.

Add 3 cups of the cooked sauce and ½ cup of the Romano cheese to the linguini; toss to combine and turn into a warm, pasta serving bowl. Sprinkle the remaining ¼ cup Romano cheese over the linguini. Cover the Romano cheese with an additional 1 cup sauce; *do not toss.* Spoon some sauce over the braciole. Serve the braciole and linguini at the table. Pass additional Romano cheese in an appropriate serving dish and additional sauce in a sauce dish.

SERVES 8

GRACE'S SPAGHETTI AND MEATBALLS

M E A T B A L L S
1½ cups commercially packaged, seasoned, Italian-style bread crumbs
2 cups freshly grated Romano cheese (page 30)
1 tablespoon dried leaf basil
¾ teaspoon salt
¼ teaspoon pepper
¾ pound lean, pure ground beef
¼ pound lean, ground pork
4 extra-large eggs
⅓ cup whole milk
2 garlic cloves, pressed
2 tablespoons snipped, fresh parsley
¼ cup vegetable oil

In a large mixing bowl, place the bread crumbs, Romano cheese, basil, salt, and pepper; stir to combine. Add the ground beef, ground pork, eggs, milk, garlic, and parsley. Using a large, metal mixing spoon, break up the ground meat and stir until the ingredients are evenly combined. Turn the mixture into an 8 × 8-inch baking dish; pat evenly into the bottom of the dish. Using a small knife, cut the mixture into 16 equal portions. Using your hands, roll each portion into a compact meatball and set aside on a piece of waxed paper.

In an electric skillet or a large, heavy-bottomed skillet on the range, heat the vegetable oil over medium-high heat (375°F in an electric skillet). Place the meatballs in the skillet and brown about 10 minutes, until medium brown in color but not crusty, turning often to retain their round shape. Place the browned meatballs in a bowl; cover and refrigerate.

TOMATO SAUCE
½ cup extra-virgin olive oil
2 garlic cloves, pressed
2 12-ounce cans tomato paste
2 8-ounce cans tomato sauce
6 cups water
1 teaspoon dried leaf sweet basil
1 teaspoon dried leaf oregano
1 bay leaf
1 teaspoon salt

Heat the olive oil in a 6- to 8-quart, heavy-bottomed kettle over medium-high heat. Place the garlic in the kettle; brown about 2 minutes in the hot oil. Remove the kettle from the heat and allow the oil to cool slightly. Then, add the tomato paste and tomato sauce; stir until the olive oil is completely blended. Add the water, basil, oregano, bay leaf, and salt; stir until well combined. Cover the kettle; bring the sauce to a fast *simmer* over medium-high heat, stirring often. Reduce the heat to low and maintain a fast simmer. Cook for 1 hour, stirring frequently and keeping the vent on the kettle lid open. If the lid does not have a vent, tilt the lid to partially cover the kettle during the last 15 minutes of cooking.

Add the meatballs to the sauce in the kettle. Cover the kettle and continue simmering the mixture for an additional 1 hour, stirring

often. Use a wooden mixing spoon to stir, and stir in a circular motion to help prevent cutting the meatballs. Continue to keep the lid vent open, or tilt the kettle lid during the last 15 minutes of cooking. If the sauce reduces to the desired thickness before the cooking time has elapsed, close the vent on the lid and keep the kettle tightly covered except when stirring. A small amount of water may be added if necessary. If the sauce is slightly thin at the end of the cooking period, remove the cover and continue simmering for a few minutes until it is reduced to the desired consistency. Remove from the heat. Remove and discard the bay leaf. Cover the kettle; set aside.

SPAGHETTI
1 pound dried spaghetti

Cook the spaghetti (page 236); drain in a sieve. Rinse under hot, running water; drain well in the sieve. (Do not add butter.)

TO SERVE
1¾ cups freshly grated Romano cheese (page 30), divided

Place the spaghetti in the bottom of a large, warm pasta bowl. Sprinkle ¾ cup of the Romano cheese over the spaghetti; set aside. Carefully remove the meatballs from the tomato sauce and place in a bowl; cover to keep warm and set aside. Ladle 1 cup of the sauce into a small sauce dish to serve at the table as extra sauce; cover to keep warm and set aside.

Pour all but approximately 1½ cups of the remaining sauce over the spaghetti and cheese; toss until evenly combined. Sprinkle ¼ cup of the Romano cheese over the spaghetti mixture. Arrange the meatballs on top of the spaghetti mixture toward one side of the bowl (to retain an uncovered surface of spaghetti for serving). Spoon the remaining 1½ cups sauce over all. Place the remaining ¾ cup Romano cheese in an appropriate serving dish to pass at the table.

SERVES 8

(Recipe continues on next page)

ACCOMPANIMENT SUGGESTIONS: Spaghetti and meatballs are traditionally served with an all-green lettuce and vegetable salad (page 102–103) tossed with Italian Salad Dressing (page 125), and Garlic Bread (page 356–357).

LASAGNA

(See photo insert page C-5)

1/3 pound Italian sausage
2/3 pound lean, pure ground beef
1 garlic clove, pressed
1 tablespoon snipped, fresh parsley
1 tablespoon snipped, fresh basil
1 teaspoon salt
1 14½-ounce can petite diced tomatoes, undrained
1 12-ounce can tomato paste
3 cups small curd, cream-style cottage cheese
2 extra-large eggs, beaten
1 teaspoon salt
½ teaspoon pepper
2 tablespoons snipped, fresh parsley
½ cup freshly grated Parmesan cheese (page 30)
10 ounces dried lasagna (about 2/3 of a 16-ounce box), cooked, rinsed in hot water, and drained (page 236)
1 pound mozzarella cheese, sliced very thinly

In an electric skillet or a large, heavy-bottomed skillet on the range, place the Italian sausage, ground beef, and garlic over medium heat (350°F in an electric skillet). Brown the meat, using a large, metal mixing spoon to break up the meat as it browns. Reduce the heat to very low (220°F in an electric skillet). When the skillet cools to the reduced temperature, add the 1 tablespoon parsley, basil, 1 teaspoon salt, tomatoes, and tomato paste; stir to combine. Simmer, uncovered, 30 minutes, until the sauce is thick, stirring occasionally.

Preheat the oven to 375°F Grease a 9 × 13-inch baking dish; set aside.

In a medium bowl, place the cottage cheese, eggs, 1 teaspoon salt, pepper, 2 tablespoons parsley, and Parmesan cheese; stir to combine; set aside. Arrange ½ of the cooked lasagna, single layer, in the bottom of the prepared baking dish. Spread ½ of the cottage cheese mixture evenly over the lasagna. Arrange ½ of the mozzarella cheese slices over the cottage cheese mixture. Spread ½ of the meat sauce over the cheese slices. Repeat the layers, using the remaining ½ of the ingredients.

Bake, uncovered, for 30 minutes. Remove from the oven and let stand 15 minutes to allow the Lasagna to set slightly. To serve, cut the Lasagna into 12 square servings with a sharp knife. Use a small spatula to remove the servings from the baking dish.

SERVES 12

MACARONI-BEEF CASSEROLE

1 tablespoon vegetable shortening
1 pound lean, pure ground beef
1 cup chopped green bell peppers
1 cup chopped onions
1 teaspoon salt
1/8 teaspoon pepper
1 10-ounce package frozen whole-kernel corn
2 quarts water
1 teaspoon salt
1½ cups dried elbow macaroni
1 14½-ounce can petite diced tomatoes, undrained
1 10¾-ounce can condensed tomato soup

In an electric skillet or a large, heavy-bottomed skillet on the range, melt the vegetable shortening over medium heat (350°F in an electric skillet). Tilt the skillet back and forth to completely cover the bottom with the melted shortening. Place the ground beef in the skillet and begin to brown. Using a large, metal mixing spoon, break up the ground beef as it heats and browns. When the meat begins to lose its red color, add the green peppers, onions, salt, and pepper; stir to combine and continue browning. When the meat is brown and the vegetables are cooked lightly, remove from the heat; set aside. Cook the corn, following directions on the package; drain in a sieve and set aside.

Preheat the oven to 350° F. Grease a 2-quart round baking dish; set aside.

Pour 2 quarts water into a medium kettle; add 1 teaspoon salt and stir to combine. Cover the kettle and bring the salted water to a rolling boil over high heat. Drop the macaroni into the boiling water and boil, uncovered, 10 minutes, until tender, stirring frequently. Do not overcook. Drain the macaroni in a colander; rinse under hot, running water and drain well; set aside.

Add the tomatoes and tomato soup to the ground beef mixture; using a metal mixing spoon, stir to blend and combine the ingredients. Add the corn and macaroni; toss carefully to evenly distribute. Turn the mixture into the prepared baking dish. Bake, covered, for 35 minutes.

SERVES 8

VARIATIONS
- Prior to baking, top the casserole with freshly grated Parmesan cheese (page 30), or shredded cheddar or mozzarella cheese.

- Substitute cooked green beans or carrots for the corn, or use one or both of them in combination with the corn (decreasing the amount of corn proportionately).

ISABEL'S NOODLE KUGEL

(See photo insert page C-6)

Noodle Kugel is a classic Jewish side dish that I first enjoyed at Isabel and Stan Levin's home. Isabel serves other versions of noodle kugel made with fruits, raisins, and additional sugar or preserves as dessert.

⅓ cup sugar*
1 teaspoon ground cinnamon**

1 teaspoon salt
8 ounces commercial sour cream
1 cup small curd, cream-style cottage cheese
4 quarts water
12 ounces extra-wide dried egg noodles
3 tablespoons butter, melted
4 extra-large eggs, beaten
3 tablespoons cornflake crumbs, commercially packaged or crumbed in a blender or food processor (page 34)
3 tablespoons butter

* *The sugar may be increased to ½ cup, if desired.*

***The cinnamon may be increased to 1¼ teaspoons, if desired.*

Preheat the oven to 350° F. Butter a 9 × 13-inch baking dish; set aside.

In a medium mixing bowl, place the sugar, cinnamon, and salt; stir to combine. Add the sour cream and cottage cheese; stir to combine; set aside.

Pour 4 quarts water into a medium kettle; cover and bring the water to a boil over high heat. Drop the noodles into the boiling water and boil, uncovered, about 10 minutes, until just tender, stirring frequently. Do not overcook. Drain the noodles in a sieve; rinse under hot, running water and drain well. Rinse and dry the cooking kettle; return the noodles to the kettle. Add 3 tablespoons melted butter; toss until the noodles are evenly coated. Add the sour cream mixture and eggs; stir to combine.

Turn the noodle mixture into the prepared baking dish; spread evenly. Sprinkle the cornflake crumbs over the top. Dot with 3 tablespoons butter. Bake for 20 minutes. Then, cover loosely with aluminum foil and bake an additional 15 minutes, until fully set.

Using a sharp knife, cut the Noodle Kugel into 15 servings. Use a small spatula to remove the servings from the baking dish.

SERVES 15

RAINBOW PASTA DINNER

4 slices bacon, cut widthwise into 1-inch
  pieces
1 large onion, chopped (about 1½ cups)
1 green bell pepper, diced (about 1¼ cups)
1 pound lean, pure ground beef
1 teaspoon salt
¼ teaspoon pepper
2 14½-ounce cans whole, peeled tomatoes,
  undrained
1 teaspoon dried leaf basil
¼ teaspoon dried leaf oregano
1 teaspoon sugar
¾ cup chili sauce
1 14½-ounce can cut wax beans, drained
2 quarts water
3 cups (8 ounces) dried rainbow rotini (also
  known as garden rotini)

In an electric skillet or a large, heavy-bottomed skillet on the range, fry the bacon pieces over medium-low heat (300°F in an electric skillet) until cooked but not overly crisp. Using a slotted spoon, remove the bacon from the skillet and place in a small bowl; set aside. Place the onions and green peppers in the skillet; fry in the bacon grease over medium-low heat (300°F in an electric skillet) until the onions are lightly browned. Add the ground beef, salt, and pepper. Using a large, metal mixing spoon, break up the ground beef and stir to combine with the onions and peppers. Continue frying over medium-low heat (300°F in an electric skillet) until the ground beef is medium browned.

Reduce the skillet heat to very low (215°F in an electric skillet). When the skillet cools to the reduced temperature, add the bacon, tomatoes, basil, oregano, sugar, and chili sauce. Using the large, metal mixing spoon, break the tomatoes into bite-sized chunks; stir to combine all the ingredients. Cover the skillet and simmer the mixture 25 minutes, stirring occasionally. Then, uncover the skillet and continue simmering about 10 to 15 minutes, until the mixture is reduced to a thick consistency. The mixture should not be runny; however, it should not be reduced to a pasty consistency. Add the wax beans; heat through.

Meanwhile, pour 2 quarts water into a medium kettle. Cover the kettle and bring the water to a rolling boil over high heat. Drop the rotini into the boiling water and boil, uncovered, 10 to 12 minutes, until tender, stirring occasionally. Drain the rotini in a colander; rinse under hot, running water and drain well.

Add the rotini to the ground beef mixture; toss lightly to combine. Serve in a large bowl.

SERVES 8

Other Pasta Recipes

One-Dish Meals

BAKED CABBAGE WITH HAMBURGER

Believe it or not, this recipe is from my grand-mother's cookbook. One might easily think it had been expressly tailored to twenty-first-century informal dining.

1 small head of cabbage, cored
1 pound lean, pure ground beef
1 extra-large egg
2 tablespoons whole milk
2 tablespoons all-purpose flour
¾ cup coarsely chopped onions
⅛ teaspoon dry mustard
½ teaspoon salt
¼ teaspoon pepper
1 tablespoon butter, melted
Dash of ground nutmeg
Chili sauce

Preheat the oven to 350°F.

Place the cabbage in the center of a roaster or Dutch oven; set aside. In a large mixing bowl, place the ground beef, egg, milk, flour, onions, dry mustard, salt, and pepper. Using a large, metal mixing spoon, break up the ground beef and stir until the ingredients are evenly combined. Spoon the ground beef mixture around the cabbage. Bake, covered, for 1¼ hours, until the cabbage is tender and the ground beef mixture is well done.

Place the cabbage in the center of a serving plate and surround it with the ground beef mixture. Just before serving, drizzle the melted butter over the cabbage and sprinkle the cabbage lightly with a dash of nutmeg.

To serve, cut the cabbage into 4 wedges and place 1 wedge on each of 4 dinner plates. Using a spoon, place ¼ of the ground beef mixture next to and touching the cabbage wedge on each plate. Place the chili sauce in a sauce dish and pass at the table.

SERVES 4

LIMA BEAN AND GROUND SIRLOIN CASSEROLE

1¾ cups dried baby lima beans
1 pound ground sirloin
1 teaspoon salt
¼ teaspoon pepper
1 teaspoon dry mustard
1 14½-ounce can whole, peeled tomatoes, undrained
½ cup chili sauce
1 tablespoon packed light brown sugar
1 teaspoon dried leaf basil
½ bay leaf
3½ cups sliced yellow onions separated into rings

Wash and sort the beans; place them in a large mixing bowl. Cover the beans with cold water and soak them overnight (or about 8 hours).

Preheat the oven to 325°F. Grease a 3-quart round baking dish; set aside.

Drain the beans and set aside. In a large mixing bowl, place the ground sirloin, salt, pepper, and dry mustard; using a large, metal mixing spoon, break up the ground sirloin and stir until the ingredients are evenly combined; set aside. In a medium mixing bowl, place the tomatoes, chili sauce, brown sugar, basil, and bay leaf; using a tablespoon, break the tomatoes into coarse pieces and stir to combine the ingredients; set aside.

In the prepared baking dish, layer in the following order: ½ of the beans, ½ of the ground sirloin mixture, ½ of the onion rings, and ½ of the tomato mixture. Repeat the layers, using the remaining ½ of the ingredients. Bake, covered, for 3 hours.

SERVES 8

LAYERED ZUCCHINI CASSEROLE

1 pound (1 large) zucchini, unpared, sliced
⅛ inch thick
2 cups thyme croutons (see Herb Croutons,
page 32)
1 large onion, sliced as thinly as possible
½ medium green bell pepper, sliced
lengthwise ⅛ inch thick
¾ pound (2 medium) fresh tomatoes,
blanched (page 29), peeled, and sliced
¼ inch thick
1 extra-large egg
1 teaspoon dried leaf basil
½ teaspoon dry mustard
½ teaspoon salt
¼ teaspoon pepper
6 slices bacon, cut widthwise into 1-inch
pieces
6 ounces Swiss cheese, thinly sliced
1 recipe (¼ cup) Buttered Cracker Crumbs
(page 33)
1 tablespoon freshly grated Parmesan cheese
(page 30)

Preheat the oven to 350° F. Butter a 7 × 11-inch baking dish; set aside.

Steam the zucchini (page 252) 3 minutes. Immediately remove the steamer basket containing the zucchini from the pan. Leave the zucchini in the steamer basket and rinse it under cold, running water to stop the cooking. Drain *well;* set aside.

In the bottom of the prepared baking dish, distribute the croutons evenly. Over the croutons, layer in the following order: the steamed zucchini, onions, green peppers, and tomatoes; set aside. In a small mixing bowl, place the egg, basil, dry mustard, salt, and pepper; using a handheld electric mixer, beat lightly on medium speed. Pour the egg mixture evenly over the tomato layer in the baking dish. Arrange the bacon, then the Swiss cheese, in layers over the top. Bake, uncovered, for 15 minutes.

Meanwhile, in a small mixing bowl, place the crumbs and Parmesan cheese; stir to combine; set aside. At the end of the 15-minute baking period, remove the baking dish from the oven. Increase the oven temperature to 375° F. Sprinkle the crumb mixture evenly over the top of the casserole; return it to the oven and bake, uncovered, an additional 30 minutes.

Remove the baking dish from the oven; place it on a wire rack and let stand 3 minutes. Using a sharp knife, cut the Layered Zucchini Casserole into 8 serving pieces. Use a spatula to remove the servings from the baking dish.

SERVES 6 TO 8

DINNER-IN-A-HURRY CASSEROLE

1 pound lean, pure ground beef
1 1-ounce package onion soup mix
1 10¾-ounce can condensed cream of celery
soup (undiluted)
1 10-ounce package frozen tiny peas,
uncooked
1 pound frozen Tater Tots potatoes, uncooked

Preheat the oven to 350°F. Grease a 2-quart round baking dish.

In the prepared baking dish, layer in the following order: the ground beef, onion soup mix, celery soup, peas, and potatoes. Bake, covered, for 1 hour.

SERVES 6

RING BOLOGNA CASSEROLE

1 1-pound ring of beef bologna
2 recipes Medium White Sauce (page 301–302)
1 10¾-ounce can condensed cream of
   mushroom soup (undiluted), or 1 recipe
   Cream of Mushroom Soup
   (page 71–72)
4 cups water
1 tablespoon plus 1 teaspoon instant beef
   bouillon granules
5 ounces (2½ cups) kluski dried egg noodles*
2 cups finely chopped onions (about 1 large
   onion)
1 tablespoon snipped, fresh parsley
½ cup fresh green beans cut into 1-inch
   pieces, cooked (page 254) and drained
2 tablespoons Buttered Bread Crumbs (page 33)

*If kluski egg noodles are not available, regu-
lar thin, narrow, dried egg noodles may be
substituted.*

Preheat the oven to 325°F. Butter a 2-quart
round baking dish; set aside.

Slice the bologna ¼ inch thick; peel off the cas-
ing. Cut each slice into quarters; set aside. Prepare
the Medium White Sauce. Add the mushroom
soup; stir to blend. Cover and set aside.

Pour 4 cups water into a large saucepan;
bring to a boil over high heat. Add the bouillon
granules; stir until dissolved. Add the noodles
and cook, uncovered, in the boiling bouillon
until tender, stirring often. Drain the noodles in
a sieve; return the noodles to the saucepan and
rinse in hot water. Drain the noodles again in
the sieve; set aside.

To the white sauce mixture, add the bologna,
noodles, onions, parsley, and green beans; stir
and fold until combined and evenly distributed.
Turn the mixture into the prepared baking dish.
Sprinkle the crumbs evenly over the top. Bake,
uncovered, for 1 hour.

SERVES 6

VARIATION: Substitute bratwurst for the ring beef
bologna.

TUNA-NOODLE CASSEROLE

2 tablespoons butter
½ cup chopped onions
⅓ cup chopped celery
1 cup sliced, fresh mushrooms
1 recipe Thin White Sauce (page 301–302),
   increasing the pepper to ¼ teaspoon
½ cup mayonnaise
½ teaspoon soy sauce
½ teaspoon dry mustard
8 ounces (4 cups) egg noodles, cooked, rinsed
   in hot water, and drained (page 236)
9-ounces (1 6-ounce can plus 1 3-ounce can)
   solid, white albacore tuna, packed in water
1 15-ounce can peas, drained
1 recipe (¼ cup) Buttered Cracker Crumbs
   made with saltines (page 33)

In a small, heavy-bottomed skillet, melt the butter over medium heat. Tilt the skillet back and
forth to completely cover the bottom with the
melted butter. Place the onions and celery in the
skillet; sauté lightly 2 minutes. Add the mushrooms; sauté 1 minute. Do not allow the vegetables to brown. Set aside.

Preheat the oven to 350°F. Butter a 2-quart
round baking dish; set aside.

Make the Thin White Sauce. Add the mayonnaise, soy sauce, and dry mustard; using a handheld electric mixer, beat over low heat until
smooth. Add the mushroom mixture with pan
juices; stir to combine. Remove from the heat
and set aside.

Turn the drained noodles into a large mixing
bowl. Add the white sauce mixture; toss to combine; set aside. Drain the tuna; cut into generous
chunks. Add the tuna chunks and drained peas
to the noodle mixture; using a wooden mixing
spoon, toss carefully to avoid crushing the tuna
and peas.

Turn the mixture into the prepared baking
dish. Sprinkle the crumbs evenly over the top.
Bake, uncovered, for 35 minutes.

SERVES 8

MARTHA COTTER'S SEVEN-LAYER DINNER

¼ cup parboiled* long-grain rice (not instant)
6 slices thick bacon
1 recipe Cream of Mushroom Soup**
    (page 71–72)
1 pound lean, pure ground beef
½ teaspoon ground marjoram
¼ teaspoon salt
⅛ teaspoon pepper
1 14½-ounce can whole, peeled tomatoes
1 teaspoon dried leaf basil
¼ teaspoon salt
⅛ teaspoon pepper
2 cups sliced, raw russet potatoes
¼ teaspoon salt
⅛ teaspoon pepper
¾ cup chopped onions
½ cup diced green bell peppers
1 cup fresh green beans cut into
    1½ inch pieces

* See Parboiled Rice, page 228

** 1 10¾-ounce can commercial, condensed cream of mushroom soup (undiluted) may be substituted.

Boil the rice (page 228); set aside. Cut the bacon widthwise into 1-inch pieces. In a medium skillet, *partially* fry the bacon over medium heat to extract some of the fat. Using a slotted spoon, remove the bacon from the skillet and place in a small bowl; cover and set aside. Make the Cream of Mushroom Soup; cover and refrigerate.

Preheat the oven to 350° F. Butter a 2½-quart, 3½-inch-deep baking casserole with straight sides; set aside.

In a medium mixing bowl, place the ground beef, marjoram, ¼ teaspoon salt, and ⅛ teaspoon pepper; using a large, metal mixing spoon, break up the ground beef and stir until the ingredients are evenly combined. Cover the ground beef mixture and set aside. Drain the tomatoes in a sieve; reserve the drained juice for

other uses. Place the tomatoes in a medium mixing bowl; using the edge of a tablespoon, break the tomatoes into coarse pieces. Do not drain off the juice which accumulates from breaking up the tomatoes. To the tomatoes, add the basil, ¼ teaspoon salt, and ⅛ teaspoon pepper; stir to combine; cover and set aside. In the prepared baking casserole, layer in the following order, the:

Potatoes
¼ teaspoon salt (sprinkle over the potatoes)
⅛ teaspoon pepper (sprinkle over the
    potatoes)
Onions
Bacon
Ground sirloin mixture (drop chunks evenly
    over the bacon layer)
Rice
Green peppers
Green beans

Pour the tomato mixture and accumulated juice evenly over the green beans. Spoon the Cream of Mushroom Soup evenly over all. Bake, covered, for 45 minutes. Uncover and bake for an additional 30 minutes.

SERVES 6 GENEROUSLY

PORK CHOP DINNER IN FOIL

(See photo insert page B-7)

A fun, one-dish meal. Take the aluminum-foil bundles directly from the oven to the picnic table on the patio or in the yard (or on the porch, balcony, or terrace if you're an apartment dweller) and delight in winsome outdoor dining with simplicity. Toss an uncomplicated green salad and if you're in the mood, pour glasses of red wine.

1 tablespoon vegetable shortening
4 loin pork chops, 1¼ inches thick
Salt and pepper to taste

(Recipe continues on next page)

4 ears of sweet corn
4 medium to small red potatoes
1 large onion, cut into 8 slices
1 teaspoon dried dillweed
Salt
¼ cup (4 tablespoons) butter

Cut four 14 × 18-inch pieces of heavy-duty aluminum foil; set aside.

Preheat an electric skillet or a large, heavy-bottomed skillet on the range to medium-high (380°F in an electric skillet). Melt the shortening in the skillet. Tilt the skillet back and forth to completely cover the bottom with the melted shortening. Place the pork chops in the skillet; sprinkle lightly with salt and pepper to taste. Brown the pork chops well (about 10 minutes on each side), turning once. Place 1 pork chop and 1 ear of corn in the center of each piece of foil; set aside.

Preheat the oven to 350°F.

Pare the potatoes and slice each potato widthwise about 3⁄16 inch thick. Next to each pork chop, place the slices of 1 potato overlapping in a fan shape. On each sheet of foil, tuck 1 slice of onion under all the slices of potato and 1 slice of onion between the slices in the middle of the potato. Sprinkle the potatoes and onions on each sheet of foil with ¼ of the dillweed and a dash of salt. Dot the potatoes, onions, and corn with the butter (1 tablespoon per foil dinner).

Wrap and seal each foil bundle tightly, leaving the pork chops, corn, and potatoes and onions flat on the bottom of the aluminum foil (do not roll the bundle contents). Place the bundles, single layer, on 1 or 2 shallow cookie pans. Bake for 1 hour, until the potatoes and onions are tender, and the pork chops have reached an internal temperature of at least 160°F as gauged on an instant thermometer (page 28–29). Unwrap the foil and transfer the dinners from the foil to individual dinner plates.

SERVES 4

Other One-Dish Meal Recipes

Vegetables

Steamed Vegetables

Most vegetables better retain their nutrients, flavor, and shape if steamed rather than boiled. To steam vegetables, pour about ¾ inch water in a saucepan. Place a steamer basket in the saucepan and arrange raw, prepared vegetables in the basket. Cover the saucepan. Bring the water to a boil over high heat; reduce the heat to low and steam the vegetables over briskly simmering water until they reach the desired doneness.

Steamer pans with a removable, perforated top section which fits into the bottom pan (like a double boiler) are also available.

For maximum nutrient and flavor retention, vegetables should be cooked until just tender but still firm. Overcooking vegetables is a common error. Nowadays, vegetables generally are not cooked as long as they were in years past.

Boiled Vegetables

Some especially firm vegetables, such as potatoes (except very small new potatoes), carrots, turnips, parsnips, and kohlrabi, are more satisfactorily cooked by boiling rather than steaming as it is difficult to get these vegetables done in a timely manner by steaming.

To boil vegetables, place the prepared vegetables in a saucepan; cover the vegetables with hot water. Cover the saucepan. Bring the vegetables to a boil over high heat; reduce the heat to medium and boil the vegetables until the desired doneness.

Asparagus Spears (page 253), Green and Wax Beans (page 254), and Beets (page 255) are among other vegetables generally cooked by boiling. Corn on the Cob is most commonly and best prepared by boiling (page 263).

Miniature Vegetables

Miniature (or baby) vegetables are colorful on the plate, fun to eat, and easy to prepare. They are served at posh dinner parties and are equally popular with family meal planners, who utilize them to add variety and spark to everyday fare.

Most appealing and fashionable when served in mixed combinations, it is left to the cook's imagination to combine varieties of miniatures which mingle compatible flavors and are color-coordinated with the rest of the meal. For example, carrots, turnips, scallopini, and tiny, red cocktail tomatoes might be served with Roast Beef Tenderloin (page 138–139), while yellow sunburst squash, leeks, kohlrabi, and eggplants could be selected to accompany Baked Walleye Deluxe (page 185–186).

The favored way of preparing miniature vegetables is simply to steam them and toss them lightly in butter. It would defeat the uniqueness of these special little morsels to bury their cunningness in sauces—they are sufficient unto themselves. As the skins of miniatures are often thicker than their full-sized counterparts, the steaming time required to tenderize these small vegetables is often longer than might be expected. For example, while full-sized green zucchini sliced ¼ inch thick steam to tenderness in 3 minutes, miniature zucchini require a full 5 minutes of steaming to reach a palatable level of doneness. Steaming times for the various varieties of miniatures are left to the vigilant cook watching over the steamer.

Miniature vegetables are available in specialty food stores and are turning up with more frequency in produce departments of top-line supermarkets. They can be specially ordered by most produce purveyors. Among the kinds of miniature vegetables available are the following:

Artichokes
Beets
Belgian Endive
Bok Choy
Broccoli
Carrots
Cauliflower
Corn
Eggplants
Kohlrabi
Leeks
Potatoes
Squash (scallopini, green summer, yellow sunburst, yellow crookneck, green zucchini, and yellow zucchini)
Tomatoes (yellow teardrop and red cocktail [tiny cherry])
Turnips

Asparagus

ASPARAGUS SPEARS

Asparagus spears are generally cooked by boiling as long spears will not lie flat in most household-sized steamers. To prepare the spears for boiling, break one spear (of typical size to the remainder of the spears) in your hands to determine the natural breaking point, above which the spear will be tender. Cut the remaining spears uniformly in this length.

To boil the asparagus, pour about ½ inch water into a skillet large enough in diameter to accommodate the spears to be cooked. Cover the skillet. Bring the water to a boil over high heat. Place the spears in the skillet; reduce the heat to medium. Cover the skillet. Return the water to a simmer and cook the asparagus about 3 minutes, depending upon their size.

To serve, drain the asparagus well and brush with a small amount of melted butter.

ASPARAGUS SPEARS AMANDINE

1 tablespoon butter, melted
¼ cup sliced almonds, toasted (page 35)
1¼ pounds fresh asparagus spears, cooked (see Asparagus Spears, above)

Melt the butter in a tiny saucepan. Add the toasted almonds and stir to coat. Arrange the cooked asparagus spears in a vegetable serving dish or on individual serving plates. Spoon the almonds and remaining butter over the asparagus.

SERVES 4

ASPARAGUS CUSTARD

2 cups fresh asparagus pieces cut diagonally into 1½-inch lengths
3 slices bacon, cut widthwise into 6 pieces
3 extra-large eggs
¼ teaspoon white pepper
1 teaspoon Worcestershire sauce
1 cup whole milk, scalded (page 9)
1 cup Fresh Bread Crumbs (page 33)
1 cup finely shredded Colby cheese

Preheat the oven to 325° F. Butter a 1½-quart round baking dish; set aside.

Pour about ½ inch water into a medium saucepan; bring to a boil over high heat. Place the asparagus pieces in the saucepan; reduce the heat to medium. Cover the saucepan. Return to a simmer and cook the asparagus 5 minutes. Drain the asparagus thoroughly in a colander; set aside. In a small, heavy skillet, fry the bacon pieces over medium heat until partially cooked; drain between several layers of paper towels and set aside.

Place the eggs in a medium mixing bowl; using an electric mixer, beat slightly on medium speed. Add the white pepper and Worcestershire sauce; stir to combine. Slowly add the scalded milk to the egg mixture, stirring constantly. Add the asparagus, bread crumbs, and cheese; stir to

(Recipe continues on next page)

combine. Place the mixture in the prepared baking dish. Top with the bacon pieces.

Place the baking dish in a 9 × 13-inch baking pan; then, pour very hot, but not boiling, water into the pan to approximately ½ the height of the baking dish. Bake, uncovered, for 1 hour, or until a table knife inserted near the center of the Asparagus Custard comes out clean.

SERVES 6

DIVINE BAKED ASPARAGUS

1 pound fresh asparagus spears
1½ recipes Medium White Sauce
   (page 301–302)
2 ounces finely shredded Swiss cheese (about
   ½ cup)
2 ounces crumbled Maytag blue cheese (about
   ½ cup)
¾ cup sliced almonds
1 recipe (¼ cup) Buttered Cracker Crumbs
   (page 33)

Wash the asparagus; trim off the lower "woody" portions of the spears. Cut the spears into 2½-inch lengths. Place the asparagus in a medium saucepan; add water to cover. Cover the saucepan. Bring the asparagus to a boil over high heat; reduce the heat and simmer 10 minutes. It is important to cook the asparagus this length of time in order to extract sufficient water from the spears to avoid a thin, runny, final baked dish. Drain the cooked asparagus well in a colander.

Preheat the oven to 350°F. Butter a 6 × 10-inch baking dish; set aside.

Prepare the Medium White Sauce; remove from the heat. Add the Swiss cheese and blue cheese; stir until the cheeses have melted and the sauce is smooth. (To facilitate the melting process, the sauce may be stirred over low heat if care is taken not to allow the sauce to reach a simmer.) When the cheeses have melted, add the almonds; stir to combine; set aside.

Arrange the asparagus pieces evenly in the prepared baking dish. Pour the cheese sauce evenly over the asparagus; top with the crumbs. Bake, uncovered, for 30 minutes. The mixture will be bubbly and the crumbs golden.

SERVES 6

Green and Wax Beans

TO COOK AND SERVE GREEN AND WAX BEANS
(See photo insert page B-5)

Wash the beans well, using a vegetable brush if necessary. Cut or snap off the ends and pull off the strings along both sides of the pods if the strings are large and tough. Leave the beans whole, or cut or snap into uniform lengths of choice. Place the prepared beans in a saucepan and cover with water. Add salt if desired. Cover the saucepan and bring the beans to a boil over high heat. Reduce the heat and simmer 10 minutes or until the beans reach the desired tenderness. To serve, drain the beans, add butter, and toss.

GREEN BEAN CASSEROLE

1 1-pound package frozen French-cut green
   beans
½ cup reserved liquid from cooked and
   drained green beans
¾ cup shredded Colby cheese
1 10¾-ounce can condensed cream of
   mushroom soup (undiluted)
¼ cup finely chopped onions
1 2-ounce jar diced pimientos, drained
   (2 tablespoons)
¾ cup commercially canned French-fried
   onions

Preheat the oven to 350°F. Grease a 6 × 10-inch baking dish; set aside.

Cook the green beans, following instructions on the packages. Drain the beans in a sieve, reserving ½ cup cooking liquid. In a large mixing bowl, place the green beans, ½ cup reserved cooking liquid, cheese, mushroom soup, chopped onions, and pimientos. Turn the mixture into the prepared baking dish. Bake, uncovered, for 25 minutes. Top with the French-fried onions and return to the oven to bake for an additional 5 minutes.

SERVES 8

GREEN BEANS WITH BACON AND ONIONS

5 slices bacon, cut widthwise into 1-inch pieces
½ cup chopped onions
½ teaspoon salt
⅛ teaspoon pepper
2 teaspoons tarragon vinegar
½ teaspoon dried leaf tarragon
1¼ pounds fresh green beans, cooked (cooked 254) and hot

In a small, heavy-bottomed skillet, fry the bacon pieces over medium heat until crisp. Using a slotted spoon, remove the bacon from the skillet and place in a small bowl (do not drain the fried bacon); set aside. Place the onions in the skillet used to fry the bacon; fry in the bacon grease over medium heat until tender (about 5 minutes). Remove the skillet from the heat. Let the skillet (with onions) stand until cooled to a low temperature. Then, place the bacon, salt, pepper, vinegar, and tarragon in the cooled skillet with the onions; stir to combine; set aside.

Drain the hot, cooked green beans. Pour the bacon and onions mixture over the beans and toss lightly to combine.

SERVES 8

GREEN BEANS WITH MARJORAM

1 pound green beans
2 packed tablespoons finely snipped, fresh marjoram or 2 teaspoons dried leaf marjoram
1 tablespoon butter

Follow To Cook and Serve Green and Wax Beans procedure (page 254), adding the marjoram to the saucepan containing the beans and water before cooking. To serve, drain the beans, add the butter, and toss.

SERVES 4

Beets

TO COOK AND SERVE BEETS

Trim away a portion of the stems and roots of beets, *leaving 1 inch of the stems and 1 inch of the roots on the beets.* Discard the portions of stems and roots trimmed away. Using a vegetable brush, scrub the beets thoroughly. Place the beets in a saucepan; add water to cover. Cover the saucepan. Bring the beets to a boil over high heat. Reduce the heat and cook at a low boil for ½ to 1 hour (depending upon the size and age of the beets), until tender. Drain the beets.

When cool enough to handle, cut off the remaining stems and roots of the beets. Then, slip the skins off the beets. Leave the beets whole or slice, dice, or cut them julienne (page 7). To serve, drizzle a small amount of melted butter over the beets and toss gently.

HARVARD BEETS

Although this recipe's name would appear to indicate its origin, such may not be the case. There is a school of thought (no pun intended) that insists these beets derived their name from the fact that they share the same color as Harvard's football jerseys. Apparently, rivalry generated another dish called "Yale Beets." It is made exactly like Harvard Beets except orange juice is substituted for the vinegar and 1½ teaspoons of lemon juice are added. To date, I have found no interpretation of the implications of these ingredient substitutions (if there are any) and I shall not venture one.

Others who dig into this sort of food lore argue that the dish was served in a mid-nineteenth-century Boston restaurant by the name of Harwood's and that the Russian proprietor, having difficulty with English, pronounced the name of his restaurant more like "Harvard."

4 cups cooked fresh beets (see To Cook Beets, page 255) sliced ³⁄₁₆ inch thick, reserving cooking liquid, or 2 14½-ounce cans commercial sliced beets, drained, reserving liquid
¼ cup sugar
2 tablespoons cornstarch
¼ teaspoon ground cloves
¼ cup plus 2 tablespoons cider vinegar
2 tablespoons butter

Measure 1¼ cups reserved beet liquid; set aside. In a medium-large saucepan, place the sugar, cornstarch, and cloves; stir to combine. Add 1¼ cups reserved beet liquid and the vinegar; stir to blend. Place the saucepan over medium-high heat and cook the mixture until thick and translucent (about 7 minutes), stirring constantly. Remove from the heat. Add the butter; stir until dissolved. Add the beets and stir to combine; heat through.

SERVES 6

Bok Choy

Bok choy or pak choi (*Brassica chinensis*) resembles a bunch of celery in form, with rather wide, thick, white stalks and broad, glossy, dark green leaves (see illustration). Bok choy is a standard vegetable in Oriental diets, and is sometimes known as "Chinese cabbage." However, this name can lead to confusion, as napa and michihli cabbages (types of *Brassica pekinensis*) are most often, if not generally, also called "Chinese cabbage." Napa and michihli cabbages resemble a tight bunch of leaf-type lettuce. Michihli cabbage is longer and more slender in form than napa cabbage. The leaves of both are comparatively thin, crinkled looking, and pale green. A knowledgeable produce department manager and the accompanying illustration will help distinguish bok choy from napa and michihli cabbages in case of question.

BOK CHOY ROULADES

This recipe uses only bok choy leaves. Use the remaining stalks in a stir-fry, or split the stalks in half lengthwise, then cut the split stalks into 2-inch-long pieces and stuff them to make a refreshingly different, crunchy hors d'oeuvre (see Bok Choy Stuffed with Red Caviar, page 48–49).

1½ dozen medium to thin, fresh asparagus spears
4 thin carrots
6 leafy bok choy stalks
3 extra-large eggs, hard-cooked (page 222) and sliced
1 recipe Mustard Hollandaise Sauce (page 303), warm

Wash the asparagus spears. Cut the spears to a uniform length of about 5 inches; set aside. Pour about ½ inch water into a skillet large enough in diameter to accommodate the spears. Cover the skillet. Bring the water to a boil over high heat. Place the spears in the skillet; reduce the heat to medium. Cover the skillet. Return the water to a simmer and simmer the spears about 2 minutes, until just tender; drain immediately and set aside.

Pare the carrots and cut them into 5-inch lengths. Quarter each carrot lengthwise. Place the carrots in a saucepan; add water to cover. Cover the saucepan. Bring the carrots to a boil over high heat. Reduce the heat to medium and simmer the carrots until tender but still rigid (about 3 to 5 minutes). Drain well; set aside.

Cut the large green leaves off the bok choy stalks at the place the stalks turn white. Reserve the white stalks for other uses. Wash the bok choy leaves. Lay the leaves flat in a large kettle; add water to cover. Cover the kettle. Bring the leaves to a boil over high heat; reduce the heat and simmer for 3 minutes or until the leaves are tender but retain their shape. Carefully remove the bok choy leaves from the kettle and place them between paper towels to drain.

Then, widthwise across each leaf near the cut end, place 3 asparagus spears, 2 carrot strips, and 2 egg slices. (Reserve the remaining egg slices for other uses.) Starting from the cut end, roll each leaf jelly-roll fashion. The asparagus spears and carrots should show on the ends of the roulades. Place the roulades, seam down, in a pan over hot water until ready to serve. Finely dice the remaining cooked carrots for garnish; set aside.

To serve, spoon the warm Mustard Hollandaise Sauce over each roulade and garnish the top with the diced carrots.

SERVES 6

Bok Choy

Broccoli

BROCCOLI CASSEROLE

8 cups fresh broccoli stalks cut 3 inches long and slit 2 or 3 times (see recipe procedures, below, for preparation)
1 recipe Cream of Mushroom Soup (page 71–72) or 1 10¾-ounce can commercial, condensed cream of mushroom soup (undiluted)
8 ounces commercial sour cream
½ cup chopped celery
1 2-ounce jar diced pimientos, drained (2 tablespoons)
1 cup shredded, sharp cheddar cheese
¼ teaspoon salt
¼ teaspoon pepper
¼ cup Whole-Wheat Onion Crumbs (recipe follows)

Preheat the oven to 350° F. Grease a 6 × 10-inch baking dish; set aside.

Cut off and discard the lower portion of the broccoli stalks, leaving 3-inch-long spears. Wash the broccoli. Cut each broccoli spear lengthwise 2 or 3 times to form uniformly slit stalks with flowerets about 1 inch in diameter. Steam the spears (page 252) until just tender (about 4 minutes). In the prepared baking dish, arrange the spears in overlapping rows to cover the bottom of the dish; set aside.

In a medium mixing bowl, place the soup, sour cream, celery, pimientos, cheese, salt, and pepper; stir well to combine. Spoon the mixture evenly over the broccoli spears, taking care to cover all the spears. Spread the mixture to the sides of the dish. Sprinkle the Whole-Wheat Onion Crumbs over the top. Bake, uncovered, for 30 minutes. The mixture will be bubbly and the crumbs will be lightly browned.

SERVES 6 TO 8

WHOLE-WHEAT ONION CRUMBS

¼ cup (4 tablespoons) butter, melted
2 teaspoons finely grated onions
1 cup coarse, dried, whole-wheat bread
  crumbs (page 33)

Melt the butter in a small saucepan over medium-low heat. Place the onions in the saucepan; sauté lightly. Remove from the heat; add the crumbs and stir until the crumbs are evenly coated with the butter mixture (see Note).

NOTE: Only ¼ cup Whole-Wheat Onion Crumbs is called for in the Broccoli Casserole recipe above. Freeze the remaining crumbs in a tightly covered, labeled, pint jar. These crumbs freeze nicely for convenient future use to top casseroles.

VEGETABLE MEDLEY

Follow the Broccoli Casserole recipe, above, substituting 8 cups steamed (page 252), mixed, fresh, cauliflower flowerets, Brussels sprouts, asparagus spears cut into 2-inch lengths, pearl onions, and broccoli (or any combination thereof) for 8 cups broccoli spears. Vegetable Medley is especially nice if you double the recipe and use a 9 × 13-inch baking dish.

BROCCOLI PUREE

2 pounds fresh broccoli
3 tablespoons butter, melted
2 tablespoons whipping cream, unwhipped
¼ teaspoon ground marjoram
¼ teaspoon salt
¼ teaspoon pepper

Cut off and discard the lower portion of the broccoli stalks. Wash the broccoli. Cut the flowerets off the stems; set the flowerets aside. Slice the stems ½ inch thick and place in a large saucepan; add water to cover. Cover the saucepan. Bring the sliced stems to a boil over high heat; reduce the heat and cook at a low boil 15 minutes. Add the flowerets; boil an additional 10 minutes. Drain the stems and flowerets well in a colander.

In a blender (see Note), place the stems and flowerets. Add the butter, whipping cream, marjoram, salt, and pepper; process until pureed. Broccoli Purée may be reheated in the top of a double boiler over simmering water. To serve, spoon into a small serving dish.

NOTE: If a blender is not available, a food processor may be used.

MAKES 2 CUPS PURÉE

Brussels Sprouts

DINNER BRUSSELS SPROUTS

4 cups fresh Brussels sprouts, trimmed
1¾ cups homemade Chicken Broth (page 70–71)
  or 1 14-ounce can commercial chicken broth
¼ teaspoon salt
⅛ teaspoon pepper
2 tablespoons butter

In a medium saucepan, place the Brussels sprouts, broth, salt, and pepper. Cover the saucepan. Bring the mixture to a boil over high heat. Reduce the heat and simmer until the Brussels sprouts are just tender and still bright green in color (about 7 minutes, depending on the size of the Brussels sprouts). Using a slotted spoon, remove the Brussels sprouts from the saucepan and place in a bowl; cover and keep warm. Boil the Brussels sprouts cooking liquid, uncovered, in the saucepan until reduced to about ½ cup. Add the butter and melt; stir to blend. Return the Brussels sprouts to the saucepan and heat through; toss well with the broth mixture.

Using a slotted spoon, place the Dinner Brussels Sprouts in a serving dish or on individual dinner plates.

SERVES 6

CREAMED BRUSSELS SPROUTS WITH CHESTNUTS

1 ½ pounds fresh Brussels sprouts, trimmed
1 recipe Medium White Sauce (page 301–302)
½ cup finely shredded Swiss cheese
¼ teaspoon ground sage
1 ½ cups shelled, skinned, and boiled whole chestnuts (page 35) or 1 8-ounce jar commercial, roasted whole chestnuts

Steam the Brussels sprouts (page 252); drain well in a colander; set aside. In a medium saucepan, prepare the Medium White Sauce. Add the cheese and sage; stir until the cheese has melted and the mixture is smooth; cover and set aside. If using canned chestnuts, drain the chestnuts in a colander; rinse and redrain. Add the Brussels sprouts and whole chestnuts to the cheese sauce; heat through over low heat. Do not allow to boil.

SERVES 8

VARIATION: The chestnuts may be chopped before adding to the cheese sauce.

Cabbage

BRAISED CABBAGE

Why don't we prepare this good-tasting, easy-to-fix dish more often? Maybe it's already in your current, standard repertoire. But if it isn't, and if you're seeking new menu ideas for retrieval from one of those cooking ruts into which we all slip, consider adding this to your rescue list of recipes.

¼ cup (4 tablespoons) butter
1 2-pound head cabbage, cored and sliced ¼ inch thick
⅔ cup chicken broth, homemade (page 70–71) or commercially canned

¼ teaspoon salt
¼ teaspoon white pepper
½ teaspoon sugar
Ground nutmeg

In an electric skillet or a heavy-bottomed skillet on the range, melt the butter over medium-low heat (260° F in an electric skillet). Place the cabbage in the skillet; sauté 2 minutes, turning the cabbage often with a spatula. Cover the skillet. Cook the cabbage 7 minutes, turning occasionally. Add the broth. Cover the skillet and braise the cabbage 5 minutes, until just tender. Avoid overcooking. Add the salt, white pepper, and sugar; toss to combine.

Place ½ of the Braised Cabbage in a serving bowl; sprinkle moderately with nutmeg. Add the remaining ½ of the Braised Cabbage; sprinkle nutmeg lightly over the top.

SERVES 8

SAUERKRAUT

Even if you think you don't like sauerkraut, give it another try using this recipe. Home-canned or fresh sauerkraut is on a much higher echelon than most commercially canned sauerkraut, and the added ingredients in this recipe blend to deliver a gourmet-like flavor you may not have expected possible in a sauerkraut dish.

2 pounds commercial, fresh sauerkraut
2 tablespoons bacon grease
1 large onion, chopped (about 1 ¼ cups)
1 cup canned vegetable broth
1 ¼ cups Riesling wine
1 tablespoon dried juniper berries
¼ teaspoon caraway seed
¼ teaspoon dried leaf marjoram
¼ teaspoon dried leaf thyme
½ bay leaf
1 tablespoon all-purpose flour
2 tablespoons water

(Recipe continues on next page)

In a sieve, drain the sauerkraut well. Place the drained sauerkraut in a large, heavy-bottomed saucepan; set aside. In a small, heavy-bottomed skillet, melt the bacon grease over medium heat. Place the chopped onions in the skillet; sauté only until a very pale, golden color (about 5 minutes). Using a slotted spoon, remove the onions from the skillet and add to the sauerkraut. Add the broth and wine to the sauerkraut; stir to combine; set aside.

Using slightly dampened cheesecloth, make a cheesecloth bag (page 28) filled with the juniper berries, caraway seed, marjoram, thyme, and bay leaf; add to the sauerkraut mixture and press under the surface of the sauerkraut. Cover the saucepan. Bring the sauerkraut mixture to a simmer over medium-high heat. Reduce the heat to low and simmer 45 minutes, stirring occasionally.

Remove the cheesecloth bag from the saucepan and discard. In a very small glass jar or plastic container with a secure lid, place the flour and 2 tablespoons water; cover and shake vigorously until blended and smooth. Add to the sauerkraut mixture; stir to blend. Simmer the sauerkraut mixture 2 minutes, until the liquid is slightly thickened, stirring constantly. Remove from the heat. If not serving immediately, cover the saucepan and let stand up to 2 hours before serving time. Otherwise, refrigerate. This sauerkraut may be made and refrigerated up to 2 days before serving.

Near serving time, reheat the Sauerkraut over medium heat, stirring often. At serving time, drain the Sauerkraut in a sieve, reserving the liquid to use in reheating any leftover Sauerkraut. Keeps in the refrigerator up to 4 days from the time it is made.

SERVES 8 AS A SIDE DISH OR 6 WHEN SERVED WITH A SAUERKRAUT-INTENSIVE ENTRÉE

RED CABBAGE WITH RED WINE

1 cup water
1 2½-pound head red cabbage, shredded
1 cup dry red wine, such as Cabernet
    Sauvignon, divided

2 large Golden Delicious apples, pared,
    quartered, cored, and sliced
¼ cup packed light brown sugar
1½ teaspoons all-purpose flour
1 teaspoon salt
Dash of pepper
¼ cup cider vinegar
3 tablespoons butter, melted

Pour 1 cup water into a medium kettle. Cover the kettle and bring the water to a boil over high heat. Place the cabbage in the kettle; cover and reduce the heat. Simmer the cabbage 15 minutes. Then, add ½ cup of the wine; simmer, covered, 5 minutes. Add the apples; simmer, covered, 5 minutes. Add the remaining ½ cup of wine; simmer, covered, 5 minutes, until the cabbage is tender.

Meanwhile, in a small mixing bowl, place the brown sugar, flour, salt, and pepper; stir to combine. Add the vinegar and butter; stir to blend and combine. When the cabbage is tender, add the brown sugar mixture and stir well; simmer, uncovered, 5 minutes, stirring often.

SERVES 6 TO 8

Carrots

CARROT PUREE

1 pound carrots, pared and sliced ½ inch thick
1 medium onion, quartered
¼ teaspoon celery salt
⅛ teaspoon white pepper
Dash of ground nutmeg
1 tablespoon butter, softened
1 tablespoon cream or whole milk
Ground nutmeg for garnish

In a medium saucepan, place the carrots and onions; add water to cover. Cover the saucepan. Bring the carrots and onions to a boil over high heat. Reduce the heat and simmer briskly until the carrots are *very* tender (about 20 minutes). Drain the carrots and onions in a sieve; remove the onions and reserve for other uses.

In a blender (see Note), place the carrots, celery salt, white pepper, nutmeg, butter, and cream; process until pureed. To serve, spoon the Pureed Carrots into a serving dish and sprinkle a little nutmeg on top for garnish. Or, using a decorating bag fit with large open-star tip number 8B (page 319), pipe a decorative portion of Pureed Carrots onto each individual plate.

NOTE: If a blender is not available, a food processor may be used.

SERVES 4

DILLED CARROT CASSEROLE

2 pounds carrots, pared and sliced diagonally
  ½ inch thick (about 4½ cups)
4 ounces shredded, sharp cheddar cheese
  (about 1 cup)
1½ recipes Dill Croutons (see Herb
  Croutons, page 33)
2 extra-large eggs
½ teaspoon salt
¼ cup half-and-half
¼ cup (4 tablespoons) butter, melted

Preheat the oven to 350°F. Butter a 6 × 10-inch baking dish; set aside.

Place the carrots in a large saucepan; add water to cover. Cover the saucepan. Bring the carrots to a boil over high heat; reduce the heat and simmer the carrots 10 minutes, until just tender. Drain the carrots thoroughly in a colander. Return the drained carrots to the saucepan. Add the cheese and croutons; toss until evenly distributed. Turn the mixture into the prepared baking dish; spread evenly; set aside.

Place the eggs in a small mixing bowl; using an electric mixer, beat slightly on medium speed. Add the salt, half-and-half, and butter; beat only until blended. Pour evenly over the carrot mixture. Bake, uncovered, for 25 minutes, until lightly brown.

SERVES 8

GLAZED CARROTS

1 pound carrots
2 tablespoons butter
¼ cup packed light brown sugar

Pare the carrots. Cut the carrots in half widthwise; then, cut each carrot half lengthwise in half or into fourths, depending upon the diameter of the carrot. Place the carrots in a large saucepan; add water to cover. Cover the saucepan. Bring the carrots to a boil over high heat. Reduce the heat and simmer the carrots briskly 10 minutes, until just tender. Drain the carrots in a colander. Return the drained carrots to the saucepan; cover and set aside on the back of the range (*not* over heat).

Melt the butter in a small saucepan over low heat. Add the brown sugar; stir continuously until the brown sugar warms, dissolves some, and completely blends with the butter. Pour the brown sugar mixture over the carrots; using a wooden spoon, toss carefully to coat. Cover and place over *warm* (not hotter) heat; let stand 5 minutes. Watch carefully—if the brown sugar commences to burn or the carrots begin to brown, immediately remove from the heat. During the 5-minute standing time, the brown sugar will fully dissolve and the glaze will become thin for better coverage of the carrots. Toss again before serving.

SERVES 6

Celery

CELERY BAKED IN ALMOND SAUCE

5 cups celery sliced ½ inch thick (about
   1 bunch celery; select celery with narrow
   stalks)
2 recipes Medium White Sauce (page
   301–302), substituting 1½ cups whole milk
   and ½ cup reserved celery cooking liquid
   (see recipe procedures below) for 2 cups
   whole milk; substituting ¾ teaspoon salt
   for 1 teaspoon salt; and using white pepper
2 leafy celery tops, chopped
¼ cup slivered almonds, toasted (page 35)
½ cup finely chopped onions
1 2-ounce jar diced pimientos, drained
   (2 tablespoons)
1 tablespoon butter
2 tablespoons Dried Bread Crumbs
   (page 33)
2 tablespoons chopped, toasted (page 35)
   slivered almonds

Place the celery in a saucepan; add water to
cover. Cover the saucepan. Bring the celery to a
boil over high heat. Reduce the heat and simmer 10 minutes, until the celery is just tender.
Drain the celery in a colander, reserving ½ cup
cooking liquid. Return the drained celery to the
saucepan; cover and set aside.

Preheat the oven to 350° F. Butter a 1½-quart
round baking dish; set aside.

Make the Medium White Sauce; remove from
the heat. Add the celery tops, ¼ cup almonds,
onions, and pimientos; stir to combine. Add the
white sauce mixture to the celery; stir to combine. Place the celery mixture in the prepared
baking dish; set aside.

In a small saucepan, melt the butter over low
heat. Remove from the heat; add the bread
crumbs and 2 tablespoons chopped almonds;
stir until the crumbs and almonds are evenly
coated with butter. Sprinkle the crumb mixture
evenly over the celery mixture. Bake, uncovered, for 25 minutes. The mixture will be bubbly and the crumb topping will be golden.

SERVES 10

BRAISED CELERY

*A wonderful green and red holiday side dish that
accompanies poultry, meats, and fish splendidly.*

1 bunch celery
3 tablespoons butter
2 tablespoons finely chopped onions
¼ teaspoon salt
⅛ teaspoon white pepper
1 cup beef broth, homemade (page 70) or
   commercially canned
1 tablespoon cornstarch
Additional ½ cup beef broth, homemade
   (page 70) or commercially canned,
   if necessary
1 tablespoon diced pimientos

Trim away the heavy root end, a small portion of
the tops of the stalks, and the leaves from the celery. Wash the celery stalks individually and dry
with a clean tea towel or paper towels. Cut the
celery-heart stalks and inner stalks into 2-inch
lengths; reserve the remaining stalks. Measure 4
cups cut celery pieces. If necessary, cut and use the
reserved celery stalks to make 4 cups celery pieces,
utilizing the innermost stalks first. The celery
pieces should be fairly uniform in width. If some
pieces are too wide, cut them in half or into thirds
lengthwise. Set 4 cups celery pieces aside. (Reserve
the remaining celery stalks for other uses.)

In a medium, heavy-bottomed skillet, melt
the butter over medium heat. Tilt the skillet
back and forth to completely cover the bottom
with the melted butter. Place the celery pieces,
onions, salt, and white pepper in the skillet;
sauté 5 minutes, being careful not to let the butter burn. Reduce the heat to low. When the skil-

let cools slightly, add 1 cup beef broth. Cover the skillet and simmer the mixture 10 minutes. Remove from the heat. Using a slotted spoon, remove the celery pieces from the skillet and place in a bowl; set aside.

In a small mixing bowl, place the cornstarch and $1/2$ cup beef broth; stir well. Add the cornstarch mixture to the liquid in the skillet; stir until smooth. Place the skillet over low heat and cook the mixture until thickened, stirring constantly. The mixture should be quite thick. Add the celery pieces and heat through. Add the pimientos; stir to evenly distribute.

SERVES 6

Corn

TO COOK AND SERVE CORN ON THE COB

For flavor perfection, Corn on the Cob should be eaten within half a day after the sweet corn is picked in the field or garden. While only a few lucky people can enjoy this gastronomic pleasure, it points out the critical importance of freshness when selecting sweet corn for preparation. Purchase fresh, *unshucked* corn. The kernels should spurt milk when pierced with a thumbnail.

Shuck the corn just before cooking. Remove all silk and cut off both ends of the ears with a sharp knife. Cook the corn just before serving; do not cook it in advance. Drop the ears into a kettle of plain (unsalted) boiling water. Boil until the milk in the kernels is just set—5 to 6 minutes. Immediately remove the corn from the boiling water and place it momentarily on several layers of paper towels to drain. Serve immediately. Small handles with pins, available commercially, may be inserted at both ends of the ears before serving, adding to the ease and pleasure of eating Corn on the Cob. At the table, pass an ample amount of melted butter with a small brush for application to the ears.

Some diners lightly salt Corn on the Cob after applying butter.

SCALLOPED CORN

1 $14^3/_4$-ounce can cream-style corn
3 tablespoons finely chopped onions
1 2-ounce jar pimientos, drained and coarsely chopped (2 tablespoons)
24 Ritz crackers, rolled medium-coarsely (1 cup)
1 extra-large egg, beaten
$1/4$ cup whole milk
$1/4$ teaspoon salt
Dash of pepper
2 teaspoons butter

Preheat the oven to 350° F. Butter a 1-quart round baking dish; set aside.

In a medium mixing bowl, place the corn, onions, pimientos, cracker crumbs, egg, milk, salt, and pepper; stir to combine. Place the mixture in the prepared baking dish. Dot with the butter. Bake, uncovered, for 30 minutes. The top will be faintly brown around the very edge and the mixture will be thick.

SERVES 6

PIGS IN A CORNFIELD

1 teaspoon vegetable shortening
8 ($3/4$ pound) link pork sausages

In a medium, heavy-bottomed skillet, melt the shortening over medium-high heat; using a spatula, spread the melted shortening over the entire bottom of the skillet. Place the sausages in the skillet; brown on all sides (about 10 minutes). Drain the sausage well between paper towels. Cut each link widthwise into sixths; set aside. Follow the Scalloped Corn recipe above, adding the sausage pieces to the ingredients before combining them.

SERVES 6

PATTY DAVIS'S SCALLOPED CORN

This recipe from the creative mind of my friend Patty Davis makes one of the most delicious corn dishes I have ever tasted.

3 11-ounce cans Niblets whole-kernel, golden
   sweet corn, drained
1 cup (½ pint) whipping cream, unwhipped
⅓ cup commercial sour cream
¼ teaspoon salt
¼ teaspoon pepper
22 very coarsely crushed saltines (crush in
   your hands) (about 1⅔ cups saltines)
1 cup sliced, fresh mushrooms
2 tablespoons butter

Preheat the oven to 350° F. Butter a 2-quart round baking dish; set aside.

In a large mixing bowl, place the corn, whipping cream, sour cream, salt, pepper, crushed saltines, and mushrooms; stir to combine. Turn the mixture into the prepared baking dish. Using the back of a spoon, push any visible mushroom slices beneath the surface of the mixture. Dot with the butter. Bake, uncovered, for 35 minutes. The mixture will be bubbly around the edge of the casserole.

SERVES 10

CORN PUDDING

4 extra-large eggs
½ teaspoon salt
⅛ teaspoon white pepper
1 teaspoon sugar
2 cups whole milk, scalded (page 9)
2 tablespoons butter
1 15¼-ounce can whole-kernel corn, drained
⅓ cup finely shredded, mild cheddar cheese

Preheat the oven to 325° F. Butter lightly a 2-quart round baking dish; set aside.

Place the eggs in a medium mixing bowl; using an electric mixer, beat slightly on medium speed. Add the salt, white pepper, and sugar; stir to combine; set aside. After scalding the milk, remove it from the heat and add the butter; stir until the butter melts. Add the milk mixture *slowly* to the egg mixture, stirring constantly. Add the corn and cheese; stir to combine. Pour into the prepared baking dish.

Place the baking dish in a 9 × 13-inch baking dish; then, pour very hot, but not boiling, water into the pan to approximately ½ the height of the baking dish. Bake, uncovered, for 1 hour, or until a table knife inserted near the center of the Corn Pudding comes out clean.

SERVES 6

SQUAW CORN

(See photo insert page C-2)

4 slices bacon, cut widthwise into 1-inch
   pieces
4 extra-large eggs
⅛ teaspoon salt
1 15-ounce can cream-style corn

In a medium, heavy-bottomed skillet, fry the bacon over medium heat until crisp. Meanwhile, in a medium mixing bowl, place the eggs and salt; using an electric mixer, beat well. Add the corn to the egg mixture; using a spoon, stir and fold to combine. When the bacon is crisp, add the corn mixture to the skillet. Using a small spatula, turn the mixture intermittently until the eggs are cooked (about 10 minutes).

SERVES 4

SERVING SUGGESTIONS: Serve Squaw Corn for an informal brunch, a late informal supper, or for a quick and tasty dinner main course.

CORN-OYSTER CASSEROLE

2 14¾-ounce cans cream-style corn
⅓ cup finely chopped onions
2 cups coarsely rolled saltines (about 36 saltines)
3 extra-large eggs, slightly beaten
¼ cup (4 tablespoons) butter, melted
¼ cup half-and-half
½ teaspoon salt
¼ teaspoon pepper
1 quart medium-sized shucked oysters, well drained
1 recipe (¼ cup) Buttered Cracker Crumbs (page 33)

Preheat the oven to 350°F. Butter well a 3-quart round baking dish; set aside.

In a large mixing bowl, place the corn, onions, rolled saltines, eggs, butter, half-and-half, salt, and pepper; stir to combine. Spoon ⅓ of the mixture into the prepared baking dish. Dot the mixture with ½ of the oysters. Repeat the layers. Then, add a layer of the remaining ⅓ of the corn mixture. Top with the buttered crumbs. Bake, uncovered, for 1 hour.

SERVES 10

Cucumbers

BAKED CUCUMBERS

2½ pounds (about 3 large) seedless cucumbers
2 tablespoons butter
1 teaspoon cornstarch
1 tablespoon snipped, fresh dillweed
½ teaspoon salt
¼ teaspoon white pepper
2 tablespoons dry white wine
1 recipe (¼ cup) Buttered Bread Crumbs (page 33)

Preheat the oven to 350°F. Butter an 8 × 8-inch baking dish; set aside.

Pare the cucumbers (page 17); slice ½ inch thick. Measure 7 cups cucumber slices and place them in a large saucepan. (Reserve any remaining cucumber slices for other uses.) Add hot water to cover the cucumber slices in the saucepan. Cover the saucepan. Bring the cucumbers to a boil over high heat. Reduce the heat and simmer 10 minutes, until the cucumbers are very tender. Drain the cucumbers in a colander; let stand to cool slightly.

In a tiny saucepan, melt the butter over warm heat. Remove from the heat. Add the cornstarch; stir until completely blended, with no lumps remaining. Then, add the dillweed, salt, and white pepper; stir to combine. Add the wine; stir in and set aside.

Place the cucumbers in the prepared baking dish. Pour the wine mixture evenly over the cucumbers. Just before baking, sprinkle the crumbs over the top. Bake, uncovered, for 30 minutes. The crumb topping will be golden.

SERVES 10

Eggplant

DELUXE EGGPLANT STUFFED WITH HAM

Church cookbooks are often like forgotten treasure chests full of precious gems. They are repositories of many wonderful recipes which deserve broader publication. The recipe that follows is adapted from a recipe which appeared in a 1976 cookbook published by the women of Plymouth Congregational United Church of Christ, Des Moines, Iowa, our family's church. The cookbook recipe bears the name of Martha Lenhart, wife of our senior minister at the time. Hints for serving are provided in the headnote preceding the recipe: "Good for a luncheon dish, served with tomato aspic or tossed salad."

1 small (¾ to 1 pound) eggplant
2 tablespoons butter
¾ cup chopped onions
1 small garlic clove, pressed
⅓ cup chopped green bell peppers
2 tablespoons butter
1 cup sliced, fresh mushrooms
¼ teaspoon salt
⅛ teaspoon pepper
¼ teaspoon dried leaf thyme
1 cup ham cubes cut ½ inch square from a
   ¼-inch slice of fully cooked ham (about
   ⅓ pound of ham)
¼ cup grated Colby cheese
½ cup hot water

Wash the eggplant and dry. Trim off the stem end. Cut the eggplant in half lengthwise; using a paring knife and spoon, cut and scoop out the pulp, leaving a ½-inch shell. Cut the pulp into approximately ½-inch cubes; set aside. Place the eggplant shells in a skillet; add about ½ inch water. Cover the skillet. Bring the eggplant shells to a boil over high heat. Reduce the heat and simmer about 5 minutes, *only* until the shells are just tender. Further cooking will cause the shells to lose their shape after they are stuffed. Remove the shells from the skillet; place on several layers of paper towels and set aside.

Preheat the oven to 375°F.

In a heavy-bottomed skillet, melt 2 tablespoons butter over medium heat. Tilt the skillet back and forth to completely cover the bottom with the melted butter. Place the onions, garlic, and green peppers in the skillet; brown lightly. Using a slotted spoon, remove the vegetables from the skillet and place in a bowl; set aside. Melt an additional 2 tablespoons butter in the skillet. Place the cubed eggplant pulp, mushrooms, salt, pepper, and thyme in the skillet; sauté until the mushrooms give up their juices and the pulp is tender (about 6 minutes), stirring frequently. Remove from the heat. Add the onion mixture and ham cubes; stir to combine.

Spoon the mixture into the eggplant shells and distribute grated cheese over the stuffing. Place the stuffed shells in a baking dish and pour ½ cup hot water into the dish. Bake, uncovered, for 20 minutes, until the stuffing is hot.

SERVES 2

EGGPLANT AND HAM CASSEROLE

Follow the Deluxe Eggplant Stuffed with Ham recipe, above, except: after trimming off the stem end of the eggplant, pare and cube the entire eggplant. Sauté the entire cubed eggplant with the mushrooms. Turn the completed ham mixture into a greased 1-quart round baking dish. Distribute the cheese over the top. Bake, uncovered, for 20 minutes at 375°F.

SERVES 2

EGGPLANT PARMESAN

2 1- to 1¼-pound eggplants
½ cup commercially packaged corn flake
   crumbs or 2½ cups cornflakes, crumbed
   (page 33)
½ cup freshly grated Parmesan cheese (page 30)
½ teaspoon salt

⅛ teaspoon white pepper
1 extra-large egg
2 tablespoons vegetable oil
1 tablespoon butter
Additional butter, if necessary
1 recipe Tomato Sauce (page 297–298), warm
Additional freshly grated Parmesan cheese

Wash the eggplants and dry. Trim off the stem ends. Cut the eggplants widthwise into ½-inch slices. Pare the skin from the eggplant slices; set aside. In a small bowl, place the crumbs, ½ cup Parmesan cheese, salt, and white pepper; stir to combine. Scatter the crumb mixture over a piece of waxed paper; set aside. Place the egg in a pie pan or other flat-bottomed dish; using a table fork, beat well; set aside.

In an electric skillet or a large, heavy-bottomed skillet on the range, heat the vegetable oil over medium heat (350°F in an electric skillet). Tilt the skillet back and forth to completely cover the bottom with the oil. Add the butter; spread to blend with the oil. Dip the eggplant slices in the egg, covering the edges as well as both sides; then, dredge the edges and both sides in the crumb mixture. Place the eggplant slices in the skillet and sauté, one layer at a time, 4 minutes on each side, until tender and well browned. Turn only once; add more butter if necessary.

Place the sautéed eggplant slices on individual plates or on a serving plate and spoon warm Tomato Sauce over the top. At the table, pass additional Parmesan cheese to sprinkle over the sauce.

SERVES 8

SERVING SUGGESTIONS
- Serve as a main course, accompanied by an all-green Tossed Salad (page 102–103) and Toasted Garlic Bread (page 356–357).

- Serve as a side dish.

SAUTÉED EGGPLANT

Follow the Eggplant Parmesan recipe, above, substituting an additional ½ cup cornflake crumbs for ½ cup freshly grated Parmesan cheese and omitting the Tomato Sauce and additional freshly grated Parmesan cheese.

Fennel

FENNEL AND TOMATOES BRAISED IN WINE

1 medium (½ to ¾ pound after removing stalks) fennel bulb
1 tablespoon extra-virgin olive oil
2 tablespoons butter
⅓ cup sliced leeks (white and greenish white parts only) (about 1 leek)
¼ teaspoon fennel seed
¼ teaspoon salt
⅛ teaspoon white pepper
1 cup dry white wine
½ pound tomatoes, blanched (page 29), stemmed, peeled, quartered, seeded and cored (page 29), and coarsely chopped (about ¾ cup)
¾ cup sliced, fresh mushrooms

Cut away the stalks and leaves from the fennel bulb. (Reserve the stalks and leaves for other uses.) Cut a thin slice off the root end of the bulb and discard. Remove and discard the outer layer of the bulb if the surface contains any brown spots. Wash the bulb and dry it. Cut the bulb in half vertically through the root end. Using a small paring knife, remove and discard the core from both halves of the bulb. Chop each bulb half coarsely; set aside.

Preheat an electric skillet or a large, heavy-bottomed skillet on the range to medium heat (350°F in an electric skillet). Add the olive oil; tilt the skillet back and forth to completely cover the bottom with the oil. Add the butter;

(Recipe continues on next page)

quickly spread to blend with the oil. Place the fennel and leeks in the skillet; sauté until lightly brown (about 5 minutes), stirring and turning often. Reduce the heat to low (220°F in an electric skillet).

When the skillet cools to the reduced temperature, add the fennel seed, salt, white pepper, and wine; stir to combine. Cover the skillet and simmer the fennel mixture 10 minutes, stirring about 2 times. Add the tomatoes and mushrooms; cover and simmer an additional 5 minutes.

SERVES 2 TO 3

Kohlrabi

While kohlrabi somewhat resembles the turnip in shape and texture, most of the similarities between these vegetables stop there. Kohlrabi is milder and sweeter in flavor than the turnip and is not a root vegetable. In fact, kohlrabi is the bulbous *stem* of the plant, and grows just above the ground. The leaves grow directly from the bulbous stem, giving kohlrabi that knobby appearance. Kohlrabi may be pale green or purple in color, although the variety carried in the produce market I frequent is consistently the pale green type. Kohlrabi is a member of the same species *(Brassica oleracea)* as head cabbage, Brussels sprouts, broccoli, cauliflower, kale, and collards. (The turnip is a member of a different species, *Brassica rapa.*)

To call kohlrabi a new vegetable would be grossly inaccurate; however, it is comparatively "new" insofar as general availability in many Midwest produce markets and inclusion in standard Midwest cooking. In addition to serving it cooked, kohlrabi may be pared and used raw (diced, shredded, or cut julienne) in salads, or as a crudité (page 5) with dips on an hors d'oeuvre tray. Nutritionally, kohlrabi is a superb source of potassium and vitamin C.

KOHLRABI WITH TARRAGON

8 ounces commercial sour cream
1 tablespoon all-purpose flour
½ teaspoon dried leaf tarragon
1½ pounds kohlrabi (about 6 medium kohlrabi)
3 tablespoons butter
¼ cup water
½ teaspoon salt

In a small mixing bowl, place the sour cream, flour, and tarragon; stir to combine. Cover and set aside. Wash the kohlrabi; cut off the ends and pare, completely removing the rather thick, fibrous layer of flesh underneath the outer skin. Cut the kohlrabi into ½-inch cubes; set aside.

In a large, heavy-bottomed skillet, melt the butter over low heat. Tilt the skillet back and forth to completely cover the bottom with the melted butter. Place the kohlrabi in the skillet and sauté over low heat 3 minutes. Add the water and salt; cover and cook over low heat 15 minutes, until just tender, turning intermittently. There should be little or no water left in the skillet at the end of the cooking period. Add the sour cream mixture; stir to combine with the kohlrabi. Then, cook over low heat about 2 minutes until the sour cream mixture is hot and fairly thick, stirring constantly.

SERVES 6

Mixed Vegetables

SNAPPY STIR-FRY VEGETABLES

(See photo insert page C-4)

1 medium (½ to ¾ pound after removing
   stalks) fennel bulb
1 cup carrots, pared and sliced diagonally
   ⅛ inch thick
1 cup coarsely chopped onions
¾ cup coarsely chopped red bell peppers
⅛ pound (about 1 cup) snow peas
¼ cup salted, whole cashews
¼ cup Sherried Dressing with Fennel and
   Thyme (page 121)
1 teaspoon cornstarch
2 tablespoons vegetable oil
½ teaspoon salt
½ teaspoon white pepper
½ recipe Perfect Boiled Rice (page 228)

Cut away the stalks and leaves from the fennel
bulb. (Reserve the stalks and leaves for other
uses.) Cut a thin slice off the root end of the
bulb and discard. Remove and discard the outer
layer of the bulb if the surface contains any
brown spots. Wash the bulb and dry it. Cut the
bulb in half vertically through the root end.
Using a small paring knife, remove and discard
the core from both halves of the bulb. Cut each
bulb half widthwise into ⅜-inch slices; place in
a small bowl and set aside.

Place the carrots, onions, and peppers in separate bowls; set aside. Remove the ends and
strings from the snow peas (page 275); wash
and dry. Place the snow peas in a separate bowl;
set aside. Measure the cashews; place in a separate bowl; set aside. In a small sauce dish, place
the sherried dressing and cornstarch. Using a
small fork (such as a salad fork), beat until the
cornstarch blends with the dressing; set aside.

Preheat a wok, electric skillet, or large, heavy-
bottomed skillet on the range to medium-high
heat (370°F if using a wok or electric skillet).

Add the vegetable oil. Tilt the wok or skillet back
and forth to completely cover the sides and bottom of the wok or the bottom of the skillet with
hot oil. Place the fennel and carrots in the wok or
skillet; stir-fry (page 10) 2 minutes (see Note),
using a spatula to move and turn the vegetables
almost constantly to prevent them from scorching. Add the onions and red peppers; stir-fry an
additional 3 minutes, continuing to move and
turn the vegetables. Add the snow peas, salt, and
white pepper; stir to combine. Reduce the heat to
low (240°F if using a wok or electric skillet).
Cover the wok or skillet. Let the vegetables cook
1 minute without uncovering.

Uncover the wok or skillet. Using the spatula,
move the vegetables to one side of the wok or
skillet. Pour the cornstarch mixture into the center of the wok or skillet; heat and cook briefly
until the mixture thickens, using a mixing spoon
to stir constantly. Then, using the mixing spoon,
combine the cornstarch mixture and vegetables.
Add the cashews; stir only until evenly distributed. When done, the vegetables should be
crispy-tender.

Spoon Snappy Stir-Fry Vegetables over rice on
individual plates or spoon the vegetables and rice
into separate serving bowls to pass at the table.

NOTE: A digital timer which indicates seconds is
helpful in achieving optimum results with stir-
fry dishes as the cooking times are so brief,
making the time spans difficult to gauge without a precise timekeeper.

SERVES 2 AS A MAIN COURSE OR 4 AS A SIDE DISH
(ELIMINATE THE RICE)

MIXED FRESH VEGETABLES WITH ROSEMARY

1 red bell pepper
6 carrots
1 small head cauliflower
2 medium kohlrabi
10 ounces pearl onions
2 medium zucchini

1 medium yellow summer squash
½ cup (¼ pound) butter
1 tablespoon snipped, fresh rosemary or
    1 teaspoon dried leaf rosemary

TO PREPARE THE VEGETABLES: Prepare the vegetables separately to preserve their individual colors and flavors. For steaming and boiling procedures, see Steamed Vegetables and Boiled Vegetables (page 252). After each vegetable is prepared, drain in a colander. Rinse under cold, running water to stop the cooking. Drain well. Place in a separate zipper-seal plastic bag and refrigerate. Prepare the vegetables as follows:

Red Bell Pepper: Cut lengthwise into ¼-inch strips. Cut away all white flesh. Cut each strip widthwise into 3 pieces. Steam 3 minutes.

Carrots: Cut off the ends and pare. Cut diagonally into ⅜-inch slices. Boil 5 minutes in water to cover.

Cauliflower: Cut into bite-sized flowerets. Steam 3 minutes.

Kohlrabi: Cut off the ends and pare. Cut into ¾-inch cubes. Boil 15 minutes in water to cover.

Pearl Onions: Peel (page 29). Steam 3 minutes.

Zucchini: Cut off the ends. Cut into ¼-inch slices. Steam 2 minutes.

TO SERVE: When ready to serve, place all the prepared vegetables in a very large mixing bowl. With your hands, toss carefully until evenly distributed. Place the mixed vegetables in the top of a large steamer pan. Steam *only* until hot. Meanwhile, in a small saucepan, melt the butter over low heat. Add the rosemary and stir to combine; set aside.

Turn the hot vegetables into a very large mixing bowl. Pour the butter mixture over the vegetables; using a wooden mixing spoon, toss lightly.

SERVES 16

VEGETABLE VARIATIONS: Any combination of vegetables may be used. Among other vegetables which might be included in a mixed vegetable combination are the following:

Asparagus: Cut into 1-inch pieces. Simmer 1 minute in water to cover.

Green, Yellow, and Purple Bell Peppers: Follow preparation of Red Bell Peppers.

Broccoli: Cut into bite-sized flowerets. Steam 3 minutes.

Small Brussels Sprouts: Trim off the stem ends. Steam 6 minutes.

Celery: Cut diagonally into ⅜-inch slices. Steam 5 minutes.

Snow Peas: Snip off the ends and pull off the strings along both sides of the pods. Steam 3 minutes.

Cherry Tomatoes: Add raw when heating the mixed vegetables before serving.

SEASONING VARIATIONS: Mixed Fresh Vegetables may be served plain, without the enhancement of butter and herbs or may be seasoned with butter or herbs alone. When butter is used, the following herbs, fresh or dried, may be substituted for rosemary: basil, chives, dillweed, marjoram, savory, tarragon, and thyme. When butter is not used, the vegetables may be seasoned with the same herbs, but the herbs should be fresh.

SUCCOTASH

2 ounces cured salt pork, cut into 4 pieces
½ cup water
¼ teaspoon salt
⅛ teaspoon pepper
1 teaspoon sugar
1 10-ounce package frozen baby lima beans
1 10-ounce package frozen whole-kernel corn
½ cup half-and-half
2 tablespoons butter

In a medium saucepan, place the salt pork, water, salt, pepper, sugar, and frozen lima beans. Cover the saucepan. Bring the mixture to a boil over high heat. Reduce the heat and simmer 15 minutes. Add the frozen corn. Cover the saucepan and return the mixture to a simmer; cook 4 minutes. Drain well, leaving the mixture in the saucepan. Remove and discard the salt pork.

Add the half-and-half and butter to the lima bean–corn mixture. Cover the saucepan and place over low heat. Heat the Succotash through, stirring intermittently to blend and combine the ingredients.

SERVES 6

VEGETABLE BUNDLES

(See photo insert page B-5)

A classy, eye-catching vegetable presentation for an upscale buffet or sit-down dinner.

Vegetable oil
About 6 medium carrots to make 18 carrot strips 3¾ inches in length (pare carrots [page 17]; cut into 3¾-inch lengths; then, cut lengthwise in half or into fourths, depending upon the diameter of the carrot)
36 small-to-medium diameter, fresh green beans averaging about 4½ inches in length (remove ends and strings [page 254]).
36 small diameter, fresh asparagus spears cut into 4½-inch lengths, using the top ends only)

18 green onion (scallion) leaves about 7 inches long (large diameter leaves may be cut in half lengthwise to make 2 ribbons)
2 tablespoons butter, melted

Pour a few drops of vegetable oil onto the bottom of a 9 × 13 × 2-inch baking dish. Using a paper towel, spread the oil over the bottom and halfway up the sides of the dish. Then, using a clean paper towel, wipe the dish nearly dry.

Place the carrot strips in a small saucepan; add water to cover. Cover the saucepan. Bring the carrots to a boil over high heat; reduce the heat slightly and boil 10 minutes. *Immediately* drain the carrots and run cold water over them in the saucepan to stop the cooking. Then, drain the carrots. Remove the carrots from the pan and set them aside on 3 layers of paper towels placed on a flat work surface, handling them carefully to prevent tearing.

Boil and process the green beans, using the same boiling time and procedures as with the carrots. Boil and process the asparagus spears, boiling only 1 minute, but otherwise following the same procedures as with the carrots.

Process the green onion leaves to make them pliable (page 34–35).

On a flat work surface, place 2 green beans, 2 asparagus spears, and 1 carrot strip across the center of each green onion ribbon. Tie each bundle together with the green onion ribbon, carefully making a knot. Using kitchen scissors, trim the ends of the green onion ribbons, leaving an artful length of ribbon ends on the bundles.

In the prepared baking dish, arrange 3 rows of 6 bundles each. Cover the dish with aluminum foil and refrigerate.

Twenty-five minutes before serving time, preheat the oven to 350°F. Remove the baking dish of Vegetable Bundles from the refrigerator. Remove the aluminum foil cover. Using a soft pastry brush, brush the melted butter over the bundles. Re-cover the dish with the aluminum-foil. Place the dish in the oven and heat the Vegetable Bundles for 15 minutes until hot.

(Recipe continues on next page)

To serve buffet style, remove the aluminum foil, cover and place the baking dish in an attractive silver or basket-type serving holder. Place it on the buffet table and provide small tongs for diners to conveniently serve themselves. For sit-down dinners, place 1 or more Vegetable Bundles in a handsome manner on each diner's plate.

SERVES 18

Mushrooms

CREAMED MUSHROOMS OVER ANGEL-HAIR PASTA

1 tablespoon butter
½ cup chopped onions
¼ teaspoon salt
⅛ teaspoon white pepper
1 tablespoon butter
¾ pound large, fresh mushrooms, sliced
2 tablespoons all-purpose flour
1 cup (½ pint) whipping cream,* unwhipped
2 tablespoons dry vermouth
8 ounces angel-hair pasta (capellini), cooked, rinsed in hot water, and drained (page 236)

   * Half-and-half may be substituted.

In a small to medium, heavy-bottomed skillet, melt 1 tablespoon butter over medium heat. Tilt the skillet back and forth to completely cover the bottom with the melted butter. Place the onions, salt, and white pepper in the skillet; sauté the onions until translucent, but not brown. Add 1 tablespoon butter and the mushrooms; continue sautéing until the mushrooms give up their juices. Remove from the heat. With a slotted spoon, remove the mushrooms and onions from the skillet and place in a bowl; set aside.

Add the flour to the liquid in the skillet; stir until completely smooth. Add the whipping cream and vermouth; stir to blend. Return the skillet to medium heat; cook the mixture until it thickens, stirring constantly. Add the mushrooms and onions; stir to combine; heat through. Serve Creamed Mushrooms over angel-hair pasta.

SERVES 4

VARIATION: Substitute ¾ cup parboiled (page 228) long-grain rice, cooked (page 228) or 8 ounces medium to narrow egg noodles, cooked, rinsed in hot water, and drained (page 236) for the angel-hair pasta.

SERVING SUGGESTIONS

• Serve on a brunch menu or as a luncheon main dish.

• Serve as an accompaniment to beef, veal, Baked Cut-up Chicken (page 170), or Roast Turkey Breast (page 179).

• Serve as a first-course appetizer. Spoon Creamed Mushrooms (substitute small mushrooms for the large mushrooms called for in recipe) into the center of tiny, unmolded, 3½-inch individual ring molds of rice (follow the Rice in Ring Mold recipe and procedure [page 229], eliminating the pine nuts).

MOREL MUSHROOMS SAUTÉED IN WHITE WINE

The morel is a prized variety of mushroom found only in the wild and is gathered in parts of the Midwest. In delicacy, desirability, and rarity, morels can be likened to fresh European truffles.

½ pound fresh morel mushrooms
4 cups cold water
1 tablespoon salt
1 extra-large egg
¼ teaspoon salt

⅛ teaspoon pepper
½ cup all-purpose flour
1 tablespoon vegetable oil
2 tablespoons butter
1 small garlic clove, pressed
2 tablespoons dry white wine

Clean the mushrooms well under cold, running water to remove soil and ants and other insects. In a large mixing bowl, place 4 cups cold water and 1 tablespoon salt; stir until the salt dissolves. Place the mushrooms in the salt solution; soak 15 minutes to remove any remaining insects. Drain the mushrooms; rinse well in clear water. Drain on several layers of paper towels. Trim off the bottoms of the stems and slice the mushrooms in half lengthwise; set aside.

In a small bowl, place the egg, ¼ teaspoon salt, and pepper; using a table fork, beat well; set aside. Sprinkle the flour over a piece of waxed paper; set aside. Dip the mushroom halves in the egg mixture and then dredge in the flour. Place the dredged mushrooms on a clean piece of waxed paper; set aside.

In a medium, heavy-bottomed skillet, heat the vegetable oil over medium heat. Using a spatula, spread the vegetable oil over the entire bottom of the skillet. Add the butter. Tilt the skillet back and forth to blend the butter with the oil. Place the mushrooms and garlic in the skillet; sauté 7 minutes until golden brown, keeping the heat low enough to prevent the oil and butter from burning. Reduce the heat; add the white wine and heat through, stirring to blend the wine with the pan juices and to coat the mushrooms with the wine sauce.

SERVES 4

SERVING SUGGESTIONS

- Especially good spooned over beef steaks or slices of beef tenderloin.

- Serve on the same plate, or as a side dish, with veal and wild game.

Onions

FRENCH-FRIED ONION RINGS

1½ pounds yellow onions (about 3 large
    onions)
½ cup all-purpose flour
¾ teaspoon salt
½ teaspoon white pepper
½ cup whole milk
1 extra-large egg, slightly beaten
1 tablespoon vegetable oil
1 quart vegetable oil

Cut off the ends and peel the onions. Cut the onions into 3/16-inch uniform slices. Carefully separate all the rings, reserving the tiny center rings for other uses; set aside. In a medium mixing bowl, place the flour, salt, and white pepper; stir to combine. Add the milk, egg, and 1 tablespoon vegetable oil. Using an electric mixer, beat on low speed only until smooth; set aside.

Pour 1 quart vegetable oil into a deep-fat fryer or an electric skillet; preheat the oil to 375° F. Drop a handful of onion rings into the batter. Using a cooking fork, turn the rings until they are completely coated. Using the fork, remove the rings from the batter and hold the rings over the mixing bowl briefly until the excess batter drips back into the bowl. Drop the coated rings into the hot oil. Repeat the coating process with additional raw onion rings, but drop only enough onion rings into the oil to maintain a single layer in the fryer (or skillet). Fry the rings about 4 minutes until they reach a light golden color. Using the fork, remove the fried onion rings from the fryer (or skillet) and place, single layer, on 3 layers of paper towels to drain. Place a single layer of paper towels over the onion rings to help absorb the oil and keep the rings hot.

Repeat the process until all the rings have been fried. Drain batches of the fried rings on fresh, unsaturated paper towels to achieve maximum

(Recipe continues on next page)

absorbency. French-Fried Onion Rings should be served as grease-free as possible.

Serve the onion rings immediately while hot. If necessary, drained onion rings may be placed in a 9 × 13-inch baking pan and placed, *uncovered,* in a 300°F oven to keep hot; however, French-Fried Onion Rings are best when not held.

SERVES 4

CREAMED ONIONS

1¼ pounds pearl onions
1 recipe Thin White Sauce (page 301–302), hot
Paprika for decoration

Peel the onions (page 29) and trim the ends. Steam the onions (page 252) until tender. Add the onions to the hot Thin White Sauce; stir to combine. Serve in small sauce dishes. Sprinkle sparingly with paprika.

SERVES 6

Peas

CREAMED PEAS

1 10-ounce package frozen peas
1 recipe Medium White Sauce (page 301–302), hot

Cook the peas briefly, following the directions on the package. Drain well in a sieve; set aside. In a medium saucepan, make the Medium White Sauce. Add the peas to the hot white sauce; stir lightly until the peas are evenly distributed.

SERVES 4

DILLED CREAMED PEAS

Follow the Creamed Peas recipe, this page, adding ½ teaspoon dried dillweed to the white sauce and stirring to combine before adding the peas.

PEAS WITH MUSHROOMS AND SHALLOTS

1 tablespoon butter
½ cup sliced, fresh mushrooms
3 tablespoons minced shallots
2 teaspoons dry sherry
½ cup water
2 teaspoons instant chicken bouillon granules
1 10-ounce package frozen peas

In a small, heavy-bottomed skillet, melt the butter over medium heat. Tilt the skillet back and forth to completely cover the bottom with the melted butter. Place the mushrooms and shallots in the skillet; sauté 3 minutes. Remove from the heat; let stand until the skillet cools slightly.

Then, add the sherry; stir to blend with the pan juices; set aside.

Pour ½ cup water into a medium to small saucepan. Cover the saucepan and bring the water to a boil over high heat. Add the bouillon granules; stir until dissolved. Add the peas. Cover the saucepan and bring the peas to a simmer. Reduce the heat and simmer 2 minutes. Drain the peas in a sieve.

Return the drained peas to the saucepan. Add the mushroom and shallot mixture, including the pan juices; stir to combine.

SERVES 4

MINTED PEAS

1 10-ounce package frozen peas
2 teaspoons butter
1 tablespoon finely snipped, fresh mint leaves

Cook the peas briefly, following the directions on the package; drain well. Add the butter and mint leaves; toss lightly until the butter melts and the ingredients are combined.

SERVES 4

TO COOK AND SERVE
SNOW PEAS

Wash the pods. Remove the ends of the pods and the strings along both sides of the pods. Steam (page 252) 3 minutes. Snow Peas are served in the pods. A small amount of butter may be tossed with the peas before serving, if desired.

TO COOK AND SERVE
SUGAR SNAP PEAS

Follow the procedures for cooking and serving snow peas (see To Cook and Serve Snow Peas, above), except steam Sugar Snap Peas about 4 minutes or until just tender.

Potatoes

TO COOK AND SERVE
BOILED POTATOES

Boiled potatoes may be served as such, or they are often used in the preparation of other dishes such as Potato Salad and Potato Dumplings. Potatoes may be boiled either pared or unpared.

BOILED PARED POTATOES: Using a vegetable parer, remove all skin and eyes from the potatoes. Immediately drop each pared potato into a saucepan of cold water. Immersion in cold water will prevent pared potatoes from discoloring. Pared potatoes may be retained in cold water 1 hour or so without harm to the prod-

uct. If the potatoes are especially large, they may be cut in half or into thirds, depending upon how the boiled potatoes will be used.

When ready to boil the potatoes, drain the cold water and replace it with hot water to cover. Cover the saucepan. Bring the potatoes to a boil over high heat; reduce the heat to medium and boil moderately until the potatoes are tender when pierced with a sharp fork (about 25 minutes, depending upon the size of the potatoes). Avoid overcooking, causing the potatoes to fragment and become mushy. When done, remove from heat and drain the potatoes immediately to avoid sogginess.

As a side dish, boiled potatoes are traditionally served with butter, gravy, natural meat juice, or sauce.

BOILED UNPARED POTATOES: Using a vegetable brush, scrub the potatoes well. Place the unpared, whole (uncut) potatoes in a saucepan and add hot water to cover. Cover the saucepan. Boil the potatoes, following the procedure for Boiled Pared Potatoes, above. When done, drain the potatoes immediately. If the potatoes are to be cooled for use in another dish, place them on wire racks. When cool enough to handle or when completely cool, the potatoes may be peeled, using a small paring knife. If the potatoes are to be sliced or cut in other exacting shapes, allow them to cool completely before peeling and slicing or cutting. Cool potatoes can be cut more uniformly and are less likely to fragment.

If not allowed to overcook, potatoes boiled unpared retain their shape and cohesion after peeling. This is important if the cooked potatoes are to be sliced or otherwise cut into uniform pieces. When potatoes are boiled *after* paring, the outside portion of the potatoes is prone to become somewhat soft and borderline mealy by the time the center is fully cooked—a quality not intolerable for dishes such as Mashed Potatoes but unsatisfactory for cooked potatoes which are to be sliced or otherwise cut for use in such dishes as Potato Salad where symmetry is important.

(Recipe continues on next page)

Boiled, unpared red potatoes retain their shape especially well after peeling; therefore, they are an excellent variety to use in Potato Salad. In contrast, russet potatoes are softer and are the more desirable variety to use in making Baked Potatoes and Mashed Potatoes.

TO COOK AND SERVE STEAMED POTATOES

Small, new potatoes may be steamed, pared or unpared. See Steamed Vegetables (page 252) for the procedure.

BAKED POTATOES

Uniformly sized russet potatoes

Preheat the oven to 450°F.

Using a vegetable brush, scrub the potatoes well; dry with paper towels. Wrap each potato tightly in a single layer of aluminum foil. Place the wrapped potatoes directly on the center rack in the oven. Bake for 45 to 60 minutes, depending upon size of the potatoes (see Note).

To serve, remove and discard the aluminum foil. Using a sharp paring knife, cut a cross in the top of each potato. Press the ends of each potato toward the center to open the cross and force some of the cooked potato flesh through the opening.

NOTE: Potatoes may be baked at a lower temperature for a longer period of time.

ACCOMPANIMENT SUGGESTIONS: Serve butter, sour cream, finely snipped chives, crumbled cooked bacon, chopped green onions, grated cheddar cheese, or any combination (or all) of these items to top the potatoes. Pass the topping(s) at the table, allowing diners to add their own.

TWICE-BAKED POTATOES

2 pounds russet potatoes, baked (see Baked Potatoes, page 276) (4 large potatoes)
2 tablespoons snipped, fresh chives
2 tablespoons butter, melted
½ cup finely shredded, extra-sharp cheddar cheese
Paprika for decoration

Immediately after baking the potatoes, remove the aluminum foil. Using a small, sharp knife, cut a thin slice lengthwise off the top of each potato. Using a teaspoon, carefully remove the cooked potato flesh from each potato, leaving a ⅛-inch lining of potato flesh adhering to the skin for stability of the shell. Place the potato flesh in a large mixing bowl; set aside. Set the shells aside. Using the teaspoon, remove the potato flesh from the cutaway slices and add it to the mixing bowl containing the potato flesh; discard the skin.

Mash the potato flesh, following the recipe for Mashed Potatoes (page 279). Add the chives to the mashed potatoes; using a mixing spoon, stir until evenly distributed.

Preheat the oven to 400°F.

Using a teaspoon and your thumb, *lightly* pack the mashed potatoes into the potato shells, rounding slightly. Smooth the tops of the mashed potatoes with your thumb. Then, draw the edge of the teaspoon diagonally across the mashed potatoes several times to make parallel rows of slight indentations.

Replace the stuffed potatoes loosely in the pieces of aluminum foil used for baking, but leave the tops of the potatoes uncovered; place in a shallow baking dish (see Note).

Pour the melted butter over the mashed potatoes. Bake, uncovered, for 25 minutes. Remove from the oven and distribute the shredded cheese over the mashed potatoes. Sprinkle the paprika over the cheese. Bake for an additional 3 minutes, until the cheese melts.

NOTE: At this point, the baking dish may be covered with plastic wrap and set aside or refrigerated for completion of the potatoes before serving later in the day.

SERVES 4

VARIATION: Substitute minced onions for the chives.

DECORATION SUGGESTION: For a more decorative appearance, reserve a portion of the mashed potatoes when packing the shells. Using a decorating bag fit with large open-star tip number 8B (page 319), pipe the reserved mashed potatoes in an attractive pattern over the top of the packed potatoes.

Eliminate making indentations in the mashed potatoes with the teaspoon. Include the addition of melted butter. The addition of shredded cheese is optional. Paprika decoration is also optional. If cheese is not added, eliminate the additional 3 minutes baking time. Instead, the potatoes may be browned quickly under the broiler, about 5 inches from the heat, if desired.

AMERICAN FRIES

1 tablespoon vegetable oil
2 tablespoons butter
2 pounds red potatoes, pared, quartered, and sliced ⅜ inch thick (about 6 medium-large potatoes)
1½ cups coarsely chopped onions
½ teaspoon salt
¼ teaspoon pepper

In an electric skillet or a large, heavy-bottomed skillet on the range, heat the vegetable oil over medium heat (350° F if using an electric skillet). Using a spatula, spread the vegetable oil over the entire bottom of the skillet. Add the butter. Tilt the skillet back and forth to blend the butter with the oil.

Place the potatoes in the skillet; fry, uncovered, 8 minutes, turning often. Add the onions, salt, and pepper; fry an additional 5 minutes, turning intermittently to achieve even browning. Reduce the skillet heat to medium-low (280° F if using an electric skillet). Cover the skillet and continue cooking the potatoes and onions 10 minutes, until tender, turning occasionally.

SERVES 4

SCALLOPED POTATOES

(See photo insert page A-8)

2 pounds red potatoes (about 6 medium potatoes)
2 recipes Medium White Sauce (page 301–302), warm
⅓ cup chopped onions
1 cup (4 ounces) shredded Colby cheese

Pare the potatoes and retain in a large bowl of cold water to prevent discoloration; set aside. Make 2 recipes of Medium White Sauce; cover and set aside.

Preheat the oven to 350° F. Grease a 2-quart round baking dish; set aside.

Slice each potato as follows: Cut the potato in half lengthwise; while holding the potato halves together, roll the potato one-quarter turn and cut the potato halves lengthwise in half or into thirds, depending upon the size of the potato. While continuing to hold the potato together, cut it widthwise into ¼-inch slices. Place ½ of the sliced potatoes in the prepared baking dish; distribute ½ of the chopped onions evenly over the potatoes. Scatter ½ of the shredded cheese evenly over the onions; cover with ½ of the warm white sauce. Repeat the layers, using the remaining ½ of the ingredients.

Cover and bake for 1 hour. Uncover and continue baking until nicely browned (about 15 minutes).

SERVES 6

SCALLOPED POTATOES WITH HAM

Cut fully cooked ham into 1½ cups of ⅜-inch cubes. Follow the Scalloped Potatoes recipe, page 277, distributing ½ of the ham cubes over each of the 2 potato layers. Bake in a greased 2½-quart round baking dish.

ALLEGRO SCALLOPED POTATOES

In music, "allegro" means to play the composition at a quick tempo and merrily, definitions which connote the speed and pleasure with which this amazing potato casserole is prepared. The recipe relies heavily on prepared foods, but don't be turned off. They'll shout "Bravissimo!" when you serve it.

1 10¾-ounce can condensed cream of chicken soup (undiluted)
8 ounces commercial sour cream
1 2-pound bag frozen hash brown potatoes, thawed
1 cup chopped onions
½ teaspoon salt
¼ teaspoon white pepper
8 ounces sharp cheddar cheese, shredded (about 2 cups)
1 tablespoon plus 2 teaspoons butter
Paprika for decoration
Sprigs of fresh parsley for decoration

Preheat the oven to 350° F. Butter well a 7 × 11-inch baking dish; set aside.

In a medium mixing bowl, place the chicken soup and sour cream; stir to combine; set aside. In the prepared baking dish, layer in the following order: ½ of the potatoes, ½ of the onions, ½ of the salt, ½ of the white pepper, ½ of the sour cream mixture (spread as evenly as possible), and ½ of the cheese. Repeat the layers, using the remaining ½ of the layered ingredients. Dot with the butter. Sprinkle the paprika lightly over the top (see Note).

Bake, uncovered, for 1 hour. When done, the top should be slightly browned. Decorate with the parsley sprigs.

NOTE: At this point, the baking dish may be covered with plastic wrap and the Allegro Scalloped Potatoes refrigerated for baking and serving later in the day.

SERVES 10

SERVING SUGGESTION: A convenient and very tasty dish to serve at buffets.

NEW POTATOES WITH PARSLEY

(See photo insert page C-1)

2 pounds small, new, red potatoes
3 tablespoons butter
1½ teaspoons freshly squeezed, strained lemon juice
2 tablespoons finely snipped, fresh parsley

Using a vegetable brush, scrub the potatoes well. Place the potatoes in a saucepan; add hot water to cover. Cover the saucepan. Bring the potatoes to a boil over high heat; reduce the heat to medium and boil moderately until the potatoes are tender when pierced with a sharp fork (about 20 minutes). Drain the potatoes; let stand until cool enough to handle.

Meanwhile, in a tiny saucepan, melt the butter over low heat. Remove from the heat. Add the lemon juice and parsley; stir to combine; set aside. Peel the potatoes and place them in a mixing bowl. Drizzle the parsley mixture over the potatoes; using a wooden mixing spoon, toss to coat the potatoes. To serve, turn into a serving bowl.

SERVES 6

Marinated Halibut Steaks, page 214;
New Potatoes with Parsley, page 278

C-1

Front to back: Squaw Corn, page 264; American Indian Fry Bread, page 375; Pecan Wild Rice, page 231

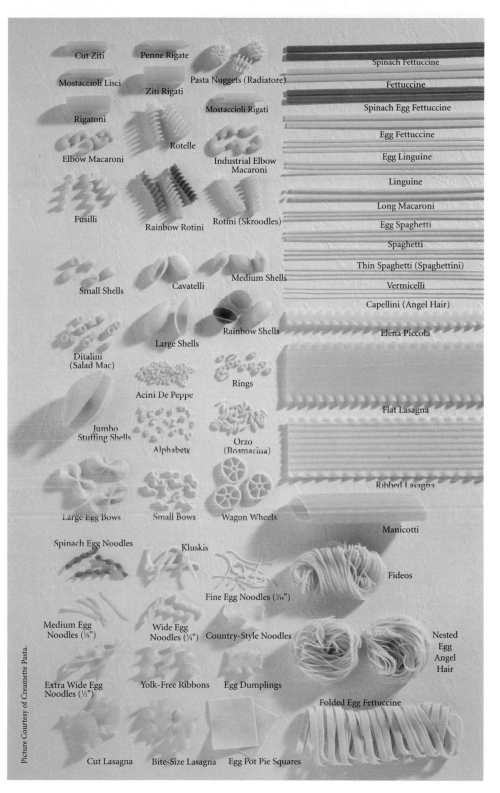

Cut Ziti
Penne Rigate
Spinach Fettuccine
Mostaccioli Lisci
Pasta Nuggets (Radiatore)
Fettuccine
Ziti Rigati
Mostaccioli Rigati
Spinach Egg Fettuccine
Rigatoni
Egg Fettuccine
Elbow Macaroni
Rotelle
Egg Linguine
Industrial Elbow Macaroni
Linguine
Fusilli
Long Macaroni
Rainbow Rotini
Rotini (Skroodles)
Egg Spaghetti
Spaghetti
Thin Spaghetti (Spaghettini)
Small Shells
Cavatelli
Medium Shells
Vermicelli
Capellini (Angel Hair)
Ditalini (Salad Mac)
Large Shells
Rainbow Shells
Elena Piccola
Acini De Peppe
Rings
Flat Lasagna
Jumbo Stuffing Shells
Alphabets
Orzo (Rosmarina)
Large Egg Bows
Small Bows
Wagon Wheels
Ribbed Lasagna
Manicotti
Spinach Egg Noodles
Kluskis
Fideos
Fine Egg Noodles (1/16")
Medium Egg Noodles (1/8")
Wide Egg Noodles (1/4")
Country-Style Noodles
Nested Egg Angel Hair
Extra Wide Egg Noodles (1/2")
Yolk-Free Ribbons
Egg Dumplings
Folded Egg Fettuccine
Cut Lasagna
Bite-Size Lasagna
Egg Pot Pie Squares

Pasta Chart

Snappy Stir-Fry Vegetables, page 269

Lasagna, page 242

Isabel's Noodle Kugel, page 243

Poached Rhubarb, page 294

Fresh Fruit Compote, page 291

Front to back: Honey-Seed Bread, page 354; White Bread, page 352

CREAMED NEW POTATOES AND PEAS WITH SNIPPED CHIVES

2 pounds small, new, red potatoes
1 10-ounce package frozen, tiny peas
1½ recipes Thin White Sauce (page 301–302), hot
1 tablespoon snipped, fresh chives

Using a vegetable brush, scrub the potatoes well. Place the potatoes in a large saucepan; add hot water to cover. Cover the saucepan. Bring the potatoes to a boil over high heat; reduce the heat to medium and boil moderately until the potatoes are tender when pierced with a sharp fork (about 20 minutes). Drain the potatoes; let stand until cool enough to handle.

Meanwhile, cook the peas briefly, following the directions on the package; set aside. Peel the potatoes and place in a mixing bowl; cover with aluminum foil to keep warm. Drain the peas and add to the potatoes; using a wooden mixing spoon, toss very gently and turn into a serving bowl. Pour the hot Thin White Sauce over the potatoes and peas; sprinkle with the chives.

SERVES 8

MASHED POTATOES

2 pounds russet potatoes (about 4 large potatoes)
3 tablespoons butter
¾ teaspoon salt
¼ cup whole milk
1 tablespoon butter

Pare the potatoes carefully, removing all skin and eyes. Immediately after paring each potato, place it in a large saucepan filled with cold water to prevent discoloration. Cut each pared potato into thirds and return to the cold water. Pared potatoes may be retained in cold water 1 hour or so before cooking.

When ready to cook the potatoes, drain the cold water and replace with hot water to cover. Cover the saucepan. Bring the potatoes to a boil over high heat; reduce the heat to medium and boil moderately until potatoes are tender when pierced with a sharp fork (about 25 minutes). Avoid overcooking, causing the potatoes to fragment and become mushy. Overcooked potatoes can result in watery mashed potatoes which lack the desired lightness and fluffiness.

Drain the potatoes *well,* leaving them in the saucepan in which they were cooked to help retain heat. Add 3 tablespoons butter, salt, and milk. Using an electric mixer, beat the potato mixture on high speed until completely smooth and fluffy, with *no lumps* (see Note).

Spoon the Mashed Potatoes into a serving bowl and top with a generous pat of butter (about 1 tablespoon).

NOTE: Mashed Potatoes are best when served immediately after mashing; however, they may be held for a short period of time by covering the pan and placing it in a larger pan of hot water over low heat.

SERVES 6

ACCOMPANIMENT SUGGESTIONS
- Serve with gravy or natural meat juice passed at the table in a gravy boat.

- Certain dishes, such as Beef and Noodles (page 136–137), Chicken and Noodles (page 175), and Dried Beef Gravy (page 140), are traditionally served over Mashed Potatoes.

MASHED POTATO PATTIES

3 cups cold, leftover mashed potatoes
1 extra-large egg
1 teaspoon vegetable oil
1 tablespoon butter

In a medium mixing bowl, place the mashed potatoes and egg; using a fork or a handheld electric mixer, mix until smooth. Using a ½-cup measuring cup, measure ½-cup portions of the

(Recipe continues on next page)

potato mixture and shape into thick patties with your hands; place the patties on a plate or in a shallow pan; set aside.

In a medium, heavy-bottomed skillet, heat the vegetable oil and butter over medium heat. Tilt the skillet back and forth to completely cover bottom with the blend of oil and butter. When the oil and butter *begin* to sizzle, carefully place the patties in the skillet, using a small spatula. Fry the patties, uncovered, until nicely browned and heated through, turning once.

MAKES 6 PATTIES

SERVING NOTE: Mashed Potato Patties are generally not served with gravy, although they may be. If desired, gravy may be passed at the table for diners who wish to ladle it over their potato patty.

MASHED POTATOES IN A CASSEROLE

A great dish for parties and buffets!

4 pounds russet potatoes (about 8 large potatoes)
8 ounces commercial sour cream
8 ounces cream cheese, softened
2 tablespoons butter
2 teaspoons finely snipped, fresh parsley

Pare the potatoes carefully, removing all skin and eyes. Immediately after paring each potato, place it in a very large saucepan filled with cold water to prevent discoloration. Cut each potato into thirds and return to the cold water. Drain the cold water and replace with hot water to cover. Cover the saucepan. Bring the potatoes to a boil over high heat; reduce the heat to medium and boil moderately until the potatoes are tender when pierced with a sharp fork (about 25 minutes).

When the potatoes are nearly done, preheat the oven to 325° F. Butter a 9 × 13-inch baking dish; set aside.

When the potatoes are done, drain *well*, leaving them in the saucepan in which they were cooked to help retain the heat. To the potatoes, add the sour cream and cream cheese. Using an electric mixer, beat the potato mixture on high speed until completely smooth, with *no lumps*.

Spoon the mashed potatoes into the prepared baking dish. With the back of a tablespoon, fashion attractive peaks in the top of the potatoes. Dot with butter in the little valleys formed between the peaks. Sprinkle parsley evenly over the potatoes. Cover with aluminum foil (see Note) and bake until heated thoroughly (about 20 to 25 minutes depending upon whether or not the casserole has been refrigerated).

NOTE: After covering the mashed potatoes with aluminum foil, the dish may be refrigerated up to 24 hours before baking.

SERVES 12

DUCHESS POTATOES

Potato finery for the main-course plate at an elegant dinner party.

2 extra-large eggs
¾ teaspoon salt
2½ pounds russet potatoes, pared, boiled, and drained (page 275–276) (about 4 very large potatoes)
3 tablespoons butter
3 tablespoons butter, melted

Preheat the oven to 350° F. Butter one 9 × 13-inch baking dish and one 6 × 10-inch baking dish; set aside.

In a small mixing bowl, place the eggs and salt; using an electric mixer, beat slightly on medium speed. To the drained potatoes, add the egg mixture and 3 tablespoons butter. Using the electric mixer, beat the potato mixture on high speed until completely smooth, with *no lumps*.

Using a decorating bag fit with large open-star tip number 8B (page 319), pipe about 20 rosettes (page 325) of the potato mixture, side by side but not touching, onto the prepared baking dishes. Drizzle 3 tablespoons melted butter over the rosettes. Bake, uncovered, 10 minutes. Brown the Duchess Potatoes quickly under the broiler, about 5 inches from the heat. Use a small spatula to carefully transfer the Duchess Potatoes from the baking dishes onto individual plates or a serving platter.

SERVES 10

OVEN-BROWNED POTATOES

Small, new, russet or red potatoes
Butter
Vegetable oil
Pan drippings

Using a vegetable brush, scrub the potatoes well; do not pare. Place the potatoes in a saucepan; add hot water to cover. Cover the saucepan. Bring the potatoes to a boil over high heat; reduce the heat to medium and boil moderately 10 minutes, until *just tender* (the potatoes will cook further during browning). Drain the potatoes; place them on a wire rack and let stand until cool enough to handle (or, optionally, until completely cool).

Preheat the oven to 350°F. Butter a shallow baking pan large enough to accommodate, single layer, the number of potatoes to be oven browned; set aside.

Peel the potatoes and place in the prepared baking pan (see Note 1). Add enough equal amounts of butter and vegetable oil to the bottom of the baking pan to very thinly cover the pan bottom when the butter melts. If roasting meat simultaneously, spoon some of the meat-pan drippings over the potatoes for flavor and to enhance browning. (Be sure to leave sufficient drippings in the meat pan to make gravy, if planned.) (See Note 2.)

Place the potatoes in the oven and brown for 25 minutes. Turn the potatoes over; baste with pan drippings and continue browning an additional 20 minutes.

NOTE 1: After the potatoes have been peeled and placed in the prepared baking pan, the baking pan may be tightly covered with plastic wrap and the potatoes refrigerated up to 24 hours before completion of cooking.

NOTE 2: Although the boiled and peeled potatoes may be browned in the bottom of a pan in which meat is being roasted rather than in a separate baking pan, meats are generally roasted on a wire rack which does not leave sufficient space on the bottom of the pan to place the potatoes. If the potatoes are browned in the meat pan (or in a separate baking pan) in a 325°F oven, allow an additional 15 minutes (1 hour total) for browning.

POTATO DUMPLINGS

3 pounds red potatoes
3 extra-large eggs
¾ cup regular (not instant) Cream of Wheat cereal, uncooked, or ¾ cup raw farina
1¼ cups all purpose flour
1¼ teaspoons salt
¾ teaspoon sugar
¼ teaspoon ground nutmeg
¼ teaspoon ground cinnamon
Water
Salt
Crumb Topping (recipe follows)

Pare and boil the potatoes (page 275–276). Drain the potatoes well and press them through a ricer into a large mixing bowl; set aside. Place the eggs in a small mixing bowl; using an electric mixer, beat slightly on medium speed. Add the Cream of Wheat, flour, salt, sugar, nutmeg, and cinnamon; stir to combine. Add the egg mixture to the potatoes; stir until well combined.

With floured hands, make uniform balls about 1¾ inches in diameter and place on a piece of

(Recipe continues on next page)

waxed paper. If the potato mixture is too sticky for easy handling, roll the balls lightly in a small amount of flour as you form them. Set aside.

Pour at least 3 quarts water into a large kettle. Add 1 teaspoon salt for each quart of water. Cover the kettle and bring the salted water to a boil over high heat. Drop the dumplings into the boiling water and simmer, uncovered, 20 minutes. Adjust the heat to maintain a simmer. Lift the dumplings out with a slotted spoon. Sprinkle Crumb Topping on each dumpling.

SERVES 10

CRUMB TOPPING

3 tablespoons butter
2 tablespoons finely minced onions
½ cup fine, Dried Bread Crumbs (page 33)

In a small, heavy-bottomed skillet, melt the butter over medium heat. Place the onions in the skillet; sauté briefly (about 5 minutes), until tender. Add the crumbs and brown lightly.

POTATO PANCAKES WITH LINGONBERRIES

2 pounds russet potatoes (about 4 large potatoes)
¼ cup all-purpose flour
¾ teaspoon salt
¼ teaspoon pepper
½ teaspoon ground nutmeg
2 extra-large eggs
½ cup medium-grated onions (about 1 medium onion)
1 tablespoon vegetable oil
2 tablespoons butter
1 tablespoon vegetable oil
2 tablespoons butter
1 cup canned wild lingonberries in sugar

Pare the potatoes. Immediately after paring each potato, place it, whole, in a large mixing bowl of cold water to prevent discoloration; set aside. In a small mixing bowl, place the flour, salt, pepper, and nutmeg; stir to combine; set aside. Place the eggs in a medium mixing bowl; using an electric mixer, beat on medium speed only until the whites and yolks are blended. Add the flour mixture; beat only until blended. Add the onions; beat briefly to combine; set aside.

Remove one potato from the water and pat it dry with paper towels or a clean tea towel. Grate the potato coarsely. Place the grated potato in a sieve over a deep pan. With the back of your hand, press the grated potato to extract as much liquid as possible. Immediately add the drained potatoes to the egg mixture; stir until the potatoes are thoroughly coated. Repeat the procedure with the 3 remaining potatoes, processing only 1 potato at a time to help prevent the potatoes from turning brown. Set the potato batter aside.

Preheat an electric skillet or a large, heavy-bottomed skillet on the range to medium-high heat (380°F in an electric skillet). Place 1 tablespoon vegetable oil in the skillet. Using a spatula, spread the vegetable oil over the entire bottom of the skillet. Add 2 tablespoons butter. Tilt the skillet back and forth to blend the butter with the oil. When the oil and butter sizzle, use a ¼-cup measuring cup to drop 4 or 5 even, ¼ cups of potato batter, uniformly distributed, onto the hot skillet surface. Using a spatula, flatten each mound of batter into a pancake approximately 4 inches in diameter. Fry the pancakes 2 minutes, until the bottoms are golden brown; turn once and fry the second side an additional 2 minutes.

Arrange the potato pancakes on a warm platter and place, uncovered, in a warm oven while frying the remaining pancakes.

Blend an additional 1 tablespoon vegetable oil and 2 tablespoons butter in the skillet before frying the remaining potato pancakes.

Serve the pancakes immediately. Place the lingonberries in a small, crystal serving dish; let each diner spoon lingonberries over his/her potato pancakes at the table.

MAKES ABOUT 10 PANCAKES

POTATO PANCAKES WITH APPLESAUCE

Follow the Potato Pancakes with Lingonberries recipe, above, substituting 1 cup Plain Applesauce (page 290) for 1 cup lingonberries.

Yams

In the United States, the vegetable we call a "yam" is a variety of sweet potato. True yams are botanically unrelated to sweet potatoes, and are widely grown and consumed in the tropics. They are available in this country principally in Latin markets. Though a national misnomer, the yams called for in this cookbook are the sweet potato variety.

What we usually label a "sweet potato" has light yellow skin, with flesh that is pale yellow in color, and when cooked, is dry and mealy in texture. Yams have copper-colored skin and deep orange flesh which is moist and sweet when cooked. I personally prefer the texture and rich flavor of yams over sweet potatoes, and admit to being further swayed by their beautiful, intense orange color.

BAKED YAMS

Uniformly sized yams
Butter
Salt
Pepper

Preheat the oven to 350° F.

Using a vegetable brush, scrub the yams well; dry them with paper towels. Wrap each yam tightly in a single layer of aluminum foil. Place the wrapped yams directly on the center rack in the oven. Bake for 45 to 50 minutes, depending upon the size of the yams, until fork-tender.

To serve, remove and discard the aluminum foil. Using a sharp paring knife, cut a cross in the top of each yam. Press the ends of each yam toward the center to open the cross and force some of the cooked yam flesh through the opening. Tuck a pat of butter slightly into the exposed flesh on the top of each yam. Pass additional butter at the table. Set the table with salt and pepper for use by diners who wish to add these seasonings to their Baked Yams.

CANDIED YAMS

3 pounds yams (about 6 medium yams)
¼ teaspoon salt
½ cup packed light brown sugar
2 tablespoons butter
⅓ cup dark corn syrup
1 cup miniature marshmallows

Using a vegetable brush, scrub the yams well. Place the unpared yams in a large saucepan; add hot water to cover. Cover the saucepan. Bring the yams to a boil over high heat; reduce the heat to medium and cook at a low boil about 15 minutes, until the yams are just tender. The cooking time will depend upon the size of the yams. Avoid overcooking, causing the yams to become mushy. Drain the yams; place on a wire rack to cool.

Butter a 7 × 11-inch baking dish; set aside.

Peel the cooled yams, removing the thin layer of flesh directly beneath the skin to reveal the bright orange flesh. Cut the yams widthwise into 1½-inch chunks and arrange, single layer, in the prepared baking dish.

IMMEDIATELY BEFORE BAKING: Preheat the oven to 350° F. Sprinkle the salt over the yams. Then, distribute the brown sugar over the yams and dot with the butter. Drizzle the syrup back and forth over top. Immediately place the yams in the oven and bake, uncovered, for 20 minutes. Remove from the oven and baste. Scatter the marshmallows evenly over the yams. Bake an additional 5 minutes. Baste and serve.

SERVES 10

(Recipe continues on next page)

TO PREPARE CANDIED YAMS IN ADVANCE: Up to 1 day before serving, Candied Yams may be prepared through arranging them in the baking dish. Cover the dish with plastic wrap and refrigerate until ready to bake. Do not add the topping until immediately before baking. Placing the topping on Candied Yams in advance of baking will result in the brown sugar dissolving and sinking to the bottom of the baking dish together with the syrup, adversely affecting the final quality of the glaze.

YAMS GRAND MARNIER WITH CRANBERRIES AND KUMQUATS

2 pounds yams (about 4 medium yams)
1 1/4 cups sugar
1/2 teaspoon ground cinnamon
1/2 teaspoon ground nutmeg
1/4 teaspoon ground mace
1 12-ounce package fresh cranberries, washed and sorted (about 3 1/2 cups)
1/3 cup kumquats halved lengthwise, seeded, and finely sliced widthwise
1/2 cup pecan halves
3 tablespoons Grand Marnier liqueur

Using a vegetable brush, scrub the yams well. Place the unpared yams in a large saucepan; add hot water to cover. Cover the saucepan. Bring the yams to a boil over high heat; reduce the heat to medium and cook at a low boil about 15 minutes, until the yams are just tender. The cooking time will depend upon the size of the yams. Avoid overcooking, causing the yams to become mushy. Drain the yams; place them on a wire rack and let stand until cool.

Peel the cooled yams, removing the thin layer of flesh directly beneath the skin to reveal the bright orange flesh. Cut the yams widthwise into 1 1/2-inch chunks; set aside.

Preheat the oven to 375° F. Butter one 1 1/2-quart round baking dish *and* one 2-quart round baking dish; set aside.

In a large mixing bowl, place the sugar, cinnamon, nutmeg, and mace; stir to combine. Add the cranberries, kumquats, and pecans; stir to combine. Turn the cranberry mixture into the prepared 1 1/2-quart baking dish; spread evenly. Bake, uncovered, for 30 minutes.

Remove the cranberry mixture from the oven. Add the Grand Marnier liqueur; stir to combine. Into the prepared 2-quart baking dish, spoon a small amount of the cranberry mixture to cover the bottom of the dish. Arrange the yams evenly over the cranberry mixture in the bottom of the 2-quart baking dish. Spoon the remaining cranberry mixture over the yams.

Cover and bake for 15 minutes, until heated through.

SERVES 8

Rutabagas

While rutabagas and turnips are related and share many characteristics, they are actually separate species in the same botanical genus as cabbage *(Brassica)*. The common variety of rutabagas (also known as yellow turnips) has yellow flesh and light gold skin which changes to a deep purple mottled with green at the stem end, while bulbous turnips have white flesh and white skin which blends into a pretty purplish rose color at the top. The purple-hued parts of rutabagas and turnips are the parts which grow above the ground. Rutabagas are larger than turnips and have firmer flesh. Their distinct flavor is somewhat sweeter than that of turnips.

STEWED RUTABAGAS WITH ROOT VEGETABLES

Our family has always enjoyed the taste of rutabagas, and I commonly serve them as a wintertime main course, using this recipe. A tossed, green salad and coarse, dark bread are good accompaniments, followed by fruit for dessert.

1¼ cups whole milk
1¼ cups water
¾ teaspoon salt
¼ teaspoon white pepper
4 cups pared rutabagas, cut into ½-inch cubes (about 1½ pounds rutabagas)
1 cup pared, sliced carrots
½ pound pared, red potatoes cut into ½-inch cubes
¾ cup sliced leeks (white and greenish white parts only) (1 large or 2 medium leeks)
¼ cup coarsely diced green bell peppers
⅓ cup sliced celery
2 tablespoons butter
¼ pound pasteurized process American cheese, shredded
¼ cup rolled saltines (5 saltines)

In a large saucepan, place the milk, water, salt, and white pepper; stir to blend. Bring the mixture to a simmer over medium heat. Add the rutabagas, carrots, potatoes, leeks, green peppers, and celery; stir to combine. Cover the saucepan and return the mixture to a simmer. Reduce the heat and cook about 20 minutes, until the vegetables are tender. Add the butter, cheese, and saltines. Stir gently over low heat until the cheese melts.

SERVES 4 AS A MAIN COURSE OR 8 AS A SIDE DISH

SERVING SUGGESTIONS: Serve in soup bowls as a main course or in sauce dishes as a side dish.

Spinach

TO COOK AND SERVE SPINACH

Remove from the spinach the stems and any yellow leaves; discard. Wash the spinach leaves twice, making certain that all the sand has been removed. Place the spinach leaves in a large kettle; add water to cover. Cover the kettle. Bring the spinach to a boil over high heat; reduce the heat and simmer 4 minutes. Drain the spinach well in a colander.

Chop the spinach on a cutting board and place in a mixing bowl. Add 1 tablespoon plus 1 teaspoon melted butter per pound of raw spinach used. Toss to coat the spinach. If necessary, rewarm the spinach in a covered saucepan over very low heat, stirring often.

Serve family style in a vegetable dish or in individual sauce dishes. Garnish with hard-cooked egg slices (page 222). Serve with lemon wedges or pass a cruet of cider vinegar at the table.

1 POUND OF RAW SPINACH SERVES 2 OR 3

Squash

BAKED ACORN SQUASH

Acorn squash are also known as Des Moines squash. They are commonly dark green and often mottled with orange. There is also an all-orange variety of acorn squash called Gold Acorn squash. Des Moines squash and Gold Acorn squash are similar in flavor.

2 acorn squash
1 tablespoon plus 1 teaspoon butter, softened
Salt (optional)
½ cup (8 tablespoons) packed dark brown
    sugar
¼ cup (4 tablespoons) butter

Preheat the oven to 400°F.

Wash the squash; dry them with paper towels. Using a large, sharp, rigid knife, cut the squash in half lengthwise. Using a tablespoon, scrape out and discard the seeds and stringy centers of the squash. Brush the yellow flesh of each squash half (including the top rims) generously with 1 teaspoon butter. Lightly sprinkle salt over the flesh, if desired. Place the squash, cut side down, in a 9 × 13-inch ungreased baking dish. Bake, uncovered, for 30 minutes.

Remove the squash from the oven and reduce the oven temperature to 350°F. Using a spatula, turn the squash cut side up. Place 2 tablespoons packed brown sugar and 1 tablespoon butter in the cavity of each squash half. Return the squash to the oven and bake, uncovered, for an additional 15 to 30 minutes, depending upon the size of the squash. Bake the squash until the flesh is fork-tender and the top rim of each squash half is golden brown. Be careful not to overbake. Serve 1 squash half per person.

SERVES 4

VARIATION: When baking Gold Acorn Squash, substitute light brown sugar for the dark brown sugar.

BAKED BUTTERNUT SQUASH

2 1¼- to 1½-pound butternut squash
1 tablespoon plus 1 teaspoon butter, softened
Salt (optional)
1/4 cup packed light brown sugar
1 tablespoon plus 1 teaspoon butter

Preheat the oven to 400°F.

Wash the squash; dry them with paper towels. Using a large, sharp, rigid knife, cut the squash in half lengthwise. Using a tablespoon, scrape out and discard the seeds and stringy centers of the squash. Brush the yellow flesh of each squash half (including the top rim) generously with 1 teaspoon butter. Lightly sprinkle salt over the flesh, if desired. Place the squash, cut side down, in a 9 × 13-inch ungreased baking dish. Bake, uncovered, for 30 minutes.

Remove the squash from the oven and reduce the oven temperature to 350°F. Using a spatula, turn the squash cut side up. Place 1 tablespoon packed light brown sugar and 1 teaspoon butter in the cavity of each squash half. Return the squash to the oven and bake, uncovered, for an additional 15 to 30 minutes until the flesh is fork-tender. Serve 1 squash half per person.

SERVES 4

ZUCCHINI AND YELLOW SUMMER SQUASH WITH WALNUTS

1 teaspoon vegetable oil
1½ tablespoons butter
¾ pound (total) zucchini and yellow summer
    squash (1 medium squash each), sliced ¼
    inch thick
⅓ cup shallots thinly sliced and separated
    into rings
3 tablespoons water
2 tablespoons dry red wine
¼ cup broken English walnuts

In a medium, heavy-bottomed skillet, heat the vegetable oil over medium heat. Using a spatula, spread the vegetable oil over the entire bottom of the skillet. Add the butter. Tilt the skillet back and forth to blend the butter with the oil. Place the zucchini, yellow summer squash, and shallots in the skillet; sauté until lightly brown (about 5 minutes). Reduce the heat to low. When the skillet cools slightly, add the water and wine; stir to blend. Simmer the mixture 3 minutes to reduce the liquid. Add the walnuts; stir to combine; heat through.

SERVES 4

Tomatoes

SCALLOPED TOMATOES

1 14½-ounce can whole, peeled tomatoes, undrained
1 tablespoon butter
½ cup minced onions
¼ cup finely chopped celery
¼ cup Dried Bread Crumbs (page 33)
1 tablespoon finely snipped, fresh parsley
½ teaspoon sugar
⅛ teaspoon pepper
¼ teaspoon salt (omit if canned tomatoes contain salt)
1 tablespoon butter, melted
1¼ cups tarragon croutons (see Herb Croutons, page 32)

Preheat the oven to 350° F. Butter a 1-quart round baking dish; set aside.

Place the undrained tomatoes in a medium mixing bowl. Using a small knife, cut the tomatoes into quarters or eighths, depending upon their size. (The tomatoes should be in large chunks.) Set aside. In a small, heavy-bottomed skillet, melt 1 tablespoon butter over medium heat. Tilt the skillet back and forth to completely cover the bottom with the melted butter. Place

the onions and celery in the skillet; sauté lightly (about 5 minutes); do not brown. Using a slotted spoon, remove the onions and celery from the skillet and place in the bowl containing the tomatoes; stir to combine; set aside.

In a small mixing bowl, place the crumbs, parsley, sugar, pepper, and salt (if used); stir to combine. Add 1 tablespoon melted butter; stir to combine. Add the crumb mixture to the tomato mixture; stir to combine.

Spoon ½ of the tomato mixture into the prepared baking dish (see Note). Scatter ½ of the croutons evenly over the tomato mixture. Repeat the layers, using the remaining ½ of the tomato mixture and croutons. Bake, uncovered, for 25 minutes. The mixture will be bubbly.

SERVES 6

NOTE: Do not assemble the ingredients in the baking dish until shortly before baking so the croutons will remain whole.

STEWED TOMATOES

1 14½-ounce can whole, peeled tomatoes, undrained
1 tablespoon finely chopped onions
1 tablespoon finely chopped green bell peppers
2 medium-sized, fresh basil leaves, finely snipped
¼ teaspoon sugar
⅛ teaspoon salt
Dash of pepper
Dash of ground nutmeg

Place the undrained tomatoes in a medium saucepan. Using a small knife, cut the tomatoes into quarters or eighths, depending upon their size. (The tomatoes should be in large chunks.) Add the onions, green peppers, basil, sugar, salt, pepper, and nutmeg; stir to combine. Cover the saucepan and bring the mixture to a boil over

(Recipe continues on next page)

medium-high heat. Reduce the heat to low and simmer 10 minutes, until the onions and green peppers are tender. Serve in individual sauce dishes.

SERVES 4

Other Vegetable Recipes

Baked Cabbage with Hamburger (page 246)
Broccoli-Rice Casserole (page 228–229)
Layered Zucchini Casserole (page 247)

Fruits

AMBROSIA

Ambrosia, the food of the Greek and Roman gods, is an appropriate name for this time-honored dessert, which apparently dates back to the nineteenth century. Worthy creations are awarded permanence.

4 medium-large oranges, sectioned
    (page 32)
Juice of 1 medium-large orange
⅓ cup flaked coconut
3 bananas

In a medium mixing bowl, place the orange sections, orange juice, and coconut. Just before serving, slice the bananas and add to the mixture; using a wooden mixing spoon, stir to combine. Spoon into crystal fruit dishes.

SERVES 8

CINNAMON APPLESAUCE

A fixture in American cooking.

2 pounds cooking apples (about 5 large
    apples) (McIntosh is an excellent variety for
    applesauce)
⅔ cup water*
½ cup sugar
1 teaspoon freshly squeezed, strained lemon
    juice
½ teaspoon ground cinnamon

  * *Reduce the water to ½ cup for extra-thick
    applesauce.*

Wash the apples. Pare, quarter, and core the apples. In a large saucepan, place the apples and water. Cover the saucepan. Bring the apples to a boil over high heat. Reduce the heat and simmer 15 to 20 minutes, until the apples are tender, stirring occasionally. Add the sugar and stir constantly until dissolved. Add the lemon juice

and cinnamon; stir to blend and combine. Remove from the heat.

Some varieties of apples remain in whole pieces after cooking, while other varieties puree when stirred during the cooking process. After the applesauce is made, press it through a food mill if desired.

MAKES ABOUT 3 CUPS

PLAIN APPLESAUCE

Follow the Cinnamon Applesauce recipe, above, eliminating the ground cinnamon.

SCALLOPED APPLES

¼ cup granulated sugar
¼ cup packed light brown sugar
1 tablespoon plus 2 teaspoons all-purpose
    flour
¼ teaspoon ground cinnamon
¼ teaspoon ground nutmeg
¼ teaspoon ground mace
8 cups Golden Delicious apples, pared,
    quartered, cored, and sliced ⅛ inch thick
    (about 6 medium apples), divided
2 tablespoons freshly squeezed, strained
    lemon juice, divided
2 tablespoons cognac
4 cups dried raisin bread cubes (page 32),
    divided
¼ cup plus 2 tablespoons (6 tablespoons)
    butter, melted
½ cup chopped, unsalted peanuts
2 tablespoons butter

Preheat the oven to 350° F. Butter a 7 × 11-inch baking dish; set aside.

In a small mixing bowl, place the granulated sugar, brown sugar, flour, cinnamon, nutmeg, and mace; stir to combine; set aside.

Pare, quarter, core, and slice 4 cups apples; place in a large mixing bowl. Sprinkle 1 tablespoon lemon juice over the apples; toss to coat.

Prepare the remaining 4 cups sliced apples; add to the mixing bowl containing the sliced apples. Sprinkle the remaining 1 tablespoon lemon juice over the apples; toss to coat. Sprinkle the cognac over the apples; toss to combine. Sprinkle the sugar mixture over the apples; toss to coat. Cover with plastic wrap; set aside.

Place the bread cubes in a large mixing bowl; drizzle the melted butter evenly over the top. Toss until the bread cubes are coated. Arrange ½ of the bread cubes evenly over the bottom of the prepared baking dish. Spoon the apple mixture evenly over the bread cubes. Scatter the peanuts evenly over the top. Dot with 2 tablespoons butter.

Cover the baking dish with aluminum foil. Bake for 45 minutes. Remove from the oven. Remove the foil and spoon the remaining ½ bread cubes evenly over the top of the apple mixture. Bake, *uncovered*, for an additional 15 minutes.

SERVES 12

FRESH FRUIT COMPOTE

(See photo insert page C-7)

1½ cups freshly squeezed orange juice
1 red apple, unpared, quartered, cored, and sliced
1 Granny Smith apple, unpared, quartered, cored, and sliced
1 ripe, juicy pear, pared, quartered, cored, and sliced
1 banana, peeled and sliced
1 large red grapefruit, peeled and sectioned (page 32)
2 large oranges, peeled and sectioned (page 32)
½ small cantaloupe, pared, cut lengthwise into 1-inch-wide strips, and sliced
½ small honeydew melon, pared, cut lengthwise into 1-inch-wide strips, and sliced
⅔ fresh pineapple, pared, cored, sliced, and cut into bite-sized pieces
1½ cups seedless red grapes

1½ cups strawberries, hulled (page 6) and cut in half lengthwise
2 kiwis, ends trimmed (cut away the core at the stem end), pared, and sliced ¼ inch thick
½ cup fresh blackberries

Pour the orange juice into a large mixing bowl. Prepare the apples, pear, and banana, and mix with the orange juice as they are prepared to prevent discoloration. Prepare the remaining ingredients and add to the mixing bowl; wait to combine until all the fruit has been prepared to help avoid tearing the fruit pieces by overhandling.

Using a wooden spoon, combine the fruit carefully and turn into a glass compote or bowl. To serve, ladle the fruit into crystal sherbet glasses or sauce dishes at the table. Place on small, doily-lined plates.

SERVES 12

OPTIONAL GARNISH: The kiwi slices may be reserved and used to garnish the compote by overlapping them around the edge of the bowl. Additional kiwi slices may be required.

ACCOMPANIMENT SUGGESTION: At the table, pass a beautiful plate on which is arranged one or more of the following cookies: Scotch Shortbread (page 565–566), Butterscotch Icebox Cookies (page 569), or Lace Cookies (page 553).

UGLI FRUIT, KIWI, AND STRAWBERRY DESSERT SUITE

Ugli (pronounced "ugly") is the trademark name of a Jamaican fruit believed to be a cross between a tangerine and a grapefruit (or, some authorities say, a pomelo). While its thick, somewhat loose-fitting skin of lime green to light orange color may not be super-glamorous, the ultra-juicy citrus fruit it encases is a radiant yellow-orange and anything but ugly. Ugli fruit ranges in size from a good-sized orange to a large grapefruit, and its flavor is best described as acid-sweet. Peel it and

(Recipe continues on next page)

eat it like a tangerine, or cut it in half and eat it as you would a grapefruit. The recipe that follows calls for the fruit to be sectioned. Available from December to about May, Ugli fruit is a superior, change-of-pace citrus for use in both desserts and salads. It is sometimes known as "uniq" fruit.

1 large Ugli fruit
2 kiwis
½ pound fresh strawberries
4 small sprigs of fresh mint for decoration

Peel the Ugli fruit; remove all remaining white membrane. Section the Ugli fruit (page 32), retaining all juice; set aside. Trim off both ends of the kiwis and cut away the core at the stem end. Pare the kiwis and slice them widthwise ¼ inch thick; set aside. Wash the strawberries; using a strawberry huller, remove the hulls (page 6). Cut the strawberries in half lengthwise; set aside.

Artistically arrange the prepared fruit in 4 crystal sherbet glasses. Pour the reserved Ugli fruit juice over the fruit in each glass. Decorate each serving with a small sprig of fresh mint and place it on a small, doily-lined plate.

SERVES 4

ACCOMPANIMENT SUGGESTIONS: Place two Coconut Macaroons (page 537), Frosted Orange Cookies (page 541), or Almond-Butter Puffs (page 534) on the doily-lined plate under each serving; or, arrange all three types of cookies on a lovely plate and pass at the table.

HOT CURRIED FRUIT

1 15-ounce can unpeeled apricot halves
1 15-ounce can pitted Royal Anne white cherries
1 15¼-ounce can sliced pears
1 15¼-ounce can cling peach halves
1 20-ounce can pineapple chunks
1 15-ounce can figs
1 15-ounce can white grapes
1 15½-ounce can pitted dark sweet cherries
1 15-ounce can gooseberries
1 cup packed light brown sugar
1 tablespoon curry powder
½ teaspoon ground ginger
2 tablespoons cornstarch
½ cup (¼ pound) butter

Preheat the oven to 350° F. Butter a 10 × 15-inch (4-quart) baking dish; set aside.

In a sieve, drain the apricots, Royal Anne cherries, pears, peaches, and pineapple chunks, reserving the mixed juice. Place the drained fruit in a very large mixing bowl; set aside. Measure 1½ cups reserved mixed juice; set aside. (Reserve any remaining mixed juice for other uses.) Then, drain the figs, grapes, and dark cherries; if desired, reserve the juices from these fruits for other uses. Add the drained fruit to the mixing bowl containing the first-drained fruit. Using a wooden mixing spoon, *carefully* combine the fruits. Turn the mixed fruits into the prepared baking dish. Drain the gooseberries and carefully distribute them over the mixed fruit; set aside.

In a small mixing bowl, place the brown sugar, curry powder, ginger, and cornstarch; stir to combine; set aside. In a small saucepan, melt the butter over low heat. Remove from the heat; add the brown sugar mixture and stir well. Add the 1½ cups reserved mixed juice; stir to combine. Cook the fruit juice mixture over medium heat until smooth and thick, stirring continuously. Pour the mixture evenly over the fruit (see Note). Bake, uncovered, 35 minutes, until completely heated and bubbly.

NOTE: At this point, the baking dish may be covered with plastic wrap and the curried fruit refrigerated up to 24 hours prior to baking. (Bake uncovered.)

SERVES 16

SERVING SUGGESTIONS
• An excellent brunch dish.

• Serve with ham, poultry, and game birds.

BROILED GRAPEFRUIT

3 large red grapefruit
3 maraschino cherries, cut in half lengthwise
2 tablespoons packed light brown sugar
2 tablespoons pure maple syrup
2 tablespoons butter, melted
2 tablespoons cream sherry (optional)

Preheat the broiler.

Cut the grapefruit in half and remove the seeds. Using a grapefruit knife, cut around the meat in each grapefruit section to loosen the fruit from the membrane. Arrange the grapefruit halves in a shallow, flat-bottomed baking dish. Place half a cherry, skin side up, in the center of each grapefruit half. Sprinkle 1 teaspoon brown sugar over each grapefruit half. Then, drizzle 1 teaspoon maple syrup evenly over each half. Lightly brush 1 teaspoon melted butter over each grapefruit half, *including the rind and the cherry.*

Broil the grapefruit, 4 inches from the heat, about 8 minutes, until golden. Watch the grapefruit closely. If they begin to overbrown, immediately remove them from the broiler. When done, remove the grapefruit from the broiler and drizzle 1 teaspoon sherry over each grapefruit half. Serve on small plates or in small sauce dishes. Place either the small plates or sauce dishes containing the Broiled Grapefruit on slightly larger, doily-lined service plates.

SERVES 6

SERVING SUGGESTION: This is nice served as a first course on a brunch or holiday breakfast menu.

BAKED FRUIT

12 bite-sized pitted prunes
1 cup water
1 20-ounce can crushed pineapple in pineapple juice, undrained
4 ounces shredded, medium cheddar cheese (1 cup)

½ cup sugar
3 tablespoons all-purpose flour
¼ teaspoon salt
¼ teaspoon ground allspice
4 canned, unpeeled apricot halves, cut into thirds vertically
1 cup Plain Croutons (page 32)

In a small saucepan, place the prunes and water. Bring the prunes to a boil, uncovered, over high heat; reduce the heat and simmer 1 minute. Remove from the heat. Cover the saucepan and let the prunes stand to cool.

Preheat the oven to 350° F. Butter a 6 × 10-inch baking dish; set aside.

In a medium mixing bowl, place the pineapple, cheese, sugar, flour, salt, and allspice; stir to combine. Turn the mixture into the prepared baking dish. Press the prunes and apricots lightly and decoratively into the pineapple mixture in the following pattern:

Make 6 rows of fruit across the 6-inch (narrow) way of the dish, using 2 prunes and 2 pieces of apricot in each row, and alternating the fruit, as follows:

First row: prune, apricot, prune, apricot
Second row: apricot, prune, apricot, prune
Repeat the 2 rows twice (see illustration).

Arrange the apricot pieces diagonally, skin side up.

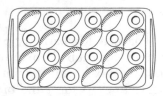

Scatter the Plain Croutons evenly over the top. Bake, uncovered, for 30 minutes.

SERVES 8

SERVING SUGGESTIONS
• A delicious accompaniment for ham, pork, and chicken.

• An excellent side dish for a buffet brunch.

POACHED RHUBARB

(See photo insert page C-6)

3 cups fresh rhubarb cut into ½-inch lengths
(slit very wide stalks in two, lengthwise,
before slicing)
¼ cup sugar
1 tablespoon water

In a medium, heavy-bottomed saucepan, place
the rhubarb, sugar, and water; using a small
mixing spoon, toss to combine. Cover the
saucepan and place it over low heat; let stand
until the sugar dissolves, stirring intermittently.
Watch closely, not allowing the mixture to burn.

When the sugar has dissolved, increase the
heat to medium low. Bring the mixture to a low
simmer and cook for 4 to 6 minutes, until the
rhubarb is tender, stirring occasionally. Some
pieces of rhubarb will have remained fairly
whole while other pieces will have completely
shredded. Remove from the heat; let stand to
cool slightly. Then, pour the Poached Rhubarb
into a plastic storage container; cover and
refrigerate. Cool before serving.

To serve, spoon the Poached Rhubarb into
small, glass sauce dishes.

SERVES 4

SERVING SUGGESTION: Spoon a very small dollop of
Whipped Cream (page 309) over each serving.

RHUBARB SAUCE

Follow the Poached Rhubarb recipe, above,
through bringing the rhubarb mixture to a low
simmer. Cook the mixture for 10 minutes, until
all the rhubarb loses its form and breaks into
shreds, stirring occasionally. Then, follow the
above recipe to conclusion.

MAKES 1 ½ CUPS (ABOUT 8 SERVINGS)

SERVING SUGGESTION: Serve over vanilla ice cream
(homemade, page 595, or commercial) in a
sauce dish. To decorate, place a sprig of fresh
mint on the inside edge of each sauce dish.

Other Fruit Recipes

Apple Brown Betty (page 574–575)
Apple Crisp (page 574)
Apple Dumplings (page 575–576)
Apricot Bavarian Cream (page 594)
Baked Apples (page 577)
Baked Nutmeg Bananas with Ice Cream and
    Caramel Sauce (page 596)
Brandied Apples (page 157–158)
Candied Grapefruit Peel (page 610)
Candied Orange Peel (page 609–610)
Cherry Cobbler (page 572–573)
Chocolate-Covered Cherries (page 604–605)
Frosted Orange Cookies (page 541)
Fruitcake Cookies (page 543)
Fruit Cocktail Dessert (page 577–578)
Fruit Pies (pages 409–419)
Fruit Salads (pages 89–100)
Glazed Pineapple (page 163)
Lemon Bars (page 520–521)
Mother's Pineapple Cookies (page 546)
Old-Fashioned Strawberry Shortcake (page 381)
Peach Bavarian Cream (page 594)
Peach Cobbler (page 573–574)
Pineapple Upside-Down Cake (page 473)
Pink Grapefruit Sorbet (page 598)
Red Raspberry Tapioca (page 581)
Rhubarb Rapture (page 578–579)
Rose Lee's Apricot Bars (page 522–523)
Strawberries, Triple Sec, and Whipped Cream
    (page 594)
Strawberry Bavarian Cream (page 594)
Strawberry Ice Cream (page 595)
Strawberry "Shortcake" (with Angel Food
    Cake) (page 485)
Strawberry Sponge-Style Shortcake (page 488)
Traditional Holiday Fruitcake (page 494–496)

NOTE: Recipes for breads, sauces, beverages, additional pies, cakes, and cookies, and other items
which include fruit may be found in the index.

Sauces and Gravies

Savory Sauces

BARBECUE SAUCE

This barbecue sauce is not precooked. It is for use with indoor cooking recipes that call for the sauce to be poured over meat, poultry, or wild game, which is then baked at medium to medium-low heat for an extended period of time. For a precooked barbecue sauce to use for outdoor cooking on the grill or in the smoker, see Barbecue Sauce for Outdoor Cooking (page 205).

2 cups tomato catsup
¾ cup chili sauce
⅔ cup packed dark brown sugar
½ cup red wine vinegar
⅓ cup freshly squeezed, strained lemon juice
3 tablespoons Heinz 57 Sauce
3 tablespoons prepared mustard
2 tablespoons Worcestershire sauce
1 tablespoon very finely grated onions
1 tablespoon vegetable oil
1 teaspoon dry mustard
1 teaspoon celery salt
1 teaspoon pepper
½ teaspoon dried leaf thyme
Dash of Tabasco pepper sauce
¾ cup beer

In a medium mixing bowl, place the catsup, chili sauce, brown sugar, vinegar, lemon juice, Heinz 57 Sauce, prepared mustard, Worcestershire sauce, onions, vegetable oil, dry mustard, celery salt, pepper, thyme, pepper sauce, and beer; using an electric mixer, beat on medium speed until well blended. *Do not cook* the Barbecue Sauce before use in recipes. Place the sauce in a glass jar; cover tightly and refrigerate up to 2 weeks.

MAKES 5¼ CUPS

VARIATION: For more spicy Barbecue Sauce, substitute commercially canned hot tomato catsup for standard tomato catsup.

SERVING SUGGESTIONS: Use this Barbecue Sauce to make Barbecued Loin Back Ribs (page 156–157), Barbecued Chicken (page 177), and barbecued butterfly pork chops.

COCKTAIL SAUCE

A favorite sauce for shrimp, whether served cold or deep-fat fried.

1 cup chili sauce
¼ cup *well-drained,* packed, prepared horseradish, homemade (page 30) or commercially canned
2 teaspoons finely grated onions
2 teaspoons celery seed
2 teaspoons celery salt
2 teaspoons Worcestershire sauce
½ teaspoon garlic salt
½ teaspoon salt
¼ teaspoon pepper
5 dashes of Tabasco pepper sauce
¼ cup sugar

In a small mixing bowl place the chili sauce, horseradish, onions, celery seed, celery salt, Worcestershire sauce, garlic salt, salt, pepper, pepper sauce, and sugar; stir well to combine. Place the sauce in a glass jar; cover tightly and refrigerate at least 2 days to blend flavors before serving. Keeps up to 2 weeks in the refrigerator.

MAKES ABOUT 1½ CUPS

HORSERADISH SAUCE

A dreamy, light sauce wonderfully served through the years with ham loaf (see Ham Loaf with Horseradish Sauce, page 163). It is also well paired with beef and fresh pork.

This recipe is from my grandmother's cookbook where it appeared in her own handwriting. The cultural heritage of food is exemplified by the fact that recipes for Horseradish Sauce in current cookbooks are very similar to hers. My grandmother's life spanned the years 1880 to 1945.

2 tablespoons well-drained, packed, prepared horseradish, homemade (page 30) or commercially canned
¼ teaspoon salt
½ cup whipping cream, whipped (with no additions)

Add the horseradish and salt to the whipped cream; fold to combine. Serve immediately or cover and refrigerate up to 3 hours.

Just before serving, lightly fold the sauce again, and spoon it attractively into a small, crystal serving dish.

MAKES ABOUT 1 CUP

TARTAR SAUCE

½ cup Miracle Whip dressing
3 tablespoons sweet pickle relish
3 tablespoons minced onions

In a small mixing bowl place the salad dressing, sweet pickle relish, and onions; stir to combine.

In a covered glass jar or plastic container, Tartar Sauce keeps up to 2 weeks in the refrigerator.

SERVES 4 AS A CONDIMENT FOR FISH OR SHELLFISH

TOMATO SAUCE

3¼ pounds ripe tomatoes (4 cups pulp; see recipe procedures below)
2 tablespoons butter
1 cup finely chopped onions (about 1 large onion)
1 large garlic clove, pressed
2 tablespoons butter
1 cup finely chopped, fresh mushrooms (about 4 ounces mushrooms)
1 teaspoon dried leaf oregano
1 tablespoon finely snipped, fresh parsley
1 bay leaf
6 whole cloves in cheesecloth bag (page 28)
1¼ teaspoons salt
¼ teaspoon pepper
2 teaspoons sugar
2 tablespoons all-purpose flour
2 tablespoons water

Wash the tomatoes. Blanch the tomatoes (page 29) 1 minute; stem, peel, quarter, seed and core (page 29). Pour off the surplus juice and reserve for other uses. Process the tomatoes in a blender (see Note), *in thirds,* for about 2 seconds only. The pulp should contain very small chunks of tomatoes. Be careful not to totally liquefy the tomatoes. Measure 4 cups pulp; set aside.

In a large, heavy-bottomed saucepan, melt 2 tablespoons butter over medium heat. Place the onions and garlic in the saucepan; sauté until translucent and tender but not brown. Spoon the onion mixture into a small bowl; set aside. Place an additional 2 tablespoons butter in the saucepan. Add the mushrooms and sauté over medium heat until they give up their juices. Remove from the heat; let stand until the mushrooms cool slightly.

Then, add the tomato pulp, onion mixture, oregano, parsley, bay leaf, cheesecloth bag of cloves, salt, pepper, and sugar to the saucepan containing the mushrooms; stir to combine. Return the saucepan to medium heat; cover and bring the mixture to a boil. Reduce the heat and

(Recipe continues on next page)

simmer the mixture slowly for 45 minutes. Remove from the heat. Remove and discard the bay leaf and cheesecloth bag of cloves. Set aside.

In a small glass jar or plastic container with a secure lid, place the flour and water; cover and shake vigorously until blended and smooth. Add the flour mixture to the mixture in the saucepan; stir to combine. Place the saucepan over low heat; return the mixture to a low boil and cook 3 minutes, until thickened, stirring constantly. In a covered glass jar or plastic container, Tomato Sauce keeps up to 1 week in the refrigerator.

NOTE: If a blender is not available, process the tomatoes in 1-cup batches in a food processor, pulsing until the pulp contains very small chunks of tomatoes. Be careful not to totally liquefy the tomatoes.

MAKES ABOUT 4 CUPS

SERVING SUGGESTIONS
- Use in Italian dishes (see Eggplant Parmesan, page 266–267).
- Serve over vegetables such as zucchini, green beans, or mixed vegetables.
- Use in pasta dishes.
- Use in casseroles.

CATSUP SAUCE

1 cup tomato catsup
1 tablespoon prepared mustard
2 tablespoons packed dark brown sugar

In a small saucepan, place the catsup, mustard, and brown sugar; stir to combine. Place the saucepan over low heat and bring the mixture to a simmer, stirring frequently. Keeps, covered, up to 1 week in the refrigerator.

MAKES ABOUT 1 CUP

SERVING SUGGESTIONS
- Spread over beef and pork during the last 15 minutes of cooking (see Mother's Meat Loaf, page 146–147).
- Serve warm in a sauce dish at the table for diners to use on hamburgers, porkburgers, hotdogs, and roast pork.

DILL SAUCE

1 cup mayonnaise
2 tablespoons dry white wine
1 teaspoon white wine Worcestershire sauce
1 teaspoon sugar
3 dashes of Tabasco pepper sauce
1 teaspoon snipped, fresh dillweed

In a small mixing bowl, place the mayonnaise, white wine, white wine Worcestershire sauce, sugar, and pepper sauce; using an electric mixer, beat on medium-high speed until smooth and blended. Add the dillweed; using a spoon, stir until evenly combined. In a covered glass jar or plastic container, Dill Sauce keeps up to 2 days in the refrigerator.

MAKES ABOUT 1 CUP

SERVING SUGGESTIONS
- Serve with cold or hot fish and shellfish.
- Serve with cold lamb or veal sandwiches.

PARSLEY SAUCE

3 tablespoons finely snipped, fresh parsley or
    1 tablespoon dried parsley
¼ teaspoon celery salt
1 recipe Medium White Sauce (page 301–302)

Add the parsley and celery salt to hot Medium White Sauce; stir to combine. Best when served immediately or soon after making; however, it may be refrigerated in a covered container up to 2 days.

MAKES ABOUT 1 CUP

SERVING SUGGESTIONS

- Serve over boiled and then peeled small, new, red potatoes (page 275–276).

- Serve with Broiled Fish Fillets (page 186).

CAPER SAUCE

¼ cup (4 tablespoons) butter
½ teaspoon cornstarch
1 tablespoon vinegar drained from bottled baby capers
2 tablespoons baby capers, drained
2 tablespoons snipped, fresh parsley
1 tablespoon freshly squeezed, strained lemon juice
1 tablespoon dry white wine
Dash of cayenne pepper

In a small saucepan, melt the butter over low heat. Remove from the heat. Add the cornstarch; stir until blended. Then, add the vinegar, capers, parsley, lemon juice, wine, and cayenne pepper; stir to blend and combine. Place over medium heat and cook the sauce until slightly thickened, stirring constantly. Serve immediately or refrigerate in a covered glass or plastic container up to 4 hours. Reheat if not served immediately.

MAKES ABOUT ½ CUP (ENOUGH TO SPOON OVER 6 ½-POUND FISH FILLETS)

SERVING SUGGESTION: Serve over broiled fish fillets (see Broiled Walleye Fillets with Caper Sauce, (page 186).

GREEN SAUCE (SAUCE VERTE)

This lovely green-colored sauce is traditionally served with Cold Poached Salmon Steaks. It may also accompany cold lobster and other cold shellfish, and poached, broiled, or baked fish served cold.

1 cup mayonnaise
2 teaspoons dry white wine
1 tablespoon finely snipped, fresh parsley
2 teaspoons finely snipped, fresh dillweed
1 teaspoon finely snipped, fresh chives

In a small blender beaker or a small food processor, place the mayonnaise, white wine, parsley, dillweed, and chives. Process until the herbs are chopped as finely as possible. In a covered glass or plastic container, Green Sauce keeps up to 2 days in the refrigerator.

JELLIED CRANBERRY SAUCE

2 12-ounce packages (7 cups) fresh cranberries
2 cups water
3⅓ cups sugar

Wash and sort the cranberries. In an 8-quart, heavy-bottomed kettle, place the cranberries and water. Cover the saucepan and bring the cranberries to a boil over high heat. Reduce the heat to medium and simmer the cranberries about 3 minutes, until the skins burst and the berries are soft, stirring occasionally. Press the cranberries and liquid through a food mill; set aside.

Clean the saucepan and pour the pressed cranberries into the pan. Add the sugar; stir well to combine. Over high heat, bring the mixture to a boil, stirring constantly. Attach a candy thermometer to the saucepan. Boil the mixture until it reaches 8°F. above the boiling point of water (page 10) and begins to sheet (see next page) (about 7 minutes), stirring continuously.

(Recipe continues on next page)

Remove from the heat; using a metal spoon, quickly skim the foam (if any) off the top of the cranberry sauce and discard. *Immediately* pour the cranberry sauce (there will be about 4 cups) into 1 or more ungreased molds. Place the mold(s) carefully on a wire cookie rack; let stand 30 minutes to cool the cranberry sauce partially. Then, refrigerate, uncovered. When the cranberry sauce is completely cool and set, cover the molds with plastic wrap.

Unmold just before serving. To unmold, insert a paring knife about 1 inch into the outer edge of the mold at 3 approximately equidistant places. Place a flat serving plate on top of the mold; hold the plate and mold together and invert. If the sauce does not unmold, lift the inverted mold slightly and insert a paring knife along the edge of the mold at one place until the sauce releases. Do not unmold Jellied Cranberry Sauce by placing the mold in warm water or applying warm towels to the mold.

Keep up to 2 days molded in the refrigerator. After unmolding and serving, leftover Jellied Cranberry Sauce may be covered and refrigerated up to 5 days, although it will weep.

MAKES ABOUT 4 CUPS

SERVING SUGGESTIONS

- A traditional accompaniment for holiday roast turkey.

- Excellent with all fowl.

SHEET: v. When a boiling jelly mixture reaches the jellying point, and two drops of the mixture flow together and break in a single sheet from a metal (previously cool) tablespoon of the mixture poured back into the kettle from the side of the tablespoon bowl held about 12 inches above the kettle (out of the steam).

APRICOT SAUCE

6 ounces dried apricots (about 1 cup packed dried apricots)
2 cups water
½ cup sugar
1 tablespoon cornstarch
2 tablespoons freshly squeezed, strained lemon juice
⅛ teaspoon ground cloves
1 tablespoon cognac

In a small saucepan, place the apricots and water. Cover the saucepan. Bring the apricots to a boil over high heat; reduce the heat and simmer 15 minutes. Place the apricots and cooking liquid in a blender (see Note); process until pureed; set aside.

In a clean, dry, small saucepan, place the sugar, cornstarch, lemon juice, and cloves; stir until completely smooth and blended. Add about ½ cup of the pureed apricots; stir to blend. Add the remainder of the pureed apricots; stir until blended. Over medium-low heat, cook the apricot mixture until clear and thick (about 6 minutes), stirring constantly. At this point, the sauce may be placed in a covered jar or plastic container and refrigerated up to 1 day before serving. Just before serving, reheat the sauce over low heat. Add the cognac and stir to blend.

NOTE: If a blender is not available, a food processor may be used.

MAKES ABOUT 2½ CUPS

SERVING SUGGESTIONS: Nice with goose (see Baked Goose with Apricot-Cognac Dressing, page 197–198), duck, and ham.

RAISIN SAUCE

Raisin Sauce is simply too good to be forgotten, but you can hardly find a recipe for it in current cookbooks. There seems to be no rhyme or reason for this in light of the fact that Raisin Sauce's extended relationship with ham has long been recognized as a shining example of the perfect food couple!

1 cup water
⅓ cup golden raisins
⅓ cup currants
3 tablespoons packed dark brown sugar
⅛ teaspoon ground ginger
⅛ teaspoon salt
1 tablespoon plus 2 teaspoons cornstarch
¼ cup port wine
1 tablespoon red wine vinegar
¼ cup water

Pour 1 cup water into a small saucepan. Cover the saucepan and bring the water to a boil over high heat. Remove from the heat. Place the raisins and currants in the saucepan of hot water. Cover the saucepan and let the raisins and currants stand to plump 30 minutes.

In a small mixing bowl, place the brown sugar, ginger, salt, and cornstarch; stir to combine. Add the wine, vinegar, and ¼ cup water; stir until smooth. Add to the raisin-water mixture; stir to mix. Place over medium heat and cook until the sauce thickens, stirring continuously. Serve hot. In a covered glass jar or plastic container, Raisin Sauce keeps up to 1 week in the refrigerator.

MAKES ABOUT 1¼ CUPS

VARIATION: ⅔ cup regular raisins may be substituted for the golden raisins and currants.

MEDIUM WHITE SAUCE

White sauce is one of the most frequently used sauces in Midwest cooking. Rarely is this sauce used alone. Rather, white sauce is ordinarily combined with other foods in dishes such as casseroles, creamed vegetables, and cream soups, and is used in making other sauces. Recipes for 5 thicknesses of white sauce are given here. Selection of thickness depends upon use of the sauce; however, Medium White Sauce is used most often.

Properly made white sauce is smooth, with absolutely no lumps. If the simple procedures are followed, completely smooth white sauce will result every time.

2 tablespoons all-purpose flour
½ teaspoon salt
⅛ teaspoon white pepper or black pepper
2 tablespoons butter
1 cup whole milk

In a small sauce dish, place the flour, salt, and pepper; stir to combine; set aside. In a small saucepan, melt the butter over low heat. Remove from the heat. Add the flour mixture and stir until the mixture is perfectly smooth. Add the milk; stir to mix. Place over medium-low heat. Cook until the mixture thickens and is just under boiling (about 8 minutes), stirring constantly. Do not allow the mixture to boil. Best when used immediately or soon after making; however, white sauce may be refrigerated in a covered container up to 2 days.

MAKES ABOUT 1 CUP

THIN WHITE SAUCE

Follow the Medium White Sauce recipe, above, increasing the milk to 1¼ cups. Makes about 1¼ cups.

EXTRA-THIN WHITE SAUCE

Follow the Medium White Sauce recipe, above, decreasing the flour and butter to 1 tablespoon each. Makes about 1 cup.

(Recipe continues on next page)

THICK WHITE SAUCE

Follow the Medium White Sauce recipe, above, increasing the flour and butter to 3 tablespoons each. Makes slightly more than 1 cup.

EXTRA-THICK WHITE SAUCE

Follow the Medium White Sauce recipe, above, increasing the flour and butter to ¼ cup each. Makes about 1¼ cups.

BÉARNAISE SAUCE

A classic French sauce.

¼ cup white wine tarragon vinegar
1 shallot, chopped
1 teaspoon snipped, fresh chervil*
1 teaspoon snipped, fresh tarragon**
⅛ teaspoon white pepper
3 extra-large egg yolks
1 tablespoon whipping cream, unwhipped
¾ cup (¼ pound plus 4 tablespoons) butter, melted
2 teaspoons very finely snipped, fresh parsley

 * *If fresh chervil is not available, a generous ¼ teaspoon dried leaf chervil may be substituted.*

** *If fresh tarragon is not available, a generous ¼ teaspoon dried leaf tarragon may be substituted.*

In a small blender beaker (or a small food processor), place the vinegar, shallots, chervil, tarragon, and white pepper; process on high speed until the herbs are chopped as finely as possible. Place the mixture in a very small saucepan. Place the saucepan over medium-low heat and simmer the mixture until it is reduced by half. (The mixture will be quite thick.) Pour the mixture into the top of a double boiler; cover and let stand until cooled to room temperature.

Then, add the egg yolks and whipping cream; using a handheld electric mixer, beat on low speed until blended. Place the top of the double boiler in the bottom pan *over* (not touching) hot (*not boiling*) water. Place over low heat. Add the melted butter *very gradually* to the egg yolk mixture while beating continuously with the electric mixer on low speed and watching carefully that the water does not boil. Continue beating until the sauce is thick and shiny like mayonnaise. Add the parsley; stir to combine. Serve immediately.

If the sauce should curdle, add an additional 1 to 2 tablespoons cold whipping cream and beat well, using the electric mixer.

MAKES ABOUT 1 CUP

SERVING SUGGESTIONS: Serve on beef, particularly broiled beef tenderloin steak (see Broiled Steak, page 141); poached, baked, or broiled fish fillets or steaks; and steamed or boiled vegetables compatible with tarragon (see Herb Chart, pages 22–25).

HOLLANDAISE SAUCE

3 extra-large egg yolks
1 tablespoon whipping cream, unwhipped
¼ teaspoon salt
Dash of cayenne pepper
1 tablespoon freshly squeezed, strained lemon juice
½ cup (¼ pound) butter, melted

In the top of a double boiler, place the egg yolks, whipping cream, salt, cayenne pepper, and lemon juice; using a handheld electric mixer, beat on medium speed until blended. Place the top of the double boiler in the bottom pan *over* (not touching) hot (*not boiling*) water. Place over low heat. Add the melted butter *very gradually* to the egg yolk mixture while beating continuously with the electric mixer on medium speed and watching carefully that the water does not boil. Continue beating until the sauce thickens. Serve immediately.

To hold the sauce for a very short period of

time, place lukewarm water in the bottom pan of the double boiler; cover the top of the double boiler and let the sauce stand over the water. If the sauce should curdle, add an additional 1 to 2 tablespoons cold whipping cream and beat well, using the electric mixer.

MAKES ABOUT ¾ CUP

MUSTARD HOLLANDAISE SAUCE

Follow the Hollandaise Sauce recipe, above, adding 1 teaspoon prepared mustard to the egg yolk mixture ingredients after adding the lemon juice.

SERVING SUGGESTIONS

• Serve over boiled or steamed asparagus, broccoli, and cauliflower.

• Serve with Poached Salmon Steaks (page 187).

• Serve with Eggs Benedict.

CHEESE SAUCE

1 recipe Thin White Sauce (page 301–302)
¼ teaspoon dry mustard (optional)
½ teaspoon Worcestershire sauce (optional)
1 cup shredded, mild cheddar cheese*

 * *For a stronger, more tangy cheese flavor, substitute sharp cheddar cheese for mild cheddar cheese.*

When making the Thin White Sauce, stir the dry mustard into the flour mixture and add the Worcestershire sauce to the milk. When the white sauce has thickened, remove from the heat and add the cheese; stir until melted and blended. Best when served immediately or soon after making; however, Cheese Sauce may be refrigerated in a covered container up to 2 days.

MAKES ABOUT 1¾ CUPS

SERVING SUGGESTIONS

• Serve over cauliflower, broccoli, and asparagus.

• Serve over ham (see Ham Pinwheels with Cheese Sauce (page 164).

HOT SWISS CHEESE SAUCE

2 tablespoons butter
1 tablespoon grated onions
3 tablespoons all-purpose flour
¾ cup plus 2 tablespoons half-and-half
¼ cup whipping cream
2 teaspoons instant chicken bouillon granules
1 cup (4 ounces) shredded Swiss cheese
½ cup freshly grated Parmesan cheese (page 30)
2 teaspoons dry sherry

In a medium, heavy-bottomed saucepan, melt the butter over medium heat. Place the onions in the saucepan; sauté 2 minutes. Do not allow the butter to brown. Remove from the heat.

Place the flour in the saucepan; stir until blended with the pan juices. Add the half-and-half, whipping cream, and bouillon granules; stir to combine. Return the saucepan to medium heat and cook the mixture until thickened, stirring constantly. Do not allow the mixture to boil. Reduce the heat to medium-low. Add the Swiss cheese and Parmesan cheese to the mixture; stir until the cheeses melt and the mixture is blended and smooth (about 10 minutes). Add the sherry; stir to blend. Best when served immediately or soon after making.

MAKES ABOUT 1½ CUPS

SERVING SUGGESTIONS

• Serve (hot) as a dip for cold shrimp (see Shrimp with Dips, page 46).

• Serve over Baked Potatoes (page 276).

• Serve over Dinner Brussels Sprouts (page 258).

GARLIC BUTTER

½ cup (¼ pound) butter, softened
4 medium to large garlic cloves, pressed

In a small mixing bowl, place butter and garlic; stir well to combine. Pack soft Garlic Butter into a fancy, small mold; cover with plastic wrap and refrigerate until hardened. To unmold, briefly dip the mold in warm water and invert onto a small serving plate; refrigerate until completely hardened. Then, cover with plastic wrap and refrigerate until ready to serve. Keeps in the refrigerator for the same length of time as plain butter (see the expiration date on the butter carton).

MAKES 8 1-TABLESPOON SERVINGS

SERVING ALTERNATIVES: See Garlic Bread (page 356–357) and Toasted Garlic Bread (page 361–362)

GARLIC BUTTER BALLS

Cover the bowl of soft Garlic Butter with plastic wrap and place in the refrigerator; let stand until slightly hardened. Then, using a 1-inch melon baller, scoop out balls of Garlic Butter and drop them into a bowl of ice water as they are made, to retain their shape. Dip the melon baller in hot water before scooping out each ball. Garlic Butter balls may be refrigerated in the ice water until served or, when hardened, they may be transferred to a plate, covered with plastic wrap, and stored in the refrigerator. Garlic Butter Balls may be ribbed (see Ribbed Butter Balls, page 331).

MAKES 8 1-TABLESPOON SERVINGS

SERVING SUGGESTION: Serve with Broiled Steak (page 141) or Grilled Steak (page 206).

ONION BUTTER

Onion Butter may be used to make attractive garnishes which melt to add a delicious flavor enhancement to foods.

¼ cup (4 tablespoons) butter, softened
2 teaspoons freshly squeezed, strained lemon juice, room temperature
1 teaspoon fresh onion juice (page 29)
1 teaspoon finely snipped, fresh parsley
⅛ teaspoon white pepper

In a small mixing bowl, place the butter, lemon juice, onion juice, parsley, and white pepper; stir until blended and smooth. Using a decorating bag fit with large open-star tip number 6B (page 319), pipe stars (page 324) of Onion Butter onto waxed paper; refrigerate until completely hardened. Then, place the Onion Butter stars on a flat plate; cover with plastic wrap and refrigerate until ready to serve.

MAKES 6 ONION BUTTER STARS

SERVING SUGGESTIONS

• Place 1 Onion Butter star on individual, piping-hot steaks (see Broiled Steak, page 141, and Grilled Steak, page 206) and serve immediately.

• Place 1 or more Onion Butter stars on serving dishes of steamed or boiled vegetables such as green beans, asparagus, carrots, peas, and mixed vegetables.

SERVING ALTERNATIVES

• Use Onion Butter to make unribbed or ribbed butter balls (see Garlic Butter Balls, page 304).

• Pack soft Onion Butter into a small sauce dish or fancy mold; cover with plastic wrap and refrigerate until hardened. To unmold, briefly dip the sauce dish or mold in warm water and invert onto a small serving plate; refrigerate until completely hardened. Then, cover with plastic wrap and refrigerate until ready to serve. Or, before serving, use a small, sharp, thin-bladed knife dipped in hot water to slice the unmolded butter attractively. Place 1 piece of the butter on each hot steak or other food before zipping to the table.

MAKES 4 1-TABLESPOON SERVINGS

ORANGE BUTTER

½ cup (¼ pound) butter, softened
1 teaspoon finely grated orange rind (page 31)
⅛ teaspoon orange extract

In a small mixing bowl, place the butter, orange rind, and orange extract; using an electric mixer, beat on high speed to combine and blend. Using a spoon, pile the Orange Butter attractively into a small serving bowl and refrigerate; cover with plastic wrap when hardened. Keeps in the refrigerator for the same length of time as plain butter (see the expiration date on butter carton).

MAKES 8 1-TABLESPOON SERVINGS

SERVING SUGGESTIONS: Serve with breads, such as Mincemeat Bread with Orange Butter (page 369–370), Whole Wheat Orange Bread (page 373–374), Baking Powder Biscuits (page 380), Waffles (page 389–390), Cranberry-Orange Muffins (page 378–379), Oat Bran Muffins (page 379), Soy Whole-Wheat Muffins (page 377), 100% Whole-Wheat Muffins (page 377), and toast.

SERVING ALTERNATIVES

• After mixing the Orange Butter, use a decorating bag fit with large open-star tip number 6B (page 319) to pipe 8 Orange Butter rosettes (page 325) onto waxed paper; refrigerate until completely hardened. Then, place the Orange Butter rosettes on a flat plate; cover with plastic wrap and refrigerate until ready to serve.

• Use Orange Butter to make Ribbed (or unribbed) Butter Balls (page 331).

MAKES 8 1-TABLESPOON SERVINGS

CLARIFIED BUTTER

Clarified butter is also called "drawn butter."

In a small saucepan, melt the butter over low heat. Remove the butter from the heat and let stand about 3 minutes until the white milk solids settle on the bottom of the pan. Using a tablespoon, skim off and discard the fat floating on the melted butter. Then, using a baster, draw off the clear, yellow clarified butter, being careful not to disturb the solids on the pan bottom. As the Clarified Butter is drawn off, place it in a clean, small saucepan. Place over low heat to warm.

The milk solids in regular butter cause it to burn at a low temperature; therefore, removal of the milk solids permits Clarified Butter to be used for cooking at higher temperatures without burning. However, Clarified Butter is less flavorful than regular butter. Elimination of the milk solids allows tightly covered Clarified Butter to be safely refrigerated for several months.

1½ CUPS (¾ POUND) OF REGULAR BUTTER MAKES ABOUT 1 CUP OF CLARIFIED BUTTER

SERVING SUGGESTIONS: Boiled or grilled whole lobsters or lobster tails are traditionally served with small, individual ramekins of warm Clarified Butter (see Boiled Whole Lobsters, page 192, and Grilled Lobster Tails Basted with Tarragon Sauce, page 216–217). Diners dip bites into the Clarified Butter.

1 CUP OF CLARIFIED BUTTER MAKES 6 SERVINGS

Other Savory Sauce Recipes

Barbecue Sauce for Outdoor Cooking
    (page 205)
Mustard-Wine Sauce (page 185)
Spiced Grape Sauce (page 200–201)
Tarragon Butter Sauce (page 217)

Dessert Sauces

CARAMEL SAUCE

¼ cup (4 tablespoons) butter
1 cup packed light brown sugar
½ cup light corn syrup
½ cup dark corn syrup
½ cup whipping cream, unwhipped
½ teaspoon pure vanilla extract

In a small saucepan, melt the butter over low heat. Remove from the heat. Add the brown sugar, light corn syrup, and dark corn syrup; stir to combine. Bring the mixture to a boil over medium heat, stirring constantly; boil 2 minutes, stirring intermittently. Remove from the heat. Add the whipping cream and vanilla; stir until blended. Let stand until cooled slightly. Then, place the Caramel Sauce in a pint jar; cover and refrigerate up to 1 week.

To serve over ice cream and many desserts (see Baked Nutmeg Bananas with Ice Cream and Caramel Sauce, page 596), place the Caramel Sauce in a small saucepan over warm heat. Warm only until thinned to the consistency of a fudge sauce, stirring often. Caramel Sauce may also be served hot, in which case it will be of thinner consistency.

MAKES ABOUT 2 CUPS

HOT FUDGE SAUCE

½ cup semisweet chocolate chips
2 tablespoons butter
½ cup sugar
1 5-ounce can (about ⅔ cup) evaporated milk
1 teaspoon pure vanilla extract

In the top of a double boiler, place the chocolate chips and butter. Place the top of the double boiler over (not touching) hot water in the bottom pan. Melt the chocolate chips and butter, stirring until completed blended. Add the sugar and evaporated milk; stir to combine. Place the double boiler over medium-high heat and bring the water in the bottom pan to a boil. Reduce the heat slightly and cook the chocolate mixture over (not touching) boiling water 15 minutes, until thick, stirring constantly.

Remove the top of the double boiler from the bottom pan and place on a wire rack. Add the vanilla; stir until blended. Store, covered, in the refrigerator up to 1 week. To serve, reheat in the top of the double boiler over boiling water. Serve over ice cream.

MAKES 1¼ CUPS (ABOUT 6 SERVINGS)

HOT BUTTERSCOTCH FUDGE

Follow the Hot Fudge sauce recipe, above, substituting ½ cup butterscotch chips for ½ cup semisweet chocolate chips, and substituting ½ cup packed light brown sugar for ½ cup (granulated) sugar. After adding the brown sugar and evaporated milk, use a handheld electric mixer to beat the mixture on low speed during the first few minutes of cooking, until the mixture is completely smooth. Butterscotch chips may become grainy during the melting process, but will smooth out when beat with the sugar and evaporated milk.

CHOCOLATE SAUCE

¼ cup unsweetened cocoa powder
¾ cup sugar
¼ cup light corn syrup
¼ cup water
⅛ teaspoon salt
¾ cup whipping cream, unwhipped
1 teaspoon pure vanilla extract

In a 2½ quart, heavy-bottomed saucepan, place the cocoa, sugar, syrup, water, and salt; stir to combine. Place the saucepan over medium heat; stir the mixture constantly until the sugar dissolves. Then, attach a candy thermometer to the saucepan. Bring the mixture to a boil over medium heat and cook, without stirring, until the temperature reaches 230°F (about 5 minutes boiling time). Remove from the heat and detach the thermometer. Add the whipping cream and vanilla; stir until blended. Refrigerate, covered, up to 1 week.

MAKES 1½ CUPS (8 3-TABLESPOON SERVINGS)

SERVING SUGGESTIONS: Serve warm or cold over ice cream, cake, or other desserts.

MAPLE BRANDY SAUCE

1 cup pure maple syrup
2 tablespoons butter
2 tablespoons brandy

In a very small saucepan, heat the syrup to nearly boiling over medium heat. Add the but-

ter and brandy; stir until the butter melts and the ingredients are fully blended. Remove from the heat and serve immediately, or let stand to cool slightly and then pour the Maple Brandy Sauce into a pint jar. Cover and refrigerate up to 1 week.

MAKES ENOUGH SAUCE FOR 8 TO 10 SERVINGS

SERVING SUGGESTIONS: Serve hot Maple Brandy Sauce over vanilla, butter pecan, or butter brickle ice cream.

LEMON SAUCE

1 tablespoon cornstarch
½ cup sugar
Dash of salt
Dash of ground nutmeg
1 cup boiling water
2 tablespoons butter
2 tablespoons plus 1½ teaspoons freshly
    squeezed, strained lemon juice
1 drop yellow liquid food coloring

In a small saucepan, place the cornstarch, sugar, salt, and nutmeg; stir to combine. Add 1 cup boiling water; stir to blend. Cook the mixture over medium heat until thick and translucent, stirring constantly. Remove from the heat. Add the butter, lemon juice, and food coloring; stir until the butter melts and the ingredients blend. Serve warm or cold. In a covered glass jar, Lemon Sauce keeps up to 3 days in the refrigerator.

MAKES ABOUT 1¼ CUPS

SERVING SUGGESTIONS

- Serve cold Lemon Sauce or Lemon Sauce with Raisins (see recipe, page 308) over bread pudding (see Bread Pudding with Lemon Sauce, page 585).

- Serve warm Lemon Sauce over Apple Brown Betty (page 574–575).

- Serve warm or cold Lemon Sauce over cake such as Gingerbread (page 474–475).

LEMON SAUCE WITH RAISINS

In a small saucepan, place ½ cup raisins and ½ cup water. Cover the saucepan. Bring the raisins to a boil over high heat. Remove from the heat; let the raisin mixture stand, covered, until cool. Then, drain the raisins well in a sieve. Add the raisins to completed Lemon Sauce (see recipe, page 307); stir to evenly distribute.

CUSTARD SAUCE

Also known as stirred custard, soft custard, and boiled custard, the sublime richness of this versatile sauce adds an elegant touch to the many desserts it enhances. Custard Sauce plays a major role in certain traditional, notable desserts, such as Snow Pudding (page 584–585) and floating island. Spooned over fresh fruit, gelatin, or cake, it turns a good dessert into a special one. Especially children are fond of it served alone.

3 extra-large egg yolks
3 tablespoons sugar
⅛ teaspoon salt
1 cup half-and-half
1 cup whole milk
1 teaspoon pure vanilla extract

Place the egg yolks in the top of a double boiler; using a handheld electric mixer, beat slightly on medium-high speed. Add the sugar and salt; stir to combine; set aside.

Into a small saucepan, pour the half-and-half and milk; place over medium heat and scald (page 9). Pour about ½ cup of the scalded milk mixture into the egg yolk mixture; stir quickly to blend. Then, pour about ½ cup additional scalded milk mixture into the egg yolk mixture; stir to blend. Pour the remaining scalded milk mixture into the egg yolk mixture; stir to blend.

Place the top of the double boiler containing the egg yolk mixture over (not touching) hot (not boiling) water in the bottom pan. While stirring constantly and watching carefully to keep the water in the bottom pan at just below the boiling point, cook the mixture until it coats the spoon (about 10 to 12 minutes). Remove the top of the double boiler from the bottom pan. Add the vanilla; stir until blended. Pour the Custard Sauce into a bowl; let stand on a wire rack for a few minutes, until cooled slightly. Then, refrigerate; cover when completely cool. Keeps up to 3 days in the refrigerator.

MAKES ABOUT 2¼ CUPS

RUM SAUCE

1 cup sugar
2 tablespoons plus 1 teaspoon cornstarch
⅛ teaspoon salt
1 cup water
¼ cup (4 tablespoons) butter
Dash of ground mace
¼ cup dark rum

In a small saucepan, place the sugar, cornstarch, and salt; stir to combine. Add the water; stir to mix. Cook the mixture over medium-high heat until thick and translucent, stirring constantly. Remove from the heat. Add the butter and mace; stir until the butter melts. Add the rum; stir until completely blended. Serve Rum Sauce warm or cold. To heat, return the sauce to medium heat; stir until warm. Do not bring to a boil. In a covered glass jar, Rum Sauce keeps up to 1 week in the refrigerator.

MAKES ABOUT 1¾ CUPS

SERVING SUGGESTIONS
- Serve warm Rum Sauce and Rum-Raisin Sauce (see recipe below) over cake such as Gingerbread (page 474–475).

- Serve cold Rum Sauce on spumoni ice cream. Serve cold Rum-Raisin Sauce (see recipe, page 309) on vanilla ice cream.

RUM-RAISIN SAUCE

In a small saucepan, place 1 cup raisins and 1¼ cups water. Cover the saucepan. Bring the raisins to a boil over high heat. Remove from the heat; let the raisin mixture stand, covered, until cool.

Then, drain the raisins in a sieve, reserving the liquid. Set the raisins aside. Strain the raisin liquid through a piece of damp cotton flannel secured, napped side up, in a small sieve over a bowl (see Note); set aside.

Follow the Rum Sauce recipe, substituting ¾ cup sugar for 1 cup sugar, and substituting the strained raisin liquid (no need to measure) for 1 cup water. Add the raisins after the rum has been blended into the sauce; stir to evenly distribute. Warm the sauce, following the procedure in the Rum Sauce recipe.

NOTE: If a piece of cotton flannel is not available, 4 layers of damp, *untreated* cheesecloth may be substituted and secured in the sieve.

WHIPPED CREAM

1 cup (½ pint) whipping cream
2 tablespoons granulated sugar
1 teaspoon pure vanilla extract

Pour the whipping cream into a cold (previously refrigerated), medium-small mixing bowl. Using an electric mixer, beat the cream on medium-high speed until it begins to stiffen. Reduce the mixer speed to medium-low. Add the sugar and vanilla; continue beating the cream until stiff but still soft and fluffy.

While the mixer is beating the cream, intermittently run a rubber spatula against the edge of the mixing bowl to move the cream in the outer portions of the bowl toward the center, helping to assure that all the cream is evenly beaten.

Watch the cream very carefully as it nears the desired stiffness, as overbeaten whipping cream turns to butter in the blink of an eye, making it less appealing in appearance and texture. Reducing the mixer speed to low in the final moments of beating helps keep the cream more controllable.

Whipped Cream is best when served immediately after whipping; however, it may be covered and kept in the refrigerator about 2 to 3 hours before liquid begins to accumulate in the bottom of the bowl and the Whipped Cream begins to stiffen. When serving Whipped Cream which has been prepared in advance, spoon it off the top to avoid including any liquid which may have accumulated at the bottom of the bowl. From a food safety standpoint, Whipped Cream may be kept refrigerated for as many days as the cream would have stayed fresh before it was whipped; however, stored Whipped Cream continues to lose its fluffiness as liquid steadily drains to the bottom of the storage container.

MAKES 2 CUPS

DECORATOR WHIPPED CREAM

1 cup (½ pint) whipping cream
¼ cup powdered sugar
1 teaspoon clear vanilla
Paste food coloring (when coloring is used)

Pour the whipping cream into a cold (previously refrigerated), medium-small mixing bowl. Using an electric mixer, beat the cream on medium-high speed until it begins to stiffen. Reduce the mixer speed to medium-low. Add the powdered sugar, vanilla, and paste food coloring (if used); continue beating the cream until stiff but still soft and fluffy.

While the mixer is beating the cream, intermittently run a rubber spatula against the edge of the mixing bowl to move the cream in the outer portions of the bowl toward the center, helping to assure that all the cream is evenly beaten.

Watch the cream very carefully as it nears the desired stiffness, as overbeaten whipping cream turns to butter in the blink of an eye, making it less appealing in appearance and texture.

(Recipe continues on next page)

Reducing the mixer speed to low in the final moments of beating helps keep the cream more controllable.

WHEN TO USE DECORATOR WHIPPED CREAM: Use Decorator Whipped Cream when whipped cream of a stiffer consistency than regular whipped cream (see Whipped Cream, page 309) is desired or required. The stiffer consistency of Decorator Whipped Cream is achieved by the substitution of powdered sugar for granulated sugar, which is used in most traditional whipped cream. Use Decorator Whipped Cream to frost pies and cakes, and to pipe whipped cream decorations using a decorating bag and tips (page 319). Decorator Whipped Cream may also be used for general purposes if you prefer it.

It is necessary that whipped cream used to pipe decorations be firm bodied to retain precise, sharp, piped decorative designs. When used to pipe decorations, Decorator Whipped Cream should be whipped to just under the point of turning to butter. Also, it is important to use paste food coloring rather than liquid food coloring to retain maximum stiffness.

For use in frosting pies and cakes, and in piping decorations, Decorator Whipped Cream should be whipped immediately before using. For best results, it should be applied to the food product within 2 to 3 hours of serving time to avert any seepage of liquid from the whipped cream.

ORANGE DECORATOR WHIPPED CREAM

Follow the Decorator Whipped Cream recipe, substituting ¼ teaspoon orange extract and ¾ teaspoon clear vanilla for 1 teaspoon clear vanilla. Using orange paste food coloring, tint the whipped cream pale orange.

CHOCOLATE DECORATOR WHIPPED CREAM

Follow the Decorator Whipped Cream recipe, adding 2 tablespoons unsweetened cocoa powder to the whipping cream after adding the powdered sugar and vanilla.

Other Dessert Sauce Recipes

Amber Sauce (page 582)
Hard Sauce (page 584)
Rhubarb Sauce (page 294)
Vanilla Sauce (page 471)

Gravies

MILK GRAVY

Even though this gravy is commonly known as "cream gravy," it is more often made with whole milk than with cream nowadays. I have written a separate recipe for Cream Gravy (see right column) which uses half-and-half and requires only half the amount of flour for thickening as that needed for Milk Gravy. These two gravies may be used interchangeably. Most people consider Milk Gravy plenty rich and tasty for general use. When you want a superluxurious gravy for entertaining or otherwise, go for the Cream Gravy, calories and all.

Milk Gravy (or Cream Gravy) is the traditional —and best—gravy to serve over mashed potatoes when panfried chicken (see Fried Chicken, page 176–177) or pork chops (see Iowa Pork Chops, page 156 are the main fare. It is also the gravy which accompanies Chicken Fried Steak (page 139.) This versatile gravy may be made with equal success using the skillet drippings and meat particles after panfrying or braising pork, veal, poultry, wildfowl, or beef.

¼ cup all-purpose flour
½ teaspoon salt
¼ teaspoon pepper
1 cup whole milk
1 cup whole milk

In a pint jar or a plastic container with a secure lid, place the flour, salt, pepper, and 1 cup milk; cover and shake vigorously until blended and smooth; set aside.

Then, pour 1 cup milk into the skillet in which the meat was cooked. Over very low heat (220°F if using an electric skillet), deglaze the skillet. Add the flour mixture; stir well to blend. Increase the skillet heat to medium (350°F if using an electric skillet). Bring the gravy to a brisk simmer, stirring constantly. Simmer the gravy 1 minute, stirring continuously. Serve immediately.

MAKES ABOUT 2 CUPS

CREAM GRAVY

Cream Gravy may be used interchangeably with Milk Gravy. See the headnote under the recipe for Milk Gravy (page 310), for a description of the many uses for this wonderful gravy. The recipe for Braised Short Ribs with Dilled Potatoes (page 145) specifically uses Cream Gravy and calls for it to be strained after making for perfect smoothness, which I find more suitable with the dilled, unmashed potatoes.

2 tablespoons all-purpose flour
½ teaspoon salt
¼ teaspoon pepper
1 cup half-and-half
1 cup half-and-half

In a pint jar or a plastic container with a secure lid, place the flour, salt, pepper, and 1 cup half-and-half; cover and shake vigorously until blended and smooth; set aside.

Then, pour 1 cup half-and-half into the skillet in which the meat was cooked. Over very low heat (220°F if using an electric skillet), deglaze the skillet. Add the flour mixture; stir well to blend. Increase the skillet heat to medium (350°F if using an electric skillet). Bring the gravy to a brisk simmer, stirring constantly. Simmer the gravy 1 minute, stirring continuously. Serve immediately.

MAKES ABOUT 2 CUPS

BEEF GRAVY

¼ cup plus 2 teaspoons flour
½ teaspoon salt
¼ teaspoon pepper
1 cup cold water
¼ cup skimmed drippings from beef roasting
    pan (see recipe procedures below)
1 cup hot water

In a pint jar or a plastic container with a secure lid, place the flour, salt, pepper, and 1 cup cold water; cover and shake vigorously until blended and smooth; set aside.

Pour the drippings from the beef roasting pan into a gravy skimmer (page 6); let stand 2 minutes. Pour off the drippings; discard the fat (see Note 1). Measure ¼ cup skimmed drippings and pour into a medium saucepan; set aside.

Pour 1 cup hot water into the beef roasting pan; place over medium heat. Using a metal mixing spoon, scrape the bottom of the roasting pan until completely deglazed. Pour the roasting pan liquid into the saucepan containing the measured drippings. Add the flour mixture. Stir to blend the ingredients. Place over medium heat. While stirring constantly, bring the gravy to a boil and boil 2 minutes (see Note 2). Pour the gravy into a gravy boat and serve immediately.

NOTE 1: If a gravy skimmer is not available, pour the drippings into a regular 1-cup glass measuring cup with a pouring spout. Let stand

(Recipe continues on next page)

about 2 minutes until the fat rises to the top. Using a baster, draw off the fat and discard.

NOTE 2: If the gravy does not appear dark enough, ¼ teaspoon Kitchen Bouquet browning and seasoning sauce may be stirred in.

MAKES ABOUT 2¼ CUPS

BEEF GRAVY/SAUCE WITH MUSHROOMS

In a small, heavy-bottomed skillet, melt 2 tablespoons butter over medium heat. Place 4 ounces fresh mushrooms, sliced ⅛ inch thick (about 1½ cups), in the skillet; sauté until the mushrooms give up their juices (about 5 minutes). Remove from the heat; set aside.

To make Beef *Gravy* with Mushrooms, follow the Beef Gravy recipe, above. Add the mushrooms and pan juices to the gravy; stir to combine and blend. Add 1 tablespoon dry sherry; stir to blend.

To make Beef *Sauce* with Mushrooms, follow the Beef Gravy recipe, above, reducing the flour to ¼ cup. Add the mushrooms and pan juices; stir to combine and blend. Add 1 tablespoon dry sherry; stir to blend.

BEEF WINE GRAVY

Follow the Beef Gravy recipe, above, substituting ¼ cup red or white wine for ¼ cup of the cold water. If wine is used in the preparation of the beef dish with which this gravy will be served, the flavor of the served fare usually will be enhanced if the same wine used in cooking the meat is used in the gravy.

POT ROAST GRAVY

(See photo insert page B-3)

¼ cup all-purpose flour
½ teaspoon salt
¼ teaspoon pepper
½ cup cold water
1½ cups skillet juices plus hot water

In a small glass jar or plastic container with a secure lid, place the flour, salt, pepper, and ½ cup cold water; cover and shake vigorously until blended and smooth; set aside.

Pour the juices from the skillet in which the pot roast was cooked into a 2-cup glass measuring cup with a pouring spout; add hot water to make 1½ cups liquid. Return the skillet juices plus added water to the skillet. Over very low heat (220°F if using an electric skillet) deglaze the skillet. Add the flour mixture; stir to blend well with the skillet liquid. Increase the skillet heat to medium-low (325°F if using an electric skillet). Bring the gravy to a simmer, stirring constantly. Simmer the gravy 2 to 3 minutes, stirring continuously.

MAKES ABOUT 2 CUPS

ROAST PORK GRAVY

¼ cup all-purpose flour
½ teaspoon salt
¼ teaspoon pepper
1 cup cold water
1 cup hot water

In a pint jar or a plastic container with a secure lid, place the flour, salt, pepper, and 1 cup cold water; cover and shake vigorously until blended and smooth; set aside.

Using a baster, draw off and discard any excess fat in the pork roasting pan. Pour 1 cup hot water into the roasting pan; place over medium heat. Using a metal mixing spoon, scrape the bottom of the roasting pan until completely deglazed. Strain the roasting pan liquid through a sieve. Pour the strained liquid into a medium saucepan. Add the flour mixture; stir to blend. Place over medium-high heat. While stirring constantly, bring the gravy to a boil and boil 2 minutes. Pour the gravy into a gravy boat and serve immediately.

MAKES ABOUT 2 CUPS

PORK WINE GRAVY

Follow the Roast Pork Gravy recipe, above, substituting ¼ cup red or white wine for ¼ cup of the cold water. If wine is used in the preparation of the pork dish with which this gravy will be served, the flavor of the served fare usually will be enhanced if the same wine used in cooking the meat is used in the gravy.

suring cup with a pouring spout. Let stand about 2 minutes until the fat rises to the top. Using a baster, draw off the fat and discard.

NOTE 2: If a piece of cotton flannel is not available, 4 layers of damp, *untreated* cheesecloth may be substituted and secured in the sieve.

MAKES ABOUT 2¼ CUPS

ROAST LAMB GRAVY

¼ cup all-purpose flour
½ teaspoon garlic salt
½ teaspoon salt
⅛ teaspoon pepper
½ cup cold water
¼ cup skimmed drippings from lamb
  roasting pan (see recipe procedures below)
1½ cups hot water

In a small glass jar or plastic container with a secure lid, place the flour, garlic salt, salt, pepper, and ½ cup cold water; cover and shake vigorously until blended and smooth; set aside.

Pour the drippings from the lamb roasting pan into a gravy skimmer (page 6); let stand 2 minutes. Pour off the drippings; discard the fat (see Note 1). Measure ¼ cup skimmed drippings and pour into a medium saucepan; set aside.

Pour 1½ cups hot water into the lamb roasting pan; place over medium heat. Using a metal mixing spoon, scrape the bottom of the roasting pan until completely deglazed. Strain the roasting pan liquid through a piece of damp cotton flannel secured, napped side up, in a sieve over a bowl (see Note 2). Pour the strained juices into the saucepan containing the measured drippings. Add the flour mixture. Stir to blend the ingredients. Place over medium heat. Bring the gravy to a brisk simmer, stirring constantly. Simmer the gravy 1 minute, stirring continously. Pour the gravy into a gravy boat and serve immediately.

NOTE 1: If a gravy skimmer is not available, pour the drippings into a regular 1-cup glass mea-

TURKEY GRAVY

½ cup all-purpose flour
1 teaspoon salt
½ teaspoon pepper
4 cups (1 quart) whole milk, divided
½ cup skimmed drippings from turkey
  roasting pan (see recipe procedures below)

When the turkey is nearly done, place the flour, salt, pepper, and about 1 cup of the milk in a pint jar or a plastic container with a secure lid; cover and shake vigorously until blended and smooth; set aside. Pour the remaining milk in a medium saucepan. Warm the milk (do not allow it to boil) over medium-low heat to help quicken the gravy-making process after the turkey is out of the oven.

Pour the drippings from the turkey roasting pan into a gravy skimmer (page 6); let stand 2 minutes. Pour off the drippings; discard the fat (see Note). Measure ½ cup skimmed drippings and add to the warm milk; stir to blend. Add the flour mixture; stir to blend. Increase the heat to medium. Bring the gravy to a brisk simmer, stirring constantly. Simmer the gravy 1 minute, stirring continously. Pour the gravy into a gravy boat and serve immediately.

NOTE: If a gravy skimmer is not available, pour the drippings into a regular 1- or 2-cup glass measuring cup with a pouring spout. Let stand about 2 minutes until the fat rises to the top. Using a baster, draw off the fat and discard.

MAKES ABOUT 4½ CUPS

TURKEY GIBLET GRAVY

Turkey giblets (heart, gizzard, and liver) and
  neck
1 celery stalk including leaves, chopped
  coarsely
1 small onion, sliced thinly
3 whole black peppercorns
1 recipe Turkey Gravy (page 313)

THE DAY BEFORE SERVING OR EARLY IN THE DAY OF
SERVING: Wash the giblets and neck under cold,
running water. Dry the liver between paper
towels. Place the dried liver on a plate; cover
and refrigerate. In a large saucepan, place the
heart, gizzard, neck, celery, onions, and peppercorns; add water to cover. Cover the saucepan;
bring the mixture to a boil over high heat.
Reduce the heat and simmer 1 hour, or until the
giblets and neck are tender. Remove the meat
from the saucepan and place it in a colander to
drain; set aside. Add the liver to the broth in the
saucepan; simmer 25 minutes, or until tender.

Meanwhile, remove the meat from the neck
bone; discard the bone. Chop the heart, gizzard,
and neck meat finely; place in a container; cover
and refrigerate. When the liver is done, place it
in the colander to drain. Chop the liver finely;
place it in the container containing the other
chopped meats; cover and refrigerate.

JUST BEFORE SERVING: Make the Turkey Gravy.
Add the chopped giblets and neck meat; heat
through and serve.

Other Gravy Recipes

Dried Beef Gravy (page 140)
Biscuits and Gravy Madeira (page 159–160)

Garnishes and Decorations

About Garnishes and Decorations

Garnishes and decorations should complement food, not detract from it or supplant it. Decorating a plate can be carried to extremes and become an end unto itself. The most beautiful, artistic decorations do not mollify ho-hum food.

Although the terms "garnish" and "decoration" are commonly used interchangeably within the context of food, I make a distinction between the two, defining each as follows:

Garnish is a small quantity of food, artistically cut, sculpted, and/or arranged on an individual or serving plate of food as an adjunct to enhance the overall appearance of the plate and as a flavor-complement to the primary food.

Decoration is a very small embellishment of food or edible flowers placed or arranged on primary food or garnish, or otherwise placed on individual or serving plates of food for the purpose of adding color, flair, and general eye appeal.

A piped deviled egg and carrot curls arranged on the edge of a Lobster-Avocado Salad (page 116) luncheon plate are examples of garnish. A tiny parsley leaf or a sprinkle of paprika on top of the deviled egg filling are examples of decoration. The assignment of one of these descriptions depends upon the quantity of food used and its purpose. Garnish generally employs a larger quantity of food than decoration. Sometimes there is a thin line between the two. If a few chocolate curls are arranged on the top of a frosted cake primarily for looks, they are a decoration. If the white frosting on a chocolate cake is covered with shaved chocolate to add flavor as well as artistic appeal, the shavings would be defined as garnish.

Whether or not a cook chooses to make a def-inition distinction between these two types of food ornamentation is, of course, a matter of personal choice. The ornamental enhancement of food is the important consideration, not what it may be labeled.

This chapter contains instructions for making thirty-eight doable garnishes and decorations which can change the complexion of served food from pedestrian to classy.

Edible Flowers

Gracing the center of the table, flowers lend majesty to dining. Edible flowers can also be exquisite decoration for the food to be savored. With new emphasis on the art of food presentation, guests in fashionable restaurants and at special dinner parties are delighting more frequently in beautifully arranged plates of food made even more breathtaking by the final, sophisticated touch of real, edible flowers.

Flowers would probably bejewel food more often if cooks had more information about the varieties which are edible. As we all know, many flowers are poisonous—among the winsome blossoms on the **poisonous** list are buttercup (*Ranunculus acris*), daffodil (*Narcissus pseudonarcissus*), lily of the valley (*Convallaria majalis*), and sweet pea (*Lathyrus odoratus*). You must know what you are doing before venturing into the garden or woods, or onto the lawn to pick flowers for human consumption. One must be absolutely sure about the safety of a flower before placing it on a plate of food. *Nonedible flowers should never be used for decorating food,* even if diners are forewarned.

Availability of flowers suitable for food is also a factor. Avant-garde cooks with a green thumb as well as an artistic flair are not only cultivating their own herb gardens, but also are tending beds of edible flowers for last-minute picking to glamorize wonderful food (see Nasturtium Salad, page 110).

A formidable barrier to flower feasting is pollution. Flowers which have been sprayed with chemical insecticides or fertilizers should not be eaten, even if they have been washed beforehand. This caveat rules out flowers commercially purchased at a florist or greenhouse. As the use of edible flowers for food grows more widespread, some varieties may become available at organic food stores or in produce markets. However, one would want assurance that they had been raised for human consumption and had not been subjected to chemical sprays. For all practical purposes, the only safe sources for edible posies are your own controlled garden and yard (provided the yard is free from pets).

Another warning must be passed along: some people are allergic to flowers. Persons subject to food allergies are best advised not to eat flowers. Whatever one's predisposition to allergies, the conservative approach is recommended for everyone eating a flower variety for the first time. Excitement over the new-found adventure of food beautification with blossoms can prompt initiates to go overboard. While it is tempting to astonish your family or friends with an unexpected, virtual bouquet salad of ravishing flowers, sound counsel suggests that such a spectacular splash be prefaced with a series of taste testings comprised of a couple of small blossoms, or two or three large petals at a time as complements to the regular daily fare.

Even when you have studied your lesson and have decided upon a specific edible flower variety for inclusion in a dish, you must be certain that the flowers ushered into the kitchen are, in fact, the intended ones. *The only safe way to identify flowers suitable for eating is by botanical name.* Common names are insufficient. A wide variety of flowers is often known by a single, common name. For example, while daylilies (*Hemerocallis fulva*) are edible, a false assumption that most or all "lilies" are edible could lead to disaster. Tiger lilies (*Lilium lancifolium*) are among members of the lily family which are poisonous. If in doubt, don't experiment.

All of the foregoing admonitions are not intended to discourage culinary pacesetters from

exploring the realm of edible flowers. Although a relatively new form of artistic culinary expression in modern American home cooking, flower cookery is ancient in practice. The use of edible flowers in cooking is meritorious and safe if properly studied and pursued.

The following flowers, listed by both their common and botanical names, are among those safe for decorating food and for consumption by most healthy people:

Apple (*Malus spp.*)
Calendula (*Calendula officinalis*)
Chrysanthemum (*Chrysanthemum × morifolium*)
Dandelion, plus leaves (*Taraxacum officinale*)
Daylily, flowers only; not the tubers (roots) (*Hemerocallis fulva*)
Elderberry (*Sambucus canadensis* [deep purple to black fruit] and *S. caerulea* [dark blue to black fruit]) (**not** *S. pubens* [red fruit])
Johnny-jump-up (*Viola tricolor*)
Mustard (*Brassica nigra, B. hirta, B. juncea,* and *B. rapa*)
Nasturtium, plus leaves (*Tropaeolum majus*)
Pansy (*Viola × Wittrockiana*)
Pink (*Dianthus spp.*)
Redbud (*Cercis canadensis*)
Red Clover (*Trifolium pratense*)
Rose, wild and domestic (*Rosa spp.*)
Squash Blossoms (*Cucurbita spp.*)
Violet, plus leaves (*Viola odorata*)

In addition to this partial list of edible flowers, the blossoms of most herbs used in cooking are edible. However, for peak flavor, herbs should not be allowed to bloom (see To Dry Herbs, page 27), so diligent herb gardeners snip the flower buds from their herb plants as soon as they appear. Even so, among dedicated herbalists, there has emerged a *corps d'elite* who know they can have their herbs and eat the flowers too. Alongside their fastidiously pruned herbs, they allow a plant or two of each variety to bloom—providing showstopping dazzlers for dishes flavored with leaves from their well-groomed, neighboring kin. One can often catch sight of herb blossoms nowadays floating in stunning bottles of upscale herb vinegars displayed in gourmet food stores.

The following are some of the herbs whose flowers are safely edible by most healthy people:

Basil (*Ocimum basilicum*)
Chervil (*Anthriscus cerefolium*)
Chives (*Allium schoenoprasum*)
Coriander (*Coriandrum sativum*)
Dill (*Anethum graveolens*)
Fennel (*Foeniculum vulgare*)
Marjoram (*Origanum majorana* and *Origanum vulgare*)
Mint (*Mentha spp.*)
Oregano (*Origanum vulgare subsp. birtum*)
Rosemary (*Rosmarinus officinalis*)
Sage (*Salvia officinalis*)
Thyme (*Thymus vulgaris*)

The preparation of edible flowers for consumption varies with the flower. While violets, Johnny-jump-ups, pansies, and nasturtiums may be eaten in their entirety (see Sugared Violets, page 343), only the petals of large calendulas, chrysanthemums, and roses are eaten. Further, the white, lower portion of the petals of chrysanthemums, pinks, roses, and certain other flowers can be bitter tasting and is often trimmed away. Especially when preparing larger flowers for eating, the pistils, stamens, and sepals (see illustration) should be removed.

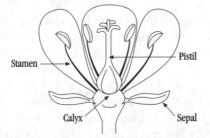

Food safety and sanitation considerations dictate that flowers be washed before being served as food; however, no matter how careful one may be, washing compromises the fresh, velvety appearance of most delicate blossoms. In the interest of public safety, I prescribe that all edible flowers be washed before being served as food. I admit to breaking this rule on occasion as I use edible flowers only from my own garden and yard, where I know they have not been subject to chemical contaminants (except natural air pollutants and the chance of wild animal pollution). In the kitchen, I meticulously examine each blossom for insects and bits of dust or dirt.

Visual ballistics—from glitter to high drama—undoubtedly are the attraction when it comes to playing matchmaker between food and flower. But flavor is not to be underestimated when orchestrating harmonious unions between food and flower eligibles. Flowers have individual flavors ranging from sweet to spicy to pungent, and vary in degree of flavor intensity from mild to strong. Successful food-flower marriages are arranged by creative, knowledgeable, and adventuresome cooks.

Using a Decorating Bag to Pipe Garnishes and Decorations

Acquiring the know-how to use a decorating bag pays off in beautiful food—as elegant to behold as it is felicitious to eat. Attractively presented food charms, tempts, and just seems to taste better.

Any interested cook can learn to pipe professional-looking borders around a cake and turn out "almost too good-looking to eat" roses to decorate the top—or, to put the finishing touch on a knockout meat platter or tantalizing casserole by piping a generous zigzag ring of fluffy mashed potatoes around the edge. There are 3 requirements: some competent instruction, good equipment, and *practice*.

My advice is to enroll in a cake-decorating

class. Continuing education programs and private cooking schools often offer such courses. Also, Wilton Enterprises sponsors cake-decorating courses in many locales across the country (see Note). Use of a decorating bag can be learned most expeditiously and satisfactorily through classes which incorporate both teacher demonstration and student practice, followed by lots of practice at home.

This section contains a brief introduction to the use of a decorating bag, as well as pictures and instructions for piping a few of the basic borders, designs, and flowers.

NOTE: For class locations and schedules, call 800-942-8881 or visit www.wilton.com.

BASIC EQUIPMENT

Good-quality equipment is essential to obtain the desired results. Sweet Celebrations Inc. and Wilton Enterprises are excellent sources for decorating equipment and supplies (see page 613 for addresses and telephone numbers). Wilton equipment and supplies are carried by retail stores in many areas.

Tip numbers called for in the instructions below and in recipes in this book are standard Wilton tip numbers. The same numbers apply to tips available from Sweet Celebrations Inc.— the difference in sizes between the two tip lines is negligible.

The following basic equipment is needed to pipe the garnishes and decorations pictured and described later in this section:

Polyester decorating bags in 8-inch, 10-inch, and 12-inch sizes
Couplers
Tips in assorted sizes
Tip storage box (to help prevent bending and denting of tips)
8-inch narrow, straight spatula
1½-inch flower nail
Pair of small scissors
4½-inch-long piece of ¼-inch dowel, sharpened in a pencil sharpener

Waxed paper cut into 2-inch squares
Paste food coloring in assorted colors
Toothpicks
Small and medium plastic containers with secure lids (for tinting and refrigerating icing)
Piping gel (to use when piping Holly Leaves; instructions, page 326)
Decorating turntable (see illustration, page 502)
Tip brush (to help clean tips)

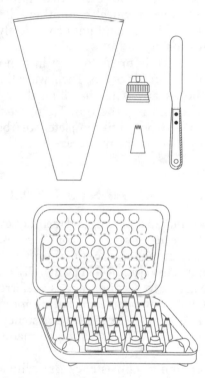

Top, clockwise from left: *Polyester decorating bag; Coupler; 8-inch narrow, straight spatula; and Tip.* Bottom: *Tip storage box.*

CARE OF EQUIPMENT

All decorating equipment should be stored in a special box or drawer to keep it in good condition, and for ready access when decorating is on the cooking agenda.

Tips should be stored in a tip storage box (see illustration) to help prevent them from becoming bent or dented. Bends or dents in tips can distort piped shapes.

Decorating bags, tips, couplers, and other decorating equipment should be washed in very hot, soapy water after use to remove all grease. Turn decorating bags inside out to thoroughly scrub the inside surfaces; then, reverse the bags and scrub the outside surfaces. Rinse the bags thoroughly in very hot water and dry them with a clean tea towel. Place each dried decorating bag tentlike over a wineglass or other tall, narrow glass and let it stand until completely dry before re-storing.

Use a special tip brush to assist in removing icing from the inside of tips. Then, wash the tips in very hot, soapy water, handling them with care. Rinse and dry the tips. Then, let them stand in a safe spot until completely dry before re-storing them in the tip storage box.

ICING CONSISTENCY

While several types of icing and techniques may be employed to frost and decorate cakes, this section is confined to the use of buttercream-type icing. This type of icing generally is used when learning to decorate, and is preferred, in general, by many people (including me) as of its good taste and very edible consistency, and as of the ease with which it is made and handled.

Proper icing consistency is critical to achieving success with cake frostings and decorations. Although a wide variety of recipes for buttercream-type icings may be used, it is recommended that cooks new to decorating use one of the following icing recipes developed especially for decorating:

Cake Decorators' White Icing (page 504)
Cake Decorators' Buttercream Icing
  (page 505)
Cake Decorators' Chocolate Icing (page 505)

These icings are excellent for frosting cakes to be decorated, as well as for the decorations themselves, because they apply nicely and make it possible to achieve a very smooth cake finish which is desirable when the surface is to be decorated. When an abundance of flowers, leaves, and other piped decorations and/or writing will be used to bedeck a cake, a smooth frosting finish is a necessity. See To Frost a Cake, page 502, for techniques to produce a smoothly frosted cake.

Different decorations require different icing consistencies. Thin icing is needed for writing, printing, stems, and leaves. Icing of medium consistency is used to pipe most borders. Stiff icing is necessary for piping roses. The three cake decorators' icings listed above are readily adaptable to various consistencies. To stiffen these icings, add additional powdered sugar; to make them thinner, add additional water.

When beating the ingredients to make icing for piped decorations, use an electric mixer speed no greater than medium-high and beat the icing only until blended and creamy. This will help diminish the incorporation of air bubbles, allowing a smoother, more continuous flow of the icing when piping.

Cake Decorators' White Icing is the warhorse of cake decorating. Made with vegetable shortening (no butter) and powdered sugar (no unsweetened cocoa powder), its consistency is particularly efficient, reliable, and adaptable. Because it is pure white, it is generally used when the icing for decorations is to be tinted.

Sometimes, more than one kind of icing is used on a cake. For example, a cake may be frosted with Cake Decorators' Chocolate Icing, piped with top and bottom borders of the same chocolate icing, and decorated with a bouquet of colorful flowers made with tinted Cake Decorators' White Icing.

CONSISTENCY OF OTHER PIPED FOODS

The same general techniques used for piping icing are used to pipe other foods. With some experience in working with a decorating bag comes the adeptness to adjust the consistency of foods to be piped. Oftentimes, it is a matter of on-the-spot trial and error. Different foods and different tips call for varied consistencies.

A number of recipes in this book suggest piping borders and other decorations using whipped cream. Whipped cream must be very thick and stable to be piped successfully. The recipe for Decorator Whipped Cream (page 309) is recommended for use in piping. This recipe produces a more stable whipped cream as it uses powdered sugar for sweetening rather than granulated sugar. When Decorator Whipped Cream is beaten as thickly as possible without allowing it to turn to butter, it holds piped shapes and patterns very well without the use of added gelatin for a stabilizer. This is especially true if, after piping, the decorated food is refrigerated for a brief period before being served.

Two flavored Decorator Whipped Cream recipes are found in this book: Orange Decorator Whipped Cream, and Chocolate Decorator Whipped Cream (page 310). Other flavored and tinted Decorator Whipped Creams may be created by using these recipes as ingredient guides.

TO TINT ICING

Paste food coloring is used to tint icing for piped decorations because it does not add liquid to change the icing consistency. Also, it is highly concentrated, so *very little* is required.

Before using paste food coloring, use a toothpick to stir the coloring in the jar. If the coloring dries out, use a few drops of glycerin (a cake-decorating supply) to restore its heavy-creamy consistency.

To tint icing, add a tiny amount of coloring to mixed icing by dipping the end of a clean toothpick into the coloring and then into the icing. Use the electric mixer to blend the color into the icing. Or, if mixing several colors of icing, place appropriate amounts of white icing in small, individual plastic containers. Then, use clean toothpicks to add coloring to the icing in each container, and vigorously stir with separate spoons until fully blended. Blend the coloring into the icing after only 1 addition of color, since paste food coloring is very concentrated. If more intense color is desired, use a *clean* toothpick to add additional coloring. Do not dip a toothpick which has been in contact with icing back into the jar of food coloring.

Substitute Cake Decorators' Chocolate Icing for dark brown colors. For best results in mixing black icing, add black paste food coloring to Cake Decorators' Chocolate Icing.

Buttercream-type icings tinted with paste food coloring continue to intensify and darken in color for about 1 to 2 hours after mixing. Keep in mind that, as a general rule, pastel decorations are more appetizing than intensely colored decorations.

PREPARING THE DECORATING BAG

Use of a coupler allows several different-sized tips to be used on a single, filled decorating bag. A coupler also helps stabilize the tip position and flow of icing. For this latter reason, use of a coupler—even when only one color of icing will be piped—is recommended.

A coupler consists of two parts: the base, which fits inside the decorating bag, and the ring, which screws onto the base on the outside of the decorating bag to hold the tip in place (see illustration, pages 319, 322).

When a coupler is used, it is usually necessary to trim the tip of a new decorating bag to make the opening at the narrow end of the bag large enough to accommodate the coupler. It is important to trim the tip of the decorating bag methodically, as follows: Place the base of the coupler in the decorating bag, narrow end first, and push it into the tip of the bag as far as you can. Then, using a pencil, mark the place on the outside of the bag where the bottom thread of the coupler base pushes against the bag. Remove the coupler base from the bag, and cut across the decorating bag at the marked place, thus making a larger opening in the bag.

Place the coupler base back in the decorating bag, and push the narrow end through the opening at the narrow end of the bag. Place the tip to be used over the exposed portion of the coupler and screw the ring onto the coupler base to hold the tip in place.

To change tips, simply unscrew the coupler ring; remove the tip and replace it with another tip; then, screw the ring back onto the coupler.

TO FILL THE DECORATING BAG

To fill the decorating bag, first fold the sides of the bag down to form a cuff and open the bag. Then, using an 8-inch narrow, straight spatula, fill the bag no more than half full of icing. Unfold the cuff. Holding the bottom of the bag with one hand, use your free hand to twist the top portion of the bag, sealing in the icing and forcing it toward the bottom of the bag. When this procedure is followed, no icing will get on the hands of the decorator or ooze out over the top of the bag while in the process of piping.

TO HOLD AND USE THE DECORATING BAG

Use both hands when decorating—for steadiness. Clasp the filled decorating bag firmly between your right thumb and index finger around the twisted portion at the top of the bag. Place the other 3 fingers of your right hand on the surface of the bag. This position allows you to keep the decorating bag sealed and also control the pressure and flow of the icing through the tip. Position your left hand near the bottom of the bag and use it to help guide the bag.

Before commencing to pipe with a newly filled decorating bag, hold the bag as described in the preceding paragraph and force the icing (or other food) to the narrow end of the bag. Then, pipe the icing (or other food) onto a piece of waxed paper until the bag "burps," releasing any air trapped in the bag during filling. This procedure will help assure a steady flow of icing (or other food) when piping.

Most garnishes and decorations are piped with the decorating bag held at a 90-degree angle to the surface being piped (perpendicular to the surface) or at a 45-degree angle to the surface being piped (halfway between perpendicular and horizontal to the surface; see illustration).

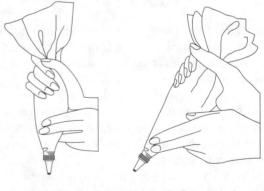

90-degree angle   45-degree angle

Pressure control is a key element in the use of a decorating bag. Different pressures are required to execute different decorations and effects. Very often, single strokes require variations of pressure as they are piped.

Pressure is controlled by your right-hand grip of the decorating bag. The amount of pressure and the steadiness of pressure regulate the size and uniformity of the decorations. Squeezing the bag with prescribed amounts of pressure, holding pressure steady, and relaxing or stopping pressure at the right times are important skills in producing piped decorations. Pressure-control dexterity is gained through practice and experience.

Proper bag position, pressure, and hand-arm movement must be simultaneously discharged when using a decorating bag. A new initiate may liken this feat to rubbing the top of the head and the stomach in opposite circles at the same time; however, focused students soon get the hang of it. Practice makes perfect.

LEFT-HANDED DECORATORS

If you are left-handed, grip the decorating bag with your left hand and guide the bag with your right hand. Use opposite hands called for in the instructions. When the instructions call for holding the top of the bag to the right, hold it to the left. Except when writing and printing, decorate from the right to the left rather than from the left to the right as with right-handed persons. When using a decorating turntable, rotate it counterclockwise. When piping a flower on a flower nail, rotate the nail clockwise in your right hand as you use your left hand to pipe. When piping roses on a stick, use tip number 97 rather than tip number 61, and rotate the stick counterclockwise as you use your left hand to pipe.

To Pipe Various Basic Decorations

DECORATIONS PIPED WITH ROUND TIPS

WRITING AND PRINTING

Use tip numbers 1 through 4 and thin icing consistency. Pipe freehanded or, if desired, use a toothpick or pattern press to draw guidelines to follow.

TO WRITE: Hold the bag at a 45-degree angle to the surface with the back of the bag to the right. The tip should lightly touch the surface as you write. Move your whole arm to write effectively with icing.

TO PRINT: Hold the bag at a 45-degree angle to the surface with the tip resting lightly on the surface. Hold the back of the bag to the right for horizontal lines and toward you for vertical lines. With steady, even pressure, squeeze out a straight line, lifting the tip off the surface to let the icing string drop. Be sure to stop squeezing before you lift the tip to end the line so a tail doesn't form.

STEMS: Use tip numbers 1 through 4 and thin icing consistency. Hold the bag at a 45-degree angle to the surface with the back of the bag to the right. Touch the tip lightly to the surface to attach the icing as you start to squeeze, but lift the tip ever so slightly above the surface as you draw out your stem so it will be rounded rather than flat. To end the line, stop squeezing and pull the tip along the surface.

DOTS: For tiny dots, use tip numbers 1 and 2 and thin icing consistency. Hold the bag at a

90-degree angle to the surface with the tip slightly above the surface. Squeeze the bag to pipe the desired dot.

For larger dots, use wider diameter round tips and medium icing consistency. Hold the bag at a 90-degree angle to the surface with the tip slightly above the surface. Squeeze the bag and keep the point of the tip in the icing until the dot is the desired size. Stop the pressure and pull the tip away. If needed or desired, use the tip to remove the point on the dot, or smooth the top of the dot with your finger which has been dipped in cornstarch. For very large dots or balls, lift the tip as you squeeze to allow greater icing buildup.

DECORATIONS PIPED WITH STAR TIPS

Star tips create some of the most popular decorations, including stars; rope, zigzag, and shell borders; and rosettes. The most often used star tips are numbers 13 through 22. Star tips range in size from small to extra large. For deep-ribbed decorations, use tip numbers 24, 25 through 31, 133, and 195. Large star tips include numbers 32, 96, 4B, 6B, and 8B. Fine-cut star tips include numbers 362 through 364, 172, and 199.

STARS

Use medium icing consistency. Hold the bag at a 90-degree angle to the surface with the tip slightly above the surface. Squeeze the bag to form a star. Then, stop the pressure and pull the tip away. Increase or decrease the pressure to change the star size. An entire cake or just one area may be covered with stars made very close together so no cake shows between the stars. Use the triple-star tip or one of the large star tips to save time.

TO PIPE STAR FLOWERS: Use medium icing consistency. Hold the bag at a 90-degree angle to the

surface with the tip slightly above the surface. Squeeze the bag and keep the tip in the icing until star petals are formed. Stop the pressure and pull the tip away. Using tip number 2 or 3, add dots in the center of the flower.

ROPE BORDERS

Use medium icing consistency. Hold the bag at a 45-degree angle to the surface with the back of the bag pointing over your right shoulder. Touch the tip to the surface. While squeezing the bag, move the tip down, up and around to the right, forming a slight S curve. Stop the pressure and pull the tip away. Then, tuck the tip under the bottom arch of the first S and repeat the procedure. Continue joining S curves to form the rope.

ZIGZAG BORDERS

Use medium icing consistency. Hold the bag at a 45-degree angle to the surface so the back of the bag points to the right, and your fingers gripping the bag are facing you. Allow the tip to touch the surface lightly. Steadily squeeze the bag and move your hand in a tight side-to-side motion. To end, stop the pressure and pull the tip away.

SHELL BORDERS

Use medium icing consistency. Hold the bag at a 45-degree angle to the surface with the back of the bag toward you and the tip slightly above the surface. Squeeze with heavy pressure and lift the tip slightly as icing builds and fans out into a full base. Gradually relax the pressure as you pull the tip slightly toward you and lower the tip until it touches the surface, making the tail. Stop the pressure completely and pull the tip away. Start each new shell slightly behind the tail of the previous shell.

REVERSE SHELL BORDERS

Use medium icing consistency. Hold the bag at a 45-degree angle to the surface with the back of the bag toward you and the tip slightly above the surface. Squeeze the bag and let the icing fan out as if you were making a typical shell (see instructions for Shell Borders above). Then, swing the tip around to the left in a semicircular motion as you relax the pressure to form the tail of the shell. Stop the pressure and pull the tip away. Continue repeating the procedure, alternating directions, for a series of reverse shells.

ROSETTES

Rosettes may be used as individual decorations, or contiguous rosettes may be used as a border.

Use medium icing consistency. Hold the bag at a 90-degree angle to the surface with the tip slightly above the surface. Squeeze the bag and move your hand to the left, up and around in a circular motion to the starting point. Stop the pressure and pull the tip away. For a fancy effect, decorate the center with a small star.

DECORATIONS PIPED WITH DROP FLOWER TIPS

Drop flowers are the easiest flowers to pipe. The number of openings on the end of the tip determines the number of petals the flower will have. Small tips include numbers 107, 108, 129, 224, and 225. Medium tips include numbers 109, 131, 140, 190, 191, and 193 through 195. For large flowers, use tip numbers 1B, 1C, 1E, 1G, 2C, 2D, 2E, and 2F.

DROP FLOWERS

Use slightly stiffer than medium icing consistency. Hold the bag at a 90-degree angle to the surface with the tip touching the surface. Squeeze the bag to form a flower. Then, stop the pressure and pull the tip away.

SWIRLED DROP FLOWERS

Swirled drop flowers cannot be made directly on a cake or other food surface. Pipe swirled drop flowers on waxed paper and let them stand until air-dried. Then, using a small spatula, loosen the flowers from the waxed paper and position them on the cake or other food surface with your hand.

Use slightly stiffer than medium icing consistency. Hold the bag at a 90-degree angle to the surface. Turn your wrist to the left (counterclockwise) as far as possible. Lightly touch the tip to the surface. As you squeeze out the icing, slowly return your wrist to its normal position. Then, stop the pressure and lift the tip away. Using tip number 2 or 3, pipe a single dot or several small dots in the center of the flower.

DECORATIONS PIPED WITH LEAF TIPS

The V-shaped opening of leaf tips gives piped leaves pointed ends. Make small leaves with center veins using tip numbers 65s and 65 through 70. For large leaves with center veins, use tip numbers 112, 113, and 115. Other popular tip numbers are 73, 75, 326, 349, and 352.

BASIC LEAVES

Use thin icing consistency. Hold the bag at a 45-degree angle to the surface with the back of the bag toward you. Touch the tip lightly to the surface, with the wide opening parallel to the surface. Squeeze the bag and hold the tip in place to let the icing fan out to form a base. Then, relax and stop the pressure as you pull the tip toward you and draw the leaf to a point.

HOLLY LEAVES

Using a pastry brush, coat the inside of the decorating bag with a thin layer of piping gel before filling the bag with icing of thin consistency. Lining the bag with piping gel results in an icing consistency more adaptable to forming leaf points. Hold the bag at a 45-degree angle to the surface with the back of the bag toward you. Touch the tip lightly to the surface, with the wide opening parallel to the surface. Squeeze the bag hard to build up a base, and at the same time, lift the tip slightly. Then, move the bag up and down in a series of quick motions to pro-duce a ruffle effect. Then, relax and stop the pressure as you pull the tip toward you and draw the leaf to a point. Before the icing begins to set, place the tip of a toothpick into the icing near the center vein of the leaf and pull up and out from the center to form the points of the leaf.

POINSETTIAS

Use tip number 352 and thin to medium icing consistency. Hold the bag at a 45-degree angle to the surface with the back of the bag toward you. Touch the tip lightly to the surface, with the wide opening parallel to the surface. To pipe the first leaf-shaped petal, squeeze the bag hard to build up a base, and at the same time, lift the tip slightly. Then, relax and stop the pressure as you pull the tip toward you and draw the leaf to a point. Pipe 5 additional leaf-shaped petals evenly spaced in a circle. Add 6 smaller leaf-shaped petals on top of, and between, the large ones. Using tip number 2, pipe several small dots in the center of the poinsettia.

TO PIPE ROSES AND ROSEBUDS

ROSES

A flower nail is used when piping most roses. For medium roses, use a 1½-inch flower nail. For small roses, a 1¼-inch flower nail may be used. For large roses, a 2- or 3-inch flower nail will be required. Use stiff icing consistency.

The key to making any flower on a flower nail is to coordinate the turning of the nail with the formulation of a petal. Hold the stem of the nail between your left thumb and index finger, so you can turn the flat nailhead at the same time you are piping a flower with your right hand.

THE BASE

Use a 1½-inch flower nail and tip number 12. (Use tip number 10 for smaller-sized roses.) Attach a 2-inch square piece of waxed paper to the nailhead with a dot of icing. Hold the bag at a 90-degree angle to the nailhead with the tip slightly above the center of the nailhead. Squeeze with heavy pressure, keeping the bottom of the tip in the icing until you have made a full, round base. Ease the pressure as you raise the tip up and away from the nailhead, narrowing the base to a dome head. The base is very important for successful rose making. Be sure that it is secure to the nail and can support all the petals.

THE CENTER BUD

Use tip number 104. (For small roses, use tip numbers 101s and 101 through 103. For large roses, use tip numbers 124 through 127. For giant roses, use tip number 127D.) Hold the bag at a 45-degree angle to the nailhead with the narrow end of the tip up. Position the tip with the wide end just below the top of the dome and the narrow end pointed in slightly. The back of the bag should be pointed over your shoulder. Now you must do 3 things simultaneously: squeeze the bag, turn the nail counterclockwise, and pull the tip up and away from the top of the dome, stretching the icing into a ribbon band. Relax the pressure as you bring the band of icing down around the dome, overlapping the point at which you started.

FIRST ROW OF 3 PETALS

Hold the bag at a 45-degree angle to the nailhead with the narrow end of tip number 104 up. Touch the wide end of the tip to the midpoint of the bud base. The back of the bag should be pointed over your shoulder. Squeeze the bag and turn the nail counterclockwise as you move the tip up and back down to the midpoint of the bud base, forming the first petal of the rose. Then, start slightly behind the end of the first petal and pipe the second petal, following the same procedure as for the first petal. Start slightly behind the end of the second petal and add a third petal, ending the third petal overlapping the starting point of the first petal.

SECOND ROW OF 5 PETALS

Touch the wide end of tip number 104 slightly below the center of a petal in the first row, angling the narrow end of the tip out slightly more than for the first row of petals. Squeeze the bag and turn the nail counterclockwise as you move the tip up and back down to form the first petal in the second row. Then, start slightly behind the end of the first petal in the second row and pipe the second petal in the second row. Repeat the procedure for a total of 5 petals, ending the fifth petal overlapping the starting point of the first petal in the second row.

THIRD ROW OF 7 PETALS

Touch the wide end of tip number 104 below the center of a petal in the second row, angling the narrow end of the tip out slightly more than for the second row of petals. Squeeze the bag and turn the nail counterclockwise as you move the tip up and back down to form the first petal in the third row. Repeat the procedure followed for the second row, piping a total of 7 petals in the third row.

Slip the square of waxed paper with the completed rose off the flower nail and place it on a flat surface. Let it stand until the rose is air-dried. Then, carefully lift the rose from the waxed paper square and position it on the cake or other food surface with your hand. If butter is an ingredient in the icing used to pipe the rose, refrigerate the rose on the waxed paper square after piping.

Alternatively, the rose may be transferred directly from the flower nail to the cake or other food surface by sliding an open pair of small scissors directly under the freshly piped rose and gently lifting the flower off the waxed paper square and flower nail. Position the rose on the cake or other food surface by slowly closing the scissors and using the stem of the flower nail to guide the base of the rose.

TO PIPE SMALL ROSES ON A STICK
Small roses may be piped more quickly using a stick rather than following the flower nail procedure. This method is particularly useful when large quantities of small roses are required; for example, when using roses to decorate cookies.

To prepare the stick, cut a ¼-inch dowel into a piece 4½ inches long. Then, sharpen one end of the cut piece in a pencil sharpener as you would a pencil. Use tip number 61 and stiff icing consistency. Hold the bag at a 45-degree angle to the stick with the narrow end of the tip up. Position the tip with the wide end just below the tip of the stick and the narrow end pointed in slightly. While squeezing the bag and turning the stick *clockwise,* pipe 3 contiguous bands of icing around the stick from the point downward. This procedure covers the end of the stick with 1 layer of icing, which will serve as the base of the rose.

THE CENTER BUD: Follow the procedure for piping the center bud of a rose on a flower nail (see Roses, page 327), except turn the stick *clockwise.*

FIRST ROW OF 3 PETALS: Follow the procedure for piping the first row of 3 petals of a rose on a flower nail (see Roses, page 327), except turn the stick *clockwise.*

SECOND ROW OF 5 PETALS: Follow the procedure for piping the second row of 5 petals of a rose on a flower nail (see Roses, page 327), except turn the stick *clockwise.*

Generally, a third row of 7 petals is not piped on small stick roses; however, if somewhat larger roses are desired, a third row of 7 petals may be added.

To remove a freshly piped rose from the stick, place a pair of small scissors around the stick and under the base of the rose. Gently move the scissors upward, removing the rose from the stick. The piped rose may be immediately positioned on the cake or other food surface, using the stick to guide the rose off the scissors. Or, use the stick to guide the rose off the scissors onto waxed paper and let the rose stand to air-dry.

ROSEBUDS
Pipe the rosebuds directly onto the cake, candy, or other food surface. Use tip numbers 101 through 104 for the petals, depending upon the size of rosebud desired. Use tip numbers 1 through 3 for the calyx and sepals (see illustration, page 329), depending upon the size of the piped petals.

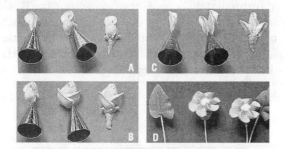

PETALS: Use tip number 104 and stiff icing consistency. To make the base petal, hold the bag at a 45-degree angle to the surface so the back of the bag points over your shoulder, and your fingertips gripping the bag are facing you. Touch the wide end of the tip to the surface and point the narrow end to the right. Squeeze the bag and move the tip forward ¼ inch along the surface; hesitate so the icing fans out, and then move the tip back to the original position, stopping the pressure about halfway back.

To make an overlapping center petal, hold the bag in the same position as for the base petal, with the wide end of the tip touching the inside right edge of the base petal and the narrow end pointing slightly up above the base petal. Squeeze the bag and lift the tip slightly. Continue squeezing as the icing catches the inside edge of the base petal and rolls to form an interlocking center petal. Stop the pressure; touch the wide end of the tip back down to the surface and pull the tip away.

CALYX AND SEPALS: Use tip number 3 and thin icing consistency. To pipe the calyx, hold the bag at a 45-degree angle to the base of the bud with the back of the bag toward you. Touch the tip to the bottom of the bud. Squeeze the bag and pull the tip up and away from the bud, relaxing the pressure as you draw the calyx to a point.

Start in the same position as for the calyx to pipe the center sepal. Squeeze the bag and let the icing build up. Then, begin to lift the bag up and away from the flower. Stop the pressure as you pull away to form the point of the sepal. Repeat the procedure, piping 1 sepal on the left and 1 sepal on the right of the center sepal.

TO PIPE LEAVES INSTEAD OF A CALYX AND SEPALS: If preferred, pipe 2 small leaves near the bottom of the bud instead of piping a calyx with sepals. Use tip numbers 65 through 67, depending upon the size of the piped petals, and follow the procedure for piping Basic Leaves, page 326.

Photographs and accompanying edited instructions courtesy of Wilton Enterprises.

BUTTER ROSES

They're butter with beauty and class.

1 cup (½ pound) cold butter

Cut the butter into approximately 16 pieces and drop into a blender beaker. Let stand, uncovered, for about 35 minutes until the butter softens just enough to process in the blender. (The butter must be very stiff to pipe successful roses.)

Process the butter in the blender until smooth.

Pipe roses, following the instructions on pages 327–329, using tip number 12 for the bases, and tip number 104 for the center buds and the petals. Place the waxed paper squares holding the piped roses on a flat plate and immediately refrigerate, uncovered. When the roses have hardened, cover them lightly with plastic wrap.

Immediately before serving peel away the waxed paper and place the roses on individual bread and butter plates, or on a flat-bottomed butter server or serving plate.

MAKES ABOUT 1 DOZEN

BUTTER CURLS

A quick-and-easy way to add further glamour to your dinner party table. You'll need a butter curler (see illustration) and a little bit of practice using it.

1 ¼-pound stick butter

Ten minutes before making Butter Curls, remove the butter from the refrigerator and place it on a flat-bottomed plate; set aside. (The butter should be only slightly soft to make well-shaped Butter Curls.)

Line the bottom of another flat-bottomed plate with waxed paper cut to the size of the bottom of the plate so it lies flat; set aside.

To make the curls, dip the butter curler (see illustration) into a glass of hot water. Shake the excess water off the curler. While holding the butter stick steady with the thumb of one hand, pull the curler toward you, down the length of the butter stick, pressing the curler gently and evenly into the butter.

With your fingers, remove the Butter Curl

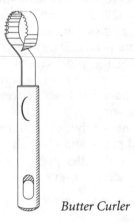

Butter Curler

from the curler and, if necessary, make any slight adjustments in the shape of the curl. Then, place the Butter Curl, seam down and single layer, on the waxed paper-lined plate. Redip the curler into the hot water before making each Butter Curl.

Refrigerate the Butter Curls, uncovered, until hardened. Then, cover with plastic wrap.

Immediately before serving, arrange the Butter Curls, single layer, on a cold serving plate; provide a small fork, such as an olive or pickle fork, for serving. Or, place 1 Butter Curl on each diner's bread and butter plate.

MAKES ABOUT 10 USABLE BUTTER CURLS

FLUTED BUTTER WEDGES

When you want generous servings of butter that still look genteel.

Dip a fluted garnishing cutter (see illustration, page 107) into hot water. Using the warm garnishing knife, cut a ⅜-inch-wide slice of butter widthwise from an uncut pound of butter. Dip a sharp, thin-bladed, standard knife into the hot water. Using the warm standard knife, cut the fluted slice of butter in half diagonally (see illustration).

Using a small spatula, place the 2 Fluted Butter Wedges on a flat plate lined with waxed paper. Repeat the process, dipping the knives into hot water before each cut. Cover the Fluted Butter Wedges with plastic wrap and refrigerate until immediately prior to serving.

1 FLUTED BUTTER WEDGE MAKES 1 SERVING

RIBBED BUTTER BALLS

A showy way to serve butter.

Place an uncut pound of butter or a ¼-pound stick of butter on a flat plate. Let the butter stand at room temperature until *slightly* soft.

Use a ⅞-inch Westmark brand butter-ball cutter or a 1-inch melon baller to cut the butter balls. Dip the cutter into boiling hot water before making each cut. To cut evenly shaped balls, press the blade face of the cutter into the slightly softened butter and then turn the cutter evenly while continuing to press. Immediately place the cut balls in a bowl of ice water.

To rib the butter balls, remove them from the ice water and roll them, one at a time, between 2 ribbed butter paddles (see illustration). Drop the Ribbed Butter Balls back into the ice water or place them, single layer, on a flat plate lined with waxed paper; refrigerate. Cover with plastic wrap when the butter fully hardens.

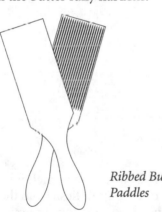

Ribbed Butter Paddles

VARIATION: Use specially blended butter, such as Onion Butter or Orange Butter (page 304), which has been refrigerated to harden in a wide, shallow bowl.

HERBED BUTTER BALLS

Sprinkle very finely snipped, fresh parsley (or other fresh herb) over a small piece of waxed paper; set aside.

Follow the Ribbed Butter Balls recipe, above.

After rolling the butter balls between the ribbed butter paddles, roll the Ribbed Butter Balls in the parsley (or other herb). Place the Herbed Butter Balls, single layer, on a flat plate lined with waxed paper; refrigerate. Cover with plastic wrap when the butter fully hardens.

ARTICHOKE BOTTOMS FILLED WITH BROCCOLI AND CARROT PUREES

For your fanciest dinner party, garnish beef, veal, lamb, fish, or poultry plates with this exquisite savory.

Drain canned artichoke bottoms. Steam (page 10) the artichoke bottoms until heated. Remove the artichokes from the steamer and brush the surfaces very lightly with melted butter.

Using a demitasse spoon, fill ½ of each artichoke bottom with warm Broccoli Puree (page 258) and the other ½ with warm Carrot Puree (page 260).

ARTICHOKE BOTTOMS FILLED WITH TINY VEGETABLES

A slightly less formal garnish than Artichoke Bottoms Filled with Broccoli and Carrot Purees (see above), but supremely elegant.

Steam (page 10), briefly and separately, frozen tiny peas; uniformly chopped red bell peppers; and peeled, tiny pearl onions (page 29). Place all the vegetables in a mixing bowl and toss lightly with a small amount of melted butter for sheen and flavor; keep warm.

Drain canned artichoke bottoms. Steam the artichoke bottoms until heated. Remove the artichokes from the steamer and brush the surfaces very lightly with melted butter. Using a

(Recipe continues on next page)

teaspoon, carefully fill the artichoke bottoms with the mixed vegetables.

SERVING SUGGESTIONS: Serve with Roast Beef Tenderloin with Mushroom Sauce (page 138), Broiled Filet Mignon (page 141), Baby Lamb Chops (page 165), Loin of Pork (page 157), and Poached Salmon Steaks (page 187).

VARIATION: Artichoke bottoms may be filled with any combination of tiny, whole vegetables and/or uniformly chopped vegetables (or any single, tiny or chopped vegetable) in coordination with the flavor and color of the food to be garnished.

APPLE-LINGONBERRY GARNISH

This outstanding garnish is a borrowed idea from Switzerland and Austria, where it is most often served on plates with wild game.

2 cups cold water
¾ teaspoon white vinegar
¾ teaspoon salt
2 cups hot water
1¼ cups sugar
1 2-inch piece stick cinnamon
1 whole clove
Up to 6 medium to large Golden Delicious
    apples
Canned wild lingonberries in sugar

In a medium mixing bowl, place 2 cups cold water, vinegar, and salt; stir until the salt dissolves; set aside.

In a medium saucepan, place 2 cups hot water and sugar. Bring the mixture to a boil over high heat, stirring constantly until the sugar dissolves. When the mixture boils, add the stick cinnamon and the clove; reduce the heat and cover the saucepan. Simmer the mixture briskly for 5 minutes. Remove from the heat; set aside.

Wash and dry the apples. Using a sharp, thin-bladed knife, cut a ⅝-inch-wide slice lengthwise

from 2 opposite sides of one of the apples (see illustration A).

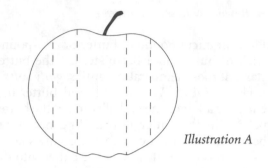

Illustration A

With a 2-inch, round, fluted cutter, cut 1 fluted apple circle from each of the 2 slices of apple. Using a ¾- to ⅝-inch round, plain (unfluted) cutter, press the cutter ¼ inch deep into the center of each fluted apple circle and then withdraw the cutter. (Do not cut completely through the fluted apple circles.) (See illustration B.)

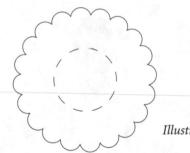

Illustration B

Using a tiny, ⅜-inch melon baller, carefully scoop out the apple flesh from the center circles to ¼ inch below the top apple surface to form a cup in each fluted apple circle. As they are prepared, drop the carved apple circles into the vinegar mixture to prevent discoloration. Repeat the process until the desired number of apple circles has been carved.

Drain and rinse the apple circles twice in clear water; set aside. Remove the cinnamon stick and clove from the syrup. Quickly bring the syrup to a boil over high heat. Drop 1 layer of apple circles at a time into the boiling syrup; boil for 3 minutes (no more). Using a slotted spoon, remove the apple circles from the syrup and drain, upside down, on 2 layers of paper towels. When drained, place the apple circles, single layer, on a flat plate; cover tightly with plastic wrap and refrigerate. If serving Apple-Lingonberry Garnish with a hot dish, remove the apple circles from the refrigerator 1 hour before serving time to allow the apple circles to reach room temperature.

Drain the lingonberries directly on 4 layers of paper towels. Shortly before serving, use a demitasse spoon to fill the cups in the apple circles with the drained lingonberries. Avoid filling the cups too far in advance, as the lingonberries may bleed into the apples.

MAKES UP TO 12

SERVING SUGGESTION: Serve with wild game, pork chops and roasts, lamb, and poultry.

CARROT CURLS

Select bright orange, medium to large, uniformly sized carrots. Cut off both ends of the carrots, cutting off enough of the small, pointed root ends to make each carrot fairly uniform in diameter. Pare the carrots. Cut a thin slice lengthwise off each carrot, creating a flat surface on which the carrots can rest solidly while cutting curls.

Place 1 carrot on a cutting board. Hold the carrot firmly with one hand. With the other hand, draw a *sharp* vegetable parer down the length of the carrot, cutting a thin strip. Roll the the carrot strip loosely around your finger to make a curl; place a toothpick through the curled carrot to secure. Repeat the process.

Place the Carrot Curls in a bowl of cold water and ice cubes; refrigerate a few hours or overnight to set the curls. Shortly before serving, drain the Carrot Curls on paper towels; *remove the toothpicks.*

SERVING SUGGESTIONS
- Makes attractive, informal garnish for tossed vegetable salads, sandwich platters, and cold luncheon plates.
- Adds color and dimension to a relish tray.

CARROT BOWS

Guests are sure to take note of this extra-special carrot decoration on their dinner salad or luncheon plates, or when used to embellish serving platters.

Follow the procedure for making Carrot Curls, left column, through cutting thin strips of carrots.

Using a sharp knife, trim each strip to make it uniform in width. Tie a knot in the center of each strip, making a bow. Using kitchen scissors, cut the ends of the bows diagonally in the shape of an inverted V, in the same manner as trimming the ends of ribbons.

Place the Carrot Bows in a bowl of cold water and ice cubes; refrigerate for a few hours or overnight to set the bows. Shortly before serving, drain the Carrot Bows on paper towels.

A BUNCH OF WHOLE, MINIATURE CARROTS

Trim miniature carrots, leaving $\frac{1}{2}$ to 1 inch of the green stems attached (length of the retained stems depends upon the size of the carrots). Pare the carrots using the scraping method if carrots are very tiny (page 29).

Boil or steam (page 10) the carrots briefly. If the carrots are boiled, drain them in a colander.

Brush the carrots lightly with melted butter for sheen, and arrange them in a fan-shaped bunch on a platter or on individual plates of food. To decorate most platters, either 5 or 3 carrots make an attractive display; however, any

(Recipe continues on next page)

number of carrots may be used (odd numbers usually look best).

CELERY BRUSHES

A splashy rendition of celery sticks.

Use small to medium stalks of celery, or cut large stalks in half lengthwise. Cut the stalks widthwise into 3½- to 5-inch pieces, depending upon the end effect desired.

Using a small, sharp knife, make parallel, lengthwise cuts through each celery piece, leaving ½ inch of the piece uncut and intact at one end. The more narrow the pieces are cut, the more fringelike will be the final appearance. Place the cut Celery Brushes in a bowl of cold water and ice cubes; refrigerate for several hours or overnight to open, curl, and set the brushes. Shortly before serving, drain the Celery Brushes on paper towels.

SERVING SUGGESTIONS
- Serve as a crudité (page 5).

- Use as a garnish for serving platters or individual plates.

CUCUMBER ROSES

This could become one of your favorite food decorations to make. One of these in the center of an hors d'oeuvre tray of Cucumber Wheels (page 49) and other goodies makes a real statement.

Cut 10 paper-thin slices from an unpared, seedless cucumber. Make 1 cut in each slice from the center to the edge. With 1 slice, make a tight cone to form the center of the rose. Build the rose with the remainder of the slices, overlapping them progressively looser. Secure the finished rose with 2 small toothpicks.

For food safety, remove the toothpicks from Cucumber Roses before placing them on indi-vidual plates of food. If one or more Cucumber Roses is used to decorate a serving platter, remove the toothpicks if there is any chance that the Cucumber Rose(s) will be eaten.

GROOVED CUCUMBER SLICES

Simple to make but you'll need a channel knife (see illustration). Use the grooved slices in salads or for garnish.

Run a channel knife (see illustration) lengthwise down an unpared, seedless cucumber. Continue cutting grooves at even intervals around the entire cucumber. Then, slice the cucumber widthwise.

GROOVED CITRUS SLICES

To make grooved lemon, lime, or orange slices, follow the procedures in Grooved Cucumber Slices above.

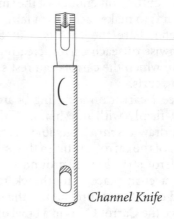

Channel Knife

MARINATED DRIED ITALIAN OLIVES

1 pound dried Italian olives
1 garlic clove, peeled and quartered lengthwise
Freshly ground pepper
1⅓ cups extra-virgin olive oil

Place the olives in a quart jar, distributing the garlic clove quarters evenly in the olives. Grind pepper over the top. Pour the olive oil into the jar to cover the olives. Place a lid on the jar. Refrigerate the olives and let stand at least 2 days before serving. Before serving, drain the olives well. Keep leftover olives refrigerated.

MAKES 1 POUND

GREEN ONION BRUSHES

Onion Brushes are principally for decoration as only ½ inch of the white root end, the part of green onions (scallions) most commonly eaten, is left uncut. Tucked between raw vegetables on a relish tray, or arranged with other food decorations on the corner of a buffet salad, the deep green, frilly appearance of Green Onion Brushes provides a stylish accent. P.S. They're a breeze to make.

Select large to medium green onions (scallions). Cut away the root ends 1½ inches from the point where the green stems commence to branch away from the solid part of the onions; reserve the root ends for other uses. Wash the onions. Remove and discard the outer layer of the onions if coarse and/or slightly discolored. Trim off enough of the green, stem ends to leave the onions about 4 inches in length.

On a cutting board, using a small, sharp knife, make straight cuts lengthwise through each onion, starting ½ inch from the root end and cutting through the green, stem end. (Leave ½ inch of the root end uncut.) Make several of

these cuts through each onion, making the strips as thin as possible. Place the cut Green Onion Brushes in a bowl of cold water and ice cubes; refrigerate for 1 hour to curl the brushes. Shortly before serving, drain the Green Onion Brushes on paper towels.

MULTICOLORED GREEN ONION FLOWERS

Add patriotic fireworks to the platter of Deviled Eggs (page 224) you take to the Fourth of July picnic with red, white, and blue Onion Flowers. Everyone will get a bang out of it!

A technique similar to that used in making Green Onion Brushes (left column) is used to make Multicolored Green Onion Flowers. Select large to medium green onions (scallions). Trim off the root ends, leaving as much of the white part of the onions as possible. Then, trim off enough of the green, stem ends to leave the onions about 4 inches in length. Remove and discard the outer layer of onions if coarse and/or slightly discolored.

On a cutting board, using a small, sharp knife, make straight cuts lengthwise through each onion, starting ½ inch from the green, stem end and cutting through the white, root end. (Leave ½ inch of the green, stem end uncut.) Make several of these cuts through each onion, making the strips as thin as possible; set aside.

Pour 4 cups cold water into a medium stainless steel or glass bowl. Add 2 teaspoons liquid food coloring; stir to blend. Add a few ice cubes to the bowl. Immerse the cut onions in the colored water. Place a plate or small, glass baking dish cover over the water and ice cubes in the bowl to function as a weight, keeping the onions completely submerged in the colored water. Refrigerate 24 hours, until the onion flowers are colored and curled. Shortly before serving, drain the onion flowers on paper towels.

Make Green Onion Flowers of as many dif-

(Recipe continues on next page)

ferent colors as desired to decorate serving plates and food displays. For more intense colors, increase the liquid food coloring to 1 tablespoon.

TO CUT LEAVES, STEMS, AND DESIGNS FROM LEEK TOPS

You'll find many applications for softened, carvable leek tops. Although a small, sharp paring knife may be used for the cutting, an X-Acto knife produces better results. I recommend adding one of these knives to your collection of kitchen tools (they're available at art supply stores) for use in making food decorations as well as accomplishing other cooking tasks such as cutting corrugated cardboard cake circles.

Cut the green tops from leeks. Wash the tops and drop them into a large saucepan of boiling water; let stand briefly until the leek tops are soft and pliable. Place 2 layers of paper towels on a wooden cutting board. Spread the softened leek tops flat on the paper towels.

Using an X-Acto knife, cut desired leaves, stems, or other designs from the leek tops.

TO CUT RIBBONS AND OUTLINE DESIGNS FROM GREEN ONION LEAVES

Cut the green leaves from green onions (scallions). Wide leaves may be cut in half lengthwise if desired. Wash the leaves; set aside. Place 2 layers of paper towels on a wooden cutting board; set aside.

Bring a medium pan of water to just under boiling; remove from the heat. Using tongs, dip the leaves into the hot water and *immediately* remove them. Avoid leaving the leaves in the hot water, causing them to become too limp and, thus, unmanageable.

Place the pliable leaves on the 2 layers of paper towels. Using an X-Acto knife (see the headnote under "To Cut Leaves, Stems, and Designs from Leek Tops," left column), fashion the leaves immediately or soon after dipping them.

LEMON, LIME, AND ORANGE TWISTS

We often see these popular citrus twists decorating all kinds of foods, from pies (see Daiquiri Pie, page 432) to fruit salads, and we have been served them as decoration on plates of food ranging from breakfast omelets (usually Orange Twists) to fish entrées. Here's how to make them in 3 short sentences (and you can make them just about as quickly).

Thinly slice widthwise an unpeeled lemon, lime, or orange. Make 1 cut in each slice from the center to the edge. Hold each slice on either side of the cut and twist in opposite directions.

VARIATION ~ GROOVED TWISTS: Prior to slicing the fruit, use a channel knife (see illustration, page 334) to cut equidistant grooves lengthwise from end to end around the fruit.

ORANGE BASKETS

Here's an idea for your next bridge (or other) luncheon: Fill daintily carved Orange Baskets with miniature pieces of fresh fruit and tie the handles with ribbons cut from leek tops (left column). Place one of these handsome baskets of fruit on each guest's plate next to Chicken Salad (page 118). Pass miniature Caramel Rolls (page 360) if you like. For a grand finale, serve stunning pieces of Black Forest Pie decorated with Chocolate Scrolls (page 342).

Select bright orange, symmetrical, uniformly sized oranges. The selected size is dependent upon how the Orange Baskets will be used. Wash the oranges, removing any stickers and stamped-on brand names or other markings (use a small amount of kitchen cleanser on a damp sponge; then, rinse the oranges well). Dry the oranges.

To make each Orange Basket, place the orange on a cutting board, with the stem and blossom ends horizontal to the board. Using a small, sharp, thin-bladed knife, make 2 parallel cuts, ⅜ inch apart, centered on the top of the orange, cutting downward *halfway* through the fruit to form the basket handle. Then, for medium to large oranges (see Note), make a horizontal cut starting ½ inch up from the base of the basket handle and continuing horizontally around the orange to the opposite side of the handle, being careful not to cut through the handle. Remove the cutaway orange piece and reserve for other uses. Repeat the same cut on the other side of the handle and remove the cutaway piece (see illustration A).

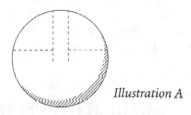

Illustration A

Using a grapefruit knife, cut the orange pulp in the basket away from the white peel membrane. Then, using a grapefruit spoon or a teaspoon, carefully remove the pulp, reserving it for other uses. Using a sharp paring knife, cut a sawtooth edge around the top edge of the basket, cutting each tooth ½ inch deep and ½ inch wide at the base (see illustration B).

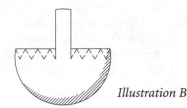

Illustration B

NOTE: For small oranges, make all the dimensions proportionately smaller.

SERVING SUGGESTIONS

- Fill Orange Baskets with fresh fruit; a conserve to accompany meat, poultry, or wild game (see Serving Suggestion, page 336); or a small serving of a fruit salad, such as Twenty-four Hour Salad (page 91) or Apple Salad (page 89). Depending upon the filling, a bow fashioned from green leek tops (page 336) or made with regular material ribbon may be tied to one side of each basket handle. Place an Orange Basket on each diner's plate as a stunning garnish.

- Fill Orange Baskets with sherbet (page 9) or sorbet (page 9) and serve for dessert.

VARIATION: The basket handles may be eliminated.

PICKLE FANS

Using a small, sharp, thin-bladed knife, cut thin, parallel slices lengthwise in a small pickle, cutting only to about ½ inch from one end of the pickle. (One end of the pickle will be uncut.) Using your fingers, spread the slices to form a fan.

Repeat the procedure to make additional Pickle Fans. If the pickles are large enough, the portion to be sliced may be pared very thinly prior to slicing for a more attractive final appearance.

SERVING SUGGESTIONS

- Use as garnish when serving sandwiches.

- Serve on cheese platters.

- Serve cornichon (a type of pickle) Pickle Fans as the traditional garnish for pâtés.

BELL PEPPER LEAVES AND FLOWER PETALS

Leaves and flower petals may be cut from green, red, yellow, orange, and purple bell peppers.

Use bell peppers. Wash the peppers; cut them lengthwise into quarters or sixths, depending upon the size of the peppers. Cut away the seeds and inner white parts of the flesh. Place the pepper sections in a saucepan (use a separate saucepan for each color of peppers); add water to cover. Cover the saucepan. Bring the peppers to a boil over high heat; reduce the heat slightly and boil about 8 minutes, until the skins peel off easily. Drain the peppers. Peel the pepper sections. Place the pepper sections on a cutting board and carefully flatten them.

Using small leaf- and petal-shaped cutters or an X-Acto knife, cut out leaves and petals. Flower stems may also be cut from green peppers.

SERVING SUGGESTIONS
- Use to decorate the tops of vegetable and meat casseroles (after baking) and vegetable salads.

- Use as decoration directly on individual plates containing meats, fish, poultry, vegetables, or vegetable salad.

- Use to decorate raw vegetable platters.

PINEAPPLE TULIPS

Using a sharp, thin-bladed paring knife or an X-Acto knife, cut very thin tulip stems from deep green celery stalks. With scissors, fashion leaves from the green, leafy celery tops. Cut the tulip blossoms from thin slices of fresh pineapple. To intensify the yellow color, dip the Pineapple Tulip blossoms in a small sauce dish of water to which a few drops of liquid yellow food coloring have been added. Remove the

blossoms from the sauce dish and place them on a paper towel to drain.

Carefully arrange the tulip parts on the food to be decorated. Pineapple blossoms may also be tinted red or orange.

SERVING SUGGESTION: Nice for decorating molded fruit salads which contain pineapple.

RADISH FANS

A fresh idea for serving some of the big crop of radishes from your garden. Or, select bright red radishes at your produce market especially for making these artful fans.

Select long, oval-shaped radishes to make Radish Fans. Wash the radishes; using a small, very sharp, thin-bladed knife, cut off both the stem and root ends. Make thin, parallel cuts *widthwise* down the entire length of each radish, cutting almost through the radish, but leaving the thin "slices" attached.

Place the cut radishes in a bowl of cold water and ice cubes; refrigerate a few hours or overnight. The radishes will open to simulate fans.

RADISH GYROSCOPES

Kids will love these atop their salads and will call them "cool."

Wash the radishes and slice off both the stem and root ends. Using a sharp, thin-bladed knife, slice the radishes widthwise $1/16$ to $1/8$ inch thick. Make a cut from the center of each slice to the edge. Make a second cut $1/16$ to $1/8$ inch from, and parallel to, the first cut. Make a tiny cut at the center of the radish slice between the two parallel cuts; remove and discard the little piece which has been cut out (see illustration A).

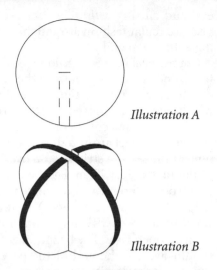

Illustration A

Illustration B

Fit 2 cut radish slices together at the points where the cutouts have been made to form a Radish Gyroscope (see illustration B). Fit the remaining radish slices together.

RADISH ROSES

These are always eye appealing to serve (see illustration on page 339). The tool suggested under Alternative, below, makes quick work out of attractive Radish Roses.

Select large, round radishes to make Radish Roses. Wash the radishes. Using a small, very sharp, thin-bladed knife, cut off the stem end of each radish, thus making a small, flat surface on which the finished rose can stand. Then, cut a tiny slice off the root end of each radish, leaving a small, white "dot" on top of each red radish.

To make each Radish Rose, cut 5, thin, evenly sized petals from the skin around the radish, as follows: cut the petals downward from the top of the radish, leaving a tiny bit of red radish skin around the center white "dot," and cutting the petals almost to the base (stem end) of the radish, but leaving them securely attached. If desired, cut 5, thin, small inner petals between the 5 large petals, cutting the small petals from the red skin which remains on the body of each radish after the 5 large petals have been cut.

Place the cut Radish Roses in a bowl of cold water and ice cubes; refrigerate for several hours or overnight. The petals will open to form attractive vegetable garnishes resembling red roses.

ALTERNATIVE: Westmark manufactures a small, combination tool which cuts Radish Roses as well as sawtooth edging on citrus fruit. Using the tool, good-looking Radish Roses are cut quickly and uniformly with a single clamping action. The cut roses should be placed in ice water and refrigerated, following the same procedure as with hand-cut Radish Roses.

STRAWBERRY FANS

Strawberry Fans look great as garnish on a summer luncheon plate featuring cold or hot poultry. And they're often the perfect decorative complement for fruit salads and desserts.

Select and wash attractive strawberries. Using a sharp, thin-bladed, paring knife, make ⅛-inch, parallel cuts lengthwise down the strawberries toward the stem end, but do not cut completely through the strawberries (the "slices" will remain attached to the stem end of the berries). With your fingers, carefully spread the slices on each strawberry in the shape of a fan.

The stems and/or green, leafy sepals may be left on the strawberries or they may be removed prior to "slicing." Do not remove the inner, center pith of the berries; if removed, the "slices" will not be firm enough to hold their shape and stay together.

BAKED TOMATOES PARMESAN

3 medium-sized, firm tomatoes, unpeeled
1 recipe (¼ cup) Buttered Cracker Crumbs
   made with Ritz crackers (page 33)
1 tablespoon freshly grated Parmesan cheese
   (page 30)
2 teaspoons finely snipped, fresh parsley
¼ teaspoon dried leaf basil or ¾ teaspoon
   finely snipped, fresh basil

Preheat the oven to 350°F.

Wash the tomatoes. Cut the tomatoes in half widthwise. Cut a thin slice off the ends of the tomatoes to make a platform on which the tomatoes can stand firmly and evenly. Place the tomato halves in an ungreased 8 × 8-inch baking dish or pan; set aside.

In a small mixing bowl, place the cracker crumbs, Parmesan cheese, parsley, and basil; stir to combine. Spoon the cheese mixture over the top of each tomato half. Using the back of a teaspoon, press the cheese mixture evenly over the top of each tomato half.

Bake the tomato halves, uncovered, for 25 minutes. Then, place them briefly under the broiler, 6 inches from the heat, until lightly brown.

MAKES 6

SERVING SUGGESTIONS: A natural accompaniment for steaks. Also nice with Brunch Eggs (page 223).

TOMATO ROSES

(See photo insert page B-5)

This is one of the most beautiful and revered food decorations.

Using a small, sharp, thin-bladed knife, pare a medium tomato in the same manner that you would pare an apple, starting at the blossom end and cutting a *thin*, ¾-inch-wide strip of peel in circular fashion around the tomato, ending at the stem end.

Cut the peel into 3-inch-long pieces. With the first 3-inch piece of peel from the blossom end of the tomato, make a tight cone, flesh side in, which will form the center of the rose. While still holding the center cone, wrap another 3-inch strip of peel around the cone. (The beginning of the second strip should overlap the end of the first strip.) Then, lay the rose facedown on a wooden board and continue wrapping the strips of peel (the rose petals) around the outside of the rose, with increasing looseness to form an open rose. The beginning of each strip should overlap the end of the previous strip. Secure the petals with one or more small toothpicks. Using a spatula, turn the rose upright. Place the Tomato Roses on a flat plate; cover loosely with plastic wrap and refrigerate until serving time. *Before placing Tomato Roses on individual plates or serving plates, carefully remove all toothpicks to assure food safety.*

TOMATO ROSEBUDS: Following the procedure for making a Tomato Rose, above, cut 2 thin, ½ × 2½-inch strips of tomato peel. Use one of the strips to form a tightly coiled center of the rosebud, and the other strip to form tight petals.

SERVING SUGGESTION: Use Tomato Roses and Tomato Rosebuds to decorate individual plates, and serving platters and dishes of meats, poultry, fish, salads, and vegetables. They are also becoming as decoration on hors d'oeuvre trays. The use of one Tomato Rose and one Tomato Rosebud together makes a particularly effective decoration. To enhance the look, arrange small sprigs of fresh coriander (cilantro), watercress, or parsley around the tomatoes. Or, using a small, sharp paring knife or an X-Acto knife, cut the blossom (not stem) end of steamed, chilled, unbuttered snow peas (page 275) in the shape of a W to simulate a ribbon. Trim away the stem ends. Then, tuck two "ribbons," in the fashion of ribbon streamers, under each rose or combination rose-rosebud.

CUTOUT TOMATO STARS

To make tiny cutout stars and other designs out of tomatoes, blanch (page 3) a firm, bright red tomato 30 to 45 seconds. Immediately immerse the tomato in cold water to stop the cooking. Carefully stem, peel, quarter, and seed and core (page 29) the tomato. Cut away the protruding inside tomato flesh to make the remaining flesh even in thickness. If necessary, cut away additional inside flesh so the remaining flesh is not only even, but somewhat thinner.

Press the tomato flesh flat on a wooden cutting board. Using a tiny star cutter (or a cutter of any desired design), cut the Tomato Stars.

Using a small spatula, move the cutout stars from the cutting board to the desired positions for food decoration or to a flat plate for later use. To store, cover with plastic wrap and refrigerate.

SERVING SUGGESTIONS

- Use cutouts of any design to decorate deviled eggs, dips, molded vegetable salads, casseroles (after baking), and other foods and dishes.

- Use cutouts in combination with other decorative foods to fashion flowers and other designs.

YELLOW SUMMER SQUASH RINGS FILLED WITH BASIL JELLY

8 unpared, yellow summer squash slices
  ¼ inch thick and 1¾ to 2 inches in diameter
4 to 6 teaspoons Jelly (see Variations)
16 to 24 small Johnny-jump-up blossoms
  (page 317) (optional)

Steam the squash slices (page 10) 3 minutes. Immediately remove the steamer basket containing the squash slices from the pan. Leave the squash slices in the steamer basket and rinse them under cold, running water to stop the cooking. Drain well.

On a cutting board, use a sharp paring knife to carefully cut around the periphery of the center seed section of each squash slice, cutting entirely through the slice. Remove and discard the center seed section of each slice, leaving the slice in the form of a ring. Briefly place the rings, single layer, on 2 layers of paper towels to drain further. Then, place the rings, single layer, in a flat-bottomed dish or plate; cover with plastic wrap. If the finished squash rings will be served within 2 hours, let them stand to cool to room temperature. Otherwise, place the rings in the refrigerator and remove them from the refrigerator about 1 hour before serving to allow them to warm to room temperature.

At serving time, arrange 1 squash ring to one side of each individual, main-course plate. Using a ½-teaspoon measuring spoon or a demitasse spoon, carefully place ½ to ¾ teaspoon (depending upon the diameter of the squash rings) jelly in the center hole of each squash ring. The jelly should mound slightly above the top surface of the rings. (Do not prewarm the plates, causing the jelly to melt quickly.) Decoratively arrange 2 or 3 (depending upon the size of the blossoms and the diameter of the squash rings) Johnny-jump-up blossoms contiguously on the outside edge of a section of each squash ring.

MAKES 8

VARIATIONS

- Substitute zucchini for yellow summer squash.

- Use jelly compatible with the food being served; for example, mint jelly with lamb, onion jelly with pork, crab apple jelly with chicken, and currant jelly with pheasant, quail, and grouse.

- Substitute another edible flower (page 316) in color harmony with the squash and jelly selected and the food being served.

CHOCOLATE CURLS

A striking decoration/garnish atop cakes, pies, and other desserts. It usually takes some practice to get the hang of making Chocolate Curls. If your first attempts don't satisfy you, break up the practice curls and use as Shaved Chocolate (see page 342).

Make Chocolate Curls from a 3-ounce or larger bar of high-quality milk chocolate. The secret to making Chocolate Curls is to have the chocolate at the proper temperature—soft enough to be pliable, but not so soft that the curls will not hold their shape. One way to warm the chocolate to the desired temperature of about 80°F is to unwrap it, place it on a piece of aluminum foil on the middle shelf of the oven, turn on the oven light, and close the oven door. The heat of the oven light will usually be sufficient to warm the chocolate within a few minutes.

Then, if using a 3-ounce chocolate bar, cut the bar in half lengthwise, using a thin, sharp knife. If using a different-sized piece of chocolate, cut it into 1½-inch-wide lengths. To help achieve precision cuts, warm the knife blade before each cut by dipping it into a tall glass of very hot water and then wiping the blade completely dry.

Place a piece of waxed paper on a cutting board, a piece of marble, or a smooth countertop. Place 1 of the pieces of chocolate, smooth side up, near the edge of the cutting board, marble, or countertop. Dip a sharp vegetable parer into the glass of very hot water and wipe it completely dry. Hold the chocolate strip in place with the thumb of one hand over a paper towel (to prevent the heat of your hand from melting the chocolate). With the other hand, *firmly* press and pull the vegetable parer toward you down the strip of chocolate to form a curl. Place a toothpick through the inside of the curl and transfer the curl to a clean piece of waxed paper. Repeat the process, dipping the vegetable parer in hot water and wiping it dry before cutting each curl. Rewarm the chocolate if necessary.

Refrigerate the Chocolate Curls a few minutes, until firm, before using.

NARROW CHOCOLATE CURLS

Warm the chocolate bar, following the procedure given in the Chocolate Curls recipe. Do not cut the chocolate into strips. Hold the entire chocolate bar in one hand with a paper towel. Using the other hand, *firmly* press and pull a warmed and dried, sharp vegetable parer toward you down the *narrow edge* of the bar to form small curls. Place the curls on a clean piece of waxed paper; refrigerate until firm.

SHAVED CHOCOLATE

Use the type and size of chocolate bar described in the procedures for making Chocolate Curls (see page 342). Do not warm the chocolate. To make Shaved Chocolate, the chocolate should be quite cool. Hold the chocolate bar in one hand with a paper towel. Using an unwarmed, sharp vegetable parer in the other hand, cut irregular chocolate shavings from the edges of the bar. Place the shavings on a clean piece of waxed paper and refrigerate. Or, if the shavings will not be used the day they are made, place them in a small container and cover tightly; refrigerate until ready to use.

CHOCOLATE SCROLLS

The scroll pattern shown in this recipe was designed especially to garnish Black Forest Pie (page 421); however, the same pattern may be used on other whipped cream-frosted or -garnished chocolate pies and cakes.

Scroll pattern
1 4-ounce German's sweet cooking chocolate
  bar

Trace the scroll pattern (see the pattern, page 343) 8 times on a piece of tissue paper; tape the tissue paper to a white, corrugated cardboard cake board. Tape waxed paper to the corrugated board over the tissue paper; set aside.

Break the chocolate into pieces and place in a tiny saucepan. Hold the tiny saucepan over (not touching) hot (not boiling) water in a small saucepan; stir until the chocolate completely melts. Refrigerate the tiny saucepan containing the melted chocolate for a few minutes until the chocolate cools to the consistency for piping.

Then, using a decorating bag fit with small round tip number 3 (page 319), pipe 8 Chocolate Scrolls on the waxed paper, following the lines in the patterns. Carefully place the board with the piped scrolls in the refrigerator for several minutes. *Refrigerate only until the scrolls are cool and set.*

With a thin spatula, remove the scrolls from the waxed paper and place them flat, single layer, on clean waxed paper lining an airtight container. Store in a cool, dry place.

MAKES 8

VARIATIONS: Follow the above procedure to pipe other designs and decorations in chocolate.

SUGARED VIOLETS

Freshly picked violets
1 extra-large egg white
½ cup superfine sugar*

* *If superfine sugar is not available, process regular granulated sugar in a blender or food processor until fine.*

Leave the stems on the violets. Carefully check each violet, making certain that it is free from any insects or specks of dust or dirt. After checking, place the violets, single layer, on a paper towel; set aside.

Separate the egg white into a small sauce dish. Using a table fork, beat the egg white only slightly, until smooth; set aside. Place a small, finely meshed hand strainer on a piece of waxed paper. Pour part of the sugar into the strainer; set aside.

With one hand, hold a single violet by the stem. With the other hand, use a small, soft, number 3 watercolor brush to paint first the back and then the front of the violet with the egg white. While continuing to hold the violet, use the strainer to sprinkle a thin layer of sugar first over the back and then the front of the violet. Make sure all surfaces of the violet are sugared. If a spot has been missed, repaint the spot with

(Recipe continues on next page)

Scroll Design (actual size)

Spatter Screen

egg white and sprinkle it with additional sugar. Lay the Sugared Violets, single layer, on a clean spatter screen (see illustration); let stand 24 hours to dry.

Then, using a thin spatula, carefully remove the Sugared Violets from the spatter screen and place them, single layer, on waxed paper in an airtight container. Freeze until ready to use. The stems may be cut off with a small pair of scissors at the time the violets are used. Violets are edible (see Edible Flowers, page 316).

SERVING SUGGESTIONS: Use to decorate pies (see Apricot Chiffon Pie with Sugared Violets, page 431); cakes; cookies; ice cream, sherbets, and sorbets; salads; and trays of hors d'oeuvres or tea sandwiches.

OTHER EDIBLE FLOWERS THAT MAY BE SUGARED: Johnny-jump-up (*Viola tricolor*), pansy (*Viola × Wittrockiana*), pink (*Dianthus spp.*), sweetheart rose (*Rosa spp.*), and petals of a rose (*Rosa spp.*) are among other edible flowers which may be sugared.

TINTED COCONUT

For use on cakes, pies, cookies, and other desserts. Go easy with the coloring—pale colors are generally the most appealing to diners.

1 7-ounce package (about 2⅔ cups) flaked coconut
½ teaspoon water
Liquid or paste food coloring

Place the coconut in a medium mixing bowl; set aside. Place the water in a small sauce dish. Add a few drops of liquid food coloring or, using a toothpick, add a small amount of paste food coloring; stir until blended. Drizzle the water mixture over the coconut; stir until the coconut is evenly tinted. Cover tightly until ready for use.

MAKES ENOUGH TO COVER THE TOP AND SIDES OF A FROSTED, 2-LAYER, 10-INCH ROUND CAKE

Other Garnish Recipes

Bok Choy Stuffed with Red Caviar (page 48)
Cherry Tomatoes Stuffed with Curried Chicken Salad (page 50)
Cucumber Wheels (page 49)
Deviled Eggs (page 225)
Miniature Vegetables, steamed (page 252)
Petite Potatoes (page 50)
Unflavored Aspic (page 55)
Vegetable Bundles (page 271)

Other Decoration Recipes

To Make an Ice Ring (page 618)

Breads and Rolls

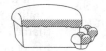

Yeast Breads and Rolls

Yeast is a microscopic plant. When used in making breads and rolls, the dough is leavened with carbon dioxide gas formed when the yeast cells metabolize fermentable sugars present in the dough.

In addition to yeast, flour, liquid, and salt are requisite ingredients in yeast dough. Sugar, fat, and eggs are optional ingredients; however, sugar and fat are generally included. The proportions of these ingredients, temperature, and the manner of mixing and handling the dough are all critical factors in the production of high-quality yeast breads and rolls.

Light, finely grained, and uniformly brown yeast breads which send forth that heavenly aroma as they bake in the oven are primarily the result of the application of good chemistry. Though not represented as a chemistry lesson on yeast breads and rolls, the suggestions and instructions given in this discussion and in the recipes in *The Blue Ribbon Country Cookbook* are based on the chemistry principles operative in yeast-bread and -roll baking. Bread-making hobbyists find the study of yeast-bread chemistry not only interesting, but also helpful in turning out superior products.

YEAST

Yeast used in making breads and rolls is available commercially in three forms: compressed cakes, active dry granules, and fast-rise dry granules. The yeast-bread and -roll recipes in this cookbook call for active dry yeast. Active dry yeast is most commonly purchased in ¼-ounce packets containing about 2¼ teaspoons of granular yeast. The packets should be stored in a cool, dry place, and used before their expiration date. Open packets should be stored in an airtight container in the refrigerator.

Active dry yeast should be dissolved in water rather than milk or some other liquid. The temperature of the water is *critical* and should be 110° to 115°F. It is important to use a food or yeast thermometer, or the temperature probe of a microwave oven to assure proper water temperature. Temperatures lower than 105°F will cause the diffusion of a substance from the yeast which will adversely affect the volume and quality of the bread. Temperatures much higher than 115°F will impair the yeast, and at 130°F, the yeast cells cannot survive.

FLOUR

Wheat flour (white or whole wheat) is a necessary ingredient in yeast breads and rolls as it is the only type of flour rich in the thick and elastic gluten. Gluten is an elastic protein which develops into strands in yeast dough as it is mixed with liquid and kneaded. Developed gluten surrounds and holds the bubbles of carbon dioxide as they form in the dough, and the gluten stretches to contain the carbon dioxide gas bubbles as they expand. This is how yeast dough rises. While other types of flour, such as rye, barley, and soy, may be used successfully in yeast breads, they must be used in combination with wheat flour.

All-purpose white flour is the most widely used flour for making yeast breads at home. Bread flour, a hard-wheat flour especially rich in strong gluten, is a choice product for bread making, and produces bread of particularly high volume and superb texture. *The Blue Ribbon Country Cookbook* bread recipes call for the use of bread flour although all-purpose flour may be used in substitution.

Recipes for yeast breads and rolls generally prescribe a range of flour quantity. This is because flour varies in moisture content and capacity to hold added liquid. The less the amount of flour used in proportion to liquid, the softer the baked product will be. Dough for rolls and most sweet breads should be as soft as will permit kneading, to produce light, fluffy end products; therefore, a minimum amount of flour in proportion to liquid should be incorporated into these products. Most nonsweet yeast breads are made with a medium-stiff dough, achieved by the incorporation of a somewhat greater proportion of flour to liquid. Some coarse breads require a stiffer dough to produce the desired texture.

As a general rule, the less the amount of flour used, within the quantity range given in a recipe, the better. Enough flour must be added to prevent the dough from being too sticky to handle and knead, but too much flour will result in heavy, compact baked goods. When stirring flour into yeast dough during the last phase of mixing, add the flour gradually and with special caution.

After the dough is mixed, cover the bowl with a tea towel and let the dough stand 5 minutes to allow time for the flour to take up additional liquid. This will decrease the stickiness of the dough, helping to make it manageable with the least amount of additional flour required.

Then, turn the mixed dough onto a *lightly floured* pastry cloth (page 38) or wooden board. Roll the dough in the flour on the cloth or board to lightly coat the entire outside surface, making it easier to knead. Knead with lightly floured hands. If your hands become sticky, flour them again. As the gluten develops during kneading, the dough will become less sticky. If the dough is too sticky to be manageable, add some flour during kneading; however, the total amount of flour in the dough should not exceed the maximum amount of flour specified in the recipe. Ideally, little additional flour should be added during kneading. No flour should be added to the dough after it has risen, as this may cause streaking and coarseness in the finished product.

LIQUID

Milk is the most common liquid used in making yeast breads and rolls. It should be scalded (page 9). Unscalded milk causes sticky dough and coarse, low-volume bread.

Plain water and potato water are also frequently used liquids in yeast breads and rolls. (It is interesting to note that milk is 87.69 percent water.) Breads made with potato water have slightly greater volume and a characteristic flavor, moistness, and tenderness.

Salt, sugar, and fat specified in yeast-bread and -roll recipes are added to the scalded milk, or other hot liquid, to be dissolved and blended. This liquid mixture should be cooled to 80 to 85°F (to measure, use a food thermometer or the temperature probe of a microwave oven that registers temperatures at least as low as 75°F) before adding the dissolved yeast and first portion of flour for mixing.

SALT

Besides providing flavor, salt has important functions in the formulation of yeast dough. Without salt, yeast dough becomes sticky and difficult to handle. Also, salt assists in controlling the yeast's production of carbon dioxide and flavor-producing components. Slowing the production of carbon dioxide helps prevent overexpansion and rupture of the air cells, adversely affecting the bread's texture. The amount of salt called for in a yeast-bread or -roll recipe should not be altered. To do so would interfere with the balance of ingredients and likely result in an inferior product.

SUGAR

In addition to adding flavor, sugar aids in raising yeast dough by providing a ready supply of food for the yeast, which results in the production of carbon dioxide gas bubbles. Sugar also helps attain beautiful browning.

FAT

Fat functions to make yeast products more tender. It also plays a role in browning as well as adding flavor. Further, fat increases the length of time yeast products remain fresh.

EGGS

Eggs not only enrich the taste of yeast breads and rolls, but also add color and provide additional protein to contribute to improved texture.

KNEADING DOUGH

Both mixing and kneading develop the gluten in yeast dough. Kneading should be done gently, yet firmly. If dough is treated too roughly, the strands of gluten will be broken. When this happens, the surface of the dough will appear rough.

To knead, start by flattening the dough slightly with your hands. Pull the far side of the dough toward you, folding the dough in half. Then, with your hands rounded over the dough, push the dough with the heels of your hands. Turn the dough one-quarter of the way around and repeat. Short, firm strokes are the most effective. Short pauses between the strokes, which allow time for the dough to relax, contribute to achieving the best dough elasticity.

Kneading by hand should be continued for at least the full time specified in a recipe. While dough may be over-kneaded, under-kneading is a common mistake in yeast-bread making. Dough may be hand-kneaded considerably longer than the time specified in most recipes before reaching the point of being overworked. Sweet dough requires more mixing and kneading than nonsweet dough as the high proportion of sugar in sweet dough causes the flour to be slower to absorb water.

Properly kneaded dough loses its stickiness. It will be smooth and elastic, and will be filled with tiny gas bubbles which can be seen beneath the surface.

RAISING DOUGH

Yeast dough must be risen in a bowl large enough to accommodate a doubling of the dough bulk. Use a pastry brush to lightly grease the bowl with vegetable shortening. After placing the dough in the bowl, turn the dough over so all surfaces of the dough are greased. Place a clean tea towel over the bowl to prevent the surface of the dough from crusting during the rising period.

Under perfect bread-making conditions, the dough and the place dough is set to rise, both will be at 80°F, the optimum temperature for the fermentation of yeast dough. The ideal temperature range for prime fermentation is 78 to 82° F. While most recipes (including those in *The Blue Ribbon Country Cookbook*) call for yeast dough to be risen in a "warm" place, it is well to remember that 80°F is less than body temperature, but warmer than the usual room temperatures for both heating and air conditioning. "Warm" is relative.

When yeast dough rises in too warm a location, it rises too quickly, causing the bread or rolls to have a yeasty, unmellowed flavor, as well as poor texture. Yeast dough will rise at temperatures lower than 78°F; however, fermentation proceeds slowly. The risk for detrimental effects on rising dough is greater when the temperature of the rising location is too high than when it is too low.

Yeast dough should rise in a location free from drafts. The oven is an excellent place. If the oven temperature is lower than 80°F, turning on the oven light in advance will generally increase the oven warmth to the desired temperature. If necessary, the oven light may be left on while the dough is rising in order to maintain the proper temperature.

Some bakers like to maintain an 80°F oven by half-filling a 9 × 13-inch baking pan with hot water and placing it on the lower rack of the oven directly beneath the bowl of unshaped dough or pan(s) of shaped dough. Usually, the baking pan must be refilled with hot water before each rising. Sometimes it is also necessary to refill the pan with hot water during the rising.

The time it takes for yeast dough to rise depends upon the temperatures of the dough and the rising location, as well as the proportions of yeast and other ingredients in the dough.

Yeast dough should rise until approximately doubled in bulk. If dough over-rises, the gluten strands overstretch, causing an elasticity loss which cannot be regained after punching down. Dough allowed to over-rise after it is shaped may flatten during baking due to inability of the overstretched gluten to contain the gas bubbles as they continue to expand during the initial baking period. Low-volume, heavy baked goods are also the consequence of under-risen dough, due to the crumb setting during baking before the gas bubbles expand adequately to obtain a light, nicely risen baked product.

Hard-wheat flour, such as bread flour, contains very strong gluten, producing yeast dough which can withstand the stress of expanding carbon dioxide bubbles better than dough made with softer wheat flour which contains weaker gluten. All-purpose flour is a blend of high gluten hard wheat and low-gluten soft wheat. While all-purpose flour is an excellent choice for use in home-baked yeast breads and rolls, it is better to let dough made with all-purpose flour rise to just under double in bulk as a precaution against over-rising. The resiliency of the gluten in dough made with bread flour warrants allowing the dough to rise until slightly more than double in bulk. A second rising before shaping produces bread with greater volume and a better, less yeasty flavor.

To test rising dough for doubling in bulk, lightly and rather quickly press two fingers approximately ½ inch into the center of the dough. If the dents remain after withdrawing your fingers, the dough has risen sufficiently. If the indentations fill in rapidly, the dough needs to rise further.

PUNCHING DOUGH DOWN

After the dough has doubled in bulk, it is punched down. Punching dough down has several purposes. Among them, it helps prevent the gluten strands surrounding the carbon dioxide gas bubbles from becoming overstretched. Also, punching down subdivides the gas bubbles into smaller bubbles, resulting in a more evenly textured baked product. Additionally, punching the dough down allows the yeast cells to come in contact with additional food for the production of further carbon dioxide.

After yeast dough has been punched down, it is important to handle it gently to avoid tearing, packing, or otherwise injuring the strands of gluten which have been separated by gas bubbles.

To punch dough down, press your fist into the center of the dough in the bowl. Lift the edges of the dough from the sides of the bowl and pull them to the center. Then, turn the dough over in the bowl.

If a recipe calls for a second rising of the dough before shaping, re-cover the bowl and let the dough rise again in the selected rising place (80° F). A second rising before shaping will take less time (usually about ½ the time) than required for the first rising. After a second rising, punch the dough down, following the same procedure as after the first rising.

After punching the dough down following the second rising, or following the first rising if a second rising is not used, turn the dough onto the pastry cloth or wooden board, cover it with a tea towel, and let it rest for 10 minutes. Resting the dough at this point makes the subsequent shaping easier.

SHAPING DOUGH

For directions on how to shape bread loaves, see To Shape Loaves of Yeast Bread (page 350). Instructions for shaping various kinds of rolls are given in the procedures for each roll recipe in this book.

After the dough has been shaped, cover the baking pans of shaped bread or roll dough with a tea towel and place the pans in the 80°F rising location. Let the shaped dough rise until nearly doubled in bulk. When the dough holds a slight indentation after pressing it lightly with your finger, it is ready for baking.

BAKING

Throughout the baking process, temperature continues to play a major role in the production of yeast breads and rolls.

When exposed to oven heat, yeast breads and rolls rise very rapidly until they reach an internal temperature of 131°F. Heat causes accelerated production of carbon dioxide in the dough, resulting in the quickened expansion of the gas bubbles. Simultaneously, the gluten surrounding the expanding gas bubbles becomes less able to withstand the pressure because heat causes the dough to become more fluid. High-quality yeast bread results when the yeast ceases to produce carbon dioxide, the dough sets, and the cells begin to leak gas *before* the gas bubbles become overinflated and begin to rupture, *but not before* the bubbles inflate sufficiently to result in a light, evenly textured baked product. Correct oven temperature is a key factor in achieving this objective.

Normally sized bread loaves should be baked in the center of a preheated oven. Most loaves of bread are properly baked at 375 or 400°F. If a bread loaf threatens to become overbrown during baking, a very loose cap of aluminum foil may be placed lightly over the top of the loaf.

Rich yeast breads and rolls, such as sweet rolls, brown more easily due to the higher ratio of sugar in the dough, and are usually baked at 350 or 375°F. The lesser volume of dough in rolls allows them to be baked at slightly lower temperatures without impairing the quality. However, when oven temperatures are too low, both yeast breads and yeast rolls will overinflate before the dough sets.

If yeast dough is overinflated before it is placed in the oven, further intense inflation generated by the heat will ultimately create an irregular texture, and may cause a bread loaf to flatten and extend over the sides of the pan as a result of gas bubbles rupturing before the crumb has set. When underinflated dough is placed in the oven, the dough will set before the gas bubbles expand sufficiently, thus producing baked goods that are dense and low in volume.

It is difficult to tell when a loaf of bread is done. A golden-brown crust does not always equate to an adequately baked interior. While the age-old test of thumping the loaf with your finger and listening for the hollow sound signaling doneness is not without merit, that sound is not a foolproof sign that the bread is done. Proper oven temperature, heed to baking time, and experience are the most valid factors in determining the doneness of bread loaves. Rolls can generally be judged done when they are golden brown.

When done, baked bread should be removed from the pan immediately and placed on a wire rack, away from drafts, to cool. If left in the pan after baking, steam is apt to cause the bread to become soggy. If bread is left to cool on a wire rack in a drafty location, the crust is in jeopardy of cracking.

To Shape Loaves of Yeast Bread

When a recipe calls for the yeast dough to be divided into portions for two or more loaves, use a sharp, thin-bladed knife to cut the dough. Shape each portion into a ball. Then, shape each ball of dough, as follows:

LOAVES TO BE BAKED IN LOAF PANS

PATTING METHOD: Pat the dough into an oblong loaf with a nicely rounded top. The loaf should be approximately the length of the loaf pan in which it will be baked. Gently pull and stretch the dough downward along the sides of the loaf, fashioning a smooth, rounded loaf. Tuck the excess dough under the loaf; seal any pleats or prominent creases on the underside of the loaf by pinching the dough together with your fingers. Place the shaped loaf in the greased loaf pan. The ends of the loaf should touch the short sides of the pan. If they don't, pat the dough gently until the ends touch the pan.

ROLLING METHOD: Some bread bakers prefer to shape bread loaves by rolling the dough. To shape a loaf of bread to be baked in a 5 × 9-inch loaf pan using the rolling method, place the dough on a *lightly floured* pastry cloth (page 38) or wooden board; using a *lightly floured* rolling pin, roll the dough into an 8 × 12-inch rectangle. Then, use your hands to tightly roll the dough, short side to short side, jelly-roll fashion, using your fingers to seal the dough after each turn. After the dough is completely rolled, seal the seam by pinching the dough together with your fingertips. Press down on each end of the dough to form a flat, sealed strip at both ends of the loaf. Fold the end strips under the loaf. Place the dough, seam down, in the greased loaf pan, making sure that the ends of the loaf touch the short sides of the pan, and making any needed adjustments to shape an attractive, symmetrical loaf.

The rolling method of shaping helps prevent holes in the baked bread by rolling excess air out of the dough; however, you can sometimes see the roll pattern in the baked crumb, which may or may not be objectionable to the bread baker. The patting method and rolling method are equally acceptable methods of shaping bread loaves entered in state fair food competition.

FREESTANDING LOAVES TO BE BAKED ON COOKIE PANS

OBLONG LOAVES: Freestanding oblong loaves may be shaped using either the Patting Method or the Rolling Method (see Loaves to Be Baked in Loaf Pans, page 350).

If using the Patting Method, pat the dough into an oblong loaf with greater width and height in the center part of the loaf, and with tapered ends. Proceed as for shaping Loaves to Be Baked in Loaf Pans using the Patting Method (see page 350). Place the shaped, freestanding loaf on a greased cookie pan.

If using the Rolling Method, follow the procedure for Shaping Loaves to Be Baked in Loaf Pans using the Rolling Method (see page 350). Before placing the rolled loaf on a greased cookie pan, shape the loaf to have greater width and height in the center, with tapered ends.

ROUND LOAVES: Freestanding round loaves must be shaped by patting. Fashion the ball of dough into a round loaf of desired diameter with a well-rounded crown. While turning the loaf, gently pull and stretch the dough downward and under the loaf to achieve a smooth finish and good symmetry. Pinch together any pleats or prominent creases on the bottom of the loaf which were created in the shaping process. Place the shaped loaf on a greased cookie pan.

To Store and Freeze Yeast Breads and Rolls

Yeast breads and rolls begin to go stale very shortly after baking, even when they have been properly stored. Consensus among food chemists has not been fully reached as to all the chemical reasons for this propensity to staleness. Stale yeast breads and rolls become more unpliable and crumbly, with leatherlike crust and a changed flavor.

STORING

After newly baked yeast breads and rolls have cooled completely, place them in zipper-seal plastic bags, with as little air as possible trapped inside the bags. Store yeast breads and rolls at room temperature even though mold is likely to grow on them if stored too long at high temperatures. Refrigeration accelerates staleness in baked yeast breads and rolls despite the fact that it may help to forestall the growth of mold. It is best to freeze yeast breads and rolls which will not be consumed within 2 or 3 days.

FREEZING

For best results in freezing yeast breads and rolls, freeze them as soon as they have cooled thoroughly after baking. Place the baked products in special zipper-seal plastic *freezer* bags (they are heavier than regular zipper-seal plastic bags), and force as much air as possible out of the bags before sealing. Store yeast breads and rolls in the freezer at 0°F or below, up to 3 months.

To thaw frozen yeast breads and rolls, leave them sealed in the zipper-seal plastic freezer bags and let them stand at room temperature 1 hour or more, until thawed. Do not apply frosting to breads and rolls before freezing. Frost breads and rolls after they have been removed from the freezer and have thawed completely.

Yeast Breads

WHITE BREAD

(See photo insert page C-8)

1½ cups whole milk
½ cup vegetable shortening, room
    temperature
½ cup sugar
1¾ teaspoons salt
2 ¼-ounce packets (about 1 tablespoon plus
    1½ teaspoons) active dry yeast
½ cup warm water (110 to 115°F)
2 extra-large eggs, room temperature
7 to 7½ cups bread flour, divided

In a small saucepan, scald the milk over medium heat (page 9). Remove from the heat. Add the vegetable shortening, sugar, and salt; stir until blended. Pour the milk mixture into a large mixing bowl; let stand until the mixture cools to 80 to 85°F. Meanwhile, in a small bowl, sprinkle the yeast over ½ cup warm water (110 to 115°F); stir until completely dissolved.

To the cooled milk mixture, add the yeast mixture, eggs, and 2 cups of the flour. Using an electric mixer, beat the mixture on low speed until combined; then, beat the mixture on medium speed until smooth (about 2 minutes). Using a large mixing spoon, gradually stir in enough of the remaining flour to form a soft dough that does not adhere to the sides of the bowl. Cover the bowl with a clean tea towel; let the dough stand 5 minutes.

Turn the dough onto a lightly floured (use bread flour) pastry cloth (page 38) or wooden board. Roll the dough on the cloth or board to lightly cover the entire outside surface with flour. Knead the dough until smooth and satiny (about 10 minutes).

Place the dough in a clean, greased bowl; turn the dough over so all surfaces are greased. Cover the bowl with the tea towel. Let the dough rise in a warm place (80°F) until doubled in bulk (about 1½ hours).

Punch the dough down. Cover the bowl with the tea towel. Let the dough rise again in the warm place (80°F) until doubled in bulk (about 45 minutes).

Punch the dough down. Turn the dough onto the pastry cloth or wooden board; cover with the tea towel. Let the dough rest 10 minutes. Meanwhile, grease two 5 × 9-inch loaf pans; set aside.

Using a sharp, thin-bladed knife, cut the dough in half. Shape each half of the dough into a loaf (page 350) and place in a prepared loaf pan. Cover the pans with tea towels. Let the bread rise in the warm place (80°F) until doubled in bulk (about 45 minutes).

Preheat the oven to 375°F.

Bake the bread loaves for 35 minutes, or until done. Immediately remove the bread from the pans and place them on wire racks to cool.

MAKES 2 LOAVES

WHOLE-WHEAT BREAD

2 ¼-ounce packets (about 1 tablespoon plus 1½ teaspoons) active dry yeast
½ cup warm water (110 to 115°F)
⅓ cup plus 1 tablespoon honey
¼ cup vegetable shortening, room temperature
2¾ teaspoons salt
1¾ cups warm water (80 to 85°F)
3 cups whole-wheat flour
3½ to 4 cups bread flour
Butter, softened

In a large mixing bowl, sprinkle the yeast over ½ cup warm water (110 to 115°F); stir until completely dissolved. Add the honey, vegetable shortening, salt, 1¾ cups warm water (80 to 85°F), and the whole-wheat flour. Using an electric mixer, beat the mixture on low speed until combined; then, beat the mixture on medium speed until smooth (about 2 minutes). Using a large mixing spoon, gradually stir in enough of the bread flour to form a dough that

does not adhere to the sides of the bowl. Cover the bowl with a clean tea towel; let the dough stand 5 minutes.

Turn the dough onto a lightly floured (use bread flour) pastry cloth (page 38) or wooden board. Roll the dough on the cloth or board to lightly cover the entire outside surface with flour. Knead the dough until smooth and elastic (about 10 minutes).

Place the dough in a clean, greased bowl; turn the dough over so all surfaces are greased. Cover the bowl with the tea towel. Let the dough rise in a warm place (80°F) until doubled in bulk (about 1 to 1¼ hours).

Punch the dough down. Turn the dough onto the pastry cloth or wooden board; cover with the tea towel. Let the dough rest 10 minutes. Meanwhile, grease two 5 × 9-inch loaf pans; set aside.

Using a sharp, thin-bladed knife, cut the dough in half. Shape each half of the dough into a loaf (page 350) and place in a prepared loaf pan. Brush the tops of the bread loaves with softened butter. Cover the pans with tea towels. Let the bread rise in the warm place (80°F) until doubled in bulk (about 1 hour).

Preheat the oven to 375°F.

Bake the bread loaves for 40 to 50 minutes, or until done. Immediately remove the bread from the pans and place them on wire racks to cool.

MAKES 2 LOAVES

LIMPA
Swedish Rye Bread

Swedish baked goods are among the world's finest, and limpa is one of the breads for which Sweden's baking artisans are best known. This wonderful rye bread may be flavored with one or more of the following: caraway seed, anise seed, fennel seed, cumin, orange rind, and lemon rind. The recipe that follows uses caraway seed. Some recipes for limpa include molasses as a sweet ingredient along with brown sugar. Limpa means "loaf" in Swedish.

(Recipe continues on next page)

½ cup water
¼ cup packed light brown sugar
2 teaspoons vegetable shortening
2 teaspoons salt
2 teaspoons caraway seed
1 cup water
½ cup warm water (110 to 115° F)
1 ¼-ounce packet (about 2¼ teaspoons)
   active dry yeast
4 cups bread flour, divided
2 cups rye flour, divided

In a small saucepan, place ½ cup water, brown sugar, vegetable shortening, salt, and caraway seed. Bring the mixture to a boil over high heat, stirring constantly; reduce the heat and simmer gently 5 minutes, stirring intermittently. Remove from the heat and pour the mixture into a large mixing bowl. Add 1 cup water and stir to blend; let stand until the mixture cools to 80 to 85°F. Meanwhile, pour ½ cup warm water (110 to 115°F) into a small bowl. Sprinkle the yeast over the water; stir until completely dissolved.

To the cooled brown sugar mixture, add the yeast mixture and 2 cups of the bread flour; using a standard-sized electric mixer, beat on low speed until combined. Add the remaining 2 cups of the bread flour; beat on medium speed until smooth (about 2 minutes). Using a large mixing spoon, gradually stir in 1½ cups of the rye flour. Cover the bowl with a clean tea towel; let the dough stand 5 minutes.

Sprinkle ¼ cup of the rye flour over a pastry cloth (page 38) or wooden board. Turn the dough onto the floured cloth or board. Roll the dough on the board cloth or to lightly cover the entire outside surface with flour. Knead the dough until smooth and satiny (about 10 minutes). If the dough feels sticky and too soft, knead in a part or all of the remaining ¼ cup rye flour.

Place the dough in a clean, greased bowl; turn the dough over so all surfaces are greased. Cover the bowl with the tea towel. Let the dough rise in a warm place (80°F) until doubled in bulk (about 1¼ hours).

Punch the dough down. Cover the bowl with the tea towel. Let the dough rise again in the warm place (80°F) until doubled in bulk (about 1 hour).

Punch the dough down. Turn the dough onto the pastry cloth or wooden board; cover with the tea towel. Let the dough rest 10 minutes. Meanwhile, lightly grease a 12 × 18 × 1-inch cookie pan; set aside.

Using a sharp, thin-bladed knife, cut the dough in half. Shape each half of the dough into a ball (see Round Loaves, page 350). Place the balls of dough 4 inches apart on the prepared cookie pan. If desired, make 3 or 4 parallel cuts about ½ inch deep across the top of each loaf, using a sharp knife. Cover the loaves with the tea towel. Let the bread rise in the warm place (80°F) until doubled in bulk (about 1 hour).

Preheat the oven to 375°F.

Bake the bread loaves for 45 to 50 minutes, until a rich brown color. Immediately remove the bread loaves from the pan and place them on wire racks to cool.

MAKES 2 LOAVES

VARIATIONS
- For a shiny crust, brush the tops of the loaves with whole milk or slightly beaten egg white after the bread has fully baked. Then, return the bread to the oven for an additional 2 minutes.

- Shape the dough into 2 regular, oblong-shaped loaves (page 350) and place in 2 greased 5 × 9-inch loaf pans.

HONEY-SEED BREAD

(See photo insert page C-8)

2 ¼-ounce packets (about 1 tablespoon plus
   1½ teaspoons) active dry yeast
½ cup warm water (110° to 115°F)
⅓ cup honey
¼ cup vegetable shortening
1 tablespoon salt
2 tablespoons poppy seed
1 tablespoon sesame seed

2 teaspoons caraway seed
1¾ cups warm water (80 to 85°F)
3 cups whole-wheat flour
¼ cup raw, hulled (unsalted) sunflower seeds
3½ to 4 cups bread flour

In a large mixing bowl, sprinkle the yeast over ½ cup warm water (110° to 115°F); stir until completely dissolved. Add the honey, vegetable shortening, salt, poppy seed, sesame seed, caraway seed, 1¾ cups warm water (80° to 85°F), and the whole-wheat flour. Using an electric mixer, beat the mixture on low speed until combined; then, beat the mixture on medium speed until smooth (about 2 minutes). Add the sunflower seeds; using a large mixing spoon, stir to evenly distribute. Using the mixing spoon, gradually stir in enough of the bread flour to form a dough that does not adhere to the sides of the bowl. Cover the bowl with a clean tea towel; let the dough stand 5 minutes.

Turn the dough onto a lightly floured (use bread flour) pastry cloth (page 38) or wooden board. Roll the dough on the cloth or board to lightly cover the entire outside surface with flour. Knead the dough until smooth and elastic (about 10 minutes).

Place the dough in a clean, greased bowl; turn the dough over so all surfaces are greased. Cover the bowl with the tea towel. Let the dough rise in a warm place (80 to 85°F) until doubled in bulk (about 1 hour).

Punch the dough down. Turn the dough onto the pastry cloth or wooden board; cover with the tea towel. Let the dough rest 10 minutes. Meanwhile, grease two 5 × 9-inch loaf pans; set aside.

Using a sharp, thin-bladed knife, cut the dough in half. Shape each half of the dough into a loaf (page 38) and place in a prepared loaf pan. Cover the pans with tea towels. Let the bread rise in the warm place (80°F) until doubled in bulk (about 1 hour).

Preheat the oven to 375°F.

Bake the bread loaves for 40 to 50 minutes, or until done. Immediately remove the bread from the pans and place them on wire racks to cool.

MAKES 2 LOAVES

PAT BERRY'S JULEKAKE
Norwegian Christmas Bread

Blue ribbon awarded to Pat Berry, 1989 Iowa State Fair.

Pat Berry is a supreme baker of yeast breads and rolls, for which she has won countless blue ribbons at the Iowa State Fair. Her presentations of Julekake are beautiful to behold. Pat now serves as a judge at the fair, and I always enjoy judging classes with her because of her broad cooking knowledge backed up by practical, applied experience.

4 ounces (½ cup) red candied cherries, cut in half
4 ounces (½ cup) green candied cherries, cut in half
½ cup golden raisins
¾ cup English walnuts, cut or broken to about 3/16 inch diameter (optional)
5½ to 6½ cups bread flour, divided
2 ¼-ounce packets (about 1 tablespoon plus 1½ teaspoons) active dry yeast
1 teaspoon salt
1 teaspoon ground cardamom
½ teaspoon ground cinnamon
1 cup whole milk
1 cup water
½ cup plus 3 tablespoons (¼ pound plus 3 tablespoons) butter
¼ cup honey
3 large eggs, room temperature
Glaze (recipe follows)
Additional red candied cherries, green candied cherries, and English walnuts (if used in bread) for garnish

In a small mixing bowl, place ½ cup red candied cherries, ½ cup green candied cherries, ½ cup raisins, and ¾ cup walnuts. Sprinkle 1 tablespoon plus 2 teaspoons of the flour over the fruits and nuts; stir until separated and combined; set aside.

In a large mixing bowl, place 2 cups of the

(Recipe continues on next page)

flour, yeast, salt, cardamom, and cinnamon; stir well to combine; set aside. In a small saucepan, place the milk, 1 cup water, and butter. Over medium heat, heat the mixture to 110 to 115°F, stirring intermittently.

To the yeast mixture, add the warm milk mixture, honey, and eggs. Using an electric mixer, beat the mixture on low speed until combined; then, beat the mixture on medium speed 3 minutes. Add the fruit and nut mixture; using a large mixing spoon, stir to combine. Using the mixing spoon, gradually stir in 3 to 3½ cups additional flour to form a soft dough. Cover the bowl with the clean tea towel; let the dough stand 5 minutes.

Turn the dough onto a lightly floured (use bread flour) pastry cloth (page 38) or wooden board. Roll the dough on the cloth or board to lightly cover the entire outside surface with flour. Knead in ½ to 1 cup additional flour until the dough is smooth and elastic (about 8 to 10 minutes).

Place the dough in a clean, greased bowl; turn the dough over so all surfaces are greased. Cover the bowl with the tea towel. Let the dough rise in a warm place (80°F) until doubled in bulk (about 55 to 60 minutes).

Punch the dough down. Turn the dough onto the pastry cloth or wooden board; cover with the tea towel. Let the dough rest 10 minutes. Meanwhile, grease two 10½ × 15½ × 1-inch cookie pans; set aside.

Using a sharp, thin-bladed knife, cut the dough into 3 equal parts. Shape each piece of dough into a ball (see Rounded Loaves, page 350). Place 2 balls of dough on one of the prepared cookie pans and 1 ball of dough on the other prepared cookie pan. Using your hand, flatten the balls slightly. Cover the loaves with tea towels. Let the bread rise in the warm place (80°F) until doubled in bulk (about 45 minutes).

Preheat the oven to 350°F.

Bake the bread loaves for 30 to 35 minutes, or until done. The loaves will be only very lightly brown when done. Immediately remove the bread loaves from the pans and place them on wire racks; let stand until completely cool.

Drizzle Glaze over the cooled loaves. Garnish the loaves attractively with red candied cherries, green candied cherries, and walnuts (if used in the bread).

MAKES 3 LOAVES

GLAZE

1½ cups powdered sugar
2½ teaspoons whole milk
¼ teaspoon almond extract

In a small mixing bowl, place the powdered sugar, milk, and almond extract; using an electric mixer, beat on high speed until blended and smooth.

TO FREEZE JULEKAKE: This bread freezes well. Freeze the loaves, unglazed and ungarnished, in separate zipper-seal plastic freezer bags. Glaze and garnish the loaves after they have completely thawed.

GARLIC BREAD

1 1-pound loaf Italian or French bread
1 recipe Garlic Butter (page 304), not molded

Slice the loaf of bread into ³/₄-inch slices, cutting almost through the loaf but leaving the slices attached (about 16 slices). Using the Garlic Butter, butter generously 1 side of each slice. Wrap the loaf in aluminum foil; set aside until a few minutes before serving time.

Near serving time, preheat the oven to 350°F.

Just before serving time, heat the Garlic Bread in the preheated oven until hot (about 5 minutes).

To serve, remove the hot loaf from the aluminum foil and place it in a long, napkin-lined basket. Diners pull off slices.

MAKES ABOUT 16 SLICES

NOTE: See Toasted Garlic Bread, page 361, for another garlic bread recipe.

Yeast Rolls

DINNER ROLLS

Butterhorn Rolls, Cloverleaf Rolls, and Parker House Rolls (see recipes below) differ from each other only in the way they are shaped. The same dough (see Dinner Rolls recipe, below) is used to make all 3 types of rolls. The shapes of Cloverleaf Rolls and Butterhorn Rolls generally would be considered more formal than the more conventional shape of Parker House Rolls.

¾ cup whole milk
¼ cup plus 2 tablespoons (6 tablespoons) butter
¼ cup sugar
1 teaspoon salt
2 ¼-ounce packets (about 1 tablespoon plus 1½ teaspoons) active dry yeast
½ cup warm water (110 to 115°F)
2 extra-large eggs, room temperature
5¾ to 6¼ cups sifted all-purpose flour (sift before measuring), divided
Butter, melted

In a small saucepan, scald the milk over medium heat (page 9). Remove from the heat. Add ¼ cup plus 2 tablespoons butter, sugar, and salt; stir until blended. Pour the milk mixture into a large mixing bowl; let stand until the mixture cools to 80 to 85°F. Meanwhile, in a small bowl, sprinkle the yeast over ½ cup warm water (110 to 115°F); stir until completely dissolved.

To the cooled milk mixture, add the yeast mixture, eggs, and 2 cups of the flour. Using an electric mixer, beat the mixture on low speed until combined; then, beat the mixture on medium speed 2 minutes. Using a large mixing spoon, gradually stir in enough of the remaining flour to form a dough that does not adhere to the sides of the bowl. Cover the bowl with a clean tea towel; let the dough stand 5 minutes.

Turn the dough onto a lightly floured pastry cloth (page 38) or wooden board. Roll the dough on the cloth or board to lightly cover the entire outside surface with flour. Knead the dough until smooth and elastic (about 8 minutes). The dough should be very soft.

Place the dough in a clean, greased bowl; turn the dough over so all surfaces are greased. Cover the bowl with the tea towel. Let the dough rise in a warm place (80°F) until doubled in bulk (about 1 to 1½ hours).

Punch the dough down. Turn the dough onto the pastry cloth or wooden board; cover with the tea towel. Let the dough rest 10 minutes. Follow the procedures, below, for shaping the type of dinner rolls desired.

After shaping the rolls, use a soft brush to brush them very lightly with melted butter. Cover the pans of rolls with tea towels. Let the rolls rise in the warm place (80°F) until nearly doubled in bulk (about 30 to 45 minutes).

Preheat the oven to 375°F.

Bake the rolls for 10 to 12 minutes. Immediately remove the rolls from the pans and place them on wire cookie racks. Serve immediately or let stand on wire racks until completely cool. Store, single layer, in an airtight container. Dinner Rolls (including all configurations) should be served hot in a roll basket (wicker, silver, or otherwise) lined and covered with a bread cloth to keep them warm. To heat rolls baked in advance and cooled, wrap them in airtight aluminum foil and place in a preheated 350°F oven for 5 to 8 minutes.

MAKES 24 TO 32 ROLLS

BUTTERHORN ROLLS

Follow the Dinner Rolls recipe, above, through resting the dough for 10 minutes after punching it down. Grease lightly four 10½ × 15½ × 1-inch cookie pans; set aside.

Using a sharp, thin-bladed knife, cut the dough

(Recipe continues on next page)

in half. Using a lightly floured rolling pin, roll each half of the dough into a 12-inch-diameter circle. Using a soft pastry brush, brush 1 tablespoon melted butter over each circle of dough. Cut each circle of dough into 16 equal wedges. Roll each wedge, starting with the wide end. Place the rolls, pointed end down, 2 inches apart on the prepared cookie pans. Resume following the procedures in the Dinner Rolls recipe to conclusion.

MAKES 32

CLOVERLEAF ROLLS

Follow the Dinner Rolls recipe, page 357, through resting the dough for 10 minutes after punching it down. Grease lightly twenty-four 3 × 1-inch muffin-pan cups; set aside.

Using a sharp, thin-bladed knife, cut the dough into 4 equal pieces. Shape each piece of dough into long rolls 1 inch in diameter. Cut each roll widthwise into 1-inch pieces. Gently pull and stretch the dough downward and under each piece of dough to form a uniform ball with a smooth top. Place 3 dough balls, smooth side up, in each prepared muffin-pan cup. Resume following the procedures in the Dinner Rolls recipe to conclusion.

MAKES 24

PARKER HOUSE ROLLS

Follow the Dinner Rolls recipe, page 357, through resting the dough for 10 minutes after punching it down. Grease lightly four 10½ × 15½ × 1-inch cookie pans; set aside.

Using a sharp, thin-bladed knife, cut the dough in half. Using a lightly floured rolling pin, roll each half of the dough to ¼-inch thickness. Using a floured, 2½-inch round cutter, cut the dough into rounds. Wipe and reflour the cutter between each cut. Reroll and cut the excess dough until all the dough is used.

Using a soft brush, brush the dough rounds with melted butter (you will need about 2 tablespoons melted butter). Using the dull side of a table knife blade, make a crease, slightly off center, across each round. Fold the large side of each round over the small side, overlapping slightly. With your fingers, firmly press the folded edge (where you made the crease) of each round. Place the rolls 2 inches apart on the prepared cookie pans. Resume following the procedures in the Dinner Rolls recipe to conclusion.

MAKES 30

HOT CROSS BUNS

Although Hot Cross Buns, piped with a white frosting cross, are a traditional roll served by Christians during the Easter season, the affiliation of cross-marked bread with religion predates Christianity. It is said that the Greeks and Romans ate bread marked with a cross at public sacrifices and that the pagan Saxons ate cross-marked bread to honor their goddess of light, Eostre. Further, it is believed that the Mexican and Peruvian peoples participated in a similar custom using cross bread. The Saxons probably introduced cross-marked bread to England, where in pre-Christian times it was made to honor the goddess of spring. Early Christians adopted the bread since it bore the cross, the symbol of their faith. The tradition migrated to the United States with the English settlers.

Hot Cross Buns contain currants (or raisins), spices, and sometimes candied citron. They are served at breakfast, coffee, and brunch, and with certain luncheon menus.

¾ **cup whole milk**
½ **cup (¼ pound) butter**
⅓ **cup sugar**
1 **teaspoon salt**
1 **¼-ounce packet plus ¼ teaspoon (about 2½ teaspoons) active dry yeast**
¼ **cup warm water (110 to 115°F)**
1 **extra-large egg, room temperature**

¾ teaspoon ground cinnamon

3½ to 4 cups sifted all-purpose flour
(sift before measuring), divided

⅔ cup currants

2 ounces (¼ cup) finely diced candied citron

1 extra-large egg white, room temperature

1 teaspoon water (approximately 80°F)

½ recipe untinted Confectioners' Frosting
(page 507)

In a small saucepan, scald the milk over medium heat (page 9). Remove from the heat. Add the butter, sugar, and salt; stir until blended. Pour the milk mixture into a large mixing bowl; let stand until the mixture cools to 80 to 85°F. Meanwhile, in a small bowl, sprinkle the yeast over ¼ cup warm water (110 to 115°F); stir until completely dissolved.

To the cooled milk mixture, add the yeast mixture, 1 egg, cinnamon, and 2 cups of the flour. Using an electric mixer, beat the mixture on low speed until combined; then, beat the mixture on medium speed 2 minutes. Add the currants and citron; using a large mixing spoon, stir to combine. Using the mixing spoon, gradually stir in enough of the remaining flour to form a dough that does not adhere to the sides of the bowl.

Place the dough in a clean, lightly greased bowl; turn the dough over so all surfaces are greased. Cover the bowl with a clean tea towel. Let the dough rise in a warm place (80°F) until doubled in bulk (about 1¼ to 1½ hours).

Punch the dough down. Turn the dough onto a lightly floured pastry cloth (page 38) or wooden board; cover with the tea towel. Let the dough rest 10 minutes. Meanwhile, grease lightly two 10½ × 15½ × 1-inch cookie pans; set aside.

Knead the dough 2 minutes. Using a lightly floured rolling pin, roll the dough to ¾-inch thickness. Using a lightly oiled, 2-inch round cutter, cut the dough into rounds and place them 1½ inches apart on the prepared cookie pans. Intermittently wipe and reoil the cutter. Reroll and cut the excess dough until all the dough is used; set aside.

In a small sauce dish, place 1 egg white and 1 teaspoon water (approximately 80°F); using a table fork, beat slightly. Using a soft brush, brush a thin layer of egg white mixture over the tops of the dough rounds (buns). Cover the pans of buns with tea towels. Let the buns rise in the warm place (80°F) until nearly doubled in bulk (about 45 minutes to 1 hour).

Preheat the oven to 350°F.

Bake the buns for 15 minutes. Immediately remove the buns from the pans and place them on wire cookie racks; let stand to cool slightly. While the buns are still warm, use a decorating bag fit with tip number 7 (pages 319–320) to pipe a cross of Confectioners' Frosting on the top of each bun. Serve immediately. Or, let the unpiped buns stand on the wire racks until completely cool; then store, single layer, in an airtight container. Just before serving, wrap the buns in airtight aluminum foil and warm in a preheated 350°F oven for about 5 minutes. Then, pipe crosses on the buns and serve.

MAKES 2 DOZEN

CINNAMON ROLLS

¾ cup whole milk

½ cup (¼ pound) butter

½ cup sugar

1 teaspoon salt

2 ¼-ounce packets (about 1 tablespoon plus 1½ teaspoons) active dry yeast

½ cup warm water (110° to 115°F)

2 extra-large eggs, room temperature

1 teaspoon pure vanilla extract

5¾ to 6¼ cups sifted all-purpose flour
(sift before measuring), divided

¾ cup sugar

1 tablespoon ground cinnamon

3 tablespoons butter, melted

1 recipe untinted Confectioners' Frosting
(page 507)

(Recipe continues on next page)

In a small saucepan, scald the milk over medium heat (page 9). Remove from the heat. Add ½ cup butter, ½ cup sugar, and salt; stir until blended. Pour the milk mixture into a large mixing bowl; let stand until the mixture cools to 80 to 85°F. Meanwhile, in a small bowl, sprinkle the yeast over ½ cup warm water (110 to 115°F); stir until completely dissolved.

To the cooled milk mixture, add the yeast mixture, eggs, vanilla, and 2 cups of the flour. Using an electric mixer, beat the mixture on low speed until combined; then, beat the mixture on medium speed 2 minutes. Using a large mixing spoon, gradually stir in enough of the remaining flour to form a dough that does not adhere to the sides of the bowl. Cover the bowl with a clean tea towel; let the dough stand 5 minutes.

Turn the dough onto a lightly floured pastry cloth (page 38) or wooden board. Roll the dough on the cloth or board to lightly cover the entire outside surface with flour. Knead the dough until smooth and elastic (about 10 minutes). The dough should be very soft.

Place the dough in a clean, greased bowl; turn the dough over so all surfaces are greased. Cover the bowl with the tea towel. Let the dough rise in a warm place (80°F) until doubled in bulk (about 1 to 1½ hours).

Punch the dough down. Turn the dough onto the pastry cloth or wooden board; cover with the tea towel. Let the dough rest 10 minutes. Meanwhile, in a small bowl, place ¾ cup sugar and cinnamon; stir to combine; set aside. Grease well two 9-inch or three 8-inch round baking pans; set aside.

Using a sharp, thin-bladed knife, cut the dough in half. Using a lightly floured rolling pin, roll each half of the dough into an 8 × 12-inch rectangle. Using a soft brush, brush 1½ tablespoons melted butter over each rectangle of dough. Sprinkle ½ of the cinnamon mixture evenly over each rectangle. Roll each rectangle, long side to long side, jelly-roll fashion. With your fingers, pinch the seam to seal. Cut each roll of dough widthwise into twelve 1-inch slices. Place the dough slices, cut side down, in the prepared baking pans. Cover the pans of rolls with the tea towel. Let the rolls rise in the warm place (80°F) until nearly doubled in bulk (about 30 to 40 minutes).

Preheat the oven to 375°F.

Bake the rolls for 20 to 25 minutes. Remove from the oven and place the pans of rolls on wire racks; cool 5 minutes. Remove the rolls from the pans and place them on wire racks over waxed paper. Frost moderately warm rolls with Confectioners' Frosting. Serve the rolls immediately or let them stand until completely cool. Store, single layer, in a airtight container.

MAKES 2 DOZEN

SERVING ALTERNATIVE: Cool and store the rolls unfrosted. Immediately before serving, wrap the rolls in airtight aluminum foil and heat in a preheated 350°F oven for about 5 minutes. Then, frost and serve warm.

VARIATION: After sprinkling ½ of the cinnamon mixture over each rectangle of dough, distribute ⅓ cup raisins evenly over each rectangle before rolling jelly-roll fashion.

CARAMEL ROLLS (STICKY ROLLS)

(See photo insert page D-1)

I like to serve Caramel Rolls warm in the morning with breakfast, midmorning coffee, and brunch, and at midday with cold, salad luncheons. As an accompaniment to hot luncheons and on most other occasions (Midwesterners sometimes eat Caramel Rolls with dinner), I prefer them at room temperature. Some diners prefer always to eat them warm.

1 recipe Cinnamon Rolls (page 359)
2 tablespoons butter
¾ cup packed light brown sugar
2 tablespoons light corn syrup
¾ cup broken pecans or pecan halves
    (optional)
3 tablespoons butter, melted

Follow the Cinnamon Rolls recipe through combining the sugar and cinnamon. Then, butter generously two 9-inch or three 8-inch round baking pans; set aside.

In a small saucepan, melt 2 tablespoons butter over low heat. Remove from the heat. Add the brown sugar and corn syrup; stir to combine. Return to low heat; cook the brown sugar until blended, stirring constantly. Pour the mixture, evenly divided, into the prepared baking pans. Divide the pecans between (among) the pans and distribute them evenly over the brown sugar mixture; set aside.

Using a sharp, thin-bladed knife, cut the dough in half. Using a lightly floured rolling pin, roll each half of the dough into an 8 × 12-inch rectangle. Using a soft brush, brush 1½ tablespoons melted butter over each rectangle of dough. Sprinkle ½ of the cinnamon mixture evenly over each rectangle. Roll each rectangle, long side to long side, jelly-roll fashion. With your fingers, pinch the seam to seal. Cut each roll of dough widthwise into twelve 1-inch slices. Place the dough slices, cut side down, directly on the brown sugar mixture in the pans. Cover the pans of rolls with the tea towel. Let the rolls rise in the warm place (80°F) until nearly doubled in bulk (about 30 to 45 minutes).

Preheat oven to 375°F.

Bake the rolls for 20 to 25 minutes. Remove from the oven and place the pans of rolls on wire racks; cool 5 minutes. Remove the rolls from the pans by inverting the pans onto wire racks over waxed paper. Serve the rolls immediately or let them stand, sticky side up, on the wire racks until completely cool. (Eliminate the Confectioners' Frosting used in the Cinnamon Rolls recipe.) Store the rolls, single layer, in an airtight container. Serve Caramel Rolls sticky side up.

MAKES 2 DOZEN

SERVING SUGGESTIONS: Caramel Rolls may be served warm or at room temperature (see headnote). To reheat, wrap the rolls in airtight aluminum foil and place them in a preheated 350°F oven for about 5 minutes.

Toast

TOASTED BACON BREAD

½ cup (¼ pound) butter, softened
1 1-pound loaf Italian or French bread, sliced
   ¾ inch thick (about 16 slices)
½ pound bacon, fried crisply, drained well
   between paper towels, and crumbled

Spread butter generously on one side of each bread slice. Place the buttered slices, single layer, in 1 or more large, shallow baking pan(s). Scatter the crumbled bacon evenly over the slices. Cover the pan(s) tightly with aluminum foil; set aside until a few minutes before serving time.

Near serving time, preheat the broiler.

Uncover the pan(s) of bacon bread and place under the broiler, about 6 inches from the heat. Leave under the broiler until the bread is toasted to a light brown (about 2 to 3 minutes). Watch very carefully. Serve immediately in a cloth-lined breadbasket.

MAKES ABOUT 16 SLICES

TOASTED GARLIC BREAD

1 recipe Garlic Butter (page 304), not molded
1 1-pound loaf Italian or French bread, sliced
   ¾ inch thick (about 16 slices)

Spread Garlic Butter generously on one side of each bread slice. Place the buttered slices, single layer, in 1 or more large, shallow baking pan(s). Cover the pan(s) tightly with aluminum foil; set aside until a few minutes before serving time.

Near serving time, preheat the broiler.

Uncover the pan(s) of garlic bread and place under the broiler, about 6 inches from the heat. Leave under the broiler until the bread is

(Recipe continues on next page)

toasted to a light brown (about 2 to 3 minutes). Watch very carefully. Serve immediately.

MAKES ABOUT 16 SLICES

SERVING SUGGESTION: Serve with Grace's Spaghetti and Meatballs (page 240) as well as many other Italian dishes.

NOTE: See Garlic Bread, page 356.

TOASTED HERB BREAD

½ cup (¼ pound) butter, softened
1 tablespoon finely snipped, fresh parsley
  leaves
1 tablespoon finely snipped, fresh chives
1 1-pound loaf French bread, sliced 1 inch
  thick (about 12 slices)

In a small bowl, place the butter, parsley, and chives; stir to combine. Spread evenly on one side of each bread slice. Place the bread slices, single layer, in 1 or more large, shallow baking pan(s). Cover the pan(s) tightly with aluminum foil; set aside until a few minutes before serving time.

Near serving time, preheat the broiler.

Uncover the pan(s) of herb bread and place under the broiler, about 6 inches from the heat. Leave under the broiler until the bread bubbles and browns (about 2 to 3 minutes). Watch carefully. Serve immediately.

MAKES ABOUT 12 SLICES

VARIATIONS: Fresh parsley or chives may be used singly or in combination with 1 or more of the following herbs: basil, chervil, dill, fennel, marjoram, rosemary, tarragon, and thyme. Combine 2 well-packed tablespoons of finely snipped, fresh herbs with each ½ cup softened butter.

Dried herbs may also be used. Use 2 teaspoons dried herbs to each ½ cup butter. When using dried herbs, soak the measured herbs in 1 tablespoon lemon juice for 5 minutes; then

press out most of juice before combining with the softened butter.

TOASTED SESAME BREAD

¼ cup (4 tablespoons) butter, softened
1 tablespoon Dijon mustard
1 tablespoon finely snipped, fresh parsley
  leaves
1 teaspoon grated onions
2 teaspoons sesame seed
1 1-pound loaf French bread, sliced ½ inch
  thick (about 24 slices)

Preheat the broiler.

In a small mixing bowl, place the butter, mustard, parsley, onions, and sesame seed; stir to combine. Spread the mixture thinly on one side of each bread slice. Place the bread slices, single layer, in 1 or more large, shallow baking pan(s).

Place the pan(s) under the broiler, about 6 inches from the heat. Leave under the broiler until the bread bubbles and browns (about 2 to 3 minutes). Watch carefully. Serve immediately.

MAKES ABOUT 24 SLICES

TOASTED PARMESAN-PARSLEY BREAD

My favorite bread to serve with steaks and pork chops. People go for toasted breads on a dinner menu, and this one especially seems to hit the spot.

½ cup (¼ pound) butter, softened
1 1-pound loaf French bread, sliced ¾ inch
  thick (about 16 slices)
¾ cup freshly grated Parmesan cheese (page 30)
¼ cup finely snipped, fresh parsley leaves

Spread butter generously on one side of each bread slice. Place the buttered slices, single layer, in 1 or more large, shallow baking pan(s). Using a teaspoon, sprinkle Parmesan cheese over the buttered slices (use all of the cheese). Using your fingers, distribute the parsley evenly over the Parmesan cheese on the slices. Cover the pan(s) tightly with aluminum foil; set aside until a few minutes before serving time.

Near serving time, preheat the broiler.

Uncover the pan(s) of parmesan-parsley bread and place under the broiler, about 6 inches from the heat. Leave under the broiler until the bread is bubbly and lightly browned (about 2 to 3 minutes). Watch carefully. Serve immediately in a covered breadbasket.

MAKES ABOUT 16 SLICES

FRENCH TOAST

2 extra-large eggs
2 tablespoons whole, lowfat, or fat-free (skim) milk
1/8 teaspoon salt
Dash of pepper
1 tablespoon butter
4 slices French bread, 3/4 to 1 inch thick
Butter
Pure maple syrup, hot

In an 8-inch round or square baking pan, place the eggs, milk, salt, and pepper; using a table fork, beat the mixture until blended.

Preheat an electric skillet, griddle, or regular skillet on the range to medium heat (350°F in an electric skillet). Melt 1 tablespoon butter in the skillet. Using a spatula, spread the butter over the entire bottom of the skillet.

Using a fork, dip 1 bread slice at a time in the egg mixture, covering both sides of the bread generously with the mixture. Immediately after dipping each slice of bread in the egg mixture, place it in the skillet. Sizzle the dipped bread slices a few minutes on each side, until a deep, golden brown. Turn only once. Serve immediately. Pass generous portions of butter and hot syrup at the table for diners to first butter their French Toast and then pour syrup over top.

SERVES 2

VARIATION: Any type of white or whole-wheat bread may be substituted for French bread. Bread used to make French Toast need not be as thick as designated in the above recipe.

SERVING SUGGESTION: Powdered sugar may be sprinkled sparingly on top of French Toast before serving (primarily as a decoration).

MILK TOAST

1 teaspoon sugar
1/4 teaspoon ground cinnamon
1 tablespoon plus 1 teaspoon butter, softened
2 slices white, whole-wheat, or raisin toast, hot
1 1/3 cups whole, lowfat, or fat-free (skim) milk, hot

In a small sauce dish, place the sugar and cinnamon; stir to combine; set aside. Spread 1/2 of the butter on each slice of hot toast. Sprinkle the cinnamon mixture equally over the buttered toast. Cut each slice of toast twice, diagonally from corner to corner, to make 4 triangular pieces.

Place 4 toast quarters in each of 2 warmed soup or chowder bowls. Pour 1/2 of the hot milk over the toast in each bowl. Serve *immediately* before the toast becomes soggy.

SERVES 2

CINNAMON TOAST

Follow the Milk Toast recipe, above, through sprinkling the toast with the cinnamon mixture. (Eliminate milk from the recipe.) Cut the Cinnamon Toast in half diagonally, and serve in lieu of plain toast.

SAUTÉED TOAST POINTS

6 slices very thin, white bread
2 tablespoons butter

Trim the crusts from the bread slices. Cut each slice twice, diagonally from corner to corner, to make 4 triangular bread points.

Preheat an electric skillet or a skillet on the range to medium-low heat (300°F in an electric skillet). Melt the butter in the skillet. Using a spatula, spread the butter over the entire bottom of the skillet. Place the bread points, single layer, in the skillet. Sauté both sides of the bread points until a deep golden brown, turning once. Remove the toast points from the skillet and place on wire cookie racks; let stand, uncovered, until serving time.

MAKES 2 DOZEN

VARIATIONS: One tablespoon finely snipped, fresh basil, parsley, or dill (or 1 teaspoon of any 1 of these herbs, dried) may be mixed with the butter in the skillet prior to sautéing the toast points.

SERVING SUGGESTIONS: Serve with hot hors d'oeuvres, first-course appetizers, soups, and salads.

Yeast Doughnuts

RAISED DOUGHNUTS

1 cup whole milk
½ cup sugar
1 teaspoon salt
1 ¼-ounce packet (about 2¼ teaspoons) active dry yeast
¼ cup warm water (110° to 115°F)
4½ cups sifted all-purpose flour (sift before measuring), divided
¼ cup vegetable oil
2 extra-large eggs, room temperature
½ teaspoon ground nutmeg
About 2 quarts (64 ounces) vegetable oil for frying

In a small saucepan, scald the milk over medium heat (page 9). Remove from the heat. Add the sugar and salt; stir until blended. Pour the milk mixture into a large mixing bowl; let stand until the mixture cools to 80° to 85°F. Meanwhile, in a small bowl, sprinkle the yeast over ¼ cup warm water (110° to 115°F); stir until completely dissolved.

To the cooled milk mixture, add the yeast mixture and 2¼ cups of the flour. Using an electric mixer, beat the mixture on low speed until combined; then, beat the mixture on medium speed until well blended and smooth (about 2 minutes). Cover the bowl with a clean tea towel. Let the yeast mixture rise in a warm place (80°F) about 1 hour.

Then, place ¼ cup vegetable oil in a small mixing bowl; using an electric mixer, add the eggs, one at a time, beating well on high speed after each addition. Add the egg mixture to the yeast mixture; using the electric mixer, beat on medium-high speed until combined; set aside. Sift the remaining 2¼ cups flour with the nutmeg. Using a large mixing spoon, gradually stir the flour mixture into the yeast mixture. Cover the bowl with the tea towel; let the dough stand 5 minutes.

Turn the dough onto a lightly floured pastry cloth or wooden board (page 38). Roll the dough on the cloth or board to lightly cover the entire outside surface with flour. Knead the dough well (about 8 minutes).

Place the dough in a clean, greased bowl; turn the dough over so all surfaces are greased. Cover the bowl with the tea towel. Let dough rise in the warm place (80°F) until doubled in bulk (about 1 hour).

Turn the dough onto the pastry cloth or wooden board. Using a stockinet-covered, then lightly floured rolling pin (page 38), roll the dough to ¾-inch thickness. Using a 2¾-inch, floured doughnut cutter, cut out the doughnuts and place them on a very lightly floured wooden board. Gather the remaining dough into a ball; roll out again and cut. Repeat until all the dough is used. Cover the doughnuts with the tea towel. Let the doughnuts rise in a warm place (80°F) until doubled in bulk (about 45 minutes).

In a deep-fat fryer or deep electric skillet, heat about 2 quarts vegetable oil to 370°F. The oil should be at least 1¼ inches deep. Using a spatula, carefully place the doughnuts, *raised side down,* in the hot oil. Fry the doughnuts 40 seconds on each side, turning once by slipping a cooking fork under the doughnuts, one at a time (do not pierce), and turning them over. Fry no more than 4 doughnuts at a time in order to control the frying time and keep the temperature of the oil as stable as possible.

When done, place the fork under the doughnuts, one at a time, and remove from the oil. Place the doughnuts on wire racks covered with paper towels to drain. To sugar or glaze the doughnuts, see the procedures below.

MAKES 2 DOZEN

TO SUGAR THE DOUGHNUTS: Place ¼ cup sugar in a zipper-seal plastic bag. Place the warm doughnuts, one at a time, in the bag; seal and shake carefully until evenly coated.

TO GLAZE THE DOUGHNUTS

1 pound (4 cups) powdered sugar
¼ cup plus 2 tablespoons water
1 teaspoon pure vanilla extract

Allow the Raised Doughnuts to completely cool. Then, in a medium mixing bowl, place the powdered sugar, water, and vanilla; using an electric mixer, beat on high speed only until blended and smooth. Place the glaze in a small, flat pan. Dip both sides of the doughnuts in the glaze to cover all surfaces and place the doughnuts on wire racks to dry.

Other Donut Recipe

Cake Doughnuts (page 386)

Quick Breads

TO TEST QUICK BREAD LOAVES FOR DONENESS

The standard procedure employed to test quick bread loaves for doneness is to insert a wooden toothpick into the center of the bread. If the toothpick comes out clean, the bread is judged to be done. This is the same method commonly used to determine the doneness of cakes.

Many quick bread loaves include a relatively large quantity of fruit or vegetable pieces which can make testing for their doneness a bit tricky. When withdrawn from a perfectly done loaf of quick bread, the testing toothpick may appear damp if it happened to have penetrated a nice, juicy piece of fruit, such as cranberry or apple. A second test in a different location on the bread may help the baker discern if the dampness of, or residue on, the first testing toothpick was due to the fruit/vegetable or less-than-done batter.

TO REMOVE QUICK BREAD LOAVES FROM LOAF PANS

Place the loaf pan of baked quick bread on a wire rack immediately after removing it from the oven. Let the bread stand exactly 10 minutes (use a timer) to cool. Then, carefully run a sharp, thin-bladed knife around the inside edges and to the bottom of the loaf pan to loosen the bread from the sides of the pan. Place a second wire rack over the pan. Securely hold both wire racks over and under the pan, and quickly invert them. The bread will fall from the pan onto the lower wire rack. Remove the top wire rack and carefully lift the pan off the bread.

To return the bread to its upright position, lightly place the extra wire rack on the exposed bottom side of the bread. Hold both wire racks and invert. Remove the top wire rack.

Let the bread stand on the wire rack until completely cool. Wrap the bread in airtight aluminum foil or place it in a properly sized, airtight container.

ABOUT THE CRACKING OF QUICK BREAD LOAVES

The top of quick bread loaves often cracks, which is normal and should not concern the baker. The cracking is caused by the center of the bread continuing to rise after the top crust sets.

Many state fair blue ribbons are placed across cracks in the top of loaves of quick bread.

Breads

APRICOT BREAD

1 6-ounce package dried apricots (about 1 cup packed apricots)
½ cup golden raisins
1 medium orange
2 cups all-purpose flour
2 teaspoons baking powder
½ teaspoon baking soda
½ teaspoon salt
1 extra-large egg
1 cup sugar
1 teaspoon pure vanilla extract
2 tablespoons butter, melted
½ cup broken pecans

Place the apricots in a small saucepan. Pour boiling water over the apricots to cover. Cover the saucepan; let stand until the apricot mixture cools. Place the raisins in a separate, small saucepan; follow the same procedure as for the apricots.

Preheat the oven to 350°F. Grease lightly a 5×9-inch loaf pan on the bottom and *only* 1 inch up the sides; set aside.

Drain the cooled apricots in a sieve, reserving the juice. Using a sharp knife, dice the apricots approximately ¼ inch square; set aside. Drain the cooled raisins in a sieve; set aside. (Reserve the raisin juice for other uses or discard.) Grate finely (page 31) the rind of the orange; set aside. Then, squeeze the juice from the orange and add enough of the reserved apricot juice to make 1 cup liquid; set aside.

Onto waxed paper, sift together the flour, baking powder, baking soda, and salt; set aside.

Place the egg in a large mixing bowl. Using an electric mixer, beat the egg briefly on high speed. Add the sugar and beat well on high speed. Add the orange rind, vanilla, and butter; beat on high speed until combined and blended. Add, alternately, the flour mixture in thirds, and the orange juice mixture in halves, beating on low speed after each addition only until blended. Add the apricots, raisins, and pecans; using a large mixing spoon, fold in until evenly distributed.

Spoon the batter into the prepared loaf pan. Using a small, narrow, angled spatula, lightly and quickly spread the batter evenly in the pan. Bake for 50 minutes, or until a wooden toothpick inserted into the center of the loaf comes out clean.

Remove the bread from the oven and place on a wire rack; cool 10 minutes. Remove the bread from the pan (page 366); let stand on a wire rack until completely cool. Wrap in airtight aluminum foil.

MAKES 1 LARGE LOAF

CRANBERRY NUT BREAD

An all-occasion holiday bread for breakfast, coffees, brunches, luncheons, and teas, and with selected dinner menus.

2 cups fresh cranberries, coarsely ground (page 34) (about 1 cup ground cranberries)
¼ cup sugar
3 cups sifted all-purpose flour (sift before measuring)
1 tablespoon plus 1 teaspoon baking power
¼ teaspoon salt
1 extra-large egg
1 cup sugar
2 tablespoons butter, melted
1 cup whole milk
½ cup chopped pecans

Preheat the oven to 350°F. Grease lightly a 5×9-inch loaf pan on the bottom and *only* 1 inch up the sides; set aside.

Place the ground cranberries in a small mixing bowl. Add ¼ cup sugar; stir to combine; set aside. Onto waxed paper, sift together the flour, baking powder, and salt; set aside.

In a large mixing bowl, place the egg and 1 cup sugar; using an electric mixer, beat well on high speed. Add the butter; beat on high speed until blended. Add, alternately, the flour mixture in thirds, and the milk in halves, beating on low speed after each addition only until blended. Add the cranberry mixture and pecans; using a large mixing spoon, fold in until evenly distributed.

Pour the batter into the prepared loaf pan. Using a small, narrow, angled spatula, spread the batter evenly in the pan. Bake for 50 minutes, or until a wooden toothpick inserted into the center of the loaf comes out clean.

Remove the bread from the oven and place on a wire rack; cool 10 minutes. Remove the bread from the pan (page 366); let stand on a wire rack until completely cool. Wrap in airtight aluminum foil.

MAKES 1 LARGE LOAF

DUTCH APPLE BREAD

This luscious-tasting and -looking bread is a specialty in Holland Dutch communities. When I go to Pella, Iowa, I always bring home a loaf or two of fantastic Apple Bread from the Jaarsma Bakery.

2 cups sifted all-purpose flour (sift before
   measuring)
2 teaspoons baking powder
½ teaspoon salt
1 cup *unpared*, quartered, and cored apples
   diced ⅜ inch square
½ cup (¼ pound) butter, softened
1 cup sugar
2 extra-large eggs
1 teaspoon pure vanilla extract
2 tablespoons whole milk
⅓ cup broken pecans
Glaze (recipe follows)

Preheat the oven to 350°F. Grease lightly a 5 × 9-inch loaf pan on the bottom and *only* 1 inch up the sides; set aside.

Reserve 3 tablespoons of the measured flour in a small sauce dish; set aside. Onto waxed paper, sift together the remaining flour, baking powder, and salt; set aside. Prepare the apples and place them in a small mixing bowl; set aside.

In a large mixing bowl, place the butter and sugar; using an electric mixer, cream well on high speed. Add the eggs, one at a time, beating well on high speed after each addition. Add the vanilla and milk; beat until blended; set aside.

Add the pecans to the apples; sprinkle the reserved 3 tablespoons flour over top and toss quickly to coat. Add the apple mixture and flour mixture to the egg mixture; using a large mixing spoon, fold in only until the flour is dampened and the apples and pecans are evenly distributed.

Spoon the batter into the prepared loaf pan. Using a small, narrow angled spatula, spread the batter evenly in the pan. Bake for 45 minutes, or until a wooden toothpick inserted into the center of the loaf comes out clean.

Remove the bread from the oven and place on a wire rack; cool 10 minutes. Remove the bread from the pan (page 366) and place on a wire rack over waxed paper; let stand until completely cool.

Then, pour the Glaze over the bread, allowing it to drip down the sides; let stand until the glaze is dry. Place the bread in an airtight container or wrap in aluminum foil.

MAKES 1 LARGE LOAF

GLAZE

½ cup powdered sugar
2 tablespoons butter, melted
2 teaspoons water

In a small mixing bowl, place the powdered sugar, butter, and water; using an electric mixer, beat on high speed only until smooth.

LEMON BREAD

1 cup broken pecans
2 cups sifted all-purpose flour (sift before
   measuring)
2 teaspoons baking soda
½ teaspoon salt
1 cup (½ pound) butter, softened
2 cups sugar
4 extra-large eggs
1 teaspoon lemon extract
1 teaspoon finely grated lemon rind
1 cup buttermilk
Glaze (recipe follows)

Preheat the oven to 350°F. Grease lightly two 4½ × 8½-inch loaf pans on the bottoms and *only* 1 inch up the sides; set aside.

Place the pecans in a small mixing bowl. Sprinkle 1 tablespoon of the measured flour over the pecans; toss until evenly dusted; set aside. Onto waxed paper, sift together the remaining flour, baking soda, and salt; set aside.

In a large mixing bowl, place the butter and sugar; using an electric mixer, beat on high speed until light and creamy. Add the eggs, one at a time, beating well on high speed after each addition. Add the lemon extract and lemon rind; beat on high speed until fluffy. Add, alternately, the flour mixture in fourths, and the buttermilk in thirds, beating on low speed after each addition only until blended. Add the pecans; using a large mixing spoon, fold in only until evenly distributed.

Spoon the batter equally into the prepared loaf pans. Using a small, narrow angled spatula, spread the batter evenly in the pans. Bake for 50 minutes, or until a wooden toothpick inserted into the center of the loaves comes out clean.

Remove the bread from the oven and place on wire racks; cool 10 minutes. Remove the bread from the pans (page 366) and place on wire racks over waxed paper; let stand while preparing the glaze.

Spoon warm Glaze, a little at a time, over the warm bread. Using a soft brush, spread the glaze evenly over the top of the bread and brush the glaze on the sides of the bread; let stand until completely cool. Wrap the loaves separately in airtight aluminum foil.

MAKES 2 MEDIUM LOAVES

GLAZE

1 cup sugar
1/3 cup freshly squeezed, strained lemon juice (about 2 lemons)

In a small saucepan, place the sugar and lemon juice; stir to combine. Over medium-high heat, heat the lemon mixture only until the sugar melts, stirring constantly.

SERVING SUGGESTIONS: A nice breakfast, brunch, or tea bread.

MINCEMEAT BREAD WITH ORANGE BUTTER

Baked in a ring mold, this bread looks appealing served at buffet-style coffees, breakfasts, and brunches. It's especially inviting and appropriate around the holidays.

1¾ cups sifted all-purpose flour (sift before measuring)
1 tablespoon baking powder
½ teaspoon salt
¼ teaspoon ground cinnamon
⅛ teaspoon ground nutmeg
2 extra-large eggs
¼ cup whole milk
3 tablespoons butter, melted
½ cup packed dark brown sugar
1 cup mincemeat
2 ounces finely diced candied orange peel (about ¼ cup packed candied orange peel), homemade (page 609) or commercial
1 recipe Orange Butter (page 305) or Ribbed Orange Butter Balls (page 331)

Preheat the oven to 350° F. Grease and flour an 8-inch ring mold; set aside.

Onto waxed paper, sift together the flour, baking powder, salt, cinnamon, and nutmeg. Place the flour mixture in a medium mixing bowl. Using a tablespoon, make a well in the center of the flour mixture; set aside.

Place the eggs in a medium-small mixing bowl. Using an electric mixer, beat the eggs slightly on medium speed. Add the milk, butter, and brown sugar; beat on medium speed only until blended. Add the mincemeat and candied orange peel; using a tablespoon, stir to combine. Pour the mincemeat mixture, all at once, into the well in the flour mixture; using a small mixing spoon, stir and fold *only* until the flour disappears and the mincemeat and candied orange peel are evenly distributed.

Spoon the batter into the prepared ring mold. Using a small, narrow, angled spatula, spread the batter evenly in the ring mold. Bake

(Recipe continues on next page)

for 45 minutes, or until a wooden toothpick inserted into the bread comes out clean.

Remove the bread from the oven and place on a wire rack; let stand 10 minutes. Then, carefully run a sharp, thin-bladed knife around the outer and inner edges of the ring mold to loosen the bread. Place a second wire rack over the top of the ring mold; hold both wire racks securely and invert. Remove the top wire rack and carefully lift the ring mold off the bread. The bread may be reinverted or left as is with the bottom side up. Let the bread stand on a wire rack until completely cool.

Using 2 spatulas, transfer the bread to a 10-inch corrugated cardboard cake circle; place in an airtight cake container.

To serve, slice the bread ring, leaving it in place on the cake circle. Place the cake circle on a cake stand or serving tray. Place a serving bowl of Orange Butter or Ribbed Orange Butter Balls in the center of the bread ring.

MAKES ABOUT 20 SLICES

POPPY SEED BREAD WITH ORANGE GLAZE

3 cups all-purpose flour
1½ teaspoons baking powder
1 teaspoon salt
1½ cups sugar
½ cup plus 2 tablespoons vegetable oil
½ cup (¼ pound) butter, melted
3 extra-large eggs
1½ teaspoons pure vanilla extract
1½ teaspoons pure almond extract
2 tablespoons poppy seed
1½ cups whole milk
Orange Glaze (recipe follows)

Preheat the oven to 340°F. Grease lightly two 4½ × 8½-inch loaf pans on the bottoms and *only* 1 inch up the sides; set aside (see Note).

Onto waxed paper, sift together the flour, baking powder, and salt; set aside.

In a large mixing bowl, place the sugar and vegetable oil; using an electric mixer, beat well on high speed. Add the butter; beat on high speed until blended. Add the eggs, one at a time, beating well on high speed after each addition. Add the vanilla, almond extract, and poppy seed; beat to blend and combine. Add, alternately, the flour mixture in thirds, and the milk in halves, beating on low speed after each addition only until blended.

Pour the batter equally into the prepared loaf pans. Using a small, narrow, angled spatula, spread the batter evenly in the pans. Bake for 1 hour, or until a wooden toothpick inserted into the center of the loaves comes out clean.

Remove the bread from the oven and place on wire racks; cool 10 minutes. Remove the bread from the pans (page 366) and place on wire racks over waxed paper. Immediately pour the hot Orange Glaze over the tops of the loaves, letting it trickle down the sides. Use a soft brush to spread the glaze over the entire top of the loaves; let stand until completely cool. Wrap the loaves separately in airtight aluminum foil.

NOTE: One 4 × 16-inch loaf pan may be substituted for two 4½ × 8½-inch loaf pans.

MAKES 2 MEDIUM LOAVES (OR 1 LONG LOAF IF 4 × 16-INCH LOAF PAN IS USED)

ORANGE GLAZE

¾ cup sugar
2 tablespoons plus 2 teaspoons freshly squeezed, strained orange juice
½ teaspoon pure almond extract

In a small saucepan, place the sugar and orange juice; stir together. Over medium-high heat, bring the mixture to a boil, stirring constantly. Remove from the heat. Add the almond extract; stir to blend.

PUMPKIN BREAD

Definitely one of the best-loved quick breads. It goes with fall and the Halloween and Thanksgiving seasons.

3⅓ cups all-purpose flour
2 teaspoons baking soda
1½ teaspoons salt
1 teaspoon ground cinnamon
1 teaspoon ground nutmeg
3 cups sugar
1 cup vegetable oil
4 extra-large eggs
1 15-ounce can pumpkin
⅔ cup water

Preheat the oven to 350° F. Grease lightly two 5 × 9-inch loaf pans on the bottoms and *only* 1 inch up the sides; set aside.

Onto waxed paper, sift together the flour, baking soda, salt, cinnamon, and nutmeg; set aside.

In a large mixing bowl, place the sugar and vegetable oil; using an electric mixer, beat on high speed until light and well blended. Add the eggs, one at a time, beating well on high speed after each addition. Add the pumpkin and water; beat until completely blended. Add the flour mixture in halves, beating on low speed after each addition only until blended.

Pour the batter equally into the prepared loaf pans. Using a small, narrow, angled spatula, spread the batter evenly in the pans. Bake for 1 hour, or until wooden toothpick inserted into center of the loaves comes out clean.

Remove the bread from the oven and place on wire racks; cool 10 minutes. Remove the bread from the pans (page 366); let stand on wire racks until completely cool. Wrap the loaves separately in airtight aluminum foil.

MAKES 2 LARGE LOAVES

RHUBARB BREAD

1½ cups fresh rhubarb diced ¼ inch square
2½ cups all-purpose flour
1 teaspoon baking powder
1 teaspoon baking soda
½ teaspoon salt
½ cup granulated sugar
1 teaspoon ground cinnamon
1 tablespoon butter, melted
1½ cups packed light brown sugar
⅔ cup vegetable oil
1 extra-large egg
1 teaspoon pure vanilla extract
1 cup buttermilk
½ cup broken pecans

Preheat the oven to 350° F. Grease lightly two 4½ × 8½-inch loaf pans on the bottoms and *only* 1 inch up the sides; set aside.

Wash the rhubarb, dry between paper towels. Dice the rhubarb and place it in a medium mixing bowl; set aside. Reserve 2 tablespoons of the measured flour in a small sauce dish; set aside. Onto waxed paper, sift together the remaining flour, baking powder, baking soda, and salt; set aside. In a small mixing bowl, place the granulated sugar and cinnamon; stir to combine. Add the butter and stir until crumbly; set aside.

In a large mixing bowl, place the brown sugar and vegetable oil; using an electric mixer, beat well on high speed. Add the egg and vanilla; beat on high speed until the mixture is well blended. Add, alternately, the flour mixture in thirds, and the buttermilk in halves, beating on low speed after each addition only until blended; set aside. Add the pecans to the rhubarb; stir until evenly combined. Sprinkle the 2 tablespoons reserved flour over the rhubarb mixture; toss to coat. Add the rhubarb mixture to the batter; fold in until the rhubarb and pecans are evenly distributed.

Spoon the batter equally into the prepared loaf pans. Using a small, narrow, angled spatula, spread the batter evenly in the pans. Using a tablespoon, sprinkle the cinnamon mixture

(Recipe continues on next page)

evenly over the batter. Bake for 50 minutes, or until a wooden toothpick inserted into the center of the loaves comes out clean.

Remove the bread from the oven and place on wire racks; cool 10 minutes. Remove the bread from the pans (page 366); let stand on wire racks until completely cool. Wrap the loaves separately in airtight aluminum foil.

MAKES 2 MEDIUM LOAVES

SERVING SUGGESTIONS: Rhubarb Bread, with its sweet, crumbly topping, is perfect for breakfast or brunch, or with a salad luncheon.

JANET STERN'S MANDEL (ALMOND) BREAD

An utterly exquisite bread for luncheons and teas.

3 cups all-purpose flour
1 tablespoon baking powder
1 teaspoon salt
¼ cup vegetable shortening
¼ cup (4 tablespoons) butter, softened
1 cup sugar
3 extra-large eggs, room temperature
2 teaspoons pure vanilla extract
½ cup chopped blanched almonds (chop slivered blanched almonds)
All-purpose flour
⅓ cup sugar
¾ teaspoon ground cinnamon
2 tablespoons butter, melted

Preheat the oven to 350° F. Using vegetable shortening, grease an insulated cookie sheet (see Note); set aside.

Onto waxed paper, sift together 3 cups flour, baking powder, and salt; set aside.

In a large mixing bowl, place the vegetable shortening, ¼ cup butter, and 1 cup sugar; using an electric mixer, cream well on high speed. Add the eggs, one at a time, beating well on high speed after each addition. Add the vanilla; beat until thoroughly blended. Add ½ of the flour mixture; beat on low speed only

until blended. Add the remaining ½ of the flour mixture and almonds; beat on low speed only until the flour mixture is blended.

Spoon ⅓ of the dough onto a well-floured pastry cloth (page 38); sprinkle the dough very lightly with flour (use only enough flour to permit handling of the dough). With floured hands, quickly shape the dough into a soft roll about 9 inches long. Place the roll to one side of the prepared cookie sheet. Following the same procedure, shape 2 more rolls, using the remaining dough. Space the 3 rolls, side by side, on the cookie sheet. Bake for 25 minutes.

Meanwhile, in a small mixing bowl, place the ⅓ cup sugar and cinnamon; stir to combine; set aside. After baking for 25 minutes, remove the bread from the oven. Using a spatula, immediately transfer the bread to a large wooden board covered with aluminum foil. Brush 2 tablespoons melted butter over the entire surface of the bread except the bottom of the loaves. Sprinkle the cinnamon mixture liberally (use all of the mixture) over the loaves and roll the loaves in the mixture which falls onto the aluminum foil. Spoon any mixture remaining on the foil onto the top of the loaves.

Then, using a sharp, thin-bladed knife, cut each loaf diagonally into 1-inch slices (about 7 to 8 slices per loaf). Using the spatula, return the cut loaves to the cookie sheet. Push each loaf together to close any space between the slices (to prevent drying). Bake for an additional 5 minutes at 350° F.

Using a spatula, remove the loaves from the cookie sheet and place them on wire cookie racks; let stand until cool. When cool, immediately wrap the loaves separately in airtight aluminum foil.

NOTE: Although not as satisfactory, a standard cookie sheet may be used if an insulated cookie sheet is not available.

MAKES ABOUT 2 DOZEN SLICES

SERVING SUGGESTIONS: Serve as a breakfast, brunch, or salad-luncheon bread. Or, cut the slices thinner and serve as a tea bread.

ZUCCHINI BREAD

The popularity of this bread can be attributed not only to its super taste, but to the big supply of zucchini from vegetable gardens.

3 cups all-purpose flour
1 teaspoon baking powder
1 teaspoon baking soda
1 teaspoon salt
1 teaspoon ground cinnamon
2 cups sugar
1 cup vegetable oil
3 extra-large eggs
2 teaspoons pure vanilla extract
3 cups unpared, cored, and coarsely shredded
  fresh zucchini
1 cup broken pecans
1 cup flaked coconut

Preheat the oven to 325°F. Grease lightly two 5 × 9-inch loaf pans on the bottoms and *only* 1 inch up the sides; set aside.

Onto waxed paper, sift together the flour, baking powder, baking soda, salt, and cinnamon; set aside.

In a large mixing bowl, place the sugar and vegetable oil; using an electric mixer, beat on high speed until light and well blended. Add the eggs, one at a time, beating well on high speed after each addition. Add the vanilla; beat until well blended. Add the flour mixture in halves, beating on low speed after each addition only until blended. Add the zucchini, pecans, and coconut; using a large mixing spoon, fold in until evenly distributed.

Pour the batter equally into the prepared loaf pans. Using a small, narrow, angled spatula, spread the batter evenly in the pans. Bake for 1 hour, or until a wooden toothpick inserted into the center of the loaves comes out clean.

Remove the bread from the oven and place on wire racks; cool 10 minutes. Remove the bread from the pans (page 366); let stand on wire racks until completely cool. Wrap the loaves separately in airtight aluminum foil.

MAKES 2 LARGE LOAVES

WHOLE-WHEAT ORANGE BREAD

¾ cup broken English walnuts
½ cup golden raisins
1½ cups all-purpose flour
¾ cup whole-wheat flour
1 teaspoon baking powder
1 teaspoon baking soda
¼ teaspoon salt
1 teaspoon ground cinnamon
½ teaspoon ground ginger
½ cup (¼ pound) butter, softened
⅔ cup sugar
¼ cup honey
2 extra-large eggs
1 tablespoon finely grated orange rind
  (page 31)
½ cup freshly squeezed, strained orange juice

Preheat the oven to 325°F. Grease lightly a 5 × 9-inch loaf pan on the bottom and *only* 1 inch up the sides; set aside.

In a small mixing bowl, place the walnuts and raisins; set aside. In a medium mixing bowl, place the all-purpose flour and whole-wheat flour; stir to combine. Sprinkle 2 tablespoons of the flour mixture over the walnut mixture; toss to coat; set aside. Onto waxed paper, sift together the remaining flour mixture, baking powder, baking soda, salt, cinnamon, and ginger; set aside.

In a large mixing bowl, place the butter, sugar, and honey; using an electric mixer, cream well on high speed. Add the eggs, one at a time, beating well on high speed after each addition. Add the orange rind; beat the mixture until light and fluffy. Add, alternately, the flour mixture in fourths, and the orange juice in thirds, beating on low speed after each addition only until blended. Add the walnut mixture; using a large mixing spoon, fold in until evenly distributed.

Pour the batter into the prepared loaf pan. Using a small, narrow, angled spatula, lightly and quickly spread the batter evenly in the pan. Bake for 1 hour, or until a wooden toothpick

(Recipe continues on next page)

inserted into the center of the loaf comes out clean.

Remove the bread from the oven and place on a wire rack; cool 10 minutes. Remove the bread from the pan (page 366); let stand on a wire rack until completely cool. Wrap in airtight aluminum foil.

MAKES 1 LARGE LOAF

WHOLE-WHEAT PRUNE BREAD

A full-flavored bread particularly good for serving in the fall and winter.

1 10-ounce package bite-sized pitted prunes
1½ cups water
½ cup reserved prune juice
1½ cups whole-wheat flour
1 teaspoon baking powder
1 teaspoon baking soda
¼ teaspoon salt
2 tablespoons butter, softened
½ cup sugar
1 extra-large egg
1 cup homemade sour milk (page 42)

In a small saucepan, place the prunes and water; cover and bring to a boil. Reduce the heat and simmer the prunes 2 minutes. Remove from the heat; let stand to cool (covered).

When cool, drain the prunes well in a sieve, reserving the juice. Measure 1 cup cooked prunes; grind coarsely (page 34); set aside. Measure ½ cup reserved prune juice; set aside. (Reserve the remaining prunes and juice for other uses.)

Preheat the oven to 350°F. Grease lightly a 5 × 9-inch loaf pan on the bottom and *only* 1 inch up the sides; set aside.

Onto waxed paper, sift together the flour, baking powder, baking soda, and salt; set aside.

In a medium mixing bowl, place the butter and sugar; using an electric mixer, cream well on high speed. Add the egg; beat well on high speed. Add approximately ¼ of the flour mix-

ture; beat on low speed only until blended. Add ½ cup prune juice; beat on low speed only until blended. Add, alternately, the remaining flour mixture in thirds, and the sour milk in halves, beating after each addition only until blended. Add 1 cup ground prunes; using a large mixing spoon, fold in until evenly distributed.

Pour the batter into the prepared loaf pan. Using a small, narrow, angled spatula, spread the batter evenly in the pan. Bake for 50 to 55 minutes, or until a wooden toothpick inserted into the center of the loaf comes out clean.

Remove the bread from the oven and place on a wire rack; cool 10 minutes. Remove the bread from the pan (page 366); let stand on a wire rack until completely cool. Wrap in airtight aluminum foil.

MAKES 1 LARGE LOAF

CORN BREAD

(See photo insert page A-3)

Midwest-style corn bread, thick in shape and made with yellow cornmeal, flour, and a bit of sugar (among other ingredients) has been a fixture in Heartland diets since the pioneer days.

Corn is truly the American grain. It is exclusively indigenous to North and South America. In fact, North American corn dates back to at least 2000 B.C. New World explorers learned about corn from the Indians for whom it was a staple, cultivated crop. From the Indians, the settlers learned to grind corn and use it to make corn bread or "Indian bread" as it was called then. Today, nearly four hundred years later, it can be said that corn bread is universally enjoyed across the Midwest—not surprising since the Midwest, sometimes referred to as the "Corn Belt," is where about 40 percent of the world's corn is grown.

Corn Bread is easy and reliable to make. You can whip up a world-class pan of this American classic at the same time you prepare dinner.

1 cup yellow cornmeal
1 cup all-purpose flour
3 tablespoons sugar
1 tablespoon plus 1 teaspoon baking powder
¾ teaspoon salt
1 extra-large egg
1½ cups whole milk
¼ cup (4 tablespoons) butter, melted

Preheat the oven to 425° F. Grease lightly an 8 ×
8-inch baking pan on the bottom and *only* ½
inch up the sides; set aside.

Onto waxed paper, sift together the cornmeal, flour, sugar, baking powder, and salt.
Place the cornmeal mixture in a medium mixing bowl; stir to combine. Using a tablespoon,
make a well in the center of the cornmeal mixture; set aside.

Place the egg in a small mixing bowl. Using
an electric mixer, beat the egg slightly on
medium speed. Add the milk and butter; beat
on medium speed only until blended. Pour the
egg mixture all at once into the well in the cornmeal mixture; using a small mixing spoon, stir
and fold *only* until the cornmeal mixture is
dampened. The batter will be lumpy.

Pour the batter into the prepared baking pan.
Bake for 20 minutes.

Remove the Corn Bread from the oven and
place on a wire rack. Cut into 9 pieces. Serve hot
(see Note).

NOTE: Corn Bread may be cooled in the pan,
then covered with aluminum foil, and reheated
before serving.

SERVES 9

SERVING SUGGESTIONS
• Serve with plenty of butter. Many Midwest-
erners also enjoy jellies and jams with Corn
Bread.

• A natural accompaniment for Bean Soup
(page 72).

AMERICAN INDIAN FRY BREAD

(See photo insert page C-2)

*Fry bread is a specialty of several American Indian
peoples, including the Ojibway or Ojibwa (also
known as Chippewa) Indians in the Minnesota
region of the Midwest. The bread dough, made of
flour, baking powder, salt, milk or water, and
sometimes sugar, is rolled into thin circles and then
is deep-fat fried. It is usually served with honey or
some other sweet spread. I prefer fry bread made
without sugar as an ingredient, and like to spread
butter over my serving of the bread before adding
honey, jam, or jelly. Our family enjoys eating
American Indian Fry Bread with dinner.*

2¼ cups all-purpose flour
1½ teaspoons baking powder
⅛ teaspoon salt
¾ cup plus 1 tablespoon whole milk, warm
Vegetable oil for frying

Onto waxed paper, sift together the flour, baking powder, and salt. Place the flour mixture in
a medium mixing bowl. Add the warm milk;
stir in quickly. Turn the mixture onto a lightly
floured pastry cloth (page 38); knead until
smooth (about 4 minutes).

Using a sharp, thin-bladed knife, cut the
dough in half. Using a stockinet-covered, then
lightly floured rolling pin (page 38), roll each
half of the dough into a circle ⅛ inch thick; let
stand.

Pour 1 inch of vegetable oil into a large electric skillet; heat to 380° F (medium-high heat).
Fry the circles, one at a time, in the hot oil. Fry
2 minutes on each side, turning once. Drain on
paper towels. To serve, diners tear off portions
of the bread at the table. Serve with butter; and
honey, jams, and jellies.

SERVES 4

VARIATION: Cut the kneaded dough into 4 parts.
Roll and fry each part, following the procedures
in the recipe. Serve each diner 1 whole portion
of fry bread.

BROWN BREAD

½ cup chopped dates
½ cup broken English walnuts
1½ cups whole-wheat flour
½ cup all-purpose flour
2 teaspoons baking soda
¼ teaspoon salt
1½ cups packed dark brown sugar
1 extra-large egg
1½ cups buttermilk
1 tablespoon plus 2 teaspoons vegetable oil

Preheat the oven to 350° F. Grease lightly a 5 × 9-inch loaf pan on the bottom and *only* 1 inch up the sides; set aside.

In a small mixing bowl, place the dates and walnuts; stir to combine; set aside. Sprinkle 1 tablespoon of the measured whole-wheat flour over the date-nut mixture; stir until evenly dusted; set aside. Onto waxed paper, sift together the remaining whole-wheat flour, the all-purpose flour, baking soda, and salt. Place the flour mixture in a large mixing bowl. Using a tablespoon, make a well in the center of the mixture; set aside.

Place the egg in a small mixing bowl. Using an electric mixer, beat the egg slightly on medium speed. Add the buttermilk and vegetable oil; beat on medium speed only until blended. Pour the egg mixture all at once into the well in the flour mixture. Using a large mixing spoon, stir and fold *only* until the flour disappears. Add the date-nut mixture; quickly fold in until evenly distributed.

Spoon the batter into the prepared loaf pan. Using a small, narrow, angled spatula, lightly and quickly spread the batter evenly in the pan. Bake for 50 to 55 minutes, or until a wooden toothpick inserted into the center of the loaf comes out clean.

Remove the bread from the oven and place on a wire rack; cool 10 minutes. Remove the bread from the pan (page 366); let stand on a wire rack until completely cool. Wrap in airtight aluminum foil.

MAKES 1 LARGE LOAF

Muffins

CORNMEAL MUFFINS

1 cup yellow cornmeal
1 cup all-purpose flour
1 tablespoon plus 1 teaspoon baking powder
½ teaspoon salt
1 extra-large egg
1¼ cups whole milk
¼ cup (4 tablespoons) butter, melted

Preheat the oven to 400° F. Using Special Grease (page 40) (see Note), grease twelve 3 × 1-inch muffin-pan cups; set aside.

Onto waxed paper, sift together the cornmeal, flour, baking powder, and salt. Place the cornmeal mixture in a medium mixing bowl. Using a tablespoon, make a well in the center of the cornmeal mixture; set aside.

Place the egg in a small mixing bowl. Using an electric mixer, beat the egg slightly on medium speed. Add the milk and butter; beat on medium speed only until blended. Pour the egg mixture all at once into the well in the cornmeal mixture; using a small mixing spoon, stir and fold *only* until the cornmeal mixture is dampened. The batter will be lumpy.

Using 2 tablespoons (1 to transport the batter and 1 to push the batter from the filled tablespoon), spoon the batter into the prepared muffin-pan cups. Each cup will be nearly full. Bake for 12 to 13 minutes.

Immediately remove the baked muffins from the cups by inverting the pan(s). Serve the muffins hot, or let them cool on wire racks.

NOTE: Although not as satisfactory, vegetable shortening may be substituted for Special Grease.

MAKES 12

100% WHOLE-WHEAT MUFFINS

2 cups whole-wheat flour
1 tablespoon plus 1 teaspoon baking powder
½ teaspoon salt
¼ cup sugar
2 extra-large eggs
1 cup whole milk
¼ cup butter, melted, *or* ¼ cup vegetable
    shortening, melted

Preheat the oven to 400° F. Using Special Grease (page 40) (see Note), grease twelve 3 × 1-inch muffin-pan cups; set aside.

Onto waxed paper, sift together the flour, baking powder, salt, and sugar. Place the flour mixture in a medium mixing bowl. Using a tablespoon, make a well in the center of the flour mixture; set aside.

Place the eggs in a small mixing bowl. Using an electric mixer, beat the eggs slightly on medium speed. Add the milk and butter; beat on medium speed only until blended. Pour the egg mixture all at once into the well in the flour mixture; using a small mixing spoon, stir and fold *only* until the flour disappears. The batter will be lumpy.

Using 2 tablespoons (1 to transport the batter and 1 to push the batter from the filled tablespoon), spoon the batter into the prepared muffin-pan cups. Each cup will be about ⅔ full. Bake for 15 minutes.

Immediately remove the baked muffins from the muffin-pan cups by inverting the pan(s). Serve the muffins hot, or let them cool on wire racks.

NOTE: Although not as satisfactory, vegetable shortening may be substituted for Special Grease.

MAKES 12

SOY WHOLE-WHEAT MUFFINS

I think you will like the flavor of these muffins which combine soy flour with whole-wheat flour.

½ cup soy flour
1½ cups whole-wheat flour
1 tablespoon baking powder
½ teaspoon salt
2 tablespoons sugar
1 extra-large egg
1 cup whole milk
3 tablespoons vegetable oil

Preheat the oven to 400° F. Using Special Grease (page 40) (see Note), grease ten 3 × 1-inch muffin-pan cups; set aside.

Onto waxed paper, sift together the soy flour, whole-wheat flour, baking powder, salt, and sugar. Place the flour mixture in a medium mixing bowl. Using a tablespoon, make a well in the center of the flour mixture; set aside.

Place the egg in a small mixing bowl. Using an electric mixer, beat the egg slightly on medium speed. Add the milk and vegetable oil; beat on medium speed only until blended. Pour the egg mixture all at once into the well in the flour mixture; using a small mixing spoon, stir and fold *only* until the flour disappears. The mixture will be lumpy.

Using 2 tablespoons (1 to transport the batter and 1 to push the batter from the filled tablespoon), spoon the batter into the prepared muffin-pan cups. Each cup will be nearly full. Bake for 12 to 15 minutes.

Immediately remove the baked muffins from the muffin-pan cups by inverting the pan(s). Serve the muffins hot, or let them cool on wire racks.

NOTE: Although not as satisfactory, vegetable shortening may be substituted for Special Grease.

MAKES 10

OAT BRAN MUFFINS

1 cup all-purpose flour
1¼ teaspoons baking soda
¼ teaspoon salt
3 tablespoons sugar
1 cup oat bran
2 extra-large eggs
8 ounces commercial sour cream
¼ cup whole milk
3 tablespoons butter, melted, *or* 3 tablespoons
    vegetable oil

Preheat the oven to 400° F. Using Special Grease (page 40) (see Note), grease ten 3 × 1-inch muffin-pan cups; set aside.

Onto waxed paper, sift together the flour, baking soda, salt, and sugar. Place the flour mixture in a medium mixing bowl. Add the oat bran; stir to combine. Using a tablespoon, make a well in the center of the flour mixture; set aside.

Place the eggs in a small mixing bowl. Using an electric mixer, beat the eggs slightly on medium speed. Add the sour cream, milk, and butter; beat on medium speed only until blended. Pour the egg mixture all at once into the well in the flour mixture; using a small mixing spoon, stir and fold *only* until the flour disappears. The batter will be lumpy.

Using 2 tablespoons (1 to transport the batter and 1 to push the batter from the filled tablespoon), spoon the batter into the prepared muffin-pan cups. Each cup will be nearly full. Bake for 15 minutes.

Immediately remove the baked muffins from the muffin-pan cups by inverting the pan(s). Serve the muffins hot, or let them cool on wire racks.

NOTE: Although not as satisfactory, vegetable shortening may be substituted for Special Grease.

MAKES 10

LINGONBERRY–OAT BRAN MUFFINS

Good tasting, good-looking, and good for you. Who could ask for anything more?

1 recipe Oat Bran Muffins, above
½ cup plus 2 tablespoons commercially
    canned wild lingonberries in sugar

Follow the Oat Bran Muffins recipe through the mixing of the ingredients. Fill the muffin-pan cups half full of the batter. Using a teaspoon, make a well in the center of the batter in each muffin-pan cup. Place 1 tablespoon lingonberries in each well. Spoon the remaining batter equally into the muffin-pan cups. Each cup will be nearly full. Resume following the Oat Bran Muffins recipe for baking.

CRANBERRY-ORANGE MUFFINS

1 tablespoon plus 1 teaspoon finely ground
    orange peel (requires about 1 medium
    orange) (see recipe procedures below)
2 cups fresh cranberries
2 cups all-purpose flour
1 tablespoon plus 1 teaspoon baking powder
1 teaspoon ground allspice
½ teaspoon salt
½ cup granulated sugar
2 extra-large eggs
1 cup whole milk
3 tablespoons butter, melted, *or* 3 tablespoons
    vegetable oil
¼ cup packed light brown sugar
1 teaspoon pure vanilla extract
½ cup broken pecans

Preheat the oven to 400° F. Using Special Grease (page 40) (see Note), grease twelve 3 × 1-inch muffin-pan cups; set aside.

Wash the orange; dry it. Using a sharp paring knife, thinly pare the orange, removing *only* the orange-colored outer peel, including as little of the white peel membrane as possible. Using a meat grinder fit with a fine blade (page 34), grind the peel. Measure 1 tablespoon plus 1 teaspoon finely ground peel; set aside.

Wash the cranberries; drain well in a sieve. Grind the cranberries finely in the meat grinder; drain in a sieve; set aside.

Onto waxed paper, sift together the flour, baking powder, allspice, salt, and granulated sugar. Place the flour mixture in a medium mixing bowl. Using a tablespoon, make a well in the center of the flour mixture; set aside.

Place the eggs in a small mixing bowl. Using an electric mixer, beat the eggs slightly on medium speed. Add the milk, butter, brown sugar, and vanilla; beat on medium speed only until blended. Pour the egg mixture all at once into the well in the flour mixture; using a small mixing spoon, make 3 or 4 folding strokes until the egg mixture begins to mix with the flour mixture. Add the orange peel, cranberries, and pecans; fold and stir *only* until the flour disappears (and the fruit and nuts are evenly distributed). The batter will be lumpy.

Using 2 tablespoons (1 to transport the batter and 1 to push the batter from the filled tablespoon), spoon the batter into the prepared muffin-pan cups. Each cup will be nearly full. Bake for 15 minutes.

Immediately remove the baked muffins from the muffin-pan cups by inverting the pan(s). Serve the muffins hot, or let them cool on wire racks.

NOTE: Although not as satisfactory, vegetable shortening may be substituted for Special Grease.

MAKES 12

BANANA MUFFINS

1½ cups all-purpose flour
1 teaspoon baking soda
1 teaspoon ground nutmeg
¾ cup sugar
1 cup mashed, very ripe bananas (about 2 large bananas)
1 extra-large egg
½ cup (¼ pound) butter, melted
1 teaspoon pure vanilla extract

Preheat the oven to 350° F. Using Special Grease (page 40) (see Note), grease twelve 3 × 1-inch muffin-pan cups; set aside.

Onto waxed paper, sift together the flour, baking soda, nutmeg, and sugar. Place the flour mixture in a medium mixing bowl. Using a tablespoon, make a well in the center of the flour mixture; set aside.

Peel the bananas; slice them into a small mixing bowl. Using a fork, mash the bananas (the bananas will be slightly lumpy); measure and set aside.

Place the egg in a small mixing bowl. Using an electric mixer, beat the egg slightly on medium speed. Add the butter and vanilla; beat on medium speed only until blended. Add the bananas; using a spoon, stir to combine. Pour the egg mixture all at once into the well in the flour mixture; using a small mixing spoon, stir and fold *only* until the flour disappears. The batter will be lumpy.

Using 2 tablespoons (1 to transport the batter and 1 to push the batter from the filled tablespoon), spoon the batter into the prepared muffin-pan cups. Each cup will be about ⅔ full. Bake for 15 to 18 minutes.

Immediately remove the baked muffins from the muffin-pan cups by inverting the pan(s). Serve the muffins hot, or let them cool on wire racks.

NOTE: Although not as satisfactory, vegetable shortening may be substituted for Special Grease.

MAKES 12

Biscuits

BAKING POWDER BISCUITS

2 cups sifted all-purpose flour (sift before
  measuring)
1 tablespoon plus 1 teaspoon baking powder
½ teaspoon salt
¼ cup plus 2 tablespoons refrigerated lard
¾ cup whole milk, cold

Preheat the oven to 400°F.

Onto waxed paper, sift together the flour, baking powder, and salt. Place the flour mixture in a medium mixing bowl. Using a table knife, quickly cut the measured lard into approximately nickel-sized (irregular) chunks and drop them onto the flour mixture. Using a pastry blender, cut the lard into the flour mixture until the mixture is the texture of coarse cornmeal. Using a table fork, make a well in the center of the flour mixture. Pour the milk all at once into the well in the flour mixture. Using the fork, stir with 25 to 30 strokes, until the flour mixture is dampened and the dough stiffens. (Biscuit dough is stirred and manipulated more than muffin batter.)

Turn the dough onto a *lightly floured* pastry cloth (page 38) or wooden board. Knead (page 348) about 20 times until the dough is cohesive and manageable. Using a *lightly floured* rolling pin, roll the dough to ½-inch thickness. Using a floured, 2-inch biscuit cutter, cut the biscuits with a straight up and down motion, dipping the cutter in flour between each cut. Wipe the cutter intermittently with a paper towel when the dough begins to cling to it. Place the cut biscuits on an ungreased cookie sheet (preferably an insulated cookie sheet). Gather the remaining dough and knead briefly; reroll and cut additional biscuits. Repeat the procedure until all the dough is used. Bake for 12 minutes, until the biscuits are lightly brown.

When done, immediately remove the biscuits from the cookie sheet to prevent the bottoms from overbrowning on the hot, cookie-sheet sur-face. Place the biscuits in a cloth-lined roll basket for immediate serving. If serving at a later time, place the biscuits on a wire cookie rack to cool. When cool, promptly arrange them, single layer, in an airtight container. Just before serving, reheat the biscuits in a microwave oven, or wrap them in airtight aluminum foil and heat them in a preheated 350°F oven.

MAKES 14

OLD-FASHIONED SERVING SUGGESTION: Set the table with a bread and butter plate at each diner's place. The diner splits a biscuit in half, places it open-faced on the bread and butter plate, then generously butters each half and pours hot maple syrup over top. This dish is eaten with a fork.

(When Baking Powder Biscuits were on my mother's family dinner menu, no matter how the biscuits were otherwise eaten with the meal, at least one biscuit always was savored this way by each of us.)

OLD-FASHIONED (BISCUIT-STYLE) SHORTCAKES

2 cups sifted all-purpose flour (sift before
  measuring)
1 tablespoon plus 1 teaspoon baking powder
½ teaspoon salt
¼ cup sugar
1 extra-large egg, cold
½ cup whole milk, cold
¼ cup plus 2 tablespoons refrigerated lard
Additional lard (about 1 teaspoon) for top of
  shortcakes

Preheat the oven to 450°F.

Onto waxed paper, sift together the flour, baking powder, salt, and sugar. Place the flour mixture in a medium mixing bowl; set aside. In a small mixing bowl, place the egg and milk; using an electric mixer, beat on medium speed until blended; set aside.

Using a table knife, quickly cut the measured lard into approximately nickel-sized (irregular) chunks and drop them onto the flour mixture. Using a pastry blender, cut the lard into the flour mixture until the mixture is the texture of coarse cornmeal. Using a table fork, make a well in the center of the flour mixture. Pour the egg mixture all at once into the well in the flour mixture. Using the fork, stir with 25 to 30 strokes, until the flour mixture is dampened and the dough stiffens.

Turn the dough onto a *lightly floured* pastry cloth (page 38) or wooden board. Knead (page 348) about 20 times until the dough is cohesive and manageable. Using a *lightly floured* rolling pin, roll the dough to ½-inch thickness. Using a floured, 2½-inch biscuit cutter, cut the shortcakes with a straight up and down motion, dipping the cutter in flour between each cut. Wipe the cutter intermittently with a paper towel when the dough begins to cling to it. Place the cut shortcakes on an ungreased cookie sheet (preferably, an insulated cookie sheet). Gather the remaining dough and knead briefly; reroll and cut additional shortcakes. Repeat the procedure until all the dough is used. Using a knife, lay about ⅛ teaspoon of lard on top of each shortcake. Bake for 11 to 12 minutes, until the shortcakes are lightly brown.

When done, immediately remove the shortcakes from the cookie sheet and place them on a wire cookie rack; let stand until lukewarm or completely cool, depending upon how the shortcakes are to be served. If allowed to completely cool, promptly arrange the shortcakes, single layer, in an airtight container.

MAKES 8

OLD-FASHIONED STRAWBERRY SHORTCAKE

In the Midwest, three different types of cakes are used to make strawberry shortcake: Old-Fashioned (Biscuit-Style) Shortcake (page 380), Sponge-Style Shortcake (page 487), and Angel Food Cake (page 484). The recipe that follows is for strawberry shortcake made with biscuit-style shortcakes. (Old-Fashioned [Biscuit-Style] Shortcakes are accurately defined as biscuits rather than cakes.)

While there are many Old-Fashioned (Biscuit-Style) Shortcake advocates, Sponge-Style Shortcake or Angel Food Cake is generally preferred by most contemporary strawberry shortcake enthusiasts.

2 pints fresh strawberries
¼ cup sugar
1 recipe Old-Fashioned (Biscuit-Style) Shortcakes (page 380), lukewarm*
¼ cup (4 tablespoons) butter, melted (optional)
1 recipe Whipped Cream (page 309)

* Shortcakes may be served completely cool, if preferred.

Wash and hull the strawberries (page 6). Reserve 8 whole strawberries for garnishing the tops of the shortcakes. Place ½ of the remaining berries in a flat-bottomed pan and crush them with a potato masher; place in a medium mixing bowl; set aside. Slice the remaining berries lengthwise ⅜ inch thick; add to the crushed berries. Add the sugar; stir to combine; set aside.

Using a sharp, thin-bladed knife, split the lukewarm shortcakes in half lengthwise. Lightly brush the melted butter over the cut side of the bottom halves of the shortcakes, and place them on individual serving plates. Spoon ½ of the strawberries equally over the bottom halves of the shortcakes. Place the top halves of the shortcakes over the berries. Spoon the remaining ½ of the berries equally over the tops of the shortcakes. Spoon a generous dollop of Whipped Cream over each shortcake and garnish with a whole strawberry.

SERVES 8

SERVING SUGGESTION: For a more decorative presentation, garnish each serving with a Strawberry Fan (page 339) instead of a whole strawberry.

OLD-FASHIONED PEACH, RASPBERRY, OR BLUEBERRY SHORTCAKE

Follow the Old-Fashioned Strawberry Short-cake recipe, above, substituting peaches, raspberries, or blueberries for the strawberries. Prepare the fruit as follows:

PEACHES: Wash, blanch (page 3) 30 seconds; peel, halve, pit, and quarter. Slice the peach quarters ⅜ inch thick. Using a potato masher, crush ½ of the peach slices. Leave the remaining ½ of the slices intact.

RASPBERRIES OR BLUEBERRIES: Wash and drain. Using a potato masher, crush ½ of the berries. Leave the remaining ½ of the berries whole.

Dumplings

DUMPLINGS

2 cups sifted all-purpose flour (sift before
   measuring)
1 tablespoon plus 1 teaspoon baking powder
½ teaspoon salt
3 tablespoons refrigerated vegetable
   shortening
1 cup whole milk, cold

Onto waxed paper, sift together the flour, baking powder, and salt. Place the flour mixture in a medium mixing bowl. Using a table knife, quickly cut the measured shortening into approximately dime-sized (irregular) chunks and drop them onto the flour mixture. Using a pastry blender, cut the shortening into the flour mixture until the mixture is the texture of coarse cornmeal. Using a table fork, make a well in the center of the flour mixture. Pour the milk, all at once, into the well in the flour mixture. Using a small mixing spoon, stir and fold until combined.

Drop the batter by the tablespoonful onto the top of boiling broth or stew. Cover the kettle; reduce the heat slightly but keep the liquid bub-

bling. Cook 15 minutes. *Do not lift the cover while the Dumplings are cooking—not even to peek.*

Remove from the heat. Uncover the kettle. Using a small spatula, remove the Dumplings and place them, single layer, in a pan; cover to keep warm.

MAKES 10

HERB DUMPLINGS

Follow the Dumplings recipe, above, sprinkling 1 tablespoon finely snipped, fresh parsley and ¼ teaspoon dried leaf summer savory over the sifted flour mixture in the mixing bowl. Using a small mixing spoon, lightly combine the herbs with the flour mixture. Then, add the shortening and proceed to follow with the Dumplings recipe.

THYME DUMPLINGS

Follow the Herb Dumplings recipe, above, substituting ¾ teaspoon finely snipped, fresh thyme for ¼ teaspoon dried leaf summer savory.

Crackers

DELUXE CRACKERS

A breeze to prepare and nice to serve when entertaining.

Small, plain water crackers
Butter, softened

Preheat the broiler.

Spread the crackers very thinly with butter and place them in a shallow baking pan. Place under the broiler about 6 inches from the heat. Leave the crackers under the broiler until the butter bubbles well (about 1 minute). Watch carefully.

Serve warm.

DELUXE SESAME SEED CRACKERS

Follow the Deluxe Cracker recipe, page 382, substituting small water crackers with sesame seeds for the small, plain water crackers.

SERVING SUGGESTIONS: Serve with soups, first-course appetizers, salads, and hors d'oeuvres.

ELEGANT CRACKERS

A step up from Deluxe Crackers (see preceding recipe), but more involved and time-consuming to prepare.

Ice cubes and water
1 dozen saltines
3 tablespoons butter, melted

Preheat the oven to 375°F.

Butter lightly the bottom of a 9 × 13-inch baking pan; set aside.

Place the ice cubes and water in a large mixing bowl to ²/₃ full. Float the crackers, 4 at a time, in the ice water. Using a slotted spatula, push the crackers under the surface of the water to immerse them briefly; then, let the crackers float in the water for a *few seconds* until puffy but not falling apart. Using the spatula, carefully remove the crackers from the water and place them, single layer (do not overlap), in the prepared pan.

Using a soft brush, brush the top of the crackers with butter. Bake for 15 minutes.

Remove the crackers from the oven. Reduce the oven heat to 275°F. Brush the crackers with additional butter; bake for an additional 15 minutes, until a deep brown color. Using a spatula, place the crackers on waxed paper to cool. Store in an airtight container.

SERVING SUGGESTIONS: Serve with soups and salads.

RICE CRACKERS

1 cup all-purpose flour
¼ teaspoon salt
¼ teaspoon white pepper
½ cup (¼ pound) butter, softened
1½ cups very finely shredded, extra-sharp cheddar cheese
1 cup Rice Krispies cereal

Preheat the oven to 350°F. Grease lightly cookie sheets; set aside.

Onto waxed paper, sift together flour, salt, and white pepper; set aside.

In a medium mixing bowl, place the butter and cheese; using an electric mixer, beat on high speed until creamy. Add the flour mixture; continue beating on high speed until the mixture is of a creamy consistency. Add the Rice Krispies; using a spoon, stir to evenly combine.

Using a 1-inch trigger scoop or melon baller, scoop portions of the dough and roll 1-inch balls of dough in your hands; place them about 2½ inches apart on the prepared cookie sheets. With the heel of your hand, flatten the balls to 2-inch-diameter crackers. Bake for 12 minutes.

Using a thin spatula, carefully transfer the crackers to waxed paper; let stand until completely cool. Store in an airtight container in single layers separated by sheets of plastic wrap.

MAKES ABOUT 3½ DOZEN

SERVING SUGGESTION: Serve with thin soups.

CHEESE STRAWS

Look no further if you're searching for the ultimate gourmet cracker to serve with a thin soup as an introduction to a beautiful dinner. These Cheese Straws are rich, delicate, and in tune with polished dining.

1 cup sifted all-purpose flour (sift before measuring)

(Recipe continues on next page)

¼ teaspoon salt
½ cup (¼ pound) butter, softened
1 cup finely shredded, sharp cheddar cheese
3 tablespoons freshly grated Parmesan cheese
(page 30)

Preheat the oven to 350°F.

Onto waxed paper, sift together the flour and salt; set aside.

Place the butter in a small mixing bowl; using an electric mixer, cream on high speed. Add the cheddar cheese; beat on high speed until well combined. Add the Parmesan cheese; continue beating on high speed until fluffy. Add the flour mixture; beat on medium speed until well blended.

Using a decorating bag fit with large (⅝ inch wide) basket-weave tip number 2B (page 319), pipe 2-inch-long, ribbed sticks onto ungreased cookie sheets. Bake for 10 to 12 minutes.

Using a thin spatula, place the Cheese Straws on waxed paper; let stand until completely cool. Store in an airtight container.

MAKES 6 DOZEN ¾-INCH-WIDE CHEESE STRAWS

ALTERNATIVE BAKING METHOD: Use a cookie press fit with a ribbon disc to press 2-inch-long, ribbed sticks onto the cookie sheets.

MAKES 3 DOZEN 1½-INCH-WIDE CHEESE STRAWS

SERVING SUGGESTION: Serve with soup appetizer courses.

Coffee Cake

CINNAMON COFFEE CAKE

Coffee cake is a choice selection for serving with breakfast, morning coffee, and brunch (provided the menu includes one or more explicitly breakfast main dishes). It is grand to serve when a morning meeting is held at your house.

1½ cups sifted all-purpose flour (sift before
measuring)
2 teaspoons baking powder
½ cup sugar
½ teaspoon salt
3 tablespoons butter, softened
1 extra-large egg
½ cup whole milk
Cinnamon Topping (recipe follows)
2 tablespoons butter

Preheat the oven to 375°F. Using Special Grease (page 40) (see Note), grease an 8 × 8-inch baking pan; set aside.

Onto waxed paper, sift together the flour, baking powder, sugar, and salt. Place the flour mixture in a medium mixing bowl. Using a table knife, cut the 3 tablespoons softened butter into about 6 chunks and drop onto the flour mixture. Using a pastry blender, cut the butter into the flour mixture until the mixture is the texture of cornmeal. Using a table fork, make a well in the center of the flour mixture; set aside.

Place the egg in a small mixing bowl. Using an electric mixer, beat the egg slightly on medium speed. Add the milk; beat on medium speed only until blended. Pour the egg mixture, all at once, into the well in the flour mixture; using a small mixing spoon, stir and fold *only* until the flour disappears. The batter will be lumpy and sticky.

Spoon the batter into the prepared baking pan. Using a small, narrow, angled spatula, quickly spread the batter evenly in the pan. Sprinkle the Cinnamon Topping evenly over the batter; dot with 2 tablespoons butter. Bake for 20 minutes. Serve hot. Cut into 9 pieces.

NOTE: Although not as satisfactory, vegetable shortening may be substituted for Special Grease.

SERVES 9

VARIATION: Add ½ teaspoon pure vanilla extract to the small mixing bowl after adding ½ cup whole milk. Then, proceed to beat only until blended.

CINNAMON TOPPING

¼ cup sugar
1 teaspoon ground cinnamon

In a small mixing bowl, place the sugar and cinnamon; stir to combine.

APPLE COFFEE CAKE

1 recipe Cinnamon Coffee Cake, page 384
1½ cups pared, quartered, cored, and thinly
   sliced cooking apples, such as Golden
   Delicious (about 1 large apple)

Follow the Cinnamon Coffee Cake recipe through spreading the batter in the baking pan. Then, distribute the apples evenly over the batter. Sprinkle Cinnamon Topping evenly over the apples; dot with 2 tablespoons butter. Bake for 25 minutes at 375° F.

CRUMB COFFEE CAKE
(STREUSEL KAFFEEKUCHEN)

1 recipe Cinnamon Coffee Cake, page 384
Crumb Topping (recipe follows)

Follow the Cinnamon Coffee Cake recipe through mixing the batter. Spoon ½ of the batter into the prepared baking pan. Using a small, narrow spatula, spread the batter evenly in the pan. Sprinkle ½ of the Crumb Topping over the batter. Spoon the remaining ½ batter over the Crumb Topping. Using the small spatula, spread the batter as evenly as possible over the topping. Sprinkle the remaining ½ Crumb Topping over the batter. (Eliminate the Cinnamon Topping and 2 tablespoons of butter for dotting the coffee cake called for in the Cinnamon Coffee Cake recipe.) Bake for 20 to 25 minutes at 375° F.

VARIATION: Place all the batter in the baking pan; halve the Crumb Topping recipe and sprinkle it evenly over the batter.

CRUMB TOPPING

½ cup packed light brown sugar
2 tablespoons all-purpose flour
1 tablespoon ground cinnamon
½ cup chopped pecans
2 tablespoons butter, melted

In a small mixing bowl, place the brown sugar, flour, cinnamon, and pecans; stir to combine. Add the butter; stir until combined.

MARIE DALBEY'S SOUR CREAM COFFEE CAKE

A truly deluxe coffee cake baked in a springform pan.

¾ cup chopped pecans
¼ cup plus 2 tablespoons sugar
½ teaspoon ground cinnamon
2 cups sifted all-purpose flour (sift before
   measuring)
1 teaspoon baking powder
½ teaspoon salt
1 cup (½ pound) butter, softened
1½ cups sugar
2 extra-large eggs
8 ounces commercial sour cream
1¼ teaspoons pure vanilla extract

Preheat the oven to 350° F. Using Special Grease (page 40) (see Note), grease a 9 × 3-inch springform pan; set aside.

In a small bowl, place the pecans, ¼ cup plus 2 tablespoons sugar, and cinnamon; stir to combine; set aside. Onto waxed paper, sift together the flour, baking powder, and salt; set aside.

In a large mixing bowl, place the butter and 1½ cups sugar; using an electric mixer, cream on high speed. While continuing to beat on high speed, add the eggs, one at a time; beat until blended and fluffy. Add the sour cream and vanilla; beat until well blended. Add the

(Recipe continues on next page)

flour mixture in halves, beating on low speed after each addition only until blended.

Spoon ½ of the batter into the prepared springform pan; spread with a small, narrow, angled spatula, slightly mounding the batter toward the center of the pan. Sprinkle ½ of the pecan mixture evenly over the batter. Spoon the remaining ½ of the batter into the pan; spread, using the previous procedure. Sprinkle with the remaining ½ pecan mixture. Bake for 50 minutes, or until a wooden toothpick inserted into the center of the coffee cake comes out clean. *Caution:* Do not open the oven door until at least 45 minutes baking time has elapsed, as opening the oven door sooner may cause this delicate coffee cake to fall.

Remove the coffee cake from the oven and place on a wire rack; cool 10 minutes. Then, carefully run a sharp, thin-bladed knife around the inside edge of the pan; remove the sides of the pan. Leave the coffee cake on the bottom of the pan and serve warm.

NOTE: Although not as satisfactory, vegetable shortening may be substituted for Special Grease.

SERVES 12

Doughnuts

CAKE DOUGHNUTS

3½ cups all-purpose flour
2 teaspoons baking powder
1 teaspoon baking soda
½ teaspoon salt
¼ teaspoon ground cinnamon
¼ teaspoon ground nutmeg
2 extra-large eggs
1 cup sugar
2 tablespoons vegetable oil
½ teaspoon pure vanilla extract
¾ cup buttermilk
About 2 quarts (64 ounces) vegetable oil for frying

Onto waxed paper, sift together the flour, baking powder, baking soda, salt, cinnamon, and nutmeg; set aside.

Place the eggs in a large mixing bowl. Using an electric mixer, beat the eggs well on medium speed. Add the sugar, 2 tablespoons vegetable oil, and vanilla; beat well on high speed. Add the buttermilk; beat on high speed until blended. Add the flour mixture all at once; beat on low speed only until blended and smooth. Cover the bowl; refrigerate the dough at least 2 hours.

Turn the dough onto a lightly floured pastry cloth (page 38). Using a stockinet-covered, then lightly floured rolling pin (page 38), roll the dough to ⅜-inch thickness. Using a 2¾-inch, floured doughnut cutter, cut out the doughnuts and place them on lightly floured cookie sheets. Dip the cutter in flour before cutting each doughnut. Intermittently, remove the excess dough which accumulates around the cutting edge of the doughnut cutter. Gather the remaining dough into a ball; roll out again and cut. Repeat until all the dough is used. Handle the dough as little as possible.

In a deep-fat fryer or deep electric skillet, heat about 2 quarts vegetable oil to 370°F. The oil should be at least 1¼ inches deep. Do not commence to fry the doughnuts until the 370°F temperature has been reached.

Using a spatula, lift the doughnuts from the cookie sheets and place them in the hot oil. Fry the doughnuts about 1½ minutes on each side, turning once by slipping a cooking fork under the doughnuts, one at a time, and turning them over. Fry no more than 6 doughnuts at a time in order to control the frying time and keep the temperature of the oil as stable as possible.

When done, place the fork under the doughnuts, one at a time, and remove them from the oil. Place the doughnuts on wire racks covered with paper towels to drain. To sugar, or frost and garnish the doughnuts, see the recipes, below.

MAKES ABOUT 2 DOZEN

CINNAMON-SUGAR DOUGHNUTS

½ cup granulated sugar
1 teaspoon ground cinnamon
1 recipe Cake Doughnuts, above

In a small bowl, place the sugar and cinnamon; stir until evenly combined. Place the cinnamon mixture in a zipper-seal plastic bag. Place the *warm* doughnuts, one at a time, in the bag; seal and shake carefully until evenly coated. Place the coated doughnuts on wire racks; let stand until completely cool.

POWDERED SUGAR DOUGHNUTS

½ cup powdered sugar
1 recipe Cake Doughnuts, above

Place the powdered sugar in a zipper-seal plastic bag. Place *cool* doughnuts, one at a time, in the bag; seal and shake carefully until fully coated.

VANILLA-FROSTED DOUGHNUTS

1 recipe Ornamental Vanilla Frosting
  (page 512)
1 recipe Cake Doughnuts, above

Using a small, narrow, angled tapered spatula, frost the tops of *cool* doughnuts and place them on wire racks until the frosting cools. Frosts 1 dozen doughnuts only.

Immediately after frosting the doughnuts, before the frosting dries, one of the following may be sprinkled on the frosting:

Flaked coconut
Chopped pecans, almonds, or hazelnuts
  (page 34)
Nonpareils (page 24)

When the frosting cools and dries, store the doughnuts in an airtight container.

CHOCOLATE-FROSTED DOUGHNUTS

1 recipe Ornamental Chocolate Frosting
  (page 512)
1 recipe Cake Doughnuts, above

Follow the Vanilla-Frosted Doughnuts recipe, above, for frosting procedures, garnishing suggestions, and storage instructions.

Other Donut Recipes

Raised Doughnuts (page 364)

Popovers

POPOVERS

3 extra-large eggs
1⅓ cups whole milk
¼ teaspoon salt
1 tablespoon butter, melted
1⅓ cups all-purpose flour

Butter 6 popover-pan cups (see Note); set aside.

Place the eggs in a medium mixing bowl. Using an electric mixer, beat the eggs slightly on medium speed. Add the milk, salt, and butter; beat on medium speed until blended. Add the flour; beat on low speed only until blended. Avoid overbeating.

Using 2 tablespoons (1 to transport the batter and 1 to push the batter from the filled tablespoon), fill the prepared popover-pan cups half full of batter. Place in a *cold* oven. Turn on the oven to 450°F and bake the popovers 15 minutes. Reduce the oven heat to 350°F and bake the popovers an additional 15 to 20 minutes. When done, the Popovers will be crisp on the outside and moist on the inside. Serve hot.

(Recipe continues on next page)

NOTE: I prefer the type of popover pan with cups measuring about 2½ inches wide and 2½ inches deep which are separated by wires. If a popover pan is not available, custard cups may be substituted.

MAKES 6

SERVING SUGGESTION: Traditionally served with Rib Roast (Standing or Rolled) (page 142).

Pancakes and Waffles

PANCAKES GEORGE

From the golden recipe book of George Dinsdale, Omaha, Nebraska, who was a culinarian par excellence.

1¼ cups sifted all-purpose flour (sift before
   measuring)
1½ teaspoons baking powder
½ teaspoon baking soda
½ teaspoon salt
1 tablespoon sugar
1 extra-large egg
1 tablespoon plus 2 teaspoons vegetable oil
1½ cups buttermilk
1 teaspoon butter
Butter
Pure maple syrup, hot

Onto waxed paper, sift together the flour, baking powder, baking soda, salt, and sugar. Place the flour mixture in a medium mixing bowl. Using a tablespoon, make a well in the center of the flour mixture; set aside.

Immediately prior to baking the pancakes, place the egg in a small mixing bowl. Using an electric mixer, beat the egg slightly on medium speed. Add the vegetable oil and buttermilk; beat on medium speed only until blended. Pour the egg mixture all at once into the well in the flour mixture; using a small mixing spoon, stir

and fold *only* until the flour disappears. The batter will be lumpy.

Preheat an electric skillet, a griddle, or a large, heavy-bottomed skillet on the range to medium-high (375° F in an electric skillet).

Place 1 teaspoon butter in the skillet; using a spatula, spread the melted butter over the entire bottom of the skillet. Using a large mixing spoon, spoon the batter onto the sizzling skillet, cooking two or three 5-inch pancakes at a time. Using the spatula, turn pancakes *once* when bubbles form and break on the top of the batter, and the underside of the pancakes is browned (cook about 1½ minutes on each side). Serve immediately.

Do not add additional butter to the skillet as you cook the rest of the pancakes even though the skillet appears to be ungreased—it is not necessary. In fact, pancakes cooked subsequent to the first batch on the skillet are considered by most pancake devotees to be superior to the first batch cooked in the freshly added butter.

Pass generous portions of butter and hot, pure maple syrup at the table for diners to place on top of their pancakes.

The recipe may be doubled.

MAKES ABOUT NINE 5-INCH PANCAKES

NOTE

- Pancake batter should be made immediately prior to cooking the pancakes. The quality of the batter deteriorates if it stands too long or is stored in the refrigerator.

- To enjoy pancakes at their best, they should be eaten immediately as they come off the skillet; therefore, it is preferable that pancakes be cooked after the diners are seated at the table. Necessarily, this means that the cook eats last.

BLUEBERRY PANCAKES

Wash fresh blueberries; spread on paper towels to dry. Follow the Pancakes George recipe, above, sprinkling blueberries on the pancakes immediately after the batter is spooned onto the skillet. Then, resume following the cooking and serving procedures in the Pancakes George recipe (see Note, below).

STRAWBERRY PANCAKES

Wash and hull fresh strawberries (page 23); dry between paper towels. Quarter or slice the berries, depending upon size. Follow the Pancakes George recipe, above, sprinkling strawberries on the pancakes immediately after the batter is spooned onto the skillet. Then, resume following the cooking and serving procedures in the Pancakes George recipe (see Note below).

PINEAPPLE PANCAKES

Drain commercially canned, unsweetened pineapple slices in a colander; reserve the juice for other uses. Dry the slices between paper towels. Follow the Pancakes George recipe, above, placing 1 pineapple slice in the center of each pancake immediately after the batter is spooned onto the skillet. Then, resume following the cooking and serving procedures in the Pancakes George recipe (see Note below).

NOTE: When baking pancakes with added fruit, add about 1 teaspoon additional butter to the skillet to prevent the fruit from sticking. The addition of fruit generally necessitates a slight increase in the cooking time for pancakes.

WAFFLES

2 cups all-purpose flour
1 tablespoon baking powder
½ teaspoon salt
1 tablespoon plus 1 teaspoon sugar
3 extra-large eggs, room temperature
1⅔ cups whole milk
¼ cup plus 2 tablespoons butter, melted and
    cooled slightly
Butter
Pure maple syrup, hot

Onto waxed paper, sift together the flour, baking powder, salt, and sugar. Place the flour mixture in a large mixing bowl. Using a tablespoon, make a well in the center of the flour mixture; set aside.

Separate the eggs, placing the whites in a medium-small mixing bowl and the yolks in a small mixing bowl; set the egg whites aside. Using an electric mixer, beat the egg yolks slightly on medium speed. Add the milk and butter; beat on medium speed only until blended; set aside. Using the electric mixer fit with clean, dry beater blades, beat the egg whites on high speed until stiff but still moist and glossy; set aside.

Pour the milk mixture all at once into the well in the flour mixture; using a large mixing spoon, stir and fold *only* until the flour disappears. The batter will be lumpy. Add the egg whites; using the mixing spoon, fold in quickly, leaving marble-sized clumps of egg whites in the batter.

Cook the waffles in an electric waffle iron, following the instructions from the manufacturer. Waffles should be cooked until they stop steaming—about 3 minutes. Set the table with plenty of butter and hot, pure maple syrup.

MAKES 7 AVERAGE-SIZED WAFFLES

NOTE: While waffles are best when served directly off the waffle iron, cooked waffles may be placed, single layer, on wire racks resting on cookie sheets or cookie pans, and kept warm for a short period of time in a 275° F oven. If a portion or all of the waffles are to be served directly off the waffle iron, they are served at informal meals when the cook stations himself/herself at the waffle iron and eats last. The usual courtesy of waiting until everyone is served before diners commence eating is best dispensed with at most waffle meals.

SERVING SUGGESTIONS: Waffles may be served for breakfast, brunch, or casual dinners. Serve them with Canadian bacon, ham, sausage, or regular bacon. Additionally, Fried Eggs (page 224) or poached eggs are an excellent accompaniment.

(Recipe continues on next page)

TO FREEZE WAFFLES: Place cooked waffles on wire racks; let stand until cool. Stack up to 3 waffles on a large piece of freezer paper, placing smaller pieces of freezer paper between the waffles. Wrap the stack of waffles airtightly in the freezer paper and seal with freezer tape. Place the package of waffles in a zipper-seal plastic freezer bag; store in the freezer.

To heat for serving, break off quarters or halves of frozen waffles and heat in a conventional toaster. Or, heat frozen, whole waffles, or frozen quarters or halves of waffles, in a microwave oven.

WHOLE-WHEAT WAFFLES

Follow the Waffles recipe, above, substituting 1 cup whole-wheat flour and 1 cup all-purpose flour for 2 cups all-purpose flour.

Fritters

CORN FRITTERS

1 cup all-purpose flour
1 teaspoon baking powder
¾ teaspoon salt
1 tablespoon plus 1 teaspoon sugar
2 extra-large eggs
¼ cup whole milk
2 tablespoons butter, melted
1½ cups drained, canned whole-kernel corn
2 tablespoons vegetable oil
1 teaspoon butter

Onto waxed paper, sift together the flour, baking powder, salt, and sugar. Place the flour mixture in a medium mixing bowl. Using a tablespoon, make a well in the center of the flour mixture; set aside.

Place the eggs in a small mixing bowl. Using an electric mixer, beat the eggs well on medium speed. Add the milk and butter; beat on medium speed until blended; set aside. Add the corn; stir in.

Preheat an electric skillet or a large, heavy-bottomed skillet on the range to medium-high (380°F in an electric skillet).

Pour the egg mixture, all at once, into the well in the flour mixture; using a small mixing spoon, fold in only until the mixture is blended and the corn is evenly combined; set aside. Place the vegetable oil in the skillet. Tilt the skillet back and forth to completely cover the bottom with the oil. Add 1 teaspoon butter; spread to blend with the oil. When the grease sizzles, drop heaping tablespoonsful of batter onto the skillet. Fry the fritters about 5 minutes, turning once.

MAKES 10

SERVING SUGGESTIONS
• Serve Corn Fritters with butter and hot, pure maple syrup as a main course, accompanied by bacon, ham, or sausage.

• Make small, dollar-sized Corn Fritters and serve them without butter and syrup as an accompaniment to ham, pork, and lamb dishes.

APPLE FRITTERS

Follow the Corn Fritters recipe, above, substituting 1½ cups pared, quartered, cored, and coarsely diced (page 29) Golden Delicious or other cooking apples for the corn. Using a small hand strainer, sprinkle powdered sugar over the fried fritters. Serve with or without butter and hot, pure maple syrup.

Pies and Tarts

To Cut and Serve Pies and Tarts

If a pie has been baked with an attractive lattice top, or has been otherwise decorated in a particularly appealing way, it is inviting to show the pie at the table before returning to the kitchen to cut it. Diners eat with their eyes as well as their palates. A tart may be displayed by removing the rim of the pan and placing the tart on a raised stand. (Leave the tart on the pan bottom.)

Use a medium to small, sharp, thin-bladed knife to cut pies and tarts. Wipe both sides of the blade on a damp sponge before each cut. When cutting, take care to cut completely through the crust—on the bottom and side of the pan as well as the fluted edge—so the slices will be neat and unfrayed when removed from the pan.

Cut meringue-topped pies with a wet blade to prevent the meringue from sticking to the knife. Dip the knife blade into a glass of tepid water, shake off the excess water (safely away from the pie), make a cut, wipe the blade on a damp sponge and repeat.

To cut ice cream pies, dip the knife blade into a glass of very hot water. Wipe the blade on a damp sponge to remove excess water; then, make one cut in the pie. Dip the blade into the hot water and wipe it on the sponge before making each cut. For very neat, even pieces of pie, go over the cuts a second time.

Use a wedge-shaped pie spatula to remove cut pie slices from the pie pan and tart slices from the tart pan bottom. Place slices on individual serving plates.

Standard pies in 8- or 9-inch pie pans cut into 7 servings. Standard pies in 10-inch pie pans cut into 8 servings. Cheese pies in 9-inch pie pans cut into 9 servings. Ice cream pies in 9-inch pie pans cut into 10 servings. Tarts in 9-inch tart pans cut into 9 servings.

Pastry

PASTRY PIECRUST

Best Pastry Piecrust, 1988 Iowa State Fair.

MAKES ENOUGH PASTRY PIECRUST FOR:
- Two 8- or 9-inch pie shells
- One 8- or 9-inch two-crust pie
- One 8- or 9-inch lattice-top pie

2¼ cups sifted all-purpose flour (sift before measuring)
1 teaspoon salt
¾ cup refrigerated lard
⅓ cup refrigerated water

Onto waxed paper, sift together the flour and salt. Place the flour mixture in a large mixing bowl. Using a pastry blender, cut ⅔ of the lard into the flour mixture until the mixture is the texture of cornmeal. Cut in the remaining ⅓ of the lard until the size of peas. Move the mixture to one side of the bowl. Sprinkle 2 or 3 teaspoons of the water over the mixture. Using the back of a table fork, lightly rake the moistened portion of the mixture to the other side of the bowl. Repeat the procedure until all the water has been added. Mix and handle the pastry as little as possible. With floured hands, form the pastry into 2 balls (don't worry if the pastry doesn't hold together well) and wrap each pastry ball fairly tightly in plastic wrap.

In your hands, quickly press 1 wrapped ball of pastry somewhat firmly to form a more solid ball. Then, leaving the pastry ball wrapped, use your hands to flatten the pastry ball into a round, pattylike shape about 3½ to 4 inches in diameter. Next, smooth the edges of the wrapped pastry as much as you can, under the constraints of quick, *minimal* handling, to help lessen splitting of the edge of the pastry when it is rolled. Immediately refrigerate the shaped, wrapped portion of the pastry. Repeat the procedure with the second ball of pastry. These procedures should all be done as fast as possible to minimize the handling of the pastry.

After about 30 minutes of refrigeration, remove one of the portions of pastry from the refrigerator (see Note). Unwrap the pastry and place it on a lightly floured pastry cloth (page 38). Let the pastry stand 1 minute or so, just until it is soft enough to roll.

Using a stockinet-covered, then lightly floured rolling pin (page 38), roll the pastry on the pastry cloth, rolling from the center to the edge, until the pastry is 1½ inches greater in diameter than the inverted pie pan to be used. Carefully run a thin spatula around and under the edge of the pastry to loosen it from the pastry cloth. Fold the pastry in half. Move the folded pastry to the ungreased pie pan, situating the fold across the center of the pan. Unfold the pastry and fit it into the pan. Do not stretch the pastry. If it is necessary to patch the pastry, place a scrap of rolled pastry over the place to be patched and lightly press the edges to seal. Then, using your finger, lightly moisten the seam with cold water.

Continue the recipe, below, according to the type of pie to be baked.

NOTE: There are two purposes for brief refrigeration of the pastry: (1) to recool the lard, and (2) to allow a little time for the moisture in the pastry to be assimilated by the flour more evenly, thereby making the pastry easier to roll and handle.

BAKED PIE SHELL: Preheat the oven to 425° F.

Using kitchen scissors, trim the edge of the pastry to 1 inch beyond the edge of the pan. Roll the edge of the pastry *under,* evenly along the top of the pan rim. Roll small sections of pastry at a time. After rolling a section, press the pastry together to form a uniform, continuous

edge in the shape of a triangular peak over and around the pie pan rim. Then, flute the edge by flouring the end of a table knife handle and pressing it into the outside of the triangular pastry edge and against the thumb and index finger of your other hand on the inside of the triangular pastry edge to form a V. Repeat, making contiguous V's around the pan.

Using a table fork, prick the pastry every 1 inch around the side of the pan and every 1½ to 1¾ inches on the bottom of the pan. Bake for 10 to 12 minutes. If any bubbles form in the pastry after a few minutes of baking, prick them with a fork. Cool on a wire rack.

MAKES ENOUGH PASTRY FOR TWO 8- OR 9-INCH PIE SHELLS

NOTE: If only one pie shell is needed, the recipe may be halved; or, prepare the second pie shell for baking, then cover it with plastic wrap and freeze it. Remove the pie shell from the freezer 5 minutes before baking.

UNBAKED PIE SHELL: Follow the Baked Pie Shell procedure, above, omitting the pricking of the pastry and the baking.

TWO-CRUST PIE: Using kitchen scissors, trim the unbaked bottom-crust pastry evenly with the edge of the pan. Lay a piece of plastic wrap over the pastry-lined pan to prevent the pastry from drying; set aside. Remove the second portion of pastry from the refrigerator. Unwrap the pastry and place it on the lightly floured pastry cloth. Let the pastry stand 1 minute or so, just until soft enough to roll. Using the stockinet-covered, then lightly floured rolling pin, roll the top-crust pastry on the pastry cloth to about 1½ inches greater in diameter than an inverted pie pan of the same size as the one being used for the pie. Let the rolled pastry stand on the pastry cloth; cover it lightly with a piece of plastic wrap.

Remove the plastic wrap covering the pie pan and fill the pie, following a specific pie recipe. Remove the plastic wrap from the rolled top-crust pastry. Carefully run a thin spatula around and under the edge of the pastry to loosen it from the pastry cloth. Fold the pastry in half. Using a small, sharp knife, make several slits through both halves of the pastry near the folded edge to allow steam to escape during baking. Slits may be made evenly or in a decorative design.

Move the top-crust pastry to the filled pie and unfold. Using kitchen scissors, trim the top-crust pastry to ½ inch beyond the edge of the pan. Fold the edge of the top-crust pastry *under* the edge of the bottom-crust pastry along the top of the rim, and press the pastry together to form a uniform, continuous edge in the shape of a triangular peak over and around the pie pan rim. Flute the edge (follow the Baked Pie Shell procedures, page 393). Bake according to a specific pie recipe.

MAKES ENOUGH PASTRY FOR ONE 8- OR 9-INCH TWO-CRUST PIE

LATTICE-TOP PIE: Using kitchen scissors, trim the unbaked bottom-crust pastry to ½ inch beyond the edge of the pan. Lay a piece of plastic wrap over the pastry-lined pan to prevent the pastry from drying; set aside. Remove the second portion of pastry from the refrigerator. Unwrap the pastry and place it on the lightly floured pastry cloth. Let the pastry stand 1 minute or so, just until soft enough to roll. Using the stockinet-covered, then lightly floured rolling pin, roll the top-crust pastry on the pastry cloth to about 1½ inches greater in diameter than an inverted pie pan of the same size as the one being used for the pie. Using a sharp, thin-bladed, floured knife, cut 14 strips of pastry ⅝ inch wide. Wipe the knife with a paper towel and reflour before each cut. Let the cut pastry stand on the pastry cloth; cover lightly with a piece of plastic wrap.

Remove the plastic wrap covering the pie pan and fill the pie, following a specific pie recipe. Remove the plastic wrap covering the pastry strips. Place the 2 longest pastry strips crosswise across the center of the pie. Arrange 3 strips on each side of, and parallel to, the lower center strip, carefully folding back the intersecting center strip before adding every other new strip to create a weave. Then, arrange 3 strips on each side of, and parallel to, the other center strip,

folding back every other intersecting strip to form a weave (see illustration).

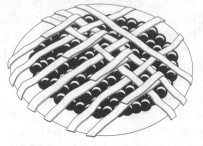

Using kitchen scissors, trim the lattice strips to ½ inch beyond the edge of the pan. Roll the bottom-crust pastry *over* the lattice strips along the top of the rim, and press the pastry together to form a uniform, continuous edge in the shape of a triangular peak over and around the pie pan rim. Flute the edge (follow the Baked Pie Shell procedures, page 461). Bake according to a specific pie recipe.

MAKES ENOUGH PASTRY FOR ONE 8- OR 9-INCH LATTICE-TOP PIE

1½ RECIPES OF PASTRY PIECRUST

3¼ cups plus 2 tablespoons sifted
    all-purpose flour (sift before measuring)
1½ teaspoons salt
1 cup plus 2 tablespoons refrigerated lard
½ cup refrigerated water

Follow the Pastry Piecrust recipe procedures.

MAKES ENOUGH PASTRY FOR ONE 8- OR 9-INCH TWO-CRUST PIE PLUS ONE 8- OR 9-INCH BAKED PIE SHELL

NOTE: For a wonderful snack, form a ball out of any leftover pastry; roll and place it on a cookie sheet or on the bottom of a pie pan. Using a table fork, prick the pastry every 1½ to 1¾ inches. Sprinkle the pastry with combined ground cinnamon and sugar (¼ teaspoon ground cinnamon per 1 teaspoon sugar). To bake, follow the Baked Pie Shell procedures, page 393. Cool on a wire rack and break off pieces to eat.

PASTRY PIECRUST TART SHELLS

Pastry Piecrust may be used to make tart shells of various sizes. These pastry shells are used to make tarts which are just small, standard pies. See page 442 for an explanation of the difference between pastry piecrust tarts and classical tarts. A recipe for Classical Tart Pastry may be found on page 401.

1 recipe Pastry Piecrust (page 392; see recipe procedures below)

Bake the tart shells in small aluminum tart pans measuring about 3 to 4½ inches in diameter, with *slanted* sides (like miniature pie pans). Aluminum-foil pans are not satisfactory.

Preheat the oven to 425° F.

Follow the Pastry Piecrust recipe through rolling the first portion of pastry as for a standard-sized pie. Invert a tart pan on, and near the edge of, the rolled pastry. Using a sharp, flour-dipped knife, cut a circle of pastry greater in diameter than the inverted pan, allowing sufficient pastry to fit into the pan and flute an edge proportionate in size to the small tart pan. Follow the Pastry Piecrust procedures for transferring and fitting the cutout pastry into the ungreased tart pan. Follow the Baked Pie Shell procedures (page 393) for forming and fluting the edge, and for pricking the pastry. The size of the V's in the fluting should be smaller, and the space between pricks in the pastry should be less than for a standard pie, and should be gauged in proportion to the size of the tart pan.

Cut and fit into the tart pans as many pastry circles as possible from the rolled pastry. Then, quickly gather the pastry scraps and lightly press them into a ball; reroll and cut additional circles. Roll the second portion of pastry and repeat the procedure. Unavoidably, the pastry rolled more than once will not be as flaky and tender as the pastry rolled only one time.

Bake the tart shells for approximately 10 minutes, depending upon the size of the pans. Watch carefully. If any bubbles form in the pastry after a few minutes of baking, prick them with a fork. The tart shells will be lightly brown when done. Cool on wire racks.

Baked Pastry Piecrust Tart Shells may be removed from the pans before or after filling. If the filling is heavy, it is safer to leave the shells in the pans until filled to avoid the risk of breaking the fragile crust even though filled tart shells are more difficult to remove from the pans. If the planned filling is light, the shells may be carefully removed from the pans after cooling and before filling.

SECRETS FOR MAKING SUCCESSFUL PASTRY PIECRUST

Many cooks consider good pastry piecrust to be one of the most difficult of all culinary undertakings. When piecrust ingredients are mixed to the optimum consistency for the production of first-class crust, the dough does not hold together well, making it difficult to gather and roll. In addition, humidity, room temperature, temperature of ingredients, and other factors affect the flour and fat, causing piecrust dough to be somewhat different each time you make it.

Nevertheless, these hurdles in no way should frighten away those who wish to master the challenge. As with most things, piecrust expertise takes study, patience, and practice, practice, practice. The satisfaction derived when family and friends rave about the incredibly luscious slice of pie you have placed in front of them, will more than offset the effort.

Many users of this cookbook are already accomplished piecrust bakers. For those readers desirous of joining the ranks, it is suggested that the recipe for Pastry Piecrust (page 392) be studied and followed carefully. The following additional hints and explanations should be of further assistance.

• The best pastry piecrust is made with lard. Fat acts to shorten the strands of gluten (the derivation of the term "shortening") in piecrust dough, thereby making the crust more tender. Lard is composed of relatively short-chain fatty acids which cover the gluten better than the longer-chain fatty acids found in hydrogenated vegetable shortening. By covering more area of gluten, short-chain fatty acids provide more tenderness.

In addition, lard adds the piquant flavor often associated with choice, homemade piecrust—a flavor which cannot be duplicated with other types of fat.

Commercial lard is readily available in most supermarkets. (If a baker does not wish to use lard, vegetable shortening may be substituted.)

- Use *cold* lard and water. Keep both refrigerated, even after measuring, until added to the piecrust mixture. Piecrust is made flaky, in part, by bits and pieces of lard melting during baking which create air spaces throughout the baked pastry. Warm lard will blend with the flour and not retain its particle integrity. Warm water will cause the lard to soften when added to the pastry mixture.

- From beginning to end, handle piecrust pastry *as little as possible.* In every step of the pastry-making procedure, this is one of the keys to retaining the distinct pieces of lard in the pastry and to preventing the lard from melting.

- Measure piecrust ingredients precisely. The ratio of ingredients is critical. Occasionally, a very slight variation in the amount of water called for in the recipe may be warranted. In a dry climate, and when the flour has low moisture content, it may be necessary to increase the water by 1 or 2 teaspoons in order to hold the dough together and roll it out without undue cracking. In addition, sometimes bits of unmoistened dough gravitate to the bottom of the bowl during mixing and remain there after the dough is gathered into balls, in which case a tiny amount of additional water may be sprinkled over the dry particles in the bottom of the bowl. Using a

fork, stir the mixture briefly; then, gather it and add it to the remainder of the dough.

In humid weather, slightly less water may be necessary than called for in the recipe. In any case, use only enough water to make workable dough. Too much water will cause the crust to be tough.

- Cut the measured lard into chunks about the diameter of a quarter before adding to the flour mixture. This will speed the cutting-in process and help achieve even distribution of the lard in the pastry.

- To cut the lard into the flour, use a pastry blender with thin, round wires (see illustration). This simple tool allows the greatest control of the cutting-in process.

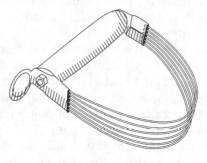

Pastry Blender

Hold the pastry blender firmly and use rapid, circular reverse folding-in motions. In other words, press the pastry blender against the front bottom of the mixing bowl to cut the lard, then push the blender away from you, about ⅔ of the way across the bottom of the bowl, and bring it up over the mixture and back toward you in a circular motion. Simultaneously, turn the mixing bowl with your free hand. Quickly cutting in the lard, using rapid motions, will keep the pastry light and airy.

Small chunks of lard will usually adhere to the wires of the pastry blender at the beginning of the cutting in process. Use a table knife to release lard stuck in the wires, and drop it back into the pastry mixture.

- It is critical to first cut in ⅔ of the lard until the mixture is the texture of cornmeal, and then to cut in the remaining ⅓ of the lard until the size of peas. The cornmeal texture is necessary for cohesion of the dough; the pea-sized pieces are necessary for flakiness. Follow closely the procedure for mixing the pastry ingredients described in the recipe for Pastry Piecrust (page 392).

- Piecrust dough of the best consistency tends to fall apart somewhat as it is gathered and formed into a ball and after the dough is placed on the pastry cloth. Cooks new to piecrust making will think the dough is too dry. However, when you commence to roll the dough, it will cohere and roll out smoothly. If the dough cracks throughout and does not hold together when rolled, it is, in fact, not moist enough. Experience is the best teacher in judging how much water to add when mixing the dough, though this is one of the biggest challenges even for expert piecrust bakers. Because of the necessity for handling the dough as little as possible, a significant measure of flakiness will be sacrificed if rolled-out dough is gathered, remixed, and rerolled.

- Roll the dough on a lightly floured pastry cloth, using a stockinet-covered, then lightly floured rolling pin (see To Use a Pastry Cloth and a Stockinet-Covered Rolling Pin, page 38).

- Roll out the dough with as few strokes as possible. Start by lightly rolling the dough to further flatten it. If needed, smooth the edges again with your hands, but only to the extent that you can do so speedily and with minimal touching of the pastry. Then, roll from the center of the dough to the edge. Let up on the pressure slightly as you reach the edge. This will help prevent the edge both from splitting and becoming too thin; however, it is virtually impossible to eliminate all edge splitting.

When a split occurs in the edge of the pastry during the rolling process, stop rolling and cut a small piece of pastry from any protruding edge of the circle of pastry. Place the cutaway piece of pastry over the split, like a patch. Carefully roll over the patch once or twice, rolling parallel with the pastry edge nearest the patch rather than rolling outward from the center. This is usually sufficient to bind the patch to the pastry without the use of water as a sealer. Final rolling of the entire pastry circle will often totally blend the patch with the remainder of the pastry, making the patched section indistinguishable.

(To illustrate the edge-splitting problem, some seasoned entrants in state fair pie competitions make 1½ recipes of dough when preparing a pie for entry. The extra dough allows the entrant to roll out a larger circle of pastry than required and cut off a significant amount of edge, thus averting the possible need to patch the edge which might be noticed by a perceptive judge.)

- Use dull, metal pie pans, such as those made of anodized aluminum. Shiny pie pans reflect heat, making it more difficult to produce properly browned, nonsoggy, bottom crusts. On the other hand, very dark pie pans should be avoided as they contribute to overbrowning. Do not use nonstick, slick-coated pie pans. Glass pie plates are acceptable to use because they absorb and distribute heat evenly; however, I prefer to use metal pie pans.

- After unfolding the pastry in the pie pan, fit it gently against the bottom and sides of the pan. Avoid stretching the pastry, which will cause it to shrink when baked. To prevent stretching, after unfolding the pastry, use one hand to lift the edge of the pastry which overhangs the pan (relieving the tautness), while fitting the pastry into the pan with the other hand. When fitting, do not press the pastry against the pan, but gently ease it into place, trying to make sure that it touches the bottom and side of the pan, and that no air pockets are trapped between the pastry and the pan. These procedures will help prevent pie shells from blistering during baking and help keep the pastry lining the side of the pie pan from slipping down during baking.

Properly pricking the bottom and sides of pie shells with a fork before baking is also an important factor in holding the pastry in place. Pricking helps prevent pockets of steam from forming between the crust and the pie pan.

Some recipes advocate the use of weights, such as beans, to hold pie shell pastry in place during baking. This procedure is counterproductive to attaining the flaky crust the baker is so laboriously trying to achieve. Flakiness results from air spaces in the baked crust; weights delete air spaces.

• To mold a fluted pastry edge on *baked and unbaked pie shells,* use your fingers to roll small sections of the overhanging pastry (about 1½ inches at a time) *under* (not over), until the rolled section is situated over the top of the pie pan rim. (The pastry seam will be *under* the rolled edge and not visible.)

Immediately after rolling a section of overhanging pastry, lightly mold it with your fingers into an upright triangular peak situated directly over the rim of the pan. Repeat the rolling and molding procedure around the pie, trying to make the continuous triangular peak as uniform in size and shape as possible.

If a section of overhanging pastry seems too long or too thick as you roll and mold the pastry around the pan, trim some of it away with kitchen scissors before commencing to roll that particular section. Should a section of overhanging pastry be too short or too thin, carefully hold a small, extra piece of rolled-out pastry *under* the overhanging pastry and roll the extra pastry into the roll.

Follow the procedures in Baked Pie Shell (page 393) to flute the molded triangular pastry peak around the pie pan, taking care to keep the fluted pastry edge directly on *top* of the rim. If the fluted pastry edge hangs over the outside of the pie pan rim, it will most likely sag over the edge of the pan during baking. Conversely, if the fluted pastry edge is too close to the inside of the pan, it may cause both the fluted edge and the pastry against the side of the pan to slip downward into the pan during baking.

• To mold a fluted pastry edge on a *two-crust pie,* fold the overhanging upper-crust pastry *under* the bottom-crust pastry, which has been trimmed evenly with the edge of the pie pan (see procedures for Two-Crust Pie, page 393). After all the overhanging upper-crust pastry has been folded under the bottom-crust pastry, use your fingers to lightly mold the pastry around the edge of the pan into an upright triangular peak situated *directly over* the rim of the pan, pressing the 2 crusts together to seal. Then, flute the triangular pastry peak. The technique for molding the triangular peak on a two-crust pie is similar to that employed when preparing a baked pie shell; the procedure for fluting is identical (see Baked Pie Shell, page 393).

• To mold a fluted pastry edge on a *lattice-top pie,* roll the overhanging bottom-crust pastry *over* the overhanging lattice strips. (Roll the edge pastry in the opposite direction from rolling the edge on a baked pie shell or a two-crust pie.) As the bottom-crust pastry and lattice strips are rolled together, gently pull the lattice strips taut to help prevent them from sinking beneath the surface of the pie filling near the outer edge of the pie. At the same time, keep the ends of the lattice strips in their straight lines as the overhanging bottom-crust pastry is rolled over them. This can be slightly tricky, as the lattice strips, laid at right angles, must be molded angularly to form the circular edge around the pan, but the know-how will be acquired after practicing a few times.

After all the edge pastry has been rolled, use your fingers to lightly mold an upright triangular peak situated *directly over* the rim of the pan, pressing the bottom-crust pastry and the lattice-top pastry together. Then, flute the triangular pastry peak, following the procedure in Baked Pie Shell (page 393).

Contrary to baked pie shells and two-crust pies, the pastry seam on the edge of a lattice-top pie is visible at the inner base of the triangular pastry peak. Fluting helps disguise the seam.

• While edge pastry must be handled more than the pastry in the rest of a pie, the cardinal rule still prevails: handle pastry as little and as quickly as possible to retain optimal flakiness. It helps to rinse your hands in cold water (wipe them completely dry) before flouring them to handle pastry. Warm hands melt the pieces of lard you are trying to retain in the pastry before baking.

• When the pie filling is to be baked in the pie, it should not be added until the last possible moment to best preserve the composition integrity of the bottom crust. Filling allowed to stand in unbaked bottom-crust pastry can cause the bottom crust to become soggy and lose much of its flakiness. At best, the bottom crust of a baked filled pie is not as flaky as the top and edge crust due to the moisture and weight of the filling on the bottom pastry during baking.

When making a two-crust or lattice-top pie, prepare the filling before commencing to mix the pastry (pastry ingredients may be premeasured, of course). Roll and fit the bottom-crust pastry in the pie pan. Then, lay a piece of plastic wrap over the pan to prevent the pastry from drying out. Quickly roll the top-crust pastry, (and cut strips if making a lattice-top pie). Lay a piece of plastic wrap over the rolled top-crust pastry. *Then,* place the filling in the pastry-lined pan, arrange the top-crust pastry, and flute the edge as expeditiously as possible. Immediately place the pie in a thoroughly preheated oven, being careful not to tilt the pie in transit, causing the filling to wash against the edge.

• Pastry-crust pies should be served the same day they are baked. Pastry crust is never as good as it is in the immediate few hours after a pie has cooled. Moisture absorbed from the pie filling and refrigeration (if required) causes the crust to lose a measure of its crispness, lightness, and flakiness. For the very best results, freshly baked pies not requiring refrigeration should be kept uncovered on wire racks—for total circulation—in a relatively cool, dry part of the house until served. Covering pies or leaving them in a steamy kitchen will allow moisture to infuse the crust. (I keep baked pies which do not require refrigeration on wire racks on the dining-room buffet until mealtime.)

Cream and custard pies must be served soon after they have cooled; otherwise, they must be refrigerated for food safety. Therefore, timing of the baking or filling of these pies must be gauged to the planned serving time if refrigeration is to be avoided. This timing factor becomes even more critical with meringue-topped pies, which not only should be eaten the day they are made, but also should not be refrigerated before serving, if possible. Refrigeration causes meringue to become tough and to shrink.

Of course, some types of pastry-crust pies require refrigeration before serving; for example, pies topped or decorated with whipped cream, and chiffon pies which all must be refrigerated to set and to retain the consistency of their fillings. Such pastry-crust pies should be stored in the refrigerator *uncovered* on a wire rack until serving time. This allows more air to circulate around the crust and generally leads to less moisture absorption than when covered. Of course, make certain that other foods stored in the refrigerator are covered to avoid the transfer of other food flavors to the pie. Whipped cream topping and decoration are especially prone to this hazard.

• If a pastry-crust pie requiring refrigeration must be made the day before serving, store it in the refrigerator on a wire rack placed in a plastic pie container. Tilt the container cover to allow for some air circulation and prevent the surface of the pie filling from drying out. Under any circumstance, whipped cream topping and decoration should be applied near the time of serving to avert the possibility of the whipped cream weeping onto the filling.

- If time restrictions require it, pastry pie shells may be baked the day before they are filled and served if they are stored at room temperature in an airtight container standing on a wire rack. Some quality will be sacrificed.

- *Unbaked* pastry pie shells may be frozen (see the Note under Baked Pie Shell, page 393); however, when baked, the crust will be less flaky and slightly tough.

- After serving, most leftover fruit pies may be stored at room temperature for 1 or 2 days. Loosely covering them in a plastic pie container will help prevent the filling from drying out. All other leftover pies should be covered and refrigerated.

TO MAKE ALUMINUM FOIL EDGE-COVERS FOR PIES

When a pie requires a lengthy period of baking, its fluted pastry edge usually overbrowns if not covered with aluminum foil during part of the baking time.

To make a foil edge-cover, cut aluminum foil into three 4 × 12-inch pieces, and one 4 × 4-inch piece. Staple the pieces together to form one continuous 4-inch-wide strip. Then, staple the two ends together to form a circle. Stand the aluminum foil circle around a 9-inch pie pan. Using your hands, *very loosely* crinkle the foil around the rim of the pie pan, fashioning a cover which can be easily dropped over the edge of pies without damaging the pastry.

TO DECORATE PASTRY PIECRUST

CUTOUT PASTRY DECORATIONS: To decorate the top of Pastry Piecrust (page 392) with applied, cutout pastry decorations, roll the pastry as for piecrust. Using flour-dipped, small cutters in the design of stars, flowers, leaves, letters of the alphabet, or other designs, carefully cut out desired pastry designs. Wipe the cutters with a paper towel and reflour before each cut. Or, using a flour-dipped X-Acto knife, cut out pastry of your own design.

Place an egg white in a small sauce dish; using a table fork, beat until foamy. Using a small, soft watercolor brush, apply a small amount of the egg white to the back of each pastry cutout and arrange on the surface of the *unbaked* pastry to be decorated, pressing softly to cement. No alteration in baking time or procedure is required. Follow the recipe for the item being prepared.

EGG WHITE GLAZE: Place an egg white in a small sauce dish; using a table fork, beat until foamy. Using a very soft brush, lightly apply a thin layer of egg white over the *unbaked* pastry, omitting any fluted edge. No alteration in baking time or procedure is required. Bake according to the recipe for the item being prepared. When the pastry has reached the desired golden color during baking, cover it lightly with a piece of aluminum foil and continue baking.

SUGAR GLAZE: Using your fingers or a very small spoon (such as a demitasse spoon), sprinkle sanding sugar (see Note) or granulated sugar over the top crust of a two-crust pie or the lattice crust of a lattice-top pie (omitting the fluted edge) 10 minutes prior to completion of baking. No alteration in baking time or procedure is required. Return the pastry to the oven and bake, uncovered, at the temperature called for in the recipe.

Sugar glaze adds a special glisten to two-crust and lattice-top fruit pies—that final touch which makes a beautifully made pie even more appealing.

NOTE: Sanding sugar has crystals larger in size than granulated sugar, and is often used by professional bakers to decorate the tops of cookies, pastry, and other baked items. Sanding sugar makes a particularly noticeable and handsome decoration. In addition to white, it is available in a host of nice colors. Your local baker may be a source for sanding sugar, or it can be ordered from Sweet Celebrations Inc. (see Product Sources, page 631).

CLASSICAL TART PASTRY

Classical Tart Pastry differs considerably from Pastry Piecrust (page 442) in the ingredients used, the techniques employed, and the texture after baking. Baked Classical Tart Pastry is similar in consistency and taste to a rich cookie. Baked in special tart pans with removable rims, it is used when making classical tarts (see page 442) for more information). Recipes for classical tarts, using this recipe, may be found on pages 401–402.

1 cup plus 1 tablespoon sifted all-purpose
    flour (sift before measuring)
2 tablespoons sugar
½ teaspoon salt
¼ cup plus 2 tablespoons (6 tablespoons)
    butter, softened
2 extra large egg yolks, slightly beaten with a
    fork
½ teaspoon pure vanilla extract

Set out a 9-inch tart pan with a removable, perpendicular, ⅞-inch-high, fluted rim.

Onto waxed paper, sift together the flour, sugar, and salt. Place the flour mixture in a medium mixing bowl. Using a tablespoon, make a well in the center of the flour mixture. Place the butter, egg yolks, and vanilla in the well. Using an electric mixer, beat on medium speed *only until all the ingredients are combined;* guard against overbeating.

Using floured hands, quickly gather the pastry into a ball, handling as little as possible. Using a stockinet-covered, then lightly floured rolling pin (page 38), roll the pastry on a lightly floured pastry cloth (page 38) to 1 inch greater in diameter than the inverted tart-pan rim. Carefully run a thin spatula around and under the edge of the pastry to loosen it from the pastry cloth.

Place the ungreased, inverted tart pan (bottom and rim) on the center of the pastry. Place a wire rack over the inverted tart pan. With both hands, hold the wire rack and the pastry cloth (pulled somewhat tautly); invert quickly. Carefully peel the pastry cloth off the pastry.

With floured hands, quickly and gently fit the pastry into the pan. Pull the extra pastry overlapping the pan back into the pan and press it into the pastry lining the pan rim, thereby making the pastry lining the rim of the pan slightly thicker than the pastry on the bottom of the pan. As you press the extra pastry against the inside of the pan rim, mold the top of the pastry to make it flat and even with the top of the rim. Do not be concerned if the rim of the pan cuts through some of the pastry when inverting the tart pan. If this happens, simply press the severed portions of pastry into the inside of the pan rim, smoothing it into the pastry lining.

Using a table fork, prick the pastry on the *bottom* of the pan at 1-inch intervals in a circle around the periphery of the pan, about ⅛ inch from the edge. Then, prick the remainder of the pastry on the *bottom* of the pan at 1½- to 1¾-inch intervals (see illustration). Do not prick the side pastry. Refrigerate the tart shell, uncovered, for 1½ hours.

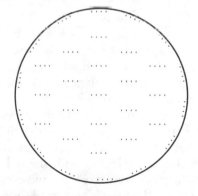

Preheat the oven to 350°F.

Remove the tart pan from the refrigerator and place it on a wire rack. Leave the tart pan on the wire rack and immediately place the tart pan *and* rack in the oven on the middle shelf. Bake for 13 to 15 minutes, until golden brown. If any bubbles form in the pastry on the bottom

(Recipe continues on next page)

of the pan after a few minutes of baking, prick them with a fork. If any pastry on the sides of the pan falls down, use a table fork to press it back into the pan rim.

Place the baked tart shell on a wire rack to cool. (To avoid scorching the countertop, use a wire rack different from the one used under the tart pan during baking.) Do not remove the pan rim until just before serving or displaying the tart. This will help prevent the side pastry from breaking off when handling and filling the tart shell. Always leave the pan bottom under the tart.

MAKES ONE 9-INCH CLASSICAL TART SHELL

TARTLET SHELLS

Made in teeny tartlet tins, these pastry shells are usually artistically filled and decorated with tantalizing hors d'oeuvre savories or seductive dessert dainties.

3 ounces cream cheese, softened
½ cup (¼ pound) butter, softened
¼ teaspoon salt
1 cup plus 2 tablespoons all-purpose flour

Preheat the oven to 400° F.

Place the cream cheese in a small mixing bowl; using an electric mixer, beat on high speed until creamy. Add the butter and salt; continue beating on high speed until blended. Add the flour; using a spoon, stir to combine.

With floured hands, form the dough into ¾-inch-diameter balls. Press each pastry ball firmly into the bottom and sides of an ungreased, tiny, 1¾-inch fluted tartlet tin with slanted sides, molding the pastry to make it flat and even with the top edge of the tin. Using a small fork, prick the pastry in each tartlet tin twice.

Place the pastry-lined tartlet tins on a cookie pan (with 1-inch sides). Bake the Tartlet Shells for 11 to 12 minutes, until golden in color. Remove from the oven and place the cookie pan on a wire rack. Cool the Tartlet Shells 2 minutes.

Remove the shells from the tins by inverting them, one at a time, in your hands. Place the Tartlet Shells on waxed paper; let stand until completely cool. Store the Tartlet Shells, single layer, in an airtight container until ready to fill.

MAKES ABOUT 3 DOZEN

SERVING SUGGESTIONS: These Tartlet Shells contain no sugar and may be filled with either nonsweet or sweet foods.

PUFF PASTRY SHELLS (PATTY SHELLS)

These pretty-looking, flaky, individual "containers" or shells made of puff pastry are filled with creamed poultry, shellfish, fish, meat, egg, or vegetable refinements and are often served as the main course for luncheons, brunches, or late suppers (see Chicken à la King, page 174; Deviled Tuna on Patty Shells, page 188; and Eggsotic Eggs, page 225). Commercial, frozen puff pastry makes light work of these poufy niceties.

1 17¼-ounce package (2 sheets) frozen puff pastry
2 extra-large egg yolks
2 teaspoons half-and-half

Remove the frozen pastry sheets from the sealed inner package and let them stand, folded, at room temperature 30 minutes to thaw. Meanwhile, in a small sauce dish, place the egg yolks and half-and-half; using a table fork, beat to blend; set aside.

Preheat the oven to 350° F.

On a lightly floured pastry cloth (page 38), carefully unfold the pastry sheets. Using a stockinet-covered, then lightly floured rolling pin (page 38), roll each pastry sheet to a 9½ × 9½-inch square. Using a floured, 3-inch round cutter, cut 9 pastry circles from each sheet of pastry. Then, using a floured, 2⅛-inch round cutter, cut an inner circle ⅔ through the pastry on each 3-inch circle (see illustration).

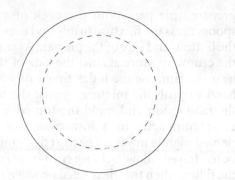

Place the 18 pastry circles on an ungreased cookie sheet. Using a soft brush, brush the *top* of the circles lightly with the egg yolk mixture. Do not allow the egg yolk mixture to drip down the sides of the pastry, as the mixture will act as an adhesive and prevent the pastry from rising evenly. Using a table fork, prick each pastry circle several times. Bake for 18 to 20 minutes, until golden in color.

Immediately upon removal from the oven, use a small, thin-bladed knife to loosen and help remove the inner circles which were cut ⅔ through the pastry on each pastry circle. A base of pastry will remain within each circle. The removed inner circles may be retained and used as lids on filled Puff Pastry Shells, if desired. Remove any damp pastry which may remain on the underside of the pastry lids. Carefully place the Puff Pastry Shells and lids on wire cookie racks; let stand until completely cool. Store, uncovered, if the shells will be used within 12 hours; otherwise, store in a container with the cover ajar to permit the circulation of air.

MAKES 1½ DOZEN 3½-INCH-ROUND PUFF PASTRY SHELLS (PATTY SHELLS)

4½-INCH-SQUARE PUFF PASTRY SHELLS

Follow the Puff Pastry Shells (Patty Shells) recipe, above, through rolling each pastry sheet to a 9½ × 9½-inch square.

Preheat the oven to 350° F.

Using a sharp, thin-bladed, floured knife and a ruler to measure, cut four 4-inch squares of pastry from each pastry sheet. Place the 8 pastry squares on an ungreased cookie sheet. Using a soft brush, brush the *top* (not the sides) of the squares lightly with the egg yolk mixture. From the remaining rolled pastry, cut:

16 pastry strips, ⅜ inch wide by 4 inches long; and

16 pastry strips, ⅜ inch wide by 3¼ inches long.

See illustration A for cutting each pastry sheet.

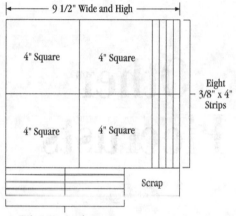

Illustration A

Lay two 4-inch pastry strips and two 3¼-inch pastry strips flat on top of each 4-inch pastry square along all 4 edges (see illustration B).

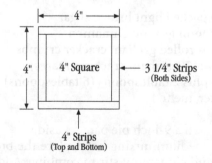

Illustration B

The pastry strips should abut but not overlap. Using a soft brush, brush the *top* (not the sides)

(Recipe continues on next page)

of the strips lightly with the egg yolk mixture. Using a table fork, prick the bottoms of the squares several times. Bake for 18 to 20 minutes, until golden in color. Check after 5 minutes of baking; if the bottoms of the shells have puffed up, prick the puffed areas with a fork.

When done, use a thin spatula to carefully place the shells on wire cookie racks to cool. Follow the Puff Pastry Shells (Patty Shells) recipe for storage procedure.

MAKES EIGHT 4½-INCH-SQUARE PUFF PASTRY SHELLS (PATTY SHELLS)

prepared pie pan. With the back of a tablespoon, press the mixture firmly and evenly over the bottom and side of the pie pan. As you press the crumb mixture against the side of the pan near the rim, use the index finger of your free hand to push the mixture against the back of the tablespoon and mold the top edge of the crust compactly in a low triangular shape slanted slightly inward. The top edge should not be left frayed, allowing loose crumbs to fall onto the filling when the pie is filled or when it is cut for serving. (Do not cover the top of the pie pan rim with the mixture.)

Refrigerate the crust; let stand in the refrigerator at least 15 minutes before filling. (This crust may be baked after filling if called for in a recipe.)

MAKES ONE 9-INCH PIE SHELL

Other Piecrusts

UNBAKED GRAHAM CRACKER CRUST

⅓ cup packed light brown sugar
½ teaspoon ground cinnamon
1½ cups rolled graham cracker crumbs (about 20 graham cracker squares)
¼ cup plus 2 tablespoons (6 tablespoons) butter, melted

Butter well a 9-inch pie pan; set aside.

In a medium mixing bowl, place the brown sugar and cinnamon; stir to combine. Add the graham cracker crumbs; stir until well combined. Add the melted butter; stir until the mixture is crumbly in texture.

Place the crumb mixture in the bottom of the

BAKED GRAHAM CRACKER CRUST

Crumb crusts are light years easier to make than Pastry Piecrust, and they're scrumptious when matched with appropriate fillings. Two of my favorite pies using the Baked Graham Cracker Crust recipe that follows are Graham Cracker Fudge Pie (page 420) and Glazed Fresh Blueberry Pie (page 411).

1½ cups rolled graham cracker crumbs (about 20 graham cracker squares)
¼ cup granulated sugar
¼ cup plus 2 tablespoons (6 tablespoons) butter, softened

Preheat the oven to 350° F.

In a medium mixing bowl, place the graham cracker crumbs and sugar; stir to combine. Cut the butter into approximately 8 pieces and drop into the bowl containing the graham cracker crumb mixture. Using a pastry blender, cut the butter into the crumb mixture until the mixture is crumbly in texture.

Place the crumb mixture in the bottom of an

ungreased 9-inch pie pan. With the back of a tablespoon, press the mixture firmly and evenly over the bottom and side of the pie pan. As you press the crumb mixture against the side of the pan near the rim, use the index finger of your free hand to push the mixture against the back of the tablespoon and mold the top edge of the crust compactly in a low triangular shape slanted slightly inward. The top edge should not be left frayed, allowing loose crumbs to fall onto the filling when the pie is filled or when it is cut for serving. (Do not cover the top of the pie pan rim with the mixture.)

Bake the crust for 8 minutes. Baking causes very little change in the appearance of the crust. Remove the piecrust from the oven and place on a wire rack to cool before filling.

MAKES ONE 9-INCH PIE SHELL

BAKED NUTMEG GRAHAM CRACKER CRUST

Follow the Baked Graham Cracker Crust recipe, above, adding 1/2 teaspoon ground nutmeg to the mixing bowl containing the graham cracker crumbs and sugar before stirring to combine.

MAKES ONE 9-INCH PIE SHELL

MERINGUE PIE SHELL

4 extra-large egg whites, room temperature
1/4 teaspoon cream of tartar
1 cup superfine sugar

Preheat the oven to 275°F. Butter *well* a 9-inch pie pan; set aside.

In a medium mixing bowl, place the egg whites and cream of tartar; using an electric mixer, beat on high speed until soft peaks hold. While continuing to beat on high speed, very gradually sprinkle the sugar over the egg white mixture. Beat until the sugar completely dissolves and the meringue is stiff but still glossy (about 3 minutes, after commencing to add the sugar).

Using a small, narrow, angled spatula, spread the meringue evenly on the bottom and up the sides (not on the rim) of the prepared pie pan, reserving enough meringue to pipe a border, if desired.

If a piped border is planned, the meringue up the side of the pan should be 1/2 inch thick with a flat, smooth, top edge, even with the rim. Using a decorating bag fit with medium-large open-star tip number 32 (page 319), pipe a zigzag border (page 324) of meringue on top of the 1/2-inch meringue edge. Do not pipe the border on the rim of the pie pan.

Bake the meringue shell for 55 minutes. When done, the meringue will be ivory colored and crusty. It is normal if the meringue cracks slightly. Cool the shell on a wire rack in a non-humid place away from drafts.

MAKES ONE 9-INCH PIE SHELL

GINGERSNAP CRUST

1 1/3 cups finely rolled gingersnap crumbs
   (about twenty 2-inch gingersnap cookies)
1/4 cup plus 2 tablespoons (6 tablespoons)
   butter, softened

Preheat the oven to 350°F.

Place the gingersnap crumbs in a medium mixing bowl. Cut the butter into approximately 8 pieces and drop into the bowl containing the gingersnap crumbs. Using a pastry blender, cut the butter into the crumbs until the mixture is crumbly in texture.

Place the crumb mixture in the bottom of an ungreased 9-inch pie pan. With the back of a tablespoon, press the mixture firmly and evenly over the bottom and side of the pie pan. As you press the crumb mixture against the side of the pan near the rim, use the index finger of your free hand to push the mixture against the back of the tablespoon and mold the top edge of the crust compactly in a low triangular shape slanted slightly inward. The top edge should not

(Recipe continues on next page)

be left frayed, allowing loose crumbs to fall onto the filling when the pie is filled or when it is cut for serving. (Do not cover the top of the pie pan rim with the mixture.)

Bake the crust for 8 minutes. Baking causes very little change in the appearance of the crust. Remove the piecrust from the oven and place on a wire rack to cool before filling.

MAKES ONE 9-INCH PIE SHELL

10-INCH GINGERSNAP CRUST PIE SHELL

1¾ cups finely rolled gingersnap crumbs
  (about 26 2-inch gingersnap cookies)
½ cup (¼ pound) butter, softened

Follow the Gingersnap Crust recipe, above, substituting a 10-inch pie pan for a 9-inch pan.

MAKES ONE 10-INCH PIE SHELL

UNBAKED VANILLA WAFER CRUST

Ice cream pies frequently are made using crumb crusts. The pleasingly rich vanilla flavor of this crumb crust pairs well with butter brickle ice cream and a touch of chunky peanut butter in Peanut Butter Brickle Ice Cream Pie (page 596) to create a just-right, refreshing finale to a substantial dinner.

1½ cups rolled vanilla wafer crumbs (about
  33 vanilla wafers)
1 teaspoon pure vanilla extract
¼ cup plus 2 tablespoons (6 tablespoons)
  butter, melted

Place the vanilla wafer crumbs in a medium mixing bowl; set aside. Add the vanilla to the melted butter; stir to blend. Pour the butter mixture over the crumbs; stir until the mixture is crumbly in texture.

Place the crumb mixture in the bottom of an ungreased 9-inch pie pan. With the back of a tablespoon, press the mixture firmly and evenly over the bottom and side of the pie pan. As you

press the crumb mixture against the side of the pan near the rim, use the index finger of your free hand to push the mixture against the back of the tablespoon and mold the top edge of the crust compactly in a low triangular shape slanted slightly inward. The top edge should not be left frayed, allowing loose crumbs to fall onto the filling when the pie is filled or when it is cut for serving. (Do not cover the top of the pie pan rim with the mixture.)

Refrigerate the crust; let stand in the refrigerator at least 15 minutes before filling.

MAKES ONE 9-INCH PIE SHELL

Meringue Pie Topping

3 extra-large egg whites, room temperature
¼ teaspoon cream of tartar
Dash of salt
½ teaspoon clear vanilla
¼ cup plus 2 tablespoons superfine sugar

Preheat the oven to 350°F.

Place the egg whites in a medium mixing bowl; using an electric mixer, beat on high speed until foamy. Add the cream of tartar and salt; continue beating on high speed until soft peaks hold. Add the vanilla. While continuing to beat on high speed, very gradually add the sugar. Beat until the sugar dissolves and the meringue is stiff but still glossy (about 2½ minutes after commencing to add the sugar).

Spoon part of the meringue onto the outer portions of slightly cooled filling (see Note) in a 9-inch pie pan. Using a small, narrow, angled spatula, spread the meringue around the edge of the pie, making certain that it touches the inner edge of the piecrust to seal the meringue and help prevent shrinkage. Mound the remainder of the meringue in the center of the pie. Using the spatula, briefly spread the meringue to distribute the topping symmetrically. Then, using the back of the spatula, swirl the meringue to form attractive peaks.

Bake the meringue-topped pie for 5 minutes. Reduce the heat to 325°F and continue baking for 7 to 10 minutes, until the meringue is golden. If the meringue reaches the desired golden color prior to baking 12 minutes, turn off the oven and leave the pie in the oven until 12 minutes have elapsed.

Remove the pie from the oven and place on a wire rack in a fairly warm location away from drafts; let stand until cool.

NOTE: The filling should still be quite warm when the meringue topping is added. This will help assure that the underside of the meringue cooks and does not weep onto the filling.

When making meringue to top a cream-type pie, let the cooked filling cool slightly on a wire rack before pouring it into the pie shell. Let the filled pie shell stand on a wire rack while immediately proceeding to make the meringue. Some degree of flakiness is sacrificed when pastry piecrust is filled with a warm to hot filling, but that is the unavoidable nature of meringue-topped pies.

MAKES ENOUGH MERINGUE TO TOP ONE 9-INCH PIE

TWO-EGG-WHITES MERINGUE

Ingredient amounts for Meringue Pie Topping for one 8-inch pie, or for use with pie recipes calling for 2 extra-large egg yolks in the filling:

2 extra-large egg whites, room temperature
¼ teaspoon cream of tartar
Dash of salt
¼ teaspoon clear vanilla
¼ cup superfine sugar

Follow the Meringue Pie Topping recipe procedures above.

MAKES ENOUGH MERINGUE TO TOP ONE 8-INCH PIE

FOUR-EGG-WHITES MERINGUE

Ingredient amounts for Meringue Pie Topping for one 10-inch pie, or for use with pie recipes calling for 4 extra-large egg yolks in the filling:

4 extra-large egg whites, room temperature
½ teaspoon cream of tartar
⅛ teaspoon salt
½ teaspoon clear vanilla
½ cup superfine sugar

Follow the Meringue Pie Topping recipe procedures above.

MAKES ENOUGH MERINGUE TO TOP ONE 10-INCH PIE

Pies

Types of Dessert Pies

Dessert pies may be classified into the following seven general types based upon their fillings:

FRUIT PIES: Standard fruit pies are filled with whole, sliced, or cut-up fruit—usually fresh—sweetened with sugar and thickened with flour, cornstarch, or quick-cooking tapioca. Most are baked with 2 crusts.

Another type of fruit pie consists of a baked pie shell in which fresh fruit is arranged and then covered with a sweet, translucent glaze. Whipped cream is often piped decoratively over portions of the glaze.

CREAM PIES: Cream pies have a soft, pudding-type filling made with egg yolks, milk, sugar, and flavoring, and thickened with cornstarch or flour. Fruits, such as bananas or peaches, may be mixed with the cream filling. Cooked cream pie fillings are poured into baked pie shells and are generally topped with meringue or whipped cream.

CUSTARD PIES: Custard pies are simply custards baked in a pie shell. The basic custard ingredients are eggs, milk, sugar, and flavoring. Other ingredients, such as pumpkin or fruits, may be added.

SYRUP-BASED NUT PIES: Syrup-based nut pies are made with syrup or molasses, eggs, butter, sugar, flavoring, and nuts. The fillings bake to a transparent, jellylike consistency, and the nuts rise to cover the top of the pies. Pecan pie is the best known example of this type of pie.

CHIFFON PIES: Chiffon pies are light, airy pies made by folding stiffly beaten egg whites—and sometimes whipped cream, as well—into a very thick mixture of egg yolks, unflavored gelatin, sugar, flavoring, and milk or other liquid, which has been cooked in a double boiler and cooled to room temperature. Pieces of fruit or other additions may also be folded into the filling. Chiffon filling is usually piled high in the pie shell and is often topped with whipped cream.

CHEESE PIES: Dessert cheese pies most often have as principal ingredients, cream cheese, eggs, sugar, and flavoring, which are beaten only until blended and smooth. The cheese filling is usually baked in a graham cracker crust which lines a standard pie pan, or occasionally, a spring-form pan. Or, the filling may be baked in a pastry shell. Fresh fruit, such as berries, is commonly arranged over the chilled filling and then covered with a translucent glaze. Some cheese pies are made with cottage cheese.

CHEESE PIE CONTRASTED WITH CHEESECAKE: While, very commonly, no distinction is made between cheese pie and cheesecake, I distinguish between the two by ascribing the following characteristics to cheesecake: Cheesecake

- Is deeper in size than cheese pie and is most always baked in a springform pan.

- Usually has a very thin crust of either a special pastry or finely ground crumbs which are often, though not always, made with zwieback.

- Often has flour as an ingredient.

- Commonly has a baked sour cream topping or is served with a fruit sauce spooned over individual servings.

(See page 588 for Cheesecake recipe.)

ICE CREAM PIES (SEE PAGE 596 FOR RECIPES): Ice cream pies consist of ice cream—plain, mixed with other ingredients, or layered with other fillings—frozen in a crumb crust or a baked pastry shell. They may be topped with crumbs, meringue, or various garnishes and decorations such as whipped cream, chopped nuts, and fruit. The toppings are added before the pie is frozen or at serving time, depending upon the type.

Fruit Pies

APPLE PIE

The All-American pie!

¾ cup sugar
2 tablespoons plus 2 teaspoons all-purpose
   flour
1 teaspoon ground cinnamon
¼ teaspoon ground nutmeg
Dash of salt
7 cups Golden Delicious apples sliced
   ⅛ inch thick (about 6 medium apples)
Pastry Piecrust for 1 9-inch lattice-top pie
   (page 393)*
2 tablespoons butter, melted
Sanding sugar (see Sugar Glaze, page 400) or
   granulated sugar to decorate lattice crust

* *If desired, a plain top crust may be substituted for a lattice top (see Two-Crust Pie, page 393).*

In a small mixing bowl, place ¾ cup sugar, flour, cinnamon, nutmeg, and salt; stir to combine; set aside. Wash the apples. Pare, quarter, core, and slice the apples. Measure 7 cups sliced apples and place in a large mixing bowl. Sprinkle the sugar mixture over the apples; using a mixing spoon, toss lightly until the apple slices are coated. Let the apple mixture stand.

Preheat the oven to 400°F.

Prepare the pastry. Line the pie pan with the bottom-crust pastry. Lay a piece of plastic wrap lightly over the pie pan to prevent the pastry from drying; set aside. Roll the top-crust pastry; cut 14 pastry strips. Leave the cut strips on the pastry cloth; cover lightly with a piece of plastic wrap; let stand.

Add the butter to the apple mixture; stir to combine. Remove the plastic wrap covering the pie pan. Spoon the apple mixture evenly over the bottom-crust pastry. Remove the plastic wrap covering the pastry strips. Arrange the lattice-top pastry on the pie and flute the edge.

Bake the pie for 1 hour. After 15 minutes baking, drop an aluminum foil edge-cover (page 400) over the fluted edge of the pie to prevent overbrowning. After 25 minutes total baking, rotate the pie 180 degrees in the oven to help achieve even browning. When the lattice crust reaches the desired golden color (after approximately 25 minutes total baking), lay a piece of aluminum foil loosely over the entire pie (including the foil edge-cover). After 50 minutes total baking, remove the foil from the top and edge of the pie. Then, remove the pie from the oven. Using your fingers or a very small spoon (such as a demitasse spoon), sprinkle the sanding sugar lightly over the lattice crust. Do not sprinkle the sugar over the fluted edge of the pie. Return the pie to the oven and bake for 10 additional minutes.

When done, remove the pie from the oven and place on a wire rack to cool.

MAKES ONE 9-INCH PIE; 7 SERVINGS

SERVING SUGGESTIONS

- Drape a thin slice of yellow cheddar cheese over one side of each piece of pie after placing the pie servings on individual plates; or,

- Place a scoop of vanilla ice cream (homemade, page 595, or commercial) next to each pie slice.

CRAN-APPLE PIE

1½ cups fresh cranberries, washed
5½ cups Golden Delicious apples sliced
   ⅛ inch thick (about 5 medium apples)
Pastry Piecrust for 1 9-inch two-crust pie
   (page 393)

(Recipe continues on next page)

Follow the Apple Pie recipe, above, substituting 1½ cups fresh cranberries and 5½ cups apples for the 7 cups apples. Make a regular top crust rather than a lattice-top crust.

MAKES ONE 9-INCH PIE; 7 SERVINGS

APPLE CRUMB PIE

Satisfy your sweet tooth with this delectable change-of-pace apple pie. Don't forget the ice cream. Apple Crumb Pie and vanilla ice cream are a duet!

⅔ cup granulated sugar
3 tablespoons all-purpose flour
¾ teaspoon ground cinnamon
6 cups Golden Delicious apples sliced
   ⅜ inch thick (about 5 medium apples)
½ cup (¼ pound) butter
1 cup all-purpose flour
½ cup packed light brown sugar
½ teaspoon ground cinnamon
1 9-inch unbaked Pastry Piecrust pie shell
   (page 393)

In a small mixing bowl, place the granulated sugar, 3 tablespoons flour, and ¾ teaspoon cinnamon; stir to combine; set aside. Wash the apples. Pare the apples and place in a large bowl of cold water as they are pared to help prevent discoloration. Quarter and core the apples. Cut each quarter in half lengthwise and slice ⅜ inch thick. Measure 6 cups sliced apples and place in a large mixing bowl. Sprinkle the sugar mixture over the apples; using a mixing spoon, toss lightly until the apple slices are coated. Let the apple mixture stand.

Preheat the oven to 400° F.

Remove the butter from the refrigerator; set aside. In a medium mixing bowl, place 1 cup flour, brown sugar, and ½ teaspoon cinnamon; stir to combine. Cut the butter into approximately 8 pieces and drop onto the flour mix-

ture. Using a pastry blender, cut the butter into the flour mixture until the mixture is the consistency of coarse crumbs; set aside.

Spoon the apples and accumulated juice evenly into the pie shell. Using a tablespoon, sprinkle the flour mixture evenly over the apples, being careful not to sprinkle the mixture on the fluted edge of the piecrust. If this should occur, use a very soft brush to brush the flour mixture off the fluted edge.

Bake the pie for 50 to 55 minutes. After 15 minutes baking, drop an aluminum foil edge-cover (page 400) over the fluted edge of the pie to prevent overbrowning. Lay a piece of aluminum foil loosely over the entire pie (including the foil edge-cover). After 15 additional minutes baking, rotate the pie 180 degrees in the oven to help achieve even browning. After 40 minutes total baking, check the brownness of the fluted edge. Remove the foil from the top and edge of the pie if the fluted edge needs further browning. Bake for 10 to 15 additional minutes.

When done, remove the pie from the oven and place on a wire rack to cool.

MAKES ONE 9-INCH PIE; 7 SERVINGS

SERVING SUGGESTION: Serve warm with a scoop of vanilla ice cream (homemade, page 595, or commercial).

BLUEBERRY PIE

¾ cup sugar
3 tablespoons all-purpose flour
4 cups fresh blueberries
Pastry Piecrust for 1 9-inch two-crust pie
   (page 393)
2 tablespoons butter
Sanding sugar (see Sugar Glaze, page 400) or
   granulated sugar to decorate top crust

In a small mixing bowl, place ¾ cup sugar and flour; stir to combine; set aside. Wash and sort the blueberries; drain in a colander. Measure 4 cups blueberries and place in a large mixing bowl. Sprinkle the sugar mixture over the blueberries; using a mixing spoon, toss lightly until the blueberries are coated. Let the blueberry mixture stand.

Preheat the oven to 400° F.

Prepare the pastry. Line the pie pan with the bottom-crust pastry. Lay a piece of plastic wrap lightly over the pie pan to prevent the pastry from drying; set aside. Roll the top-crust pastry. Leave the top-crust pastry on the pastry cloth; cover lightly with a piece of plastic wrap; let stand.

Remove the plastic wrap covering the pie pan. Spoon the blueberry mixture evenly over the bottom-crust pastry; dot with butter. Remove the plastic wrap covering the top-crust pastry. Fold and slit the top-crust pastry; arrange on the pie and flute the edge.

Bake the pie for 45 minutes. After 15 minutes baking, drop an aluminum foil edge-cover (page 400) over the fluted edge of the pie to prevent overbrowning. After 25 minutes total baking, rotate the pie 180 degrees in the oven to help achieve even browning. If the top crust reaches the desired golden color prior to completion of baking, lay a piece of aluminum foil loosely over the entire pie (including the foil edge-cover). After 35 minutes total baking, remove the foil from the top (if used) and edge of the pie. Then, remove the pie from the oven. Using your fingers or a very small spoon (such as a demitasse

spoon), sprinkle the sanding sugar lightly over the top crust. Do not sprinkle the sugar over the fluted edge of the pie. Return the pie to the oven and bake for 10 additional minutes.

When done, remove the pie from the oven and place on a wire rack to cool.

MAKES ONE 9-INCH PIE; 7 SERVINGS

GLAZED FRESH BLUEBERRY PIE

½ cup sugar
3 tablespoons cornstarch
½ teaspoon ground cinnamon
⅛ teaspoon salt
1 cup water
1 quart fresh blueberries,* divided
2 tablespoons freshly squeezed, strained
   lemon juice
1 9-inch Baked Graham Cracker Crust pie
   shell (page 404)
1 recipe Decorator Whipped Cream
   (page 309)

If fresh blueberries are not available, 2 15-ounce cans of commercial blueberries may be substituted. Drain the blueberries well in a sieve, reserving the juice. Substitute blueberry juice for water in the above recipe ingredients, adding water, if necessary, to make 1 cup liquid. Do not add any blueberries to the glaze mixture during the cooking process; add all of the blueberries after removing the mixture from the heat and stirring in the lemon juice.

In a medium saucepan, place the sugar, cornstarch, cinnamon, and salt; stir to combine. Add the water; stir well. Bring the cornstarch mixture to a simmer over medium heat, stirring constantly. Add 1 cup blueberries. Return the mixture to a simmer and cook until thick and translucent (about 2 minutes), stirring continuously. Remove from the heat and place the saucepan on a wire rack.

(Recipe continues on next page)

Add the lemon juice; stir to blend. Add the remaining 3 cups blueberries; stir to evenly distribute. Let the mixture stand until cooled to room temperature.

Spoon the blueberry mixture into the pie shell; using a small, narrow, angled spatula, spread smoothly. Refrigerate until the filling is cold and set.

Using a decorating bag fit with large open-star tip number 6B (page 319) decorate the top of the pie with piped Decorator Whipped Cream, allowing some of the blueberry filling to show. Refrigerate the pie and keep stored in the refrigerator.

MAKES ONE 9-INCH PIE; 7 SERVINGS

ALTERNATIVE TOPPING: Using a small, narrow, angled spatula, spread Decorator Whipped Cream evenly over the entire surface of the filling. Decorate the top of the pie with fresh blueberries.

CHERRY PIE

Across America, cherry pie is associated with George Washington, "The Father of His Country." Serving cherry pie in February is one of the ways we celebrate Washington's birthday and honor our first president.

In the Midwest, cherry pie is also a celebratory food on another important national holiday, the Fourth of July, and for two well-founded reasons: at that time of the summer, the tart, bright red cherries used in making cherry pies are ripe and ready for picking off the cherry trees growing in town and city yards, and on farms. Plus, the brilliant red color of the fruit, which fades little with the baking, becomes part of the decoration on picnic tables parading red, white, and blue.

4 cups pitted, tart, fresh (or frozen and
    thawed) red cherries
1 ⅓ cups sugar*
2 tablespoons quick-cooking tapioca
Dash of salt

Pastry Piecrust for 1 9-inch lattice-top pie
    (page 394)**
2 tablespoons butter, melted
Sanding sugar (see Sugar Glaze, page 400) or
    granulated sugar to decorate lattice crust

* *Use 1½ cups sugar if the cherries are especially tart.*

** *If desired, a plain top crust may be substituted for a lattice top (see Two-Crust Pie, page 393).*

In a medium mixing bowl, place the cherries, 1⅓ cups sugar, tapioca, and salt; stir to combine. Let the cherry mixture stand.

Preheat the oven to 400° F.

Prepare the pastry. Line the pie pan with the bottom-crust pastry. Lay a piece of plastic wrap lightly over the pie pan to prevent the pastry from drying; set aside. Roll the top-crust pastry; cut 14 pastry strips. Leave the cut strips on the pastry cloth; cover lightly with a piece of plastic wrap; let stand.

Add the butter to the cherry mixture; stir to blend the liquids. Remove the plastic wrap covering the pie pan. Spoon the cherry mixture over the bottom-crust pastry, distributing the cherries evenly over the entire bottom of the pastry-lined pie pan. Remove the plastic wrap covering the pastry strips. Arrange the lattice-top pastry on the pie and flute the edge.

Bake the pie for 45 minutes. After 15 minutes baking, drop an aluminum foil edge-cover (page 400) over the fluted edge of the pie to prevent overbrowning. After 25 minutes total baking, rotate the pie 180 degrees in the oven to help achieve even browning. If the lattice crust reaches the desired golden color prior to completion of baking, lay a piece of aluminum foil loosely over the entire pie (including the foil edge-cover). After 35 minutes total baking, remove the foil from the top (if used) and edge of the pie. Then, remove the pie from the oven. Using your fingers or a very small spoon (such as a demitasse spoon), sprinkle the sanding sugar lightly over the lattice crust. Do not sprinkle the sugar over the fluted edge of the pie.

Return the pie to the oven and bake for 10 additional minutes, until the filling has gently bubbled for about 2 minutes.

When done, remove the pie from the oven and place on a wire rack to cool.

MAKES ONE 9-INCH PIE; 7 SERVINGS

GOOSEBERRY-DATE PIE

Gooseberries are old hat to most Midwest natives, who have eaten them in pies for as long as they can remember. Gooseberries are small, very tart green berries which develop reddish purple tinges when they ripen. They are gathered mainly in the wild, where they grow on prickly bushes. In the early summer, I often gather wild raspberries with my friend, Betty Baker, who several years ago divulged to me her secret gathering place. As we head into the woods, we always take along an extra pail for gooseberries, which we find most years. (Sometimes weather conditions affect the wild berry crop.)

4½ cups fresh gooseberries"
½ cup sugar
2 tablespoons cornstarch
1 teaspoon ground cinnamon
¼ teaspoon salt
1 cup cooking juice from gooseberries
1 cup seeded dates cut into pieces (cut
    medium-sized dates into eighths)
    OR 1 cup commercially packaged
    prechopped dates
1 9-inch baked Pastry Piecrust pie shell (page
    393)
1 recipe Decorator Whipped Cream (page 309)

If fresh gooseberries are not available, 2 15-ounce cans of commercial gooseberries in light syrup may be substituted. Drain the gooseberries well in a sieve, reserving 1 cup syrup to use in substitution for 1 cup cooking juice from gooseberries in the recipe ingredients above. Place the drained gooseberries in a medium mixing bowl; set aside. Then, follow the recipe commencing with the second paragraph of the procedures.

Wash and sort the gooseberries. Place the gooseberries in a medium saucepan; add water to cover. Cover the saucepan. Bring the gooseberries to a low simmer over medium-low heat; uncover and simmer 3 minutes. Drain the gooseberries in a sieve, reserving the juice. Measure 1 cup reserved juice; set aside. Place the drained gooseberries in a medium mixing bowl; set aside.

In a small saucepan, place the sugar, cornstarch, cinnamon, and salt; stir to combine. Add the 1 cup reserved cooking juice from the gooseberries; stir well. Bring the cornstarch mixture to a boil over medium heat, stirring constantly. Reduce the heat and continue boiling until the mixture is thick and translucent (about 2 minutes), stirring continuously. Remove from the heat. Add the dates and the hot cornstarch mixture to the gooseberries; using a wooden mixing spoon, stir carefully, only until combined. Place the mixing bowl containing the gooseberry-date filling on a wire rack; let stand until lukewarm.

Spoon the lukewarm gooseberry-date filling evenly into the pie shell; let stand on a wire rack until completely cool.

Shortly before serving, pipe a lattice pattern and border on the top of the pie (see pages 324–325 for border pictures and procedures), using a decorating bag fit with medium-large open-star tip number 32 (page 319) and filled with Decorator Whipped Cream. Refrigerate the pie until served.

MAKES ONE 9-INCH PIE; 7 SERVINGS

GOOSEBERRY PIE

6 cups fresh gooseberries*
¾ cup sugar

If fresh gooseberries are not available, 3 15-ounce cans of commercial gooseberries in light syrup may be substituted. Drain the gooseberries well in a sieve, reserving 1 cup syrup in substitution for 1 cup cooking juice

(Recipe continues on next page)

from gooseberries in the Gooseberry-Date Pie recipe above. Place the drained gooseberries in a medium mixing bowl; set aside. Substitute ⅔ cup sugar (rather than substituting ¾ cup sugar) for ½ cup sugar in the Gooseberry-Date Pie recipe and follow the Gooseberry-Date Pie recipe commencing with the second paragraph of the procedures.

Follow the Gooseberry-Date Pie recipe, above, substituting 6 cups fresh gooseberries for 4½ cups fresh gooseberries, and ¾ cup sugar for ½ cup sugar. Eliminate the dates.

MAKES ONE 9-INCH PIE; 7 SERVINGS

PEACH PIE

Without a doubt, fresh Peach Pie is one of the high points of summer dining. When your eyes catch sight of the golden peaches peaking through the tender lattice crust, anticipation of that soothing, yet fruity, taste seems to have a near-tranquilizing effect.

½ cup sugar
3 tablespoons all-purpose flour
¼ teaspoon ground cinnamon
5 cups peeled, halved, pitted, quartered, and sliced fresh peaches
1 tablespoon freshly squeezed, strained lemon juice
Pastry Piecrust for 1 9-inch lattice-top pie (page 394)*
2 tablespoons butter, melted
Sanding sugar (see Sugar Glaze, page 400) or granulated sugar to decorate lattice crust

* If desired, a plain top crust may be substituted for a lattice top (see Two-Crust Pie, page 393).

In a small mixing bowl, place ½ cup sugar, flour, and cinnamon; stir to combine; set aside. Wash the peaches; peel, halve, pit, quarter, and slice. Measure 5 cups sliced peaches and place in a large mixing bowl. Sprinkle lemon juice over the sliced peaches 2 or 3 times during preparation to prevent discoloration. Add any remaining lemon juice; using a wooden mixing spoon, stir *carefully* to assure that all the peach slices are coated with lemon juice. Sprinkle the sugar mixture evenly over the peaches; toss lightly. Let the peach mixture stand.

Preheat the oven to 400°F.

Prepare the pastry. Line the pie pan with the bottom-crust pastry. Lay a piece of plastic wrap lightly over the pie pan to prevent the pastry from drying; set aside. Roll the top-crust pastry; cut 14 pastry strips. Leave the cut strips on the pastry cloth; cover lightly with a piece of plastic wrap; let stand.

Add the butter to the peach mixture; stir to combine. Remove the plastic wrap covering the pie pan. Spoon the peach mixture evenly over the bottom-crust pastry; dot with butter. Remove the plastic wrap covering the pastry strips. Arrange the lattice-top pastry on the pie and flute the edge.

Bake the pie for 45 minutes. After 15 minutes baking, drop an aluminum foil edge-cover (page 400) over the fluted edge of the pie to prevent overbrowning. After 25 minutes total baking, rotate the pie 180 degrees in the oven to help achieve even browning. If the lattice crust reaches the desired golden color prior to completion of baking, lay a piece of aluminum foil loosely over the entire pie (including the foil edge-cover). After 35 minutes total baking, remove the foil from the top (if used) and edge of the pie. Then, remove the pie from the oven. Using your fingers or a very small spoon (such as a demitasse spoon), sprinkle the sanding sugar lightly over the lattice crust. Do not sprinkle the sugar over the fluted edge of the pie. Return the pie to the oven and bake for 10 additional minutes.

When done, remove the pie from the oven and place on a wire rack to cool.

MAKES ONE 9-INCH PIE; 7 SERVINGS

PEACH-RED RASPBERRY PIE

3½ cups peeled, halved, pitted, quartered, and
    sliced fresh peaches
1½ cups fresh red raspberries

Follow the Peach Pie recipe, page 414, substituting 3½ cups sliced peaches and 1½ cups red
raspberries for 5 cups sliced peaches. Keep the
sliced peaches and raspberries in separate bowls.
Sprinkle the entire sugar mixture over the sliced
peaches; add no sugar mixture to the raspberries.

To fill the pie, spoon ½ of the peach mixture
evenly over the bottom-crust pastry. Distribute
the raspberries evenly over the peach layer.
Spoon the remaining ½ of the peach mixture
evenly over the raspberries.

FRESH PEAR PIE

*While pears are a fairly common fruit used in
making tarts, pear pies are not frequently
encountered. If you're wondering whether Pear
Pie is really good and whether you should try one,
the answers are "yes" and "yes."*

½ cup granulated sugar
2 tablespoons quick-cooking tapioca
½ teaspoon ground cinnamon
Dash of ground mace
8 cups cold water
1 tablespoon white vinegar
1 tablespoon salt
4 to 5 large, fresh Bartlett pears (5 cups sliced
    pears; see recipe procedures below)
3 tablespoons freshly squeezed, strained
    lemon juice
½ cup (¼ pound) butter
¾ cup all-purpose flour
½ cup packed light brown sugar
½ teaspoon ground ginger
1 9-inch unbaked Pastry Piecrust pie shell
    (page 393)

In a small mixing bowl, place the granulated
sugar, tapioca, cinnamon, and mace; stir to
combine; set aside. In a small kettle or large
mixing bowl, place 8 cups water, vinegar, and
salt; stir until the salt dissolves; set aside.

Wash, halve, core, and pare the pears. As the
pear halves are prepared, drop them into the
vinegar solution to prevent discoloration.
Drain and rinse the pear halves twice. Then,
carefully place the pears in a colander to fully
drain. Cut the pear halves in half lengthwise.
Slice each pear quarter widthwise into ⅜-inch
slices. Measure 5 cups sliced pears and place in
a large mixing bowl. Sprinkle the lemon juice
over the pears; using a wooden mixing spoon,
toss to coat all slices. Add the tapioca mixture;
toss until the pear slices are coated. Let the pear
mixture stand for 15 minutes.

Preheat the oven to 375° F.

While the pear mixture is standing, remove
the butter from the refrigerator; set aside. In a
medium mixing bowl, place the flour, brown
sugar, and ginger; stir to combine. Cut the butter into approximately 8 pieces and drop onto
the flour mixture. Using a pastry blender, cut the
butter into the flour mixture until the mixture is
the consistency of very coarse crumbs; set aside.

Spoon the pear slices and accumulated juice
evenly into the pie shell, mounding the pear
slices slightly in the center of the pie. Using a
tablespoon, sprinkle the flour mixture evenly
over the pears, being careful not to sprinkle the
mixture on the fluted edge of the piecrust. If
this should occur, use a very soft brush to brush
the flour mixture off the fluted edge. The flour
mixture should cover all the pears and be
slightly mounded in the center of the pie.

Bake the pie for 50 minutes. After 15 minutes
baking, drop an aluminum foil edge-cover
(page 400) over the fluted edge of the pie to prevent overbrowning. After 25 minutes total baking, rotate the pie 180 degrees in the oven to
help achieve even browning. When the topping
on the pie reaches the desired brownness, lay a
piece of aluminum foil loosely over the entire
pie (including the foil edge-cover). After 40
minutes total baking, check the brownness of

(Recipe continues on next page)

the fluted edge. Remove the foil from the top and edge of the pie if the fluted edge needs further browning. Bake for 10 additional minutes.

When done, remove the pie from the oven and place on a wire rack to cool.

MAKES ONE 9-INCH PIE; 7 SERVINGS

SERVING SUGGESTIONS

- Serve warm with a small scoop of vanilla ice cream (homemade, page 595, or commercial).

- Serve at room temperature topped with a dollop of Whipped Cream (page 309).

RHUBARB PIE

Rhubarb Pie: an old-time (and modern-time, too) pie rite of spring—the season when you have more rhubarb growing than you know what to do with. This does not mean to infer that Rhubarb Pie is remotely inferior, only that you might wish the generous bounty were harvestable over a longer period of time so you could spread out the joy of eating fresh rhubarb dishes. The availability hurdle is cleared by some rhubarb fanciers who wash, cut, and freeze part of their abundant crop in zipper-seal plastic freezer bags for later delivery in off-season rhubarb desserts.

1⅔ cups sugar
⅓ cup all-purpose flour
½ teaspoon ground nutmeg
4 cups fresh (or frozen) rhubarb cut into ½-inch lengths
Pastry Piecrust for 1 9-inch two-crust pie (page 393)
2 tablespoons butter

In a medium mixing bowl, place the sugar, flour, and nutmeg; stir to combine; set aside. Place the rhubarb in a large mixing bowl. Sprinkle the sugar mixture over the rhubarb; using a mixing spoon, toss lightly until the rhubarb is coated. Let the rhubarb mixture stand for 15 minutes.
Preheat the oven to 400° F.

While the rhubarb mixture is standing, prepare the pastry. Line the pie pan with the bottom-crust pastry. Lay a piece of plastic wrap lightly over the pie pan to prevent the pastry from drying; set aside. Roll the top-crust pastry. Leave the top-crust pastry on the pastry cloth; cover lightly with a piece of plastic wrap; let stand.

Remove the plastic wrap covering the pie pan. Spoon the rhubarb mixture over the bottom-crust pastry, distributing the rhubarb evenly; dot with butter. Remove the plastic wrap covering the top-crust pastry. Fold and slit the top-crust pastry; arrange on the pie and flute the edge.

Bake the pie for 40 to 50 minutes. After 15 minutes baking, drop an aluminum foil edge-cover (page 400) over the fluted edge of the pie to prevent overbrowning. After 25 minutes total baking, rotate the pie 180 degrees in the oven to help achieve even browning. If the top crust reaches the desired golden color prior to completion of baking, lay a piece of aluminum foil loosely over the entire pie (including the foil edge-cover). After 35 minutes total baking, remove the foil from the top (if used) and edge of the pie. Bake for 5 to 10 additional minutes.

When done, remove the pie from the oven and place on a wire rack to cool.

MAKES ONE 9-INCH PIE; 7 SERVINGS

SERVING SUGGESTIONS

- Serve with a scoop of vanilla ice cream (homemade, page 595, or commercial).

- Top each slice of pie with a generous dollop of Whipped Cream (page 309).

STRAWBERRY-RHUBARB PIE

1 cup sugar
¼ cup plus 1 tablespoon all-purpose flour
1 tablespoon plus 1 teaspoon cornstarch
½ teaspoon ground mace
2 cups hulled (page 6), halved or quartered
   (depending upon size) fresh strawberries
2 cups fresh rhubarb cut into ¾-inch lengths
Pastry Piecrust for 1 9-inch lattice-top pie
   (page 394)*
1 5-ounce can (½ cup plus 2 tablespoons)
   evaporated milk
Sanding sugar (see Sugar Glaze, page 400) or
   granulated sugar to decorate lattice crust

 * If desired, a plain top crust may be substituted for a lattice top (see Two-Crust Pie,
   page 393).

In a small mixing bowl, place 1 cup sugar, flour,
cornstarch, and mace; stir to combine; set aside.
In a large mixing bowl, place the strawberries
and rhubarb; stir until evenly distributed; set
aside.

Preheat the oven to 400° F.

Prepare the pastry. Line the pie pan with the
bottom-crust pastry. Lay a piece of plastic wrap
lightly over the pie pan to prevent the pastry
from drying; set aside. Roll the top crust pastry;
cut 14 pastry strips. Leave the cut strips on the
pastry cloth; cover lightly with a piece of plastic
wrap; let stand.

Add the evaporated milk to the sugar mixture; stir until completely blended; set aside.
Remove the plastic wrap covering the pie pan.
Spoon the strawberry-rhubarb mixture evenly
over the bottom-crust pastry. Pour the evaporated milk mixture evenly over the strawberries
and rhubarb in the pie. Remove the plastic wrap
covering the pastry strips. Arrange the lattice-
top pastry on the pie and flute the edge.

Bake the pie for 55 minutes. After 15 minutes
baking, drop an aluminum foil edge-cover
(page 400) over the fluted edge of the pie to prevent overbrowning. After 25 minutes total baking, rotate the pie 180 degrees in the oven to

help achieve even browning. If the lattice crust
reaches the desired golden color prior to the
completion of baking, lay a piece of aluminum
foil loosely over the entire pie (including the foil
edge-cover). After 45 minutes total baking,
remove the foil from the top (if used) and edge
of the pie. Then, remove the pie from the oven.
Using your fingers or a very small spoon (such
as a demitasse spoon), sprinkle the sanding
sugar lightly over the lattice crust. Do not sprinkle the sugar over the fluted edge of the pie.
Return the pie to the oven and bake for 10 additional minutes.

When done, remove the pie from the oven
and place on a wire rack to cool.

MAKES ONE 9-INCH PIE; 7 SERVINGS

GLAZED STRAWBERRY PIE

(See picture on front jacket)

*Huge, gorgeous strawberries arranged under
shiny glaze with no-holds-barred amounts of
whipped cream piped like white puffy clouds on
the top — all of this makes a spring and summertime pie indulgence that is too satisfying to resist.*

8 cups (about 2¼ pounds) hulled (page 6),
   whole, fresh strawberries
¾ cups sugar
3 tablespoons cornstarch
½ cup plus 2 tablespoons water
12 drops red liquid food coloring
1 9-inch baked Pastry Piecrust pie shell (page
   393)
1 recipe Decorator Whipped Cream
   (page 309)

Place 2 cups of the strawberries in a blender
beaker; using the blender, purée; set aside. Distribute the remaining 6 cups strawberries on
paper towels to completely drain; set aside.

In a medium saucepan, place the sugar and
cornstarch; stir to combine. Add the water; stir
well. Add the puréed strawberries; stir to combine.

(Recipe continues on next page)

Bring the strawberry mixture to a boil over medium heat, stirring constantly. Reduce the heat and continue boiling and stirring until the mixture is thick and translucent (about 2 minutes). Remove from the heat and place the saucepan on a wire rack. Add the food coloring; stir until evenly blended. Let the mixture stand to cool slightly, stirring occasionally.

Meanwhile, arrange the whole strawberries, stem end down, in the pie shell. If the strawberries are especially large, cut them in half lengthwise, and arrange them, cut-side down, in the pie shell. Slightly mound the strawberries in the center of the pie for a more attractive final appearance.

Pour the cooked strawberry mixture evenly over the strawberries in the pie shell; refrigerate until cold.

Using a decorating bag fit with large open-star tip number 6B (page 319), pipe two wide, contiguous borders of Decorator Whipped Cream on top of the pie around the outside edge (see pages 324–325 for pictures and procedures for borders), leaving the center portion of the pie free of topping. Refrigerate the pie and keep stored in the refrigerator.

MAKES ONE 9-INCH PIE; 7 SERVINGS

ALTERNATIVE GARNISH: If a decorating bag is not available, spoon small, uniform mounds of the Decorator Whipped Cream around the edge of the pie.

RASPBERRY PIE

¾ cup sugar
3 tablespoons cornstarch
⅛ teaspoon salt
5 cups fresh red or black raspberries
Pastry Piecrust for 1 9-inch two-crust pie
    (page 393)
2 tablespoons butter
Sanding sugar (see Sugar Glaze, page 400) or
    granulated sugar to decorate top crust

In a small mixing bowl, place ¾ cup sugar, cornstarch, and salt; stir to combine; set aside. Using gentle handling to retain the wholeness of the raspberries, rinse, drain in a colander, and measure the berries. Place the raspberries in a large mixing bowl. Sprinkle the sugar mixture evenly over the berries; using a wooden mixing spoon, toss *minimally* to coat the berries. Let the raspberry mixture stand.

Preheat the oven to 400°F.

Prepare the pastry. Line the pie pan with the bottom-crust pastry. Lay a piece of plastic wrap lightly over the pie pan to prevent the pastry from drying; set aside. Roll the top-crust pastry. Leave the top-crust pastry on the pastry cloth; cover lightly with a piece of plastic wrap; let stand.

Remove the plastic wrap covering the pie pan. Turn the raspberry mixture into the bottom-crust pastry; using the wooden mixing spoon, spread the raspberries carefully and evenly. Dot the raspberry filling with butter. Remove the plastic wrap covering the top-crust pastry. Fold and slit the top-crust pastry; arrange on the pie and flute the edge.

Bake the pie for 45 minutes. After 15 minutes baking, drop an aluminum foil edge-cover (page 400) over the fluted edge of the pie to prevent overbrowning. After 25 minutes total baking, rotate the pie 180 degrees in the oven to help achieve even browning. If the top crust reaches the desired golden color prior to completion of baking, lay a piece of aluminum foil loosely over the entire pie (including the foil edge-cover). After 35 minutes total baking, remove the foil from the top (if used) and edge of the pie. Then, remove the pie from the oven. Using your fingers or a very small spoon (such as a demitasse spoon), sprinkle the sanding sugar lightly over the top crust. Do not sprinkle the sugar over the fluted edge of the pie. Return the pie to the oven and bake for 10 additional minutes.

When done, remove the pie from the oven and place on a wire rack to cool.

MAKES ONE 9-INCH PIE; 7 SERVINGS

FRESH PLUM PIE

1 cup sugar
¼ cup cornstarch
1 teaspoon ground cinnamon
5 cups fresh, pitted plums cut into quarters or
    sixths lengthwise, depending upon size
Pastry Piecrust for 1 9-inch two-crust pie
    (page 393)
2 tablespoons butter
Sanding sugar (see Sugar Glaze, page 400) or
    granulated sugar to decorate top crust

In a medium saucepan, place 1 cup sugar, corn-starch, and cinnamon; stir to combine. Add the plums; stir to combine. Bring the plum mixture to a simmer over medium heat, stirring constantly. Reduce the heat to medium-low and cook until the mixture is thick and translucent, stirring continuously. Remove from the heat; set aside.

Preheat the oven to 400°F.

Prepare the pastry. Line the pie pan with the bottom-crust pastry. Lay a piece of plastic wrap lightly over the pie pan to prevent the pastry from drying; set aside. Roll the top-crust pastry. Leave the top-crust pastry on the pastry cloth; cover lightly with a piece of plastic wrap; let stand.

Remove the plastic wrap covering the pie pan. Spoon the plum mixture evenly over the bottom-crust pastry; dot with butter. Remove the plastic wrap covering the top-crust pastry. Fold and slit the top-crust pastry; arrange on the pie and flute the edge.

Bake the pie for 45 minutes. After 15 minutes baking, drop an aluminum foil edge-cover (page 400) over the fluted edge of the pie to prevent overbrowning. After 25 minutes total baking, rotate the pie 180 degrees in the oven to help achieve even browning. If the top crust reaches the desired golden color prior to completion of baking, lay a piece of aluminum foil loosely over the entire pie (including the foil edge-cover). After 35 minutes total baking, remove the foil from the top (if used) and edge

of the pie. Then, remove the pie from the oven. Using your fingers or a very small spoon (such as a demitasse spoon), sprinkle the sanding sugar lightly over the top crust. Do not sprinkle the sugar over the fluted edge of the pie. Return the pie to the oven and bake for 10 additional minutes.

When done, remove the pie from the oven and place on a wire rack to cool.

MAKES ONE 9-INCH PIE; 7 SERVINGS

BRANDIED MINCEMEAT PIE

1 quart (4 cups) mincemeat
2 tablespoons good brandy
Pastry Piecrust for 1 9-inch two-crust pie
    (page 393)
1 extra-large egg white

Preheat the oven to 400°F.

In a medium mixing bowl, place the mincemeat and brandy; stir to combine; set aside.

Line the pie pan with the bottom-crust pastry. Lay a piece of plastic wrap lightly over the pie pan to prevent the pastry from drying; set aside. Roll the top-crust pastry. Leave the top-crust pastry on the pastry cloth; cover lightly with a piece of plastic wrap; let stand.

Remove the plastic wrap covering the pie pan. Spoon the mincemeat mixture evenly over the bottom-crust pastry. Remove the plastic wrap covering the top-crust pastry. Fold and slit the top-crust pastry; arrange on the pie and flute the edge; set aside.

Place the egg white in a small sauce dish; using a table fork, beat until foamy. Using a very soft brush, apply lightly a thin layer of egg white over the top-crust pastry, *omitting* the fluted edge.

Bake the pie for 45 minutes. After 15 minutes baking, drop an aluminum foil edge-cover (page 400) over the fluted edge of the pie to prevent overbrowning. After 25 minutes total baking,

(Recipe continues on next page)

rotate the pie 180 degrees in the oven to help achieve even browning. When the top of the pie reaches the desired golden color, lay a piece of aluminum foil loosely over the entire pie (including the foil edge-cover). After 40 minutes total baking, remove the foil from the top and edge of the pie. Bake for 5 additional minutes.

When done, remove the pie from the oven and place on a wire rack. Serve at room temperature or hot (cut slices may be heated in a microwave oven). Store leftover pie in the refrigerator. If the pie is baked well in advance of serving, it should be refrigerated as it contains meat.

MAKES ONE 9-INCH PIE; 7 SERVINGS

HOLIDAY DECORATION: The top crust of the pie may be decorated with cutout pastry stars applied prior to baking the pie. See To Decorate Pastry Piecrust (page 400) for instructions.

Cream Pies

GRAHAM CRACKER FUDGE PIE

"Calling all chocolate lovers!" Satisfy your craving with this super-duper pie which borders on a confection. The recipe came from longtime friend Dora Smith, who lives in Melcher, Iowa. The tattered card bearing this recipe has been in my recipe box ever since Dora served this awesome pie at a party years ago. I've served it over and over. How can such a phenomenal pie be so easy to make? Don't ask—just enjoy! (I cut this rich 9-inch pie into 8 servings rather than the usual 7.)

½ cup whole milk
6 1.45-ounce (8.7 ounces total) Hershey's milk chocolate with almond bars, broken into chunks
28 large marshmallows

1 cup (½ pint) whipping cream, unwhipped
1 9-inch Baked Graham Cracker Crust pie shell (page 404)
1 recipe Decorator Whipped Cream (page 309)
Shaved Chocolate (page 343) for decoration

In the top of a double boiler, place the milk, chocolate bar chunks, and marshmallows. Place the top of the double boiler over (not touching) hot (not simmering) water in the bottom pan on the range. Stir continuously until the chocolate and marshmallows melt and the mixture blends.

Remove the top of the double boiler from the bottom pan and place it on a wire rack. Let the mixture stand until cooled to room temperature, stirring occasionally.

Meanwhile, pour 1 cup whipping cream into a medium-small mixing bowl. Using an electric mixer, beat the cream on medium-high speed until it begins to stiffen. Reduce the mixer speed to medium-low and continue beating the cream until stiff, but still soft and fluffy; cover and refrigerate.

When the chocolate mixture cools to room temperature, add the whipped cream; fold in. Pour the filling mixture into the pie shell; using a small, narrow, angled spatula, spread evenly, slightly mounding the mixture in the center of the pie. Refrigerate the pie until the filling is cold and set.

Then, spoon the Decorator Whipped Cream over the top of the pie; using a clean, small, narrow, angled spatula, spread evenly and smoothly over the entire surface of the filling. Sprinkle the Shaved Chocolate over the top. Refrigerate the pie and keep stored in the refrigerator.

MAKES ONE 9-INCH PIE; 8 SERVINGS

BLACK FOREST PIE

A glamorous pie.

3 ounces (3 squares) unsweetened chocolate
¼ cup water
2 extra-large eggs, slightly beaten
Dash of salt
½ cup (¼ pound) butter, softened
¾ cup sugar
1 teaspoon pure vanilla extract
1 9-inch baked Pastry Piecrust pie shell
  (page 393)
1 recipe Cherry Glaze (recipe follows)
1 recipe Decorator Whipped Cream (page 309)
6 Chocolate Scrolls (page 342) (optional)
Shaved Chocolate (page 342)

In the top of a double boiler, place the chocolate and water. Place the top of the double boiler over (not touching) hot (not simmering) water in the bottom pan on the range. Stir the chocolate-water mixture until the chocolate melts and blends with the water.

Add the eggs and salt. Using a handheld electric mixer, beat the mixture on low speed until the mixture reaches 160°F. Use a candy thermometer to assure the proper temperature. When the mixture reaches 160°F, immediately remove the top of the double boiler from the bottom pan and place it in a bowl of cold water to cool the mixture quickly. Using the electric mixer, intermittently beat the mixture on low speed until it cools to room temperature—*not cooler.*

Meanwhile, in a medium mixing bowl, place the butter and sugar; using a standard-sized electric mixer, beat 4 minutes on high speed to cream well. Add the chocolate mixture and vanilla; continue beating on high speed until the mixture is completely blended and fluffy.

Turn the mixture into the pie shell; using a small, narrow, angled spatula, spread smoothly. Refrigerate the pie until the filling is cold and set.

Then, spoon the Cherry Glaze, cooled to room temperature, evenly over the cold chocolate pie filling. Refrigerate until the glaze is cold and set.

Using a decorating bag fit with large open-star tip number 6B (page 319) and filled with Decorator Whipped Cream, pipe a border and decorative center on the top of the pie (see pages 324–325 for pictures and procedures). The Cherry Glaze should remain visible between the whipped cream border and the center.

Arrange the Chocolate Scrolls (if used) at even intervals in spokelike fashion around the pie, pressing one of the long edges of each scroll into the whipped cream border and center to hold it in place. The wide end of the scrolls should be pressed into the border, and the narrow, pointed end should be pressed into the center.

Sprinkle the Shaved Chocolate sparingly on the whipped cream between the scrolls in the center of the pie (see illustration). Refrigerate the pie and keep stored in the refrigerator.

MAKES ONE 9-INCH PIE; 7 SERVINGS

Black Forest Pie

CHERRY GLAZE

2 cups pitted, tart, fresh (or frozen and
  thawed) red cherries
⅓ cup sugar
2 tablespoons plus 2 teaspoons cornstarch
¼ teaspoon almond extract

(Recipe continues on next page)

In a medium mixing bowl, place the cherries and sugar; stir to combine. Let stand at room temperature until the sugar dissolves and the cherries give juice.

Pour the juice off the cherries, reserving the juice. Set the drained cherries aside. Measure 1 cup reserved juice (add water, if necessary, to make 1 cup liquid). Pour the juice into a small saucepan. Add the cornstarch; stir to combine. Bring the juice mixture to a simmer over medium heat and cook until thick and translucent (about 2 minutes), stirring constantly. Remove from the heat and place the saucepan on a wire rack.

Add the almond extract; stir until blended. Add the cherries; stir to combine. Let the mixture stand until cooled to room temperature.

BUTTERSCOTCH PIE

One of my all-time favorite pies.

1½ cups packed light brown sugar
¼ cup all-purpose flour
¼ cup cornstarch
¼ teaspoon salt
3 extra-large egg yolks
2 cups whole milk, scalded (page 9)
1 tablespoon butter
1 teaspoon pure vanilla extract
1 9-inch baked Pastry Piecrust pie shell
  (page 393)
1 recipe Decorator Whipped Cream (page
  309) or 1 recipe Meringue Pie Topping (use
  3 extra-large egg whites; page 406)

In a medium mixing bowl, place the brown sugar, flour, cornstarch, and salt; stir to combine; set aside.

Place the egg yolks in the top of a double boiler. Using a handheld electric mixer, beat the egg yolks slightly on medium speed. Add the flour mixture; beat on medium speed until combined. Add about ⅓ cup of the hot, scalded milk; beat on medium speed to blend. While

beating continuously, slowly add the remaining scalded milk. Place the top of the double boiler over low boiling water in the bottom pan. Cook the mixture until thick (about 10 minutes), constantly beating with the electric mixer on low speed or stirring with a spoon.

Remove the top of the double boiler from the bottom pan and place it on a wire rack. Add the butter and vanilla; stir until blended.

Proceed, following one of the alternatives below:

WHIPPED CREAM TOPPING (My preferred topping): Let the butterscotch mixture stand until cooled to room temperature, stirring occasionally. If the mixture becomes slightly lumpy, beat briefly with the electric mixer on low speed until smooth.

Spoon the butterscotch mixture into the pie shell; using a small, narrow, angled spatula, spread evenly. Refrigerate the pie until the filling is cold and set.

Then, spoon the Decorator Whipped Cream over the top of the pie; using a small, narrow, angled spatula, spread evenly and smoothly over the entire surface of the filling. Refrigerate the pie and keep stored in the refrigerator.

MERINGUE TOPPING: Let the butterscotch mixture stand only until cooled slightly. Pour the warm to hot butterscotch mixture into the pie shell; using a small, narrow, angled spatula, spread evenly. Cover the filling with the Meringue Pie Topping and bake, following the Meringue Pie Topping recipe.

Remove the pie from the oven and place it on a wire rack in a fairly warm location away from drafts; let stand until cool. Serve soon after cool; otherwise, the pie must be refrigerated and kept stored in the refrigerator.

MAKES ONE 9-INCH PIE; 7 SERVINGS

Caramel Rolls (Sticky Rolls), page 360

Carrot Cake, page 466

Pineapple Upside-Down Cake, page 473

Front to back: Lemon Bars, page 520; Pumpkin Bars with Cashew Frosting, page 519; Cream Cheese Brownies, page 529

Clockwise from top left: Triple-Layer Pinwheels, page 565; Peanut Butter Cookies, page 555; Frosted Chocolate Cookies, page 541; Lace Cookies, page 553; Coconut Macaroons, page 537; Artist's Palette Thumbprints, page 548; Monster Cookies, page 540

D-5

Apple Crisp, page 574; Vanilla Ice Cream, page 595

Date Pudding with Amber Sauce, page 581

Fudge, page 610; Peanut Brittle, page 605; Divinity, page 602

CHOCOLATE CREAM PIE

1 cup sugar
⅓ cup all-purpose flour
¼ teaspoon salt
3 extra-large egg yolks
2¼ cups whole milk, scalded (page 9)
2½ ounces (2½ squares) unsweetened
   chocolate, cut into pieces
2 tablespoons butter
1 teaspoon pure vanilla extract
1 9-inch baked Pastry Piecrust pie shell
   (page 393)
1 recipe Meringue Pie Topping (use
   3 extra-large egg whites; page 406)

In a small mixing bowl, place the sugar, flour, and salt; stir to combine; set aside.

Place the egg yolks in the top of a double boiler. Using a handheld electric mixer, beat the egg yolks slightly on medium speed. Add the flour mixture; beat on medium speed until combined. Add about ⅓ cup of the hot, scalded milk; beat on medium speed to blend. While beating continuously, slowly add the remaining scalded milk. Add the chocolate; stir to combine (it is not necessary to stir until the chocolate dissolves). Place the top of the double boiler over low boiling water in the bottom pan. Cook the mixture 15 minutes, or until thick and smooth, beating with the electric mixer on low speed during the first 5 minutes of cooking, and stirring continuously with a spoon during the last 10 minutes of cooking. If lumps form during the last 10 minutes of cooking, beat intermittently with the electric mixer.

Remove the top of the double boiler from the bottom pan and place it on a wire rack. Add the butter and vanilla; stir until blended. Let the mixture stand only until cooled slightly. Then, using the electric mixer, beat briefly on low speed until smooth.

Pour the warm to hot chocolate mixture into the pie shell; using a small, narrow, angled spatula, spread the filling, slightly mounding it in the center of the pie. Cover the filling with the Meringue Pie Topping and bake, following the Meringue Pie Topping recipe.

Remove the pie from the oven and place it on a wire rack in a fairly warm location away from drafts; let stand until cool. Serve soon after cool; otherwise, the pie must be refrigerated and kept stored in the refrigerator.

MAKES ONE 9-INCH PIE; 7 SERVINGS

VARIATION: Chocolate Cream Pie may be topped with 1 recipe Decorator Whipped Cream (page 309) rather than Meringue Pie Topping.

After the additions of butter and vanilla to the cooked filling, let the mixture stand until cooled to room temperature, stirring occasionally. Then, using the electric mixer, beat briefly on low speed until smooth.

Spoon the filling mixture into the pie shell; using a small, narrow, angled spatula, spread evenly. Refrigerate the pie until the filling is cold and set.

Then, spoon the Decorator Whipped Cream over the top of the pie; using a small, narrow, angled spatula, spread smoothly over the entire surface of the filling. The pie may be decorated with Shaved Chocolate (page 342) distributed over the whipped cream topping. Refrigerate the pie and keep stored in the refrigerator.

COCONUT CREAM PIE

½ cup plus 1 tablespoon sugar
¼ cup cornstarch
¼ teaspoon salt
2¼ cups whole milk
3 extra-large egg yolks, slightly beaten
2 tablespoons butter
1 teaspoon pure vanilla extract
¾ cup shredded coconut
1 9-inch baked Pastry Piecrust pie shell
   (page 393)
1 recipe Meringue Pie Topping (use
   3 extra-large egg whites; page 406)
3 tablespoons shredded coconut

(Recipe continues on next page)

In the top of a double boiler, place the sugar, cornstarch, and salt; stir to combine. Add the milk; stir well. Place the top of the double boiler over boiling water in the bottom pan. Cook the cornstarch mixture until thick (about 8 minutes), constantly beating with a handheld electric mixer on low speed or stirring with a spoon. Add about 1/2 cup of the hot cornstarch mixture to the egg yolks and quickly stir in. Then, add the egg yolk mixture to the remaining cornstarch mixture and stir vigorously to blend. Cook the mixture 2 minutes, beating constantly with the electric mixer on low speed.

Remove the top of the double boiler from the bottom pan and place it on a wire rack. Add the butter and vanilla; using the electric mixer, beat on low speed until blended. Let the filling mixture stand only until cooled slightly, stirring occasionally. Then, add 3/4 cup coconut; stir to combine.

Pour the warm-to-hot filling mixture into the pie shell; using a small, narrow, angled spatula, spread evenly. Cover the filling with the Meringue Pie Topping. Sprinkle 3 tablespoons coconut over the meringue. Bake, following the Meringue Pie Topping recipe.

Remove the pie from the oven and place it on a wire rack in a fairly warm location away from drafts; let stand until cool. Serve soon after cool; otherwise the pie must be refrigerated and kept stored in the refrigerator.

MAKES ONE 9-INCH PIE; 7 SERVINGS

BANANA CREAM PIE

2 bananas

Follow the Coconut Cream Pie recipe, above, through slightly cooling the filling. Eliminate the coconut.

Spoon a small amount of warm-to-hot filling into the pie shell to cover the bottom of the crust. Slice 1 banana evenly over the filling in the pie shell; cover the banana slices with 1/2 of the remaining filling. Slice the second banana evenly over the filling in the pie; cover the banana slices with the remaining filling. Cover

the filling with the Meringue Pie Topping. Eliminate the coconut garnish. Bake, following the Meringue Pie Topping recipe.

Remove the pie from the oven and place it on a wire rack in a fairly warm location away from drafts; let stand until cool. Serve soon after cool; otherwise, the pie must be refrigerated and kept stored in the refrigerator.

MAKES ONE 9-INCH PIE; 7 SERVINGS

VARIATION: Banana Cream Pie may be topped with 1 recipe Decorator Whipped Cream (page 309) rather than Meringue Pie Topping.

After the additions of butter and vanilla to the cooked filling, let the mixture stand until cooled to room temperature, stirring occasionally. Then, using the electric mixer, beat briefly on low speed until smooth.

Fill the pie shell, following the procedure in the Banana Cream Pie recipe. Refrigerate the pie until the filling is cold and set.

Then, spoon the Decorator Whipped Cream over the top of the pie; using a small, narrow, angled spatula, spread smoothly over the entire surface of the filling. Refrigerate the pie and keep stored in the refrigerator.

PEACH CREAM PIE

1 9-inch baked Gingersnap Crust pie shell (page 405)
2 cups peeled, halved, pitted, quartered, and sliced fresh peaches
1 recipe Decorator Whipped Cream (page 309)

Follow the Coconut Cream Pie recipe, above, through the additions of butter and vanilla to the cooked filling. Let the filling mixture stand until cooled to room temperature, stirring occasionally. Then, using the electric mixer, beat briefly on low speed until smooth. Eliminate the coconut.

Substitute the Gingersnap Crust pie shell for the baked Pastry Piecrust pie shell. Assemble the filling and peaches in the pie shell, following the procedure in the Banana Cream Pie recipe, above, substituting 1 cup sliced peaches for each banana. Eliminate the Meringue Pie Topping. Refrigerate the pie until the filling is cold and set.

Then, spoon the Decorator Whipped Cream over the top of the pie; using a small, narrow, angled spatula, spread smoothly over the entire surface of the filling. Refrigerate the pie and keep stored in the refrigerator.

MAKES ONE 9-INCH PIE; 7 SERVINGS

FRENCH SILK PIE

In years past, French Silk Pie contained uncooked eggs; however, new food safety guidelines caution against eating raw eggs (see Egg Safety, page 220). I reworked the outdated method of making French Silk Pie and devised this recipe, which calls for cooking the eggs in the chocolate mixture to 160° F, the recommended safe temperature to which eggs should be cooked. I don't think any of the desirable texture and flavor of the original French Silk Pie has been sacrificed with the change in preparation procedure. Hope you agree.

3 ounces (3 squares) unsweetened chocolate
⅓ cup water
3 extra-large eggs, slightly beaten
⅛ teaspoon salt
¾ cup (¼ pound plus 4 tablespoons) butter, softened
1 cup sugar
1¼ teaspoons pure vanilla extract
1 9-inch baked Pastry Piecrust pie shell (page 393)
1 recipe Decorator Whipped Cream (page 309)
Chocolate Curls (page 342) for decoration

In the top of a double boiler, place the chocolate and water. Place the top of the double boiler over (not touching) hot (not simmering) water in the bottom pan on the range. Stir the chocolate-water mixture until the chocolate melts and blends with the water.

Add the eggs and salt. Using a handheld electric mixer, beat the mixture on low speed until the mixture reaches 160° F. Use a candy thermometer to assure the proper temperature. When the mixture reaches 160° F, immediately remove the top of the double boiler from the bottom pan and place it on a wire rack. Using the electric mixer, intermittently beat the mixture on low speed until it cools to room temperature—*not cooler.*

Meanwhile, in a medium mixing bowl, place the butter and sugar; using a standard-sized electric mixer, beat 4 minutes on high speed to cream well. Add the chocolate mixture and vanilla; continue beating on high speed until the mixture is completely blended and fluffy.

Turn the mixture into the pie shell; using a small, narrow, angled spatula, spread smoothly. Refrigerate the pie until the filling is cold and set.

Then, spoon the Decorator Whipped Cream over the top of the pie, reserving enough whipped cream to pipe a border. Using the small, narrow, angled spatula, spread the whipped cream smoothly over the entire surface of the chocolate filling. Using a decorating bag fit with medium-large open-star tip number 32 (page 309), pipe a rope border (page 324) of Decorator Whipped Cream around the edge of the filling. Arrange the Chocolate Curls over the top of the pie. Refrigerate the pie and keep stored in the refrigerator.

MAKES ONE 9-INCH PIE; 7 SERVINGS

LEMON ANGEL PIE

Angel pies, which are made with Meringue Pie Shells, could not have been more appropriately named. They are truly heavenly—especially Lemon Angel Pie, the best-known angel pie. The light, mildly crunchy meringue shell and pleasantly tart lemon filling spread with a layer of whipped cream and sprinkled with pale yellow coconut translate into a perfect summer luncheon dessert.

(Recipe continues on next page)

4 extra-large egg yolks
½ cup sugar
¼ cup freshly squeezed, strained lemon juice
2 teaspoons finely grated lemon rind (page
   311) (rind of about 2 lemons)
2 recipes Decorator Whipped Cream
   (page 309)
1 9-inch baked Meringue Pie Shell
   (page 405)
½ cup pale yellow Tinted Coconut
   (page 344)

Place the egg yolks in a small mixing bowl. Using a standard-sized electric mixer, beat the egg yolks on high speed 4 minutes, until thick and lemon colored. In the top of a double boiler, place the beaten egg yolks, sugar, lemon juice, and lemon rind; stir to combine. Place the top of the double boiler over (not touching) simmering water in the bottom pan. Cook the lemon mixture until thick (about 7 to 8 minutes), beating continuously with a handheld electric mixer on the lowest speed. When done, the mixture will very softly mound when spooned.

Remove the top of the double boiler from the bottom pan and refrigerate it until the lemon mixture cools to slightly under room temperature.

Then, spoon ½ of the Decorator Whipped Cream into the Meringue Pie Shell; using a small, narrow, angled spatula, spread evenly. Spoon the lemon mixture over the whipped cream in the pie shell; using a clean, small, narrow, angled spatula, spread evenly. Spoon the remaining ½ of the whipped cream over the lemon mixture; using a clean, small, narrow, angled spatula, spread evenly. Refrigerate the pie, uncovered; let stand at least 6 hours before serving.

Just before cutting and serving, sprinkle the Tinted Coconut evenly over the top of the pie. Keep the pie stored in the refrigerator.

MAKES ONE 9-INCH PIE; 7 SERVINGS

VARIATION: Just before filling the Meringue Pie Shell, fold ¾ of the Decorator Whipped Cream into the lemon mixture. Spoon the lemon mixture into the pie shell; using a small, clean, nar-

row, angled spatula, spread evenly. Refrigerate the pie until the filling is cold and set. Then, spoon the remaining ¼ of the Decorator Whipped Cream over the pie filling; using a clean, small, narrow, angled spatula, spread evenly. Refrigerate the pie until the whipped cream topping sets. Sprinkle the Tinted Coconut evenly over the top of the pie just before cutting and serving. Keep the pie stored in the refrigerator.

LEMON MERINGUE PIE

1 cup sugar
¼ cup plus 2 teaspoons cornstarch
Dash of salt
1⅓ cups cold water
3 extra-large egg yolks, slightly beaten
¼ cup freshly squeezed, strained lemon juice
1 tablespoon butter
1 teaspoon finely grated lemon rind (page 31)
   (rind of about 1 lemon)
1 8-inch baked Pastry Piecrust pie shell (page
   393)
1 recipe Meringue Pie Topping (use 3 extra-
   large egg whites; page 406)

In a medium saucepan, place the sugar, cornstarch, and salt; stir to combine. Add the water; stir well. Bring the cornstarch mixture to a boil over medium heat, stirring constantly. Reduce the heat and cook the mixture until thick (about 3 minutes), stirring continuously. Add about ½ cup of the hot cornstarch mixture to the egg yolks and quickly stir in. Then, add the egg yolk mixture and lemon juice to the remaining cornstarch mixture and stir vigorously to blend. Return the mixture to a low boil and cook 2 minutes, stirring constantly.

Remove the saucepan from the heat and place it on a wire rack. Add the butter and lemon rind; stir to blend and combine. Let the lemon mixture stand only until cooled slightly, stirring occasionally.

Pour the warm to hot lemon mixture into the pie shell; using a small, narrow, angled spatula, spread evenly. Cover the filling with the Meringue Pie Topping and bake, following the Meringue Pie Topping recipe.

Remove the pie from the oven and place it on a wire rack in a fairly warm location away from drafts; let stand until cool. Serve soon after cool; otherwise, the pie must be refrigerated and kept stored in the refrigerator.

MAKES ONE 8-INCH PIE; 7 SERVINGS

ORANGE MERINGUE PIE

This is similar to Lemon Meringue Pie but less tart.

1 cup sugar
½ cup all-purpose flour
2 tablespoons cornstarch
¼ teaspoon salt
1 cup freshly squeezed, strained orange juice
1 cup water
3 extra-large egg yolks, slightly beaten
2 tablespoons finely grated orange rind (page 31)
2 tablespoons freshly squeezed, strained lemon juice
1 9-inch baked Pastry Piecrust pie shell (page 393)
1 recipe Meringue Pie Topping (use 3 extra-large egg whites; page 406)

In the top of a double boiler, place the sugar, flour, cornstarch, and salt; stir to combine. Add the orange juice and water; stir well. Place the top of the double boiler over boiling water in the bottom pan. Cook the orange mixture until it begins to thicken, continuously stirring with a spoon or beating with a handheld electric mixer on the lowest speed. If stirring the mixture with a spoon, intermittent beating of the mixture with an electric mixer will help keep the mixture smooth, without lumps. Add about ½ cup of the hot orange mixture to the egg yolks and quickly stir in. Then, add the egg yolk

mixture and orange rind to the remaining orange mixture and stir vigorously to blend and combine. Continue cooking the orange mixture 5 minutes, constantly stirring or beating with the electric mixer on low speed.

Remove the top of the double boiler from the bottom pan and place it on a wire rack. Add the lemon juice; using the electric mixer, beat on low speed until blended. Let the orange mixture stand only until cooled slightly, stirring occasionally.

Pour the warm to hot orange mixture into the pie shell; using a small, narrow, angled spatula, spread evenly. Cover the filling with the Meringue Pie Topping and bake, following the Meringue Pie Topping recipe.

Remove the pie from the oven and place it on a wire rack in a fairly warm location away from drafts; let stand until cool. Serve soon after cool; otherwise, the pie must be refrigerated and kept stored in the refrigerator.

MAKES ONE 9-INCH PIE; 7 SERVINGS

SOUR CREAM RAISIN PIE

An oldie with a big fan club that never diminishes in number.

⅔ cup sugar
1 teaspoon ground cinnamon
½ teaspoon ground cloves
3 extra-large egg yolks
8 ounces commercial sour cream
¾ cup baking raisins*
1 8-inch baked Pastry Piecrust pie shell (page 393)
1 recipe Meringue Pie Topping (use 3 extra-large egg whites; page 406)

 * *The raisins may be chopped, if desired (page 4).*

In a small mixing bowl, place the sugar, cinnamon, and cloves; stir to combine; set aside.

Place the egg yolks in the top of a double boiler. Using a handheld electric mixer, beat the

(Recipe continues on next page)

egg yolks slightly on medium speed. Add the sour cream; using a spoon, stir vigorously until blended. Add the sugar mixture; stir to combine. Place the top of the double boiler over simmering water in the bottom pan. Cook the mixture until thick (about 7 minutes), stirring constantly.

Remove the top of the double boiler from the bottom pan and place it on a wire rack. Add the raisins; stir until evenly distributed. Let the mixture stand only until cooled slightly, stirring occasionally.

Pour the warm to hot raisin mixture into the pie shell; using a small, narrow, angled spatula, spread evenly. Cover the filling with the Meringue Pie Topping and bake, following the Meringue Pie Topping recipe.

Remove the pie from the oven and place it on a wire rack in a fairly warm location away from drafts; let stand until cool. Serve soon after cool; otherwise, the pie must be refrigerated and kept stored in the refrigerator.

MAKES ONE 8-INCH PIE; 7 SERVINGS.

1 9-inch unbaked Pastry Piecrust pie shell (page 393)
1 recipe Whipped Cream (page 309)

Preheat the oven to 400°F.

In a medium mixing bowl, place the brown sugar, granulated sugar, salt, cinnamon, ginger, cloves, and nutmeg; stir to combine. Add the pumpkin; stir vigorously until well blended. Add the whole milk, evaporated milk, and eggs; stir until blended and smooth. Pour the pumpkin mixture into the pie shell.

Bake the pie for 15 minutes. Reduce the oven temperature to 350°F and continue baking for 55 additional minutes, or until a table knife inserted into the pumpkin filling halfway between the edge and the center of the pie comes out clean.

Remove the pie from the oven and place it on a wire rack to cool. To serve, spoon a large dollop of the Whipped Cream on top of each pie slice. After serving, leftover pie must be refrigerated.

MAKES ONE 9-INCH PIE; 7 SERVINGS

Custard Pies

PUMPKIN PIE

½ cup packed light brown sugar
½ cup granulated sugar
½ teaspoon salt
1¼ teaspoons ground cinnamon
1 teaspoon ground ginger
½ teaspoon ground cloves
½ teaspoon ground nutmeg
1½ cups canned pumpkin
1 cup whole milk
1 5-ounce can (½ cup plus 2 tablespoons) evaporated milk
3 extra-large eggs, slightly beaten

CUSTARD PIE

Baking the pie shell for 7 minutes prior to adding the custard filling, as called for in the recipe that follows, helps reduce the perennial custard pie problem of a soggy bottom crust. Avoiding use of a shiny metal pie pan which reflects the heat will also aid in overcoming the soggy bottom crust difficulty when making custard pies (see page 397 for more on this subject).

Some custard pie bakers advocate baking the pie shell and the custard in separate pie pans and then slipping the baked custard into the baked pie shell. This procedure never appealed to me as a very viable way to beat the soggy bottom crust problem, but some cooks may find it workable.

4 extra-large eggs
⅔ cup sugar
½ teaspoon salt

1½ teaspoons pure vanilla extract
1 9-inch unbaked Pastry Piecrust pie shell
(page 393), pricked on the side and bottom
(see Baked Pie Shell, page 393, for pricking
procedure)
2½ cups whole milk, scalded (page 9)
Ground nutmeg

Preheat the oven to 425°F.

Place the eggs in a medium mixing bowl.
Using an electric mixer, beat the eggs slightly on
medium speed. Add the sugar, salt, and vanilla;
using a spoon, stir until blended; set aside.

Place the unbaked pie shell in the oven and
bake for 7 minutes. If any bubbles form in the
pastry after a few minutes of baking, prick them
with a fork. Meanwhile, scald the milk and pour
it slowly into the egg mixture, stirring constantly.

After baking for 7 minutes, remove the pie
shell from the oven and place it on a wire rack.
Reduce the oven temperature to 350°F. Pour the
egg mixture into the pie shell; sprinkle the egg
mixture filling with the nutmeg.

Bake the pie for 30 minutes, until a table knife
inserted into the custard filling halfway between
the edge and the center of the pie comes out
clean. The custard will continue cooking after
removal of the pie from the oven, and the center of the pie will fully set. Overbaking will
cause the custard to become porous and watery.

Remove the pie from the oven and place it on
a wire rack. Let the pie stand until cool; then,
refrigerate it immediately. Keep the pie stored in
the refrigerator.

MAKES ONE 9-INCH PIE; 7 SERVINGS

SERVING SUGGESTION: Cooled Custard Pie may be
garnished with Decorator Whipped Cream
(page 309) spooned or piped (using a decorating bag fit with a tip of choice, page 319) over
the top. The whipped cream may be sprinkled
with ground nutmeg for decoration.

RHUBARB CUSTARD PIE

1⅓ cups sugar
¼ teaspoon salt
¼ teaspoon ground nutmeg
4 cups fresh rhubarb cut into ¾-inch lengths
1 tablespoon all-purpose flour
3 extra-large eggs
¼ cup half-and-half
½ teaspoon pure vanilla extract
1 9-inch unbaked Pastry Piecrust pie shell
(page 393), pricked on the side and bottom
(see Baked Pie Shell, page 393, for pricking
procedure)

Preheat the oven to 425°F.

In a small mixing bowl, place the sugar, salt,
and nutmeg; stir to combine; set aside. Place the
rhubarb in a large mixing bowl. Sprinkle the
flour over the rhubarb; toss to coat; set aside.

Place the eggs in a small mixing bowl. Using
an electric mixer, beat the eggs slightly on
medium speed. Add the half-and-half and
vanilla; stir to blend. Add the sugar mixture; stir
to combine; set aside.

Place the unbaked pie shell in the oven and
bake for 5 minutes. If any bubbles form in the
pastry after a few minutes of baking, prick them
with a fork. Then, remove the pie shell from the
oven and place it on a wire rack; let stand.
Reduce the oven temperature to 350°F. Pour the
egg mixture over the rhubarb; stir to combine.
Spoon the rhubarb mixture evenly into the pie
shell.

Bake the pie for 50 to 55 minutes, or until the
custard is set. When the fluted edge of the
piecrust reaches the desired golden color, cover
it with an aluminum foil edge-cover (page 400)
to prevent overbrowning. During the last 15
minutes of baking, a piece of aluminum foil
may be laid loosely over the entire pie (including the foil edge-cover) to prevent the top of the
pie from overbrowning.

When the pie is done, remove the foil from
the top (if used) and edge of the pie. Then,
remove the pie from the oven and place it on a

(Recipe continues on next page)

wire rack. Let the pie stand until cool; then, refrigerate it immediately. Keep the pie stored in the refrigerator.

MAKES ONE 9-INCH PIE; 7 SERVINGS

SERVING SUGGESTION: After the pie has thoroughly cooled in the refrigerator, use a decorating bag fit with large open-star tip number 6B (page 319) and filled with Decorator Whipped Cream (page 309) to pipe attractive garnish on the top of the pie (see pages 318–329 for pictures and procedures).

Syrup-Based Nut Pies

PECAN PIE

4 extra-large eggs
¾ cup sugar
¼ teaspoon salt
1 cup light corn syrup
¼ cup plus 2 tablespoons (6 tablespoons) butter, melted
1 9-inch unbaked Pastry Piecrust pie shell (page 392)
2 cups (8 ounces) uniformly sized pecan halves
1 tablespoon butter, melted

Preheat the oven to 400°F.

Place the eggs in a medium mixing bowl. Using an electric mixer, beat the eggs slightly on medium speed. Add the sugar and salt; beat on medium speed to combine. Add the syrup and 6 tablespoons melted butter; beat until blended. Pour the mixture into the pie shell.

Bake the pie for 10 minutes. Meanwhile, place the pecan halves in a small mixing bowl. Pour 1 tablespoon melted butter over the pecans; toss to coat, being careful not to break or nick the pecans.

After baking for 10 minutes, remove the pie from the oven and place it on a wire rack.

Reduce the oven temperature to 350°F. Arrange the pecan halves, side by side in concentric circles, on top of the pie.

Return the pie to the oven and bake for 35 minutes, until a table knife inserted into the filling halfway between the edge and the center of the pie comes out clean. The filling will continue cooking after removal of the pie from the oven, and the center of the pie will fully set.

Remove the pie from the oven and place it on a wire rack to cool. Serve the pie at room temperature. After serving, leftover pie should be refrigerated.

MAKES ONE 9-INCH PIE; 7 SERVINGS

VARIATIONS: For a quicker but less decorative way to make this Pecan Pie, do not coat the pecans with 1 tablespoon melted butter, nor otherwise use the 1 tablespoon butter in the recipe. Add the uncoated pecan halves to the egg mixture after all the other ingredients have been blended; using a spoon, stir and fold until the pecans are evenly distributed.

Pour the pecan mixture into the pie shell. Bake the pie at 350°F for 45 to 50 minutes, or until the filling is set. During baking, the pecan halves will rise to the top of the filling in a random pattern.

BLACK WALNUT PIE

Follow the Pecan Pie recipe, substituting 1 cup dark corn syrup for 1 cup light corn syrup and substituting 2 cups very coarsely broken black walnuts for 2 cups pecan halves. Follow the procedure in Variations, above.

CHOCOLATE PECAN PIE

People who like both pecan pie and chocolate flavor will experience double delight when they savor this double delicious Chocolate Pecan Pie.

¾ cup sugar
1¼ cups dark corn syrup
2 ounces (2 squares) unsweetened chocolate
¼ cup (4 tablespoons) butter
4 extra-large eggs, slightly beaten
1 tablespoon Myers's (dark) rum
2 cups (8 ounces) pecan halves
1 9-inch unbaked Pastry Piecrust pie shell
  (page 393)
1 recipe Whipped Cream (page 309)

Preheat the oven to 375°F.

In a medium saucepan, place the sugar and syrup; stir to combine. Slowly bring the syrup mixture to a boil over medium-low heat, stirring constantly. Remove from the heat. Add the chocolate and butter; stir until melted and blended. Add about ½ cup of the hot chocolate mixture to the eggs and quickly stir in. Then, add the egg mixture to the remaining chocolate mixture; using a handheld electric mixer, beat on low speed only until blended. Add the rum; using a spoon, stir to blend. Add the pecans; stir to combine. Pour the mixture into the pie shell.

Place the pie in the oven and immediately reduce the oven temperature to 350°F. Bake the pie for 45 to 50 minutes, or until a table knife inserted into the filling halfway between the edge and the center of the pie comes out clean. The filling will continue cooking after removal of the pie from the oven, and the center of the pie will fully set.

Remove the pie from the oven and place it on a wire rack to cool. Serve the pie at room temperature, with a dollop of the Whipped Cream spooned on top of each slice. After serving, leftover pie should be refrigerated.

MAKES ONE 9-INCH PIE; 7 SERVINGS

Chiffon Pies

APRICOT CHIFFON PIE WITH SUGARED VIOLETS

This elegant-looking and -tasting pie is suitable for elaborate dinners and luncheons.

Note: This recipe contains uncooked egg whites (see page 220).

1 6-ounce package dried apricots (about
  1 cup packed apricots)
¾ cup water
¼ cup sugar
¼ teaspoon salt
2 teaspoons (1 envelope) unflavored gelatin
3 extra-large eggs, room temperature,
  separated
2 tablespoons freshly squeezed, strained
  lemon juice
¼ cup whipping cream, unwhipped
5 drops almond extract
½ cup sugar
1 8-inch baked Pastry Piecrust pie shell
  (page 393)
1 recipe Decorator Whipped Cream
  (page 309)
3 dozen Sugared Violets (page 343)

In a small saucepan, place the apricots and ¾ cup water; cover and let stand 1 hour. Then, bring the covered apricot mixture to a boil over high heat; reduce the heat and simmer 12 minutes. Place the apricots and cooking liquid in a blender beaker; using the blender, puree. Measure 1 cup pureed apricots and set aside. (Reserve any remainder for other uses.)

In a small mixing bowl, place ¼ cup sugar, salt, and gelatin; stir to combine; set aside. Place the egg yolks in the top of a double boiler. Using a handheld electric mixer, beat the egg yolks slightly on medium speed. Add the 1 cup pureed apricots and lemon juice; using a spoon, stir to blend. Add the sugar mixture; stir to combine. Place the

(Recipe continues on next page)

top of the double boiler over boiling water in the bottom pan. Cook the apricot mixture until thick (about 5 minutes), stirring constantly.

Remove the top of the double boiler from the bottom pan; refrigerate only until the mixture does not feel warm, stirring occasionally during the cooling period.

Meanwhile, pour ¼ cup whipping cream into a small mixing bowl. Using the electric mixer fit with clean, dry blades, beat the cream on medium-high speed until it begins to stiffen. Reduce the mixer speed to medium-low. Add the almond extract; continue beating the cream until stiff, but still soft and fluffy. Cover and refrigerate.

When the apricot mixture has cooled, immediately remove it from the refrigerator; set aside. Place the egg whites in a large mixing bowl. Using a standard-sized electric mixer, beat the egg whites on high speed until soft peaks hold. While continuing to beat on high speed, very gradually add ½ cup sugar and continue beating the egg white mixture until stiff, but still moist and glossy. Pour the apricot mixture over the egg white mixture. Add the almond-flavored whipped cream. Using a large mixing spoon, fold together.

Turn the filling mixture into the pie shell; using a small, narrow, angled spatula, spread evenly. Refrigerate the pie until the filling is cold and set.

Then, using a decorating bag fit with medium open-star tip number 21 (page 319) and filled with Decorator Whipped Cream, pipe a border of rosettes (page 325) around the edge of the pie, and a circle of swags in the center of the pie. Place a Sugared Violet on top of each rosette, and arrange a few Sugared Violets artistically on the whipped cream swags. Refrigerate the pie and keep stored in the refrigerator.

MAKES ONE 8-INCH PIE; 7 SERVINGS

ALTERNATIVE TOPPING: Using the small, narrow, angled spatula, spread the Decorator Whipped Cream attractively over the entire pie filling. Cut the pie into 7 servings and arrange 5 Sugared Violets on each serving.

DAIQUIRI PIE

A warm-weather pie, coinciding with the time daiquiris are served.

NOTE: *This recipe contains uncooked egg whites (see page 220).*

3 tablespoons cold water
2 teaspoons (1 envelope) **unflavored gelatin**
4 **extra-large eggs, room temperature, separated**
½ **cup sugar**
Dash of salt
2 teaspoons **finely grated lime rind (page 31)**
¼ **cup freshly squeezed, strained lime juice**
½ **cup light rum**
5 drops green liquid food coloring (optional)
½ **cup sugar**
1 9-inch baked Pastry Piecrust pie shell (page 393)
1 recipe Decorator Whipped Cream (page 309)
7 Lime Twists (page 336) for decoration

Pour 3 tablespoons cold water into a small sauce dish. Sprinkle the gelatin over the water; let stand 15 minutes.

Place the egg yolks in the top of a double boiler. Using a handheld electric mixer, beat the egg yolks slightly on medium speed. Add ½ cup sugar, salt, lime rind, lime juice, and the gelatin mixture; stir to combine. Place the top of the double boiler over boiling water in the bottom pan. Cook the lime mixture until very thick (about 7 minutes), stirring constantly.

Remove the top of the double boiler from the bottom pan and place it on a wire rack; let stand until the lime mixture cools to room temperature, stirring intermittently. (The lime mixture may be refrigerated to hasten cooling; however, watch carefully to prevent it from becoming too cool and gelling; stir intermittently.)

When the lime mixture has cooled to room temperature, add the rum and food coloring;

stir until completely blended; set aside. Place the egg whites in a large mixing bowl. Using a standard-sized electric mixer, beat the egg whites on high speed until soft peaks hold. While continuing to beat on high speed, very gradually add ½ cup sugar and continue beating the egg white mixture until stiff, but still moist and glossy. Pour the lime mixture over the egg white mixture; using a large mixing spoon, fold in.

Turn the filling mixture into the pie shell; using a small, narrow, angled spatula, spread smoothly. Refrigerate the pie until the filling is cold and set.

Then, spoon the Decorator Whipped Cream over the top of the pie; using the small, narrow, angled spatula, spread attractively over the entire surface of the filling. Arrange the 7 Lime Twists uniformly around the top of the pie in such a way that 1 Twist will be centered on the top of each of 7 slices of pie. (Or, place 1 Lime Twist on the top of each serving of pie after it is cut.) Refrigerate the pie and keep stored in the refrigerator.

MAKES ONE 9-INCH PIE; 7 SERVINGS

BLACK BOTTOM PIE

NOTE: This recipe contains uncooked egg whites (see page 220).

¼ cup cold water
2 teaspoons (1 envelope) unflavored gelatin
1½ ounces (1½ squares) unsweetened
    chocolate
4 extra-large eggs, room temperature
½ cup sugar
1 tablespoon plus 1 teaspoon cornstarch
2 cups whole milk, scalded (page 9)
1 teaspoon pure vanilla extract
1 10-inch baked Gingersnap Crust pie shell
    (page 405)
2 tablespoons Myers's (dark) rum
½ cup sugar

½ recipe Decorator Whipped Cream
    (page 309)
Shaved Chocolate (page 342) for decoration

Pour ¼ cup water into a small sauce dish. Sprinkle the gelatin over the water; set aside. Cut the unsweetened chocolate into small pieces; place in a small mixing bowl; set aside. Separate the eggs, placing the egg whites in a large mixing bowl and the egg yolks in a small mixing bowl. Set the egg whites aside. Using an electric mixer, beat the egg yolks slightly on medium speed; set aside.

In the top of a double boiler, place ½ cup sugar and cornstarch; stir to combine. Add the scalded milk; stir well. Place the top of the double boiler over boiling water in the bottom pan. Cook the cornstarch mixture until it thickens (about 5 minutes), stirring constantly.

Remove the entire double boiler pan from the heat; let stand. Add about ½ cup of the hot cornstarch mixture to the egg yolks and quickly stir in. Then, add the egg yolk mixture to the remaining cornstarch mixture and stir vigorously to blend. Return the entire double boiler pan to the heat. While stirring constantly, cook the mixture over simmering water until the mixture coats a spoon (about 2 minutes).

Remove the entire double boiler pan from the heat. Add 1 measured cup of the hot cornstarch mixture to the chocolate pieces; stir until the chocolate melts. Add the vanilla; stir until blended.

Pour the chocolate mixture into the pie shell. Place the pie on a wire rack; set aside.

Add the gelatin mixture to the remaining cornstarch mixture; stir until the gelatin fully dissolves. Remove the top of the double boiler from the bottom pan and place it on a wire rack. Add the rum; stir until well blended. Let the rum mixture stand until cooled to room temperature, stirring occasionally. (The rum mixture may be refrigerated to expedite cooling; however, watch carefully to prevent it from becoming too cool and gelling; stir intermittently.)

Then, using the electric mixer fit with clean, dry blades, beat the egg whites on high speed

(Recipe continues on next page)

until soft peaks hold. While continuing to beat on high speed, very gradually add ½ cup sugar and continue beating the egg white mixture until stiff, but still moist and glossy. Pour the rum mixture over the egg white mixture; using a large mixing spoon, fold in, carefully and quickly.

Place the egg white mixture over the chocolate layer in the pie shell; using a small, narrow, angled spatula, spread evenly. Refrigerate the pie until the filling is cold and set.

Then, using a decorating bag fit with large open-star tip number 6B (page 319) and filled with Decorator Whipped Cream, pipe a shell border (page 324) around the edge of the pie and a large rosette (page 325) in the center of the pie. Scatter the Shaved Chocolate over the pie filling between the piped whipped cream border and the center. Refrigerate the pie and keep stored in the refrigerator.

MAKES ONE 10-INCH PIE; 8 SERVINGS

ALTERNATIVE TOPPING: Spoon the Decorator Whipped Cream over the top of the pie; using the small, narrow, angled spatula, spread smoothly over the entire surface of the filling. Decorate with the Shaved Chocolate, if desired.

EGGNOG CHIFFON PIE

An elegant holiday menu item with a modern tone.

NOTE: *This recipe contains uncooked egg whites (see page 220).*

¼ cup cold water
1 tablespoon (exactly) **unflavored gelatin**
4 extra-large eggs, room temperature
¼ cup sugar
¼ teaspoon salt
1¼ cups whole milk, scalded (page 9)
⅓ cup light rum (or 2 teaspoons rum flavoring)
½ teaspoon ground nutmeg
½ cup sugar
1 9-inch Baked Nutmeg Graham Cracker Crust pie shell (page 405)
1 recipe Decorator Whipped Cream (page 309)
Ground nutmeg for decoration

Pour ¼ cup cold water into a small sauce dish. Sprinkle the gelatin over the water; let stand 15 minutes. Separate the eggs, placing the egg whites in a large mixing bowl and the egg yolks in a small mixing bowl. Set the egg whites aside. Using an electric mixer, beat the egg yolks slightly on medium speed; set aside.

In the top of a double boiler, place ¼ cup sugar, salt, and hot, scalded milk; stir well to combine. Add about ½ cup of the hot milk mixture to the egg yolks and quickly stir in. Then, add the egg yolk mixture to the remaining milk mixture and stir vigorously to blend. Place the top of the double boiler over simmering water in the bottom pan. Cook the mixture 3 minutes, stirring constantly. (The mixture will be slightly thickened.) Do not overcook the mixture, causing it to curdle (see Note).

Remove the top of the double boiler from the bottom pan and place it on a wire rack. Add the gelatin mixture to the hot mixture; stir until the gelatin fully dissolves. Add the rum and ½ teaspoon nutmeg; stir until well blended and combined. Refrigerate the rum mixture and stir intermittently until the mixture mounds when dropped from the spoon (about 1½ hours). Be careful not to let the mixture fully set.

Remove the rum mixture from the refrigerator. Using a handheld electric mixer, beat the mixture briefly on high speed until smooth; set aside.

Using the electric mixer fit with clean, dry blades, beat the egg whites on high speed until soft peaks hold. While continuing to beat on high speed, very gradually add ½ cup sugar and continue beating the egg white mixture until stiff, but still moist and glossy. Pour the rum mixture over the egg white mixture; using a large mixing spoon, fold in.

Turn the filling mixture into the pie shell; using a small, narrow, angled spatula, spread smoothly, mounding slightly in the center of the pie. Refrigerate the pie until the filling is cold and set.

Then, spoon the Decorator Whipped Cream over the top of the pie; using a clean small, narrow, angled spatula, spread attractively over the entire surface of the filling. Sprinkle the nutmeg sparingly over the whipped cream topping. Refrigerate the pie and keep stored in the refrigerator.

NOTE: Despite careful timing, if the mixture should begin to curdle, immediately remove the top of the double boiler from the bottom pan and beat the mixture until smooth, using a handheld electric mixer on high speed.

MAKES ONE 9-INCH PIE; 7 SERVINGS

OPTIONAL DECORATION: Reserve ½ of the Decorator Whipped Cream. Using the small, narrow, angled spatula, spread the remaining ½ of the Decorator Whipped Cream smoothly over the pie filling. Sprinkle the nutmeg sparingly over the center ⅔ of the whipped cream-topped pie. Using a decorating bag fit with medium-large open-star tip number 32 (page 319) and filled with the reserved Decorator Whipped Cream, pipe 2 small, contiguous shell borders (page 324) around the edge of the pie, over the whipped cream topping.

MELINDA'S PUMPKIN CHIFFON PIE

This is a rich, smashing alternative to conventional pumpkin pie.

Note: This recipe contains uncooked egg whites (see page 220).

¼ cup whole milk
2 teaspoons (1 envelope) unflavored gelatin
3 extra-large eggs, room temperature, separated
¾ cup packed light brown sugar
½ teaspoon salt
1 teaspoon ground cinnamon
½ teaspoon ground nutmeg
¼ teaspoon ground ginger
½ cup whole milk
1¼ cups canned pumpkin
½ cup granulated sugar
1 9-inch Baked Graham Cracker Crust pie shell (page 404)
1 recipe Decorator Whipped Cream (page 309)
Ground nutmeg for decoration

Pour ¼ cup milk into a small sauce dish. Sprinkle the gelatin over the milk; let stand for 15 minutes.

Place the egg yolks in the top of a double boiler. Using a handheld electric mixer, beat the egg yolks slightly on medium speed. Add the brown sugar, salt, cinnamon, ½ teaspoon nutmeg, and the ginger; stir to combine. Add ½ cup milk; stir well. Place the top of the double boiler over simmering water in the bottom pan. Cook the mixture until thick (about 8 minutes), alternately and constantly stirring with a spoon and beating with the electric mixer on low speed. Add the gelatin mixture; stir until well blended.

Remove the top of the double boiler from the bottom pan and place it on a wire rack. Add the pumpkin; stir until evenly blended. Refrigerate

(Recipe continues on next page)

the pumpkin mixture until cooled to room temperature.

Then, remove the pumpkin mixture from the refrigerator; set aside. Place the egg whites in a large mixing bowl. Using a standard-sized electric mixer, beat the egg whites on high speed until soft peaks hold. While continuing to beat on high speed, very gradually add ½ cup granulated sugar and continue beating the egg white mixture until stiff, but still moist and glossy. Pour the pumpkin mixture over the egg white mixture; using a large mixing spoon, fold in.

Turn the filling mixture into the pie shell; using a small, narrow, angled spatula, spread evenly, mounding slightly in the center of the pie. Refrigerate the pie until the filling is cold and set.

Reserve a portion of the Decorator Whipped Cream; using a clean, small, narrow, angled spatula, swirl the remainder over the pie filling. Using a decorating bag fit with large open-star tip number 6B (page 319) and filled with the reserved Decorator Whipped Cream, pipe a zigzag border (page 324) around the pie. Using your fingers, sprinkle the nutmeg very sparingly over the center of the pie. Refrigerate the pie and keep stored in the refrigerator.

To serve, cut smaller than usual pieces of this rich pie.

MAKES ONE 9-INCH PIE; 8 OR 9 SERVINGS

LEMON CHIFFON PIE

I have served this pie more often at dinner parties than any other pie. It is my favorite, and it won the blue ribbon for Best Chiffon Pie at the 1988 Iowa State Fair.

Note: This recipe contains uncooked egg whites (see page 220).

⅓ **cup cold water**
2¼ **teaspoons (exactly) unflavored**
   gelatin
4 **extra-large eggs, room temperature,**
   separated

1 **teaspoon finely grated lemon rind (page 31)**
   (rind of about 1 lemon)
3 **tablespoons freshly squeezed, strained**
   lemon juice
Dash of salt
½ **cup sugar**
½ **cup sugar**
1 **9-inch baked Pastry Piecrust pie shell**
   (page 393)
1 **recipe Decorator Whipped Cream**
   (page 309)

Pour ⅓ cup cold water into a small sauce dish. Sprinkle the gelatin over the water; let stand 15 minutes.

In the top of a double boiler, place the egg yolks, lemon rind, lemon juice, and salt; using a handheld electric mixer, beat slightly on medium speed. Add ½ cup sugar; beat on low speed to blend. Place the top of the double boiler over boiling water in the bottom pan. Cook the lemon mixture until very thick (about 5 minutes), stirring constantly. Add the gelatin mixture; stir until completely dissolved and blended.

Remove the top of the double boiler from the bottom pan; refrigerate until the lemon mixture cools to room temperature, stirring occasionally.

Then, remove the lemon mixture from the refrigerator; set aside. Place the egg whites in a large mixing bowl. Using a standard-sized electric mixer, beat the egg whites on high speed until soft peaks hold. While continuing to beat on high speed, very gradually add ½ cup sugar and continue beating the egg white mixture until stiff, but still moist and glossy. Pour the lemon mixture over the egg white mixture; using a large mixing spoon, fold in.

Using the mixing spoon, pile the filling mixture high into the pie shell, mounding in the center; using a small, narrow, angled spatula, smooth the surface. Refrigerate the pie until the filling is cold and set.

Then, spoon Decorator Whipped Cream over the pie filling; using a clean, small, narrow, angled spatula, spread smoothly. Refrigerate the pie and keep stored in the refrigerator.

MAKES ONE 9-INCH PIE; 7 SERVINGS

OPTIONAL DECORATION: Reserve a portion of the Decorator Whipped Cream; using a small, narrow, angled spatula, spread the remainder smoothly over the top of the pie. Using paste food coloring, tint part of the reserved whipped cream pale yellow. Fit 2 decorating bags with medium-large open-star tips number 32 (page 319). Fill 1 decorating bag with white whipped cream and the other with pale yellow whipped cream. Pipe a white, shell border around the edge of the pie and a large rosette in the center of the pie. Then, pipe pale yellow decorations of choice on the pie. (See pages 324–325 for illustrations and procedures for the shell border, the rosette, and other decorations.)

NOTE: For a super-high Lemon Chiffon Pie, double the ingredients for the filling mixture.

PINEAPPLE CHIFFON PIE

NOTE: This recipe contains uncooked egg whites (see page 220).

1 8-ounce can crushed pineapple in its own juice
⅓ cup cold water
1 tablespoon (exactly) unflavored gelatin
4 extra-large eggs, room temperature, separated
⅓ cup granulated sugar
¼ teaspoon salt
1 tablespoon freshly squeezed, strained lemon juice
1 cup (½ pint) whipping cream, unwhipped
½ cup granulated sugar
1 9-inch baked Pastry Piecrust pie shell (page 393)
2 tablespoons powdered sugar
½ teaspoon pure vanilla extract

Place the crushed pineapple, including the syrup, in a blender beaker; using the blender, puree; set aside. Pour ⅓ cup cold water into a small sauce dish. Sprinkle the gelatin over the water; let stand 15 minutes.

Place the egg yolks in the top of a double boiler. Using a handheld electric mixer, beat the egg yolks slightly on medium speed. Add ⅓ cup granulated sugar, salt, lemon juice, and pureed pineapple; beat on low speed to blend. Place the top of the double boiler over boiling water in the bottom pan. Cook the pineapple mixture until thick (about 5 minutes), stirring constantly. Add the gelatin mixture; stir until well blended.

Remove the top of the double boiler from the bottom pan; refrigerate until the pineapple mixture is slightly cooler than room temperature, stirring occasionally.

Meanwhile, pour the whipping cream into a medium mixing bowl. Using a standard-sized electric mixer, beat the cream on medium-high speed until it begins to stiffen. Reduce the mixer speed to medium-low and continue beating the

(Recipe continues on next page)

cream until stiff, but still soft and fluffy; cover and refrigerate.

When the pineapple mixture has cooled to slightly cooler than room temperature, remove it from the refrigerator; set aside. Place the egg whites in a large mixing bowl. Using the standard-sized electric mixer fit with clean, dry blades, beat the egg whites on high speed until soft peaks hold. While continuing to beat on high speed, very gradually add ½ cup granulated sugar and continue beating the egg white mixture until stiff, but still moist and glossy. Spoon ½ of the whipped cream over the egg white mixture. Cover and refrigerate the remaining ½ of the whipped cream. Pour the pineapple mixture over the egg white mixture and whipped cream; using a large mixing spoon, quickly fold together.

Turn the filling mixture into the pie shell; using a small, narrow, angled spatula, spread evenly, mounding slightly in the center of the pie. Refrigerate the pie until the filling is cold and set.

Then, remove the reserved ½ of the whipped cream from the refrigerator. Add the powdered sugar and vanilla; using the standard-sized electric mixer fit with clean, dry blades, beat *briefly* on low speed to blend. Spoon the whipped cream over the pie filling; using a clean, small, narrow, angled spatula, spread smoothly and evenly. Refrigerate the pie and keep stored in the refrigerator.

MAKES ONE 9-INCH PIE; 7 SERVINGS

OPTIONAL DECORATION: Using paste food coloring, tint ½ recipe Decorator Whipped Cream (page 309) pale yellow. Using a decorating bag fit with medium-large open-star tip number 32 (page 319) and filled with the tinted Decorator Whipped Cream, decorate the whipped cream-topped pie with piped rosettes (page 325) and/or swags.

TANGERINE CHIFFON PIE

Just the name of this pie sounds inviting, and the results fulfill expectations.

NOTE: This recipe contains uncooked egg whites (see page 220).

1¼ cup freshly squeezed, strained tangerine juice (about 8 medium-sized Clementine tangerines [mandarins]*), divided
2½ teaspoons (exactly) unflavored gelatin
2 teaspoons finely grated tangerine rind (page 31)
1 tablespoon freshly squeezed, strained lemon juice
2 tablespoons sugar
¼ teaspoon salt
4 extra-large eggs, room temperature, separated
Orange-colored paste food coloring
⅓ cup sugar
1 9-inch baked Pastry Piecrust pie shell (page 393)
1 recipe Orange Decorator Whipped Cream (page 310)
1 11-ounce can mandarin orange segments, well drained

* *Clementine is a variety of mandarins; however, mandarins are popularly known as tangerines in the United States. If Clementine tangerines are not available, any other variety of tangerines may be substituted.*

Pour ¼ cup tangerine juice into a small sauce dish. Sprinkle the gelatin over the juice; let stand 15 minutes.

In the top of a double boiler, place the remaining 1 cup tangerine juice, tangerine rind, lemon juice, 2 tablespoons sugar, salt, and egg yolks; using a handheld electric mixer, beat on medium speed until well combined. Place the top of the double boiler over boiling water in the bottom pan. Cook the tangerine mixture until thick (about 8 minutes), stirring constantly. Add the gelatin mixture; stir until completely dissolved and blended.

Remove the top of the double boiler from the bottom pan and place it on a wire rack. Add a *very small* amount of orange food coloring; using the electric mixer, beat on medium speed until the mixture is uniformly colored. Refrigerate the tangerine mixture until slightly cooler than room temperature, stirring occasionally.

Then, remove the tangerine mixture from the refrigerator; set aside. Place the egg whites in a large mixing bowl. Using a standard-sized electric mixer, beat the egg whites on high speed until soft peaks hold. While continuing to beat on high speed, very gradually add ⅓ cup sugar and continue beating the egg white mixture until stiff, but still moist and glossy. Pour the tangerine mixture over the egg white mixture; using a large mixing spoon, quickly fold in until evenly combined.

Spoon the tangerine mixture into the pie shell; using a small, narrow, angled spatula, spread smoothly, mounding in the center of the pie. Refrigerate the pie until the filling is cold and set.

Then, spoon the Orange-Flavored Decorator Whipped Cream over the pie filling; using a clean, small, narrow, angled spatula, spread attractively over the pie. Place the mandarin orange segments randomly over the whipped cream topping. (Reserve the remaining mandarin orange segments for other uses.) Refrigerate the pie and keep stored in the refrigerator.

MAKES ONE 9-INCH PIE; 7 SERVINGS

KAHLÚA PIE

Note: This recipe contains uncooked egg whites (see page 220).

½ cup strong, brewed coffee, cold
2 teaspoons (1 envelope) unflavored gelatin
4 extra-large eggs, room temperature, separated
⅓ cup sugar
Dash of salt
3 tablespoons Kahlúa (page 7)
3 tablespoons Irish whiskey
½ cup whipping cream, unwhipped
⅓ cup sugar
1 9-inch Baked Nutmeg Graham Cracker Crust pie shell (page 405)
1 recipe Decorator Whipped Cream (page 309)
Powdered instant coffee for decoration (to powder instant coffee, process in blender*)

If a blender is not available, a food processor may be used; however, it is difficult to achieve a fine powder using a food processor. Reserve any remaining powdered instant coffee for other uses, such as flavoring whipped cream (see Filling recipe, page 191).

Pour the coffee into a small sauce dish. Sprinkle the gelatin over the coffee; let stand 15 minutes.

Place the egg yolks in the top of a double boiler. Using a handheld electric mixer, beat the egg yolks slightly on medium speed. Add ⅓ cup sugar, salt, and gelatin mixture; using the electric mixer, beat briefly on low speed until blended. Place the top of the double boiler over boiling water in the bottom pan. Cook the mixture until very thick (about 7 minutes), stirring constantly.

Remove the top of the double boiler from the bottom pan and place it on a wire rack. Add the Kahlúa and Irish whiskey; using the electric mixer, beat on low speed only until blended. Refrigerate the Kahlúa mixture until lukewarm, stirring occasionally; do not allow the mixture to gel.

Meanwhile, pour ½ cup whipping cream into

(Recipe continues on next page)

a small mixing bowl. Using a standard-sized electric mixer, beat the cream on medium-high speed until it begins to stiffen. Reduce the mixer speed to medium-low and continue beating the cream until stiff, but still soft and fluffy; cover and refrigerate.

When the Kahlúa mixture cools to lukewarm, remove it from the refrigerator; set aside. Place the egg whites in a large mixing bowl. Using the standard-sized electric mixer fit with clean, dry blades, beat the egg whites on high speed until soft peaks hold. While continuing to beat on high speed, very gradually add ⅓ cup sugar and continue beating the egg white mixture until stiff, but still moist and glossy. Add the whipped cream and Kahlúa mixture to the egg white mixture; using a large mixing spoon, fold together.

Spoon the filling mixture into the pie shell; using a small, narrow, angled spatula, spread evenly and smoothly, mounding slightly in the center of the pie. Refrigerate the pie until the filling is cold and set.

Then, using a decorating bag fit with large open-star tip number 6B (page 319), pipe a reverse shell border (page 325) of Decorator Whipped Cream around the edge of the pie and in a small circle around the center of the pie. Sprinkle the powdered instant coffee sparingly over the piped whipped cream. Refrigerate the pie and keep stored in the refrigerator. Cut the pie into 8 servings, as it is very rich.

MAKES ONE 9-INCH PIE; 8 SERVINGS

ALTERNATIVE TOPPING: Spoon the Decorator Whipped Cream over the top of the pie; using a clean, small, narrow, angled spatula, spread evenly over the entire surface of the filling. Sprinkle the powdered instant coffee over the whipped cream topping.

Cheese Pies

CHERRY CHEESE PIE

For years, I made these Cherry Cheese Pies in disposable aluminum pie pans at Christmastime and delivered them to close friends for their holiday dining. If you decide to do the same, coax your commercial baker into selling you plastic pie containers. Just before you leave to deliver your goodies, place the pies in the containers and decorate the tops with a few red and green satin ribbons. Once you initiate this tradition, your friends will hope for repeat performances year after year.

12 ounces cream cheese, softened
½ cup sugar
2 extra-large eggs
½ teaspoon pure vanilla extract
1 9-inch Unbaked Graham Cracker Crust pie shell (page 404)
Cherry Topping (recipe follows)

Preheat the oven to 350° F.

In a medium mixing bowl, place the cream cheese and sugar; using an electric mixer, beat on high speed only until the mixture is completely smooth. Stop the electric mixer. Add the eggs and vanilla; beat on medium speed only until blended. Pour the cheese mixture into the pie shell.

Bake the pie for 30 minutes, until set. Remove the pie from the oven and place it on a wire rack. Let stand to cool slightly; then refrigerate.

When the pie is cold, make the Cherry Topping. When the topping has cooled, remove the pie from the refrigerator and spoon the topping over the cheese filling. Distribute the cherries and glaze evenly over the pie. Refrigerate the pie. Allow the topping to set before serving. Keep the pie stored in the refrigerator.

MAKES ONE 9-INCH PIE; 9 SERVINGS

NOTE: Cherry Cheese Pie may be made the day before serving. It keeps very well for 2 or 3 days.

CHERRY TOPPING

2 cups pitted, tart, fresh red cherries (or 1
    1-pound bag frozen red cherries, thawed)
½ cup juice drained from cherries
2 tablespoons sugar
1 tablespoon cornstarch
¼ teaspoon almond extract
Red liquid food coloring (optional)

Drain the cherries well in a sieve, reserving the juice. Measure ½ cup reserved juice, adding water, if necessary, to make ½ cup liquid; set aside.

In a small saucepan, place the sugar and cornstarch; stir to combine. Add the ½ cup reserved juice; stir well. Bring the mixture to a simmer over medium heat, stirring constantly. Simmer the mixture until thick and translucent (about 1½ minutes), stirring continuously. Remove from the heat and place the saucepan on a wire rack. Add the cherries and almond extract; stir to combine. Add a few drops of red food coloring; stir to blend. Let the mixture stand to cool until close to room temperature.

OPTIONAL DECORATION: After the Cherry Topping has set, pipe small, contiguous rosettes (page 325) around the edge of the pie, using a decorating bag fit with medium-small open-star tip number 18 (page 319) and filled with 8 ounces of soft-style cream cheese.

STRAWBERRY CHEESE PIE

1 recipe Cherry Cheese Pie (recipe, above)
Strawberry Topping (recipe follows)

Follow the Cherry Cheese Pie recipe, substituting Strawberry Topping for Cherry Topping.

STRAWBERRY TOPPING

4 cups fresh strawberries cut in half,
    lengthwise
2 tablespoons sugar
2 teaspoons cornstarch
Red liquid food coloring (optional)

Arrange 2½ cups of the strawberries, cut-side down, in concentric circles on top of the cold cheese pie; refrigerate.

Place the remaining 1½ cups of the strawberries in a blender beaker; using the blender, puree. Strain the pureed strawberries through a piece of damp cotton flannel secured, napped side up, in a sieve over a bowl. Measure ½ cup strawberry juice, adding water, if necessary, to make ½ cup liquid; set aside.

In a small saucepan, place the sugar and cornstarch; stir to combine. Add the ½ cup strawberry juice; stir well. Bring the mixture to a simmer over medium heat, stirring constantly. Simmer the mixture until thick and translucent (about 1½ minutes), stirring continuously. Remove from the heat and place the saucepan on a wire rack. Add a few drops of red food coloring; stir to blend. Let the mixture stand to cool slightly.

Spoon the slightly cooled glaze evenly over the cold pie. Refrigerate the pie and keep stored in the refrigerator.

MAKES ONE 9-INCH PIE; 9 SERVINGS

RED RASPBERRY CHEESE PIE

1 recipe Strawberry Cheese Pie (recipe, above)
4 cups whole, fresh red raspberries

Follow the Strawberry Cheese Pie recipe, substituting 4 cups red raspberries for 4 cups strawberries. Cover the top of the cheese pie with raspberries arranged, stem end down, in concentric circles. Puree the remainder of the raspberries in a blender and follow the Strawberry Topping recipe, using the same juice, sugar, and cornstarch quantities. The addition of red food coloring is optional.

MAKES ONE 9-INCH PIE; 9 SERVINGS

BLUEBERRY CHEESE PIE

1 recipe Strawberry Cheese Pie (recipe,
    above)
4 cups whole, fresh blueberries

(Recipe continues on next page)

Follow the Strawberrry Cheese Pie recipe, substituting 4 cups blueberries for 4 cups strawberries. Cover the top of the cheese pie with a single layer of blueberries. Puree the remainder of the blueberries in a blender and follow the Strawberry Topping recipe, using the same juice, sugar, and cornstarch quantities. Eliminate the food coloring.

MAKES ONE 9-INCH PIE; 9 SERVINGS

Tarts

TYPES OF DESSERT TARTS

The word "tart" is used to describe two types of pastry desserts. Neither type rivals standard pie in popularity across the Midwest.

CLASSICAL TARTS: Classical tarts are European-style, pielike pastries made with a rich, buttery, single crust similar in composition and texture to a cookie. The sides of the crust are short in height (about ¾ to 1 inch), often fluted, and are perpendicular to the bottom of the tart. Classical tarts are commonly made in special, round tart pans with removable bottoms. These special pans are available in many sizes. Classical tarts also may be made in a flan ring placed on a cookie sheet, which serves as the bottom of the pan. Flan rings are available in round, rectangular, and square shapes.

Classical tarts are generally filled with large pieces of artistically arranged poached or fresh fruit which are covered with a translucent glaze. Often, the fruit is arranged over a medium-thin layer of cream filling (commonly, vanilla flavor) spread over the bottom of the crust.

SMALL, STANDARD PIES: The word "tart" is commonly used to describe individual serving-sized standard pies made in regular, small pie pans of 3 to 4½ inches diameter with slanted sides. The crusts and fillings for these tarts are identical to those used in making standard-sized pies. They are simply prepared in small pie pans.

VANILLA CREAM TART FILLING

Classical tarts often contain a layer of rich vanilla cream underneath a top layer of beautifully arranged glazed fruit (see Classical Tarts, page 401). The recipe for vanilla cream that follows is especially for that use. It is made more rich than the vanilla cream used in making standard cream pies such as Coconut Cream Pie (page 423) and Banana Cream Pie (page 424), by substituting half-and-half for whole milk, and by using proportionately more egg yolks, sugar, and flavoring. This Vanilla Cream Tart Filling recipe is called for in the recipes for Apple Tart (page 443), Pear Tart (page 444), Strawberry Tart (page 444), and Three-Fruit Tart with Peach Schnapps Glaze (page 446).

⅓ **cup sugar**
2 **tablespoons plus 2 teaspoons cornstarch**
⅛ **teaspoon salt**
1 **cup half-and-half**
3 **extra-large egg yolks, slightly beaten**
2 **teaspoons butter**
1½ **teaspoons pure vanilla extract**
¼ **teaspoon pure almond extract**

In the top of a double boiler, place the sugar, cornstarch, and salt; stir to combine. Add the half-and-half; stir well. Place the top of the double boiler over boiling water in the bottom pan. Cook the cornstarch mixture until very thick (about 4 to 5 minutes), constantly beating with a handheld electric mixer on low speed or stirring with a spoon. Add about ⅓ cup of the hot cornstarch mixture to the egg yolks and quickly stir in. Then, add the egg yolk mixture to the remaining cornstarch mixture and stir vigorously to blend. Cook the mixture 2 minutes, beating constantly with the electric mixer on low speed.

Remove the top of the double boiler from the bottom pan and place it on a wire rack. Add the butter, vanilla, and almond extract; using the electric mixer, beat on medium speed until blended. Refrigerate the mixture until cooled to room temperature, stirring occasionally.

Then, remove the mixture from the refrigerator. Spoon the mixture into the baked tart shell, following the procedures in a particular tart recipe.

Tarts containing Vanilla Cream Tart Filling must be kept refrigerated.

MAKES ENOUGH FOR USE IN ONE 9-INCH TART

APPLE TART

Exercise your artistic inclinations by creating a picture-perfect arrangement of apples on this exquisite tart.

8 cups cold water
1 tablespoon white vinegar
1 tablespoon salt
1 pound Golden Delicious apples (about
   3 large apples)
5 cups water
1 cup sugar
1 9-inch baked Classical Tart Pastry shell
   (pages 401–402)
1 recipe Vanilla Cream Tart FIlling
   (pages 442–443)
1 tablespoon cold water
1½ teaspoons (exactly) unflavored gelatin
1 teaspoon sugar
½ teaspoon arrowroot (page 13)
½ cup apple jelly
1 recipe Decorator Whipped Cream
   (pages 309–310)
Ground cinnamon for garnish

THE DAY BEFORE SERVING: In a small kettle or large mixing bowl, place 8 cups cold water, vinegar, and salt; stir until the salt dissolves; set aside. Wash the apples; pare and immediately drop them into the vinegar solution to prevent discoloration. Quarter and core the apples, continuing to retain the prepared fruit in the vinegar solution; set aside.

In a large saucepan, place 5 cups water and 1 cup sugar; stir to combine. Bring the mixture to a boil over high heat, stirring until the sugar dissolves. Reduce the heat and simmer the syrup 3 minutes, stirring occasionally. Then, increase the heat to high and return the syrup to a full boil.

Meanwhile, drain the apples and *thoroughly rinse* them twice in cold water. Place the rinsed apples in the boiling syrup. When the syrup returns to a boil, boil the apples 5 minutes, using a wooden mixing spoon to turn the apples occasionally.

Drain the apples in a colander, reserving the syrup. Run cold water over the apples to stop the cooking. Place the drained apples in a bowl or plastic storage container. Let the apples stand, uncovered, until cooled to nearly room temperature. Let the reserved syrup stand in a separate container, also to cool to nearly room temperature. When the apples and syrup have cooled, pour the syrup over the apples; cover and refrigerate.

The Classical Tart Pastry shell may be baked the day before serving, if desired. If baked a day in advance, let the baked tart shell stand on a wire rack until completely cool. Then, place the tart shell (pan rim and bottom *unremoved*) in an airtight container; store at room temperature.

THE DAY OF SERVING: Make the Vanilla Cream Tart Filling. Spoon the room-temperature filling into the baked tart shell, leaving the removable rim on the tart pan; using a small, narrow, angled spatula, spread evenly. Refrigerate, uncovered, until the filling is cold and set.

Drain the apple quarters in the colander, reserving the syrup for other uses. Place the drained apples between 3 layers of paper towels

(Recipe continues on next page)

to dry. On a cutting board, using a small, sharp, thin-bladed knife, carefully cut the apple quarters *lengthwise* into thin, uniform slices ¼ inch thick on the outside, wide edge of the slices. Arrange the apple slices in 2 concentric circles over the cream tart filling, overlapping the slices and completely covering the filling; set aside.

Place 1 tablespoon cold water in a small sauce dish. Sprinkle the gelatin over the water; let stand 15 minutes to soften. In a separate small sauce dish, place 1 teaspoon sugar and the arrowroot; stir to combine; set aside.

Place the apple jelly in a small saucepan. Bring the jelly to a boil over medium heat, stirring constantly. Boil 1 minute only, stirring continuously. Remove from the heat and add the gelatin mixture; stir until completely dissolved and blended. Immediately add the arrowroot mixture; stir briefly until blended and thick.

Drizzle the apple jelly glaze over the tart, being careful not to get glaze on the tart shell edge. Using a soft brush, spread the glaze completely over the apples and any tiny portions of cream filling showing between the apple slices. Refrigerate the tart, uncovered.

Remove the tart pan rim just before serving or briefly displaying the tart before serving; leave the pan bottom under the tart. To serve, place a slice of Apple Tart toward one side of each individual serving plate. Using a decorating bag fit with large open-star tip number 6B (page 319), pipe Decorator Whipped Cream in a line of continuous swirls down the side of each serving plate, parallel to, but not touching the tart slice. Sprinkle cinnamon sparingly over the whipped cream. Cover and refrigerate the leftover tart on the pan bottom.

MAKES ONE 9-INCH TART; 9 SERVINGS

PEAR TART

3 medium, ripe, fresh Bartlett pears
Ground nutmeg for garnish

Follow the Apple Tart recipe, above, substituting fresh pears for fresh apples. Wash, halve, core, and pare the pears, immediately dropping them into the vinegar solution. Cook the pears single layer. Slice the pears lengthwise. Substitute nutmeg for cinnamon to garnish the whipped cream.

MAKES ONE 9-INCH TART; 9 SERVINGS

STRAWBERRY TART

1 recipe Vanilla Cream Tart Filling
   (pages 442–443)
1 9-inch baked Classical Tart Pastry
   shell (pages 401–402)
1 recipe Strawberry Topping (page 441)

Spoon the room-temperature Vanilla Cream Tart Filling into the baked tart shell, leaving the removable rim on the tart pan; using a small, narrow, angled spatula, spread evenly. Refrigerate, uncovered, until the filling is cold and set.

Follow the Strawberry Topping recipe to arrange the strawberries over the cold cream filling in the tart shell, and to prepare and apply the glaze. Refrigerate the tart, uncovered, allowing sufficient time for the glaze to set before serving.

Remove the tart pan rim just before serving or briefly displaying the tart before serving; leave the pan bottom under the tart. Cover and refrigerate the leftover tart on the pan bottom.

MAKES ONE 9-INCH TART; 9 SERVINGS

GRAPEFRUIT AND ORANGE TART

2 cups red grapefruit sections with juice (page 32) (about 3 large grapefruit)
3 tablespoons sugar
1 cup orange sections with juice (page 32) (about 3 medium-large oranges)
1 tablespoon sugar
1 9-inch baked Classical Tart Pastry shell (pages 401–402)
⅔ cup ground English walnuts (page 34)
Freshly squeezed, strained orange juice
1 cup sugar
3 tablespoons cornstarch
Dash of salt
1 tablespoon butter
¼ teaspoon clear vanilla
1 recipe Whipped Cream (page 309)

THE NIGHT BEFORE SERVING: Section the grapefruit; measure 2 cups grapefruit sections and place in a glass bowl. With your hands, squeeze the juice from the unused grapefruit parts into the bowl containing the grapefruit sections. Sprinkle 3 tablespoons sugar over the grapefruit sections; cover with plastic wrap and refrigerate. Following the same procedure, prepare 1 cup orange sections and juice, placing them in a separate glass bowl and sprinkling with 1 tablespoon sugar.

THE DAY OF SERVING: Leave the removable rim on the tart pan containing the baked tart shell. Sprinkle the ground walnuts over the bottom of the tart shell. Using the back of a spoon or your hand, carefully pat the walnuts into the tart shell; set aside.

Remove the grapefruit and orange mixtures from the refrigerator. If sugar remains on top of either mixture, stir with a wooden mixing spoon, being careful not to tear the fruit sections. Drain the grapefruit and orange sections, side by side, in a colander, reserving the juice and letting it mix in a bowl under the colander. Strain the reserved juice in a sieve. Strain enough addi-

tional freshly squeezed orange juice to measure 1¼ cups total strained juice; set aside.

In a small saucepan, place the 1 cup sugar, cornstarch, and salt; stir to combine. Add the 1¼ cups strained juice; stir well. Bring the juice mixture to a simmer over medium heat, stirring constantly. Simmer the mixture until thick and translucent (about 2 minutes), stirring continuously. Remove from the heat and place the saucepan on a wire rack. Add the butter and vanilla; stir until completely blended. Let the juice glaze stand only a few minutes until cooled slightly.

Then, spoon sufficient juice glaze into the tart shell to generously cover the walnuts and provide an even base for the fruit sections to be arranged on top; set the remaining juice glaze aside.

Arrange the grapefruit sections, slightly overlapping, around the outside of the tart, with the ends of the sections pointing toward the rim and the center of the tart. Arrange the orange sections in similar fashion in a concentric circle around the center of the tart (see illustration).

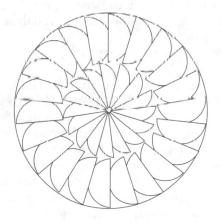

Spoon sufficient juice glaze over the tart to glaze the fruit sections and fill any spaces between the sections, being careful not to get glaze on the tart shell edge. (Reserve any remaining juice glaze for other uses.) Let the tart stand on a wire rack in a cool, dry place until cool and set.

Remove the tart pan rim just before serving

(Recipe continues on next page)

or briefly displaying the tart before serving; leave the pan bottom under the tart. Place the Whipped Cream in an attractive bowl; pass at the table for diners to spoon a dollop over or beside their individual tart servings. Cover and refrigerate the leftover tart on the pan bottom.

MAKES ONE 9-INCH TART; 9 SERVINGS

THREE-FRUIT TART WITH PEACH SCHNAPPS GLAZE

Food, like music, can evoke warm memories of past happy events. Tarts like this one remind me of the beautiful tarts savored on wonderful trips to France, Switzerland, and Austria.

1 recipe Vanilla Cream Tart Filling
   (pages 442–443)
1 9-inch baked Classical Tart Pastry shell
   (pages 401–402)
1 15-ounce can sliced, yellow cling peaches
1 15¼-ounce can sliced Bartlett pears
1 15¼-ounce can unpeeled apricot halves
½ cup peach jam
2 teaspoons peach schnapps

Spoon the room-temperature Vanilla Cream Tart Filling into the baked tart shell, leaving the removable rim on the tart pan; using a small, narrow, angled spatula, spread evenly. Refrigerate, uncovered, until the filling is cold and set.

Separately, drain the peaches, pears, and apricots in a colander, being careful not to tear the fruit. Place the drained fruit between 3 layers of paper towels to further drain and dry.

Over the cream filling in the tart shell, arrange attractively the peach slices, pear slices, and apricot halves, in that order, each in a concentric circle beginning at the outside edge of the tart; set aside.

Place ½ cup peach jam in a small saucepan; bring the jam just to boiling over medium-low heat, stirring constantly. Strain the hot jam through a sieve. Measure ¼ cup strained jam

and place in a tiny, clean saucepan. Over low heat, heat the strained jam until warm, stirring constantly. Remove from the heat and add the peach schnapps; stir until blended.

Spoon the peach schnapps glaze evenly over the tart, being careful not to get glaze on the tart shell edge. If necessary, use a small, very soft brush to spread the glaze over all exposed portions of the fruit and cream filling. Refrigerate the tart, uncovered, allowing sufficient time for the glaze to set before serving.

Carefully remove the tart pan rim just before serving or briefly displaying the tart before serving; leave the pan bottom under the tart. Cover and refrigerate the leftover tart on the pan bottom.

MAKES ONE 9-INCH TART; 9 SERVINGS

Cakes and Frostings

Cakes

TYPES OF CAKES

Cakes may be classified into the following nine general types based upon their form or content:

LAYER CAKES: Layer cakes consist of individually baked cakes—usually two or three—of the same size which are stacked, with frosting or a thickened filling spread between the layers. The top and sides of layer cakes are often frosted and then may be garnished or decorated with frosting designs, nuts, coconut, chocolate curls, other food products, or edible flowers.

SHEET CAKES: Sheet cakes are single-layer cakes which are generally baked in a 2-inch-deep pan. When baked at home, they are often cooled and frosted in the baking pan, remaining in the pan until cut and served. After cooling, sheet cakes may be cut into individual servings, which are then iced on the top and sides. Petits fours are an example.

LOAF AND BUNDT CAKES: Loaf and Bundt cakes are deep, unlayered cakes baked in a loaf pan, Bundt pan, ring mold pan, or tube pan. Cakes in this classification usually include among their contents traditional cake ingredients, i.e., fat, sugar, eggs, flour, leaven, liquid, and flavoring.

ANGEL FOOD CAKES: Angel food cakes are very light, airy, tall cakes made with many egg whites, cake flour, sugar, cream of tartar, and flavoring, with air and steam serving as the primary leavening agents. Angel food cakes contain no shortening. They are usually baked in a special tube pan with a removable bottom and tube section, and cooling legs.

SPONGE CAKES: Sponge cakes are similar to angel food cakes in that they have a light, airy consistency and contain similar ingredients, including no shortening. They differ from angel food cakes in that they have egg yolks and a small amount of water as ingredients, and contain fewer egg whites. Like angel food cakes, air and steam are the primary leavening agents in sponge cakes; however, baking powder may be included, if desired. While often baked in a tube pan, sponge cakes are baked in a cookie pan when used in making jelly rolls, Yule logs, and similar cakes. They also may be baked in other types of pans when called for in recipes for particular style cakes.

CHIFFON CAKES: Chiffon cakes are a cousin of sponge cakes. In addition to the ingredients in sponge cakes, chiffon cakes include vegetable oil as an added ingredient, and they always contain baking powder. Due to the inclusion of oil, the egg whites in chiffon cakes must be beaten until extraordinarily stiff. Chiffon cakes are generally baked in a tube pan.

FRUITCAKES: Fruitcakes are dense, heavy cakes whose primary ingredients are a selected combination of candied fruits, raisins, nuts, dates, figs, and other dried fruits bound together with a minimum amount of cake batter. These rich cakes are best when aged in liquor-soaked cloths, and are generally baked in loaf or tube pans. Fruitcakes are traditionally served during the Christmas holiday season.

TORTES: Tortes are elegant, delicate cakes usually containing many eggs and, often, ground nuts and/or bread crumbs in substitution for part or all of the flour. Tortes generally consist of several layers of cake often infused with liqueur. Among the ingredients frequently included in the fillings between the layers are jam, whipped cream, and finely chopped nuts. Or, a buttercream frosting may be used to sandwich the layers. Tortes are commonly iced with a buttercream frosting or a glaze, and then decorated ornately.

CUPCAKES: Cupcakes are small, round, single-serving-sized cakes baked in muffin-pan cups which are greased or lined with paper baking cups. Most standard cake batters may be used to make cupcakes. The tops of cupcakes are usually frosted with a buttercream frosting. They frequently are decorated with chopped or whole nuts, coconut, nonparcils (page 24), crushed candy, piped frosting, or other decorations compatible with the cake flavor, frosting, and serving occasion.

SECRETS FOR BAKING SUCCESSFUL CAKES

I would like to help dispel the modern notion that cakes come from boxes. The truth is, cakes result from the mixing and baking of proportionate amounts of certain ingredients such as flour, sugar, eggs, leavening, milk, flavoring, and, commonly, fat.

Contrary to the impression held by some, cakes made with fresh ingredients are quick and easy to prepare from scratch. And the delectable results are umatched by anything to be found in the colorful boxes on aisle 4.

The hardest, most time-consuming part about baking a cake is frosting it—especially layer cakes (see To Frost a Cake, page 501). But the task of frosting must be accomplished whether the icing comes from a plastic container off the shelf or from a bowl of fluffy sweetness made at home almost before the baker can say "Jack Robinson." Luscious frosting is not difficult to make. Why not spend the time spreading one's own superior product?

Primed with the requisite equipment, proper ingredients, an understanding of a few simple basics of preparation, and a reliable recipe, any cook rapidly can learn to turn out gratifying, praiseworthy fare for the cake stand.

To label the following information "secrets" is really a misnomer. What follows are some of the fundamental principles and procedures in baking good cakes based on food science and practical experience gained through decades of American cake baking. The pointers and suggestions given here are in addition to those found within the recipes and in other articles in this chapter.

EQUIPMENT

Proper equipment has much to do with the outcome of a cake. Accumulate the right equipment before expending the energy and quelling the enthusiasm for cake baking on a predictable failure due to faulty equipment.

The following basic equipment will take the baker through years of blue ribbon cake baking:

- A standard-sized, substantial, upright electric mixer.

- Top-quality, anodized aluminum cake pans of various sizes.

  Wilton Enterprises carries an excellent line of cake pans available in many stores and by mail order. A nearly inexhaustible line of high-grade cake pans of every size and description also can be found in the Sweet Celebrations Inc. catalog. (See Product Sources, page 631, for addresses and telephone numbers.)

  Do not use cake pans with nonstick or slick-coated surfaces often displayed in cookware sections. Also, dark-colored pans should not be used because they absorb heat too readily and cause overbrowning. Shiny, stainless steel pans are not good selections because they do not conduct heat well.

- A level, calibrated oven.

  Most modern ranges are made with leveling feet. The installation manual accompanying the range describes how to adjust them to achieve a level oven.

  A properly calibrated oven is a must. Temperature control is all-important to successful cake baking. In fact, accurate temperature control is critical to all baking and cooking.

  While oven thermometers are helpful in determining the accuracy of oven temperature, I have found that the most satisfactory and reliable way to calibrate an oven is to call the consumer service number of the range manufacturer and have an experienced person sent to do it professionally. Even new ranges require oven calibration.

- Fundamental measuring utensils (see To Measure Ingredients, page 36).

- A regular-sized (preferably 5-cup) sifter and a 1-cup sifter (see To Sift Flour, page 40).

- A pastry brush, flour scoop, regular-sized rubber spatula, large mixing spoon, timer, large spatula, and sharp, thin-bladed knife; stainless steel mixing bowls; waxed paper; bake-even cake strips (see To Use Bake-Even Cake Strips, page 452); regular tableware knives (for leveling measured dry ingredients) and tablespoons and teaspoons (for mixing); long, wooden toothpicks; 3 wire racks; and frosting tools (page 501).

Assemble all the needed equipment before commencing to measure and mix the ingredients for a cake.

PROPER INGREDIENTS

- Use only fresh, high-quality ingredients (see Notes about Recipe Ingredients, page 1).

- Review the recipe well in advance of preparing a cake, making sure that all the necessary ingredients are on hand.

- Have all the cake ingredients at room temperature before starting to combine them.

Depending upon the kitchen temperature, remove butter or vegetable shortening from the refrigerator about 2 hours in advance of commencing to mix a cake.

Remove eggs from the refrigerator 1 hour in advance. Let the eggs stand in the shells and break them immediately before adding them to the batter. If the recipe calls for the eggs to be separated, place the part of the eggs not immediately used in the batter (usually the whites) in a bowl and cover with plastic wrap. Let stand at room temperature until used, a short time later, in the preparation of the batter.

I do not like to let milk, half-and-half, or cream stand unrefrigerated too long, so I remove from the refrigerator and measure any of these required products immediately after assembling the needed equipment for baking the cake, and then return the unneeded portion to the refrigerator. By the time the liquid ingredient is added to the batter, it will have warmed considerably, albeit not quite to room temperature.

TIPS FOR MIXING AND BAKING SHORTENED CAKES (CAKES CONTAINING FAT) (SEE NOTE, PAGES 19–20)

- Before commencing to mix a cake:

  ~ Complete any required preparation of ingredients (such as chopping nuts).

  ~ Measure all ingredients (except vanilla or other such liquid flavoring, which can readily be measured when added to the batter).

  ~ Prepare the cake pan(s).

  ~ Sift the flour (usually with added leavening and salt).

- When you begin to mix the cake, proceed uninterrupted until the cake(s) is(are) in the oven.

- When the electric mixer is running during the mixing process, use a rubber spatula to scrape the side of the mixing bowl, moving the batter from the side to the center of the bowl as the mixer is beating. This helps assure even mixture of the ingredients. I like to hold the spatula in one hand while manually controlling the turning of the mixing bowl with the other hand.

- It is highly important to cream the fat and sugar adequately. Creaming incorporates air, helping to produce light cakes. When sufficiently creamed, the fat-sugar mixture will be fluffy and light.

- If more than one whole egg (or egg yolk) is called for, add the eggs (or egg yolks) one at a time and beat very well after adding each. This procedure achieves thorough blending of the whole eggs (or egg yolks) with the creamed fat and sugar, and effects further aeration of the batter.

- After adding vanilla (or other flavoring), beat the batter well on medium-high speed, not only to blend the flavoring, but also to incorporate as much additional air as possible into the batter before adding the flour mixture and liquid.

- Add the sifted flour mixture and liquid alternately, usually in fourths and thirds, depending on the recipe, always beginning and ending with the dry ingredients (flour mixture). Use a flour scoop to transport estimated portions of the flour mixture from the waxed paper to the mixing bowl. When measuring the liquid before commencing to mix the cake (described, above), my preference is to use fractional measuring cups (and measuring spoons, if required) for measuring, and then to pour the measured liquid into a glass measuring cup with a pouring spout. The glass measuring cup makes estimated additions of liquid to the batter more efficient and the pouring spout reduces the risk of spilling measured liquid.

  After each addition of both the flour mixture and the liquid, beat the batter on low speed only until the added flour mixture or liquid is blended. On my mixer, I use speed 2 and beat approximately 20 seconds after adding ¼ of the flour mixture for an average-sized cake, and approximately 12 seconds after adding ⅓ of the liquid. Of course, these numbers will vary, depending upon the mixer and the volume of ingredients.

  After all the flour mixture and liquid additions have been made and blended, beat the batter *very briefly* (about 20 seconds) on low speed, but slightly faster than the speed used after the flour mixture and liquid additions. I use speed 3 on my electric mixer. The purpose of this final, short beating is to help make certain that all ingredients are evenly blended.

- Many cake recipes call for the eggs to be separated and the egg whites to be beaten and folded into the cake batter as the last procedure in mixing. Beaten egg whites lose their volume quickly when left to stand; therefore, when beaten egg whites are to be incorporated into cake batter, they should not be beaten until the remainder of the batter has been mixed. Unless a kitchen is equipped with 2 standard-sized electric mixers, it is necessary that the beater blades be removed from the mixer, thoroughly washed and dried, and reinserted into the mixer before beating the egg whites. (Do not use a blender or food processor for beating egg whites.)

  Beat the egg whites on high speed until soft peaks hold. Soft peaks of beaten egg whites bend to the side when the beater blades are lifted from the egg whites. Continue beating the egg whites on high speed while simultaneously and *very slowly* sprinkling the measured sugar over the egg white mixture. Beat the egg white mixture until stiff peaks hold, but the mixture is still moist and glossy. Stiff peaks of beaten egg whites remain upright when the beater blades are lifted from the mixture. Sugar is usually added to the egg whites during beating to help stabilize the foam and to produce a mixture consistency which allows the beaten egg whites to be more readily folded into the batter.

  Using a large mixing spoon, fold the egg white mixture into the batter with care, but quickly, to minimize the loss of air (see definition of "Fold," page 6).

- If baking a layer cake, use a large mixing spoon to place large spoonsful of the batter *alternately* into the prepared cake pans. By following this procedure, approximately equal amounts of batter will be placed in each pan, resulting in uniformly sized cake layers. Then, use a small, narrow, angled spatula (see illustration, page 502) to lightly and quickly spread the batter in the pans, mounding the batter ever so slightly in the center.

- Bake the cake(s) on the center shelf of the preheated oven. Do not open the oven door until near the end of the baking period, as the cooling effect on the batter may cause the cake(s) to fall. Jolts to the oven may also cause the cake(s) to fall.

• Near the end of the baking time, check the cake for doneness. Avoid overbaking. Cakes dry when left in the oven for even a few minutes after they are done.

NOTE: Mixing and baking procedures for other types of cakes, such as angel food and sponge cakes, are found in the recipe procedures for those cakes.

RELIABLE RECIPES

The ingredients must be balanced properly to produce a successful cake; therefore, accurate measuring is very important. Carefully measure the ingredients and closely follow the procedures given in the cake recipes in this chapter or in other tested recipes, applying generally accepted principles of skillful cake baking. Wonderful cakes will be the reward!

TO USE BAKE-EVEN CAKE STRIPS *

A level top surface can be maintained on most cakes during baking by wrapping bake-even cake strips around the outside of the cake pans prior to baking. A level top surface is required on lower layers of layered cakes and on the tops of cakes to be decorated with piped frosting. Bake-even cake strips work by helping to control heat distribution in the pan during baking.

To use bake-even cake strips, immerse them in cold water and let them stand at least 5 minutes. Just before commencing to mix the ingredients to bake a cake, remove the strips from the water and run them tightly between your index and middle fingers to extract excess water. (Do not wring the strips.)

Wrap one strip, aluminized side out, tightly around the *outside* of each prepared cake pan. Overlap the strip ends and secure with a pin supplied in the package with the strips. Bake-even cake strips are available in several lengths; however, they may be overlapped and pinned

---

* *A product of Wilton Enterprises (see Product Sources, page 631).*

together around larger pans. Overlapping of the strips does not interfere with their performance efficiency.

Spoon the batter into the pans and bake the cakes as usual. Remove the strips immediately after removing the cakes from the oven and placing them on wire racks. Follow the standard procedure of letting the cakes stand 10 minutes on wire racks to partially cool before removing them from the pans. Hang the strips on a towel bar to completely dry before refolding them for storage. They may be reused over and over.

Use of bake-even cake strips generally makes it unnecessary to level cakes after baking.

Bake-even cake strips fit best around 2-inch-deep cake pans with straight (not slanted) sides. They should not be used around cakes which contain large proportions of ground nuts and/or bread crumbs in substitution for part, or all, of the flour (as in many tortes). These cakes do not develop crowns during baking

Cake recipes in this chapter indicate when the use of bake-even cake strips is recommended.

TO LEVEL A BAKED CAKE

When a baked cake is to be used as a lower layer of a finished cake, or when the top layer of a cake is to be piped with decoration, it is necessary that the top surface of the cake be flat and level. If baking has produced a crown on the cake, it must be removed to achieve the needed level surface (see Note).

To level a cake, place it on a corrugated cardboard cake circle. Place the cake circle (with cake) on a decorating turntable. (See illustration, page 502.) While slowly rotating the turntable with one hand, move a serrated knife horizontally back and forth in sawing motions across the top of the cake to remove the crown. The crown should be removed at eye level to assure that the finished cake surface is parallel with the bottom of the cake.

Or, to level a cake with greater ease and accuracy, cake levelers are commercially available from Sweet Celebrations Inc. and Wilton Enterprises (see Product Sources, page 631). Cake levelers horizontally level cakes or split them into layers with precision. These simple kitchen tools adjust to desired heights and operate as a saw which is pulled through the cake. Cake levelers are available in several styles, varying in cost from reasonable to pricey.

NOTE: Special bake-even cake strips may be placed on cake pans prior to baking most cakes to produce cakes without crowns (see To Use Bake-Even Cake Strips, page 452).

TO SPLIT A CAKE INTO LAYERS

Baked cakes may be split horizontally to make 2 or more layers. Cakes with several thin layers are most often made by splitting each of 2 or 3 baked cake layers in half to make 4 or 6 layers, respectively.

To split a cake into layers, a procedure similar to that used to level a baked cake is employed (see To Level a Baked Cake, page 452). Follow the same procedure for placing the cake to be split on a corrugated cardboard cake circle and then on a decorating turntable. Level the top of the cake, if required, as described above. Then, with the knife blade parallel to the bottom of the cake, hold a serrated knife against the side of the cake at the place where you wish to make the cut. To split the cake, move the knife back and forth in sawing motions while slowly rotating the turntable with your other hand. As in leveling a cake, a cake should be split at eye level to help assure that it is cut parallel with the bottom of the cake.

After making the cut, carefully slide a corrugated cardboard cake circle between the split layers and remove the top layer.

As described in To Level a Baked Cake, a cake leveler kitchen tool also may be used to split cakes into layers.

TO CUT AND SERVE CAKES

After taking the time to bake and carefully frost a delectable cake, the same diligence should be applied to cutting and serving it in order to render the individual servings as tantalizing as the whole, uncut cake.

Proper, meticulous cake cutting takes a little time and patience. Pride in the professional-looking results will deem the bit of extra effort well worth it. As my wonderful first-grade teacher, Miss Cameron, engraved on our minds: "Anything worth doing, is worth doing well."

TO CUT ROUND LAYER CAKES AND TORTES: Dip a sharp, *thin-bladed* knife into a tall glass or pitcher of hot water. Shake off the excess water (away from the cake) and make a cut from the center to the edge of the cake. Hold the knife at a slight angle (handle upward) when you cut into the cake so the point of the knife will cut down the center and to the bottom of the cake in a straight, vertical line; then, pull the knife handle fully downward to complete the cut. This procedure will help assure a pointed, unfrayed edge at the center end of the cut piece.

After making the cut, wipe the knife on a damp sponge or cloth, redip the knife in hot water, shake off the excess water, and make the second cut. Repeat the procedure for each cut.

Exercise care to make the cuts at right angles to the bottom of the cake so the slices will not be slanted. Also, gauge the cuts to make sure that servings arriving at the table are uniform in size (unless a family member requests a smaller —or larger—piece).

Cut the number of pieces to be served before removing any of the servings from the cake. Use a triangular pie/cake server to remove the cut slices. Carefully push the server under the bottom of a cake slice all the way to the center; lift straight up and transfer the cut piece to an individual serving plate.

TO CUT SHEET CAKES AND SQUARE LAYER CAKES: To achieve servings of uniform size, hold a ruler against the edges of the cake pan (or close to the edges of the cake, if it has been removed from the pan) and make tiny marks in the frosting with the point of a sharp knife at measured places along the edges of the cake where you wish to make cuts. Before marking, you must decide what size pieces you desire and do some arithmetic vis-à-vis the pan size.

Measure and mark all four sides of the cake. Shortcutting the process by marking only two sides of the cake more often than not results in slightly slanted cut lines, producing irregular pieces of cake.

To cut marked cakes, dip a sharp, *thin-bladed* knife into a tall glass or pitcher of hot water. Shake off the excess water (away from the cake) and, in a nonstop motion, make a cut from one side of the cake to the opposite side. Do not use back-and-forth sawing motions when cutting, or lift the knife from the cake before the full cut is made. These actions will cause raggedy frosting edges as well as possible crumbling of the cut edges of the cake. After making the cut, wipe the knife on a damp sponge or cloth, redip the knife in hot water, shake off the excess water, and make the next cut. Repeat the procedure for each cut.

When cutting rectangular sheet cakes, make the lengthwise cuts before the widthwise cuts. By following this sequence, the cake will be more stable when the long, more difficult cuts are made. If cutting a cake in the pan, run the knife along the inside edges of the pan to loosen the cake from the pan *after* making the other cuts. By loosening the cake from the pan last, the cake will better hold its position when making the previous cuts.

To remove the cut pieces from the pan (or cake board), use a small spatula as close to the size of the cut pieces of cake as possible. Push the spatula completely under a cut piece of cake and lift straight upward to remove.

TO CUT LOAF AND BUNDT CAKES: Dip a sharp, *thin-bladed* knife into a tall glass or pitcher of hot water. Shake off the excess water (away from the cake) and make a single cut in the cake. Wipe the knife on a damp sponge or cloth, redip the knife in hot water, shake off the excess water, and make the second cut. Repeat the procedure

for each cut. Cut the number of pieces to be served before removing any of the servings from the cake.

Remove cut slices from the cake using a spatula or pie/cake server appropriate for the size and shape of the cut pieces.

TO CUT ANGEL FOOD CAKES, SPONGE CAKES, AND CHIFFON CAKES: To cut the first slice of cake, dip a pronged cake cutter (see illustration) into a small, deep pan of hot water. Shake off the excess water (away from the cake) and plunge the cutter into the cake where you wish to make a cut. Pull the cutter straight up and out of the cake. Wipe the cutter on a damp sponge or cloth. Redip the cutter in hot water, shake off the excess water, and plunge the cutter into the cake where you wish to make the second cut for the first slice. Pull the cutter straight up and out of the cake.

Then, dip a long, sharp, *thin-bladed* (nonserrated) knife into a tall glass or pitcher of hot water and shake off the excess water (away from the cake). Using light, sawing motions with the knife, complete the cuts at the two places pierced with the cutter. Use a triangular pie/cake server to remove the first cut slice from the cake.

Wipe the pronged cake cutter on a damp sponge or cloth, redip the cutter in hot water, shake off the excess water, and plunge the cutter into the cake where you wish to make the next cut. Leaving the cutter in the cake, rotate the top of the cutter away from the cake to break the next slice from the cake. Transfer the cut slice to an individual serving plate. Wipe the cutter, redip it in hot water, and shake off the excess water before piercing the cake and breaking away each slice.

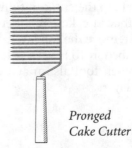

Pronged Cake Cutter

If a pronged cake cutter is not available, slices may be cut using light, sawing motions with a long, sharp, *thin-bladed* (nonserrated) knife. Wipe the knife on a damp sponge or cloth, dip the knife in hot water, and shake off the excess water before making each cut.

TO CUT FRUITCAKES: For precision pieces, fruitcakes should be refrigerated and chilled before slicing. Dip a sharp, *thin-bladed* knife into a tall glass or pitcher of hot water, shake off the excess water (away from the cake), and make a cut. Wipe the knife on a damp sponge or cloth, redip the knife in hot water, shake off the excess water, and make the second cut. Repeat the procedure for each subsequent cut. Cut the number of pieces to be served before removing any of the servings from the cake.

SERVINGS

While the number of servings from a particular-sized cake depends upon how the cake will be served, the dining occasion, the appetites of the diners, and the richness and nature of the cake, the following may serve as general guidelines:

Cake Description	Number of Servings
2- or 3-layer, 8-inch round or square cake	10
2- or 3-layer, 9-inch round or square cake	12
2- or 3-layer, 10-inch round or square cake	16
7 × 11-inch sheet cake	12
9 × 13-inch sheet cake	15
5 × 9-inch loaf cake	12
10-inch Bundt cake	14
10 × 4-inch tube-pan angel food, sponge, or chiffon cake	12
8-inch round torte	12
9-inch round torte	14

Layer Cakes

TO REMOVE LAYER CAKES FROM CAKE PANS

Immediately upon removing from the oven, place baked layer cakes on separate wire racks. Remove the bake-even cake strips, if used, from the pans (page 452). Let the cakes stand in the pans exactly 10 minutes (use a timer) to partially cool.

Then, carefully run a sharp, thin-bladed knife around the inside edge of the pans to completely loosen the side of the cakes from the pans. Place a wire rack over one of the pans. Firmly hold both the wire rack under the pan and the wire rack over the pan and, in a single motion, invert the wire racks (and pan). The cake will drop onto the lower rack provided the right type of pan has been used (see Equipment, page 449) and properly prepared, and the cake has been correctly baked.

Remove the upper wire rack and carefully lift the pan off the cake. Lightly place the extra wire rack over the exposed bottom side of the cake, hold the wire racks on both sides of the cake, and invert to return the cake to its upright position. Remove the upper wire rack and let the cake stand on the lower wire rack. Repeat the procedure with the other layer(s).

Let the cakes stand on the wire racks until completely cool. Then, immediately frost the cake (see To Frost a Cake, page 501), or place the layers on separate corrugated cardboard cake circles and store in separate airtight cake containers to prevent drying.

Follow the recipe procedures for removal of other types of cakes from their pans.

WHITE CAKE

2½ cups sifted cake flour (sift before
  measuring)
1 tablespoon plus ¼ teaspoon baking powder
½ teaspoon salt
⅔ cup vegetable shortening, softened
1¼ cups sugar
1½ teaspoons clear vanilla
1 cup whole milk
4 extra-large egg whites, room temperature
¼ cup sugar
Frosting of choice (see Frosting Suggestion
  below)

Preheat the oven to 375°F. Grease well and
flour lightly two 8 × 2-inch *or* two 9 × 1½- or 2-
inch round cake pans; set aside (see Note).

Onto wax paper, sift together the flour, baking powder, and salt; set aside.

In a large mixing bowl, place the vegetable
shortening and 1¼ cups sugar; using an electric
mixer, cream well on medium-high speed. Add
the vanilla; continue beating on medium-high
speed until blended. Add, alternately, the flour
mixture in fourths, and the milk in thirds, beating on low speed after each addition only until
blended; set aside.

Place the egg whites in a large mixing bowl.
Using the electric mixer fit with clean, dry
blades, beat the egg whites on high speed until
soft peaks hold. While continuing to beat on
high speed, very gradually add ¼ cup sugar and
continue beating the egg white mixture until
stiff, but still moist and glossy. Add the egg
white mixture to the cake batter; using a large
mixing spoon, fold in.

Using the large mixing spoon, spoon the batter equally into the 2 prepared cake pans. Using
a small, narrow, angled spatula, lightly and
quickly spread the batter evenly in the pans.
Bake the cakes for 17 to 18 minutes, or until a
wooden toothpick inserted into the center of
the cakes comes out clean.

Remove the cakes from the oven and place on
wire racks; let stand to cool 10 minutes. Remove
the cakes from the pans (page 455); let stand on
wire racks until completely cool.

Then, frost between the layers and the top
and side of the cake with frosting of choice (see
To Frost a Cake, page 501). Let the cake stand
until the frosting sets. Then, place the cake in an
airtight container.

NOTE: Do not wrap bake-even cake strips (page
452) around the cake pans when using this
recipe.

**MAKES ONE 8- OR 9-INCH, 2-LAYER ROUND CAKE;
10 SERVINGS**

FROSTING SUGGESTION: This cake was a blue ribbon winner frosted with Fluff Frosting (page
511) garnished with Pink-Tinted Coconut
(page 344). Immediately after frosting the cake
with Fluff Frosting, spoon Tinted Coconut
(pink or another color of choice) over the top
and side of the cake, pressing the coconut
lightly into the frosting with your hand only
until it holds in place. Let the cake stand 1 hour
to allow the frosting to dry slightly. Then, place
the cake in an airtight container.

3-LAYER WHITE CAKE

3¾ cups sifted cake flour (sift before
  measuring)
1 tablespoon plus 1¾ teaspoons baking
  powder
¾ teaspoon salt
1 cup vegetable shortening, softened
1¾ cups plus 2 tablespoons sugar
2¼ teaspoons clear vanilla
1½ cups whole milk
6 extra-large egg whites, room temperature
¼ cup plus 2 tablespoons sugar

Follow the procedures in the White Cake recipe,
above, using three 8 × 2-inch *or* three 9 × 1½-
or 2-inch round cake pans and the ingredient
amounts for a 3-Layer White Cake.

**MAKES ONE 8- OR 9-INCH, 3-LAYER ROUND CAKE;
10 OR 12 SERVINGS**

SHADOW CAKE

A shadow of mellifluous chocolate trickling down over billowy, white Boiled Frosting gives this gorgeous, delectable cake its name. Underneath the picturesque frosting, a white middle layer "shadows" two chocolate outer ones (see illustration, page 447).

3 tablespoons sugar
¼ teaspoon baking soda
¼ teaspoon salt
2½ ounces (2½ squares) unsweetened chocolate
¼ cup boiling water
2½ cups sifted cake flour (sift before measuring)
2½ teaspoons baking powder
½ teaspoon salt
½ cup (¼ pound) butter, softened
1 cup sugar
1 extra-large egg plus 2 extra-large egg yolks
1½ teaspoons pure vanilla extract
¾ cup whole milk
1 recipe Boiled Frosting (page 506)
2 ounces (2 squares) unsweetened chocolate
2 teaspoons butter

Preheat the oven to 350°F. Using Special Grease (page 40), grease three 8 × 2-inch round cake pans (see Note); set aside. Place 3 bake-even cake strips (page 452) in cold water; let stand.

In a small sauce dish, place 3 tablespoons sugar, baking soda, and ¼ teaspoon salt; stir to combine; set aside.

Place 2½ ounces chocolate in the top of a double boiler over (not touching) simmering water in the bottom pan. Melt the chocolate, stirring constantly. Add the sugar mixture; stir to combine. Remove the top of the double boiler from the bottom pan. Add the boiling water to the chocolate mixture; stir until blended; set aside.

Onto waxed paper, sift together the flour, baking powder, and ½ teaspoon salt; set aside.

Extract the excess water from the bake-even cake strips. Wrap and pin the strips around the prepared cake pans; set aside.

In a large mixing bowl, place the butter and 1 cup sugar; using an electric mixer cream well on medium-high speed. Add the whole egg and egg yolks, one at a time, beating well on medium-high speed after each addition. Add the vanilla; continue beating on medium-high speed until light and fluffy. Add, alternately, the flour mixture in fourths, and the milk in thirds, beating on low speed after each addition only until blended. Using a large mixing spoon, spoon ⅓ of the cake batter into 1 prepared cake pan. Using a small, narrow, angled spatula, lightly and quickly spread the batter evenly in the pan; set aside.

Add the chocolate mixture to the remaining batter; using the electric mixer, beat on low speed only until blended. Using a clean, large mixing spoon, spoon the batter equally into the 2 remaining prepared cake pans; using a clean, small, narrow, angled spatula, spread the batter evenly in the pans. Bake the cakes for 20 to 25 minutes, or until a wooden toothpick inserted into the center of the cakes comes out clean.

Remove the cakes from the oven and place on wire racks; remove the cake strips. Let the cakes stand to cool 10 minutes. Remove the cakes from the pans (page 455); let stand on wire racks until completely cool.

Then, with the Boiled Frosting, frost between the layers of the cake, using the light-colored cake as the center layer (see To Frost a Cake, page 501); frost the top of the cake quite smoothly; frost the side of the cake and then swirl the *side* frosting attractively (see To Swirl Frosting, page 504). Let the cake stand until the frosting sets.

Then, in a tiny saucepan, place 2 ounces chocolate and 2 teaspoons butter. Melt the chocolate and butter over *warm* (no hotter) heat, stirring constantly and until completely blended. Cool the chocolate mixture *slightly*. Using a tablespoon, spoon the chocolate mixture onto the top of the cake and let it trickle down the sides. Let the cake stand until the chocolate topping sets. Then, place the cake in an airtight container.

(Recipe continues on next page)

NOTE: Although not as satisfactory, the pans may be greased and floured using the traditional method (page 40) in substitution for using Special Grease.

**MAKES ONE 8-INCH, 3-LAYER ROUND CAKE;
10 SERVINGS**

OPTIONAL DECORATION: For additional elegance, decorate the top of the cake with 3 fresh, white roses placed in the center (see Edible Flowers, page 316).

WHITE AND CHOCOLATE 2-LAYER CAKE

To satisfy all preferences, this cake sports one white layer and one chocolate layer, and uses both white and chocolate frostings.

2 tablespoons sugar
¼ teaspoon baking soda
2 ounces (2 squares) unsweetened chocolate
3 tablespoons boiling water
Ingredients for 1 recipe White Cake
   (page 456) (see recipe procedures, below)
½ recipe Cake Decorators' White Icing
   (page 504)
½ recipe Cake Decorators' Chocolate Icing
   (page 505)

Preheat the oven to 375° F. Grease well and flour lightly two 8 × 2-inch round baking pans; set aside (see Note).

In a small sauce dish, place the sugar and baking soda; stir to combine; set aside. Place the chocolate in a tiny saucepan. Hold the tiny pan over (not touching) low simmering water in a small saucepan until the chocolate melts, stirring intermittently. Remove the tiny pan from the heat. Add the baking soda mixture to the melted chocolate; stir to combine. Add the boiling water; stir until blended; set aside.

Follow the White Cake recipe through the additions of the flour mixture and milk. Using a large mixing spoon, spoon the cake batter equally into 2 medium mixing bowls. Add the chocolate mixture to one of the bowls of batter; using the electric mixer, beat on low speed only until completely blended; set aside.

Follow the White Cake recipe to beat 4 egg whites, adding ¼ cup sugar. Using a table knife, cut the beaten egg white mixture in half. Quickly and carefully spoon ½ of the egg white mixture into each bowl of batter. Using a separate, large mixing spoon for each bowl, fold in.

Spoon each bowl of batter into one of the prepared cake pans. Using a small, narrow, angled spatula, lightly and quickly spread the batter evenly in one of the pans. Then, clean and dry the spatula, and spread the batter in the second pan. Bake the cakes for 17 to 18 minutes, or until a wooden toothpick inserted into the center of the cakes comes out clean.

Remove the cakes from the oven and place on wire racks; let stand to cool 10 minutes. Remove the cakes from the pans (page 455); let stand on wire racks until completely cool.

Then, frost between the layers of the cake with the Cake Decorators' White Icing, using the chocolate cake as the bottom layer (see To Frost a Cake, page 501). Frost the top and side of the cake with the Cake Decorators' Chocolate Icing. Let the cake stand until the frosting sets. Then, place the cake in an airtight container.

NOTE: Do not wrap bake-even cake strips (page 452) around the cake pans when using this recipe.

**MAKES ONE 8-INCH, 2-LAYER ROUND CAKE;
10 SERVINGS**

OPTIONAL DECORATION: Reserve a portion of both the Cake Decorators' White Icing and the Cake Decorators' Chocolate Icing to decorate the cake. Fit 2 decorating bags each with a medium open-star tip number 21 (page 319). Fill one of the bags with Cake Decorators' White Icing, and the other bag with Cake Decorators' Chocolate Icing. Pipe a shell border (page 324) around the bottom and top of the cake, alternating white and chocolate shells. Arrange piped, white roses (pages 327–329) on the top of the cake. Using medium leaf tip number 67, pipe chocolate leaves (page 326) around the roses.

CHECKERBOARD CAKE

Each slice looks like a chocolate and yellow cake checkerboard. A special Checkerboard Cake Set (three 9-inch round baking pans and a divider), available commercially, is required to make this fun dessert.

2 1/2 ounces (2 1/2 squares) unsweetened chocolate
4 cups sifted cake flour (sift before measuring)
3 tablespoons plus 2 teaspoons baking powder
1 teaspoon salt
3/4 cup (1/4 pound plus 4 tablespoons) butter, softened
2 cups sugar
2 extra-large eggs
2 teaspoons pure vanilla extract
1 1/2 cups plus 2 tablespoons whole milk
1 recipe Cake Decorators' Chocolate Icing (page 505)

Preheat the oven to 350°F. Grease and flour lightly the three 9-inch round cake pans in a Checkerboard Cake Set (see headnote); set aside.

Place the chocolate in a tiny saucepan. Hold the tiny pan over (not touching) low simmering water in a small saucepan until the chocolate melts, stirring intermittently. Remove the tiny pan from the heat; set aside.

Onto waxed paper, sift together the flour, baking powder, and salt; set aside.

In a large mixing bowl, place the butter and sugar; using an electric mixer, cream well on medium-high speed. Add the eggs, one at a time, beating well on medium-high speed after each addition. Add the vanilla; beat on medium-high speed until light and fluffy. Add, alternately, the flour mixture in fourths, and the milk in thirds, beating on low speed after each addition only until blended.

Using a large mixing spoon, spoon slightly less than 1/2 of the cake batter into a medium mixing bowl; set aside. Add the melted chocolate to the remaining batter; using the electric mixer, beat on low speed until blended.

Place the checkerboard cake divider in one of the prepared cake pans (the top layer of the cake). The divider separates the cake into 3 sections (see illustration A).

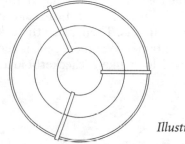

Illustration A

Use one hand to press down on the divider and hold it firmly against the bottom of the pan to help prevent seepage of batter between the sections. Using a tableware teaspoon, carefully spoon chocolate batter into the outside and the center sections of the pan until approximately 1/2 full. Using a small, narrow, angled spatula spread the batter evenly. Then, using a clean teaspoon, spoon yellow batter into the middle section of the pan until approximately 1/2 full. Using a clean, small, narrow, angled spatula, spread the batter evenly. All batter in the pan should be the same depth.

Remove the divider; rinse and dry it. Wipe off any excess batter around the inside edge of the pan; carefully regrease (but don't reflour) the edge of the pan, if necessary, taking care not to touch the batter with grease.

Repeat the exact procedure to fill the second pan with batter (the bottom layer of the cake).

Using the same procedure, fill the third pan (the middle layer of the cake), placing the yellow batter in the outside and the center sections, and the chocolate batter in the middle section.

Bake the cakes for 18 to 20 minutes, or until

(Recipe continues on next page)

a wooden toothpick inserted into the center of the cakes comes out clean.

Remove the cakes from the oven and place on wire racks; let stand to cool 10 minutes. Remove the cakes from the pans (page 455); let stand on wire racks until completely cool.

Frost between the layers of the cake with the Cake Decorators' Chocolate Icing, using the layer with yellow cake in the outside and center sections as the middle layer. Then, frost the top and side of the cake as smoothly as possible with Cake Decorators' Chocolate Icing (see To Frost a Cake, page 501). Let the cake stand until the frosting sets. Then, place the cake in an airtight container. When the cake is served, each slice will look like a checkerboard (see Illustration B).

Illustration B

MAKES ONE 9-INCH, 3-LAYER ROUND CAKE;
12 SERVINGS

OPTIONAL DECORATION:
½ recipe Cake Decorators' Buttercream Icing (page 505)

Before frosting the cake, reserve 1½ cups of the Cake Decorators' Chocolate Icing; set aside. After frosting the cake, let the cake stand only until the frosting partially sets.

Then, using a 1-inch-square cookie cutter (see Note), lightly mark rows of squares in the frosting over the entire top surface of the cake. Using a decorating bag fit with very small round tip number 2 (page 319) and filled with Cake Decorators' Buttercream Icing, outline every other square. Using the same icing and small round tip number 5, fill in alternate outlined squares, in checkerboard fashion. To fin-

ish the cake, use a decorating bag fit with medium open-star tip number 21 and filled with the reserved Cake Decorators' Chocolate Icing to pipe shell borders (page 505) around the bottom and top of the cake. Let the cake stand until the frosting sets. Then, place the cake in an airtight container.

NOTE: If not available commercially, the cutter may be made from a suitable gauge of aluminum flashing material available at hardware stores.

CHOCOLATE CAKE

Lion among cakes!

3 ounces (3 squares) unsweetened chocolate
2 cups sifted cake flour (sift before measuring)
1 teaspoon baking soda
½ teaspoon salt
½ cup (¼ pound) butter *or* vegetable shortening, softened
1½ cups sugar
2 extra-large eggs
1 teaspoon pure vanilla extract
1 cup whole milk
1 recipe Chocolate Frosting (page 508)
Chocolate Curls (page 342) for decoration

Preheat the oven to 350° F. Using Special Grease (page 40), grease two 8 × 2-inch round cake pans (see Note); set aside. Place 2 bake-even cake strips (page 452) in cold water; let stand.

Place the chocolate in a tiny saucepan. Hold the tiny pan over (not touching) low simmering water in a small saucepan until the chocolate melts, stirring intermittently. Remove the tiny pan from the heat; set aside.

Onto waxed paper, sift together the flour, baking soda, and salt; set aside.

Extract the excess water from the bake-even cake strips. Wrap and pin the strips around the prepared cake pans; set aside.

In a large mixing bowl, place the butter and sugar; using an electric mixer, cream well on medium-high speed. Add the eggs, one at a time, beating well on medium-high speed after each addition. Add the vanilla and melted chocolate; beat on medium-high speed until completely blended. Add, alternately, the flour mixture in fourths, and the milk in thirds, beating on low speed after each addition only until blended.

Using a large mixing spoon, spoon the cake batter equally into the 2 prepared cake pans. Using a small, narrow, angled spatula, lightly and quickly spread the batter evenly in the pans. Bake the cakes for 25 minutes, or until a wooden toothpick inserted into the center of the cakes comes out clean.

Remove the cakes from the oven and place on wire racks; remove the cake strips. Let the cakes stand to cool 10 minutes. Remove the cakes from the pans (page 455); let stand on wire racks until completely cool.

Then, frost between the layers, and the top and side of the cake with the Chocolate Frosting (see To Frost a Cake, page 501). Let the cake stand until the frosting sets. Then, place the cake in an airtight container.

NOTE: Although not as satisfactory, the pans may be greased and floured using the traditional method (page 40) in substitution for using Special Grease.

MAKES ONE 8-INCH, 2-LAYER ROUND CAKE; 10 SERVINGS

VARIATION: A frosting of choice may be substituted for the Chocolate Frosting.

CHOCOLATE BANANA CAKE WITH BANANA-NUT FROSTING

Chocolate adds a new twist to this banana cake.

2 cups sifted cake flour (sift before measuring)
1 ½ teaspoons baking powder
¾ teaspoon baking soda
¾ teaspoon salt
¾ cup mashed bananas (see procedures below) (about 2 very ripe bananas)
2 ounces (2 squares) unsweetened chocolate
½ cup (¼ pound) butter *or* vegetable shortening, softened
1 ½ cups packed light brown sugar
¾ cup homemade sour milk (page 42)
2 extra-large eggs
1 teaspoon pure vanilla extract
1 recipe Banana-Nut Frosting (page 509)
Pecan halves for decoration

Preheat the oven to 350° F. Using Special Grease (page 40), grease two 8 × 2-inch round cake pans (see Note 1); set aside (see Note 2).

Onto waxed paper, sift together the flour, baking powder, baking soda, and salt; set aside. Slice the bananas into a medium-small mixing bowl; using a table fork, mash well. Measure ¾ cup mashed bananas; set aside.

Place the chocolate in a tiny saucepan. Hold the tiny pan over (not touching) low simmering water in a small saucepan until the chocolate melts, stirring intermittently. Remove the tiny pan from the heat; set aside.

In a large mixing bowl, place the butter and brown sugar; using an electric mixer, beat well on medium-high speed. Add the eggs, one at a time, beating well on medium-high speed after each addition. Add the vanilla; continue beating on medium-high speed until light and fluffy. Add the bananas; beat well. Add the melted chocolate; beat until blended. Add, alternately, the flour mixture in fourths, and the sour milk in thirds, beating on low speed after each addition only until blended.

Using a large mixing spoon, spoon the cake

(Recipe continues on next page)

batter equally into the 2 prepared cake pans. Using a small, narrow, angled spatula, lightly and quickly spread the batter evenly in the pans. Bake the cakes for 30 minutes, or until a wooden toothpick inserted into the center of the cakes comes out clean.

Remove the cakes from the oven and place on wire racks; let stand to cool 10 minutes. Remove the cakes from the pans (page 455); let stand on wire racks until completely cool.

Then, frost between the layers, and the top and side of the cake with the Banana-Nut Frosting (see To Frost a Cake, page 501). Arrange the pecan halves, side by side widthwise, on top of the cake around the outer edge. Let the cake stand until the frosting sets. Then, place the cake in an airtight container.

NOTE 1: Although not as satisfactory, the pans may be greased and floured using the traditional method (page 40) in substitution for using Special Grease.

NOTE 2: Do not wrap bake-even cake strips (page 40) around the cake pans when using this recipe.

MAKES ONE 8-INCH, 2-LAYER ROUND CAKE;
10 SERVINGS

GERMAN CHOCOLATE CAKE

Sweet chocolate and frosting loaded with coconut and pecans distinguish this 3-layer, ever-popular cake. By tradition, the side of German Chocolate Cake usually is not frosted.

1 4-ounce German's sweet chocolate bar for cooking, broken into several pieces
½ cup water
2¼ cups sifted cake flour (sift before measuring)
1½ teaspoons baking soda
½ teaspoon salt
¾ cup (¼ pound plus 4 tablespoons) butter, softened
1¼ cups sugar
4 extra-large eggs, room temperature, separated

1½ teaspoons pure vanilla extract
1 cup buttermilk
¼ cup sugar
1 recipe Coconut-Pecan Frosting I
  (page 510)

Preheat the oven to 350° F. Using Special Grease (page 40), grease three 8 × 2-inch round cake pans (see Note); set aside. Place 3 bake-even cake strips (page 452) in cold water; let stand.

In a small saucepan, place the chocolate pieces and water; place over medium-low heat and stir continuously until the chocolate melts. Remove from the heat; let stand to cool to room temperature.

Onto waxed paper, sift together the flour, baking soda, and salt; set aside.

Extract the excess water from the bake-even cake strips. Wrap and pin the strips around the prepared cake pans; set aside.

In a large mixing bowl, place the butter and 1¼ cups sugar; using an electric mixer, cream well on medium-high speed. Add the egg yolks, one at a time, beating well on medium-high speed after each addition. The batter should be very light and fluffy. Add the vanilla and melted chocolate; beat on medium-high speed until completely blended. Add, alternately, the flour mixture in fourths, and the buttermilk in thirds, beating on low speed after each addition only until blended; set aside.

Place the egg whites in a large mixing bowl. Using the electric mixer fit with clean, dry blades, beat the egg whites on high speed until soft peaks hold. While continuing to beat on high speed, very gradually add ¼ cup sugar and continue beating the egg white mixture until stiff, but still moist and glossy. Add the egg white mixture to the cake batter; using a large mixing spoon, fold in. (If the bowl in which the batter was mixed is not large enough, quickly and carefully transfer the batter to a larger mixing bowl before adding the egg white mixture.)

Using the large mixing spoon, spoon the batter equally into the 3 prepared cake pans. Using a small, narrow, angled spatula, lightly and quickly spread the batter evenly in the pans. Bake the cakes for 30 minutes, or until a wooden toothpick inserted into the center of the cakes comes out clean.

Remove the cakes from the oven and place on wire racks; remove the cake strips. Let the cakes stand to cool 10 minutes. Remove the cakes from the pans (page 455); let stand on wire racks until completely cool.

Then, frost between the layers, and the top, *but not the side,* of the cake with the Coconut-Pecan Frosting I (see To Frost a Cake, page 501). Let the cake stand until the frosting sets. Then, place the cake in an airtight container and refrigerate.

NOTE: Although not as satisfactory, the pans may be greased and floured in substitution for using Special Grease.

MAKES ONE 8-INCH, 3-LAYER ROUND CAKE; 10 SERVINGS

YELLOW CAKE

In contrast to White Cake, which uses egg whites and vegetable shortening to maintain its pure whiteness, Yellow Cake contains egg yolks and butter, which give this cake its warm, sunny hue. While Chocolate Frosting is customarily used on Yellow Cake, as called for in the recipe that follows, other frostings may be substituted, if you prefer (see Variation below).

3 cups sifted cake flour (sift before measuring)
1 tablespoon plus ¾ teaspoon baking powder
¾ teaspoon salt
½ cup (¼ pound) butter
1½ cups sugar
2 extra-large eggs
1½ teaspoons pure vanilla extract
1 cup whole milk
1 recipe Chocolate Frosting (page 508), *or* other frosting of choice

Preheat the oven to 350°F. Using Special Grease (page 40), grease two 9 × 2-inch round cake pans (see Note); set aside. Place 2 bake-even cake strips (page 452) in cold water; let stand.

Onto waxed paper, sift together the flour, baking powder, and salt; set aside.

Extract the excess water from the bake-even cake strips. Wrap and pin the strips around the prepared cake pans; set aside.

In a large mixing bowl, place the butter and sugar; using an electric mixer, cream well on medium-high speed. Add the eggs, one at a time, beating well on medium-high speed after each addition. Add the vanilla; continue beating on medium-high speed until very light and fluffy. Add, alternately, the flour mixture in fourths, and the milk in thirds, beating on low speed after each addition only until blended.

Using a large mixing spoon, spoon the cake batter equally into the 2 prepared cake pans. Using a small, narrow, angled spatula, lightly and quickly spread the batter evenly in the pans. Bake the cakes for 18 to 20 minutes, or until a wooden toothpick inserted into the center of the cakes comes out clean.

Remove the cakes from the oven and place on wire racks; remove the cake strips. Let the cakes stand to cool 10 minutes. Remove the cakes from the pans (page 455); let stand on wire racks until completely cool.

Then, frost between the layers, and the top and side of the cake with the Chocolate Frosting (see To Frost a Cake, page 501). Let the cake stand until the frosting sets. Then, place the cake in an airtight container.

NOTE: Although not as satisfactory, the pans may be greased and floured using the traditional method (page 40) in substitution for using Special Grease.

MAKES ONE 9-INCH, 2-LAYER ROUND CAKE; 12 SERVINGS

VARIATION: Add ¾ teaspoon lemon extract after adding the vanilla. Frost the cake with 1 recipe Lemon Buttercream Frosting (page 505).

BURNT-SUGAR CAKE

A longtime member of the cake hall of fame, Burnt-Sugar Cake's seductive, caramelized flavor continues to win its well-deserved praise and adoration.

2½ cups sifted cake flour (sift before
   measuring)
1 tablespoon baking powder
1 cup cold water
¼ cup cool Burnt-Sugar Syrup (recipe
   follows)
½ cup (¼ pound) butter, softened
1¼ cups sugar
2 extra-large eggs, room temperature,
   separated
1 teaspoon pure vanilla extract
¼ cup sugar
1 recipe Burnt-Sugar Frosting (page 507)

Preheat the oven to 350°F. Using Special Grease (page 40), grease two 9 × 2-inch round cake pans (see Note); set aside. Place 2 bake-even cake strips (page 452) in cold water; let stand.

Onto waxed paper, sift together the flour and baking powder; set aside. Into a small mixing bowl, pour the cold water and Burnt-Sugar Syrup; stir until blended; set aside.

Extract the excess water from the bake-even cake strips. Wrap and pin the strips around the prepared cake pans; set aside.

In a large mixing bowl, place the butter and 1¼ cups sugar; using an electric mixer, cream well on medium-high speed. Add the egg yolks, one at a time, beating well on medium-high speed after each addition. Add the vanilla; continue beating on medium-high until the batter is fluffy. Add, alternately, the flour mixture in fourths, and the burnt-sugar mixture in thirds, beating on low speed after each addition only until blended; set aside.

Place the egg whites in a medium mixing bowl. Using the electric mixer fit with clean, dry blades, beat the egg whites on high speed until soft peaks hold. While continuing to beat on high speed, very gradually add ¼ cup sugar and continue beating the egg white mixture until it is stiff and cuts with a table knife, but is still moist and glossy. Add the egg white mixture to the cake batter; using a large mixing spoon, fold in.

Using the large mixing spoon, spoon the batter equally into the 2 prepared cake pans. Using a small, narrow, angled spatula, lightly and quickly spread the batter evenly in the pans. Bake the cakes for 25 minutes, or until a wooden toothpick inserted into the center of the cakes comes out clean.

Remove the cakes from the oven and place on wire racks; remove the cake strips. Let the cakes stand to cool 10 minutes. Remove the cakes from the pans (page 455); let stand on wire racks until completely cool.

Then, frost between the layers, and the top and side of the cake with the Burnt-Sugar Frosting (see To Frost a Cake, page 501). Let the cake stand until the frosting sets. Then, place the cake in an airtight container.

NOTE: Although not as satisfactory, the pans may be greased and floured using the traditional method (page 40) in substitution for using Special Grease.

**MAKES ONE 9-INCH, 2-LAYER ROUND CAKE;
12 SERVINGS**

BURNT-SUGAR SYRUP

⅔ cup sugar
⅔ cup boiling water

Place the sugar in a small, heavy saucepan over medium heat. Melt the sugar, stirring constantly. Continue stirring until the melted sugar is deep brown in color. Remove from the heat. Add the boiling water; stir until completely blended. Return the saucepan to medium heat. Bring the mixture to a boil and cook, without stirring, until the mixture is the consistency of syrup and reduced to ½ cup. Remove from the heat and cool at room temperature.

MAKES ½ CUP. ENOUGH FOR USE IN THE BURNT-SUGAR CAKE, ABOVE, AND 1 RECIPE OF BURNT-SUGAR FROSTING (PAGE 507).

HARVEST MOON CAKE

I resurrected this recipe from Mother's old three-ring recipe book (a treasure trove, believe me). She says Harvest Moon Cake was popular when she was young (that would have been in the 1930s). Why this grand-tasting cake made with brown sugar has been in hibernation is hard to fathom. The frosting, which matches the cake in color and name, is really Seven-Minute Frosting made with brown sugar rather than granulated sugar. I can't figure out how this cake got its name because it is very light brown in color—not gold, the color associated with the full harvest moon.

3 cups sifted cake flour (sift before
    measuring)
1 tablespoon baking powder
¼ teaspoon salt
¾ cup (¼ pound plus 4 tablespoons) butter,
    softened
1 cup plus 2 tablespoons packed light brown
    sugar
3 extra-large egg yolks
1½ teaspoons pure vanilla extract
1 cup whole milk
1 recipe Harvest Moon Frosting (page 507)
⅓ cup sliced, unblanched almonds, toasted
    (page 34) and chopped (page 34)

Preheat the oven to 350° F. Using Special Grease (page 40), grease two 8 × 2-inch round cake pans (see Note); set aside. Place 2 bake-even cake strips (page 452) in cold water; let stand.

Onto waxed paper, sift together the flour, baking powder, and salt; set aside.

Extract the excess water from the bake-even cake strips. Wrap and pin the strips around the prepared cake pans; set aside.

In a large mixing bowl, place the butter and brown sugar; using an electric mixer, cream well on medium-high speed. Add the egg yolks, one at a time, beating on medium-high speed after each addition. Add the vanilla; continue beating until completely blended. Add, alter-

nately, the flour mixture in fourths, and the milk in thirds, beating on low speed after each addition only until blended.

Using a large mixing spoon, spoon the cake batter equally into the 2 prepared cake pans. Using a small, narrow, angled spatula, lightly and quickly spread the batter evenly in the pans. Bake the cakes for 20 to 25 minutes, or until a wooden toothpick inserted into the center of the cakes comes out clean.

Remove the cakes from the oven and place on wire racks; remove the cake strips. Let the cakes stand to cool 10 minutes. Remove the cakes from the pans (page 455); let stand on wire racks until completely cool.

Then, frost between the layers, and the top and side of the cake with the Harvest Moon Frosting (see To Frost a Cake, page 501).

Sprinkle the chopped almonds in the form of a circle to resemble a full moon on the top of the cake. The perimeter of the moon should be about 1 inch from the outside edge of the cake. To achieve a well-formed moon with a sharp edge, make a stencil by using an X-Acto knife to cut a 6-inch-diameter circle out of the center of an 8-inch-diameter corrugated cardboard cake circle. With one hand, hold the stencil close to the frosting surface and, with the other hand, sprinkle the almonds evenly inside the circle.

Let the cake stand until the frosting sets. Then, place the cake in an airtight container.

NOTE: Although not as satisfactory, the pans may be greased and floured using the traditional method (page 40) in substitution for using Special Grease.

**MAKES ONE 8-INCH, 2-LAYER ROUND CAKE;
10 SERVINGS**

CARROT CAKE

(See photo insert page D-2)

2 cups sifted all-purpose flour (sift before
    measuring)
1¾ teaspoons baking soda
1 teaspoon ground cinnamon
½ teaspoon salt
2 cups sugar
1½ cups vegetable oil
4 extra-large eggs
1 teaspoon pure vanilla extract
3 cups pared and medium-finely shredded
    carrots
1 cup broken pecans
Cream Cheese Frosting (recipe follows)

Preheat the oven to 350°F. Grease and lightly
flour two 9 × 2-inch round cake pans; set aside.

Onto waxed paper, sift together the flour,
baking soda, cinnamon, and salt. Place the flour
mixture in a large mixing bowl. Add the sugar;
using a large mixing spoon, stir to combine.
Using the mixing spoon, make a well in the center of the flour mixture.

Pour the vegetable oil, all at once, into the well
in the flour mixture; using an electric mixer,
beat on medium-high speed until blended.
While continuing to beat on medium-high
speed, add the eggs, one at a time, beating after
each addition until blended. Add the vanilla;
beat on medium-high speed until blended. Add
the carrots; beat on medium speed until evenly
combined. Add the pecans; using the large mixing spoon, stir and fold until evenly distributed.

Using the large mixing spoon, spoon the cake
batter equally into the 2 prepared cake pans.
Using a small, narrow, angled spatula, lightly
and quickly spread the batter evenly in the pans.
Bake the cakes for 35 minutes, or until a wooden
toothpick inserted into the center of the cakes
comes out clean.

Remove the cakes from the oven and place on
wire racks; let stand to cool 10 minutes. Remove
the cakes from the pans (page 455); let stand on
wire racks until completely cool.

Then, frost between the layers, and the top
and side of the cake with the Cream Cheese
Frosting (see To Frost a Cake, page 501). Let the
cake stand until the frosting sets. Then, place
the cake in an airtight container and store in the
refrigerator.

**MAKES ONE 9-INCH, 2-LAYER ROUND CAKE;
12 SERVINGS**

CREAM CHEESE FROSTING

8 ounces cream cheese, softened
½ cup (¼ pound) butter, softened
1 teaspoon pure vanilla extract
1 pound (4 cups) powdered sugar
½ cup chopped pecans
½ cup baking raisins, quartered

In a medium mixing bowl, place the cream
cheese and butter; using an electric mixer, beat
on high speed until completely blended and
smooth. Add the vanilla; beat on medium-high
speed until blended. Add the powdered sugar;
mix on low speed and then beat on medium-
high speed only until blended and fluffy. Add
the pecans and raisins; using a large spoon, stir
until evenly distributed.

OPTIONAL DECORATION

¼ recipe Cake Decorators' White Icing
    (page 504)
Orange and leaf green paste food coloring

Tint ½ of the Cake Decorators' White Icing
orange and the remaining ½ of the icing leaf
green (see To Tint Icing, page 321). Place the
orange-tinted icing in a decorating bag fit with
small round tip number 5 (page 319) and the
leaf green-tinted icing in a decorating bag fit
with very small round tip number 2.

Pipe 5 or more orange carrots with green,
leafy tops around the top of the cake, with the
small end of the carrots pointing toward the
center of the cake.

PINK CHAMPAGNE CAKE

This fashionable Midwest cake derives its name more from its color and elegance than from the champagne it contains. Actually, only 1 tablespoon of champagne is used in the custard filling, and none is included among the other cake ingredients. That leaves the remainder of the bottle to pour into fluted champagne glasses and raise in a toast to a luxurious dessert.

2¼ cups sifted cake flour (sift before
   measuring)
1 tablespoon baking powder
¾ teaspoon salt
1 cup superfine sugar
⅓ cup vegetable oil
½ cup whole milk
2 extra-large eggs, room temperature,
   separated
1 teaspoon clear vanilla
1 dot, pink paste food coloring
½ cup whole milk
½ cup superfine sugar
Champagne Custard Filling (recipe follows)
1 recipe Cake Decorators' White Icing (page
   504)
Pink paste food coloring

Preheat the oven to 325° F. Grease well and flour lightly two 9 × 2-inch round cake pans; set aside. Place 2 bake-even cake strips (page 452) in cold water; let stand.

Onto waxed paper, sift together the flour, baking powder, and salt.

Extract the excess water from the bake-even cake strips. Wrap and pin the strips around the prepared cake pans; set aside.

Place the flour mixture in a large mixing bowl. Add 1 cup sugar; using a large mixing spoon, stir to combine. Using the mixing spoon, make a well in the center of the flour mixture.

Pour the vegetable oil and ½ cup milk into the well in the flour mixture; using an electric mixer, beat on medium speed until blended. Add the egg yolks, one at a time, beating well on medium-high speed after each addition. Add the vanilla, dot of pink food coloring (use a toothpick), and ½ cup milk; continue beating on medium-high speed until well blended; set aside.

Place the egg whites in a large mixing bowl. Using the electric mixer fit with clean, dry blades, beat the egg whites on high speed until soft peaks hold. While continuing to beat on high speed, very gradually add ½ cup sugar and continue beating the egg white mixture until stiff, but still moist and glossy. Add the egg white mixture to the cake batter; using a large mixing spoon, fold in until blended and the color is even.

Using the large mixing spoon, spoon the batter equally into the 2 prepared cake pans. Using a small, narrow, angled spatula, lightly and quickly spread the batter evenly in the pans. Bake the cakes for 30 to 35 minutes, or until a wooden toothpick inserted the into center of the cakes comes out clean.

Remove the cakes from the oven and place on wire racks; remove the cake strips. Let the cakes stand to cool 10 minutes. Remove the cakes from the pans (page 455); let stand on wire racks until completely cool.

Then, spread the Champagne Custard Filling between the cake layers (see To Frost a Cake, page 501); set aside. Reserve 1½ cups of the Cake Decorators' White Icing. Tint the remainder of the icing pale pink (see To Tint Icing, page 321). Use the pink-tinted icing to frost smoothly the top and side of the cake. Using a decorating bag fit with medium open-star tip number 19 (page 319), pipe a shell border (page 324) of the reserved white icing around the bottom of the cake, and a reverse shell border (page 325) of the reserved white icing around the top edge of the cake.

Let the cake stand until the frosting sets. Then, place the cake in an airtight container and store in refrigerator.

**MAKES ONE 9-INCH, 2-LAYER ROUND CAKE;
12 SERVINGS**

CHAMPAGNE CUSTARD FILLING

¼ cup granulated sugar
1 tablespoon plus 2 teaspoons cornstarch
Dash of salt
⅔ cup whole milk
1 extra-large egg yolk, slightly beaten
2 teaspoons butter
½ teaspoon pure vanilla extract
2 tablespoons butter, softened
1 cup powdered sugar
Dash of salt
½ teaspoon pure vanilla extract
1 tablespoon champagne
1¼ teaspoons cognac
¾ cup powdered sugar

In the top of a double boiler, place the granulated sugar, cornstarch, and dash of salt; stir to combine. Add the milk; stir well. Place the top of the double boiler over simmering water in the bottom pan. Cook the mixture until thick (about 2 to 3 minutes), constantly beating with a handheld electric mixer on low speed or stirring with a spoon. Add about ¼ cup of the hot cornstarch mixture to the egg yolk and quickly stir in. Then, add the egg yolk mixture to the remaining cornstarch mixture and stir vigorously to blend. Cook the mixture 2 minutes, beating constantly with the electric mixer on low speed.

Remove the top of the double boiler from the bottom pan and place on a wire rack. Add 2 teaspoons butter and ½ teaspoon vanilla; using the electric mixer, beat on low speed until blended. Let the custard mixture stand until cooled to room temperature, stirring occasionally.

Then, in a small mixing bowl, place 2 tablespoons softened butter, 1 cup powdered sugar, dash of salt, ½ teaspoon vanilla, champagne, and cognac; using the electric mixer, beat on high speed until blended and fluffy. Add the custard mixture and ¾ cup powdered sugar; beat on high speed until blended.

LADY BALTIMORE CAKE

This is a cake with a history, although that history has several versions. The gist of the story is that the cake was baked by a Charleston, South Carolina lady for Owen Wister, a novelist who then described the cake in his 1906 book Lady Baltimore. *While there are varying accounts of the cake's origin, everyone agrees on how it should be made: It is a three-layer white cake filled with figs, raisins, nuts, and candied cherries in white Boiled Frosting, all of which is iced with the remainder of the frosting. It's a glamorous, wonderful delicacy!*

1 recipe Boiled Frosting (page 506)
½ cup chopped dried figs (page 30)
½ cup chopped raisins (page 30)
4 ounces (½ cup) red candied cherries,
    chopped (page 30)
½ cup broken English walnuts
Baked cake layers for one 8-inch, 3-layer
    White Cake (page 456), substituting
    1 teaspoon clear vanilla and ½ teaspoon
    almond extract for 1½ teaspoons clear
    vanilla
2 tablespoons chopped raisins, page 30
3 tablespoons chopped English walnuts
2 tablespoons quartered, red candied cherries

In a medium mixing bowl, place 2 cups of the Boiled Frosting, figs, ½ cup chopped raisins, 4 ounces chopped cherries, and ½ cup walnuts; stir to combine and evenly distribute the fruits and nuts. Spread the frosting mixture between the cake layers, but not on the top or side of the cake (see To Frost a Cake, page 501). Using the remaining plain Boiled Frosting, frost the top and side of the cake.

Sprinkle the top of the cake with 2 tablespoons chopped raisins and 3 tablespoons chopped walnuts. Then, randomly distribute 2 tablespoons quartered cherries over the top of the cake. Let the cake stand until the frosting sets. Then, place the cake in an airtight container.

**MAKES ONE 8-INCH, 3-LAYER ROUND CAKE;
10 SERVINGS**

WHIPPED CREAM CAKE WITH CRÈME DE MENTHE FROSTING

I decided to try making a whipped cream cake when I noticed it listed among the cake classes to be judged at the 1990 Iowa State Fair. After studying whipped cream cakes and two or three testings, I wrote the recipe that follows. I'm happy to report that the end result garnered a blue ribbon.

3 cups sifted cake flour (sift before
  measuring)
1 tablespoon baking powder
½ teaspoon salt
1½ cups sugar
1½ cups whipping cream, unwhipped
1½ teaspoons pure vanilla extract
3 extra-large eggs, room temperature
1 recipe Crème de Menthe Whipped Cream
  Frosting (page 510)
Sprig(s) of fresh mint leaves for decoration

Preheat the oven to 350° F. Grease well and flour lightly two 8 × 2-inch round cake pans; set aside. Place 2 bake-even cake strips (page 452) in cold water; let stand.

Onto waxed paper, sift together the flour, baking powder, salt, and sugar; set aside.

Pour the whipping cream into a medium mixing bowl. Using an electric mixer, beat the cream on medium-high speed until it begins to stiffen. Reduce the mixer speed to medium-low. Add the vanilla and continue beating the cream until stiff, but still soft and fluffy; cover and refrigerate.

Extract the excess water from the bake-even cake strips. Wrap and pin the strips around the prepared cake pans; set aside.

Place the eggs in a small mixing bowl. Using the electric mixer fit with clean, dry blades, beat the eggs on high speed 5 minutes, until thick and lemon colored; set aside. Turn the whipped cream into a large mixing bowl. Pour the beaten eggs over the whipped cream; using a large mixing spoon, fold in thoroughly but quickly.

Sprinkle the flour mixture, about 1 cup at a time, over the whipped cream mixture and fold in after each addition, using the large mixing spoon.

Using the large mixing spoon, spoon the cake batter equally into the 2 prepared cake pans. Using a small, narrow, angled spatula, lightly and quickly spread the batter evenly in the pans. Bake the cakes for 25 to 30 minutes, or until a wooden toothpick inserted into the center of the cakes comes out clean.

Remove the cakes from the oven and place on wire racks; remove the cake strips. Let the cakes stand to cool 10 minutes. Remove the cakes from the pans (page 455); let stand on wire racks until completely cool.

Then, frost between the layers, and the top and side of cake with the Crème de Menthe Whipped Cream Frosting (see To Frost a Cake, page 501). Place the cake in an airtight container and store in the refrigerator.

Just before displaying the cake prior to serving, place a sprig of mint leaves in the center of the cake; or, place slices of cake on individual plates and decorate each plate with a small sprig of mint leaves.

**MAKES ONE 8-INCH, 2-LAYER ROUND CAKE;
10 SERVINGS**

VARIATIONS

- For an attractive holiday cake, decorate the cake with red maraschino cherries which have been cut in half lengthwise, then rinsed under cold, running water and dried between paper towels. Add small sprigs of fresh mint leaves, if desired.

- Frost the cake with Whipped Cream-Coconut Frosting (page 509).

SPICE CAKE

Caramel Frosting and chopped hazelnuts top this two-layer Spice Cake.

2¼ cups sifted cake flour (sift before
   measuring)
1 teaspoon baking powder
1 teaspoon baking soda
½ teaspoon salt
1 teaspoon ground cinnamon
¼ teaspoon ground nutmeg
¼ teaspoon ground cloves
½ cup (¼ pound) butter, softened
¾ cup granulated sugar
⅔ cup packed light brown sugar
3 extra-large eggs
1 cup buttermilk
1 recipe Caramel Frosting (page 508)
3 tablespoons chopped hazelnuts
   (page 34)

Preheat the oven to 350° F. Using Special Grease (page 40), grease two 9 × 2-inch round cake pans (see Note); set aside. Place 2 bake-even cake strips (page 452) in cold water; let stand.

Onto waxed paper, sift together the flour, baking powder, baking soda, salt, cinnamon, nutmeg, and cloves; set aside.

Extract the excess water from the bake-even cake strips. Wrap and pin the strips around the prepared cake pans; set aside.

In a large mixing bowl, place the butter, granulated sugar, and brown sugar; using an electric mixer, beat on medium-high speed until creamed. Add the eggs, one at a time, beating well on medium-high speed after each addition. Add, alternately, the flour mixture in fourths, and the buttermilk in thirds, beating on low speed after each addition only until blended.

Using a large mixing spoon, spoon the cake batter equally into the 2 prepared cake pans. Using a small, narrow, angled spatula, lightly and quickly spread the batter evenly in the pans. Bake the cakes for 30 minutes, or until a wooden toothpick inserted into the center of the cakes comes out clean.

Remove the cakes from the oven and place on wire racks; remove the cake strips. Let the cakes stand to cool 10 minutes. Remove the cakes from the pans (page 455); let stand on wire racks until completely cool.

Then, frost between the layers, and the top and side of cake with the Caramel Frosting (see To Frost a Cake, page 501). Sprinkle the chopped hazelnuts over the top of the cake. Let the cake stand until the frosting sets. Then, place the cake in an airtight container.

NOTE: Although not as satisfactory, the pans may be greased and floured using the traditional method (page 40) in substitution for using Special Grease.

**MAKES ONE 9-INCH, 2-LAYER ROUND CAKE;
12 SERVINGS**

VARIATION: Powdered Sugar Frosting (page 508) is also excellent on Spice Cake.

Sheet Cakes

APPLESAUCE CAKE WITH VANILLA SAUCE

A delicious, golden oldie from the recipe file of Ada Goreham, originally from Grinnell, Iowa, and mother of Dee Staples, my sister-in-law.

1 cup golden raisins, plumped (page 30)
½ cup broken pecans
2 cups sifted cake flour (sift before
   measuring)
1 teaspoon baking soda
¼ teaspoon salt
¾ teaspoon ground cinnamon
½ teaspoon ground nutmeg
½ teaspoon ground cloves
⅓ cup vegetable shortening, softened

1 cup sugar

1 extra-large egg

1½ cups puree-style, unsweetened, Plain Applesauce, homemade (page 290) or commercially canned

Vanilla Sauce (recipe follows)

Drain the plumped raisins in a sieve; distribute over paper towels to dry.

Preheat the oven to 350°F. Using Special Grease (page 40), grease a 7 × 11 × 2-inch baking pan (see Note); set aside.

In a small mixing bowl, place the dry raisins and pecans; stir to combine; set aside. Sprinkle 1 tablespoon of the measured flour over the raisin-pecan mixture; stir until evenly dusted; set aside. Onto waxed paper, sift together the remaining flour, baking soda, salt, cinnamon, nutmeg, and cloves; set aside.

In a large mixing bowl, place the vegetable shortening and sugar; using an electric mixer, cream well on medium-high speed. Add the egg; beat well on medium-high speed. Add, alternately, the flour mixture in fourths, and the applesauce in thirds, beating on low speed after each addition only until blended.

Pour the cake batter into the prepared baking pan. Using a small, narrow, angled spatula, lightly and quickly spread the batter evenly in the pan. Bake the cake for 30 to 35 minutes, or until a wooden toothpick inserted into the center of the cake comes out clean.

Remove the cake from the oven and place on a wire rack. Serve the cake warm, with the warm Vanilla Sauce spooned over individual servings.

NOTE: Although not as satisfactory, the pan may be greased and floured using the traditional method (page 40) in substitution for using Special Grease.

MAKES ONE 7 × 11-INCH SHEET CAKE; 12 SERVINGS

VANILLA SAUCE

½ cup sugar

2 tablespoons cornstarch

¼ teaspoon salt

2 cups water

¼ cup (4 tablespoons) butter

2 teaspoons clear vanilla

In a small saucepan, place the sugar, cornstarch, and salt; stir to combine. Add the water; stir well. Bring the mixture to a full boil over medium heat, stirring constantly. Reduce the heat and cook the mixture until thick, stirring continuously. Remove from the heat. Add the butter and vanilla; stir until blended. Serve warm.

RHUBARB CAKE

When rhubarb is cut and brought into the house for the preparation of eagerly awaited rhubarb dishes, it's a sure sign that spring has arrived at last. When most Midwesterners see the rosy red stalks being washed and cut in the kitchen, they anticipate delighting in pies, crunchy desserts, and quick breads (see Rhubarb Pie, page 416; Strawberry-Rhubarb Pie, page 417; Rhubarb Rapture, page 578; and Rhubarb Bread, page 371). For variety during the next rhubarb-feasting season, surprise everyone with this tasty Rhubarb Cake with tantalizing Buttercream Frosting.

2 cups cake flour

1 teaspoon baking soda

¼ teaspoon salt

½ cup (¼ pound) butter, softened

1½ cups sugar

1 extra-large egg

1¼ teaspoons pure vanilla extract

1 cup whole milk

2 cups fresh rhubarb, diced ¼ inch square

1 recipe Buttercream Frosting (page 505)

(Recipe continues on next page)

Preheat the oven to 350° F. Using Special Grease (page 40), grease a 7 × 11 × 2-inch baking pan (see Note); set aside.

Reserve 1 tablespoon of the measured flour in a small sauce dish. Onto waxed paper, sift together the remaining flour, baking soda, and salt; set aside.

In a large mixing bowl, place the butter and sugar; using an electric mixer, cream well on medium-high speed. Add the egg and vanilla; beat on medium-high speed until light and fluffy. Add, alternately, the flour mixture in fourths, and the milk in thirds, beating on low speed after each addition only until blended; set aside.

Place the rhubarb in a medium mixing bowl. Sprinkle the 1 tablespoon reserved flour over the rhubarb; toss until the rhubarb is coated. Add the rhubarb to the cake batter; using a large mixing spoon, fold in only until evenly distributed.

Turn the batter into the prepared baking pan. Using a small, narrow, angled spatula, lightly and quickly spread the batter evenly in the pan. Bake the cake for 40 to 45 minutes.

Remove the cake from the oven and place on a wire rack to cool.

When completely cool, leave the cake in the pan and frost it with the Buttercream Frosting. Let the cake stand until the frosting sets. Then, cover the cake with aluminum foil.

NOTE: Although not as satisfactory, the pan may be greased and floured using the traditional method (page 40) in substitution for using Special Grease.

**MAKES ONE 7 × 11-INCH SHEET CAKE;
12 SERVINGS**

FRUIT COCKTAIL CAKE

1 15¼-ounce can fruit cocktail in heavy syrup
2 cups all-purpose flour
2 teaspoons baking soda
2 tablespoons butter, softened
1½ cups sugar
2 extra-large eggs
1 recipe Coconut-Pecan Frosting II
  (page 510)

Preheat the oven to 350° F. Using Special Grease (page 40), grease a 9 × 13 × 2-inch baking pan (see Note); set aside.

Drain the fruit cocktail in a sieve, reserving the syrup. Place the fruit in a small mixing bowl and pour the syrup into a glass measuring cup with pouring spout; set aside.

Reserve 2 tablespoons of the measured flour in a small sauce dish; set aside. Onto waxed paper, sift together the remaining flour and baking soda; set aside.

In a large mixing bowl, place the butter and sugar; using an electric mixer, beat on medium-high speed until the mixture is the texture of crumbs. Add the eggs, one at a time, beating well on medium-high speed after each addition. Add, alternately, the flour mixture in fourths, and the fruit syrup in thirds, beating on low speed after each addition only until blended; set aside.

Sprinkle the 2 tablespoons reserved flour over the fruit and quickly toss to coat. Add the fruit to the cake batter; using a large mixing spoon, fold in only until evenly distributed.

Pour the batter into the prepared baking pan. Using a small, narrow, angled spatula, lightly and quickly spread the batter evenly in the pan. Bake the cake for 30 minutes.

Remove the cake from the oven and place on a wire rack; let stand to cool 30 minutes. While the cake is still warm, frost it in the pan with the Coconut-Pecan Frosting II. Let the cake stand on the wire rack until completely cool. Then, cover the cake with aluminum foil or a baking pan cover.

NOTE: Although not as satisfactory, the pan may be greased and floured using the traditional method (page 40) in substitution for using Special Grease.

MAKES ONE 9 × 13-INCH SHEET CAKE; 18 SERVINGS

PINEAPPLE UPSIDE-DOWN CAKE

(See photo insert page D-3)

1 20-ounce can pineapple slices in
   unsweetened pineapple juice
½ cup juice drained from pineapple slices
2 tablespoons plus 2 teaspoons butter
½ cup packed dark brown sugar
3 red maraschino cherries, cut in half
   lengthwise
1¼ cups sifted all-purpose flour (sift before
   measuring)
2 teaspoons baking powder
¼ cup plus 2 tablespoons (6 tablespoons)
   butter, softened
½ cup sugar
1 extra-large egg
1 teaspoon pure vanilla extract
1 recipe Whipped Cream (page 309)

Preheat the oven to 350°F.

Drain the pineapple slices well in a sieve, reserving the juice. Measure ½ cup of the reserved pineapple juice. Set the pineapple slices and reserved juice aside.

Place 2 tablespoons plus 2 teaspoons butter in an *ungreased* 8 × 8 × 2-inch baking pan. Place the baking pan over warm heat; let stand until the butter melts. Remove from the heat. Tilt the pan back and forth to spread the melted butter over the entire bottom of the pan. Sprinkle the brown sugar evenly over the butter in the bottom of the pan. Over the brown sugar, arrange 1 pineapple slice near each of the corners of the pan, and 1 pineapple slice in the center of the pan. Place ½ of a maraschino cherry,

cut side up, in the center of each pineapple slice. If desired, an additional ¼ slice of pineapple and 1 maraschino cherry half may be placed on each side of the pan between the slices, allowing each serving of cake to be topped with pineapple and a cherry half when the cake is cut into 9 servings; set aside.

Onto waxed paper, sift together the flour and baking powder; set aside.

In a medium mixing bowl, place ¼ cup plus 2 tablespoons butter and sugar; using an electric mixer, cream well on medium-high speed. Add the egg; beat on medium-high speed until fluffy. Add the vanilla; continue beating on medium-high speed until well blended. Add, alternately, the flour mixture in thirds, and the reserved pineapple syrup in halves, beating on low speed after each addition only until blended.

Using a large mixing spoon, spoon the cake batter over the pineapple slices in the bottom of the pan. Using a small, narrow, angled spatula, spread the batter evenly over the entire bottom of the pan, being careful not to disturb the arrangement of the pineapple slices and cherries. Bake the cake for 40 minutes.

Remove the cake from the oven and place on a wire rack; let stand to cool 10 minutes. Then, run a sharp, thin-bladed knife along the inside edges of the cake pan. Invert the cake onto a serving plate. Carefully lift the pan off the cake. Let the cake stand until completely cool. Then, cover the cake with an airtight dome or place it in an airtight container.

Pass the Whipped Cream in an inviting serving bowl at the table.

MAKES ONE 8-INCH-SQUARE SHEET-TYPE CAKE; 9 SERVINGS

WACKY CAKE

So unorthodox are the mixing procedures for this fun cake, it has been dubbed "Wacky Cake." Who has ever heard of making holes in the flour mixture in the pan and pouring a different ingredient into each of them? Well, it works. When you're looking for a little cooking levity, you're sure to get a kick out of baking this good-tasting, maverick cake.

1½ cups cake flour
1 teaspoon baking soda
½ teaspoon salt
3 tablespoons unsweetened cocoa powder
1 cup sugar
1 tablespoon cider vinegar
1 teaspoon pure vanilla extract
¼ cup plus 2 tablespoons (6 tablespoons)
    butter, melted
1 cup water
½ recipe Buttercream Frosting (page 505) *or*
    ½ recipe Chocolate Frosting
    (page 508)

Preheat the oven to 350°F.

Into an *ungreased* 8 × 8 × 2-inch baking pan, sift together the flour, baking soda, salt, cocoa, and sugar; using a small, narrow, angled spatula, spread evenly in the pan. Using a tablespoon, make 2 small holes and 1 large hole in the flour mixture, making the holes in a triangular pattern around the central part of the cake pan. Into 1 of the small holes, pour the vinegar. Into the other small hole, pour the vanilla. Into the large hole, pour the melted butter. Pour 1 cup water over all. Using a tablespoon, stir and beat the mixture well, until blended. The cake batter will be very slightly lumpy.

Using a damp sponge, remove the excess batter from the sides of the pan above the batter. Bake the cake for 30 minutes, or until a wooden toothpick inserted into the center of the cake comes out clean.

Remove the cake from the oven and place on a wire rack to cool.

When completely cool, leave the cake in the pan and frost it with the Buttercream Frosting or the Chocolate Frosting. Let the cake stand until the frosting sets. Then, cover the cake with aluminum foil.

MAKES ONE 8-INCH-SQUARE SHEET CAKE; 10 SERVINGS

GINGERBREAD

Counter the cool breezes of fall and the winds of winter with warm pieces of gingerbread, enhanced, if you like, with Rum or Lemon Sauce spooned over the top.

1 cup water
2 teaspoons baking soda
2½ cups sifted all-purpose flour (sift before
    measuring)
1 teaspoon ground ginger
1 teaspoon ground cinnamon
1 teaspoon ground cloves
½ teaspoon ground allspice
½ cup (¼ pound) butter, softened
½ cup sugar
1 cup light (mild) molasses
2 extra-large eggs

Preheat the oven to 350°F. Grease and flour lightly a 7 × 11 × 2-inch baking pan; set aside.

Pour 1 cup water into a very small saucepan. Bring the water to a boil over high heat. Remove from the heat. Add the baking soda; stir to dissolve; set aside.

Onto waxed paper, sift together the flour, ginger, cinnamon, cloves, and allspice; set aside.

In a large mixing bowl, place the butter and sugar; using an electric mixer, cream well on medium-high speed. Add the molasses; beat on medium-high until blended. Add the eggs, one at a time, beating well on medium-high speed after each addition. Add, alternately, the flour mixture in fourths, and the baking soda mixture in thirds, beating on low speed after each addition only until blended.

Pour the Gingerbread batter into the prepared pan. Using a small, narrow, angled spatula, lightly and quickly spread the batter evenly in the pan. Bake the Gingerbread for 35 to 40 minutes, or until a wooden toothpick inserted into the center of the Gingerbread comes out clean.

Remove the Gingerbread from the oven and place on a wire rack to cool. When completely cool, cover the Gingerbread with aluminum foil.

**MAKES ONE 7 × 11-INCH SHEET CAKE;
12 SERVINGS**

SERVING SUGGESTIONS
- Spoon warm Rum Sauce (page 308) or Lemon Sauce (page 307) over individual servings.
- Serve Gingerbread with a generous dollop of Whipped Cream (page 309) on each slice.

SOUR CREAM SPICE CAKE

Here is the recipe for one of the cakes my mother made the most often when we were kids. It was— and still is—my brother's favorite.

3 cups all-purpose flour
2 teaspoons baking soda
½ teaspoon cream of tartar
½ teaspoon salt
2 teaspoons ground cinnamon
½ teaspoon ground cloves
½ teaspoon ground nutmeg
1 cup golden* raisins
1 cup broken English walnuts
2 cups sugar
2 cups homemade sour cream (page 42)
4 extra-large eggs
1 recipe Powdered Sugar Frosting
   (page 508)

* *If preferred, 1 cup of dark baking raisins
   may be substituted for 1 cup golden raisins.*

Preheat the oven to 350°F. Using Special Grease (page 40), grease a 9 × 13 × 2-inch baking pan (see Note); set aside.

Reserve 1 tablespoon of the measured flour in a small sauce dish. Onto waxed paper, sift together the remaining flour, baking soda, cream of tartar, salt, cinnamon, cloves, and nutmeg; set aside.

In a medium mixing bowl, place the raisins and walnuts. Sprinkle the 1 tablespoon reserved flour over the raisins and walnuts; toss until lightly dusted and evenly distributed; set aside.

In a large mixing bowl, place the sugar and sour cream; using an electric mixer, blend well on medium-high speed. Add the eggs, one at a time, beating well on medium-high speed after each addition. Continue beating the mixture on medium-high until fluffy. Add the flour mixture; beat on low speed only until well blended. Add the raisins and walnuts; using a large mixing spoon, fold in.

Turn the cake batter into the prepared baking pan. Using a large, narrow, angled spatula, lightly and quickly spread the batter evenly in the pan. Bake the cake for 30 to 35 minutes, or until a wooden toothpick inserted into the center of the cake comes out clean.

Remove the cake from the oven and place on a wire rack to cool.

When completely cool, leave the cake in the pan and frost it with the Powdered Sugar Frosting. Let the cake stand until the frosting sets. Then, cover the cake with aluminum foil or a baking pan cover.

NOTE: Although not as satisfactory, the pan may be greased and floured using the traditional method (page 40) in substitution for using Special Grease.

**MAKES ONE 9 × 13-INCH SHEET CAKE;
15 SERVINGS**

OATMEAL CAKE

A rich, lush, dessert-type cake.

1½ cups water
1 cup quick-cooking rolled oats, uncooked
1½ cups sifted cake flour (sift before
   measuring)
1 teaspoon baking soda
½ teaspoon salt
1 teaspoon ground cinnamon
½ cup vegetable shortening, softened
1 cup granulated sugar
1 cup packed light brown sugar
2 extra-large eggs
Topping (recipe follows)
¾ cup whipping cream, unwhipped
1 tablespoon granulated sugar
½ teaspoon pure vanilla extract

Preheat the oven to 325° F. Using Special Grease (page 40), grease a 9 × 13 × 2-inch baking pan (see Note); set aside.

Pour 1½ cups water into a medium saucepan; bring the water to a boil over high heat. Add the oats; stir to combine. Remove from the heat; let stand.

Onto waxed paper, sift together the flour, baking soda, salt, and cinnamon; set aside.

In a large mixing bowl, place the vegetable shortening, 1 cup granulated sugar, and brown sugar; using an electric mixer, cream well on medium-high speed. Add the eggs, one at a time, beating well on medium-high speed after each addition. Add the flour mixture; beat on low speed only until blended. Add the oatmeal mixture; beat on low speed only until combined.

Pour the cake batter into the prepared baking pan. Using a small, narrow, angled spatula, lightly and quickly spread the batter evenly in the pan. Bake the cake for 35 minutes, or until a wooden toothpick inserted into the center of the cake comes out clean.

Remove the cake from the oven and place on a wire rack. Increase the oven temperature to 400° F. Spoon the Topping over the hot cake in the pan; using a clean, small, narrow, angled spatula, spread as evenly as possible, being careful not to crush the cake. Return the cake to the oven; bake for 8 additional minutes.

Remove the cake from the oven and place on the wire rack; let stand until completely cool. Then, cover the cake with aluminum foil or a baking pan cover.

Shortly before serving, pour the whipping cream into a small mixing bowl. Using the electric mixer fit with clean, dry blades, beat the cream on medium-high speed until it begins to stiffen. Reduce the mixer speed to medium-low. Add 1 tablespoon granulated sugar and vanilla; continue beating the cream until stiff, but still soft and fluffy; cover and refrigerate. Spoon a small dollop of whipped cream over individual pieces of Oatmeal Cake at serving time.

NOTE: Although not as satisfactory, the pan may be greased and floured using the traditional method (page 40) in substitution for using Special Grease.

**MAKES ONE 9 × 13-INCH SHEET CAKE;
15 SERVINGS**

TOPPING

½ cup (¼ pound) butter
½ cup packed light brown sugar
¼ cup whipping cream, unwhipped
1 teaspoon pure vanilla extract
1 cup chopped pecans
1 cup flaked coconut

In a small saucepan, melt the butter over low heat. Remove from the heat. Add the brown sugar; using an electric mixer, beat on medium speed until blended. Add the whipping cream and vanilla; beat to blend. Add the pecans and coconut; using a spoon, stir until evenly combined.

COLA CAKE

Would you believe? Your favorite cola is an ingredient in both this yummy chocolate cake and its nutty, chocolate frosting. Wonders never cease.

2 cups cake flour
2 cups sugar
½ cup (¼ pound) butter
1 cup Coca-Cola Classic cola *or* regular
    Pepsi-Cola cola
3 tablespoons unsweetened cocoa powder
½ cup buttermilk
2 extra-large eggs, well beaten
1 teaspoon baking soda
1 teaspoon pure vanilla extract
1½ cups miniature marshmallows
Cola Icing (recipe follows)

Preheat the oven to 350°F. Using Special Grease (page 40), grease a 9 × 13 × 2-inch baking pan (see Note); set aside.

Onto waxed paper, sift together the flour and sugar. Place the flour mixture in a large mixing bowl; set aside.

In a small saucepan, place the butter, cola, and cocoa; stir. Bring the cola mixture to the boiling point over medium heat, stirring constantly. Pour the cola mixture over the flour mixture; using an electric mixer, beat well on medium-high speed. Add the buttermilk, eggs, baking soda, vanilla, and marshmallows; beat well.

Pour the cake batter into the prepared baking pan. Using a small, narrow, angled spatula, lightly and quickly spread the batter evenly in the pan. Bake the cake for 40 minutes, or until a wooden toothpick inserted into the center of the cake comes out clean.

Remove the cake from the oven and place on a wire rack. Spread the Cola Icing over the *hot* cake in the pan. Let the cake stand on the wire rack until completely cool. Then, cover the cake with aluminum foil or a baking pan cover.

NOTE: Although not as satisfactory, the pan may be greased and floured using the traditional method (page 40) in substitution for using Special Grease.

**MAKES ONE 9 × 13-INCH SHEET CAKE;
15 SERVINGS**

COLA ICING

1 pound (4 cups) powdered sugar
½ cup (¼ pound) butter
¼ cup plus 2 tablespoons Coca-Cola Classic
    cola *or* regular Pepsi-Cola cola
3 tablespoons unsweetened cocoa powder
1 cup chopped pecans

Place the powdered sugar in a medium mixing bowl; set aside. In a small saucepan, place the butter, cola, and cocoa; stir. Bring the cola mixture to the boiling point over medium heat, stirring constantly. Pour the hot cola mixture over the powdered sugar; using an electric mixer, beat on high speed only until well blended and fluffy.

AUNT TELL'S DEVIL'S FOOD CAKE

My Aunt Fauntell, who lived in Creston, Iowa, was an excellent cook. This was her specialty cake —always known as "Aunt Tell's Cake" in our family (when we were little, my brother and I couldn't pronounce her name, so we called her "Aunt Tell").

2 cups sifted cake flour (sift before measuring)
1 teaspoon baking soda
¼ teaspoon salt
½ cup (¼ pound) butter, softened
1¼ cups sugar
3 extra-large eggs, room temperature, separated
1 teaspoon pure vanilla extract
½ cup unsweetened cocoa powder
1 cup cold water
½ cup sugar
1 recipe Chocolate Frosting (page 508)

Preheat the oven to 350° F. Using Special Grease (page 40), grease a 9 × 13 × 2-inch baking pan (see Note); set aside.

Onto waxed paper, sift together the flour, baking soda, and salt; set aside.

In a large mixing bowl, place the butter and 1¼ cups sugar; using an electric mixer, cream well on medium-high speed. Add the egg yolks, one at a time, beating well on medium-high speed after each addition. Add the vanilla; continue beating on medium-high speed until completely blended. Add the cocoa; beat on medium-high speed until blended. Add, alternately, the flour mixture in fourths, and the water in thirds, beating on low speed after each addition only until blended; set aside.

Place the egg whites in a large mixing bowl. Using the electric mixer fit with clean, dry blades, beat the egg whites on high speed until soft peaks hold. While continuing to beat on high speed, gradually add ½ cup sugar and continue beating the egg white mixture until stiff, but still moist and glossy. Add the egg white mixture to the cake batter; using a large mixing spoon, fold in.

Using the large mixing spoon, spoon the batter into the prepared baking pan. Using a small, narrow, angled spatula, lightly and quickly spread the batter evenly in the pan. Bake the cake for 30 minutes, or until a wooden toothpick inserted into the center of the cake comes out clean.

Remove the cake from the oven and place on a wire rack to cool.

When completely cool, leave the cake in the pan and frost it with the Chocolate Frosting. Let the cake stand until the frosting sets. Then, cover the cake with aluminum foil or a baking pan cover.

NOTE: Although not as satisfactory, the pan may be greased and floured using the traditional method (page 40) in substitution for using Special Grease.

MAKES ONE 9 × 13-INCH SHEET CAKE; 15 SERVINGS

VARIATION: If a white frosting is desired, frost with Marshmallow Cloud Frosting (page 512).

Loaf and Bundt Cakes

JERRI GOREHAM'S CHOCOLATE-NUT BUNDT CAKE

Jerri Goreham, an Iowa relative who now lives in La Jolla, California, is a cookbooknik with an unfathomable collection. Wherever she goes, it's a good bet that she will return home with one or more additions to her ever-increasing library. But you won't find this recipe in any bound book on Jerri's shelves—it was passed down from her mother, who hailed from Tipton, Iowa.

1 cup plus 2 tablespoons water
1 cup chopped dates
2 cups sifted all-purpose flour (sift before
    measuring)
1 teaspoon baking soda
1 tablespoon unsweetened cocoa powder
1 12-ounce package (2 cups) semisweet
    chocolate chips
1 cup broken pecans
1 cup (½ pound) butter, softened
1 cup sugar
2 extra-large eggs
1 teaspoon pure vanilla extract
2 recipes Chocolate Glaze (page 513)

Preheat the oven to 350° F. Using Special Grease (page 40), grease a 10-inch (12-cup) Bundt pan (see Note); set aside.

Pour 1 cup plus 2 tablespoons water into a small saucepan. Bring the water to a boil over high heat. Remove from the heat. Add the dates and stir to combine; let stand until cool.

Reserve 1 tablespoon of the measured flour in a small sauce dish. Then, onto waxed paper, sift together the remaining flour, baking soda, and cocoa; set aside. In a medium mixing bowl, place the chocolate chips and pecans. Sprinkle the 1 tablespoon reserved flour over the chocolate chips and pecans; toss until lightly dusted and evenly distributed; set aside.

In a large mixing bowl, place the butter and sugar; using an electric mixer, beat on medium-high speed until light and fluffy. Add the eggs, one at a time, beating well on medium-high speed after each addition. Add the vanilla; continue beating on medium-high speed until blended. Add, alternately, the flour mixture in fourths, and the date mixture (including the liquid) in thirds, beating on low speed after each addition only until blended; set aside. Measure ½ cup of the chocolate chip–pecan mixture; set aside. Add the remaining chocolate chip–pecan mixture to the cake batter; using a large mixing spoon, fold in.

Using the large mixing spoon, spoon the cake batter into the prepared Bundt pan. Scatter the ½ cup reserved chocolate chip–pecan mixture

evenly over the batter. Bake the cake for 40 to 45 minutes, or until a wooden toothpick inserted into the cake comes out clean. (*Caution*: If the testing toothpick pierces chocolate chips or dates when inserted into the cake, the toothpick may not be clean when removed from cake even though the cake crumb is done.)

Remove the cake from the oven and place on a wire rack; let stand to cool 10 minutes. Very carefully, run a small, sharp, thin-bladed knife around the inside edge of the pan ⅛ inch below the top surface of the cake. Place a wire rack over the cake pan and invert. Carefully lift the pan off the cake. Let the cake stand on the wire rack until completely cool.

Then, place the wire rack holding the cake on a piece of waxed paper. Using a teaspoon, spoon the Chocolate Glaze over the top of the cake, letting it trickle down the sides. Let the cake stand until the glaze sets. Then, transfer the cake to a perfectly flat serving plate or a corrugated cardboard cake circle. Cover the cake with an airtight dome or place it in an airtight container.

NOTE: Although not as satisfactory, the pan may be greased and floured using the traditional method (page 40) in substitution for using Special Grease.

MAKES ONE 10-INCH BUNDT CAKE; 14 SERVINGS

VARIATION: The cake may be topped with sprinkled powdered sugar rather than the Chocolate Glaze. Place 1 tablespoon powdered sugar in a small hand strainer and sprinkle the powdered sugar evenly over the top of the cool cake.

SERVING SUGGESTIONS
- Serve with Vanilla Ice Cream, homemade (page 595) or commercial.

- Pass an attractive serving bowl of Whipped Cream (page 309) at the table.

MARBLE CAKE

This distinctive cake is made in a loaf pan to give it greater depth for showing off the swirls of chocolate and white cake. Served slices are most appealing.

1 tablespoon plus 1 teaspoon sugar
⅛ teaspoon baking soda
1½ ounces (1½ squares) unsweetened
   chocolate
2 tablespoons boiling water
1⅔ cups sifted cake flour (sift before
   measuring)
2¼ teaspoons baking powder
½ teaspoon salt
½ cup vegetable shortening, softened
¾ cup sugar
1 teaspoon clear vanilla
⅔ cup whole milk
3 extra-large egg whites, room temperature
¼ cup sugar
1 recipe Chocolate Frosting (page 508)

Preheat the oven to 350°F. Grease and flour lightly a 5 × 9 × 2¾-inch loaf pan; set aside.

In a small sauce dish, place 1 tablespoon plus 1 teaspoon sugar and baking soda; stir to combine; set aside. Place the chocolate in a tiny saucepan. Hold the tiny pan over (not touching) low simmering water in a small saucepan until the chocolate melts, stirring intermittently. Remove the tiny pan from the heat. Add the baking soda mixture to the melted chocolate; stir to combine. Add the boiling water; stir until blended; set aside.

Onto waxed paper, sift together the flour, baking powder, and salt; set aside.

In a large mixing bowl, place the vegetable shortening and ¾ cup sugar; using an electric mixer, beat on medium-high speed until fluffy. Add the vanilla; beat on medium-high speed until blended. Add, alternately, the flour mixture in fourths, and the milk in thirds, beating on low speed after each addition only until blended. Using a large mixing spoon, carefully spoon ½ of the cake batter into another large mixing bowl. Add the chocolate mixture to one of the bowls of batter; using the electric mixer, beat on low speed only until blended; set aside.

Place the egg whites in a medium mixing bowl. Using the electric mixer fit with clean, dry blades, beat the egg whites on high speed until soft peaks hold. While continuing to beat on high speed, very gradually add ¼ cup sugar and continue beating the egg white mixture until stiff, but still moist and glossy. Using a table knife, cut the egg white mixture in half. Quickly and carefully, spoon ½ of the egg white mixture over the white batter, and the remaining ½ of the egg white mixture over the chocolate batter. Using separate, large mixing spoons, fold in.

Alternately place large spoons of white and chocolate batter side by side in the prepared loaf pan. Zigzag a table knife through the batter (to the bottom of the pan) to create a marble effect in the baked cake. Using a small, narrow, angled spatula, lightly even the top of the batter in the pan. Bake the cake for 45 minutes, or until a wooden toothpick inserted into the center of the cake comes out clean.

Remove the cake from the oven and place on a wire rack; let stand to cool 10 minutes. Remove the cake from the pan, following the same procedure as for removing a layer cake from a cake pan (page 455); let stand on the wire rack until completely cool.

Then, frost the top and sides of the cake with the Chocolate Frosting (see To Frost a Cake, page 501). Let the cake stand until the frosting sets. Then, cover the cake with an airtight dome or place it in an airtight container.

MAKES ONE 5 × 9-INCH LOAF CAKE; 12 SERVINGS

OPTIONAL DECORATION
1 recipe Ornamental Vanilla Frosting made
   with whole milk (page 512)
1 recipe Chocolate Glaze (page 513)

Immediately after frosting the cake with the Chocolate Frosting, fit 2 decorating bags each with a small round tip number 2 (page 319). Fill one of the bags with Ornamental Vanilla Frosting and the other with Chocolate Glaze. Then, pipe vanilla and chocolate swirls randomly, but artistically, over the top of the cake. Lastly, pipe a shell border (page 324) of Chocolate Frosting around the bottom and top of the cake, using a decorating bag fit with medium open-star tip number 21 (reserve sufficient Chocolate Frosting before frosting the cake).

MILKY WAY CAKE

Ridiculously rich; incredibly luscious.

3 cups sifted all-purpose flour (sift before
   measuring)
½ teaspoon baking soda
8 2.05-ounce Milky Way candy bars
½ cup (¼ pound) butter
½ cup (¼ pound) butter, softened
2 cups sugar
4 extra-large eggs
1¼ cups buttermilk
1 cup broken pecans
1 recipe Supreme Chocolate Icing
   (page 513)

Preheat the oven to 325° F. Using Special Grease (page 40), grease a 10 × 4-inch tube pan (see Note 1); set aside.

Onto waxed paper, sift together the flour and baking soda; set aside.

In the top of a double boiler, place the Milky Way bars and ½ cup butter. Place the top of the double boiler over (not touching) simmering water in the bottom pan. Stir the candy-butter mixture until melted and completely blended. (The mixture will be thick.) Remove the top of the double boiler from the bottom pan; set aside.

In a large mixing bowl, place ½ cup softened butter and sugar; using an electric mixer, cream well on medium-high speed. Add the eggs, one at a time, beating well on medium-high speed after each addition. Add, alternately, the flour

mixture in fourths, and the buttermilk in thirds, beating on low speed after each addition only until blended. Add the chocolate mixture; beat on medium speed only until blended. Add the pecans; using a large mixing spoon, fold in.

Turn the cake batter into the prepared tube pan. Using a small, narrow, angled spatula, lightly and quickly spread the batter evenly in the pan. Bake the cake for 1 hour and 10 to 15 minutes. When done, this cake will be dense and very slightly moist. Insert a long, wooden toothpick into the cake to help determine doneness.

Remove the cake from the oven and place the upright pan on a wire rack; let stand to cool 15 minutes. Then, carefully run a sharp, thin-bladed knife around the inside edge of the pan (not around the tube) to loosen the cake. Place a 12-inch corrugated cardboard cake circle over the top of the pan (see Note 2). Hold the cake circle and the pan together securely and invert. Carefully lift the pan off the cake. Place the cake circle (and cake) on the wire rack; let stand until the cake is completely cool.

Then, frost the top and side of the cake with the Supreme Chocolate Icing. Let the cake stand until the frosting sets. Then, place the cake in an airtight container.

NOTE 1: Although not as satisfactory, the pan may be greased and floured using the traditional method (page 40) in substitution for using Special Grease.

NOTE 2: If a corrugated cardboard cake circle is not available, a perfectly flat serving plate may be substituted.

MAKES ONE 10 × 4-INCH TUBE CAKE; 20 SERVINGS

SERVING SUGGESTION: A small scoop of vanilla ice cream (homemade, page 595, or commercial) complements Milky Way Cake well. Serve the ice cream next to the cake serving (not on top of it).

POUND CAKE

Pound cake is an old, historic cake which derives its name from the traditional ingredients; 1 pound each of butter, flour, sugar, and eggs (plus flavoring, such as lemon or vanilla extract, or mace). The following recipe makes an authentic pound cake with the exception that I have taken the liberty of adding a bit of baking powder (only 1 teaspoon) for added leavening. For flavoring, I like the combination of vanilla and lemon extract; however, the baker may adjust the flavoring to suit his/her personal preferences.

Although small versions of Pound Cake are often baked in loaf pans, the original, full-sized Pound Cake is traditionally baked in a tube pan.

1 pound butter (2 cups), **softened to cool
    room temperature (about 70°F)**
1 pound cake flour (4½ cups sifted cake flour;
    sift before measuring)
1 teaspoon baking powder
1 pound sugar (2¼ cups)
1 pound eggs (7 extra-large eggs), room
    temperature
1 teaspoon baking powder
1 teaspoon pure vanilla extract
1 teaspoon lemon extract

Place the butter in a very large mixing bowl; set aside.

Preheat the oven to 325°F. Grease and flour a 10 × 4-inch tube pan; set aside.

Onto waxed paper, sift together the flour and baking powder; set aside.

Using an electric mixer, cream the butter on medium-high speed. While continuing to beat on medium-high speed, add the sugar in fourths, creaming well after each addition (about 5 minutes total beating time to add and cream the sugar). While continuing to beat on medium-high, add the eggs, one at a time, beating well after each addition (about 5 minutes total beating time to add the eggs). Add the vanilla and lemon extract; beat on medium-high speed until blended. Add the flour mixture in fourths, beating on low speed after each addition only until blended (about 5 minutes total beating time to add the flour mixture).

Using a large mixing spoon, spoon the cake batter into the prepared tube pan. Using a small, narrow, angled spatula, lightly and quickly spread the batter evenly in the pan. Bake the cake for 1 hour to 1 hour and 10 minutes, or until a long, wooden toothpick inserted into the cake comes out clean.

Remove the cake from the oven and place the upright pan on a wire rack; let stand to cool 15 minutes. Then, carefully run a sharp, thin-bladed knife around the inside edge of the pan (not around the tube) to loosen the cake. Place a 12-inch corrugated cardboard cake circle over the top of the pan (see Note). Hold the cake circle and the pan together securely and invert. Carefully lift the pan off the cake. Place the cake circle (and cake) on a wire rack; let stand until the cake is completely cool. Then, place the cake in an airtight container.

NOTE: If a corrugated cardboard cake circle is not available, a perfectly flat serving plate may be substituted.

MAKES ONE 10 × 4-INCH TUBE CAKE; 20 SERVINGS

OPTIONAL DECORATION: When cool, the cake may be dusted with powdered sugar, if desired. Place 1 tablespoon powdered sugar in a small hand strainer and sprinkle the powdered sugar over the top of the cake.

SCRIPTURE CAKE

Scripture Cake is so named because it is made from ingredients referred to in the Bible.

1½ cups sifted all-purpose flour (sift before measuring) (1 Kings 4:22)
2 teaspoons baking powder (1 Corinthians 5:6)
2 teaspoons ground cinnamon (1 Kings 10:10)
1 teaspoon ground nutmeg (1 Kings 10:10)
½ teaspoon ground ginger (1 Kings 10:2)
½ teaspoon ground cloves (1 Kings 10:2)
⅛ teaspoon salt (Leviticus 2:13)
2 cups chopped, dried figs (1 Samuel 30:12)
2 cups chopped, unblanched almonds (chop slivered, unblanched almonds; page 50) (Genesis 43:11)
2 cups baking raisins (1 Samuel 30:12)
½ cup (¼ pound) butter, softened (Judges 5:25)
1⅔ cups sugar (Jeremiah 6:20)
2 tablespoons honey (Exodus 16:31)
6 extra-large eggs, room temperature, separated (Isaiah 10:14)
½ cup whole milk (Judges 4:19)
⅓ cup sugar (Jeremiah 6:20)
1 tablespoon powdered sugar for decoration

Preheat the oven to 300° F. Using Special Grease (page 40), grease a 10-inch (12-cup) Bundt pan (see Note 1); set aside.

Reserve 3 tablespoons of the measured flour in a small sauce dish; set aside. Then, onto waxed paper, sift together the remaining flour, baking powder, cinnamon, nutmeg, ginger, cloves, and salt; set aside. In a medium mixing bowl, place the figs, almonds, and raisins; stir to combine. Sprinkle the 3 tablespoons reserved flour over the fig mixture; toss until well dusted; cover and set aside.

In a large mixing bowl, place the butter, 1⅔ cups sugar, and honey; using an electric mixer, cream well on medium-high speed. Add the egg yolks, one at a time, beating well on medium-high speed after each addition. Add, alternately, the flour mixture in fourths, and the milk in thirds, beating on low speed after each addition only until blended; set aside.

Place the egg whites in a large mixing bowl. Using the electric mixer fit with clean, dry blades, beat the egg whites on high speed until soft peaks hold. While continuing to beat on high speed, very gradually add ⅓ cup sugar and continue beating the egg white mixture until stiff, but still moist and glossy; set aside. Add the fig mixture to the flour batter; using a large mixing spoon, fold in only until evenly distributed. Add the egg white mixture; quickly fold in.

Using the large mixing spoon, spoon the cake batter into the prepared Bundt pan. Bake the cake for 1 hour and 50 minutes, or until a wooden toothpick inserted into the cake comes out clean. (*Caution:* If the testing toothpick happens to pierce a piece of fruit when inserted into cake, the toothpick may not be clean when removed from cake even though the cake crumb is done.)

Remove the cake from the oven and place on a wire rack; let stand to cool 10 minutes. Very carefully, run a small, sharp, thin-bladed knife around the inside edge of the pan ⅛ inch below the top surface of the cake. Place a 10- or 12-inch corrugated cardboard cake circle over the top of the pan (see Note 2). Hold the cake circle and the pan together securely and invert. Carefully lift the pan off the cake. Place the cake circle (and cake) on a wire rack; let stand until the cake is completely cool.

Then, place the powdered sugar in a small hand strainer and sprinkle over the top of the cake. Place the cake in an airtight container.

NOTE 1: Although not as satisfactory, the pan may be greased and floured using the traditional method (page 40) in substitution for using Special Grease.

NOTE 2: If a corrugated cardboard cake circle is not available, a perfectly flat serving plate may be substituted.

MAKES ONE 10-INCH BUNDT CAKE; 14 SERVINGS

Angel Food Cakes

ANGEL FOOD CAKE

Lighter-than-a-feather Angel Food Cake has been popular and fashionable in America since the last quarter of the nineteenth century, when this sublimely delicious repast provided a propitious way to put extra egg whites to use. (This recipe calls for 1½ cups of egg whites.)

Although it was the sweet taste and satiny texture that won Angel Food Cake permanence in the best-loved desserts inner circle, present-day health awareness has harkened Angel Food Cake center stage, owing to the absence of egg yolks and shortening among its ingredients. Burdened with no cholesterol whatsoever, and virtually no fat (just 1 gram in the cake flour), this culinary centenarian is as "in" as any cake could hope to be. But don't forget: there are 193 calories in each piece of this food fit for the angels (when a 10-inch cake is cut into 12 servings). Nothing is perfect.

1 cup sifted cake flour (sift before measuring)
1 cup superfine sugar
1½ cups egg whites (about 10 extra-large egg whites*), room temperature
1½ teaspoons cream of tartar
½ teaspoon salt
1 teaspoon pure vanilla extract
½ teaspoon almond extract
½ cup superfine sugar

* About 12 large egg whites.

Preheat the oven to 350°F.

Onto waxed paper, sift together the flour and 1 cup sugar 4 times. (If you are using a triple sifter [page 41] go ahead and sift the flour mixture 4 times through the triple sifter.) Return the sifted flour mixture to the top of the sifter; set aside.

Place the egg whites in an extra-large mixing bowl. Using an electric mixer, beat the egg whites on high speed until foamy. Add the cream of tartar and salt; continue beating on high speed just until soft peaks hold. Add the vanilla and almond extract. While beating on medium speed, very gradually sprinkle ½ cup sugar over the egg white mixture; beat only until the sugar is blended.

If necessary, use a large rubber spatula to quickly and carefully push the egg white mixture into a larger mixing bowl for more expeditious folding in of the flour mixture, which is the next procedure.

Sift the flour mixture in fourths over the egg white mixture, using a large mixing spoon to fold in after each addition only until the flour disappears.

Push the cake batter into an *ungreased* 10 × 4-inch tube pan with a removable bottom. Using a small, narrow, angled spatula, lightly and quickly smooth the top of the batter. Then, carefully run a narrow, rubber spatula once around the center of the batter in the pan to remove any large air pockets. Place the cake on the lowest shelf in the oven. Bake the cake for 40 minutes, or until a long, wooden toothpick inserted into the cake comes out clean.

Remove the cake from the oven. Immediately invert the pan and let it stand on the cooling legs until the cake is *completely cool* (about 2 hours). If the pan does not have cooling legs, place the center tube over the neck of a bottle and let the cake stand until cool.

When the cake is cool, carefully run a very sharp, very thin-bladed knife in a continuous motion first around the inside edge and then around the center tube of the pan to loosen the cake. Hold the knife against the side of the pan (and the center tube) to help prevent tearing the cake. Avoid up-and-down sawing motions, which will spoil the outside appearance of the cake. Lift the center tube section, with the cake, out of the pan. Then, run the knife around the bottom of the tube section under the cake. Invert the cake onto a 12-inch corrugated cardboard cake circle or a perfectly flat serving plate. Carefully lift the tube section off the cake. Place the cake in an airtight container.

MAKES ONE 10 × 4-INCH TUBE CAKE; 12 SERVINGS

GEORGE WASHINGTON ICEBOX CAKE

Made-to-order for serving on George Washington's Birthday, this decorative cake derives its name from the generous amount of maraschino cherries used in making it. But it's perfectly suitable for serving any time of the year.

¾ cup red maraschino cherries cut in half lengthwise, divided
1 Angel Food Cake (page 484) *or* 1 Sponge Cake (page 486)
1½ recipes Decorator Whipped Cream (page 309)
1 7-ounce package (2⅔ cups) flaked coconut, divided
¾ cup broken English walnuts
1 recipe Decorator Whipped Cream (page 309)

Place the maraschino cherries in a sieve; rinse under cold, running water. Place the cherries, single layer, between several layers of paper towels; let stand to dry.

With your fingers, tear the cake into pieces approximately 1 to 1½ inches square and place them in a large mixing bowl. Add 1½ recipes of Decorator Whipped Cream, 1⅓ cups of the coconut (cover the remaining coconut and set aside), ½ cup of the maraschino cherries (cover the remaining maraschino cherries and refrigerate), and all of the walnuts. Using a large mixing spoon, fold together carefully.

Transfer the mixture to a large mixing bowl approximately 9 inches in diameter which has been lined with plastic wrap. Using the back of the mixing spoon, press the mixture lightly into the bowl; cover with plastic wrap and refrigerate at least 6 hours.

Invert the bowl onto a flat serving plate. Lift the bowl off the cake and peel off the plastic wrap.

Frost the cake with 1 recipe of Decorator Whipped Cream. Spoon the remaining 1 cup of coconut over the entire cake, using your hand to lightly press the coconut into the whipped cream to hold it in place. Then, lightly press the remaining ¼ cup maraschino cherries randomly into the whipped cream frosting. Refrigerate the cake.

This cake is eye-appealing and should be served at the table. To serve, use a sharp, thin-bladed knife to cut 12 wedge-shaped servings. Using a triangular pie/cake server, remove the servings from the cake and place them, cut side down, on individual serving plates.

SERVES 12

STRAWBERRY "SHORTCAKE" (WITH ANGEL FOOD CAKE)

Angel Food Cake is often substituted for Old-Fashioned (Biscuit-Style) Shortcake (page 380) or Sponge-Style Shortcake (page 487) when serving Strawberry Shortcake. (See the headnote for Old-Fashioned Strawberry Shortcake, page 381.)

2 pints fresh strawberries
12 whole, fresh strawberries for garnish (in addition to the 2 pints)
1 recipe Angel Food Cake (page 484)
2 recipes Whipped Cream (page 309)

Wash the 2 pints strawberries; using a strawberry huller, remove the hulls (page 6). Cut the hulled strawberries in half or into quarters lengthwise, depending upon the size of the berries; place in a bowl and set aside. Wash and hull the 12 whole strawberries; place in a bowl and set aside.

Cut the Angel Food Cake into 12 servings and place each serving on an individual dessert plate. Spoon about ⅓ cup of the sliced, fresh strawberries over each serving of cake. Top each serving with a generous dollop of the Whipped Cream. Place 1 of the whole strawberries atop the Whipped Cream on each serving.

SERVES 12

VARIATIONS: Fresh raspberries, blueberries, or sliced peaches may be substituted for the strawberries.

Sponge and Chiffon Cakes

SPONGE CAKE

2¼ cups sifted cake flour (sift before measuring)
½ teaspoon salt
8 extra-large eggs,* room temperature, separated
1¾ cups superfine sugar
½ cup plus 2 tablespoons water
1 tablespoon freshly squeezed, strained lemon juice
1½ teaspoons very finely grated lemon rind (page 31)
1 teaspoon pure vanilla extract
1½ teaspoons cream of tartar
½ cup superfine sugar

* If extra-large eggs are not available, 10 large eggs may be substituted.

Preheat the oven to 325°F.

Onto waxed paper, sift together the flour and salt; set aside.

Place the egg yolks in a medium mixing bowl. Using an electric mixer, beat the egg yolks on high speed about 8 minutes, until very thick and butter colored. While continuing to beat the egg yolks on high speed, very gradually add 1¾ cups sugar (about 3 minutes additional beating time). Add the water, lemon juice, lemon rind, and vanilla; beat on high speed until blended. Transfer the egg yolk mixture to a large mixing bowl. Add the flour mixture in thirds, using a large mixing spoon to fold in after each addition only until the flour disappears; set aside.

Place the egg whites in a large mixing bowl. Using the electric mixer fit with clean, dry blades, beat the egg whites on high speed until foamy. Add the cream of tartar; continue beating on high speed until soft peaks hold. While continuing to beat on high speed, very gradu-ally add ½ cup sugar and continue beating the egg white mixture until stiff, but still moist and glossy. Quickly, with as little disturbance as possible to the mixture, transfer the egg white mixture to an extra-large mixing bowl. Pour the egg yolk mixture back and forth over the egg white mixture; using the large mixing spoon, fold in carefully and quickly.

Pour the cake batter into an *ungreased* 10 × 4-inch tube pan with a removable bottom. Using a small, narrow, angled spatula, lightly spread the batter evenly in the pan. Then, carefully run a narrow, rubber spatula once around the center of the batter in the pan to remove any large air pockets. Bake the cake for 50 to 60 minutes. When done, the inside of the cracks on the top of the cake will appear dry, not moist, and the cake will spring back when pressed lightly with your finger.

Remove the cake from the oven. Immediately invert the pan and let it stand on the cooling legs until the cake is *completely cool* (about 2 hours). If the pan does not have cooling legs, place the center tube over the neck of a bottle and let the cake stand until cool.

When the cake is cool, carefully run a sharp, very thin-bladed knife in a continuous motion first around the inside edge and then around the center tube of the pan to loosen the cake. Hold the knife against the side of the pan (and the center tube) to help prevent tearing the cake. Avoid up-and-down sawing motions, which will spoil the outside appearance of the cake. Lift the center tube section, with the cake, out of the pan. Then, run the knife around the bottom of the tube section under the cake. Invert the cake onto a 12-inch corrugated card-board cake circle or a perfectly flat serving plate. Carefully lift the tube section off the cake. Place the cake in an airtight container.

MAKES ONE 10 × 4-INCH TUBE CAKE; 12 SERVINGS

SERVING SUGGESTIONS
• Serve plain.

• Spoon fresh fruit over individual servings; top with Whipped Cream (page 3090).

- Spoon Glaze (page 513) over the top of the cake and let it trickle down the sides.

LEMON-FILLED SPONGE CAKE

1 baked Sponge Cake (recipe above)
Lemon Filling (recipe follows)
1½ recipes Lemon Buttercream Frosting
(page 505)

Using a serrated knife or a cake leveler, split the Sponge Cake in half horizontally, making 2 layers (see To Split a Cake into Layers, page 453). Using a large spatula, carefully transfer the top layer to another 12-inch corrugated cardboard cake circle.

Spoon the cold Lemon Filling over the bottom cake layer. Using a small, narrow, angled spatula, spread the filling evenly to within ¼ inch of the outside and inside edges of the cake. Using the large spatula, position the top layer of the cake over the Lemon Filling.

Frost the top and side of the cake with the Lemon Buttercream Frosting (see To Frost a Cake, page 501). Let the cake stand until the frosting sets. Then, place the cake in an airtight container and refrigerate. Use light, sawing motions with a sharp, very thin bladed knife to cut the cake into serving portions.

LEMON FILLING

¾ cup sugar
¼ cup all-purpose flour
⅛ teaspoon salt
1 extra-large egg
3 tablespoons water
2 tablespoons butter
¼ cup freshly squeezed, strained lemon juice
½ teaspoon finely grated lemon rind
(page 31)

In a small mixing bowl, place the sugar, flour, and salt; stir to combine; set aside.

Place the egg in the top of a double boiler; using a handheld electric mixer, beat well on medium-high speed. Add the water; beat on medium-high speed until blended. Add the flour mixture; using a spoon, stir to combine. Place the top of the double boiler over boiling water in the bottom pan. Cook the mixture until very thick (about 8 minutes), constantly stirring with a spoon or beating with the electric mixer on low speed.

Remove the top of the double boiler from the bottom pan and place on a wire rack; using the electric mixer, beat briefly on medium speed to remove any lumps. Add the butter, lemon juice, and lemon rind; beat on medium speed until blended and combined.

Let the Lemon Filling stand on the wire rack until cooled slightly. Then, place a piece of plastic wrap directly on the filling and refrigerate. Wait until the filling is cold before using it to fill the cake. Cakes filled with Lemon Filling must be kept refrigerated.

SPONGE-STYLE SHORTCAKES

½ cup sifted cake flour (sift before
measuring)
½ teaspoon baking powder
⅛ teaspoon salt
3 extra-large eggs,* room temperature,
separated
½ teaspoon pure vanilla extract
¼ teaspoon very finely grated lemon rind
(page 31)
1 teaspoon freshly squeezed, strained lemon
juice
¼ cup superfine sugar
¼ teaspoon cream of tartar
¼ cup superfine sugar

If extra-large eggs are not available, 4 large eggs may be substituted.

Preheat the oven to 325° F. Grease well and flour lightly twelve 3½-inch-diameter by 1-inch-deep shortcake pan molds. (Shortcake pans sometimes contain 6 molds for individual shortcakes. In such case, 2 pans will be required.)

(Recipe continues on next page)

Onto waxed paper, sift together the flour, baking powder, and salt. Return the sifted flour mixture to the top of the sifter; set aside.

Place the egg yolks in a small mixing bowl. Using an electric mixer, beat the egg yolks on high speed 5 minutes, until thick and lemon colored. Add the vanilla, lemon rind, and lemon juice; beat on high speed until blended. While continuing to beat the egg yolk mixture on high speed, very gradually add ¼ cup sugar; beat 1 additional minute after adding the sugar. *Sift* the flour mixture over the egg yolk mixture; using a mixing spoon, fold in only until the flour disappears; set aside.

Place the egg whites in a large mixing bowl. Using the electric mixer fit with clean, dry blades, beat the egg whites on high speed until foamy. Add the cream of tartar; continue beating on high speed until soft peaks hold. While continuing to beat on high speed, very gradually add ¼ cup sugar and continue beating the egg white mixture until stiff, but still moist and glossy. Pour the egg yolk mixture back and forth over the egg white mixture; using a large mixing spoon, fold in carefully and quickly.

Spoon the cake batter into the 12 prepared shortcake pan molds. Using a small, narrow, angled spatula, lightly and quickly spread the batter evenly to within about ⅜ inch of the top of each mold. Bake the shortcakes 10 minutes, until the top surface of the cakes springs back when touched lightly.

Remove the pans from the oven and place on wire racks. *Immediately* run a small, sharp, thin-bladed knife around the inside edge of each mold to loosen the shortcakes. Place a wire rack over one pan at a time and invert to unmold the shortcakes. Let the shortcakes stand on wire racks only until cool.

Meanwhile, cut a piece of waxed paper to fit the bottom of an airtight storage container. Place the waxed paper in the storage container and dust the waxed paper with a small amount of powdered sugar to prevent the shortcakes from sticking to it. The small amount of powdered sugar which will adhere to the bottoms of the shortcakes during storage will also pre-vent them from sticking to the serving plates. Place the cooled shortcakes in the storage container and cover tightly.

MAKES TWELVE 3½ × 1-INCH SHORTCAKES;
12 SERVINGS

STRAWBERRY SPONGE-STYLE SHORTCAKE

Strawberry Shortcake also may be made using Old-Fashioned (Biscuit-Style) Shortcake (page 380) or Angel Food Cake (page 484) instead of Sponge-Style Shortcake. (See the headnote for Old-Fashioned Strawberry Shortcake, page 381)

2 pints fresh strawberries
12 baked Sponge-Style Shortcakes (left column)
2 recipes Whipped Cream (page 309)

Wash the strawberries; using a strawberry huller, remove the hulls (page 6). Reserve 12 uniform, whole strawberries and cut the remainder in half or into quarters lengthwise, depending upon the size of the berries; place in a bowl and set aside. Place the shortcakes on individual dessert plates. Spoon the sliced strawberries equally over the shortcakes. Top each serving with a generous dollop of the Whipped Cream. Place 1 of the reserved whole strawberries atop the Whipped Cream on each serving.

SERVES 12

VARIATIONS: Fresh raspberries, blueberries, or sliced peaches may be substituted for the strawberries.

JELLY ROLL

Jelly rolls are a traditional cake dating back to the middle 1800s. They consist of a thin sponge cake rolled, historically, around a jelly filling and sprinkled with powdered sugar. When sliced for serving, the attractive pinwheel design is revealed. A wide variety of fillings is used nowadays in jelly rolls, ranging from jams to fruited frostings and flavored whipped cream (see Filling Suggestions, below).

¾ cup sifted cake flour (sift before
  measuring)
1 teaspoon baking powder
¼ teaspoon salt
4 extra-large eggs,* room temperature,
  separated
1 teaspoon pure vanilla extract
½ cup superfine sugar
¼ cup superfine sugar
Powdered sugar
1½ cups jelly, jam, frosting, or other filling
  (see Filling Suggestions below)

* If extra-large eggs are not available, 5 large eggs may be substituted.

Preheat the oven to 350° F. Grease and flour lightly a 10½ × 15½ × 1-inch jelly-roll (cookie) pan. Line the bottom of the pan with waxed paper. Grease the waxed paper; set aside.

Onto a piece of clean waxed paper, sift together the flour, baking powder, and salt. Return the sifted flour mixture to the top of the sifter; set aside.

Place the egg yolks in a small mixing bowl. Using an electric mixer, beat the egg yolks on high speed 5 minutes, until thick and lemon colored. Add the vanilla; beat on high speed until blended. While continuing to beat the egg yolk mixture on high speed, very gradually add ½ cup sugar and continue beating until completely blended and creamy. *Sift* the flour mixture over the egg yolk mixture; using a mixing spoon, fold in only until the flour disappears; set aside.

Place the egg whites in a large mixing bowl. Using the electric mixer fit with clean, dry blades, beat the egg whites on high speed until soft peaks hold. While continuing to beat on high speed, very gradually add ¼ cup sugar and continue beating the egg white mixture until stiff, but still moist and glossy. Spoon the egg yolk mixture *evenly* over the egg white mixture; using a large mixing spoon, fold in carefully and quickly.

Turn the cake batter into the prepared jelly-roll pan. Using a large, narrow, angled spatula, carefully spread the batter evenly over the pan. Bake the cake for 12 minutes or until the top surface of the cake springs back when touched lightly.

Meanwhile, lay a clean kitchen hand towel on a flat surface and dust it with sifted powdered sugar (page 42); let stand.

Remove the cake from the oven and place on a wire rack. *Immediately* run a sharp, thin-bladed knife along the inside edges of the pan to loosen the cake. Place the dusted hand towel over the cake pan, dusted side down. Pull the towel tautly over the pan and invert the towel and pan. Lay the inverted towel and pan on the flat surface. Lift the pan off the cake and peel the waxed paper off the bottom of the cake. Beginning at one of the short sides of the cake, roll the warm cake and towel together. Place the rolled cake on a wire rack, seam down, and let stand until completely cool.

Then, unroll the cake. Spoon teaspoonsful of jelly evenly over the surface of the cake. Using a clean, small, narrow, angled spatula, lightly spread the jelly to within ¼ inch of the edges of the cake. Roll the cake short side to short side (without the towel). Using a small hand strainer, dust the top of the Jelly Roll with additional powdered sugar. Cover tightly until serving time.

SERVES 10

FILLING SUGGESTIONS: Any jelly, jam, conserve, flavored whipped cream, or frosting may be used to fill the Jelly Roll. Nuts; chopped, fresh or canned fruits; or candied fruits may be used in combination with any whipped cream or frosting. The following are a few suggested fillings:

• Red Raspberry Jelly

• Apricot Jam

(Recipe continues on next page)

- Rhubarb-Strawberry Conserve
- 1½ recipes Chocolate Decorator Whipped Cream (page 310). ¾ cup chopped pecans may be folded into the whipped cream, if desired.
- 1 8-ounce can crushed pineapple in its own juice, well drained, combined with 1 recipe Buttercream Frosting (page 505).

YULE LOG
Bûche de Noël

In many parts of the United States, this cake is known by its French name: Bûche de Noël. The English translation is Yule log, the name by which this famous French Christmas cake is best known in the Midwest. The cake is made to resemble the Yule log, which in earlier times was placed in the fireplace on Christmas Eve to serve as the foundation for the fire. Often, Yule log cakes are piped and decorated to further carry out the holiday theme.

1 baked Jelly Roll cake without filling (page 489), rolling cake in hand towel and letting stand until completely cool
Filling (recipe follows)
1 recipe Mocha Buttercream Frosting (page 506), reserving ¾ cup frosting before adding cocoa and coffee to remainder of frosting
¼ recipe Cake Decorators' White Icing (page 504) for decoration
Ivory, bright red, kelly green, and yellow-orange paste food coloring

Cut an 8 × 14-inch piece of corrugated cardboard cake board; set aside.

Unroll the Jelly Roll and towel. Using a very sharp, thin-bladed knife, cut a 1-inch strip of cake off one of the short sides of the Jelly Roll. Cut the strip in half widthwise; roll each half and secure with a toothpick. Then, unroll the strips and, using a small, narrow, angled spatula,

spread them with Filling. Reroll the strips and resecure with toothpicks; place in a zipper-seal plastic bag and refrigerate. (These 2 pieces will later be attached to the Yule Log to simulate branch stumps.)

Spoon the remainder of the Filling over the Jelly Roll. Using the small, narrow, angled spatula, spread the filling evenly to within ¼ inch of the edges of the cake. Roll the cake short side to short side (without the towel). Place the cake, seam down, on the cut piece of corrugated cardboard cake board. Slip strips of waxed paper under the bottom edges of the Jelly Roll to prevent unwanted frosting from getting on the exposed border of the cake board when frosting the Yule Log; set aside.

Using ivory-colored paste food coloring, tint the ¾ cup reserved light-colored Mocha Buttercream Frosting to simulate the inner color of cut logs; cover and set aside. Using a clean, small, narrow, angled spatula, frost the log, except the ends, with the dark-colored Mocha Buttercream Frosting, reserving a small amount of the frosting. Apply the frosting liberally and smoothly. Then, pull a wide-toothed decorating comb (see illustration, page 498) down the length of the log several times and contiguously until the entire log is grooved to simulate bark; set aside.

Remove the 2 rolled cake strips from the refrigerator. Using a very sharp, thin-bladed knife, cut a thin triangular piece off one of the ends of each strip (see illustration). Discard (or eat) the cutaway triangular pieces.

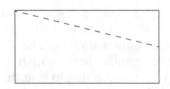

Apply a very generous amount of the reserved dark-colored Mocha Buttercream Frosting to the surface from which the triangular piece was cut away on each rolled strip. Press the frosted surface of one of the rolled strips into the frosting on one side of the log to affix the rolled strip to the log and simulate a branch stump. Affix the other rolled strip to the opposite side, and at the opposite end, of the log. Then, apply the reserved dark-colored Mocha Buttercream Frosting only to the *edge* (the bark) of the stumps. Run the decorating comb around the frosting on the edge of the stumps in a single, circular motion.

Using a clean, small, narrow, angled spatula, frost the ends of the log and stumps with the light-colored Mocha Buttercream Frosting, making circular swirls with the spatula to simulate the rings of a cut log.

With quick motions, pull the strips of waxed paper from under the Yule Log. Make any necessary, small repairs to the frosting around the bottom of the log. Refrigerate the Yule Log until the frosting sets.

To decorate the Yule Log (see illustration), use paste food coloring to tint portions of the Cake Decorators' White Icing bright red, kelly green, and yellow-orange (for the center of the poinsettias). Place each of the 3 tinted icings in a separate decorating bag. Fit the decorating bags (page 318) with the numbered tips indicated below, and pipe the word "Noel" in red across the log; then, decorate the Yule Log with piped holly (green leaves and red berries) and poinsettias (red petals, 3 yellow-orange dots in center of petals, and green leaves) (see Writing and Printing, page 323; Holly Leaves, page 326; and Poinsettias, page 326, for piping procedures).

"Noel"—small round tip number 3
Holly—medium leaf tip number 68 (leaves) and small round tip number 3 (berries)
Poinsettias—medium leaf tip number 352 (petals), tiny round tip number 2 (center dots), and small leaf tip number 66 (leaves)

Yule Log

Refrigerate the Yule Log and let the frosting decorations set before serving. Keep the Yule Log refrigerated.

SERVES 10

FILLING

1½ recipes Decorator Whipped Cream (page 309)
2 teaspoons unsweetened cocoa powder
2 teaspoons powdered instant coffee (to powder instant coffee, process in blender*)

* If a blender is not available, a food processor may be used; however, it is difficult to achieve a fine powder using a food processor. Reserve any remaining powdered instant coffee for other uses.

When preparing the Decorator Whipped Cream, add the cocoa and powdered instant coffee after adding the powdered sugar; cover and refrigerate.

DOUBLE-LENGTH YULE LOG

Double all ingredients in the Yule Log recipe, above, except continue to reserve only ¾ cup Mocha Buttercream Frosting.

Cut an 8 × 28-inch piece of corrugated cardboard cake board; set aside.

Make 2 separate Jelly Roll cakes, following the Yule Log recipe, above. Cut 2 1-inch strips from only 1 of the Jelly Rolls. (2 simulated branches are sufficient for a double-length Yule Log.) Fill

(Recipe continues on next page)

and refrigerate the 2 strips, and fill each Jelly Roll, following the recipe.

Place the 2 filled Jelly Rolls, seam down, and end to end as snugly as possible without crushing the cakes, on the cut piece of corrugated cardboard cake board. Then, continue to follow the recipe, frosting as smoothly as possible over the place where the Jelly Rolls abut in order to disguise the seam.

Follow the recipe to the end, attaching the 2 simulated branch stumps. Of course, for an attractive appearance, it will be necessary to pipe more decoration on a Double-Length Yule Log.

SERVES 20

BOSTON CREAM PIE

Although called a "pie," this lush dessert bears no resemblance to one. Boston Cream Pie is definitely a cake, made with two layers of sponge cake and a rich custard filling. The top of this yummy creation is iced with a thin chocolate coating, which I allow to trickle down the sides. By any name, it's really good!

1 cup sifted cake flour (sift before measuring)
1 teaspoon baking powder
¼ teaspoon salt
3 extra-large eggs,* room temperature
1 cup superfine sugar
½ teaspoon finely grated lemon rind (page 31)
2 teaspoons freshly squeezed, strained lemon juice
¼ cup plus 2 tablespoons hot (not scalded) milk
Custard Filling (recipe follows)
1 recipe Chocolate Coating (page 514)
Chocolate Curls (page 342)

* *If extra-large eggs are not available, 4 large eggs may be substituted.*

Preheat the oven to 350°F. Line the bottoms of 2 *ungreased* 8-inch round cake pans with waxed paper; set aside.

Onto a piece of waxed paper, sift together the flour, baking powder, and salt; set aside.

Place the eggs in a large mixing bowl. Using an electric mixer, beat the eggs on high speed 5 minutes, until very thick. While continuing to beat on high speed, very gradually add the sugar. Add the lemon rind and lemon juice; beat on high speed until combined and blended. Add the flour mixture in fourths, using a large mixing spoon to fold in after each addition only until the flour disappears. Add the milk all at once; using the large mixing spoon, quickly fold and stir in.

Using the large mixing spoon, spoon the cake batter equally into the 2 prepared cake pans. Using a small, narrow, angled spatula, lightly and quickly spread the batter evenly in the pans. Bake the cakes for 20 minutes, or until the top surface of the cake springs back when touched lightly.

Remove the cakes from the oven and place on wire racks; let stand in the pans until completely cool.

Then, run a sharp, thin-bladed knife around the inside edge of the pans to loosen the cakes. Invert one cake (the bottom layer) onto a perfectly flat serving plate; carefully lift the pan off the cake and peel the waxed paper off the bottom of the cake. Invert the other cake onto a wire rack and follow the same procedure.

Spoon the Custard Filling over the bottom cake layer on the serving plate. Using a clean, small, narrow, angled spatula, spread the filling evenly to within ¼ inch of the outside edge of the cake. Using a large spatula, position the top layer of the cake, bottom side up, over the Custard Filling.

Spoon the Chocolate Coating over the cake and let it run down the sides. If necessary, use a clean, small, narrow, angled spatula to help spread the Chocolate Coating over the entire edge of the cake. Carefully wipe any excess Chocolate Coating off the serving plate. Decorate the top of the cake with the Chocolate Curls. Let the cake stand until the Chocolate Coating sets. Then, place the cake in an airtight container and refrigerate.

**MAKES ONE 8-INCH, 2-LAYER ROUND CAKE;
10 TO 12 SERVINGS**

CUSTARD FILLING

¾ cup half-and-half
¼ cup sugar
⅛ teaspoon salt
¼ cup half-and-half
2 tablespoons cornstarch
2 egg yolks, slightly beaten
¾ teaspoon pure vanilla extract
½ cup whipping cream, unwhipped

Pour ¾ cup half-and-half into a medium saucepan; place over medium heat and let stand until bubbles begin to form around the edge of the pan. Add the sugar and salt; stir until dissolved. Remove from the heat; cover and set aside.

In a small mixing bowl, place ¼ cup half-and-half and cornstarch; stir until smooth and blended. Add the egg yolks; stir to blend. Add about ⅓ cup of the hot half-and-half mixture to the egg mixture; stir to blend. Add the egg mixture to the remaining, hot half-and-half mixture; stir until blended. Over medium-low heat, cook the mixture until it thickens, stirring constantly.

Remove the custard mixture from the heat and place on a wire rack. Add the vanilla; stir until blended. Let the custard mixture stand until cooled slightly; then, refrigerate until cooled to room temperature, stirring occasionally.

Meanwhile, pour the whipping cream into a small mixing bowl. Using an electric mixer, beat the cream on medium-high speed until it begins to stiffen. Reduce the mixer speed to medium-low and continue beating the cream until stiff, but still soft and fluffy; cover and refrigerate.

When the custard mixture cools to room temperature, add the whipped cream; using a mixing spoon, fold in. Cover and keep refrigerated.

ORANGE-COCONUT CHIFFON CAKE

When a professional baker invented chiffon cake in the late 1940's, it was all the rage, and it has stood the test of a half-century's time. Similar to a sponge cake, chiffon cake includes vegetable oil as an added ingredient, and it always contains baking powder (see Types of Cakes, page 448). The light texture, refreshing orange flavor, flaky coconut appliqué, and subdued color of this Orange-Coconut Chiffon Cake make for a perfect summertime dessert.

2¼ cups sifted cake flour (sift before measuring)
1 tablespoon baking powder
1 teaspoon salt
1½ cups superfine sugar
½ cup vegetable oil
6 extra-large egg yolks,* room temperature
¼ cup finely grated orange rind (page 31) (rind of about 3 extra-large oranges)
¾ cup freshly squeezed, strained orange juice
½ teaspoon pure vanilla extract
1 cup egg whites (about 7 extra-large egg whites**), room temperature
½ teaspoon cream of tartar
1 recipe Orange Fluff Frosting (page 511), tinted *very pale* orange
1 recipe Tinted Coconut (page 344), tinted light orange
Orange-colored paste food coloring (to tint Orange Fluff Frosting and Tinted Coconut)

 * *If extra-large egg yolks are not available, 7 large egg yolks may be substituted.*

**About 8 large egg whites.*

Preheat the oven to 325°F.

Onto waxed paper, sift together the flour, baking powder, salt, and sugar. Place the flour mixture in a large mixing bowl. With a large mixing spoon, make a well in the center of the

(Recipe continues on next page)

flour mixture. Into the well, place the vegetable oil, egg yolks, orange rind, orange juice, and vanilla; using an electric mixer, beat on medium speed until well blended and very smooth; set aside.

Place the egg whites in a large mixing bowl. Using the electric mixer fit with clean, dry blades, beat the egg whites on high speed until foamy. Add the cream of tartar; continue beating on high speed until the egg white mixture is *very stiff* and dry. (Do not worry about over-beating.) Pour the egg yolk mixture back and forth over the egg white mixture; using a large mixing spoon, fold in carefully and quickly.

Pour the cake batter into an *ungreased* 10 × 4-inch tube pan with a removable bottom. Using a small, narrow, angled spatula, lightly spread the batter evenly in the pan. Bake the cake for 50 to 55 minutes, or until a long, wooden toothpick inserted into the cake comes out clean.

Remove the cake from the oven. Immediately invert the pan and let it stand on the cooling legs until the cake is *completely cool* (about 2 hours). If the pan does not have cooling legs, place the center tube over the neck of a bottle and let the cake stand until cool.

When the cake is cool, carefully run a very sharp, very thin-bladed knife in a continuous motion first around the inside edge and then around the center tube of the pan to loosen the cake. Hold the knife against the side of the pan (and the center tube) to help prevent tearing the cake. Avoid up-and-down, sawing motions, which will spoil the outside appearance of the cake. Lift the center tube section, with the cake, out of the pan. Then, run the knife around the bottom of the tube section under the cake. Invert the cake onto a 12-inch corrugated cardboard cake circle or a perfectly flat serving plate. Carefully lift the tube section off the cake.

Frost the top and side of the cake with the Orange Fluff Frosting (see To Frost a Cake, page 501). Immediately after frosting the cake, spoon the Tinted Coconut over the top and side of the cake, pressing the coconut lightly into the frosting on the side of the cake with your hand only until it holds in place. Let the cake stand 1 hour

to allow the frosting to dry slightly. Then, place the cake in an airtight container.

MAKES ONE 10 × 4-INCH TUBE CAKE; 12 SERVINGS

Fruitcakes

TRADITIONAL HOLIDAY FRUITCAKE

Get in the holiday spirit early by making this exquisite fruitcake. You may make it in either 7 small loaf pans (for gift giving) or 1 large tube pan. The cakes (or cake) are wrapped in cognac-soaked cloths and left to season for 6 weeks before serving.

8 ounces (1 cup) candied pineapple slices sliced thinly
8 ounces (1 cup) diced candied orange peel
8 ounces (1 cup) diced candied citron
4 ounces (½ cup) red candied cherries, cut in half
4 ounces (½ cup) green candied cherries, cut in half
1 8-ounce package pitted dates, quartered (1 cup packed dates)
1 9-ounce package dried figs, stems removed and cut into eighths (1 cup plus 2 tablespoons packed figs)
1 15-ounce box (2½ cups) raisins
1 cup currants
1 cup coarsely broken pecans
1 cup coarsely broken English walnuts
2 cups sifted all-purpose flour (sift before measuring)
2 teaspoons baking powder
1 teaspoon salt
1 teaspoon ground allspice
½ teaspoon ground cloves
½ teaspoon ground nutmeg
¼ cup freshly squeezed, strained orange juice
¼ cup cognac

1 cup (½ pound) butter, softened
½ cup sugar
½ cup honey
5 extra-large eggs
2¼ cups cognac, divided
½ cup light corn syrup

DECORATION INGREDIENTS
4 ounces (½ cup) red candied cherries
4 ounces (½ cup) candied pineapple slices cut
    into wedges
35 pecan halves (5 per fruitcake)

Cut seven 13-inch-square pieces of clean, dry, white cotton cloth; set aside.

Prepare the fruits and nuts (the first 11 ingredients); set aside in separate, covered bowls.

Preheat the oven to 275°F. Grease seven 3 × 5¾ × 2⅛-inch loaf pans; set aside.

Reserve ¾ cup of the measured flour in a small mixing bowl; set aside. Onto waxed paper, sift together the remaining flour, baking powder, salt, allspice, cloves, and nutmeg; set aside.

Place the prepared fruits and nuts (the first 11 ingredients) in an extra-large mixing bowl or kettle. Sprinkle the ¾ cup reserved flour over the fruits and nuts; mix with your hands until the fruits and nuts are coated with flour and evenly distributed; set aside.

In a small mixing bowl, pour the orange juice and ¼ cup cognac; stir to blend; set aside.

In a large mixing bowl, place the butter and sugar; using an electric mixer, cream well on medium-high speed. Add the honey and beat on medium-high speed until fluffy. Add the eggs, one at a time, beating well on medium-high speed after each addition. Add, alternately, the flour mixture in fourths, and the orange juice mixture in thirds, beating on low speed after each addition only until blended. Pour the cake batter over the fruits and nuts mixture; using a large mixing spoon, fold and stir until combined.

Spoon the fruitcake batter equally into the 7 prepared loaf pans. With the back of a tablespoon, smooth lightly the top of the batter in the pans. Place the fruitcakes on the middle shelf in the oven. Then, place a 7 × 11 × 2-inch pan of very hot (not boiling) water (from the teakettle) on the oven shelf beneath the fruitcakes. Bake the fruitcakes for 1½ hours. When done, the cakes will spring back when pressed lightly with your finger.

Remove the fruitcakes from the oven and place on wire racks; let stand in the pans until *completely* cool.

Then, carefully run a sharp, thin-bladed knife along the inside edges of the pans to loosen the cakes. Remove the fruitcakes from the pans by inverting the pans, one at a time, in your hand or onto a wire rack. Let the cakes stand in the upright position.

Pour ¾ cup cognac into a large mixing bowl. Place the 7 pieces of cut cotton cloth in the bowl and saturate them in the cognac. Wrap each fruitcake in one of the cognac-soaked cloths. Then, wrap each fruitcake in airtight aluminum foil lined with plastic wrap. Place the fruitcakes, single layer, on a tray or cookie pan and store in a cool place such as the basement.

In 7 days, unwrap the fruitcakes; place the cloths in a large mixing bowl and sprinkle them with ½ cup cognac. Rewrap the fruitcakes, as before, and re-store them. Repeat the process of unwrapping the fruitcakes, resoaking the cloths, rewrapping the fruitcakes, and re-storing them 2 additional times at 7- to 10-day intervals.

Six weeks after baking, unwrap the fruitcakes, leaving the cloths wrapped around the sides of the fruitcakes to prevent them from drying while glazing and decorating the tops of the cakes.

Place the syrup in a very small saucepan. Over medium-low heat, heat the syrup until warm. Using a soft brush, paint the top of the fruitcakes with warm syrup. Arrange the red candied cherries, candied pineapple wedges, and pecan halves in a design or randomly on the top of the fruitcakes. Then, brush warm syrup on all sides of the decorations and brush a second layer of syrup on the remaining undecorated portions of the top of the cakes. Let the fruitcakes stand 45 minutes for the glaze to dry. Remove the cloths wrapped around the

(Recipe continues on next page)

sides of the fruitcakes and store the fruitcakes in airtight containers or wrap them in plastic wrap.

See To Cut Fruitcakes (page 455) for the procedure to cut the fruitcakes into serving portions.

MAKES SEVEN 1-POUND FRUITCAKES; 8 SERVINGS PER FRUITCAKE

ALTERNATIVE BAKING PAN: Traditional Holiday Fruitcake may be baked in a 10 × 4-inch tube pan with a removable bottom. Grease the pan; line the pan with aluminum foil, fitting the foil as smoothly as possible to the pan to prevent creases in the cake. Then, grease the aluminum foil. Bake the fruitcake for 3 hours at 275° F.

Remove the fruitcake from the oven and place on a wire rack; let stand upright in the pan until *completely* cool.

When cool, remove the fruitcake from the pan by lifting out the center tube section and then lifting the cake off the tube section. Carefully remove the aluminum foil and place the fruitcake on a *flat,* nonmetallic plate or tray.

Use one 22-inch-square piece of clean, dry, white cotton cloth for saturating in cognac and wrapping the fruitcake. (If necessary, the fruitcake may be left on the plate or tray if it is too difficult to transport the fruitcake and place it on the soaked cloth. Wrap the soaked cloth snugly around the fruitcake on the plate or tray.)

MAKES ONE 7-POUND FRUITCAKE; 56 SERVINGS

Tortes

JOY MCFARLAND'S MILE-HIGH TORTE

Blue ribbon awarded to Joy McFarland, 1992 Iowa State Fair.

Joy McFarland is one of the prodigious winners of blue ribbons at the Iowa State Fair. This divine entry of hers not only won a blue ribbon at the 1992 Iowa State Fair, but also was named Best Overall Cake at the fair that year. Joy and her husband, David, farm near Ellston, Iowa, and are one of the state's largest breeders of purebred Angus cattle.

2¼ cups cake flour
2 teaspoons baking soda
⅛ teaspoon salt
½ cup (¼ pound) butter, softened
2 cups packed light brown sugar
3 extra-large eggs
1 teaspoon pure vanilla extract
3 1-ounce packages Choco Bake chocolate
8 ounces commercial sour cream
1 cup water
½ cup seedless red raspberry jam
6 tablespoons Chambord raspberry
   liqueur, divided
Raspberry Frosting (recipe follows)
Fresh red raspberries for decoration
Chocolate Curls (page 342) for decoration
Additional seedless red raspberry jam for
   glazing raspberries

Preheat the oven to 350° F. Using Special Grease (page 40), grease three 8 × 2-inch round cake pans (see Note 1); set aside. Place 3 bake-even cake strips (page 452) in cold water; let stand (see Note).

Onto waxed paper, sift together the flour, baking soda, and salt; set aside.

Extract the excess water from the bake-even

cake strips. Wrap and pin the strips around the prepared cake pans; set aside.

In a large mixing bowl, place the butter and brown sugar; using an electric mixer, cream well on medium-high speed. While continuing to beat on medium-high speed, add the eggs one at a time; beat until fluffy. Add the vanilla and Choco Bake; beat on medium-high speed until completely blended. Add the sour cream; beat on medium-high speed until blended. Add, alternately, the flour mixture in fourths, and the water in thirds, beating on low speed after each addition only until blended.

Using a large mixing spoon, spoon the cake batter equally into the 3 prepared cake pans. Using a small, narrow, angled spatula, lightly and quickly spread the batter evenly in the pans. Bake the cakes for 25 minutes, or until a wooden toothpick inserted into the center of the cakes comes out clean.

Remove the cakes from the oven and place on wire racks; remove the cake strips. Let the cakes stand to cool 10 minutes. Remove the cakes from the pans (page 455); let stand on wire racks until completely cool.

If necessary, level the cakes to remove the crowns (page 452) (if bake-even cake strips were not used).

To assemble, fill, and frost the torte (procedure to follow), following the techniques described in To Frost a Cake (page 501). Assemble all 3 cake layers *underside up* to provide spongelike surfaces which will absorb the liqueur filling when added.

In a small saucepan, melt ½ cup raspberry jam over low heat; set aside. Slowly drizzle 2 tablespoons of the Chambord evenly over the bottom torte layer; let stand a few moments until the Chambord soaks in. Spread ½ of the melted raspberry jam over the bottom torte layer. Then, carefully spread 1 cup of the Raspberry Frosting over the jam. Place the middle torte layer evenly over the bottom layer. Repeat the filling and frosting procedure.

Place the top torte layer evenly over the middle layer. Drizzle the remaining 2 tablespoons Chambord over the top layer. (Melted rasp-

berry jam is *not* applied to the top layer.) Frost the top and side of the torte with Raspberry Frosting. Decorate the top of the torte with the fresh red raspberries and Chocolate Curls. In a small saucepan, melt a small amount of additional raspberry jam over low heat. Using a small, soft watercolor brush, paint the fresh raspberries with the melted jam to glaze them. Let the torte stand until the frosting sets. Then, place the torte in an airtight container and refrigerate.

NOTE 1: Although not as satisfactory, the pans may be greased and floured using the traditional method (page 40) in substitution for using Special Grease.

NOTE 2: The use of bake-even cake strips is optional with this recipe, but it is recommended in order to achieve evenly topped torte layers that do not require leveling.

MAKES ONE 8-INCH, 3-LAYER ROUND TORTE;
12 SERVINGS

RASPBERRY FROSTING

2 cups (1 pound) butter, softened
2 pounds (8 cups) powdered sugar
¾ cup unsweetened cocoa powder
1 cup (½ pint) whipping cream,
    unwhipped
¼ cup Chambord raspberry liqueur

Place the butter in a very large mixing bowl; using an electric mixer, beat on medium-high speed until fluffy. Add the powdered sugar, cocoa, whipping cream, and Chambord. Beat on low speed until partially mixed; then, beat on medium speed only until blended and fluffy.

OPTIONAL FROSTING DECORATION: After frosting smoothly the side of the torte, immediately run a decorating comb (see illustrations) around the side frosting to form small, parallel lines of decorative frosting ridges.

(Recipe continues on next page)

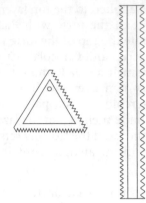

Two Styles of Decorating Combs

Using a decorating bag fit with medium open-star tip number 21 (page 319), pipe a shell border (page 324) of Raspberry Frosting around the bottom and top of the torte. (When frosting the torte, reserve about 1½ cups of the Raspberry Frosting for piping the borders.) Arrange a circle of fresh red raspberries around the top of the torte close to, but not touching, the shell border. Then, pipe an additional shell border of Raspberry Frosting around the torte, inside the circle of raspberries. Place a large raspberry in the center of the torte and arrange Chocolate Curls, in spoke fashion, around it (see illustration). Glaze the raspberries, following the procedure in the recipe.

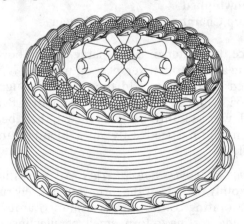

Joy McFarland's Mile-High Torte

BLACK FOREST CHERRY TORTE
Schwarzwälder Kirschtorte

This is one of the great, grand German desserts from the Black Forest region where tart, red cherries grow. Between the three layers of this infatuating chocolate cake is a lush cherry filling spiked with Kirschwasser (cherry brandy). More Kirschwasser flavors the whipped cream swirled lavishly over the top. As a final indulgence, shaved chocolate and maraschino cherries are added as adornment to the whipped cream. It's fun to make and glorious to eat!

3 ounces (3 squares) unsweetened chocolate
¼ cup sugar
½ cup whole milk
2¼ cups sifted cake flour (sift before measuring)
1 teaspoon baking soda
½ teaspoon salt
½ cup (¼ pound) butter, softened
1¼ cups sugar
3 extra-large eggs
1 teaspoon pure vanilla extract
1 cup whole milk
Cherry Filling (recipe follows)
Kirschwasser Whipped Cream (recipe follows)
Shaved Chocolate (page 342)
Maraschino cherries, rinsed, drained, and dried between paper towels, for decoration

Preheat the oven to 350° F. Using Special Grease (page 40), grease three 8 × 2-inch round cake pans (see Note); set aside. Place 3 bake-even cake strips (page 452) in cold water; let stand.

In the top of a double boiler, place the chocolate, ¼ cup sugar, and ½ cup milk. Place the top of the double boiler over (not touching) simmering water in the bottom pan. Stir the mixture constantly until the chocolate melts and the mixture is completely blended and smooth. Remove the top of the double boiler from the bottom pan; set aside.

Onto waxed paper, sift together the flour, baking soda, and salt; set aside.

Extract the excess water from the bake-even cake strips. Wrap and pin the strips around the prepared cake pans; set aside.

In a large mixing bowl, place the butter and 1¼ cups sugar; using an electric mixer, beat on medium-high speed until light and fluffy. Add the eggs, one at a time, beating well on medium-high speed after each addition. Add the chocolate mixture and vanilla; beat on medium-high speed until blended. Add, alternately, the flour mixture in fourths, and 1 cup milk in thirds, beating on low speed after each addition only until blended.

Using a large mixing spoon, spoon the cake batter equally into the 3 prepared cake pans. Using a small, narrow, angled spatula, lightly and quickly spread the batter evenly in the pans. Bake the cakes for 25 minutes, or until a wooden toothpick inserted into the center of the cakes comes out clean.

Remove the cakes from the oven and place on wire racks; remove the cake strips. Let the cakes stand to cool 10 minutes. Remove the cakes from the pans (page 455); let stand on wire racks until completely cool.

Then, spread ½ of the Cherry Filling between the bottom and middle torte layers; spread the remaining ½ of the Cherry Filling between the middle and top torte layers (see To Frost a Cake, page 501). Spread the Kirschwasser Whipped Cream attractively over the top of the torte, leaving the side of the cake unfrosted.

Decorate the top of the torte with the Shaved Chocolate and the maraschino cherries. Place the torte in an airtight cake container and refrigerate.

NOTE: Although not as satisfactory, the pans may be greased and floured using the traditional method (page 40) in substitution for using Special Grease.

MAKES ONE 8-INCH, 3-LAYER ROUND TORTE; 12 SERVINGS

CHERRY FILLING

2 cups pitted, tart, fresh (or frozen and thawed) red cherries
1 cup plus 3 tablespoons sugar
1 cup juice drained from cherries
3 tablespoons cornstarch
Red liquid food coloring (optional)
¼ cup Kirschwasser (cherry brandy; page 7)

Cut the cherries in half lengthwise, and place in a medium mixing bowl. Add the sugar and stir to combine; let stand 1 hour, stirring occasionally.

Drain the cherries in a sieve, reserving the juice. Measure 1 cup reserved juice, adding water, if necessary, to make 1 cup liquid. Place the cherries in a medium saucepan. Add the 1 cup reserved juice and cornstarch; stir to combine. Bring the cherry mixture to a simmer over medium heat and cook until thick and translucent, stirring constantly.

Remove the saucepan from the heat and place on a wire rack. Add a few drops of food coloring (if used); stir until evenly blended. Add the Kirschwasser; stir to blend. Let the Cherry Filling stand until cooled to room temperature before spreading.

KIRSCHWASSER WHIPPED CREAM

1 cup (½ pint) whipping cream
⅓ cup powdered sugar, sifted (page 42)
1 tablespoon plus 2 teaspoons Kirschwasser (cherry brandy; page 7)

Pour the whipping cream into a cold (previously refrigerated), medium-small mixing bowl. Using an electric mixer, beat the cream on medium-high speed until it begins to stiffen. Reduce the mixer speed to medium-low. While continuing to beat, sprinkle the powdered sugar over the cream. Then, sprinkle in the Kirschwasser. Continue beating the cream until stiff but still soft and fluffy.

HAZELNUT TORTE

This famous old-world torte is a good example of a European baking procedure, which uses large quantities of ground nuts in combination with flour. Sometimes, European-style baked goods are made with ground nuts and no flour at all (see Zimtsterne cookies, page 563).

¾ pound (about 2¼ cups) shelled hazelnuts, toasted and skinned (page 35)
¾ cup sifted cake flour (sift before measuring)
¾ teaspoon powdered instant coffee (to powder instant coffee, process in blender*)
¾ teaspoon unsweetened cocoa powder
9 extra-large eggs,** room temperature, separated
1 cup superfine sugar
1½ teaspoons Myers's (dark) rum
1½ teaspoons finely grated lemon rind (page 31)
1 teaspoon pure vanilla extract
½ cup superfine sugar
Hazelnut Frosting (recipe follows)
3 tablespoons toasted, skinned, and chopped hazelnuts for decoration (chop with a knife)

　* *If a blender is not available, a food processor may be used; however, it is difficult to achieve a fine powder using a food processor. Reserve any remaining powdered instant coffee for other uses, such as flavored whipped cream (see Filling recipe, page 491).*

***If extra-large eggs are not available, 12 large eggs may be substituted.*

In a food processor, process ¾ pound hazelnuts for *a few seconds* until ground. Be careful not to overprocess, reducing the nuts to butter. Set the ground nuts aside.

Preheat the oven to 350° F. Grease the bottoms of two 9-inch springform pans; set aside (see Note).

Onto waxed paper, sift together the flour, cof-fee, and cocoa. Place the flour mixture in a medium mixing bowl. Add the ground hazelnuts; stir to combine; set aside.

Place the egg yolks in a large mixing bowl. Using an electric mixer, beat the egg yolks on high speed about 8 minutes, or until very thick and butter colored. While continuing to beat the egg yolks on high speed, very gradually add 1 cup sugar (about 3 minutes additional beating time). Add the rum, lemon rind, and vanilla; beat on high speed 2 additional minutes, until very thick. Add the flour mixture in thirds, using a large mixing spoon to fold in after each addition only until the flour disappears; set aside.

Place the egg whites in a large mixing bowl. Using the electric mixer fit with clean, dry blades, beat the egg whites on high speed until soft peaks hold. While continuing to beat on high speed, very gradually add ½ cup sugar and continue beating the egg white mixture until stiff, but still moist and glossy. Pour the egg yolk mixture back and forth over the egg white mixture; using the large mixing spoon, fold in carefully and quickly.

Pour ⅓ of the cake batter into one of the prepared springform pans. Pour the remaining ⅔ of the batter into the other springform pan. Using a small, narrow, angled spatula, lightly spread the batter evenly in the pans. Then, carefully run a narrow, rubber spatula once in a circle around the batter in each pan halfway between the edge and the center of the pans to remove any large air pockets. Bake the cakes for 20 to 25 minutes, or until the cakes spring back when touched lightly with your finger. (The thicker cake will take longer to bake.)

Remove the cakes from the oven and place on wire racks; let the cakes stand in the pans until completely cool.

When the cakes are cool, run a sharp, very thin-bladed knife in a continuous motion around the inside edge of the pans to loosen the cakes. Then, remove the sides of the pans. Invert each cake onto a wire rack and carefully remove the pan bottoms. Split the thicker cake in half horizontally to form 2 layers (see To Split a

Cake into Layers, page 453). (The thinner, single cake is the third layer.)

Reserve about 1½ cups of the Hazelnut Frosting to decorate the torte. With the remainder of the frosting, frost between the layers, and the top and side of the torte (see To Frost a Cake, page 501). Sprinkle the 3 tablespoons chopped hazelnuts over the top of the torte. With the 1½ cups reserved Hazelnut Frosting, pipe rope borders (page 324) around the bottom and top of the torte using a decorating bag fit with medium open-star tip number 21 (page 319). Let the torte stand until the frosting sets. Then, place the torte in an airtight container and refrigerate.

NOTE: Do not wrap bake-even cake strips (page 452) around the cake pans when using this recipe.

MAKES ONE 9-INCH, 3-LAYER ROUND TORTE; 14 SERVINGS

HAZELNUT FROSTING

¼ pound (about ¾ cup) shelled hazelnuts, toasted and skinned (page 35)
1 cup sugar
¾ teaspoon cornstarch
8 extra-large egg yolks*
1 cup (½ pint) whipping cream, unwhipped
2¾ teaspoons pure vanilla extract
2 cups (1 pound) butter

* If extra-large egg yolks are not available, 9 large egg yolks may be substituted.

In a food processor, process the hazelnuts for *a few seconds* until ground. Be careful not to overprocess, reducing the nuts to butter. Set the ground nuts aside. In a small mixing bowl, place the sugar and cornstarch; stir to combine; set aside.

Place the egg yolks in a medium mixing bowl. Using an electric mixer, beat the egg yolks on high speed about 8 minutes, until very thick and butter colored. While continuing to beat the egg yolks on high speed, very gradually add the sugar mixture; beat until blended. While continuing to beat on high speed, gradually add the whipping cream; beat until blended. With the aid of a rubber spatula, place the egg yolk mixture in the top of a double boiler. Place the top of the double boiler over simmering water in the bottom pan. Cook the egg yolk mixture until thick (about 15 to 20 minutes), stirring constantly.

Remove the top of the double boiler from the bottom pan and place it on a wire rack. Add the vanilla; stir until blended. Let the mixture stand until cooled slightly; then, refrigerate until cold, stirring occasionally.

Remove the butter from the refrigerator and place it in a large mixing bowl; let stand 5 minutes only. Using the electric mixer fit with clean, dry blades, beat the butter on high speed until fluffy. Add the cold egg yolk mixture; beat on high speed until well blended. Add the ground hazelnuts; beat to combine. Use the Hazelnut Frosting immediately. Food frosted with Hazelnut Frosting must be kept refrigerated.

Frostings

TO FROST A CAKE

EQUIPMENT FOR FROSTING A CAKE
With the following items, you will be well equipped to frost most types of cakes made in the home kitchen (see illustration):

    Corrugated cardboard cake circles and
      boards
    1 decorating turntable
    1 8-inch, narrow, angled spatula
    1 12-inch, narrow, angled spatula

(Continues on next page)

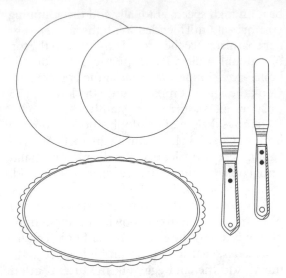

Clockwise from bottom: *Decorating Turntable; Corrugated Cardboard Cake Circles; 12-Inch Narrow, Angled Spatula; and 8-Inch Narrow, Angled Spatula.*

The above equipment is available from Wilton Enterprises and Sweet Celebrations Inc. (see Product Sources, page 631, for addresses and telephone numbers).

FROSTING CONSISTENCY

Proper frosting consistency is critical to the successful frosting of a cake. With a tinge of facetiousness, the instruction is: "Frosting should not be too thick, nor should it be too thin." Frosting which is too thick will not spread easily and attractively, and will pull at the surface of the cake, causing crumbling. Frosting which is too thin will run, and cannot be spread thick enough to smoothly cover the cake. Extremely thin frosting may permeate the cake, causing soggy texture.

The knack of achieving correct frosting consistency is gained by experience—trial and error. Reliable, tested frosting recipes generally produce frostings of satisfactory consistency; however, factors such as room temperature, softness of the butter or shortening, and humidity may create the need for tiny adjustments to thicken or thin the frosting.

Bowls of frosting should be covered immediately after making and should be kept covered as much as possible during the frosting process to prevent drying.

STEPS PREPARATORY TO FROSTING (other than sheet cakes frosted in the baking pan)

1. If frosting a layered cake, level the lower layer(s) if necessary (see To Level a Baked Cake, page 452). Level the top layer if necessary or required because of planned decoration. Some cakes frosted more informally—for example, with swirls of Boiled Frosting (page 506) or Seven-Minute Frosting (page 507)—may be considered more eye-appealing if the top layer has an unleveled crown.

2. Brush the cake surfaces lightly with a soft pastry brush to remove any loose crumbs which would otherwise mingle with the frosting as it is applied.

3. Place the lower layer of the cake (or the entire cake, if not layered) on a corrugated cardboard cake circle (or board) which is approximately 2 inches greater in diameter (or length and width) than the diameter (or length and width) of the cake; in other words, use a 10-inch cake circle under an 8-inch round cake. (While it is strongly recommended that a cake circle [or board] be used to achieve good results and for ease of handling, a *perfectly flat* plate with little or no rim may be substituted.)

4. Place the cake circle which holds the lowest cake layer (or the entire single-layered cake) on a decorating turntable. Slip three 4-inch × 1-foot strips of waxed paper under the bottom edge of the cake around the cardboard cake circle to prevent unwanted frosting from getting on the exposed border of the cake circle during the frosting process. The waxed paper will be removed after the cake is frosted.

FROSTING PROCEDURE

To help prevent cake crumbs from mixing with the frosting as it is applied, always keep the spatula on the frosting and avoid letting it touch the surface of the cake.

To frost the lower layer of a cake, place tablespoonsful of frosting (or other filling) over the central surface of the cake. Using the small spatula, spread the frosting very evenly and smoothly to within ¼ inch of the outside edge of the cake. The weight of the top layer(s) will press the frosting to the edge of the cake. It is important to maintain an even thickness of frosting between the layers and to finish the surface smoothly in order to produce a symmetrical cake which does not tilt. Carefully place the top (or next) cake layer over the frosting (or filling) covering the bottom layer, taking great care to position it evenly over the bottom layer. Repeat the process if stacking more than 2 layers. If desired, the top cake layer may be inverted, thereby positioning the bottom side of the layer at the top of the whole cake to provide a smoother surface for frosting.

Spoon frosting over the top of the cake; using the large spatula, spread the frosting evenly over the top surface, pushing the surplus frosting over the edge and down the side of the cake.

Using the small spatula, transport frosting from the bowl to the side of the cake, spreading small vertical areas at a time. Then, if a smooth finish is desired, hold the small spatula in a stationary, vertical position perpendicular to the cardboard cake circle and lightly against the frosting on the side of the cake. Slowly turn the decorating turntable; return excess frosting accumulated on the spatula to the bowl.

Finally, if a smooth finish is desired on the top of a level-topped cake, make fan-type sweeping motions with the edge of the large spatula from the top edge of the cake toward the center, returning any excess frosting to the bowl. Rotate the decorating turntable before making each sweep. Then, using either the large or small spatula, smooth the frosting in the center of the cake. As a last step, very lightly pull the edge of the large spatula over the entire top of the cake. If the frosting on the cake becomes too dry and unpliable before the finishing process is completed, intermittently dip the spatula in very hot water and wipe it dry as you hurry to complete the smoothing procedure. The heat of the spatula will help soften the frosting. Or, with extreme care, the spatula may be left slightly damp after dipping in the hot water. The tiny bit of water will thin the surface of the frosting, making it easier to rework, and also will help restore a shiny finish. *This technique should not be used on frostings which contain egg whites.*

To achieve a smooth frosting finish employing the techniques described above, a buttercream-style frosting is generally used.

After the top and side of the cake are frosted, use quick motions to pull the strips of waxed paper from under the cake. Make any necessary small repairs to the frosting around the bottom of the cake. Make certain that the frosting on the side of the cake touches the cake circle in order to completely seal the cake with frosting to prevent loss of moisture. This also can be accomplished by piping a border around the bottom of the cake (see pages 324–325 for illustrations and procedures for piping borders). Piping borders around the bottom and top of a cake not only endows it with a professional flair, but also helps mask any flaws in the application of frosting.

Allow the newly frosted cake to stand for a short time until the frosting sets; then, place it in an airtight cake container. Leave the frosted cake on the cake circle throughout, including serving.

For an even more perfect job of frosting, first frost the cake with a very thin layer of frosting to contain the crumbs. Let the frosting dry for a few minutes before applying the main layer of frosting.

To achieve a completely smooth finish to the frosting on the top of the cake, which is especially desirable if the cake is to be decorated with piped flowers and/or lettering, or other piped frosting decorations, let the newly frosted cake stand only until the frosting is dry to

(Continues on next page)

touch. Then, place a piece of parchment baking paper or a paper towel over the top of the cake. Lightly roll a pizza roller back and forth over the parchment or paper towel to smooth the frosting surface. Or, draw the edge of the large spatula lightly across the parchment or paper towel to achieve the same result. This smoothing procedure should be used only on buttercream-style frostings. It is particularly effective when Cake Decorators' Icing (this page) has been used to frost the cake. The consistency of some frostings is not conducive to the successful application of this smoothing procedure.

TO SWIRL FROSTING: The consistency of Boiled Frosting (page 506), Seven-Minute Frosting (page 507), and other frostings made with beaten egg whites lends itself best to a swirled finish. In fact, these frostings, skillfully applied in swirls, can render a cake almost too glamorous to eat! Most buttercream-style frostings also can be swirled successfully.

While frostings made with beaten egg whites generally are not used when a smooth finish is desired, there are exceptions. For example, the recipe for Shadow Cake (page 457) calls for Boiled Frosting to be applied smoothly to the top of the cake and swirled on the sides.

For a swirled frosting finish, spoon frosting over the top of the cake. Using the small spatula, spread the frosting to cover the top surface. Then, use the small spatula to sculpt quick, random C's on the frosting surface. Additional portions of frosting may be added as you sculpt the C's to produce a decorative, symmetrical appearance.

Use the small spatula to apply frosting over small vertical areas at a time on the side of the cake. After applying the frosting to each small area, swirl the frosting just applied.

When the cake is completely frosted, do any necessary touching up with further swirls and added bits of frosting where needed.

CAKE DECORATORS' ICINGS

Use Cake Decorators' Icings to pipe flowers and other decorations, including lettering, for/on cakes. Also use Cake Decorators' Icings to frost such decorated cakes, as a very smooth finish can be achieved with this icing. A flat, smooth frosting surface on which to apply piped icing decorations is essential to produce an attractive and professional-looking decorated cake. (See To Frost a Cake, page 501, for procedures.)

CAKE DECORATORS' WHITE ICING

½ cup nonfat dry milk
½ cup cool water
½ teaspoon clear vanilla
½ teaspoon almond extract
1 teaspoon salt
1⅓ cups vegetable shortening, softened
2 pounds (8 cups) powdered sugar
Paste food coloring (optional)

In a large mixing bowl, place the dry milk, water, vanilla, almond extract, and salt; stir until completely blended. Add the vegetable shortening and powdered sugar; using an electric mixer, beat on medium-high speed only until blended and creamy.

To tint the icing, use a toothpick to add a tiny amount of paste food coloring; beat the icing on medium-high speed only until the color is evenly blended.

Or, if mixing more than one color, spoon the desired amounts of white icing into separate plastic containers. Then, using toothpicks, add a tiny amount of paste food coloring to the icing in each container. Using separate, small spoons, stir the icing in each container vigorously until the color is completely blended and even.

Use the frosting immediately or place it in an

airtight plastic storage container and refrigerate. Keeps well up to one week in the refrigerator.

MAKES ENOUGH TO FROST BETWEEN THE LAYERS, AND THE TOP AND SIDES, AND TO DECORATE ONE 2- OR 3-LAYER, 8- OR 9-INCH ROUND OR SQUARE CAKE

¼ RECIPE CAKE DECORATORS' WHITE ICING (MINUS ALMOND EXTRACT FOR SMALL DECORATING TASKS)

2 tablespoons dry milk
2 tablespoons cool water
¼ teaspoon clear vanilla
¼ teaspoon salt
¼ cup plus 1 tablespoon plus 1 teaspoon
   vegetable shortening, softened
2 cups powdered sugar

Use a small mixing bowl and follow the recipe.

CAKE DECORATORS' BUTTER-CREAM ICING

⅔ cup (¼ pound plus 2 tablespoons plus
   2 teaspoons) butter, softened
⅔ cup vegetable shortening, softened

Follow the Cake Decorators' White Icing recipe, above, substituting ⅔ cup butter and ⅔ cup vegetable shortening for 1⅓ cups vegetable shortening. (In general, Cake Decorators' *White* Icing should be used when the icing is to be tinted.)

CAKE DECORATORS' CHOCOLATE ICING

¼ cup nonfat dry milk
½ cup cool water
1 teaspoon pure vanilla extract
1 cup (½ pound) butter, softened
2 pounds (8 cups) powdered sugar
1 cup unsweetened cocoa powder

In a small mixing bowl, place the dry milk, water, and vanilla; stir until completely blended; set aside. In a large mixing bowl, place the butter, powdered sugar, cocoa, and dry milk mixture; using an electric mixer, beat on medium-high speed only until blended and creamy.

Use the frosting immediately or place it in an airtight plastic storage container and refrigerate. Keeps well up to one week in the refrigerator.

MAKES ENOUGH TO FROST BETWEEN THE LAYERS, AND THE TOP AND SIDES, AND TO DECORATE ONE 2- OR 3-LAYER, 8- OR 9-INCH ROUND OR SQUARE CAKE

BUTTERCREAM FROSTING

½ cup (¼ pound) butter, softened
1 pound (4 cups) powdered sugar
¼ teaspoon salt
2 teaspoons pure vanilla extract
¼ cup half-and-half

In a medium mixing bowl, place the butter, powdered sugar, salt, vanilla, and half-and-half. Using an electric mixer, beat the mixture on medium-high speed only until blended and fluffy.

MAKES ENOUGH TO FROST BETWEEN THE LAYERS, AND THE TOP AND SIDES OF ONE 2-LAYER, 8- OR 9-INCH ROUND OR SQUARE CAKE, OR THE TOP OF ONE 9 × 13-INCH SHEET CAKE

LEMON BUTTERCREAM FROSTING

½ cup (¼ pound) butter, softened
1 pound (4 cups) powdered sugar
¼ cup freshly squeezed, strained lemon juice
¼ teaspoon lemon extract
Lemon-colored paste food coloring

In a medium mixing bowl, place the butter, powdered sugar, lemon juice, and lemon extract. Using an electric mixer, beat the ingredients on low speed to combine; then, increase the mixer speed to medium-high and continue

(Recipe continues on next page)

beating only until blended and smooth. To lightly tint the frosting, use a toothpick to add a tiny amount of paste food coloring; beat the frosting on medium-high speed only until the color is evenly blended.

If thinner frosting is desired, add water, 1 or 2 teaspoons at a time, until the desired consistency is achieved.

MAKES ENOUGH TO FROST BETWEEN THE LAYERS, AND THE TOP AND SIDES OF ONE 2-LAYER, 8- OR 9-INCH ROUND OR SQUARE CAKE, OR THE TOP OF ONE 9 × 13-INCH SHEET CAKE

MOCHA BUTTERCREAM FROSTING

½ cup (¼ pound) butter, softened
1 pound (4 cups) powdered sugar
¼ teaspoon salt
½ teaspoon pure vanilla extract
2 tablespoons half-and-half
1 tablespoon unsweetened cocoa powder
2 tablespoons strong, brewed coffee, room temperature

In a medium mixing bowl, place the butter, powdered sugar, salt, vanilla, half-and-half, cocoa, and coffee. Using an electric mixer, beat the mixture on medium-high speed only until blended and fluffy.

MAKES ENOUGH TO FROST BETWEEN THE LAYERS, AND THE TOP AND SIDES OF ONE 2-LAYER, 8- OR 9-INCH ROUND OR SQUARE CAKE, THE TOP OF ONE 9 × 13-INCH SHEET CAKE, OR THE SIDE OF ONE ROLLED 10½ × 15½-INCH JELLY-ROLL CAKE

CREAMY CINNAMON FROSTING

1 pound plus 1 cup (5 cups) powdered sugar
1½ teaspoons ground cinnamon
½ teaspoon salt
½ cup vegetable shortening
¼ cup plus 2 tablespoons half-and-half
1¼ teaspoons pure vanilla extract

In a medium mixing bowl, place the powdered

sugar, cinnamon, salt, vegetable shortening, half-and-half, and vanilla. Using an electric mixer, beat the mixture on medium-high speed only until smooth and creamy.

MAKES ENOUGH TO FROST BETWEEN THE LAYERS, AND THE TOP AND SIDES, AND TO DECORATE ONE 2-LAYER, 8- OR 9-INCH ROUND OR SQUARE CAKE, OR THE TOP OF ONE 9 × 13-INCH SHEET CAKE

BOILED FROSTING

Note: This recipe contains uncooked egg whites (see page 220).

2¼ cups sugar
1 cup water
2 tablespoons light corn syrup
⅛ teaspoon salt
3 extra-large egg whites, room temperature
1 teaspoon clear vanilla

In a large, heavy saucepan, place the sugar, water, syrup, and salt; stir to combine. Over low heat, stir the mixture until the sugar dissolves. Attach a candy thermometer. Increase the heat to medium-high. Bring the mixture to a boil and cook, *without stirring,* until the temperature reaches 240°F (see Note).

Meanwhile, place the egg whites in a large mixing bowl. Using an electric mixer, beat the egg whites on high speed until stiff peaks hold; let stand.

When the syrup reaches 240°F (see Note), remove from the heat and detach the thermometer. While beating constantly with the electric mixer on high speed, *slowly* trickle the hot syrup into the beaten egg whites. Add the vanilla and continue beating on high speed until the frosting is thick enough to hold stiff peaks.

NOTE: This temperature is for use at sea-level locations. To adjust the temperature for preparation of this recipe at higher elevations, see Boiled Candies and Frostings, page 19.

MAKES ENOUGH TO FROST BETWEEN THE LAYERS, AND THE TOP AND SIDES OF ONE 2- OR 3-LAYER, 8- OR 9-INCH ROUND OR SQUARE CAKE, OR THE TOP OF ONE 9 × 13-INCH SHEET CAKE

BURNT-SUGAR FROSTING

Follow the Boiled Frosting recipe, above, substituting ¼ cup Burnt-Sugar Syrup (page 464) for 2 tablespoons light corn syrup.

CONFECTIONERS' FROSTING

1 pound (4 cups) powdered sugar
¼ cup plus 1 tablespoon half-and-half
2 teaspoons clear vanilla
Paste food coloring (optional)

In a medium mixing bowl, place the powdered sugar, half-and-half, and vanilla; using an electric mixer, beat on medium-high speed only until well blended. To tint the frosting, use a toothpick to add a tiny amount of paste food coloring. Using a spoon, stir the frosting vigorously until the color is completely blended and uniform.

Use the frosting immediately. While using the frosting, place a piece of plastic wrap over half of the bowl to help keep the frosting moist.

MAKES ENOUGH TO FROST 5 DOZEN LARGE COOKIES; TO DECORATE 15 DOZEN MEDIUM COOKIES; OR TO FROST 2 DOZEN CINNAMON ROLLS

SERVING SUGGESTIONS

- Use plain or tinted Confectioners' Frosting to frost cutout cookies which will be decorated with colored sugar, nonpareils (page 7), and other edible decorations (see To Decorate Cutout Cookies, page 561).

- Use Confectioners' Frosting to pipe decorations on cookies (see Gingerbread People, page 559).

SEVEN-MINUTE FROSTING

1¾ cups sugar
½ cup cold water
1 tablespoon light corn syrup
2 extra-large egg whites, room temperature
⅛ teaspoon salt
1 teaspoon clear vanilla

In the top of a double boiler with at least an 8-cup (top pan) capacity, place the sugar, water, syrup, egg whites, and salt; using a handheld electric mixer, beat 1 minute on high speed. Place the top of the double boiler over (not touching) boiling water in the bottom pan. While beating constantly with the electric mixer on high speed, cook the mixture 7 minutes, until stiff peaks hold. If the frosting threatens to spill over the edge of the double boiler top pan during the cooking process, spoon some of the frosting out of the pan and discard. (This recipe makes ample frosting for the cake recipes in *The Blue Ribbon Country Cookbook* that specify its use.)

Remove the top of the double boiler from the bottom pan and transfer the frosting mixture to a large mixing bowl. Add the vanilla. Using a standard-sized electric mixer, beat the frosting on high speed until stiff enough to spread.

MAKES ENOUGH TO FROST BETWEEN THE LAYERS, AND THE TOP AND SIDES OF ONE 2-LAYER, 8- OR 9-INCH ROUND OR SQUARE CAKE, OR THE TOP OF ONE 9 × 13-INCH SHEET CAKE

SUGGESTION FOR USE OF LEFTOVER FROSTING: This recipe makes a generous amount of frosting. Leftover frosting may be used to frost commercially purchased vanilla or chocolate wafers. Top each frosted wafer with a pecan half, an English walnut half, or a hazelnut.

HARVEST MOON FROSTING

Follow the Seven-Minute Frosting recipe, above, substituting 1¾ cups packed light brown sugar for 1¾ cups granulated sugar, and substituting 1 teaspoon pure vanilla extract for 1 teaspoon clear vanilla.

CHOCOLATE FROSTING

This wonderful, basic Chocolate Frosting recipe is my mother's. I've enjoyed it my whole life on cakes, brownies, and cookies, and have never found a better chocolate buttercream frosting. The fresh, strong, brewed coffee in this frosting gives it a richness and depth of flavor which make it a standout. (Be sure to use real butter.)

1 pound (4 cups) powdered sugar
1/3 cup unsweetened cocoa powder
1/2 cup (1/4 pound) butter, melted
1/4 cup strong, brewed coffee, room
    temperature
2 teaspoons pure vanilla extract

In a medium mixing bowl, place the powdered sugar, cocoa, butter, coffee, and vanilla. Using an electric mixer, beat the mixture on high speed only until completely smooth.

MAKES ENOUGH TO FROST BETWEEN THE LAYERS, AND THE TOP AND SIDES OF ONE 2-LAYER, 8- OR 9-INCH ROUND OR SQUARE CAKE, THE TOP OF ONE 9 × 13-INCH SHEET CAKE, THE TOP AND SIDES OF ONE 5 × 9-INCH LOAF CAKE, OR 7 DOZEN MEDIUM COOKIES

CARAMEL FROSTING

3/4 cup (1/4 pound plus 4 tablespoons) butter
1 1/2 cups packed light brown sugar
1/3 cup half-and-half
3 1/4 cups powdered sugar, sifted (page 42)

In a medium-small, heavy saucepan, melt the butter over low heat. Add the brown sugar; stir to combine. Over medium heat, bring the brown sugar mixture to a boil, stirring constantly. Boil the mixture 2 minutes, stirring continuously. Remove from the heat. Add the half-and-half; stir vigorously to blend. Return the mixture to a boil over medium heat, stirring constantly. Remove from the heat.

Leave the brown sugar mixture in the saucepan and refrigerate it until the mixture is cooled to slightly warm (about 40 minutes), stirring intermittently.

Then, remove the mixture from the refrigerator; set aside. Place the powdered sugar in a medium mixing bowl. Add the brown sugar mixture; using an electric mixer, beat on medium-high speed only until blended and smooth.

MAKES ENOUGH TO FROST ONE 2-LAYER, 8- OR 9-INCH ROUND OR SQUARE CAKE, OR THE TOP OF ONE 9 × 13-INCH SHEET CAKE

POWDERED SUGAR FROSTING

A primary frosting used in the Midwest to frost cakes and cookies.

1 pound (4 cups) powdered sugar
1/4 cup plus 2 tablespoons (6 tablespoons)
    butter, melted
1/4 cup half-and-half *or* whole milk
2 teaspoons clear vanilla

In a medium mixing bowl, place the powdered sugar, butter, half-and-half (or milk), and vanilla. Using an electric mixer, beat the mixture on medium-high speed only until blended and fluffy.

MAKES ENOUGH TO FROST BETWEEN THE LAYERS, AND THE TOP AND SIDES OF ONE 2-LAYER, 8- OR 9-INCH ROUND OR SQUARE CAKE, THE TOP OF ONE 9 × 13-INCH SHEET CAKE, OR 7 DOZEN MEDIUM COOKIES

ORANGE FROSTING

2 cups powdered sugar
2 tablespoons butter, melted
2 tablespoons freshly squeezed, strained
    orange juice
1 tablespoon very finely grated orange rind
    (page 31)
Orange-colored paste food coloring
    (optional)

In a medium mixing bowl, place the powdered sugar, butter, orange juice, orange rind, and a tiny amount of food coloring (if used). Using an electric mixer, beat the mixture on medium-high speed only until blended and smooth.

MAKES ENOUGH TO FROST 6 DOZEN MEDIUM COOKIES. DOUBLE THE RECIPE TO FROST BETWEEN THE LAYERS, AND THE TOP AND SIDES OF ONE 2-LAYER, 8- OR 9-INCH ROUND OR SQUARE CAKE, OR THE TOP OF ONE 9 × 13-INCH SHEET CAKE

BANANA-NUT FROSTING

1 pound (4 cups) powdered sugar
¼ cup plus 2 tablespoons (6 tablespoons)
    butter, melted
¼ cup half-and-half
1½ teaspoons clear vanilla
¼ teaspoon banana flavoring
½ cup chopped pecans

In a medium mixing bowl, place the powdered sugar, butter, half-and-half, vanilla, and banana flavoring. Using an electric mixer, beat the mixture on medium-high speed only until blended and smooth. Add the pecans; beat on medium speed until evenly distributed.

MAKES ENOUGH TO FROST BETWEEN THE LAYERS, AND THE TOP AND SIDES OF ONE 2-LAYER, 8- OR 9-INCH ROUND OR SQUARE CAKE, OR THE TOP OF ONE 9 × 13-INCH SHEET CAKE

WHIPPED CREAM–COCONUT FROSTING

1 cup (½ pint) whipping cream
¼ cup powdered sugar
½ teaspoon clear vanilla
½ cup shredded coconut

Pour the whipping cream into a cold (previously refrigerated), medium-small mixing bowl. Using an electric mixer, beat the cream on medium-high speed until it begins to stiffen. Reduce the mixer speed to medium-low. Add the powdered sugar and vanilla; continue beating the cream until stiff but still soft and fluffy.

Frost the top and sides of a white or yellow cake with the whipped cream. Then, sprinkle the coconut on the frosted top and sides of the cake, pressing the coconut lightly into the frosting on the sides of the cake with your hand only until it holds in place. Refrigerate the cake after frosting.

MAKES ENOUGH TO FROST THE TOP AND SIDES OF ONE 1-LAYER, 8- OR 9-INCH ROUND OR SQUARE CAKE

VARIATION: After applying the coconut to the frosted cake, garnish the top of the cake with fresh raspberries, strawberries, or blueberries, or in combination.

NOTE: To frost between the layers, and the top and sides of one 2-layer, 8- or 9-inch round or square cake, double the recipe. Use coconut between the layers as well as on top of the cake. Use fruit only on the top of the cake (see Variation above).

COCONUT-PECAN FROSTING I

½ cup (¼ pound) butter
1 cup sugar
1 cup evaporated milk
3 extra-large egg yolks, slightly beaten
1 teaspoon pure vanilla extract
1¼ cups flaked coconut
1 cup chopped pecans

In a small saucepan, melt the butter over low heat. Add the sugar, evaporated milk, and egg yolks. Increase the heat to medium; cook the mixture until thick (about 10 minutes), stirring constantly. Do not allow the mixture to boil.

Remove the saucepan from the heat and place on a wire rack. Add the vanilla; stir until blended. Add the coconut and pecans; stir to combine. Let stand until the frosting is cooled to spreading consistency, stirring occasionally. Cakes frosted with Coconut-Pecan Frosting I must be kept refrigerated.

MAKES ENOUGH TO FROST BETWEEN THE LAYERS, AND THE TOP OF ONE 3-LAYER, 8-INCH ROUND OR SQUARE CAKE, OR THE TOP OF ONE 9 × 13-INCH SHEET CAKE

COCONUT-PECAN FROSTING II

½ cup (¼ pound) butter
¾ cup sugar
½ cup evaporated milk
1 teaspoon pure vanilla extract
1 cup flaked coconut
1 cup broken pecans

In a small saucepan, melt the butter over low heat. Remove from the heat. Add the sugar and evaporated milk; stir to combine. Bring the mixture to a rapid boil over medium-high heat, stirring constantly. Reduce the heat slightly and continue boiling rapidly 5 minutes, stirring continuously.

Remove the saucepan from the heat. Add the

vanilla; stir to blend. Add the coconut; stir to combine. Then, add the pecans; stir to combine.

MAKES ENOUGH TO FROST THE TOP OF ONE 9 × 13-INCH SHEET CAKE

CRÈME DE MENTHE BUTTER FROSTING

½ cup (¼ pound) butter, softened
1 pound (4 cups) powdered sugar
¼ cup plus 2 tablespoons green crème de menthe

In a medium mixing bowl, place the butter, powdered sugar, and crème de menthe. Using an electric mixer, beat the mixture on medium-high speed only until blended and fluffy.

MAKES ENOUGH TO FROST BETWEEN THE LAYERS, AND THE TOP AND SIDES OF ONE 2-LAYER, 8- OR 9-INCH ROUND OR SQUARE CAKE, OR THE TOP OF ONE 9 × 13-INCH SHEET CAKE

SERVING SUGGESTIONS

- Particularly good with chocolate cake. The frosted cake may be decorated with Chocolate Curls (page 342).

- Makes a nice green frosting for Christmas and St. Patrick's Day cakes and cookies.

CRÈME DE MENTHE WHIPPED CREAM FROSTING

2½ cups miniature marshmallows
⅓ cup whole milk
¼ cup green crème de menthe
2 cups (1 pint) whipping cream
½ cup powdered sugar, sifted (page 42)

In a medium saucepan, place the marshmallows and milk. Over medium heat, stir the mixture constantly until the marshmallows *completely* melt (about 5 minutes). Remove the saucepan from the heat and place on a wire rack. Let the mixture stand until cooled to room temperature, stirring occasionally.

Then, add the crème de menthe; stir until completely blended; set aside. Pour the whipping cream into a cold (previously refrigerated), medium mixing bowl. Using an electric mixer, beat the cream on medium-high speed until it begins to stiffen. Reduce the mixer speed to medium-low. Add the powdered sugar; continue beating the cream until stiff but still soft and fluffy.

Pour the crème de menthe mixture back and forth over the whipped cream; using a mixing spoon, fold in until evenly blended. Refrigerate the cake after frosting.

MAKES ENOUGH TO FROST BETWEEN THE LAYERS, AND THE TOP AND SIDES OF ONE 2- OR 3-LAYER, 8- OR 9-INCH ROUND OR SQUARE CAKE

HONEY-CREAM CHEESE FROSTING

3 ounces cream cheese, softened
2 teaspoons honey
1 teaspoon clear vanilla
¾ cup powdered sugar

Place the cream cheese in a small mixing bowl. Using an electric mixer, beat the cream cheese on high speed until creamy. Add the honey and vanilla; beat on medium-high speed until blended. Add the powdered sugar; beat on medium-high speed until smooth.

Place the uncovered food frosted with Honey-Cream Cheese Frosting in the refrigerator; let stand 2 hours, or until the frosting sets. (Even when set, this frosting is slightly soft.) Then, cover the food and store in the refrigerator for food safety due to the cream cheese ingredient.

MAKES ENOUGH TO DECORATE 5 DOZEN MEDIUM COOKIES

SERVING SUGGESTION: Using a decorating bag fit with small round tip number 2 (page 319), pipe close, parallel stripes of Honey–Cream Cheese Frosting back and fourth across the tops of cookies for an attractive decoration.

FLUFF FROSTING

Note: This recipe contains uncooked egg whites (see page 220).

1 cup plus 2 tablespoons light corn syrup
2 extra-large egg whites, room temperature
⅛ teaspoon salt
1¼ teaspoons clear vanilla

Place the syrup in a small saucepan. Bring the syrup to a boil over medium heat, stirring constantly. Remove from the heat; set aside.

Place the egg whites in a medium mixing bowl. Using an electric mixer, beat the egg whites on high speed until stiff peaks hold. Add the salt and vanilla. While continuing to beat on high speed, pour the hot syrup in a slow, steady stream into the egg white mixture and continue beating until the frosting is fluffy and of spreading consistency.

MAKES ENOUGH TO FROST BETWEEN THE LAYERS, AND THE TOP AND SIDES OF ONE 8- OR 9-INCH ROUND OR SQUARE CAKE, THE TOP OF ONE 9 × 13-INCH SHEET CAKE, OR THE TOP AND SIDES OF ONE 10 × 4-INCH TUBE CAKE

ORANGE FLUFF FROSTING

Follow the Fluff Frosting recipe, with the following modifications:

After removing the syrup from the heat, use a toothpick to add a tiny amount of orange-colored paste food coloring; stir to blend. Reduce the clear vanilla to ¾ teaspoon and add 1 teaspoon orange extract.

MARSHMALLOW CLOUD FROSTING

Note: This recipe contains uncooked egg whites (see page 220).

1 cup sugar
¼ teaspoon cream of tartar
⅛ teaspoon salt
⅓ cup water
2 extra-large egg whites, room temperature
1 cup miniature marshmallows
1 teaspoon clear vanilla

In a small, heavy saucepan, place the sugar, cream of tartar, salt, and water; stir to combine. Over low heat, stir the mixture until the sugar dissolves. Attach a candy thermometer. Increase the heat to medium-high. Bring the mixture to a boil and cook, *without stirring,* until the temperature reaches 240°F (see Note).

Meanwhile, place the egg whites in a medium mixing bowl. Using an electric mixer, beat the egg whites on high speed until stiff peaks hold; let stand.

When the syrup reaches 240°F (see Note), remove from the heat and detach the thermometer. Immediately add the marshmallows; stir quickly to dissolve the marshmallows and blend with the syrup. While beating constantly with the electric mixer on high speed, *slowly* trickle the hot marshmallow syrup into the beaten egg whites. Add the vanilla and continue beating on high speed until the frosting is thick enough to hold stiff peaks.

NOTE: This temperature is for use at sea-level locations. To adjust the temperature for preparation of this recipe at higher elevations, see Boiled Candies and Frostings, page 19.

MAKES ENOUGH TO FROST BETWEEN THE LAYERS, AND THE TOP AND SIDES OF ONE 2-LAYER, 8- OR 9-INCH ROUND OR SQUARE CAKE, OR THE TOP OF ONE 9 × 13-INCH SHEET CAKE

ORNAMENTAL VANILLA FROSTING

1½ cups powdered sugar
1 teaspoon clear vanilla
1 tablespoon plus 1 teaspoon water

In a small mixing bowl, place the powdered sugar, vanilla, and water. Using an electric mixer, beat the mixture on medium-high speed only until blended and smooth.

MAKES ENOUGH TO FROST 1 DOZEN CAKE DOUGHNUTS

SERVING SUGGESTION: Use Ornamental Vanilla Frosting to pipe stripes and other simple line-type decorations over cakes, bars, and other cookies.

VARIATION: Whole milk may be substituted for the water.

ORNAMENTAL CHOCOLATE FROSTING

1 cup powdered sugar
2 tablespoons butter
1½ ounces (1½ squares) unsweetened chocolate
2 tablespoons hot water
½ teaspoon pure vanilla extract

Place the powdered sugar in a small mixing bowl; set aside. In a tiny saucepan, place the butter and chocolate. Hold the tiny pan over (not touching) low simmering water in a small saucepan until the butter and chocolate melt, stirring intermittently. Remove the tiny pan from the heat and stir the melted butter and chocolate vigorously until blended.

Add the chocolate mixture, hot water, and vanilla to the powdered sugar. Using an electric mixer, beat the mixture on medium-high speed only until blended and smooth.

MAKES ENOUGH TO FROST 1 DOZEN CAKE DOUGHNUTS

SUPREME CHOCOLATE ICING

2½ cups sugar
1 cup evaporated milk
1 6-ounce package (1 cup) semisweet
  chocolate chips
1 cup marshmallow cream
½ cup (¼ pound) butter

Butter the sides of a medium-large, heavy-bottomed saucepan. Place the sugar and milk in the saucepan; stir to combine. Bring the mixture to a boil over medium heat, stirring constantly. Attach a candy thermometer. Continue boiling the mixture until the temperature reaches 234°F (see Note), stirring often.

Remove the saucepan from the heat; detach the thermometer. Add the chocolate chips, marshmallow cream, and butter; using a spoon, stir vigorously until all the ingredients completely melt and the icing is perfectly smooth.

Place the saucepan on a wire rack; let the icing stand to cool at room temperature, stirring occasionally to break up the crust which forms on the top of the icing. To achieve a smooth appearance on a frosted cake, cool the icing to lukewarm.

When cooled to lukewarm, carefully pour the icing over the top and edge of the cake, letting it trickle down the side. Using a small, narrow, angled spatula, apply additional icing to any remaining unfrosted sections on the side of the cake. Cut away extra icing which trickles onto the serving plate or waxed paper covering the corrugated cardboard cake circle (board) around the bottom of the cake.

NOTE: This temperature is for use at sea-level locations. To adjust the temperature for preparation of this recipe at higher elevations, see Boiled Candies and Frostings, page 19.

MAKES ENOUGH TO FROST THE TOP AND SIDES OF ONE 10 × 4-INCH TUBE CAKE

VARIATION: To use Supreme Chocolate Icing to frost a cake in the conventional manner (that is, by spreading the icing with a spatula), allow the icing to cool to room temperature before spreading.

SUGGESTION FOR USE OF LEFTOVER ICING: Leftover icing may be used to frost commercially purchased vanilla or chocolate wafers. Pecan halves may be placed on the top of each frosted cookie.

GLAZE

1½ cups powdered sugar
1 tablespoon plus 2 teaspoons water
1 teaspoon clear vanilla

In a medium mixing bowl, place the powdered sugar, water, and vanilla. Using an electric mixer, beat the mixture on low speed until the powdered sugar is moistened; then, increase the mixer speed to high and continue beating only until blended and smooth.

MAKES ENOUGH TO GLAZE 4 DOZEN LARGE COOKIES

CHOCOLATE GLAZE

2 ounces (2 squares) semisweet chocolate
2 teaspoons butter

In the top of a double boiler, place the chocolate and butter. Place the top of the double boiler over (not touching) hot (not boiling) water in the bottom pan; stir constantly until the chocolate and butter melt and blend.

TO USE CHOCOLATE GLAZE FOR PIPING: If Chocolate Glaze is to be used for decorative piping, allow it to cool to a workable consistency.

MAKES ENOUGH TO DECORATE ONE 10-INCH BUNDT CAKE OR ONE 5 × 9-INCH LOAF CAKE

CHOCOLATE COATING

2 ounces (2 squares) semisweet chocolate
2 tablespoons butter
3 tablespoons half-and-half
1 cup sifted powdered sugar (page 42) (sift
   before measuring)
½ teaspoon pure vanilla extract

In the top of a double boiler, place the chocolate
and butter. Place the top of the double boiler
over (not touching) hot (not boiling) water in
the bottom pan; stir constantly until the chocolate and butter melt and blend. Add the half-
and-half; continue stirring until blended and
warm.

Remove the top of the double boiler from the
bottom pan. Add the powdered sugar and
vanilla; using a spoon, stir until blended and
smooth.

**MAKES ENOUGH TO COAT THE TOP OF ONE 8-INCH
ROUND OR SQUARE CAKE**

Cookies

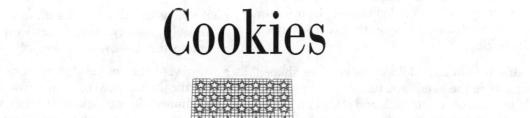

TYPES OF COOKIES

Cookies may be classified into the following six general types based upon the process by which they are made:

BAR COOKIES: Bar cookies are dense, moist, and usually cakelike. The batter/dough is spread/pressed into a pan, baked, and cut into rectangles, squares, or triangles when cool.

DROP COOKIES: The dough of drop cookies is scooped from the mixing bowl in a spoon, trigger scoop, or melon baller and dropped or pushed with a second spoon onto cookie sheets for baking.

MOLDED COOKIES: Molded cookies are shaped usually in the hands and usually before baking. Many are rolled into balls and placed on cookie sheets for baking. In some instances, the balls of dough are then flattened or pressed in various ways. The dough of some types of molded cookies is rolled into pencil-like sticks and then twisted into various shapes. Certain cookies, such as Lace Cookies (page 553), are molded into prescribed shapes after baking.

ROLLED COOKIES: The dough of rolled cookies is gathered into a ball, rolled out with a rolling pin, and cut into cookies, generally using cookie cutters. Sometimes the dough is chilled to facilitate rolling and cutting.

REFRIGERATOR COOKIES: Refrigerator cookie dough is shaped into large, thick rolls (usually about 1 to 2 inches in diameter), wrapped in plastic wrap, and refrigerated overnight or until completely cold. The rolls are then sliced into cookies and baked on cookie sheets.

PRESSED COOKIES: Pressed cookies are made by forcing the dough through a cookie press fit with disks of various designs and shapes, or by piping the dough with a decorating bag fit with selected tips, onto cookie sheets for baking.

SECRETS FOR BAKING SUCCESSFUL COOKIES

- Bake cookies (except bar cookies, of course) on shiny, aluminum cookie sheets without sides. Pans with sides deflect oven heat. Insulated cookie sheets help prevent the bottoms of cookies from overbrowning. Bake bar cookies in good-quality aluminum pans. (Wilton Enterprises [see Product Sources, page 631] carries excellent aluminum baking pans.) Do not use nonstick cookie sheets or baking pans.

- Take pains to make cookies uniform in size. Not only are they more attractive-looking, but also, they bake more uniformly.

- To prevent the cookie dough from drying, keep the mixing bowl of dough covered with aluminum foil or plastic wrap when not filling cookie sheets with batches of cookies for baking.

- Bake cookies in the *top half* of the oven to prevent the bottoms from becoming too brown. In most standard ovens with four shelf positions, bake cookies at the *second* shelf position from the top.

- Use a timer when baking cookies, and watch the cookies closely while they are baking. Avoid the pitfall of filling cookie sheets when you should be watching the cookies baking in the oven. The baking of attractive, uniform cookies requires time and concentration.

- Use a thin, sharp, medium to small spatula to remove baked cookies from cookie sheets. Use of the proper spatula will prevent the bottoms of baked cookies from crumbling when they are transferred from the cookie sheets for cooling.

- Cool baked cookies on pieces of waxed paper spread on the kitchen counter, or on wire cookie racks, depending upon the type of cookie. Most cookies are best cooled on waxed paper because the bottoms remain perfectly flat during the cooling process. Certain special cookies such as Kringla (page

549) and Lace Cookies (page 553) preferably are cooled on wire cookie racks which allow the air to circulate around all surfaces of the cookies. Special wire cookie racks are made with close-set wires strung in the pattern of small squares which provide even support for small cookies. The wires on general utility wire racks are set too far apart to provide uniform support under warm cookies.

• After removing baked cookies from a cookie sheet, immediately scrape the cookie sheet, while it is still hot, with a wide spatula to remove crumbs and excess grease. Then, wipe the cookie sheet with a paper towel. Place the cookie sheet in a cool place such as the basement to hasten cooling. Wait until the cookie sheet is *completely cool* before filling it with another batch of cookies for baking. Regrease the cookie sheet, if necessary.

• As soon as baked cookies have cooled thoroughly, arrange them, single layer with plastic wrap between the layers, in an airtight container.

• Cookie sheets and baking pans should be washed by hand to retain their finish for even baking results. Insulated cookie sheets should not be immersed in water.

TO GREASE COOKIE SHEETS

To bake most cookies, either soft vegetable shortening or vegetable oil should be used to grease the cookie sheets. To apply vegetable shortening, use a pastry brush to spread a light, even coat over the surface of the cookie sheets. To use vegetable oil, pour a very small amount from the bottle directly onto the cookie sheets; then, use a pastry brush to spread evenly. Wipe away any excess oil with a paper towel.

To bake certain cookies, Special Grease (page 40) is recommended for greasing the cookie sheets because of its particular nonstick attribute; however, Special Grease is not recommended for general use in the baking of most cookies (see When To Use Special Grease, page 40).

Parchment baking paper is sometimes used to line cookie sheets in lieu of greasing. When used in the baking of appropriate cookies, it helps prevent the bottoms from overbrowning. Parchment baking paper affords the additional advantage of producing baked cookies with no trace of grease residue on the bottoms.

Cookie recipes in *The Blue Ribbon Country Cookbook* specify when other than vegetable shortening or vegetable oil is recommended for greasing the cookie sheets. Of course, some cookies are baked on ungreased cookie sheets.

Depending upon the cookies, it is often necessary to very lightly regrease the cookie sheets after baking each batch (see Secrets for Baking Successful Cookies, page 516).

Bar Cookies

TO GREASE BAKING PANS FOR BAR COOKIES

Unless otherwise specified in the recipe, use vegetable shortening to grease baking pans for baking bar cookies.

TO CUT AND SERVE BAR COOKIES

After investing the time to bake a pan of delicious-tasting bars, it is worth the extra effort to cut them in an eye-appealing way. For very uniform, professional-looking bars, use a ruler to determine the exact places for cutting. Carefully hold the ruler against the edges of the baking pan and, with the point of a sharp knife, make tiny marks along the top edges of the bars where you plan to cut. Mark all four sides of the bars to help prevent making slanted cuts.

To cut marked bars, dip a sharp, *thin-bladed* knife into a tall glass of hot water. Then, partially dry the knife on a damp sponge or cloth. In a nonstop motion, make a cut from one side of the bars to the opposite side. Do not use back-and-forth sawing motions to cut, nor lift the knife from the bars before the full cut is made. After making each cut, wipe the knife blade clean on the damp sponge or cloth, redip the knife in hot water, and partially dry it on the damp sponge or cloth. If the pan is rectangular, make the long cuts first; then, make the short cuts. Make each cut twice to assure precision cutting.

After making the cuts across the pan in both directions, run the knife along the inside edges of the pan to loosen the sides of the bars from the pan. If the sides are not loosened until last, the bars will not shift as readily during cutting, making it easier to cut straight lines.

To remove the cut bars from the pan, use a small spatula as close in size to the bars as possible. Push the spatula completely under one bar at a time and lift straight upward to remove.

RAISIN BARS

1 14-ounce can (1¼ cups) sweetened condensed milk
2 teaspoons finely grated lemon rind (page 31) (rind of about 2 lemons)
1 tablespoon freshly squeezed, strained lemon juice
1 cup all-purpose flour
½ teaspoon baking soda
¼ teaspoon salt (optional)
2½ cups Quaker MultiGrain cereal, uncooked (found at the supermarket with the oatmeal)
1½ cups broken pecans
1 cup (½ pound) butter, softened
1⅓ cups packed light brown sugar
1½ teaspoons pure vanilla extract
2 6-ounce packages (2 cups) baking raisins

In a medium, heavy-bottomed saucepan, place the condensed milk, lemon rind, and lemon juice; stir to blend and combine. Over medium heat, scald the milk mixture (page 9), stirring constantly. Remove from the heat. Cover and let stand until cooled to room temperature.

Preheat the oven to 350°F. Grease a 9 × 13 × 2-inch baking pan; set aside.

Onto waxed paper, sift together the flour, baking soda, and salt (if included); set aside. In a medium mixing bowl, place the MultiGrain and pecans; stir until evenly distributed; set aside.

In a large mixing bowl, place the butter and brown sugar; using an electric mixer, beat on medium-high speed until fluffy. Add the vanilla; beat on medium-high speed until blended. Add the flour mixture; beat on low speed only until blended. Add the MultiGrain mixture; using a large mixing spoon, stir until evenly combined and crumbly.

Reserve 2 cups of the flour batter; spoon the remaining batter into the prepared baking pan. Using the back of a tablespoon, press the batter evenly into the bottom of the pan; set aside.

Add the raisins to the milk mixture; stir to combine. Pour the raisin mixture back and forth over the flour batter in the baking pan. Using a large, narrow, angled spatula, spread the raisin mixture to within ½ inch of the sides of the pan. Sprinkle the 2 cups reserved flour mixture over the raisin mixture; pat lightly with the back of the tablespoon. Bake for 30 minutes, or until lightly golden.

Remove from the oven and place the baking pan on a wire rack. Let stand until the uncut bars completely cool.

Then, cut into 45 bars (page 517). Arrange the bars in an airtight container.

MAKES 45

DATE BARS

Date Bars, packed with dates and English walnuts and sprinkled with powdered sugar, are as old as the hills but every bit as good and voguish today as they were way back when. Mother added the recipe that follows to her recipe notebook before I was born, and I continue to whip up this family favorite to the present time.

1 cup all-purpose flour
1 teaspoon baking powder
⅛ teaspoon salt
¼ teaspoon ground cloves
¼ teaspoon ground cinnamon
3 extra-large eggs
1 cup sugar
1 teaspoon pure vanilla extract
2 8-ounce packages chopped dates (2 cups packed dates)
1 cup chopped English walnuts
3 tablespoons powdered sugar

Preheat the oven to 325° F. Grease a 9 × 13 × 2-inch baking pan; set aside.

Onto waxed paper, sift together the flour, baking powder, salt, cloves, and cinnamon; set aside.

Place the eggs in a large mixing bowl. Using an electric mixer, beat the eggs well on medium-high speed. Add the sugar and vanilla; beat well on medium-high speed. Add the flour mixture; beat on low speed only until blended. Add the dates and walnuts; using a large mixing spoon, stir and fold in.

Using the large mixing spoon, spoon the batter into the prepared baking pan. Using a large, narrow, angled spatula, quickly spread the batter evenly in the pan. Bake for 25 minutes, until golden and the bars just begin to pull away slightly from the sides of the pan.

Remove from the oven and place the baking pan on a wire rack. Let stand until the uncut bars completely cool.

Then, place the powdered sugar in a small hand strainer. Sprinkle the powdered sugar over the uncut bars. Cut into forty 1 × 2-inch bars (page 517). Arrange the bars in an airtight container.

MAKES 40

OPTIONAL DECORATION: Using your fingers, sprinkle a faint amount of ground cinnamon on each bar.

PUMPKIN BARS WITH CASHEW FROSTING

(See photo insert page D-4)

In this recipe, cashews complement the pumpkin flavor to give the traditional cream cheese frosting a new and delicious twist.

2 cups all-purpose flour
2 teaspoons baking soda
¼ teaspoon salt
1½ teaspoons ground cinnamon
½ teaspoon ground ginger
¼ teaspoon ground cloves
¼ teaspoon ground nutmeg
½ cup (¼ pound) butter, melted
2 cups sugar
½ cup vegetable oil
4 extra-large eggs
1 15-ounce can pumpkin
Cashew Frosting (recipe follows)

Preheat the oven to 350° F. Using Special Grease (page 40), grease a 10½ × 15½ × 1-inch cookie pan (see Note); set aside.

Onto waxed paper, sift together the flour, baking soda, salt, cinnamon, ginger, cloves, and nutmeg; set aside.

In a large mixing bowl, place the butter, sugar, and vegetable oil; using an electric mixer, beat well on medium-high speed. Add the eggs, one at a time, beating well on medium-high speed after each addition. Add the pumpkin; beat on medium-high speed until completely blended. Add the flour mixture in halves, beating on low speed after each addition only until blended.

(Recipe continues on next page)

Using a large mixing spoon, spoon the batter into the prepared cookie pan. Using a large, narrow, angled spatula, quickly spread the batter evenly in the pan. Bake for 25 minutes, or until a wooden toothpick inserted into the center comes out clean.

Remove from the oven and place the cookie pan on a wire rack. Let stand until the uncut bars completely cool.

Then, using a clean large, narrow, angled spatula, frost smoothly the uncut bars in the pan with the Cashew Frosting. Place the uncut bars, uncovered, in the refrigerator; let stand only until the frosting sets.

Cut into 48 bars (page 517). Arrange the bars in an airtight container and keep refrigerated.

NOTE: Although not as satisfactory, the pan may be greased and floured using the traditional method (page 40) in substitution for using Special Grease.

MAKES 48

CASHEW FROSTING

3 ounces cream cheese, softened
¼ cup (4 tablespoons) butter, softened
1 tablespoon plus 2 teaspoons whole milk
1 teaspoon pure vanilla extract
3 cups powdered sugar
½ cup chopped, unsalted cashews

In a medium mixing bowl, place the cream cheese and butter; using an electric mixer, beat on high speed until blended and smooth. Add the milk and vanilla; beat on medium-high speed until creamy. Add the powdered sugar; beat on medium-high speed until fluffy. Add the cashews; beat on medium speed only until combined.

SERVING SUGGESTION: At Thanksgiving time, for something different or to serve a large gathering, serve Pumpkin Bars with Cashew Frosting instead of traditional Pumpkin Pie.

LEMON BARS

(See photo insert page D-4)

Lemon lovers go for these. A generous measure of coconut gives these Lemon Bars an extra-special flavor and sets them apart from usual renditions.

½ cup (¼ pound) butter
1 cup sifted all-purpose flour (sift before measuring)
¼ cup powdered sugar
2 extra-large eggs
1 cup granulated sugar
2 teaspoons finely grated lemon rind (page 31) (rind of about 2 lemons)
3 tablespoons freshly squeezed, strained lemon juice
2 tablespoons all-purpose flour
⅛ teaspoon salt
1 cup flaked coconut
2 tablespoons powdered sugar
Lemon zest (page 31) for decoration (optional)

Preheat the oven to 350°F. Butter lightly an 8 × 8 × 2-inch baking pan; set aside.

Remove the butter from the refrigerator; let stand. Onto waxed paper, sift together 1 cup flour and ¼ cup powdered sugar. Place the flour mixture in a medium mixing bowl. Using a knife, cut the butter into approximately 8 pieces and drop into the bowl containing the flour mixture. Using a pastry blender, cut the butter into the flour mixture until approximately ⅔ of the mixture is the texture of coarse cornmeal and ⅓ of the mixture is the size of small peas.

Turn the mixture into the prepared baking pan. Using the back of a tablespoon, pat the mixture evenly and firmly into the bottom of the pan. Bake for 10 minutes. The crust will be pale and unbrowned.

Remove from the oven and place the baking pan on a wire rack. Let stand until the baked crust completely cools.

Then, preheat the oven to 350°F.

Carefully rebutter lightly the sides of the baking pan *above* the baked crust; set aside.

Place the eggs in a medium mixing bowl. Using an electric mixer, beat the eggs well on medium-high speed. Add the granulated sugar, lemon rind, and lemon juice; beat well on medium-high speed. Add 2 tablespoons flour and salt; beat until blended. Add the coconut; using a large mixing spoon, fold in.

Pour the lemon mixture over the baked crust in the pan. Bake for 25 minutes. The edges will be lightly browned.

Remove from the oven and place the baking pan on the wire rack; let stand. Place 2 tablespoons powdered sugar in a small hand strainer. Sprinkle the powdered sugar over the hot lemon bars to evenly dust the surface. Return the lemon bars to the oven; bake for an additional 2 minutes.

Remove from the oven and place the baking pan on the wire rack. Let stand until the uncut bars completely cool.

Then, cut into 18 bars (page 517). Arrange the bars in an airtight container. The top of each bar may be decorated with a few tiny pieces of lemon zest, if desired.

MAKES 18

3-LAYER CHERRY CHIP BARS

All kinds of new chips, from raspberry to peanut butter to mint, can be found in the baking aisle of supermarkets today. This recipe features cherry-flavored chips which combine in the middle layer of the bars with crushed pineapple and coconut for a summery, even Hawaiian-like, flair.

NOTE: *This recipe contains an uncooked egg white (see page 220).*

BOTTOM LAYER
1 cup (½ pound) butter
2 cups all-purpose flour
¼ cup plus 2 tablespoons powdered sugar

Remove 1 cup butter from the refrigerator and let stand 10 minutes before use in the recipe.

Preheat the oven to 350°F.

In a medium mixing bowl, place 2 cups flour and ¼ cup plus 2 tablespoons powdered sugar; stir to combine. Using a knife, cut the butter into approximately tablespoon-sized pieces and drop into the bowl containing the flour mixture. Using a pastry blender, cut the butter into the flour mixture until the mixture is the texture of coarse cornmeal.

Turn the mixture into an ungreased 9 × 13 × 2-inch baking pan. Using a tablespoon, spread the mixture evenly over the bottom of the pan. Then, with lightly floured hands, pat the mixture tightly into the bottom of the pan. Bake for 15 minutes, until lightly golden.

Remove from the oven and place the baking pan on a wire rack. Let stand until the baked crust completely cools.

MIDDLE LAYER
1 cup (6 ounces) cherry baking chips
¾ cup flaked coconut
2 tablespoons all-purpose flour
¼ cup plus 2 tablespoons all-purpose flour
1 teaspoon baking powder
¼ teaspoon salt
4 extra-large eggs
1⅔ cups granulated sugar
2 teaspoons pure vanilla extract
1 8¼-ounce can crushed pineapple, drained

Preheat the oven to 350°F. Butter lightly the sides of the baking pan *above* the baked crust; set aside.

In a small mixing bowl, place the cherry chips and coconut; sprinkle 2 tablespoons flour over top. Using a tablespoon, toss to coat the cherry chips and coconut; set aside. Onto waxed paper, sift together ¼ cup plus 2 tablespoons flour, baking powder, and salt; set aside.

Place the eggs in a large mixing bowl. Using an electric mixer, beat the eggs well on medium-high speed. Add the granulated sugar and vanilla; beat on medium-high speed until blended. Add the flour mixture; beat on low

(Recipe continues on next page)

speed only until blended. Add the cherry chip mixture and drained pineapple; using a large mixing spoon, fold in until evenly combined.

Pour the batter over the baked crust in the pan. Using a small, narrow, angled spatula, quickly spread the batter evenly. Bake for 30 minutes, until golden.

Remove from the oven and place the baking pan on the wire rack. Let stand until the uncut bars completely cool.

TOP LAYER (FROSTING)

2 cups powdered sugar
2 tablespoons butter, melted
2 tablespoons maraschino cherry juice (pour off juice from canned red maraschino cherries)
1 extra-large egg white

In a medium mixing bowl, place 2 cups powdered sugar, 2 tablespoons butter, cherry juice, and egg white. Using the electric mixer fit with clean, dry blades, beat the mixture on high speed until smooth.

Spoon the frosting over the Middle Layer in the pan. Using a large, narrow, angled spatula, spread the frosting evenly. Let the uncut bars stand until the frosting sets.

Then, cut into 35 bars (page 517). Arrange the bars in an airtight container and keep refrigerated.

MAKES 35

OPTIONAL DECORATION: Each bar may be decorated with ¼ red candied cherry.

ROSE LEE'S APRICOT BARS

Talk about melt-in-your-mouth goodies . . . Rose Lee Pomerantz baked these bars for a press party we held years ago to unveil a new apartment building built by her husband, Marvin, my brother, and my husband. They were such a smash hit, they nearly upstaged the beautiful building.

½ cup (¼ pound) butter
1 6-ounce package (about 1 packed cup) dried apricots
1 cup sifted all-purpose flour (sift before measuring)
¼ cup granulated sugar
⅓ cup sifted all-purpose flour (sift before measuring)
½ teaspoon baking powder
¼ teaspoon salt
2 extra-large eggs
1 cup packed light brown sugar
½ teaspoon pure vanilla extract
½ cup broken pecans
2 tablespoons powdered sugar

Preheat the oven to 350°F.

Remove the butter from the refrigerator; set aside. Cut the apricots into small pieces approximately ¼ inch square (page 517); set aside.

In a large mixing bowl, place 1 cup flour and granulated sugar; stir to combine. Using a knife, cut the butter into approximately 10 pieces and drop into the bowl containing the flour mixture. Using a pastry blender, cut the butter into the flour mixture until the mixture is the texture of coarse cornmeal.

Turn the mixture into an ungreased 9 × 13 × 2-inch baking pan. Using the back of a tablespoon and your hand, press the mixture evenly into the bottom of the pan. Bake for 15 minutes, until lightly golden.

Remove from the oven and place the baking pan on a wire rack; let stand. Leave the oven on at 350°F.

Onto waxed paper, sift together ⅓ cup flour, baking powder, and salt; set aside.

Place the eggs in a large mixing bowl. Using an electric mixer, beat the eggs well on medium-high speed. While continuing to beat on medium-high speed, gradually add the brown sugar. Add the vanilla; beat on medium-high speed until completely blended. Add the flour mixture; beat on low speed only until blended. Add the apricots and pecans; using a large mixing spoon, fold in until evenly distributed; set aside.

Butter lightly the sides of the baking pan *above* the baked crust. Pour the batter over the baked crust. Using a small, narrow, angled spatula, spread the batter evenly. Bake for 20 to 25 minutes, until lightly golden.

Remove from the oven and place the baking pan on the wire rack. Let stand until the uncut bars completely cool.

Then, place the powdered sugar in a small hand strainer. Sprinkle the powdered sugar evenly over the uncut bars. Cut into 27 bars (page 517). Arrange the bars in an airtight container.

MAKES 27

JANHAGEL KOEKJES
Johnny Buckshot Cookies

Janhagel Koekjes are a historical Holland Dutch cookie named after mercenary soldiers, nick-named Jan Hagels, who were hired by the Dutch. The chopped almonds sprinkled over the top of these cookies are said to resemble buckshot.

2 cups all-purpose flour
¼ teaspoon baking soda
¼ teaspoon salt
1 cup (½ pound) butter, softened
2 cups sugar
1 extra-large egg, separated
¾ teaspoon sugar
¾ teaspoon ground cinnamon
¾ cup chopped, slivered blanched almonds
  (page 35)

Preheat the oven to 350° F. Grease a 10½ × 15½ × 1-inch cookie pan; set aside.

Onto waxed paper, sift together the flour, baking soda, and salt; set aside.

In a large mixing bowl, place the butter and 2 cups sugar; using an electric mixer, cream well on medium-high speed. Add the egg yolk; beat on medium-high speed until very light and fluffy. Add the flour mixture; using a pastry blender, cut the butter mixture into the flour mixture.

Using a large mixing spoon, spoon the dough into the prepared cookie pan. With your hands, spread the dough and press as evenly as possible into the bottom of the pan; set aside. Place the egg white in a small sauce dish. Using a table fork, beat the egg white slightly until frothy. Using a soft pastry brush, brush the egg white over the dough in the cookie pan; set aside. Place ¾ teaspoon sugar and cinnamon in a small sauce dish; stir to combine. Using a teaspoon, sprinkle the cinnamon mixture over the egg-brushed dough. Then, sprinkle the almonds evenly over the top. Press the almonds very lightly into the dough. Bake for 20 minutes, until lightly golden.

Remove from the oven and place the cookie pan on a wire rack. While warm, cut the uncut baked cookies into 48 small squares (page 517). Remove the cookies from the pan and place on wire cookie racks; let stand until completely cool.

Then, arrange the cookies in an airtight container.

MAKES 48

BUTTERSCOTCH MAGIC BARS WITH BRAZIL NUTS

This is an adaptation of the old, familiar recipe for Magic Bars, sometimes called "Hello Dollies" in regional cookbooks. I have no idea why these bars were dubbed Hello Dollies in some circles, but I do know why they were called "magic." Houdini would have had his hands full coming up with an easier, more mystifying way to materialize a delicious bar cookie. You simply place the six ingredients directly in the pan, in layers, and bake. I have used butterscotch chips rather than chocolate chips which are often called for in these recipes, and have specified Brazil nuts for the nut layer.

At Christmastime, my grandmothers and mother always placed on the coffee table or a side table a wooden nut dish full of mixed, unshelled nuts. These nut dishes were made with a center wooden post covered on top with a piece of metal on which the snacker cracked the nuts with a matching wooden mallet resembling a gavel. You supplied nut dishes with a nut pick and sometimes a small, metal nutcracker for those who preferred that method of cracking over the mallet mode (if you weren't careful, your fingers holding a nut on the post could be hit by the mallet). There were always almonds, pecans, hazelnuts (filberts), English walnuts, and Brazil nuts in the Christmas nut bowl. The Brazil nuts were the big ones and the hardest to crack.

½ cup (¼ pound) butter
20 graham cracker squares, rolled finely
　(about 1½ cups crumbs)
1 14-ounce can (1¼ cups) sweetened
　condensed milk
1 cup (6 ounces) butterscotch chips
1 cup chopped Brazil nuts (page 34)
1 cup flaked coconut

Preheat the oven to 325°F.

Place the butter in a 9 × 13 × 2-inch baking pan. Place the baking pan in the oven to melt the butter. Watch carefully and do not allow the butter to brown. Remove from the oven. Tilt the pan back and forth to completely cover the bottom with the melted butter.

Spoon the graham cracker crumbs evenly over the butter; using the back of a tablespoon, press to form a compact and even layer. Pour the condensed milk evenly over the crumbs. If necessary, use a small, narrow, angled spatula to carefully distribute the milk over the entire surface of the crumbs.

Sprinkle the butterscotch chips evenly over the condensed milk. Then, spoon the nuts evenly over the surface. Sprinkle the coconut evenly over the top. Bake for 30 minutes, until lightly browned.

Remove from the oven and place the baking pan on a wire rack. Let stand until the uncut bars completely cool.

Then, cut into 30 bars (page 517). Arrange the bars in an airtight container.

MAKES 30

BLACK WALNUT BARS

These distinctively flavored native American nuts, plentiful across the central and eastern parts of the Midwest, have a very difficult shell to crack; otherwise, they surely would be used more often in cookies, cakes, and other foods. Another deterrent is the thick, chartreuse-colored husks in which the shells are encased. Many Midwesterners have found that the easiest way to remove these husks is to let the walnuts stand for a period of time after gathering and then to run them through an old-fashioned, hand-cranked, or a motor-driven corn sheller. After removal of the husks, various devices are employed to crack the ultrahard shells. For a number of years, a man sold a viselike apparatus for this purpose at the Iowa State Fair, but I haven't seen him there the last few years.

Shelled, native black walnuts are occasionally found at farmers' markets or in produce sections of local supermarkets. In the past few years, commercial black walnuts have become available in the regular section where nuts are displayed at the supermarket. When you locate and invest in good black walnuts (or gather and shell them yourself), store them in the freezer to retain their freshness (see To Store Nuts, page 35).

2¾ cups sifted all-purpose flour (sift before
　measuring)
2½ teaspoons baking powder
¾ teaspoon salt
¾ cup (¼ pound plus 4 tablespoons) butter,
　melted
1 pound light brown sugar (2¼ cups packed
　sugar)
3 extra-large eggs
½ teaspoon pure vanilla extract
½ teaspoon black walnut flavoring
1 cup broken black walnuts
1 6-ounce package (1 cup) semisweet
　chocolate chips

Preheat the oven to 350°F. Grease a 10½ × 15½ × 1-inch cookie pan; set aside.

Onto waxed paper, sift together the flour, baking powder, and salt; set aside.

In a large mixing bowl, place the butter and brown sugar; using an electric mixer, beat well on medium-high speed. Add the eggs, one at a time, beating well on medium-high speed after each addition. Add the vanilla and walnut flavoring; beat on medium-high speed until fluffy. Add the flour mixture; beat on low speed only until blended. Add the walnuts and chocolate chips; using a large mixing spoon, fold in until evenly distributed.

Turn the batter into the prepared cookie pan. Using a large, narrow, angled spatula, quickly spread the batter evenly in the pan. Bake for 20 minutes, or until a wooden toothpick inserted into the center comes out clean.

Remove from the oven and place the cookie pan on a wire rack. Let stand until the uncut bars completely cool.

Then, cut into 48 bars (page 517). Arrange the bars in an airtight container.

MAKES 48

TRAIL MIX BARS

Pack along these nourishing bars, chockful of healthful ingredients, when you head for a hike in the woods. (But don't let the name of these bars confine the pleasure of eating them only to outdoor occasions.)

1 cup commercially packaged trail mix (fruits and nuts)
2/3 cup sifted whole-wheat flour (sift before measuring)
1/2 teaspoon baking powder
1/2 teaspoon baking soda
1/2 cup (1/4 pound) butter, softened
1/3 cup packed light brown sugar
1/2 cup honey
1 extra-large egg
1 teaspoon pure vanilla extract
1 cup quick-cooking rolled oats, uncooked

Preheat the oven to 350°F. Grease a 9 × 13 × 2-inch baking pan; set aside.

Place the trail mix in a small mixing bowl. Sprinkle 2 teaspoons of the measured flour over the trail mix; stir to coat the trail mix; set aside. Onto waxed paper, sift together the remaining flour, baking powder, and baking soda; set aside.

In a large mixing bowl, place the margarine and brown sugar; using an electric mixer, beat on medium-high speed until creamed. Add the honey; beat on medium-high speed until well blended. Add the egg and vanilla; continue beating on medium-high speed until blended. Add the flour mixture; beat on low speed only until blended. Add the oats; beat on low speed only until combined. Add the trail mix; using a large mixing spoon, fold in.

Using a large mixing spoon, spoon the batter into the prepared baking pan. Using a large, narrow, angled spatula, quickly spread the batter evenly in the pan. Bake for 20 minutes, or until a wooden toothpick inserted into the center comes out clean.

Remove from the oven and place the baking pan on a wire rack. Let stand until the uncut bars completely cool.

Then, cut into 30 bars (page 517). Arrange the bars in an airtight container.

MAKES 30

DREAM BARS

1/2 cup (1/4 pound) butter
1 cup all-purpose flour
1/2 cup packed light brown sugar
2 extra-large eggs
1 cup packed light brown sugar
1 teaspoon pure vanilla extract
1 tablespoon all-purpose flour
1/2 teaspoon baking powder
Dash of salt
1 cup flaked coconut
1 cup chopped pecans

(Recipe continues on next page)

Remove the butter from the refrigerator and let stand 5 minutes before use in the recipe.

Preheat the oven to 350° F.

Onto waxed paper, sift together 1 cup flour and ½ cup brown sugar. Place the flour mixture in a large mixing bowl. Using a knife, cut the butter into approximately 8 pieces and drop into the bowl containing the flour mixture. Using a pastry blender, cut the butter into the flour mixture until the mixture is the texture of coarse cornmeal interspersed with some pieces the size of small peas.

Turn the mixture into an ungreased 9 × 13 × 2-inch baking pan. Using the back of a tablespoon and your hand, pat the mixture evenly into the bottom of the pan. Bake for 10 minutes.

Remove from the oven and place the baking pan on a wire rack; let stand for approximately 3 to 5 minutes.

Meanwhile, place the eggs in a medium mixing bowl. Using an electric mixer, beat the eggs well on medium-high speed. Add 1 cup brown sugar; beat on medium-high speed until well blended. Add the vanilla, 1 tablespoon flour, baking powder, and salt; beat on medium speed only until blended. Add the coconut and pecans; using a large mixing spoon, fold in until evenly combined.

Using a large mixing spoon, spoon the mixture over the baked crust. Using a small, narrow, angled spatula, spread the mixture evenly. Bake for 20 minutes, or until a wooden toothpick inserted into the center comes out clean.

Remove from the oven and place the baking pan on the wire rack. Let stand until the uncut bars completely cool.

Then, cut into 44 bars (page 517). Arrange the bars in an airtight container.

MAKES 44

LEBKUCHEN
Spiced Honey Cake

Notwithstanding the renowned, international reputation of Bavaria's age-old specialties, *namely, Weisswurst (veal sausage) and beer, Nuremberg's Lebkuchen probably is the masterpiece that has captured the region's greatest culinary fame. In medieval times, Nuremberg was a center of spice trade, and there was an abundance of honey available from Franconia in the northern part of Bavaria. Access to spices and honey, key ingredients in Lebkuchen, prompted creation of this legendary Deutschland classic.*

2¼ cups sifted all-purpose flour (sift before measuring)
½ teaspoon baking soda
½ teaspoon ground cinnamon
½ teaspoon ground cloves
½ teaspoon ground allspice
¼ teaspoon ground nutmeg
½ cup warm, very strong, brewed coffee (double strength)
½ cup honey
¼ cup vegetable shortening
½ cup packed dark brown sugar
1 extra-large egg
2 ounces (¼ cup) diced candied citron
2 ounces (¼ cup) diced candied orange peel
2 ounces (¼ cup) diced candied lemon peel
¾ cup finely chopped, sliced unblanched almonds
Orange Glaze (recipe follows)

Preheat the oven to 350° F. Grease a 10½ × 15½ × 1-inch cookie pan; set aside.

Onto waxed paper, sift together the flour, baking soda, cinnamon, cloves, allspice, and nutmeg; set aside. In a small mixing bowl, place the coffee and honey; stir to blend; set aside.

In a medium mixing bowl, place the vegetable shortening and brown sugar; using an electric mixer, beat on medium-high speed until creamed. Add the egg; continue beating on medium-high speed until well blended. Add, alternately, the flour mixture in fourths, and the honey mixture in thirds, beating on low speed after each addition only until blended. Add the citron, orange peel, lemon peel, and almonds; using a large mixing spoon, fold in until evenly distributed.

Using the large mixing spoon, spoon the batter into the prepared cookie pan. Using a large, narrow, angled spatula, quickly spread the batter evenly in the pan. Bake for 20 minutes, or until a wooden toothpick inserted into the center comes out clean.

Remove from the oven and place the cookie pan on a wire rack. Let stand until the uncut Lebkuchen completely cools.

Then, drizzle the Orange Glaze over the uncut Lebkuchen; using a soft pastry brush, spread the glaze over the entire top surface. Before the glaze completely dries, cut the Lebkuchen into forty-two 1½ × 2½-inch bars (page 517); let stand until the glaze dries. Then, arrange the bars in an airtight container.

MAKES 42

ORANGE GLAZE

1½ cups powdered sugar
3 tablespoons water
½ teaspoon orange extract

In a small mixing bowl, place the powdered sugar, water, and orange extract. Using an electric mixer, beat the mixture on medium-high speed until smooth.

HOLIDAY DECORATION: Cut green candied cherries and red candied cherries in the fashion of holly leaves and berries. Immediately after cutting the Lebkuchen and before the glaze completely dries, arrange the cut cherries in the form of a holly sprig on the top of each bar.

CHARLOTTE'S BUTTER RUM CHEESE BARS

A native of Montgomery County, Ohio, Charlotte Watkins was one wonderful cook! Charlotte once served these too-luscious-for-words bars at the end of a fabulous dinner, and I took home the recipe, which still stands in my recipe box. These scrumptious bars took the red ribbon in the always large, two-layer bar class at the 1992 Iowa State Fair.

BOTTOM LAYER

1 cup all-purpose flour
¼ teaspoon cream of tartar
¼ teaspoon baking soda
¼ cup (4 tablespoons) butter, softened
½ cup packed light brown sugar
½ extra-large egg (slightly beat 1 egg; use ½)
   or 1 small (no larger) egg
¼ teaspoon pure vanilla extract
¼ cup broken pecans

Preheat the oven to 350°F. Butter lightly a 7 × 11 × 2-inch baking pan; set aside.

Onto waxed paper, sift together the flour, cream of tartar, and baking soda; set aside.

In a medium mixing bowl, place the butter and brown sugar; using an electric mixer, beat on medium-high speed until creamed. Add ½ egg and vanilla; beat on medium-high speed until fluffy. Add the flour mixture; beat on low speed only until blended. Add the pecans; using a mixing spoon, fold in until evenly distributed.

Turn the mixture into the prepared baking pan. With lightly floured hands, pat the mixture evenly into the bottom of the pan. Bake for 15 minutes.

Remove from the oven and place the baking pan on a wire rack. Let stand until the bottom layer of the bars completely cools.

TOP LAYER

8 ounces cream cheese, softened
½ cup granulated sugar
1 extra-large egg
1 teaspoon rum flavoring
¼ teaspoon pure vanilla extract
2½ dozen unblemished pecan halves

When the bottom layer of the bars has completely cooled, preheat the oven to 375°F.

In a small mixing bowl, place the cream cheese and granulated sugar; using the electric

(Recipe continues on next page)

mixer fit with clean, dry blades, beat on high speed until creamed. Add the egg and rum flavoring; beat on medium-high speed until blended and smooth.

Spoon the cream cheese mixture over the bottom layer of the bars. Using a small, narrow, angled spatula, spread the cream cheese mixture evenly. Bake for 20 minutes, until lightly golden.

Remove from the oven and place the baking pan on the wire rack. Let stand until the uncut bars cool slightly. Then, refrigerate, uncovered, and on a wire rack, at least 1 hour.

Cut into 30 bars (page 517). Decorate the top of each bar with a pecan half. Arrange the bars in an airtight container and keep refrigerated.

MAKES 30

HOLIDAY DECORATION: For the holidays, decorate the top of each bar with ½ red candied cherry rather than ½ pecan.

CRÈME DE MENTHE BARS

These pretty-to-look-at bars feature a chocolate-flavored bottom layer and a green-hued, crème de menthe-flavored top layer made with cream cheese. Yum! The top layer is unbaked, simplifying the preparation. To further fancify the appearance of these minty bars, pipe a crisscross chocolate decoration on top, as described and illustrated below.

BOTTOM LAYER
1 cup all-purpose flour
½ teaspoon baking powder
½ cup unsweetened cocoa powder
1 cup (½ pound) butter, softened
2 cups sugar
4 extra-large eggs, beaten
2 teaspoons pure vanilla extract

Preheat the oven to 375° F. Grease a 9 × 13 × 2-inch baking pan; set aside.

Onto waxed paper, sift together the flour, baking powder, and cocoa; set aside.

In a large mixing bowl, place the butter and sugar; using an electric mixer, cream well on medium-high speed. Add the eggs; continue beating on medium-high speed until well blended. Add the vanilla; beat on medium-high speed until blended. Add the flour mixture in halves, beating on low speed after each addition only until blended.

Using a large mixing spoon, spoon the batter into the prepared baking pan. Using a large, narrow, angled spatula, spread the batter evenly in the pan. Bake for 20 minutes, until a wooden toothpick inserted into the center comes out clean.

Remove from the oven and place the baking pan on a wire rack. Let stand until the bottom layer of the bars completely cools.

TOP LAYER
3 ounces cream cheese, softened
¼ cup (4 tablespoons) butter, softened
1 pound (4 cups) powdered sugar
¼ cup green crème de menthe

In a medium mixing bowl, place the cream cheese and butter; using the electric mixer fit with clean, dry blades, beat on high speed until blended and smooth. Add the powdered sugar and crème de menthe; beat on low speed to combine; then, beat on medium-high speed until completely blended.

Spoon the crème de menthe mixture over the bottom layer of the bars. Using a large, narrow, angled spatula, spread the crème de menthe mixture evenly. Let stand only until the top layer sets.

DECORATION
½ cup (3 ounces) semisweet chocolate chips
2 tablespoons butter

In the top of a double boiler, place the chocolate chips and butter. Place the top of the double boiler over (not touching) hot (not simmering) water in the bottom pan. Stir the chocolate chips and butter until melted and blended.

Remove the top of the double boiler from the bottom pan. Using a decorating bag fit with small round tip number 3 (page 319), pipe the chocolate mixture in a diagonal crisscross pattern over the top of the second layer. Pipe the lines about ½ inch apart (see illustration).

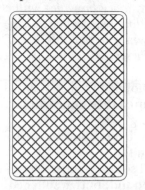

Refrigerate the uncut bars, uncovered, until set. Then, cut into 32 bars (page 517). Arrange the bars in an airtight container and keep refrigerated.

MAKES 32

FROSTED BROWNIES

Brownies probably go unchallenged as America's number one bar cookie. This version, with a thick layer of frosting, carries chocolate extravagance to the limit.

1¼ cups sifted all-purpose flour (sift before measuring)
½ teaspoon baking powder
½ teaspoon salt
4 ounces (4 squares) unsweetened chocolate
1 cup (½ pound) butter
2 cups sugar
4 extra-large eggs
1 teaspoon pure vanilla extract
1 cup broken English walnuts
1 recipe Chocolate Frosting (page 508)

Preheat the oven to 375° F. Grease a 9 × 13 × 2-inch baking pan; set aside.

Onto waxed paper, sift together the flour, baking powder, and salt; set aside.

In the top of a double boiler, place the chocolate and butter. Place the top of the double boiler over (not touching) simmering water in the bottom pan. Stir the chocolate and butter constantly until melted and blended.

Remove the top of the double boiler from the bottom pan. Add the sugar; stir to combine. Transfer the chocolate mixture to a large mixing bowl. Add the eggs, one at a time, beating well with an electric mixer on medium-high speed after each addition. Add the vanilla; continue beating on medium-high until well blended. Add the flour mixture; beat on low speed only until blended. Add the walnuts; using a large mixing spoon, fold in.

Pour the batter into the prepared baking pan. Using a large, narrow, angled spatula, lightly and quickly spread the batter evenly in the pan. Bake for 20 minutes, or until a wooden toothpick inserted into the center comes out clean (see Note).

Remove from the oven and place the baking pan on a wire rack. Let stand until the uncut brownies completely cool.

Then, using a clean, large, narrow, angled spatula, frost the brownies in the pan with the Chocolate Frosting. Let the brownies stand until the frosting sets.

Then, cut into 33 bars (page 517). Arrange the brownies in an airtight container.

NOTE: For more moist brownies, bake for about 17 minutes, or until a wooden toothpick inserted into the center comes out barely moist.

MAKES 33

CREAM CHEESE BROWNIES

(See photo insert page D-4)

8 ounces cream cheese, softened
½ cup sugar
2 extra-large eggs
1 teaspoon pure vanilla extract
1 recipe Frosted Brownies, above (see recipe procedures below)

(Recipe continues on next page)

Preheat the oven to 375°F (see Note). Grease a 9 × 13 × 2-inch baking pan; set aside.

In a medium-small mixing bowl, place the cream cheese and sugar; using an electric mixer, beat on high speed until creamy and *completely* smooth. Add the eggs, one at a time, beating well on medium-high speed after each addition. Add the vanilla; beat on medium-high speed until well blended; set aside.

Follow the recipe for Frosted Brownies through spreading the brownie batter in the baking pan. Then, slowly pour the cream cheese mixture back and forth over the brownie batter. If necessary, use a small, narrow, angled spatula to spread the cream cheese mixture over any uncovered portion of the brownie batter. Bake for 40 minutes. The top of the cream cheese layer will be golden in the center of the pan and fairly brown around the edges.

Remove from the oven and place the baking pan on a wire rack. Let stand only until the uncut brownies completely cool. Then, cover and refrigerate.

When cold, using a large, narrow, angled spatula, frost the brownies in the pan with the Chocolate Frosting. Let the brownies stand only until the frosting sets. Then, cover the uncut brownies tightly with aluminum foil or a baking pan cover, and store in the refrigerator.

Before serving, cut into 33 bars (page 517). Keep stored in the refrigerator.

MAKES 33

OPTIONAL DECORATION: After the Chocolate Frosting sets, pipe stripes (page 323) of Ornamental Vanilla Frosting (page 512) back and forth over the Chocolate Frosting, using a decorating bag fit with small round tip number 2 (page 319). Cover and store in the refrigerator. Let the piped decoration set well before cutting into bars.

MARBLE BROWNIES WITH FEATHER ICING

These fancy, fancy brownies with chocolate and white marbling and feathered icing carry traditional brownies to new heights. They're haute enough to be served on most any occasion.

1½ cups chopped English walnuts
1½ cups sifted cake flour (sift before measuring)
½ teaspoon baking powder
½ teaspoon salt
2 ounces (2 squares) unsweetened chocolate
1 cup (½ pound) butter, softened
1⅔ cups sugar
4 extra-large eggs, room temperature, separated
2 teaspoons pure vanilla extract
⅓ cup sugar
Chocolate Icing (recipe follows)
White Icing (recipe follows)

Preheat the oven to 350°F. Grease a 9 × 13 × 2-inch baking pan; set aside.

Place the walnuts in a small mixing bowl. Sprinkle 2 teaspoons of the measured flour over the walnuts; toss until well coated; set aside. Onto waxed paper, sift together the remaining flour, baking powder, and salt; set aside.

Place the chocolate in a tiny saucepan. Hold the tiny pan over (not touching) low simmering water in a small saucepan until the chocolate melts, stirring intermittently. Remove the tiny pan from the heat; set aside.

In a large mixing bowl, place the butter and 1⅔ cups sugar; using an electric mixer, beat on medium-high speed until fluffy. Add the egg yolks, one at a time, beating well on medium-high after each addition. Add the vanilla; beat on medium-high speed until blended. Add the flour mixture; beat on low speed only until blended. Add the walnuts; using a large mixing spoon, stir and fold in until evenly distributed.

Using the large mixing spoon, spoon ½ of the

batter into another large mixing bowl. Add the melted chocolate to one of the bowls of batter; using the electric mixer, beat on low speed only until blended; set aside.

Place the egg whites in a medium mixing bowl. Using the electric mixer fit with clean, dry blades, beat the egg whites on high speed until soft peaks hold. While continuing to beat on high speed, very gradually add ⅓ cup sugar and continue beating the egg white mixture until stiff, but still moist and glossy.

Using a table knife, cut the beaten egg white mixture in half. Quickly and carefully spoon ½ of the egg white mixture over the white batter, and the remaining ½ of the egg white mixture over the chocolate batter. Using separate mixing spoons, fold the egg white mixture into the 2 batters.

Alternately place heaping tablespoons of white and chocolate batter side by side in the prepared baking pan. Zigzag a table knife through the batter to create a marble effect in the baked brownies. Using a small, narrow, angled spatula, lightly even the top of the batter in the pan. Bake for 30 minutes, or until a wooden toothpick inserted into the center comes out clean.

Remove from the oven and place the baking pan on a wire rack. Let stand until the uncut brownies completely cool.

For Feather Icing, spoon the Chocolate Icing over the cooled, uncut brownies in the pan. Using a clean, small, narrow, angled spatula, quickly spread the icing evenly. Using a decorating bag fit with small round tip number 3 (page 319) and filled with White Icing, immediately pipe even, parallel lines (page 323) of White Icing, ⅝ inch apart, on top of the Chocolate Icing widthwise across the brownies. Immediately, starting at one of the short sides of the pan, lightly draw a table knife over the surface of the icing, in parallel lines 1¼ inches apart, lengthwise across the brownies. Turn the pan, and starting from the other short side, draw the knife over the surface of the icing, in parallel lines 1¼ inches apart, centered between the lines pulled from the opposite side. In other words, pull parallel lines ⅝ inch apart, in alter-

nate directions lengthwise across the brownies, to produce a feathered effect with the White Icing (see illustration). Wipe the knife on a damp sponge after pulling each line. Avoid pressing the knife deeply into the Chocolate Icing when making the lines. It is necessary to work quickly before the icing sets.

Let the uncut brownies stand in the pan on the wire rack until the icing completely sets.

Then, cut into 48 approximately square bars (page 517). Arrange the brownies in an airtight container.

MAKES 40

VARIATION: Marble Brownies may be frosted with the Chocolate Icing alone, eliminating the White Icing and feathering.

CHOCOLATE ICING

3 cups powdered sugar
¼ cup unsweetened cocoa powder
¼ cup plus 2 tablespoons (6 tablespoons) butter, melted
3 tablespoons plus 1 teaspoon warm, strong, brewed coffee
1 teaspoon pure vanilla extract

In a medium mixing bowl, place the powdered sugar, cocoa, butter, coffee, and vanilla. Using an electric mixer, beat the mixture on medium-high speed only until completely smooth.

(Recipe continues on next page)

WHITE ICING

¾ cup powdered sugar
2¼ teaspoons water
½ teaspoon clear vanilla

In a small mixing bowl, place the powdered sugar, water, and vanilla. Using an electric mixer, beat the mixture on medium-high speed only until completely smooth.

GRAHAM CRACKER GOODIES

Good after-school snacks.

¾ cup packed light brown sugar
¼ teaspoon ground cinnamon
½ cup (¼ pound) butter, melted
⅓ cup chopped pecans
30 graham cracker squares

Preheat the oven to 350°F.

In a medium-small mixing bowl, place the brown sugar and cinnamon; stir to combine. Add the butter; stir well. Add the pecans; stir until evenly combined.

Spread the brown sugar mixture over the center of the graham cracker squares (the topping will spread to cover the graham crackers during baking).

Place the graham crackers on ungreased cookie sheets. Bake for 10 minutes.

Using a thin spatula, place the baked Graham Cracker Goodies on waxed paper to cool.

MAKES 30

SAINT AND SINNER CRUNCHIES

1 cup sugar
1 cup light corn syrup
2 tablespoons butter
6 cups Special K cereal
1 12-ounce jar (about 1½ cups) chunky peanut butter

1 12-ounce package (2 cups) semisweet chocolate chips
1 cup (6 ounces) butterscotch chips
2 teaspoons butter

Butter a 10½ × 15½ × 1-inch cookie pan; set aside.

In a large saucepan, place the sugar, syrup, and 2 tablespoons butter; stir to combine. Bring the mixture to a boil over medium heat, stirring constantly. Remove from the heat. Add the cereal; stir until well coated. Add the peanut butter; stir to combine.

Turn the mixture into the prepared cookie pan. Using the back of a tablespoon, pat the mixture evenly into the bottom of the pan; set aside.

In the top of a double boiler, place the chocolate chips and butterscotch chips. Place the top of the double boiler over (not touching) hot (not simmering) water in the bottom pan on the range. Stir continuously to expedite the melting of the chips and to blend. Add 2 teaspoons butter; stir until melted and blended.

Pour the chocolate mixture back and forth over the cereal mixture in the cookie pan. Using a small, narrow, angled spatula, spread the chocolate mixture evenly. Refrigerate the uncut Saint and Sinner Crunchies, uncovered, until set.

Then, cut into seventy 1½-inch squares. Cover the cookie pan tightly with aluminum foil. Store either in the refrigerator or at room temperature.

MAKES 70

COLETTE WORTMAN'S DANISH PUFF

These Danish Puffs are nothing short of exquisite!

PASTRY
½ cup (¼ pound) butter
1 cup sifted all-purpose flour (sift before measuring)
2 tablespoons refrigerated water

Remove the butter from the refrigerator and let stand 10 minutes before use in the recipe. Grease a cookie sheet (preferably an insulated cookie sheet); set aside.

Resift the flour into a medium mixing bowl. Using a knife, cut the butter into approximately 8 pieces and drop into the bowl containing the flour. Using a pastry blender, cut the butter into the flour until the mixture is the texture of cornmeal interspersed with some pieces the size of small peas.

Tilt the mixing bowl and gently shake the flour mixture to one side of the bowl. Sprinkle about 1½ teaspoons of the water over the mixture; using a table fork, lightly rake the moistened portion of the mixture to the other side of the bowl. Repeat the procedure until all the water has been added.

With floured hands, divide the pastry in half. On the prepared cookie sheet and with floured hands, pat each ½ of the dough into a long, 3 × 12-inch strip. Lay a piece of plastic wrap lightly over the pastry; set aside.

TOPPING

1 cup sifted all-purpose flour (sift before measuring)
½ cup (¼ pound) butter
1 cup water
1 teaspoon almond extract
3 extra-large eggs, room temperature

Preheat the oven to 350°F.

Resift the flour onto waxed paper; set aside. In a small saucepan, place the butter and water. Over high heat, bring the butter and water to a rolling boil. Remove from the heat. Add the almond extract; stir to blend. Add the flour all at once; using a small mixing spoon, stir vigorously until the mixture forms a soft ball.

Transfer the mixture to a medium mixing bowl. Add the eggs, one at a time, beating with an electric mixer on medium-high speed after each addition until well blended.

Remove the plastic wrap from the pastry. Spoon ½ of the topping mixture over each of the pastry strips. Using a small, narrow, angled

spatula, spread the topping as evenly and smoothly, and as close to the edges of the pastry, as possible. Bake for 50 to 55 minutes. The topping will rise and then fall during baking, like some cookies. When done, the topping will be crisp and browned.

Remove from the oven and place the cookie sheet on a wire rack. Let the baked strips stand 15 minutes to cool slightly before frosting.

FROSTING AND NUTS

½ recipe Powdered Sugar Frosting (page 508), substituting ½ teaspoon almond extract and ½ teaspoon clear vanilla for 1 teaspoon clear vanilla
⅓ cup finely chopped blanched almonds (run slivered blanched almonds through a nut chopper 3 times [see page 34])

Leave the baked strips on the cookie sheet. Divide the Powdered Sugar Frosting in half. Spoon ½ of the frosting over each baked strip and spread with a small, narrow, angled spatula. Sprinkle ½ of the nuts over each frosted strip. Let the cookie sheet stand on the wire rack until the baked strips completely cool and the frosting sets.

Then, carefully run a large, thin spatula underneath the strips to loosen them from the cookie sheet. Using a sharp, thin-bladed knife, cut each strip in half lengthwise, and then into twelfths widthwise, thus cutting each strip into 24 bars. Arrange the bars in an airtight container.

MAKES 48

Drop Cookies

BUTTER BRICKLE COOKIES

1½ cups all-purpose flour
½ teaspoon baking soda
½ teaspoon salt

(Recipe continues on next page)

½ cup (¼ pound) butter, softened
¾ cup packed light brown sugar
1 extra-large egg
1 teaspoon pure vanilla extract
1 8-ounce package Heath Bits 'O Brickle
    Toffee Bits
⅓ cup broken pecans

Preheat the oven to 350°F. Grease 2 or 3 cookie sheets (page 517); set aside.

Onto waxed paper sift together the flour, baking soda, and salt; set aside.

In a large mixing bowl, place the butter and brown sugar; using an electric mixer, cream well on medium-high speed. Add the egg and vanilla; beat on medium-high speed until smooth and creamy. Add the flour mixture; beat on low speed only until blended. Add the baking chips and pecans; using a large mixing spoon, stir and fold in until evenly combined.

Drop the dough by rounded tablespoonsful, 2 inches apart, onto the prepared cookie sheets. Bake for 8 to 10 minutes, until lightly golden.

Using a thin spatula, place the baked cookies on waxed paper spread on the kitchen counter; let stand until completely cool.

Then, store the cookies in an airtight container.

MAKES ABOUT 42

ALMOND-BUTTER PUFFS

Food finery at its delicate best.

1¼ cups (½ pound plus 4 tablespoons)
    butter, softened
1½ cups powdered sugar
1 cup bread flour (page 17)
¼ teaspoon salt
1 extra-large egg plus 1 extra-large egg yolk
2 cups bread flour
1 *tablespoon* pure vanilla extract
1 cup finely chopped, slivered blanched
    almonds (page 35)

Preheat the oven to 350°F. Oil lightly 2 or 3 cookie sheets (page 517); set aside.

In a large mixing bowl, place the butter and powdered sugar; using an electric mixer, cream well on medium-high speed. Add 1 cup of the flour and salt; beat on medium speed until blended. Add 1 egg plus 1 egg yolk and vanilla; beat well on medium speed. Add 2 cups flour and almonds; beat on low speed only until blended.

Drop the dough by rounded teaspoonsful, 1 inch apart, onto the prepared cookie sheets. Bake for 10 minutes, until faintly golden.

Using a thin spatula, place the baked cookies on waxed paper spread on the kitchen counter; let stand until completely cool.

Then, store the cookies in an airtight container.

MAKES 96

VARIATION: Shape the dough into ¾-inch-diameter balls and place, 3 inches apart, on lightly oiled cookie sheets. Using a table fork, press the top of each ball until the dough is about 1¼ inches in diameter. Lightly press a blanched almond sliver into the top of each cookie. Bake as above.

BUTTERSCOTCH OATMEAL COOKIES

Take your choice of either butterscotch or chocolate chips when you make these good, basic cookies.

1 cup all-purpose flour
½ teaspoon baking soda
½ cup butter, softened
⅓ cup granulated sugar
⅓ cup packed light brown sugar
2 extra-large eggs
½ teaspoon pure vanilla extract
1 cup quick-cooking rolled oats, uncooked
1 cup (6 ounces) butterscotch chips
½ cup broken English walnuts (optional)

Preheat the oven to 375° F. Grease lightly 2 or 3 cookie sheets (page 517); set aside.

Onto waxed paper, sift together the flour and baking soda; set aside.

In a large mixing bowl, place the butter, granulated sugar, and brown sugar; using an electric mixer, cream well on medium-high speed. Add the eggs, one at a time, beating well on medium-high speed after each addition. Add the vanilla; beat well on medium speed. Add the flour mixture; beat on low speed only until blended. Add the oats; beat on low speed only until combined. Add the butterscotch chips and walnuts (if included); using a large mixing spoon, stir and fold in until evenly combined.

Drop the dough by rounded tablespoonsful, 2 inches apart, onto the prepared cookie sheets. Bake for 7 minutes, until lightly golden.

Using a thin spatula, place the baked cookies on waxed paper spread on the kitchen counter; let stand until completely cool.

Then, store the cookies in an airtight container.

MAKES ABOUT 40

VARIATION: Chocolate chips may be substituted for the butterscotch chips.

CHOCOLATE CHIP COOKIES

2½ cups all-purpose flour
1 teaspoon baking soda
1 teaspoon salt
1 cup (½ pound) butter, softened
¾ cup granulated sugar
¾ cup packed light brown sugar
2 extra-large eggs
1¼ teaspoons pure vanilla extract
1 12-ounce package (2 cups) semisweet
   chocolate chips
1 cup broken pecans*

 * *Broken black walnuts or coarsely chopped
   hazelnuts or macadamia nuts may be
   substituted.*

Preheat the oven to 375° F.

Onto waxed paper, sift together the flour, baking soda, and salt; set aside.

In a large mixing bowl, place the butter, granulated sugar, and brown sugar; using an electric mixer, cream well on medium-high speed. Add the eggs, one at a time, beating well on medium-high speed after each addition. Add the vanilla; beat well on medium speed. Add the flour mixture in halves, beating on low speed after each addition only until blended. Add the chocolate chips and pecans; using a large mixing spoon, stir and fold in until evenly combined.

Drop the dough by rounded teaspoonsful, 2 inches apart, onto ungreased cookie sheets. Bake for 9 to 10 minutes, until lightly golden.

Using a thin spatula, place the baked cookies on waxed paper spread on the kitchen counter; let stand until completely cool.

Then, store the cookies in an airtight container.

MAKES ABOUT 84

M&M'S CHOCOLATE CHIP COOKIES

Follow the Chocolate Chip Cookies recipe, above, substituting 1 12-ounce package (1¾ cups) M&M's semisweet chocolate mini baking bits for the chocolate chips and eliminating the pecans.

QUICK-AS-A-WINK CHOCOLATE-COCONUT COOKIES

Simple, and simply delicious.

2 ounces (2 squares) unsweetened chocolate
1 14-ounce can (1¼ cups) sweetened
   condensed milk
1 7-ounce package (2⅔ cups) flaked coconut
⅓ cup chopped pecans

Preheat the oven to 350° F. Using Special Grease (page 40), grease 2 or 3 cookie sheets; set aside.

Place the chocolate in a tiny saucepan. Hold

(Recipe continues on next page)

the tiny pan over (not touching) low simmering water in a small saucepan until the chocolate melts, stirring intermittently. Remove the tiny pan from the heat; set aside.

In a medium mixing bowl, place the condensed milk, coconut, pecans, and melted chocolate; stir until blended and evenly combined.

Drop the mixture by rounded teaspoonsful, 2 inches apart, onto the prepared cookie sheets. Bake for 12 minutes, until set.

Using a thin spatula, immediately place the baked cookies on waxed paper spread on the kitchen counter; let stand until completely cool.

Then, store the cookies in an airtight container.

MAKES ABOUT 48

COCONUT OATMEAL COOKIES

1½ cups all-purpose flour
½ teaspoon baking soda
½ cup (¼ pound) butter, softened
½ cup granulated sugar
½ cup packed light brown sugar
2 extra-large eggs
½ teaspoon pure vanilla extract
1 cup quick-cooking rolled oats, uncooked
¾ cup flaked coconut
½ cup chopped pecans

Preheat the oven to 350° F. Grease 2 or 3 cookie sheets (page 517); set aside.

Onto waxed paper, sift together the flour and baking soda; set aside.

In a large mixing bowl, place the butter, granulated sugar, and brown sugar; using an electric mixer, cream well on medium-high speed. Add the eggs, one at a time, beating well on medium-high speed after each addition. Add the vanilla; beat on medium-high speed until fluffy. Add the oats; beat on medium speed until combined. Add the flour mixture; beat on low speed only until blended. Add the coconut and

pecans; using a large mixing spoon, stir and fold in until evenly distributed.

Drop the dough by rounded teaspoonsful, 2 inches apart, onto the prepared cookie sheets. Bake for 8 minutes, until lightly golden.

Using a thin spatula, place the baked cookies on waxed paper spread on the kitchen counter; let stand until completely cool.

Then, store the cookies in an airtight container.

MAKES ABOUT 60

EASTER EGG NESTS

Cute-looking and easy as pie to make, Easter Egg Nests are an ideal treat to make with children as assistant cooks.

1 cup (6 ounces) milk chocolate chips
1 cup (6 ounces) butterscotch chips
1 5-ounce can chow mein noodles
½ cup flaked coconut, tinted green (page 344)
About 10½ dozen small jelly beans in
    assorted colors

Line 2 cookie sheets with waxed paper; set aside.

In the top of a double boiler, place the chocolate chips and butterscotch chips. Place the top of the double boiler over (not touching) hot (not simmering) water in the bottom pan. Stir continuously to expedite the melting of the chips and to blend.

Remove the top of the double boiler from the bottom pan. Add the chow mein noodles to the melted chips; using a spoon, stir to combine, crushing the noodles into smaller pieces with the edge of the spoon as you mix.

Drop the mixture by rounded teaspoonsful onto the prepared cookie sheets, forming each cookie into a little nest with a slight indentation on the top. With your fingers, sprinkle a small amount of coconut over the center of each nest to simulate grass. Press 3 jelly beans of varied color into the coconut on each cookie to simulate eggs.

Place the cookie sheets of Easter Egg Nests in the refrigerator for a few minutes until set.

Then, store the cookies in an airtight container.

MAKES ABOUT 42

COCONUT MACAROONS

(See photo insert page D-5)

Often included on platters of gaily decorated Christmas cookies are Coconut Macaroons topped with ½ red candied cherry in keeping with the season.

2 tablespoons all-purpose flour
⅛ teaspoon salt
2 extra-large egg whites, room temperature
½ cup powdered sugar
1 teaspoon clear vanilla
7 ounces (2⅔ cups) flaked coconut

Preheat the oven to 300°F. Grease 2 or 3 cookie sheets (page 517); set aside.

In a small sauce dish, place the flour and salt; stir to combine; set aside.

Place the egg whites in a medium mixing bowl. Using an electric mixer, beat the egg whites on high speed until stiff peaks hold. While continuing to beat on high speed, slowly add the powdered sugar, then the flour mixture, and then the vanilla. Beat on high speed until well blended. Add the coconut; using a mixing spoon, fold in.

Drop the dough by rounded teaspoonsful, 2 inches apart, onto the prepared cookie sheets. Bake for 20 minutes. When done, the macaroons will be a light golden color.

Using a thin spatula, place the baked cookies on waxed paper spread on the kitchen counter; let stand until completely cool.

Store the cookies overnight in an airtight container before serving. Keep stored in an airtight container.

MAKES ABOUT 30

HOLIDAY DECORATION: Prior to baking, place ½ red candied cherry on the top of each mound of dough on the cookie sheet.

CORNFLAKES MACAROONS

Recipes for these supergood cookies appear fairly consistently in old cookbooks, and they pop up occasionally in current cookbooks. Cornflakes Macaroons will probably remain popular not only because they are great tasting, but also because their ingredients are consistent with healthful eating trends (no egg yolks and no added shortening).

2 extra-large egg whites, room temperature
1 cup sugar
½ teaspoon clear vanilla
2 cups cornflakes
½ cup broken pecans
1 cup flaked coconut

Preheat the oven to 325°F. Grease 2 or 3 cookie sheets (page 517); set aside.

Place the egg whites in a medium mixing bowl; using an electric mixer, beat the egg whites on high speed until soft peaks form. While continuing to beat on high speed, very gradually add the sugar and then the vanilla. Continue beating the egg white mixture on high speed until stiff, but still moist and glossy. Add the cornflakes, pecans, and coconut; using a large mixing spoon, fold in until evenly distributed.

Drop the dough by rounded teaspoonsful, 2 inches apart, onto the prepared cookie sheets. Bake for 15 minutes. When done, the cookies will not be brown.

Using a thin spatula, place the baked cookies on waxed paper spread on the kitchen counter; let stand until completely cool.

Then, store the cookies in an airtight container.

MAKES 48

BRAN FLAKES COOKIES

2 cups all-purpose flour
2 teaspoons baking powder
½ teaspoon baking soda
½ teaspoon salt
1 cup baking raisins
1 cup flaked coconut
1 cup vegetable shortening, softened
1 cup granulated sugar
1 cup packed light brown sugar
2 extra-large eggs
2 tablespoons whole milk
1 teaspoon pure vanilla extract
2 cups bran flakes

Preheat the oven to 350° F.

Onto waxed paper, sift together the flour, baking powder, soda, and salt; set aside. In a medium mixing bowl, place the raisins and coconut; stir to combine; cover and set aside.

In a large mixing bowl, place the vegetable shortening, granulated sugar, and brown sugar; using an electric mixer, cream well on medium-high speed. Add the eggs, one at a time, beating well on medium-high speed after each addition. Add the milk and vanilla; beat on medium-high speed until fluffy. Add the flour mixture; beat on low speed only until blended. Add the raisin mixture and bran flakes; using a large mixing spoon, stir and fold in until evenly distributed throughout the dough.

Drop the dough by rounded tablespoonsful, 2 inches apart, onto ungreased cookie sheets. Bake for 10 minutes. The cookies will fall when done; do not remove them from the oven too soon.

Using a thin spatula, place the baked cookies on waxed paper spread on the kitchen counter; let stand until completely cool.

Then, store the cookies in an airtight container.

MAKES 72

VARIATION: This recipe may be conveniently cut in half.

HONEY-GRANOLA COOKIES

1½ cups whole-wheat flour
1½ cups all-purpose flour
½ teaspoon baking powder
1 teaspoon baking soda
¾ teaspoon salt
2 teaspoons ground ginger
½ teaspoon ground nutmeg
1 extra-large egg
⅔ cup packed light brown sugar
⅔ cup honey
½ cup (¼ pound) butter, softened
4 cups granola, homemade (page 67) or
　　1 13-ounce commercial package
Whole, blanched almonds (optional)

Preheat the oven to 350° F. Using Special Grease (page 40), grease 2 or 3 cookie sheets; set aside.

Onto waxed paper, sift together the whole-wheat flour, all-purpose flour, baking powder, baking soda, salt, ginger, and nutmeg; set aside.

Place the egg in a large mixing bowl; using an electric mixer, beat the egg well on medium-high speed. Add the brown sugar and honey; beat well on medium-high speed. Add the butter; continue beating on medium-high speed until well blended. Add the flour mixture in halves, beating on low speed after each addition only until blended. Add the granola; using a large mixing spoon, stir and fold in.

Drop the dough by heaping teaspoonsful, 2 inches apart, onto the prepared cookie sheets. If desired, place a whole, blanched almond in the center of each mound of cookie dough. Bake for 7 to 8 minutes, until golden.

Remove the cookies from the oven and let stand on the cookie sheets 1 minute. Then, using a thin spatula, place the cookies on waxed paper spread on the kitchen counter; let stand until completely cool.

Then, store the cookies in an airtight container.

MAKES ABOUT 96

OATMEAL-DATE COOKIES

2 cups all-purpose flour
½ teaspoon baking soda
¼ teaspoon salt
½ teaspoon ground cloves
½ teaspoon ground cinnamon
¼ teaspoon ground nutmeg
1 cup quick-cooking rolled oats, uncooked
½ cup (¼ pound) butter, softened
1 cup packed light brown sugar
2 extra-large eggs
1 cup dates chopped very finely
½ cup homemade sour milk (page 42)

Preheat the oven to 375° F. Grease 2 or 3 cookie sheets (page 517); set aside.

Onto waxed paper, sift together the flour, baking soda, salt, cloves, cinnamon, and nutmeg. Place the flour mixture in a large mixing bowl. Add the oats; stir to combine; set aside.

In a large mixing bowl, place the butter and brown sugar; using an electric mixer, cream well on medium-high speed. Add the eggs, one at a time, beating well on medium-high speed after each addition. Add the dates; beat on medium speed only until combined. Add, alternately, the flour mixture in thirds, and the sour milk in halves, beating on low speed after each addition only until blended.

Drop the dough by rounded tablespoonsful, 2 inches apart, onto the prepared cookie sheets. Bake for 8 minutes, until lightly golden.

Using a thin spatula, place the baked cookies on waxed paper spread on the kitchen counter; let stand until completely cool.

Then, store the cookies in an airtight container.

MAKES ABOUT 60

OAT BRAN COOKIES

1½ cups all-purpose flour
½ teaspoon baking soda
½ cup vegetable shortening, softened
½ cup granulated sugar
½ cup packed light brown sugar
2 extra-large eggs
½ teaspoon pure vanilla extract
1 cup oat bran
½ cup flaked coconut
½ cup broken pecans

Preheat the oven to 350° F.

Onto waxed paper, sift together the flour and baking soda; set aside.

In a medium mixing bowl, place the vegetable shortening, granulated sugar, and brown sugar; using an electric mixer, cream well on medium-high speed. Add the eggs, one at a time, beating well on medium-high speed after each addition. Add the vanilla; beat on medium-high speed until well blended. Add the oat bran; beat on medium speed until combined. Add the flour mixture in halves, beating on low speed after each addition only until blended. Add the coconut and pecans; using a large mixing spoon, stir and fold in until evenly combined.

Drop the dough by rounded teaspoonfuls, 2 inches apart, onto ungreased cookie sheets. Bake for 8 minutes, until lightly golden.

Using a thin spatula, place the baked cookies on waxed paper spread on the kitchen counter; let stand until completely cool.

Then, store the cookies in an airtight container.

MAKES 60

MONSTER COOKIES

(See photo insert page D-5)

There's something to suit just about all cookie lovers in these behemoths, but there isn't any flour. Well, something had to give. Instructions for making these cookies in a more normal size are also given.

½ cup (¼ pound) butter, softened
1 cup granulated sugar
1 cup packed light brown sugar
3 extra-large eggs
2 teaspoons baking soda
1 tablespoon pure vanilla extract
1 12-ounce jar (1⅓ cups) creamy peanut
   butter
4½ cups quick-cooking rolled oats, uncooked
1 6-ounce package (1 cup) semisweet
   chocolate chips
1 ¼ cups milk chocolate M&M's candies

Preheat the oven to 325° F.

In a large mixing bowl, place the butter, granulated sugar, and brown sugar; using an electric mixer, cream well on medium-high speed. Add the eggs, one at a time, beating well on medium-high speed after each addition. Add the baking soda and vanilla; beat on medium-high speed until well blended. Add the peanut butter; beat on medium-high speed until blended. Add the oats; beat on medium-low speed until combined. Add the chocolate chips and M&M's; using a large mixing spoon, stir and fold in until evenly distributed.

Drop the dough by heaping tablespoonsful, 3 inches apart, onto ungreased cookie sheets. Bake for 10 to 12 minutes, until very lightly golden.

Remove the cookies from the oven and let stand on the cookie sheets until cooled slightly. Then, using a thin spatula, place the cookies on waxed paper spread on the kitchen counter; let stand until completely cool.

Then, store them in an airtight container.

MAKES ABOUT 36 MONSTER-SIZED COOKIES

VARIATION: For smaller cookies substitute 1 cup M&M's milk chocolate mini baking bits for 1 ¼ cups milk chocolate M&M's candies. Drop the dough by heaping teaspoonsful, 2 inches apart, onto ungreased cookie sheets. Bake for 10 minutes at 325° F. Makes about 120 smaller-sized cookies.

SOUR CREAM DROP COOKIES

2¾ cups all-purpose flour
½ teaspoon baking powder
½ teaspoon baking soda
¼ teaspoon salt
½ cup (¼ pound) butter or vegetable
   shortening, softened
1½ cups sugar
2 extra-large eggs
1 teaspoon pure vanilla extract
1 cup homemade sour cream (page 42)

Onto waxed paper, sift together the flour, baking powder, baking soda, and salt; set aside.

In a large mixing bowl, place the butter and sugar; using an electric mixer, cream well on medium-high speed. Add the eggs, one at a time, beating well on medium-high speed after each addition. Add the vanilla; beat on medium-high speed until blended. Add, alternately, the flour mixture in thirds, and the sour cream in halves, beating on low speed after each addition only until blended. Cover the mixing bowl with aluminum foil and refrigerate the dough 1 hour.

Preheat the oven to 350° F. Grease well 2 or 3 cookie sheets (page 517); set aside.

Remove the dough from the refrigerator and drop it by rounded teaspoonsful, 2 inches apart, onto the prepared cookie sheets. Bake for 8 minutes, until lightly golden.

Using a thin spatula, place the baked cookies on waxed paper spread on the kitchen counter; let stand until completely cool.

Then, store the cookies in an airtight container.

MAKES ABOUT 156

FROSTED CHOCOLATE COOKIES

(See photo insert page D-5)

Ever popular and ever good, Frosted Chocolate Cookies are a staple in the world of cookies.

1½ cups all-purpose flour
1 teaspoon baking powder
½ teaspoon baking soda
¼ cup unsweetened cocoa powder
½ cup (¼ pound) butter, softened
1 cup packed light brown sugar
1 extra-large egg
½ teaspoon pure vanilla extract
½ cup homemade sour milk (page 42)
1 cup chopped pecans
1 recipe Chocolate Frosting (page 508)

Preheat the oven to 350°F. Grease lightly 2 or 3 cookie sheets (page 517); set aside.

Onto waxed paper, sift together the flour, baking powder, baking soda, and cocoa; set aside.

In a large mixing bowl, place the butter and brown sugar; using an electric mixer, cream well on medium-high speed. Add the egg and vanilla; beat on medium-high speed until fluffy. Add, alternately, the flour mixture in thirds, and the sour milk in halves, beating on low speed after each addition only until blended. Add the pecans; using a large mixing spoon, stir and fold in until evenly combined.

Drop the dough by rounded teaspoonsful, 2 inches apart, onto the prepared cookie sheets. Bake for 8 minutes, until set.

Using a thin spatula, place the baked cookies on waxed paper spread on the kitchen counter; let stand until completely cool.

Then, using a small, narrow, angled, and tapered spatula, frost the cookies with the Chocolate Frosting. Let the cookies stand until the frosting sets.

Store the cookies, single layer, separated by plastic wrap, in an airtight container.

MAKES 84

FROSTED ORANGE COOKIES

1¾ cups all-purpose flour
1 teaspoon baking powder
½ teaspoon baking soda
½ teaspoon salt
½ cup (¼ pound) butter, softened
¾ cup packed light brown sugar
1 extra-large egg
½ teaspoon orange extract
1 tablespoon plus 1 teaspoon very finely
    grated orange rind (page 31)
½ cup homemade sour milk (page 42)
1 recipe Orange Frosting (page 509)
Snipped orange gumdrops for decoration

Preheat the oven to 350°F. Oil lightly 2 or 3 cookie sheets (page 517); set aside.

Onto waxed paper, sift together the flour, baking powder, soda, and salt; set aside.

In a large mixing bowl, place the butter and brown sugar; using an electric mixer, cream well on medium-high speed. Add the egg; beat on medium-high speed until well blended. Add the orange extract and orange rind; beat on medium-high speed until blended and combined. Add, alternately, the flour mixture in thirds, and the sour milk in halves, beating on low speed after each addition only until blended.

Drop the dough by rounded teaspoonsful, 2 inches apart, onto the prepared cookie sheets. Bake for 8 to 9 minutes, until set.

Remove the cookies from the oven and let stand on the cookie sheets 1 minute. Then, using a thin spatula, place the cookies on wire cookie racks. Let the cookies stand until completely cool.

Then, using a small, narrow, angled, and tapered spatula, frost the cookies with the Orange Frosting. Decorate the top of each frosted cookie with a small, snipped piece of orange gumdrop. Let the cookies stand until the frosting sets.

Store the cookies, single layer, separated by plastic wrap, in an airtight container.

MAKES ABOUT 72

FROSTED MOLASSES COOKIES

Molasses is a product which results from the manufacture of cane and beet sugar. In the manufacture of cane sugar, the sugar-bearing juice is extracted from the cane by means of chopping and crushing or by diffusion, after which the extracted juice is clarified. The clarified sugarcane juice is then processed through a series of three boilings and evaporations which result in a mixture of crystallized raw sugar and a brown syrup which is molasses. The molasses is separated from the sugar crystals by means of centrifuging.

Molasses obtained after the first boiling contains a greater percentage of sugar and is lighter in color than molasses obtained after the second and third boilings. Molasses obtained from the first extraction is called light (or mild-flavored) molasses, and molasses obtained from the second extraction is called dark (or robust- or full-flavored) molasses. The very dark, heavy, and somewhat bitter syrup obtained after the third boiling is called blackstrap molasses. While blackstrap molasses is available on supermarket shelves for consumers who include it in their diets for its high iron content, it is used primarily in animal feed, for fermentation into alcohol, and for other commercial purposes. I recall that in the late 1940s molasses was mixed with a grain fed to our purebred Shorthorn cattle being fattened for show purposes as an inducement for them to eat abundantly. Molasses obtained from sugar beets is very low in sugar and generally is considered to be inedible.

Molasses was one of the provisions supplied to the Midwest frontier, sometimes arriving, with other foodstuffs, by steamboat up the Mississippi River during warm navigable months. As sugar was in short supply, molasses was consistently used as a sweetener substitute. Molasses cookies were a pioneer food. Some of the very old recipes for molasses cookies call for them to be made with vinegar and require no shortening (vinegar molasses cookies). Other old molasses cookie recipes still in use today commonly call for lard as the shortening which helps to give the cookies that deep, rich, beloved flavor. This recipe is one of those old, incomparable ones handed down in my sister-in-law's family. The appeal of these cookies to modern palates has not diminished.

4½ cups all-purpose flour
2 teaspoons baking soda
1 teaspoon salt
1 teaspoon ground cinnamon
½ teaspoon ground nutmeg
½ teaspoon ground ginger
1 cup lard, softened
1½ cups packed light brown sugar
½ cup light (mild-flavored) molasses
3 extra-large eggs
1 teaspoon pure vanilla extract
½ cup homemade sour milk (page 42)
1 recipe Powdered Sugar Frosting (page 508)

Preheat the oven to 350°F. Grease 2 or 3 cookie sheets (page 517); set aside.

Onto waxed paper, sift together the flour, baking soda, salt, cinnamon, nutmeg, and ginger; set aside.

In a large mixing bowl, place the lard and brown sugar; using an electric mixer, cream well on medium-high speed. Add the molasses; beat on medium-high speed until blended. Add the eggs, one at a time, beating well on medium-high speed after each addition. Add the vanilla; beat on medium-high speed until blended. Add, alternately, the flour mixture in thirds, and the sour milk in halves, beating on low speed after each addition only until blended.

Drop the dough by rounded tablespoonsful, 2 inches apart, onto the prepared cookie sheets. Bake for 10 minutes, until lightly golden.

Using a thin spatula, place the baked cookies on waxed paper spread on the kitchen counter; let stand until completely cool.

Then, using a small, narrow, angled, and tapered spatula, frost the cookies with the Powdered Sugar Frosting. Let the cookies stand until the frosting sets.

Store the cookies, single layer, separated by plastic wrap, in an airtight container.

MAKES ABOUT 96

FRUITCAKE COOKIES

If you like really good fruitcake but don't have time to make it this holiday season, make these cookies instead. This big recipe yields about 13 dozen cookies—enough for gift giving as well as your own family's enjoyment. The recipe came from my grandmother's cookbook (your guarantee as to its excellence).

16 ounces diced candied mixed fruits
½ cup baking raisins
½ cup golden raisins
1 cup broken English walnuts
¼ cup all-purpose flour
3 cups all-purpose flour
1 tablespoon baking powder
¼ teaspoon salt
2 teaspoons ground cinnamon
½ teaspoon ground cloves
½ teaspoon ground nutmeg
1 cup (½ pound) butter, softened
2 cups sugar
2 extra-large eggs
¾ cup whole milk
4 ounces candied red cherries, quartered
   lengthwise, for decoration

Preheat the oven to 375° F. Grease 2 or 3 cookie sheets (page 517); set aside.

In a medium mixing bowl, place the candied mixed fruits, raisins, golden raisins, and walnuts; stir until evenly distributed. Add ¼ cup flour; toss to coat the fruits and nuts; set aside.

Onto waxed paper, sift together 3 cups flour, baking powder, salt, cinnamon, cloves, and nutmeg; set aside.

In a large mixing bowl, place the butter and sugar; using an electric mixer, cream well on medium-high speed. Add the eggs, one at a time, beating well on medium-high speed after each addition. Continue beating the mixture on medium-high speed until the mixture is light and fluffy. Add, alternately, the flour mixture in thirds, and the milk in halves, beating on low speed after each addition only until blended.

Add the fruits and nuts mixture; using a large mixing spoon, stir and fold in until evenly distributed.

Drop the dough by rounded teaspoonsful, 2 inches apart, onto the prepared cookie sheets. Place a candied red cherry quarter in the center of each mound of cookie dough. Bake for 9 to 10 minutes, until lightly golden.

Using a thin spatula, place the baked cookies on waxed paper spread on the kitchen counter; let stand until completely cool.

Then, store the cookies in an airtight container.

MAKES ABOUT 156

HAYSTACKS

For those readers less familiar with farming, "hay" is a general term used to mean any number of dried herbaceous plant crops used for animal feed that supply both important nutrients and roughage. While alfalfa and red clover are the primary crops raised for hay in the Midwest, various grasses are used for hay in some sections of the Heartland.

These cookies are so named because they resemble stacks of dry hay. The marshmallows provide height and the coconut gives the appearance of stems protruding from the haystacks.

1 ounce (1 square) unsweetened chocolate
3 ounces cream cheese, softened
2 tablespoons half-and-half
1 teaspoon crème de cacao (cacao bean- and
   vanilla-flavored liqueur)
2 cups powdered sugar, sifted (page 42) (sift
   after measuring)
2 cups miniature marshmallows
1 cup flaked coconut

Line a cookie sheet with waxed paper; set aside.

Place the chocolate in a tiny saucepan. Hold the tiny pan over (not touching) low simmering water in a small saucepan until the chocolate melts, stirring intermittently. Remove the tiny pan from the heat; set aside.

(Recipe continues on next page)

Place the cream cheese in a medium mixing bowl. Using an electric mixer, beat the cream cheese on high speed only until smooth. Add the half-and-half; beat on medium-high speed until blended. Add the crème de cacao and melted chocolate; continue beating on medium-high speed until fluffy. Add the powdered sugar; beat on low speed to combine; then, beat on medium-high speed until completely blended and smooth. Add the marshmallows and coconut; using a small mixing spoon, stir and fold in until evenly distributed.

Drop the mixture by rounded teaspoonsful onto the prepared cookie sheet. Refrigerate, uncovered, until the cookies are firm (about 3 hours).

Then, store the cookies, single layer, separated by plastic wrap, in an airtight container; keep refrigerated.

MAKES ABOUT 42

SUNFLOWER SEED COOKIES

While the use of hulled sunflower seeds as a cooking ingredient might seem contemporary to some of us, American Indians grew sunflowers for food long before the Europeans came to this land. The Indians dried sunflower seeds and then ground them, unshelled, into a meal. The common sunflower, Helianthus annuus, *is native to North America, especially the western tier of Midwest states and the west-central section of the United States. In 1996, the top four sunflower-producing states, by rank, were North Dakota, South Dakota, Kansas, and Minnesota. (The sunflower is the official state flower of Kansas.) Sunflower-seed oil, pressed from the seeds and used in salad dressings and for cooking, is low in saturated fat and high in polyunsaturated fat.*

The appearance of sunflowers, with their yellow-petaled flower heads resembling sunbursts, is familiar to everyone. However, the huge size of the flower heads of cultivated sunflowers, which can be as much as one foot or more in diameter, is astonishing when you see these flowers for the first time. (The size of one I saw at our local farmers' market last Saturday amazed me.)

Hulled sunflower seeds are rich in nutrients and are usually available in the section of supermarkets where nuts are displayed. The recipe that follows makes sunflower seed cookies that are high in fiber and tops in taste. For a yeast bread containing sunflower seeds, see Honey-Seed Bread (page 354).

½ cup raw, hulled (unsalted) sunflower seeds
½ cup flaked coconut
1 cup Quaker MultiGrain cereal, uncooked (found at the supermarket near oatmeal)
1 cup all-purpose flour
¼ teaspoon baking powder
½ teaspoon baking soda
½ cup (¼ pound) butter, softened
½ cup granulated sugar
½ cup packed light brown sugar
1 extra-large egg
½ teaspoon pure vanilla extract
1 recipe Honey-Cream Cheese Frosting (page 511) (optional)

Preheat the oven to 350° F. Grease 2 or 3 cookie sheets (page 517); set aside.

In a medium mixing bowl, place the sunflower seeds, coconut, and MultiGrain cereal; stir to evenly combine; cover and set aside. Onto waxed paper, sift together the flour, baking powder, and baking soda; set aside.

In a large mixing bowl, place the butter, granulated sugar, and brown sugar; using an electric mixer, cream well on medium-high speed. Add the egg and vanilla; beat on medium-high speed until light and fluffy. Add the flour mixture; beat on low speed only until blended. Add the sunflower seed mixture; using a large mixing spoon, stir until evenly combined and all dry ingredients are dampened.

Drop the dough by heaping teaspoonsful, 2 inches apart, onto the prepared cookie sheets. Bake for 7 to 8 minutes, until lightly golden.

Using a thin spatula, place the baked cookies on waxed paper spread on the kitchen counter; let stand until completely cool.

Then, if desired, using a decorating bag fit with small round tip number 2 (page 319), pipe stripes (page 323) of Honey-Cream Cheese Frosting back and forth across the top of the cookies. Place the cookies, single layer, uncovered, in a container(s) with a lid(s). Refrigerate 2 hours, or until the frosting sets; then, cover. For food safety, keep the cookies refrigerated due to the cream cheese in the frosting.

MAKES ABOUT 60

MACADAMIA NUT COOKIES

Although the tree Macadamia ternifolia *was originally native to Australia, we associate macadamia nuts, the seeds of this tree, with Hawaii, where they are one of our fiftieth state's largest crops. I like macadamia nuts in these thin, delicate cookies, which I first made with macadamia nuts brought home from an Hawaiian vacation.*

1⅓ cups all-purpose flour
1¼ cups (½ pound plus 4 tablespoons) butter, softened
1¼ cups powdered sugar
1 extra-large egg
1¾ teaspoons pure vanilla extract
1 7-ounce jar (1½ cups) macadamia nuts, chopped

Preheat the oven to 350° F. Grease lightly 2 or 3 cookies sheets (page 517); set aside.

Sift the floor onto waxed paper; set aside.

In a medium mixing bowl, place the butter and powdered sugar; using an electric mixer, cream well on medium-high speed. Add the egg and vanilla; beat on medium-high speed until well blended. Add the flour; beat on low speed only until blended. Add the nuts; using a medium mixing spoon, stir and fold in until evenly distributed.

Drop the dough by rounded teaspoonsful, 2 inches apart, onto the prepared cookie sheets. Bake for 10 to 12 minutes. Watch the cookies closely during baking. When done, the cookies

should be golden brown around the edges. Be careful not to let these cookies get too brown, as it will ruin their delicate taste.

Using a thin spatula, place the baked cookies on waxed paper spread on the kitchen counter; let stand until completely cool.

Then, store the cookies in an airtight container.

MAKES ABOUT 48

HEALTH NUT COOKIES

These cookies contain all kinds of ingredients that are good for you.

2½ cups quick-cooking rolled oats, uncooked
1 cup broken pecans
½ cup golden raisins
1 cup whole-wheat flour
¾ teaspoon salt
1 teaspoon ground cinnamon
½ teaspoon ground nutmeg
2 extra-large eggs
¾ cup vegetable oil
1¼ cups honey
1 teaspoon pure vanilla extract
1½ cups untoasted (raw) wheat germ
½ cup nonfat dry milk
6½ dozen pecan halves
Honey-Cinnamon Glaze (recipe follows)

Preheat the oven to 325° F. Grease 2 or 3 cookie sheets (page 517); set aside.

In a medium mixing bowl, place the oats, pecans, and raisins; sir to combine; cover and set aside. Onto waxed paper, sift together the flour, salt, cinnamon, and nutmeg; set aside.

Place the eggs in a large mixing bowl. Using an electric mixer, beat the eggs well on medium-high speed. Add the vegetable oil and honey; beat on medium-high speed until well blended. Add the vanilla; beat on medium-high speed until blended. Add the wheat germ; beat on low speed until blended. Add the flour mixture and dry milk; beat on low speed only until blended.

(Recipe continues on next page)

Add the oats mixture; using a large mixing spoon, stir and fold in until evenly distributed. Cover the mixing bowl containing the cookie dough with plastic wrap; let stand 5 minutes to allow the dough to thicken.

Drop the dough by rounded teaspoonsful, 2 inches apart, onto the prepared cookie sheets. Place a pecan half in the center of each mound of cookie dough. Using a small, soft watercolor brush, brush a thin coat of the Honey-Cinnamon Glaze over each pecan half. Bake for 9 to 10 minutes, until golden.

Remove the cookies from the oven and let stand on the cookie sheets 2 minutes. Then, using a thin spatula, place the cookies on waxed paper spread on the kitchen counter; let stand until completely cool.

Store the cookies, single layer, separated by plastic wrap in an airtight container.

MAKES ABOUT 78

HONEY-CINNAMON GLAZE

1 tablespoon honey
Dash of ground cinnamon

In a tiny saucepan, place the honey and cinnamon; stir to combine. Over low heat, heat the mixture until thin, stirring intermittently.

MOTHER'S PINEAPPLE COOKIES

When we were growing up, the cookies Mother made the most often were these Pineapple Cookies, our very favorite. Mother always put any leftover frosting on Ritz crackers (an unlikely but swell-tasting, "down-home" combination) and topped them with half a pecan. Whenever I have extra Powdered Sugar Frosting, I make these homespun treats for my brother.

1 8-ounce can crushed pineapple in its own juice
2 cups all-purpose flour

1 teaspoon baking powder
¼ teaspoon baking soda
¼ teaspoon salt
½ cup (¼ pound) butter, softened
½ cup granulated sugar
½ cup packed light brown sugar
1 extra-large egg
1 teaspoon pure vanilla extract
½ cup broken pecans
Frosting (recipe instructions below)

Preheat the oven to 325° F. Grease lightly 2 or 3 cookie sheets (page 517); set aside.

Drain the pineapple in a sieve, reserving the juice for use in the frosting; set aside. Onto waxed paper, sift together the flour, baking powder, baking soda, and salt; set aside.

In a large mixing bowl, place the butter, granulated sugar, and brown sugar; using an electric mixer, cream well on medium-high speed. Add the egg and vanilla; beat on medium-high speed until thoroughly blended. Add the flour mixture; beat on low speed only until blended. The dough will be quite stiff. Add the drained pineapple and pecans; using a large mixing spoon, stir and fold in until evenly combined.

Drop the dough by rounded teaspoonsful, 2 inches apart, onto the prepared sheets. Bake for 12 to 14 minutes, until lightly golden brown.

Using a thin spatula, place the baked cookies on waxed paper spread on the kitchen counter; let stand until completely cool.

Then, using a small, narrow, angled, and tapered spatula, frost the cookies. Let stand until frosting sets.

Store the cookies, single layer, separated by plastic wrap, in an airtight container.

MAKES ABOUT 72

FROSTING: Frost the cookies with 1 recipe of Powdered Sugar Frosting (page 508), substituting ¼ cup reserved pineapple juice for ¼ cup half-and-half or whole milk. If the reserved juice measures less than ¼ cup, add water to make ¼ cup liquid.

NIGHTY NIGHTS

They bake overnight; plus, they're great for a bedtime treat. (It's also okay to have one for breakfast.)

1 cup (6 ounces) mint-flavored semisweet
   chocolate chips
1 cup chopped pecans
2 extra-large egg whites, room temperature
⅔ cup sugar
½ teaspoon clear vanilla

Preheat the oven to 350°F. Line 2 cookie sheets smoothly with aluminum foil; set aside.

In a small mixing bowl, place the chocolate chips and pecans; stir to combine; set aside.

Place the egg whites in a medium mixing bowl. Using an electric mixer, beat the egg whites on high speed until soft peaks hold. While continuing to beat on high speed, very gradually add the sugar and then the vanilla. Continue beating the egg white mixture on high speed until very stiff. Add the chocolate chip mixture; using a spoon, fold in until evenly distributed.

Drop the meringue mixture by heaping teaspoonsful, 2 inches apart, onto the prepared cookie sheets. Place the cookie sheets in the top half of the oven. Turn off the oven and leave the cookies overnight without opening the oven door until morning.

Store the cookies, single layer, separated by plastic wrap, in an airtight container.

MAKES 42

MADELEINES

Although they are usually classified as cookies, Madeleines are really delicate, rich little cakes leavened by air and steam, and are similar in texture to tiny sponge cakes. They are French in origin and are traditionally baked in molds the shape of scallop shells. Madeleines are the perfect tea cake.

I classify Madeleines as drop cookies (page 516) even though the batter is dropped into molds rather than onto cookies sheets.

¼ cup (4 tablespoons) butter
½ cup sifted cake flour (sift before
   measuring)
2 extra-large eggs, room temperature
⅛ teaspoon salt
⅓ cup superfine sugar
½ teaspoon pure vanilla extract
2 tablespoons powdered sugar

In a tiny saucepan, melt the butter over low heat. Remove the saucepan from the heat and allow the butter to cool at room temperature.

Preheat the oven to 375°F. Grease well and flour lightly twenty-four 2 × 3-inch Madeleine molds (see note); set aside.

Place the measured sifted flour in the top of the sifter; set aside.

In a medium mixing bowl, place the eggs and salt; using an electric mixer, beat on the highest speed until the mixture is frothy. While continuing to beat on the highest speed, gradually add the sugar and continue beating until the mixture is stiff and holds ribbons when you lift the beater from the mixing bowl. Add the vanilla; beat on the highest speed until blended. Remove the mixing bowl from the mixer.

Promptly *sift* the flour in fourths over the egg mixture, using a medium mixing spoon to fold in after each addition only until the flour disappears. Add the melted butter, 1 tablespoon at a time, using the mixing spoon to fold in as expeditiously as possible after each addition.

Using 2 teaspoons (1 to transport the batter

(Recipe continues on next page)

and 1 to push the batter from the filled teaspoon), immediately spoon the batter into each prepared Madeleine mold to about ²/₃ full. Fill all of the molds quickly, preparing to bake all of the Madeleines at once, as the quality of the batter declines rapidly. (When baked in batches, Madeleines baked subsequent to the first batch are compact and rubbery.) Bake for 10 minutes, until the top surface of the madeleines springs back when touched lightly.

Remove the Madeleines from the oven. Using the pointed tip of a paring knife, immediately remove the Madeleines from the molds and place them, scalloped side up, on wire cookie racks; let stand until cool.

When completely cool, arrange the Madeleines, single layer, in airtight containers lined with waxed paper. Place the powdered sugar in a small hand strainer, and dust the Madeleines with powdered sugar. Store the Madeleines securely covered.

MAKES 24

NOTE: 2×3-inch Madeleine molds come in single tins containing 12 molds. It is important to have 24 molds so that all of the Madeleines may be baked at one time. Although tins of very small Madeleine molds measuring 1¹/₄ × 1⁵/₈ inches are available, I find the Madeleines baked in these molds too small for satisfactory serving and eating.

Molded Cookies

ARTIST'S PALETTE THUMBPRINTS

(See photo insert page D-5)

Thumbprint cookies derive their name from the fact that the baker's thumb becomes an implement to make a depression in the top of each unbaked cookie into which jam (or jelly) is placed after baking. This particular recipe is entitled

"Artist's Palette Thumbprints" because I am suggesting that the indentations be filled with jams (or jellies) in a variety of colors to create an especially attractive and appealing array of cookies.

1½ cups all-purpose flour
½ teaspoon salt
½ cup plus 3 tablespoons butter, softened
½ cup sifted powdered sugar (page 42)
  (sift before measuring)
1 extra-large egg yolk
2 teaspoons pure vanilla extract
2 extra-large egg whites
1¾ cups chopped English walnuts
At least 4 kinds of jams in various colors, such
  as strawberry, peach, pineapple, plum,
  cherry, blueberry, and apricot

Onto waxed paper, sift together the flour and salt; set aside.

In a medium mixing bowl, place the butter and powdered sugar; using an electric mixer, beat on medium-high speed until blended and creamy. Add the egg yolk; beat well on medium-high speed. Add the vanilla; continue beating on medium-high speed until blended. Add ½ of the flour mixture; beat on low speed only until blended. Add the remaining ½ of the flour mixture; beat on low speed only until the flour mixture is fully blended and the dough is smooth. Cover the mixing bowl with aluminum foil and refrigerate the dough 45 minutes, until cool enough to mold into balls easily. (If the dough becomes too stiff, let it stand, covered, at room temperature until it warms to the desired consistency.)

Meanwhile, place the egg whites in a small sauce dish; using a table fork, beat slightly; set aside. Distribute the walnuts over a piece of waxed paper; set aside.

Preheat the oven to 350° F. Line 2 or 3 cookie sheets with parchment baking paper. (If parchment baking paper is not available, the cookie sheets may be greased, page 517.) Set aside.

Using a 1-inch trigger scoop or melon baller, scoop portions of dough from the mixing bowl and roll in the palms of your hands to form 1-

inch-diameter balls. Drop the balls of dough into the slightly beaten egg whites to coat; then, roll them in the nuts until they are fully and generously covered.

Place the nut-covered balls, 1½ inches apart, on the prepared cookie sheets. Press down on the top of each ball with your thumb, forming a deep cup in which jam will be placed *after* baking. The thumbprinting procedure will flatten the dough balls slightly. Bake for 15 minutes, until a very pale golden color.

Using a thin spatula, place the baked cookies on waxed paper spread on the kitchen counter; let stand until completely cool.

Then, fill the thumbprint cup in each cookie with about ⅛ teaspoon of one of the vari-colored jams. A tiny salt spoon or a demitasse spoon is excellent for use in filling the cups.

Store the cookies, single layer, separated by plastic wrap, in a loose container.

MAKES ABOUT 36

VARIATION: The thumbprint cups may be filled with jellies. Mint and cherry or strawberry jellies are attractive during the holiday season.

KRINGLA

These large Norwegian cookies, shaped in the form of a figure eight, border on a sweet bread in consistency and taste. Though not common, Kringla may be glazed, as indicated in the recipe that follows. Some Norwegian people like to eat Kringla buttered.

3 cups all-purpose flour
1 tablespoon baking powder
1 teaspoon baking soda
½ teaspoon salt
½ cup (¼ pound) butter, softened
1 cup sugar
1 extra-large egg
1 teaspoon pure vanilla extract
1 cup buttermilk
1 recipe Glaze (page 513) (optional)

AFTERNOON OF THE FIRST DAY: Onto waxed paper, sift together the flour, baking powder, baking soda, and salt; set aside.

In a large mixing bowl, place the butter and sugar; using an electric mixer, cream well on medium-high speed. Add the egg and vanilla; beat on medium-high speed until well blended and fluffy. Add, alternately, the flour mixture in thirds, and the buttermilk in halves, beating on low speed after each addition only until blended. Using a rubber spatula, quickly turn the dough into a medium mixing bowl; cover tightly and refrigerate overnight.

THE NEXT DAY: Preheat the oven to 500° F.

Remove the dough from the refrigerator and divide it in half. On a floured pastry cloth (page 38), using floured hands, roll each half of the dough into a log about 12 inches long. Wrap one log in plastic wrap and refrigerate.

Using a sharp, floured knife, cut the remaining log into 20 equal pieces. On the floured pastry cloth, using floured hands, roll each piece of dough into a pencil-like stick 7 to 8 inches long. Carefully lift each dough stick to an ungreased cookie sheet and form it into a figure eight. To make a figure eight, lay the stick of dough on the cookie sheet in the shape of the bottom loop (see illustration A).

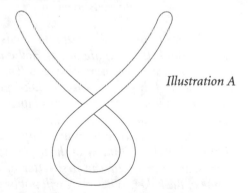

Illustration A

Bring the ends of the dough together to complete the figure eight. Lightly push the ends of the dough together; there is no need to pinch the dough and interfere with the uniformity of the shape (see Illustration B).

(Recipe continues on next page)

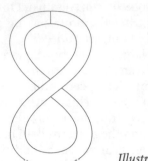

Illustration B

Bake the cookies for 5 minutes. The cookies will be pale.

Using a thin spatula, immediately place the baked Kringla on wire cookie racks; let stand until completely cool.

When cool, the Kringla may be glazed, if desired. Using a soft watercolor brush, apply the Glaze to the tops of the Kringla, following the figure eight; let stand on the wire racks until the glaze sets.

Store the Kringla, single layer, separated by plastic wrap, in an airtight container.

MAKES 40

DUTCH LETTERS
Banketstaven

In a litany of outstanding national foods, Dutch Letters (Banketstaven) are one of Holland's best-known and -loved culinary creations. The exquisite almond filling encased in flaky pastry is formed into long rolls which are shaped into letters of the alphabet before baking. In Holland, Dutch Letters traditionally are shaped into the first letter of the last name of the person to whom they will be given or the first letter of the last name of the baker. When they will not be given as gifts, Dutch Letters are usually made in the shape of the letter S.

2 cups (1 pound) butter
4 cups sifted all-purpose flour (sift before measuring)
1 cup refrigerated water

1 pound almond paste
2 extra-large eggs plus 1 extra-large egg yolk (reserve 1 extra-large egg white)
1 teaspoon pure vanilla extract
2 cups sugar
Crystal sugar* or granulated sugar for decoration

* Crystal sugar has larger grains than either granulated sugar or sanding sugar (page 400). You may be able to secure crystal sugar from your baker, or it is available from Sweet Celebrations Inc. (see Product Sources, page 631).

AFTERNOON OF THE FIRST DAY: Remove the butter from the refrigerator and let stand 10 minutes before use in the recipe. (If the kitchen is especially warm, reduce the standing time to 5 minutes.)

Place the flour in a large mixing bowl. Using a knife, cut the butter into approximately tablespoon-sized pieces and drop into the bowl containing the flour. Using a pastry blender, cut the butter into the flour until the mixture is the texture of very coarse cornmeal interspersed with some pieces the size of small peas.

Tilt the mixing bowl and gently shake the flour mixture to one side of the bowl. Sprinkle about 2 tablespoons of the water over the mixture; using a table fork, lightly rake the moistened portion of the mixture to the other side of the bowl. Repeat the procedure until all the water has been added.

With floured hands, divide the pastry in half and quickly form each half into a ball. The pastry will be quite dry; do not be concerned if it does not hold together well in a ball. Wrap each half of the pastry in plastic wrap. Using your hand, slightly flatten each ball of pastry in the plastic wrap and then refrigerate overnight. Handle the pastry as little as possible.

EARLY THE NEXT DAY: Place the almond paste in a large mixing bowl. Using an electric mixer, beat the almond paste on high speed to smooth it as much as possible. Add 2 eggs plus 1 egg yolk, one at a time, beating well on medium-high speed after each addition. Add the vanilla; beat on medium-high speed until the mixture is smooth. Add 2 cups sugar; beat on medium-high speed until well blended. Cover the bowl with aluminum foil; refrigerate 2 to 3 hours until the almond paste mixture is well chilled.

Preheat the oven to 400° F. Grease 3 or more cookie sheets (page 517); set aside.

Using a sharp knife, cut the chilled almond paste mixture into 14 equal portions. On a buttered marble slab or countertop, using buttered hands, roll 7 of the almond paste portions into 13-inch-long rolls, each. Cover and refrigerate the remaining 7 portions.

Remove 1 ball of pastry from the refrigerator and remove the plastic wrap. Using a sharp knife, mark the pastry into 7 equal portions. Cut away, *in one piece,* 3 of the pastry portions. Wrap the remainder of the pastry in plastic wrap and set aside.

On a floured pastry cloth, using a stockinet-covered, then lightly floured rolling pin (page 38), roll the cutaway pastry into a 14 × 15-inch rectangle. Using a sharp, floured knife, cut the rolled pastry into three 5 × 14-inch strips. Place one of the almond paste rolls lengthwise down the center of each pastry strip.

Using a small, soft watercolor brush, brush a ¼-inch strip of water down one of the 14-inch sides of each rolled strip. Roll each strip of pastry lengthwise fairly tightly around the filling and toward the wet edge (making three 14-inch-long rolls). The wet edge will help seal the seam on each roll. Pinch the ends of the rolls to seal.

Arrange each roll, seam side down, in the shape of the letter S (or any desired letter), on a prepared cookie sheet. Repeat the procedure with the remaining almond paste rolls and pastry. (Press the last 2 portions of pastry together and roll into a 14 × 10-inch rectangle; cut into 2 pastry strips.) Let the filled cookie sheets stand.

Place the reserved egg white in a small mixing bowl. Using a handheld electric mixer, beat the egg white slightly on medium speed. Using the soft watercolor brush, brush the tops of the letters with beaten egg white. Then, sprinkle the letters generously with crystal (or granulated) sugar. Using a sharp fork, prick the tops of the letters every 2 inches. Bake for 18 to 20 minutes, until lightly golden.

Using a large, thin spatula, place the baked Dutch Letters on wire cookie racks; let stand until completely cool.

Store the Dutch Letters in a loose container.

To eat, use your fingers to break off desired portions of your served Dutch Letter and eat in the same manner as a cookie.

MAKES FOURTEEN 8-INCH-HIGH S LETTERS

GIFT IDEA: For a special gift, bake Dutch Letters in the initials of the favored person's name.

CHRISTMAS HOLLY WREATHS

Holidays are times for special, shared family activities. Children can participate in the fun and satisfaction of Christmastime baking by helping to make these pretty (and good-tasting, as well) holly wreaths. They're unbaked, and the procedures for making them present opportunities for children of various ages to assist.

3½ cups cornflakes
½ cup flaked coconut
½ cup (¼ pound) butter
30 large marshmallows
¼ teaspoon green liquid food coloring
Cinnamon Imperials candy (red hots)

In a large mixing bowl, place the cornflakes and coconut; using a large mixing spoon, stir until combined; set aside.

In the top of a double boiler, place the butter and marshmallows. Place the top of the double boiler over simmering water in the bottom pan. Stir the butter and marshmallows intermittently until melted and blended. Remove the double boiler from the heat, leaving the top of the double boiler in the bottom pan. Add the

(Recipe continues on next page)

food coloring; stir vigorously until blended thoroughly.

Immediately pour the green mixture over the cornflakes mixture; using the large mixing spoon, toss until the cornflakes and coconut are completely coated with the green mixture.

Spoon heaping tablespoons of the mixture onto waxed paper spread on the kitchen counter. Butter your fingers and form wreaths about 2 inches in diameter. Lightly press 3 red hots, close together, into each wreath to simulate holly berries. Let the wreaths stand on the waxed paper 6 hours to partially dry.

Then, using a thin spatula, place the wreaths, single layer, in containers lined with waxed paper. Let the wreaths stand, uncovered, an additional 2 hours to continue drying. Then, cover the containers.

MAKES 20

PFEFFERNÜSSE
Peppernuts

These small, round, nut-shaped German Christmas cookies contain several spices, including black pepper, the ingredient for which they are named. After baking, Pfeffernüsse are stored in an airtight container (preferably a tin), where they are left to season at least one week before they are served.

⅓ cup slivered blanched almonds
2 cups sifted all-purpose flour (sift before measuring)
1 teaspoon baking powder
¼ teaspoon salt
¼ teaspoon black pepper
1 teaspoon ground cinnamon
½ teaspoon ground nutmeg
¼ teaspoon ground cloves
Dash of ground mace
2 extra-large eggs
1 cup sugar
¼ cup (2 ounces) chopped candied citron
Brandy

Preheat the oven to 350°F. Grease 2 cookie sheets (page 517); set aside.

In a food processor, process the almonds *a few seconds* until ground. Be careful not to overprocess, reducing the nuts to butter. Place the ground almonds in a small mixing bowl; set aside.

Onto waxed paper, sift together the flour, baking powder, salt, pepper, cinnamon, nutmeg, cloves, and mace. Place the flour mixture in a medium mixing bowl. Add the ground almonds; stir to combine; set aside.

Place the eggs in a medium mixing bowl. Using an electric mixer, beat the eggs on high speed until very thick (about 5 minutes). While continuing to beat on high speed, very gradually add the sugar. Add the flour mixture in thirds, beating on low speed after each addition only until blended. Add the citron; using a mixing spoon, stir and fold in until evenly combined.

Using a small melon baller, scoop small portions of dough from the mixing bowl and, with damp hands, roll into small balls about ½ inch in diameter. Place the balls of dough, 1½ inches apart, on the prepared cookie sheets. Using an eye dropper, place 1 drop of brandy on the top of each ball. Bake for 12 to 13 minutes, until lightly browned.

Using a thin spatula, place the baked cookies on waxed paper spread on the kitchen counter; let stand until completely cool.

Store the cookies in an airtight container (such as a tin) for at least 1 week before serving.

MAKES ABOUT 84

VARIATION: If you prefer softer Pfeffernüsse, place a small slice of apple in the airtight container (tin) with the cookies. To prevent the apple slice from touching the cookies directly, place it on a tiny piece of plastic wrap. Replace the apple slice frequently.

RUM BALLS

½ cup powdered sugar
1½ cups rolled vanilla wafer crumbs (about 33 vanilla wafers)
8 ounces English walnuts, ground (page 34) (about 2 cups ground walnuts)
¼ cup Myers's (dark) rum
¼ cup honey

Place the powdered sugar in a sauce dish; set aside.

In a medium mixing bowl, place the vanilla wafer crumbs and walnuts; stir to combine. Add the rum and honey; stir to combine well.

Using a 1-inch trigger scoop or melon baller, scoop even portions of the mixture from the mixing bowl and, with damp hands, roll into balls 1 inch in diameter. Place the rolled balls on waxed paper spread on the kitchen counter. Then, roll the balls in the sauce dish of powdered sugar to coat.

Store the Rum Balls in an airtight container lined with waxed paper.

MAKES 60

LACE COOKIES

(See photo insert page D-5)

1 cup all-purpose flour
1 cup finely chopped pecans
½ teaspoon ground cinnamon (optional)
½ cup (¼ pound) butter
⅔ cup packed light brown sugar
½ cup light corn syrup
½ teaspoon pure vanilla extract

Have ready a clean piece of ⅝-inch-diameter wooden dowel cut to approximately 7½ inches in length.

Preheat the oven to 350° F. Using Special Grease (page 40), grease lightly 2 or 3 cookie sheets; set aside.

In a small mixing bowl, place the flour, pecans, and cinnamon (if desired); stir to combine; set aside.

In a small saucepan, melt the butter over low heat. Remove from the heat. Add the brown sugar and corn syrup; stir vigorously to blend. Over medium-high heat, bring the butter mixture to a boil, stirring constantly. Remove from the heat. Add the flour mixture; stir to blend and combine. Add the vanilla; stir well to blend.

Using a lightly greased measuring teaspoon to measure the batter and a lightly greased tableware teaspoon to push the batter off the measuring teaspoon, drop the batter for 5 or 6 cookies only, by even teaspoons, 3 inches apart, onto a prepared cookie sheet. Intermittently wash the teaspoons and regrease when the batter begins to stick to the spoons. Bake the cookies for 6 to 7 minutes, until lightly browned. The cookies will spread thinly and bubble during baking. While each batch of cookies is baking, cover the saucepan of remaining batter and place on top of the range (not over heat) to keep the batter warm and soft. If the batter becomes too stiff, heat slightly over medium heat, stirring constantly.

Remove the cookie sheet from the oven and place on a wooden board; let stand 1 minute. While the cookies are still warm and pliable, use a thin spatula to remove one cookie at a time from the cookie sheet and, using your hands, carefully roll it around the wooden dowel. Remove the dowel from the rolled cookie and place the cookie on waxed paper spread on the kitchen counter; let stand until cool. Bake only 5 to 6 cookies at a time and roll them quickly, as they cool rapidly and become impossible to roll without breaking.

When completely cool, store the cookies in an airtight container. Lace Cookies are better the day after baking because they become somewhat drier and more crispy.

MAKES ABOUT 72

VARIATION: Lace Cookies may be left unrolled, in which case, slightly less than 1 teaspoon of batter produces a smaller, more desirably sized flat cookie.

GRACE'S PEANUT CRISPIES

No bake; no fuss.

½ cup sugar
½ cup light corn syrup
½ cup chunky peanut butter
2 cups Rice Krispies cereal

In a small saucepan, place the sugar and syrup; stir to combine. Over low heat, stir the mixture constantly until the sugar dissolves. Remove from the heat. Add the peanut butter; stir to combine. Return to low heat and stir only until the peanut butter completely melts and blends; do not overcook. Remove from the heat. Add the cereal; stir until evenly combined.

Using a 1½-inch trigger scoop (see Note), quickly drop the mixture by even scoops onto waxed paper spread on the kitchen counter. Using your hands, immediately roll each portion into a ball and replace on the waxed paper; let stand until completely cool.

Then, store the cookies in an airtight container.

NOTE: A tablespoon may be substituted.

MAKES ABOUT 30

CRISPY COOKIES

2 cups all-purpose flour
½ teaspoon baking powder
1 teaspoon baking soda
½ teaspoon salt
½ cup vegetable shortening, softened
½ cup (¼ pound) butter, softened
1 cup granulated sugar
1 cup packed light brown sugar
2 extra-large eggs
2 cups quick-cooking rolled oats, uncooked
2 cups Rice Krispies cereal
1 cup flaked coconut

Preheat the oven to 375° F.

Onto waxed paper, sift together the flour, baking powder, baking soda, and salt; set aside.

In a large mixing bowl, place the vegetable shortening, butter, granulated sugar, and brown sugar; using an electric mixer, cream well on medium-high speed. Add the eggs, one at a time, beating well on medium-high speed after each addition. Add the flour mixture in halves, beating on low speed after each addition only until blended. Add the oats; beat on medium-low speed only until evenly combined.

Add the cereal and coconut; using a mixing spoon, work in until evenly distributed throughout the dough. The dough will be crumbly.

Using a small melon baller, scoop portions of dough from the mixing bowl and roll in the palms of your hands to form ¾-inch-diameter balls. Place the balls of dough, 1½ inches apart, on ungreased cookie sheets. Bake for 8 to 10 minutes, until lightly golden.

Using a thin spatula, place the baked cookies on waxed paper spread on the kitchen counter; let stand until completely cool.

Then, store the cookies in an airtight container.

MAKES ABOUT 108

PEANUT COOKIES

3 cups bread flour (page 17)
¼ teaspoon baking soda
½ teaspoon salt
¾ cup lard or vegetable shortening, softened
2 cups sugar
¼ cup creamy peanut butter
3 extra-large eggs
1 teaspoon pure vanilla extract
1 cup unsalted peanuts without skins, chopped
¼ cup unsalted peanut halves without skins

Preheat the oven to 350° F.

Onto waxed paper, sift together the flour, baking soda, and salt; set aside.

In a large mixing bowl, place the lard, sugar, and peanut butter; using an electric mixer, beat on medium-high speed until light and fluffy. Add the eggs, one at a time, beating well on medium-high speed after each addition. Add the vanilla; beat on medium-high speed until blended. Add the flour mixture in halves, beating on low speed after each addition only until blended. Add the chopped peanuts; beat on medium speed only until evenly distributed.

Using a 1-inch trigger scoop or melon baller, scoop portions of dough from the mixing bowl and roll in the palms of your hands to form 1-inch-diameter balls. Place the balls of dough, 3 inches apart, on ungreased cookie sheets.

Using the bottom of a dampened, rigid spatula or drinking glass, flatten the dough balls to 1½ inches in diameter. Press a peanut half into the center of each unbaked cookie. Bake for 12 minutes, until lightly golden.

Using a thin spatula, place the baked cookies on waxed paper spread on the kitchen counter; let stand until completely cool.

Then, store the cookies in an airtight container.

MAKES 72

PEANUT BUTTER COOKIES

(See photo insert page D-5)

1 cup all-purpose flour
¾ teaspoon baking soda
¼ teaspoon salt
½ cup vegetable shortening
½ cup granulated sugar
½ cup packed light brown sugar
½ cup creamy peanut butter
1 extra-large egg
½ teaspoon pure vanilla extract

Preheat the oven to 375° F.

Onto waxed paper, sift together the flour, baking soda, and salt; set aside.

In a medium mixing bowl, place the vegetable shortening, granulated sugar, brown sugar, and peanut butter; using an electric mixer, cream well on medium-high speed. Add

the egg and vanilla; beat on medium-high speed until light and fluffy. Add the flour mixture; beat on low speed only until blended.

Using a 1-inch trigger scoop or melon baller, scoop portions of dough from the mixing bowl and roll in the palms of your hands to form 1-inch-diameter balls. Place the balls of dough, 2 inches apart, on ungreased cookie sheets.

Using the tines of a table fork, flatten each ball of dough by pressing it twice, at right angles, to form a crisscross pattern (see illustration).

Bake for 8 to 10 minutes, or until very lightly browned.

Using a thin spatula, place the baked cookies on waxed paper spread on the kitchen counter; let stand until completely cool.

Then, store the cookies in an airtight container.

MAKES ABOUT 54

CHOCOLATE PEANUT BUTTER BALLS

1 9-ounce package commercial chocolate wafers, rolled finely (2⅓ cups crumbs)
2½ cups powdered sugar, sifted (page 42) (sift after measuring)
1 cup (½ pound) butter
1 12-ounce jar (1⅓ cups) creamy peanut butter
3 11.5-ounce packages milk chocolate chips

Line 2 cookie sheets with waxed paper; set aside.

In a medium mixing bowl, place the chocolate wafer crumbs and powdered sugar; stir to combine; set aside.

In a medium saucepan, melt the butter over low heat. Add the peanut butter. Stir until the

(Recipe continues on next page)

peanut butter melts and blends with the butter. Remove from the heat. Add the crumb mixture; stir until thoroughly combined. Cover the saucepan and refrigerate the mixture until cooled to room temperature (about 35 minutes).

Then, using a 1-inch trigger scoop or melon baller, scoop portions of the mixture from the saucepan and roll in the palms of your hands to form 1-inch-diameter balls. Place the balls of dough on the prepared cookie sheets; refrigerate, uncovered, for 30 minutes.

Then, place the chocolate chips in the top of a double boiler. Place the top of the double boiler over hot (not simmering) water in the bottom pan. Stir until the chocolate chips completely melt and the chocolate is smooth.

Remove the cookie sheets of rolled balls from the refrigerator. Using a candy-dipping fork or a table fork, dip the rolled balls in the chocolate, one at a time, to coat. Replace the coated balls on the waxed paper-lined cookie sheets. Leave the top of the double boiler over hot (not simmering) water in the bottom pan during the dipping process to retain the proper consistency of the chocolate.

Refrigerate the coated balls until the chocolate hardens.

MAKES ABOUT 108

SNICKERDOODLES

Snickerdoodles: a nonsense name for no-nonsense cookies with wide taste appeal. When you bake them, the surface—covered with a cinnamon-sugar mixture—cracks, giving Snickerdoodles a distinct identity. Research reveals that these cookies originated in New England in the 1800s, with nuts, raisins, and currants among the ingredients then.

2¾ cups all-purpose flour
1 teaspoon baking soda
½ teaspoon salt
2 teaspoons cream of tartar
2 tablespoons sugar
2 teaspoons ground cinnamon
½ cup (¼ pound) butter, softened

½ cup vegetable shortening, softened
1½ cups sugar
2 extra-large eggs

Preheat the oven to 400° F.

Onto waxed paper, sift together the flour, baking soda, salt, and cream of tartar; set aside. In a small sauce dish, place 2 tablespoons sugar and the cinnamon; stir well to combine; set aside.

In a large mixing bowl, place the butter, vegetable shortening, and 1½ cups sugar; using an electric mixer, cream well on medium-high speed. Add the eggs, one at a time, beating well on medium-high speed after each addition. Continue beating on medium-high speed until light and fluffy. Add the flour mixture in halves, beating on low speed after each addition only until blended.

Using a 1½-inch trigger scoop, measure level scoops of dough from the mixing bowl and roll in the palms of your hands to form balls (see Note). Place the balls of dough on waxed paper spread on the kitchen counter. Roll the balls in the cinnamon mixture to coat, and then place them, 2 inches apart, on ungreased cookie sheets (12 cookies to a 12 × 15½-inch cookie sheet). Bake for 9 minutes. The cookies will flatten during baking. The tops will have a cracked, cut glass appearance when baked.

Using a thin spatula, place the baked cookies on clean waxed paper spread on the kitchen counter; let stand until completely cool.

Then, store the cookies in an airtight container

NOTE: If a 1½-inch trigger scoop is not available, shape tablespoonsful of dough into balls the size of table tennis balls.

MAKES ABOUT 48

WHOLE-WHEAT OATMEAL COOKIES

1¼ cups whole-wheat flour
½ teaspoon baking soda
½ cup (¼ pound) butter, softened
1 cup sugar

1 extra-large egg
½ teaspoon pure vanilla extract
½ cup quick-cooking rolled oats, uncooked
½ cup packed baking raisins
¾ cup broken English walnuts

Preheat the oven to 375°F.

Onto waxed paper, sift together flour and soda; set aside.

In a medium mixing bowl, place the butter and sugar; using an electric mixer, cream well on medium-high speed. Add the egg; beat on medium-high speed until blended. Add the vanilla; continue beating on medium-high speed until fluffy. Add the flour mixture; beat on low speed only until blended. Add the oats; beat on medium speed only until combined. Add the raisins and walnuts; using a mixing spoon, stir and fold in until evenly combined.

Using a 1-inch trigger scoop or melon baller, scoop portions of dough from the mixing bowl and roll in the palms of your hands to form 1-inch-diameter balls. Place the balls of dough, 2 inches apart, on ungreased cookie sheets. Using a small, rigid spatula, flatten the balls of dough to ¼-inch thickness. Bake for 8 to 10 minutes, until lightly golden.

Using a thin spatula, place the baked cookies on waxed paper spread on the kitchen counter; let stand until completely cool.

Then, store the cookies in an airtight container.

MAKES ABOUT 36

VARIATION: For 24 large cookies, increase the diameter of the dough balls to about 1¼ inches.

JERRY'S GINGERSNAPS

One of the ingredients called for in this recipe is unsulphured, light (or mild-flavored) molasses. Unsulphured molasses is molasses processed without the use of sulphur. For more information about molasses, see the headnote for Frosted Molasses Cookies (page 542).

2 cups all-purpose flour
2 teaspoons baking soda
¼ teaspoon salt
1 teaspoon ground cinnamon
½ teaspoon ground ginger
½ teaspoon ground cloves
¼ teaspoon ground allspice
1 cup sugar
¾ cup vegetable oil
1 extra-large egg
¼ cup unsulphured, light (mild-flavored) molasses
½ cup sugar

Preheat the oven to 375°F. Using Special Grease (page 40), grease 2 or 3 cookie sheets; set aside.

Onto waxed paper, sift together the flour, baking soda, salt, cinnamon, ginger, cloves, and allspice; set aside.

In a large mixing bowl, place 1 cup sugar and the vegetable oil; using an electric mixer, beat well on medium-high speed. Add the egg; beat on medium-high speed until blended. Add the molasses; beat on medium-high speed until completely blended. Add the flour mixture; beat on low speed only until blended; set aside.

Place ½ cup sugar in a small sauce dish; set aside.

Using a 1-inch trigger scoop or melon baller dipped into sugar, scoop even portions of dough from the mixing bowl and roll into 1-inch-diameter balls using lightly sugared hands. Roll the balls of dough in the sauce dish of sugar to coat, and then place them, 2 inches apart, on the prepared cookie sheets. Dip the trigger scoop or melon baller into sugar before scooping each portion of dough. Bake for 8 to 9 minutes, or until set. The tops of the cookies will be cracked.

Remove the cookies from the oven and let stand on the cookie sheets 1 minute. Then, using a thin spatula, place the cookies on waxed paper spread on the kitchen counter; let stand until completely cool.

Then, store the cookies in an airtight container

MAKES ABOUT 66

UNBAKED WHEAT GERM BALLS

A bounty of different-flavored, healthful wheat germ cookies may be made in a wink from the basic recipe that follows. Three flavor versions are given after the basic recipe, and creative cooks can come up with many more to suit their own taste fancies. It's easy—just follow the basic recipe, using 1 cup of dried or candied fruits and/or nuts plus complementary flavoring, and then roll the Wheat Germ Balls in a compatible topping.

Wheat germ is the small embryo within a kernel of wheat from which the grain sprouts. Untoasted (raw) wheat germ, as used in this recipe, is an extremely rich source of vitamins E and B6. Untoasted wheat germ also contains large quantities of protein and important minerals and vitamins, and it is high in fiber. Wheat germ should be refrigerated after it is opened. A quart glass jar with a lid makes a good container for storing it. For another recipe using untoasted wheat germ, see Granola (page 67).

Follow the Basic Recipe to make the various-flavored Wheat Germ Balls given below.

BASIC RECIPE
2 cups untoasted (raw) wheat germ
Filling ingredients (from selected recipe, below)
⅓ cup whole milk
1¼ cups sugar
¼ cup plus 2 tablespoons (6 tablespoons) margarine or butter
Flavoring ingredient (from selected recipe below)
Topping ingredient (from selected recipe below)

In a medium mixing bowl, place the wheat germ and filling ingredient(s); stir to combine; set aside.

In a small saucepan, place the milk and sugar; stir to combine. Add the margarine. Over medium-high heat, bring the milk mixture to a rolling boil, stirring constantly. Pour the milk mixture over the wheat germ mixture. Add the flavoring ingredient. Stir until the mixture is well combined.

Drop the mixture by tablespoonsful onto waxed paper spread on the kitchen counter; let stand until cool.

Then, in the palms of your hands, roll each mound of cooled dough into a ball about 1 inch in diameter and replace on the waxed paper.

Sprinkle the topping ingredient over a clean piece of waxed paper. Roll the balls of dough in the topping until well covered.

Store the wheat germ balls in an airtight container for at least 12 hours before serving.

MAKES ABOUT 24

UNBAKED WHEAT GERM RAISIN BALLS

FILLING
½ cup raisins
½ cup broken pecans
1 tablespoon unsweetened cocoa powder
FLAVORING
½ teaspoon pure vanilla extract
TOPPING
½ cup powdered sugar

Follow the Basic Recipe above.

UNBAKED WHEAT GERM APRICOT-NUT BALLS

FILLING
1 6-ounce package (about 1 packed cup) dried apricots, diced (page 22) finely
½ teaspoon ground cinnamon
⅛ teaspoon ground nutmeg
FLAVORING
½ teaspoon pure vanilla extract
TOPPING
¾ cup finely chopped pecans

Follow the Basic Recipe, above.

UNBAKED WHEAT GERM PINEAPPLE-COCONUT BALLS

FILLING
8 ounces (1 cup) candied pineapple slices chopped finely

FLAVORING
2 teaspoons white rum *or* ½ teaspoon pure
  vanilla extract
TOPPING
1 cup flaked coconut

Follow the Basic Recipe above.

Rolled Cookies

OLD-FASHIONED SUGAR COOKIES

3 cups sifted all-purpose flour (sift before
  measuring)
½ teaspoon baking soda
½ teaspoon salt
1 cup (½ pound) butter, softened
1½ cups sugar
2 extra-large eggs
1 teaspoon pure vanilla extract
3 tablespoons homemade sour cream (page
  42) (make ¼ cup sour cream; use only
  3 tablespoons)
Sugar for top of cookies

Onto waxed paper, sift together the flour, baking soda, and salt; set aside.

In a large mixing bowl, place the butter and
sugar; using an electric mixer, cream well on
medium-high speed. Add the eggs, one at a time,
beating well on medium-high speed after each
addition. Add the vanilla; beat on medium-high
speed until light and fluffy. Add the sour cream;
beat on medium speed until blended. Add the
flour mixture in thirds, beating on low speed
after each addition only until blended.

Divide the dough into thirds; wrap each third
in plastic wrap and refrigerate at least 2 hours.

Preheat the oven to 400° F.

Remove 1 package of dough from the refrigerator. If the dough is too stiff to roll, let it stand,
briefly, at room temperature in the plastic wrap

until it is pliable. On a well-floured pastry cloth,
using a stockinet-covered, then floured rolling
pin (page 38), roll the dough to ³⁄₁₆-inch
thickness.

Using a 2-inch round cutter dipped in flour,
cut out the cookies. After each cut, wipe the
excess dough off the cutter and redip it in flour.
Using a thin spatula, place the cutout cookies, 2
inches apart, on ungreased cookie sheets.
Gather the remaining dough on the pastry cloth
into a ball; rewrap it in the plastic wrap and
refrigerate. Sprinkle each cutout cookie with
sugar. Bake for 5 minutes, until the edge of the
cookies is lightly golden.

Remove the cookies from the oven and let
stand on the cookie sheets until cooled slightly.
Then, using a thin spatula, place the cookies on
waxed paper spread on the kitchen counter; let
stand until completely cool.

Repeat the procedure with the remaining 2
packages of dough. Then, combine all the
remaining dough from the 3 packages and continue making cookies until all the dough is used.

Store the cookies in an airtight container.

MAKES ABOUT 84

GINGERBREAD PEOPLE

2¾ cups sifted all-purpose flour (sift before
  measuring)
1 teaspoon baking soda
½ teaspoon salt
1 teaspoon ground ginger
1½ teaspoons ground cinnamon
½ cup (¼ pound) butter, softened
½ cup sugar
½ cup light (mild-flavored) molasses
½ cup buttermilk
Currants
½ recipe Confectioners' Frosting (page 507)

Onto waxed paper, sift together the flour, baking soda, salt, ginger, and cinnamon; set aside.

In a large mixing bowl, place the butter and

(Recipe continues on next page)

sugar; using an electric mixer, cream well on medium-high speed. Add the molasses; beat well on medium-high speed. Add, alternately, the flour mixture in thirds, and the buttermilk in halves, beating on low speed after each addition only until blended.

Divide the dough in half; wrap each half in plastic wrap and refrigerate at least 2 hours.

Preheat the oven to 375°F. Grease 2 or 3 cookie sheets (page 517); set aside.

Remove 1 package of dough from the refrigerator. On a floured pastry cloth, using a stockinet-covered, then floured rolling pin (page 38), roll the dough to ¼-inch thickness.

Using a gingerbread-person cookie cutter dipped in flour, cut out the cookies. After each cut, wipe the excess dough off the cutter and redip it in flour. Using a thin spatula, place the cutout cookies, 2 inches apart, on the prepared cookie sheets. Gather the remaining dough on the pastry cloth into a ball; rewrap it in the plastic wrap and refrigerate. Decorate part of the cookies with currants replicating eyes, noses, and buttons. Bake for 7 minutes, until the edges just begin to brown. Do not overbake.

Using a thin spatula, place the baked cookies on waxed paper spread on the kitchen counter; let stand until completely cool.

Repeat the procedure with the remaining ½ of the cookie dough. Then, combine all the remaining dough and continue making cookies until all the dough is used; refrigerate the dough intermittently if it becomes too soft.

When the cookies have completely cooled, decorate them imaginatively with the Confectioners' Frosting, using a decorating bag fit with small round tip number 2 (page 319). Some suggestions: pipe hair, eyes, noses, mouths, shirt collars and cuffs, neckties, belts and buckles, trouser cuffs, skirts with ruffled trim, and short-sleeved blouses; pipe names of family members and friends on Gingerbread People (page 559). Let the cookies stand until the frosting sets.

Store the cookies, single layer, separated by plastic wrap, in an airtight container.

MAKES ABOUT 36 5-INCH-TALL GINGERBREAD PEOPLE

CUTOUT COOKIES

Select cookie cutters in patterns appropriate for various holidays and occasions, and then have fun turning out festive, decorated cookies using this basic cutout cookie recipe. See To Decorate Cutout Cookies at the end of the recipe for general decorating instructions and suggestions. Let your imagination take it from there.

4 cups cake flour
1 teaspoon baking soda
¾ teaspoon salt
½ cup vegetable shortening, softened
½ cup (¼ pound) butter, softened
1 cup sugar
2 extra-large eggs
2 teaspoons pure vanilla extract
¼ cup whole milk

Onto waxed paper, sift together the flour, baking soda, and salt; set aside.

In a large mixing bowl, place the vegetable shortening, butter, and sugar; using an electric mixer, cream well on medium-high speed. Add the eggs, one at a time, beating well on medium-high speed after each addition. Add the vanilla; beat on medium-high speed until light and fluffy. Add, alternately, the flour mixture in thirds, and the milk in halves, beating on low speed after each addition only until blended.

Divide the dough into thirds; wrap each third in plastic wrap and refrigerate at least 2 hours.

Preheat the oven to 350°F. Oil lightly 2 or 3 cookie sheets; set aside.

Remove 1 package of dough from the refrigerator. On a well-floured pastry cloth, using a stockinet-covered, then floured rolling pin (page 38), roll the dough to ⅛-inch thickness.

Dip the cutting edge of the cookie cutter of choice in flour; cut out the cookies. After each cut, wipe the excess dough off the cutter and redip it in flour. Using a thin spatula, place the cutout cookies, 2 inches apart, on the prepared cookie sheets. Gather the remaining dough on the pastry cloth into a ball; rewrap it in the plastic wrap and refrigerate. Bake the cookies for 9 to 10 minutes, or just until set. The bottoms will be pale or a very pale golden color. Do not overbake.

Using a thin spatula, place the baked cookies on waxed paper spread on the kitchen counter; let stand until completely cool.

Repeat the procedure with the remaining 2 packages of dough. Then, combine all the remaining dough from the 3 packages and continue making cookies until all the dough is used.

Store the cookies in an airtight container.

MAKES ABOUT 54 3-INCH CUTOUT COOKIES

TO DECORATE CUTOUT COOKIES

- Using a small, narrow, angled, tapered spatula, frost baked Cutout Cookies with Confectioners' Frosting (page 507) tinted in one or more colors of choice. Immediately after frosting the cookies, before the frosting dries, decorate them with colored sugar, nonpareils (page 7), cinnamon imperials (candy red hots), nuts, candied fruits, or other edible decorations.

- To decorate *unfrosted* Cutout Cookies, sprinkle or place colored sugar, nonpareils, nuts, etc. on the cookies before baking.

VALENTINE CUTOUT COOKIES

1 recipe Confectioners' Frosting (page 507)
Red and pink paste food coloring
1 recipe Cutout Cookies (page 560) made
    with a 3-inch, heart-shaped cookie cutter
½ recipe Cake Decorators' White Icing (page
    504)

Tint ⅓ of the Confectioners' Frosting red and ⅓ of the frosting pink; leave the remaining ⅓ of the frosting untinted (white). Using the Confectioners' Frosting and a small, narrow, angled and tapered spatula, frost ⅓ of the baked, heart-shaped Cutout Cookies with red frosting, ⅓ with pink frosting, and ⅓ with white frosting; let stand until the frosting sets.

Tint ⅓ of the Cake Decorators' White Icing red; leave the remaining ⅔ of the icing untinted (white). Fill one decorating bag with the red Cake Decorators' Icing and one decorating bag with the untinted Cake Decorators' White Icing. Using medium-small open-star tip number 16 (page 319), outline the frosting on the cookies with a shell border (page 324), piping a white border on the red- and pink-frosted cookies, and a red border on the white-frosted cookies. Let the cookies stand.

Using medium petal tip number 61 and a stick, pipe small white roses and red roses (page 327).

Place a rose in the center of each cookie, placing a white rose on red- and pink-frosted cookies, and a red rose on white- and pink-frosted cookies. (To attach the roses to the cookies, use small round tip number 3 to place a small dot of frosting in the center of each heart; then, position a rose on the dot of frosting on each heart to hold the rose in place. Pipe the dots 4 cookies at a time, and in the same color of frosting as the roses to be placed thereon.) Let the cookies stand until the frosting sets.

Then, store the cookies, single layer, in airtight containers.

MAKES ABOUT 54

SPRINGERLE

These beautiful, but very firm, traditional German Christmas cookies, imprinted with intricate Christmas designs and scenes, are often dunked in coffee when eaten. Sometimes they are allowed to become extremely dry and are drilled with tiny holes for hanging them on the Christmas tree.

3½ cups all-purpose flour
¼ teaspoon baking powder
⅛ teaspoon salt
4 extra-large eggs, room temperature
2 cups sugar
1 tablespoon finely grated lemon rind (page 31) (rind of about 3 lemons)
3 tablespoons anise seed
Additional sifted all-purpose flour
2 teaspoons anise seed (for storage container)

THE FIRST DAY: Onto waxed paper, sift together 3½ cups flour, baking powder, and salt; set aside.

Place the eggs in a large mixing bowl. Using an electric mixer, beat the eggs on high speed 8 minutes until thick. While continuing to beat on high speed, very gradually add the sugar (8 minutes additional beating time). Add the lemon rind; beat on high speed until evenly combined. Add the flour mixture in thirds, beating on low speed after each addition only until blended. The dough will be very thick and pasty. Cover the bowl and refrigerate the mixture 1 hour.

Grease lightly 3 cookie sheets. Sprinkle each greased cookie sheet evenly with 1 tablespoon anise seed; set aside.

On a lightly floured pastry cloth (page 38), knead the dough (pages 7, 348) about 5 minutes until pliable and smooth, kneading in additional sifted flour if necessary to make the dough stiff enough to hold the molded designs. Using a lightly floured rolling pin, roll the dough to ⅜-inch thickness. Sprinkle sifted flour lightly over the rolled dough. Using your fingers, spread the flour evenly and thinly over the surface of the dough; let stand. Flour individual, wooden springerle molds; tap the molds to remove the excess flour. Press the molds very firmly into the rolled dough to imprint designs (see Note). Do not remove any excess flour from the tops of the cookies.

Using a sharp, thin-bladed knife dipped in flour, carefully cut out the cookies. Clean the knife intermittently when the dough begins to stick to it; then, redip it in flour. Using a thin spatula, place the cookies, 1 inch apart, on the prepared cookie sheets. Gather any remaining dough and knead briefly; reroll, impress designs, and cut. Repeat the procedure until all the dough is used. Let the unbaked cookies stand, *uncovered,* at room temperature, 24 hours to dry.

NOTE: A floured, carved Springerle rolling pin may also be used to imprint the cookies; however, the impressions made in the dough using the special rolling pin are usually not as precise as those achieved using individual molds. One of my prize culinary possessions is an antique German Springerle rolling pin, given to me by my dear German friend, Gertrud Acksen (mother of Siegfried Hoerner, one of those to whom this cookbook is dedicated). Gertrud also gave me several lovely, modern, individual Springerle molds which she purchased in Stuttgart.

24 HOURS LATER: The surface of the cookies should be dry and quite hard.

Preheat the oven to 300°F.

Using a soft, ½-inch watercolor brush, brush a small amount of water on the bottom of each cookie, taking extreme care not to get *any* water on the top of the cookies. Replace the cookies on the cookie sheets. Bake the cookies for 15 minutes, until a faint straw color. (The cookies will be nearly white.)

Using a thin spatula, place the baked cookies on wire cookie racks. Brush the cookies lightly with a dry, soft brush to remove any excess flour; let stand until completely cool.

Sprinkle 2 teaspoons anise seed over the bottom of an airtight container (such as a tin); store the cookies in the container. (The additional anise seed in the storage container will enhance the anise flavor of the cookies.) Allow Springerle to season at least 1 week before serving.

MAKES ABOUT 48 TO 60, DEPENDING UPON THE SIZE OF THE COOKIES

ZIMTSTERNE
Cinnamon Stars

A German Christmas cookie.

2 cups slivered blanched almonds
1 *tablespoon* ground cinnamon
1 teaspoon finely grated lemon rind
    (page 47) (rind of about 1 lemon)
1/3 cup egg whites (about 2 extra-large egg
    whites*), room temperature
Dash of salt
2 cups powdered sugar, sifted (page 42) (sift
    after measuring)
1/2 cup to 1 cup powdered sugar, sifted
    (sift after measuring)

 * *About 3 large egg whites.*

In a food processor, process the almonds for *a few seconds* until ground. Be careful not to overprocess, reducing the nuts to butter. Place the ground almonds in a medium mixing bowl. Add the cinnamon; stir to combine. Add the lemon rind; stir to combine. Cover the bowl and set aside.

In a medium mixing bowl, place the egg whites and salt; using an electric mixer, beat on high speed until soft peaks hold. While continuing to beat on high speed, very gradually add 2 cups powdered sugar; beat well on high speed.

Measure 1/2 cup of the egg white mixture and place in a small container; cover tightly and set aside. Add the almond mixture the to remaining egg white mixture; using a small mixing spoon, fold in until combined. Cover and let stand 30 minutes to allow time for the almonds to absorb some of the moisture.

Meanwhile, line 3 cookie sheets with the parchment baking paper; set aside. Using powdered sugar, dust well a pastry cloth and stockinet-covered rolling pin (page 38).

Preheat the oven to 325°F.

Turn the almond mixture (dough) onto the pastry cloth. Dust your hands with powdered sugar and knead (pages 7, 348) just enough powdered sugar (about 1/2 cup to 1 cup) into the dough to make it stiff enough to roll and cut. Roll the dough to 1/4-inch thickness. Avoid rolling the dough any thicker, as this may cause the cookies to lose their shape during baking.

Using a 2-inch star cutter dipped in powdered sugar, cut out the cookies. After each cut, wipe the excess dough off the cutter and redip in powdered sugar. Using a thin spatula, place the cutout cookies, 1 inch apart, on the prepared cookie sheets. Gather the remaining dough on the pastry cloth into a ball; reroll and cut out additional cookies. Repeat the procedure until all the dough is used. Cover the cutout cookies with plastic wrap after each cookie sheet is filled.

Using a small, narrow, angled, and tapered spatula, frost the cookies with a thin layer of the reserved egg white mixture. To frost each cookie, use the spatula to place a small amount of the egg white mixture in the center of the cookie. Using a circular motion with the spatula, spread the mixture to form a small circle. Then, pull the mixture toward the points of the star. Replace the frosted cookies on the lined cookie sheets. Bake for 12 to 15 minutes. When done, Zimtsterne should be just slightly brown on the outside and chewy on the inside.

Using a thin spatula, place the baked cookies on wire cookie racks; let stand until completely cool.

Then, store the cookies in an airtight container.

MAKES ABOUT 66

PINWHEEL COOKIES

Pinwheel cookies are made in one of two ways: (1) rolled-out dough is spread with a filling, after which the dough (with filling) is rolled and then sliced into cookies ready for baking; or (2) two or three layers of rolled-out dough, each in a different color and sometimes a different flavor, are stacked, after which they are rolled together and then sliced into cookies ready for baking. The pinwheel design of the cookies created by either of these techniques stays intact after baking.

The recipes that follow use the second technique for making three different styles of stacked-dough pinwheel cookies: (1) the primary recipe makes two-layer pinwheel cookies with color as the only variation between the layers; (2) the Chocolate Pinwheels recipe makes two-layer pinwheel cookies with one of the layers chocolate flavored (and chocolate colored); and (3) the Triple-Layer Pinwheels recipe makes attractive three-colored cookies, with the option of flavoring one of the layers with chocolate.

3 cups sifted all-purpose flour (sift before
　　measuring)
½ teaspoon baking powder
¾ teaspoon salt
1 cup (½ pound) butter, softened
1 cup sugar
2 extra-large eggs
2 teaspoons pure vanilla extract
Pink paste food coloring*

* *Any color of paste food coloring may be
　substituted.*

AFTERNOON OF THE FIRST DAY: Onto waxed paper, sift together flour, baking powder, and salt; set aside.

In a large mixing bowl, place the butter and sugar; using an electric mixer, cream well on medium-high speed. Add the eggs, one at a time, beating well on medium-high speed after each addition. Add the vanilla; beat on medium-high speed until light and fluffy. Add the flour mixture in halves, beating on low speed after each addition only until blended.

Divide the dough in half in the mixing bowl. Remove ½ of the dough from the mixing bowl and wrap it in plastic wrap; refrigerate. Using a toothpick, add a small amount of food coloring to the remaining ½ of the dough; using the electric mixer, beat on low speed only until evenly tinted. Wrap the tinted dough in plastic wrap; refrigerate. Refrigerate all the dough 1 hour.

Then, remove the package of untinted dough from the refrigerator. On well-floured waxed paper, using a stockinet-covered, then floured rolling pin (page 38), roll the dough into a 10 × 14-inch rectangle. If necessary, patch the dough during rolling to achieve an accurately sized rectangle. Slide the waxed paper with the rolled dough onto a cookie sheet; cover it with plastic wrap and refrigerate.

Repeat the rolling and refrigerating procedure using the tinted dough. Refrigerate all the rolled dough 15 minutes.

Then, remove the plastic wrap covering the dough on both cookie sheets. Quickly invert the tinted dough on top of the untinted dough; peel the waxed paper off the tinted dough. Using the rolling pin, very lightly roll the top of the layered dough to slightly seal the layers.

Using a sharp, thin-bladed knife dipped in flour, cut the rectangle of dough in half widthwise, dividing the layered dough into two 7 × 10-inch rectangles. Using floured hands, tightly roll each rectangle, jelly-roll fashion, from the 7-inch side of the rectangles. Lift the waxed paper under the dough to assist in rolling it forward. (Do not roll the waxed paper into the dough.) After rolling each rectangle of dough, carefully press the seam to seal.

Wrap each 7-inch-long roll tightly in plastic wrap. Very lightly roll each plastic-covered roll on the counter to achieve even circles of dough; refrigerate overnight.

THE NEXT DAY: Preheat the oven to 400° F.

On a floured board, remove the plastic wrap from the rolls of cookie dough. Using a sharp, thin-bladed knife dipped in flour, slice the cookies a scant ¼ inch thick. Intermittently wipe the knife and redip it in flour. Place the sliced cookies, 1½ inches apart, on ungreased cookie sheets. Bake for about 7 minutes. Do not allow the cookies to brown, as browning will detract from the colors of the cookies.

Using a thin spatula, place the baked cookies on waxed paper spread on the kitchen counter; let stand until completely cool.

Then, store the cookies in an airtight container.

MAKES ABOUT 66

CHOCOLATE PINWHEELS

Place 1 ounce (1 square) semisweet chocolate in a tiny saucepan. Hold the tiny pan over (not touching) low simmering water in a small saucepan until the chocolate melts, stirring intermittently. Remove the tiny pan from the heat; set aside. Follow the Pinwheels Cookies recipe, above, substituting the melted chocolate for the pink paste food coloring (add it to the second ½ of the dough).

TRIPLE-LAYER PINWHEELS
(See photo insert page D-5)

Follow the Pinwheel Cookies recipe, above, dividing the dough into thirds rather than halves. Tint 2 or 3 of the thirds of the dough. If one of the thirds is to be chocolate, use ½ ounce (½ square) semisweet chocolate and follow the procedure in the Chocolate Pinwheels recipe.

Roll each third of the dough into a 10 × 10-inch rectangle. Stack all 3 rectangles of the dough together. Do not cut the layered dough in half before rolling; in other words, make only one pinwheel roll of dough.

SCOTCH SHORTBREAD

Scotland has given us this wonderfully rich, buttery cookie, which in that country was traditionally served on Christmas and New Year's Eve (there called Hogmanay). In American cooking nomenclature, Scotch Shortbread is definitely a cookie and does not remotely resemble bread, as its name implies. Shortbread is made with three ingredients: flour, sugar, and much butter (margarine won't do). Sometimes a scant amount of salt is added. I have chosen not to use salt but have taken the liberty of adding just a bit of baking powder, which I think makes the crisp texture of these tender cookies even lighter and more delicate.

Traditionally, shortbread was made one of two ways: (1) the dough was cut into round cookies that were notched on the edges to look like sun rays, or (2) the dough was pressed into a large, round, engraved mold, and after baking, the warm shortbread was cut into serving-sized wedges. Nowadays, Scotch Shortbread is made in all sorts of shapes, but I like making it in the shape of rectangular cookies, and adding a bit of tradition by imprinting a fluted design on the top of each cookie using the side of a fluted garnishing cutter.

2 cups sifted all-purpose flour (sift before measuring)
¼ teaspoon baking powder
1 cup (½ pound) butter, softened
½ cup powdered sugar

Onto waxed paper, sift together the flour and baking powder; set aside.

In a medium mixing bowl, place the butter and powdered sugar; using an electric mixer, beat on medium-high speed until *very* fluffy. Add the flour mixture; beat on low speed only until blended. Wrap the dough in plastic wrap and refrigerate about 2 hours.

Preheat the oven to 350° F.

Remove the dough from the refrigerator. If the dough is too stiff to roll, let it stand at room temperature in the plastic wrap for a few minutes. On a floured pastry cloth, using a stockinet-covered, then floured rolling pin (page 38), roll the dough to ⅜-inch thickness.

Using a ruler to measure, and a sharp, thin-bladed knife dipped in flour, cut the dough into precise 1¼ × 2-inch cookies. Using a small, thin

(Recipe continues on n0ext page)

spatula, carefully separate the cookies. Then, using the wide side of a floured, fluted garnishing cutter (see illustration, page 107), impress a wavy surface on the top of each cookie.

Using a thin spatula, place the cookies, 1½ inches apart, on ungreased cookie sheets. Gather the remaining dough into a ball, reroll, cut additional cookies, and impress the tops until all the dough is used. Bake the cookies for about 13 minutes. The cookies should be light in color.

Using a thin spatula, place the baked cookies on waxed paper spread on the kitchen counter. Handle carefully, as Scotch Shortbread breaks easily. Let them stand until completely cool.

Then, store the cookies in an airtight container.

MAKES ABOUT 24

DESIGNER FILLED COOKIES

These filled cookies are basically two cookies pressed together around the edge to contain a filling of jam, conserve, or mincemeat. The filling shows through a small round-, star-, or other-shaped opening cut out of the center of the top cookie.

4½ cups all-purpose flour
1½ teaspoons baking soda
½ teaspoon salt
1½ cups (¾ pound) butter, softened
2 cups sugar
4 extra-large eggs
2½ teaspoons pure vanilla extract
2 cups jam or conserve (page 4) of choice, or mincemeat
¼ cup sugar for decoration

Onto waxed paper, sift together the flour, baking soda, and salt; set aside.

In a large mixing bowl, place the butter and 2 cups sugar; using an electric mixer, cream well on medium-high speed. Add the eggs, one at a time, beating well on medium-high speed after each addition. Add the vanilla; continue beating on medium-high speed until fluffy. Add the

flour mixture in thirds, beating on low speed after each addition only until blended.

Divide the dough into fourths; wrap each fourth in plastic wrap and refrigerate at least 4 hours or overnight.

Preheat the oven to 375°F.

Remove 1 package of dough from the refrigerator. On a well-floured pastry cloth, using a stockinet-covered, then floured rolling pin (page 38), roll the dough to ⅛-inch thickness.

Using a 2¼-inch round cutter dipped in flour, cut out the cookie bottoms. After each cut, wipe the excess dough off the cutter and redip it in flour. Using a thin spatula, place the cutout cookie bottoms, 2 inches apart, on an ungreased cookie sheet. Gather the remaining dough on the pastry cloth into a ball; rewrap it in the plastic wrap and refrigerate.

Place ½ teaspoon conserve, mincemeat, or jam in the center of each cutout cookie bottom; set aside.

Remove another package of dough from the refrigerator and roll it to ⅛-inch thickness.

Using the 2¼-inch round cutter dipped in flour, cut out the cookie tops, leaving them on the pastry cloth. Then, using a floured ¾-inch round cutter (or any other small cutter, such as a scalloped or star-shaped cutter), make a cut in the center of each cutout cookie top. Using the spatula, place the cookie tops (minus the cutout centers) over the filled cookie bottoms. Using your fingers, lightly press the outside edge of the cookie tops to seal, maintaining the round shape of the cookies. Gather the remaining dough on the pastry cloth into a ball; rewrap it in the plastic wrap and refrigerate. Bake the cookies for 9 minutes. The edge of the cookies will be very lightly golden.

Using a thin spatula, place the baked cookies on waxed paper spread on the kitchen counter; let stand until completely cool.

Repeat the procedure with the remaining 2 packages of dough. Then, combine all the remaining dough and continue making cookies until all the dough is used.

Sprinkle a tiny amount of sugar around the top edge of the cool cookies, being careful not to sprinkle any sugar on the filling. Using a small, soft, watercolor brush, spread the sugar evenly around the top surface of each cookie.

Store the cookies in a loose container.

MAKES ABOUT 84

CHRISTMAS DESIGNER FILLED COOKIES

Follow the Designer Filled Cookies recipe above, using a 2½-inch star cutter and a 1-inch round, tiny-scalloped cutter to cut the cookies. Fill the cookies with any red-colored jam or conserve.

CREAM-FILLED PASTRY FLUFFS

Tint the cream filling of these dainty sandwich cookies in a soft, pastel shade to match your tea table, or make them in a color and flavor to complement selected fruit or ice cream for a nice party dessert. See Variations at the end of the recipe for several color/flavor suggestions.

¾ cup (¼ pound plus 4 tablespoons) butter
2 cups all-purpose flour
1 teaspoon salt
½ cup plus 2 teaspoons half-and-half
3 tablespoons sugar
Cream Filling (recipe below)

Preheat the oven to 375°F.

Remove the butter from the refrigerator and let stand 5 minutes before use in the recipe.

Onto waxed paper, sift together the flour and salt. Place the flour mixture in a large mixing bowl. Using a knife, cut the butter into approximately tablespoon-sized pieces and drop into the bowl containing the flour mixture. Using a pastry blender, cut the butter into the flour mixture until the mixture is the texture of very coarse cornmeal.

Tilt the mixing bowl and gently shake the flour mixture to one side of the bowl. Sprinkle 1 to 2 tablespoons of the half-and-half over the mixture; using a table fork, lightly rake the

moistened portion of the mixture to the other side of the bowl. Repeat the procedure until all the half-and-half has been added.

With floured hands, gather the pastry into a ball and place it on a floured pastry cloth. Using a stockinet-covered, then lightly floured rolling pin (page 38), roll the pastry to ⅛-inch thickness.

Using a 2-inch round, tiny-scalloped cookie cutter dipped in flour, cut the cookies. Using a small, thin spatula, carefully place the cookies, 1 inch apart, on an ungreased cookie sheet. Gather the remaining pastry on the pastry cloth into a ball; reroll and cut additional cookies. Repeat the procedure until all the pastry is used.

Using a table fork, deeply prick each cookie 3 times in 3 neat, parallel rows to form a square design. Using your fingers, sprinkle the cookies lightly with sugar. Bake for 10 minutes. Remove the cookies from the oven before they brown.

Using a thin spatula, carefully place the cookies on wire cookie racks; let stand until completely cool.

Then, using a small, narrow, tapered spatula, spread a small amount of the Cream Filling on the non-sugar-glazed side of ½ of the cookies. Cover the filled cookies with the remaining ½ of the cookies, sugar-glazed side up, to make sandwiches. Let the cookies stand on the wire cookie racks until the filling sets.

Then, store the cookies in a loose container.

MAKES ABOUT 36

CREAM FILLING

1 cup powdered sugar, sifted (page 42)
  (sift after measuring)
1 tablespoon plus 1 teaspoon butter, melted
2 teaspoons half-and-half
½ teaspoon clear vanilla
12 drops peppermint extract
1 drop green liquid food coloring

In a small mixing bowl, place the powdered sugar, butter, half-and-half, vanilla, peppermint

(Recipe continues on next page)

extract, and food coloring. Using an electric mixer, beat the mixture on medium-high speed only until blended and smooth.

VARIATIONS

- Substitute pink paste food coloring for the green liquid food coloring.

- To make Vanilla Cream Filling, increase the clear vanilla to ¾ teaspoon, and eliminate the peppermint extract and green liquid food coloring.

- To make Lemon Cream Filling, substitute lemon extract and yellow liquid food coloring for the peppermint extract and green liquid food coloring.

- To make Orange Cream Filling, substitute orange extract and orange paste food coloring for the peppermint extract and green liquid food coloring.

Refrigerator Cookies

OATMEAL REFRIGERATOR COOKIES

¾ cup all-purpose flour
½ teaspoon baking soda
½ teaspoon salt
½ cup (¼ pound) butter, softened
½ cup granulated sugar
½ cup packed light brown sugar
1 extra-large egg
½ teaspoon pure vanilla extract
1½ cups quick-cooking *or* old-fashioned rolled oats, uncooked
⅓ cup red maraschino cherries cut into eighths
¼ cup broken pecans

Onto waxed paper, sift together the flour, baking soda, and salt; set aside.

In a large mixing bowl, place the butter, granulated sugar, and brown sugar; using an electric mixer, cream well on medium-high speed. Add the egg and vanilla; beat on medium-high speed until well blended. Add the flour mixture; beat on low speed only until blended. Add the oatmeal, cherries, and pecans; using a large mixing spoon, stir and fold in until evenly combined.

Divide the dough in half. On a lightly floured pastry cloth (page 38), using floured hands, shape each half of the dough into a roll approximately 1¼ inches in diameter. Wrap each roll in plastic wrap. Refrigerate the rolls at least 2 hours. (The rolls may be refrigerated overnight.)

Preheat the oven to 350° F.

Remove the rolls of dough from the refrigerator and unwrap. Using a sharp, thin-bladed knife, cut the rolls into ¼-inch slices. Place the slices, 2 inches apart, on 3 ungreased cookie sheets. Bake for 10 minutes, until lightly golden.

Using a thin spatula, place the baked cookies on waxed paper spread on the kitchen counter; let stand until completely cool.

Then, store the cookies in an airtight container.

MAKES ABOUT 40

HOLIDAY VARIATION: For Christmas cookies, substitute ¼ cup red maraschino cherries and ¼ cup green maraschino cherries (cut into eighths) for ⅓ cup red maraschino cherries.

GUMDROP-OATMEAL COOKIES

Kids love them!

1 13-ounce package (2 cups) small gumdrops in assorted colors and flavors
1½ cups all-purpose flour
1 teaspoon baking soda
½ teaspoon salt
1 cup (½ pound) butter, softened
1 cup granulated sugar
1 cup packed light brown sugar

2 extra-large eggs
1 teaspoon pure vanilla extract
3 cups quick-cooking rolled oats, uncooked
½ cup broken pecans

THE FIRST DAY: Using kitchen scissors with wet blades, cut each gumdrop into 3 pieces; set aside. Onto waxed paper, sift together the flour, baking soda, and salt; set aside.

In a large mixing bowl, place the butter, granulated sugar, and brown sugar; using an electric mixer, cream well on medium-high speed. Add the eggs, one at a time, beating well on medium-high speed after each addition. Add the vanilla; continue beating on medium-high speed until fluffy. Add the flour mixture; beat on low speed only until blended. Add the oats; beat on medium speed only until combined. Add the gumdrops and pecans; using a large mixing spoon, stir and fold in until evenly distributed.

Divide the dough in half. On a lightly floured pastry cloth (page 38), using floured hands, shape each half of the dough into a roll approximately 14 inches long and 2¼ inches in diameter. Wrap each roll in plastic wrap. Refrigerate the rolls overnight.

THE NEXT DAY: Preheat the oven to 350°F.

Remove the rolls of dough from the refrigerator and unwrap. Using a sharp, thin-bladed knife, cut the rolls into ⅜-inch slices. Using your hands, reshape the circular form of the slices, if necessary. Place the slices, 2 inches apart, on ungreased cookie sheets. Bake for 12 minutes, until lightly golden.

Using a thin spatula, place the baked cookies on waxed paper spread on the kitchen counter; let stand until completely cool.

Then, store the cookies in an airtight container.

MAKES ABOUT 66

BUTTERSCOTCH ICEBOX COOKIES

2 cups all-purpose flour
½ teaspoon baking soda
½ teaspoon cream of tartar
½ cup (¼ pound) butter, softened
1 cup packed light brown sugar
1 extra-large egg
½ teaspoon pure vanilla extract
½ cup broken pecans

Onto waxed paper, sift together the flour, baking soda, and cream of tartar; set aside.

In a large mixing bowl, place the butter and brown sugar; using an electric mixer, cream well on medium-high speed. Add the egg and vanilla; continue beating on medium-high speed until fluffy. Add the flour mixture in halves, beating on low speed after each addition only until blended. Add the pecans; using a mixing spoon, stir and fold in until evenly distributed.

Divide the dough in half. On a lightly floured pastry cloth (page 38), using floured hands, shape each half of the dough into a roll approximately 10 inches long and 1¼ inches in diameter. Wrap each roll in plastic wrap. Refrigerate the rolls at least 2 hours.

Preheat the oven to 350°F.

Remove the rolls of dough from the refrigerator and unwrap. Using a sharp, thin-bladed knife, cut the rolls into ¼-inch slices. Place the slices, 2½-inches apart, on ungreased cookie sheets. Bake for 8 to 10 minutes. Watch closely; bake until golden, but not brown.

Using a thin spatula, place the baked cookies on waxed paper spread on the kitchen counter; let stand until completely cool.

Then, store the cookies in an airtight container.

MAKES ABOUT 72

Pressed Cookies

SPRITZ

Gaily decorated, Scandinavian Spritz cookies, pressed in many shapes, go hand in hand with Christmas. They are made by forcing the dough through a special cookie press. I suggest using a good-quality, manually operated cookie press rather than a battery-operated model, which I have found difficult to control. Wilton Enterprises (see Product Sources, page 631) makes an excellent manually operated cookie press.

2¾ cups all-purpose flour
¼ teaspoon salt
1 cup (½ pound) butter, softened
⅔ cup sugar
1 extra-large egg
½ teaspoon pure vanilla extract
½ teaspoon pure almond extract
Red- and green-colored sugar, nonpareils
   (page 7), red and green candied cherries,
   whole almonds, and pecan halves for
   decoration
Liquid or paste food coloring (optional)

Preheat the oven to 400°F.

Onto waxed paper, sift together the flour and salt; set aside.

In a medium mixing bowl, place the butter and sugar; using an electric mixer, cream well on medium-high speed. Add the egg; beat on medium-high speed until well blended. Add the vanilla and almond extracts; beat on medium-high speed until completely blended. Add the flour mixture in halves, beating on low speed after each addition only until blended.

Force the dough through a special cookie press for making spritz cookies onto ungreased cookie sheets, following the instructions which accompany the cookie press. Press the cookies 1 inch apart, using various disks of choice to make cookies of different shapes and designs.

If desired, part (or all) of the cookie dough may be tinted in a pale color (usually pale pink or pale green) before forcing it through the cookie press. To tint the dough, add a tiny amount of food coloring to the portion of dough to be tinted. Then, using the electric mixer, beat on low speed only until the dough is evenly colored.

Decorate the unbaked cookies attractively, using the suggested decorations in the ingredients list, above, or other decorative, edible items. If the dough is not moist enough to hold a particular decoration, use a small, soft, watercolor brush to brush a drop of water on the unbaked cookie where the decoration is to be placed.

After decorating the cookies, bake for 7 minutes. Watch the cookies closely and do not allow them to brown.

Using a thin spatula, place the baked cookies on waxed paper spread on the kitchen counter; let stand until completely cool.

Then, store the cookies in an airtight container.

MAKES ABOUT 90

Desserts and
Ice Cream

Desserts

CHERRY COBBLER

A cobbler is a thickened fruit mixture (like pie fill-ing) spread in a baking dish with batter spooned over the top, all of which is baked until the shortcake-like topping is golden and has risen over the bubbly fruit. Cobblers are cut into indi-vidual servings and served warm, preferably before they cool from baking. While any number of fruits, such as apples, blueberries, and pears, may be used to make cobblers, cherry and peach cobblers are the most Midwest-typical. (See the recipe for Peach Cobbler, page 573)

¼ cup (4 tablespoons) butter
1 cup sifted all-purpose flour (sift before
   measuring)
1½ teaspoons baking powder
½ teaspoon salt
2 tablespoons sugar
4 cups pitted, tart, fresh (or frozen and
   thawed) red cherries
1 cup juice drained from cherries (adding
   water if necessary) (see recipe procedures
   below)
1¼ cups sugar
2 tablespoons plus 2 teaspoons quick-cooking
   tapioca
⅛ teaspoon salt
2 tablespoons butter
1 extra-large egg
¼ cup whole milk
¼ teaspoon pure vanilla extract

Remove ¼ cup butter from the refrigerator and let stand 10 minutes before use in the recipe.

Onto waxed paper, sift together the flour, baking powder, ½ teaspoon salt, and 2 table-spoons sugar. Place the flour mixture in a large mixing bowl. Using a knife, cut the butter into approximately 12 pieces and drop into the bowl containing the flour mixture. Using a pastry blender, cut the butter into the flour mixture until the mixture is the texture of coarse crumbs. Cover the bowl and refrigerate.

Preheat the oven to 400° F.

Drain the cherries in a sieve, reserving the juice. Let the cherries stand. Measure 1 cup of the natural cherry juice, adding water, if neces-sary, to make 1 cup liquid. Pour the liquid into a large saucepan. Add 1¼ cups sugar, tapioca, and ⅛ teaspoon salt; stir to combine. Over medium-high heat, bring the mixture to a rolling boil (page 9), stirring constantly. Boil the mixture briskly 5 minutes, stirring almost constantly. Remove from the heat and add the cherries. Over medium-high heat, return the mixture to a rolling boil and boil an additional 5 minutes, continuing to stir. The mixture will be thickened and cooked. Remove from the heat. Add 2 table-spoons butter. Stir the cherry mixture until the butter melts and blends; set aside.

Place the egg in a very small mixing bowl. Using an electric mixer, beat the egg slightly on medium speed. Add the milk and vanilla; beat on medium speed only until blended; set aside. Remove the flour mixture from the refrigerator. Using a tablespoon, make a well in the center of the flour mixture. Pour the egg mixture, all at once, into the well in the flour mixture; using a small mixing spoon, stir and fold *only* until the flour mixture is moistened; set aside.

Pour the hot cherry mixture evenly into an ungreased 7 × 11 × 1½-inch baking dish. Using a mixing spoon, drop 8 approximately equal spoonfuls of the flour mixture, evenly spaced (2 rows of 4 spoonfuls each), over the cherry mixture. Do not spread or touch the flour mixture. It is not necessary to completely cover the cherry mixture, as the flour mixture will spread during baking, creating 8 distinct servings. Bake, uncovered, for 18 minutes. The topping will be golden.

Remove from the oven and place the baking dish on a wire rack.

Serve Cherry Cobbler warm (see Note). Cut

the cobbler into 8 servings and serve on individual plates.

NOTE: Cobbler is at its best when served warm shortly after baking rather than rewarmed at a later time.

SERVES 8

SERVING SUGGESTION: Vanilla ice cream (homemade, page 595, or commercial) may be served as an accompaniment.

PEACH COBBLER

See the headnote for Cherry Cobbler, page 572.

¼ cup (4 tablespoons) butter
1 cup sifted all-purpose flour (sift before measuring)
1½ teaspoons baking powder
½ teaspoon salt
2 tablespoons sugar
⅓ cup plus 2 tablespoons sugar
2 tablespoons plus 1 teaspoon cornstarch
¼ teaspoon ground nutmeg
½ cup plus 1 tablespoon water
4 cups peeled, halved, pitted, quartered, and sliced fresh peaches (about 5 large peaches)
2 tablespoons butter
1 extra-large egg
¼ cup whole milk
¼ teaspoon pure vanilla extract

Remove ¼ cup butter from the refrigerator and let stand 10 minutes before use in the recipe.

Onto waxed paper, sift together the flour, baking powder, salt, and 2 tablespoons sugar. Place the flour mixture in a large mixing bowl. Using a knife, cut the butter into approximately 12 pieces and drop into the bowl containing the flour mixture. Using a pastry blender, cut the butter into the flour mixture until the mixture is the texture of coarse crumbs. Cover the bowl and refrigerate.

Preheat the oven to 400°F.

In a large saucepan, place ⅓ cup plus 2 table-spoons sugar, cornstarch, nutmeg, and water; stir to combine. Place the cornstarch mixture over medium heat; stir constantly until the sugar melts and the mixture is smooth. Remove from the heat and set aside.

Prepare the peaches per ingredients list, above, and add the cornstarch mixture; using a wooden mixing spoon (to help avoid cutting the peach slices), stir briefly to combine. Over medium heat, bring the peach mixture to a simmer, stirring almost continuously using the wooden mixing spoon. Simmer the mixture until thickened (about 6 minutes), stirring almost continuously. Remove from the heat. Add the butter. Stir the peach mixture until the butter melts and blends; set aside.

Place the egg in a very small mixing bowl. Using an electric mixer, beat the egg slightly on medium speed. Add the milk and vanilla; beat on medium speed only until blended; set aside. Remove the flour mixture from the refrigerator. Using a tablespoon, make a well in the center of the flour mixture. Pour the egg mixture, all at once, into the well in the flour mixture; using a small mixing spoon, stir and fold *only* until the flour mixture is moistened; set aside.

Pour the hot peach mixture evenly into an ungreased 7 × 11 × 1½-inch baking dish. Using a mixing spoon, drop 8 approximately equal spoonfuls of the flour mixture, evenly spaced (2 rows of 4 spoonfuls each), over the peach mixture. Do not spread or touch the flour mixture. It is not necessary to completely cover the peach mixture, as the flour mixture will spread during baking, creating 8 distinct servings. Bake, uncovered, for 18 minutes. The topping will be golden.

Remove from the oven and place the baking dish on a wire rack.

Serve Peach Cobbler warm (see Note). Cut the cobbler into 8 servings and serve on individual plates.

NOTE: Cobbler is at its best when served warm shortly after baking rather than rewarmed at a later time.

SERVES 8

(Continues on next page)

SERVING SUGGESTIONS: Vanilla ice cream (home-made, page 595, or commercial) may be served as an accompaniment.

APPLE CRISP

(See photo insert page D-6)

When apple tree branches are so laden with juicy, ripe fruit that they threaten to break under the burden, apple desserts are as plentiful as the golden autumn leaves swirling gently in the cool winds. Of course, Apple Pie (page 409) is a Mid-west institution, but I dare say that nearly as many bubbling Apple Crisps fill the fall air with that captivating spicy-sweet fragrance. That's because Apple Crisp is so simple to make and the flavor so closely resembles Apple Pie. While Apple Pie reigns on a culinary throne, Apple Crisp is one of the handsome princes in the court.

½ cup (¼ pound) butter
½ cup granulated sugar
1 teaspoon ground cinnamon
¼ teaspoon ground nutmeg
5 cups pared, quartered, cored, and sliced
     apples* (about 4 large apples)
1 cup all-purpose flour
½ cup packed light brown sugar

  * *Golden Delicious apples are especially good for use in this recipe.*

Remove the butter from the refrigerator; let stand.

Preheat the oven to 350°F. Butter a 6 × 10-inch baking dish; set aside.

In a small mixing bowl, place the granulated sugar, cinnamon, and nutmeg; stir to combine; set aside.

As the apples are prepared, place them in a large mixing bowl. Sprinkle the cinnamon-nutmeg mixture over the apples; toss to combine. Turn the apple mixture into the prepared baking dish; spread evenly; set aside.

In a medium mixing bowl, place the flour

and brown sugar; stir to combine. Using a knife, cut the butter into approximately 16 pieces and drop into the bowl. Using a pastry blender, cut the butter into the flour mixture until it is the texture of coarse crumbs. Spoon the mixture evenly over the apples; do not press the mixture into the apples and do not be concerned about the mixture mounding considerably above the sides of the baking dish. The dessert will bake down and will not bubble over in the oven. Bake, uncovered, for 40 minutes, or until the apples are tender.

Serve warm or cool.

SERVES 8

SERVING SUGGESTIONS: Serve with Whipped Cream (page 309), vanilla ice cream (homemade, page 595, or commercial), or half-and-half.

VARIATION: Sprinkle ½ cup broken pecans, ½ cup plumped raisins (page 30), or ¼ cup of each over the apples prior to adding the flour mixture.

APPLE BROWN BETTY

Like Apple Crisp (page 574), Apple Brown Betty is baked in a baking dish. The principal difference between the two desserts is that a flour mixture is spooned over the top of Apple Crisp prior to bak-ing, while a bread crumb mixture is layered with the spicy apple mixture in Apple Brown Betty. Brown Betty is an American dessert dating back to the nineteenth century. The origin of the name is unknown. While Brown Betty may be made with peaches, pears, apricots, and other fruits, Apple Brown Betty is the most popular and tra-ditional way of making this great old dish.

½ cup sugar
½ teaspoon ground cinnamon
2 cups Fresh Bread Crumbs (page 33)
¼ cup (4 tablespoons) butter, melted
5 cups pared, quartered, cored, and sliced
     apples (about 4 large apples)
½ teaspoon finely grated lemon rind (page 31)

¼ cup water
1 tablespoon freshly squeezed, strained lemon juice

Preheat the oven to 375°F. Grease a 1½-quart round baking dish; set aside.

In a small mixing bowl, place the sugar and cinnamon; stir to combine; set aside. Place the bread crumbs in a medium mixing bowl. Drizzle the melted butter over the crumbs; toss lightly; set aside.

As the apples are prepared, place them in a large mixing bowl. Sprinkle the sugar mixture and lemon rind over the apples; toss to combine; set aside.

Distribute ⅓ of the bread crumb mixture evenly over the bottom of the prepared baking dish. Spread ½ of the apple mixture evenly over the bread crumb mixture. Cover the apple mixture with an additional ⅓ of the bread crumb mixture. Spread the remaining ½ of the apple mixture over the bread crumb mixture. Cover the apple mixture with the remaining ⅓ of the bread crumb mixture; set aside.

Pour the water and lemon juice into a glass measuring cup with a pouring spout; stir to blend. Pour evenly over the layered mixture in the baking dish. Bake, covered, for 30 minutes. Uncover and bake for an additional 20 minutes, or until the apples are tender.

SERVES 8

SERVING SUGGESTIONS

- Serve warm with a generous dollop of Whipped Cream (page 309) sprinkled sparingly with ground cinnamon for decoration.

- Place individual servings in large-sized sauce dishes or cereal bowls. Pass half-and-half in a medium-small pitcher at the table.

- Serve warm with warm Lemon Sauce (page 307).

APPLE DUMPLINGS

Whose heart is not warmed by the endearment "My sweet apple dumpling" from a loved one? The affectionate expression clearly derives from this dessert, which has been cherished through the years. In Horst Scharfenberg's cookbook The Cuisines of Germany, *there is an old recipe for apple dumplings, dated 1844, that calls for diced apples and grated white bread to be mixed with other ingredients and formed into balls (dumplings), which are then cooked in salted water. The dumplings are served with a wine sauce. But Apple Dumplings, as we know them, are whole, pared, and cored apples filled in the center with a spicy raisin mixture, and then wrapped in pastry and baked in a syrup that is often rose colored. They are usually served warm.*

What, exactly, are "dumplings"? Dumplings take many forms and are somewhat complex to define. See the definition on page 5 for various kinds of foods that may be categorized as dumplings.

2 cups water
1 cup sugar
¼ teaspoon ground cinnamon
¼ teaspoon ground nutmeg
3 tablespoons butter
3 drops red liquid food coloring (optional)
2 tablespoons sugar
⅛ teaspoon ground cinnamon
⅛ teaspoon ground nutmeg
¼ cup baking raisins
¼ cup golden raisins, plumped (page 30) and drained well
2 tablespoons packed light brown sugar
8 cups cold water
1 tablespoon white vinegar
1 tablespoon salt
6 medium-sized (not too large) apples
2 cups all-purpose flour
1 teaspoon baking powder
1 teaspoon salt
⅔ cup refrigerated lard
½ cup whole milk

(Recipe continues on next page)

1 tablespoon plus 2 teaspoons butter
2 teaspoons sugar

In a medium saucepan, place 2 cups water, 1 cup sugar, ¼ teaspoon cinnamon, and ¼ teaspoon nutmeg; stir to combine. Over high heat, bring the sugar mixture to a boil, stirring constantly. Remove from the heat. Add 3 tablespoons butter and the food coloring; stir until the butter melts and the mixture blends. Cover the syrup mixture and set aside.

In a small sauce dish, place 2 tablespoons sugar, ⅛ teaspoon cinnamon, and ⅛ teaspoon nutmeg; stir to combine; set aside. In a small mixing bowl, place the raisins, golden raisins, and brown sugar; stir to combine; set aside.

In a small kettle or large mixing bowl, place 8 cups water, vinegar, and salt; stir until the salt dissolves; set aside.

Wash and pare the apples (leave the apples whole). As the apples are prepared, drop them into the vinegar solution to prevent discoloration. Then, using an apple corer, core the apples and drop them back into the vinegar solution; set aside.

Preheat the oven to 375° F. Butter a 9 × 13-inch baking dish; set aside.

Onto waxed paper, sift together the flour, baking powder, and salt. Place the flour mixture in a large mixing bowl. Using a knife, cut the lard into approximately 12 pieces and drop about ⅔ of the pieces into the bowl. Using a pastry blender, cut the lard into the flour mixture until the mixture is the texture of cornmeal. Add the remaining ⅓ of the pieces of the lard; using the pastry blender, cut into the flour mixture until the size of small peas. Add the milk all at once; quickly stir only until the mixture is evenly moistened.

Using floured hands, gather the pastry into a ball and place it on a well-floured pastry cloth. Using a stockinet-covered, then floured rolling pin (page 38), roll the pastry into a rectangular shape, ⅛ inch thick. Using a ruler and a sharp, thin-bladed knife dipped in flour, cut the pastry into six 7-inch squares (it probably will be necessary to reroll the pastry scraps); set aside.

Drain the apples and rinse twice in clear water; drain well in a colander. Place the drained apples on 2 layers of paper towels and quickly dry them fairly well with additional paper towels.

Place 1 apple, stem side up, in the center of each pastry square. Loosely pack the raisin mixture into the core cavities of the apples, even with the top of the apples. Sprinkle 1 teaspoon of the cinnamon-nutmeg mixture over the top of each apple. Dot the top of the apples with the 1 tablespoon plus 2 teaspoons butter (slightly less than 1 teaspoon of butter per apple).

Bring the corners of the pastry together over the top of each apple; pinch together well to seal. Pinch the pastry edges together tightly to form pastry wings. Lightly fold the sealed wings against the side of each pastry-covered apple, folding each of the 4 wings in the same direction around the apple.

Place the dumplings, about 1 inch apart, in the prepared baking dish. Pour some of the syrup mixture over the dumplings and pour the remainder in the baking dish around the dumplings. Sprinkle the 2 teaspoons sugar over the dumplings (about ⅓ teaspoon of sugar per dumpling). Bake, uncovered, for 35 minutes, until the pastry is golden and the apples are tender.

Remove from the oven and place the baking dish on a wire rack. Serve 1 Apple Dumpling per person. Best served warm.

SERVES 6

SERVING SUGGESTIONS

- Serve alone on dessert plates.

- Serve in bowls and pass half-and-half in a pitcher at the table.

- Serve a small dish of vanilla ice cream (homemade, page 595, or commercial) on the side.

BAKED APPLES

Baked Apples are similar to Apple Dumplings (page 575); however, Baked Apples are not wrapped in pastry and are only partially pared. The cores of these Baked Apples are filled with applejack-soaked currants, dates, and walnuts, and the apples are baked in a spice-flavored, buttery, maple syrup mixture—a perfect dessert for informal, company fare.

¼ cup currants, plumped (page 30) and drained well
¼ cup chopped dates, plumped (page 30) and drained well
2 tablespoons finely broken English walnuts
1 tablespoon packed light brown sugar
¼ cup applejack (page 2)
1 cup pure maple syrup
½ teaspoon ground cinnamon
¼ teaspoon ground nutmeg
2 tablespoons butter
8 cups cold water
1 tablespoon white vinegar
1 tablespoon salt
6 medium-sized red-skinned apples
1 tablespoon plus 2 teaspoons butter
2 cups (1 pint) half-and-half
½ recipe Whipped Cream (page 309)

In a small mixing bowl, place the currants, dates, walnuts, brown sugar, and applejack; stir to combine. Cover the bowl with plastic wrap; set aside.

In a small saucepan, place the maple syrup, cinnamon, and nutmeg; stir to combine. Over medium-high heat, bring the syrup mixture to a boil, stirring constantly. Remove from the heat. Add 2 tablespoons butter; stir until the butter melts. Cover the syrup mixture and set aside.

Preheat the oven to 350°F. Butter a 7 × 11-inch baking dish; set aside.

In a small kettle or large mixing bowl, place 8 cups water, vinegar, and salt; stir until the salt dissolves; set aside.

Wash the apples and leave them whole; do not pare. Using an apple corer, core the apples. As the apples are cored, drop them into the vinegar solution to prevent discoloration.

Then, starting at the stem end, pare approximately the top ¼ of each apple, leaving the skin on the lower ¾ of each apple. As the apples are pared, drop them back into the vinegar solution.

Drain the apples and rinse twice in clear water; drain well in a colander. Place the drained apples on 2 layers of paper towels and quickly dry them fairly well with additional paper towels.

Place the apples, stem side up, in the prepared baking dish. Pack the currant mixture into the core cavities of the apples. Strain the remaining currant mixture liquid in a small sieve. Pour the strained liquid into the packed core cavities and over the tops of the apples.

Spoon some of the syrup mixture over the apples and pour the remainder in the baking dish around the apples. Dot the top of the apples with the 1 tablespoon plus 2 teaspoons butter (slightly less than 1 teaspoon of butter per apple). Bake, uncovered, until fork-tender (about 30 to 40 minutes, depending upon the size and type of apples). Baste 2 or 3 times during baking.

Serve the Baked Apples warm in individual bowls. Spoon some of the liquid in the baking dish over each apple. Pass a small pitcher of half-and-half and a bowl of Whipped Cream at the table; diners may prefer one or the other or both. Some prefer to eat Baked Apples plain.

SERVES 6

FRUIT COCKTAIL DESSERT

This is a perfect choice for a dessert party, such as a shower, when nothing else but coffee or tea will be served. It's rich and wonderful enough to carry the day. If guests ask you to share the recipe—and

(Recipe continues on next page)

it's a sure bet they will—more than likely they will be surprised when you disclose that this delectable contains canned fruit cocktail.

1 17-ounce can fruit cocktail in heavy syrup
¼ cup reserved fruit cocktail syrup
10 red maraschino cherries, cut in half lengthwise
¾ cup packed light brown sugar
¾ cup broken English walnuts
1 cup granulated sugar
1 cup all-purpose flour
1 teaspoon baking soda
¼ teaspoon salt
2 extra-large eggs
1 teaspoon pure vanilla extract
1 8-ounce can crushed pineapple in its own juice
1 recipe Whipped Cream (page 309)
8 red maraschino cherries, cut in half, for decoration

Preheat the oven to 350°F. Grease and flour (page 517) a 9 × 13 × 2-inch baking pan; set aside.

Drain the fruit cocktail well in a sieve, reserving ¼ cup syrup. Set the reserved syrup aside. Add the 10 halved maraschino cherries to the fruit cocktail; set aside. In a small mixing bowl, place the brown sugar and walnuts; stir to combine; set aside.

Onto waxed paper, sift together the granulated sugar, flour, baking soda, and salt. Place the flour mixture in a large mixing bowl; stir briefly to completely combine. Using the spoon, make a well in the center of the flour mixture; set aside.

Place the eggs in a medium mixing bowl. Using an electric mixer, beat the eggs briefly on medium speed. Add the vanilla and ¼ cup reserved syrup; beat on medium speed to blend. Add the fruit cocktail (and cherries); using a large mixing spoon, stir to combine.

Pour the fruit cocktail mixture, all at once, into the well in the flour mixture; using the large mixing spoon, stir and fold only until the mixture blends and the fruit cocktail is evenly distributed.

Turn the mixture into the prepared baking pan; using a small, narrow, angled spatula, spread evenly. Using a tablespoon, sprinkle the brown sugar mixture evenly over the top of the mixture in the baking pan. Bake for 30 minutes, until golden.

Remove from the oven and place the baking pan on a wire rack; let stand until the dessert completely cools. Then, cover the dessert tightly with aluminum foil or a baking-pan cover. Store at room temperature.

Shortly before serving, drain the pineapple in a small sieve. Using the back of a tablespoon, press and stir the pineapple until as much additional syrup as possible has been extracted. (Reserve the syrup for other uses.) Add the drained pineapple to the Whipped Cream; using a spoon, fold in until evenly combined.

To serve, cut the dessert into 15 servings and place the servings on individual plates. Spoon the whipped cream mixture over each serving. Decorate the whipped cream mixture on each serving with ½ maraschino cherry.

SERVES 15

RHUBARB RAPTURE

This rapturous dessert baked in a pan is composed of a fresh rhubarb mixture, with eggs and flour as thickeners, baked over a flaky, sweetened crust made with butter. Rhubarb has never been so lusciously ensconced! Go all the way and crown the top of each serving with a spoonful of whipped cream, or serve vanilla ice cream on the side.

¼ cup (4 tablespoons) butter
1 cup all-purpose flour
¼ cup plus 1 tablespoon powdered sugar
4 cups fresh rhubarb cut diagonally into 1½-inch lengths
1 cup all-purpose flour
2 cups granulated sugar
Dash of salt
3 extra-large eggs, beaten

Remove the butter from the refrigerator and let stand 10 minutes before use in the recipe.

Preheat the oven to 325° F.

Onto waxed paper, sift together 1 cup flour and the powdered sugar. Place the flour mixture in a large mixing bowl. Using a knife, cut the butter into approximately 8 pieces and drop into the bowl containing the flour. Using a pastry blender, cut the butter into the flour mixture until the mixture is the texture of coarse cornmeal interspersed with some pieces the size of small peas.

Turn the mixture into an ungreased 9 × 13 × 2-inch baking pan. Using the back of a tablespoon, pat the mixture firmly into the bottom of the pan. Bake for 10 minutes, until golden brown.

Remove from the oven and place the baking pan on a wire rack; let stand until the baked crust completely cools.

Preheat the oven to 350° F.

Place the rhubarb in a large mixing bowl; set aside.

Carefully butter the sides of the baking pan *above* the cooled, baked crust; set aside.

In a medium mixing bowl, place 1 cup flour, granulated sugar, and salt; stir to combine. Add the eggs; stir only until combined. Pour the flour mixture over the rhubarb (with accumulated juice); stir lightly.

Using a large mixing spoon, spoon the rhubarb mixture evenly and carefully over the baked crust. Bake for 35 to 40 minutes. The top will be golden.

Remove from the oven and place the baking pan on the wire rack; let stand until the dessert completely cools.

To serve, cut the dessert into 15 servings and place on individual plates.

SERVES 12

SERVING SUGGESTIONS: Serve with vanilla ice cream (homemade, page 595, or commercial) or Whipped Cream (page 309).

CREAMY RICE PUDDING

1 cup whole milk
1 cup water
¾ cup parboiled* long-grain rice (not instant)
1 tablespoon butter
¼ teaspoon salt
2 extra-large eggs
¾ cup whole milk
½ cup half-and-half
½ cup sugar
¼ teaspoon finely grated lemon rind (page 31)
1 teaspoon pure vanilla extract
½ cup baking raisins
Ground cinnamon for garnish

See Parboiled Rice, page 228.

Preheat the oven to 325° F. Butter a 1½-quart round or oval baking dish; set aside.

Into a medium saucepan, pour 1 cup milk and 1 cup water; stir to blend. Bring the mixture to a boil over medium heat. Add the rice, butter, and salt; stir to combine. Cover the saucepan and reduce the heat. Bring the rice mixture to a simmer, stirring occasionally. Simmer the rice mixture, covered, for 20 minutes, continuing to stir occasionally.

Remove the rice mixture from the heat; let stand, covered, until the liquid is completely absorbed (about 10 minutes).

Meanwhile, place the eggs in a medium mixing bowl. Using an electric mixer, beat the eggs slightly on medium speed. Add ¾ cup milk, half-and-half, sugar, lemon rind, and vanilla; stir to blend and combine. Add about 1 cup of the rice to the egg mixture; stir to combine. Add the remaining rice; stir to combine. Add the raisins; stir until evenly distributed.

Turn the mixture into the prepared baking dish. Carefully stir the mixture to assure that the rice and raisins are evenly distributed in the dish. Sprinkle the cinnamon lightly over the mixture. Place the baking dish in a 9 × 13 × 2-inch baking pan. Then, pour approximately 1¼ inches of very hot (not boiling) water into the

(Recipe continues on next page)

pan around the baking dish. Bake, uncovered, for 45 to 50 minutes, or until a table knife inserted into the pudding near the center of the baking dish comes out clean.

Remove the baking dish from the baking pan and place on a wire rack.

Creamy Rice Pudding is best when served warm; however, it may also be served cold (store the pudding, covered, in the refrigerator).

SERVES 8

SERVING SUGGESTION: Whether served warm or cold, individual servings of pudding may be topped with Whipped Cream (page 309) and sprinkled sparingly with ground cinnamon.

VARIATION: Ground nutmeg may be substituted for ground cinnamon.

OLD-FASHIONED RICE PUDDING (NO EGGS)

½ cup parboiled* long-grain rice (not instant)
4 cups (1 quart) whole milk
⅓ cup sugar
½ teaspoon salt
1 tablespoon butter
½ cup baking raisins
¼ teaspoon ground cinnamon
1 teaspoon pure vanilla extract
Additional ground cinnamon for decoration

***See Parboiled Rice, page 228.**

Preheat the oven to 300°F. Butter a 1½-quart round or oval baking dish; set aside.

In a medium mixing bowl, place the rice, milk, sugar, and salt; stir to combine. Add the butter in a single piece.

Pour the mixture into the prepared baking dish. Bake for 1 hour, stirring the mixture every 15 minutes.

Remove from the oven. Add the raisins and ¼ teaspoon cinnamon; stir to combine. Return to the oven. Bake for an additional 1 hour, stirring the mixture after 30 minutes.

Remove from the oven. Add the vanilla; stir to blend. Sprinkle the cinnamon over the top of the pudding to decorate.

Return the pudding to the oven; bake for an additional 30 minutes, undisturbed. Serve warm or cold.

SERVES 6

SERVING SUGGESTION: Whether served warm or cold, the pudding may be topped with a dollop of Whipped Cream (page 309).

TAPIOCA PUDDING

NOTE: This recipe contains uncooked egg whites (see page 220).

2 EXTRA-LARGE EGGS, SEPARATED
⅓ cup quick-cooking tapioca
⅓ cup sugar
¼ teaspoon salt
4 cups (1 quart) whole milk
1½ teaspoons pure vanilla extract
2 tablespoons sugar

Place the egg yolks in the top of a double boiler. Using a handheld electric mixer, beat the egg yolks slightly on medium speed; set aside. In a small mixing bowl, place the tapioca, ⅓ cup sugar, and salt; stir to combine; set aside.

Pour the milk into a medium saucepan. Scald the milk (page 9). Add about ½ cup of the scalded milk to the egg yolks and quickly stir in. Add the tapioca mixture to the egg yolk mixture; stir to combine. Add the remaining scalded milk; stir to blend. Place the top of the double boiler over boiling water in the bottom pan. Cook the tapioca mixture until thick (about 10 minutes), stirring frequently.

Remove the top of the double boiler from the bottom pan and place it on a wire rack. Add the vanilla; stir until fully blended. Let the mixture stand until cooled slightly; then, refrigerate until cooled to room temperature, stirring occasionally.

Remove the tapioca mixture from the refrigerator; set aside. Place the egg whites in a medium mixing bowl. Using an electric mixer, beat the egg whites on high speed until soft peaks hold. While continuing to beat on high speed, very gradually add 2 tablespoons sugar and continue beating the egg white mixture until stiff, but still moist and glossy. Spoon the tapioca mixture over the egg white mixture; using a large mixing spoon, quickly fold in. Refrigerate, uncovered, until chilled. Then, cover and keep refrigerated.

SERVES 8

SERVING SUGGESTIONS

• Top individual servings with Whipped Cream (page 309). Place ½ red maraschino cherry atop the whipped cream on each serving.

• Top individual servings with sliced fresh peaches or other fruit and a dollop of Whipped Cream (page 309).

RED RASPBERRY TAPIOCA

1 cup fresh red raspberries
½ cup sugar
¼ cup quick-cooking tapioca
Dash of salt
1 tablespoon freshly squeezed, strained lemon juice
1 recipe Whipped Cream (page 309)
6 whole raspberries for decoration
6 small, fresh mint leaves for decoration

Place 1 cup raspberries in a flat-bottomed pan. Using a potato masher, crush the raspberries. Add the sugar; stir to combine. Let the raspberry mixture stand 1 hour.

Then, turn the raspberry mixture (including the liquid) into a sieve placed over a deep pan; drain well. Let the crushed raspberries stand in the sieve. Add enough water to the drained liquid to make 2 cups liquid. Pour the measured liquid into the top of a double boiler; set aside.

Press the crushed raspberries in the sieve through a food mill to remove the seeds; set aside the raspberry pulp (with the additional accumulated juice).

Add the tapioca and salt to the liquid in the top of the double boiler; stir to combine. Place the top of the double boiler over simmering water in the bottom pan. Cook the mixture until the tapioca is transparent (about 15 minutes), stirring constantly.

Remove the top of the double boiler from the bottom pan and place it on a wire rack. Add the raspberry pulp and lemon juice; stir to combine. Refrigerate the tapioca, uncovered, until chilled. Then, cover and keep refrigerated.

To serve, spoon the Red Raspberry Tapioca into footed goblets. Top with the Whipped Cream. Decorate each serving with a whole raspberry and a small mint leaf. Place each goblet on a small (bread and butter–sized), doily-lined plate.

SERVES 6

DATE PUDDING WITH AMBER SAUCE

(See photo insert page D 7)

Awarded first place overall in the Recipes of Yesteryear division (29 classes) at the 1989 Iowa State Fair.

The food that comes to mind when most of us think of pudding is a thick, soft, creamy dessert made with eggs, milk, sugar, flavoring, and a thickener—most commonly flour, cornstarch, or tapioca. However, other foods also are designated as "pudding" in culinary nomenclature. One of the types of foods historically called pudding is a dense, rich, cakelike dessert that is either baked or steamed and often is served with a sauce; for example, this classic Date Pudding with Amber Sauce, which is baked, and traditional English Plum Pudding (page 582), which is steamed.

(Recipe continues on next page)

1 8-ounce package chopped dates (1 cup
   packed dates)
1 teaspoon baking soda
1 cup boiling water
1½ cups sifted cake flour (sift before measuring)
½ teaspoon salt
2 tablespoons butter, softened
1 cup sugar
1 extra-large egg
1 teaspoon pure vanilla extract
½ cup broken English walnuts
Amber Sauce (recipe follows)

Place the dates in a small saucepan. Sprinkle the baking soda over the dates. Add the boiling water; cover and let stand until cool.

Then, preheat the oven to 325°F. Using Special Grease (page 40), grease an 8 × 8 × 2-inch baking pan (see Note); set aside.

Onto waxed paper, sift together the flour and salt; set aside.

In a medium mixing bowl, place the butter and sugar; using an electric mixer, cream well on medium-high speed. Add the egg and vanilla; beat on medium-high speed until blended. Add, alternately, the flour mixture in thirds, and the date mixture (including the liquid) in halves, beating on low speed after each addition only until blended. Add the walnuts; using a medium mixing spoon, stir and fold in until evenly distributed.

Turn the batter into the prepared baking pan. Using a small, narrow, angled spatula, lightly and quickly spread the batter evenly in the pan. Bake for 40 to 45 minutes, or until a wooden toothpick inserted into the center of the pudding comes out clean.

Remove the pudding from the oven and place on a wire rack.

Serve the Date Pudding warm, with warm Amber Sauce spooned over each serving. Cut the pudding into 9 servings.

NOTE: Although not as satisfactory, the pan may be greased and floured in substitution for using Special Grease.

SERVES 9

AMBER SAUCE

¼ cup (4 tablespoons) butter
1 cup packed light brown sugar
½ cup light corn syrup
½ cup half-and-half
1 teaspoon pure vanilla extract

In a small saucepan, melt the butter over low heat. Remove from the heat. Add the brown sugar and corn syrup; stir to combine. Add the half-and-half; stir well. Return to low heat. Cook slowly until the sugar dissolves and the sauce is thick, stirring constantly. Add the vanilla; stir to blend.

VARIATION: The Date Pudding and Amber Sauce recipes may be doubled. Bake the pudding in a 9 × 13 × 2-inch baking pan.

ENGLISH PLUM PUDDING

English Plum Pudding is a historical Christmas pudding steamed in a tall mold. (For more information about this type of pudding, see the headnote for Date Pudding with Amber Sauce, page 581.) Among the traditional ingredients in English Plum Pudding are raisins, currants, candied fruits, almonds, suet, bread crumbs, spices, and brandy. So why no plums in plum pudding? Research reveals that raisins used in desserts were called plums in the seventeenth century.

For the full beauty and grandeur of this aristocratic dessert, brandy is customarily poured over the top of it and ignited at the table before the pudding is sliced. Hard sauce traditionally is spooned over the individual servings—a snowy white foil for the dark pudding.

1½ cups raisins
1½ cups currants
1 cup cognac (page 4)
2 tablespoons diced candied citron
2 tablespoons diced candied orange peel
2 tablespoons diced candied lemon peel
1 cup chopped, slivered blanched almonds
   (page 35)

1½ cups fine, Fresh Bread Crumbs (page 33) (about 3 slices of bread)

1 cup (about ¼ pound) finely ground beef suet

1¾ cups unpared, quartered, cored, and medium-coarsely grated Golden Delicious apples (about 2 large apples)

1 cup all-purpose flour

½ cup sugar

½ teaspoon salt

1 teaspoon ground cinnamon

½ teaspoon ground allspice

½ teaspoon ground cloves

3 extra-large eggs

1 cup light (mild-flavored) molasses

1½ teaspoons very finely grated lemon rind (page 31) (rind of about 1 large lemon)

1 recipe Hard Sauce (recipe follows)

EVENING OF FIRST DAY: In a medium glass bowl, place the raisins and currants; stir to combine. Add the cognac; stir until the fruits are coated. Cover the bowl tightly with plastic wrap; then, cover securely with aluminum foil. Let the mixture stand at room temperature.

THE NEXT DAY: Using vegetable shortening, grease well a 2-liter or 2-quart pudding steamer with cover (do not grease the cover); set aside.

Place a wire rack in the bottom of a large (such as 12-quart) kettle. On the wire rack, spread a 4-layer, damp piece of cheesecloth to prevent the pudding steamer from moving during the steaming process. Cover the kettle and set aside.

Turn the soaked raisins and currants, together with the cognac liquid, into a sieve placed over a deep pan. Using the back of a spoon, press the fruits against the sieve to extract as much liquid as possible. Let the fruits stand in the sieve to continue draining while preparing the other pudding ingredients.

In a large mixing bowl, place the citron, orange peel, lemon peel, and almonds; stir to combine. Cover the bowl with plastic wrap; set aside. In a medium mixing bowl, place the bread crumbs and suet; using your hands, rub the crumbs and suet together. Add the bread crumb mixture to the candied fruits mixture; stir to combine. Re-cover and set aside.

Prepare the apples; set aside. Transfer the raisins and currants from the sieve to a large mixing bowl; set aside. Reserve the cognac liquid.

Place the flour in a small mixing bowl. Sprinkle 2 tablespoons of the flour over the candied fruits-bread crumb mixture; stir to evenly coat; set aside. Sprinkle another 2 tablespoons of the flour over the raisin-currant mixture; stir to evenly coat; set aside. Onto waxed paper, sift together the remaining flour, sugar, salt, cinnamon, allspice, and cloves; set aside.

Place the eggs in an *extra-large* mixing bowl. Using an electric mixer, beat the eggs well on medium-high speed. Add the molasses, lemon rind, and reserved cognac liquid; beat on medium-high speed until completely blended. Add the flour mixture; beat on low speed only until blended. Add the apples; using a large mixing spoon, fold in until evenly combined. Add the candied fruits-bread crumb mixture and raisin-currant mixture; using the large mixing spoon, fold in and stir until evenly combined.

Spoon and gently press the batter into the prepared pudding steamer. The steamer should be about ¾ (or slightly more) full. Place the cover on the steamer and secure it closed. Place the steamer on the damp cheesecloth spread over the wire rack in the kettle. Pour boiling water into the kettle around the steamer until the surface of the water is approximately 2 inches below the top rim of the steamer. Cover the kettle.

Over high heat, bring the water in the kettle to a low simmer. Immediately reduce the heat to warm or low to maintain a low simmer. Steam the pudding for 6 hours. If necessary, add *boiling* water to the kettle once or twice to maintain the water depth. *Do not uncover the pudding steamer during the entire steaming period.*

At the end of the steaming period, remove the steamer from the kettle and place on a wire rack. Uncover the steamer; let stand 15 minutes.

Then, run a sharp, thin-bladed knife around the inside edge of the steamer and then around the center tube, running the knife only about ½ inch below the surface of the pudding. Quickly

(Recipe continues on next page)

dip the steamer in and out of a kettle of cold water, being careful not to get any water on the pudding. Using a kitchen towel, quickly wipe the outside of the steamer to remove the excess water.

Place a silver or other attractive serving tray over the top of the steamer; invert and carefully lift the steamer off the pudding.

Using a sharp, thin-bladed knife dipped in hot water, slice the pudding like a cake and serve hot. (English Plum Pudding is very rich, so guard against cutting the servings too large.) Let the diners spoon a dollop of the Hard Sauce over their servings of pudding.

NOTE: English Plum Pudding is best when ripened 24 hours after steaming. This procedure achieves a better blend of the flavors. To ripen, proceed as follows:

Remove the steamer from the kettle after steaming and place on a wire rack. Uncover the steamer; let stand 2 hours. Re-cover and let stand until completely cool. Then, store the steamer containing the pudding on the wire rack in a cold place. (The pudding may be stored in the refrigerator.)

To reheat before serving, replace the covered steamer on the dampened piece of cheesecloth spread over the wire rack in the kettle. Carefully pour the boiling water into the kettle, following the same procedure as when previously steaming the pudding. Steam the pudding for 1 hour. Then, follow the recipe.

SERVES 16

HARD SAUCE

½ cup (¼ pound) **butter, softened**
1 teaspoon **pure vanilla extract**
1 cup **powdered sugar, sifted (page 42)**
  (sift after measuring)

Place the butter in a medium-small mixing bowl. Using an electric mixer, beat the butter on medium-high speed until *very* fluffy. Add the vanilla; beat on medium-high speed until blended. While continuing to beat on medium-high speed, slowly add the powdered sugar, 1 heaping tablespoon at a time, and continue beating the mixture until light and smooth.

Spoon the Hard Sauce into a small crystal or silver bowl. Serve soon after making; do not refrigerate.

TO FLAME THE PUDDING AT SERVING TIME: The English Plum Pudding may be flamed at serving time, if desired.

1 teaspoon **butter**
6 cubes **sugar**
¼ cup **hot cognac**

Unmold the pudding on a *hot* silver or ovenproof serving plate. Dot the top of the pudding with the butter. Place the sugar cubes equidistant from each other around the top of the pudding. Place the serving plate on a hot pad to protect the serving table; lower the lights in the room. Pour the hot cognac evenly over the top of the pudding and ignite with a match. Immediately begin basting the pudding with the ignited cognac and lightly pressing the sugar cubes to prolong the flaming. When the flames stop, remove any remaining sugar cubes. Slice the pudding and serve.

SNOW PUDDING

Elegantly understated, Snow Pudding is an egg-white foam delicately lemon flavored, with thin Custard Sauce gracefully spooned over the top like the winter sun over crystalline snow.

NOTE: This recipe contains uncooked egg whites (see page 220).

¼ cup cold water
2 teaspoons (1 envelope) unflavored gelatin
½ cup sugar
1 cup boiling water
3 tablespoons freshly squeezed, strained
   lemon juice
3 extra-large egg whites (reserve yolks for the
   Custard Sauce)
¼ cup sugar
1 recipe Custard Sauce (page 308)

Place ¼ cup cold water in a small mixing bowl. Sprinkle the gelatin over the water; let stand 15 minutes.

Then, add ½ cup sugar and 1 cup boiling water to the gelatin mixture; stir until the sugar completely dissolves. Add the lemon juice; stir to blend. Refrigerate the gelatin mixture until it begins to set and is the consistency of unbeaten egg whites, stirring occasionally.

Then, remove the gelatin mixture from the refrigerator; set aside. Place the egg whites in a medium mixing bowl. Using an electric mixer, beat the egg whites on high speed until soft peaks hold. While continuing to beat on high speed, very gradually add ¼ cup sugar and continue beating the egg white mixture until stiff, but still moist and glossy.

Pour the gelatin mixture over the egg white mixture; using a large mixing spoon, fold in until nearly blended. Using the electric mixer, beat the mixture *briefly* on high speed to thoroughly blend.

Turn the mixture into a bowl; refrigerate until cold and set. Then, cover the bowl.

To serve, spoon the gelatin mixture (snow) into sherbet glasses; spoon Custard Sauce generously over the gelatin mixture. Place each glass on a small (bread and butter-sized), doily-lined plate.

SERVES 8

ALTERNATIVE SERVING PROCEDURE: To serve the Snow Pudding on a buffet or at the table, turn the gelatin mixture into a *very* lightly oiled 1-quart mold (see To Lightly Oil a Salad Mold, page 89) after blending. Unmold (page 89) on a

flat, crystal plate. Serve the Custard Sauce alongside, in an attractive sauce dish with a ladle.

BREAD PUDDING WITH LEMON SAUCE

4 cups (1 quart) whole milk
2 cups Dried Bread Cubes (page 32)
   (cut good-quality, unsliced white bread into
   ⅝-inch-square cubes)
¾ cup sugar
½ teaspoon salt
1 tablespoon butter, melted
4 extra-large eggs
1 teaspoon pure vanilla extract
1 recipe Lemon Sauce with Raisins
   (page 308)

Preheat the oven to 350°F. Butter a 1½-quart round or oval baking dish; set aside.

Pour the milk into a medium saucepan. Scald the milk (page 9). Remove from the heat. Add the bread cubes; stir carefully, only until the bread cubes are coated with milk. Let the mixture stand 5 minutes.

Then, add the sugar, salt, and butter to the bread cube mixture; stir well; set aside.

Place the eggs in a small mixing bowl. Using an electric mixer, beat the eggs slightly on medium speed. Pour approximately ¼ cup liquid from the bread cube mixture over the eggs; stir quickly to blend. Then, add the egg mixture to the remaining bread cube mixture; stir to blend with the liquid in the bread cube mixture. Add the vanilla; stir to blend.

Pour the bread cube mixture into the prepared baking dish. Place the baking dish in a 9 × 13 × 2-inch baking pan. Then, pour very hot (not boiling) water into the pan to approximately ½ the height of the baking dish. Bake, uncovered, for 1 hour, or until a table knife inserted into the pudding near the center of the baking dish comes out clean.

(Recipe continues on next page)

Remove the baking dish from the baking pan and place on a wire rack. Let the pudding stand until cooled slightly; then, refrigerate. When the pudding is cold, cover; keep refrigerated.

Serve the Bread Pudding cold in individual sauce dishes. Spoon cold Lemon Sauce with Raisins over each serving.

SERVES 8

CHOCOLATE-CHERRY SOUFFLÉ

Concealed under this puffy chocolate soufflé you whisk from the oven to the table, are cherry preserves. This is a sophisticated, seductive dessert to say the least. You will need a 1½-quart, straight-sided soufflé dish to make it. (For the definition of Soufflé, see page 9.)

½ cup cherry preserves
3 tablespoons unsweetened cocoa powder
2 tablespoons powdered sugar
4 extra-large eggs, room temperature
1 teaspoon pure vanilla extract
1 recipe Custard Sauce (page 308)

Preheat the oven to 375° F. Butter a 7½ × 3-inch (1½-quart) ovenproof, round soufflé dish with straight sides. Using granulated sugar, sugar the inside of the dish as you would flour a baking pan (page 40).

Spread the cherry preserves evenly over the bottom of the prepared soufflé dish; set aside. In a small mixing bowl, place the cocoa and powdered sugar; stir to combine; set aside.

Separate the eggs, placing the egg yolks in a small mixing bowl and the egg whites in a large mixing bowl. Set the egg whites aside. Add the vanilla to the egg yolks; using an electric mixer, beat on medium speed only until smooth and blended; set aside. Using the electric mixer fit with clean, dry blades, beat the egg whites on high speed until soft peaks hold. While continuing to beat on high speed, very gradually add the cocoa mixture and continue beating the egg white mixture until stiff, but still moist and glossy. Add the egg yolk mixture; using a large mixing spoon, quickly and gently fold in.

Turn the mixture into the soufflé dish (over the cherry preserves). Using a small, narrow, angled spatula, lightly and quickly spread the mixture evenly. Place the soufflé dish in the center of an oven rack on the lowest shelf level in the oven. Bake for 23 to 25 minutes, or until the soufflé rises. Watch carefully, as both overbaking and underbaking can cause the soufflé to fall.

When done, remove the soufflé from the oven, and *quickly* cut into 4 servings using a sharp, thin-bladed knife. Using a small spatula, carefully remove the servings from the soufflé dish and place on individual plates. Spoon a small amount of the Custard Sauce over each serving and *serve immediately*. Time is of the essence when serving soufflés, as they begin to fall after only a few minutes out of the oven. The baking of soufflés must precisely coincide with the time they are to be served. Soufflés are customarily taken directly from the oven to the table, where they are quickly displayed and then immediately cut, served, and consumed before time plays havoc with these evanescent delicacies.

SERVES 4

VARIATION: The Custard Sauce may be omitted, in which case the top of the soufflé should be sprinkled very lightly with powdered sugar before being presented at the table. To sprinkle the top of the soufflé, place 1 tablespoon powdered sugar in a very small hand strainer and shake it back and forth over the soufflé until the top is lightly decorated.

BAKED CUSTARD

3 extra-large eggs
¼ cup plus 1 tablespoon sugar
¼ teaspoon salt
¾ teaspoon pure vanilla extract
2 cups whole milk, scalded (page 9)
Ground nutmeg for garnish

Preheat the oven to 325°F.

Place the eggs in a medium mixing bowl. Using an electric mixer, beat the eggs only until blended on medium speed. Add the sugar, salt, and vanilla. Using a large spoon, stir to combine. Slowly add the scalded milk, stirring constantly.

Ladle the mixture into five 6-ounce oven-proof glass custard cups. Sprinkle nutmeg lightly over the mixture in each custard cup.

Place the filled custard cups in a $9 \times 13 \times 2$-inch baking pan. Then, pour very hot (not boiling) water into the pan to slightly more than $\frac{1}{2}$ the height of the custard cups. Bake for 40 minutes, or until a table knife inserted into the custard halfway between the edge and the center of a custard cup comes out clean. The custard will continue cooking after removal from the oven, and the center of the custard will fully set. Avoid overbaking, causing the custard to become porous and watery.

Remove the custard cups from the baking pan and place on a wire cookie rack (see Note). Let the custard stand until cooled slightly; then, refrigerate. When the custard is cold, cover each custard cup with aluminum foil; keep refrigerated.

Serve Baked Custard cold, in the custard cups.

NOTE: The close-set wires of a cookie rack will keep the custard cups level while allowing for full air circulation.

SERVES 5

SERVING SUGGESTION: Each serving may be garnished with a small amount of Whipped Cream (page 309) at serving time. Spoon or pipe the Whipped Cream onto the center of each custard cup; if piped, use a decorating bag fit with large open-star tip number 6B (page 309).

CRÉME CARAMEL

A standard French dessert, this esteemed meal-time finale consists of a silky custard baked over a thin, golden, caramel syrup (caramelized sugar).

Served cold, it is unmolded and inverted onto the serving plate just before serving, allowing the luscious syrup to trickle down and around the side of the custard. Equally appropriate on formal and informal menus, Créme Caramel enjoys universal appeal.

½ **cup sugar**
1 **recipe Baked Custard (page 586),**
  eliminating the ground nutmeg (see recipe procedures below)

Preheat the oven to 325°F. Place five 6-ounce ovenproof glass custard cups, evenly distributed, in a $9 \times 13 \times 2$-inch baking pan; set aside.

In a 7- to 8-inch heavy-bottomed skillet, place ½ cup sugar; distribute evenly over the bottom of the skillet. Place the skillet over medium to medium-high heat. Using a wooden mixing spoon, stir the sugar intermittently as it heats, keeping the unmelted sugar evenly distributed over the bottom of the skillet. When the sugar begins to melt, reduce the heat to medium-low and stir the sugar continuously until all the sugar granules and lumps that have formed are dissolved and the caramel syrup is a medium-golden color. Immediately remove the skillet from the heat and, using a measuring spoon, pour approximately 1 tablespoon of the syrup into the bottom of each custard cup. (Wear a rubber glove on the hand you use for measuring as the syrup will cause the metal measuring spoon to become extremely hot.) The syrup will soon extend to cover the bottoms of the custard cups; let stand at least 10 minutes while you mix the Baked Custard ingredients. The caramel syrup will harden in the custard cups, but will dissolve to a thin, water-like syrup during baking, and will remain thin during refrigeration of the finished Créme Caramel.

Ladle the mixed Baked Custard ingredients into the custard cups over the hardened caramel syrup. Then, pour very hot (not boiling) water into the baking pan to slightly more than ½ the height of the custard cups. Bake for 40 minutes, following the recipe for Baked Custard. Avoid

(Recipe continues on next page)

overbaking in order to achieve a smooth, tender custard.

Follow the Baked Custard recipe for removing the custard cups from the baking pan and for cooling and refrigerating the Créme Caramel.

Serve the Créme Caramel cold. Unmold immediately before serving. To unmold each serving, run a sharp, thin-bladed knife around the edge of the custard cup to the bottom of the cup, keeping the knife as close to the side of the cup as possible. Then, place a 6-inch serving plate (bread-and-butter size) upside down over the custard cup; hold the plate and custard cup together and invert. Lift the custard cup off the Créme Caramel and let all the caramel syrup flow over the custard and onto the plate around the custard. The top of the inverted Créme Caramel will be a light, golden brown color, and the extra caramel syrup will be quite thin. If the Créme Caramel does not drop from the custard cup onto the plate when inverted, lift one side of the custard cup slightly above the plate and carefully slide a small, thin-bladed paring knife about 1/2 inch into the outer edge of the custard cup at a single place. This will release the Créme Caramel onto the plate.

Serve with a spoon.

SERVES 5

NOTE: This recipe may be doubled or tripled, in which case, use a 9-inch, heavy-bottomed skillet when making the caramel syrup and as many baking pans as required.

SERVING SUGGESTION: For added elegance, pipe a very small mound of Decorator Whipped Cream (page 309) onto the center of each serving of Créme Caramel, using a decorating bag fit with medium-large open-star tip number 32 (page 319).

CHEESECAKE

PASTRY
½ cup (¼ pound) butter
1 cup all-purpose flour
¼ cup sugar
½ teaspoon finely grated lemon rind
   (page 31)
1 extra-large egg yolk
¼ teaspoon pure vanilla extract

Remove the butter from the refrigerator and let stand 10 minutes before use in the recipe.

Preheat the oven to 400° F. Butter the bottom and side of a 9 × 3-inch springform pan; set aside.

In a large mixing bowl, place the flour, sugar, and lemon rind; stir to combine; set aside. In a small mixing bowl, place the egg yolk and vanilla; using a table fork, beat to blend; set aside. Using a knife, cut the butter into approximately 8 pieces and drop into the bowl containing the flour mixture. Using a pastry blender, cut the butter into the flour mixture until the mixture is the texture of coarse cornmeal interspersed with some pieces the size of small peas. Add the egg yolk mixture; using a table fork, quickly stir to combine.

With floured hands, gather ⅔ of the pastry into a ball and wrap in plastic wrap; refrigerate.

Remove the side of the prepared springform pan; set aside. Gather the remaining ⅓ of the pastry into a ball and place on a floured pastry cloth. Using a stockinet-covered, then floured rolling pin (page 38), roll the pastry to ⅛-inch thickness and into a circle slightly larger in diameter than the springform pan bottom. Place the buttered side of the springform pan bottom on the rolled pastry. Carefully invert the pastry cloth, pastry, and pan bottom; remove the pastry cloth. Run a sharp, thin-bladed knife dipped in flour around the edge of the springform pan bottom to remove the extra pastry. Gather the extra pastry into a ball; wrap in plastic wrap and refrigerate. Bake the bottom crust 4 to 5 minutes, or until light golden.

Remove from the oven and place the pan bottom (with crust) on a wire rack. Let stand until the crust completely cools.

Then, lock the side of the pan onto the pan bottom (leaving the crust on the pan bottom). Remove from the refrigerator the balls containing the remaining ⅔ of the pastry and the extra pastry; let stand at room temperature, in the plastic wrap, 10 minutes.

Unwrap the balls of pastry and press together to form one ball, handling the pastry minimally.

Roll the pastry (in a circle) to ⅛-inch thickness. Using the sharp, thin-bladed knife dipped in flour, cut the pastry into 2½-inch-wide strips. Cut and fit the pastry strips to cover the side of the pan, use your fingers to press the strips to the side of the pan. Patching may be necessary. Set aside while proceeding to make the Filling (recipe follows).

FILLING

36 ounces cream cheese, softened
1½ cups sugar
2 tablespoons plus 2 teaspoons all-purpose
**   flour**
1 teaspoon finely grated orange rind
**   (page 31)**
½ teaspoon finely grated lemon rind
**   (page 31)**
4 extra-large eggs plus 2 extra-large egg yolks
½ teaspoon pure vanilla extract
¼ cup whipping cream, unwhipped

Preheat the oven to 475°F.

In a large mixing bowl, place the cream cheese, sugar, flour, orange rind, and lemon rind; using an electric mixer, beat on high speed *only* until the cream cheese is *completely* smooth. Stop the electric mixer. Add the eggs, egg yolks, and vanilla; beat on medium speed *only* until blended. Do not overbeat the cream cheese mixture, which will incorporate too much air and cause the cheesecake to inflate, fall, and crack during baking. Add the cream; using a large mixing spoon, stir *only* until blended.

Pour the cream cheese mixture into the pastry-lined pan. Bake for 10 minutes. Reduce the oven heat to 200°F. and bake for an additional 1 hour. To test for doneness, gently shake the cheesecake; the very center will jiggle slightly when done.

Remove the cheesecake from the oven and place on a wire rack; let stand to cool in the pan 30 minutes. Shortly before the 30-minute cooling period is over, prepare the Sour Cream Topping.

SOUR CREAM TOPPING

16 ounces commercial sour cream
¼ cup sugar
1 teaspoon clear vanilla

Preheat the oven to 475°F.

In a medium mixing bowl, place the sour cream, sugar, and vanilla; using a spoon, stir until well blended.

When the cheesecake has cooled 30 minutes, use a small, narrow, angled spatula to spread the topping as evenly as possible over the top. Bake for 10 minutes. (The topping will completely set when the cheesecake is cold.)

Remove the cheesecake from the oven and place on a wire rack; let stand to cool in the pan 15 minutes. Then, carefully run a sharp, very thin-bladed knife around the inside edge of the pan to loosen the side of the cheesecake from the pan. Let the cheesecake stand in the pan on the wire rack to cool an additional 3 hours.

Then, carefully remove the side of the pan. Leave the cheesecake on the pan bottom. Using kitchen scissors and your fingers, carefully remove any crust which may extend higher than the top surface of the cake. Place the cheesecake (on the pan bottom) in an airtight container and refrigerate 24 hours before serving. Keep stored in the refrigerator.

SERVES 16

OPTIONAL DECORATION: Thoroughly cold cheesecake may be decorated with tinted or untinted flowers, designs, and borders (page 324) made of cream cheese. Place 12 ounces of softened cream cheese in a medium-small mixing bowl. Using an electric mixer, beat the cream cheese

(Recipe continues on next page)

on high speed only until fluffy. If desired, tint the beaten cream cheese, using paste food coloring. Place the cream cheese in a decorating bag(s) fit with an appropriate tip(s) and follow the same piping procedures employed when decorating cakes with piped icing (page 318).

MRS. DOWELL'S DESSERT

Of all desserts, this vanilla-flavored mousse, made with a scandalous amount of whipped cream, and chilled between dustings of graham cracker crumbs, is one of my very favorites.

NOTE: *This recipe contains uncooked egg whites (see page 220).*

1¼ cups finely rolled graham cracker crumbs (about 16 graham cracker squares), **divided**
½ cup whole milk
2 teaspoons (1 envelope) **unflavored gelatin**
2 extra-large eggs, room temperature, separated
¾ cup sugar
¼ teaspoon salt
2 teaspoons pure vanilla extract
2 cups (1 pint) **whipping cream, unwhipped**
¼ cup sugar

Distribute ½ of the graham cracker crumbs evenly over the bottom of a 7 × 11 × 2-inch baking pan; set aside. Set aside the remaining ½ of the graham cracker crumbs. Pour the milk into a small sauce dish. Sprinkle the gelatin over the milk; let stand 15 minutes.

Meanwhile, place the egg yolks in the top of a double boiler. Using a handheld electric mixer, beat the egg yolks slightly on medium speed. Add ¾ cup sugar and the salt; beat on medium speed to combine. Add the gelatin mixture; stir to blend. Place the top of the double boiler over boiling water in the bottom pan. Cook the egg yolk mixture until thick (about 12 minutes), stirring constantly.

Remove the top of the double boiler from the bottom pan and place it on a wire rack. Add the vanilla; stir until blended. Refrigerate the egg yolk mixture until cooled to room temperature, stirring occasionally. Be careful not to let the mixture cool until set.

Meanwhile, pour the whipping cream into a medium mixing bowl. Using a standard-sized electric mixer, beat the cream on medium-high speed until it begins to stiffen. Reduce the mixer speed to medium-low and continue beating the cream until stiff, but still soft and fluffy; cover and refrigerate.

When the egg yolk mixture cools to room temperature, remove it from the refrigerator; set aside. Place the egg whites in a medium mixing bowl. Using the standard-sized electric mixer fit with clean, dry blades, beat the egg whites on high speed until soft peaks hold. While continuing to beat on high speed, very gradually add ¼ cup sugar and continue beating the egg white mixture until stiff, but still moist and glossy; set aside.

Remove the whipped cream from the refrigerator. Measure ½ cup whipped cream; cover and refrigerate for use as decoration.

Turn the remainder of the whipped cream into a large mixing bowl. Add the egg yolk mixture; using a large mixing spoon, fold together until combined and uniform in color. Add the egg white mixture; quickly and carefully fold in only until combined.

Using a large mixing spoon, spoon the mixture into the baking pan over the graham cracker crumbs; using a small, narrow, angled spatula, lightly spread the mixture evenly. Using a teaspoon, sprinkle the remaining ½ of the graham cracker crumbs evenly over the mixture. Refrigerate the dessert, uncovered. As soon as the dessert is cold and set, cover with aluminum foil; keep refrigerated.

To serve, use a sharp, thin-bladed knife to cut the dessert into 12 servings. Using a decorating bag fit with medium open-star tip number 21 (page 319) and filled with the ½ cup reserved whipped cream, pipe a small rosette (page 325) atop each serving.

SERVES 12

OPTIONAL DECORATION: If a decorating bag and tip are not available, use a teaspoon to carefully place a small dollop of the reserved whipped cream atop and in the center of each serving.

MAPLE NUT MOUSSE

Note: This recipe contains uncooked egg whites (see page 220).

1 cup cold water
2 tablespoons (3 envelopes) unflavored gelatin
4 extra-large eggs, room temperature, separated
1½ cups (12 ounces) pure maple syrup
2 cups (1 pint) whipping cream
2 cups rolled vanilla wafer crumbs (about 44 vanilla wafers)
1½ cups chopped pecans
2 cups miniature marshmallows
½ cup quartered red maraschino cherries

Oil very lightly a 10-inch (12-cup) Bundt pan (see To Lightly Oil a Salad Mold, page 89); set aside.

Pour 1 cup cold water into a small sauce dish. Sprinkle gelatin over the water; let stand 15 minutes.

Meanwhile, place the egg yolks in the top of a double boiler. Using a handheld electric mixer, beat the egg yolks slightly on medium speed. Add the syrup; beat on low speed only until blended. Place the top of the double boiler over boiling water in the bottom pan. Cook the syrup mixture until thick (about 18 minutes), beating twice during the cooking period with the electric mixer to retain complete smoothness, and otherwise stirring constantly. Add the gelatin mixture; stir well to blend.

Remove the top of the double boiler from the bottom pan and place it on a wire rack; let stand until the syrup mixture cools slightly. Then, refrigerate the syrup mixture *only* until cooled to room temperature, stirring intermittently. Do not allow the syrup mixture to cool until gelled.

Meanwhile, pour the whipping cream into a medium mixing bowl. Using a standard-sized electric mixer, beat the cream on medium-high speed until it begins to stiffen. Reduce the mixer speed to medium-low and continue beating the cream until stiff, but still soft and fluffy; cover and refrigerate.

When the syrup mixture cools to room temperature, remove it from the refrigerator; set aside. Place the egg whites in a large mixing bowl. Using the standard-sized electric mixer fit with clean, dry blades, beat the egg whites on high speed until stiff, but still moist and glossy. Add the syrup mixture, vanilla wafer crumbs, pecans, marshmallows, and cherries; using a large mixing spoon, gently fold in until evenly combined. Add the whipped cream; fold in.

Turn the mixture into the prepared Bundt pan; using a small, narrow, angled spatula, smooth the surface. Refrigerate the mousse until cold and set. Keep refrigerated.

At serving time, unmold the mousse onto an attractive cake stand (see To Remove Salads from Large Molds, page 89). Slice and serve at the table.

SERVES 14

CONCERTO FOR DATES AND NUTS

Preparation time: Allegro
Consumption time: Presto

A richly orchestrated score which will receive a standing ovation.

¼ cup (4 tablespoons) butter
1 cup packed dark brown sugar

(Recipe continues on next page)

2 cups water
1 cup all-purpose flour
2 teaspoons baking powder
¼ teaspoon salt
1 cup sugar
½ cup whole milk
1 cup very coarsely cut, pitted dates (cut small
    dates into 3 pieces)
¾ cup broken English walnuts
1 recipe Whipped Cream (page 309)

Preheat the oven to 350° F. Using Special Grease (page 40), grease a 7 × 11-inch baking dish (see Note); set aside.

In a small saucepan, melt the butter over low heat. Remove from the heat. Add the brown sugar and water; stir to combine. Bring the mixture to a boil over medium-high heat, stirring constantly. Boil the mixture 1 minute, stirring continuously. Remove from the heat. Place the saucepan in a large bowl of cold water to cool the mixture; set aside.

Meanwhile, onto waxed paper, sift together the flour, baking powder, and salt. Place the flour mixture in a medium mixing bowl. Add the sugar; stir to combine. Using a tablespoon, make a well in the center of the flour mixture. Pour the milk, all at once, into the well in the flour mixture; using an electric mixer, beat on low speed only until blended. Add the dates and walnuts; using a mixing spoon, stir and fold in only until combined and evenly distributed; set aside.

Pour the brown sugar mixture into the prepared baking dish. Using the mixing spoon, spoon the date mixture over the brown sugar mixture. Using a small, narrow, angled spatula, smooth the mixture some. Bake for 50 minutes. The top will be golden.

Remove from the oven and place the baking dish on a wire rack; let stand until the dessert completely cools. Then, cover the dessert with aluminum foil. Store at room temperature.

To serve, cut the dessert into 15 servings and spoon a generous dollop of the Whipped Cream on each serving.

NOTE: Although not as satisfactory, the pan may be greased and floured using the traditional method (page 40) in substitution for using Special Grease.

SERVES 15

PISTACHIO ARABESQUE

This tantalizing dessert combines fresh, from-scratch ingredients with instant pudding and a small can of crushed pineapple. The pretty, pale-green mixture is chilled over a baked crust of shortbread crumbs, chopped pistachio nuts, and butter. But pistachios are not confined to the crust. These popular nuts also are used in the dessert filling and as the topping.

2 cups rolled shortbread cookie crumbs (use
    homemade Scotch Shortbread cookies, page
    565, or about ¾ of a
    10-ounce package of Lorna Doone
    Shortbread Cookies)
⅔ cup chopped, non-artificially colored
    pistachio nuts, divided
½ cup (¼ pound) butter, melted
8 ounces cream cheese, softened
1 14-ounce can (1¼ cups) sweetened
    condensed milk
¼ cup freshly squeezed, strained lime juice
1 3.4-ounce package instant pistachio-
    flavored pudding and pie filling
1 8-ounce can crushed pineapple in its own
    juice
1 cup (½ pint) whipping cream, unwhipped

Preheat the oven to 350° F. Butter well a 9 × 13-inch baking dish; set aside.

In a medium mixing bowl, place the cookie crumbs and 3 tablespoons of the pistachio nuts; stir to combine. Add the melted butter; stir until the crumbs and nuts are coated. Spoon the mixture into the prepared baking dish. Using the back of a tablespoon, press the mixture firmly and evenly over the bottom of the dish. Bake for 8 to 10 minutes, until lightly golden.

Remove from the oven and place the baking

dish on a wire rack; let stand until the baked crust completely cools.

Then, place the cream cheese in a large mixing bowl. Using an electric mixer, beat the cream cheese on high speed until smooth and fluffy. Add the condensed milk and lime juice; beat on medium-high speed until blended. Add the pudding and pie filling; beat on medium-high speed until smooth; set aside.

Place 2 tablespoons of the remaining pistachio nuts in a small sauce dish; set aside for topping. Add the remaining pistachio and pineapple (undrained) to the cream cheese mixture; using a large mixing spoon, stir and fold in until evenly distributed; set aside.

Pour the whipping cream into a medium-small mixing bowl. Using the electric mixer fit with clean, dry blades, beat the cream on medium-high speed until it begins to stiffen. Reduce the mixer speed to medium-low and continue beating the cream until stiff, but still soft and fluffy. Add the whipped cream to the cream cheese mixture; using the large mixing spoon, fold in.

Spoon the mixture over the baked crust; using a long, narrow, angled spatula, spread evenly. Sprinkle the reserved 2 tablespoons pistachio nuts evenly over the top. Refrigerate the dessert, uncovered; cover with aluminum foil when completely cold and set.

To serve, cut the dessert into 15 servings, using a sharp, thin-bladed knife dipped in moderately hot water and then dried. Redip the knife in the water and dry before making each cut.

SERVES 15

KAHLÚA ICEBOX DESSERT

When simplicity of preparation is the goal, new and experienced cooks alike will find this recipe appealing. Kahlúa and easy-to-make chocolate curls dress up this version of a time-honored dessert standby.

1 recipe Chocolate Decorator Whipped Cream (page 310)
¼ cup Kahlúa liqueur (page 7)
1 9-ounce package commercial, thin chocolate wafers
1 recipe Decorator Whipped Cream (plain) (page 309)
Narrow Chocolate Curls (page 342)

Make the Chocolate Decorator Whipped Cream and add the Kahlúa near the end of beating. Using a small, narrow, angled spatula, frost the wafers on the flat side with the chocolate whipped cream mixture. Assemble the frosted wafers, sandwich style, in a long, continuous roll (about 14 inches long) on a serving plate; refrigerate while making the (plain) Decorator Whipped Cream.

Using a clean, small, narrow, angled spatula, frost the outside of the roll, including the ends, with the Decorator Whipped Cream. Sprinkle some Narrow Chocolate Curls evenly over the top of the roll. Then, lightly press additional curls into the side and ends of roll. Refrigerate the finished dessert at least 4 hours before serving to allow sufficient time for the wafers to soften.

To serve, slice diagonally at a 45-degree angle into 8 servings.

SERVES 8

STRAWBERRIES, TRIPLE SEC, AND WHIPPED CREAM

Fresh strawberries, hulled (page 6) and cut in
  half lengthwise
Triple Sec liqueur (page 10)
Whipped Cream (page 309)

Place individual servings of strawberries in
crystal sherbet glasses. Pour about ½ ounce
Triple Sec over each serving. Spoon a dollop of
Whipped Cream over the strawberries in each
serving. Place each sherbet glass on a small
(bread and butter-sized), doily-lined plate.

VARIATION: Grand Marnier liqueur (page 6) may
be substituted for the Triple Sec.

STRAWBERRY BAVARIAN CREAM

*The fruit Bavarian creams in the recipes that fol-
low are made with flavored gelatin, whipped
cream, and fresh fruit. They're marvelous tasting
and as easy as falling off a log to make. While this
style of fruit Bavarian cream often is served for
informal dining in the Midwest, more classical
Bavarian cream consists of custard, gelatin,
whipped cream, and flavoring, which may be
pureed fruit.*

1 3-ounce package wild strawberry-
  flavored gelatin
1 cup boiling water
½ cup cold water
2½ cups hulled (page 6) and halved or
  quartered (depending upon size),
  lengthwise, fresh strawberries
1 recipe Whipped Cream (page 309)

Place the gelatin in a medium mixing bowl. Add
1 cup boiling water; stir until the gelatin completely dissolves. Add ½ cup cold water; stir to
blend. Refrigerate the gelatin mixture until it
begins to set and is the consistency of unbeaten
egg whites.

Then, remove the gelatin mixture from the
refrigerator. Add the strawberries and the
Whipped Cream; using a medium mixing
spoon, fold in, leaving a slight rippled effect.

Spoon the mixture into a glass serving bowl
or into 8 individual, crystal sherbet glasses;
refrigerate. When cold and set, cover the bowl
or sherbet glasses with aluminum foil; keep
refrigerated.

SERVES 8

OPTIONAL DECORATION: Decorate with additional
Whipped Cream and fresh strawberries, and
small sprigs of fresh mint.

APRICOT BAVARIAN CREAM

1 3-ounce package apricot-flavored gelatin
2½ cups halved, pitted, and coarsely cut fresh
  apricots

Follow the Strawberry Bavarian Cream recipe,
above, substituting apricot-flavored gelatin and
fresh apricots for the wild strawberry–flavored
gelatin and fresh strawberries.

PEACH BAVARIAN CREAM

1 3-ounce package peach-flavored gelatin
2½ cups peeled, halved, pitted, quartered, and
  sliced fresh peaches (if peaches are large,
  split peach quarters in half lengthwise
  before slicing)

Follow the Strawberry Bavarian Cream recipe,
above, substituting the peach-flavored gelatin
and fresh peaches for the wild strawberry-
flavored gelatin and fresh strawberries.

Ice Cream

VANILLA ICE CREAM

(See photo insert page D-6)

1 ½ cups sugar
¼ cup plus 2 tablespoons all-purpose flour
⅛ teaspoon salt
¼ cup whole milk
2 ¾ cups whole milk
6 extra-large eggs, slightly beaten
2 tablespoons pure vanilla extract
4 cups (1 quart) whipping cream, unwhipped
4 cups (1 quart) half-and-half
About 2 cups whole milk
Crushed ice
Rock salt

Have ready a 6-quart electric ice cream freezer.

In the top of a double boiler, place the sugar, flour, and salt; stir to combine. Add ¼ cup milk; stir until smooth. Add 2¾ cups milk; stir to blend. Place the top of the double boiler over boiling water in the bottom pan. Cook the milk mixture until thick (about 10 minutes), constantly stirring with a spoon or beating with a handheld electric mixer on low speed. Add about ½ cup of the hot milk mixture to the eggs and quickly stir in. Then, add the egg mixture to the remaining milk mixture and stir vigorously to blend. Continue cooking the mixture 2 minutes, beating constantly with the electric mixer on low speed.

Remove the top of the double boiler from the bottom pan and place on a wire rack; let stand until the mixture cools to moderately warm.

Then, transfer the mixture to a large mixing bowl. Add the vanilla, whipping cream, and half-and-half; using the electric mixer; beat on low speed only until blended. Cover the bowl and refrigerate the ice cream mixture until cold.

Then, pour the ice cream mixture into the ice cream freezer can. Add milk (about 2 cups) to the full line. To make ice cream, use crushed ice and rock salt, and follow the freezer instructions.

NOTE: The ice cream mixture may be made and refrigerated 1 day in advance of making the ice cream.

STRAWBERRY ICE CREAM

6 cups hulled (page 6) fresh strawberries, divided
½ cup sugar

Place 3 cups of the strawberries in a flat-bottomed pan. Using a potato masher, mash the strawberries. Place the mashed strawberries in a medium mixing bowl; set aside. Cut the remaining strawberries in half or into quarters, lengthwise, depending upon the size of the berries. (If the strawberries are small, leave them whole.) Add the strawberries to the mashed berries. Add ½ cup sugar; stir to combine.

Follow the Vanilla Ice Cream recipe, above, adding the strawberry mixture to the ice cream mixture just before making the ice cream; stir until evenly distributed. (Less than 2 cups milk will be required to fill the ice cream freezer can to the full line.)

HOT FUDGE SUNDAE

Spoon Hot Fudge (page 306) over vanilla ice cream (homemade, left column, or commercial). Sprinkle with coarsely chopped cashews or pecans. Add a dollop of Whipped Cream (page 309) and top with 1 red maraschino cherry with stem.

HOT BUTTERSCOTCH SUNDAE

Follow the Hot Fudge Sundae recipe, above, substituting Hot Butterscotch Fudge (page 306) for Hot Fudge. Butter brickle or butter pecan

(Recipe continues on next page)

ice cream may be substituted for the vanilla ice cream.

Sauces and Toppings for Ice Cream

Caramel Sauce (page 306)
Cherry Sauce (page 441)
Cherry Sauce with Kirschwasser (page 499)
Chocolate Sauce (page 307)
Hot Butterscotch Fudge (page 306)
Hot Fudge (page 306)
Maple Brandy Sauce (page 307)
Rhubarb Sauce (page 294)
Rum Sauce (page 308)
Rum-Raisin Sauce (page 309)

BAKED NUTMEG BANANAS WITH ICE CREAM AND CARAMEL SAUCE

3 tablespoons butter
3 tablespoons packed light brown sugar
2 tablespoons freshly squeezed, strained
   lemon juice
1 tablespoon light corn syrup
¼ teaspoon ground nutmeg
3 firm, but ripe, bananas
¾ cup Caramel Sauce (page 306)
1 pint vanilla ice cream, homemade
   (page 595) or commercial

Preheat the oven to 325° F. Butter a 7 × 11-inch baking dish; set aside.

In a small saucepan, melt the butter over low heat. Remove from the heat. Add the brown sugar, lemon juice, syrup, and nutmeg; stir to combine. Bring the mixture to a boil over medium heat, stirring constantly. When the mixture reaches the boiling point, the sugar should be dissolved and all the ingredients completely blended. Remove the syrup mixture from the heat; set aside.

Peel the bananas; cut them in half widthwise. Then, cut each half in two lengthwise. Place the bananas, flat side down and single layer, in the prepared baking dish. Pour the hot syrup mixture over the bananas. Bake, uncovered, for 5 minutes.

Remove the baking dish from the oven. Using a small spatula, carefully turn the bananas over; baste with the syrup in the baking dish. Return to the oven and bake for an additional 5 minutes, until the bananas are just soft. Time the baking carefully, as overbaking will cause the bananas to become too soft and not hold their shape when removed from the baking dish.

Meanwhile, place the Caramel Sauce in a small saucepan. Over warm heat, warm the Caramel Sauce only until it is the consistency of a hot fudge. Remove from the heat.

When the baking time has elapsed, remove the baking dish of bananas from the oven; baste. Using a spatula, place 2 banana quarters, flat side up, on each of 6 medium dessert plates. Place the bananas to one side of each plate. Place a scoop of vanilla ice cream next to the bananas on each plate. (Do not place the ice cream on top of the bananas as the heat from the bananas will melt the ice cream too quickly.) Using a spoon, drizzle ribbons of the Caramel Sauce back and forth over both the bananas and ice cream. Serve immediately.

SERVES 6

PEANUT BUTTER BRICKLE ICE CREAM PIE

1 9-inch Unbaked Vanilla Wafer Crust pie
   shell (page 406)
1 quart butter brickle ice cream
1 cup (½ pint) whipping cream, unwhipped
½ teaspoon pure vanilla extract
½ cup chunky peanut butter, room
   temperature
2 tablespoons chopped, unsalted peanuts

Place the pie shell in the freezer until ready to fill. Let the ice cream stand at room temperature, in the container, *only* until slightly soft.

Meanwhile, pour the whipping cream into a medium-small mixing bowl. Using an electric mixer, beat the cream on medium-high speed until it begins to stiffen. Reduce the mixer speed to medium-low. Add the vanilla and continue beating the cream until stiff, but still soft and fluffy; cover and refrigerate.

In a large mixing bowl, place the softened ice cream and peanut butter; using the electric mixer, beat on medium speed only until combined, but not until the ice cream melts. Add the whipped cream; using a large mixing spoon, fold in.

Remove the pie shell from the freezer. Using the large mixing spoon, spoon the ice cream mixture into the pie shell; using a small, narrow, angled spatula, spread evenly. Sprinkle the top of the pie filling with the chopped peanuts. Place the pie, uncovered, in the freezer. When firm, place the pie in a dome-topped, airtight container. Keep the pie in the freezer until ready to cut and serve (see To Cut and Serve Pies and Tarts, page 392, for procedure.)

SERVES 10

PEPPERMINT STICK DESSERT

Here is a nice recipe which features peppermint stick ice cream in a sophisticated dessert. The refreshing flavor and coolness of the ice cream make it a welcome and appropriate finale to a heavy dinner. Over graham cracker crumbs, you freeze a layer of rich chocolate cream before spreading the softened ice cream generously over all. As the final touch, you garnish the top with Narrow Chocolate Curls. Allow at least 24 hours for this appealing concoction to freeze solidly before serving. Make-ahead desserts like this one go a long way toward relieving entertainment-day cooking fatigue.

¾ cup finely rolled graham cracker crumbs (about 10 graham cracker squares)
3 extra-large eggs
¼ cup whole milk
½ cup (¼ pound) butter
1 6-ounce package (1 cup) semisweet chocolate chips
2 cups powdered sugar
2 quarts peppermint stick ice cream
Narrow Chocolate Curls (page 342)

Spread the graham cracker crumbs evenly over the bottom of a 9 × 13 × 2-inch baking pan; set aside. In a small mixing bowl, place the eggs and milk; using a handheld electric mixer, beat on medium speed only until blended; set aside.

In the top of a double boiler, place the butter and chocolate chips. Place the top of the double boiler over simmering water in the bottom pan. Stir the butter and chocolate chips until melted and blended. Add about 2 tablespoons of the hot, chocolate mixture to the egg mixture and quickly stir in. Then, add the egg mixture to the remaining chocolate mixture and stir vigorously to blend. Cook the chocolate mixture 2 minutes over simmering water, beating constantly with the electric mixer on low speed.

Remove the top of the double boiler from the bottom pan. Add the powdered sugar; using the electric mixer, beat on low speed until blended. Pour the chocolate mixture evenly over the graham cracker crumbs in the baking pan; using a small, narrow, angled spatula, spread the mixture, being careful not to move the crumbs. Place the baking pan, uncovered, in the freezer; let stand until the chocolate mixture is firm.

Then, remove the ice cream from the freezer. Remove the ice cream from the container and place it in a large mixing bowl. Let stand until the ice cream is just soft enough to beat. (Do not allow the ice cream to melt.) Using a standard-sized electric mixer, beat the ice cream on medium speed until smooth.

Spoon the ice cream over the firm chocolate mixture; using a clean, small, narrow angled spatula, spread evenly. Sprinkle the Narrow Chocolate Curls over the top. Place the dessert in

(Recipe continues on next page)

the freezer. When firm, cover tightly with aluminum foil. Let stand 24 hours to freeze solidly before serving.

To serve, use a sharp, thin-bladed knife to cut the dessert. Before making each cut, dip the knife blade into a glass of very hot water and then wipe the blade on a damp sponge to remove the excess water. (Serve frozen.)

MAKES 15 LARGE SERVINGS OR 30 SMALL SERVINGS

PINK GRAPEFRUIT SORBET

NOTE: This recipe contains an uncooked egg white (see page 220).

¼ cup sugar
2 cups water
1 cup freshly squeezed, strained, pink (or red) grapefruit juice
1 teaspoon finely grated grapefruit rind (page 31)
1 drop (no more) red liquid food coloring
1 extra-large egg white, room temperature
Grapefruit zest (page 31)

In a small saucepan, place the sugar and water; stir to combine. Over low heat, stir the mixture until the sugar completely dissolves. Remove from the heat and place the saucepan on a wire rack. Let stand until the syrup is cool.

Then, add the grapefruit juice and grapefruit rind; stir to blend and combine. Add the food coloring; stir until completely blended.

Pour the mixture into an 8 × 8 × 2-inch baking pan; place in the freezer for 2 hours.

Remove from the freezer and spoon the mixture into a blender beaker. Using the blender, puree the mixture until slushy. Transfer the mixture back to the baking pan and repeat the freezing and pureeing procedures.

Freeze the mixture a third time and, again, remove from the freezer after 2 hours; let stand. Place the egg white in a small mixing bowl. Using an electric mixer, beat the egg white on high speed until soft peaks hold. Place the beaten egg white in the blender beaker with the sorbet mixture for the final pureeing.

Pour the sorbet into a 6-inch-diameter × 2-inch-deep round cake pan. Cover the pan and freeze the sorbet until ready to serve.

Shortly before serving, remove the sorbet from the freezer and let stand to soften slightly. Decorate each serving with a tiny amount of grapefruit zest.

SERVING SUGGESTION: Nice to serve between dinner courses to cleanse the palate (intermezzo, page 6). As intermezzo, serve the sorbet in crystal sherbet glasses or saucer champagne glasses. Using a 1½-inch trigger scoop, place a small serving of sorbet in each glass and decorate the top of each serving very sparingly with grapefruit zest. Place the glasses of sorbet on small (bread and butter-sized), doily-lined plates. Provide small teaspoons for the diners.

Other Dessert Recipes

Candies

SOURCES FOR CANDY-MAKING SUPPLIES

High-quality candy-making tools, molds, oil-based candy flavorings and colors, and other supplies are available from Wilton Enterprises and Sweet Celebrations Inc. (see Product Sources, page 631).

TEMPERING CHOCOLATE

PURPOSES FOR TEMPERING CHOCOLATE

There are three purposes for tempering chocolate:

- Preventing white streaks in the finished product.

- Achieving a shiny finish on the finished product.

- Achieving a firm set up of the chocolate.

WHAT IS TEMPERING?

Tempering chocolate is a three-step process:

- Melting the chocolate.

- Cooling the chocolate.

- Reheating the chocolate to the desired, usable temperature.

When chocolate is melted, the cocoa butter separates from the chocolate liquor (both are products of the cocoa bean). During the cooling process, the cocoa butter and liquor reblend. The reblended chocolate is then carefully increased in temperature to a usable consistency. Tempering requires some time and patience, but the results are worth the effort.

WHEN SHOULD CHOCOLATE BE TEMPERED?

Tempering is most often employed in making candy; for example, chocolate-dipped candies, chocolate-covered nuts, and molded chocolates. For the best results, chocolate used to make decorations for cakes, pies, and cookies should also be tempered.

TYPES OF CHOCOLATE WHICH ARE TEMPERED

In general, two types of chocolate are used in recipes which call for tempering:

- Real semisweet chocolate.

- Real milk chocolate.

Real white chocolate is a superior, ivory-colored product made with cocoa butter. It contains no chocolate liquor. White chocolate should be tempered when used in most candy making.

Confectioners' coating, also known as almond bark, candy coating, summer coating, and by various commercial names, contains little or no cocoa butter. It is made with a vegetable fat base. It need not be tempered; however, tempering results in a more shiny end product.

HOW TO TEMPER CHOCOLATE

1. Using a sharp knife, coarsely shave the chocolate. Place the shaved chocolate in the top of a double boiler and set aside. Pour water into the bottom pan of the double boiler to ½ inch from the bottom of the double boiler top when in place. Cover the bottom pan of the double boiler (without the double boiler top pan). Over medium heat, heat the water until hot (not simmering).

2. Remove the pan from the heat. Remove the cover and place the top of the double boiler over the hot water in the bottom pan. (The water should not be touching the bottom of the double boiler top.) Stir constantly until the chocolate just melts.

3. Replace the hot water in the bottom pan of the double boiler with cool (about 60°F) water. Use a candy thermometer to assure the proper water temperature. Stir the melted chocolate until it cools to 85°F. Use the candy thermometer to determine the temperature. The chocolate will be very thick. If the water in the bottom pan of the double boiler becomes too warm during the cooling

process due to the initial high temperature of the chocolate, thus making it difficult to reduce the chocolate temperature to 85°F, replace the warm water with fresh 60°F water and continue stirring.

4. When the chocolate cools to 85°F, replace the water in the bottom pan of the double boiler with 90°F water. Stir the chocolate constantly until it reaches suitable dipping temperature (about 88 to 90°F). Keep the chocolate (in the double boiler top) over 90°F water to maintain the dipping temperature. Stir the chocolate often during the dipping process to keep the cocoa butter properly blended. Replace the water if it becomes too cool, causing the chocolate to begin to thicken beyond a desirable dipping consistency. If the temperature of the chocolate is allowed to drop below 80°F, it will be necessary to retemper it.

5. Be careful not to get any water or moisture in the chocolate.

TO DIP CHOCOLATES

It is important to dip chocolates on a dry day in a cool (about 65°F) kitchen. The candy centers should be 65 to 70°F (room temperature) for dipping.

Drop one center at a time into 1 to 2 pounds of tempered chocolate (see Tempering Chocolate, page 600). (It is difficult to control the temperature of more than 2 pounds of dipping chocolate.) Lift the center out of the chocolate with a candy-dipping fork. Remove the excess chocolate by scraping the dipping fork on the edge of the pan (double boiler top). Place the dipped chocolate on waxed paper spread on the kitchen counter, and make an attractive swirl on top of the candy with the excess chocolate on the fork.

Allow the chocolates to stand until cool and set. Then, place them in an airtight container and store in a cool, dry place. Most chocolate-dipped candies may be stored for several weeks.

BOURBON BALLS

2½ cups (about 58) *finely rolled* vanilla wafers
2 tablespoons unsweetened cocoa powder
1 cup powdered sugar, sifted (page 42) (sift after measuring)
1 cup finely chopped English walnuts
2 tablespoons light corn syrup
⅓ cup bourbon
½ cup powdered sugar, sifted (sift after measuring)

In a large mixing bowl, place the vanilla wafer crumbs, cocoa, 1 cup powdered sugar, and the walnuts; stir to combine. Add the syrup and bourbon; stir until all particles are moistened.

Using a wet, 1-inch trigger scoop, scoop even portions of the mixture from the mixing bowl and, with damp hands, roll into balls. Place the shaped balls on a piece of waxed paper. Rinse the trigger scoop and your hands often in warm water.

Place ½ cup powdered sugar in a sauce dish. Roll each ball in the powdered sugar to coat.

Place the Bourbon Balls, single layer, on a clean piece of waxed paper in an airtight container; let stand to ripen 2 days.

If necessary, reroll the Bourbon Balls in additional sifted powdered sugar to coat before serving.

MAKES ABOUT 54

CARAMEL PUFF BALLS

You don't need to get out the candy thermometer and other specialized candy-making paraphernalia to prepare these puffy confections.

8 cups (7.2 ounces) Rice Krispies cereal
½ cup (¼ pound) butter
1 14-ounce package commercial caramels
1 14-ounce can (1¼ cups) sweetened condensed milk
1 16-ounce package standard-sized marshmallows

(Recipe continues on next page)

Place 2 cups cereal in a medium mixing bowl; set aside. In a medium, heavy-bottomed saucepan, melt the butter over low heat. Add the caramels and condensed milk. Increase the heat to medium-low and stir constantly until the caramels melt and the mixture is creamy. Remove from the heat.

Butter your hands for easier handling. Using a small cooking fork, dip one marshmallow at a time in the caramel mixture and then roll it in the cereal until coated. Using a toothpick, push the coated marshmallows off the fork and onto waxed paper. Return the caramel mixture to low heat whenever it begins to thicken; stir until the creamy consistency is restored. Replenish the cereal in the bowl, 2 cups at a time, as needed.

Let the candy stand to dry about 1½ hours.

Then, store the candy, single layer, on clean waxed paper in airtight containers.

MAKES ABOUT 48

PECAN CARAMELS

1 cup (½ pound) butter
2 cups sugar
1¾ cups light corn syrup
1 cup (½ pint) whipping cream, unwhipped
1 cup (½ pint) half-and-half
1 cup broken pecans
1 teaspoon pure vanilla extract

Butter an 8 × 8 × 2-inch baking pan; set aside.

In a 3½-quart, heavy saucepan, melt 1 cup butter over low heat. Remove from the heat. Add the sugar, syrup, whipping cream, and half-and-half; stir to combine. Over medium-high heat, bring the mixture to a boil, stirring constantly. Reduce the heat to medium and attach a candy thermometer to the saucepan. Continue cooking the mixture at a moderate boil which covers the complete surface, *without stirring*, until the temperature reaches 236°F (see Note).

Remove from the heat and detach the thermometer. Add the pecans and vanilla; stir until the pecans are evenly distributed.

Pour the mixture into the prepared baking pan. Place the baking pan on a wire rack. Let stand until the mixture completely cools.

Then, cover the baking pan with aluminum foil and refrigerate until the candy chills and sets.

Remove the candy from the refrigerator. Remove the aluminum foil and let stand at room temperature for a few minutes until the candy warms very slightly for easier cutting. Using a sharp, thin-bladed paring knife, cut the candy into 49 square pieces. If the uncut candy becomes too soft to cut sharp edges, refrigerate it for a few minutes.

Wrap each caramel neatly in a 3 × 5-inch piece of plastic wrap.

NOTE: This temperature is for use at sea-level locations. To adjust the temperature for preparation of this recipe at higher elevations, see Boiled Candies and Frostings, page 19.

MAKES 49

DIVINITY

(See photo insert page D-8)

NOTE: This recipe contains uncooked egg whites (see page 220).

2 extra-large egg whites, room temperature
2½ cups sugar
½ cup water
½ cup light corn syrup
¼ teaspoon salt
1 teaspoon pure vanilla extract
½ cup chopped pecans

Place the egg whites in a medium mixing bowl; set aside.

In a 3½-quart, heavy saucepan, place the sugar, water, syrup, and salt; stir to combine. Place the saucepan over medium heat. Stir the mixture constantly only until the sugar dissolves. Avoid splashing the mixture on the side of the saucepan to prevent the formation of crystals. Discontinue stirring after the sugar dissolves. Bring the mixture to a boil and attach a candy thermometer to the saucepan. Continue boiling the mixture over medium heat, *without stirring,* until the temperature reaches 250°F (see Note) (about 15 minutes boiling time). During the boiling process, the syrup should bubble quite briskly over the entire surface. When the syrup temperature reaches 245°F (see Note), use an electric mixer to beat the egg whites on high speed until stiff; set aside.

When the syrup temperature reaches 250°F (see Note), remove from the heat and detach the thermometer. While beating with the electric mixer on high speed, pour the syrup in a tiny, steady stream into the beaten egg whites. This will take about 3½ to 4 minutes. While continuing to beat the mixture on high speed, add the vanilla. Continue beating on high speed until the mixture just *begins* to lose its gloss (about 4 to 5 minutes beating time after adding the vanilla). Test the candy by dropping a teaspoonful onto waxed paper. If the candy holds its form and does not flatten, it is ready. If the candy flattens, beat it another 20 to 30 seconds and test again.

When the candy is ready, add the pecans and fold in quickly, using a mixing spoon. Using 2 lightly buttered teaspoons (1 to transport the candy and 1 to push the candy), drop teaspoonsful of the candy onto waxed paper. Work quickly. If the candy becomes too stiff and chunky, add a *few drops* of hot water and, using the electric mixer, beat it until smooth.

Allow the candy to stand until it sets and loses its stickiness. Store in airtight containers.

Divinity should not be made when the weather or kitchen is humid.

NOTE: These temperatures are for use at sea-level locations. To adjust the temperatures for preparation of this recipe at higher elevations, see Boiled Candies and Frostings, page 19.

MAKES ABOUT 48

CHOCOLATE-ALMOND TOFFEE

Toffee is a hard but still crunchy candy made by boiling butter, sugar, and a bit of water to the hard-crack stage (295 to 310°F). I boil this toffee to 300°F at sea level (see note*). The cooled and hardened candy is broken irregularly into serving-sized pieces. This recipe reflects one of the most popular ways of making toffee—with almonds and a layer of chocolate melted over the top.*

1 cup unblanched, whole almonds
1½ cups (¾ pound) butter
1½ cups sugar
¼ cup water
¾ cup milk chocolate chips
½ cup sliced, unblanched almonds, ground finely (page 35)

Butter well a 9 × 13 × 2-inch baking pan; set aside. Butter the side of a 2½-quart heavy saucepan; set aside.

Scatter 1 cup whole almonds evenly over the bottom of the prepared baking pan. Place the baking pan on a wire rack; set aside.

Place 1½ cups butter in the prepared saucepan. Melt the butter over low heat. Remove from the heat. Add the sugar and water; stir to combine. Over medium to medium-high heat, bring the mixture to a boil, stirring constantly. Attach a candy thermometer to the saucepan and continue boiling the mixture until the temperature reaches 300°F (see Note) (about 12 to 15 minutes boiling time), stirring continuously.

Quickly pour the hot mixture over the almonds in the baking pan. Using the back of a spoon, spread the mixture evenly. Let the mixture stand 5 minutes, or until the surface firms slightly.

Then, refrigerate the mixture, uncovered on a wire rack, for 30 minutes, or until partially hardened.

Remove the candy mixture from the refrigerator; set aside. Place the chocolate chips in a very small saucepan. Hold the small saucepan over (not touching) hot water in a medium saucepan

(Recipe continues on next page)

until the chocolate chips melt, stirring intermittently. Remove the small saucepan from the heat. Drizzle the melted chocolate back and forth over the candy mixture; using a small, narrow, angled spatula, spread evenly. Refrigerate the candy a few minutes until the chocolate *begins* to harden.

Then, remove the candy from the refrigerator. Using a teaspoon, sprinkle the ground almonds evenly over the chocolate. Using the back of the teaspoon, *very lightly* press the ground almonds against the chocolate to facilitate adherence. Refrigerate, uncovered on the wire rack, for 2 hours, or until the candy hardens.

Remove the candy from the refrigerator; let stand 10 minutes at room temperature.

Then, run a sharp, thin-bladed knife along the inside edges of the pan to loosen the sides of the candy from the pan. Using a spatula, lift the candy from the pan in one or more blocks. If the candy does not easily release from the pan, use the knife to cut out a small chunk of candy to facilitate running the spatula under the sheet of toffee. Place the sheet (or large chunks) of toffee on a piece of waxed paper. Using your hands, break the toffee into irregular, serving-sized pieces.

Store the toffee in an airtight container (such as a tin) lined with plastic wrap; keep refrigerated.

NOTE: This temperature is for use at sea-level locations. To adjust the temperature for preparation of this recipe at higher elevations, see Boiled Candies and Frostings, page 19.

MAKES ABOUT 2 POUNDS

CHOCOLATE-COVERED CHERRIES

Give yourself a midwinter lift by making beloved Chocolate-Covered Cherries for Valentine's Day or George Washington's birthday. One of the beauties of cooking is the satisfaction and feeling of personal worth derived from the creation of wonderful food. (And who can deny that we all can use a little praise from others now and then?)

Note: This recipe contains an uncooked egg white (see page 220).

2 cups sugar
½ cup plus 2 tablespoons water
2 tablespoons light corn syrup
1 extra-large egg white
5 drops cherry-flavored, oil-based candy
  flavoring
2 10-ounce jars small, red maraschino
  cherries, drained, rinsed, and thoroughly
  dried between several layers of paper towels
1 pound (16 squares) semisweet chocolate,
  tempered (page 600)

Butter lightly the side of a 3½-quart, heavy saucepan, starting from the top of the pan and buttering down the side about 3 inches only.

In the prepared saucepan, place the sugar, water, and syrup; stir to combine. Place the saucepan over medium-high heat. Stir the mixture only until the sugar melts; then, discontinue stirring, and cover the saucepan. Bring the mixture to a boil and boil 1 minute to allow time for any sugar which may have crystallized on the side of the pan to wash down. Uncover the saucepan and attach a candy thermometer. Continue cooking the mixture at a brisk boil, *without stirring,* until the temperature reaches 234°F (see Note 1) (about 7 additional minutes).

Remove from the heat and detach the thermometer. Without stirring the mixture or scraping the side of the pan, pour the mixture onto a marble slab (see Note 2). Allow the mixture (fondant) to stand undisturbed until it cools to 110° F (warm to the touch); the fondant will be translucent.

Then, place the egg white in a medium-small mixing bowl. Using an electric mixer, beat the egg white on high speed until stiff. Spoon the beaten egg white over the fondant on the marble slab. Using a small, narrow, angled spatula, spread the egg white evenly over the fondant. (The egg white will cause the fondant to liquefy after the centers are dipped in chocolate.) Using a wide, firm spatula, work the fondant by scraping under the mixture from the outside edge to the center, and turning it over. Continue to work the fondant until it becomes white, opaque, and creamy in consistency (about 15 minutes). Then, take the fondant in your hands and knead it by folding it in half and pressing, until the fondant is completely smooth and free of lumps (about 5 minutes). During the kneading process, knead in 5 drops of cherry flavoring.

Shape the fondant into a ½-inch-diameter pencil. Cut the fondant pencil into ½-inch slices (or slices large enough to provide sufficient fondant to cover one cherry). With your hands, roll each slice of fondant around a maraschino cherry.

Then, dip the centers in the tempered chocolate following the procedures described in To Dip Chocolates (page 601). (Fondant made with egg white must be molded and dipped immediately after making.)

When cool, place the Chocolate-Covered Cherries in a covered container and refrigerate. These candies must be kept refrigerated because they contain uncooked egg white.

NOTE 1: This temperature is for use at sea-level locations. To adjust the temperature for preparation of this recipe at higher elevations, see Boiled Candies and Frostings, page 19.

NOTE 2: If a marble slab is not available, pour the mixture onto a laminated plastic counter or a platter which has been cooled with ice cubes and then thoroughly dried.

MAKES ABOUT 54

PEANUT BRITTLE

(See photo insert page D-8)

2 cups sugar
½ cup water
1 cup light corn syrup
2¼ cups (12 ounces) raw Spanish peanuts
1 tablespoon plus 2 teaspoons butter
1½ teaspoons clear vanilla
2 teaspoons sifted baking soda

Butter the side of a 3½-quart, heavy saucepan; set aside. Butter lightly a 12 × 18 × 1-inch cookie pan; set aside. Butter lightly the back of a mixing spoon; set aside and reserve for spreading the Peanut Brittle mixture in the cookie pan.

In the prepared saucepan, place the sugar, water, and syrup; stir to combine. Over medium-high heat, bring the mixture to a boil, stirring constantly. Attach a candy thermometer to the saucepan. Reduce the heat to medium and continue cooking the mixture at a moderate boil that covers the complete surface, stirring occasionally, until the temperature reaches 250°F (see Note). Add the butter and peanuts; stir to blend the butter and combine the peanuts. Continue cooking at a moderate boil, stirring almost constantly, until the temperature reaches 305°F (See Note).

Remove from the heat and detach the thermometer. Quickly add the vanilla; do not stir. Sprinkle the baking soda over the mixture, stirring constantly (the mixture will foam). Stir very quickly but well, until the baking soda completely blends.

Then, immediately pour the mixture into the prepared cookie pan; using the back of the buttered mixing spoon, spread very quickly. Place the cookie pan on a wire rack. Let stand until the Peanut Brittle completely cools.

Using a medium-to-small spatula, release the Peanut Brittle from the pan. The Peanut Brittle will break into large pieces when released. Using paper towels, wipe any excess butter off the bottom side of the Peanut Brittle. Then, using

(Recipe continues on next page)

your hands or the handle of a heavy cooking utensil such as a large fork, break the Peanut Brittle into pieces. Store the candy in an airtight container.

Peanut brittle must be made and stored in an environment with low humidity in order to achieve and maintain its dry, brittle composition.

NOTE: These temperatures are for use at sea-level locations. To adjust the temperatures for preparation of this recipe at higher elevations, see Boiled Candies and Frostings, page 19.

MAKES ABOUT 2 POUNDS

PEANUT CLUSTERS

Our family loves Peanut Clusters made from this recipe of my sister-in-law's. Dee uses ½ semisweet chocolate and ½ white confectioners' coating. Tempering the combination chocolate and confectioners' coating, properly hardens the clusters and makes them shiny.

12 ounces (12 squares) semisweet chocolate
12 ounces white confectioners' coating
  (almond bark), wafers or block style
2 12-ounce cans salted, whole peanuts
  without skins

Cover 2 cookie sheets with aluminum foil; smooth to remove any wrinkles; set aside.

Using a sharp knife, cut the chocolate and confectioners' coating into thin shavings and then chop. Place the chocolate and confectioners' coating in the top of a double boiler.

Temper the chocolate and confectioners' coating together, following the procedures described in How to Temper Chocolate (page 600). Bring the tempered mixture to 90°F. Then, add the peanuts and quickly stir to evenly distribute.

Drop the candy by rounded teaspoonful onto the prepared cookie sheets while leaving the top of the double boiler over the warm water in the bottom pan and stirring occasionally. Let the candy stand until completely cool and set.

Then, peel the Peanut Clusters off the aluminum foil and place in an airtight container.

MAKES ABOUT 84

PEANUT BARS

2½ tablespoons butter
1⅔ cups (10 ounces) peanut butter baking
  chips
1 14-ounce can (1¼ cups) sweetened
  condensed milk
3 cups miniature marshmallows
2 12-ounce cans salted peanuts without skins,
  divided

Butter a 9 × 13 × 2-inch baking pan; set aside.

In a medium saucepan, melt the butter over very low heat. Add the peanut butter chips; stir until melted. Remove from the heat and transfer the mixture to a medium mixing bowl. Add the condensed milk; using an electric mixer, beat on medium speed until blended. Add the marshmallows; using a spoon, stir to combine; set aside.

Place one 12-ounce can of peanuts in the prepared baking pan. Spread the peanuts evenly over the bottom of the pan.

Spread the marshmallow mixture evenly over the peanuts in the baking pan using 2 spoons (one to transport the marshmallow mixture and one to push the mixture into the baking pan). The marshmallow mixture will be heavy and difficult to handle. If it sticks to the spoons, first dip the spoons in water. Spread the remaining 12-ounce can of peanuts evenly over the marshmallow mixture. With your hands, press the candy firmly. Let the candy stand until completely set.

Then, using a sharp, thin-bladed knife, cut the candy into 54 approximately 1½-inch squares. Cover the baking pan with aluminum foil or a baking pan cover to store the bars.

MAKES 54

TURTLE BARS

Revel in this irresistible confection made similarly to traditional turtle candies, with pecans, chocolate, and caramel, but cut into bars. In a departure from usual candy-making techniques, this candy is baked. After you make these Turtle Bars the first time, I think you'll find yourself making them again and again.

1ST LAYER
2 cups all-purpose flour
1 cup packed light brown sugar
½ cup (¼ pound) butter, softened

2ND LAYER
1 cup coarsely broken pecans

3RD LAYER
½ cup (¼ pound) plus 3 tablespoons butter
½ cup packed light brown sugar

4TH LAYER
1 cup milk chocolate chips

DECORATION
48 pecan halves

Preheat the oven to 350° F.

In a large mixing bowl, place the flour and 1 cup brown sugar; stir to combine. Using a knife, cut ½ cup softened butter into approximately 8 pieces and drop into the bowl. Using a pastry blender, cut the butter into the flour mixture until the mixture is the texture of coarse crumbs.

Turn the mixture into an ungreased 9 × 13 × 2-inch baking pan. Using a tablespoon, spread the mixture evenly. Then, using the back of the tablespoon, pat the mixture firmly into the pan.

Sprinkle 1 cup broken pecans evenly over the mixture; set aside.

In a small saucepan, melt ½ cup plus 3 tablespoons butter over low heat. Add ½ cup brown sugar; stir to combine. Increase the heat to medium. Bring the mixture to a boil, stirring constantly. Boil the mixture 1 minute, stirring continuously.

Pour the mixture back and forth evenly over the crust and pecans in the baking pan. Use a small, narrow, angled spatula to spread the mixture, if necessary. Bake for 18 minutes. The third layer of the bars still will be bubbling when the baking time elapses.

Remove from the oven and place the baking pan on a wire rack. Immediately sprinkle the chocolate chips evenly over the hot candy. When the chocolate chips have melted, use a clean, small, narrow, angled spatula to spread the chocolate evenly. Let the candy stand 15 minutes.

Then, lightly press the pecan halves into the top of the uncut candy, situating them in what will be the center of each of the bars when cut.

When completely cool, use a sharp, thin-bladed knife to cut the candy into 48 bars. Cover the baking pan with aluminum foil or a baking pan cover to store the bars.

MAKES 48

CREAM CHEESE MINTS

Party-perfect molded Cream Cheese Mints in pure white or rainbow colors are a snap to make. Of course, if you decide to go all out and pipe little decorations on them, more skill and time will be entailed.

3 ounces cream cheese, softened
¼ teaspoon plus ⅛ teaspoon peppermint-
**   flavored, oil-based candy flavoring**
2¾ cups plus 2 tablespoons powdered sugar,
**   sifted (page 42) (sift after measuring)**
¼ cup granulated sugar

In a medium mixing bowl, place the cream cheese and peppermint flavoring; using an electric mixer, beat on high speed until smooth and blended. Add the powdered sugar; beat on low speed until combined. Then, beat on high speed only until blended.

Knead the mixture in your hands until smooth; set aside.

(Recipe continues on next page)

Place the granulated sugar in a small sauce dish. With your fingers, pinch off pieces of the candy mixture and roll into balls the size of marbles. Roll the balls of candy mixture in the granulated sugar and press the balls into ungreased, clear plastic, mint candy molds. Using a small paring knife, remove any excess candy mixture above the surface level of the molds. Immediately unmold the mints onto a clean kitchen hand towel by inverting and flexing the molds. Hold the molds close to the hand towel to help prevent the mints from denting when they fall onto the towel.

Place the mints, single layer, in an airtight container; refrigerate (they must be kept refrigerated because they contain cream cheese).

MAKES ABOUT 72

OPTIONAL DECORATION
Paste food coloring in pale green, plus other pale colors of choice
¼ recipe Cake Decorators' White Icing, using ¼ teaspoon clear vanilla and no almond extract (page 504)

When the mints are cold, use paste food coloring to tint portions of the Cake Decorators' White Icing pale green and one or more other pale colors of choice for rosebuds. Using decorating bags filled with the tinted icings (page 321), pipe a tiny rosebud (page 327) with pale green leaves (page 326) on each mint. Use small petal tip number 101 to pipe the rosebuds and small leaf tip number 65 to pipe the leaves. Let the mints stand briefly until the decorations set. Then, replace the mints in the airtight container and refrigerate.

VARIATIONS
- Using oil-based candy flavoring, flavor the mints with other flavorings of choice.

- Using oil-based candy coloring, tint the mints in preferably pale (or other) colors of choice in keeping with the flavor of the mints. Add a few drops of coloring to the candy mixture after beating the mixture on low speed to combine the powdered sugar. Then, beat the candy mixture on high speed only until the powdered sugar and coloring are blended into the mixture.

PINK PEPPERMINTS

The finest mints are made with tempered confectioners' coating. While entitled Pink Peppermints, this recipe tells how to make these creamy-smooth mints in other colors and flavors. With a tiny rosebud meticulously piped on top, they're exquisite!

14 ounces white confectioners' coating (almond bark), wafers or block style
10 drops peppermint-flavored, oil-based candy flavoring
4 drops red, oil-based candy coloring

If using block-style confectioners' coating, shave it coarsely with a sharp knife.

Temper the confectioners' coating, following the procedures described in How to Temper Chocolate (page 600), with the following exceptions:

- Add the flavoring and coloring immediately after the confectioners' coating melts (end of step 2, page 600); stir until blended.

- In step 4 (page 601), replace the water in the bottom pan of the double boiler with 100°F (rather than 90°F) water. Bring the temperature of the confectioners' coating to 98 to 100°F (rather than 88 to 90°F) and retain it at 98 to 100°F while filling the molds.

Fill ungreased, clear plastic, mint candy molds with the confectioners' coating mixture using 2 teaspoons (one to transport the coating mixture and one to push the coating mixture into the molds). Be careful not to fill the molds too full, resulting in stands (excess candy on the bottom of the finished mints). Tap the bottom of the filled molds on the kitchen counter until air bubbles no longer surface on the candy. Refrigerate the filled molds until the candy is set, or place the filled molds in the freezer for just a few minutes until the candy is set.

When the candy is set, invert and flex the molds over a clean kitchen hand towel to remove the mints. Hold the molds close to the hand towel to help prevent the mints from denting when they fall onto the towel. Using a small, sharp, thin-bladed knife, carefully trim away any excess candy around the bottom of the mints (stands).

Place the Pink Peppermints, single layer, separated by waxed paper, in an airtight container. Store in a cool, dry place.

MAKES ABOUT 72

OPTIONAL DECORATION
Paste food coloring in pale green, plus other pale colors of choice
¼ recipe Cake Decorators' White Icing, using ¼ teaspoon clear vanilla and no almond extract (page 504)

Use paste food coloring to tint portions of the Cake Decorators' White Icing pale green and one or more other pale colors of choice for rosebuds. Using decorating bags filled with the tinted icings (page 321), pipe a tiny rosebud (page 327) with pale green leaves (page 326) on each mint. Use small petal tip number 101 to pipe the rosebuds and small leaf tip number 65 to pipe the leaves. Plain white rosebuds with pale green leaves are also effective on the pink mints. Let the mints stand until the decorations set. Then, place the mints, single layer, in airtight containers and store in a cool, dry place.

VARIATIONS
- Leave the mints untinted or, using oil-based candy coloring, tint the mints in other colors (preferably pale) of choice.

- Using oil-based candy flavoring, flavor the mints with other flavorings of choice, such as crème de menthe, cinnamon, and amaretto. The flavoring and coloring of individual mints should be compatible.

CANDIED ORANGE PEEL

7 small navel oranges
4 cups granulated sugar
1 cup water
1 cup superfine sugar
6 ounces milk chocolate (bar or 1 cup chips)

Wash the oranges well, removing any brand names or other marking stamped or taped on the skins. Using a small, sharp, thin-bladed knife, cut each orange lengthwise, only through the outer peel and white membrane, into fourths. (Cut 2 circles around each orange which transect both ends of the fruit.) With your fingers or the back of a spoon, detach each quarter of the peel (including the white membrane) from the pulp. (Reserve the pulp for other uses.)

Place the quarters of the peel in a large nonmetallic bowl and cover with cold water. Place a nonmetallic plate directly on top of the peels. Weight the plate with a covered pint jar of water to hold the peels under the water. Cover the bowl with plastic wrap; let stand at cool room temperature about 18 hours.

Drain the peels in a colander. Place the peels in a large saucepan. Add water to cover the peels. Cover the saucepan. Over high heat, bring the peels to a boil. Immediately drain the peels in the colander. Repeat the boiling and draining process 2 more times to help remove the bitterness from the peels.

Then, using a small, sharp knife, cut the peels lengthwise into ¼-inch-wide strips; set aside.

In a clean, large, heavy saucepan, place 4 cups granulated sugar and 1 cup water; stir to combine. Over medium-low heat, bring the mixture to a boil, stirring constantly. Add the peels and continue cooking the mixture at a moderate boil which covers the complete surface. Reduce

(Recipe continues on next page)

the heat to low as the mixture thickens. Cook the peels until translucent (about 30 minutes total cooking time), stirring occasionally.

Drain the peels in the colander and let stand until lukewarm and still sticky. Place 1 cup superfine sugar in a small mixing bowl. Roll each peel in the sugar and place on a wire cookie rack. Let the peels stand 2 to 3 hours until dry.

Then, if the chocolate is in bar form, use a sharp knife to chop it.

Place the chopped chocolate or chocolate chips in a very small saucepan. Hold the small saucepan over (not touching) hot water in a medium saucepan until the chocolate melts, stirring intermittently. Remove the small saucepan from the heat.

Dip about ½ inch of one end of each peel into the chocolate to coat; place on waxed paper. Reheat the chocolate if it becomes too thick. Let the coated peels stand until the chocolate completely sets. Six ounces of chocolate will coat the ends of approximately ½ of the peels. Because some people prefer candied peel uncoated, serve both chocolate-coated and uncoated peel on the same candy plate.

Store the chocolate-coated peel and the uncoated peel in separate airtight containers.

MAKES 120 TO 144, DEPENDING UPON THE SIZE OF THE ORANGES

CANDIED GRAPEFRUIT PEEL

Follow the Candied Orange Peel recipe, above, substituting 3 medium grapefruit for the oranges.

FUDGE

(See photo insert page D-8)

4 cups sugar
2 5-ounce cans (1¼ cups) evaporated milk
¾ cup (¼ pound plus 4 tablespoons) butter
1 12-ounce package (2 cups) semisweet chocolate chips
1 7-ounce jar marshmallow creme
1 teaspoon pure vanilla extract
1 cup broken pecans

Butter the side of a 3½ quart, heavy saucepan; set aside. Butter a 9 × 13 × 2-inch baking pan; set aside.

In the prepared saucepan, place the sugar and evaporated milk; stir to combine. Add the butter. Over *medium* heat (higher heat may cause the mixture to scorch), bring the mixture to a boil, stirring constantly. Attach a candy thermometer to the saucepan and continue boiling the mixture until the temperature reaches 236°F (see Note) (about 8 minutes boiling time), stirring occasionally.

Remove from the heat and detach the thermometer. Add the chocolate chips, marshmallow creme, and vanilla. Using a handheld electric mixer, quickly beat the mixture on *low* speed until the chocolate chips melt and the mixture blends. Add the pecans; using a spoon, quickly stir to evenly distribute.

Pour the mixture into the prepared baking pan. Place the baking pan on a wire rack. Let stand until the Fudge completely cools.

Then, using a sharp, thin-bladed knife, cut the Fudge into 70 squares. Do not allow the Fudge to stand for an extended period of time before cutting as the drying of the candy (even if covered) may cause the surface to crack slightly when cut. Store the Fudge, single layer, in an airtight container.

NOTE: This temperature is for use at sea-level locations. To adjust the temperature for preparation of this recipe at higher elevations, see Boiled Candies and Frostings, page 19.

MAKES 70

HOLLY DECORATION
¼ recipe Cake Decorators' White Icing, using
   ¼ teaspoon clear vanilla and no almond
   extract (page 504)
Bright green and red paste food coloring

For the holidays, a sprig of holly may be piped
on each piece of Fudge, using the Cake Decorators' White Icing tinted green and red with paste
food coloring. Using a decorating bag fit with
small leaf tip number 65 (page 319), pipe 2
green holly leaves (page 326) on a corner of
each piece of candy. Then, using a decorating
bag fit with tiny round tip number 1, pipe 3
small red berries (see Dots, page 324) between
the stem ends of the leaves.

PENUCHE

*Penuche (pronounced puh-new'-chee) is a fudge
made with brown sugar.*

3 cups granulated sugar
2 cups packed light brown sugar
1⅓ cups half-and-half
¼ cup (4 tablespoons) butter, cut into 4 pieces
2 teaspoons pure vanilla extract
1½ cup broken pecans

Butter the side of a 3½-quart, heavy saucepan;
set aside. Butter an 8 × 8 × 2-inch baking pan;
set aside.

In the prepared saucepan, place the granulated sugar, brown sugar, and half-and-half; stir
to combine. Over medium-high heat, bring the
mixture to a boil, stirring constantly. Avoid
splashing the mixture on the side of the
saucepan to prevent the formation of crystals.
Reduce the heat to medium and attach a candy
thermometer to the saucepan. Continue cooking the mixture at a moderate boil which covers
the complete surface, *without stirring,* until the
temperature reaches 234°F (see Note) (about
15 minutes boiling time).

Remove from the heat and place the saucepan
on a wire rack. Do not detach the thermometer.
Add the butter and vanilla, but *do not stir.* Let the
mixture stand, *without stirring,* until cooled to
110°F.

Then, detach the thermometer and transfer
the mixture to a medium mixing bowl. Using an
electric mixer, beat the mixture on high speed
until it just *begins* to lose its gloss (approximately 3 to 4 minutes). Quickly add the pecans;
using a spoon, stir to evenly combine.

Turn the mixture into the prepared baking
pan; using a small, narrow, angled spatula,
spread evenly. Place the baking pan on the wire
rack. Let stand until the Penuche cools slightly.

Then, while still warm, use a sharp, thin-bladed
knife to score the Penuche into 64 squares.
Replace the baking pan on the wire rack. Let
stand until the Penuche completely cools.

When completely cool, cut the Penuche into
squares along the scored lines. Store the
Penuche, single layer, in an airtight container.

NOTE: This temperature is for use at sea-level
locations. To adjust the temperature for preparation of this recipe at higher elevations, see
Boiled Candies and Frostings, page 19.

MAKES 64

PEANUT BUTTER FUDGE

1½ cups granulated sugar
2 cups packed light brown sugar
¼ cup light corn syrup
1 cup (½ pint) whipping cream, unwhipped
½ cup chunky peanut butter
2 tablespoons butter, softened
1 teaspoon pure vanilla extract
¼ cup chopped, unsalted peanuts without
   skins

Butter the side of a 3½-quart, heavy saucepan; set aside. Butter an 8 × 8 × 2-inch baking pan; set aside.

In the prepared saucepan, place the granulated sugar, brown sugar, syrup, and whipping cream; stir to combine. Over medium-high heat, bring the mixture to a boil, stirring constantly. Attach a candy thermometer to the saucepan. Reduce the heat to medium-low and continue boiling the mixture, *without stirring,* until the temperature reaches 234°F (see Note) (about 10 minutes total boiling time).

Remove from the heat and place the saucepan on a wire rack. Do not detach the thermometer. Let the mixture stand, *without stirring,* until cooled to 110°F.

Then, detach the thermometer and transfer the mixture to a medium mixing bowl. Add the peanut butter, butter, and vanilla; using an electric mixer, beat on high speed until blended. Continue beating on high speed until the mixture becomes very thick, but is still glossy (about 4 minutes total beating time).

Quickly turn the mixture into the prepared baking pan and sprinkle evenly with the chopped peanuts. Place the baking pan on a wire rack. Let stand until the fudge completely cools.

Then, using a sharp, thin-bladed knife, cut the fudge into 36 squares. Store the fudge, single layer, in an airtight container.

NOTE: This temperature is for use at sea-level locations. To adjust the temperature for preparation of this recipe at higher elevations, see Boiled Candies and Frostings, page 19.

MAKES 36

VARIATION: For smooth fudge, substitute creamy peanut butter for chunky peanut butter and eliminate the chopped peanuts. After turning the mixture into the baking pan, let the fudge stand on a wire rack until cooled slightly. Then, while still warm, use a sharp, thin-bladed knife to score the fudge into 36 squares. If desired, place an unsalted peanut half in the center of each square. Replace the baking pan on the wire rack. Let stand until the fudge completely cools. When completely cool, cut the fudge into squares along the scored lines.

CHRISTMAS DECORATION: Whether chunky- or smooth-style Peanut Butter Fudge, decorate the center of each fudge square with ½ red candied cherry. (Use of chopped peanuts on chunky-style fudge is optional.)

SPICED PECANS

Use fresh, large, unbroken, and unnicked pecan halves when making these Spiced Pecans. Each year, I like to order lovely, orchard-fresh pecans right after they are harvested in Georgia in October. I store them in the freezer for use in making these sweetened nuts and pecan pies and for all my baking and cooking (see To Store Nuts, page 35). My source for pecans is Sunnyland Farms in Albany, Georgia (see Product Sources, page 631). They have a good catalog.

1 pound pecan halves
½ cup sugar
½ teaspoon ground cinnamon
¼ teaspoon ground nutmeg
¼ teaspoon plus ⅛ teaspoon salt
1 extra-large egg white
1 teaspoon water

Preheat the oven to 225°F. Butter a 10½ × 15½ × 1-inch cookie pan; set aside.

Sort the pecans, using only unbroken halves; set aside. In a small mixing bowl, place the sugar, cinnamon, nutmeg, and salt; stir to combine; set aside.

In a medium mixing bowl, place the egg white and water; using an electric mixer, beat on high speed until very frothy, but not stiff. Add the pecans; using a spoon, stir until completely coated. Add the cinnamon mixture; stir until thoroughly mixed.

Spread the pecans on the prepared cookie pan. Bake for 1 hour, using a large spatula to turn the pecans every 15 minutes.

Remove from the oven and turn the pecans once more. Place the cookie pan on a wire rack. Let the pecans stand until completely cool.

Then, store the Spiced Pecans in an airtight container.

MAKES 1 POUND

POPCORN BALLS

1 cup unpopped yellow popcorn (not microwave popcorn)
2 cups sugar
1 cup water
½ cup light corn syrup
¼ teaspoon salt
3 tablespoons butter, cut into 3 or more pieces
1 teaspoon pure vanilla extract
6 drops red liquid food coloring* (optional)

Popcorn Balls may be tinted red, green, orange, or any desired color.

Butter the side of a 3½-quart, heavy saucepan; set aside.

Pop the corn in an electric corn popper; make no additions, such as salt or butter. Place the popped corn in a 12- to 16-quart kettle; set aside.

In the prepared saucepan, place the sugar, water, syrup, and salt; stir to combine. Place the saucepan over medium-high heat. Stir the mixture constantly until the sugar dissolves. Then, discontinue stirring. Bring the mixture to a boil and attach a candy thermometer to the saucepan. Continue boiling the mixture, *without stirring*, until the temperature reaches 260°F (see Note) (about 15 minutes boiling time).

Remove from the heat and detach the thermometer. Add the butter, vanilla, and food coloring; stir briskly until the butter melts and the color is evenly blended.

Pour the mixture, in thirds, over the popcorn, carefully and quickly tossing with a large mixing spoon after each addition to coat the popcorn. Try to avoid breaking the popped kernels.

With buttered hands, shape large handsful of the popcorn into balls, pressing slightly until the balls hold their shape. Place the shaped balls on waxed paper. Keep your hands well buttered. Let the balls stand 2 hours, or until dry.

Then, for gifts or an attractive presentation, wrap each Popcorn Ball in clear cellophane and tie with a narrow, red satin ribbon. Otherwise, wrap each ball snugly in clear plastic wrap.

NOTE: This temperature is for use at sea-level locations. To adjust the temperature for preparation of this recipe at higher elevations, see Boiled Candies and Frostings, page 19.

MAKES ABOUT 14

POPCORN CAKE

It's made in a tube pan in the shape of a big cake, but Popcorn Cake is made of popped corn, small gumdrops, and honey-roasted peanuts, all held together with a yummy syrup. Children and adult "kids" go for this conversation-piece candy, which you cut just like a cake.

⅔ cup unpopped yellow popcorn (not microwave popcorn)
1 13-ounce package (2 cups) small gumdrops in assorted colors and flavors
1 12-ounce can honey roasted peanuts
2 cups sugar
1 cup water
½ cup light corn syrup
¼ teaspoon salt
3 tablespoons butter, cut into 3 or more pieces
1 teaspoon pure vanilla extract

Butter the side of a 3½-quart, heavy saucepan; set aside. Butter well a 10 × 4-inch tube pan with a removable bottom; set aside.

Pop the corn in an electric corn popper; make no additions, such as salt or butter. Place the popped corn in a very large kettle or mixing bowl. Add the gumdrops and peanuts; using your hands, toss to combine evenly, being careful not to crush the popcorn; set aside.

In the prepared saucepan, place the sugar, water, syrup, and salt; stir to combine. Place the saucepan over medium-high heat. Stir the mixture constantly until the sugar dissolves. Then, discontinue stirring. Bring the mixture to a boil and attach a candy thermometer to the saucepan. Continue boiling the mixture, *without stirring,* until the temperature reaches 260° F (see Note) (about 15 minutes boiling time).

Remove from the heat and detach the thermometer. Add the butter and vanilla; stir briskly until the butter melts and the vanilla blends.

Pour the syrup mixture, in halves, over the popcorn mixture, carefully and quickly tossing with a large mixing spoon after each addition to coat the popcorn mixture. Try to avoid breaking the popped kernels.

With buttered hands, lightly press large handsful of the popcorn mixture into the prepared tube pan. Place the tube pan on a wire rack. Let the cake stand 2 hours.

Then, run a sharp, thin-bladed knife around the inside edge and the center tube of the pan to loosen the cake. Lift the center tube section, with the cake, out of the pan. Then, run the knife around the bottom of the tube section under the cake. Invert the cake onto a 12-inch corrugated cardboard cake circle. Carefully lift the tube section off the cake. Store the cake in an airtight container.

At serving time, place the cake (on the cardboard cake circle) on a cake stand or serving tray and present the cake uncut. Using a sharp knife, cut pieces of the cake for diners, or let the diners cut their own.

NOTE: This temperature is for use at sea-level locations. To adjust the temperature for preparation of this recipe at higher elevations, see Boiled Candies and Frostings, page 19.

MAKES APPROXIMATELY 14 FULL SERVINGS

CARAMEL CORN

An old-time to current-age Midwest favorite, I remember eating lots of caramel corn at my grandparents' house when we were kids. No wonder caramel corn is a Midwest candy icon—about 90 percent of the popcorn grown in the United States comes from the Heartland. Indiana is the largest popcorn-producing state.

This recipe, made with peanuts, reminds me of Cracker Jack, that special caramel corn delight of tykes when we were growing up. Those boxes of Cracker Jack are still made, and there's still a prize in every box.

1¼ cups unpopped yellow popcorn (not microwave popcorn)
2¼ cups (12 ounces) salted Spanish peanuts (with skins)
1 cup (½ pound) butter
2 cups packed light brown sugar
½ cup light corn syrup
¾ teaspoon salt
½ teaspoon baking soda
1 teaspoon pure vanilla extract

Butter the side of a 3½-quart, heavy saucepan, starting from the top of the pan and buttering down the side about 3 inches only; set aside.

Pop the popcorn in a standard-sized electric corn popper; make no additions, such as salt or butter. Place the popped corn in a 12- to 16-quart kettle. Sprinkle the peanuts over the popcorn; set aside.

Preheat the oven to 250° F.

In the prepared saucepan, melt 1 cup butter over low heat. Remove from the heat. Add the brown sugar, syrup, and salt; stir to combine. Place the saucepan over medium heat. Stir the mixture constantly until the sugar dissolves. Attach a candy thermometer to the saucepan. Increase the heat to medium-high and bring the mixture to a boil, stirring constantly. Continue cooking the mixture at a brisk boil, stirring occasionally, until the temperature reaches 240° F (see Note).

Remove from the heat and detach the thermometer. Add the baking soda and vanilla; stir to blend.

Pour ½ of the caramel mixture over the popcorn and peanuts; using a large mixing spoon, stir to coat. Using the mixing spoon, bring the uncoated popcorn and peanuts from the bottom of the kettle to the top. Add the remaining ½ of the caramel mixture and continue stirring until all the popcorn and peanuts are coated.

Spread the caramel corn equally and evenly in two 12 × 18 × 1-inch or two 10½ × 15½ × 1-inch cookie pans. Bake for 1 hour, stirring every 15 minutes. The caramel coating will be crisp.

Remove from the oven and place the cookie pans on wire racks. Let the Caramel Corn stand until completely cool. Then, store the Caramel Corn in an airtight container.

NOTE: This temperature is for use at sea-level locations. To adjust the temperature for preparation of this recipe at higher elevations, see Boiled Candies and Frostings, page 19.

MAKES ABOUT 7 QUARTS

SERVING SUGGESTION: Place Caramel Corn in individual, colorful paper or cellophane bags and serve for dessert at a tailgate lunch or a teenage buffet before a football game.

GIFT SUGGESTION: Place Caramel Corn in large, colorful tin containers with covers and give as holiday gifts.

CHOCOLATE CRACKER SNACKS

1 1-pound package Town House crackers,
    divided
1 12-ounce jar (about 1½ cups) chunky
    peanut butter
24 ounces white confectioners' coating
    (almond bark), wafers or block style
1 12-ounce package (2 cups) semisweet
    chocolate chips

Cover 2 cookie sheets with aluminum foil;
smooth to remove any wrinkles; set aside.

Spread the peanut butter generously to cover
one side of ½ of the crackers. Cover each spread
cracker with a plain cracker to make sandwiches (use the remaining ½ of the crackers);
set aside.

Using a sharp knife, shave the confectioners'
coating coarsely and place it in the top of a double boiler. Add the chocolate chips.

Temper the confectioners' coating and chocolate chips together, following the procedures
described in How to Temper Chocolate (page
600). Bring the tempered mixture to 90° F.

Using a candy-dipping fork or a table fork,
dip the sandwiches, completely, in the tempered
mixture and place them on the prepared cookie
sheets. Let the dipped sandwiches stand until
completely cool and set.

Then, peel the Chocolate Cracker Snacks off
the aluminum foil and place, single layer, in an
airtight container(s).

MAKES ABOUT 72

Beverages

TO MAKE AN ICE RING

Many bowls of punch may be made especially glamorous and appealing by floating a beautifully arranged ice ring atop. Place your work of art in your bowl of irresistible punch just moments before the guests arrive.

To make a plain ice ring, fill an 8-inch ring mold with water, and freeze. To unmold, dip the mold briefly in warm water and invert.

To freeze decorative arrangements of strawberries, raspberries, grapes, or other edible foods in the ice ring, pour about ¼ inch cold water in the bottom of the mold, and freeze.

Arrange the fruit or other foods on top of the frozen water, placing the front of the fruit toward the bottom of the mold. Carefully pour about ⅛ inch additional cold water into the mold around the fruit. Guard against adding too much water, causing the fruit to float and the arrangement to be lost.

Place the mold in the freezer and let stand only until the fruit freezes in place. Then, add cold water to the top of the mold, and freeze.

Edible flowers (page 316) may be frozen in an ice ring, following the same procedures as for fruit.

COCOA

Swift and easy to make; warm and satisfying to drink.

3 tablespoons unsweetened cocoa powder
⅓ cup sugar
Dash of ground cinnamon
⅓ cup water
4 cups (1 quart) whole milk
¼ teaspoon pure vanilla extract
½ recipe Whipped Cream (page 373)
1 cup miniature marshmallows

In a medium saucepan, place the cocoa, sugar, and cinnamon; stir to combine. Add the water; stir to combine. Over medium heat, bring the mixture to a boil, stirring constantly. Add the milk; stir to blend. Increase the heat to medium-high and bring the mixture to just under boiling, stirring frequently.

Remove from the heat. Add the vanilla; stir to blend.

Pour the hot Cocoa into mugs. In two separate, small bowls with accompanying small serving spoons, serve the Whipped Cream and marshmallows for topping the Cocoa.

MAKES 4 SERVINGS

EGGNOG

The holidays hardly would seem complete without at least one cup of eggnog. Eggnogs have a long history, dating back to 1775 in America. "Nog" is an old English word for an ale; however, it is said that the English often made their eggnog with red wine. In America, this annual, festive indulgence is usually made with rum, brandy, or bourbon. Some recipes use both brandy and bourbon, but I prefer the smooth flavor of white rum blended with the eggs and whipped cream.

Although eggnog traditionally has been made with raw eggs, today's more informed food safety standards warn that it should be made either with a cooked custard base, as in this recipe, or with pasteurized eggs, as in commercial eggnog (see Egg Safety, page 220, for more on this subject).

6 extra-large eggs
½ cup sugar
Dash of salt
4 cups (1 quart) whole milk
1 teaspoon pure vanilla extract
2 cups (1 pint) whipping cream, unwhipped
¼ cup powdered sugar
1 teaspoon pure vanilla extract
1 cup white rum (optional)
Ground nutmeg for garnish

Place the eggs in the top of a double boiler. Using a handheld electric mixer, beat the eggs slightly on medium speed. Add the sugar and salt; using a spoon, stir to combine; set aside.

Pour the milk into a medium saucepan. Over medium heat, heat the milk until hot, but do not scald. Remove from the heat. Gradually add the hot milk to the egg mixture, beating constantly with the electric mixer on medium speed. Place the top of the double boiler over (not touching) low simmering water in the bottom pan. Cook the mixture until it reaches 160° F. on a candy thermometer (about 8 minutes), stirring continuously. (When the mixture reaches 160° F., it will just coat the spoon.)

Remove the top of the double boiler from the bottom pan. Add 1 teaspoon vanilla; stir to blend. Cool the custard mixture quickly by placing the top of the double boiler in a large mixing bowl of ice water and stirring the mixture constantly for 10 minutes. Cover the top of the double boiler tightly with plastic wrap; then, cover securely with aluminum foil and refrigerate until the custard mixture is completely cold.

Near serving time, pour the whipping cream into a medium mixing bowl. Using a standard-sized electric mixer, beat the cream on medium-high speed until it begins to stiffen. Reduce the mixer speed to medium-low. Add the powdered sugar and 1 teaspoon vanilla; continue beating the cream until stiff, but still soft and fluffy. Cover the whipped cream and refrigerate.

Shortly before serving, pour the cold custard mixture into a large mixing bowl. Add the rum; stir to blend; set aside. Reserve 1 cup of the refrigerated whipped cream in a small bowl; cover and refrigerate. Add the remaining whipped cream to the custard mixture; using a large mixing spoon, stir and fold in, leaving small lumps of whipped cream in the Eggnog. To serve, ladle the Eggnog into punch cups, spoon a small dollop of the reserved whipped cream on top, and sprinkle with nutmeg.

To serve buffet style, pour the Eggnog into a punch bowl. Spoon the reserved whipped cream into a small, attractive silver or crystal bowl and supply a small silver spoon. Fill a clean, decorative salt shaker with nutmeg. Serve the Eggnog for the guests, or let the guests serve themselves.

MAKES ABOUT 2 QUARTS; 12 SERVINGS

EGGNOG COFFEE

6 cups hot, freshly brewed coffee, regular or decaffeinated
¾ cup eggnog, homemade (page 618) or commercial
¼ cup plus 2 tablespoons Myers's (dark) rum
½ recipe Whipped Cream (page 309)
Ground nutmeg for garnish

Pour the hot coffee into 6 mugs. To each mug of coffee, add 2 tablespoons eggnog and 1 tablespoon rum; stir to blend. Top with a dollop of the Whipped Cream. Sprinkle the nutmeg over the Whipped Cream.

MAKES 6 SERVINGS

LEMONADE

Lemonade has played a longtime role in coping with Midwest summer heat. When I was young, I remember my Aunt Tell making gallons of fresh lemonade which we would pour into quart canning jars over lots of ice and deliver to the several hired men cultivating corn on my Uncle Joe's large farm near Creston, Iowa. Aunt Tell would drive through the gates of the various fields, and I would run with the lemonade down the end rows of corn and wait at the particular rows where each worker was on his tractor cultivating. The men were all smiles when they spotted me waiting to hand them the cold, icy drink—a welcome relief in the blistering sun. Of course, that was in the days before air-conditioned tractor cabs, now fairly common, and modern herbicides which make cultivation of today's hybrid corn unnecessary for the most part. But Midwest summers are still scorchers, and we still love lemonade!

The Iowa State Fair just wouldn't be complete for me without several trips to one of the Brafford lemonage stands (my favorite), where your order is made from real lemons as you wait, thirsting for a swig of that ambrosial, sour-sweet nectar splashing around the frosty ice cubes.

¾ cup freshly squeezed lemon juice (about 3 to 4 lemons)
½ cup sugar (superfine or granulated)
4 cups water
Sprigs of fresh mint for decoration (optional)

In a large pitcher, place the lemon juice, sugar, and water; stir until the sugar dissolves. Pour into tall glasses filled with ice cubes. Each glass may be decorated with a sprig of fresh mint.

MAKES 5 TO 6 SERVINGS

VARIATION: ½ cup freshly squeezed orange juice may be added to the mixture to produce a slightly less tart taste.

GRAPE JUICE–GINGER ALE REFRESHER

½ 12-ounce can (¾ cup) undiluted, frozen grape juice, thawed
¾ cup cold water
1 12-ounce can cold ginger ale

In a small pitcher, place the grape juice and water; stir to blend; set aside.

Fill 4 tall glasses nearly full of ice cubes. Into each glass, pour ¼ cup plus 2 tablespoons of the grape juice mixture (¼ of the grape juice mixture) and ¼ cup plus 2 tablespoons ginger ale (¼ of the ginger ale); stir briefly.

MAKES 4 SERVINGS

CHAMPAGNE PUNCH

If heretofore you have found most champagne punches to be disappointing, lacking in both "champagne" and "punch," a cup of this lively cheer should prove that champagne punch can live up to its name.

4 cups (1 quart) freshly squeezed, strained, cold orange juice
1 12-ounce can undiluted, frozen pineapple juice, thawed
1 cup cognac
½ cup Triple Sec liqueur (page 10)
1 1-liter bottle cold sparkling water
2 750-milliliter bottles cold champagne

Place a punch bowl in a larger bowl of small ice cubes or shaved ice. Pour some cold water over the ice cubes or shaved ice in the larger bowl. Into the punch bowl, pour the orange juice, pineapple juice, cognac, and Triple Sec liqueur; stir to blend.

Just before serving, add the sparkling water and champagne; stir, gently and briefly, to blend. Let the punch stand 1 or 2 minutes until the foam on top dissipates. Ladle into punch cups.

MAKES 3 1/2 QUARTS; 20 SERVINGS

CRANBERRY-VODKA PUNCH

Cranberry-Vodka Punch is a gorgeous bright red color, particularly suitable for Christmas, Valentine's Day, or a patriotic occasion. If you serve it during the holiday season, freeze fresh cranberries in the ice ring you float atop the punch. (If the punch will be served over a rather long period of time, remove the ice ring before it melts to the point of releasing the cranberries into the punch. Raw cranberries are too tart to be enjoyed in the drink.)

8 cups (2 quarts) cold cranberry juice
1 12-ounce can undiluted, frozen pink
  lemonade, thawed
1 750-milliliter bottle vodka
1 2-liter bottle cold ginger ale
Ice ring (page 618)

Into a punch bowl, pour the cranberry juice and lemonade; stir to blend. Add the vodka; stir to blend. Add the ginger ale; stir until just blended. Unmold the ice ring and float it in the punch. Serve the punch immediately.

MAKES 5 QUARTS; 30 SERVINGS

DES MOINES CLUB PUNCH

1 12-ounce can undiluted, frozen orange
  juice, partially thawed
1/3 cup undiluted, frozen lemonade, partially
  thawed
1/3 cup undiluted, frozen limeade, partially
  thawed
1/2 cup grenadine (alcoholic or nonalcoholic)
1 2/3 cups vodka (optional)
1 2-liter bottle plus 1 12-ounce can (about 2 1/2
  quarts total) cold 7UP
Small ice cubes

Into a punch bowl, pour the orange juice, lemonade, limeade, grenadine, and vodka; stir until the juices completely thaw and all the ingredients blend. Add the 7UP and ice cubes; stir briefly to blend. Serve immediately.

MAKES 3 1/2 QUARTS; 20 SERVINGS

BREAKFAST PUNCH

You will become known as a punch virtuoso when you serve this one at your next brunch or special breakfast.

¾ cup freshly squeezed, strained orange juice
¾ cup (6 ounces) undiluted, frozen pineapple juice, thawed
¾ cup water
1 medium-sized, ripe banana, peeled and cut into 1-inch chunks
1 ½ cups vodka

In a blender beaker, place the orange juice, pineapple juice, water, and banana chunks; process in the blender until the banana chunks blend with the juice. Add the vodka; process briefly until blended.

Pour the punch into a glass pitcher; cover with plastic wrap and refrigerate until ready to serve.

Then, stir the punch and place the pitcher in a wine cooler of ice to keep cold. To serve, pour the punch over ice cubes in 10-ounce rock glasses.

MAKES 8 SERVINGS

VARIATION: The amount of vodka may be reduced or it may be left out entirely; substitute additional water for the amount of vodka omitted.

ICEBERG PUNCH (ORANGE)

Little clumps of sherbet float like icebergs on top of this pretty, pale-colored punch. Each of the four versions of Iceberg Punch features a different sherbet, fruit juice, and optional liquor.

½ gallon orange sherbet
1 ½ cups freshly squeezed, strained orange juice
1 cup Grand Marnier liqueur (optional)
1 2-liter bottle cold sparkling water

Let the orange sherbet stand at room temperature, in the container, until softened (about 30 minutes).

Then, remove the softened sherbet from the container and place it in a large mixing bowl. Add the orange juice and Grand Marnier liqueur; stir to combine, leaving golf ball–sized chunks of sherbet.

Turn the mixture into a punch bowl. Add the ginger ale; stir briefly to blend. Serve immediately. Chunks of sherbet will float to the top of the punch, both in the punch bowl and in the punch cups when served, simulating icebergs.

MAKES 4 QUARTS; 24 SERVINGS

ICEBERG PUNCH (LEMON)

½ gallon lemon sherbet
¾ cup (6 ounces) undiluted, frozen lemonade, thawed
1 ½ cups (12 ounces) cold water
1 cup vodka (optional)
1 2-liter bottle cold sparkling water

Follow the Iceberg Punch (Orange) recipe, above, substituting lemon sherbet for the orange sherbet, ¾ cup (6 ounces) undiluted, frozen lemonade plus 1 ½ cups (12 ounces) water for the orange juice, and vodka for the Grand Marnier.

ICEBERG PUNCH (LIME)

½ gallon lime sherbet
¾ cup (6 ounces) undiluted, frozen limeade,
  thawed
1½ cups (12 ounces) cold water
1 cup white rum (optional)
1 2-liter bottle cold sparkling water

Follow the Iceberg Punch (Orange) recipe, above, substituting lime sherbet for the orange sherbet, ¾ cup (6 ounces) frozen limeade plus 1½ cups (12 ounces) water for the orange juice, and white rum for the Grand Marnier.

ICEBERG PUNCH (RASPBERRY)

½ gallon raspberry sherbet
¾ cup (½ 12-ounce can) undiluted, frozen
  cranberry-raspberry juice, thawed
1½ cups (12 ounces) cold water
1 cup Chambord raspberry liqueur (optional)
1 2-liter bottle cold sparkling water

Follow the Iceberg Punch (Orange) recipe, above, substituting raspberry sherbet for the orange sherbet, ¾ cup (6 ounces) frozen undiluted cranberry-raspberry juice plus 1½ cups (12 ounces) water for the orange juice, and Chambord for the Grand Marnier.

SPRITZER PUNCH

A spritzer is a drink made of wine (usually white) and soda water. The added fruit juice makes this drink what I call Spritzer Punch.

1 750-milliliter bottle, cold German
  Riesling–Auslese (white) wine*
2 cups freshly squeezed, strained orange juice
1 11.5-ounce can undiluted, frozen white
  grape juice, thawed
1 1-liter bottle cold sparkling water
Small ice cubes

* *Auslese is a category of high-quality German wines which are made from fully ripened grapes. Wines that are labeled "Auslese" have a naturally high sugar content but contain no added sugar.*

Place a punch bowl in a larger, attractive bowl of crushed ice standing on a serving tray. Into the punch bowl, pour the wine, orange juice, and grape juice; stir to blend. Add the sparkling water; stir briefly to blend. Drop a small number of ice cubes into the punch. Serve immediately, ladling the punch into widemouthed (to facilitate serving) wine glasses or punch cups

MAKES 2¾ QUARTS; 16 SERVINGS

HOT SPICED CIDER WITH APPLEJACK

2 2-inch pieces stick cinnamon
1 teaspoon whole allspice
10 whole cloves
8 cups (2 quarts) cider
¼ cup packed light brown sugar
¾ cup applejack (page 2) (optional)

Tie the stick cinnamon, allspice, and cloves in a damp cheesecloth bag (page 28); set aside. Pour the cider into a large saucepan or kettle. Add the brown sugar; stir to combine. Add the cheesecloth bag of spices. Over high heat, stir the mixture until the brown sugar dissolves. Cover and bring the mixture to a boil. Reduce the heat and simmer the mixture 15 minutes.

Remove from the heat. Remove and discard the cheesecloth bag of spices. Strain the hot cider through a piece of damp flannel secured, napped side up, in a sieve over a deep pan; let stand.

Clean the saucepan or kettle used to boil the cider to eliminate any remaining spice fragments. Pour the strained cider back into the saucepan or kettle. Add the applejack; stir to blend. Reheat, if necessary, but do not boil.

Ladle the spiced cider into mugs. Keep the remainder warm in the covered saucepan or kettle over very low heat.

MAKES 10 SERVINGS

TO SERVE IN A PUNCH BOWL: Pour the cider into a punch bowl which has been warmed with hot water. *Caution:* Do not pour hot water or hot cider into a cut glass or delicate crystal punch bowl (or any nonheatproof glass punch bowl). Float a few kumquats, each studded with 3 whole cloves, in the hot cider.

Permissions and Courtesies

Edited extractions from *Publication N-2857: What's in a Recipe?*, prepared by Phyllis Olson and Diane Nelson. Published March 1986 by Iowa State University, Cooperative Extension Service. By permission of the publisher.

Information and extractions from *Pamphlet 41: High Altitude Food Preparation*, prepared by Pat Kendall. Revised. Published January 1995 by Colorado State University Cooperative Extension. By permission of the publisher.

Information and extractions from *Bulletin 497A: High Altitude Baking* by Pat Kendall and Willene Dilsaver. Revised. Published April 1992 by Colorado State University Cooperative Extension. By permission of the publisher.

Picture of retail cuts of pork, copyright © 2007 by the Pork Checkoff. Reprinted by permission of the Pork Checkoff.

Picture of retail cuts beef and veal, copyright © 2005 by The Beef Checkoff Program. Reprinted by permission of The Beef Checkoff Program.

Grilled Iowa Pork Chops recipe. Courtesy of the Iowa Pork Producers Association.

Picture of pasta types, from *A Passion for Pasta!*, copyright © 1995 by Borden, Inc. By permission of the publisher.

Adaptation of the recipe "Ham-Stuffed Eggplant" from *'76 Cook Book*, Women of Plymouth Church, editors, published 1976 by Plymouth Congregational United Church of Christ, Des Moines, Iowa. By permission of the publisher.

Edited extractions from *The Wilton Method: Basic Cake Decorating Course*, copyright © 1987 by Wilton Enterprises, Inc. By permission of the publisher.

Edited extractions and photographs of piped holly leaves and piped poinsettia from *The Wilton Method: Cake Decorating Course 2*, copyright © 1987 by Wilton Enterprises, Inc. By permission of the publisher.

Photographs of piped borders, designs, and flowers, and accompanying edited instructions from *Wilton Cake Decorating: 1998 Wilton Yearbook*, copyright © 1996 by Wilton Enterprises, Inc. By permission of the publisher.

Illustrations on pages 319 and 322 based upon adaptations of pictures and illustrations in Wilton Enterprises publications. By permission of the publisher.

Edited version of recipe for Jule Kage by Pat Hatch from *Fun Fest Favorites: Recipes from the Iowa State Fair*, copyright © 1990 by the Iowa State Fair, and recipe for Julekake by Pat Hatch from *The Only Cookbook of Its Kind: Recipes from the Iowa State Fair*, copyright © 1993 by the Iowa State Fair. By permission of the publisher.

Recipe for Pat Berry's Julekake (Norwegian Christmas Bread). By permission of Pat Berry.

Edited version of recipe for Chocolate Raspberry Torte by Joy McFarland from *The Only Cookbook of Its Kind: Recipes from the Iowa State Fair*, copyright © 1993 by the Iowa State Fair. By permission of the publisher.

Recipe for Joy McFarland's Mile-High Torte. By permission of Joy McFarland.

Edited versions of recipes by Diane S. Roupe from *Fun Fest Favorites: Recipes from the Iowa State Fair*, copyright © 1990 by the Iowa State Fair. By permission of the publisher.

Edited versions of recipes by Diane S. Roupe from *The Only Cookbook of Its Kind: Recipes from the Iowa State Fair*, copyright © 1993 by the Iowa State Fair. By permission of the publisher.

Sources Consulted

VOLUME AND WEIGHT MEASURES

U.S. Department of Commerce. National Institute of Standards and Technology. *NIST Handbook 44: Specifications, Tolerances, and Other Technical Requirements for Weighing and Measuring Devices.* 1994 ed. Edited by Henry V. Oppermann and Tina G. Butcher. Washington, D.C., October 1993.

SPECIAL SECTIONS

Food Safety

American Egg Board. *Eggcyclopedia.* 3d ed., rev. Park Ridge, Ill., April 1994.

American Egg Board. *Salmonella & Egg Safety.* Park Ridge, Ill., May 1995.

American Egg Board. *The Egg Handling & Care Guide.* rev. Park Ridge, Ill., September 1994.

Carr, Tom. "Trichinosis: Risk and Prevention," *Facts from the Meat Board: Meat Science: Series FS/MS 004.* Chicago: National Live Stock and Meat Board, Meat Science Department, 1992.

Gentsch, Cynthia C., and Susan Templin Conley. "From USDA's Meat and Poultry Hotline: A Barbeque Handbook." *Food News for Consumers* (Summer 1991); reprint, Washington, D.C.: U.S. Department of Agriculture, Food Safety and Inspection Service, n.d.

National Pork Producers Council. Pork Information Bureau. *National Survey Confirms Millions of Consumers Are Cooking Pork Wrong.* Des Moines, January 1992.

National Pork Producers Council. Pork Information Bureau. *Pork Industry to Mom: Teach Your Children Medium—Not Well.* Minneapolis, January 1992.

Parmley, Mary Ann. "Researching Microwave Safety." *Food News for Consumers* (Summer 1990); reprint, Washington, D.C.: U.S. Department of Agriculture. Food Safety and Inspection Service, n.d.

Parmley, Mary Ann, and Diane VanLonkhuyzen. "The Whys Behind USDA's Food Safety Rules," *Food News for Consumers* (Spring 1991); reprint, Washington, D.C.: U.S. Department of Agriculture, Food Safety and Inspection Service, n.d.

Templin, Susan, CiCi Williamson, and Marilyn Johnston. "How to Microwave Safely." *Food News for Consumers* (Spring 1990); reprint, Washington, D.C.: U.S. Department of Agriculture, Food Safety and Inspection Service, n.d.

U.S. Department of Agriculture. Agriculture Marketing Service. *Home and Garden Bulletin Number 263: How to Buy Poultry.* Washington, D.C., July 1995.

U.S. Department of Agriculture. Agriculture Marketing Service. *Home and Garden Bulletin Number 264: How to Buy Eggs.* Washington, D.C., July 1995.

U.S. Department of Agriculture. Food and Drug Administration. *Consumer Bulletin AMS-602: Handling Eggs Safetly at Home.* rev. Washington, D.C., January 1992.

U.S. Department of Agriculture. Food Safety and Inspection Service. Cooperative State Research, Education and Extension Service. *Take the Guesswork Out of Roasting a Turkey.* Washington, D.C., n.d.

U.S. Department of Agriculture. Food Safety and Inspection Service. "Focus On: Egg Products." *Food Safety Focus: From USDA's Meat and Poultry Hotline.* Washington, D.C., n.d.

U.S. Department of Agriculture. Food Safety and Inspection Service. Food Safety & Consumer Education Office. "Turkey Basics: Safe Defrosting." *Consumer Information from USDA.* Washington, D.C., November 1996.

U.S. Department of Agriculture. Food Safety and Inspection Service. Food Safety & Consumer Education Office. "Turkey Basics: Stuffing." *Consumer Information from USDA.* Washington, D.C., November 1996.

U.S. Department of Agriculture. Food Safety and Inspection Service. "From USDA's Meat and Poultry Hotline: Pack-Up-And-Go with Summer Foods." *Food News for Consumers* (Summer 1991); reprint, Washington, D.C., n.d.

U.S. Department of Agriculture. Food Safety and Inspection Service. *Home and Garden Bulletin No. 248: A Quick Consumer Guide to Safe Food Handling.* Washington, D.C., August 1995.

U.S. Department of Agriculture. Food Safety and Inspection Service. "Safe Food to Go—For Lunches and Picnics." *Food News for Consumers* (Summer 1988); condensed reprint, Washington, D.C., May 1988.

Williamson, CiCi. "Why the Experts Say Cook It." *Food News for Consumers* (Spring 1991); reprint, Washington, D.C.: U.S. Department of Agriculture Food Safety and Inspection Service, n.d.

The Functions of Ingredients in Batters and Doughs

Iowa State University, Cooperative Extension Service. *Publication N-2857: What's in a Recipe?*, prepared by Phyllis Olson and Diane Nelson. Ames, March 1986.

McComber, Diane, Associate Professor of Food Science and Human Nutrition, Iowa State University, Ames. Consultation and correspondence with author, June 1994.

To Cook and Bake at High Altitudes

Charley, Helen. *Food Science.* 2d ed. New York: Macmillan Publishing Co., 1982.

Colorado State University Cooperation Extension. *Pamphlet 41: High Altitude Food Preparation,* rev., prepared by Pat Kendall. Fort Collins, January 1995.

Johnson, Jeff, Coordination Meteorologist, U.S. Department of Commerce, National Oceanic and Atmospheric Administration, Johnston, Iowa. Telephone interview by author, 11 January 1997.

Kendall, Pat, Professor and Extension Food and Nutrition Specialist, Colorado State University, Fort Collins. Telephone interview by author, 9 January 1997 and correspondence with author, January 1997.

Kendall, Pat, and Willene Dilsaver. *Bulletin 497A: High Altitude Baking.* rev. Fort Collins: Colorado State University Cooperative Extension, April 1992.

Kendrick, Ruth A., and Pauline H. Atkinson. *Candymaking.* Los Angeles: HPBooks, 1987.

The American Home Economics Association. *Handbook of Food Preparation.* 8th ed. Alexandria, Va., 1980.

To Use Herbs

Hollis, Sarah. *The Country Diary Herbal.* New York: Henry Holt and Co., 1990.

Kowalchik, Claire, and William H. Hylton, eds. *Rodale's Illustrated Encyclopedia of Herbs.* Emmaus, Pa.: Rodale Press, 1987.

Tone Bros., Inc. *Spice Advice Chart.* Des Moines, 1989.

Today's Leaner Meats

National Live Stock and Meat Board and National Pork Board. *Possibilities with Pork.* Chicago, 1991.

National Live Stock and Meat Board in cooperation with the American Heart Association. *Meat Nutrient Facts.* Chicago, 1995.

Savell, J. W., H. R. Cross, D. S. Hale, and Lisa Beasley. *National Beef Market Basket Survey: Final Report to the National Cattlemen's Foundation, Inc.* n.p.: Texas A&M University, Department of Animal Science, Meats & Muscle Biology Section, June 1988.

U.S. Department of Agriculture. Human Nutrition Information Service. *Agriculture Handbook Number 8-10: Composition of Foods: Pork Products,* rev., by Nutrition Minitoring Division. Principal investigator: Barbara A. Anderson. Assisted by: Lynn E. Dickey and I. Margaret Hoke. Washington, D.C.: Government Printing Office, December 1992.

U.S. Department of Agriculture. Human Nutrition Information Service. *Agriculture Handbook Number*

8-13: Composition of Foods: Beef Products, rev., by Nutrition Monitoring Division. Principal investigators: Barbara A. Anderson and I. Margaret Hoke. Washington, D.C.: Government Printing Office, May 1990.

U.S. Department of Agriculture. Science and Education Administration. *Agriculture Handbook Number 8-5: Composition of Foods: Poultry Products,* rev., by Consumer and Food Economics Institute. Principal investigator: Linda P. Posati. Washington, D.C.: Government Printing Office, August 1979.

Edible Flowers

Creasy, Rosalind. *Cooking from the Garden.* San Francisco: Sierra Club Books, 1988.

Duke, James A., Economic Botanist, U.S. Department of Agriculture, Agricultural Research Service, Beltsville, Maryland (retired). Writings on the subject of edible flowers and correspondence with author 1995 and 1996.

Elias, Thomas S., and Peter A. Dykeman. *Edible Wild Plants: A North American Field Guide.* New York: Sterling Publishing Co., 1990.

Holis, Sarah. *The Country Diary Herbal.* New York: Henry Holt and Co., 1990.

Kowalchik, Claire, and William H. Hylton, eds. *Rodale's Illustrated Encyclopedia of Herbs.* Emmaus, Pa.: Rodale Press, 1987.

Young, Kay. *Wild Seasons: Gathering and Cooking Wild Plants of the Great Plains.* Lincoln: University of Nebraska Press, 1993.

Using a Decorating Bag to Pipe Garnishes and Decorations

Wilton Enterprises, Inc. *The Wilton Method: Basic Cake Decorating Course.* Woodridge, Ill., 1987.

Wilton Enterprises, Inc. *The Wilton Method: Basic Cake Decorating Course 2.* Woodridge, Ill., 1987.

Wilton Enterprises. *Wilton Cake Decorating: 1998 Wilton Yearbook.* Woodridge, Ill., 1997.

Baking Yeast Breads and Rolls

Berry, Pat. Urbandale, Iowa. Consultation with author, 1995 and 1996.

Better Homes and Gardens. *Homemade Bread Cook Book.* Des Moines: Meredith Corp., 1973.

Better Homes and Gardens. *Old-Fashioned Home Baking.* Des Moines: Meredith Corp., 1990.

Charley, Helen. *Food Science.* 2d ed. New York: Macmillan Publishing Co., 1982.

Farm Journal Food Editors. *Homemade Bread.* Edited by Nell B. Nichols. Garden City, N.Y.: Doubleday and Co., 1969.

McComber, Diane, Associate Professor of Food Science and Human Nutrition, Iowa State University, Ames. Consultation and correspondence with author, 1995 and 1996.

Secrets for Making Successful Pastry Piecrust

McComber, Diane, Associate Professor of Food Science and Human Nutrition, Iowa State University, Ames. Consultation and correspondence with author, December 1993 and January 1994.

GENERAL

All Saints Parish. *All Saints 1914–1989: Celebrating 75 Years of Faith* [cookbook]. Des Moines, 1990.

American Egg Board. *Encyclopedia.* 3rd ed., rev. Park Ridge, Ill., April 1994.

Anderson, Beth. *Wild Rice for All Seasons Cookbook.* Minneapolis: Beth Anderson Associates, 1984.

Anderson, Kenneth N., and Lois E. Anderson. *The International Dictionary of Food & Nutrition.* New York: John Wiley & Sons, Inc., 1993.

Atwood, Mary S. *A Taste of India.* Boston: Houghton Mifflin Co., 1969.

Austin, Elizabeth S., and Oliver L. Austin, Jr. *The Random House Book of Birds.* New York: Random House, 1970.

Baker, Mina, and Betty J. Bergman, eds. *Pella Collectors Cook Book,* 8th ed. Pella, Iowa: Central College Auxiliary, 1982.

Beard, James. *James Beard's American Cookery.* Boston: Little, Brown and Co., 1972.

Beef Checkoff Program, The. *Beef Made Easy: Retail Cuts and Recommended Cooking Methods.* Photograph. Centennial, CO, 2005.

Beef Checkoff Program, The. *Veal Retail Cuts.* Photograph. Centennial, CO, 2005.

Better Homes and Gardens. *All-Time Favorite Vegetable Recipes.* Des Moines: Meredith Corp., 1977.

Better Home and Gardens. *Candy.* Des Moines: Meredith Corp., 1984.

Better Homes and Gardens. *Cookies for Christmas.* Des Moines: Meredith Corp., 1985.

Better Homes and Gardens. *Old-Fashioned Home Baking.* Des Moines: Meredith Corp., 1990.

Better Homes and Gardens. *Pies and Cakes.* New York: Meredith Press, 1996.

Better Homes and Gardens Creative Ideas. *Holiday Cooking.* (1986.)

Better Homes and Gardens Creative Ideas. *Holiday Desserts.* (1988.)

Better Homes and Gardens Editors. *Salad Book.* Des Moines: Meredith Publishing Co., 1958.

Biller, Rudolf. *Garnishing and Decoration.* n.p.: Virtue & Co., n.d.

Birkby, Evelyn, ed. *KMA Festival Cookie Book.* Shenandoah, Iowa: KMA Radio, 1983.

Brand, Mildred. *Ideals Candy Cookbook.* n.p.: Ideals, 1979.

Brennan, Georgeanne, Isaac Cronin, and Charlotte Glenn. *The New American Vegetable Cookbook: The Definitive Guide to America's Exotic & Traditional Vegetables.* Berkeley, Calif.: Aris Books, 1985.

Brethren Publishing House. *Granddaughter's Inglenook Cookbook.* Elgin, Ill., 1942.

Brown & Bigelow. *A Merry Christmas at Your House.* St. Paul, Minn., 1956.

Brown & Bigelow. *Game & Fish: Their Preparation and Special Cooking.* St. Paul, Minn., 1960.

Budgen, June. *The Book of Garnishes.* Tucson: HPBooks, 1986.

Charley, Helen. *Food Science.* 2d ed. New York: Macmillan Publishing Co., 1982.

Claiborne, Craig, ed. *The New York Times Cook Book.* New York: Harper and Row, 1961.

Collier's Encyclopedia, 1993 ed. S.v. "George Washington," by Esmond Wright.

Committee from St. Cecilia's Church and St. Michael's Church. *Hastings Catholic Community Cookbook.* Hastings, Nebr.: Vaughan's Printers, n.d.

Crowley, Jerry. *The Fine Art of Garnishing.* Baltimore: Lieba Inc., 1978.

Culinary Arts Institute. *The German & Viennese Cookbook.* Chicago, 1956.

Culinary Arts Institute. *The Gourmet Foods Cookbook.* Chicago, 1955.

Cunningham, Marion. *The Fannie Farmer Cookbook.* 13th ed. New York: Alfred A. Knopf, 1990.

Dinsmore, James J. *A Country So Full of Game: The Story of Wildlife in Iowa.* Iowa City: University of Iowa Press, 1994.

Elias, Thomas S., and Peter A. Dykeman. *Edible Wild Plants: A North American Field Guide.* New York: Sterling Publishing Co., 1990.

Encyclopaedia Brittanica, 1967 ed. S.v. "Brazil Nuts," "Bun," and "Corn," by Paul C. Mangelsdorf.

Farm Journal Food Editors. *America's Best Vegetable Recipes: 666 Ways to Make Vegetables Irresistible.* Edited by Nell B. Nichols. Garden City, N.Y.: Doubleday and Co., 1970.

Farm Journal Food Editors. *Great Home Cooking in America: Heirloom Recipes Treasures for Generations.* Garden City, N.Y.: Doubleday and Co., 1976.

Farm Journal Food Editors. *Homemade Bread.* Edited by Nell B. Nichols. Garden City, N.Y.: Doubleday and Co., 1969.

Farm Journal Food Editors. *Homemade Cookies.* Edited by Nell B. Nichols. Garden City, N.Y.: Doubleday and Co., 1971.

General Mills, Inc. *Betty Crocker's Christmas Cookbook.* New York: Golden Press, 1983.

Gerhard, Frank. *Kulinarische Streifzüge durch Schwaben.* Künzelsau, Germany: Sigloch Edition, 1979.

Gifts O' the Wild. *Original Minnesota Ojibway (Chippewa) Indian Recipes.* Guthrie, Minn., 1983.

Herbst, Sharon Tyler. *Food Lover's Companion.* Hauppauge, N.Y.: Barron's, 1990.

Hodgson Mill, Inc. *Recipes for Unprocessed Wheat Bran and Untoasted Wheat Germ.* Effingham, Ill., n.d.

Huck, Virginia, and Ann H. Anderson, eds. *100 Years of Good Cooking.* St. Paul: The Minnesota Historical Society, 1958.

Iowa Department of Agriculture & Land Stewardship in Cooperation with Iowa Honey Producers Association. *Honey Recipe Book.* Des Moines, 1971.

Iowa Pork Producers Association. *Ground Pork Instead.* Des Moines, n.d.

Iowa Pork Producers Association. *Iowa Pork Tent Recipes: Iowa Chops.* Des Moines, 1984.

Iowa State Fair. *Fun Fest Favorites: Recipes from the Iowa State Fair.* Des Moines, 1990.

Iowa State Fair. *Prize Winning Recipes: From the Iowa State Fair!* 2d ed. Des Moines, n.d.

Iowa State Fair. *Recipes to Savor: Iowa State Fair Cookbook.* Des Moines, 1988.

Iowa State Fair. *The Only Cookbook of Its Kind: Recipes from the Iowa State Fair.* Des Moines, 1993.

Iowa State Fair. *Winners Every One!* [cookbook]. Des Moines, 1986.

Jamison, Cheryl and Bill. *Smoke & Spice.* Rev. ed. Boston: The Harvard Common Press, 2003.

Kappa Alpha Theta Alumnae of Des Moines. *Noel Nibbles.* Des Moines, 1973.

Kendrick, Ruth A., and Pauline H. Atkinson. *Candymaking.* Los Angeles: HPBooks, 1987.

Kirk, Paul, and Bob Lyon. *Paul Kirk's Championship Barbecue.* Boston: The Harvard Common Press, 2004

Kreidberg, Marjorie. *Food on the Frontier.* St. Paul: Minnesota Historical Society Press, 1975.

Larousse, David Paul. *Edible Art: Forty-Eight Garnishes for the Professional.* New York: Van Nostrand Reinhold, 1987.

Mariani, John F. *The Dictionary of American Food and Drink.* New Haven: Ricknor & Fields, 1983.

Marsh, Dorothy B., ed. *Good Housekeeping Cook Book.* New York: Rinehart & Co., 1955.

Meredith Corporation. *Better Homes and Gardens Meat Cook Book.* Des Moines: Meredith Press, 1969.

Meredith Corporation. *Better Homes and Gardens New Cook Book.* 10th ring-bound ed. Des Moines: Meredith Corp., 1989.

Meredith Publishing Company. *Better Homes and Gardens New Cook Book.* Des Moines: Meredith Publishing Co., 1953.

Michigan United Conservation Clubs. *Wildlife Chef.* 2d ed., rev. and enl. Lansing, 1981.

North American Meat Processors Association. *The Meat Buyers Guide.* 2d printing, August 2000. Reston, Virginia: North American Meat Processors Association, 1997.

Nichols, Nell B., ed. *Farm Journal's Complete Pie Cookbook.* Garden City, N.Y.: Doubleday and Co., 1965.

Peace Lutheran Church. *The Lord's Harvest.* Hastings, Nebr.: Fundcraft Publishing, 1978.

Peck, Paula. *The Art of Fine Baking.* New York: Barnes & Noble Books, 1993.

Polushkin, Maria. *The Dumpling Cookbook.* New York: Workman Publishing Company, Inc., 1997.

Pork Checkoff, The. *Pork Basics.* Photograph. Des Moines, 2007.

Pullen, Pauline Evans. *The Missouri Sampler: A Collection of Favorite Recipes from All Counties.* Springfield: Pauline E. Pullen, 1987.

Raichlen, Steven. *The Barbecue! Bible.* New York: Workman Publishing, 1998.

Robbins, Chandler S., Bertel Bruun, and Herbert S. Zim. *A Guide to Field Identification: Birds of North America.* New York: Golden Press, 1966.

Roemig, Sue, ed. *German Recipes: Old World Specialties from the Amana Colonies.* Iowa City: Penfield Press, 1985.

Rombauer, Irma S., and Marion Rombauer Becker. *Joy of Cooking.* New York: Bobbs-Merrill, 1975.

Rubash, Joyce. *Master Dictionary of Food and Wine.* New York: Van Nostrand Reinhold, 1990.

Scharfenberg, Horst. *The Cuisines of Germany: Regional Specialties and Traditional Home Cooking.* New York: Poseidon Press, 1989.

Schik, Susan, ed. *Schik Family Recipe Book.* Hastings, Nebr.: Tom Schik, n.d.

Schneider, Elizabeth. *Uncommon Fruits & Vegetables: A Commonsense Guide.* New York: Harper and Row, 1986.

Small, Marvin. *The World's Best Recipes.* n.p.: Hawthorn Books, 1955; reprint, New York: Pocket Books, Cardinal ed. 1957.

Stephenson's Apple Farm Restaurant. *Stephenson's Old Apple Farm Receipts.* Kansas City, Mo., 1967.

Sully Christian School Circle. [Cookbook]. Iowa Falls: General Publishing and Binding, 1970.

The American Home Economics Association. *Handbook of Food Preparation.* 8th ed. Alexandria, Va., 1980.

The Chapel by the Sea, United Presbyterian Church. *Women's Association Cook Book II.* Fort Myers Beach, Fla., 1979.

The New Encyclopaedia Brittanica, 15th ed. S.v. "Food Processing: Sugar" by Margaret A. Clarke and "Molasses."

The Popcorn Institute. *Popcorn Production Study 1995.* Chicago: The Popcorn Institute, 18 January 1996.

Time Incorporated. *Picture Cook Book.* New York, 1958.

"Two Good Layer Cakes," *Woman's Day* (February 1940): 36.

Van Klompenburg, Carol. *Delightfully Dutch: Recipes and Traditions.* Iowa City: Penfield Press, 1984.

Van Klompenburg, Carol, comp. *Dutch Treats: Recipes, Folklore, Proverbs.* Iowa City: Penfield Press, 1987.

What Cheer Methodist Church, Mary Circle. *Methodist Church Cook Book.* What Cheer, Iowa, 1964.

Williams, Sallie Y. *The Art of Presenting Food.* New York: Hearst Books, 1982.

Women of Plymouth Church, eds. *'76 Cook Book.* Des Moines: Plymouth Congregational United Church of Christ, 1976.

Ying, Mildred, ed. *The New Good Housekeeping Cookbook.* New York: Hearst Books, 1986.

Product Sources

Sunnyland Farms, Inc.
Jane Willson
Willson Road at Pecan City
P.O. Box 8200
Albany, Georgia 31706-8200
800-999-2488
Website: www.sunnylandfarms.com

Sweet Celebrations, Inc.
P.O. Box 39426
Edina, Minnesota 55439-0426
800-328-6722
Website: www.sweetc.com

Wilton Enterprises
2240 West 75th Street
Woodridge, Illinois 60517-0750
800-794-5866
Website: www.wilton.com

Acknowledgments

Our world is interdependent—humankind's works result from collaboration. Personal creative products are an amalgamation of the maker's family, childhood, teachers, friends, advisers, and life experiences, interfused with his/her own efforts and unique, individual spirit.

While *The Blue Ribbon Country Cookbook* carries my name as "author," "catalyst" would be a more appropriate designation. Those to whom this cookbook is dedicated have influenced my life in special ways which led to and made possible the writing of the book. Immense credit is due many other people, organizations, and agencies who shared their knowledge, talents, and time to culminate in this volume. My thank you to those recognized below for their gracious help and meaningful contributions.

I am most grateful to Larry Stone, Geoff Stone, and Pamela Clements at Thomas Nelson Publishers for producing this new edition of *The Blue Ribbon Country Cookbook*. It has been a real pleasure working with them. A big thanks also to Belinda Bass, Emily Prather, Damon Goude, Beth Hood, Kay Meadows, and all those at the publishing house who have worked so diligently on the revision and marketing of the book.

My wonderful agent, Coleen O'Shea, teamed *The Blue Ribbon Country Cookbook* with Thomas Nelson, and I am deeply appreciative of her insightful and propitious pairing.

Featured in this new edition are 36 stunning food photographs by master photographer Mike Dieter, whose pictures artfully couple clear recipe depiction with style and beauty. The recipe-precise food was prepared expertly, while at the same time elegantly, by food stylist Jill Lust assisted by Sally Benson. Prop stylist, Sue Mitchell, skillfully designed the attractive, appropriate settings to stage the food. My thanks to you all for so seamlessly combining your exceptional talents to produce the beautiful pictures.

Plaudits to Sharon Soder whose instructional, detail-perfect illustrations continue to punctuate the recipes in this volume. What a talented artist!

Abiding gratitude to Lauren Shakely, Katie Workman, and my many friends at Clarkson Potter and Crown who believed in *The Blue Ribbon Country Cookbook* and published the successful first edition. And my continuing appreciation to Angela Miller who was the instrumental in bringing my original dream for this cookbook into reality.

Other key players who so earnestly and graciously helped steer the first edition of the book down the road to publication are my dear friends, Tom Wells and Lee Tannen; and Alix Nelson, Al Lowman, and Cici Winant. Profound and enduring thanks to each of you.

Many notable scholars generously shared their knowledge to assist in the development of certain technical explanations in the cookbook. I particularly want to thank:

Diane McComber, associate professor emeritus, Food Science Human Nutrition, Iowa State University; Pat Kendall, professor and extension food and nutrition specialist, Colorado State University; and James A. Duke, noted authority on edible flowers.

My special appreciation to Candace Manroe, Arlette Hollister, Kathie Swift, Pat Berry, Joy McFarland, Louise Piper, Grace Montognese, and Sharon Willmore who each contributed to *The Blue Ribbon Country Cookbook* in important ways.

Sincere thanks to the following agencies, corporations, and organizations, and named personnel therein, who will find the fruits of their assistance and efforts on the pages of this book and/or the first edition of it. Some of the people whose names are listed have retired or currently hold other positions; however, positions are listed as held when contributions to the first or new edition of the book were made:

Alltrista Consumer Products Company

American Lamb Council:
Priscilla Root

Borden Foods Corporation:
Becky S. Honigford, Administrative Secretary, Product Publicity

Borden, Inc.:
North American Pasta and Sauce—Lynn Anderson, Manager of Corporate Communications; North American Pasta Products —Jeanne W. Fox, Manager of Media Communications

Cooks'Ware:
Nancy and Dick Sanders, Owners

Dahl's Food Marts:
Ed Beltrame, Don Bennett, Barry Brauch, Steve Goodrich, Don Hart, John Hawxby, Wally Hawxby, Kevin Helm, Jim Hubbartt, Denny Johnson, Cliff Nelson, Don Relph, Dave Richards, Charles Thyberg, Dave Wilson

Des Moines Club:
Kevin Robinson, General Manager

Des Moines Public Library

Hawgeyes BBQ:
Mike Tucker, Bret Wram

Hershey Foods Corporation:
Cheryl A. Reitz, Senior Consumer Food Publicist

Hodgson Mill, Inc.:
Kristin Dougherty, Hope R. Yingst

International Association of Fairs and Expositions:
Lewis Miller, Executive Vice President

International Dairy Foods Association:
Linda A. Leger, Assistant Director

Iowa Association of Electric Cooperatives:
Jody Garlock, Managing Editor

Iowa Department of Natural Resources:
Marion Conover, Chief of Fisheries; Terry Little, Wildlife Research Supervisor; Jan Myers; Irene Ray; Terry Z. Riley, Ph.D., Upland Wildlife Research Biologist

Iowa Pork Producers Association:
Joyce Hoppes, Consumer Information Director; Jeff Schnell, Public Policy Director; Marty Schwager, Consumer Education Director

Iowa State Fair:
Arlette Hollister, Superintendent, Food Department; Kathie Swift, Marketing Director

Illinois State Fair:
Janet Mathis, Deputy Superintendent; Suzanne Moss, Manager, Promotional Events

Indiana State Fair:
William H. Stinson, Executive Director; Cynthia C. Hoye, Marketing Director

Kansas State Fair:
Robert A. Gottschalk, General Mgr.; Joan R. Brown, Opeations Manager

Michigan State Fair:
John C. Hertel, General Manger; Alice Diefenthaler, Community Arts Coordinator; Joan Schwedt

Minnesota State Fair:
Susan Ritt, Marketing Director

Missouri State Fair:
Gary D. Slater, Director; Wendy Baker, Public Information Specialist; Heather Willard, Marketing/Publicity

Nebraska State Fair:
John Skold, General Manager

New York State Fair

North Dakota State Fair:
Leslie S. Herslip, Marketing Director;
Renae Korslien

Ohio State Fair

South Dakota State Fair:
Milo Rypkema, Commission Chairman;
Christine Duxbury, Sr. Secretary;
Holly Hornung

Wisconsin State Fair:
Julie Carlson, Director of Public Relations

Iowa State University:
Dr. Joseph C. Cordray; Professor of Animal
Science and Extension Meat Specialist.
Stephen W. Bryant; Assistant Meat Labora-
tory Manager. Cooperative Extension Ser-
vice—Dr. William Edwards; Susan B. Klein,
Nutrition and Health Field Specialist; Diane
Nelson, Extension Communication Systems.
Plant Introduction Station—Mark Widr-
lechner, Ph.D., Horticulturist

Italian Importing Co.:
Mary and John Sitroneto, Owners

Knapp Properties Inc.:
R. Stephen Vilmain, President, Restaurant
Division; Jody Valentine

Kraft General Foods, Inc.

Libbey Glass Inc.:
Lucille Lee

Mayo Clinic Health Letter:
Christopher Frye, Managing Editor; Marie
Cranor, Secretary

National Cattlemen's Beef Association:
Marietta J. Buyck, Director of Producer
Education; Terence R. Dockerty, Ph.D.,
Director of Research Information; Kim
First, Director of Customer Service; Jim
Gibb, Ph.D., Vice President, Center for
Quality; H. Kenneth Johnson, Executive
Director, Value Based Meat Systems; James
O. Reagan, Ph.D., Executive Director, Sci-
ence and Technology; Melissa Taylor

National Corn Growers Association:
KayAnn Miller, Manager, Public Relations

National 4-H Council:
Rachel Nestor, Marketing Assistant

National Pork Producers Council:
Robin Kline, M.S., R.D., Director of Consumer Affairs

National Rifle Association of America:
Billy R. Templeton, Wildlife Management
Specialist

Nebraska Soybean Board:
Phyllis Staats,
Consumer Information Specialist

Pennsylvania State University:
Thomas S. Dimick, Research Support Staff,
Food Science Department

**Plymouth Congregational United
Church of Christ:**
Nancy Wallace, President,
Women's Fellowship

Random House, Inc.:
Patricia Flynn, Director,
Copyright & Permissions

Red Star Yeast & Products

State Library of Iowa:
Beth Henning, Coordinator,
State Data Center

Sweet Celebrations Inc.:
Christine Dalquist

The Fine Arts Museums of San Francisco:
Mary Haas

**The Northcentral Section of The Wildlife
Society:**
Gary E. Potts, President;
David J. Case, Past President

The Popcorn Institute:
Kristin Stromberg, Marketing Coordinator

The Quaker Oats Company:
Susan Regal

The University of Georgia:
Cooperative Extension Service—Elizabeth
L. Andress, Extension Leader for Food,
Nutrition, and Health

The Windrow Restaurant:
Janet and Bill Hayes, Owners;
Kelly Bellcock, Chef

Tone Brothers, Inc.:
Diane M. Ward, Certified Home Economist

United States Department of Agriculture:

Agricultural Research Service:
Bernadette McAuliffe, Writer; Judy Ducellier, Plant Germplasm Program Assistant; Mary Y. Hama, Economist

Center for Nutrition Policy and Promotion:
John S. Webster, Director, Public Information; Jackie Haven, Nutritionist

Cooperative State Research, Education, and Extension Service:
Virginia C. Gobeli, Ed.D., National 4-H Program Leader, Families, 4-H, and Nutrition; Jan Singleton, Ph.D., R.D. National Program Leader, Food Science and Nutrition

Economic Research Service:
Arthur Daugherty, Agricultural Economist; Mark J. Gehlhar Ph.D., Economist; Stephen A. MacDonald, Agricultural Economist; Judy Putnam, Economist; Roger P. Strickland, Head, Farm Sector Income Accounts

Food Safety and Inspection Service:
Susan Templin Conley, Director, Food Safety Education and Communications Staff; Charles R. Edwards, Director, Labeling, Product and Technology Standards Division; Diane VanLonkhuyzen, Manager, Meat and Poultry Hotline; Kathy Brenard; Project Coordinator, Meat and Poultry Hotline; Meat and Poultry Hotline Technical Information Specialists

Foreign Agricultural Service:
Joel L. Greene, Agricultural Economist

National Agricultural Statistics Service:
Doyle R. Fuchs, Deputy State Statistician, Texas Agricultural Statistics Service; Howard R. Holden, Deputy State Statistician, Iowa Agricultural Statistics Service; Muriel Laliberte, Secretary, Livestock and Economics Branch

Rural Electrification Administration:
James L. McKenna

United States Department of Commerce:
National Institute of Standards and Technology:
Joan Koenig, Weights and Measures Coordinator

National Oceanic and Atmospheric Administration:
Jeff Johnson, Warning Coordination Meteorologist, Johnston, Iowa

United States Bureau of the Census:
Nancy White, Program Assistant

United States Department of Health and Human Services:
Food and Drug Administration:
Tina Gilliam, Printing Specialist

National Institutes of Health:
National Heart, Lung, and Blood Institute

United States Department of the Interior:
Fish and Wildlife Service:
Janet L. Miller, Editor, Office of Public Affairs; Robert B. Dahlgren, Ph.D., Biologist, Retired

General Services Administration:
Consumer Information Center:
Carole Collins, Senior Media Specialist

Van Nostrand Reinhold Company Inc.:
Carl Maddalone, Permission Manager

West Des Moines Public Library

Whitetails Unlimited, Inc.:
Peter Gerl, Executive Director

Wilton Enterprises:
Zella Junkin, Manager, Consumer Affairs

People often ask, "Where did you get the recipes for the book?" Many were handed down in our immediate family, others are the result of research, some are original dishes, and a good number of recipes and ideas came from friends, family members, and acquaintances whose names appear in the list that follows. Some of the persons are deceased, and I am happy that *The Blue Ribbon Country Cookbook* can help serve as a vehicle for the perpetuation and recognition of their contributions to the

American cooking tradition. In addition, several of the people listed assisted with the book in ways other than via recipes. My appreciation is extended to each and every one of you for your important contributions to the first and/or new edition of The Blue Ribbon Country Cookbook:

Julie A. Abbott, M.D., M.P.H., Gertrud Acksen, Kelly Adams, Susan Albaugh, Tommy Allen, Barbara Amend, Nancy Amend

Florence Barns, Chris Bening, Mary Berndt, Alice Bernstein, Teri Bognanno, Joanne Brown, Mary and Dave Brown, Mary Burgess, Marlene Bushman

Martha Cotter, Pauline Crenshaw

Marie Dalbey, Peg Danielson, Patty Davis, Dorothy Davison, Kay DeWitt, Elizabeth and George Dinsdale, Belle Dowell, Rebecca Bowlsby Duncan, Miriam Dunlap

Jeri Extok Janet and Charles Fillman, Floy Flanders

Jean Yvonne Galloway, Denise Goode, Ada Goreham, Anna Goreham, Jerri Goreham, Nancy and Dick Goreham, Tiss Goreham, Ethel Graaff, Werner Greiner, Kathy Griffin

Brent Halling, Scott Halling, Gayle Hamilton, Ruth Henss, Josephine Herndon, Hank Higdon, Joy Holmquist

Margaret Johnson, Teri Johnson, Marj Jordan

Jim Kascoutas, Bill Keefer, Sylvia Keefer, Karen King

Jane LaMair, Mary Ann Lane, David Paul Larousse, Shirley and Lou Lauro, Ken Lepley, Isabel Levin, Irene and George Loder

Carol Mapes, Alpha Markell, Dorothy Martin, Judy Merrill, Barbara Millington

Meredith Noble, Dianna Nolin

Dan Perkins, Rose Lee Pomerantz, Jerome J. Pratt

Mina Baker Roelofs, Ellen Roupe, Don Roush, Jesse Roush

Bernice Safris, Opal Sallow, Donna Sandin, Jacalyn See, M.S., R.D., Ernie Seneca, Edith Shelley, Shirlie and Keith Simmer, Christie Smith, Dora Smith, Jeannie Snyder, Bret Staples, Nina Staples, Dave Stephenson, Janet Stern, June Street

Sharon Teale, Barbara Telleen, Ellen Thomas Laura Van Sant, Melinda von Reis

Charlotte Watkins, Susan and Chuck Weiss, Emma Whitlock, Paula Wilcher, Connie Wilson, Linda Wilson, Colette Wortman, Fauntell Wray, Lynne Wright

Gene Zefron

Index

VOLUME AND WEIGHT MEASURES

VOLUME MEASURES

U.S. Customary Measures			Metric Measures[1]
Dash[2]	=	Less than 1/8 tsp	
1/4 tsp	=	15 drops	.04 fl oz	1.23 mL
1/2 tsp	=	30 drops	.08 fl oz	2.46 mL
3/4 tsp	=	45 drops	.13 fl oz	3.70 mL
1 tsp	=	60 drops	1/6 fl oz	4.929 mL
1/4 Tbsp	=	3/4 tsp	.13 fl oz	3.70 mL
1/3 Tbsp	=	1 tsp	1/6 fl oz	4.929 mL
3/8 Tbsp	=	1 1/8 tsp	.19 fl oz	5.55 mL
1/2 Tbsp	=	1 1/2 tsp	1/4 fl oz	7.39 mL
5/8 Tbsp	=	1 7/8 tsp (1 3/4 tsp + 1/8 tsp)	.31 fl oz	9.24 mL
2/3 Tbsp	=	2 tsp	1/3 fl oz	9.86 mL
3/4 Tbsp	=	2 1/4 tsp	.37 fl oz	11.09 mL
7/8 Tbsp	=	2 1/2 tsp	.44 fl oz	12.94 mL
1 Tbsp	=	3 tsp	1/2 fl oz	14.787 mL
1/8 cup	=	2 Tbsp	1 fl oz	29.574 mL
1/4 cup	=	4 Tbsp	2 fl oz	59.15 mL
1/3 cup	=	5 1/3 Tbsp (5 Tbsp + 1 tsp)	2 2/3 fl oz	78.85 mL
3/8 cup	=	6 Tbsp	3 fl oz	88.72 mL
1/2 cup	=	8 Tbsp	4 fl oz	118.29 mL
5/8 cup	=	10 Tbsp	5 fl oz	147.87 mL
2/3 cup	=	10 2/3 Tbsp (10 Tbsp + 2 tsp)	5 1/3 fl oz	157.71 mL
3/4 cup	=	12 Tbsp	6 fl oz	177.44 mL
7/8 cup	=	14 Tbsp	7 fl oz	207.01 mL
1 cup (liq)	=	16 Tbsp	8 fl oz	236.582 mL
1/2 pt (dry)	=	1 cup		275.31 mL
1/2 pt (liq)	=	1 cup (liq)	8 fl oz	236.589 mL
1 pt (dry)	=	2 cups		550.610 mL
1 pt (liq)	=	2 cups (liq)	16 fl oz	473.177 mL
1 qt (dry)	=	2 pt (dry) or 4 cups (dry)		1.101 L
1 qt (liq)	=	2 pt (liq) or 4 cups (liq)	32 fl oz	0.946 L
1 gal (dry)	=	4 qt or 8 pt		4.405 L
1 gal (liq)	=	4 qt (liq) or 8 pt (liq)	128 fl oz	3.785 L
1 peck (dry)	=	2 gal (dry) or 8 qt (dry)		8.810 L
1 bu (dry) (struck[3])	=	4 pecks (dry) or 8 gal (dry)		35.239 L

[1]Approximate measures.
[2]Not a standard volume measure.
[3]Struck measure. A **heaped** bushel is equal to 1 1/4 **struck** bushels.

See page 661 for Metric Conversion Tables.

WEIGHT MEASURES

U.S. Ounces and Pounds (Avoirdupois Weight)			Metric Measures[1]
1/4 oz	=		7.087 g
1/2 oz	=		14.175 g
3/4 oz	=		21.262 g
1 oz	=		28.350 g
16 oz	=	1 lb	453.592 g
1 lb	=		0.4536 kg
2 lbs	=		0.9072 kg

[1]Approximate measures.

METRIC CONVERSIONS

Metric Measures		U.S. Measures[1]
1 milliliter	=	0.203 tsp
		0.0676 Tbsp
		0.0338 fl oz
		0.0042 cups
		0.0021 pt (liq)
		0.0011 qt (liq)
		0.00026 gal (liq)
1 liter	=	33.8140 fl oz
		4.2268 cups
		1.8162 pt (dry)
		2.1134 pt (liq)
		0.9081 qt (dry)
		1.0567 qt (liq)
		0.2270 gal (dry)
		0.2642 gal (liq)
		0.1135 peck (dry)
		0.0284 bu (dry)
1 gram	=	0.0353 oz (avdp)
1 kilogram	=	2.2046 lb (avdp)

[1]Approximate measures.

ABBREVIATIONS[1]

Avoirdupois	avdp	Milliliter	mL
Bushel	bu	Ounce	oz
Fluid Ounce	fl oz	Peck	pk
Gallon	gal	Pint	pt
Gram	g	Pound	lb
Kilogram	kg	Quart	qt
Liquid	liq	Tablespoon	Tbsp
Liter	L	Teaspoon	tsp

[1]These abbreviations are used for both singular and plural items.

METRIC CONVERSION TABLES

To Convert (U.S.)	To (Metric)	Multiply By[1]
Teaspoons	Milliliters	4.9289
Tablespoons	Milliliters	14.787
Fluid Ounces	Milliliters	29.5735
Cups (Liquid)	Milliliters	236.5882
Fluid Ounces	Liters	0.0296
Pints (Dry)	Liters	0.5506
Pints (Liquid)	Liters	0.4732
Quarts (Dry)	Liters	1.1012
Quarts (Liquid)	Liters	0.9464
Gallons (Dry)	Liters	4.4048
Gallons (Liquid)	Liters	3.7854
Pecks (Dry)	Liters	8.8098
Bushels (Dry) (Struck[2])	Liters	35.2391
Ounces (Avoirdupois)	Grams	28.3495
Pounds (Avoirdupois)	Grams	453.5924
Ounces (Avoirdupois)	Kilograms	0.0283
Pounds (Avoirdupois)	Kilograms	0.4536

To Convert (Metric)	To (U.S.)	Multiply By[1]
Milliliters	Teaspoons	0.2029
Milliliters	Tablespoons	0.0676
Milliliters	Fluid Ounces	0.0338
Milliliters	Cups (Liquid)	0.0042
Liters	Fluid Ounces	33.8140
Liters	Pints (Dry)	1.8162
Liters	Pints (Liquid)	2.1134
Liters	Quarts (Dry)	0.9081
Liters	Quarts (Liquid)	1.0567
Liters	Gallons (Dry)	0.2270
Liters	Gallons (Liquid)	0.2642
Liters	Pecks (Dry)	0.1135
Liters	Bushels (Dry) (Struck[2])	0.0284
Grams	Ounces (Avoirdupois)	0.0353
Grams	Pounds (Avoirdupois)	0.0022
Kilograms	Ounces (Avoirdupois)	35.274
Kilograms	Pounds (Avoirdupois)	2.2046

To Convert (Metric)	To (Metric)	Multiply By[1]
Milliliters	Liters	0.001
Liters	Milliliters	1000.0
Grams	Kilograms	0.001
Kilograms	Grams	1000.0

[1]Approximate factors.
[2]Struck measure. A **heaped** bushel is equal to 1 1/4 **struck** bushels.

See Volume and Weight Measures, page 662.